HARPER COLLINS
SPANISH
DICTIONARY

W9-AGA-863

HARPER COLLINS
SPANISH
DICTIONARY
SPANISH·ENGLISH ENGLISH·SPANISH

HarperResource
An Imprint of HarperCollins*Publishers*

ISBN 0-06-273749-X

The HarperCollins website address is
www.harpercollins.com

The HarperCollins UK website address is
www.fireandwater.com

Harper*Resource*   A Division of HarperCollins*Publishers*
10 East 53rd Street, New York, N.Y. 10022

first published 1990
second edition 2000

First Harper*Resource* printing: 2000

Typeset by Morton Word Processing Ltd, Scarborough
Printed in the United States of America

Harper*Resource* and colophons are trademarks of
HarperCollins*Publishers*

ÍNDICE   CONTENTS

Marcas Registradas

Las marcas que creemos que constituyen marcas registradas las denominamos como tales. Sin embargo, no debe considerarse que la presencia o la ausencia de esta designación tenga que ver con la situación legal de ninguna marca.

Note on trademarks

Words which we have reason to believe constitute trademarks have been designated as such. However, neither the presence nor the absence of such designation should be regarded as affecting the legal status of any trademark.

INTRODUCCIÓN

Estamos muy satisfechos de que hayas decidido comprar el Diccionario de Inglés Collins y esperamos que lo disfrutes y que te sirva de gran ayuda ya sea en el colegio, en el trabajo, en tus vacaciones o en casa.

Esta introducción pretende darte algunas indicaciones para ayudarte a sacar el mayor provecho de este diccionario; no sólo de su extenso vocabulario, sino de toda la información que te proporciona cada entrada. Esta te ayudará a leer y comprender — y también a comunicarte y a expresarte — en inglés moderno.

El Diccionario de Inglés Collins comienza con una lista de abreviaturas utilizadas en el texto y con una ilustración de los sonidos representados por los símbolos fonéticos. Al final del diccionario encontrarás una tabla de los verbos irregulares del inglés, y para terminar, una sección sobre el uso de los números y de las expresiones de tiempo.

EL MANEJO DE TU DICCIONARIO COLLINS

La amplia información que te ofrece este diccionario aparece presentada en distintas tipografías, con caracteres de diversos tamaños y con distintos símbolos, abreviaturas y paréntesis. Los apartados siguientes explican las reglas y símbolos utilizados.

Entradas

Las palabras que consultas en el diccionario — las "entradas" — aparecen ordenadas alfabéticamente y en **caracteres gruesos** para una identificación más rápida. Las dos palabras que ocupan el margen superior de cada página indican la primera y la última entrada de la página en cuestión.

La información sobre el uso o la forma de determinadas entradas aparece entre paréntesis, detrás de la transcripción fonética, y generalmente en forma abreviada y en cursiva (p.ej.: (*fam*), (*COM*)).

En algunos casos se ha considerado oportuno agrupar palabras de una misma familia (**nación, nacionalismo; accept, acceptance**) bajo una misma entrada, en caracteres gruesos de tamaño algo más pequeño que los de la entrada principal.
Las expresiones de uso corriente en las que aparece una entrada se dan en negrita (p.ej.: **to be in a hurry**).

Símbolos fonéticos

La transcripción fonética de cada entrada (que indica su pronunciación) aparece entre corchetes, inmediatamente después de la entrada (p.ej.: **knead** [ni:d]). En la página xiii encontrarás una lista de los símbolos fonéticos utilizados en este diccionario.

Traducciones

Las traducciones de las entrades aparecen en caracteres normales, y en los casos en los que existen significados o usos diferentes, éstos aparecen separados mediante un punto y coma. A menudo encontrarás también otras palabras en cursiva y entre paréntesis antes de las traducciones. Estas sugieren contextos en los que la entrada podría aparecer (p.ej.: **rough** (*voice*) o (*weather*)) o proporcionan sinónimos (p.ej.: **rough** (*violent*)).

Palabras clave

Particular relevancia reciben ciertas palabras inglesas y españolas que han sido consideradas palabras "clave" en cada lengua. Estas pueden, por ejemplo, ser de utilización muy corriente o tener distintos usos (**de, haber; get, that**). La combinación de rombos ♦ y números te permitirá distinguir las diferentes categorías gramaticales y los diferentes significados. Las indicaciones en cursiva y entre paréntesis proporcionan además importante información adicional.

Información gramatical

Las categorías gramaticales aparecen en forma abreviada y en cursiva después de la transcripción fonética de cada entrada (*vt, adv, conj*).

También se indican la forma femenina y los plurales irregulares de los sustantivos del ingeIs (**child, ~ren**).

INTRODUCTION

We are delighted you have decided to buy the Collins Spanish Dictionary and hope you will enjoy and benefit from using it at school, at home, on holiday or at work.

This introduction gives you a few tips on how to get the most out of your dictionary — not simply from its comprehensive wordlist but also from the information provided in each entry. This will help you to read and understand modern Spanish, as well as communicate and express yourself in the language.

The Collins Spanish Dictionary begins by listing the abbreviations used in the text and illustrating the sounds shown by the phonetic symbols. You will find Spanish verb tables at the back, followed by a final section on numbers and time expressions.

USING YOUR COLLINS DICTIONARY

A wealth of information is presented in the dictionary, using various type-faces, sizes of type, symbols, abbreviations and brackets. The conventions and symbols used are explained in the following sections.

Headwords

The words you look up in a dictionary — "headwords" — are listed alpha-betically. They are printed in **bold type** for rapid identification. The two headwords appearing at the top of each page indicate the first and last word dealt with on the page in question.

Information about the usage or form of certain headwords is given in brackets after the phonetic spelling. This usually appears in abbreviated form and in italics (e.g. *(fam)*, *(COMM)*).

Where appropriate, words related to headwords are grouped in the same entry (**nación, nacionalismo; accept, acceptance**) in a slightly smaller bold type than the headword.

Common expressions in which the headword appears are shown in a different bold roman type (e.g. **hacer calor**).

Phonetic spellings

The phonetic spelling of each headword (indicating its pronunciation) is given in square brackets immediately after the headword (e.g. **dónde** ['donde]). A list of these symbols is given on page xiii.

Translations

Headword translations are given in ordinary type and, where more than one meaning or usage exists, these are separated by a semi-colon. You will often find other words in italics in brackets before the translations. These offer suggested contexts in which the headword might appear (e.g.

grande (*de tamaño*) or provide synonyms (e.g. **grande** (*alto*) *o* (*distinguido*)).

"Key" words

Special status is given to certain Spanish and English words which are considered as "key" words in each language. They may, for example, occur very frequently or have several types of usage (e.g. **de, haber**). A combination of lozenges ◆ and numbers helps you to distinguish different parts of speech and different meanings. Further helpful information is provided in brackets and in italics.

Grammatical information

Parts of speech are given in abbreviated form in italics after the phonetic spellings of headwords (e.g. *vt, adv, conj*).

Genders of Spanish nouns are indicated as follows: *nm* for a masculine and *nf* for a feminine noun. Feminine and irregular plural forms of nouns are also shown (**irlandés, esa; luz,** (*pl* **luces**)).

ABREVIATURAS

ABBREVIATIONS

abreviatura	ab(b)r	abbreviation
adjetivo, locución adjetiva	adj	adjective, adjectival phrase
administración	ADMIN	administration
adverbio, locución adverbial	adv	adverb, adverbial phrase
agricultura	AGR	agriculture
América Latina	AM	Latin America
anatomía	ANAT	anatomy
arquitectura	ARQ, ARCH	architecture
el automóvil	AUT(O)	the motor car and motoring
aviación, viajes aéreos	AVIAT	flying, air travel
biología	BIO(L)	biology
botánica, flores	BOT	botany
inglés británico	BRIT	British English
química	CHEM	chemistry
comercio, finanzas, banca	COM(M)	commerce, finance, banking
informática	COMPUT	computers
conjunción	conj	conjunction
construcción	CONSTR	building
compuesto	cpd	compound element
cocina	CULIN	cookery
economía	ECON	economics
electricidad, electrónica	ELEC	electricity, electronics
enseñanza, sistema escolar y universitario	ESCOL	schooling, schools and universities
España	Esp	Spain
especialmente	esp	especially
exclamación, interjección	excl	exclamation, interjection
femenino	f	feminine
lengua familiar (! vulgar)	fam (!)	colloquial usage (! particularly offensive)
ferrocarril	FERRO	railways
uso figurado	fig	figurative use
fotografía	FOTO	photography
(verbo inglés) del cual la partícula es inseparable	fus	(phrasal verb) where the particle is inseparable
generalmente	gen	generally
geografía, geología	GEO	geography, geology
geometría	GEOM	geometry
uso familiar (! vulgar)	inf (!)	colloquial usage (! particularly offensive)
infinitivo	infin	infinitive
informática	INFORM	computers
invariable	inv	invariable
irregular	irreg	irregular
lo jurídico	JUR	law
América Latina	LAM	Latin America
gramática, lingüística	LING	grammar, linguistics
masculino	m	masculine

ABREVIATURAS

ABBREVIATIONS

matemáticas	MATH	mathematics
masculino/femenino	m/f	masculine/feminine
medicina	MED	medicine
lo militar, ejército	MIL	military matters
música	MUS	music
sustantivo, nombre	n	noun
navegación, náutica	NAUT	sailing, navigation
sustantivo numérico	num	numeral noun
complemento	obj	(grammatical) object
	o.s.	oneself
peyorativo	pey, pej	derogatory, pejorative
fotografía	PHOT	photography
fisiología	PHYSIOL	physiology
plural	pl	plural
política	POL	politics
participio de pasado	pp	past participle
preposición	prep	preposition
pronombre	pron	pronoun
psicología, psiquiatría	PSICO, PSYCH	psychology, psychiatry
tiempo pasado	pt	past tense
química	QUÍM	chemistry
ferrocarril	RAIL	railways
religión	REL	religion
	sb	somebody
enseñanza, sistema escolar y universitario	SCH	schooling, schools and universities
singular	sg	singular
España	SP	Spain
	sth	something
sujeto	su(b)j	(grammatical) subject
subjuntivo	subjun	subjunctive
tauromaquia	TAUR	bullfighting
también	tb	also
técnica, tecnología	TEC(H)	technical term, technology
telecomunicaciones	TELEC, TEL	telecommunications
imprenta, tipografía	TIP, TYP	typography, printing
televisión	TV	television
universidad	UNIV	university
inglés norteamericano	US	American English
verbo	vb	verb
verbo intransitivo	vi	intransitive verb
verbo pronominal	vr	reflexive verb
verbo transitivo	vt	transitive verb
zoología	ZOOL	zoology
marca registrada	®	registered trademark
indica un equivalente cultural	≈	introduces a cultural equivalent

SPANISH PRONUNCIATION

Consonants

c	[k]	caja	c before *a, o* or *u* is pronounced as in cat
ce, ci	[θe, θi]	cero cielo	c before *e* or *i* is pronounced as in thin
ch	[tʃ]	chiste	ch is pronounced as ch in chair
d	[d, ð]	danés ciudad	at the beginning of a phrase or after *l* or *n*, d is pronounced as in English. In any other position it is pronounced like th in the
g	[g, ɤ]	gafas paga	g before *a, o* or *u* is pronounced as in gap, if at the beginning of a phrase or after *n*. In other positions the sound is softened
ge, gi	[xe, xi]	gente girar	g before *e* or *i* is pronounced similar to ch in Scottish loch
h		haber	h is always silent in Spanish
j	[x]	jugar	j is pronounced similar to ch in Scottish loch
ll	[ʎ]	talle	ll is pronounced like the lli in million
ñ	[ɲ]	niño	ñ is pronounced like the ni in onion
q	[k]	que	q is pronounced as k in king
r, rr	[r, rr]	quitar garra	r is always pronounced in Spanish, unlike the silent r in dancer. rr is trilled, like a Scottish r
s	[s]	quizás isla	s is usually pronounced as in pass, but before *b, d, g, l, m* or *n* it is pronounced as in rose
v	[b, ß]	vía dividir	v is pronounced something like b. At the beginning of a phrase or after *m* or *n* it is pronounced as b in boy. In any other position the sound is softened
z	[θ]	tenaz	z is pronounced as th in thin

b, f, k, l, m, n, p, t and x are pronounced as in English.

Vowels

a	[a]	p*a*ta	not as long as *a* in f*a*r. When followed by a consonant in the same syllable (i.e. in a closed syllable), as in am*a*nte, the *a* is short, as in b*a*t
e	[e]	m*e*	like *e* in th*e*y. In a closed syllable, as in g*e*nte, the *e* is short as in p*e*t
i	[i]	p*i*no	as in m*ea*n or mach*i*ne
o	[o]	l*o*	as in l*o*cal. In a closed syllable, as in c*o*ntrol, the *o* is short as in c*o*t
u	[u]	l*u*nes	as in r*u*le. It is silent after *q*, and in *gue, gui*, unless marked *güe, güi* e.g. anti*güe*dad

Diphthongs

ai, ay	[ai]	b*ai*le	as *i* in r*i*de
au	[au]	*au*to	as *ou* in sh*ou*t
ei, ey	[ei]	bu*ey*	as *ey* in gr*ey*
eu	[eu]	d*eu*da	both elements pronounced independently |e|/|u|
oi, oy	[oi]	h*oy*	as *oy* in t*oy*

Stress

The rules of stress in Spanish are as follows:
(a)   when a word ends in a vowel or in *n* or *s*, the second last syllable is stressed: pat*a*ta, pat*a*tas, c*o*me, c*o*men
(b)   when a word ends in a consonant other than *n* or *s*, the stress falls on the last syllable: par*e*d, habl*a*r
(c)   when the rules set out in a and b are not applied, an acute accent appears over the stressed vowel: com*ú*n, geograf*í*a, ingl*é*s

In the phonetic transcription, the symbol |'| precedes the syllable on which the stress falls.

PRONUNCIACIÓN INGLESA

Vocales y diptongos

	Ejemplo inglés	Ejemplo español/explicación
ɑ:	father	Entre a de padre y o de noche
ʌ	but, come	a muy breve
æ	man, cat	Se mantienen los labios en la posición de e en pena y luego se pronuncia el sonido a
ə	father, ago	Sonido indistinto parecido a una e u o casi mudas
ə:	bird, heard	Entre e abierta, y o cerrada, sonido alargado
ɛ	get, bed	como en perro
ɪ	it, big	Más breve que en si
i:	tea, see	Como en fino
ɔ	hot, wash	Como en torre
ɔ:	saw, all	Como en por
u	put, book	Sonido breve, más cerrado que burro
u:	too, you	Sonido largo, como en uno
aɪ	fly, high	Como en fraile
au	how, house	Como en pausa
ɛə	there, bear	Casi como en vea, pero el sonido a se mezcla con el indistinto [ə]
eɪ	day, obey	e cerrada seguida por una i débil
ɪə	here, hear	Como en manía, mezclándose el sonido a con el indistinto [ə]
əu	go, note	[ə] seguido por una breve u
ɔɪ	boy, oil	Como en voy
uə	poor, sure	u bastante larga más el sonido indistinto [ə]

Consonantes

	Ejemplo inglés	*Ejemplo español/explicación*
d	men*d*ed	Como en con*d*e, an*d*ar
g	*g*o, *g*et, bi*g*	Como en *g*rande, *g*ol
dʒ	*g*in, *j*udge	Como en la *ll* andaluza y en *G*eneralitat (catalán)
ŋ	si*ng*	Como en ví*n*culo
h	*h*ouse, *h*e	Como la jota hispanoamericana
j	*y*oung, *y*es	Como en *y*a
k	*c*ome, mo*ck*	Como en *c*aña, Es*c*ocia
r	*r*ed, t*r*ead	Se pronuncia con la punta de la lengua hacia atrás y sin hacerla vibrar
s	*s*and, ye*s*	Como en *c*asa, *s*esión
z	ro*s*e, *z*ebra	Como en de*s*de, mi*s*mo
ʃ	*sh*e, ma*ch*ine	Como en *ch*ambre (francés), ro*x*o (portugués)
tʃ	*ch*in, ri*ch*	Como en *ch*ocolate
v	*v*alley	Como en f, pero se retiran los dientes superiores vibrándolos contra el labio inferior
w	*w*ater, *wh*ich	Como en la *u* de h*u*evo, p*u*ede
ʒ	vi*s*ion	Como en *j*ournal (francés)
θ	*th*ink, my*th*	Como en re*c*eta, *z*apato
ð	*th*is, *th*e	Como en la *d* de habla*d*o, verda*d*

b, p, f, m, n, l, t iguales que en español

El signo * indica que la r final escrita apenas se pronuncia en inglés británico cuando la palabra siguiente empieza con vocal.

El signo [ˈ] indica la sílaba acentuada.

ESPAÑOL – INGLÉS

SPANISH – ENGLISH

A, a

PALABRA CLAVE

a |a| (*a + el = al*) *prep* **1** (*dirección*) to; **fueron ~ Madrid/Grecia** they went to Madrid/Greece; **me voy ~ casa** I'm going home

2 (*distancia*): **está ~ 15 km de aquí** it's 15 km from here

3 (*posición*): **estar ~ la mesa** to be at table; **al lado de** next to, beside; *ver tb* **puerta**

4 (*tiempo*): **~ las 10/~ medianoche** at 10/ midnight; **~ la mañana siguiente** the following morning; **~ los pocos días** after a few days; **estamos ~ 9 de julio** it's the ninth of July; **~ los 24 años** at the age of 24; **al año/~ la semana** (*AM*) a year/week later

5 (*manera*): **~ la francesa** the French way; **~ caballo** on horseback; **~ oscuras** in the dark

6 (*medio, instrumento*): **~ lápiz** in pencil; **~ mano** by hand; **cocina ~ gas** gas stove

7 (*razón*): **~ 30 ptas el kilo** at 30 pesetas a kilo; **~ más de 50 km/h** at more than 50 km per hour

8 (*dativo*): **se lo di ~ él** I gave it to him; **vi al policía** I saw the policeman; **se lo compré ~ él** I bought it from him

9 (*tras ciertos verbos*): **voy ~ verle** I'm going to see him; **empezó ~ trabajar** he started working o to work

10 (+ *infin*): **al verle, le reconocí inmediata- mente** when I saw him I recognized him at once; **el camino ~ recorrer** the distance we (*etc*) have to travel; **¡~ callar!** keep quiet!; **¡~ comer!** let's eat!

---

abad, esa [a'ßað, 'ðesa] *nm/f* abbot/abbess; **~ía** *nf* abbey

abajo [a'ßaxo] *adv* (*situación*) (down) below, underneath; (*en edificio*) downstairs; (*dirección*) down, downwards; **el piso de ~** the downstairs flat; **la parte de ~** the lower part; **¡~ el gobierno!** down with the government!; **cuesta/río ~** downhill/ downstream; **de arriba ~** from top to bottom; **el ~ firmante** the undersigned; **más ~** lower o further down

abalanzarse [aßalan'θarse] *vr*: **~ sobre** o **contra** to throw o.s. at

abandonado, a [aßando'naðo, a] *adj* derelict; (*desatendido*) abandoned; (*desierto*) deserted; (*descuidado*) neglected

abandonar [aßando'nar] *vt* to leave; (*persona*) to abandon, desert; (*cosa*) to abandon, leave behind; (*descuidar*) to neglect; (*renunciar a*) to give up; (*INFORM*) to quit; **~se** *vr*: **~se a** to abandon o.s. to; **abandono** *nm* (*acto*) desertion, abandonment; (*estado*) abandon, neglect; (*renuncia*) withdrawal, retirement; **ganar por abandono** to win by default

abanicar [aßani'kar] *vt* to fan; **abanico** *nm* fan; (*NAUT*) derrick

abaratar [aßara'tar] *vt* to lower the price of; **~se** *vr* to go o come down in price

abarcar [aßar'kar] *vt* to include, embrace; (*AM*) to monopolize

abarrotado, a [aßarro'taðo, a] *adj* packed

abarrotar [aßarro'tar] *vt* (*local, estadio, teatro*) to fill, pack

abarrotero, a [aßarro'tero, a] (*AM*) *nm/f* grocer; **abarrotes** *nmpl* (*AM*) groceries, provisions

abastecer [aßaste'θer] *vt*: **~ (de)** to supply (with); **abastecimiento** *nm* supply

abasto [a'ßasto] *nm* supply; **no dar ~ a** to be unable to cope with

abatido, a [aßa'tiðo, a] *adj* dejected, downcast

abatimiento [aßati'mjento] *nm* (*depresión*) dejection, depression

abatir [aßa'tir] *vt* (*muro*) to demolish; (*pájaro*) to shoot o bring down; (*fig*) to depress; **~se** *vr* to get depressed; **~se sobre** to swoop o pounce on

abdicación [aßðika'θjon] *nf* abdication

abdicar [aßði'kar] *vi* to abdicate

abdomen [aß'ðomen] *nm* abdomen; **abdominales** *nmpl* (*tb*: *ejercicios abdominales*) sit-ups

abecedario [aßeθe'ðarjo] *nm* alphabet

abedul [aße'ðul] *nm* birch

abeja [a'ßexa] *nf* bee

abejorro [aße'xorro] *nm* bumblebee

abertura [aßer'tura] *nf* = **apertura**

abeto [a'ßeto] *nm* fir

abierto, a [a'ßjerto, a] *pp de* **abrir** ♦ *adj* open; (*AM*) generous

abigarrado, a [aßiva'rraðo, a] *adj* multi- coloured

abismal [aßis'mal] *adj* (*fig*) vast, enormous

abismar [aßis'mar] *vt* to humble, cast down;

~se vr to sink; **~se en** (fig) to be plunged into
abismo [a'βismo] nm abyss
abjurar [aβxu'rar] vi: ~ **de** to abjure, forswear
ablandar [aβlan'dar] vt to soften; **~se** vr to get softer
abnegación [aβneɣa'θjon] nf self-denial
abnegado, a [aβne'ɣaðo, a] adj self-sacrificing
abocado, a [aβo'kaðo, a] adj: **verse ~ al desastre** to be heading for disaster
abochornar [aβotʃor'nar] vt to embarrass
abofetear [aβofete'ar] vt to slap (in the face)
abogado, a [aβo'ɣaðo, a] nm/f lawyer; (notario) solicitor; (en tribunal) barrister (BRIT), attorney (US); ~ **defensor** defence lawyer o attorney (US)
abogar [aβo'ɣar] vi: ~ **por** to plead for; (fig) to advocate
abolengo [aβo'lengo] nm ancestry, lineage
abolición [aβoli'θjon] nf abolition
abolir [aβo'lir] vt to abolish; (cancelar) to cancel
abolladura [aβoʎa'ðura] nf dent
abollar [aβo'ʎar] vt to dent
abominable [aβomi'naβle] adj abominable
abonado, a [aβo'naðo, a] adj (deuda) paid(-up) ♦ nm/f subscriber
abonar [aβo'nar] vt (deuda) to settle; (terreno) to fertilize; (idea) to endorse; **~se** vr to subscribe; **abono** nm payment; fertilizer; subscription
abordar [aβor'ðar] vt (barco) to board; (asunto) to broach
aborigen [aβo'rixen] nm/f aborigine
aborrecer [aβorre'θer] vt to hate, loathe
abortar [aβor'tar] vi (al malparir) to have a miscarriage; (deliberadamente) to have an abortion; **aborto** nm miscarriage; abortion
abotonar [aβoto'nar] vt to button (up), do up
abovedado, a [aβoβe'ðaðo, a] adj vaulted, domed
abrasar [aβra'sar] vt to burn (up); (AGR) to dry up, parch
abrazar [aβra'θar] vt to embrace, hug
abrazo [a'βraθo] nm embrace, hug; **un ~** (en carta) with best wishes
abrebotellas [aβreβo'teʎas] nm inv bottle opener
abrecartas [aβre'kartas] nm inv letter opener
abrelatas [aβre'latas] nm inv tin (BRIT) o can opener
abreviar [aβre'βjar] vt to abbreviate; (texto) to abridge; (plazo) to reduce; **abreviatura** nf abbreviation
abridor [aβri'ðor] nm bottle opener; (de latas) tin (BRIT) o can opener
abrigar [aβri'ɣar] vt (proteger) to shelter; (suj: ropa) to keep warm; (fig) to cherish

abrigo [a'βriɣo] nm (prenda) coat, overcoat; (lugar protegido) shelter
abril [a'βril] nm April
abrillantar [aβriʎan'tar] vt to polish
abrir [a'βrir] vt to open (up) ♦ vi to open; **~se** vr to open (up); (extenderse) to open out; (cielo) to clear; **~se paso** to find o force a way through
abrochar [aβro'tʃar] vt (con botones) to button (up); (zapato, con broche) to do up
abrumar [aβru'mar] vt to overwhelm; (sobrecargar) to weigh down
abrupto, a [a'βrupto, a] adj abrupt; (empinado) steep
absceso [aβs'θeso] nm abscess
absentismo [aβsen'tismo] nm absenteeism
absolución [aβsolu'θjon] nf (REL) absolution; (JUR) acquittal
absoluto, a [aβso'luto, a] adj absolute; **en ~** adv not at all
absolver [aβsol'βer] vt to absolve; (JUR) to pardon; (: acusado) to acquit
absorbente [aβsor'βente] adj absorbent; (interesante) absorbing
absorber [aβsor'βer] vt to absorb; (embeber) to soak up
absorción [aβsor'θjon] nf absorption; (COM) takeover
absorto, a [aβ'sorto, a] pp de **absorber** ♦ adj absorbed, engrossed
abstemio, a [aβs'temjo, a] adj teetotal
abstención [aβsten'θjon] nf abstention
abstenerse [aβste'nerse] vr: ~ **(de)** to abstain o refrain (from)
abstinencia [aβsti'nenθja] nf abstinence; (ayuno) fasting
abstracción [aβstrak'θjon] nf abstraction
abstracto, a [aβ'strakto, a] adj abstract
abstraer [aβstra'er] vt to abstract; **~se** vr to be o become absorbed
abstraído, a [aβstra'iðo, a] adj absent-minded
absuelto [aβ'swelto] pp de **absolver**
absurdo, a [aβ'surðo, a] adj absurd
abuchear [aβutʃe'ar] vt to boo
abuelo, a [a'βwelo, a] nm/f grandfather/mother; **~s** nmpl grandparents
abulia [a'βulja] nf apathy
abultado, a [aβul'taðo, a] adj bulky
abultar [aβul'tar] vi to be bulky
abundancia [aβun'danθja] nf: **una ~ de** plenty of; **abundante** adj abundant, plentiful
abundar [aβun'dar] vi to abound, be plentiful
aburguesarse [aβurɣe'sarse] vr to become middle-class
aburrido, a [aβu'rriðo, a] adj (hastiado) bored; (que aburre) boring; **aburrimiento**

nm boredom, tedium

aburrir [aβu'rrir] *vt* to bore; **~se** *vr* to be bored, get bored

abusar [aβu'sar] *vi* to go too far; **~ de** to abuse

abusivo, a [aβu'siβo, a] *adj* (*precio*) exorbitant

abuso [a'βuso] *nm* abuse

abyecto, a [aβ'jekto, a] *adj* wretched, abject

acá [a'ka] *adv* (*lugar*) here; **¿de cuándo ~?** since when?

acabado, a [aka'βaðo, a] *adj* finished, complete; (*perfecto*) perfect; (*agotado*) worn out; (*fig*) masterly ♦ *nm* finish

acabar [aka'βar] *vt* (*llevar a su fin*) to finish, complete; (*consumir*) to use up; (*rematar*) to finish off ♦ *vi* to finish, end; **~se** *vr* to finish, stop; (*terminarse*) to be over; (*agotarse*) to run out; **~ con** to put an end to; **~ de llegar** to have just arrived; **~ por hacer** to end (up) by doing; **¡se acabó!** it's all over!; (*¡basta!*) that's enough!

acabóse [aka'βose] *nm*: **esto es el ~** this is the last straw

academia [aka'ðemja] *nf* academy; **académico, a** *adj* academic

acaecer [akae'θer] *vi* to happen, occur

acallar [aka'ʎar] *vt* (*persona*) to silence; (*protestas, rumores*) to suppress

acalorado, a [akalo'raðo, a] *adj* (*discusión*) heated

acalorarse [akalo'rarse] *vr* (*fig*) to get heated

acampar [akam'par] *vi* to camp

acantilado [akanti'laðo] *nm* cliff

acaparar [akapa'rar] *vt* to monopolize; (*acumular*) to hoard

acariciar [akari'θjar] *vt* to caress; (*esperanza*) to cherish

acarrear [akarre'ar] *vt* to transport; (*fig*) to cause, result in

acaso [a'kaso] *adv* perhaps, maybe; **(por) si ~** (just) in case

acatamiento [akata'mjento] *nm* respect; (*ley*) observance

acatar [aka'tar] *vt* to respect; (*ley*) obey

acatarrarse [akata'rrarse] *vr* to catch a cold

acaudalado, a [akauða'laðo, a] *adj* well-off

acaudillar [akauði'ʎar] *vt* to lead, command

acceder [akθe'ðer] *vi*: **~ a** (*petición etc*) to agree to; (*tener acceso a*) to have access to; (*INFORM*) to access

accesible [akθe'siβle] *adj* accessible

acceso [ak'θeso] *nm* access, entry; (*camino*) access, approach; (*MED*) attack, fit

accesorio, a [akθe'sorjo, a] *adj, nm* accessory

accidentado, a [akθiðen'taðo, a] *adj* uneven; (*montañoso*) hilly; (*azaroso*) eventful

♦ *nm/f* accident victim

accidental [akθiðen'tal] *adj* accidental; **accidentarse** *vr* to have an accident

accidente [akθi'ðente] *nm* accident; **~s** *nmpl* (*de terreno*) unevenness *sg*

acción [ak'θjon] *nf* action; (*acto*) action, act; (*COM*) share; (*JUR*) action, lawsuit; **accionar** *vt* to work, operate; (*INFORM*) to drive

accionista [akθjo'nista] *nm/f* shareholder, stockholder

acebo [a'θeβo] *nm* holly; (*árbol*) holly tree

acechar [aθe'tʃar] *vt* to spy on; (*aguardar*) to lie in wait for; **acecho** *nm*: **estar al acecho (de)** to lie in wait (for)

aceitar [aθei'tar] *vt* to oil, lubricate

aceite [a'θeite] *nm* oil; (*de oliva*) olive oil; **~ra** *nf* oilcan; **aceitoso, a** *adj* oily

aceituna [aθei'tuna] *nf* olive

acelerador [aθelera'ðor] *nm* accelerator

acelerar [aθele'rar] *vt* to accelerate

acelga [a'θelɣa] *nf* chard, beet

acento [a'θento] *nm* accent; (*acentuación*) stress

acentuar [aθen'twar] *vt* to accent; to stress; (*fig*) to accentuate

acepción [aθep'θjon] *nf* meaning

aceptable [aθep'taβle] *adj* acceptable

aceptación [aθepta'θjon] *nf* acceptance; (*aprobación*) approval

aceptar [aθep'tar] *vt* to accept; (*aprobar*) to approve

acequia [a'θekja] *nf* irrigation ditch

acera [a'θera] *nf* pavement (*BRIT*), sidewalk (*US*)

acerca [a'θerka]: **~ de** *prep* about, concerning

acercar [aθer'kar] *vt* to bring o move nearer; **~se** *vr* to approach, come near

acerico [aθe'riko] *nm* pincushion

acero [a'θero] *nm* steel

acérrimo, a [a'θerrimo, a] *adj* (*partidario*) staunch; (*enemigo*) bitter

acertado, a [aθer'taðo, a] *adj* correct; (*apropiado*) apt; (*sensato*) sensible

acertar [aθer'tar] *vt* (*blanco*) to hit; (*solución*) to get right; (*adivinar*) to guess ♦ *vi* to get it right, be right; **~ a** to manage to; **~ con** to happen o hit on

acertijo [aθer'tixo] *nm* riddle, puzzle

achacar [atʃa'kar] *vt* to attribute

achacoso, a [atʃa'koso, a] *adj* sickly

achantar [atʃan'tar] (*fam*) *vt* to scare, frighten; **~se** *vr* to back down

achaque *etc* [a'tʃake] *vb ver* **achacar** ♦ *nm* ailment

achicar [atʃi'kar] *vt* to reduce; (*NAUT*) to bale out

achicharrar [atʃitʃa'rrar] *vt* to scorch, burn

achicoria [atʃi'korja] *nf* chicory

aciago, a [a'θjaɣo, a] *adj* ill-fated, fateful

acicalar |aθika'lar| vt to polish; (persona) to dress up; ~se vr to get dressed up

acicate |aθi'kate| nm spur

acidez |aθi'ðeθ| nf acidity

ácido, a |'aθiðo, a| adj sour, acid ♦ nm acid

acierto etc |a'θjerto| vb ver **acertar** ♦ nm success; (buen paso) wise move; (solución) solution; (habilidad) skill, ability

aclamación |aklama'θjon| nf acclamation; (aplausos) applause

aclamar |akla'mar| vt to acclaim; (aplaudir) to applaud

aclaración |aklara'θjon| nf clarification, explanation

aclarar |akla'rar| vt to clarify, explain; (ropa) to rinse ♦ vi to clear up; ~se vr (explicarse) to understand; ~se la garganta to clear one's throat

aclaratorio, a |aklara'torjo, a| adj explanatory

aclimatación |aklimata'θjon| nf acclimatization

aclimatar |aklima'tar| vt to acclimatize; ~se vr to become acclimatized

acné |ak'ne| nm acne

acobardar |akoβar'ðar| vt to intimidate

acodarse |ako'ðarse| vr: ~ en to lean on

acogedor, a |akoxe'ðor, a| adj welcoming; (hospitalario) hospitable

acoger |ako'xer| vt to welcome; (abrigar) to shelter; ~se vr to take refuge

acogida |ako'xiða| nf reception; refuge

acometer |akome'ter| vt to attack; (emprender) to undertake; **acometida** nf attack, assault

acomodado, a |akomo'ðaðo, a| adj (persona) well-to-do

acomodador, a |akomoða'ðor, a| nm/f usher(ette)

acomodar |akomo'ðar| vt to adjust; (alojar) to accommodate; ~se vr to conform; (instalarse) to install o.s.; (adaptarse) ~se (a) to adapt (to)

acompañar |akompa'nar| vt to accompany; (documentos) to enclose

acondicionar |akondiθjo'nar| vt to arrange, prepare; (pelo) to condition

acongojar |akongo'xar| vt to distress, grieve

aconsejar |akonse'xar| vt to advise, counsel; ~se vr: ~se con to consult

acontecer |akonte'θer| vi to happen, occur; **acontecimiento** nm event

acopio |a'kopjo| nm store, stock

acoplamiento |akopla'mjento| nm coupling, joint; **acoplar** vt to fit; (ELEC) to connect; (vagones) to couple

acorazado, a |akora'θaðo, a| adj armour-plated, armoured ♦ nm battleship

acordar |akor'ðar| vt (resolver) to agree,

resolve; (recordar) to remind; ~se vr to agree; ~se (de algo) to remember (sth); **acorde** adj (MUS) harmonious; **acorde con** (medidas etc) in keeping with ♦ nm chord

acordeón |akorðe'on| nm accordion

acordonado, a |akorðo'naðo, a| adj (calle) cordoned-off

acorralar |akorra'lar| vt to round up, corral

acortar |akor'tar| vt to shorten; (duración) to cut short; (cantidad) to reduce; ~se vr to become shorter

acosar |ako'sar| vt to pursue relentlessly; (fig) to hound, pester; **acoso** nm harassment; **acoso sexual** sexual harassment

acostar |akos'tar| vt (en cama) to put to bed; (en suelo) to lay down; ~se vr to go to bed; to lie down; ~se con uno to sleep with sb

acostumbrado, a |akostum'braðo, a| adj usual; ~ a used to

acostumbrar |akostum'brar| vt: ~ a uno a algo to get sb used to sth ♦ vi: ~ (a) hacer to be in the habit of doing; ~se vr: ~se a to get used to

acotación |akota'θjon| nf marginal note; (GEO) elevation mark; (de límite) boundary mark; (TEATRO) stage direction

ácrata |'akrata| adj, nmf anarchist

acre |'akre| adj (olor) acrid; (fig) biting ♦ nm acre

acrecentar |akreθen'tar| vt to increase, augment

acreditar |akreði'tar| vt (garantizar) to vouch for, guarantee; (autorizar) to authorize; (dar prueba de) to prove; (COM: abonar) to credit; (embajador) to accredit; ~se vr to become famous

acreedor, a |akree'ðor, a| adj: ~ de worthy of ♦ nm/f creditor

acribillar |akriβi'ʎar| vt: ~ a balazos to riddle with bullets

acróbata |a'kroβata| nm/f acrobat

acta |'akta| nf certificate; (de comisión) minutes pl, record; ~ de nacimiento/de matrimonio birth/marriage certificate; ~ notarial affidavit

actitud |akti'tuð| nf attitude; (postura) posture

activar |akti'ßar| vt to activate; (acelerar) to speed up

actividad |aktißi'ðað| nf activity

activo, a |ak'tißo, a| adj active; (vivo) lively ♦ nm (COM) assets pl

acto |'akto| nm act, action; (ceremonia) ceremony; (TEATRO) act; **en el ~** immediately

actor |ak'tor| nm actor; (JUR) plaintiff ♦ adj: **parte ~a** prosecution

actriz |ak'triθ| nf actress

actuación |aktwa'θjon| nf action; (comportamiento) conduct, behaviour; (JUR) proceedings pl; (desempeño) performance

actual [ak'twal] adj present(-day), current;
~idad nf present; **~idades** nfpl (noticias) news
sg; **en la ~idad** at present; (hoy día)
nowadays

actualizar [aktwali'θar] vt to update,
modernize

actualmente [aktwal'mente] adv at present;
(hoy día) nowadays

actuar [ak'twar] vi (obrar) to work, operate;
(actor) to act, perform ♦ vt to work, operate;
~ de to act as

acuarela [akwa'rela] nf watercolour

acuario [a'kwarjo] nm aquarium;
(ASTROLOGÍA): **A~** Aquarius

acuartelar [akwarte'lar] vt (MIL) to confine
to barracks

acuático, a [a'kwatiko, a] adj aquatic

acuchillar [akutʃi'ʎar] vt (TEC) to plane
(down), smooth

acuciante [aku'θjante] adj urgent

acuciar [aku'θjar] vt to urge on

acudir [aku'ðir] vi (asistir) to attend; (ir) to
go; **~ a** (fig) to turn to; **~ en ayuda de** to go
to the aid of

acuerdo etc [a'kwerðo] vb ver **acordar** ♦ nm
agreement; **¡de ~!** agreed!; **de ~ con**
(persona) in agreement with; (acción,
documento) in accordance with; **estar de ~ to**
be agreed, agree

acumular [akumu'lar] vt to accumulate,
collect

acuñar [aku'ɲar] vt (moneda) to mint; (frase)
to coin

acupuntura [akupun'tura] nf acupuncture

acurrucarse [akurru'karse] vr to crouch;
(ovillarse) to curl up

acusación [akusa'θjon] nf accusation

acusar [aku'sar] vt to accuse; (revelar) to
reveal; (denunciar) to denounce

acuse [a'kuse] nm: **~ de recibo**
acknowledgement of receipt

acústica [a'kustika] nf acoustics pl

acústico, a [a'kustiko, a] adj acoustic

adaptación [aðapta'θjon] nf adaptation

adaptador [aðapta'ðor] nm (ELEC) adapter

adaptar [aðap'tar] vt to adapt; (acomodar) to
fit

adecuado, a [aðe'kwaðo, a] adj (apto)
suitable; (oportuno) appropriate

adecuar [aðe'kwar] vt to adapt; to make
suitable

a. de J.C. abr (= antes de Jesucristo) B.C.

adelantado, a [aðelan'taðo, a] adj
advanced; (reloj) fast; **pagar por ~** to pay in
advance

adelantamiento [aðelanta'mjento] nm
(AUTO) overtaking

adelantar [aðelan'tar] vt to move forward;

(avanzar) to advance; (acelerar) to speed up;
(AUTO) to overtake ♦ vi to go forward,
advance; **~se** vr to go forward, advance

adelante [aðe'lante] adv forward(s), ahead
♦ excl come in!; **de hoy en ~** from now on;
más ~ later on; (más allá) further on

adelanto [aðe'lanto] nm advance; (mejora)
improvement; (progreso) progress

adelgazar [aðelɣa'θar] vt to thin (down)
♦ vi to get thin; (con régimen) to slim down,
lose weight

ademán [aðe'man] nm gesture; **ademanes**
nmpl manners; **en ~ de** as if to

además [aðe'mas] adv besides; (por otra
parte) moreover; (también) also; **~ de**
besides, in addition to

adentrarse [aðen'trarse] vr: **~ en** to go into,
get inside; (penetrar) to penetrate (into)

adentro [a'ðentro] adv inside, in; **mar ~** out
at sea; **tierra ~** inland

adepto [a'ðepto, a] nm/f supporter

aderezar [aðere'θar] vt (ensalada) to dress;
(comida) to season; **aderezo** nm dressing;
seasoning

adeudar [aðeu'ðar] vt to owe; **~se** vr to run
into debt

adherirse [aðe'rirse] vr: **~ a** to adhere to;
(partido) to join

adhesión [aðe'sjon] nf adhesion; (fig)
adherence

adicción [aðik'θjon] nf addiction

adición [aði'θjon] nf addition

adicto, a [a'ðikto, a] adj: **~ a** addicted to;
(dedicado) devoted to ♦ nm/f supporter,
follower; (toxicómano etc) addict

adiestrar [aðjes'trar] vt to train, teach;
(conducir) to guide, lead; **~se** vr to practise;
(enseñarse) to train o.s.

adinerado, a [aðine'raðo, a] adj wealthy

adiós [a'ðjos] excl (para despedirse) goodbye!,
cheerio!; (al pasar) hello!

aditivo [aði'tiβo] nm additive

adivinanza [aðiβi'nanθa] nf riddle

adivinar [aðiβi'nar] vt to prophesy;
(conjeturar) to guess; **adivino, a** nm/f
fortune-teller

adj abr (= adjunto) encl.

adjetivo [aðxe'tiβo] nm adjective

adjudicación [aðxuðika'θjon] nf award;
adjudication

adjudicar [aðxuði'kar] vt to award; **~se** vr:
~se algo to appropriate sth

adjuntar [aðxun'tar] vt to attach, enclose;
adjunto, a adj attached, enclosed ♦ nm/f
assistant

administración [aðministra'θjon] nf
administration; (dirección) management;
administrador, a nm/f administrator;
manager(ess)

administrar [aðminis'trar] vt to administer;
 administrativo, a adj administrative
admirable [aðmi'raßle] adj admirable
admiración [aðmira'θjon] nf admiration;
 (asombro) wonder; (LING) exclamation mark
admirar [aðmi'rar] vt to admire; (extrañar) to
 surprise; **~se** vr to be surprised
admisible [aðmi'sißle] adj admissible
admisión [aðmi'sjon] nf admission;
 (reconocimiento) acceptance
admitir [aðmi'tir] vt to admit; (aceptar) to
 accept
admonición [aðmoni'θjon] nf warning
adobar [aðo'ßar] vt (CULIN) to season
adobe [a'ðoße] nm adobe, sun-dried brick
adoctrinar [aðoktri'nar] vt: **~ en** to
 indoctrinate with
adolecer [aðole'θer] vi: **~ de** to suffer from
adolescente [aðoles'θente] nm/f adolescent,
 teenager
adonde [a'ðonde] conj (to) where
adónde [a'ðonde] adv = **dónde**
adopción [aðop'θjon] nf adoption
adoptar [aðop'tar] vt to adopt
adoptivo, a [aðop'tißo, a] adj (padres)
 adoptive; (hijo) adopted
adoquín [aðo'kin] nm paving stone
adorar [aðo'rar] vt to adore
adormecer [aðorme'θer] vt to put to sleep;
 ~se vr to become sleepy; (dormirse) to fall
 asleep
adornar [aðor'nar] vt to adorn
adorno [a'ðorno] nm ornament; (decoración)
 decoration
adosado, a [aðo'saðo, a] adj: **casa adosada**
 semi-detached house
adquiero etc vb ver **adquirir**
adquirir [aðki'rir] vt to acquire, obtain
adquisición [aðkisi'θjon] nf acquisition
adrede [a'ðreðe] adv on purpose
adscribir [aðskri'ßir] vt to appoint
adscrito pp de **adscribir**
aduana [a'ðwana] nf customs pl
aduanero, a [aðwa'nero, a] adj customs cpd
 ♦ nm/f customs officer
aducir [aðu'θir] vt to adduce; (dar como
 prueba) to offer as proof
adueñarse [aðwe'narse] vr: **~ de** to take
 possession of
adulación [aðula'θjon] nf flattery
adular [aðu'lar] vt to flatter
adulterar [aðulte'rar] vt to adulterate
adulterio [aðul'terjo] nm adultery
adúltero, a [a'ðultero, a] adj adulterous
 ♦ nm/f adulterer/adulteress
adulto, a [a'ðulto, a] adj, nm/f adult
adusto, a [a'ðusto, a] adj stern; (austero)
 austere
advenedizo, a [aðßene'ðiθo, a] nm/f

upstart
advenimiento [aðßeni'mjento] nm arrival;
 (al trono) accession
adverbio [að'ßerßjo] nm adverb
adversario, a [að'ßer'sarjo, a] nm/f adversary
adversidad [aðßersi'ðað] nf adversity;
 (contratiempo) setback
adverso, a [að'ßerso, a] adj adverse
advertencia [aðßer'tenθja] nf warning;
 (prefacio) preface, foreword
advertir [aðßer'tir] vt to notice; (avisar): **~ a
 uno de** to warn sb about o of
Adviento [að'ßjento] nm Advent
advierto etc vb ver **advertir**
adyacente [aðja'θente] adj adjacent
aéreo, a [a'ereo, a] adj aerial
aerobic [ae'roßik] nm aerobics sg
aerodeslizador [aeroðesli'θa'ðor] nm
 hovercraft
aeromozo, a [aero'moθo, a] (AM) nm/f air
 steward(ess)
aeronáutica [aero'nautika] nf aeronautics sg
aeronave [aero'naße] nm spaceship
aeroplano [aero'plano] nm aeroplane
aeropuerto [aero'pwerto] nm airport
aerosol [aero'sol] nm aerosol
afabilidad [afaßili'ðað] nf friendliness;
 afable adj affable
afamado, a [afa'maðo, a] adj famous
afán [a'fan] nm hard work; (deseo) desire
afanar [afa'nar] vt to harass; (fam) to pinch;
 ~se vr: **~se por hacer** to strive to do
afear [afe'ar] vt to disfigure
afección [afek'θjon] nf (MED) disease
afectación [afekta'θjon] nf affectation;
 afectado, a adj affected
afectar [afek'tar] vt to affect
afectísimo, a [afek'tisimo, a] adj
 affectionate; **suyo ~** yours truly
afectivo, a [afek'tißo, a] adj (problema etc)
 emotional
afecto [a'fekto] nm affection; **tenerle ~ a uno**
 to be fond of sb
afectuoso, a [afek'twoso, a] adj affectionate
afeitar [afei'tar] vt to shave; **~se** vr to shave
afeminado, a [afemi'naðo, a] adj effeminate
Afganistán [afɣanis'tan] nm Afghanistan
afianzamiento [afjanθa'mjento] nm
 strengthening; security
afianzar [afjan'θar] vt to strengthen; to
 secure; **~se** vr to become established
afiche [a'fitʃe] (AM) nm poster
afición [afi'θjon] nf fondness, liking; **la ~** the
 fans pl; **pinto por ~** I paint as a hobby;
 aficionado, a adj keen, enthusiastic; (no
 profesional) amateur ♦ nm/f enthusiast, fan;
 amateur; **ser aficionado a algo** to be very
 keen on o fond of sth
aficionar [afiθjo'nar] vt: **~ a uno a algo** to

make sb like sth; **~se** *vr*: **~se a algo** to grow fond of sth

afilado, a [afi'laðo, a] *adj* sharp

afilar [afi'lar] *vt* to sharpen

afiliarse [afi'ljarse] *vr* to affiliate

afín [a'fin] *adj* (*parecido*) similar; (*conexo*) related

afinar [afi'nar] *vt* (*TEC*) to refine; (*MUS*) to tune ♦ *vi* (*tocar*) to play in tune; (*cantar*) to sing in tune

afincarse [afin'karse] *vr* to settle

afinidad [afini'ðað] *nf* affinity; (*parentesco*) relationship; **por ~** by marriage

afirmación [afirma'θjon] *nf* affirmation

afirmar [afir'mar] *vt* to affirm, state; **afirmativo, a** *adj* affirmative

aflicción [aflik'θjon] *nf* affliction; (*dolor*) grief

afligir [afli'xir] *vt* to afflict; (*apenar*) to distress; **~se** *vr* to grieve

aflojar [aflo'xar] *vt* to slacken; (*desatar*) to loosen, undo; (*relajar*) to relax ♦ *vi* to drop; (*bajar*) to go down; **~se** *vr* to relax

aflorar [aflo'rar] *vi* to come to the surface, emerge

afluente [aflu'ente] *adj* flowing ♦ *nm* tributary

afluir [aflu'ir] *vi* to flow

afmo, a *abr* (= *afectísimo(a) suyo(a)*) Yours

afónico, a [a'foniko, a] *adj*: **estar ~** to have a sore throat; to have lost one's voice

aforo [a'foro] *nm* (*de teatro etc*) capacity

afortunado, a [afortu'naðo, a] *adj* fortunate, lucky

afrancesado, a [afranθe'saðo, a] *adj* francophile; (*pey*) Frenchified

afrenta [a'frenta] *nf* affront, insult; (*deshonra*) dishonour, shame

África ['afrika] *nf* Africa; **africano, a** *adj*, *nm/f* African

afrontar [afron'tar] *vt* to confront; (*poner cara a cara*) to bring face to face

afuera [a'fwera] *adv* out, outside; **~s** *nfpl* outskirts

agachar [aɣa'tʃar] *vt* to bend, bow; **~se** *vr* to stoop, bend

agalla [a'ɣaʎa] *nf* (*ZOOL*) gill; **tener ~s** (*fam*) to have guts

agarradera [aɣarra'ðera] (*esp AM*) *nf* handle

agarrado, a [aɣa'rraðo, a] *adj* mean, stingy

agarrar [aɣa'rrar] *vt* to grasp, grab; (*AM*) to take, catch; (*recoger*) to pick up ♦ *vi* (*planta*) to take root; **~se** *vr* to hold on (tightly)

agarrotar [aɣarro'tar] *vt* (*persona*) to squeeze tightly; (*reo*) to garrotte; **~se** *vr* (*motor*) to seize up; (*MED*) to stiffen

agasajar [aɣasa'xar] *vt* to treat well, fête

agazaparse [aɣaθa'parse] *vr* to crouch down

agencia [a'xenθja] *nf* agency; **~ inmobiliaria** estate (*BRIT*) o real estate (*US*) agent's

(office); **~ de viajes** travel agency

agenciarse [axen'θjarse] *vr* to obtain, procure

agenda [a'xenda] *nf* diary

agente [a'xente] *nm/f* agent; (*de policía*) policeman/policewoman; **~ inmobiliario** estate agent (*BRIT*), realtor (*US*); **~ de seguros** insurance agent

ágil ['axil] *adj* agile, nimble; **agilidad** *nf* agility, nimbleness

agilizar [axili'θar] *vt* (*trámites*) to speed up

agitación [axita'θjon] *nf* (*de mano etc*) shaking, waving; (*de líquido etc*) stirring; (*fig*) agitation

agitado, a [axi'taðo, a] *adj* hectic; (*viaje*) bumpy

agitar [axi'tar] *vt* to wave, shake; (*líquido*) to stir; (*fig*) to stir up, excite; **~se** *vr* to get excited; (*inquietarse*) to get worried o upset

aglomeración [aɣlomera'θjon] *nf*: **~ de tráfico/gente** traffic jam/mass of people

aglomerar [aɣlome'rar] *vt* to crowd together; **~se** *vr* to crowd together

agnóstico, a [aɣ'nostiko, a] *adj*, *nm/f* agnostic

agobiar [aɣo'βjar] *vt* to weigh down; (*oprimir*) to oppress; (*cargar*) to burden

agolparse [aɣol'parse] *vr* to crowd together

agonía [aɣo'nia] *nf* death throes *pl*; (*fig*) agony, anguish

agonizante [aɣoni'θante] *adj* dying

agonizar [aɣoni'θar] *vi* to be dying

agosto [a'ɣosto] *nm* August

agotado, a [aɣo'taðo, a] *adj* (*persona*) exhausted; (*libros*) out of print; (*acabado*) finished; (*COM*) sold out

agotador, a [aɣota'ðor, a] *adj* exhausting

agotamiento [aɣota'mjento] *nm* exhaustion

agotar [aɣo'tar] *vt* to exhaust; (*consumir*) to drain; (*recursos*) to use up, deplete; **~se** *vr* to be exhausted; (*acabarse*) to run out; (*libro*) to go out of print

agraciado, a [aɣra'θjaðo, a] *adj* (*atractivo*) attractive; (*en sorteo etc*) lucky

agradable [aɣra'ðaβle] *adj* pleasant, nice

agradar [aɣra'ðar] *vt*: **él me agrada** I like him

agradecer [aɣraðe'θer] *vt* to thank; (*favor etc*) to be grateful for; **agradecido, a** *adj* grateful; **¡muy agradecido!** thanks a lot!; **agradecimiento** *nm* thanks *pl*; gratitude

agradezco *etc vb ver* **agradecer**

agrado [a'ɣraðo] *nm*: **ser de tu etc ~** to be to your *etc* liking

agrandar [aɣran'dar] *vt* to enlarge; (*fig*) to exaggerate; **~se** *vr* to get bigger

agrario, a [a'ɣrarjo, a] *adj* agrarian, land *cpd*; (*política*) agricultural, farming

agravante [aɣra'βante] *adj* aggravating ♦ *nm*: **con el ~ de que ...** with the further difficulty that ...

agravar [aɣra'ßar] vt (pesar sobre) to make heavier; (irritar) to aggravate; ~se vr to worsen, get worse

agraviar [aɣra'ßjar] vt to offend; (ser injusto con) to wrong; ~se vr to take offence; **agravio** nm offence; wrong; (JUR) grievance

agredir [aɣre'ðir] vt to attack

agregado, a [aɣre'ɣaðo, a] nm/f: A~ ≈ teacher (who is not head of department) ♦ nm aggregate; (persona) attaché

agregar [aɣre'ɣar] vt to gather; (añadir) to add; (persona) to appoint

agresión [aɣre'sjon] nf aggression

agresivo, a [aɣre'sißo, a] adj aggressive

agriar [a'ɣrjar] vt to (turn) sour; ~se vr to turn sour

agrícola [a'ɣrikola] adj farming cpd, agricultural

agricultor, a [aɣrikul'tor, a] nm/f farmer

agricultura [aɣrikul'tura] nf agriculture, farming

agridulce [aɣri'ðulθe] adj bittersweet; (CULIN) sweet and sour

agrietarse [aɣrje'tarse] vr to crack; (piel) to chap

agrimensor, a [aɣrimen'sor, a] nm/f surveyor

agrio, a [ˈaɣrjo, a] adj bitter

agrupación [aɣrupa'θjon] nf group; (acto) grouping

agrupar [aɣru'par] vt to group

agua [ˈaɣwa] nf water; (NAUT) slope of a roof; ~s nfpl (de piedra) water sg, sparkle sg; (MED) water sg, urine sg; (NAUT) waters; ~s abajo/arriba downstream/ upstream; ~ bendita/destilada/potable holy/ distilled/drinking water; ~ caliente hot water; ~ corriente running water; ~ de colonia eau de cologne; ~ mineral (con/sin gas) (carbonated/uncarbonated) mineral water; ~ oxigenada hydrogen peroxide; ~s jurisdiccionales territorial waters

aguacate [aɣwa'kate] nm avocado (pear)

aguacero [aɣwa'θero] nm (heavy) shower, downpour

aguado, a [a'ɣwaðo, a] adj watery, watered down

aguafiestas [aɣwa'fjestas] nm/f inv spoilsport, killjoy

aguanieve [aɣwa'njeße] nf sleet

aguantar [aɣwan'tar] vt to bear, put up with; (sostener) to hold up ♦ vi to last; ~se vr to restrain o.s.; **aguante** nm (paciencia) patience; (resistencia) endurance

aguar [a'ɣwar] vt to water down

aguardar [aɣwar'ðar] vt to wait for

aguardiente [aɣwar'ðjente] nm brandy, liquor

aguarrás [aɣwa'rras] nm turpentine

agudeza [aɣu'ðeθa] nf sharpness; (ingenio) wit

agudizar [aɣuði'θar] vt (crisis) to make worse; ~se vr to get worse

agudo, a [a'ɣuðo, a] adj sharp; (voz) high-pitched, piercing; (dolor, enfermedad) acute

agüero [a'ɣwero] nm: **buen/mal** ~ good/bad omen

aguijón [aɣi'xon] nm sting; (fig) spur

águila [ˈaɣila] nf eagle; (fig) genius

aguileño, a [aɣi'leɲo, a] adj (nariz) aquiline; (rostro) sharp-featured

aguinaldo [aɣi'naldo] nm Christmas box

aguja [a'ɣuxa] nf needle; (de reloj) hand; (ARQ) spire; (TEC) firing-pin; ~s nfpl (ZOOL) ribs; (FERRO) points

agujerear [aɣuxere'ar] vt to make holes in

agujero [aɣu'xero] nm hole

agujetas [aɣu'xetas] nfpl stitch sg; (rigidez) stiffness sg

aguzar [aɣu'θar] vt to sharpen; (fig) to incite

ahí [a'i] adv there; **de ~ que** so that, with the result that; ~ **llega** here he comes; **por ~ that way; (allá) over there; 200 o por ~ 200 or so

ahijado, a [ai'xaðo, a] nm/f godson/daughter

ahínco [a'inko] nm earnestness

ahogar [ao'ɣar] vt to drown; (asfixiar) to suffocate, smother; (fuego) to put out; ~se vr (en el agua) to drown; (por asfixia) to suffocate

ahogo [a'oɣo] nm breathlessness; (fig) financial difficulty

ahondar [aon'dar] vt to deepen, make deeper; (fig) to study thoroughly ♦ vi: ~ en to study thoroughly

ahora [a'ora] adv now; (hace poco) a moment ago, just now; (dentro de poco) in a moment; ~ **voy** I'm coming; ~ **mismo** right now; ~ **bien** now then; **por ~ for the present

ahorcar [aor'kar] vt to hang

ahorita [ao'rita] (fam: esp AM) adv right now

ahorrar [ao'rrar] vt (dinero) to save; (esfuerzos) to save, avoid; **ahorro** nm (acto) saving; **ahorros** nmpl (dinero) savings

ahuecar [awe'kar] vt to hollow (out); (voz) to deepen; ~se vr to give o.s. airs

ahumar [au'mar] vt to smoke, cure; (llenar de humo) to fill with smoke ♦ vi to smoke; ~se vr to fill with smoke

ahuyentar [aujen'tar] vt to drive off, frighten off; (fig) to dispel

airado, a [ai'raðo, a] adj angry

airar [ai'rar] vt to anger; ~se vr to get angry

aire [ˈaire] nm air; (viento) wind; (corriente) draught; (MUS) tune; ~s nmpl: **darse ~s** to give o.s. airs; **al ~ libre** in the open air; ~ **acondicionado** air conditioning; **airearse** vr (persona) to go out for a breath of fresh air;

airoso, a *adj* windy; draughty; (*fig*) graceful

aislado, a [ais'laðo, a] *adj* isolated; (*incomunicado*) cut-off; (*ELEC*) insulated

aislar [ais'lar] *vt* to isolate; (*ELEC*) to insulate

ajardinado, a [axarði'naðo, a] *adj* landscaped

ajedrez [axe'ðreθ] *nm* chess

ajeno, a [a'xeno, a] *adj* (*que pertenece a otro*) somebody else's; ~ a foreign to

ajetreado, a [axetre'aðo, a] *adj* busy

ajetreo [axe'treo] *nm* bustle

ají [a'xi] (*AM*) *nm* chil(l)i, red pepper; (*salsa*) chil(l)i sauce

ajillo [a'xiλo] *nm*: **gambas al ~** garlic prawns

ajo ['axo] *nm* garlic

ajuar [a'xwar] *nm* household furnishings *pl*; (*de novia*) trousseau; (*de niño*) layette

ajustado, a [axus'taðo, a] *adj* (*tornillo*) tight; (*cálculo*) right; (*ropa*) tight(-fitting); (*resultado*) close

ajustar [axus'tar] *vt* (*adaptar*) to adjust; (*encajar*) to fit; (*TEC*) to engage; (*IMPRENTA*) to make up; (*apretar*) to tighten; (*concertar*) to agree (on); (*reconciliar*) to reconcile; (*cuentas, deudas*) to settle ♦ *vi* to fit; ~se *vr*: ~se a (*precio etc*) to be in keeping with, fit in with; ~ las cuentas a uno to get even with sb

ajuste [a'xuste] *nm* adjustment; (*COSTURA*) fitting; (*acuerdo*) compromise; (*de cuenta*) settlement

al [al] (= a + el) *ver* a

ala ['ala] *nf* wing; (*de sombrero*) brim; (*futbolista*) winger; ~ **delta** *nf* hang-glider

alabanza [ala'ßanθa] *nf* praise

alabar [ala'ßar] *vt* to praise

alacena [ala'θena] *nf* kitchen cupboard (*BRIT*), kitchen closet (*US*)

alacrán [ala'kran] *nm* scorpion

alambique [alam'bike] *nm* still

alambrada [alam'braða] *nf* wire fence; (*red*) wire netting

alambrado [alam'braðo] *nm* = **alambrada**

alambre [a'lambre] *nm* wire; ~ **de púas** barbed wire

alameda [ala'meða] *nf* (*plantío*) poplar grove; (*lugar de paseo*) avenue, boulevard

álamo ['alamo] *nm* poplar; ~ **temblón** aspen

alarde [a'larðe] *nm* show, display; **hacer ~ de** to boast of

alargador [alarxa'ðor] *nm* (*ELEC*) extension lead

alargar [alar'xar] *vt* to lengthen, extend; (*paso*) to hasten; (*brazo*) to stretch out; (*cuerda*) to pay out; (*conversación*) to spin out; ~se *vr* to get longer

alarido [ala'riðo] *nm* shriek

alarma [a'larma] *nf* alarm

alarmar *vt* to alarm; ~se to get alarmed; **alarmante** [alar'mante] *adj* alarming

alba ['alßa] *nf* dawn

albacea [alßa'θea] *nm/f* executor/executrix

albahaca [al'ßaka] *nf* basil

Albania [al'ßanja] *nf* Albania

albañil [alßa'ɲil] *nm* bricklayer; (*cantero*) mason

albarán [alßa'ran] *nm* (*COM*) delivery note, invoice

albaricoque [alßari'koke] *nm* apricot

albedrío [alße'ðrio] *nm*: **libre ~** free will

alberca [al'ßerka] *nf* reservoir; (*AM*) swimming pool

albergar [alßer'var] *vt* to shelter

albergue *etc* [al'ßerve] *vb ver* **albergar** ♦ *nm* shelter, refuge; ~ **juvenil** youth hostel

albóndiga [al'ßondixa] *nf* meatball

albornoz [alßor'noθ] *nm* (*de los árabes*) burnous; (*para el baño*) bathrobe

alborotar [alßoro'tar] *vi* to make a row ♦ *vt* to agitate, stir up; ~se *vr* to get excited; (*mar*) to get rough; **alboroto** *nm* row, uproar

alborozar [alßoro'θar] *vt* to gladden; ~se *vr* to rejoice

alborozo [alßo'roθo] *nm* joy

álbum ['alßum] (*pl* ~**s**, ~**es**) *nm* album; ~ **de recortes** scrapbook

alcachofa [alka'tʃofa] *nf* artichoke

alcalde, esa [al'kalde, esa] *nm/f* mayor(ess)

alcaldía [alkal'dia] *nf* mayoralty; (*lugar*) mayor's office

alcance *etc* [al'kanθe] *vb ver* **alcanzar** ♦ *nm* reach; (*COM*) adverse balance

alcantarilla [alkanta'riλa] *nf* (*de aguas cloacales*) sewer; (*en la calle*) gutter

alcanzar [alkan'θar] *vt* (*algo: con la mano, el pie*) to reach; (*alguien: en el camino etc*) to catch up (with); (*autobús*) to catch; (*suj: bala*) to hit, strike ♦ *vi* (*ser suficiente*) to be enough; ~ a hacer to manage to do

alcaparra [alka'parra] *nf* caper

alcayata [alka'jata] *nf* hook

alcázar [al'kaðar] *nm* fortress; (*NAUT*) quarter-deck

alcoba [al'koßa] *nf* bedroom

alcohol [al'kol] *nm* alcohol; ~ **metílico** methylated spirits *pl* (*BRIT*), wood alcohol (*US*); **alcohólico, a** *adj*, *nm/f* alcoholic

alcoholímetro [alko'limetro] *nm* Breathalyser ® (*BRIT*), drunkometer (*US*)

alcoholismo [alko'lismo] *nm* alcoholism

alcornoque [alkor'noke] *nm* cork tree; (*fam*) idiot

alcurnia [al'kurnja] *nf* lineage

aldaba [al'daßa] *nf* (*door*) knocker

aldea [al'dea] *nf* village; ~**no, a** *adj* village *cpd* ♦ *nm/f* villager

aleación [alea'θjon] *nf* alloy

aleatorio, a [alea'torjo, a] *adj* random

aleccionar [alek0jo'nar] vt to instruct; (adiestrar) to train

alegación [aleɣa'θjon] nf allegation

alegar [ale'ɣar] vt to claim; (JUR) to plead ♦ vi (AM) to argue

alegato [ale'ɣato] nm (JUR) allegation; (AM) argument

alegoría [aleɣo'ria] nf allegory

alegrar [ale'ɣrar] vt (causar alegría) to cheer (up); (fuego) to poke; (fiesta) to liven up; ~se vr (fam) to get merry o tight; ~se de to be glad about

alegre [a'leɣre] adj happy, cheerful; (fam) merry, tight; (chiste) risqué, blue; **alegría** nf happiness; merriment

alejamiento [alexa'mjento] nm removal; (distancia) remoteness

alejar [ale'xar] vt to remove; (fig) to estrange; ~se vr to move away

alemán, ana [ale'man, ana] adj, nm/f German ♦ nm (LING) German

Alemania [ale'manja] nf: ~ Occidental/ Oriental West/East Germany

alentador, a [alenta'ðor, a] adj encouraging

alentar [alen'tar] vt to encourage

alergia [a'lerxja] nf allergy

alero [a'lero] nm (de tejado) eaves pl; (de carruaje) mudguard

alerta [a'lerta] adj, nm alert

aleta [a'leta] nf (de pez) fin; (de ave) wing; (de foca, DEPORTE) flipper; (AUTO) mudguard

aletargar [aletar'ɣar] vt to make drowsy; (entumecer) to make numb; ~se vr to grow drowsy; to become numb

aletear [alete'ar] vi to flutter

alevín [ale'ßin] nm fry, young fish

alevosía [aleßo'sia] nf treachery

alfabeto [alfa'ßeto] nm alphabet

alfalfa [al'falfa] nf alfalfa, lucerne

alfarería [alfare'ria] nf pottery; (tienda) pottery shop; **alfarero, a** nm/f potter

alféizar [al'feiθar] nm window-sill

alférez [al'fereθ] nm (MIL) second lieutenant; (NAUT) ensign

alfil [al'fil] nm (AJEDREZ) bishop

alfiler [alfi'ler] nm pin; (broche) clip

alfiletero [alfile'tero] nm needlecase

alfombra [al'fombra] nf carpet; (más pequeña) rug; **alfombrar** vt to carpet; **alfombrilla** nf rug, mat; (INFORM) mouse mat o pad

alforja [al'forxa] nf saddlebag

algarabía [alɣara'ßia] (fam) nf gibberish; (griterío) hullabaloo

algas ['alɣas] nfpl seaweed

álgebra ['alxeßra] nf algebra

álgido, a ['alxiðo, a] adj (momento etc) crucial, decisive

algo ['alɣo] pron something; anything ♦ adv somewhat, rather; ¿~ más? anything else?; (en tienda) is that all?; por ~ será there must be some reason for it

algodón [alɣo'ðon] nm cotton; (planta) cotton plant; ~ de azúcar candy floss (BRIT), cotton candy (US); ~ hidrófilo cotton wool (BRIT), absorbent cotton (US)

algodonero, a [alɣoðo'nero, a] adj cotton cpd ♦ nm/f cotton grower ♦ nm cotton plant

alguacil [alɣwa'θil] nm bailiff; (TAUR) mounted official

alguien ['alxjen] pron someone, somebody; (en frases interrogativas) anyone, anybody

alguno, a [al'ɣuno, a] adj (delante de nm: algún) some; (después de n): no tiene talento ~ he has no talent, he doesn't have any talent ♦ pron (alguien) someone, somebody; algún que otro libro some book or other; algún día iré I'll go one o some day; sin interés ~ without the slightest interest; ~ que otro an occasional one; ~s piensan some (people) think

alhaja [a'laxa] nf jewel; (tesoro) precious object, treasure

alhelí [ale'li] nm wallflower, stock

aliado, a [a'ljaðo, a] adj allied

alianza [a'ljanθa] nf alliance; (anillo) wedding ring

aliar [a'ljar] vt to ally; ~se vr to form an alliance

alias ['aljas] adv alias

alicates [ali'kates] nmpl pliers; ~ de uñas nail clippers

aliciente [ali'θjente] nm incentive; (atracción) attraction

alienación [aljena'θjon] nf alienation

aliento [a'ljento] nm breath; (respiración) breathing; sin ~ breathless

aligerar [alixe'rar] vt to lighten; (reducir) to shorten; (aliviar) to alleviate; (mitigar) to ease; (paso) to quicken

alijo [a'lixo] nm consignment

alimaña [ali'maɲa] nf pest

alimentación [alimenta'θjon] nf (comida) food; (acción) feeding; (tienda) grocer's (shop); **alimentador** nm: **alimentador de papel** sheet-feeder

alimentar [alimen'tar] vt to feed; (nutrir) to nourish; ~se vr to feed

alimenticio, a [alimen'tiθjo, a] adj food cpd; (nutritivo) nourishing, nutritious

alimento [ali'mento] nm food; (nutrición) nourishment

alineación [alinea'θjon] nf alignment; (DEPORTE) line-up

alinear [aline'ar] vt to align; ~se vr (DEPORTE) to line up; ~se en to fall in with

aliñar [ali'ɲar] vt (CULIN) to season; **aliño** nm (CULIN) dressing

alioli [ali'oli] *nm* garlic mayonnaise

alisar [ali'sar] *vt* to smooth

aliso [a'liso] *nm* alder

alistarse [alis'tarse] *vr* to enlist; *(inscribirse)* to enrol

aliviar [ali'βjar] *vt (carga)* to lighten; *(persona)* to relieve; *(dolor)* to relieve, alleviate

alivio [a'liβjo] *nm* alleviation, relief

aljibe [al'xiβe] *nm* cistern

allá [a'ʎa] *adv (lugar)* there; *(por ahí)* over there; *(tiempo)* then; ~ **abajo** down there; **más** ~ further on; **más** ~ **de** beyond; **¡~ tú!** that's your problem!

allanamiento [aʎana'mjento] *nm*: ~ **de morada** burglary

allanar [aʎa'nar] *vt* to flatten, level (out); *(igualar)* to smooth (out); *(fig)* to subdue; *(JUR)* to burgle, break into

allegado, a [aʎe'ɣaðo, a] *adj* near, close ♦ *nm/f* relation

allí [a'ʎi] *adv* there; ~ **mismo** right there; **por** ~ over there; *(por ese camino)* that way

alma ['alma] *nf* soul; *(persona)* person

almacén [alma'θen] *nm (depósito)* warehouse, store; *(MIL)* magazine; *(AM)* shop; **(grandes) almacenes** *nmpl* department store *sg;* **almacenaje** *nm* storage

almacenar [almaθe'nar] *vt* to store, put in storage; *(proveerse)* to stock up with; **almacenero** *nm (AM)* shopkeeper

almanaque [alma'nake] *nm* almanac

almeja [al'mexa] *nf* clam

almendra [al'mendra] *nf* almond; **almendro** *nm* almond tree

almíbar [al'miβar] *nm* syrup

almidón [almi'ðon] *nm* starch; **almidonar** *vt* to starch

almirante [almi'rante] *nm* admiral

almirez [almi'reθ] *nm* mortar

almizcle [al'miθkle] *nm* musk

almohada [almo'aða] *nf* pillow; *(funda)* pillowcase; **almohadilla** *nf* cushion; *(TEC)* pad; *(AM)* pincushion

almohadón [almoa'ðon] *nm* large pillow; bolster

almorranas [almo'rranas] *nfpl* piles, haemorrhoids

almorzar [almor'θar] *vt*: ~ **una tortilla** to have an omelette for lunch ♦ *vi* to (have) lunch

almuerzo *etc* [al'mwerθo] *vb ver* **almorzar** ♦ *nm* lunch

alocado, a [alo'kaðo, a] *adj* crazy

alojamiento [aloxa'mjento] *nm* lodging(s) *(pl);* *(viviendas)* housing

alojar [alo'xar] *vt* to lodge; ~**se** *vr* to lodge, stay

alondra [a'londra] *nf* lark, skylark

alpargata [alpar'ɣata] *nf* rope-soled sandal, espadrille

Alpes ['alpes] *nmpl:* **los** ~ the Alps

alpinismo [alpi'nismo] *nm* mountaineering, climbing; **alpinista** *nm/f* mountaineer, climber

alpiste [al'piste] *nm* birdseed

alquilar [alki'lar] *vt (suj: propietario: inmuebles)* to let, rent (out); *(: coche)* to hire out; *(: TV)* to rent (out); *(suj: alquilador: inmuebles, TV)* to rent; *(: coche)* to hire; **"se alquila casa"** "house to let *(BRIT)* o for rent *(US)*"

alquiler [alki'ler] *nm* renting; letting; hiring; *(arriendo)* rent; hire charge; ~ **de automóviles** car hire; **de** ~ for hire

alquimia [al'kimja] *nf* alchemy

alquitrán [alki'tran] *nm* tar

alrededor [alreðe'ðor] *adv* around, about; ~ **de** around, about; **mirar a su** ~ to look (round) about one; ~**es** *nmpl* surroundings

alta ['alta] *nf (certificate of) discharge;* **dar de** ~ to discharge

altanería [altane'ria] *nf* haughtiness, arrogance; **altanero, a** *adj* arrogant, haughty

altar [al'tar] *nm* altar

altavoz [alta'βoθ] *nm* loudspeaker; *(amplificador)* amplifier

alteración [altera'θjon] *nf* alteration; *(alboroto)* disturbance

alterar [alte'rar] *vt* to alter; to disturb; ~**se** *vr (persona)* to get upset

altercado [alter'kaðo] *nm* argument

alternar [alter'nar] *vt* to alternate ♦ *vi* to alternate; *(turnar)* to take turns; ~**se** *vr* to alternate; to take turns; ~ **con** to mix with; **alternativa** *nf* alternative; *(elección)* choice; **alternativo, a** *adj* alternative; *(alterno)* alternating; **alterno, a** *adj* alternate; *(ELEC)* alternating

Alteza [al'teθa] *nf (tratamiento)* Highness

altibajos [alti'βaxos] *nmpl* ups and downs

altiplanicie [altipla'niθje] *nf* high plateau

altiplano [alti'plano] *nm* = **altiplanicie**

altisonante [altiso'nante] *adj* high-flown, high-sounding

altitud [alti'tuð] *nf* height; *(AVIAT, GEO)* altitude

altivez [alti'βeθ] *nf* haughtiness, arrogance; **altivo, a** *adj* haughty, arrogant

alto, a ['alto, a] *adj* high; *(persona)* tall; *(sonido)* high, sharp; *(noble)* high, lofty ♦ *nm* halt; *(MUS)* alto; *(GEO)* hill; *(AM)* pile ♦ *adv (de sitio)* high; *(de sonido)* loud, loudly ♦ *excl* halt!; **la pared tiene 2 metros de** ~ the wall is 2 metres high; **en alta mar** on the high seas; **en voz alta** in a loud voice; **las altas horas de la noche** the small o wee hours; **en lo** ~ **de** at

the top of; **pasar por ~** to overlook
altoparlante [altopar'lante] (*AM*) *nm*
loudspeaker
altruismo [altru'ismo] *nm* altruism
altura [al'tura] *nf* height; (*NAUT*) depth; (*GEO*)
latitude; **la pared tiene 1.80 de ~** the wall is 1
metre 80cm high; **a estas ~s** at this stage; **a
estas ~s del año** at this time of the year
alubia [a'luβja] *nf* bean
alucinación [aluθina'θjon] *nf* hallucination
alucinar [aluθi'nar] *vi* to hallucinate ♦ *vt* to
deceive; (*fascinar*) to fascinate
alud [a'luð] *nm* avalanche; (*fig*) flood
aludir [alu'ðir] *vi*: **~ a** to allude to; **darse por
aludido** to take the hint
alumbrado [alum'braðo] *nm* lighting;
alumbramiento *nm* lighting; (*MED*)
childbirth, delivery
alumbrar [alum'brar] *vt* to light (up) ♦ *vi*
(*MED*) to give birth
aluminio [alu'minjo] *nm* aluminium (*BRIT*),
aluminum (*US*)
alumno, a [a'lumno, a] *nm/f* pupil, student
alunizar [aluni'θar] *vi* to land on the moon
alusión [alu'sjon] *nf* allusion
alusivo, a [alu'siβo, a] *adj* allusive
aluvión [alu'βjon] *nm* alluvium; (*fig*) flood
alverja [al'βerxa] (*AM*) *nf* pea
alza [ˈalθa] *nf* rise; (*MIL*) sight
alzada [al'θaða] *nf* (*de caballos*) height; (*JUR*)
appeal
alzamiento [alθa'mjento] *nm* (*rebelión*)
rising
alzar [al'θar] *vt* to lift (up); (*precio, muro*) to
raise; (*cuello de abrigo*) to turn up; (*AGR*) to
gather in; (*IMPRENTA*) to gather; **~se** *vr* to get
up, rise; (*rebelarse*) to revolt; (*COM*) to go
fraudulently bankrupt; (*JUR*) to appeal
ama [ˈama] *nf* lady of the house; (*dueña*)
owner; (*institutriz*) governess; (*madre
adoptiva*) foster mother; **~ de casa** housewife;
~ de llaves housekeeper
amabilidad [amaβili'ðað] *nf* kindness;
(*simpatía*) niceness; **amable** *adj* kind; nice;
es usted muy amable that's very kind of you
amaestrado, a [amaes'traðo, a] *adj*
(*animal: en circo etc*) performing
amaestrar [amaes'trar] *vt* to train
amago [a'maxo] *nm* threat; (*gesto*)
threatening gesture; (*MED*) symptom
amainar [amai'nar] *vi* (*viento*) to die down
amalgama [amal'xama] *nf* amalgam;
amalgamar *vt* to amalgamate; (*combinar*)
to combine, mix
amamantar [amaman'tar] *vt* to suckle,
nurse
amanecer [amane'θer] *vi* to dawn ♦ *nm*
dawn; **~ afiebrado** to wake up with a fever
amanerado, a [amane'raðo, a] *adj* affected

amansar [aman'sar] *vt* to tame; (*persona*) to
subdue; **~se** *vr* (*persona*) to calm down
amante [a'mante] *adj*: **~ de** fond of ♦ *nm/f*
lover
amapola [ama'pola] *nf* poppy
amar [a'mar] *vt* to love
amargado, a [amar'xaðo, a] *adj* bitter
amargar [amar'xar] *vt* to make bitter; (*fig*) to
embitter; **~se** *vr* to become embittered
amargo, a [a'marxo, a] *adj* bitter;
amargura *nf* bitterness
amarillento, a [amari'Áento, a] *adj*
yellowish; (*tez*) sallow; **amarillo, a** *adj, nm*
yellow
amarrar [ama'rrar] *vt* to moor; (*sujetar*) to
tie up
amarras [a'marras] *nfpl*: **soltar ~** to set sail
amasar [ama'sar] *vt* (*masa*) to knead;
(*mezclar*) to mix, prepare; (*confeccionar*) to
concoct; **amasijo** *nm* kneading; mixing;
(*fig*) hotchpotch
amateur [ˈamatur] *nm/f* amateur
amazona [ama'θona] *nf* horsewoman; **A~s**
nm: **el A~s** the Amazon
ambages [am'baxes] *nmpl*: **sin ~** in plain
language
ámbar [ˈambar] *nm* amber
ambición [ambi'θjon] *nf* ambition;
ambicionar *vt* to aspire to; **ambicioso, a**
adj ambitious
ambidextro, a [ambi'ðekstro, a] *adj*
ambidextrous
ambientación [ambjenta'θjon] *nf* (*CINE,
TEATRO etc*) setting; (*RADIO*) sound effects
ambiente [am'bjente] *nm* (*tb fig*)
atmosphere; (*medio*) environment
ambigüedad [ambixwe'ðað] *nf* ambiguity;
ambiguo, a *adj* ambiguous
ámbito [ˈambito] *nm* (*campo*) field; (*fig*)
scope
ambos, as [ˈambos, as] *adj pl, pron pl* both
ambulancia [ambu'lanθja] *nf* ambulance
ambulante [ambu'lante] *adj* travelling *cpd*,
itinerant
ambulatorio [ambula'torjo] *nm* state
health-service clinic
amedrentar [ameðren'tar] *vt* to scare
amén [a'men] *excl* amen; **~ de** besides
amenaza [ame'naθa] *nf* threat
amenazar [amena'θar] *vt* to threaten ♦ *vi*:
~ con hacer to threaten to do
amenidad [ameni'ðað] *nf* pleasantness
ameno, a [a'meno, a] *adj* pleasant
América [a'merika] *nf* America; **~ del Norte/
del Sur** North/South America; **~ Central/
Latina** Central/Latin America; **americana** *nf*
coat, jacket; *ver tb* **americano; americano, a**
adj, nm/f American
amerizar [ameri'θar] *vi* (*avión*) to land (on

the sea)

ametralladora [ametraʎaˈðora] nf machine gun

amianto [aˈmjanto] nm asbestos

amigable [amiˈvaßle] adj friendly

amígdala [aˈmivðala] nf tonsil; **amigdalitis** nf tonsillitis

amigo, a [aˈmivo, a] adj friendly ♦ nm/f friend; (amante) lover; **ser ~ de algo** to be fond of sth; **ser muy ~s** to be close friends

amilanar [amilaˈnar] vt to scare; **~se** vr to get scared

aminorar [aminoˈrar] vt to diminish; (reducir) to reduce; **~ la marcha** to slow down

amistad [amisˈtað] nf friendship; **~es** nfpl (amigos) friends; **amistoso, a** adj friendly

amnesia [amˈnesja] nf amnesia

amnistía [amnisˈtia] nf amnesty

amo [ˈamo] nm owner; (jefe) boss

amodorrarse [amoðoˈrrarse] vr to get sleepy

amoldar [amolˈdar] vt to mould; (adaptar) to adapt

amonestación [amonestaˈθjon] nf warning; **amonestaciones** nfpl (REL) marriage banns

amonestar [amonesˈtar] vt to warn; (REL) to publish the banns of

amontonar [amontoˈnar] vt to collect, pile up; **~se** vr to crowd together; (acumularse) to pile up

amor [aˈmor] nm love; (amante) lover; **hacer el ~** to make love; **~ propio** self-respect

amoratado, a [amoraˈtaðo, a] adj purple

amordazar [amorðaˈθar] vt to muzzle; (fig) to gag

amorfo, a [aˈmorfo, a] adj amorphous, shapeless

amoroso, a [amoˈroso, a] adj affectionate, loving

amortajar [amortaˈxar] vt to shroud

amortiguador [amortigwaˈðor] nm shock absorber; (parachoques) bumper; **~es** nmpl (AUTO) suspension sg

amortiguar [amortiˈɣwar] vt to deaden; (ruido) to muffle; (color) to soften

amortización [amortiθaˈθjon] nf (de deuda) repayment; (de bono) redemption

amotinar [amotiˈnar] vt to stir up, incite (to riot); **~se** vr to mutiny

amparar [ampaˈrar] vt to protect; **~se** vr to seek protection; (de la lluvia etc) to shelter; **amparo** nm help, protection; **al amparo de** under the protection of

amperio [amˈperjo] nm ampère, amp

ampliación [ampljaˈθjon] nf enlargement; (extensión) extension

ampliar [amˈpljar] vt to enlarge; to extend

amplificación [amplifikaˈθjon] nf enlargement; **amplificador** nm amplifier

amplificar [amplifiˈkar] vt to amplify

amplio, a [ˈampljo, a] adj spacious; (de falda etc) full; (extenso) extensive; (ancho) wide; **amplitud** nf spaciousness; extent; (fig) amplitude

ampolla [amˈpoʎa] nf blister; (MED) ampoule

ampuloso, a [ampuˈloso, a] adj bombastic, pompous

amputar [ampuˈtar] vt to cut off, amputate

amueblar [amweˈßlar] vt to furnish

amurallar [amuraˈʎar] vt to wall up o in

anacronismo [anakroˈnismo] nm anachronism

anales [aˈnales] nmpl annals

analfabetismo [analfaßeˈtismo] nm illiteracy; **analfabeto, a** adj, nm/f illiterate

analgésico [analˈxesiko] nm painkiller, analgesic

análisis [aˈnalisis] nm inv analysis

analista [anaˈlista] nm/f (gen) analyst

analizar [analiˈθar] vt to analyse

analogía [analoˈxia] nf analogy

analógico, a [anaˈloxiko, a] adj (INFORM) analog; (reloj) analogue (BRIT), analog (US)

análogo, a [aˈnalovo, a] adj analogous, similar

ananá(s) [anaˈna(s)] (AM) nm pineapple

anaquel [anaˈkel] nm shelf

anarquía [anarˈkia] nf anarchy; **anarquismo** nm anarchism; **anarquista** nm/f anarchist

anatomía [anatoˈmia] nf anatomy

anca [ˈanka] nf rump, haunch; **~s** nfpl (fam) behind sg

ancho, a [ˈantʃo, a] adj wide; (falda) full; (fig) liberal ♦ nm width; (FERRO) gauge; **ponerse ~** to get conceited; **estar a sus anchas** to be at one's ease

anchoa [anˈtʃoa] nf anchovy

anchura [anˈtʃura] nf width; (extensión) wideness

anciano, a [anˈθjano, a] adj old, aged ♦ nm/f old man/woman; elder

ancla [ˈankla] nf anchor; **~dero** nm anchorage; **anclar** vi to (drop) anchor

andadura [andaˈðura] nf gait; (de caballo) pace

Andalucía [andaluˈθia] nf Andalusia; **andaluz, a** adj, nm/f Andalusian

andamiaje [andaˈmjaxe] nm = andamio

andamio [anˈdamjo] nm scaffold(ing)

andar [anˈdar] vt to go, cover, travel ♦ vi to go, walk, travel; (funcionar) to go, work; (estar) to be ♦ nm walk, gait, pace; **~se** vr to go away; **~ a pie/a caballo/en bicicleta** to go on foot/on horseback/by bicycle; **~ haciendo algo** to be doing sth; **¡anda!** (sorpresa) go on!; **anda por o en los 40** he's about 40

andén [anˈden] nm (FERRO) platform; (NAUT) quayside; (AM: de la calle) pavement (BRIT), sidewalk (US)

Andes ['andes] nmpl: **los ~** the Andes

Andorra [an'dorra] nf Andorra

andrajo [an'draxo] nm rag; **~so, a** adj ragged

anduve etc [an'duße] vb ver **andar**

anécdota [a'nekðota] nf anecdote, story

anegar [ane'xar] vt to flood; (ahogar) to drown; **~se** vr to drown; (hundirse) to sink

anejo, a [a'nexo, a] adj, nm = **anexo**

anemia [a'nemja] nf anaemia

anestesia [anes'tesja] nf (sustancia) anaesthetic; (proceso) anaesthesia

anexar [anek'sar] vt to annex; (documento) to attach; **anexión** nf annexation; **anexionamiento** nm annexation; **anexo, a** adj attached ♦ nm annexe

anfibio, a [an'fißjo, a] adj amphibious ♦ nm amphibian

anfiteatro [anfite'atro] nm amphitheatre; (TEATRO) dress circle

anfitrión, ona [anfi'trjon, ona] nm/f host(ess)

ángel ['anxel] nm angel; **~ de la guarda** guardian angel; **tener ~** to be charming; **angelical** adj, **angélico, a** adj angelic(al)

angina [an'xina] nf (MED) inflammation of the throat; **~ de pecho** angina; **tener ~s** to have tonsillitis

anglicano, a [angli'kano, a] adj, nm/f Anglican

anglosajón, ona [anglosa'xon, ona] adj Anglo-Saxon

angosto, a [an'gosto, a] adj narrow

anguila [an'gila] nf eel

angula [an'gula] nf elver, baby eel

ángulo ['angulo] nm angle; (esquina) corner; (curva) bend

angustia [an'gustja] nf anguish; **angustiar** vt to distress, grieve

anhelar [ane'lar] vt to be eager for; (desear) to long for, desire ♦ vi to pant, gasp; **anhelo** nm eagerness; desire

anidar [ani'ðar] vi to nest

anillo [a'niʎo] nm ring; **~ de boda** wedding ring

animación [anima'θjon] nf liveliness; (vitalidad) life; (actividad) activity; bustle

animado, a [ani'maðo, a] adj lively; (vivaz) animated; **animador, a** nm/f (TV) host(ess), compère; (DEPORTE) cheerleader

animadversión [animaðßer'sjon] nf ill-will, antagonism

animal [ani'mal] adj animal; (fig) stupid ♦ nm (fig) fool; (bestia) brute

animar [ani'mar] vt (BIO) to animate, give life to; (fig) to liven up, brighten up, cheer up; (estimular) to stimulate; **~se** vr to cheer up; to feel encouraged; (decidirse) to make up

one's mind

ánimo ['animo] nm (alma) soul; (mente) mind; (valentía) courage ♦ excl cheer up!

animoso, a [ani'moso, a] adj brave; (vivo) lively

aniquilar [aniki'lar] vt to annihilate, destroy

anís [a'nis] nm aniseed; (licor) anisette

aniversario [anißer'sarjo] nm anniversary

anoche [a'notʃe] adv last night; **antes de ~** the night before last

anochecer [anotʃe'θer] vi to get dark ♦ nm nightfall, dark; **al ~** at nightfall

anodino, a [ano'ðino, a] adj dull, anodyne

anomalía [anoma'lia] nf anomaly

anonadado, a [anona'ðaðo, a] adj: **estar/ quedar/sentirse ~** to be overwhelmed o amazed

anonimato [anoni'mato] nm anonymity

anónimo, a [a'nonimo, a] adj anonymous; (COM) limited ♦ nm (carta) anonymous letter; (: maliciosa) poison-pen letter

anormal [anor'mal] adj abnormal

anotación [anota'θjon] nf note; annotation

anotar [ano'tar] vt to note down; (comentar) to annotate

anquilosamiento [ankilosa'mjento] nm (fig) paralysis; stagnation

anquilosarse [ankilo'sarse] vr (fig: persona) to get out of touch; (método, costumbres) to go out of date

ansia ['ansja] nf anxiety; (añoranza) yearning; **ansiar** vt to long for

ansiedad [ansje'ðað] nf anxiety

ansioso, a [an'sjoso, a] adj anxious; (anhelante) eager; **~ de** o **por algo** greedy for sth

antagónico, a [anta'yoniko, a] adj antagonistic; (opuesto) contrasting; **antagonista** nm/f antagonist

antaño [an'taɲo] adv long ago, formerly

Antártico [an'tartiko] nm: **el ~** the Antarctic

ante ['ante] prep before, in the presence of; (problema etc) faced with ♦ nm (piel) suede; **~ todo** above all

anteanoche [antea'notʃe] adv the night before last

anteayer [antea'jer] adv the day before yesterday

antebrazo [ante'ßraθo] nm forearm

antecedente [anteθe'ðente] adj previous ♦ nm antecedent; **~s** nmpl (JUR): **~s penales** criminal record; (procedencia) background

anteceder [anteθe'ðer] vt to precede, go before

antecesor, a [anteθe'sor, a] nm/f predecessor

antedicho, a [ante'ðitʃo, a] adj afore-mentioned

antelación [antela'θjon] nf: **con ~** in

advance

antemano [ante'mano]: **de ~** *adv* beforehand, in advance

antena [an'tena] *nf* antenna; (*de televisión etc*) aerial; **~ parabólica** satellite dish

anteojo [ante'oxo] *nm* eyeglass; **~s** *nmpl* (*AM*) glasses, spectacles

antepasados [antepa'saðos] *nmpl* ancestors

anteponer [antepo'ner] *vt* to place in front; (*fig*) to prefer

anteproyecto [antepro'jekto] *nm* preliminary sketch; (*fig*) blueprint

anterior [ante'rjor] *adj* preceding, previous; **~idad** *nf*: **con ~idad a** prior to, before

antes ['antes] *adv* (*con prioridad*) before ♦ *prep*: **~ de** before ♦ *conj*: **~ de ir/de que te vayas** before going/before you go; **~ bien** (but) rather; **dos días ~** two days before o previously; **no quiso venir ~** she didn't want to come any earlier; **tomo el avión ~ que el barco** I take the plane rather than the boat; **~ que yo** before me; **lo ~ posible** as soon as possible; **cuanto ~ mejor** the sooner the better

antiaéreo, a [antia'ereo, a] *adj* anti-aircraft

antibalas [anti'ßalas] *adj inv*: **chaleco ~** bullet-proof jacket

antibiótico [anti'ßjotiko] *nm* antibiotic

anticiclón [antiθi'klon] *nm* anticyclone

anticipación [antiθipa'θjon] *nf* anticipation; **con 10 minutos de ~** 10 minutes early

anticipado, a [antiθi'paðo, a] *adj* (*pago*) advance; **por ~** in advance

anticipar [antiθi'par] *vt* to anticipate; (*adelantar*) to bring forward; (*COM*) to advance; **~se** *vr*: **~se a su época** to be ahead of one's time

anticipo [anti'θipo] *nm* (*COM*) advance

anticonceptivo, a [antikonθep'tißo, a] *adj, nm* contraceptive

anticongelante [antikonxe'lante] *nm* antifreeze

anticuado, a [anti'kwaðo, a] *adj* out-of-date, old-fashioned; (*desusado*) obsolete

anticuario [anti'kwarjo] *nm* antique dealer

anticuerpo [anti'kwerpo] *nm* (*MED*) antibody

antidepresivo [antiðepre'sißo] *nm* antidepressant

antídoto [an'tiðoto] *nm* antidote

antiestético, a [anties'tetiko, a] *adj* unsightly

antifaz [anti'faθ] *nm* mask; (*velo*) veil

antigualla [anti'ɣwaʎa] *nf* antique; (*reliquia*) relic

antiguamente [antiɣwa'mente] *adv* formerly; (*hace mucho tiempo*) long ago

antigüedad [antiɣwe'ðað] *nf* antiquity; (*artículo*) antique; (*rango*) seniority

antiguo, a [an'tiɣwo, a] *adj* old, ancient; (*que fue*) former

Antillas [an'tiʎas] *nfpl*: **las ~** the West Indies

antílope [an'tilope] *nm* antelope

antinatural [antinatu'ral] *adj* unnatural

antipatía [antipa'tia] *nf* antipathy, dislike; **antipático, a** *adj* disagreeable, unpleasant

antirrobo [anti'rroßo] *adj inv* (*alarma etc*) anti-theft

antisemita [antise'mita] *adj* anti-Semitic ♦ *nm/f* anti-Semite

antiséptico, a [anti'septiko, a] *adj* antiseptic ♦ *nm* antiseptic

antítesis [an'titesis] *nf inv* antithesis

antojadizo, a [antoxa'ðiθo, a] *adj* capricious

antojarse [anto'xarse] *vr* (*desear*): **se me antoja comprarlo** I have a mind to buy it; (*pensar*): **se me antoja que** I have a feeling that

antojo [an'toxo] *nm* caprice, whim; (*rosa*) birthmark; (*lunar*) mole

antología [antolo'xia] *nf* anthology

antorcha [an'tortʃa] *nf* torch

antro ['antro] *nm* cavern

antropófago, a [antro'pofaɣo, a] *adj, nm/f* cannibal

antropología [antropolo'xia] *nf* anthropology

anual [a'nwal] *adj* annual

anuario [a'nwarjo] *nm* yearbook

anudar [anu'ðar] *vt* to knot, tie; (*unir*) to join; **~se** *vr* to get tied up

anulación [anula'θjon] *nf* annulment; (*cancelación*) cancellation

anular [anu'lar] *vt* (*contrato*) to annul, cancel; (*ley*) to revoke, repeal; (*suscripción*) to cancel ♦ *nm* ring finger

Anunciación [anunθja'θjon] *nf* (*REL*) Annunciation

anunciante [anun'θjante] *nm/f* (*COM*) advertiser

anunciar [anun'θjar] *vt* to announce; (*proclamar*) to proclaim; (*COM*) to advertise

anuncio [a'nunθjo] *nm* announcement; (*señal*) sign; (*COM*) advertisement; (*cartel*) poster

anzuelo [an'θwelo] *nm* hook; (*para pescar*) fish hook

añadidura [aɲaði'ðura] *nf* addition, extra; **por ~** besides, in addition

añadir [aɲa'ðir] *vt* to add

añejo, a [a'ɲexo, a] *adj* old; (*vino*) mellow

añicos [a'ɲikos] *nmpl*: **hacer ~** to smash, shatter

añil [a'ɲil] *nm* (*BOT, color*) indigo

año ['aɲo] *nm* year; **¡Feliz A~ Nuevo!** Happy New Year!; **tener 15 ~s** to be 15 (years old); **los ~s 90** the nineties; **~ bisiesto/escolar** leap/school year; **el ~ que viene** next year

añoranza [aɲoˈranθa] nf nostalgia; (anhelo) longing

apabullar [apaβuˈʎar] vt (tb fig) to crush, squash

apacentar [apaθenˈtar] vt to pasture, graze

apacible [apaˈθiβle] adj gentle, mild

apaciguar [apaθiˈɣwar] vt to pacify, calm (down)

apadrinar [apaðriˈnar] vt to sponsor, support; (REL) to be godfather to

apagado, a [apaˈɣaðo, a] adj (volcán) extinct; (color) dull; (voz) quiet; (sonido) muted, muffled; (persona: apático) listless; **estar ~** (fuego, luz) to be out; (RADIO, TV etc) to be off

apagar [apaˈɣar] vt to put out; (ELEC, RADIO, TV) to turn off; (sonido) to silence, muffle; (sed) to quench

apagón [apaˈɣon] nm blackout; power cut

apalabrar [apalaˈβrar] vt to agree to; (contratar) to engage

apalear [apaleˈar] vt to beat, thrash

apañar [apaˈɲar] vt to pick up; (asir) to take hold of, grasp; (reparar) to mend, patch up; **~se** vr to manage, get along

aparador [aparaˈðor] nm sideboard; (AM: escaparate) shop window

aparato [apaˈrato] nm apparatus; (máquina) machine; (doméstico) appliance; (boato) ostentation; **~ de facsímil** facsimile (machine), fax; **~ digestivo** (ANAT) digestive system; **~so, a** adj showy, ostentatious

aparcamiento [aparkaˈmjento] nm car park (BRIT), parking lot (US)

aparcar [aparˈkar] vt, vi to park

aparear [apareˈar] vt (objetos) to pair, match; (animales) to mate; **~se** vr to make a pair; to mate

aparecer [apareˈθer] vi to appear; **~se** vr to appear

aparejado, a [apareˈxaðo, a] adj fit, suitable; **llevar o traer ~** to involve; **aparejador, a** nm/f (ARQ) master builder

aparejo [apaˈrexo] nm harness, rigging; (de poleas) block and tackle

aparentar [aparenˈtar] vt (edad) to look; (fingir): **~ tristeza** to pretend to be sad

aparente [apaˈrente] adj apparent; (adecuado) suitable

aparezco etc vb ver **aparecer**

aparición [apariˈθjon] nf appearance; (de libro) publication; (espectro) apparition

apariencia [apaˈrjenθja] nf (outward) appearance; **en ~** outwardly, seemingly

apartado, a [aparˈtaðo, a] adj separate; (lejano) remote ♦ nm (tipográfico) paragraph; **~ (de correos)** post office box

apartamento [apartaˈmento] nm apartment, flat (BRIT)

apartamiento [apartaˈmjento] nm separation; (aislamiento) remoteness, isolation; (AM) apartment, flat (BRIT)

apartar [aparˈtar] vt to separate; (quitar) to remove; **~se** vr to separate, part; (irse) to move away; to keep away

aparte [aˈparte] adv (separadamente) separately; (además) besides ♦ nm aside; (tipográfico) new paragraph

aparthotel [apartoˈtel] nm serviced apartments

apasionado, a [apasjoˈnaðo, a] adj passionate

apasionar [apasjoˈnar] vt to excite; **le apasiona el fútbol** she's crazy about football; **~se** vr to get excited

apatía [apaˈtia] nf apathy

apático, a [aˈpatiko, a] adj apathetic

Apdo abr (= Apartado (de Correos)) PO Box

apeadero [apeaˈðero] nm halt, stop, stopping place

apearse [apeˈarse] vr (jinete) to dismount; (bajarse) to get down o out; (AUTO, FERRO) to get off o out

apechugar [apetʃuˈɣar] vr: **~ con algo** to face up to sth

apedrear [apeðreˈar] vt to stone

apegarse [apeˈɣarse] vr: **~ a** to become attached to; **apego** nm attachment, devotion

apelación [apelaˈθjon] nf appeal

apelar [apeˈlar] vi to appeal; **~ a** (fig) to resort to

apellidar [apeʎiˈðar] vt to call, name; **~se** vr: **se apellida Pérez** her (sur)name's Pérez

apellido [apeˈʎiðo] nm surname

apelmazarse [apelmaˈθarse] vr (masa, arroz) to go hard; (prenda de tana) to shrink

apenar [apeˈnar] vt to grieve, trouble; (AM: avergonzar) to embarrass; **~se** vr to grieve; (AM) to be embarrassed

apenas [aˈpenas] adv scarcely, hardly ♦ conj as soon as, no sooner

apéndice [aˈpendiθe] nm appendix; **apendicitis** nf appendicitis

aperitivo [aperiˈtiβo] nm (bebida) aperitif; (comida) appetizer

apero [aˈpero] nm (AGR) implement; **~s** nmpl farm equipment sg

apertura [aperˈtura] nf opening; (POL) liberalization

apesadumbrar [apesaðumˈbrar] vt to grieve, sadden; **~se** vr to distress o.s.

apestar [apesˈtar] vt to infect ♦ vi: **~ (a)** to stink (of)

apetecer [apeteˈθer] vt: **¿te apetece un café?** do you fancy a (cup of) coffee?; **apetecible** adj desirable; (comida) appetizing

apetito [apeˈtito] nm appetite; **~so, a** adj

appetizing; (*fig*) tempting

apiadarse [apja'ðarse] *vr*: ~ **de** to take pity on

ápice ['apiθe] *nm* whit, iota

apilar [api'lar] *vt* to pile o heap up; ~**se** *vr* to pile up

apiñarse [api'narse] *vr* to crowd o press together

apio ['apjo] *nm* celery

apisonadora [apisona'ðora] *nf* steamroller

aplacar [apla'kar] *vt* to placate; ~**se** *vr* to calm down

aplanar [apla'nar] *vt* to smooth, level; (*allanar*) to roll flat, flatten

aplastante [aplas'tante] *adj* overwhelming; (*lógica*) compelling

aplastar [aplas'tar] *vt* to squash (flat); (*fig*) to crush

aplatanarse [aplata'narse] *vr* to get lethargic

aplaudir [aplau'ðir] *vt* to applaud

aplauso [a'plauso] *nm* applause; (*fig*) approval, acclaim

aplazamiento [aplaθa'mjento] *nm* postponement

aplazar [apla'θar] *vt* to postpone, defer

aplicación [aplika'θjon] *nf* application; (*esfuerzo*) effort

aplicado, a [apli'kaðo, a] *adj* diligent, hard-working

aplicar [apli'kar] *vt* (*ejecutar*) to apply; ~**se** *vr* to apply o.s.

aplique *etc* [a'plike] *vb ver* **aplicar** ♦ *nm* wall light

aplomo [a'plomo] *nm* aplomb, self-assurance

apocado, a [apo'kaðo, a] *adj* timid

apodar [apo'ðar] *vt* to nickname

apoderado [apoðe'raðo] *nm* agent, representative

apoderarse [apoðe'rarse] *vr*: ~ **de** to take possession of

apodo [a'poðo] *nm* nickname

apogeo [apo'xeo] *nm* peak, summit

apolillarse [apoli'ʎarse] *vr* to get moth-eaten

apología [apolo'xia] *nf* eulogy; (*defensa*) defence

apoltronarse [apoltro'narse] *vr* to get lazy

apoplejía [apople'xia] *nf* apoplexy, stroke

apoquinar [apoki'nar] (*fam*) *vt* to fork out, cough up

aporrear [aporre'ar] *vt* to beat (up)

aportar [apor'tar] *vt* to contribute ♦ *vi* to reach port; ~**se** *vr* (AM: *llegar*) to arrive, come

aposento [apo'sento] *nm* lodging; (*habitación*) room

aposta [a'posta] *adv* deliberately, on purpose

apostar [apos'tar] *vt* to bet, stake; (*tropas etc*) to station, post ♦ *vi* to bet

apóstol [a'postol] *nm* apostle

apóstrofo [a'postrofo] *nm* apostrophe

apoyar [apo'jar] *vt* to lean, rest; (*fig*) to support, back; ~**se** *vr*: ~**se en** to lean on; **apoyo** *nm* (*gen*) support; backing, help

apreciable [apre'θjaβle] *adj* considerable; (*fig*) esteemed

apreciar [apre'θjar] *vt* to evaluate, assess; (COM) to appreciate, value; (*persona*) to respect; (*tamaño*) to gauge, assess; (*detalles*) to notice

aprecio [a'preθjo] *nm* valuation, estimate; (*fig*) appreciation

aprehender [apreen'der] *vt* to apprehend, detain

apremiante [apre'mjante] *adj* urgent, pressing

apremiar [apre'mjar] *vt* to compel, force ♦ *vi* to be urgent, press; **apremio** *nm* urgency

aprender [apren'der] *vt, vi* to learn

aprendiz, a [apren'diθ, a] *nm/f* apprentice; (*principiante*) learner; ~ **de conductor** learner driver; ~**aje** *nm* apprenticeship

aprensión [apren'sjon] *nm* apprehension, fear; **aprensivo, a** *adj* apprehensive

apresar [apre'sar] *vt* to seize; (*capturar*) to capture

aprestar [apres'tar] *vt* to prepare, get ready; (TEC) to prime, size; ~**se** *vr* to get ready

apresurado, a [apresu'raðo, a] *adj* hurried, hasty; **apresuramiento** *nm* hurry, haste

apresurar [apresu'rar] *vt* to hurry, accelerate; ~**se** *vr* to hurry, make haste

apretado, a [apre'taðo, a] *adj* tight; (*escritura*) cramped

apretar [apre'tar] *vt* to squeeze; (TEC) to tighten; (*presionar*) to press together, pack ♦ *vi* to be too tight

apretón [apre'ton] *nm* squeeze; ~ **de manos** handshake

aprieto [a'prjeto] *nm* squeeze; (*dificultad*) difficulty; **estar en un** ~ to be in a fix

aprisa [a'prisa] *adv* quickly, hurriedly

aprisionar [aprisjo'nar] *vt* to imprison

aprobación [aproβa'θjon] *nf* approval

aprobar [apro'βar] *vt* to approve (of); (*examen, materia*) to pass ♦ *vi* to pass

apropiación [apropja'θjon] *nf* appropriation

apropiado, a [apro'pjaðo, a] *adj* appropriate

apropiarse [apro'pjarse] *vr*: ~ **de** to appropriate

aprovechado, a [aproβe'tfaðo, a] *adj* industrious, hard-working; (*económico*) thrifty; (*pey*) unscrupulous; **aprovechamiento** *nm* use; exploitation

aprovechar [aproβe'tfar] *vt* to use; (*explotar*) to exploit; (*experiencia*) to profit from; (*oferta, oportunidad*) to take advantage of ♦ *vi* to progress, improve; ~**se** *vr*: ~**se de** to make use of; to take advantage of; **¡que aproveche!** enjoy your meal!

aproximación [aproksima'θjon] nf approximation; (de lotería) consolation prize; **aproximado, a** adj approximate

aproximar [aproksi'mar] vt to bring nearer; **~se** vr to come near, approach

apruebo etc vb ver **aprobar**

aptitud [apti'tuð] nf aptitude

apto, a ['apto, a] adj suitable

apuesta [a'pwesta] nf bet, wager

apuesto, a [a'pwesto, a] adj neat, elegant

apuntador [apunta'ðor] nm prompter

apuntalar [apunta'lar] vt to prop up

apuntar [apun'tar] vt (con arma) to aim at; (con dedo) to point at o to; (anotar) to note (down); (TEATRO) to prompt; **~se** vr (DEPORTE: tanto, victoria) to score; (ESCOL) to enrol

apunte [a'punte] nm note

apuñalar [apuɲa'lar] vt to stab

apurado, a [apu'raðo, a] adj needy; (difícil) difficult; (peligroso) dangerous; (AM) hurried, rushed

apurar [apu'rar] vt (agotar) to drain; (recursos) to use up; (molestar) to annoy; **~se** vr (preocuparse) to worry; (darse prisa) to hurry

apuro [a'puro] nm (aprieto) fix, jam; (escasez) want, hardship; (vergüenza) embarrassment; (AM) haste, urgency

aquejado, a [ake'xaðo, a] adj: **~ de** (MED) afflicted by

aquél, aquélla [a'kel, a'keʎa] (pl aquéllos, as) pron that (one); (pl) those (ones)

aquel, aquella [a'kel, a'keʎa] (pl aquellos, as) adj that; (pl) those

aquello [a'keʎo] pron that, that business

aquí [a'ki] adv (lugar) here; (tiempo) now; **~ arriba** up here; **~ mismo** right here; **~ yace** here lies; **de ~ a siete días** a week from now

aquietar [akje'tar] vt to quieten (down), calm (down)

ara ['ara] nf: **en ~s de** for the sake of

árabe ['araβe] adj, nm/f Arab ♦ nm (LING) Arabic

Arabia [a'raβja] nf: **~ Saudí** o **Saudita** Saudi Arabia

arado [a'raðo] nm plough

Aragón [ara'ɣon] nm Aragon; **aragonés, esa** adj, nm/f Aragonese

arancel [aran'θel] nm tariff, duty; **~ de aduanas** customs (duty)

arandela [aran'dela] nf (TEC) washer

araña [a'raɲa] nf (ZOOL) spider; (lámpara) chandelier

arañar [ara'ɲar] vt to scratch

arañazo [ara'ɲaθo] nm scratch

arar [a'rar] vt to plough, till

arbitraje [arβi'traxe] nm arbitration

arbitrar [arβi'trar] vt to arbitrate in; (DEPORTE) to referee ♦ vi to arbitrate

arbitrariedad [arβitrarje'ðað] nf arbitrariness; (acto) arbitrary act; **arbitrario, a** adj arbitrary

arbitrio [ar'βitrjo] nm free will; (JUR) adjudication, decision

árbitro ['arβitro] nm arbitrator; (DEPORTE) referee; (TENIS) umpire

árbol ['arβol] nm (BOT) tree; (NAUT) mast; (TEC) axle, shaft; **arbolado, a** adj wooded; (camino etc) tree-lined ♦ nm woodland

arboleda [arβo'leða] nf grove, plantation

arbusto [ar'βusto] nm bush, shrub

arca ['arka] nf chest, box

arcada [ar'kaða] nf arcade; (de puente) arch, span; **~s** nfpl (náuseas) retching sg

arcaico, a [ar'kaiko, a] adj archaic

arce ['arθe] nm maple tree

arcén [ar'θen] nm (de autopista) hard shoulder; (de carretera) verge

archipiélago [artʃi'pjelaxo] nm archipelago

archivador [artʃiβa'ðor] nm filing cabinet

archivar [artʃi'βar] vt to file (away); **archivo** nm file, archive(s) (pl)

arcilla [ar'θiʎa] nf clay

arco ['arko] nm arch; (MAT) arc; (MIL, MUS) bow; **~ iris** rainbow

arder [ar'ðer] vi to burn; **estar que arde** (persona) to fume

ardid [ar'ðið] nm ploy, trick

ardiente [ar'ðjente] adj burning, ardent

ardilla [ar'ðiʎa] nf squirrel

ardor [ar'ðor] nm (calor) heat; (fig) ardour; **~ de estómago** heartburn

arduo, a ['arðwo, a] adj arduous

área ['area] nf area; (DEPORTE) penalty area

arena [a'rena] nf sand; (de una lucha) arena; **~ movedizas** quicksand sg

arenal [are'nal] nm (arena movediza) quicksand

arengar [aren'gar] vt to harangue

arenisca [are'niska] nf sandstone; (cascajo) grit

arenoso, a [are'noso, a] adj sandy

arenque [a'renke] nm herring

argamasa [arɣa'masa] nf mortar, plaster

Argel [ar'xel] n Algiers; **Argelia** nf Algeria; **argelino, a** adj, nm/f Algerian

Argentina [arxen'tina] nf: **(la) ~** Argentina

argentino, a [arxen'tino, a] adj Argentinian; (de plata) silvery ♦ nm/f Argentinian

argolla [ar'ɣoʎa] nf (large) ring

argot [ar'xo] (pl **~s**) nm slang

argucia [ar'ɣuθja] nf subtlety, sophistry

argüir [ar'ɣwir] vt to deduce; (discutir) to argue; (indicar) to indicate, imply; (censurar) to reproach ♦ vi to argue

argumentación [arɣumenta'θjon] nf (line of) argument

argumentar [arɣumen'tar] vt, vi to argue

argumento [arɣu'mento] *nm* argument;
(*razonamiento*) reasoning; (*de novela etc*)
plot; (*CINE, TV*) storyline

aria ['arja] *nf* aria

aridez [ari'ðeθ] *nf* aridity, dryness

árido, a ['ariðo, a] *adj* arid, dry; **~s** *nmpl*
(*COM*) dry goods

Aries ['arjes] *nm* Aries

ario, a ['arjo, a] *adj* Aryan

arisco, a [a'risko, a] *adj* surly; (*insociable*)
unsociable

aristócrata [aris'tokrata] *nm/f* aristocrat

aritmética [arit'metika] *nf* arithmetic

arma ['arma] *nf* arm; **~s** *nfpl* arms; **~ blanca**
blade, knife; (*espada*) sword; **~ de fuego**
firearm; **~s cortas** small arms

armada [ar'maða] *nf* armada; (*flota*) fleet

armadillo [arma'ðiʎo] *nm* armadillo

armado, a [ar'maðo, a] *adj* armed; (*TEC*)
reinforced

armador [arma'ðor] *nm* (*NAUT*) shipowner

armadura [arma'ðura] *nf* (*MIL*) armour; (*TEC*)
framework; (*ZOOL*) skeleton; (*FÍSICA*) armature

armamento [arma'mento] *nm* armament;
(*NAUT*) fitting-out

armar [ar'mar] *vt* (*soldado*) to arm;
(*máquina*) to assemble; (*navío*) to fit out; **~la,
~ un lío** to start a row, kick up a fuss

armario [ar'marjo] *nm* wardrobe; (*de cocina,
baño*) cupboard

armatoste [arma'toste] *nm* (*mueble*)
monstrosity; (*máquina*) contraption

armazón [arma'θon] *nf o m* body, chassis;
(*de mueble etc*) frame; (*ARQ*) skeleton

armería [arme'ria] *nf* gunsmith's

armiño [ar'miɲo] *nm* stoat; (*piel*) ermine

armisticio [armis'tiθjo] *nm* armistice

armonía [armo'nia] *nf* harmony

armónica [ar'monika] *nf* harmonica

armonioso, a [armo'njoso, a] *adj*
harmonious

armonizar [armoni'θar] *vt* to harmonize;
(*diferencias*) to reconcile ♦ *vi*: **~ con** (*fig*) to
be in keeping with; (*colores*) to tone in with,
blend

arnés [ar'nes] *nm* armour; **arneses** *nmpl* (*de
caballo etc*) harness *sg*

aro ['aro] *nm* ring; (*tejo*) quoit; (*AM: pendiente*) earring

aroma [a'roma] *nm* aroma, scent

aromático, a [aro'matiko, a] *adj* aromatic

arpa ['arpa] *nf* harp

arpía [ar'pia] *nf* shrew

arpillera [arpi'ʎera] *nf* sacking, sackcloth

arpón [ar'pon] *nm* harpoon

arquear [arke'ar] *vt* to arch, bend; **~se** *vr* to
arch, bend

arqueología [arkeolo'xia] *nf* archaeology;
arqueólogo, a *nm/f* archaeologist

arquero [ar'kero] *nm* archer, bowman

arquetipo [arke'tipo] *nm* archetype

arquitecto [arki'tekto] *nm* architect;
arquitectura *nf* architecture

arrabal [arra'ßal] *nm* suburb; (*AM*) slum; **~es**
nmpl (*afueras*) outskirts

arraigado, a [arrai'ʋaðo, a] *adj* deep-rooted;
(*fig*) established

arraigar [arrai'var] *vt* to establish ♦ *vi* to take
root; **~se** *vr* to take root; (*persona*) to settle

arrancar [arran'kar] *vt* (*sacar*) to extract, pull
out; (*arrebatar*) to snatch (away); (*INFORM*)
to boot; (*fig*) to extract ♦ *vi* (*AUTO, máquina*)
to start; (*ponerse en marcha*) to get going;
~ de to stem from

arranque *etc* [a'rranke] *vb ver* **arrancar** ♦ *nm*
sudden start; (*AUTO*) start; (*fig*) fit, outburst

arrasar [arra'sar] *vt* (*aplanar*) to level, flatten;
(*destruir*) to demolish

arrastrado, a [arras'traðo, a] *adj* poor,
wretched; (*AM*) servile

arrastrar [arras'trar] *vt* to drag (along); (*fig*)
to drag down, degrade; (*suj: agua, viento*) to
carry away ♦ *vi* to drag, trail on the ground;
~se *vr* to crawl; (*fig*) to grovel; **llevar algo
arrastrado** to drag sth along

arrastre [a'rrastre] *nm* drag, dragging

arre ['arre] *excl* gee up!

arrear [arre'ar] *vt* to drive on, urge on ♦ *vi* to
hurry along

arrebatado, a [arreßa'taðo, a] *adj* rash,
impetuous; (*repentino*) sudden, hasty

arrebatar [arreßa'tar] *vt* to snatch (away),
seize; (*fig*) to captivate; **~se** *vr* to get carried
away, get excited

arrebato [arre'ßato] *nm* fit of rage, fury;
(*éxtasis*) rapture

arrecife [arre'θife] *nm* (*tb: ~ de coral*) reef

arredrarse [arre'ðrarse] *vr*: **~ (ante algo)** to
be intimidated (by sth)

arreglado, a [arre'ʋlaðo, a] *adj* (*ordenado*)
neat, orderly; (*moderado*) moderate,
reasonable

arreglar [arre'ʋlar] *vt* (*poner orden*) to tidy
up; (*algo roto*) to fix, repair; (*problema*) to
solve; **~se** *vr* to reach an understanding;
arreglárselas (*fam*) to get by, manage

arreglo [a'rreʋlo] *nm* settlement; (*orden*)
order; (*acuerdo*) agreement; (*MUS*)
arrangement, setting

arrellanarse [arreʎa'narse] *vr*: **~ en** to sit
back in/on

arremangar [arreman'gar] *vt* to roll up, turn
up; **~se** *vr* to roll up one's sleeves

arremeter [arreme'ter] *vi*: **~ contra** to attack,
rush at

arrendamiento [arrenda'mjento] *nm*
letting; (*alquilar*) hiring; (*contrato*) lease;
(*alquiler*) rent; **arrendar** *vt* to let, lease; to

rent; **arrendatario, a** nm/f tenant

arreos [a'rreos] nmpl (de caballo) harness sg, trappings

arrepentimiento [arrepenti'mjento] nm regret, repentance

arrepentirse [arrepen'tirse] vr to repent; **~ de** to regret

arrestar [arres'tar] vt to arrest; (encarcelar) to imprison; **arresto** nm arrest; (MIL) detention; (audacia) boldness, daring; **arresto domiciliario** house arrest

arriar [a'rrjar] vt (velas) to haul down; (bandera) to lower, strike; (cable) to pay out

---

PALABRA CLAVE
---

arriba [a'rrißa] adv 1 (posición) above; **desde ~ from** above; **~ de todo** at the very top, right on top; **Juan está ~** Juan is upstairs; **lo ~ mencionado** the aforementioned

2 (dirección): **calle ~** up the street

3: de ~ abajo from top to bottom; **mirar a uno de ~ abajo** to look sb up and down

4: para ~: de 5000 pesetas para ~ from 5000 pesetas up(wards)

♦ adj: **de ~: el piso de ~** the upstairs flat (BRIT) o apartment; **la parte de ~** the top o upper part

♦ prep: **~ de** (AM) above; **~ de 200 dólares** more than 200 dollars

♦ excl: **¡~! up!; ¡manos ~!** hands up!; **¡~ España!** long live Spain!

---

arribar [arri'ßar] vi to put into port; (llegar) to arrive

arribista [arri'ßista] nm/f parvenu(e), upstart

arriendo etc [a'rrjendo] vb ver **arrendar** ♦ nm = arrendamiento

arriero [a'rrjero] nm muleteer

arriesgado, a [arrjes'vaðo, a] adj (peligroso) risky; (audaz) bold, daring

arriesgar [arrjes'xar] vt to risk; (poner en peligro) to endanger; **~se** vr to take a risk

arrimar [arri'mar] vt (acercar) to bring close; (poner de lado) to set aside; **~se** vr to come close o closer; **~se a** to lean on

arrinconar [arrinko'nar] vt (colocar) to put in a corner; (enemigo) to corner; (fig) to put on one side; (abandonar) to push aside

arrodillarse [arroði'Áarse] vr to kneel (down)

arrogancia [arro'vanθja] nf arrogance; **arrogante** adj arrogant

arrojar [arro'xar] vt to throw, hurl; (humo) to emit, give out; (COM) to yield, produce; **~se** vr to throw o hurl o.s.

arrojo [a'rroxo] nm daring

arrollador, a [arroÁa'ðor, a] adj overwhelming

arrollar [arro'Áar] vt (AUTO etc) to run over,

knock down; (DEPORTE) to crush

arropar [arro'par] vt to cover, wrap up; **~se** vr to wrap o.s. up

arroyo [a'rrojo] nm stream; (de la calle) gutter

arroz [a'rroθ] nm rice; **~ con leche** rice pudding

arruga [a'rruxa] nf (de cara) wrinkle; (de vestido) crease

arrugar [arru'xar] vt to wrinkle; to crease; **~se** vr to get creased

arruinar [arrwi'nar] vt to ruin, wreck; **~se** vr to be ruined, go bankrupt

arrullar [arru'Áar] vi to coo ♦ vt to lull to sleep

arsenal [arse'nal] nm naval dockyard; (MIL) arsenal

arsénico [ar'seniko] nm arsenic

arte ['arte] (gen m en sg y siempre f en pl) nm art; (maña) skill, guile; **~s** nfpl (bellas ~s) arts

artefacto [arte'fakto] nm appliance

arteria [ar'terja] nf artery

artesanía [artesa'nia] nf craftsmanship; (artículos) handicrafts pl; **artesano, a** nm/f artisan, craftsman/woman

ártico, a ['artiko, a] adj Arctic ♦ nm: **el Á~** the Arctic

articulación [artikula'θjon] nf articulation; (MED, TEC) joint; **articulado, a** adj articulated; jointed

articular [artiku'lar] vt to articulate; to join together

artículo [ar'tikulo] nm article; (cosa) thing, article; **~s** nmpl (COM) goods

artífice [ar'tifiθe] nm/f (fig) architect

artificial [artifi'θjal] adj artificial

artificio [arti'fiθjo] nm art, skill; (astucia) cunning

artillería [artiÁe'ria] nf artillery

artillero [arti'Áero] nm artilleryman, gunner

artilugio [arti'luxjo] nm gadget

artimaña [arti'maɲa] nf trap, snare; (astucia) cunning

artista [ar'tista] nm/f (pintor) artist, painter; (TEATRO) artist, artiste; **~ de cine** film actor/actress; **artístico, a** adj artistic

artritis [ar'tritis] nf arthritis

arveja [ar'ßexa] (AM) nf pea

arzobispo [arθo'ßispo] nm archbishop

as [as] nm ace

asa ['asa] nf handle; (fig) lever

asado [a'saðo] nm roast (meat); (AM: barbacoa) barbecue

asador [asa'ðor] nm spit

asadura [asa'ðura] nf entrails pl, offal

asalariado, a [asala'rjaðo, a] adj paid, salaried ♦ nm/f wage earner

asaltante [asal'tante] nm/f attacker

asaltar [asal'tar] vt to attack, assault; (fig) to

assail; **asalto** nm attack, assault; (DEPORTE) round

asamblea [asam'blea] nf assembly; (reunión) meeting

asar [a'sar] vt to roast

asbesto [as'ßesto] nm asbestos

ascendencia [asθen'denθja] nf ancestry; (AM) ascendancy; **de ~ francesa** of French origin

ascender [asθen'der] vi (subir) to ascend, rise; (ser promovido) to gain promotion ♦ vt to promote; **~ a** to amount to; **ascendiente** nm influence ♦ nm/f ancestor

ascensión [asθen'sjon] nf ascent; (REL): la A~ the Ascension

ascenso [as'θenso] nm ascent; (promoción) promotion

ascensor [asθen'sor] nm lift (BRIT), elevator (US)

ascético, a [as'θetiko, a] adj ascetic

asco ['asko] nm: **¡qué ~!** how revolting o disgusting!; **el ajo me da ~** I hate o loathe garlic; **estar hecho un ~** to be filthy

ascua ['askwa] nf ember; **estar en ~s** to be on tenterhooks

aseado, a [ase'aðo, a] adj clean; (arreglado) tidy; (pulcro) smart

asear [ase'ar] vt to clean, wash; to tidy (up)

asediar [ase'ðjar] vt (MIL) to besiege, lay siege to; (fig) to chase, pester; **asedio** nm siege; (COM) run

asegurado, a [aseɣu'raðo, a] adj insured

asegurador, a nm/f insurer

asegurar [aseɣu'rar] vt (consolidar) to secure, fasten; (dar garantía de) to guarantee; (preservar) to safeguard; (afirmar, dar por cierto) to assure, affirm; (tranquilizar) to reassure; (tomar un seguro) to insure; **~se** vr to assure o.s., make sure

asemejarse [aseme'xarse] vr to be alike; **~ a** to be like, resemble

asentado, a [asen'taðo, a] adj established, settled

asentar [asen'tar] vt (sentar) to seat, sit down; (poner) to place, establish; (alisar) to level, smooth down o out; (anotar) to note down ♦ vi to be suitable, suit

asentir [asen'tir] vi to assent, agree; **~ con la cabeza** to nod (one's head)

aseo [a'seo] nm cleanliness; **~s** nmpl (servicios) toilet sg (BRIT), cloakroom sg (BRIT), restroom sg (US)

aséptico, a [a'septiko, a] adj germ-free, free from infection

asequible [ase'kißle] adj (precio) reasonable; (meta) attainable; (persona) approachable

aserradero [aserra'ðero] nm sawmill; **aserrar** vt to saw

asesinar [asesi'nar] vt to murder; (POL) to

assassinate; **asesinato** nm murder; assassination

asesino, a [ase'sino, a] nm/f murderer, killer; (POL) assassin

asesor, a [ase'sor, a] nm/f adviser, consultant

asesorar [aseso'rar] vt (JUR) to advise, give legal advice to; (COM) to act as consultant to; **~se** vr: **~se con o de** to take advice from, consult; **asesoría** nf (cargo) consultancy; (oficina) consultant's office

asestar [ases'tar] vt (golpe) to deal, strike

asfalto [as'falto] nm asphalt

asfixia [as'fiksja] nf asphyxia, suffocation

asfixiar [asfik'sjar] vt to asphyxiate, suffocate; **~se** vr to be asphyxiated, suffocate

asgo etc vb ver **asir**

así [a'si] adv (de esta manera) in this way, like this, thus; (aunque) although; (tan pronto como) as soon as; **~ que** so; **~ como** as well as; **~ y todo** even so; **¿no es ~?** isn't it?, didn't you? etc; **~ de grande** this big

Asia ['asja] nf Asia; **asiático, a** adj, nm/f Asian, Asiatic

asidero [asi'ðero] nm handle

asiduidad [asiðwi'ðað] nf assiduousness; **asiduo, a** adj assiduous; (frecuente) frequent ♦ nm/f regular (customer)

asiento [a'sjento] nm (mueble) seat, chair; (de coche, en tribunal etc) seat; (localidad) seat, place; (fundamento) site; **~ delantero/ trasero** front/back seat

asignación [asiɣna'θjon] nf (atribución) assignment; (reparto) allocation; (sueldo) salary; **~ (semanal)** pocket money

asignar [asiɣ'nar] vt to assign, allocate

asignatura [asiɣna'tura] nf subject; course

asilado, a [asi'laðo, a] nm/f inmate; (POL) refugee

asilo [a'silo] nm (refugio) asylum, refuge; (establecimiento) home, institution; **~ político** political asylum

asimilación [asimila'θjon] nf assimilation

asimilar [asimi'lar] vt to assimilate

asimismo [asi'mismo] adv in the same way, likewise

asir [a'sir] vt to seize, grasp

asistencia [asis'tenθja] nf audience; (MED) attendance; (ayuda) assistance; **asistente** nm/f assistant; **los asistentes** those present; **asistente social** social worker

asistido, a [a'sis'tiðo, a] adj: **~ por ordenador** computer-assisted

asistir [asis'tir] vt to assist, help ♦ vi: **~ a** to attend, be present at

asma ['asma] nf asthma

asno ['asno] nm donkey; (fig) ass

asociación [asoθja'θjon] nf association; (COM) partnership; **asociado, a** adj associate ♦ nm/f associate; (COM) partner

asociar [aso'θjar] vt to associate

asolar [aso'lar] vt to destroy

asomar [aso'mar] vt to show, stick out ♦ vi to appear; **~se** vr to appear, show up; **~ la cabeza por la ventana** to put one's head out of the window

asombrar [asom'brar] vt to amaze, astonish; **~se** vr (sorprenderse) to be amazed; (asustarse) to get a fright; **asombro** nm amazement, astonishment; (susto) fright; **asombroso, a** adj astonishing, amazing

asomo [a'somo] nm hint, sign

aspa ['aspa] nf (cruz) cross; (de molino) sail; **en ~** X-shaped

aspaviento [aspa'ßjento] nm exaggerated display of feeling; (fam) fuss

aspecto [as'pekto] nm (apariencia) look, appearance; (fig) aspect

aspereza [aspe'reθa] nf roughness; (agrura) sourness; (de carácter) surliness; **áspero, a** adj rough; bitter, sour; harsh

aspersión [asper'sjon] nf sprinkling

aspiración [aspira'θjon] nf breath, inhalation; (MUS) short pause; **aspiraciones** nfpl (ambiciones) aspirations

aspirador [aspira'ðor] nm = **aspiradora**

aspiradora [aspira'ðora] nf vacuum cleaner, Hoover ®

aspirante [aspi'rante] nm/f (candidato) candidate; (DEPORTE) contender

aspirar [aspi'rar] vt to breathe in ♦ vi: **~ a** to aspire

aspirina [aspi'rina] nf aspirin

asquear [aske'ar] vt to sicken ♦ vi to be sickening; **~se** vr to feel disgusted; **asqueroso, a** adj disgusting, sickening

asta ['asta] nf lance; (arpón) spear; (mango) shaft, handle; (ZOOL) horn; **a media ~** at half mast

asterisco [aste'risko] nm asterisk

astilla [as'tiʎa] nf splinter; (pedacito) chip; **~s** nfpl (leña) firewood sg

astillero [asti'ʎero] nm shipyard

astringente [astrin'xente] adj, nm astringent

astro ['astro] nm star

astrología [astrolo'xia] nf astrology; **astrólogo, a** nm/f astrologer

astronauta [astro'nauta] nm/f astronaut

astronave [astro'naße] nm spaceship

astronomía [astrono'mia] nf astronomy; **astrónomo, a** nm/f astronomer

astucia [as'tuθja] nf astuteness; (ardid) clever trick

asturiano, a [astu'rjano, a] adj, nm/f Asturian

astuto, a [as'tuto, a] adj astute; (taimado) cunning

asumir [asu'mir] vt to assume

asunción [asun'θjon] nf assumption; (REL): **A~** Assumption

asunto [a'sunto] nm (tema) matter, subject; (negocio) business

asustar [asus'tar] vt to frighten; **~se** vr to be (o become) frightened

atacar [ata'kar] vt to attack

atadura [ata'ðura] nf bond, tie

atajar [ata'xar] vt (enfermedad, mal) to stop ♦ vi (persona) to take a short cut

atajo [a'taxo] nm short cut

atañer [ata'ɲer] vi: **~ a** to concern

ataque etc [a'take] vb ver **atacar** ♦ nm attack; **~ cardíaco** heart attack

atar [a'tar] vt to tie, tie up

atardecer [atarðe'θer] vi to get dark ♦ nm evening; (crepúsculo) dusk

atareado, a [atare'aðo, a] adj busy

atascar [atas'kar] vt to clog up; (obstruir) to jam; (fig) to hinder; **~se** vr to stall; (cañería) to get blocked up; **atasco** nm obstruction; (AUTO) traffic jam

ataúd [ata'uð] nm coffin

ataviar [ata'ßjar] vt to deck, array; **~se** vr to dress up

atavío [ata'ßio] nm attire, dress; **~s** nmpl finery sg

atemorizar [atemori'θar] vt to frighten, scare; **~se** vr to get scared

Atenas [a'tenas] n Athens

atención [aten'θjon] nf attention; (bondad) kindness ♦ excl (be) careful!, look out!

atender [aten'der] vt to attend to, look after ♦ vi to pay attention

atenerse [ate'nerse] vr: **~ a** to abide by, adhere to

atentado [aten'taðo] nm crime, illegal act; (asalto) assault; **~ contra la vida de uno** attempt on sb's life

atentamente [atenta'mente] adv: **Le saluda ~** Yours faithfully

atentar [aten'tar] vi: **~ a o contra** to commit an outrage against

atento, a [a'tento, a] adj attentive, observant; (cortés) polite, thoughtful

atenuante [ate'nwante] adj extenuating

atenuar [ate'nwar] vt (disminuir) to lessen, minimize

ateo, a [a'teo, a] adj atheistic ♦ nm/f atheist

aterciopelado, a [aterθjope'laðo, a] adj velvety

aterido, a [ate'riðo, a] adj: **~ de frío** frozen stiff

aterrador, a [aterra'ðor, a] adj frightening

aterrar [ate'rrar] vt to frighten; to terrify

aterrizaje [aterri'θaxe] nm landing

aterrizar [aterri'θar] vi to land

aterrorizar [aterrori'θar] vt to terrify

atesorar [ateso'rar] vt to hoard

atestado, a [ates'taðo, a] adj packed ♦ nm

(*JUR*) affidavit

atestar [atesˈtar] *vt* to pack, stuff; (*JUR*) to attest, testify to

atestiguar [atestiˈɣwar] *vt* to testify to, bear witness to

atiborrar [atiβoˈrrar] *vt* to fill, stuff; **~se** *vr* to stuff o.s.

ático [ˈatiko] *nm* attic; **~ de lujo** penthouse (flat (*BRIT*) o apartment)

atinado, a [atiˈnaðo, a] *adj* (*sensato*) wise; (*correcto*) right, correct

atinar [atiˈnar] *vi* (*al disparar*): **~ al blanco** to hit the target; (*fig*) to be right

atisbar [atisˈβar] *vt* to spy on; (*echar una ojeada*) to peep at

atizar [atiˈθar] *vt* to poke; (*horno etc*) to stoke; (*fig*) to stir up, rouse

atlántico, a [atˈlantiko, a] *adj* Atlantic ♦ *nm*: **el (océano) A~** the Atlantic (Ocean)

atlas [ˈatlas] *nm* atlas

atleta [atˈleta] *nm* athlete; **atlético, a** *adj* athletic; **atletismo** *nm* athletics *sg*

atmósfera [atˈmosfera] *nf* atmosphere

atolladero [atoʎaˈðero] *nm* (*fig*) jam, fix

atolondramiento [atolondraˈmjento] *nm* bewilderment; (*insensatez*) silliness

atómico, a [aˈtomiko, a] *adj* atomic

atomizador [atomiθaˈðor] *nm* atomizer; (*de perfume*) spray

átomo [ˈatomo] *nm* atom

atónito, a [aˈtonito, a] *adj* astonished, amazed

atontado, a [atonˈtaðo, a] *adj* stunned; (*bobo*) silly, daft

atontar [atonˈtar] *vt* to stun; **~se** *vr* to become confused

atormentar [atormenˈtar] *vt* to torture; (*molestar*) to torment; (*acosar*) to plague, harass

atornillar [atorniˈʎar] *vt* to screw on o down

atosigar [atosiˈɣar] *vt* to harass, pester

atracador, a [atrakaˈðor, a] *nm/f* robber

atracar [atraˈkar] *vt* (*NAUT*) to moor; (*robar*) to hold up, rob ♦ *vi* to moor; **~se** *vr*: **~se (de)** to stuff o.s. (with)

atracción [atrakˈθjon] *nf* attraction

atraco [aˈtrako] *nm* holdup, robbery

atracón [atraˈkon] *nm*: **darse** o **pegarse un ~ (de)** (*fam*) to stuff o.s. (with)

atractivo, a [atrakˈtiβo, a] *adj* attractive ♦ *nm* appeal

atraer [atraˈer] *vt* to attract

atragantarse [atraɣanˈtarse] *vr*: **~ (con)** to choke (on); **se me ha atragantado el chico** I can't stand the boy

atrancar [atranˈkar] *vt* (*puerta*) to bar, bolt

atrapar [atraˈpar] *vt* to trap; (*resfriado etc*) to catch

atrás [aˈtras] *adv* (*movimiento*) back(wards);

(*lugar*) behind; (*tiempo*) previously; **ir hacia ~** to go back(wards); to go to the rear; **estar ~** to be behind o at the back

atrasado, a [atraˈsaðo, a] *adj* slow; (*pago*) overdue, late; (*país*) backward

atrasar [atraˈsar] *vi* to be slow; **~se** *vr* to remain behind; (*tren*) to be o run late; **atraso** *nm* slowness; lateness, delay; (*de país*) backwardness; **atrasos** *nmpl* (*COM*) arrears

atravesar [atraβeˈsar] *vt* (*cruzar*) to cross (over); (*traspasar*) to pierce; to go through; (*poner al través*) to lay o put across; **~se** *vr* to come in between; (*intervenir*) to interfere

atravieso *etc vb ver* **atravesar**

atrayente [atraˈjente] *adj* attractive

atreverse [atreˈβerse] *vr* to dare; (*insolentarse*) to be insolent; **atrevido, a** *adj* daring; insolent; **atrevimiento** *nm* daring; insolence

atribución [atriβuˈθjon] *nf*: **atribuciones** (*POL*) powers; (*ADMIN*) responsibilities

atribuir [atriβuˈir] *vt* to attribute; (*funciones*) to confer

atribular [atriβuˈlar] *vt* to afflict, distress

atributo [atriˈβuto] *nm* attribute

atril [aˈtril] *nm* (*para libro*) lectern; (*MUS*) music stand

atrocidad [atroθiˈðað] *nf* atrocity, outrage

atropellar [atropeˈʎar] *vt* (*derribar*) to knock over o down; (*empujar*) to push (aside); (*AUTO*) to run over, run down; (*agraviar*) to insult; **~se** *vr* to act hastily; **atropello** *nm* (*AUTO*) accident; (*empujón*) push; (*agravio*) wrong; (*atrocidad*) outrage

atroz [aˈtroθ] *adj* atrocious, awful

ATS *nmf abr* (= *Ayudante Técnico Sanitario*) nurse

atto, a *abr* = **atento**

atuendo [aˈtwendo] *nm* attire

atún [aˈtun] *nm* tuna

aturdir [aturˈðir] *vt* to stun; (*de ruido*) to deafen; (*fig*) to dumbfound, bewilder

atusar [atuˈsar] *vt* to smooth (down)

audacia [auˈðaθja] *nf* boldness, audacity; **audaz** *adj* bold, audacious

audible [auˈðiβle] *adj* audible

audición [auðiˈθjon] *nf* hearing; (*TEATRO*) audition

audiencia [auˈðjenθja] *nf* audience; **A~** (*JUR*) High Court

audífono [auˈðifono] *nm* (*para sordos*) hearing aid

auditor [auðiˈtor] *nm* (*JUR*) judge advocate; (*COM*) auditor

auditorio [auðiˈtorjo] *nm* audience; (*sala*) auditorium

auge [ˈauxe] *nm* boom; (*clímax*) climax

augurar [auɣuˈrar] *vt* to predict; (*presagiar*)

to portend
augurio [au'ɣurjo] nm omen
aula ['aula] nf classroom; (en universidad etc) lecture room
aullar [au'ʎar] vi to howl, yell
aullido [au'ʎiðo] nm howl, yell
aumentar [aumen'tar] vt to increase; (precios) to put up; (producción) to step up; (con microscopio, anteojos) to magnify ♦ vi to increase, be on the increase; ~se vr to increase, be on the increase; **aumento** nm increase; rise
aun [a'un] adv even; ~ así even so; ~ más even o yet more
aún [a'un] adv: ~ está aquí he's still here; ~ no lo sabemos we don't know yet; ¿no ha venido ~? hasn't she come yet?
aunque [a'unke] conj though, although, even though
aúpa [a'upa] excl come on!
aureola [aure'ola] nf halo
auricular [auriku'lar] nm (TEL) earpiece, receiver; ~es nmpl (para escuchar música etc) headphones
aurora [au'rora] nf dawn
auscultar [auskul'tar] vt (MED: pecho) to listen to, sound
ausencia [au'senθja] nf absence
ausentarse [ausen'tarse] vr to go away; (por poco tiempo) to go out
ausente [au'sente] adj absent
auspicios [aus'piθjos] nmpl auspices
austeridad [austeri'ðað] nf austerity; **austero, a** adj austere
austral [aus'tral] adj southern ♦ nm monetary unit of Argentina
Australia [aus'tralja] nf Australia; **australiano, a** adj, nm/f Australian
Austria ['austrja] nf Austria; **austríaco, a** adj, nm/f Austrian
auténtico, a [au'tentiko, a] adj authentic
auto ['auto] nm (JUR) edict, decree; (: orden) writ, (AUTO) car; ~s nmpl (JUR) proceedings; (: acta) court record sg
autoadhesivo [autoaðe'siβo] adj self-adhesive; (sobre) self-sealing
autobiografía [autoβjoɣra'fia] nf autobiography
autobronceador [autoβronθea'ðor] adj self-tanning
autobús [auto'βus] nm bus
autocar [auto'kar] nm coach (BRIT), (passenger) bus (US)
autóctono, a [au'toktono, a] adj native, indigenous
autodefensa [autoðe'fensa] nf self-defence
autodeterminación [autoðetermina'θjon] nf self-determination
autodidacta [autoði'ðakta] adj self-taught

autoescuela [autoes'kwela] nf driving school
autógrafo [au'toɣrafo] nm autograph
autómata [au'tomata] nm automaton
automático, a [auto'matiko, a] adj automatic ♦ nm press stud
automotor, triz [automo'tor, 'triθ] adj self-propelled ♦ nm diesel train
automóvil [auto'moβil] nm (motor) car (BRIT), automobile (US); **automovilismo** nm (actividad) motoring; (DEPORTE) motor racing; **automovilista** nm/f motorist, driver; **automovilístico, a** adj (industria) motor cpd
autonomía [autono'mia] nf autonomy; **autónomo, a** (ESP), **autonómico, a** (ESP) adj (POL) autonomous
autopista [auto'pista] nf motorway (BRIT), freeway (US); ~ **de peaje** toll road (BRIT), turnpike road (US)
autopsia [au'topsja] nf autopsy, postmortem
autor, a [au'tor, a] nm/f author
autoridad [autori'ðað] nf authority; **autoritario, a** adj authoritarian
autorización [autoriθa'θjon] nf authorization; **autorizado, a** adj authorized; (aprobado) approved
autorizar [autori'θar] vt to authorize; (aprobar) to approve
autorretrato [autorre'trato] nm self-portrait
autoservicio [autoser'βiθjo] nm (tienda) self-service shop (BRIT) o store (US); (restaurante) self-service restaurant
autostop [auto'stop] nm hitch-hiking; **hacer** ~ to hitch-hike; ~**ista** nm/f hitch-hiker
autosuficiencia [autosufi'θjenθja] nf self-sufficiency
autovía [auto'βia] nf ≈ A-road (BRIT), dual carriageway (BRIT), ≈ state highway (US)
auxiliar [auksi'ljar] vt to help ♦ nm/f assistant; **auxilio** nm assistance, help; **primeros auxilios** first aid sg
Av abr (= Avenida) Av(e).
aval [a'βal] nm guarantee; (persona) guarantor
avalancha [aβa'lantʃa] nf avalanche
avance [a'βanθe] nm advance; (pago) advance payment; (CINE) trailer
avanzar [aβan'θar] vt, vi to advance
avaricia [aβa'riθja] nf avarice, greed; **avaricioso, a** adj avaricious, greedy
avaro, a [a'βaro, a] adj miserly, mean ♦ nm/f miser
avasallar [aβasa'ʎar] vt to subdue, subjugate
Avda abr (= Avenida) Av(e).
AVE ['aβe] nm abr (= Alta Velocidad Española) ≈ bullet train
ave ['aβe] nf bird; ~ **de rapiña** bird of prey
avecinarse [aβeθi'narse] vr (tormenta, fig)

to be on the way

avellana [aβe'ʎana] nf hazelnut; **avellano** nm hazel tree

avemaría [aβema'ria] nm Hail Mary, Ave Maria

avena [a'βena] nf oats pl

avenida [aβe'niða] nf (calle) avenue

avenir [aβe'nir] vt to reconcile; **~se** vr to come to an agreement, reach a compromise

aventajado, a [aβenta'xaðo, a] adj outstanding

aventajar [aβenta'xar] vt (sobrepasar) to surpass, outstrip

aventura [aβen'tura] nf adventure; **aventurado, a** adj risky; **aventurero, a** adj adventurous

avergonzar [aβerxon'θar] vt to shame; (desconcertar) to embarrass; **~se** vr to be ashamed; to be embarrassed

avería [aβe'ria] nf (TEC) breakdown, fault

averiado, a [aβe'rjaðo, a] adj broken down; "**~**" "out of order"

averiguación [aβeriɣwa'θjon] nf investigation; (descubrimiento) ascertainment

averiguar [aβeri'ɣwar] vt to investigate; (descubrir) to find out, ascertain

aversión [aβer'sjon] nf aversion, dislike

avestruz [aβes'truθ] nm ostrich

aviación [aβja'θjon] nf aviation; (fuerzas aéreas) air force

aviador, a [aβja'ðor, a] nm/f aviator, airman/woman

avicultura [aβikul'tura] nf poultry farming

avidez [aβi'ðeθ] nf avidity, eagerness; **ávido, a** adj avid, eager

avinagrado, a [aβina'ɣraðo, a] adj sour, acid

avión [a'βjon] nm aeroplane; (ave) martin; **~ de reacción** jet (plane)

avioneta [aβjo'neta] nf light aircraft

avisar [aβi'sar] vt (advertir) to warn, notify; (informar) to tell; (aconsejar) to advise, counsel; **aviso** nm warning; (noticia) notice

avispa [a'βispa] nf wasp

avispado, a [aβis'paðo, a] adj sharp, clever

avispero [aβis'pero] nm wasp's nest

avispón [aβis'pon] nm hornet

avistar [aβis'tar] vt to sight, spot

avituallar [aβitwa'ʎar] vt to supply with food

avivar [aβi'βar] vt to strengthen, intensify; **~se** vr to revive, acquire new life

axila [ak'sila] nf armpit

axioma [ak'sjoma] nm axiom

ay [ai] excl (dolor) ow!, ouch!; (aflicción) oh!, oh dear!; **¡~ de mi!** poor me!

aya ['aja] nf governess; (niñera) nanny

ayer [a'jer] adv, nm yesterday; **antes de ~** the day before yesterday

ayote [a'jote] (AM) nm pumpkin

ayuda [a'juða] nf help, assistance ♦ nm page; **ayudante, a** nm/f assistant, helper; (ESCOL) assistant; (MIL) adjutant

ayudar [aju'ðar] vt to help, assist

ayunar [aju'nar] vi to fast; **ayunas** nfpl: **estar en ayunas** to be fasting; **ayuno** nm fast; fasting

ayuntamiento [ajunta'mjento] nm (consejo) town (o city) council; (edificio) town (o city) hall

azabache [aθa'βatʃe] nm jet

azada [a'θaða] nf hoe

azafata [aθa'fata] nf air stewardess

azafrán [aθa'fran] nm saffron

azahar [aθa'ar] nm orange/lemon blossom

azar [a'θar] nm (casualidad) chance, fate; (desgracia) misfortune, accident; **por ~** by chance; **al ~** at random

azoramiento [aθora'mjento] nm alarm; (confusión) confusion

azorar [aθo'rar] vt to alarm; **~se** vr to get alarmed

Azores [a'θores] nfpl: **las ~** the Azores

azotar [aθo'tar] vt to whip, beat; (pegar) to spank; **azote** nm (látigo) whip; (latigazo) lash, stroke; (en las nalgas) spank; (calamidad) calamity

azotea [aθo'tea] nf (flat) roof

azteca [aθ'teka] adj, nm/f Aztec

azúcar [a'θukar] nm sugar; **azucarado, a** adj sugary, sweet

azucarero, a [aθuka'rero, a] adj sugar cpd ♦ nm sugar bowl

azucena [aθu'θena] nf white lily

azufre [a'θufre] nm sulphur

azul [a'θul] adj, nm blue; **~ marino** navy blue

azulejo [aθu'lexo] nm tile

azuzar [aθu'θar] vt to incite, egg on

B, b

B.A. abr (= Buenos Aires) B.A.

baba ['baβa] nf spittle, saliva; **babear** vi to drool, slaver

babero [ba'βero] nm bib

babor [ba'βor] nm port (side)

baboso, a [ba'βoso, a] (AM: fam) adj silly

baca ['baka] nf (AUTO) luggage o roof rack

bacalao [baka'lao] nm cod(fish)

bache ['batʃe] nm pothole, rut; (fig) bad patch

bachillerato [batʃiʎe'rato] nm higher secondary school course

bacteria [bak'terja] nf bacterium, germ

báculo ['bakulo] nm stick, staff

bagaje [ba'ɣaxe] nm baggage, luggage

Bahama [ba'ama]: **las (Islas) ~** nfpl the Bahamas

bahía [ba'ia] nf bay

bailar [bai'lar] vt, vi to dance; **~ín, ina** nm/f
(ballet) dancer; **baile** nm dance; (formal)
ball

baja ['baxa] nf drop, fall; (MIL) casualty; **dar de
~** (soldado) to discharge; (empleado) to
dismiss

bajada [ba'xaða] nf descent; (camino) slope;
(de aguas) ebb

bajar [ba'xar] vi to go down, come down;
(temperatura, precios) to drop, fall ♦ vt
(cabeza) to bow; (escalera) to go down,
come down; (precio, voz) to lower; (llevar
abajo) to take down; **~se** vr (de coche) to get
out; (de autobús, tren) to get off; **~ de**
(coche) to get out of; (autobús, tren) to get
off

bajeza [ba'xeθa] nf baseness no pl; (una ~)
vile deed

bajío [ba'xio] nm (AM) lowlands pl

bajo, a ['baxo, a] adj (mueble, número, precio)
low; (piso) ground; (de estatura) small, short;
(color) pale; (sonido) faint, soft, low; (voz: en
tono) deep; (metal) base; (humilde) low,
humble ♦ adv (hablar) softly, quietly; (volar)
low ♦ prep under, below, underneath ♦ nm
(MUS) bass; **~ la lluvia** in the rain

bajón [ba'xon] nm fall, drop

bakalao [baka'lao] (fam) nm rave (music)

bala ['bala] nf bullet

balance [ba'lanθe] nm (COM) balance;
(: libro) balance sheet; (: cuenta general)
stocktaking

balancear [balanθe'ar] vt to balance ♦ vi to
swing (to and fro); (vacilar) to hesitate; **~se**
vr to swing (to and fro); to hesitate;
balanceo nm swinging

balanza [ba'lanθa] nf scales pl, balance;
(ASTROLOGÍA): **B~ Libra**; **~ comercial** balance of
trade; **~ de pagos** balance of payments

balar [ba'lar] vi to bleat

balaustrada [balaus'traða] nf balustrade;
(pasamanos) banisters pl

balazo [ba'laθo] nm (golpe) shot; (herida)
bullet wound

balbucear [balβuθe'ar] vi, vt to stammer,
stutter; **balbuceo** nm stammering, stuttering

balbucir [balβu'θir] vi, vt to stammer, stutter

balcón [bal'kon] nm balcony

balde ['balde] nm bucket, pail; **de ~** (for) free,
for nothing; **en ~** in vain

baldío, a [bal'dio, a] adj uncultivated;
(terreno) waste ♦ nm waste land

baldosa [bal'dosa] nf (azulejo) floor tile;
(grande) flagstone; **baldosín** nm (small) tile

Baleares [bale'ares] nfpl: **las (Islas) ~** the
Balearic Islands

balido [ba'liðo] nm bleat, bleating

baliza [ba'liθa] nf (AVIAT) beacon; (NAUT)

buoy

ballena [ba'ʎena] nf whale

ballesta [ba'ʎesta] nf crossbow; (AUTO) spring

ballet [ba'le] (pl **~s**) nm ballet

balneario, a [balne'arjo, a] adj: **estación
balnearia** (AM) (bathing) resort ♦ nm spa,
health resort

balón [ba'lon] nm ball

baloncesto [balon'θesto] nm basketball

balonmano [balon'mano] nm handball

balonvolea [balombo'lea] nm volleyball

balsa ['balsa] nf raft; (BOT) balsa wood

bálsamo ['balsamo] nm balsam, balm

baluarte [ba'lwarte] nm bastion, bulwark

bambolear [bambole'ar] vi to swing, sway;
(silla) to wobble; **~se** vr to swing, sway; to
wobble; **bamboleo** nm swinging, swaying,
wobbling

bambú [bam'bu] nm bamboo

banana [ba'nana] (AM) nf banana; **banano**
(AM) nm banana tree

banca ['banka] nf (COM) banking

bancario, a [ban'karjo, a] adj banking cpd,
bank cpd

bancarrota [banka'rrota] nf bankruptcy;
hacer ~ to go bankrupt

banco ['banko] nm bench; (ESCOL) desk;
(COM) bank; (GEO) stratum; **~ de crédito/de
ahorros** credit/savings bank; **~ de arena**
sandbank; **~ de datos** databank

banda ['banda] nf band; (pandilla) gang;
(NAUT) side, edge; **la B~ Oriental** Uruguay;
~ sonora soundtrack

bandada [ban'daða] nf (de pájaros) flock; (de
peces) shoal

bandazo [ban'daθo] nm: **dar ~s** to sway from
side to side

bandeja [ban'dexa] nf tray

bandera [ban'dera] nf flag

banderilla [bande'riʎa] nf banderilla

banderín [bande'rin] nm pennant, small flag

bandido [ban'diðo] nm bandit

bando ['bando] nm (edicto) edict,
proclamation; (facción) faction; **los ~s** (REL)
the banns

bandolera [bando'lera] nf: **llevar en ~** to
wear across one's chest

bandolero [bando'lero] nm bandit, brigand

banquero [ban'kero] nm banker

banqueta [ban'keta] nf stool; (AM: en la
calle) pavement (BRIT), sidewalk (US)

banquete [ban'kete] nm banquet; (para
convidados) formal dinner

banquillo [ban'kiʎo] nm (JUR) dock,
prisoner's bench; (banco) bench; (para los
pies) footstool

bañador [baɲa'ðor] nm swimming costume
(BRIT), bathing suit (US)

bañar [ba'ɲar] vt to bath, bathe; (objeto) to

dip; (*de barniz*) to coat; **~se** *vr* (*en el mar*) to
bathe, swim; (*en la bañera*) to have a bath
bañera [ba'ɲera] *nf* bath(tub)
bañero, a [ba'ɲero, a] (*AM*) *nm/f* lifeguard
bañista [ba'ɲista] *nm/f* bather
baño ['baɲo] *nm* (*en bañera*) bath; (*en río*)
dip, swim; (*cuarto*) bathroom; (*bañera*)
bath(tub); (*capa*) coating
baqueta [ba'keta] *nf* (*MUS*) drumstick
bar [bar] *nm* bar
barahúnda [bara'unda] *nf* uproar, hubbub
baraja [ba'raxa] *nf* pack (of cards); **barajar**
vt (*naipes*) to shuffle; (*fig*) to jumble up
baranda [ba'randa] *nf* = **barandilla**
barandilla [baran'diʎa] *nf* rail, railing
baratija [bara'tixa] *nf* trinket
baratillo [bara'tiʎo] *nm* (*tienda*) junkshop;
(*subasta*) bargain sale; (*conjunto de cosas*)
secondhand goods *pl*
barato, a [ba'rato, a] *adj* cheap ♦ *adv* cheap,
cheaply
baraúnda [bara'unda] *nf* = **barahúnda**
barba ['barβa] *nf* (*mentón*) chin; (*pelo*) beard
barbacoa [barβa'koa] *nf* (*parrilla*) barbecue;
(*carne*) barbecued meat
barbaridad [barβari'ðað] *nf* barbarity; (*acto*)
barbarism; (*atrocidad*) outrage; **una ~** (*fam*)
loads; **¡qué ~!** (*fam*) how awful!
barbarie [bar'βarje] *nf* barbarism, savagery;
(*crueldad*) barbarity
barbarismo [barβa'rismo] *nm* = **barbarie**
bárbaro, a ['barβaro, a] *adj* barbarous, cruel;
(*grosero*) rough, uncouth ♦ *nm/f* barbarian
♦ *adv*: **lo pasamos ~** (*fam*) we had a great
time; **¡qué ~!** (*fam*) how marvellous!; **un éxito
~** (*fam*) a terrific success; **es un tipo ~** (*fam*)
he's a great bloke
barbecho [bar'βetʃo] *nm* fallow land
barbero [bar'βero] *nm* barber, hairdresser
barbilla [bar'βiʎa] *nf* chin, tip of the chin
barbo ['barβo] *nm* barbel; **~ de mar** red
mullet
barbotear [barβote'ar] *vt, vi* to mutter,
mumble
barbudo, a [bar'βuðo, a] *adj* bearded
barca ['barka] *nf* (small) boat; **~ pesquera**
fishing boat; **~ de pasaje** ferry; **~za** *nf* barge;
~za de desembarco landing craft
Barcelona [barθe'lona] *n* Barcelona
barcelonés, esa [barθelo'nes, esa] *adj* of o
from Barcelona
barco ['barko] *nm* boat; (*grande*) ship; **~ de
carga** cargo boat; **~ de vela** sailing ship
baremo [ba'remo] *nm* (*MAT, fig*) scale
barítono [ba'ritono] *nm* baritone
barman ['barman] *nm* barman
Barna *n* = **Barcelona**
barniz [bar'niθ] *nm* varnish; (*en la loza*)
glaze; (*fig*) veneer; **~ar** *vt* to varnish; (*loza*)

to glaze
barómetro [ba'rometro] *nm* barometer
barquero [bar'kero] *nm* boatman
barquillo [bar'kiʎo] *nm* cone, cornet
barra ['barra] *nf* bar, rod; (*de un bar, café*)
bar; (*de pan*) French stick; (*palanca*) lever;
~ de carmín o **de labios** lipstick; **~ libre** free
bar
barraca [ba'rraka] *nf* hut, cabin
barranco [ba'rranko] *nm* ravine; (*fig*)
difficulty
barrena [ba'rrena] *nf* drill; **barrenar** *vt* to
drill (through), bore; **barreno** *nm* large drill
barrer [ba'rrer] *vt* to sweep; (*quitar*) to sweep
away
barrera [ba'rrera] *nf* barrier
barriada [ba'rrjaða] *nf* quarter, district
barricada [barri'kaða] *nf* barricade
barrida [ba'rriða] *nf* sweep, sweeping
barrido [ba'rriðo] *nm* = **barrida**
barriga [ba'rriɣa] *nf* belly; (*panza*) paunch;
barrigón, ona *adj* potbellied; **barrigudo, a**
adj potbellied
barril [ba'rril] *nm* barrel, cask
barrio ['barrjo] *nm* (*vecindad*) area,
neighborhood (*US*); (*en las afueras*) suburb;
~ chino red-light district
barro ['barro] *nm* (*lodo*) mud; (*objetos*)
earthenware; (*MED*) pimple
barroco, a [ba'rroko, a] *adj, nm* baroque
barrote [ba'rrote] *nm* (*de ventana*) bar
barruntar [barrun'tar] *vt* (*conjeturar*) to
guess; (*presentir*) to suspect; **barrunto** *nm*
guess; suspicion
bartola [bar'tola]: **a la ~** *adv*: **tirarse a la ~** to
take it easy, be lazy
bártulos ['bartulos] *nmpl* things, belongings
barullo [ba'ruʎo] *nm* row, uproar
basar [ba'sar] *vt* to base; **~se** *vr*: **~se en** to be
based on
báscula ['baskula] *nf* (*platform*) scales
base ['base] *nf* base; **a ~ de** on the basis of;
(*mediante*) by means of; **~ de datos** (*INFORM*)
database
básico, a ['basiko, a] *adj* basic
basílica [ba'silika] *nf* basilica

┌─────────────────────────┐
│ **PALABRA CLAVE** │
└─────────────────────────┘

bastante [bas'tante] *adj* **1** (*suficiente*)
enough; **~ dinero** enough o sufficient money;
~s libros enough books
2 (*valor intensivo*): **~ gente** quite a lot of
people; **tener ~ calor** to be rather hot
♦ *adv*: **~ bueno/malo** quite good/rather bad;
~ rico pretty rich; **(lo) ~ inteligente (como)
para hacer algo** clever enough o sufficiently
clever to do sth

bastar [bas'tar] *vi* to be enough o sufficient;

~se *vr* to be self-sufficient; **~ para** to be enough to; **¡basta!** (that's) enough!

bastardilla [bastar'ðiʎa] *nf* italics

bastardo, a [bas'tarðo, a] *adj, nm/f* bastard

bastidor [basti'ðor] *nm* frame; (*de coche*) chassis; (*TEATRO*) wing; **entre ~es** (*fig*) behind the scenes

basto, a ['basto, a] *adj* coarse, rough; **~s** *nmpl* (*NAIPES*) ≈ clubs

bastón [bas'ton] *nm* stick, staff; (*para pasear*) walking stick

bastoncillo [baston'θiʎo] *nm* cotton bud

basura [ba'sura] *nf* rubbish (*BRIT*), garbage (*US*)

basurero [basu'rero] *nm* (*hombre*) dustman (*BRIT*), garbage man (*US*); (*lugar*) dump; (*cubo*) (rubbish) bin (*BRIT*), trash can (*US*)

bata ['bata] *nf* (*gen*) dressing gown; (*cubretodo*) smock, overall; (*MED, TEC etc*) lab(oratory) coat

batalla [ba'taʎa] *nf* battle; **de ~** (*fig*) for everyday use

batallar [bata'ʎar] *vi* to fight

batallón [bata'ʎon] *nm* battalion

batata [ba'tata] *nf* sweet potato

batería [bate'ria] *nf* battery; (*MUS*) drums; **~ de cocina** kitchen utensils

batido, a [ba'tiðo, a] *adj* (*camino*) beaten, well-trodden ♦ *nm* (*CULIN*): **~ (de leche)** milk shake

batidora [bati'ðora] *nf* beater, mixer; **~ eléctrica** food mixer, blender

batir [ba'tir] *vt* to beat, strike; (*vencer*) to beat, defeat; (*revolver*) to beat, mix; **~se** *vr* to fight; **~ palmas** to clap, applaud

batuta [ba'tuta] *nf* baton; **llevar la ~** (*fig*) to be the boss, be in charge

baúl [ba'ul] *nm* trunk; (*AUTO*) boot (*BRIT*), trunk (*US*)

bautismo [bau'tismo] *nm* baptism, christening

bautizar [bauti'θar] *vt* to baptize, christen; (*fam: diluir*) to water down; **bautizo** *nm* baptism, christening

baya ['baja] *nf* berry

bayeta [ba'jeta] *nf* floorcloth

bayoneta [bajo'neta] *nf* bayonet

baza ['baθa] *nf* trick; **meter ~** to butt in

bazar [ba'θar] *nm* bazaar

bazofia [ba'θofja] *nf* trash

BCE *nm abr* (= *Banco Central Europeo*) ECB

beato, a [be'ato, a] *adj* blessed; (*piadoso*) pious

bebé [be'ße] (*pl* **~s**) *nm* baby

bebedor, a [beße'ðor, a] *adj* hard-drinking

beber [be'ßer] *vt, vi* to drink

bebida [be'ßiða] *nf* drink; **bebido, a** *adj* drunk

beca ['beka] *nf* grant, scholarship

becario, a [be'karjo, a] *nm/f* scholarship holder, grant holder

bedel [be'ðel] *nm* (*ESCOL*) janitor; (*UNIV*) porter

béisbol ['beisßol] *nm* (*DEPORTE*) baseball

belén [be'len] *nm* (*de navidad*) nativity scene, crib; **B~** Bethlehem

belga ['belxa] *adj, nm/f* Belgian

Bélgica ['belxika] *nf* Belgium

bélico, a ['beliko, a] *adj* (*actitud*) warlike; **belicoso, a** *adj* (*guerrero*) warlike; (*agresivo*) aggressive, bellicose

beligerante [belixe'rante] *adj* belligerent

belleza [be'ʎeθa] *nf* beauty

bello, a ['beʎo, a] *adj* beautiful, lovely; **Bellas Artes** Fine Art

bellota [be'ʎota] *nf* acorn

bemol [be'mol] *nm* (*MUS*) flat; **esto tiene ~es** (*fam*) this is a tough one

bencina [ben'θina] *nf* (*AM*) (*gasolina*) petrol (*BRIT*), gasoline (*US*)

bendecir [bende'θir] *vt* to bless

bendición [bendi'θjon] *nf* blessing

bendito, a [ben'dito, a] *pp de* **bendecir** ♦ *adj* holy; (*afortunado*) lucky; (*feliz*) happy; (*sencillo*) simple ♦ *nm/f* simple soul

beneficencia [benefi'θenθja] *nf* charity

beneficiar [benefi'θjar] *vt* to benefit, be of benefit to; **~se** *vr* to benefit, profit; **~io, a** *nm/f* beneficiary

beneficio [bene'fiθjo] *nm* (*bien*) benefit, advantage; (*ganancia*) profit, gain; **~so, a** *adj* beneficial

benéfico, a [be'nefiko, a] *adj* charitable

beneplácito [bene'plaθito] *nm* approval, consent

benevolencia [beneßo'lenθja] *nf* benevolence, kindness; **benévolo, a** *adj* benevolent, kind

benigno, a [be'niɣno, a] *adj* kind; (*suave*) mild; (*MED: tumor*) benign, non-malignant

berberecho [berße'retʃo] *nm* (*ZOOL, CULIN*) cockle

berenjena [beren'xena] *nf* aubergine (*BRIT*), eggplant (*US*)

Berlín [ber'lin] *n* Berlin; **berlinés, esa** *adj* of o from Berlin ♦ *nm/f* Berliner

bermudas [ber'muðas] *nfpl* Bermuda shorts

berrear [berre'ar] *vi* to bellow, low

berrido [be'rriðo] *nm* bellow(ing)

berrinche [be'rrintʃe] (*fam*) *nm* temper, tantrum

berro ['berro] *nm* watercress

berza ['berθa] *nf* cabbage

besamel [besa'mel] *nf* (*CULIN*) white sauce, bechamel sauce

besar [be'sar] *vt* to kiss; (*fig: tocar*) to graze; **~se** *vr* to kiss (one another); **beso** *nm* kiss

bestia ['bestja] *nf* beast, animal; (*fig*) idiot;

~ **de carga** beast of burden
bestial [bes'tjal] *adj* bestial; (*fam*) terrific;
  ~**idad** *nf* bestiality; (*fam*) stupidity
besugo [be'suɣo] *nm* sea bream; (*fam*) idiot
besuquear [besuke'ar] *vt* to cover with
  kisses; ~**se** *vr* to kiss and cuddle
betún [be'tun] *nm* shoe polish; (*QUÍM*)
  bitumen
biberón [biβe'ron] *nm* feeding bottle
Biblia ['biβlja] *nf* Bible
bibliografía [biβljoɣra'fia] *nf* bibliography
biblioteca [biβljo'teka] *nf* library; (*mueble*)
  bookshelves; ~ **de consulta** reference library;
  ~**rio, a** *nm/f* librarian
bicarbonato [bikarβo'nato] *nm* bicarbonate
bicho ['bitʃo] *nm* (*animal*) small animal;
  (*sabandija*) bug, insect; (*TAUR*) bull
bici ['biθi] (*fam*) *nf* bike
bicicleta [biθi'kleta] *nf* bicycle, cycle; **ir en** ~
  to cycle
bidé [bi'ðe] (*pl* ~**s**) *nm* bidet
bidón [bi'ðon] *nm* (*de aceite*) drum; (*de
gasolina*) can

PALABRA CLAVE
---

bien [bjen] *nm* 1 (*bienestar*) good; **te lo digo
por tu** ~ I'm telling you for your own good; **el
~ y el mal** good and evil
  2 (*posesión*) ~**es** goods; ~**es de consumo**
consumer goods; ~**es inmuebles** o **raíces/~es
muebles** real estate *sg*/personal property *sg*
  ♦ *adv* 1 (*de manera satisfactoria, correcta etc*)
well; **trabaja/come** ~ she works/eats well;
contestó ~ he answered correctly; **me siento**
~ I feel fine; **no me siento** ~ I don't feel very
well; **se está** ~ **aquí** it's nice here
  2 (*frases*): **hiciste** ~ **en llamarme** you were
right to call me
  3 (*valor intensivo*) very; **un cuarto** ~ **caliente**
a nice warm room; ~ **se ve que ...** it's quite
clear that ...
  4: **estar** ~: **estoy muy** ~ **aquí** I feel very happy
here; **está** ~ **que vengan** it's all right for them
to come; **¡está** ~! **lo haré** oh all right, I'll do it
  5 (*de buena gana*): **yo** ~ **que iría pero ...** I'd
gladly go but ...
  ♦ *excl*: **¡~!** (*aprobación*) O.K.!; **¡muy ~!** well
done!
  ♦ *adj inv* (*matiz despectivo*): **niño** ~ rich kid;
gente ~ posh people
  ♦ *conj* 1: ~ **... ~:** ~ **en coche** ~ **en tren** either
by car or by train
  2: **no** ~ (*esp AM*): **no** ~ **llegue te llamaré** as
soon as I arrive I'll call you
  3: **si** ~ even though; *ver tb* **más**

---

bienal [bje'nal] *adj* biennial
bienaventurado, a [bjenaβentu'raðo, a]
  adj (*feliz*) happy, fortunate

bienestar [bjenes'tar] *nm* well-being, welfare
bienhechor, a [bjene'tʃor, a] *adj* beneficent
  ♦ *nm/f* benefactor/benefactress
bienvenida [bjembe'niða] *nf* welcome; **dar
la** ~ **a uno** to welcome sb
bienvenido [bjembe'niðo] *excl* welcome!
bife ['bife] (*AM*) *nm* steak
bifurcación [bifurka'θjon] *nf* fork
bifurcarse [bifur'karse] *vr* (*camino, carretera,
río*) to fork
bigamia [bi'vamja] *nf* bigamy; **bígamo, a**
  adj bigamous ♦ *nm/f* bigamist
bigote [bi'vote] *nm* moustache; **bigotudo, a**
  adj with a big moustache
bikini [bi'kini] *nm* bikini; (*CULIN*) toasted ham
and cheese sandwich
bilbaíno, a [bilβa'ino, a] *adj* from o of Bilbao
bilingüe [bi'lingwe] *adj* bilingual
billar [bi'ʎar] *nm* billiards *sg*; (*lugar*) billiard
hall; (*mini-casino*) amusement arcade;
~ **americano** pool
billete [bi'ʎete] *nm* ticket; (*de banco*)
(bank)note (*BRIT*), bill (*US*); (*carta*) note;
~ **sencillo**, ~ **de ida solamente** single (*BRIT*) o
one-way (*US*) ticket; ~ **de ida y vuelta** return
(*BRIT*) o round-trip (*US*) ticket; ~ **de 20 libras**
£20 note
billetera [biʎe'tera] *nf* wallet
billetero [biʎe'tero] *nm* = **billetera**
billón [bi'ʎon] *nm* billion
bimensual [bimen'swal] *adj* twice monthly
bimotor [bimo'tor] *adj* twin-engined ♦ *nm*
twin-engined plane
bingo ['bingo] *nm* bingo
biodegradable [bioðeɣra'ðaβle] *adj*
biodegradable
biografía [bjoɣra'fia] *nf* biography;
biógrafo, a *nm/f* biographer
biología [bjolo'xia] *nf* biology; **biológico, a**
  adj biological; (*cultivo, producto*) organic;
biólogo, a *nm/f* biologist
biombo ['bjombo] *nm* (*folding*) screen
biopsia [bi'opsja] *nf* biopsy
biquini [bi'kini] *nm* bikini
birlar [bir'lar] (*fam*) *vt* to pinch
Birmania [bir'manja] *nf* Burma
birria ['birrja] *nf*: **ser una** ~ (*película, libro*) to
be rubbish
bis [bis] *excl* encore! ♦ *adv*: **viven en el 27** ~
they live at 27a
bisabuelo, a [bisa'βwelo, a] *nm/f* great-
grandfather/mother
bisagra [bi'saɣra] *nf* hinge
bisiesto [bi'sjesto] *adj*: **año** ~ leap year
bisnieto, a [bis'njeto, a] *nm/f* great-
grandson/daughter
bisonte [bi'sonte] *nm* bison
bisté [bis'te] *nm* = **bistec**
bistec [bis'tek] *nm* steak

bisturí [bistu'ri] nm scalpel

bisutería [bisute'ria] nf imitation o costume jewellery

bit [bit] nm (INFORM) bit

bizco, a ['biθko, a] adj cross-eyed

bizcocho [biθ'kotʃo] nm (CULIN) sponge cake

bizquear [biθke'ar] vi to squint

blanca ['blanka] nf (MUS) minim; **estar sin ~** to be broke; ver tb blanco

blanco, a ['blanko, a] adj white ♦ nm/f white man/woman, white ♦ nm (color) white; (en texto) blank; (MIL, fig) target; **en ~** blank; **noche en ~** sleepless night

blancura [blan'kura] nf whiteness

blandir [blan'dir] vt to brandish

blando, a ['blando, a] adj soft; (tierno) tender, gentle; (carácter) mild; (fam) cowardly; **blandura** nf softness; tenderness; mildness

blanquear [blanke'ar] vt to whiten; (fachada) to whitewash; (paño) to bleach ♦ vi to turn white; **blanquecino, a** adj whitish

blasfemar [blasfe'mar] vi to blaspheme, curse; **blasfemia** nf blasphemy

blasón [bla'son] nm coat of arms

bledo ['bleðo] nm: **me importa un ~** I couldn't care less

blindado, a [blin'daðo, a] adj (MIL) armour-plated; (antibala) bullet-proof; **coche** (ESP) o **carro** (AM) **~** armoured car

blindaje [blin'daxe] nm armour, armour-plating

bloc [blok] (pl ~s) nm writing pad

bloque ['bloke] nm block; (POL) bloc; **~ de cilindros** cylinder block

bloquear [bloke'ar] vt to blockade; **bloqueo** nm blockade; (COM) freezing, blocking

blusa ['blusa] nf blouse

boato [bo'ato] nm show, ostentation

bobada [bo'ßaða] nf foolish action; foolish statement; **decir ~s** to talk nonsense

bobería [boße'ria] nf = **bobada**

bobina [bo'ßina] nf (TEC) bobbin; (FOTO) spool; (ELEC) coil

bobo, a ['boßo, a] adj (tonto) daft, silly; (cándido) naïve ♦ nm/f fool, idiot ♦ nm (TEATRO) clown, funny man

boca ['boka] nf mouth; (de crustáceo) pincer; (de cañón) muzzle; (entrada) mouth, entrance; **~s** nfpl (de río) mouth sg; **~ abajo/arriba** face down/up; **se me hace agua la ~** my mouth is watering

bocacalle [boka'kaʎe] nf (entrance to a) street; **la primera ~** the first turning o street

bocadillo [boka'ðiʎo] nm sandwich

bocado [bo'kaðo] nm mouthful, bite; (de caballo) bridle; **~ de Adán** Adam's apple

bocajarro [boka'xarro]: **a ~** adv (disparar,

preguntar) point-blank

bocanada [boka'naða] nf (de vino) mouthful, swallow; (de aire) gust, puff

bocata [bo'kata] (fam) nm sandwich

bocazas [bo'kaθas] (fam) nm inv bigmouth

boceto [bo'θeto] nm sketch, outline

bochorno [bo'tʃorno] nm (vergüenza) embarrassment; (calor): **hace ~** it's very muggy; **~so, a** adj muggy; embarrassing

bocina [bo'θina] nf (MUS) trumpet; (AUTO) horn; (para hablar) megaphone

boda ['boða] nf (tb: ~s) wedding, marriage; (fiesta) wedding reception; **~s de plata/de oro** silver/golden wedding

bodega [bo'ðeɣa] nf (de vino) (wine) cellar; (depósito) storeroom; (de barco) hold

bodegón [boðe'ɣon] nm (ARTE) still life

bofe ['bofe] nm (tb: ~s: de res) lights

bofetada [bofe'taða] nf slap (in the face)

bofetón [bofe'ton] nm = **bofetada**

boga ['boɣa] nf: **en ~** (fig) in vogue

bogar [bo'ɣar] vi (remar) to row; (navegar) to sail

bogavante [boɣa'ßante] nm lobster

Bogotá [boɣo'ta] n Bogotá

bohemio, a [bo'emjo, a] adj, nm/f Bohemian

boicot [boi'kot] (pl ~s) nm boycott; **~ear** vt to boycott; **~eo** nm boycott

boina ['boina] nf beret

bola ['bola] nf ball; (canica) marble; (NAIPES) (grand) slam; (betún) shoe polish; (mentira) tale, story; **~s** (AM) nfpl bolas sg; **~ de billar** billiard ball; **~ de nieve** snowball

bolchevique [boltʃe'ßike] adj, nm/f Bolshevik

boleadoras [bolea'ðoras] (AM) nfpl bolas sg

bolera [bo'lera] nf skittle o bowling alley

boleta [bo'leta] (AM) nf (billete) ticket; (permiso) pass, permit

boletería [bolete'ria] (AM) nf ticket office

boletín [bole'tin] nm bulletin; (periódico) journal, review; **~ de noticias** news bulletin

boleto [bo'leto] nm ticket

boli ['boli] (fam) nm Biro ®, pen

bolígrafo [bo'liɣrafo] nm ball-point pen, Biro ®

bolívar [bo'lißar] nm monetary unit of Venezuela

Bolivia [bo'lißja] nf Bolivia; **boliviano, a** adj, nm/f Bolivian

bollería [boʎe'ria] nf cakes pl and pastries pl

bollo ['boʎo] nm (pan) roll; (bulto) bump, lump; (abolladura) dent

bolo ['bolo] nm skittle; (píldora) (large) pill; (juego de) **~s** nmpl skittles sg

bolsa ['bolsa] nf (AM) bag; (ANAT) pocket; (COM) stock exchange; (MINERÍA) cavity, sac; (COM) stock exchange; (MINERÍA) pocket; **~ de ~** pocket cpd; **~ de agua caliente** hot water bottle; **~ de aire** air pocket; **~ de**

papel paper bag; **~ de plástico** plastic bag
bolsillo [bol'siʎo] nm pocket; (cartera) purse; **de ~** pocket(-size)
bolsista [bol'sista] nm/f stockbroker
bolso ['bolso] nm (bolsa) bag; (de mujer) handbag
bomba ['bomba] nf (MIL) bomb; (TEC) pump ♦ (fam) adj: **noticia ~** bombshell ♦ (fam) adv: **pasarlo ~** to have a great time; **~ atómica/de humo/de efecto retardado** atomic/smoke/time bomb
bombardear [bombarðe'ar] vt to bombard; (MIL) to bomb; **bombardeo** nm bombardment; bombing
bombardero [bombar'ðero] nm bomber
bombear [bombe'ar] vt (agua) to pump (out o up); **~se** vr to warp
bombero [bom'bero] nm fireman
bombilla [bom'biʎa] (ESP) nf (light) bulb
bombín [bom'bin] nm bowler hat
bombo ['bombo] nm (MUS) bass drum; (TEC) drum
bombón [bom'bon] nm chocolate
bombona [bom'bona] nf (de butano, oxígeno) cylinder
bonachón, ona [bona'tʃon, ona] adj good-natured, easy-going
bonanza [bo'nanθa] nf (NAUT) fair weather; (fig) bonanza; (MINERÍA) rich pocket o vein
bondad [bon'daθ] nf goodness, kindness; **tenga la ~ de** (please) be good enough to; **~oso, a** adj good, kind
bonificación [bonifika'θjon] nf bonus
bonito, a [bo'nito, a] adj pretty; (agradable) nice ♦ nm (atún) tuna (fish)
bono ['bono] nm voucher; (FIN) bond
bonobús [bono'ßus] (ESP) nm bus pass
bonoloto [bono'loto] nf state-run weekly lottery
boquerón [boke'ron] nm (pez) (kind of) anchovy; (agujero) large hole
boquete [bo'kete] nm gap, hole
boquiabierto, a [bokia'ßjerto, a] adj: **quedar ~** to be amazed o flabbergasted
boquilla [bo'kiʎa] nf (para riego) nozzle; (para cigarro) cigarette holder; (MUS) mouthpiece
borbotón [borßo'ton] nm: **salir a borbotones** to gush out
borda ['borða] nf (NAUT) (ship's) rail; **tirar algo/caerse por la ~** to throw sth/fall overboard
bordado [bor'ðaðo] nm embroidery
bordar [bor'ðar] vt to embroider
borde ['borðe] nm edge, border; (de camino etc) side; (en la costura) hem; **al ~ de** (fig) on the verge o brink of; **ser ~** (ESP: fam) to be rude; **~ar** vt to border
bordillo [bor'ðiʎo] nm kerb (BRIT), curb (US)

bordo ['borðo] nm (NAUT) side; **a ~** on board
borinqueño, a [borin'kenjo, a] adj, nm/f Puerto Rican
borla ['borla] nf (adorno) tassel
borrachera [borra'tʃera] nf (ebriedad) drunkenness; (orgía) spree, binge
borracho, a [bo'rratʃo, a] adj drunk ♦ nm/f (habitual) drunkard, drunk; (temporal) drunk, drunk man/woman
borrador [borra'ðor] nm (escritura) first draft, rough sketch; (goma) rubber (BRIT), eraser
borrar [bo'rrar] vt to erase, rub out
borrasca [bo'rraska] nf storm
borrico, a [bo'rriko, a] nm/f donkey/she-donkey; (fig) stupid man/woman
borrón [bo'rron] nm (mancha) stain
borroso, a [bo'rroso, a] adj vague, unclear; (escritura) illegible
bosque ['boske] nm wood; (grande) forest
bosquejar [boske'xar] vt to sketch; **bosquejo** nm sketch
bostezar [boste'θar] vi to yawn; **bostezo** nm yawn
bota ['bota] nf (calzado) boot; (para vino) leather wine bottle; **~s de agua, ~s de goma** Wellingtons
botánica [bo'tanika] nf (ciencia) botany; ver tb botánico
botánico, a [bo'taniko, a] adj botanical ♦ nm/f botanist
botar [bo'tar] vt to throw, hurl; (NAUT) to launch; (AM) to throw out ♦ vi to bounce
bote ['bote] nm (salto) bounce; (golpe) thrust; (vasija) tin, can; (embarcación) boat; **de ~ en ~** packed, jammed full; **~ de la basura** (AM) dustbin (BRIT), trashcan (US); **~ salvavidas** lifeboat
botella [bo'teʎa] nf bottle; **botellín** nm small bottle
botica [bo'tika] nf chemist's (shop) (BRIT), pharmacy; **~rio, a** nm/f chemist (BRIT), pharmacist
botijo [bo'tixo] nm (earthenware) jug
botín [bo'tin] nm (calzado) half boot; (polaina) spat; (MIL) booty
botiquín [boti'kin] nm (armario) medicine cabinet; (portátil) first-aid kit
botón [bo'ton] nm button; (BOT) bud; **~ de oro** buttercup
botones [bo'tones] nm inv bellboy (BRIT), bellhop (US)
bóveda ['boßeða] nf (ARQ) vault
boxeador [boksea'ðor] nm boxer
boxear [bokse'ar] vi to box
boxeo [bok'seo] nm boxing
boya ['boja] nf (NAUT) buoy; (de caña) float
boyante [bo'jante] adj prosperous
bozal [bo'θal] nm (de caballo) halter; (de perro) muzzle

bracear [braθe'ar] vi (agitar los brazos) to wave one's arms

bracero [bra'θero] nm labourer; (en el campo) farmhand

bragas [bra'veta] nfpl (de mujer) panties, knickers (BRIT)

bragueta [bra'veta] nf fly, flies pl

braille [breil] nm braille

bramar [bra'mar] vi to bellow, roar; **bramido** nm bellow, roar

brasa ['brasa] nf live o hot coal

brasero [bra'sero] nm brazier

Brasil [bra'sil] nm: (el) ~ Brazil; **brasileño, a** adj, nm/f Brazilian

bravata [bra'ßata] nf boast

braveza [bra'ßeθa] nf (valor) bravery; (ferocidad) ferocity

bravío, a [bra'ßio, a] adj wild; (feroz) fierce

bravo, a ['braßo, a] adj (valiente) brave; (feroz) ferocious; (salvaje) wild; (mar etc) rough, stormy ♦ excl bravo!; **bravura** nf bravery; ferocity

braza ['braθa] nf fathom; **nadar a la ~** to swim (the) breast-stroke

brazada [bra'θaða] nf stroke

brazado [bra'θaðo] nm armful

brazalete [braθa'lete] nm (pulsera) bracelet; (banda) armband

brazo ['braθo] nm arm; (ZOOL) foreleg; (BOT) limb, branch; **luchar a ~ partido** to fight hand-to-hand; **ir cogidos del ~** to walk arm in arm

brea ['brea] nf pitch, tar

brebaje [bre'ßaxe] nm potion

brecha ['bretʃa] nf (hoyo, vacío) gap, opening; (MIL, fig) breach

brega ['breva] nf (lucha) struggle; (trabajo) hard work

breva ['breßa] nf early fig

breve ['breße] adj short, brief ♦ nf (MUS) breve; **~dad** nf brevity, shortness

brezo ['breθo] nm heather

bribón, ona [bri'ßon, ona] adj idle, lazy ♦ nm/f (pícaro) rascal, rogue

bricolaje [briko'laxe] nm do-it-yourself, DIY

brida ['briða] nf bridle, rein; (TEC) clamp; **a toda ~** at top speed

bridge [britʃ] nm bridge

brigada [bri'vaða] nf (unidad) brigade; (trabajadores) squad, gang ♦ nm ≈ staff-sergeant, sergeant-major

brillante [bri'ʎante] adj brilliant ♦ nm diamond

brillar [bri'ʎar] vi (tb fig) to shine; (joyas) to sparkle

brillo ['briʎo] nm shine; (brillantez) brilliance; (fig) splendour; **sacar ~ a** to polish

brincar [brin'kar] vi to skip about, hop about, jump about; **está que brinca** he's hopping mad

brinco ['brinko] nm jump, leap

brindar [brin'dar] vi: **~ a** o **por** to drink (a toast) to ♦ vt to offer, present

brindis ['brindis] nm inv toast

brío ['brio] nm spirit, dash; **brioso, a** adj spirited, dashing

brisa ['brisa] nf breeze

británico, a [bri'taniko, a] adj British ♦ nm/f Briton, British person

brizna ['briθna] nf (de hierba, paja) blade; (de tabaco) leaf

broca ['broka] nf (TEC) drill, bit

brocal [bro'kal] nm rim

brocha ['brotʃa] nf (large) paintbrush; **~ de afeitar** shaving brush

broche ['brotʃe] nm brooch

broma ['broma] nf joke; **en ~** in fun, as a joke; **~ pesada** practical joke; **bromear** vi to joke

bromista [bro'mista] adj fond of joking ♦ nm/f joker, wag

bronca ['bronka] nf row; **echar una ~ a uno** to tick sb off

bronce ['bronθe] nm bronze; **~ado, a** adj bronze; (por el sol) tanned ♦ nm (sun)tan; (TEC) bronzing

bronceador [bronθea'ðor] nm suntan lotion

broncearse [bronθe'arse] vr to get a suntan

bronco, a ['bronko, a] adj (manera) rude, surly; (voz) harsh

bronquio ['bronkjo] nm (ANAT) bronchial tube

bronquitis [bron'kitis] nf inv bronchitis

brotar [bro'tar] vi (BOT) to sprout; (aguas) to gush (forth); (MED) to break out

brote ['brote] nm (BOT) shoot; (MED, fig) outbreak

bruces ['bruθes]: **de ~** adv: **caer** o **dar de ~** to fall headlong, fall flat

bruja ['bruxa] nf witch; **brujería** nf witchcraft

brujo ['bruxo] nm wizard, magician

brújula ['bruxula] nf compass

bruma ['bruma] nf mist; **brumoso, a** adj misty

bruñir [bru'ɲir] vt to polish

brusco, a ['brusko, a] adj (súbito) sudden; (áspero) brusque

Bruselas [bru'selas] n Brussels

brutal [bru'tal] adj brutal

brutalidad [brutali'ðað] nf brutality

bruto, a ['bruto, a] adj (idiota) stupid; (bestial) brutish; (peso) gross; **en ~** raw, unworked

Bs.As. abr (= Buenos Aires) B.A.

bucal [bu'kal] adj oral; **por vía ~** orally

bucear [buθe'ar] vi to dive ♦ vt to explore; **buceo** nm diving

bucle ['bukle] nm curl

budismo [bu'ðismo] *nm* Buddhism

buen [bwen] *adj m ver* **bueno**

buenamente [bwena'mente] *adv* (*fácilmente*) easily; (*voluntariamente*) willingly

buenaventura [bwenaßen'tura] *nf* (*suerte*) good luck; (*adivinación*) fortune

---
PALABRA CLAVE
---

bueno, a ['bweno, a] *adj* (*antes de nmsg:* **buen**) **1** (*excelente etc*) good; **es un libro ~, es un buen libro** it's a good book; **hace ~, hace buen tiempo** the weather is fine, it is fine; **el ~ de Paco** good old Paco; **fue muy ~ conmigo** he was very nice o kind to me

2 (*apropiado*) **ser ~ para** to be good for; **creo que vamos por buen camino** I think we're on the right track

3 (*irónico*) **le di un buen rapapolvo** I gave him a good o real ticking off; **¡buen conductor estás hecho!** some o a fine driver you are!; **¡estaría ~ que ...!** a fine thing it would be if ...!

4 (*atractivo, sabroso*) **está ~ este bizcocho** this sponge is delicious; **Carmen está muy buena** Carmen is gorgeous

5 (*saludos*) **¡buen día!, ¡~s días!** (good) morning!; **¡buenas (tardes)!** (good) afternoon!; (*más tarde*) (good) evening!; **¡buenas noches!** good night!

6 (*otras locuciones*) **estar de buenas** to be in a good mood; **por las buenas o por las malas** by hook or by crook; **de buenas a primeras** all of a sudden

♦ *excl*: **¡~!** all right!; **~, ¿y qué?** well, so what?

Buenos Aires *nm* Buenos Aires

buey [bwei] *nm* ox

búfalo ['bufalo] *nm* buffalo

bufanda [bu'fanda] *nf* scarf

bufar [bu'far] *vi* to snort

bufete [bu'fete] *nm* (*despacho de abogado*) lawyer's office

buffer ['bufer] *nm* (*INFORM*) buffer

bufón [bu'fon] *nm* clown

buhardilla [buar'ðiʎa] *nf* attic

búho ['buo] *nm* owl; (*fig*) hermit, recluse

buhonero [buo'nero] *nm* pedlar

buitre ['bwitre] *nm* vulture

bujía [bu'xia] *nf* (*vela*) candle; (*ELEC*) candle (power); (*AUTO*) spark plug

bula ['bula] *nf* (*papal*) bull

bulbo ['bulβo] *nm* bulb

bulevar [bule'ßar] *nm* boulevard

Bulgaria [bul'yarja] *nf* Bulgaria; **búlgaro, a** *adj, nm/f* Bulgarian

bulla ['buʎa] *nf* (*ruido*) uproar; (*de gente*) crowd

bullicio [bu'ʎiθjo] *nm* (*ruido*) uproar; (*movimiento*) bustle

bullir [bu'ʎir] *vi* (*hervir*) to boil; (*burbujear*) to bubble

bulto ['bulto] *nm* (*paquete*) package; (*fardo*) bundle; (*tamaño*) size, bulkiness; (*MED*) swelling, lump; (*silueta*) vague shape

buñuelo [bu'nwelo] *nm* ≈ doughnut (*BRIT*), ≈ donut (*US*); (*fruta de sartén*) fritter

BUP [bup] *nm abr* (*ESP*: = *Bachillerato Unificado Polivalente*) secondary education and leaving certificate for 14–17 age group

buque ['buke] *nm* ship, vessel

burbuja [bur'ßuxa] *nf* bubble; **burbujear** *vi* to bubble

burdel [bur'ðel] *nm* brothel

burdo, a ['burðo, a] *adj* coarse, rough

burgués, esa [bur'ves, esa] *adj* middle-class, bourgeois; **burguesía** *nf* middle class, bourgeoisie

buria ['burla] *nf* (*mofa*) gibe; (*broma*) joke; (*engaño*) trick

burladero [burla'ðero] *nm* (*bullfighter's*) refuge

burlar [bur'lar] *vt* (*engañar*) to deceive ♦ *vi* to joke; **~se** *vr* to joke; **~se de** to make fun of

burlesco, a [bur'lesko, a] *adj* burlesque

burlón, ona [bur'lon, ona] *adj* mocking

burocracia [buro'kraθja] *nf* civil service

burócrata [bu'rokrata] *nm/f* civil servant

burrada [bu'rraða] *nf*: **decir/soltar ~s** to talk nonsense; **hacer ~s** to act stupid; **una ~** (*mucho*) a (hell of a) lot

burro, a ['burro, a] *nm/f* donkey/she-donkey; (*fig*) ass, idiot

bursátil [bur'satil] *adj* stock-exchange *cpd*

bus [bus] *nm* bus

busca ['buska] *nf* search, hunt ♦ *nm* (*TEL*) bleeper; **en ~ de** in search of

buscar [bus'kar] *vt* to look for, search for, seek ♦ *vi* to look, search, seek; **se busca secretaria** secretary wanted

busque *etc vb ver* **buscar**

búsqueda ['buskeða] *nf* = **busca** *nf*

busto ['busto] *nm* (*ANAT, ARTE*) bust

butaca [bu'taka] *nf* armchair; (*de cine, teatro*) stall, seat

butano [bu'tano] *nm* butane (gas)

buzo ['buθo] *nm* diver

buzón [bu'θon] *nm* (*en puerta*) letter box; (*en la calle*) pillar box

C, c

C. *abr* (= *centígrado*) C; (= *compañía*) Co.

c. *abr* (= *capítulo*) ch.

C/ *abr* (= *calle*) St

c.a. *abr* (= *corriente alterna*) AC

cabal [ka'ßal] *adj* (*exacto*) exact; (*correcto*) right, proper; (*acabado*) finished, complete;

~es *nmpl*: **estar en sus ~es** to be in one's right mind

cábalas ['kaβalas] *nfpl*: **hacer ~** to guess

cabalgar [kaβal'γar] *vt, vi* to ride

cabalgata [kaβal'γata] *nf* procession

caballa [ka'βaλa] *nf* mackerel

caballeresco, a [kaβaλe'resko, a] *adj* noble, chivalrous

caballería [kaβaλe'ria] *nf* mount; (*MIL*) cavalry

caballeriza [kaβaλe'riθa] *nf* stable; **caballerizo** *nm* groom, stableman

caballero [kaβa'λero] *nm* gentleman; (*de la orden de caballería*) knight; (*trato directo*) sir

caballerosidad [kaβaλerosi'ðað] *nf* chivalry

caballete [kaβa'λete] *nm* (*ARTE*) easel; (*TEC*) trestle

caballito [kaβa'λito] *nm* (*caballo pequeño*) small horse, pony; **~s** *nmpl* (*en verbena*) roundabout, merry-go-round

caballo [ka'βaλo] *nm* horse; (*AJEDREZ*) knight; (*NAIPES*) queen; **ir en ~** to ride; **~ de vapor** o **de fuerza** horsepower; **~ de carreras** racehorse

cabaña [ka'βaɲa] *nf* (*casita*) hut, cabin

cabaré [kaβa're] (*pl* **~s**) *nm* cabaret

cabaret [kaβa're] (*pl* **~s**) *nm* cabaret

cabecear [kaβeθe'ar] *vt, vi* to nod

cabecera [kaβe'θera] *nf* head; (*IMPRENTA*) headline

cabecilla [kaβe'θiλa] *nm* ringleader

cabellera [kaβe'λera] *nf* (head of) hair; (*de cometa*) tail

cabello [ka'βeλo] *nm* (*tb*: **~s**) hair

caber [ka'βer] *vi* (*entrar*) to fit, go; **caben 3 más** there's room for 3 more

cabestrillo [kaβes'triλo] *nm* sling

cabestro [ka'βestro] *nm* halter

cabeza [ka'βeθa] *nf* head; (*POL*) chief, leader; **~ rapada** skinhead; **~da** *nf* (*golpe*) butt; **dar ~das** to nod off; **cabezón, ona** *adj* (*vino*) heady; (*fam*: *persona*) pig-headed

cabida [ka'βiða] *nf* space

cabildo [ka'βildo] *nm* (*de iglesia*) chapter; (*POL*) town council

cabina [ka'βina] *nf* cabin; (*de camión*) cab; **~ telefónica** telephone box (*BRIT*) o booth

cabizbajo, a [kaβiθ'βaxo, a] *adj* crestfallen, dejected

cable ['kaβle] *nm* cable

cabo ['kaβo] *nm* (*de objeto*) end, extremity; (*MIL*) corporal; (*NAUT*) rope, cable; (*GEO*) cape; **al ~ de 3 días** after 3 days

cabra ['kaβra] *nf* goat

cabré *etc vb ver* **caber**

cabrear [kaβre'ar] (*fam*) *vt* to bug; **~se** *vr* (*enfadarse*) to fly off the handle

cabrío, a [ka'βrio, a] *adj* goatish; **macho ~** (he-)goat, billy goat

cabriola [ka'βrjola] *nf* caper

cabritilla [kaβri'tiλa] *nf* kid, kidskin

cabrito [ka'βrito] *nm* kid

cabrón [ka'βron] *nm* cuckold; (*fam!*) bastard (!)

caca ['kaka] (*fam*) *nf* pooh

cacahuete [kaka'wete] (*ESP*) *nm* peanut

cacao [ka'kao] *nm* cocoa; (*BOT*) cacao

cacarear [kakare'ar] *vi* (*persona*) to boast; (*gallina*) to crow

cacería [kaθe'ria] *nf* hunt

cacerola [kaθe'rola] *nf* pan, saucepan

cachalote [katʃa'lote] *nm* (*ZOOL*) sperm whale

cacharro [ka'tʃarro] *nm* earthenware pot; **~s** *nmpl* pots and pans

cachear [katʃe'ar] *vt* to search, frisk

cachemir [katʃe'mir] *nm* cashmere

cacheo [ka'tʃeo] *nm* searching, frisking

cachete [ka'tʃete] *nm* (*ANAT*) cheek; (*bofetada*) slap (in the face)

cachiporra [katʃi'porra] *nf* truncheon

cachivache [katʃi'βatʃe] *nm* (*trasto*) piece of junk; **~s** *nmpl* junk *sg*

cacho ['katʃo] *nm* (small) bit; (*AM*: *cuerno*) horn

cachondeo [katʃon'deo] (*fam*) *nm* farce, joke

cachondo, a [ka'tʃondo, a] *adj* (*ZOOL*) on heat; (*fam*: *sexualmente*) randy; (: *gracioso*) funny

cachorro, a [ka'tʃorro, a] *nm/f* (*perro*) pup, puppy; (*león*) cub

cacique [ka'θike] *nm* chief, local ruler; (*POL*) local party boss; **caciquismo** *nm* system of control by the local boss

caco ['kako] *nm* pickpocket

cacto ['kakto] *nm* cactus

cactus ['kaktus] *nm inv* cactus

cada ['kaða] *adj inv* each; (*antes de número*) every; **~ día** each day, every day; **~ dos días** every other day; **~ uno/a** each one, every one; **~ vez más/menos** more and more/less and less; **uno de ~ diez** one out of every ten

cadalso [ka'ðalso] *nm* scaffold

cadáver [ka'ðaβer] *nm* (dead) body, corpse

cadena [ka'ðena] *nf* chain; (*TV*) channel; **trabajo en ~** assembly line work; **~ perpetua** (*JUR*) life imprisonment

cadencia [ka'ðenθja] *nf* rhythm

cadera [ka'ðera] *nf* hip

cadete [ka'ðete] *nm* cadet

caducar [kaðu'kar] *vi* to expire; **caduco, a** *adj* expired; (*persona*) very old

caer [ka'er] *vi* to fall (down); **~se** *vr* to fall (down); **me cae bien/mal** I get on well with him/I can't stand him; **~ en la cuenta** to realize; **su cumpleaños cae en viernes** her birthday falls on a Friday

café [ka'fe] (*pl* **~s**) *nm* (*bebida, planta*) coffee;

(*lugar*) café ♦ *adj* (*color*) brown; ~ **con leche** white coffee; ~ **solo** black coffee

cafetera [kafe'tera] *nf* coffee pot

cafetería [kafete'ria] *nf* (*gen*) café

cafetero, a [kafe'tero, a] *adj* coffee *cpd*; **ser muy** ~ to be a coffee addict

cagar [ka'xar] (*fam!*) *vt* to bungle, mess up ♦ *vi* to have a shit (*!*)

caída [ka'iða] *nf* fall; (*declive*) slope; (*disminución*) fall, drop

caído, a [ka'iðo, a] *adj* drooping

caiga *etc vb ver* **caer**

caimán [kai'man] *nm* alligator

caja ['kaxa] *nf* box; (*para reloj*) case; (*de ascensor*) shaft; (*COM*) cashbox; (*donde se hacen los pagos*) cashdesk; (: *en super-mercado*) checkout, till; ~ **de ahorros** savings bank; ~ **de cambios** gearbox; ~ **fuerte**, ~ **de caudales** safe, strongbox

cajero, a [ka'xero, a] *nm/f* cashier; ~ **automático** cash dispenser

cajetilla [kaxe'tiʎa] *nf* (*de cigarrillos*) packet

cajón [ka'xon] *nm* big box; (*de mueble*) drawer

cal [kal] *nf* lime

cala [ˈkala] *nf* (*GEO*) cove, inlet; (*de barco*) hold

calabacín [kalaβa'θin] *nm* (*BOT*) baby marrow; (: *más pequeño*) courgette (*BRIT*), zucchini (*US*)

calabaza [kala'βaθa] *nf* (*BOT*) pumpkin

calabozo [kala'βoθo] *nm* (*cárcel*) prison; (*celda*) cell

calada [ka'laða] *nf* (*de cigarrillo*) puff

calado, a [ka'laðo, a] *adj* (*prenda*) lace *cpd* ♦ *nm* (*NAUT*) draught

calamar [kala'mar] *nm* squid *no pl*

calambre [ka'lambre] *nm* (*tb*: ~**s**) cramp

calamidad [kalami'ðað] *nf* calamity, disaster

calar [ka'lar] *vt* (*mojar*) to soak, drench; (*penetrar*) to pierce, penetrate; (*comprender*) to see through; (*vela*) to lower; ~**se** *vr* (*AUTO*) to stall; ~**se las gafas** to stick one's glasses on

calavera [kala'βera] *nf* skull

calcar [kal'kar] *vt* (*reproducir*) to trace; (*imitar*) to copy

calcetín [kalθe'tin] *nm* sock

calcinar [kalθi'nar] *vt* (*MAT*) to burn, blacken

calcio ['kalθjo] *nm* calcium

calcomanía [kalkoma'nia] *nf* transfer

calculador, a [kalkula'ðor, a] *adj* (*persona*) calculating

calculadora [kalkula'ðora] *nf* calculator

calcular [kalku'lar] *vt* (*calcular*) to calculate, compute; ~ **que** ... to reckon that ...; **cálculo** *nm* calculation

caldear [kalde'ar] *vt* to warm (up), heat (up)

caldera [kal'dera] *nf* boiler

calderilla [kalde'riʎa] *nf* (*moneda*) small

change

caldero [kal'dero] *nm* small boiler

caldo ['kaldo] *nm* stock; (*consomé*) consommé

calefacción [kalefak'θjon] *nf* heating; ~ **central** central heating

calendario [kalen'darjo] *nm* calendar

calentador [kalenta'ðor] *nm* heater

calentamiento [kalenta'mjento] *nm* (*DEPORTE*) warm-up

calentar [kalen'tar] *vt* to heat (up); ~**se** *vr* to heat up, warm up; (*fig: discusión etc*) to get heated

calentura [kalen'tura] *nf* (*MED*) fever, (high) temperature

calibrar [kali'ßrar] *vt* to gauge, measure; **calibre** *nm* (*de cañón*) calibre, bore; (*diámetro*) diameter; (*fig*) calibre

calidad [kali'ðað] *nf* quality; **de** ~ quality *cpd*; **en** ~ **de** in the capacity of, as

cálido, a ['kaliðo, a] *adj* hot; (*fig*) warm

caliente *etc* [ka'ljente] *vb ver* **calentar** ♦ *adj* hot; (*fig*) fiery; (*disputa*) heated; ´(*fam: cachondo*) randy

calificación [kalifika'θjon] *nf* qualification; (*de alumno*) grade, mark

calificar [kalifi'kar] *vt* to qualify; (*alumno*) to grade, mark; ~ **de** to describe as

calima [ka'lima] *nf* (*cerca del mar*) mist

cáliz ['kaliθ] *nm* chalice

caliza [ka'liθa] *nf* limestone

calizo, a [ka'liθo, a] *adj* lime *cpd*

callado, a [ka'ʎaðo, a] *adj* quiet

callar [ka'ʎar] *vt* (*asunto delicado*) to keep quiet about, say nothing about; (*persona, opinión*) to silence ♦ *vi* to keep quiet, be silent; ~**se** *vr* to keep quiet, be silent; **¡cállate!** be quiet!, shut up!

calle ['kaʎe] *nf* street; (*DEPORTE*) lane; ~ **arriba/abajo** up/down the street; ~ **de un solo sentido** one-way street

calleja [ka'ʎexa] *nf* alley, narrow street; **callejear** *vi* to wander (about) the streets; **callejero, a** *adj* street *cpd* ♦ *nm* street map; **callejón** *nm* alley, passage; **callejón sin salida** cul-de-sac; **callejuela** *nf* side-street, alley

callista [ka'ʎista] *nm/f* chiropodist

callo ['kaʎo] *nm* callus; (*en el pie*) corn; ~**s** *nmpl* (*CULIN*) tripe *sg*

calma ['kalma] *nf* calm

calmante [kal'mante] *nm* sedative, tranquillizer

calmar [kal'mar] *vt* to calm, calm down ♦ *vi* (*tempestad*) to abate; (*mente etc*) to become calm

calmoso, a [kal'moso, a] *adj* calm, quiet

calor [ka'lor] *nm* heat; (*agradable*) warmth; **hace** ~ it's hot; **tener** ~ to be hot

caloría [kalo'ria] *nf* calorie

calumnia [ka'lumnja] nf calumny, slander; **calumnioso, a** adj slanderous

caluroso, a [kalu'roso, a] adj hot; (sin exceso) warm; (fig) enthusiastic

calva ['kalßa] nf bald patch; (en bosque) clearing

calvario [kal'ßarjo] nm stations pl of the cross

calvicie [kal'ßiθje] nf baldness

calvo, a ['kalßo, a] adj bald; (terreno) bare, barren; (tejido) threadbare

calza ['kalθa] nf wedge, chock

calzada [kal'θaða] nf roadway, highway

calzado, a [kal'θaðo, a] adj shod ♦ nm footwear

calzador [kalθa'ðor] nm shoehorn

calzar [kal'θar] vt (zapatos etc) to wear; (un mueble) to put a wedge under; **~se** vr: **~se los zapatos** to put on one's shoes; **¿qué (número) calza?** what size do you take?

calzón [kal'θon] nm (tb: calzones nmpl) shorts; (AM: de hombre) (under)pants; (: de mujer) panties

calzoncillos [kalθon'θiʎos] nmpl underpants

cama ['kama] nf bed; **~ individual/de matrimonio** single/double bed

camafeo [kama'feo] nm cameo

camaleón [kamale'on] nm chameleon

cámara ['kamara] nf chamber; (habitación) room; (sala) hall; (CINE) cinema; (fotográfica) camera; **~ de aire** inner tube; **~ de comercio** chamber of commerce; **~ frigorífica** cold-storage room

camarada [kama'raða] nm comrade, companion

camarera [kama'rera] nf (en restaurante) waitress; (en casa, hotel) maid

camarero [kama'rero] nm waiter

camarilla [kama'riʎa] nf clique

camarón [kama'ron] nm shrimp

camarote [kama'rote] nm cabin

cambiable [kam'bjaßle] adj (variable) changeable, variable; (intercambiable) interchangeable

cambiante [kam'bjante] adj variable

cambiar [kam'bjar] vt to change; (dinero) to exchange ♦ vi to change; **~se** vr (mudarse) to move; (de ropa) to change; **~ de idea** to change one's mind; **~ de ropa** to change (one's clothes)

cambio ['kambjo] nm change; (trueque) exchange; (COM) rate of exchange; (oficina) bureau de change; (dinero menudo) small change; **en ~** on the other hand; (en lugar de) instead; **~ de divisas** foreign exchange; **~ de velocidades** gear lever

camelar [kame'lar] vt to sweet-talk

camello [ka'meʎo] nm camel; (fam: traficante) pusher

camerino [kame'rino] nm dressing room

camilla [ka'miʎa] nf (MED) stretcher

caminante [kami'nante] nm/f traveller

caminar [kami'nar] vi (marchar) to walk, go ♦ vt (recorrer) to cover, travel

caminata [kami'nata] nf long walk; (por el campo) hike

camino [ka'mino] nm way, road; (sendero) track; **a medio ~** halfway (there); **en el ~** on the way, en route; **~ de** on the way to; **~ particular** private road

camión [ka'mjon] nm lorry (BRIT), truck (US); **~ cisterna** tanker; **camionero, a** nm/f lorry o truck driver

camioneta [kamjo'neta] nf van, light truck

camisa [ka'misa] nf shirt; (BOT) skin; **~ de fuerza** straitjacket; **camisería** nf outfitter's (shop)

camiseta [kami'seta] nf (prenda) tee-shirt; (: ropa interior) vest; (de deportista) top

camisón [kami'son] nm nightdress, nightgown

camorra [ka'morra] nf: **buscar ~** to look for trouble

campamento [kampa'mento] nm camp

campana [kam'pana] nf bell; **~ de cristal** jar; **~da** nf peal; **~rio** nm belfry

campanilla [kampa'niʎa] nf small bell

campaña [kam'paɲa] nf (MIL, POL) campaign

campechano, a [kampe'tʃano, a] adj (franco) open

campeón, ona [kampe'on, ona] nm/f champion; **campeonato** nm championship

campesino, a [kampe'sino, a] adj country cpd, rural; (gente) peasant cpd ♦ nm/f countryman/woman; (agricultor) farmer

campestre [kam'pestre] adj country cpd, rural

camping ['kampin] (pl ~s) nm camping; (lugar) campsite; **ir de o hacer ~** to go camping

campo ['kampo] nm (fuera de la ciudad) country, countryside; (AGR, ELEC) field; (de fútbol) pitch; (de golf) course; (MIL) camp; **~ de batalla** battlefield; **~ de deportes** sports ground, playing field

camposanto [kampo'santo] nm cemetery

camuflaje [kamu'flaxe] nm camouflage

cana ['kana] nf white o grey hair; **tener ~s** to be going grey

Canadá [kana'ða] nm Canada; **canadiense** adj, nm/f Canadian ♦ nf fur-lined jacket

canal [ka'nal] nm canal; (GEO) channel, strait; (de televisión) channel; (de tejado) gutter; **~ de Panamá** Panama Canal; **~izar** vt to channel

canalla [ka'naʎa] nf rabble, mob ♦ nm swine

canalón [kana'lon] nm (conducto vertical) drainpipe; (del tejado) gutter

canapé [kana'pe] (pl ~s) nm sofa, settee;

(*CULIN*) canapé

Canarias [ka'narjas] *nfpl*: (**las Islas**) ~ the Canary Islands, the Canaries

canario, a [ka'narjo, a] *adj, nm/f* (native) of the Canary Isles ♦ *nm* (*ZOOL*) canary

canasta [ka'nasta] *nf* (round) basket; **canastilla** *nf* small basket; (*de niño*) layette

canasto [ka'nasto] *nm* large basket

cancela [kan'θela] *nf* gate

cancelación [kanθela'θjon] *nf* cancellation

cancelar [kanθe'lar] *vt* to cancel; (*una deuda*) to write off

cáncer ['kanθer] *nm* (*MED*) cancer; (*ASTROLOGÍA*): **C~** Cancer

cancha ['kantʃa] *nf* (*de baloncesto, tenis etc*) court; (*AM: de fútbol*) pitch

canciller [kanθi'ʎer] *nm* chancellor

canción [kan'θjon] *nf* song; ~ **de cuna** lullaby; **cancionero** *nm* song book

candado [kan'daðo] *nm* padlock

candente [kan'dente] *adj* red-hot; (*fig: tema*) burning

candidato, a [kandi'ðato, a] *nm/f* candidate

candidez [kandi'ðeθ] *nf* (*sencillez*) simplicity; (*simpleza*) naiveté; **cándido, a** *adj* simple; naive

candil [kan'dil] *nm* oil lamp; **~ejas** *nfpl* (*TEATRO*) footlights

candor [kan'dor] *nm* (*sinceridad*) frankness; (*inocencia*) innocence

canela [ka'nela] *nf* cinnamon

canelones [kane'lones] *nmpl* cannelloni

cangrejo [kan'grexo] *nm* crab

canguro [kan'guro] *nm* kangaroo; **hacer de ~** to babysit

caníbal [ka'niβal] *adj, nm/f* cannibal

canica [ka'nika] *nf* marble

canijo, a [ka'nixo, a] *adj* frail, sickly

canino, a [ka'nino, a] *adj* canine ♦ *nm* canine (tooth)

canjear [kanxe'ar] *vt* to exchange

cano, a ['kano, a] *adj* grey-haired, white-haired

canoa [ka'noa] *nf* canoe

canon ['kanon] *nm* canon; (*pensión*) rent; (*COM*) tax

canónigo [ka'noniɣo] *nm* canon

canonizar [kanoni'θar] *vt* to canonize

canoso, a [ka'noso, a] *adj* grey-haired

cansado, a [kan'saðo, a] *adj* tired, weary; (*tedioso*) tedious, boring

cansancio [kan'sanθjo] *nm* tiredness, fatigue

cansar [kan'sar] *vt* (*fatigar*) to tire, tire out; (*aburrir*) to bore; (*fastidiar*) to bother; **~se** *vr* to tire, get tired; (*aburrirse*) to get bored

cantábrico, a [kan'taβriko, a] *adj* Cantabrian; **mar C~** Bay of Biscay

cantante [kan'tante] *adj* singing ♦ *nm/f* singer

cantar [kan'tar] *vt* to sing ♦ *vi* to sing; (*insecto*) to chirp ♦ *nm* (*acción*) singing; (*canción*) song; (*poema*) poem

cántara ['kantara] *nf* large pitcher

cántaro ['kantaro] *nm* pitcher, jug; **llover a ~s** to rain cats and dogs

cante ['kante] *nm*: ~ **jondo** flamenco singing

cantera [kan'tera] *nf* quarry

cantidad [kanti'ðað] *nf* quantity, amount

cantimplora [kantim'plora] *nf* (*frasco*) water bottle, canteen

cantina [kan'tina] *nf* canteen; (*de estación*) buffet

canto ['kanto] *nm* singing; (*canción*) song; (*borde*) edge, rim; (*de un cuchillo*) back; ~ **rodado** boulder

cantor, a [kan'tor, a] *nm/f* singer

canturrear [kanturre'ar] *vi* to sing softly

canuto [ka'nuto] *nm* (*tubo*) small tube; (*fam: droga*) joint

caña ['kaɲa] *nf* (*BOT: tallo*) stem, stalk; (*carrizo*) reed; (*vaso*) tumbler; (*de cerveza*) glass of beer; (*ANAT*) shinbone; ~ **de azúcar** sugar cane; ~ **de pescar** fishing rod

cañada [ka'ɲaða] *nf* (*entre dos montañas*) gully, ravine; (*camino*) cattle track

cáñamo ['kaɲamo] *nm* hemp

cañería [kaɲe'ria] *nf* (*tubo*) pipe

caño ['kaɲo] *nm* (*tubo*) tube, pipe; (*de albañal*) sewer; (*MUS*) pipe; (*de fuente*) jet

cañón [ka'ɲon] *nm* (*MIL*) cannon; (*de fusil*) barrel; (*GEO*) canyon, gorge

caoba [ka'oβa] *nf* mahogany

caos ['kaos] *nm* chaos

cap. *abr* (= *capítulo*) ch.

capa ['kapa] *nf* cloak, cape; (*GEO*) layer, stratum; **so ~ de** under the pretext of; ~ **de ozono** ozone layer

capacidad [kapaθi'ðað] *nf* (*medida*) capacity; (*aptitud*) capacity, ability

capacitar [kapaθi'tar] *vt*: ~ **a algn para** (*hacer*) to enable sb to (do)

capar [ka'par] *vt* to castrate, geld

caparazón [kapara'θon] *nm* shell

capataz [kapa'taθ] *nm* foreman

capaz [ka'paθ] *adj* able, capable; (*amplio*) capacious, roomy

capcioso, a [kap'θjoso, a] *adj* wily, deceitful

capellán [kape'ʎan] *nm* chaplain; (*sacerdote*) priest

caperuza [kape'ruθa] *nf* hood

capicúa [kapi'kua] *adj inv* (*número, fecha*) reversible

capilla [ka'piʎa] *nf* chapel

capital [kapi'tal] *adj* capital ♦ *nm* (*COM*) capital ♦ *nf* (*ciudad*) capital; ~ **social** share o authorized capital

capitalismo [kapita'lismo] *nm* capitalism; **capitalista** *adj, nm/f* capitalist

capitán [kapi'tan] nm captain

capitanear [kapitane'ar] vt to captain

capitulación [kapitula'θjon] nf (rendición) capitulation, surrender; (acuerdo) agreement, pact; **capitulaciones (matrimoniales)** nfpl marriage contract sg

capitular [kapitu'lar] vi to make an agreement

capítulo [ka'pitulo] nm chapter

capó [ka'po] nm (AUTO) bonnet

capón [ka'pon] nm (gallo) capon

capota [ka'pota] nf (de mujer) bonnet; (AUTO) hood (BRIT), top (US)

capote [ka'pote] nm (abrigo: de militar) greatcoat; (: de torero) cloak

capricho [ka'pritʃo] nm whim, caprice; **~so, a** adj capricious

Capricornio [kapri'kornjo] nm Capricorn

cápsula ['kapsula] nf capsule

captar [kap'tar] vt (comprender) to understand; (RADIO) to pick up; (atención, apoyo) to attract

captura [kap'tura] nf capture; (JUR) arrest; **capturar** vt to capture; to arrest

capucha [ka'putʃa] nf hood, cowl

capullo [ka'puʎo] nm (BOT) bud; (ZOOL) cocoon; (fam) idiot

caqui ['kaki] nm khaki

cara ['kara] nf (ANAT, de moneda) face; (de disco) side; (descaro) boldness; **~ a** facing; **de ~** opposite, facing; **dar la ~** to face the consequences; **¿~ o cruz?** heads or tails?; **¡qué ~ (más dura)!** what a nerve!

carabina [kara'ßina] nf carbine, rifle; (persona) chaperone

Caracas [ka'rakas] n Caracas

caracol [kara'kol] nm (ZOOL) snail; (concha) (sea) shell

carácter [ka'rakter] (pl **caracteres**) nm character; **tener buen/mal ~** to be good natured/bad tempered

característica [karakte'ristika] nf characteristic

característico, a [karakte'ristiko, a] adj characteristic

caracterizar [karakteri'θar] vt to characterize, typify

caradura [kara'ðura] nm/f: **es un ~** he's got a nerve

carajillo [kara'xiʎo] nm coffee with a dash of brandy

carajo [ka'raxo] (fam!) nm: **¡~!** shit! (!)

caramba [ka'ramba] excl good gracious!

carámbano [ka'rambano] nm icicle

caramelo [kara'melo] nm (dulce) sweet; (azúcar fundida) caramel

caravana [kara'ßana] nf caravan; (fig) group; (AUTO) tailback

carbón [kar'ßon] nm coal; **papel ~** carbon paper; **carboncillo** nm (ARTE) charcoal; **carbonero, a** nm/f coal merchant; **carbonilla** [-'niʎa] nf coal dust

carbonizar [karßoni'θar] vt to carbonize; (quemar) to char

carbono [kar'ßono] nm carbon

carburador [karßura'ðor] nm carburettor

carburante [karßu'rante] nm (para motor) fuel

carcajada [karka'xaða] nf (loud) laugh, guffaw

cárcel ['karθel] nf prison, jail; (TEC) clamp; **carcelero, a** adj prison cpd ♦ nm/f warder

carcoma [kar'koma] nf woodworm

carcomer [karko'mer] vt to bore into, eat into; (fig) to undermine; **~se** vr to become worm-eaten; (fig) to decay

cardar [kar'ðar] vt (pelo) to backcomb

cardenal [karðe'nal] nm (REL) cardinal; (MED) bruise

cardíaco, a [kar'ðiako, a] adj cardiac, heart cpd

cardinal [karði'nal] adj cardinal

cardo ['karðo] nm thistle

carearse [kare'arse] vr to come face to face

carecer [kare'θer] vi: **~ de** to lack, be in need of

carencia [ka'renθja] nf lack; (escasez) shortage; (MED) deficiency

carente [ka'rente] adj: **~ de** lacking in, devoid of

carestía [kares'tia] nf (escasez) scarcity, shortage; (COM) high cost

careta [ka'reta] nf mask

carga ['karɣa] nf (peso, ELEC) load; (de barco) cargo, freight; (MIL) charge; (responsabilidad) duty, obligation

cargado, a [kar'ɣaðo, a] adj loaded; (ELEC) live; (café, té) strong; (cielo) overcast

cargamento [karɣa'mento] nm (acción) loading; (mercancías) load, cargo

cargar [kar'ɣar] vt (barco, arma) to load; (ELEC) to charge; (COM: algo en cuenta) to charge; (INFORM) to load ♦ vi (MIL) to charge; (AUTO) to load (up); **~ con** to pick up, carry away; (peso, fig) to shoulder, bear; **~se** (fam) vr (estropear) to break; (matar) to bump off

cargo ['karɣo] nm (puesto) post, office; (responsabilidad) duty, obligation; (JUR) charge; **hacerse ~ de** to take charge of o responsibility for

carguero [kar'ɣero] nm freighter, cargo boat; (avión) freight plane

Caribe [ka'rißee] nm: **el ~** the Caribbean; **del ~** Caribbean

caribeño, a [kari'ßeɲo, a] adj Caribbean

caricatura [karika'tura] nf caricature

caricia [ka'riθja] nf caress

caridad [kari'ðað] nf charity

caries ['karjes] nf inv tooth decay

cariño [ka'riɲo] nm affection, love; (caricia) caress; (en carta) love ...; **tener ~ a** to be fond of; **~so, a** adj affectionate

carisma [ka'risma] nm charisma

caritativo, a [karita'tißo, a] adj charitable

cariz [ka'riθ] nm: **tener o tomar buen/mal ~** to look good/bad

carmesí [karme'si] adj, nm crimson

carmín [kar'min] nm lipstick

carnal [kar'nal] adj carnal; **primo ~** first cousin

carnaval [karna'ßal] nm carnival

carne ['karne] nf flesh; (CULIN) meat; **~ de cerdo/cordero/ternera/vaca** pork/lamb/veal/beef; **~ de gallina** (fig): **se me pone la ~ de gallina sólo verlo** I get the creeps just seeing it

carné [kar'ne] (pl **~s**) nm: **~ de conducir** driving licence (BRIT), driver's license (US); **~ de identidad** identity card

carnero [kar'nero] nm sheep, ram; (carne) mutton

carnet [kar'ne] (pl **~s**) nm = **carné**

carnicería [karniθe'ria] nf butcher's (shop); (fig: matanza) carnage, slaughter

carnicero, a [karni'θero, a] adj carnivorous ♦ nm/f (tb fig) butcher; (carnívoro) carnivore

carnívoro, a [kar'nißoro, a] adj carnivorous

carnoso, a [kar'noso, a] adj beefy, fat

caro, a ['karo, a] adj dear; (COM) dear, expensive ♦ adv dear, dearly

carpa ['karpa] nf (pez) carp; (de circo) big top; (AM: de camping) tent

carpeta [kar'peta] nf folder, file

carpintería [karpinte'ria] nf carpentry, joinery; **carpintero** nm carpenter

carraspear [karraspe'ar] vi to clear one's throat

carraspera [karras'pera] nf hoarseness

carrera [ka'rrera] nf (acción) run(ning); (espacio recorrido) run; (competición) race; (trayecto) course; (profesión) career; (ESCOL) course

carreta [ka'rreta] nf wagon, cart

carrete [ka'rrete] nm reel, spool; (TEC) coil

carretera [karre'tera] nf (main) road, highway; **~ de circunvalación** ring road; **~ nacional** ≈ A road (BRIT), ≈ state highway (US)

carretilla [karre'tiʎa] nf trolley; (AGR) (wheel)barrow

carril [ka'rril] nm furrow; (de autopista) lane; (FERRO) rail

carrillo [ka'rriʎo] nm (ANAT) cheek; (TEC) pulley

carrito [ka'rrito] nm trolley

carro ['karro] nm cart, wagon; (MIL) tank; (AM: coche) car

carrocería [karroθe'ria] nf bodywork,

coachwork

carroña [ka'rroɲa] nf carrion no pl

carroza [ka'rroθa] nf (carruaje) coach

carrusel [karru'sel] nm merry-go-round, roundabout

carta ['karta] nf letter; (CULIN) menu; (naipe) card; (mapa) map; (JUR) document; **~ de ajuste** (TV) test card; **~ de crédito** credit card; **~ certificada** registered letter; **~ marítima** chart; **~ verde** (AUTO) green card

cartabón [karta'ßon] nm set square

cartel [kar'tel] nm (anuncio) poster, placard; (ESCOL) wall chart; (COM) cartel; **~era** nf hoarding, billboard; (en periódico) entertainments guide; **"en ~era"** "showing"

cartera [kar'tera] nf (de bolsillo) wallet; (de colegial, cobrador) satchel; (de señora) handbag; (para documentos) briefcase; (COM) portfolio; **ocupa la ~ de Agricultura** she is Minister of Agriculture

carterista [karte'rista] nm/f pickpocket

cartero [kar'tero] nm postman

cartilla [kar'tiʎa] nf primer, first reading book; **~ de ahorros** savings book

cartón [kar'ton] nm cardboard; **~ piedra** papier-mâché

cartucho [kar'tutʃo] nm (MIL) cartridge

cartulina [kartu'lina] nf card

casa ['kasa] nf house; (hogar) home; (COM) firm, company; **en ~** at home; **~ consistorial** town hall; **~ de huéspedes** boarding house; **~ de socorro** first aid post

casado, a [ka'saðo, a] adj married ♦ nm/f married man/woman

casamiento [kasa'mjento] nm marriage, wedding

casar [ka'sar] vt to marry; (JUR) to quash, annul; **~se** vr to marry, get married

cascabel [kaska'ßel] nm (small) bell

cascada [kas'kaða] nf waterfall

cascanueces [kaska'nweθes] nm inv nutcrackers pl

cascar [kas'kar] vt to crack, split, break (open); **~se** vr to crack, split, break (open)

cáscara ['kaskara] nf (de huevo, fruta seca) shell; (de fruta) skin; (de limón) peel

casco ['kasko] nm (de bombero, soldado) helmet; (NAUT: de barco) hull; (ZOOL: de caballo) hoof; (botella) empty bottle; (de ciudad): **el ~ antiguo** the old part; **el ~ urbano** the town centre; **los ~s azules** the UN peace-keeping force, the blue berets

cascote [kas'kote] nm rubble

caserío [kase'rio] nm hamlet; (casa) country house

casero, a [ka'sero, a] adj (pan etc) home-made ♦ nm/f (propietario) landlord/lady; **ser muy ~** to be home-loving; **"comida casera"** "home cooking"

caseta [ka'seta] nf hut; (*para bañista*) cubicle; (*de feria*) stall

casete [ka'sete] nm o f cassette

casi ['kasi] adv almost, nearly; ~ **nada** hardly anything; ~ **nunca** hardly ever, almost never; ~ **te caes** you almost fell

casilla [ka'siʎa] nf (*casita*) hut, cabin; (*AJEDREZ*) square; (*para cartas*) pigeonhole; **casillero** nm (*para cartas*) pigeonholes pl

casino [ka'sino] nm club; (*de juego*) casino

caso ['kaso] nm case; **en ~ de ...** in case of ...; **en ~ de que ...** in case ...; **el ~ es que** the fact is that; **en ese ~** in that case; **hacer ~ a** to pay attention to; **hacer o venir al ~** to be relevant

caspa ['kaspa] nf dandruff

cassette [ka'sete] nm o f = **casete**

casta ['kasta] nf caste; (*raza*) breed; (*linaje*) lineage

castaña [kas'taɲa] nf chestnut

castañetear [kastaɲete'ar] vi (*dientes*) to chatter

castaño, a [kas'taɲo, a] adj chestnut (-coloured), brown ♦ nm chestnut tree

castañuelas [kasta'ɲwelas] nfpl castanets

castellano, a [kaste'ʎano, a] adj, nm/f Castilian ♦ nm (*LING*) Castilian, Spanish

castidad [kasti'ðað] nf chastity, purity

castigar [kasti'ɣar] vt to punish; (*DEPORTE*) to penalize; **castigo** nm punishment; (*DEPORTE*) penalty

Castilla [kas'tiʎa] nf Castile

castillo [kas'tiʎo] nm castle

castizo, a [kas'tiθo, a] adj (*LING*) pure

casto, a ['kasto, a] adj chaste, pure

castor [kas'tor] nm beaver

castrar [kas'trar] vt to castrate

castrense [kas'trense] adj (*disciplina, vida*) military

casual [ka'swal] adj chance, accidental; ~**idad** nf chance, accident; (*combinación de circunstancias*) coincidence; ¡qué ~**idad!** what a coincidence!

cataclismo [kata'klismo] nm cataclysm

catador, a [kata'ðor, a] nm/f wine taster

catalán, ana [kata'lan, ana] adj, nm/f Catalan ♦ nm (*LING*) Catalan

catalizador [kataliθa'ðor] nm catalyst; (*AUT*) catalytic convertor

catalogar [katalo'ɣar] vt to catalogue; ~ **a algn (de)** (*fig*) to categorize sb (as)

catálogo [ka'taloɣo] nm catalogue

Cataluña [kata'luɲa] nf Catalonia

catar [ka'tar] vt to taste, sample

catarata [kata'rata] nf (*GEO*) waterfall; (*MED*) cataract

catarro [ka'tarro] nm catarrh; (*constipado*) cold

catástrofe [ka'tastrofe] nf catastrophe

catear [kate'ar] (*fam*) vt (*examen, alumno*) to fail

cátedra ['kateðra] nf (*UNIV*) chair, professorship

catedral [kate'ðral] nf cathedral

catedrático, a [kate'ðratiko, a] nm/f professor

categoría [kateɣo'ria] nf category; (*rango*) rank, standing; (*calidad*) quality; **de ~** (*hotel*) top-class

categórico, a [kate'ɣoriko, a] adj categorical

cateto, a ['kateto, a] (*pey*) nm/f peasant

catolicismo [katoli'θismo] nm Catholicism

católico, a [ka'toliko, a] adj, nm/f Catholic

catorce [ka'torθe] num fourteen

cauce ['kauθe] nm (*de río*) riverbed; (*fig*) channel

caucho ['kautʃo] nm rubber; (*AM*: llanta) tyre

caución [kau'θjon] nf bail; **caucionar** vt (*JUR*) to bail, go bail for

caudal [kau'ðal] nm (*de río*) volume, flow; (*fortuna*) wealth; (*abundancia*) abundance; ~**oso, a** adj (*río*) large

caudillo [kau'ðiʎo] nm leader, chief

causa ['kausa] nf cause; (*razón*) reason; (*JUR*) lawsuit, case; **a ~ de** because of

causar [kau'sar] vt to cause

cautela [kau'tela] nf caution, cautiousness; **cauteloso, a** adj cautious, wary

cautivar [kauti'ßar] vt to capture; (*atraer*) to captivate

cautiverio [kauti'ßerjo] nm captivity

cautividad [kautißi'ðað] nf = **cautiverio**

cautivo, a [kau'tißo, a] adj, nm/f captive

cauto, a ['kauto, a] adj cautious, careful

cava ['kaßa] nm champagne-type wine

cavar [ka'ßar] vt to dig

caverna [ka'ßerna] nf cave, cavern

cavidad [kaßi'ðað] nf cavity

cavilar [kaßi'lar] vt to ponder

cayado [ka'jaðo] nm (*de pastor*) crook; (*de obispo*) crozier

cayendo etc vb ver **caer**

caza ['kaθa] nf (*acción: gen*) hunting; (: *con fusil*) shooting; (*una ~*) hunt, chase; (*animales*) game ♦ nm (*AVIAT*) fighter

cazador, a [kaθa'ðor, a] nm/f hunter; **cazadora** nf jacket

cazar [ka'θar] vt to hunt; (*perseguir*) to chase; (*prender*) to catch

cazo ['kaθo] nm saucepan

cazuela [ka'θwela] nf (*vasija*) pan; (*guisado*) casserole

CD abbr (= compact disc) CD

CD-ROM abbr m CD-ROM

CE nf abr (= Comunidad Europea) EC

cebada [θe'ßaða] nf barley

cebar [θe'ßar] vt (*animal*) to fatten (up); (*anzuelo*) to bait; (*MIL, TEC*) to prime

cebo ['θeßo] nm (*para animales*) feed, food;

(*para peces, fig*) bait; (*de arma*) charge

cebolla [θe'βoʎa] *nf* onion; **cebolleta** *nf* spring onion; **cebollín** *nm* spring onion

cebra ['θeβra] *nf* zebra

cecear [θeθe'ar] *vi* to lisp; **ceceo** *nm* lisp

ceder [θe'ðer] *vt* to hand over, give up, part with ♦ *vi* (*renunciar*) to give in, yield; (*disminuir*) to diminish, decline; (*romperse*) to give way

cedro ['θeðro] *nm* cedar

cédula ['θeðula] *nf* certificate, document

cegar [θe'xar] *vt* to blind; (*tubería etc*) to block up, stop up ♦ *vi* to go blind; **~se** *vr*: **~se (de)** to be blinded (by)

ceguera [θe'vera] *nf* blindness

CEI *abbr* (= *Confederación de Estados Independientes*) CIS

ceja ['θexa] *nf* eyebrow

cejar [θe'xar] *vi* (*fig*) to back down

celador, a [θela'ðor, a] *nm/f* (*de edificio*) watchman; (*de museo etc*) attendant

celda ['θelda] *nf* cell

celebración [θeleβra'θjon] *nf* celebration

celebrar [θele'βrar] *vt* to celebrate; (*alabar*) to praise ♦ *vi* to be glad; **~se** *vr* to occur, take place

célebre ['θeleβre] *adj* famous

celebridad [θeleβri'ðað] *nf* fame; (*persona*) celebrity

celeste [θe'leste] *adj* (*azul*) sky-blue

celestial [θeles'tjal] *adj* celestial, heavenly

celibato [θeli'βato] *nm* celibacy

célibe ['θeliβe] *adj, nm/f* celibate

celo¹ ['θelo] *nm* zeal; (*REL*) fervour; (*ZOOL*): **en ~** on heat; **~s** *nmpl* jealousy *sg*; **tener ~s** to be jealous

celo² ® ['θelo] *nm* Sellotape ®

celofán [θelo'fan] *nm* cellophane

celoso, a [θe'loso, a] *adj* jealous; (*trabajador*) zealous

celta ['θelta] *adj* Celtic ♦ *nm/f* Celt

célula ['θelula] *nf* cell; **~ solar** solar cell

celulitis [θelu'litis] *nf* cellulite

celuloide [θelu'loiðe] *nm* celluloid

cementerio [θemen'terjo] *nm* cemetery, graveyard

cemento [θe'mento] *nm* cement; (*hormigón*) concrete; (*AM: cola*) glue

cena ['θena] *nf* evening meal, dinner

cenagal [θena'val] *nm* bog, quagmire

cenar [θe'nar] *vt* to have for dinner ♦ *vi* to have dinner

cenicero [θeni'θero] *nm* ashtray

cenit [θe'nit] *nm* zenith

ceniza [θe'niθa] *nf* ash, ashes *pl*

censo ['θenso] *nm* census; **~ electoral** electoral roll

censura [θen'sura] *nf* (*POL*) censorship

censurar [θensu'rar] *vt* (*idea*) to censure;

(*cortar: película*) to censor

centella [θen'teʎa] *nf* spark

centellear [θenteʎe'ar] *vi* (*metal*) to gleam; (*estrella*) to twinkle; (*fig*) to sparkle

centenar [θente'nar] *nm* hundred

centenario, a [θente'narjo, a] *adj* centenary; hundred-year-old ♦ *nm* centenary

centeno [θen'teno] *nm* (*BOT*) rye

centésimo, a [θen'tesimo, a] *adj* hundredth

centígrado [θen'tixraðo] *adj* centigrade

centímetro [θen'timetro] *nm* centimetre (*BRIT*), centimeter (*US*)

céntimo ['θentimo] *nm* cent

centinela [θenti'nela] *nm* sentry, guard

centollo [θen'toʎo] *nm* spider crab

central [θen'tral] *adj* central ♦ *nf* head office; (*TEC*) plant; (*TEL*) exchange; **~ eléctrica** power station; **~ nuclear** nuclear power station; **~ telefónica** telephone exchange

centralita [θentra'lita] *nf* switchboard

centralizar [θentrali'θar] *vt* to centralize

centrar [θen'trar] *vt* to centre

céntrico, a ['θentriko, a] *adj* central

centrifugar [θentrifu'var] *vt* to spin-dry

centrista [θen'trista] *adj* centre *cpd*

centro ['θentro] *nm* centre; **~ comercial** shopping centre; **~ juvenil** youth club; **~ de llamadas** call centre

centroamericano, a [θentroameri'kano, a] *adj, nm/f* Central American

ceñido, a [θe'ɲiðo, a] *adj* (*chaqueta, pantalón*) tight(-fitting)

ceñir [θe'ɲir] *vt* (*rodear*) to encircle, surround; (*ajustar*) to fit (tightly)

ceño ['θeɲo] *nm* frown, scowl; **fruncir el ~** to frown, knit one's brow

CEOE *nf abr* (*ESP*: = *Confederación Española de Organizaciones Empresariales*) ≈ CBI (*BRIT*), employers' organization

cepillar [θepi'ʎar] *vt* to brush; (*madera*) to plane (down)

cepillo [θe'piʎo] *nm* brush; (*para madera*) plane; **~ de dientes** toothbrush

cera ['θera] *nf* wax

cerámica [θe'ramika] *nf* pottery; (*arte*) ceramics

cerca ['θerka] *nf* fence ♦ *adv* near, nearby, close; **~ de** near, close to

cercanías [θerka'nias] *nfpl* (*afueras*) outskirts, suburbs

cercano, a [θer'kano, a] *adj* close, near

cercar [θer'kar] *vt* to fence in; (*rodear*) to surround

cerciorar [θerθjo'rar] *vt* (*asegurar*) to assure; **~se** *vr* (*asegurarse*) to make sure

cerco ['θerko] *nm* (*AGR*) enclosure; (*AM*) fence; (*MIL*) siege

cerdo, a ['θerðo, a] *nm/f* pig/sow

cereal [θere'al] *nm* cereal; **~es** *nmpl* cereals,

grain sg

cerebro [θe'reβro] nm brain; (fig) brains pl

ceremonia [θere'monja] nf ceremony; **ceremonial** adj, nm ceremonial; **ceremonioso, a** adj ceremonious

cereza [θe'reθa] nf cherry

cerilla [θe'riʎa] nf (fósforo) match

cernerse [θer'nerse] vr to hover

cero ['θero] nm nothing, zero

cerrado, a [θe'rraðo, a] adj closed, shut; (con llave) locked; (tiempo) cloudy, overcast; (curva) sharp; (acento) thick, broad

cerradura [θerra'ðura] nf (acción) closing; (mecanismo) lock

cerrajero [θerra'xero] nm locksmith

cerrar [θe'rrar] vt to close, shut; (paso, carretera) to close; (grifo) to turn off; (cuenta, negocio) to close ♦ vi to close, shut; (la noche) to come down; **~se** vr to close, shut; **~ con llave** to lock; **~ un trato** to strike a bargain

cerro ['θerro] nm hill

cerrojo [θe'rroxo] nm (herramienta) bolt; (de puerta) latch

certamen [θer'tamen] nm competition, contest

certero, a [θer'tero, a] adj (gen) accurate

certeza [θer'teθa] nf certainty

certidumbre [θerti'ðumßre] nf = **certeza**

certificado [θertifi'kaðo] nm certificate

certificar [θertifi'kar] vt (asegurar, atestar) to certify

cervatillo [θer'ßa'tiʎo] nm fawn

cervecería [θerßeθe'ria] nf (fábrica) brewery; (bar) public house, pub

cerveza [θer'ßeθa] nf beer

cesante [θe'sante] adj redundant

cesar [θe'sar] vi to cease, stop ♦ vt (funcionario) to remove from office

cesárea [θe'sarea] nf (MED) Caesarean operation o section

cese ['θese] nm (de trabajo) dismissal; (de pago) suspension

césped ['θespeð] nm grass, lawn

cesta ['θesta] nf basket

cesto ['θesto] nm (large) basket, hamper

cetro ['θetro] nm sceptre.

cfr abr (= confróntese) cf.

chabacano, a [tʃaßa'kano, a] adj vulgar, coarse

chabola [tʃa'ßola] nf shack; **barrio de ~s** shanty town sg

chacal [tʃa'kal] nm jackal

chacha ['tʃatʃa] (fam) nf maid

cháchara ['tʃatʃara] nf chatter; **estar de ~** to chatter away

chacra ['tʃakra] (AM) nf smallholding

chafar [tʃa'far] vt (aplastar) to crush; (plan etc) to ruin

chal [tʃal] nm shawl

chalado, a [tʃa'lado, a] (fam) adj crazy

chalé [tʃa'le] (pl ~s) nm villa; ≈ detached house

chaleco [tʃa'leko] nm waistcoat, vest (US); **~ salvavidas** life jacket

chalet [tʃa'le] (pl ~s) nm = **chalé**

champán [tʃam'pan] nm champagne

champaña [tʃam'paɲa] nm = **champán**

champiñón [tʃampi'ɲon] nm mushroom

champú [tʃam'pu] (pl champúes, champús) nm shampoo

chamuscar [tʃamus'kar] vt to scorch, sear, singe

chance ['tʃanθe] (AM) nm chance

chancho, a ['tʃantʃo, a] (AM) nm/f pig

chanchullo [tʃan'tʃuʎo] (fam) nm fiddle

chandal [tʃan'dal] nm tracksuit

chantaje [tʃan'taxe] nm blackmail

chapa ['tʃapa] nf (de metal) plate, sheet; (de madera) board, panel; (AM: AUTO) number (BRIT) o license (US) plate; **~do, a** adj: **~do en oro** gold-plated

chaparrón [tʃapa'rron] nm downpour, cloudburst

chapotear [tʃapote'ar] vi to splash about

chapurrear [tʃapurre'ar] vt (idioma) to speak badly

chapuza [tʃa'puθa] nf botched job

chapuzón [tʃapu'θon] nm: **darse un ~** to go for a dip

chaqueta [tʃa'keta] nf jacket

chaquetón [tʃake'ton] nm long jacket

charca ['tʃarka] nf pond, pool

charco ['tʃarko] nm pool, puddle

charcutería [tʃarkute'ria] nf (tienda) shop selling chiefly pork meat products; (productos) cooked pork meats pl

charla ['tʃarla] nf talk, chat; (conferencia) lecture

charlar [tʃar'lar] vi to talk, chat

charlatán, ana [tʃarla'tan, ana] nm/f (hablador) chatterbox; (estafador) trickster

charol [tʃa'rol] nm varnish; (cuero) patent leather

chascarrillo [tʃaska'rriʎo] (fam) nm funny story

chasco ['tʃasko] nm (desengaño) disappointment

chasis ['tʃasis] nm inv chassis

chasquear [tʃaske'ar] vt (látigo) to crack; (lengua) to click; **chasquido** nm crack; click

chatarra [tʃa'tarra] nf scrap (metal)

chato, a ['tʃato, a] adj flat; (nariz) snub

chaval, a [tʃa'ßal, a] nm/f kid, lad/lass

checo, a ['tʃeko, a] adj, nm/f Czech ♦ nm (LING) Czech

checo(e)slovaco, a [tʃeko(e)slo'ßako, a] adj, nm/f Czech, Czechoslovak

Checo(e)slovaquia [tʃeko(e)sloˈßakja] nf Czechoslovakia

cheque [ˈtʃeke] nm cheque (BRIT), check (US); ~ **de viajero** traveller's cheque (BRIT), traveler's check (US)

chequeo [tʃeˈkeo] nm (MED) check-up; (AUTO) service

chequera [tʃeˈkera] (AM) nf chequebook (BRIT), checkbook (US)

chicano, a [tʃiˈkano, a] adj, nm/f chicano

chícharo [ˈtʃitʃaro] (AM) nm pea

chichón [tʃiˈtʃon] nm bump, lump

chicle [ˈtʃikle] nm chewing gum

chico, a [ˈtʃiko, a] adj small, little ♦ nm/f (niño) child; (muchacho) boy/girl

chiflado, a [tʃiˈflaðo, a] adj crazy

chiflar [tʃiˈflar] vt to hiss, boo

Chile [ˈtʃile] nm Chile; **chileno, a** adj, nm/f Chilean

chile [ˈtʃile] nm chilli pepper

chillar [tʃiˈʎar] vi (persona) to yell, scream; (animal salvaje) to howl; (cerdo) to squeal

chillido [tʃiˈʎiðo] nm (de persona) yell, scream; (de animal) howl

chillón, ona [tʃiˈʎon, ona] adj (niño) noisy; (color) loud, gaudy

chimenea [tʃimeˈnea] nf chimney; (hogar) fireplace

China [ˈtʃina] nf: (la) ~ China

chinche [ˈtʃintʃe] nf (insecto) (bed)bug; (TEC) drawing pin (BRIT), thumbtack (US) ♦ nm/f nuisance, pest

chincheta [tʃinˈtʃeta] nf drawing pin (BRIT), thumbtack (US)

chino, a [ˈtʃino, a] adj, nm/f Chinese ♦ nm (LING) Chinese

chipirón [tʃipiˈron] nm (ZOOL, CULIN) squid

Chipre [ˈtʃipre] nf Cyprus; **chipriota** adj, nm/f Cypriot

chiquillo, a [tʃiˈkiʎo, a] nm/f (fam) kid

chirimoya [tʃiriˈmoja] nf custard apple

chiringuito [tʃirinˈvito] nm small open-air bar

chiripa [tʃiˈripa] nf fluke

chirriar [tʃiˈrrjar] vi to creak, squeak

chirrido [tʃiˈrriðo] nm creak(ing), squeak(ing)

chis [tʃis] excl sh!

chisme [ˈtʃisme] nm (habladurías) piece of gossip; (fam: objeto) thingummyjig

chismoso, a [tʃisˈmoso, a] adj gossiping ♦ nm/f gossip

chispa [ˈtʃispa] nf spark; (fig) sparkle; (ingenio) wit; (fam) drunkenness

chispear [tʃispeˈar] vi (lloviznar) to drizzle

chisporrotear [tʃisporroteˈar] vi (fuego) to throw out sparks; (leña) to crackle; (aceite) to hiss, splutter

chiste [ˈtʃiste] nm joke, funny story

chistoso, a [tʃisˈtoso, a] adj funny, amusing

chivo, a [ˈtʃißo, a] nm/f (billy-/nanny-) goat; ~ **expiatorio** scapegoat

chocante [tʃoˈkante] adj startling; (extraño) odd; (ofensivo) shocking

chocar [tʃoˈkar] vi (coches etc) to collide, crash ♦ vt to shock; (sorprender) to startle; ~ **con** to collide with; (fig) to run into, run up against; ¡**chócala!** (fam) put it there!

chochear [tʃotʃeˈar] vi to dodder, be senile

chocho, a [ˈtʃotʃo, a] adj doddering, senile; (fig) soft, doting

chocolate [tʃokoˈlate] adj, nm chocolate; **chocolatina** nf chocolate

chofer [tʃoˈfer] nm = **chófer**

chófer [ˈtʃofer] nm driver

chollo [ˈtʃoʎo] (fam) nm bargain, snip

choque etc [ˈtʃoke] vb ver **chocar** ♦ nm (impacto) impact; (golpe) jolt; (AUTO) crash; (fig) conflict; ~ **frontal** head-on collision

chorizo [tʃoˈriθo] nm hard pork sausage, (type of) salami

chorrada [tʃoˈrraða] (fam) nf: **¡es una ~!** that's crap! (!); **decir ~s** to talk crap (!)

chorrear [tʃorreˈar] vi to gush (out), spout (out); (gotear) to drip, trickle

chorro [ˈtʃorro] nm jet; (fig) stream

choza [ˈtʃoθa] nf hut, shack

chubasco [tʃuˈßasko] nm squall

chubasquero [tʃußasˈkero] nm lightweight raincoat

chuchería [tʃutʃeˈria] nf trinket

chuleta [tʃuˈleta] nf chop, cutlet

chulo [ˈtʃulo] nm (de prostituta) pimp

chupar [tʃuˈpar] vt to suck; (absorber) to absorb; ~**se** vr to grow thin

chupete [tʃuˈpete] nm dummy (BRIT), pacifier (US)

chupito [tʃuˈpito] (fam) nm shot

churro [ˈtʃurro] nm (type of) fritter

chusma [ˈtʃusma] nf rabble, mob

chutar [tʃuˈtar] vi to shoot (at goal)

Cía abr (= compañía) Co.

cianuro [θjaˈnuro] nm cyanide

cibercafé [θißerkaˈfe] nm cybercafé

cicatriz [θikaˈtriθ] nf scar; ~**arse** vr to heal (up), form a scar

ciclismo [θiˈklismo] nm cycling

ciclista [θiˈklista] adj cycle cpd ♦ nm/f cyclist

ciclo [ˈθiklo] nm cycle; ~**turismo** nm: **hacer ~turismo** to go on a cycling holiday

ciclón [θiˈklon] nm cyclone

ciego, a [ˈθjexo, a] adj blind ♦ nm/f blind man/woman

cielo [ˈθjelo] nm sky; (REL) heaven; ¡~**s**! good heavens!

ciempiés [θjemˈpjes] nm inv centipede

cien [θjen] num ver **ciento**

ciénaga [ˈθjenaxa] nf marsh, swamp

ciencia ['θjenθja] nf science; **~s** nfpl (ESCOL) science sg; **~-ficción** nf science fiction

cieno ['θjeno] nm mud, mire

científico, a [θjen'tifiko, a] adj scientific ♦ nm/f scientist

ciento ['θjento] (tb: cien) num hundred; **pagar al 10 por ~** to pay at 10 per cent

cierre etc ['θjerre] vb ver **cerrar** ♦ nm closing, shutting; (con llave) locking; **~ de cremallera** zip (fastener)

cierro etc vb ver **cerrar**

cierto, a ['θjerto, a] adj sure, certain; (un tal) a certain; (correcto) right, correct; **~ hombre** a certain man; **ciertas personas** certain o some people; **si, es ~** yes, that's correct

ciervo ['θjerβo] nm deer; (macho) stag

cierzo ['θjerθo] nm north wind

cifra ['θifra] nf number; (secreta) code

cifrar [θi'frar] vt to code, write in code

cigala [θi'yala] nf Norway lobster

cigarra [θi'yarra] nf cicada

cigarrillo [θiya'rriʎo] nm cigarette

cigarro [θi'yarro] nm cigarette; (puro) cigar

cigüeña [θi'ɣweɲa] nf stork

cilíndrico, a [θi'lindriko, a] adj cylindrical

cilindro [θi'lindro] nm cylinder

cima ['θima] nf (de montaña) top, peak; (de árbol) top; (fig) height

cimbrearse [θimbre'arse] vr to sway

cimentar [θimen'tar] vt to lay the foundations of; (fig: fundar) to found

cimiento [θi'mjento] nm foundation

cinc [θink] nm zinc

cincel [θin'θel] nm chisel; **~ar** vt to chisel

cinco ['θinko] num five

cincuenta [θin'kwenta] num fifty

cine ['θine] nm cinema

cineasta [θine'asta] nm/f film director

cinematográfico, a [θinemato'yrafiko, a] adj cine-, film cpd

cínico, a ['θiniko, a] adj cynical ♦ nm/f cynic

cinismo [θi'nismo] nm cynicism

cinta ['θinta] nf band, strip; (de tela) ribbon; (película) reel; (de máquina de escribir) ribbon; **~ adhesiva** sticky tape; **~ de vídeo** videotape; **~ magnetofónica** tape; **~ métrica** tape measure

cintura [θin'tura] nf waist

cinturón [θintu'ron] nm belt; **~ de seguridad** safety belt

ciprés [θi'pres] nm cypress (tree)

circo ['θirko] nm circus

circuito [θir'kwito] nm circuit

circulación [θirkula'θjon] nf circulation; (AUTO) traffic

circular [θirku'lar] adj, nf circular ♦ vi, vt to circulate ♦ vi (AUTO) to drive; **"circule por la derecha"** "keep (to the) right"

círculo ['θirkulo] nm circle; **~ vicioso** vicious circle

circuncidar [θirkunθi'dar] vt to circumcise

circundar [θirkun'dar] vt to surround

circunferencia [θirkunfe'renθja] nf circumference

circunscribir [θirkunskri'βir] vt to circumscribe; **~se** vr to be limited

circunscripción [θirkunskrip'θjon] nf (POL) constituency

circunspecto, a [θirkuns'pekto, a] adj circumspect, cautious

circunstancia [θirkuns'tanθja] nf circumstance

cirio ['θirjo] nm (wax) candle

ciruela [θi'rwela] nf plum; **~ pasa** prune

cirugía [θiru'xia] nf surgery; **~ estética** o **plástica** plastic surgery

cirujano [θiru'xano] nm surgeon

cisne ['θisne] nm swan

cisterna [θis'terna] nf cistern, tank

cita ['θita] nf appointment, meeting; (de novios) date; (referencia) quotation

citación [θita'θjon] nf (JUR) summons sg

citar [θi'tar] vt (gen) to make an appointment with; (JUR) to summons; (un autor, texto) to quote; **~se** vr: **se citaron en el cine** they arranged to meet at the cinema

cítricos ['θitrikos] nmpl citrus fruit(s)

ciudad [θju'ðað] nf town; (más grande) city; **~anía** nf citizenship; **~ano, a** nm/f citizen

cívico, a ['θiβiko, a] adj civic

civil [θi'βil] adj civil ♦ nm (guardia) policeman

civilización [θiβiliθa'θjon] nf civilization

civilizar [θiβili'θar] vt to civilize

civismo [θi'βismo] nm public spirit

cizaña [θi'θaɲa] nf (fig) discord

cl. abr (= centilitro) cl.

clamar [kla'mar] vt to clamour for, cry out for ♦ vi to cry out, clamour

clamor [kla'mor] nm clamour, protest

clandestino, a [klandes'tino, a] adj clandestine; (POL) underground

clara ['klara] nf (de huevo) egg white

claraboya [klara'βoja] nf skylight

clarear [klare'ar] vi (el día) to dawn; (el cielo) to clear up, brighten up; **~se** vr to be transparent

clarete [kla'rete] nm rosé (wine)

claridad [klari'ðað] nf (del día) brightness; (de estilo) clarity

clarificar [klarifi'kar] vt to clarify

clarinete [klari'nete] nm clarinet

clarividencia [klariβi'ðenθja] nf clairvoyance; (fig) far-sightedness

claro, a ['klaro, a] adj clear; (luminoso) bright; (color) light; (evidente) clear, evident; (poco espeso) thin ♦ nm (en bosque) clearing ♦ adv clearly ♦ excl (tb: **~ que sí**) of course!

clase ['klase] nf class; **~ alta/media/obrera**

upper/middle/working class; **~s particulares** private lessons, private tuition *sg*

clásico, a ['klasiko, a] *adj* classical

clasificación [klasifika'θjon] *nf* classification; (*DEPORTE*) league (table)

clasificar [klasifi'kar] *vt* to classify

claudicar [klauði'kar] *vi* to give in

claustro ['klaustro] *nm* cloister

cláusula ['klausula] *nf* clause

clausura [klau'sura] *nf* closing, closure; **clausurar** *vt* (*congreso etc*) to bring to a close

clavar [kla'βar] *vt* (*clavo*) to hammer in; (*cuchillo*) to stick, thrust

clave ['klaβe] *nf* key; (*MUS*) clef

clavel [kla'βel] *nm* carnation

clavícula [kla'βikula] *nf* collar bone

clavija [kla'βixa] *nf* peg, dowel, pin; (*ELEC*) plug

clavo ['klaβo] *nm* (*de metal*) nail; (*BOT*) clove

claxon ['klakson] (*pl* **~s**) *nm* horn

clemencia [kle'menθja] *nf* mercy, clemency

cleptómano, a [klep'tomano, a] *nm/f* kleptomaniac

clérigo ['kleriɣo] *nm* priest

clero ['klero] *nm* clergy

cliché [kli'tʃe] *nm* cliché; (*FOTO*) negative

cliente, a ['kljente, a] *nm/f* client, customer

clientela [kljen'tela] *nf* clientele, customers *pl*

clima ['klima] *nm* climate

climatizado, a [klimati'θaðo, a] *adj* air-conditioned

clímax ['klimaks] *nm inv* climax

clínica ['klinika] *nf* clinic; (*particular*) private hospital

clip [klip] (*pl* **~s**) *nm* paper clip

clítoris ['klitoris] *nm inv* (*ANAT*) clitoris

cloaca [klo'aka] *nf* sewer

cloro ['kloro] *nm* chlorine

club [klub] (*pl* **~s o ~es**) *nm* club; **~ de jóvenes** youth club

cm *abr* (= *centímetro, centímetros*) cm

C.N.T. (*ESP*) *abr* = *Confederación Nacional de Trabajo*

coacción [koak'θjon] *nf* coercion, compulsion; **coaccionar** *vt* to coerce

coagular [koaɣu'lar] *vt* (*leche, sangre*) to clot; **~se** *vr* to clot; **coágulo** *nm* clot

coalición [koali'θjon] *nf* coalition

coartada [koar'taða] *nf* alibi

coartar [koar'tar] *vt* to limit, restrict

coba ['koβa] *nf*: **dar ~ a uno** to soft-soap sb

cobarde [ko'βarðe] *adj* cowardly ♦ *nm* coward; **cobardía** *nf* cowardice

cobaya [ko'βaja] *nf* guinea pig

cobertizo [koβer'tiθo] *nm* shelter

cobertura [koβer'tura] *nf* cover

cobija [ko'βixa] (*AM*) *nf* blanket

cobijar [koβi'xar] *vt* (*cubrir*) to cover; (*proteger*) to shelter; **cobijo** *nm* shelter

cobra ['koβra] *nf* cobra

cobrador, a [koβra'ðor, a] *nm/f* (*de autobús*) conductor/conductress; (*de impuestos, gas*) collector

cobrar [ko'βrar] *vt* (*cheque*) to cash; (*sueldo*) to collect, draw; (*objeto*) to recover; (*precio*) to charge; (*deuda*) to collect ♦ *vi* to be paid; **cóbrese al entregar** cash on delivery

cobre ['koβre] *nm* copper; **~s** *nmpl* (*MUS*) brass instruments

cobro ['koβro] *nm* (*de cheque*) cashing; **presentar al ~** to cash

cocaína [koka'ina] *nf* cocaine

cocción [kok'θjon] *nf* (*CULIN*) cooking; (*en agua*) boiling

cocear [koθe'ar] *vi* to kick

cocer [ko'θer] *vt, vi* to cook; (*en agua*) to boil; (*en horno*) to bake

coche ['kotʃe] *nm* (*AUTO*) car (*BRIT*), automobile (*US*); (*de tren, de caballos*) coach, carriage; (*para niños*) pram (*BRIT*), baby carriage (*US*); **ir en ~** to drive; **~ celular** Black Maria, prison van; **~ de bomberos** fire engine; **~ fúnebre** hearse; **coche-cama** (*pl* **coches-cama**) *nm* (*FERRO*) sleeping car, sleeper

cochera [ko'tʃera] *nf* garage; (*de autobuses, trenes*) depot

coche restaurante (*pl* **coches restaurante**) *nm* (*FERRO*) dining car, diner

cochinillo [kotʃi'niʎo] *nm* (*CULIN*) suckling pig, sucking pig

cochino, a [ko'tʃino, a] *adj* filthy, dirty ♦ *nm/f* pig

cocido [ko'θiðo] *nm* stew

cocina [ko'θina] *nf* kitchen; (*aparato*) cooker, stove; (*acto*) cookery; **~ eléctrica/de gas** electric/gas cooker; **~ francesa** French cuisine; **cocinar** *vt, vi* to cook

cocinero, a [koθi'nero, a] *nm/f* cook

coco ['koko] *nm* coconut

cocodrilo [koko'ðrilo] *nm* crocodile

cocotero [koko'tero] *nm* coconut palm

cóctel ['koktel] *nm* cocktail

codazo [ko'ðaθo] *nm*: **dar un ~ a uno** to nudge sb

codicia [ko'ðiθja] *nf* greed; **codiciar** *vt* to covet; **codicioso, a** *adj* covetous

código ['koðiɣo] *nm* code; **~ de barras** bar code; **~ civil** common law; **~ de (la) circulación** highway code; **~ postal** postcode

codillo [ko'ðiʎo] *nm* (*ZOOL*) knee; (*TEC*) elbow (joint)

codo ['koðo] *nm* (*ANAT, de tubo*) elbow; (*ZOOL*) knee

codorniz [koðor'niθ] *nf* quail

coerción [koer'θjon] *nf* coercion

coetáneo, a [koe'taneo, a] *adj, nm/f* contemporary

coexistir [koe(k)sis'tir] vi to coexist
cofradía [kofra'ðia] nf brotherhood, fraternity
cofre ['kofre] nm (de joyas) case; (de dinero) chest
coger [ko'xer] (ESP) vt to take (hold of); (objeto caído) to pick up; (frutas) to pick, harvest; (resfriado, ladrón, pelota) to catch ♦ vi: ~ por el buen camino to take the right road; ~se vr (el dedo) to catch; ~se a algo to get hold of sth
cogollo [ko'ɣoʎo] nm (de lechuga) heart
cogote [ko'ɣote] nm back o nape of the neck
cohabitar [koaßi'tar] vi to live together, cohabit
cohecho [ko'etʃo] nm (acción) bribery; (soborno) bribe
coherente [koe'rente] adj coherent
cohesión [koe'sjon] nm cohesion
cohete [ko'ete] nm rocket
cohibido, a [koi'ßiðo, a] adj (PSICO) inhibited; (tímido) shy
cohibir [koi'ßir] vt to restrain, restrict
coincidencia [koinθi'ðenθja] nf coincidence
coincidir [koinθi'ðir] vi (en idea) to coincide, agree; (en lugar) to coincide
coito ['koito] nm intercourse, coitus
coja etc vb ver **coger**
cojear [koxe'ar] vi (persona) to limp, hobble; (mueble) to wobble, rock
cojera [ko'xera] nf limp
cojín [ko'xin] nm cushion; **cojinete** nm (TEC) ball bearing
cojo, a etc ['koxo, a] vb ver **coger** ♦ adj (que no puede andar) lame, crippled; (mueble) wobbly ♦ nm/f lame person, cripple
cojón [ko'xon] (fam) nm: ¡cojones! shit! (!); **cojonudo, a** (fam) adj great, fantastic
col [kol] nf cabbage; ~es de Bruselas Brussels sprouts
cola ['kola] nf tail; (de gente) queue; (lugar) end, last place; (para pegar) glue, gum; hacer ~ to queue (up)
colaborador, a [kolaßora'ðor, a] nm/f collaborator
colaborar [kolaßo'rar] vi to collaborate
colada [ko'laða] nf: hacer la ~ to do the washing
colador [kola'ðor] nm (de líquidos) strainer; (para verduras etc) colander
colapso [ko'lapso] nm collapse; ~ nervioso nervous breakdown
colar [ko'lar] vt (líquido) to strain off; (metal) to cast ♦ vi to ooze, seep (through); ~se vr to jump the queue; ~se en to get into without paying; (fiesta) to gatecrash
colcha ['koltʃa] nf bedspread
colchón [kol'tʃon] nm mattress; ~ inflable o neumático air bed, air mattress
colchoneta [koltʃo'neta] nf (en gimnasio)

mat; (de playa) air bed
colección [kolek'θjon] nf collection; **coleccionar** vt to collect; **coleccionista** nm/f collector
colecta [ko'lekta] nf collection
colectivo, a [kolek'tißo, a] adj collective, joint ♦ nm (AM) (small) bus
colega [ko'leɣa] nm/f colleague
colegial, a [kole'xjal, a] nm/f schoolboy/girl
colegio [ko'lexjo] nm college; (escuela) school; (de abogados etc) association; ~ electoral polling station; ~ mayor hall of residence
colegir [kole'xir] vt to infer, conclude
cólera ['kolera] nf (ira) anger; (MED) cholera; **colérico, a** [ko'leriko, a] adj irascible, bad-tempered
colesterol [koleste'rol] nm cholesterol
coleta [ko'leta] nf pigtail
colgante [kol'ɣante] adj hanging ♦ nm (joya) pendant
colgar [kol'ɣar] vt to hang (up); (ropa) to hang out ♦ vi to hang; (TELEC) to hang up
cólico ['koliko] nm colic
coliflor [koli'flor] nf cauliflower
colilla [ko'liʎa] nf cigarette end, butt
colina [ko'lina] nf hill
colisión [koli'sjon] nf collision; ~ de frente head-on crash
collar [ko'ʎar] nm necklace; (de perro) collar
colmar [kol'mar] vt to fill to the brim; (fig) to fulfil, realize
colmena [kol'mena] nf beehive
colmillo [kol'miʎo] nm (diente) eye tooth; (de elefante) tusk; (de perro) fang
colmo ['kolmo] nm: ¡es el ~! it's the limit!
colocación [koloka'θjon] nf (acto) placing; (empleo) job, position
colocar [kolo'kar] vt to place, put, position; (dinero) to invest; (poner en empleo) to find a job for; ~se vr to get a job
Colombia [ko'lombja] nf Colombia; **colombiano, a** adj, nm/f Colombian
colonia [ko'lonja] nf colony; (de casas) housing estate; (agua de ~) cologne
colonización [koloniθa'θjon] nf colonization; **colonizador, a** [koloniθa'ðor, a] adj colonizing ♦ nm/f colonist, settler
colonizar [koloni'θar] vt to colonize
coloquio [ko'lokjo] nm conversation; (congreso) conference
color [ko'lor] nm colour
colorado, a [kolo'raðo, a] adj (rojo) red; (LAM: chiste) rude
colorante [kolo'rante] nm colouring
colorear [kolore'ar] vt to colour
colorete [kolo'rete] nm blusher
colorido [kolo'riðo] nm colouring
columna [ko'lumna] nf column; (pilar) pillar;

(*apoyo*) support

columpiar [kolum'pjar] *vt* to swing; **~se** *vr* to swing; **columpio** *nm* swing

coma ['koma] *nf* comma ♦ *nm* (MED) coma

comadre [ko'maðre] *nf* (*madrina*) godmother; (*chismosa*) gossip; **comadrona** *nf* midwife

comandancia [koman'danθja] *nf* command

comandante [koman'dante] *nm* commandant

comarca [ko'marka] *nf* region

comba ['komba] *nf* (*curva*) curve; (*cuerda*) skipping rope; **saltar a la ~** to skip

combar [kom'bar] *vt* to bend, curve

combate [kom'bate] *nm* fight; **combatiente** *nm* combatant

combatir [komba'tir] *vt* to fight, combat

combinación [kombina'θjon] *nf* combination; (QUÍM) compound; (*prenda*) slip

combinar [kombi'nar] *vt* to combine

combustible [kombus'tiβle] *nm* fuel

combustión [kombus'tjon] *nf* combustion

comedia [ko'meðja] *nf* comedy; (TEATRO) play, drama

comediante [kome'ðjante] *nm/f* (*comic*) actor/actress

comedido, a [kome'ðiðo, a] *adj* moderate

comedor, a [kome'ðor, a] *nm* (*habitación*) dining room; (*cantina*) canteen

comensal [komen'sal] *nm/f* fellow guest (*o* diner)

comentar [komen'tar] *vt* to comment on

comentario [komen'tarjo] *nm* comment, remark; (*literario*) commentary; **~s** *nmpl* (*chismes*) gossip *sg*

comentarista [komenta'rista] *nm/f* commentator

comenzar [komen'θar] *vt, vi* to begin, start; **~ a hacer algo** to begin *o* start doing sth

comer [ko'mer] *vt* to eat; (DAMAS, AJEDREZ) to take, capture ♦ *vi* to eat; (*almorzar*) to have lunch; **~se** *vr* to eat up

comercial [komer'θjal] *adj* commercial; (*relativo al negocio*) business *cpd*; **comercializar** *vt* (*producto*) to market; (*pey*) to commercialize

comerciante [komer'θjante] *nm/f* trader, merchant

comerciar [komer'θjar] *vi* to trade, do business

comercio [ko'merθjo] *nm* commerce, trade; (*negocio*) business; (*fig*) dealings *pl*; **~ electrónico** e-commerce

comestible [komes'tiβle] *adj* eatable, edible; **~s** *nmpl* food *sg*, foodstuffs

cometa [ko'meta] *nm* comet ♦ *nf* kite

cometer [kome'ter] *vt* to commit

cometido [kome'tiðo] *nm* task, assignment

comezón [kome'θon] *nf* itch, itching

cómic ['komik] *nm* comic

comicios [ko'miθjos] *nmpl* elections

cómico, a ['komiko, a] *adj* comic(al) ♦ *nm/f* comedian

comida [ko'miða] *nf* (*alimento*) food; (*almuerzo, cena*) meal; (*de mediodía*) lunch

comidilla [komi'ðiʎa] *nf*: **ser la ~ de la ciudad** to be the talk of the town

comienzo *etc* [ko'mjenθo] *vb ver* **comenzar** ♦ *nm* beginning, start

comillas [ko'miʎas] *nfpl* quotation marks

comilona [komi'lona] (*fam*) *nf* blow-out

comino [ko'mino] *nm*: **(no) me importa un ~** I don't give a damn

comisaría [komisa'ria] *nf* (*de policía*) police station; (MIL) commissariat

comisario [komi'sarjo] *nm* (MIL *etc*) commissary; (POL) commissar

comisión [komi'sjon] *nf* commission

comité [komi'te] (*pl* **~s**) *nm* committee

comitiva [komi'tiβa] *nf* retinue

como ['komo] *adv* as; (*tal* ~) like; (*aproximadamente*) about, approximately ♦ *conj* (*ya que, puesto que*) as, since; **¡~ no!** of course!; **~ no lo haga hoy** unless he does it today; **~ si** as if; **es tan alto ~ ancho** it is as high as it is wide

cómo ['komo] *adv* how?, why? ♦ *excl* what?, I beg your pardon? ♦ *nm*: **el ~ y el porqué** the whys and wherefores

cómoda ['komoða] *nf* chest of drawers

comodidad [komoði'ðað] *nf* comfort; **venga a su ~** come at your convenience

comodín [komo'ðin] *nm* joker

cómodo, a ['komoðo, a] *adj* comfortable; (*práctico, de fácil uso*) convenient

compact disc *nm* compact disk player

compacto, a [kom'pakto, a] *adj* compact

compadecer [kompaðe'θer] *vt* to pity, be sorry for; **~se** *vr*: **~se de** to pity, be *o* feel sorry for

compadre [kom'paðre] *nm* (*padrino*) godfather; (*amigo*) friend, pal

compañero, a [kompa'nero, a] *nm/f* companion; (*novio*) boy/girlfriend; **~ de clase** classmate

compañía [kompa'nia] *nf* company

comparación [kompara'θjon] *nf* comparison; **en ~ con** in comparison with

comparar [kompa'rar] *vt* to compare

comparecer [kompare'θer] *vi* to appear (in court)

comparsa [kom'parsa] *nm/f* (TEATRO) extra

compartimiento [komparti'mjento] *nm* (FERRO) compartment

compartir [kompar'tir] *vt* to share; (*dinero, comida etc*) to divide (up), share (out)

compás [kom'pas] *nm* (MUS) beat, rhythm;

(MAT) compasses *pl;* *(NAUT etc)* compass

compasión [kompa'sjon] *nf* compassion, pity

compasivo, a [kompa'siβo, a] *adj* compassionate

compatibilidad [kompatiβili'ðað] *nf* compatibility

compatible [kompa'tiβle] *adj* compatible

compatriota [kompa'trjota] *nm/f* compatriot, fellow countryman/woman

compendiar [kompen'djar] *vt* to summarize; **compendio** *nm* summary

compenetrarse [kompene'trarse] *vr* to be in tune

compensación [kompensa'θjon] *nf* compensation

compensar [kompen'sar] *vt* to compensate

competencia [kompe'tenθja] *nf* *(incumbencia)* domain, field; *(JUR, habilidad)* competence; *(rivalidad)* competition

competente [kompe'tente] *adj* competent

competición [kompeti'θjon] *nf* competition

competir [kompe'tir] *vi* to compete

compilar [kompi'lar] *vt* to compile

complacencia [kompla'θenθja] *nf* *(placer)* pleasure; *(tolerancia excesiva)* complacency

complacer [kompla'θer] *vt* to please; **~se** *vr* to be pleased

complaciente [kompla'θjente] *adj* kind, obliging, helpful

complejo, a [kom'plexo, a] *adj, nm* complex

complementario, a [komplemen'tarjo, a] *adj* complementary

completar [komple'tar] *vt* to complete

completo, a [kom'pleto, a] *adj* complete; *(perfecto)* perfect; *(lleno)* full ♦ *nm* full complement

complicado, a [kompli'kaðo, a] *adj* complicated; **estar ~ en** to be mixed up in

cómplice ['kompliθe] *nm/f* accomplice

complot [kom'plo(t)] *(pl* **~s***) nm* plot

componer [kompo'ner] *vt* *(MUS, LITERATURA, IMPRENTA)* to compose; *(algo roto)* to mend, repair; *(arreglar)* to arrange; **~se** *vr:* **~se de** to consist of; **componérselas para hacer algo** to manage to do sth

comportamiento [komporta'mjento] *nm* behaviour, conduct

comportarse [kompor'tarse] *vr* to behave

composición [komposi'θjon] *nf* composition

compositor, a [komposi'tor, a] *nm/f* composer

compostura [kompos'tura] *nf* *(actitud)* composure

compra ['kompra] *nf* purchase; **ir de ~s** to go shopping; **comprador, a** *nm/f* buyer, purchaser

comprar [kom'prar] *vt* to buy, purchase

comprender [kompren'der] *vt* to understand; *(incluir)* to comprise, include

comprensión [kompren'sjon] *nf* understanding; **comprensivo, a** *adj* *(actitud)* understanding

compresa [kom'presa] *nf:* **~ higiénica** sanitary towel *(BRIT)* o napkin *(US)*

comprimido, a [kompri'miðo, a] *adj* compressed ♦ *nm (MED)* pill, tablet

comprimir [kompri'mir] *vt* to compress

comprobante [kompro'ßante] *nm* proof; *(COM)* voucher; **~ de recibo** receipt

comprobar [kompro'ßar] *vt* to check; *(probar)* to prove; *(TEC)* to check, test

comprometer [komprome'ter] *vt* to compromise; *(poner en peligro)* to endanger; **~se** *vr (involucrarse)* to get involved

compromiso [kompro'miso] *nm* *(obligación)* obligation; *(cometido)* commitment; *(convenio)* agreement; *(apuro)* awkward situation

compuesto, a [kom'pwesto, a] *adj:* **~ de** composed of, made up of ♦ *nm* compound

computador [komputa'ðor] *nm* computer; **~ central** mainframe computer; **~ personal** personal computer

computadora [komputa'ðora] *nf* = **computador**

cómputo ['komputo] *nm* calculation

comulgar [komul'var] *vi* to receive communion

común [ko'mun] *adj* common ♦ *nm:* **el ~** the community

comunicación [komunika'θjon] *nf* communication; *(informe)* report

comunicado [komuni'kaðo] *nm* announcement; **~ de prensa** press release

comunicar [komuni'kar] *vt, vi* to communicate; **~se** *vr* to communicate; **está comunicando** *(TEL)* the line's engaged *(BRIT)* o busy *(US)*; **comunicativo, a** *adj* communicative

comunidad [komuni'ðað] *nf* community; **~ autónoma** *(POL)* autonomous region; **C~ Económica Europea** European Economic Community

comunión [komu'njon] *nf* communion

comunismo [komu'nismo] *nm* communism; **comunista** *adj, nm/f* communist

---

PALABRA CLAVE

con [kon] *prep* **1** *(medio, compañía)* with; **comer ~ cuchara** to eat with a spoon; **pasear ~ uno** to go for a walk with sb

2 *(a pesar de):* **~ todo, merece nuestros respetos** all the same, he deserves our respect

3 *(para ~):* **es muy bueno para ~ los niños** he's very good with (the) children

4 (+ *infin*): **~ llegar tan tarde se quedó sin comer** by arriving so late he missed out on eating
♦ *conj:* **~ que: será suficiente ~ que le escribas** it will be sufficient if you write to her

conato [ko'nato] *nm* attempt; **~ de robo** attempted robbery

concebir [konθe'ßir] *vt, vi* to conceive

conceder [konθe'ðer] *vt* to concede

concejal, a [konθe'xal, a] *nm/f* town councillor

concentración [konθentra'θjon] *nf* concentration

concentrar [konθen'trar] *vt* to concentrate; **~se** *vr* to concentrate

concepción [konθep'θjon] *nf* conception

concepto [kon'θepto] *nm* concept

concernir [konθer'nir] *vi* to concern; **en lo que concierne a ... as** far as ... is concerned; **en lo que a mí concierne** as far as I'm concerned

concertar [konθer'tar] *vt* (*MUS*) to harmonize; (*acordar: precio*) to agree; (: *tratado*) to conclude; (*trato*) to arrange, fix up; (*combinar: esfuerzos*) to coordinate ♦ *vi* to harmonize, be in tune

concesión [konθe'sjon] *nf* concession

concesionario [konθesjo'narjo] *nm* (licensed) dealer, agent

concha ['kontʃa] *nf* shell

conciencia [kon'θjenθja] *nf* conscience; **tener/tomar ~ de** to be/become aware of; **tener la ~ limpia/tranquila** to have a clear conscience

concienciar [konθjen'θjar] *vt* to make aware; **~se** *vr* to become aware

concienzudo, a [konθjen'θuðo, a] *adj* conscientious

concierto *etc* [kon'θjerto] *vb ver* **concertar** ♦ *nm* concert; (*obra*) concerto

conciliar [konθi'ljar] *vt* to reconcile

concilio [kon'θiljo] *nm* council

conciso, a [kon'θiso, a] *adj* concise

concluir [konklu'ir] *vt, vi* to conclude; **~se** *vr* to conclude

conclusión [konklu'sjon] *nf* conclusion

concluyente [konklu'jente] *adj* (*prueba, información*) conclusive

concordar [konkor'ðar] *vt* to reconcile ♦ *vi* to agree, tally

concordia [kon'korðja] *nf* harmony

concretar [konkre'tar] *vt* to make concrete, make more specific; **~se** *vr* to become more definite

concreto, a [kon'kreto, a] *adj, nm* (*AM*) concrete; **en ~** (*en resumen*) to sum up; (*específicamente*) specifically; **no hay nada en ~** there's nothing definite

concurrencia [konku'rrenθja] *nf* turnout

concurrido, a [konku'rriðo, a] *adj* (*calle*) busy; (*local, reunión*) crowded

concurrir [konku'rrir] *vi* (*juntarse: ríos*) to meet, come together; (: *personas*) to gather, meet

concursante [konkur'sante] *nm/f* competitor

concurso [kon'kurso] *nm* (*de público*) crowd; (*ESCOL, DEPORTE, competencia*) competition; (*ayuda*) help, cooperation

condal [kon'dal] *adj:* **la Ciudad C~** Barcelona

conde ['konde] *nm* count

condecoración [kondekora'θjon] *nf* (*MIL*) medal

condecorar [kondeko'rar] *vt* (*MIL*) to decorate

condena [kon'dena] *nf* sentence

condenación [kondena'θjon] *nf* condemnation; (*REL*) damnation

condenar [konde'nar] *vt* to condemn; (*JUR*) to convict; **~se** *vr* (*REL*) to be damned

condensar [konden'sar] *vt* to condense

condesa [kon'desa] *nf* countess

condición [kondi'θjon] *nf* condition; **condicional** *adj* conditional

condicionar [kondiθjo'nar] *vt* (*acondicionar*) to condition; **~ algo a** to make sth conditional on

condimento [kondi'mento] *nm* seasoning

condolerse [kondo'lerse] *vr* to sympathize

condón [kon'don] *nm* condom

conducir [kondu'θir] *vt* to take, convey; (*AUTO*) to drive ♦ *vi* to drive; (*fig*) to lead; **~se** *vr* to behave

conducta [kon'dukta] *nf* conduct, behaviour

conducto [kon'dukto] *nm* pipe, tube; (*fig*) channel

conductor, a [konduk'tor, a] *adj* leading, guiding ♦ *nm* (*FÍSICA*) conductor; (*de vehículo*) driver

conduje *etc vb ver* **conducir**

conduzco *etc vb ver* **conducir**

conectado, a [konek'taðo, a] *adj* (*INFORM*) on-line

conectar [konek'tar] *vt* to connect (up); (*enchufar*) plug in

conejillo [kone'xiʎo] *nm:* **~ de Indias** (*ZOOL*) guinea pig

conejo [ko'nexo] *nm* rabbit

conexión [konek'sjon] *nf* connection

confección [konfe(k)'θjon] *nf* preparation; (*industria*) clothing industry

confeccionar [konfekθjo'nar] *vt* to make (up)

confederación [konfeðera'θjon] *nf* confederation

conferencia [konfe'renθja] *nf* conference; (*lección*) lecture; (*TEL*) call

conferir [konfe'rir] vt to award
confesar [konfe'sar] vt to confess, admit
confesión [konfe'sjon] nf confession
confesionario [konfesjo'narjo] nm confessional
confeti [kon'feti] nm confetti
confiado, a [kon'fjaðo, a] adj (crédulo) trusting; (seguro) confident
confianza [kon'fjanθa] nf trust; (seguridad) confidence; (familiaridad) intimacy, familiarity
confiar [kon'fjar] vt to entrust ♦ vi to trust
confidencia [konfi'ðenθja] nf confidence
confidencial [konfiðen'θjal] adj confidential
confidente [konfi'ðente] nm/f confidant/e; (policial) informer
configurar [konfiɣu'rar] vt to shape, form
confín [kon'fin] nm limit; **confines** nmpl confines, limits
confinar [konfi'nar] vi to confine; (desterrar) to banish
confirmar [konfir'mar] vt to confirm
confiscar [konfis'kar] vt to confiscate
confite [kon'fite] nm sweet (BRIT), candy (US)
confitería [konfite'ria] nf (tienda) confectioner's (shop)
confitura [konfi'tura] nf jam
conflictivo, a [konflik'tiβo, a] adj (asunto, propuesta) controversial; (país, situación) troubled
conflicto [kon'flikto] nm conflict; (fig) clash
confluir [kon'flwir] vi (ríos) to meet; (gente) to gather
conformar [konfor'mar] vt to shape, fashion ♦ vi to agree; ~se vr to conform; (resignarse) to resign o.s.
conforme [kon'forme] adj (correspondiente): ~ con in line with; (de acuerdo): estar ~s (con algo) to be in agreement (with sth) ♦ adv as ♦ excl agreed! ♦ prep: ~ a in accordance with; quedarse ~ (con algo) to be satisfied (with sth)
conformidad [konformi'ðað] nf (semejanza) similarity; (acuerdo) agreement; **conformista** adj, nm/f conformist
confortable [konfor'taβle] adj comfortable
confortar [konfor'tar] vt to comfort
confrontar [konfron'tar] vt to confront; (dos personas) to bring face to face; (cotejar) to compare
confundir [konfun'dir] vt (equivocar) to mistake, confuse; (turbar) to confuse; ~se vr (turbarse) to get confused; (equivocarse) to make a mistake; (mezclarse) to mix
confusión [konfu'sjon] nf confusion
confuso, a [kon'fuso, a] adj confused
congelado, a [konxe'laðo, a] adj frozen; ~s nmpl frozen food(s); **congelador** nm (aparato) freezer, deep freeze
congelar [konxe'lar] vt to freeze; ~se vr

(sangre, grasa) to congeal
congeniar [konxe'njar] vi to get on (BRIT) o along (US) well
congestión [konxes'tjon] nf congestion
congestionar [konxestjo'nar] vt to congest
congoja [kon'goxa] nf distress, grief
congraciarse [kongra'θjarse] vr to ingratiate o.s.
congratular [kongratu'lar] vt to congratulate
congregación [kongreɣa'θjon] nf congregation
congregar [kongre'ɣar] vt to gather together; ~se vr to gather together
congresista [kongre'sista] nm/f delegate, congressman/woman
congreso [kon'greso] nm congress
congrio ['kongrjo] nm conger eel
conjetura [konxe'tura] nf guess; **conjeturar** vt to guess
conjugar [konxu'ɣar] vt to combine, fit together; (LING) to conjugate
conjunción [konxun'θjon] nf conjunction
conjunto, a [kon'xunto, a] adj joint, united ♦ nm whole; (MUS) band; en ~ as a whole
conjurar [konxu'rar] vt (REL) to exorcise; (fig) to ward off ♦ vi to plot
conmemoración [konmemora'θjon] nf commemoration
conmemorar [konmemo'rar] vt to commemorate
conmigo [kon'miɣo] pron with me
conmoción [konmo'θjon] nf shock; (fig) upheaval; ~ cerebral (MED) concussion
conmovedor, a [konmoβe'ðor, a] adj touching, moving; (emocionante) exciting
conmover [konmo'βer] vt to shake, disturb; (fig) to move
conmutador [konmuta'ðor] nm switch; (AM: TEL: centralita) switchboard; (: central) telephone exchange
cono ['kono] nm cone
conocedor, a [konoθe'ðor, a] adj expert, knowledgeable ♦ nm/f expert
conocer [kono'θer] vt to know; (por primera vez) to meet, get to know; (entender) to know about; (reconocer) to recognize; ~se vr (una persona) to know o.s.; (dos personas) to (get to) know each other
conocido, a [kono'θiðo, a] adj (well-) known ♦ nm/f acquaintance
conocimiento [konoθi'mjento] nm knowledge; (MED) consciousness; ~s nmpl (saber) knowledge sg
conozco etc vb ver **conocer**
conque ['konke] conj and so, so then
conquista [kon'kista] nf conquest; **conquistador, a** adj conquering ♦ nm conqueror

conquistar [konkis'tar] vt to conquer

consagrar [konsa'ɣrar] vt (REL) to consecrate; (fig) to devote

consciente [kons'θjente] adj conscious

consecución [konseku'θjon] nf acquisition; (de fin) attainment

consecuencia [konse'kwenθja] nf consequence, outcome; (coherencia) consistency

consecuente [konse'kwente] adj consistent

consecutivo, a [konseku'tiβo, a] adj consecutive

conseguir [konse'ɣir] vt to get, obtain; (objetivo) to attain

consejero, a [konse'xero, a] nm/f adviser, consultant; (POL) councillor

consejo [kon'sexo] nm advice; (POL) council; ~ de administración (COM) board of directors; ~ de guerra court martial; ~ de ministros cabinet meeting

consenso [kon'senso] nm consensus

consentimiento [konsenti'mjento] nm consent

consentir [konsen'tir] vt (permitir, tolerar) to consent to; (mimar) to pamper, spoil; (aguantar) to put up with ♦ vi to agree, consent; ~ que uno haga algo to allow sb to do sth

conserje [kon'serxe] nm caretaker; (portero) porter

conservación [konserβa'θjon] nf conservation; (de alimentos, vida) preservation

conservador, a [konserβa'ðor, a] adj (POL) conservative ♦ nm/f conservative

conservante [konser'βante] nm preservative

conservar [konser'βar] vt to conserve, keep; (alimentos, vida) to preserve; ~se vr to survive

conservas [kon'serβas] nfpl canned food(s) (pl)

conservatorio [konserβa'torjo] nm (MUS) conservatoire, conservatory

considerable [konsiðe'raβle] adj considerable

consideración [konsiðera'θjon] nf consideration; (estimación) respect

considerado, a [konsiðe'raðo, a] adj (atento) considerate; (respetado) respected

considerar [konsiðe'rar] vt to consider

consigna [kon'siɣna] nf (orden) order, instruction; (para equipajes) left-luggage office

consigo etc [kon'siɣo] vb ver **conseguir** ♦ pron (m) with him; (f) with her; (Vd) with you; (reflexivo) with o.s.

consiguiendo etc vb ver **conseguir**

consiguiente [konsi'ɣjente] adj consequent; por ~ and so, therefore, consequently

consistente [konsis'tente] adj consistent; (sólido) solid, firm; (válido) sound

consistir [konsis'tir] vi: ~ en (componerse de) to consist of

consola [kon'sola] nf (mueble) console table; (de videojuegos) console

consolación [konsola'θjon] nf consolation

consolar [konso'lar] vt to console

consolidar [konsoli'ðar] vt to consolidate

consomé [konso'me] {pl ~s} nm consommé, clear soup

consonante [konso'nante] adj consonant, harmonious ♦ nf consonant

consorcio [kon'sorθjo] nm consortium

conspiración [konspira'θjon] nf conspiracy

conspirador, a [konspira'ðor, a] nm/f conspirator

conspirar [konspi'rar] vi to conspire

constancia [kon'stanθja] nf constancy; dejar ~ de to put on record

constante [kons'tante] adj, nf constant

constar [kons'tar] vi (evidenciarse) to be clear o evident; ~ de to consist of

constatar [konsta'tar] vt to verify

consternación [konsterna'θjon] nf consternation

constipado, a [konsti'paðo, a] adj: estar ~ to have a cold ♦ nm cold

constitución [konstitu'θjon] nf constitution; **constitucional** adj constitutional

constituir [konstitu'ir] vt (formar, componer) to constitute, make up; (fundar, erigir, ordenar) to constitute, establish

constituyente [konstitu'jente] adj constituent

constreñir [konstre'nir] vt (restringir) to restrict

construcción [konstruk'θjon] nf construction, building

constructor, a [konstruk'tor, a] nm/f builder

construir [konstru'ir] vt to build, construct

construyendo etc vb ver **construir**

consuelo [kon'swelo] nm consolation, solace

cónsul ['konsul] nm consul; **consulado** nm consulate

consulta [kon'sulta] nf consultation; (MED): horas de ~ surgery hours

consultar [konsul'tar] vt to consult

consultorio [konsul'torjo] nm (MED) surgery

consumar [konsu'mar] vt to complete, carry out; (crimen) to commit; (sentencia) to carry out

consumición [konsumi'θjon] nf consumption; (bebida) drink; (comida) food; ~ mínima cover charge

consumidor, a [konsumi'ðor, a] nm/f consumer

consumir [konsu'mir] vt to consume; ~se vr

to be consumed; (*persona*) to waste away

consumismo [konsu'mismo] *nm* consumerism

consumo [kon'sumo] *nm* consumption

contabilidad [kontaβili'ðað] *nf* accounting, book-keeping; (*profesión*) accountancy; **contable** *nm/f* accountant

contacto [kon'takto] *nm* contact; (*AUTO*) ignition

contado, a [kon'taðo, a] *adj*: **~s** (*escasos*) numbered, scarce, few ♦ *nm*: **pagar al ~** to pay (in) cash

contador [konta'ðor] *nm* (*aparato*) meter; (*AM*: *contante*) accountant

contagiar [konta'xjar] *vt* (*enfermedad*) to pass on, transmit; (*persona*) to infect; **~se** *vr* to become infected

contagio [kon'taxjo] *nm* infection; **contagioso, a** *adj* infectious; (*fig*) catching

contaminación [kontamina'θjon] *nf* contamination; (*polución*) pollution

contaminar [kontami'nar] *vt* to contaminate; (*aire, agua*) to pollute

contante [kon'tante] *adj*: **dinero ~ (y sonante)** cash

contar [kon'tar] *vt* (*páginas, dinero*) to count; (*anécdota, chiste etc*) to tell ♦ *vi* to count; **~ con** to rely on, count on

contemplación [kontempla'θjon] *nf* contemplation

contemplar [kontem'plar] *vt* to contemplate; (*mirar*) to look at

contemporáneo, a [kontempo'raneo, a] *adj, nm/f* contemporary

contendiente [konten'djente] *nm/f* contestant

contenedor [kontene'ðor] *nm* container

contener [konte'ner] *vt* to contain, hold; (*retener*) to hold back, contain; **~se** *vr* to control o restrain o.s.

contenido, a [konte'niðo, a] *adj* (*moderado*) restrained; (*risa etc*) suppressed ♦ *nm* contents *pl*, content

contentar [konten'tar] *vt* (*satisfacer*) to satisfy; (*complacer*) to please; **~se** *vr* to be satisfied

contento, a [kon'tento, a] *adj* (*alegre*) pleased; (*feliz*) happy

contestación [kontesta'θjon] *nf* answer, reply

contestador [kontesta'ðor] *nm*: **~ automático** answering machine

contestar [kontes'tar] *vt* to answer, reply; (*JUR*) to corroborate, confirm

contexto [kon'te(k)sto] *nm* context

contienda [kon'tjenda] *nf* contest

contigo [kon'tiyo] *pron* with you

contiguo, a [kon'tiywo, a] *adj* adjacent, adjoining

continente [konti'nente] *adj, nm* continent

contingencia [kontin'xenθja] *nf* contingency; (*riesgo*) risk; **contingente** *adj, nm* contingent

continuación [kontinwa'θjon] *nf* continuation; **a ~** then, next

continuar [konti'nwar] *vt* to continue, go on with ♦ *vi* to continue, go on; **~ hablando** to continue talking o to talk

continuidad [kontinwi'ðað] *nf* continuity

continuo, a [kon'tinwo, a] *adj* (*sin interrupción*) continuous; (*acción perseverante*) continual

contorno [kon'torno] *nm* outline; (*GEO*) contour; **~s** *nmpl* neighbourhood *sg*, surrounding area *sg*

contorsión [kontor'sjon] *nf* contortion

contra ['kontra] *prep, ad* against ♦ *nm* inv **con ♦** *nf*: **la C~** (*de Nicaragua*) the Contras *pl*

contraataque [kontraa'take] *nm* counterattack

contrabajo [kontra'βaxo] *nm* double bass

contrabandista [kontraβan'dista] *nm/f* smuggler

contrabando [kontra'βando] *nm* (*acción*) smuggling; (*mercancías*) contraband

contracción [kontrak'θjon] *nf* contraction

contracorriente [kontrako'rrjente]: **(a) ~** *adv* against the current

contradecir [kontraðe'θir] *vt* to contradict

contradicción [kontraðik'θjon] *nf* contradiction

contradictorio, a [kontraðik'torjo, a] *adj* contradictory

contraer [kontra'er] *vt* to contract; (*limitar*) to restrict; **~se** *vr* to contract; (*limitarse*) to limit o.s.

contraluz [kontra'luθ] *nf*: **a ~** against the light

contrapartida [kontrapar'tiða] *nf*: **como ~ (de)** in return (for)

contrapelo [kontra'pelo]: **a ~** *adv* the wrong way

contrapesar [kontrape'sar] *vt* to counterbalance; (*fig*) to offset; **contrapeso** *nm* counterweight

contraportada [kontrapor'taða] *nf* (*de revista*) back cover

contraproducente [kontraproðu'θente] *adj* counterproductive

contrariar [kontra'rjar] *vt* (*oponerse*) to oppose; (*poner obstáculo*) to impede; (*enfadar*) to vex

contrariedad [kontrarje'ðað] *nf* (*obstáculo*) obstacle, setback; (*disgusto*) vexation, annoyance

contrario, a [kon'trarjo, a] *adj* contrary; (*persona*) opposed; (*sentido, lado*) opposite ♦ *nm/f* enemy, adversary; (*DEPORTE*) opponent; **al/por el ~** on the contrary; **de lo ~** otherwise

contrarreloj [kontrarre'lo] *nf* (*tb: prueba ~*) time trial

contrarrestar [kontrarres'tar] *vt* to counteract

contrasentido [kontrasen'tiðo] *nm*: **es un ~ que él ...** it doesn't make sense for him to ...

contraseña [kontra'sena] *nf* (*INFORM*) password

contrastar [kontras'tar] *vt*, *vi* to contrast

contraste [kon'traste] *nm* contrast

contratar [kontra'tar] *vt* (*firmar un acuerdo para*) to contract for; (*empleados, obreros*) to hire, engage; **~se** *vr* to sign on

contratiempo [kontra'tjempo] *nm* setback

contratista [kontra'tista] *nm/f* contractor

contrato [kon'trato] *nm* contract

contravenir [kontraße'nir] *vi*: **~ a** to contravene, violate

contraventana [kontraßen'tana] *nf* shutter

contribución [kontrißu'θjon] *nf* (*municipal etc*) tax; (*ayuda*) contribution

contribuir [kontrißu'ir] *vt*, *vi* to contribute; (*COM*) to pay (in taxes)

contribuyente [kontrißu'jente] *nm/f* (*COM*) taxpayer; (*que ayuda*) contributor

contrincante [kontrin'kante] *nm* opponent

control [kon'trol] *nm* control; (*inspección*) inspection, check; **~ador, a** *nm/f* controller; **~ador aéreo** air-traffic controller

controlar [kontro'lar] *vt* to control; (*inspeccionar*) to inspect, check

controversia [kontro'ßersja] *nf* controversy

contundente [kontun'dente] *adj* (*instrumento*) blunt; (*argumento, derrota*) overwhelming

contusión [kontu'sjon] *nf* bruise

convalecencia [kombale'θenθja] *nf* convalescence

convalecer [kombale'θer] *vi* to convalesce, get better

convaleciente [kombale'θjente] *adj, nm/f* convalescent

convalidar [kombali'ðar] *vt* (*título*) to recognize

convencer [komben'θer] *vt* to convince

convencimiento [kombenθi'mjento] *nm* (*certidumbre*) conviction

convención [komben'θjon] *nf* convention

conveniencia [kombe'njenθja] *nf* suitability; (*conformidad*) agreement; (*utilidad, provecho*) usefulness; **~s** *nfpl* (*convenciones*) conventions; (*COM*) property *sg*

conveniente [kombe'njente] *adj* suitable; (*útil*) useful

convenio [kom'benjo] *nm* agreement, treaty

convenir [kombe'nir] *vi* (*estar de acuerdo*) to agree; (*venir bien*) to suit, be suitable

convento [kom'bento] *nm* convent

convenza *etc vb ver* **convencer**

converger [komber'xer] *vi* to converge

convergir [komber'xir] *vi* = **converger**

conversación [kombersa'θjon] *nf* conversation

conversar [komber'sar] *vi* to talk, converse

conversión [komber'sjon] *nf* conversion

convertir [komber'tir] *vt* to convert

convicción [kombik'θjon] *nf* conviction

convicto, a [kom'bikto, a] *adj* convicted

convidado, a [kombi'ðaðo, a] *nm/f* guest

convidar [kombi'ðar] *vt* to invite

convincente [kombin'θente] *adj* convincing

convite [kom'bite] *nm* invitation; (*banquete*) banquet

convivencia [kombi'ßenθja] *nf* coexistence, living together

convivir [kombi'ßir] *vi* to live together

convocar [kombo'kar] *vt* to summon, call (together)

convocatoria [komboka'torja] *nf* (*de oposiciones, elecciones*) notice; (*de huelga*) call

convulsión [kombul'sjon] *nf* convulsion

conyugal [konju'val] *adj* conjugal; **cónyuge** ['konjuxe] *nm/f* spouse

coñac [ko'na(k)] (*pl ~s*) *nm* cognac, brandy

coño ['kono] (*fam!*) *excl* (*enfado*) shit! (*!*); (*sorpresa*) bloody hell! (*!*)

cooperación [koopera'θjon] *nf* cooperation

cooperar [koope'rar] *vi* to cooperate

cooperativa [koopera'tißa] *nf* cooperative

coordinadora [koorðina'ðora] *nf* (*comité*) coordinating committee

coordinar [koorði'nar] *vt* to coordinate

copa ['kopa] *nf* cup; (*vaso*) glass; (*bebida*): (**tomar una**) **~** (to have a) drink; (*de árbol*) top; (*de sombrero*) crown; **~s** *nfpl* (*NAIPES*) ≈ hearts

copia ['kopja] *nf* copy; **~ de respaldo** o **seguridad** (*INFORM*) back-up copy; **copiar** *vt* to copy

copioso, a [ko'pjoso, a] *adj* copious, plentiful

copla ['kopla] *nf* verse; (*canción*) (*popular*) song

copo ['kopo] *nm*: **~ de nieve** snowflake; **~s de maíz** cornflakes

coqueta [ko'keta] *adj* flirtatious, coquettish; **coquetear** *vi* to flirt

coraje [ko'raxe] *nm* courage; (*ánimo*) spirit; (*ira*) anger

coral [ko'ral] *adj* choral ♦ *nf* (*MUS*) choir ♦ *nm* (*ZOOL*) coral

coraza [ko'raθa] *nf* (*armadura*) armour; (*blindaje*) armour-plating

corazón [kora'θon] *nm* heart

corazonada [koraθo'naða] *nf* impulse; (*presentimiento*) hunch

corbata [kor'ßata] *nf* tie

corchete [kor'tʃete] nm catch, clasp

corcho ['kortʃo] nm cork; (PESCA) float

cordel [kor'ðel] nm cord, line

cordero [kor'ðero] nm lamb

cordial [kor'ðjal] adj cordial; ~idad nf warmth, cordiality

cordillera [korði'ʎera] nf range (of mountains)

Córdoba ['korðoβa] n Cordova

cordón [kor'ðon] nm (cuerda) cord, string; (de zapatos) lace; (MIL etc) cordon

cordura [kor'ðura] nf: con ~ (obrar, hablar) sensibly

corneta [kor'neta] nf bugle

cornisa [kor'nisa] nf (ARQ) cornice

coro ['koro] nm chorus; (conjunto de cantores) choir

corona [ko'rona] nf crown; (de flores) garland; coronación nf coronation; coronar vt to crown

coronel [koro'nel] nm colonel

coronilla [koro'niʎa] nf (ANAT) crown (of the head)

corporación [korpora'θjon] nf corporation

corporal [korpo'ral] adj corporal, bodily

corpulento, a [korpu'lento a] adj (persona) heavily-built

corral [ko'rral] nm farmyard

correa [ko'rrea] nf strap; (cinturón) belt; (de perro) lead, leash

corrección [korrek'θjon] nf correction; (represión) rebuke; correccional nm reformatory

correcto, a [ko'rrekto, a] adj correct; (persona) well-mannered

corredizo, a [korre'ðiθo, a] adj (puerta etc) sliding

corredor, a [korre'ðor, a] nm (pasillo) corridor; (balcón corrido) gallery; (COM) agent, broker ♦ nm/f (DEPORTE) runner

corregir [korre'xir] vt (error) to correct; ~se vr to reform

correo [ko'rreo] nm post, mail; (persona) courier; C~s nmpl Post Office sg; ~ aéreo airmail; ~ electrónico electronic mail, e-mail

correr [ko'rrer] vt to run; (cortinas) to draw; (cerrojo) to shoot ♦ vi to run; (líquido) to run, flow; ~se vr to slide, move; (colores) to run

correspondencia [korrespon'denθja] nf correspondence; (FERRO) connection

corresponder [korrespon'der] vi to correspond; (convenir) to be suitable; (pertenecer) to belong; (concernir) to concern; ~se vr (por escrito) to correspond; (amarse) to love one another

correspondiente [korrespon'djente] adj corresponding

corresponsal [korrespon'sal] nm/f correspondent

corrida [ko'rriða] nf (de toros) bullfight

corrido, a [ko'rriðo, a] adj (avergonzado) abashed; 3 noches corridas 3 nights running; un kilo ~ a good kilo

corriente [ko'rrjente] adj (agua) running; (dinero etc) current; (común) ordinary, normal ♦ nf current ♦ nm current month; ~ eléctrica electric current

corrija etc vb ver corregir

corrillo [ko'rriʎo] nm ring, circle (of people); (fig) clique

corro ['korro] nm ring, circle (of people)

corroborar [korroβo'rar] vt to corroborate

corroer [korro'er] vt to corrode; (GEO) to erode

corromper [korrom'per] vt (madera) to rot; (fig) to corrupt

corrosivo, a [korro'siβo, a] adj corrosive

corrupción [korrup'θjon] nf rot, decay; (fig) corruption

corsé [kor'se] nm corset

cortacésped [korta'θespeð] nm lawn mower

cortado, a [kor'taðo, a] adj (gen) cut; (leche) sour; (tímido) shy; (avergonzado) embarrassed ♦ nm coffee (with a little milk)

cortar [kor'tar] vt to cut; (suministro) to cut off; (un pasaje) to cut out ♦ vi to cut; ~se vr (avergonzarse) to become embarrassed; (leche) to turn, curdle; ~se el pelo to have one's hair cut

cortauñas [korta'uɲas] nm inv nail clippers pl

corte ['korte] nm cut, cutting; (de tela) piece, length ♦ nf: las C~s the Spanish Parliament; ~ y confección dressmaking; ~ de luz power cut

cortejar [korte'xar] vt to court

cortejo [kor'texo] nm entourage; ~ fúnebre funeral procession

cortés [kor'tes] adj courteous, polite

cortesía [korte'sia] nf courtesy

corteza [kor'teθa] nf (de árbol) bark; (de pan) crust

cortijo [kor'tixo] nm farm, farmhouse

cortina [kor'tina] nf curtain

corto, a ['korto, a] adj (breve) short; (tímido) bashful; ~ de luces not very bright; ~ de vista short-sighted; estar ~ de fondos to be short of funds; ~circuito nm short circuit; ~metraje nm (CINE) short

cosa ['kosa] nf thing; ~ de about; eso es ~ mía that's my business

coscorrón [kosko'rron] nm bump on the head

cosecha [ko'setʃa] nf (AGR) harvest; (de vino) vintage

cosechar [kose'tʃar] vt to harvest, gather (in)

coser [ko'ser] vt to sew

cosmético, a [kos'metiko, a] adj, nm cosmetic

cosquillas [kos'kiʎas] *nfpl*: **hacer ~** to tickle; **tener ~** to be ticklish

costa ['kosta] *nf* (GEO) coast; **C~ Brava** Costa Brava; **C~ Cantábrica** Cantabrian Coast; **C~ del Sol** Costa del Sol; **a toda ~** at all costs

costado [kos'taðo] *nm* side

costar [kos'tar] *vt* (*valer*) to cost; **me cuesta hablarle** I find it hard to talk to him

Costa Rica *nf* Costa Rica; **costarricense** *adj, nm/f* Costa Rican; **costarriqueño, a** *adj, nm/f* Costa Rican

coste ['koste] *nm* = **costo**

costear [koste'ar] *vt* to pay for

costero, a [kos'tero, a] *adj* (*pueblecito, camino*) coastal

costilla [kos'tiʎa] *nf* rib; (CULIN) cutlet

costo ['kosto] *nm* cost, price; **~ de la vida** cost of living; **~so, a** *adj* costly, expensive

costra ['kostra] *nf* (*corteza*) crust; (MED) scab

costumbre [kos'tumbre] *nf* custom, habit

costura [kos'tura] *nf* sewing, needlework; (*zurcido*) seam

costurera [kostu'rera] *nf* dressmaker

costurero [kostu'rero] *nm* sewing box *o* case

cotejar [kote'xar] *vt* to compare

cotidiano, a [koti'ðjano, a] *adj* daily, day to day

cotilla [ko'tiʎa] *nm/f* (*fam*) gossip; **cotillear** *vi* to gossip; **cotilleo** *nm* gossip(ing)

cotización [kotiθa'θjon] *nf* (COM) quotation, price; (*de club*) dues *pl*

cotizar [koti'θar] *vt* (COM) to quote, price; **~se** *vr*: **~se a** to sell at, fetch; (BOLSA) to stand at, be quoted at

coto ['koto] *nm* (*terreno cercado*) enclosure; (*de caza*) reserve

cotorra [ko'torra] *nf* parrot

COU [kou] (ESP) *nm abr* (= Curso de Orientación Universitaria) 1 year course leading to final school-leaving certificate and university entrance examinations

coyote [ko'jote] *nm* coyote, prairie wolf

coyuntura [kojun'tura] *nf* juncture, occasion

coz [koθ] *nf* kick

crack *nm* (*droga*) crack

cráneo ['kraneo] *nm* skull, cranium

cráter ['krater] *nm* crater

creación [krea'θjon] *nf* creation

creador, a [krea'ðor, a] *adj* creative ♦ *nm/f* creator

crear [kre'ar] *vt* to create, make

crecer [kre'θer] *vi* to grow; (*precio*) to rise

creces ['kreθes]: **con ~** *adv* amply, fully

crecido, a [kre'θiðo, a] *adj* (*persona, planta*) full-grown; (*cantidad*) large

creciente [kre'θjente] *adj* growing; (*cantidad*) increasing; (*luna*) crescent ♦ *nm* crescent

crecimiento [kreθi'mjento] *nm* growth;

(*aumento*) increase

credenciales [kreðen'θjales] *nfpl* credentials

crédito ['kreðito] *nm* credit

credo ['kreðo] *nm* creed

crédulo, a ['kreðulo, a] *adj* credulous

creencia [kre'enθja] *nf* belief

creer [kre'er] *vt, vi* to think, believe; **~se** *vr* to believe o.s. (to be); **~ en** to believe in; **¡ya lo creo!** I should think so!

creíble [kre'iβle] *adj* credible, believable

creído, a [kre'iðo, a] *adj* (*engreído*) conceited

crema ['krema] *nf* cream; **~ pastelera** (confectioner's) custard

cremallera [krema'ʎera] *nf* zip (fastener)

crematorio [krema'torjo] *nm* (tb: *horno* ~) crematorium

crepitar [krepi'tar] *vi* to crackle

crepúsculo [kre'puskulo] *nm* twilight, dusk

cresta ['kresta] *nf* (GEO, ZOOL) crest

creyendo *vb ver* **creer**

creyente [kre'jente] *nm/f* believer

creyó *etc vb ver* **creer**

crezco *etc vb ver* **crecer**

cría *etc* ['kria] *vb ver* **criar** ♦ *nf* (*de animales*) rearing, breeding; (*animal*) young; *ver tb* **crio**

criadero [kria'ðero] *nm* (ZOOL) breeding place

criado, a [kri'aðo, a] *nm* servant ♦ *nf* servant, maid

criador [kria'ðor] *nm* breeder

crianza [kri'anθa] *nf* rearing, breeding; (*fig*) breeding

criar [kri'ar] *vt* (*educar*) to bring up; (*producir*) to grow, produce; (*animales*) to breed

criatura [kria'tura] *nf* creature; (*niño*) baby, (small) child

criba ['kriβa] *nf* sieve; **cribar** *vt* to sieve

crimen ['krimen] *nm* crime

criminal [krimi'nal] *adj, nm/f* criminal

crin [krin] *nf* (tb: **~es** *nfpl*) mane

crío, a ['krio, a] (*fam*) *nm/f* (*niño*) kid

crisis ['krisis] *nf inv* crisis; **~ nerviosa** nervous breakdown

crispar [kris'par] *vt* (*nervios*) to set on edge

cristal [kris'tal] *nm* crystal; (*de ventana*) glass, pane; (*lente*) lens; **~ino, a** *adj* crystalline; (*fig*) clear ♦ *nm* lens (of the eye); **~izar** *vt, vi* to crystallize

cristiandad [kristjan'daθ] *nf* Christendom

cristianismo [kristja'nismo] *nm* Christianity

cristiano, a [kris'tjano, a] *adj, nm/f* Christian

Cristo ['kristo] *nm* Christ; (*crucifijo*) crucifix

criterio [kri'terjo] *nm* criterion; (*juicio*) judgement

crítica ['kritika] *nf* criticism; *ver tb* **crítico**

criticar [kriti'kar] *vt* to criticize

crítico, a ['kritiko, a] *adj* critical ♦ *nm/f* critic

Croacia *nf* Croatia

croar [kro'ar] *vi* to croak

cromo ['kromo] nm chrome

crónica ['kronika] nf chronicle, account

crónico, a ['kroniko, a] adj chronic

cronómetro [kro'nometro] nm stopwatch

croqueta [kro'keta] nf croquette

cruce etc ['kruθe] vb ver **cruzar** ♦ nm crossing; (de carreteras) crossroads

crucificar [kruθifi'kar] vt to crucify

crucifijo [kruθi'fixo] nm crucifix

crucigrama [kruθi'vrama] nm crossword (puzzle)

crudo, a ['kruðo, a] adj raw; (no maduro) unripe; (petróleo) crude; (rudo, cruel) cruel ♦ nm crude (oil)

cruel [krwel] adj cruel; **~dad** nf cruelty

crujido [kru'xiðo] nm (de madera etc) creak

crujiente [kru'xjente] adj (galleta etc) crunchy

crujir [kru'xir] vi (madera etc) to creak; (dedos) to crack; (dientes) to grind; (nieve, arena) to crunch

cruz [kruθ] nf cross; (de moneda) tails sg; **~ gamada** swastika

cruzada [kru'θaða] nf crusade

cruzado, a [kru'θaðo, a] adj crossed ♦ nm crusader

cruzar [kru'θar] vt to cross; **~se** vr (líneas etc) to cross; (personas) to pass each other

Cruz Roja nf Red Cross

cuaderno [kwa'ðerno] nm notebook; (de escuela) exercise book; (NAUT) logbook

cuadra ['kwaðra] nf (caballeriza) stable; (AM) block

cuadrado, a [kwa'ðraðo, a] adj square ♦ nm (MAT) square

cuadrar [kwa'ðrar] vt to square ♦ vi: **~ con** to square with, tally with; **~se** vr (soldado) to stand to attention

cuadrilátero [kwaðri'latero] nm (DEPORTE) boxing ring; (GEOM) quadrilateral

cuadrilla [kwa'ðriʎa] nf party, group

cuadro ['kwaðro] nm square; (ARTE) painting; (TEATRO) scene; (diagrama) chart; (DEPORTE, MED) team; **de ~s** checked (BRIT) o chequered (US) material

cuádruple ['kwaðruple] adj quadruple

cuajar [kwa'xar] vt (leche) to curdle; (sangre) to congeal; (CULIN) to set; **~se** vr to curdle; to congeal; to set; (llenarse) to fill up

cuajo ['kwaxo] nm: **de ~** (arrancar) by the roots; (cortar) completely

cual [kwal] adv like, as ♦ pron: **el ~** etc which; (persona: sujeto) who; (: objeto) whom ♦ adj such as; **cada ~** each one; **déjalo tal ~** leave it just as it is

cuál [kwal] pron interr which (one)

cualesquier(a) [kwales'kjer(a)] pl de **cualquier(a)**

cualidad [kwali'ðað] nf quality

cualquier [kwal'kjer] adj ver **cualquiera**

cualquiera [kwal'kjera] (pl **cualesquiera**) adj (delante de nm y f: **cualquier**) any ♦ pron anybody; **un coche ~ servirá** any car will do; **no es un hombre ~** he isn't just anybody; **cualquier día/libro** any day/book; **eso ~ lo sabe hacer** anybody can do that; **es un ~** he's a nobody

cuando ['kwando] adv when; (aún si) if, even if ♦ conj (puesto que) since ♦ prep: **yo, ~ niño ...** when I was a child ...; **~ no sea así** even if it is not so; **~ más** at (the) most; **~ menos** at least; **~ no** if not, otherwise; **de ~ en ~** from time to time

cuándo ['kwando] adv when; **¿desde ~?, ¿de ~ acá?** since when?

cuantía [kwan'tia] nf (importe: de pérdidas, deuda, daños) extent

cuantioso, a [kwan'tjoso, a] adj substantial

PALABRA CLAVE

cuanto, a ['kwanto, a] adj **1** (todo): **tiene todo ~ desea** he's got everything he wants; **le daremos ~s ejemplares necesite** we'll give him as many copies as o all the copies he needs; **~s hombres la ven** all the men who see her

2: **unos ~s**: **había unos ~s periodistas** there were a few journalists

3 (+ más): **~ más vino bebes peor te sentirás** the more wine you drink the worse you'll feel ♦ pron: **tiene ~ desea** he has everything he wants; **tome ~/~s quiera** take as much/many as you want

♦ adv: **en ~**: **en ~ profesor** as a teacher; **en ~ a mí** as for me; ver tb **antes**

♦ conj **1**: **~ más gana menos gasta** the more he earns the less he spends; **~ más joven más confiado** the younger you are the more trusting you are

2: **en ~**: **en ~ llegue/llegué** as soon as I arrive/arrived

---

cuánto, a ['kwanto, a] adj (exclamación) what a lot of; (interr: sg) how much?; (: pl) how many? ♦ pron, adv how; (interr: sg) how much?; (: pl) how many?; **¡cuánta gente!** what a lot of people!; **¿~ cuesta?** how much does it cost?; **¿a ~s estamos?** what's the date?; **Señor no sé ~** Mr. So-and-So

cuarenta [kwa'renta] num forty

cuarentena [kwaren'tena] nf quarantine

cuaresma [kwa'resma] nf Lent

cuarta ['kwarta] nf (MAT) quarter, fourth; (palmo) span

cuartel [kwar'tel] nm (MIL) barracks pl; **~ general** headquarters pl

cuarteto [kwar'teto] nm quartet

cuarto, a ['kwarto, a] adj fourth ♦ nm (MAT) quarter, fourth; (habitación) room; **~ de baño**

bathroom; **~ de estar** living room; **~ de hora** quarter (of an) hour; **~ de kilo** quarter kilo

cuatro ['kwatro] *num* four

Cuba ['kuβa] *nf* Cuba; **cubano, a** *adj, nm/f* Cuban

cuba ['kuβa] *nf* cask, barrel

cubata [ku'βata] *nm* (*fam*) large drink (*of rum and coke etc*)

cúbico, a ['kuβiko, a] *adj* cubic

cubierta [ku'βjerta] *nf* cover, covering; (*neumático*) tyre; (*NAUT*) deck

cubierto, a [ku'βjerto, a] *pp de* **cubrir** ♦ *adj* covered ♦ *nm* cover; (*lugar en la mesa*) place; **~s** *nmpl* cutlery *sg*; **a ~** under cover

cubil [ku'βil] *nm* den; **~ete** *nm* (*en juegos*) cup

cubito [ku'βito] *nm*: **~ de hielo** ice-cube

cubo ['kuβo] *nm* (*MATH*) cube; (*balde*) bucket, tub; (*TEC*) drum

cubrecama [kuβre'kama] *nm* bedspread

cubrir [ku'βrir] *vt* to cover; **~se** *vr* (*cielo*) to become overcast

cucaracha [kuka'ratʃa] *nf* cockroach

cuchara [ku'tʃara] *nf* spoon; (*TEC*) scoop; **~da** *nf* spoonful; **~dita** *nf* teaspoonful

cucharilla [kutʃa'riʎa] *nf* teaspoon

cucharón [kutʃa'ron] *nm* ladle

cuchichear [kutʃitʃe'ar] *vi* to whisper

cuchilla [ku'tʃiʎa] *nf* (large) knife; (*de arma blanca*) blade; **~ de afeitar** razor blade

cuchillo [ku'tʃiʎo] *nm* knife

cuchitril [kutʃi'tril] *nm* hovel

cuclillas [ku'kliʎas] *nfpl*: **en ~** squatting

cuco, a ['kuko, a] *adj* pretty; (*astuto*) sharp ♦ *nm* cuckoo

cucurucho [kuku'rutʃo] *nm* cornet

cuello ['kweʎo] *nm* (*ANAT*) neck; (*de vestido, camisa*) collar

cuenca ['kwenka] *nf* (*ANAT*) eye socket; (*GEO*) bowl, deep valley

cuenco ['kwenko] *nm* bowl

cuenta *etc* ['kwenta] *vb ver* **contar** ♦ *nf* (*cálculo*) count, counting; (*en café, restaurante*) bill (*BRIT*), check (*US*); (*COM*) account; (*de collar*) bead; **a fin de ~s** in the end; **caer en la ~** to catch on; **darse ~ de** to realize; **tener en ~** to bear in mind; **echar ~s** to take stock; **~ corriente/de ahorros** current/ savings account; **~ atrás** countdown; **~kilómetros** *nm inv* ≈ milometer; (*de velocidad*) speedometer

cuento *etc* ['kwento] *vb ver* **contar** ♦ *nm* story

cuerda ['kwerða] *nf* rope; (*fina*) string; (*de reloj*) spring; **dar ~ a un reloj** to wind up a clock; **~ floja** tightrope

cuerdo, a ['kwerðo, a] *adj* sane; (*prudente*) wise, sensible

cuerno ['kwerno] *nm* horn

cuero ['kwero] *nm* leather; **en ~s** stark naked;

~ cabelludo scalp

cuerpo ['kwerpo] *nm* body

cuervo ['kwerβo] *nm* crow

cuesta *etc* ['kwesta] *vb ver* **costar** ♦ *nf* slope; (*en camino etc*) hill; **~ arriba/abajo** uphill/ downhill; **a ~s** on one's back

cueste *etc vb ver* **costar**

cuestión [kwes'tjon] *nf* matter, question, issue

cueva ['kweβa] *nf* cave

cuidado [kwi'ðaðo] *nm* care, carefulness; (*preocupación*) care, worry ♦ *excl* careful!, look out!

cuidadoso, a [kwiða'ðoso, a] *adj* careful; (*preocupado*) anxious

cuidar [kwi'ðar] *vt* (*MED*) to care for; (*ocuparse de*) to take care of, look after ♦ *vi*: **~ de** to take care of, look after; **~se** *vr* to look after o.s.; **~se de hacer algo** to take care to do sth

culata [ku'lata] *nf* (*de fusil*) butt

culebra [ku'leβra] *nf* snake

culebrón [kule'βron] (*fam*) *nm* (*TV*) soap(-opera)

culinario, a [kuli'narjo, a] *adj* culinary, cooking *cpd*

culminación [kulmina'θjon] *nf* culmination

culo ['kulo] *nm* bottom, backside; (*de vaso, botella*) bottom

culpa ['kulpa] *nf* fault; (*JUR*) guilt; **por ~ de** because of; **tener la ~ (de)** to be to blame (for); **~bilidad** *nf* guilt; **~ble** *adj* guilty ♦ *nm/f* culprit

culpar [kul'par] *vt* to blame; (*acusar*) to accuse

cultivar [kulti'βar] *vt* to cultivate

cultivo [kul'tiβo] *nm* (*acto*) cultivation; (*plantas*) crop

culto, a ['kulto, a] *adj* (*que tiene cultura*) cultured, educated ♦ *nm* (*homenaje*) worship; (*religión*) cult

cultura [kul'tura] *nf* culture

culturismo [kultu'rismo] *nm* body-building

cumbre ['kumbre] *nf* summit, top

cumpleaños [kumple'aɲos] *nm inv* birthday

cumplido, a [kum'pliðo, a] *adj* (*abundante*) plentiful; (*cortés*) courteous ♦ *nm* compliment; **visita de ~** courtesy call

cumplidor, a [kumpli'ðor, a] *adj* reliable

cumplimentar [kumplimen'tar] *vt* to congratulate

cumplimiento [kumpli'mjento] *nm* (*de un deber*) fulfilment; (*acabamiento*) completion

cumplir [kum'plir] *vt* (*orden*) to carry out, obey; (*promesa*) to carry out, fulfil; (*condena*) to serve ♦ *vi*: **~ con** (*deberes*) to carry out, fulfil; **~se** *vr* (*plazo*) to expire; **hoy cumple dieciocho años** he is eighteen today

cúmulo ['kumulo] *nm* heap

cuna ['kuna] nf cradle, cot

cundir [kun'dir] vi (noticia, rumor, pánico) to spread; (rendir) to go a long way

cuneta [ku'neta] nf ditch

cuña ['kuɲa] nf wedge

cuñado, a [ku'naðo, a] nm/f brother-/sister-in-law

cuota ['kwota] nf (parte proporcional) share; (cotización) fee, dues pl

cupe etc vb ver **caber**

cupiera etc vb ver **caber**

cupo ['kupo] vb ver **caber** ♦ nm quota

cupón [ku'pon] nm coupon

cúpula ['kupula] nf dome

cura ['kura] nf (curación) cure; (método curativo) treatment ♦ nm priest

curación [kura'θjon] nf cure; (acción) curing

curandero, a [kuran'dero, a] nm/f quack

curar [ku'rar] vt (MED: herida) to treat, dress; (: enfermo) to cure; (CULIN) to cure, salt; (cuero) to tan; **~se** vr to get well, recover

curiosear [kurjose'ar] vt to glance at, look over ♦ vi to look round, wander round; (explorar) to poke about

curiosidad [kurjosi'ðað] nf curiosity

curioso, a [ku'rjoso, a] adj curious ♦ nm/f bystander, onlooker

currante [ku'rrante] (fam) nm/f worker

currar [ku'rrar] (fam) vi to work

currículo [ku'rrikulo] = **curriculum**

curriculum [ku'rrikulum] nm curriculum vitae

cursi ['kursi] (fam) adj affected

cursillo [kur'siʎo] nm short course

cursiva [kur'siβa] nf italics pl

curso ['kurso] nm course; **en ~** (año) current; (proceso) going on, under way

cursor [kur'sor] nm (INFORM) cursor

curtido, a [kur'tiðo, a] adj (cara etc) weather-beaten; (fig: persona) experienced

curtir [kur'tir] vt (cuero etc) to tan

curva ['kurβa] nf curve, bend

cúspide ['kuspiðe] nf (GEO) peak; (fig) top

custodia [kus'toðja] nf safekeeping; custody; **custodiar** vt (conservar) to take care of; (vigilar) to guard

cutis ['kutis] nm inv skin, complexion

cutre ['kutre] (fam) adj (lugar) grotty

cuyo, a ['kujo, a] pron (de quien) whose; (de que) whose, of which; **en ~ caso** in which case

C.V. abr (= caballos de vapor) H.P.

D, d

D. abr (= Don) Esq.

Da. abr = **Doña**

dádiva ['daðiβa] nf (donación) donation;

(regalo) gift; **dadivoso, a** adj generous

dado, a ['daðo, a] pp de **dar** ♦ nm die; **~s** nmpl dice; **~ que** given that

daltónico, a [dal'toniko, a] adj colour-blind

dama ['dama] nf (gen) lady; (AJEDREZ) queen; **~s** nfpl (juego) draughts sg

damnificar [damnifi'kar] vt to harm; (persona) to injure

danés, esa [da'nes, esa] adj Danish ♦ nm/f Dane

danzar [dan'θar] vt, vi to dance

dañar [da'ɲar] vt (objeto) to damage; (persona) to hurt; **~se** vr (objeto) to get damaged

dañino, a [da'ɲino, a] adj harmful

daño ['daɲo] nm (a un objeto) damage; (a una persona) harm, injury; **~s y perjuicios** (JUR) damages; **hacer ~ a** to damage; (persona) to hurt, injure; **hacerse ~** to hurt o.s.

PALABRA CLAVE

---

dar [dar] vt **1** (gen) to give; (obra de teatro) to put on; (film) to show; (fiesta) to hold; **~ algo a uno** to give sb sth o sth to sb; **~ de beber a uno** to give sb a drink

2 (producir: intereses) to yield; (fruta) to produce

3 (locuciones + n): **da gusto escucharle** it's a pleasure to listen to him; ver tb **paseo** y otros sustantivos

4 (+ n: = perífrasis de verbo): **me da asco** it sickens me

5 (considerar): **~ algo por descontado/ entendido** to take sth for granted/as read; **~ algo por concluido** to consider sth finished

6 (hora): **el reloj dio las 6** the clock struck 6 (o'clock)

7: **me da lo mismo** it's all the same to me; ver tb **igual, más**

♦ vi **1**: **~ con**: **dimos con él dos horas más tarde** we came across him two hours later; **al final di con la solución** I eventually came up with the answer

2: **~ en** (blanco, suelo) to hit; **el sol me da en la cara** the sun is shining (right) on my face

3: **~ de sí** (zapatos etc) to stretch, give

♦ **~se** vr **1**: **~se por vencido** to give up

2 (ocurrir): **se han dado muchos casos** there have been a lot of cases

3: **~se a**: **se ha dado a la bebida** he's taken to drinking

4: **se me dan bien/mal las ciencias** I'm good/ bad at science

5: **dárselas de**: **se las da de experto** he fancies himself o poses as an expert

---

dardo ['darðo] nm dart

datar [da'tar] vi: **~ de** to date from

dátil ['datil] nm date

dato ['dato] nm fact, piece of information; **~s personales** personal details

DC abbr m (= disco compacto) CD

dcha. abbr (= derecha) r.h.

d. de J.C. abr (= después de Jesucristo) A.D.

PALABRA CLAVE

de [de] prep (de + el = del) **1** (posesión) of; **la casa ~ Isabel/mis padres** Isabel's/my parents' house; **es ~ ellos** it's theirs

2 (origen, distancia, con números) from; **soy ~ Gijón** I'm from Gijón; **~ 8 a 20** from 8 to 20; **salir del cine** to go out o leave the cinema; **~ 2 en 2** 2 by 2, 2 at a time

3 (valor descriptivo): **una copa ~ vino** a glass of wine; **la mesa ~ la cocina** the kitchen table; **un billete ~ 1000 pesetas** a 1000 peseta note; **un niño ~ tres años** a three-year-old (child); **una máquina ~ coser** a sewing machine; **ir vestido ~ gris** to be dressed in grey; **la niña del vestido azul** the girl in the blue dress; **trabaja ~ profesora** she works as a teacher; **~ lado** sideways; **~ atrás/delante** rear/front

4 (hora, tiempo): **a las 8 ~ la mañana** at 8 o'clock in the morning; **~ día/noche** by day/night; **~ hoy en ocho días** a week from now; **~ niño era gordo** as a child he was fat

5 (comparaciones): **más/menos ~ cien personas** more/less than a hundred people; **el más caro ~ la tienda** the most expensive in the shop; **menos/más ~ lo pensado** less/more than expected

6 (causa): **del calor** from the heat; **~ puro tonto** out of sheer stupidity

7 (tema) about; **clases ~ inglés** English classes; **¿sabes algo ~ él?** do you know anything about him?; **un libro ~ física** a physics book

8 (adj + de + infin): **fácil ~ entender** easy to understand

9 (oraciones pasivas): **fue respetado ~ todos** he was loved by all

10 (condicional + infin) if; **~ ser posible** if possible; **~ no terminarlo hoy** if I etc don't finish it today

dé vb ver dar

deambular [deambu'lar] vi to wander

debajo [de'ßaxo] adv underneath; **~ de** below, under; **por ~ de** beneath

debate [de'ßate] nm debate; **debatir** vt to debate

deber [de'ßer] nm duty ♦ vt to owe ♦ vi: **debe (de)** it must, it should; **~es** nmpl (ESCOL) homework; **debo hacerlo** I must do it; **debe de ir** he should go; **~se** vr: **~se a** to be owing o due to

debido, a [de'ßiðo, a] adj proper, just; **~ a** due to, because of

débil ['deßil] adj (persona, carácter) weak; (luz) dim; **debilidad** nf weakness; dimness

debilitar [deßili'tar] vt to weaken; **~se** vr to grow weak

debutar [deßu'tar] vi to make one's debut

década ['dekaða] nf decade

decadencia [deka'ðenθja] nf (estado) decadence; (proceso) decline, decay

decaer [deka'er] vi (declinar) to decline; (debilitarse) to weaken

decaído, a [deka'iðo, a] adj: **estar ~** (abatido) to be down

decaimiento [dekai'mjento] nm (declinación) decline; (desaliento) discouragement; (MED: estado débil) weakness

decano, a [de'kano, a] nm/f (de universidad etc) dean

decapitar [dekapi'tar] vt to behead

decena [de'θena] nf: **una ~** ten (or so)

decencia [de'θenθja] nf decency

decente [de'θente] adj decent

decepción [deθep'θjon] nf disappointment

decepcionar [deθepθjo'nar] vt to disappoint

decidir [deθi'ðir] vt, vi to decide; **~se** vr: **~se a** to make up one's mind to

décimo, a [de'θimo, a] adj tenth ♦ nm tenth

decir [de'θir] vt to say; (contar) to tell; (hablar) to speak ♦ nm saying; **~se** vr: **se dice que** it is said that; **~ para o entre sí** to say to o.s.; **querer ~** to mean; **¡dígame!** (TEL) hello!; (en tienda) can I help you?

decisión [deθi'sjon] nf (resolución) decision; (firmeza) decisiveness

decisivo, a [deθi'siβo, a] adj decisive

declaración [deklara'θjon] nf (manifestación) statement; (de amor) declaration; **~ de ingresos** o **de la renta** o fiscal income-tax return

declarar [dekla'rar] vt to declare ♦ vi to declare; (JUR) to testify; **~se** vr to propose

declinar [dekli'nar] vt (gen) to decline; (JUR) to reject ♦ vi (el día) to draw to a close

declive [de'kliße] nm (cuesta) slope; (fig) decline

decodificador [dekoðifika'ðor] nm decoder

decolorarse [dekolo'rarse] vr to become discoloured

decoración [dekora'θjon] nf decoration

decorado [deko'raðo] nm (CINE, TEATRO) scenery, set

decorar [deko'rar] vt to decorate; **decorativo, a** adj ornamental, decorative

decoro [de'koro] nm (respeto) respect; (dignidad) decency; (recato) propriety; **~so, a** adj (decente) decent; (modesto) modest; (digno) proper

decrecer [dekre'θer] vi to decrease, diminish

decrépito, a [de'krepito, a] adj decrepit

decretar [dekre'tar] vt to decree; **decreto** nm decree

dedal [de'ðal] nm thimble

dedicación [deðika'θjon] nf dedication

dedicar [deði'kar] vt (libro) to dedicate; (tiempo, dinero) to devote; (palabras: decir, consagrar) to dedicate, devote; **dedicatoria** nf (de libro) dedication

dedo ['deðo] nm finger; ~ **(del pie)** toe; ~ **pulgar** thumb; ~ **índice** index finger; ~ **corazón** middle finger; ~ **anular** ring finger; ~ **meñique** little finger; **hacer** ~ (fam) to hitch (a lift)

deducción [deðuk'θjon] nf deduction

deducir [deðu'θir] vt (concluir) to deduce, infer; (COM) to deduct

defecto [de'fekto] nm defect, flaw; **defectuoso, a** adj defective, faulty

defender [defen'der] vt to defend

defensa [de'fensa] nf defence ♦ nm (DEPORTE) defender, back; **defensivo, a** adj defensive; **a la defensiva** on the defensive

defensor, a [defen'sor, a] adj defending ♦ nm/f (abogado ~) defending counsel; (protector) protector

deficiencia [defi'θjenθja] nf deficiency

deficiente [defi'θjente] adj (defectuoso) defective; ~ **en** lacking o deficient in; **ser un ~ mental** to be mentally handicapped

déficit ['defiθit] (pl ~s) nm deficit

definición [defini'θjon] nf definition

definir [defi'nir] vt (determinar) to determine, establish; (decidir) to define; (aclarar) to clarify; **definitivo, a** adj definitive; **en definitiva** definitively; (en resumen) in short

deformación [deforma'θjon] nf (alteración) deformation; (RADIO etc) distortion

deformar [defor'mar] vt (gen) to deform; ~**se** vr to become deformed; **deforme** adj (informe) deformed; (feo) ugly; (malhecho) misshapen

defraudar [defrau'ðar] vt (decepcionar) to disappoint; (estafar) to defraud

defunción [defun'θjon] nf death, demise

degeneración [dexenera'θjon] nf (de las células) degeneration; (moral) degeneracy

degenerar [dexene'rar] vi to degenerate

degollar [deyo'ʎar] vt to behead; (fig) to slaughter

degradar [deyra'ðar] vt to debase, degrade; ~**se** vr to demean o.s.

degustación [deyusta'θjon] nf sampling, tasting

deificar [deifi'kar] vt to deify

dejadez [dexa'ðeθ] nf (negligencia) neglect; (descuido) untidiness, carelessness

dejar [de'xar] vt to leave; (permitir) to allow, let; (abandonar) to abandon, forsake; (beneficios) to produce, yield ♦ vi: ~ **de** (parar) to stop; (no hacer) to fail to; **no dejes de comprar un billete** make sure you buy a ticket; ~ **a un lado** to leave o set aside

dejo ['dexo] nm (LING) accent

del [del] (= de + el) ver **de**

delantal [delan'tal] nm apron

delante [de'lante] adv in front, (enfrente) opposite; (adelante) ahead; ~ **de** in front of, before

delantera [delan'tera] nf (de vestido, casa etc) front part; (DEPORTE) forward line; **llevar la ~ (a uno)** to be ahead (of sb)

delantero, a [delan'tero, a] adj front ♦ nm (DEPORTE) forward, striker

delatar [dela'tar] vt to inform on o against, betray; **delator, a** nm/f informer

delegación [deleɣa'θjon] nf (acción, delegados) delegation; (COM: oficina) office, branch; ~ **de policía** police station

delegado, a [dele'ɣaðo, a] nm/f delegate; (COM) agent

delegar [dele'ɣar] vt to delegate

deletrear [deletre'ar] vt to spell (out)

deleznable [deleθ'naβle] adj brittle; (excusa, idea) feeble

delfín [del'fin] nm dolphin

delgadez [delɣa'ðeθ] nf thinness, slimness

delgado, a [del'ɣaðo, a] adj thin; (persona) slim, thin; (tela etc) light, delicate

deliberación [deliβera'θjon] nf deliberation

deliberar [deliβe'rar] vt to debate, discuss

delicadeza [delika'ðeθa] nf (gen) delicacy; (refinamiento, sutileza) refinement

delicado, a [deli'kaðo, a] adj (gen) delicate; (sensible) sensitive; (quisquilloso) touchy

delicia [de'liθja] nf delight

delicioso, a [deli'θjoso, a] adj (gracioso) delightful; (exquisito) delicious

delimitar [delimi'tar] vt (funciones, responsabilidades) to define

delincuencia [delin'kwenθja] nf delinquency; **delincuente** nm/f delinquent; (criminal) criminal

delineante [deline'ante] nm/f draughtsman/woman

delinear [deline'ar] vt (dibujo) to draw; (fig, contornos) to outline

delinquir [delin'kir] vi to commit an offence

delirante [deli'rante] adj delirious

delirar [deli'rar] vi to be delirious, rave

delirio [de'lirjo] nm (MED) delirium; (palabras insensatas) ravings pl

delito [de'lito] nm (gen) crime; (infracción) offence

delta ['delta] nm delta

demacrado, a [dema'kraðo, a] adj: **estar ~** to look pale and drawn, be wasted away

demagogo, a [dema'ɣoɣo, a] nm/f

demagogue

demanda [de'manda] nf (pedido, COM) demand; (petición) request; (JUR) action, lawsuit

demandante [deman'dante] nm/f claimant

demandar [deman'dar] vt (gen) to demand; (JUR) to sue, file a lawsuit against

demarcación [demarka'θjon] nf (de terreno) demarcation

demás [de'mas] adj: los ~ niños the other children, the remaining children ♦ pron: los/las ~ the others, the rest (of them); lo ~ the rest (of it)

demasía [dema'sia] nf (exceso) excess, surplus; comer en ~ to eat to excess

demasiado, a [dema'sjaðo, a] adj: ~ vino too much wine ♦ adv (antes de adj, adv) too; ~s libros too many books; ¡esto es ~! that's the limit!; hace ~ calor it's too hot; ~ despacio too slowly; ~s too many

demencia [de'menθja] nf (locura) madness; **demente** nm/f lunatic ♦ adj mad, insane

democracia [demo'kraθja] nf democracy

demócrata [de'mokrata] nm/f democrat; **democrático, a** adj democratic

demoler [demo'ler] vt to demolish; **demolición** nf demolition

demonio [de'monjo] nm devil, demon; ¡~s! hell!, damn!; ¿cómo ~s? how the hell?

demora [de'mora] nf delay; **demorar** vt (retardar) to delay, hold back; (detener) to hold up ♦ vi to linger, stay on; ~se vr to be delayed

demos vb ver **dar**

demostración [demostra'θjon] nf (MAT) proof; (de afecto) show, display

demostrar [demos'trar] vt (probar) to prove; (mostrar) to show; (manifestar) to demonstrate

demudado, a [demu'ðaðo, a] adj (rostro) pale

den vb ver **dar**

denegar [dene'ɣar] vt (rechazar) to refuse; (JUR) to reject

denigrar [deni'ɣrar] vt (desacreditar, infamar) to denigrate; (injuriar) to insult

denotar [deno'tar] vt to denote

densidad [densi'ðað] nf density; (fig) thickness

denso, a ['denso, a] adj dense; (espeso, pastoso) thick; (fig) heavy

dentadura [denta'ðura] nf (set of) teeth pl; ~ postiza false teeth pl

dentera [den'tera] nf (sensación desagradable) the shivers pl

dentífrico, a [den'tifriko, a] adj dental ♦ nm toothpaste

dentista [den'tista] nm/f dentist

dentro ['dentro] adv inside ♦ prep: ~ de in,

inside, within; por ~ (on the) inside; mirar por ~ to look inside; ~ de tres meses within three months

denuncia [de'nunθja] nf (delación) denunciation; (acusación) accusation; (de accidente) report; **denunciar** vt to report; (delatar) to inform on o against

departamento [departa'mento] nm (sección administrativa) department, section; (AM: apartamento) flat (BRIT), apartment

dependencia [depen'denθja] nf dependence; (POL) dependency; (COM) office, section

depender [depen'der] vi: ~ de to depend on

dependienta [depen'djenta] nf saleswoman, shop assistant

dependiente [depen'djente] adj dependent ♦ nm salesman, shop assistant

depilar [depi'lar] vt (con cera) to wax; (cejas) to pluck; **depilatorio** nm hair remover

deplorable [deplo'raßle] adj deplorable

deplorar [deplo'rar] vt to deplore

deponer [depo'ner] vt to lay down ♦ vi (JUR) to give evidence; (declarar) to make a statement

deportar [depor'tar] vt to deport

deporte [de'porte] nm sport; hacer ~ to play sports; **deportista** adj sports cpd ♦ nm/f sportsman/woman; **deportivo, a** adj (club, periódico) sports cpd ♦ nm sports car

depositar [deposi'tar] vt (dinero) to deposit; (mercancías) to put away, store; ~se vr to settle; ~io, a nm/f trustee

depósito [de'posito] nm (gen) deposit; (almacén) warehouse, store; (de agua, gasolina etc) tank; ~ de cadáveres mortuary

depreciar [depre'θjar] vt to depreciate, reduce the value of; ~se vr to depreciate, lose value

depredador, a [depreða'ðor, a] adj predatory ♦ nm predator

depresión [depre'sjon] nf depression

deprimido, a [depri'miðo, a] adj depressed

deprimir [depri'mir] vt to depress; ~se vr (persona) to become depressed

deprisa [de'prisa] adv quickly, hurriedly

depuración [depura'θjon] nf purification; (POL) purge

depurar [depu'rar] vt to purify; (purgar) to purge

derecha [de'retʃa] nf right(-hand) side; (POL) right; a la ~ (estar) on the right; (torcer etc) (to the) right

derecho, a [de'retʃo, a] adj right, right-hand ♦ nm (privilegio) right; (lado) right(-hand) side; (leyes) law ♦ adv straight, directly; ~s nmpl (de aduana) duty sg; (de autor) royalties; tener ~ a to have a right to

deriva [de'rißa] nf: ir o estar a la ~ to drift, be

adrift

derivado [deri'ßaðo] nm (COM) by-product

derivar [deri'ßar] vt to derive; (desviar) to direct ♦ vi to derive, be derived; (NAUT) to drift; ~se vr to derive, be derived; to drift

derramamiento [derrama'mjento] nm (dispersión) spilling; ~ **de sangre** bloodshed

derramar [derra'mar] vt to spill; (verter) to pour out; (esparcir) to scatter; ~se vr to pour out; ~ **lágrimas** to weep

derrame [de'rrame] nm (de líquido) spilling; (de sangre) shedding; (de tubo etc) overflow; (pérdida) leakage; (MED) discharge

derredor [derre'ðor] adv: **al** o **en ~ de** around, about

derretido, a [derre'tiðo, a] adj melted; (metal) molten

derretir [derre'tir] vt (gen) to melt; (nieve) to thaw; ~se vr to melt

derribar [derri'ßar] vt to knock down; (construcción) to demolish; (persona, gobierno, político) to bring down

derrocar [derro'kar] vt (gobierno) to bring down, overthrow

derrochar [derro'tʃar] vt to squander; **derroche** nm (despilfarro) waste, squandering

derrota [de'rrota] nf (NAUT) course; (MIL, DEPORTE etc) defeat, rout; **derrotar** vt (gen) to defeat; **derrotero** nm (rumbo) course

derruir [derru'ir] vt (edificio) to demolish

derrumbar [derrum'bar] vt (edificio) to knock down; ~se vr to collapse

derruyendo etc vb ver **derruir**

des vb ver **dar**

desabotonar [desaßoto'nar] vt to unbutton, undo; ~se vr to come undone

desabrido, a [desa'ßriðo, a] adj (comida) insipid, tasteless; (persona) rude, surly; (respuesta) sharp; (tiempo) unpleasant

desabrochar [desaßro'tʃar] vt (botones, broches) to undo, unfasten; ~se vr (ropa etc) to come undone

desacato [desa'kato] nm (falta de respeto) disrespect; (JUR) contempt

desacertado, a [desaθer'taðo, a] adj (equivocado) mistaken; (inoportuno) unwise

desacierto [desa'θjerto] nm mistake, error

desaconsejado, a [desakonse'xaðo, a] adj ill-advised

desaconsejar [desakonse'xar] vt to advise against

desacreditar [desakreði'tar] vt (desprestigiar) to discredit, bring into disrepute; (denigrar) to run down

desacuerdo [desa'kwerðo] nm disagreement, discord

desafiar [desa'fjar] vt (retar) to challenge; (enfrentarse a) to defy

desafilado, a [desafi'laðo, a] adj blunt

desafinado, a [desafi'naðo, a] adj: **estar ~** to be out of tune

desafinar [desafi'nar] vi (al cantar) to be o go out of tune

desafío etc [desa'fio] vb ver **desafiar** ♦ nm (reto) challenge; (combate) duel; (resistencia) defiance

desaforado, a [desafo'raðo, a] adj (grito) ear-splitting; (comportamiento) outrageous

desafortunadamente [desafortunaða'mente] adv unfortunately

desafortunado, a [desafortu'naðo, a] adj (desgraciado) unfortunate, unlucky

desagradable [desaɣra'ðaßle] adj (fastidioso, enojoso) unpleasant; (irritante) disagreeable

desagradar [desaɣra'ðar] vi (disgustar) to displease; (molestar) to bother

desagradecido, a [desaɣraðe'θiðo, a] adj ungrateful

desagrado [desa'ɣraðo] nm (disgusto) displeasure; (contrariedad) dissatisfaction

desagraviar [desaɣra'ßjar] vt to make amends fo

desagüe [des'aɣwe] nm (de un líquido) drainage; (cañería) drainpipe; (salida) outlet, drain

desaguisado [desaɣi'saðo] nm outrage

desahogado, a [desao'ɣaðo, a] adj (holgado) comfortable; (espacioso) roomy, large

desahogar [desao'ɣar] vt (aliviar) to ease, relieve; (ira) to vent; ~se vr (relajarse) to relax; (desfogarse) to let off steam

desahogo [desa'oɣo] nm (alivio) relief; (comodidad) comfort, ease

desahuciar [desau'θjar] vt (enfermo) to give up hope for; (inquilino) to evict; **desahucio** nm eviction

desairar [desai'rar] vt (menospreciar) to slight, snub

desaire [des'aire] nm (menosprecio) slight; (falta de garbo) unattractiveness

desajustar [desaxus'tar] vt (desarreglar) to disarrange; (desconcertar) to throw off balance; ~se vr to get out of order; (aflojarse) to loosen

desajuste [desa'xuste] nm (de máquina) disorder; (situación) imbalance

desalentador, a [desalenta'ðor, a] adj discouraging

desalentar [desalen'tar] vt (desanimar) to discourage

desaliento etc [desa'ljento] vb ver **desalentar** ♦ nm discouragement

desaliño [desa'liɲo] nm slovenliness

desalmado, a [desal'maðo, a] adj (cruel) cruel, heartless

desalojar [desalo'xar] vt (*expulsar, echar*) to eject; (*abandonar*) to move out of ♦ vi to move out

desamor [desa'mor] nm (*frialdad*) indifference; (*odio*) dislike

desamparado, a [desampa'raðo, a] adj (*persona*) helpless; (*lugar: expuesto*) exposed; (*desierto*) deserted

desamparar [desampa'rar] vt (*abandonar*) to desert, abandon; (*JUR*) to leave defenceless; (*barco*) to abandon

desandar [desan'dar] vt: ~ **lo andado** o **el camino** to retrace one's steps

desangrar [desan'grar] vt to bleed; (*fig: persona*) to bleed dry; ~**se** vr to lose a lot of blood

desanimado, a [desani'maðo, a] adj (*persona*) downhearted; (*espectáculo, fiesta*) dull

desanimar [desani'mar] vt (*desalentar*) to discourage; (*deprimir*) to depress; ~**se** vr to lose heart

desapacible [desapa'θiβle] adj (*gen*) unpleasant

desaparecer [desapare'θer] vi (*gen*) to disappear; (*el sol, la luz*) to vanish; **desaparecido, a** adj missing; **desaparición** nf disappearance

desapasionado, a [desapasjo'naðo, a] adj dispassionate, impartial

desapego [desa'peɣo] nm (*frialdad*) coolness; (*distancia*) detachment

desapercibido, a [desaperθi'βiðo, a] (*desprevenido*) unprepared; **pasar ~** to go unnoticed

desaprensivo, a [desapren'siβo, a] adj unscrupulous

desaprobar [desapro'βar] vt (*reprobar*) to disapprove of; (*condenar*) to condemn; (*no consentir*) to reject

desaprovechado, a [desaproβe'tʃaðo, a] adj (*oportunidad, tiempo*) wasted; (*estudiante*) slack

desaprovechar [desaproβe'tʃar] vt to waste

desarmar [desar'mar] vt (*MIL, fig*) to disarm; (*TEC*) to take apart, dismantle; **desarme** nm disarmament

desarraigar [desarrai'ɣar] vt to uproot; **desarraigo** nm uprooting

desarreglar [desarre'ɣlar] vt (*desordenar*) to disarrange; (*trastocar*) to upset, disturb

desarreglo [desa'rreɣlo] nm (*de casa, persona*) untidiness; (*desorden*) disorder

desarrollar [desarro'ʎar] vt (*gen*) to develop; ~**se** vr to develop; (*ocurrir*) to take place; (*FOTO*) to develop; **desarrollo** nm development

desarticular [desartiku'lar] vt (*hueso*) to dislocate; (*objeto*) to take apart; (*fig*) to

break up

desasir [desa'sir] vt to loosen

desasosegar [desasose'ɣar] vt (*inquietar*) to disturb, make uneasy; ~**se** vr to become uneasy

desasosiego etc [desaso'sjeɣo] vb ver **desasosegar** ♦ nm (*intranquilidad*) uneasiness, restlessness; (*ansiedad*) anxiety

desastrado, a [desas'traðo, a] adj (*desaliñado*) shabby; (*sucio*) dirty

desastre [de'sastre] nm disaster; **desastroso, a** adj disastrous

desatado, a [desa'taðo, a] adj (*desligado*) untied; (*violento*) violent, wild

desatar [desa'tar] vt (*nudo*) to untie; (*paquete*) to undo; (*separar*) to detach; ~**se** vr (*zapatos*) to come untied; (*tormenta*) to break

desatascar [desatas'kar] vt (*cañería*) to unblock, clear

desatender [desaten'der] vt (*no prestar atención a*) to disregard; (*abandonar*) to neglect

desatento, a [desa'tento, a] adj (*distraído*) inattentive; (*descortés*) discourteous

desatinado, a [desati'naðo, a] adj foolish, silly; **desatino** nm (*idiotez*) foolishness, folly; (*error*) blunder

desatornillar [desatorni'ʎar] vt to unscrew

desatrancar [desatran'kar] vt (*puerta*) to unbolt; (*cañería*) to clear, unblock

desautorizado, a [desautori'θaðo, a] adj unauthorized

desautorizar [desautori'θar] vt (*oficial*) to deprive of authority; (*informe*) to deny

desavenencia [desaβe'nenθja] nf (*desacuerdo*) disagreement; (*discrepancia*) quarrel

desayunar [desaju'nar] vi to have breakfast ♦ vt to have for breakfast; **desayuno** nm breakfast

desazón [desa'θon] nf anxiety

desazonarse [desaθo'narse] vr to worry, be anxious

desbandarse [desβan'darse] vr (*MIL*) to disband; (*fig*) to flee in disorder

desbarajuste [desβara'xuste] nm confusion, disorder

desbaratar [desβara'tar] vt (*deshacer, destruir*) to ruin

desbloquear [desβloke'ar] vt (*negociaciones, tráfico*) to get going again; (*COM: cuenta*) to unfreeze

desbocado, a [desβo'kaðo, a] adj (*caballo*) runaway

desbordar [desβor'ðar] vt (*sobrepasar*) to go beyond; (*exceder*) to exceed; ~**se** vr (*río*) to overflow; (*entusiasmo*) to erupt

descabalgar [deskaβal'ɣar] vi to dismount

descabellado, a [deskaße'ʎaðo, a] *adj*
(*disparatado*) wild, crazy

descafeinado, a [deskafei'naðo, a] *adj*
decaffeinated ♦ *nm* decaffeinated coffee

descalabro [deska'laßro] *nm* blow;
(*desgracia*) misfortune

descalificar [deskalifi'kar] *vt* to disqualify;
(*desacreditar*) to discredit

descalzar [deskal'θar] *vt* (*zapato*) to take off;
descalzo, a *adj* barefoot(ed)

descambiar [deskam'bjar] *vt* to exchange

descaminado, a [deskami'naðo, a] *adj*
(*equivocado*) on the wrong road; (*fig*)
misguided

descampado [deskam'paðo] *nm* open space

descansado, a [deskan'saðo, a] *adj* (*gen*)
rested; (*que tranquiliza*) restful

descansar [deskan'sar] *vt* (*gen*) to rest ♦ *vi*
to rest, have a rest; (*echarse*) to lie down

descansillo [deskan'siʎo] *nm* (*de escalera*)
landing

descanso [des'kanso] *nm* (*reposo*) rest;
(*alivio*) relief; (*pausa*) break; (*DEPORTE*)
interval, half time

descapotable [deskapo'taßle] *nm* (*tb: coche*
~) convertible

descarado, a [deska'raðo, a] *adj* shameless;
(*insolente*) cheeky

descarga [des'karva] *nf* (*ARQ, ELEC, MIL*)
discharge; (*NAUT*) unloading

descargar [deskar'var] *vt* to unload; (*golpe*)
to let fly; ~**se** *vr* to unburden o.s.; **descargo**
nm (*COM*) receipt; (*JUR*) evidence

descaro [des'karo] *nm* nerve

descarriar [deska'rrjar] *vt* (*descaminar*) to
misdirect; (*fig*) to lead astray; ~**se** *vr*
(*perderse*) to lose one's way; (*separarse*) to
stray; (*pervertirse*) to err, go astray

descarrilamiento [deskarrila'mjento] *nm*
(*de tren*) derailment

descarrilar [deskarri'lar] *vi* to be derailed

descartar [deskar'tar] *vt* (*rechazar*) to reject;
(*eliminar*) to rule out; ~**se** *vr* (*NAIPES*) to
discard; ~**se de** to shirk

descascarillado, a [deskaskari'ʎaðo, a] *adj*
(*paredes*) peeling

descendencia [desθen'denθja] *nf* (*origen*)
origin, descent; (*hijos*) offspring

descender [desθen'der] *vt* (*bajar: escalera*)
to go down ♦ *vi* to descend; (*temperatura,
nivel*) to fall, drop; ~ **de** to be descended
from

descendiente [desθen'djente] *nm/f*
descendant

descenso [des'θenso] *nm* descent; (*de
temperatura*) drop

descifrar [desθi'frar] *vt* to decipher;
(*mensaje*) to decode

descolgar [deskol'var] *vt* (*bajar*) to take

down; (*teléfono*) to pick up; ~**se** *vr* to let o.s.
down

descolorido, a [deskolo'riðo, a] *adj* faded;
(*pálido*) pale

descompasado, a [deskompa'saðo, a] *adj*
(*sin proporción*) out of all proportion;
(*excesivo*) excessive

descomponer [deskompo'ner] *vt*
(*desordenar*) to disarrange, disturb; (*TEC*) to
put out of order; (*dividir*) to break down
(into parts); (*fig*) to provoke; ~**se** *vr*
(*corromperse*) to rot, decompose; (*TEC*) to
break down

descomposición [deskomposi'θjon] *nf* (*de
un objeto*) breakdown; (*de fruta etc*)
decomposition; ~ **de vientre** stomach upset,
diarrhoea

descompuesto, a [deskom'pwesto, a] *adj*
(*corrompido*) decomposed; (*roto*) broken

descomunal [deskomu'nal] *adj* (*enorme*)
huge

desconcertado, a [deskonθer'taðo, a] *adj*
disconcerted, bewildered

desconcertar [deskonθer'tar] *vt* (*confundir*)
to baffle; (*incomodar*) to upset, put out; ~**se**
vr (*turbarse*) to be upset

desconchado, a [deskon'tʃaðo, a] *adj*
(*pintura*) peeling

desconcierto *etc* [deskon'θjerto] *vb ver*
desconcertar ♦ *nm* (*gen*) disorder;
(*desorientación*) uncertainty; (*inquietud*)
uneasiness

desconectar [deskonek'tar] *vt* to disconnect

desconfianza [deskon'fjanθa] *nf* distrust

desconfiar [deskon'fjar] *vi* to be distrustful;
~ **de** to distrust, suspect

descongelar [deskonxe'lar] *vt* to defrost;
(*COM, POL*) to unfreeze

descongestionar [deskonxestjo'nar] *vt*
(*cabeza, tráfico*) to clear

desconocer [deskono'θer] *vt* (*ignorar*) not
to know, be ignorant of

desconocido, a [deskono'θiðo, a] *adj*
unknown ♦ *nm/f* stranger

desconocimiento [deskonoθi'mjento] *nm*
(*falta de conocimientos*) ignorance

desconsiderado, a [deskonsiðe'raðo, a]
adj inconsiderate; (*insensible*) thoughtless

desconsolar [deskonso'lar] *vt* to distress;
~**se** *vr* to despair

desconsuelo *etc* [deskon'swelo] *vb ver*
desconsolar ♦ *nm* (*tristeza*) distress;
(*desesperación*) despair

descontado, a [deskon'taðo, a] *adj*: **dar por
~ (que)** to take (it) for granted (that)

descontar [deskon'tar] *vt* (*deducir*) to take
away, deduct; (*rebajar*) to discount

descontento, a [deskon'tento, a] *adj*
dissatisfied ♦ *nm* dissatisfaction, discontent

descorazonar [deskoraθo'nar] *vt* to
discourage, dishearten

descorchar [deskor'tʃar] *vt* to uncork

descorrer [desko'rrer] *vt* (*cortinas, cerrojo*) to
draw back

descortés [deskor'tes] *adj* (*mal educado*)
discourteous; (*grosero*) rude

descoser [desko'ser] *vt* to unstitch; **~se** *vr* to
come apart (at the seams)

descosido, a [desko'siðo, a] *adj* (*COSTURA*)
unstitched

descrédito [des'kreðito] *nm* discredit

descreído, a [deskre'iðo, a] *adj* (*incrédulo*)
incredulous; (*falto de fe*) unbelieving

descremado, a [deskre'maðo, a] *adj*
skimmed

describir [deskri'ßir] *vt* to describe;
descripción [deskrip'θjon] *nf* description

descrito [des'krito] *pp de* **describir**

descuartizar [deskwarti'θar] *vt* (*animal*) to
cut up

descubierto, a [desku'ßjerto, a] *pp de*
descubrir ♦ *adj* uncovered, bare; (*persona*)
bareheaded **♦** *nm* (*bancario*) overdraft; **al ~** in
the open

descubrimiento [deskußri'mjento] *nm*
(*hallazgo*) discovery; (*revelación*) revelation

descubrir [desku'ßrir] *vt* to discover, find;
(*inaugurar*) to unveil; (*vislumbrar*) to detect;
(*revelar*) to reveal, show; (*destapar*) to
uncover; **~se** *vr* to reveal o.s.; (*quitarse
sombrero*) to take off one's hat; (*confesar*) to
confess

descuento *etc* [des'kwento] *vb ver* **descontar
♦** *nm* discount

descuidado, a [deskwi'ðaðo, a] *adj* (*sin
cuidado*) careless; (*desordenado*) untidy;
(*olvidadizo*) forgetful; (*dejado*) neglected;
(*desprevenido*) unprepared

descuidar [deskwi'ðar] *vt* (*dejar*) to neglect;
(*olvidar*) to overlook; **~se** *vr* (*distraerse*) to be
careless; (*abandonarse*) to let o.s. go;
(*desprevenirse*) to drop one's guard;
¡descuida! don't worry!; **descuido** *nm*
(*dejadez*) carelessness; (*olvido*) negligence

PALABRA CLAVE
---

desde ['desðe] *prep* **1** (*lugar*) from; **~ Burgos
hasta mi casa hay 30 km** it's 30 kms from
Burgos to my house

2 (*posición*): **hablaba ~ el balcón** she was
speaking from the balcony

3 (*tiempo: + ad, n*): **~ ahora** from now on;
~ la boda since the wedding; **~ niño** since I
etc was a child; **~ 3 años atrás** since 3 years
ago

4 (*tiempo: + vb, fecha*) since; for; **nos
conocemos ~ 1992/~ hace 20 años** we've
known each other since 1992/for 20 years;

no le veo ~ 1997/~ hace 5 años I haven't seen
him since 1997/for 5 years

5 (*gama*): **~ los más lujosos hasta los más
económicos** from the most luxurious to the
most reasonably priced

6: **~ luego (que no)** of course (not)

♦ *conj*: **~ que**: **~ que recuerdo** for as long as I
can remember; **~ que llegó no ha salido** he
hasn't been out since he arrived

---

desdecirse [desðe'θirse] *vr* to retract; **~ de**
to go back on

desdén [des'ðen] *nm* scorn

desdeñar [desðe'ɲar] *vt* (*despreciar*) to scorn

desdicha [des'ðitʃa] *nf* (*desgracia*)
misfortune; (*infelicidad*) unhappiness;
desdichado, a *adj* (*sin suerte*) unlucky;
(*infeliz*) unhappy

desdoblar [desðo'ßlar] *vt* (*extender*) to
spread out; (*desplegar*) to unfold

desear [dese'ar] *vt* to want, desire, wish for

desecar [dese'kar] *vt* to dry up; **~se** *vr* to dry
up

desechar [dese'tʃar] *vt* (*basura*) to throw out
o away; (*ideas*) to reject, discard; **desechos**
nmpl rubbish *sg*, waste *sg*

desembalar [desemba'lar] *vt* to unpack

desembarazar [desembara'θar] *vt*
(*desocupar*) to clear; (*desenredar*) to free; **~se**
vr: **~se de** to free o.s. of, get rid of

desembarcar [desembar'kar] *vt* (*mercancías
etc*) to unload **♦** *vi* to disembark; **~se** *vr* to
disembark

desembocadura [desemboka'ðura] *nf* (*de
río*) mouth; (*de calle*) opening

desembocar [desembo'kar] *vi* (*río*) to flow
into; (*fig*) to result in

desembolso [desem'bolso] *nm* payment

desembragar [desembra'ɣar] *vi* to declutch

desembrollar [desembro'ʎar] *vt* (*madeja*)
to unravel; (*asunto, malentendido*) to sort out

desemejanza [deseme'xanθa] *nf*
dissimilarity

desempaquetar [desempake'tar] *vt*
(*regalo*) to unwrap; (*mercancía*) to unpack

desempatar [desempa'tar] *vi* to replay, hold
a play-off; **desempate** *nm* (*FÚTBOL*) replay,
play-off; (*TENIS*) tie-break(er)

desempeñar [desempe'ɲar] *vt* (*cargo*) to
hold; (*papel*) to perform; (*lo empeñado*) to
redeem; **~ un papel** (*fig*) to play (a role)

desempeño [desem'peɲo] *nm* redeeming;
(*de cargo*) occupation

desempleado, a [desemple'aðo, a] *nm/f*
unemployed person; **desempleo** *nm*
unemployment

desempolvar [desempol'ßar] *vt* (*muebles
etc*) to dust; (*lo olvidado*) to revive

desencadenar [desenkaðe'nar] *vt* to

unchain; (*ira*) to unleash; **~se** *vr* to break loose; (*tormenta*) to burst; (*guerra*) to break out

desencajar [desenka'xar] *vt* (*hueso*) to dislocate; (*mecanismo, pieza*) to disconnect, disengage

desencanto [desen'kanto] *nm* disillusionment

desenchufar [desentʃu'far] *vt* to unplug

desenfadado, a [desenfa'ðaðo, a] *adj* (*desenvuelto*) uninhibited; (*descarado*) forward; **desenfado** *nm* (*libertad*) freedom; (*comportamiento*) free and easy manner; (*descaro*) forwardness

desenfocado, a [desenfo'kaðo, a] *adj* (*FOTO*) out of focus

desenfrenado, a [desenfre'naðo, a] *adj* (*descontrolado*) uncontrolled; (*inmoderado*) unbridled; **desenfreno** *nm* wildness; (*de las pasiones*) lack of self-control

desenganchar [desengan'tʃar] *vt* (*gen*) to unhook; (*FERRO*) to uncouple

desengañar [desenga'ɲar] *vt* to disillusion; **~se** *vr* to become disillusioned; **desengaño** *nm* disillusionment; (*decepción*) disappointment

desenlace [desen'laθe] *nm* outcome

desenmarañar [desenmara'ɲar] *vt* (*fig*) to unravel

desenmascarar [desenmaska'rar] *vt* to unmask

desenredar [desenre'ðar] *vt* (*pelo*) to untangle; (*problema*) to sort out

desenroscar [desenros'kar] *vt* to unscrew

desentenderse [desenten'derse] *vr*: **~ de** to pretend not to know about; (*apartarse*) to have nothing to do with

desenterrar [desente'rrar] *vt* to exhume; (*tesoro, fig*) to unearth, dig up

desentonar [desento'nar] *vi* (*MUS*) to sing (o play) out of tune; (*color*) to clash

desentrañar [desentra'ɲar] *vt* (*misterio*) to unravel

desentumecer [desentume'θer] *vt* (*pierna etc*) to stretch

desenvoltura [desenßol'tura] *nf* ease

desenvolver [desenßol'ßer] *vt* (*paquete*) to unwrap; (*fig*) to develop; **~se** *vr* (*desarrollarse*) to unfold, develop; (*arreglárselas*) to cope

deseo [de'seo] *nm* desire, wish; **~so, a** *adj*: **estar ~so de** to be anxious to

desequilibrado, a [desekili'ßraðo, a] *adj* unbalanced

desertar [deser'tar] *vi* to desert

desértico, a [de'sertiko, a] *adj* desert *cpd*

desesperación [desespera'θjon] *nf* (*impaciencia*) desperation, despair; (*irritación*) fury

desesperar [desespe'rar] *vt* to drive to despair; (*exasperar*) to drive to distraction ♦ *vi*: **~ de** to despair of; **~se** *vr* to despair, lose hope

desestabilizar [desestaßili'θar] *vt* to destabilize

desestimar [desesti'mar] *vt* (*menospreciar*) to have a low opinion of; (*rechazar*) to reject

desfachatez [desfatʃa'teθ] *nf* (*insolencia*) impudence; (*descaro*) rudeness

desfalco [des'falko] *nm* embezzlement

desfallecer [desfaʎe'θer] *vi* (*perder las fuerzas*) to become weak; (*desvanecerse*) to faint

desfasado, a [desfa'saðo, a] *adj* (*anticuado*) old-fashioned; **desfase** *nm* (*diferencia*) gap

desfavorable [desfaßo'raßle] *adj* unfavourable

desfigurar [desfiɣu'rar] *vt* (*cara*) to disfigure; (*cuerpo*) to deform

desfiladero [desfila'ðero] *nm* gorge

desfilar [desfi'lar] *vi* to parade; **desfile** *nm* procession

desfogarse [desfo'ɣarse] *vr* (*fig*) to let off steam

desgajar [desɣa'xar] *vt* (*arrancar*) to tear off; (*romper*) to break off; **~se** *vr* to come off

desgana [des'ɣana] *nf* (*falta de apetito*) loss of appetite; (*apatía*) unwillingness; **~do, a** *adj*: **estar ~do** (*sin apetito*) to have no appetite; (*sin entusiasmo*) to have lost interest

desgarrador, a [desɣarra'ðor, a] *adj* (*fig*) heartrending

desgarrar [desɣa'rrar] *vt* to tear (up); (*fig*) to shatter; **desgarro** *nm* (*en tela*) tear; (*aflicción*) grief

desgastar [desɣas'tar] *vt* (*deteriorar*) to wear away o down; (*estropear*) to spoil; **~se** *vr* to get worn out; **desgaste** *nm* wear (and tear)

desglosar [desɣlo'sar] *vt* (*factura*) to break down

desgracia [des'ɣraθja] *nf* misfortune; (*accidente*) accident; (*vergüenza*) disgrace; (*contratiempo*) setback; **por ~** unfortunately

desgraciado, a [desɣra'θjaðo, a] *adj* (*sin suerte*) unlucky, unfortunate; (*miserable*) wretched; (*infeliz*) miserable

desgravación [desɣraßa'θjon] *nf* (*COM*): **~ fiscal** tax relief

desgravar [desɣra'ßar] *vt* (*impuestos*) to reduce the tax o duty on

deshabitado, a [desaßi'taðo, a] *adj* uninhabited

deshacer [desa'θer] *vt* (*casa*) to break up; (*TEC*) to take apart; (*enemigo*) to defeat; (*diluir*) to melt; (*contrato*) to break; (*intriga*) to solve; **~se** *vr* (*disolverse*) to melt; (*despedazarse*) to come apart o undone; **~se de** to get rid of; **~se en lágrimas** to burst into

tears
desharrapado, a [desarra'paðo, a] *adj* (*persona*) shabby

deshecho, a [des'etʃo, a] *adj* undone; (*roto*) smashed; (*persona*): **estar ~** to be shattered

desheredar [desere'ðar] *vt* to disinherit

deshidratar [desiðra'tar] *vt* to dehydrate

deshielo [des'jelo] *nm* thaw

deshonesto, a [deso'nesto, a] *adj* indecent

deshonra [des'onra] *nf* (*deshonor*) dishonour; (*vergüenza*) shame

deshora [des'ora]: **a ~** *adv* at the wrong time

deshuesar [deswe'sar] *vt* (*carne*) to bone; (*fruta*) to stone

desierto, a [de'sjerto, a] *adj* (*casa, calle, negocio*) deserted ♦ *nm* desert

designar [desiɣ'nar] *vt* (*nombrar*) to designate; (*indicar*) to fix

designio [de'siɣnjo] *nm* plan

desigual [desi'ɣwal] *adj* (*terreno*) uneven; (*lucha etc*) unequal

desilusión [desilu'sjon] *nf* disillusionment; (*decepción*) disappointment; **desilusionar** *vt* to disillusion; to disappoint; **desilusionarse** *vr* to become disillusioned

desinfectar [desinfek'tar] *vt* to disinfect

desinflar [desin'flar] *vt* to deflate

desintegración [desinteɣra'θjon] *nf* disintegration

desinterés [desinte'res] *nm* (*desgana*) lack of interest; (*altruismo*) unselfishness

desintoxicarse [desintoksi'karse] *vr* (*drogadicto*) to undergo detoxification

desistir [desis'tir] *vi* (*renunciar*) to stop, desist

desleal [desle'al] *adj* (*infiel*) disloyal; (*COM: competencia*) unfair; **~tad** *nf* disloyalty

desleír [desle'ir] *vt* (*líquido*) to dilute; (*sólido*) to dissolve

deslenguado, a [deslen'gwaðo, a] *adj* (*grosero*) foul-mouthed

desligar [desli'ɣar] *vt* (*desatar*) to untie, undo; (*separar*) to separate; **~se** *vr* (*de un compromiso*) to extricate o.s.

desliz [des'liθ] *nm* (*fig*) lapse; **~ar** *vt* to slip, slide

deslucido, a [deslu'θiðo, a] *adj* dull; (*torpe*) awkward, graceless; (*deslustrado*) tarnished

deslumbrar [deslum'brar] *vt* to dazzle

desmadrarse [desma'ðrarse] (*fam*) *vr* (*descontrolarse*) to run wild; (*divertirse*) to let one's hair down; **desmadre** (*fam*) *nm* (*desorganización*) chaos; (*jaleo*) commotion

desmán [des'man] *nm* (*exceso*) outrage; (*abuso de poder*) abuse

desmandarse [desman'darse] *vr* (*portarse mal*) to behave badly; (*excederse*) to get out of hand; (*caballo*) to bolt

desmantelar [desmante'lar] *vt* (*deshacer*) to dismantle; (*casa*) to strip

desmaquillador [desmakiʎa'ðor] *nm* make-up remover

desmayar [desma'jar] *vi* to lose heart; **~se** *vr* (*MED*) to faint; **desmayo** *nm* (*MED: acto*) faint; (: *estado*) unconsciousness

desmedido, a [desme'ðiðo, a] *adj* excessive

desmejorar [desmexo'rar] *vt* (*dañar*) to impair, spoil; (*MED*) to weaken

desmembrar [desmem'brar] *vt* (*MED*) to dismember; (*fig*) to separate

desmemoriado, a [desmemo'rjaðo, a] *adj* forgetful

desmentir [desmen'tir] *vt* (*contradecir*) to contradict; (*refutar*) to deny

desmenuzar [desmenu'θar] *vt* (*deshacer*) to crumble; (*carne*) to chop; (*examinar*) to examine closely

desmerecer [desmere'θer] *vt* to be unworthy of ♦ *vi* (*deteriorarse*) to deteriorate

desmesurado, a [desmesu'raðo, a] *adj* disproportionate

desmontable [desmon'taβle] *adj* (*que se quita: pieza*) detachable; (*que se puede plegar etc*) collapsible, folding

desmontar [desmon'tar] *vt* (*deshacer*) to dismantle; (*tierra*) to level ♦ *vi* to dismount

desmoralizar [desmorali'θar] *vt* to demoralize

desmoronar [desmoro'nar] *vt* to wear away, erode; **~se** *vr* (*edificio, dique*) to collapse; (*economía*) to decline

desnatado, a [desna'taðo, a] *adj* skimmed

desnivel [desni'βel] *nm* (*de terreno*) unevenness

desnudar [desnu'ðar] *vt* (*desvestir*) to undress; (*despojar*) to strip; **~se** *vr* (*desvestirse*) to get undressed; **desnudo, a** *adj* naked ♦ *nm/f* nude; **desnudo de** devoid o bereft of

desnutrición [desnutri'θjon] *nf* malnutrition; **desnutrido, a** *adj* undernourished

desobedecer [desoβeðe'θer] *vt, vi* to disobey; **desobediencia** *nf* disobedience

desocupado, a [desoku'paðo, a] *adj* at leisure; (*desempleado*) unemployed; (*deshabitado*) empty, vacant

desocupar [desoku'par] *vt* to vacate

desodorante [desoðo'rante] *nm* deodorant

desolación [desola'θjon] *nf* (*de lugar*) desolation; (*fig*) grief

desolar [deso'lar] *vt* to ruin, lay waste

desorbitado, a [desorβi'taðo, a] *adj* (*excesivo: ambición*) boundless; (*deseos*) excessive; (: *precio*) exorbitant

desorden [des'orðen] *nm* confusion; (*político*) disorder, unrest

desorganizar [desorɣani'θar] *vt* (*desordenar*) to disorganize;

desorganización nf (de persona) disorganization; (en empresa, oficina) disorder, chaos

desorientar [desorjen'tar] vt (extraviar) to mislead; (confundir, desconcertar) to confuse; ~se vr (perderse) to lose one's way

despabilado, a [despaβi'laðo, a] adj (despierto) wide-awake; (fig) alert, sharp

despabilar [despaβi'lar] vt (el ingenio) to sharpen ♦ vi to wake up; (fig) to get a move on; ~se vr to wake up; to get a move on

despachar [despa'tʃar] vt (negocio) to do, complete; (enviar) to send, dispatch; (vender) to sell, deal in; (billete) to issue; (mandar ir) to send away

despacho [des'patʃo] nm (oficina) office; (de paquetes) dispatch; (venta) sale; (comunicación) message

despacio [des'paθjo] adv slowly

desparpajo [despar'paxo] nm self-confidence; (pey) nerve

desparramar [desparra'mar] vt (esparcir) to scatter; (líquido) to spill

despavorido, a [despaβo'riðo, a] adj terrified

despecho [des'petʃo] nm spite; **a ~ de** in spite of

despectivo, a [despek'tiβo, a] adj (despreciativo) derogatory; (LING) pejorative

despedazar [despeða'θar] vt to tear to pieces

despedida [despe'ðiða] nf (adiós) farewell; (de obrero) sacking

despedir [despe'ðir] vt (visita) to see off, show out; (empleado) to dismiss; (inquilino) to evict; (objeto) to hurl; (olor etc) to give out o off; ~se vr: ~se de to say goodbye to

despegar [despe'var] vt to unstick ♦ vi (avión) to take off; ~se vr to come loose, come unstuck; **despego** nm detachment

despegue etc [des'peve] vb ver **despegar** ♦ nm takeoff

despeinado, a [despei'naðo, a] adj dishevelled, unkempt

despejado, a [despe'xaðo, a] adj (lugar) clear, free; (cielo) clear; (persona) wide-awake, bright

despejar [despe'xar] vt (gen) to clear; (misterio) to clear up ♦ vi (el tiempo) to clear; ~se vr (tiempo, cielo) to clear (up); (misterio) to become clearer; (cabeza) to clear

despellejar [despeʎe'xar] vt (animal) to skin

despensa [des'pensa] nf larder

despeñadero [despeɲa'ðero] nm (GEO) cliff, precipice

despeñarse [despe'narse] vr to hurl o.s. down; (coche) to tumble over

desperdicio [desper'ðiθjo] nm (despilfarro) squandering; ~s nmpl (basura) rubbish sg

(BRIT), garbage sg (US); (residuos) waste sg

desperdigarse [desperði'xarse] vr (rebaño, familia) to scatter, spread out; (granos de arroz, semillas) to scatter

desperezarse [despere'θarse] vr to stretch

desperfecto [desper'fekto] nm (deterioro) slight damage; (defecto) flaw, imperfection

despertador [desperta'ðor] nm alarm clock

despertar [desper'tar] nm awakening ♦ vt (persona) to wake up; (recuerdos) to revive; (sentimiento) to arouse ♦ vi to awaken, wake up; ~se vr to awaken, wake up

despiadado, a [despja'ðaðo, a] adj (ataque) merciless; (persona) heartless

despido etc [des'piðo] vb ver **despedir** ♦ nm dismissal, sacking

despierto, a etc [des'pjerto, a] vb ver **despertar** ♦ adj awake; (fig) sharp, alert

despilfarro [despil'farro] nm (derroche) squandering; (lujo desmedido) extravagance

despistar [despis'tar] vt to throw off the track o scent; (confundir) to mislead, confuse; ~se vr to take the wrong road; (confundirse) to become confused

despiste [des'piste] nm absent-mindedness; **un ~** a mistake, slip

desplazamiento [desplaθa'mjento] nm displacement

desplazar [despla'θar] vt to move; (NAUT) to displace; (INFORM) to scroll; (fig) to oust; ~se vr (persona) to travel

desplegar [desple'var] vt (tela, papel) to unfold, open out; (bandera) to unfurl; **despliegue** etc [des'pleve] vb ver **desplegar** ♦ nm display

desplomarse [desplo'marse] vr (edificio, gobierno, persona) to collapse

desplumar [desplu'mar] vt (ave) to pluck; (fam: estafar) to fleece

despoblado, a [despo'βlaðo, a] adj (sin habitantes) uninhabited

despojar [despo'xar] vt (alguien: de sus bienes) to divest of, deprive of; (casa) to strip, leave bare; (alguien: de su cargo) to strip of

despojo [des'poxo] nm (acto) plundering; (objetos) plunder, loot; ~s nmpl (de ave, res) offal sg

desposado, a [despo'saðo, a] adj, nm/f newly-wed

desposar [despo'sar] vt to marry; ~se vr to get married

desposeer [despose'er] vt: ~ **a uno de** (puesto, autoridad) to strip sb of

déspota ['despota] nm/f despot

despreciar [despre'θjar] vt (desdeñar) to despise, scorn; (afrentar) to slight; **desprecio** nm scorn, contempt; slight

desprender [despren'der] vt (broche) to

unfasten; (*olor*) to give off; **~se** *vr* (*botón: caerse*) to fall off; (*broche*) to come unfastened; (*olor, perfume*) to be given off; **~se de algo que ...** to draw from sth that ...

desprendimiento [desprendi'mjento] *nm* (*gen*) loosening; (*generosidad*) disinterestedness; (*de tierra, rocas*) landslide

despreocupado, a [despreoku'paðo, a] *adj* (*sin preocupación*) unworried, nonchalant; (*negligente*) careless

despreocuparse [despreoku'parse] *vr* not to worry; **~ de** to have no interest in

desprestigiar [despresti'xjar] *vt* (*criticar*) to run down; (*desacreditar*) to discredit

desprevenido, a [despreße'niðo, a] *adj* (*no preparado*) unprepared, unready

desproporcionado, a [despropor-θjo'naðo, a] *adj* disproportionate, out of proportion

desprovisto, a [despro'ßisto, a] *adj*: **~ de** devoid of

después [des'pwes] *adv* afterwards, later; (*próximo paso*) next; **~ de comer** after lunch; **un año ~** a year later; **~ se debatió el tema** next the matter was discussed; **~ de corregido el texto** after the text had been corrected; **~ de todo** after all

desquiciado, a [deski'θjaðo, a] *adj* deranged

desquite [des'kite] *nm* (*satisfacción*) satisfaction; (*venganza*) revenge

destacar [desta'kar] *vt* to emphasize, point up; (*MIL*) to detach, detail ♦ *vi* (*resaltarse*) to stand out; (*persona*) to be outstanding o exceptional; **~se** *vr* to stand out; to be outstanding o exceptional

destajo [des'taxo] *nm*: **trabajar a ~** to do piecework

destapar [desta'par] *vt* (*botella*) to open; (*cacerola*) to take the lid off; (*descubrir*) to uncover; **~se** *vr* (*revelarse*) to reveal one's true character

destartalado, a [destarta'laðo, a] *adj* (*desordenado*) untidy; (*ruinoso*) tumbledown

destello [des'teʎo] *nm* (*de estrella*) twinkle; (*de faro*) signal light

destemplado, a [destem'plaðo, a] *adj* (*MUS*) out of tune; (*voz*) harsh; (*MED*) out of sorts; (*tiempo*) unpleasant, nasty

desteñir [deste'ɲir] *vt* to fade ♦ *vi* to fade; **~se** *vr* to fade; **esta tela no destiñe** this fabric will not run

desternillarse [desterni'ʎarse] *vr*: **~ de risa** to split one's sides laughing

desterrar [deste'rrar] *vt* (*exilar*) to exile; (*fig*) to banish, dismiss

destiempo [des'tjempo] : **a ~** *adv* out of turn

destierro *etc* [des'tjerro] *vb ver* **desterrar** ♦ *nm* exile

destilar [desti'lar] *vt* to distil; **destilería** *nf* distillery

destinar [desti'nar] *vt* (*funcionario*) to appoint, assign; (*fondos*): **~ (a)** to set aside (for)

destinatario, a [destina'tarjo, a] *nm/f* addressee

destino [des'tino] *nm* (*suerte*) destiny; (*de avión, viajero*) destination

destituir [destitu'ir] *vt* to dismiss

destornillador [destorniʎa'ðor] *nm* screwdriver

destornillar [destorni'ʎar] *vt* (*tornillo*) to unscrew; **~se** *vr* to unscrew

destreza [des'treθa] *nf* (*habilidad*) skill; (*maña*) dexterity

destrozar [destro'θar] *vt* (*romper*) to smash, break (up); (*estropear*) to ruin; (*nervios*) to shatter

destrozo [des'troθo] *nm* (*acción*) destruction; (*desastre*) smashing; **~s** *nmpl* (*pedazos*) pieces; (*daños*) havoc *sg*

destrucción [destruk'θjon] *nf* destruction

destruir [destru'ir] *vt* to destroy

desuso [des'uso] *nm* disuse; **caer en ~** to become obsolete

desvalido, a [desßa'liðo, a] *adj* (*desprotegido*) destitute; (*sin fuerzas*) helpless

desvalijar [desßali'xar] *vt* (*persona*) to rob; (*casa, tienda*) to burgle; (*coche*) to break into

desván [des'ßan] *nm* attic

desvanecer [desßane'θer] *vt* (*disipar*) to dispel; (*borrar*) to blur; **~se** *vr* (*humo etc*) to vanish, disappear; (*color*) to fade; (*recuerdo, sonido*) to fade away; (*MED*) to pass out; (*duda*) to be dispelled

desvanecimiento [desßaneθi'mjento] *nm* (*desaparición*) disappearance; (*de colores*) fading; (*evaporación*) evaporation; (*MED*) fainting fit

desvariar [desßa'rjar] *vi* (*enfermo*) to be delirious; **desvarío** *nm* delirium

desvelar [desße'lar] *vt* to keep awake; **~se** *vr* (*no poder dormir*) to stay awake; (*preocuparse*) to be vigilant o watchful

desvelos [des'ßelos] *nmpl* worrying *sg*

desvencijado, a [desßenθi'xaðo, a] *adj* (*silla*) rickety; (*máquina*) broken-down

desventaja [desßen'taxa] *nf* disadvantage

desventura [desßen'tura] *nf* misfortune

desvergonzado, a [desßerɣon'θaðo, a] *adj* shameless

desvergüenza [desßer'ɣwenθa] *nf* (*descaro*) shamelessness; (*insolencia*) impudence; (*mala conducta*) effrontery

desvestir [desßes'tir] *vt* to undress; **~se** *vr* to undress

desviación [desßja'θjon] *nf* deviation; (*AUTO*) diversion, detour

desviar → diesel 70

desviar [des'ßjar] vt to turn aside; (río) to alter the course of; (navío) to divert, re-route; (conversación) to sidetrack; **~se** vr (apartarse del camino) to turn aside; (: barco) to go off course

desvío etc [des'ßio] vb ver **desviar** ♦ nm (desviación) detour, diversion; (fig) indifference

desvirtuar [desßir'twar] vt to distort

desvivirse [desßi'ßirse] vr: ~ por (anhelar) to long for, crave for; (hacer lo posible por) to do one's utmost for

detallar [deta'ʎar] vt to detail

detalle [de'taʎe] nm detail; (gesto) gesture, token; al ~ in detail; (COM) retail

detallista [deta'ʎista] nm/f (COM) retailer

detective [detek'tiße] nm/f detective

detener [dete'ner] vt (gen) to stop; (JUR) to arrest; (objeto) to keep; **~se** vr to stop; (demorarse): **~se** en to delay over, linger over

detenidamente [deteniða'mente] adv (minuciosamente) carefully; (extensamente) at great length

detenido, a [dete'niðo, a] adj (arrestado) under arrest ♦ nm/f person under arrest, prisoner

detenimiento [deteni'mjento] nm: con ~ thoroughly; (observar, considerar) carefully

detergente [deter'xente] nm detergent

deteriorar [deterjo'rar] vt to spoil, damage; **~se** vr to deteriorate; **deterioro** nm deterioration

determinación [determina'θjon] nf (empeño) determination; (decisión) decision; **determinado, a** adj specific

determinar [determi'nar] vt (plazo) to fix; (precio) to settle; **~se** vr to decide

detestar [detes'tar] vt to detest

detractor, a [detrak'tor, a] nm/f slanderer, libeller

detrás [de'tras] adv behind; (atrás) at the back; ~ de behind

detrimento [detri'mento] nm: en ~ de to the detriment of

deuda ['deuða] nf debt

devaluación [deßalwa'θjon] nf devaluation

devastar [deßas'tar] vt (destruir) to devastate

devoción [deßo'θjon] nf devotion

devolución [deßolu'θjon] nf (reenvío) return, sending back; (reembolso) repayment; (JUR) devolution

devolver [deßol'ßer] vt to return; (lo extraviado, lo prestado) to give back; (carta al correo) to send back; (COM) to repay, refund ♦ vi (vomitar) to be sick

devorar [deßo'rar] vt to devour

devoto, a [de'ßoto, a] adj devout ♦ nm/f admirer

devuelto pp de **devolver**

devuelva etc vb ver **devolver**

di vb ver **dar; decir**

día ['dia] nm day; ¿qué ~ es? what's the date?; estar/poner al ~ to be/keep up to date; el ~ de hoy/de mañana today/tomorrow; al ~ siguiente (on) the following day; vivir al ~ to live from hand to mouth; de ~ by day, in daylight; en pleno ~ in full daylight; D~ de Reyes Epiphany; ~ festivo (ESP) o feriado (AM) holiday; ~ libre day off

diabetes [dja'ßetes] nf diabetes

diablo ['djaßlo] nm devil; **diablura** nf prank

diadema [dja'ðema] nf tiara

diafragma [dja'fraxma] nm diaphragm

diagnosis [djav'nosis] nf inv diagnosis

diagnóstico [djav'nostiko] nm = **diagnosis**

diagonal [djavo'nal] adj diagonal

diagrama [dja'vrama] nm diagram; ~ de flujo flowchart

dial [djal] nm dial

dialecto [dja'lekto] nm dialect

dialogar [djalo'var] vi: ~ con (POL) to hold talks with

diálogo ['djalovo] nm dialogue

diamante [dja'mante] nm diamond

diana ['djana] nf (MIL) reveille; (de blanco) centre, bull's-eye

diapositiva [djaposi'tißa] nf (FOTO) slide, transparency

diario, a ['djarjo, a] adj daily ♦ nm newspaper; a ~ daily; de ~ everyday

diarrea [dja'rrea] nf diarrhoea

dibujar [dißu'xar] vt to draw, sketch; **dibujo** nm drawing; **dibujos animados** cartoons

diccionario [dikθjo'narjo] nm dictionary

dice etc vb ver **decir**

dicho, a ['ditʃo, a] pp de decir ♦ adj: en ~s países in the aforementioned countries ♦ nm saying

dichoso, a [di'tʃoso, a] adj happy

diciembre [di'θjembre] nm December

dictado [dik'taðo] nm dictation

dictador [dikta'ðor] nm dictator; **dictadura** nf dictatorship

dictamen [dik'tamen] nm (opinión) opinion; (juicio) judgment; (informe) report

dictar [dik'tar] vt (carta) to dictate; (JUR: sentencia) to pronounce; (decreto) to issue; (AM: clase) to give

didáctico, a [di'ðaktiko, a] adj educational

diecinueve [djeθi'nweße] num nineteen

dieciocho [djeθi'otʃo] num eighteen

dieciséis [djeθi'seis] num sixteen

diecisiete [djeθi'sjete] num seventeen

diente ['djente] nm (ANAT, TEC) tooth; (ZOOL) fang; (: de elefante) tusk; (de ajo) clove; hablar entre ~s to mutter, mumble

diera etc vb ver **dar**

diesel ['disel] adj: motor ~ diesel engine

diestro, a ['djestro, a] *adj (derecho)* right; *(hábil)* skilful

dieta ['djeta] *nf* diet; **dietética** *nf*: **tienda de dietética** health food shop; **dietético, a** *adj* diet *(atr)*, dietary

diez [djeθ] *num* ten

diezmar [djeθ'mar] *vt (población)* to decimate

difamar [difa'mar] *vt (JUR: hablando)* to slander; *(: por escrito)* to libel

diferencia [dife'renθja] *nf* difference; **diferenciar** *vt* to differentiate between ♦ *vi* to differ; **diferenciarse** *vr* to differ, be different; *(distinguirse)* to distinguish o.s.

diferente [dife'rente] *adj* different

diferido [dife'riðo] *nm*: **en ~** *(TV etc)* recorded

difícil [di'fiθil] *adj* difficult

dificultad [difikul'taθ] *nf* difficulty; *(problema)* trouble

dificultar [difikul'tar] *vt (complicar)* to complicate, make difficult; *(estorbar)* to obstruct

difteria [dif'terja] *nf* diphtheria

difundir [difun'dir] *vt (calor, luz)* to diffuse; *(RADIO, TV)* to broadcast; **~ una noticia** to spread a piece of news; **~se** *vr* to spread (out)

difunto, a [di'funto, a] *adj* dead, deceased ♦ *nm/f* deceased (person)

difusión [difu'sjon] *nf (RADIO, TV)* broadcasting

diga *etc vb ver* **decir**

digerir [dixe'rir] *vt* to digest; *(fig)* to absorb; **digestión** *nf* digestion; **digestivo, a** *adj* digestive

digital [dixi'tal] *adj* digital

dignarse [dix'narse] *vr* to deign to

dignatario, a [dixna'tarjo, a] *nm/f* dignitary

dignidad [dixni'ðað] *nf* dignity

digno, a ['dixno, a] *adj* worthy

digo *etc vb ver* **decir**

dije *etc vb ver* **decir**

dilapidar [dilapi'ðar] *vt (dinero, herencia)* to squander, waste

dilatar [dila'tar] *vt (cuerpo)* to dilate; *(prolongar)* to prolong

dilema [di'lema] *nm* dilemma

diligencia [dili'xenθja] *nf* diligence; *(ocupación)* errand, job; **~s** *nfpl (JUR)* formalities; **diligente** *adj* diligent

diluir [dilu'ir] *vt* to dilute

diluvio [di'lußjo] *nm* deluge, flood

dimensión [dimen'sjon] *nf* dimension

diminuto, a [dimi'nuto, a] *adj* tiny, diminutive

dimitir [dimi'tir] *vi* to resign

dimos *vb ver* **dar**

Dinamarca [dina'marka] *nf* Denmark

dinámico, a [di'namiko, a] *adj* dynamic

dinamita [dina'mita] *nf* dynamite

dínamo ['dinamo] *nf* dynamo

dineral [dine'ral] *nm* large sum of money, fortune

dinero [di'nero] *nm* money; **~ contante, ~ efectivo** (ready) cash; **~ suelto** (loose) change

dio *vb ver* **dar**

dios [djos] *nm* god; **¡D~ mío!** (oh,) my God!

diosa ['djosa] *nf* goddess

diploma [di'ploma] *nm* diploma

diplomacia [diplo'maθja] *nf* diplomacy; *(fig)* tact

diplomado, a [diplo'maðo, a] *adj* qualified

diplomático, a [diplo'matiko, a] *adj* diplomatic ♦ *nm/f* diplomat

diputación [diputa'θjon] *nf (tb: ~ provincial)* ≈ county council

diputado, a [dipu'taðo, a] *nm/f* delegate; *(POL)* ≈ member of parliament *(BRIT)*, ≈ representative *(US)*

dique ['dike] *nm* dyke

diré *etc vb ver* **decir**

dirección [direk'θjon] *nf* direction; *(señas)* address; *(AUTO)* steering; *(gerencia)* management; *(POL)* leadership; **~ única/ prohibida** one-way street/no entry

directa [di'rekta] *nf (AUT)* top gear

directiva [direk'tißa] *nf (DEP, tb: junta ~)* board of directors

directo, a [di'rekto, a] *adj* direct; *(RADIO, TV)* live; **transmitir en ~** to broadcast live

director, a [direk'tor, a] *adj* leading ♦ *nm/f* director; *(ESCOL)* head(teacher) *(BRIT)*, principal *(US)*; *(gerente)* manager(ess); *(PRENSA)* editor; **~ de cine** film director; **~ general** managing director

dirigente [diri'xente] *nm/f (POL)* leader

dirigir [diri'xir] *vt* to direct; *(carta)* to address; *(obra de teatro, film)* to direct; *(MUS)* to conduct; *(negocio)* to manage; **~se** *vr*: **~se a** to go towards, make one's way towards; *(hablar con)* to speak to

dirija *etc vb ver* **dirigir**

discernir [disθer'nir] *vt* to discern

disciplina [disθi'plina] *nf* discipline

discípulo, a [dis'θipulo, a] *nm/f* disciple

disco ['disko] *nm* disc; *(DEPORTE)* discus; *(TEL)* dial; *(AUTO: semáforo)* light; *(MUS)* record; *(INFORM)*: **~ flexible/rígido** floppy/hard disk; **~ compacto/de larga duración** compact disc/ long-playing record; **~ de freno** brake disc

disconforme [diskon'forme] *adj* differing; **estar ~ (con)** to be in disagreement (with)

discordia [dis'korðja] *nf* discord

discoteca [disko'teka] *nf* disco(theque)

discreción [diskre'θjon] *nf* discretion; *(reserva)* prudence; **comer a ~** to eat as much as one wishes; **discrecional** *adj (facultativo)* discretionary

discrepancia [diskre'panθja] nf (diferencia)
discrepancy; (desacuerdo) disagreement

discreto, a [dis'kreto, a] adj discreet

discriminación [diskrimina'θjon] nf
discrimination

disculpa [dis'kulpa] nf excuse; (pedir perdón)
apology; **pedir ~s a/por** to apologize to/for;
disculpar vt to excuse, pardon; **disculparse**
vr to excuse o.s.; to apologize

discurrir [disku'rrir] vi (pensar, reflexionar) to
think, meditate; (el tiempo) to pass, go by

discurso [dis'kurso] nm speech

discusión [disku'sjon] nf (diálogo)
discussion; (riña) argument

discutir [disku'tir] vt (debatir) to discuss;
(pelear) to argue about; (contradecir) to
argue against ♦ vi (debatir) to discuss;
(pelearse) to argue

disecar [dise'kar] vt (conservar: animal) to
stuff; (: planta) to dry

diseminar [disemi'nar] vt to disseminate,
spread

diseñar [dise'nar] vt, vi to design

diseño [di'seno] nm design

disfraz [dis'fraθ] nm (máscara) disguise;
(excusa) pretext; **~ar** vt to disguise; **~arse** vr:
~arse de to disguise o.s. as

disfrutar [disfru'tar] vt to enjoy ♦ vi to enjoy
o.s.; **~ de** to enjoy, possess

disgregarse [disɣre'varse] vr (muchedumbre)
to disperse

disgustar [disɣus'tar] vt (no gustar) to
displease; (contrariar, enojar) to annoy, upset;
~se vr (enfadarse) to get upset; (dos
personas) to fall out

disgusto [dis'ɣusto] nm (contrariedad)
annoyance; (tristeza) grief; (riña) quarrel

disidente [disi'ðente] nm dissident

disimular [disimu'lar] vt (ocultar) to hide,
conceal ♦ vi to dissemble

disipar [disi'par] vt to dispel; (fortuna) to
squander; **~se** vr (nubes) to vanish;
(indisciplinarse) to dissipate

dislocarse [dislo'karse] vr (articulación) to
sprain, dislocate

disminución [disminu'θjon] nf decrease,
reduction

disminuido, a [disminu'iðo, a] nm/f:
~ mental/físico mentally/physically
handicapped person

disminuir [disminu'ir] vt to decrease,
diminish

disociarse [diso'θjarse] vr: **~ (de)** to
dissociate o.s. (from)

disolver [disol'ßer] vt (gen) to dissolve; **~se**
vr to dissolve; (COM) to go into liquidation

dispar [dis'par] adj different

disparar [dispa'rar] vt, vi to shoot, fire

disparate [dispa'rate] nm (tontería) foolish
remark; (error) blunder; **decir ~s** to talk
nonsense

disparo [dis'paro] nm shot

dispensar [dispen'sar] vt to dispense;
(disculpar) to excuse

dispersar [disper'sar] vt to disperse; **~se** vr to
scatter

disponer [dispo'ner] vt (arreglar) to arrange;
(ordenar) to put in order; (preparar) to
prepare, get ready ♦ vi: **~ de** to have, own;
~se vr: **~se a o para hacer** to prepare to do

disponible [dispo'nißle] adj available

disposición [disposi'θjon] nf arrangement,
disposition; (INFORM) layout; **a la ~ de** at the
disposal of; **~ de ánimo** state of mind

dispositivo [disposi'tißo] nm device,
mechanism

dispuesto, a [dis'pwesto, a] pp de **disponer**
♦ adj (arreglado) arranged; (preparado)
disposed

disputar [dispu'tar] vt (carrera) to compete
in

disquete [dis'kete] nm floppy disk, diskette

distancia [dis'tanθja] nf distance

distanciar [distan'θjar] vt to space out; **~se**
vr to become estranged

distante [dis'tante] adj distant

distar [dis'tar] vi: **dista 5km de aquí** it is 5km
from here

diste vb ver **dar**

disteis ['disteis] vb ver **dar**

distensión [disten'sjon] nf (en las relaciones)
relaxation; (POL) détente; (muscular) strain

distinción [distin'θjon] nf distinction;
(elegancia) elegance; (honor) honour

distinguido, a [distin'giðo, a] adj
distinguished

distinguir [distin'gir] vt to distinguish;
(escoger) to single out; **~se** vr to be
distinguished

distintivo [distin'tißo] nm badge; (fig)
characteristic

distinto, a [dis'tinto, a] adj different; (claro)
clear

distracción [distrak'θjon] nf distraction;
(pasatiempo) hobby, pastime; (olvido)
absent-mindedness, distraction

distraer [distra'er] vt (atención) to distract;
(divertir) to amuse; (fondos) to embezzle; **~se**
vr (entretenerse) to amuse o.s.; (perder la
concentración) to allow one's attention to
wander

distraído, a [distra'iðo, a] adj (gen) absent-
minded; (entretenido) amusing

distribuidor, a [distrißui'ðor, a] nm/f
distributor; **distribuidora** nf (COM) dealer,
agent; (CINE) distributor

distribuir [distrißui'ir] vt to distribute

distrito [dis'trito] *nm* (*sector, territorio*) region; (*barrio*) district

disturbio [dis'turßjo] *nm* disturbance; (*desorden*) riot

disuadir [diswa'ðir] *vt* to dissuade

disuelto [di'swelto] *pp de* **disolver**

disyuntiva [disjun'tißa] *nf* dilemma

DIU *nm abr* (= *dispositivo intrauterino*) IUD

diurno, a ['djurno, a] *adj* day *cpd*

divagar [dißa'ɣar] *vi* (*desviarse*) to digress

diván [di'ßan] *nm* divan

divergencia [dißer'xenθja] *nf* divergence

diversidad [dißersi'ðað] *nf* diversity, variety

diversificar [dißersifi'kar] *vt* to diversify

diversión [dißer'sjon] *nf* (*gen*) entertainment; (*actividad*) hobby, pastime

diverso, a [di'ßerso, a] *adj* diverse; ~s **libros** several books; ~s *nmpl* sundries

divertido, a [dißer'tiðo, a] *adj* (*chiste*) amusing; (*fiesta etc*) enjoyable

divertir [dißer'tir] *vt* (*entretener, recrear*) to amuse; ~**se** *vr* (*pasarlo bien*) to have a good time; (*distraerse*) to amuse o.s.

dividendos [dißi'ðendos] *nmpl* (COM) dividends

dividir [dißi'ðir] *vt* (*gen*) to divide; (*distribuir*) to distribute, share out

divierta *etc vb ver* **divertir**

divino, a [di'ßino, a] *adj* divine

divirtiendo *etc vb ver* **divertir**

divisa [di'ßisa] *nf* (*emblema*) emblem, badge; ~s *nfpl* foreign exchange *sg*

divisar [dißi'sar] *vt* to make out, distinguish

división [dißi'sjon] *nf* (*gen*) division; (*de partido*) split; (*de país*) partition

divorciar [dißor'θjar] *vt* to divorce; ~**se** *vr* to get divorced; **divorcio** *nm* divorce

divulgar [dißul'ɣar] *vt* (*ideas*) to spread; (*secreto*) to divulge

DNI (ESP) *nm abr* (= *Documento Nacional de Identidad*) national identity card

Dña. *abr* (= *doña*) Mrs

do [do] *nm* (MUS) do, C

dobladillo [doßla'ðiʎo] *nm* (*de vestido*) hem; (*de pantalón: vuelta*) turn-up (BRIT), cuff (US)

doblar [do'ßlar] *vt* to double; (*papel*) to fold; (*caño*) to bend; (*la esquina*) to turn, go round; (*film*) to dub ♦ *vi* to turn; (*campana*) to toll; ~**se** *vr* (*plegarse*) to fold (up), crease; (*encorvarse*) to bend

doble ['doßle] *adj* double; (*de dos aspectos*) dual; (*fig*) two-faced ♦ *nm* double ♦ *nm/f* (TEATRO) double, stand-in; ~s *nmpl* (DEPORTE) doubles *sg*; **con sentido** ~ with a double meaning

doblegar [doßle'ɣar] *vt* to fold, crease; ~**se** *vr* to yield

doblez [do'ßleθ] *nm* fold, hem ♦ *nf* insincerity, duplicity

doce ['doθe] *num* twelve; ~**na** *nf* dozen

docente [do'θente] *adj*: **centro/personal** ~ teaching establishment/staff

dócil ['doθil] *adj* (*pasivo*) docile; (*obediente*) obedient

docto, a ['dokto, a] *adj*: ~ **en** instructed in

doctor, a [dok'tor, a] *nm/f* doctor

doctorado [dokto'raðo] *nm* doctorate

doctrina [dok'trina] *nf* doctrine, teaching

documentación [dokumenta'θjon] *nf* documentation, papers *pl*

documental [dokumen'tal] *adj, nm* documentary

documento [doku'mento] *nm* (*certificado*) document; ~ **national de identidad** identity card

dólar ['dolar] *nm* dollar

doler [do'ler] *vt, vi* to hurt; (*fig*) to grieve; ~**se** *vr* (*de su situación*) to grieve, feel sorry; (*de las desgracias ajenas*) to sympathize; **me duele el brazo** my arm hurts

dolor [do'lor] *nm* pain; (*fig*) grief, sorrow; ~ **de cabeza** headache; ~ **de estómago** stomachache

domar [do'mar] *vt* to tame

domesticar [domesti'kar] *vt* = **domar**

doméstico, a [do'mestiko, a] *adj* (*vida, servicio*) home; (*tareas*) household; (*animal*) tame, pet

domiciliación [domiθilia'θjon] *nf*: ~ **de pagos** (COM) standing order

domicilio [domi'θiljo] *nm* home; ~ **particular** private residence; ~ **social** (COM) head office; **sin** ~ **fijo** of no fixed abode

dominante [domi'nante] *adj* dominant; (*persona*) domineering

dominar [domi'nar] *vt* (*gen*) to dominate; (*idiomas*) to be fluent in ♦ *vi* to dominate, prevail; ~**se** *vr* to control o.s.

domingo [do'mingo] *nm* Sunday

dominio [do'minjo] *nm* (*tierras*) domain; (*autoridad*) power, authority; (*de las pasiones*) grip, hold; (*de idiomas*) command

don [don] *nm* (*talento*) gift; ~ **Juan Gómez** Mr Juan Gómez, Juan Gómez Esq (BRIT)

donaire [do'naire] *nm* charm

donar [do'nar] *vt* to donate

donativo [dona'tißo] *nm* donation

doncella [don'θeʎa] *nf* (*criada*) maid

donde ['donde] *adv* where ♦ *prep*: **el coche está allí** ~ **el farol** the car is over there by the lamppost o where the lamppost is; **en** ~ where, in which

dónde ['donde] *adv interrogativo* where?; ¿**a** ~ **vas?** where are you going (to)?; ¿**de** ~ **vienes?** where have you been?; ¿**por** ~? where?, whereabouts?

dondequiera [donde'kjera] *adv* anywhere; **por** ~ everywhere, all over the place ♦ *conj*:

~ **que** wherever

doña |'doɲa| *nf:* ~ **Alicia** Alicia; ~ **Victoria Benito** Mrs Victoria Benito

dorado, a |do'raðo, a| *adj (color)* golden; *(TEC)* gilt

dormir |dor'mir| *vt:* ~ **la siesta** to have an afternoon nap ♦ *vi* to sleep; ~**se** *vr* to fall asleep

dormitar |dormi'tar| *vi* to doze

dormitorio |dormi'torjo| *nm* bedroom; ~ **común** dormitory

dorsal |dor'sal| *nm (DEPORTE)* number

dorso |'dorso| *nm (de mano)* back; *(de hoja)* other side

dos |dos| *num* two

dosis |'dosis| *nf inv* dose, dosage

dotado, a |do'taðo, a| *adj* gifted; ~ **de** endowed with

dotar |do'tar| *vt* to endow; **dote** *nf* dowry; **dotes** *nfpl (talentos)* gifts

doy *vb ver* **dar**

dragar |dra'var| *vt (río)* to dredge; *(minas)* to sweep

drama |'drama| *nm* drama

dramaturgo |drama'turxo| *nm* dramatist, playwright

drástico, a |'drastiko, a| *adj* drastic

drenaje |dre'naxe| *nm* drainage

droga |'droɣa| *nf* drug

drogadicto, a |droɣa'ðikto, a| *nm/f* drug addict

droguería |droɣe'ria| *nf* hardware shop *(BRIT)* o store *(US)*

ducha |'dutʃa| *nf (baño)* shower; *(MED)* douche; **ducharse** *vr* to take a shower

duda |'duða| *nf* doubt; **dudar** *vt, vi* to doubt; **dudoso, a** |du'ðoso, a| *adj (incierto)* hesitant; *(sospechoso)* doubtful

duela *etc vb ver* **doler**

duelo |'dwelo| *vb ver* **doler** ♦ *nm (combate)* duel; *(luto)* mourning

duende |'dwende| *nm* imp, goblin

dueño, a |'dweɲo, a| *nm/f (propietario)* owner; *(de pensión, taberna)* landlord/lady; *(empresario)* employer

duermo *etc vb ver* **dormir**

dulce |'dulθe| *adj* sweet ♦ *adv* gently, softly ♦ *nm* sweet

dulzura |dul'θura| *nf* sweetness; *(ternura)* gentleness

duna |'duna| *nf (GEO)* dune

dúo |'duo| *nm* duet

duplicar |dupli'kar| *vt (hacer el doble de)* to duplicate; ~**se** *vr* to double

duque |'duke| *nm* duke; ~**sa** *nf* duchess

duración |dura'θjon| *nf (de película, disco etc)* length; *(de pila etc)* life; *(curso: de acontecimientos etc)* duration

duradero, a |dura'ðero, a| *adj (tela etc)* hard-wearing; *(fe, paz)* lasting

durante |du'rante| *prep* during

durar |du'rar| *vi* to last; *(recuerdo)* to remain

durazno |du'raθno| *(AM) nm (fruta)* peach; *(árbol)* peach tree

durex |'dureks| *(AM) nm (tira adhesiva)* Sellotape ® *(BRIT)*, Scotch tape ® *(US)*

dureza |du'reθa| *nf (calidad)* hardness

duro, a |'duro, a| *adj* hard; *(carácter)* tough ♦ *adv* hard ♦ *nm (moneda)* five peseta coin o piece

DVD *nm abr (= disco de vídeo digital)* DVD

E, e

E *abr (= este)* E

e |e| *conj* and

ebanista |eßa'nista| *nm/f* cabinetmaker

ébano |'eßano| *nm* ebony

ebrio, a |'eßrjo, a| *adj* drunk

ebullición |eßuʎi'θjon| *nf* boiling

eccema |ek'θema| *nf (MED)* eczema

echar |e'tʃar| *vt* to throw; *(agua, vino)* to pour (out); *(empleado: despedir)* to fire, sack; *(hojas)* to sprout; *(cartas)* to post; *(humo)* to emit, give out ♦ *vi:* ~ **a correr/llorar** to run off/burst into tears; ~**se** *vr* to lie down; ~ **llave a** to lock (up); ~ **abajo** *(gobierno)* to overthrow; *(edificio)* to demolish; ~ **mano a** to lay hands on; ~ **una mano a uno** *(ayudar)* to give sb a hand; ~ **de menos** to miss

eclesiástico, a |ekle'sjastiko, a| *adj* ecclesiastical

eclipse |e'klipse| *nm* eclipse

eco |'eko| *nm* echo; **tener** ~ to catch on

ecología |ekolo'via| *nf* ecology; **ecológico, a** *adj (producto, método)* environmentally-friendly; *(agricultura)* organic; **ecologista** *adj* ecological, environmental ♦ *nm/f* environmentalist

economato |ekono'mato| *nm* cooperative store

economía |ekono'mia| *nf (sistema)* economy; *(carrera)* economics

económico, a |eko'nomiko, a| *adj (barato)* cheap, economical; *(ahorrativo)* thrifty; *(COM: año etc)* financial; *(: situación)* economic

economista |ekono'mista| *nm/f* economist

ECU |eku| *nm* ECU

ecuador |ekwa'ðor| *nm* equator; **(el) E~** Ecuador

ecuánime |e'kwanime| *adj (carácter)* level-headed; *(estado)* calm

ecuatoriano, a |ekwato'rjano, a| *adj, nm/f* Ecuadorian

ecuestre |e'kwestre| *adj* equestrian

eczema |ek'θema| *nm* = **eccema**

edad |e'ðað| *nf* age; **¿qué ~ tienes?** how old

are you?; **tiene ocho años de ~** he is eight (years old); **de ~ mediana/avanzada** middle-aged/advanced in years; **la E~ Media** the Middle Ages

edición [eði'θjon] *nf* (*acto*) publication; (*ejemplar*) edition

edificar [eðifi'kar] *vt, vi* to build

edificio [eði'fiθjo] *nm* building; (*fig*) edifice, structure

Edimburgo [eðim'burɣo] *nm* Edinburgh

editar [eði'tar] *vt* (*publicar*) to publish; (*preparar textos*) to edit

editor, a [eði'tor, a] *nm/f* (*que publica*) publisher; (*redactor*) editor ♦ *adj*: **casa ~a** publishing house, publisher; **~ial** *adj* editorial ♦ *nm* leading article, editorial; **casa ~ial** publishing house, publisher

edredón [eðre'ðon] *nm* duvet

educación [eðuka'θjon] *nf* education; (*crianza*) upbringing; (*modales*) (good) manners *pl*

educado, a [eðu'kaðo, a] *adj*: **bien/mal ~** well/badly behaved

educar [eðu'kar] *vt* to educate; (*criar*) to bring up; (*voz*) to train

EE. UU. *nmpl abr* (= *Estados Unidos*) US(A)

efectista [efek'tista] *adj* sensationalist

efectivamente [efectiβa'mente] *adv* (*como respuesta*) exactly, precisely; (*verdaderamente*) really; (*de hecho*) in fact

efectivo, a [efek'tiβo, a] *adj* effective; (*real*) actual, real ♦ *nm*: **pagar en ~** to pay (in) cash; **hacer ~ un cheque** to cash a cheque

efecto [e'fekto] *nm* effect, result; **~s** *nmpl* (~*s personales*) effects; (*bienes*) goods; (*COM*) assets; **en ~** in fact; (*respuesta*) exactly, indeed; **~ 2000** millennium bug; **~ invernadero** greenhouse effect

efectuar [efek'twar] *vt* to carry out; (*viaje*) to make

eficacia [efi'kaθja] *nf* (*de persona*) efficiency; (*de medicamento etc*) effectiveness

eficaz [efi'kaθ] *adj* (*persona*) efficient; (*acción*) effective

eficiente [efi'θjente] *adj* efficient

efusivo, a [efu'siβo, a] *adj* effusive; **mis más efusivas gracias** my warmest thanks

EGB (*ESP*) *nf abr* (*ESCOL*) = *Educación General Básica*

egipcio, a [e'xipθjo, a] *adj, nm/f* Egyptian

Egipto [e'xipto] *nm* Egypt

egoísmo [evo'ismo] *nm* egoism

egoísta [evo'ista] *adj* egoistical, selfish ♦ *nm/f* egoist

egregio, a [e'vrexjo, a] *adj* eminent, distinguished

Eire ['eire] *nm* Eire

ej. *abr* (= *ejemplo*) eg

eje ['exe] *nm* (*GEO, MAT*) axis; (*de rueda*) axle;

(*de máquina*) shaft, spindle

ejecución [exeku'θjon] *nf* execution; (*cumplimiento*) fulfilment; (*MUS*) performance; (*JUR*: *embargo de deudor*) attachment

ejecutar [exeku'tar] *vt* to execute, carry out; (*matar*) to execute; (*cumplir*) to fulfil; (*MUS*) to perform; (*JUR*: *embargar*) to attach, distrain (on)

ejecutivo, a [exeku'tiβo, a] *adj* executive; **el (poder) ~** the executive (power)

ejemplar [exem'plar] *adj* exemplary ♦ *nm* example; (*ZOOL*) specimen; (*de libro*) copy; (*de periódico*) number, issue

ejemplo [e'xemplo] *nm* example; **por ~** for example

ejercer [exer'θer] *vt* to exercise; (*influencia*) to exert; (*un oficio*) to practise ♦ *vi* (*practicar*): **~ (de)** to practise (as)

ejercicio [exer'θiθjo] *nm* exercise; (*período*) tenure; **~ comercial** financial year

ejército [e'xerθito] *nm* army; **entrar en el ~** to join the army, join up

ejote [e'xote] (*AM*) *nm* green bean

PALABRA CLAVE

el [el] (*f* **la**, *pl* **los, las**, *neutro* **lo**) *art def* **1** the; **el libro/la mesa/los estudiantes** the book/table/students

2 (*con n abstracto: no se traduce*): **el amor/la juventud** love/youth

3 (*posesión: se traduce a menudo por adj posesivo*): **romperse el brazo** to break one's arm; **levantó la mano** he put his hand up; **se puso el sombrero** she put her hat on

4 (*valor descriptivo*): **tener la boca grande/los ojos azules** to have a big mouth/blue eyes

5 (*con días*) on; **me iré el viernes** I'll leave on Friday; **los domingos suelo ir a nadar** on Sundays I generally go swimming

6 (*lo + adj*): **lo difícil/caro** what is difficult/expensive; (= *cuán*): **no se da cuenta de lo pesado que es** he doesn't realise how boring he is

♦ *pron demos* **1**: **mi libro y el de usted** my book and yours; **los de Pepe son mejores** Pepe's are better; **no la(s) blanca(s) sino la(s) gris(es)** not the white one(s) but the grey one(s)

2: **lo de**: **lo de ayer** what happened yesterday; **lo de las facturas** that business about the invoices

♦ *pron relativo*: **el que** *etc* **1** (*indef*): **el (los) que quiera(n) que se vaya(n)** anyone who wants to can leave; **llévese el que más le guste** take the one you like best

2 (*def*): **el que compré ayer** the one I bought yesterday; **los que se van** those who leave

3: **lo que**: **lo que pienso yo/más me gusta**

what I think/like most

♦ *conj*: **el que: el que lo diga** the fact that he says so; **el que sea tan vago me molesta** his being so lazy bothers me

♦ *excl*: **¡el susto que me diste!** what a fright you gave me!

♦ *pron personal* **1** (*persona: m*) him; (: *f*) her; (: *pl*) them; **lo/las veo** I can see him/them **2** (*animal, cosa: sg*) it; (: *pl*) them; **lo** (*o* **la**) **veo** I can see it; **los** (*o* **las**) **veo** I can see them

3: lo (*como sustituto de frase*): **no lo sabía** I didn't know; **ya lo entiendo** I understand now

él [el] *pron* (*persona*) he; (*cosa*) it; (*después de prep: persona*) him; (: *cosa*) it; **de ~** his

elaborar [elaβo'rar] *vt* (*producto*) to make, manufacture; (*preparar*) to prepare; (*madera, metal etc*) to work; (*proyecto etc*) to work on *o* out

elasticidad [elastiθi'ðað] *nf* elasticity

elástico, a [e'lastiko, a] *adj* elastic; (*flexible*) flexible ♦ *nm* elastic; (*un ~*) elastic band

elección [elek'θjon] *nf* election; (*selección*) choice, selection

electorado [elekto'raðo] *nm* electorate, voters *pl*

electricidad [elektriθi'ðað] *nf* electricity

electricista [elektri'θista] *nm/f* electrician

eléctrico, a [e'lektriko, a] *adj* electric

electro... [elektro] *prefijo* electro...; **~cardiograma** *nm* electrocardiogram; **~cutar** *vt* to electrocute; **~do** *nm* electrode; **~domésticos** *nmpl* (*electrical*) household appliances; **~magnético, a** *adj* electromagnetic

electrónica [elek'tronika] *nf* electronics *sg*

electrónico, a [elek'troniko, a] *adj* electronic

elefante [ele'fante] *nm* elephant

elegancia [ele'ɣanθja] *nf* elegance, grace; (*estilo*) stylishness

elegante [ele'sante] *adj* elegant, graceful; (*estiloso*) stylish, fashionable

elegir [ele'xir] *vt* (*escoger*) to choose, select; (*optar*) to opt for; (*presidente*) to elect

elemental [elemen'tal] *adj* (*claro, obvio*) elementary; (*fundamental*) elemental, fundamental

elemento [ele'mento] *nm* element; (*fig*) ingredient; **~s** *nmpl* elements, rudiments

elepé [ele'pe] (*pl*: **elepés**) *nm* L.P.

elevación [eleβa'θjon] *nf* elevation; (*acto*) raising, lifting; (*de precios*) rise; (*GEO etc*) height, altitude

elevar [ele'βar] *vt* to raise, lift (up); (*precio*) to put up; **~se** *vr* (*edificio*) to rise; (*precios*) to go up

eligiendo *etc vb ver* **elegir**

elija *etc vb ver* **elegir**

eliminar [elimi'nar] *vt* to eliminate, remove

eliminatoria [elimina'torja] *nf* heat, preliminary (round)

elite [e'lite] *nf* elite

ella ['eʎa] *pron* (*persona*) she; (*cosa*) it; (*después de prep: persona*) her; (: *cosa*) it; **de ~ hers**

ellas ['eʎas] *pron* (*personas y cosas*) they; (*después de prep*) them; **de ~ theirs**

ello ['eʎo] *pron* it

ellos ['eʎos] *pron* they; (*después de prep*) them; **de ~ theirs**

elocuencia [elo'kwenθja] *nf* eloquence

elogiar [elo'xjar] *vt* to praise; **elogio** *nm* praise

elote [e'lote] (*AM*) *nm* corn on the cob

eludir [elu'ðir] *vt* to avoid

emanar [ema'nar] *vi*: **~ de** to emanate from, come from; (*derivar de*) to originate in

emancipar [emanθi'par] *vt* to emancipate; **~se** *vr* to become emancipated, free o.s.

embadurnar [embaður'nar] *vt* to smear

embajada [emba'xaða] *nf* embassy

embajador, a [embaxa'ðor, a] *nm/f* ambassador/ambassadress

embalaje [emba'laxe] *nm* packing

embalar [emba'lar] *vt* to parcel, wrap (up); **~se** *vr* to go fast

embalsamar [embalsa'mar] *vt* to embalm

embalse [em'balse] *nm* (*presa*) dam; (*lago*) reservoir

embarazada [embara'θaða] *adj* pregnant ♦ *nf* pregnant woman

embarazo [emba'raθo] *nm* (*de mujer*) pregnancy; (*impedimento*) obstacle, obstruction; (*timidez*) embarrassment;

embarazoso, a *adj* awkward, embarrassing

embarcación [embarka'θjon] *nf* (*barco*) boat, craft; (*acto*) embarkation, boarding

embarcadero [embarka'ðero] *nm* pier, landing stage

embarcar [embar'kar] *vt* (*cargamento*) to ship, stow; (*persona*) to embark, put on board; **~se** *vr* to embark, go on board

embargar [embar'ɣar] *vt* (*JUR*) to seize, impound

embargo [em'barɣo] *nm* (*JUR*) seizure; (*COM, POL*) embargo

embargue [em'barɣe] *etc vb ver* **embargar**

embarque *etc* [em'barke] *vb ver* **embarcar** ♦ *nm* shipment, loading

embaucar [embau'kar] *vt* to trick, fool

embeber [embe'βer] *vt* (*absorber*) to absorb, soak up; (*empapar*) to saturate ♦ *vi* to shrink; **~se** *vr*: **~se en un libro** to be engrossed *o* absorbed in a book

embellecer [embeʎe'θer] *vt* to embellish, beautify

embestida [embes'tiða] nf attack, onslaught; (carga) charge

embestir [embes'tir] vt to attack, assault; to charge, attack ♦ vi to attack

emblema [em'blema] nm emblem

embobado, a [embo'βaðo, a] adj (atontado) stunned, bewildered

embolia [em'bolja] nf (MED) clot

émbolo ['embolo] nm (AUTO) piston

embolsar [embol'sar] vt to pocket, put in one's pocket

emborrachar [emborra'tʃar] vt to make drunk, intoxicate; ~se vr to get drunk

emboscada [embos'kaða] nf ambush

embotar [embo'tar] vt to blunt, dull; ~se vr (adormecerse) to go numb

embotellamiento [emboteʎa'mjento] nm (AUTO) traffic jam

embotellar [embote'ʎar] vt to bottle

embrague [em'braɣe] nm (tb: pedal de ~) clutch

embriagar [embrja'βar] vt (emborrachar) to make drunk; ~se vr (emborracharse) to get drunk

embrión [em'brjon] nm embryo

embrollar [embro'ʎar] vt (el asunto) to confuse, complicate; (implicar) to involve, embroil; ~se vr (confundirse) to get into a muddle o mess

embrollo [em'broʎo] nm (enredo) muddle, confusion; (aprieto) fix, jam

embrujado, a [embru'xaðo, a] adj bewitched; **casa embrujada** haunted house

embrutecer [embrute'θer] vt (atontar) to stupefy; ~se vr to be stupefied

embudo [em'buðo] nm funnel

embuste [em'buste] nm (mentira) lie; ~ro, a adj lying, deceitful ♦ nm/f (mentiroso) liar

embutido [embu'tiðo] nm (CULIN) sausage; (TEC) inlay

emergencia [emer'xenθja] nf emergency; (surgimiento) emergence

emerger [emer'xer] vi to emerge, appear

emigración [emiɣra'θjon] nf emigration; (de pájaros) migration

emigrar [emi'ɣrar] vi (personas) to emigrate; (pájaros) to migrate

eminencia [emi'nenθja] nf eminence; **eminente** adj eminent, distinguished; (elevado) high

emisario [emi'sarjo] nm emissary

emisión [emi'sjon] nf (acto) emission; (COM etc) issue; (RADIO, TV: acto) broadcasting; (: programa) broadcast, programme (BRIT), program (US)

emisora [emi'sora] nf radio o broadcasting station

emitir [emi'tir] vt (olor etc) to emit, give off; (moneda etc) to issue; (opinión) to express; (RADIO) to broadcast

emoción [emo'θjon] nf emotion; (excitación) excitement; (sentimiento) feeling

emocionante [emoθjo'nante] adj (excitante) exciting, thrilling

emocionar [emoθjo'nar] vt (excitar) to excite, thrill; (conmover) to move, touch; (impresionar) to impress

emotivo, a [emo'tiβo, a] adj emotional

empacar [empa'kar] vt (gen) to pack; (en caja) to bale, crate

empacho [em'patʃo] nm (MED) indigestion; (fig) embarrassment

empadronarse [empaðro'narse] vr (POL: como elector) to register

empalagoso, a [empala'ɣoso, a] adj cloying, (fig) tiresome

empalmar [empal'mar] vt to join, connect ♦ vi (dos caminos) to meet, join; **empalme** nm joint, connection; junction; (de trenes) connection

empanada [empa'naða] nf pie, pasty

empantanarse [empanta'narse] vr to get swamped; (fig) to get bogged down

empañarse [empa'ɲarse] vr (cristales etc) to steam up

empapar [empa'par] vt (mojar) to soak, saturate; (absorber) to soak up, absorb; ~se vr: ~se de to soak up

empapelar [empape'lar] vt (paredes) to paper

empaquetar [empake'tar] vt to pack, parcel up

empastar [empas'tar] vt (embadurnar) to paste; (diente) to fill

empaste [em'paste] nm (de diente) filling

empatar [empa'tar] vi to draw, tie; **empate** nm draw, tie

empecé etc vb ver **empezar**

empedernido, a [empeðer'niðo, a] adj hard, heartless; (fumador) inveterate

empedrado, a [empe'ðraðo, a] adj paved ♦ nm paving

empeine [em'peine] nm (de pie, zapato) instep

empellón [empe'ʎon] nm push, shove

empeñado, a [empe'ɲaðo, a] adj (persona) determined; (objeto) pawned

empeñar [empe'ɲar] vt (objeto) to pawn, pledge; (persona) to compel; ~se vr (endeudarse) to get into debt; ~se en to be set on, be determined to

empeño [em'peɲo] nm (determinación, insistencia) determination, insistence; **casa de ~s** pawnshop

empeorar [empeo'rar] vt to make worse, worsen ♦ vi to get worse, deteriorate

empequeñecer [empekeɲe'θer] vt to dwarf; (minusvalorar) to belittle

emperador [empera'ðor] nm emperor;
emperatriz nf empress
empezar [empe'θar] vt, vi to begin, start
empiece etc vb ver **empezar**
empiezo etc vb ver **empezar**
empinar [empi'nar] vt to raise; **~se** vr
(persona) to stand on tiptoe; (animal) to rear
up; (camino) to climb steeply
empírico, a [em'piriko, a] adj empirical
emplasto [em'plasto] nm (MED) plaster
emplazamiento [emplaθa'mjento] nm site,
location; (JUR) summons sg
emplazar [empla'θar] vt (ubicar) to site,
place, locate; (JUR) to summons; (convocar)
to summon
empleado, a [emple'aðo, a] nm/f (gen)
employee; (de banco etc) clerk
emplear [emple'ar] vt (usar) to use, employ;
(dar trabajo a) to employ; **~se** vr (conseguir
trabajo) to be employed; (ocuparse) to
occupy o.s.
empleo [em'pleo] nm (puesto) job; (puestos:
colectivamente) employment; (uso) use,
employment
empobrecer [empoβre'θer] vt to
impoverish; **~se** vr to become poor o
impoverished
empollar [empo'ʎar] (fam) vt, vi to swot
(up); **empollón, ona** (fam) nm/f swot
emporio [em'porjo] nm (AM: gran almacén)
department store
empotrado, a [empo'traðo, a] adj (armario
etc) built-in
emprender [empren'der] vt (empezar) to
begin, embark on; (acometer) to tackle, take
on
empresa [em'presa] nf (de espíritu etc)
enterprise; (COM) company, firm; **~rio, a**
nm/f (COM) businessman/woman
empréstito [em'prestito] nm (public) loan
empujar [empu'xar] vt to push, shove
empujón [empu'xon] nm push, shove
empuñar [empu'nar] vt (asir) to grasp, take
(firm) hold of
emular [emu'lar] vt to emulate; (rivalizar) to
rival

PALABRA CLAVE

---

en [en] prep **1** (posición) in; (: sobre) on; **está
~ el cajón** it's in the drawer; **~ Argentina/La
Paz** in Argentina/La Paz; **~ la oficina/el
colegio** at the office/school; **está ~ el suelo/
quinto piso** it's on the floor/the fifth floor
2 (dirección) into; **entró ~ el aula** she went
into the classroom; **meter algo ~ el bolso** to
put sth into one's bag
3 (tiempo) in; on; **~ 1605/3 semanas/invierno**
in 1605/3 weeks/winter; **~ (el mes de) enero**
in (the month of) January; **~ aquella**

ocasión/época on that occasion/at that time
4 (precio) for; **lo vendió ~ 20 dólares** he sold
it for 20 dollars
5 (diferencia) by; **reducir/aumentar ~ una
tercera parte/un 20 por ciento** to reduce/
increase by a third/20 per cent
6 (manera): **~ avión/autobús** by plane/bus;
escrito ~ inglés written in English
7 (después de vb que indica gastar etc) on;
han cobrado demasiado ~ dietas they've
charged too much to expenses; **se le va la
mitad del sueldo ~ comida** he spends half his
salary on food
8 (tema, ocupación): **experto ~ la materia**
expert on the subject; **trabaja ~ la
construcción** he works in the building
industry
9 (adj + en + infin): **lento ~ reaccionar** slow
to react

---

enaguas [e'naɣwas] nfpl petticoat sg,
underskirt sg
enajenación [enaxena'θjon] nf: **~ mental**
mental derangement
enajenar [enaxe'nar] vt (volver loco) to drive
mad
enamorado, a [enamo'raðo, a] adj in love
♦ nm/f lover
enamorar [enamo'rar] vt to win the love of;
~se vr: **~se de alguien** to fall in love with sb
enano, a [e'nano, a] adj tiny ♦ nm/f dwarf
enardecer [enarðe'θer] vt (pasiones) to fire,
inflame; (persona) to fill with enthusiasm; **~se**
vr: **~se por** to get excited about; (entusiasmarse) to get enthusiastic about
encabezamiento [enkaβeθa'mjento] nm
(de carta) heading; (de periódico) headline
encabezar [enkaβe'θar] vt (movimiento,
revolución) to lead, head; (lista) to head, be
at the top of; (carta) to put a heading to
encadenar [enkaðe'nar] vt to chain
(together); (poner grilletes a) to shackle
encajar [enka'xar] vt (ajustar): **~ (en)** to fit
(into); (fam: golpe) to take ♦ vi to fit (well);
(fig: corresponder a) to match; **~se** vr: **~se en
un sillón** to squeeze into a chair
encaje [en'kaxe] nm (labor) lace
encalar [enka'lar] vt (pared) to whitewash
encallar [enka'ʎar] vi (NAUT) to run aground
encaminar [enkami'nar] vt to direct, send;
~se vr: **~se a** to set out for
encantado, a [enkan'taðo, a] adj
(hechizado) bewitched; (muy contento)
delighted; **¡~!** how do you do, pleased to
meet you
encantador, a [enkanta'ðor, a] adj
charming, lovely ♦ nm/f magician,
enchanter/enchantress
encantar [enkan'tar] vt (agradar) to charm,

delight; (*hechizar*) to bewitch, cast a spell on; **me encanta eso** I love that; **encanto** *nm* (*hechizo*) spell, charm; (*fig*) charm, delight

encarcelar [enkarθe'lar] *vt* to imprison, jail

encarecer [enkare'θer] *vt* to put up the price of; **~se** *vr* to get dearer

encarecimiento [enkareθi'mjento] *nm* price increase

encargado, a [enkar'γaðo, a] *adj* in charge ♦ *nm/f* agent, representative; (*responsable*) person in charge

encargar [enkar'γar] *vt* to entrust; (*recomendar*) to urge, recommend; **~se** *vr*: **~se de** to look after, take charge of

encargo [en'karγo] *nm* (*tarea*) assignment, job; (*responsabilidad*) responsibility; (*COM*) order

encariñarse [enkari'narse] *vr*: **~ con** to grow fond of, get attached to

encarnación [enkarna'θjon] *nf* incarnation, embodiment

encarnizado, a [enkarni'θaðo, a] *adj* (*lucha*) bloody, fierce

encarrilar [enkarri'lar] *vt* (*tren*) to put back on the rails; (*fig*) to correct, put on the right track

encasillar [enkasi'ʎar] *vt* (*tb fig*) to pigeonhole; (*actor*) to typecast

encauzar [enkau'θar] *vt* to channel

encendedor [enθende'ðor] *nm* lighter

encender [enθen'der] *vt* (*con fuego*) to light; (*luz, radio*) to put on, switch on; (*avivar: pasiones*) to inflame; **~se** *vr* to catch fire; (*excitarse*) to get excited; (*de cólera*) to flare up; (*el rostro*) to blush

encendido [enθen'diðo] *nm* (*AUTO*) ignition

encerado [enθe'raðo] *nm* (*ESCOL*) blackboard

encerar [enθe'rar] *vt* (*suelo*) to wax, polish

encerrar [enθe'rrar] *vt* (*confinar*) to shut in, shut up; (*comprender, incluir*) to include, contain

encharcado, a [entʃar'kaðo, a] *adj* (*terreno*) flooded

encharcarse [entʃar'karse] *vr* to get flooded

enchufado, a [entʃu'faðo, a] (*fam*) *nm/f* well-connected person

enchufar [entʃu'far] *vt* (*ELEC*) to plug in; (*TEC*) to connect, fit together; **enchufe** *nm* (*ELEC: clavija*) plug; (: *toma*) socket; (*de dos tubos*) joint, connection; (*fam: influencia*) contact, connection; (: *puesto*) cushy job

encía [en'θia] *nf* gum

encienda *etc vb ver* **encender**

encierro *etc* [en'θjerro] *vb ver* **encerrar** ♦ *nm* shutting in, shutting up; (*calabozo*) prison

encima [en'θima] *adv* (*sobre*) above, over; (*además*) besides; **~ de** (*en*) on, on top of; (*sobre*) above, over; (*además de*) besides, on top of; **por ~ de** over; **¿llevas dinero ~?** have

you (got) any money on you?; **se me vino ~** it took me by surprise

encina [en'θina] *nf* holm oak

encinta [en'θinta] *adj* pregnant

enclenque [en'klenke] *adj* weak, sickly

encoger [enko'xer] *vt* to shrink, contract; **~se** *vr* to shrink, contract; (*fig*) to cringe; **~se de hombros** to shrug one's shoulders

encolar [enko'lar] *vt* (*engomar*) to glue, paste; (*pegar*) to stick down

encolerizar [enkoleri'θar] *vt* to anger, provoke; **~se** *vr* to get angry

encomendar [enkomen'dar] *vt* to entrust, commend; **~se** *vr*: **~se a** to put one's trust in

encomiar [enko'mjar] *vt* to praise, pay tribute to

encomienda *etc* [enko'mjenda] *vb ver* **encomendar** ♦ *nf* (*encargo*) charge, commission; (*elogio*) tribute; **~ postal** (*AM*) parcel post

encontrado, a [enkon'traðo, a] *adj* (*contrario*) contrary, conflicting

encontrar [enkon'trar] *vt* (*hallar*) to find; (*inesperadamente*) to meet, run into; **~se** *vr* to meet (each other); (*situarse*) to be (situated); **~se con** to meet; **~se bien (de salud)** to feel well

encrespar [enkres'par] *vt* (*cabellos*) to curl; (*fig*) to anger, irritate; **~se** *vr* (*el mar*) to get rough; (*fig*) to get cross, get irritated

encrucijada [enkruθi'xaða] *nf* crossroads *sg*

encuadernación [enkwaðerna'θjon] *nf* binding

encuadernador, a [enkwaðerna'ðor, a] *nm/f* bookbinder

encuadrar [enkwa'ðrar] *vt* (*retrato*) to frame; (*ajustar*) to fit, insert; (*contener*) to contain

encubrir [enku'ßrir] *vt* (*ocultar*) to hide, conceal; (*criminal*) to harbour, shelter

encuentro *etc* [en'kwentro] *vb ver* **encontrar** ♦ *nm* (*de personas*) meeting; (*AUTO etc*) collision, crash; (*DEPORTE*) match, game; (*MIL*) encounter

encuesta [en'kwesta] *nf* inquiry, investigation; (*sondeo*) (public) opinion poll; **~ judicial** post mortem

encumbrar [enkum'brar] *vt* (*persona*) to exalt

endeble [en'deßle] *adj* (*argumento, excusa, persona*) weak

endémico, a [en'demiko, a] *adj* (*MED*) endemic; (*fig*) rife, chronic

endemoniado, a [endemo'njaðo, a] *adj* possessed (of the devil); (*travieso*) devilish

enderezar [endere'θar] *vt* (*poner derecho*) to straighten (out); (: *verticalmente*) to set upright; (*situación*) to straighten o sort out; (*dirigir*) to direct; **~se** *vr* (*persona sentada*) to straighten up

endeudarse [endeuˈðarse] vr to get into debt

endiablado, a [endjaˈβlaðo, a] adj devilish, diabolical; (*travieso*) mischievous

endilgar [endilˈɣar] (*fam*) vt: **~le algo a uno** to lumber sb with sth; **~le un sermón a uno** to lecture sb

endiñar [endiˈɲar] (*fam*) vt (*bofetón*) to land, belt

endosar [endoˈsar] vt (*cheque etc*) to endorse

endulzar [endulˈθar] vt to sweeten; (*suavizar*) to soften

endurecer [endureˈθer] vt to harden; **~se** vr to harden, grow hard

enema [eˈnema] nm (*MED*) enema

enemigo, a [eneˈmixo, a] adj enemy, hostile ♦ nm/f enemy

enemistad [enemisˈtað] nf enmity

enemistar [enemisˈtar] vt to make enemies of, cause a rift between; **~se** vr to become enemies; (*amigos*) to fall out

energía [enerˈxia] nf (*vigor*) energy, drive; (*empuje*) push; (*TEC, ELEC*) energy, power; **~ eólica** wind power; **~ solar** solar energy/power

enérgico, a [eˈnerxiko, a] adj (*gen*) energetic; (*voz, modales*) forceful

energúmeno, a [enerˈxumeno, a] (*fam*) nm/f (*fig*) madman/woman

enero [eˈnero] nm January

enfadado, a [enfaˈðaðo, a] adj angry, annoyed

enfadar [enfaˈðar] vt to anger, annoy; **~se** vr to get angry o annoyed

enfado [enˈfaðo] nm (*enojo*) anger, annoyance; (*disgusto*) trouble, bother

énfasis [ˈenfasis] nm emphasis, stress

enfático, a [enˈfatiko, a] adj emphatic

enfermar [enferˈmar] vt to make ill ♦ vi to fall ill, be taken ill

enfermedad [enfermeˈðað] nf illness; **~ venérea** venereal disease

enfermera [enferˈmera] nf nurse

enfermería [enfermeˈria] nf infirmary; (*de colegio etc*) sick bay

enfermero [enferˈmero] nm (male) nurse

enfermizo, a [enferˈmiθo, a] adj (*persona*) sickly, unhealthy; (*fig*) unhealthy

enfermo, a [enˈfermo, a] adj ill, sick ♦ nm/f invalid, sick person; (*en hospital*) patient

enflaquecer [enflakeˈθer] vt (*adelgazar*) to make thin; (*debilitar*) to weaken

enfocar [enfoˈkar] vt (*foto etc*) to focus; (*problema etc*) to approach

enfoque etc [enˈfoke] vb ver **enfocar** ♦ nm focus.

enfrascarse [enfrasˈkarse] vr: **~ en algo** to bury o.s. in sth

enfrentar [enfrenˈtar] vt (*peligro*) to face (up to), confront; (*oponer*) to bring face to face; **~se** vr (*dos personas*) to face o confront each other; (*DEPORTE: dos equipos*) to meet; **~se a** o **con** to face up to, confront

enfrente [enˈfrente] adv opposite; **la casa de ~** the house opposite, the house across the street; **~ de** opposite, facing

enfriamiento [enfriaˈmjento] nm chilling, refrigeration; (*MED*) cold, chill

enfriar [enfriˈar] vt (*alimentos*) to cool, chill; (*algo caliente*) to cool down; **~se** vr to cool down; (*MED*) to catch a chill; (*amistad*) to cool

enfurecer [enfureˈθer] vt to enrage, madden; **~se** vr to become furious, fly into a rage; (*mar*) to get rough

engalanar [engalaˈnar] vt (*adornar*) to adorn; (*ciudad*) to decorate; **~se** vr to get dressed up

enganchar [enganˈtʃar] vt to hook; (*dos vagones*) to hitch up; (*TEC*) to couple, connect; (*MIL*) to recruit; **~se** vr (*MIL*) to enlist, join up

enganche [enˈgantʃe] nm hook; (*TEC*) coupling, connection; (*acto*) hooking (up); (*MIL*) recruitment, enlistment; (*AM: depósito*) deposit

engañar [engaˈɲar] vt to deceive; (*estafar*) to cheat, swindle; **~se** vr (*equivocarse*) to be wrong; (*disimular la verdad*) to deceive o.s.

engaño [enˈgaɲo] nm deceit; (*estafa*) trick, swindle; (*error*) mistake, misunderstanding; (*ilusión*) delusion; **~so, a** adj (*tramposo*) crooked; (*mentiroso*) dishonest, deceitful; (*aspecto*) deceptive; (*consejo*) misleading

engarzar [engarˈθar] vt (*joya*) to set, mount; (*fig*) to link, connect

engatusar [engatuˈsar] (*fam*) vt to coax

engendrar [enxenˈdrar] vt to breed; (*procrear*) to beget; (*causar*) to cause, produce; **engendro** nm (*BIO*) foetus; (*fig*) monstrosity

englobar [engloˈβar] vt to include, comprise

engordar [engorˈðar] vt to fatten ♦ vi to get fat, put on weight

engorroso, a [engoˈrroso, a] adj bothersome, trying

engranaje [engraˈnaxe] nm (*AUTO*) gear

engrandecer [engrandeˈθer] vt to enlarge, magnify; (*alabar*) to praise, speak highly of; (*exagerar*) to exaggerate

engrasar [engraˈsar] vt (*TEC: poner grasa*) to grease; (: *lubricar*) to lubricate, oil; (*manchar*) to make greasy

engreído, a [engreˈiðo, a] adj vain, conceited

engrosar [engroˈsar] vt (*ensanchar*) to enlarge; (*aumentar*) to increase; (*hinchar*) to

swell
enhebrar [ene'ßrar] *vt* to thread
enhorabuena [enora'ßwena] *excl*: ¡~!
congratulations! ♦ *nf*: **dar la ~ a** to
congratulate
enigma [e'nixma] *nm* enigma; (*problema*)
puzzle; (*misterio*) mystery
enjabonar [enxaßo'nar] *vt* to soap; (*fam:
adular*) to soft-soap
enjambre [en'xambre] *nm* swarm
enjaular [enxau'lar] *vt* to (put in a) cage;
(*fam*) to jail, lock up
enjuagar [enxwa'xar] *vt* (*ropa*) to rinse (out)
enjuague *etc* [en'xwaxe] *vb ver* **enjuagar**
♦ *nm* (*MED*) mouthwash; (*de ropa*) rinse,
rinsing
enjugar [enxu'xar] *vt* to wipe (off);
(*lágrimas*) to dry; (*déficit*) to wipe out
enjuiciar [enxwi'θjar] *vt* (*JUR: procesar*) to
prosecute, try; (*fig*) to judge
enjuto, a [en'xuto, a] *adj* (*flaco*) lean, skinny
enlace [en'laθe] *nm* link, connection;
(*relación*) relationship; (*tb*: ~ **matrimonial**)
marriage; (*de carretera, trenes*) connection; ~
sindical shop steward
enlatado, a [enla'taðo, a] *adj* (*comida,
productos*) tinned, canned
enlazar [enla'θar] *vt* (*unir con lazos*) to bind
together; (*atar*) to tie; (*conectar*) to link,
connect; (*AM*) to lasso
enlodar [enlo'ðar] *vt* to cover in mud; (*fig:
manchar*) to stain; (: *rebajar*) to debase
enloquecer [enloke'θer] *vt* to drive mad
♦ *vi* to go mad; ~**se** *vr* to go mad
enlutado, a [enlu'taðo, a] *adj* (*persona*) in
mourning
enmarañar [enmara'ɲar] *vt* (*enredar*) to
tangle (up), entangle; (*complicar*) to
complicate; (*confundir*) to confuse; ~**se** *vr*
(*enredarse*) to become entangled;
(*confundirse*) to get confused
enmarcar [enmar'kar] *vt* (*cuadro*) to frame
enmascarar [enmaska'rar] *vt* to mask; ~**se**
vr to put on a mask
enmendar [enmen'dar] *vt* to emend,
correct; (*constitución etc*) to amend;
(*comportamiento*) to reform; ~**se** *vr* to reform,
mend one's ways; **enmienda** *nf* correction;
amendment; reform
enmohecerse [enmoe'θerse] *vr* (*metal*) to
rust, go rusty; (*muro, plantas*) to get mouldy
enmudecer [enmuðe'θer] *vi* (*perder el
habla*) to fall silent; (*guardar silencio*) to
remain silent
ennegrecer [ennexre'θer] *vt* (*poner negro*)
to blacken; (*oscurecer*) to darken; ~**se** *vr* to
turn black; (*oscurecerse*) to get dark, darken
ennoblecer [ennoßle'θer] *vt* to ennoble
enojar [eno'xar] *vt* (*encolerizar*) to anger;

(*disgustar*) to annoy, upset; ~**se** *vr* to get
angry; to get annoyed
enojo [e'noxo] *nm* (*cólera*) anger; (*irritación*)
annoyance; ~**so, a** *adj* annoying
enorgullecerse [enorχuʎe'θerse] *vr* to be
proud; ~ **de** to pride o.s. on, be proud of
enorme [e'norme] *adj* enormous, huge; (*fig*)
monstrous; **enormidad** *nf* hugeness,
immensity
enrarecido, a [enrare'θiðo, a] *adj*
(*atmósfera, aire*) rarefied
enredadera [enreða'ðera] *nf* (*BOT*) creeper,
climbing plant
enredar [enre'ðar] *vt* (*cables, hilos etc*) to
tangle (up), entangle; (*situación*) to
complicate, confuse; (*meter cizaña*) to sow
discord among o between; (*implicar*) to
embroil, implicate; ~**se** *vr* to get entangled,
get tangled (up); (*situación*) to get
complicated; (*persona*) to get embroiled;
(*AM: fam*) to meddle
enredo [en'reðo] *nm* (*maraña*) tangle;
(*confusión*) mix-up, confusion; (*intriga*)
intrigue
enrejado [enre'xaðo] *nm* fence, railings *pl*
enrevesado, a [enreße'saðo, a] *adj* (*asunto*)
complicated, involved
enriquecer [enrike'θer] *vt* to make rich,
enrich; ~**se** *vr* to get rich
enrojecer [enroxe'θer] *vt* to redden ♦ *vi*
(*persona*) to blush; ~**se** *vr* to blush
enrolar [enro'lar] *vt* (*MIL*) to enlist; (*reclutar*)
to recruit; ~**se** *vr* (*MIL*) to join up; (*afiliarse*) to
enrol
enrollar [enro'ʎar] *vt* to roll (up), wind (up)
enroscar [enros'kar] *vt* (*torcer, doblar*) to coil
(round), wind; (*tornillo, rosca*) to screw in;
~**se** *vr* to coil, wind
ensalada [ensa'laða] *nf* salad; **ensaladilla
(rusa)** *nf* Russian salad
ensalzar [ensal'θar] *vt* (*alabar*) to praise,
extol; (*exaltar*) to exalt
ensamblaje [ensam'blaxe] *nm* assembly;
(*TEC*) joint
ensanchar [ensan'tʃar] *vt* (*hacer más ancho*)
to widen; (*agrandar*) to enlarge, expand;
(*COSTURA*) to let out; ~**se** *vr* to get wider,
expand; **ensanche** *nm* (*de calle*) widening
ensangrentar [ensangren'tar] *vt* to stain
with blood
ensañar [ensa'ɲar] *vt* to enrage; ~**se** *vr*: ~**se
con** to treat brutally
ensartar [ensar'tar] *vt* (*cuentas, perlas etc*) to
string (together)
ensayar [ensa'jar] *vt* to test, try (out);
(*TEATRO*) to rehearse
ensayo [en'sajo] *nm* test, trial; (*QUÍM*)
experiment; (*TEATRO*) rehearsal; (*DEPORTE*) try;
(*ESCOL, LITERATURA*) essay

enseguida [ense'viða] adv at once, right away

ensenada [ense'naða] nf inlet, cove

enseñanza [ense'nanθa] nf (educación) education; (acción) teaching; (doctrina) teaching, doctrine

enseñar [ense'nar] vt (educar) to teach; (mostrar, señalar) to show

enseres [en'seres] nmpl belongings

ensillar [ensi'ʎar] vt to saddle (up)

ensimismarse [ensimis'marse] vr (abstraerse) to become lost in thought; (AM) to become conceited

ensombrecer [ensombre'θer] vt to darken, cast a shadow over; (fig) to overshadow, put in the shade

ensordecer [ensorðe'θer] vt to deafen ♦ vi to go deaf

ensortijado, a [ensorti'xaðo, a] adj (pelo) curly

ensuciar [ensu'θjar] vt (manchar) to dirty, soil; (fig) to defile; **~se** vr to get dirty; (niño) to wet o.s.

ensueño [en'sweɲo] nm (sueño) dream, fantasy; (ilusión) illusion; (soñando despierto) daydream

entablar [enta'ßlar] vt (recubrir) to board (up); (AJEDREZ, DAMAS) to set up; (conversación) to strike up; (JUR) to file ♦ vi to draw

entablillar [entaßli'ʎar] vt (MED) to (put in a) splint

entallar [enta'ʎar] vt (traje) to tailor ♦ vi: **el traje entalla bien** the suit fits well

ente ['ente] nm (organización) body, organization; (fam: persona) odd character

entender [enten'der] vt (comprender) to understand; (darse cuenta) to realize ♦ vi to understand; (creer) to think, believe; **~se** vr (comprenderse) to be understood; (2 personas) to get on together; (ponerse de acuerdo) to agree, reach an agreement; **~ de** to know all about; **~ algo de** to know a little about; **~ en** to deal with, have to do with; **~se mal** (2 personas) to get on badly

entendido, a [enten'diðo, a] adj (comprendido) understood; (hábil) skilled; (inteligente) knowledgeable ♦ nm/f (experto) expert ♦ excl agreed!; **entendimiento** nm (comprensión) understanding; (inteligencia) mind, intellect; (juicio) judgement

enterado, a [ente'raðo, a] adj well-informed; **estar ~ de** to know about, be aware of

enteramente [entera'mente] adv entirely, completely

enterar [ente'rar] vt (informar) to inform, tell; **~se** vr to find out, get to know

entereza [ente'reθa] nf (totalidad) entirety; (fig: carácter) strength of mind; (: honradez) integrity

enternecer [enterne'θer] vt (ablandar) to soften; (apiadar) to touch, move; **~se** vr to be touched, be moved

entero, a [en'tero, a] adj (total) whole, entire; (fig: honesto) honest; (: firme) firm, resolute ♦ nm (COM: punto) point; (AM: pago) payment

enterrador [enterra'ðor] nm gravedigger

enterrar [ente'rrar] vt to bury

entibiar [enti'ßjar] vt (enfriar) to cool; (calentar) to warm; **~se** vr (fig) to cool

entidad [enti'ðað] nf (empresa) firm, company; (organismo) body; (sociedad) society; (FILOSOFÍA) entity

entiendo etc vb ver **entender**

entierro [en'tjerro] nm (acción) burial; (funeral) funeral

entonación [entona'θjon] nf (LING) intonation

entonar [ento'nar] vt (canción) to intone; (colores) to tone; (MED) to tone up ♦ vi to be in tune

entonces [en'tonθes] adv then, at that time; **desde ~** since then; **en aquel ~** at that time; **(pues) ~** and so

entornar [entor'nar] vt (puerta, ventana) to half close, leave ajar; (los ojos) to screw up

entorpecer [entorpe'θer] vt (entendimiento) to dull; (impedir) to obstruct, hinder; (: tránsito) to slow down, delay

entrada [en'traða] nf (acción) entry, access; (sitio) entrance, way in; (INFORM) input; (COM) receipts pl, takings pl; (CULIN) starter; (DEPORTE) innings sg; (TEATRO) house, audience; (billete) ticket; (COM): **~s y salidas** income and expenditure; (TEC): **~ de aire** air intake o inlet; **de ~** from the outset

entrado, a [en'traðo, a] adj: **~ en años** elderly; **una vez ~ el verano** in the summer(time), when summer comes

entramparse [entram'parse] vr to get into debt

entrante [en'trante] adj next, coming; **mes/año ~** next month/year; **~s** nmpl starters

entraña [en'traɲa] nf (fig: centro) heart, core; (raíz) root; **~s** nfpl (ANAT) entrails; (fig) heart sg; **sin ~s** (fig) heartless; **entrañable** adj close, intimate; **entrañar** vt to entail

entrar [en'trar] vt (introducir) to bring in; (INFORM) to input ♦ vi (meterse) to go in, come in, enter; (comenzar): **~ diciendo** to begin by saying; **hacer ~** to show in; **no me entra** I can't get the hang of it

entre ['entre] prep (dos) between; (más de dos) among(st)

entreabrir [entrea'ßrir] vt to half-open, open halfway

entrecejo [entre'θexo] nm: **fruncir el ~** to

frown
entrecortado, a [entrekor'taðo, a] *adj*
(*respiración*) difficult; (*habla*) faltering
entredicho [entre'ðitʃo] *nm* (*JUR*) injunction;
poner en ~ to cast doubt on; **estar en ~** to be
in doubt
entrega [en'treɣa] *nf* (*de mercancías*)
delivery; (*de novela etc*) instalment
entregar [entre'ɣar] *vt* (*dar*) to hand (over),
deliver; **~se** *vr* (*rendirse*) to surrender, give in,
submit; (*dedicarse*) to devote o.s.
entrelazar [entrela'θar] *vt* to entwine
entremeses [entre'meses] *nmpl* hors
d'œuvres
entremeter [entreme'ter] *vt* to insert, put
in; **~se** *vr* to meddle, interfere;
entremetido, a *adj* meddling, interfering
entremezclar [entremeθ'klar] *vt* to
intermingle; **~se** *vr* to intermingle
entrenador, a [entrena'ðor, a] *nm/f* trainer,
coach
entrenarse [entre'narse] *vr* to train
entrepierna [entre'pjerna] *nf* crotch
entresacar [entresa'kar] *vt* to pick out, select
entresuelo [entre'swelo] *nm* mezzanine
entretanto [entre'tanto] *adv* meanwhile,
meantime
entretejer [entrete'xer] *vt* to interweave
entretener [entrete'ner] *vt* (*divertir*) to
entertain, amuse; (*detener*) to hold up, delay;
~se *vr* (*divertirse*) to amuse o.s.; (*retrasarse*)
to delay, linger; **entretenido, a** *adj*
entertaining, amusing; **entretenimiento** *nm*
entertainment, amusement
entrever [entre'ßer] *vt* to glimpse, catch a
glimpse of
entrevista [entre'ßista] *nf* interview;
entrevistar *vt* to interview; **entrevistarse** *vr*
to have an interview
entristecer [entriste'θer] *vt* to sadden,
grieve; **~se** *vr* to grow sad
entrometerse [entrome'terse] *vr*: **~ (en)** to
interfere (in o with)
entroncar [entron'kar] *vi* to be connected o
related
entumecer [entume'θer] *vt* to numb,
benumb; **~se** *vr* (*por el frío*) to go o become
numb; **entumecido, a** *adj* numb, stiff
enturbiar [entur'ßjar] *vt* (*el agua*) to make
cloudy; (*fig*) to confuse; **~se** *vr* (*oscurecerse*)
to become cloudy; (*fig*) to get confused,
become obscure
entusiasmar [entusjas'mar] *vt* to excite, fill
with enthusiasm; (*gustar mucho*) to delight;
~se *vr*: **~se con** *o* **por** to get enthusiastic *o*
excited about
entusiasmo [entu'sjasmo] *nm* enthusiasm;
(*excitación*) excitement
entusiasta [entu'sjasta] *adj* enthusiastic

♦ *nm/f* enthusiast
enumerar [enume'rar] *vt* to enumerate
enunciación [enunθja'θjon] *nf* enunciation
enunciado [enun'θjaðo] *nm* enunciation
envainar [embai'nar] *vt* to sheathe
envalentonar [embalento'nar] *vt* to give
courage to; **~se** *vr* (*pey: jactarse*) to boast,
brag
envanecer [embane'θer] *vt* to make
conceited; **~se** *vr* to grow conceited
envasar [emba'sar] *vt* (*empaquetar*) to pack,
wrap; (*enfrascar*) to bottle; (*enlatar*) to can;
(*embolsar*) to pocket
envase [em'base] *nm* (*en paquete*) packing,
wrapping; (*en botella*) bottling; (*en lata*)
canning; (*recipiente*) container; (*paquete*)
package; (*botella*) bottle; (*lata*) tin (*BRIT*), can
envejecer [embexe'θer] *vt* to make old, age
♦ *vi* (*volverse viejo*) to grow old; (*parecer
viejo*) to age; **~se** *vr* to grow old; to age
envenenar [embene'nar] *vt* to poison; (*fig*)
to embitter
envergadura [emberɣa'ðura] *nf* (*fig*) scope,
compass
envés [em'bes] *nm* (*de tela*) back, wrong side
enviar [em'bjar] *vt* to send
enviciarse [embi'θjarse] *vr*: **~ (con)** to get
addicted to
envidia [em'biðja] *nf* envy; **tener ~ a** to envy,
be jealous of; **envidiar** *vt* to envy
envío [em'bio] *nm* (*acción*) sending; (*de
mercancías*) consignment; (*de dinero*)
remittance
enviudar [embju'ðar] *vi* to be widowed
envoltura [embol'tura] *nf* (*cobertura*) cover;
(*embalaje*) wrapper, wrapping; **envoltorio**
nm package
envolver [embol'ßer] *vt* to wrap (up);
(*cubrir*) to cover; (*enemigo*) to surround;
(*implicar*) to involve, implicate
envuelto [em'bwelto] *pp de* **envolver**
enyesar [enje'sar] *vt* (*pared*) to plaster;
(*MED*) to put in plaster
enzarzarse [enθar'θarse] *vr*: **~ en** (*pelea*) to
get mixed up in; (*disputa*) to get involved in
épica ['epika] *nf* epic
épico, a ['epiko, a] *adj* epic
epidemia [epi'ðemja] *nf* epidemic
epilepsia [epi'lepsja] *nf* epilepsy
epílogo [e'piloɣo] *nm* epilogue
episodio [epi'soðjo] *nm* episode
epístola [e'pistola] *nf* epistle
época ['epoka] *nf* period, time; (*HISTORIA*)
age, epoch; **hacer ~** to be epoch-making
equilibrar [ekili'ßrar] *vt* to balance;
equilibrio *nm* balance, equilibrium;
equilibrista *nm/f* (*funámbulo*) tightrope
walker; (*acróbata*) acrobat
equipaje [eki'paxe] *nm* luggage; (*avíos*):

~ **de mano** hand luggage

equipar [eki'par] vt (*proveer*) to equip

equipararse [ekipa'rarse] vr: ~ **con** to be on a level with

equipo [e'kipo] nm (*conjunto de cosas*) equipment; (*DEPORTE*) team; (*de obreros*) shift

equis ['ekis] nf inv (the letter) X

equitación [ekita'θjon] nf horse riding

equitativo, a [ekita'tiβo, a] adj equitable, fair

equivalente [ekiβa'lente] adj, nm equivalent

equivaler [ekiβa'ler] vi to be equivalent o equal

equivocación [ekiβoka'θjon] nf mistake, error

equivocado, a [ekiβo'kaðo, a] adj wrong, mistaken

equivocarse [ekiβo'karse] vr to be wrong, make a mistake; ~ **de camino** to take the wrong road

equívoco, a [e'kiβoko, a] adj (*dudoso*) suspect; (*ambiguo*) ambiguous ♦ nm ambiguity; (*malentendido*) misunderstanding

era ['era] vb ver **ser** ♦ nf era, age

erais vb ver **ser**

éramos vb ver **ser**

eran vb ver **ser**

erario [e'rarjo] nm exchequer (*BRIT*), treasury

eras vb ver **ser**

erección [erek'θjon] nf erection

eres vb ver **ser**

erguir [er'xir] vt to raise, lift; (*poner derecho*) to straighten; ~**se** vr to straighten up

erigir [eri'xir] vt to erect, build; ~**se** vr: ~**se en** to set o.s. up as

erizarse [eri'θarse] vr (*pelo: de perro*) to bristle; (: *de persona*) to stand on end

erizo [e'riθo] nm (*ZOOL*) hedgehog; ~ **de mar** sea-urchin

ermita [er'mita] nf hermitage

ermitaño, a [ermi'taɲo, a] nm/f hermit

erosión [ero'sjon] nf erosion

erosionar [erosjo'nar] vt to erode

erótico, a [e'rotiko, a] adj erotic; **erotismo** nm eroticism

erradicar [erraði'kar] vt to eradicate

errante [e'rrante] adj wandering, errant

errar [e'rrar] vi (*vagar*) to wander, roam; (*equivocarse*) to be mistaken ♦ vt: ~ **el camino** to take the wrong road; ~ **el tiro** to miss

erróneo, a [e'rroneo, a] adj (*equivocado*) wrong, mistaken

error [e'rror] nm error, mistake; (*INFORM*) bug; ~ **de imprenta** misprint

eructar [eruk'tar] vt to belch, burp

erudito, a [eru'ðito, a] adj erudite, learned

erupción [erup'θjon] nf eruption; (*MED*) rash

es vb ver **ser**

esa ['esa] (pl **esas**) adj demos ver **ese**

ésa ['esa] (pl **ésas**) pron ver **ése**

esbelto, a [es'βelto, a] adj slim, slender

esbozo [es'βoθo] nm sketch, outline

escabeche [eska'βetʃe] nm brine; (*de aceitunas etc*) pickle; **en ~** pickled

escabroso, a [eska'βroso, a] adj (*accidentado*) rough, uneven; (*fig*) tough, difficult, (: *atrevido*) risqué

escabullirse [eskaβu'ʎirse] vr to slip away, to clear out

escafandra [eska'fandra] nf (*buzo*) diving suit; (~ **espacial**) space suit

escala [es'kala] nf (*proporción, MUS*) scale; (*de mano*) ladder; (*AVIAT*) stopover; **hacer ~ en** to stop o call in at

escalafón [eskala'fon] nm (*escala de salarios*) salary scale, wage scale

escalar [eska'lar] vt to climb, scale

escalera [eska'lera] nf stairs pl, staircase; (*escala*) ladder; (*NAIPES*) run; ~ **mecánica** escalator; ~ **de caracol** spiral staircase

escalfar [eskal'far] vt (*huevos*) to poach

escalinata [eskali'nata] nf staircase

escalofriante [eskalo'frjante] adj chilling

escalofrío [eskalo'frio] nm (*MED*) chill; ~**s** nmpl (*fig*) shivers

escalón [eska'lon] nm step, stair; (*de escalera*) rung

escalope [eska'lope] nm (*CULIN*) escalope

escama [es'kama] nf (*de pez, serpiente*) scale; (*de jabón*) flake; (*fig*) resentment

escamar [eska'mar] vt (*fig*) to make wary o suspicious

escamotear [eskamote'ar] vt (*robar*) to lift, swipe; (*hacer desaparecer*) to make disappear

escampar [eskam'par] vb impers to stop raining

escandalizar [eskandali'θar] vt to scandalize, shock; ~**se** vr to be shocked; (*ofenderse*) to be offended

escándalo [es'kandalo] nm scandal; (*alboroto, tumulto*) row, uproar; **escandaloso, a** adj scandalous, shocking

escandinavo, a [eskandi'naβo, a] adj, nm/f Scandinavian

escaño [es'kaɲo] nm bench; (*POL*) seat

escapar [eska'par] vi (*gen*) to escape, run away; (*DEPORTE*) to break away; ~**se** vr to escape, get away; (*agua, gas*) to leak (out)

escaparate [eskapa'rate] nm shop window

escape [es'kape] nm (*de agua, gas*) leak; (*de motor*) exhaust

escarabajo [eskara'βaxo] nm beetle

escaramuza [eskara'muθa] nf skirmish

escarbar [eskar'βar] vt (*tierra*) to scratch

escarceos [eskar'θeos] nmpl (*fig*): **en mis ~ con la política** ... in my dealings with politics ...; ~ **amorosos** love affairs

escarcha [es'kartʃa] *nf* frost

escarchado, a [eskar'tʃaðo, a] *adj* (CULIN: *fruta*) crystallized

escarlata [eskar'lata] *adj inv* scarlet; **escarlatina** *nf* scarlet fever

escarmentar [eskarmen'tar] *vt* to punish severely ♦ *vi* to learn one's lesson

escarmiento *etc* [eskar'mjento] *vb ver* **escarmentar** ♦ *nm* (*ejemplo*) lesson; (*castigo*) punishment

escarnio [es'karnjo] *nm* mockery; (*injuria*) insult

escarola [eska'rola] *nf* endive

escarpado, a [eskar'paðo, a] *adj* (*pendiente*) sheer, steep; (*rocas*) craggy

escasear [eskase'ar] *vi* to be scarce

escasez [eska'seθ] *nf* (*falta*) shortage, scarcity; (*pobreza*) poverty

escaso, a [es'kaso, a] *adj* (*poco*) scarce; (*raro*) rare; (*ralo*) thin, sparse; (*limitado*) limited

escatimar [eskati'mar] *vt* to skimp (on), be sparing with

escayola [eska'jola] *nf* plaster

escena [es'θena] *nf* scene

escenario [esθe'narjo] *nm* (TEATRO) stage; (CINE) set; (*fig*) scene; **escenografía** *nf* set design

escepticismo [esθepti'θismo] *nm* scepticism; **escéptico, a** *adj* sceptical ♦ *nm/f* sceptic

escisión [esθi'sjon] *nf* (*de partido, secta*) split

esclarecer [esklare'θer] *vt* (*misterio, problema*) to shed light on

esclavitud [esklaβi'tuð] *nf* slavery

esclavizar [esklaβi'θar] *vt* to enslave

esclavo, a [es'klaβo, a] *nm/f* slave

esclusa [es'klusa] *nf* (*de canal*) lock; (*compuerta*) floodgate

escoba [es'koβa] *nf* broom; **escobilla** *nf* brush

escocer [esko'θer] *vi* to burn, sting; ~**se** *vr* to chafe, get chafed

escocés, esa [esko'θes, esa] *adj* Scottish ♦ *nm/f* Scotsman/woman, Scot

Escocia [es'koθja] *nf* Scotland

escoger [esko'xer] *vt* to choose, pick, select; **escogido, a** *adj* chosen, selected

escolar [esko'lar] *adj* school *cpd* ♦ *nm/f* schoolboy/girl, pupil

escollo [es'koʎo] *nm* (*obstáculo*) pitfall

escolta [es'kolta] *nf* escort; **escoltar** *vt* to escort

escombros [es'kombros] *nmpl* (*basura*) rubbish *sg*; (*restos*) debris *sg*

esconder [eskon'der] *vt* to hide, conceal; ~**se** *vr* to hide; **escondidas** (AM) *nfpl*: a **escondidas** secretly; **escondite** *nm* hiding place; (*juego*) hide-and-seek; **escondrijo** *nm* hiding place, hideout

escopeta [esko'peta] *nf* shotgun

escoria [es'korja] *nf* (*de alto horno*) slag; (*fig*) scum, dregs *pl*

Escorpio [es'korpjo] *nm* Scorpio

escorpión [eskor'pjon] *nm* scorpion

escotado, a [esko'taðo, a] *adj* low-cut

escote [es'kote] *nm* (*de vestido*) low neck; **pagar a** ~ to share the expenses

escotilla [esko'tiʎa] *nf* (NAUT) hatch(way)

escozor [esko'θor] *nm* (*dolor*) sting(ing)

escribir [eskri'ßir] *vt, vi* to write; ~ **a máquina** to type; **¿cómo se escribe?** how do you spell it?

escrito, a [es'krito, a] *pp de* **escribir** ♦ *nm* (*documento*) document; (*manuscrito*) text, manuscript; **por** ~ in writing

escritor, a [eskri'tor, a] *nm/f* writer

escritorio [eskri'torjo] *nm* desk

escritura [eskri'tura] *nf* (*acción*) writing; (*caligrafía*) (hand)writing; (JUR: *documento*) deed

escrúpulo [es'krupulo] *nm* scruple; (*minuciosidad*) scrupulousness; **escrupuloso, a** *adj* scrupulous

escrutar [eskru'tar] *vt* to scrutinize, examine; (*votos*) to count

escrutinio [eskru'tinjo] *nm* (*examen atento*) scrutiny; (POL: *recuento de votos*) count(ing)

escuadra [es'kwaðra] *nf* (MIL *etc*) squad; (NAUT) squadron; (*de coches etc*) fleet; **escuadrilla** *nf* (*de aviones*) squadron; (AM: *de obreros*) gang

escuadrón [eskwa'ðron] *nm* squadron

escuálido, a [es'kwaliðo, a] *adj* skinny, scraggy; (*sucio*) squalid

escuchar [esku'tʃar] *vt* to listen to ♦ *vi* to listen

escudilla [esku'ðiʎa] *nf* bowl, basin

escudo [es'kuðo] *nm* shield

escudriñar [eskuðri'ɲar] *vt* (*examinar*) to investigate, scrutinize; (*mirar de lejos*) to scan

escuela [es'kwela] *nf* school; ~ **de artes y oficios** (ESP) ≈ technical college; ~ **normal** teacher training college

escueto, a [es'kweto, a] *adj* plain; (*estilo*) simple

escuincle [es'kwinkle] (AM: *fam*) *nm/f* kid

esculpir [eskul'pir] *vt* to sculpt; (*grabar*) to engrave; (*tallar*) to carve; **escultor, a** *nm/f* sculptor/tress; **escultura** *nf* sculpture

escupidera [eskupi'ðera] *nf* spittoon

escupir [esku'pir] *vt, vi* to spit (out)

escurreplatos [eskurre'platos] *nm inv* plate rack

escurridizo, a [eskurri'ðiθo, a] *adj* slippery

escurridor [eskurri'ðor] *nm* colander

escurrir [esku'rrir] *vt* (*ropa*) to wring out; (*verduras, platos*) to drain ♦ *vi* (*líquidos*) to drip; **~se** vr (secarse) to drain; (resbalarse) to slip, slide; (escaparse) to slip away

ese ['ese] (f esa, pl esos, esas) adj demos (sg) that; (pl) those

ése ['ese] (f ésa, pl ésos, ésas) pron (sg) that (one); (pl) those (ones); **~ ... éste ...** the former ... the latter ...; **no me vengas con ésas** don't give me any more of that nonsense

esencia [e'senθja] nf essence; **esencial** adj essential

esfera [es'fera] nf sphere; (de reloj) face; **esférico, a** adj spherical

esforzarse [esfor'θarse] vr to exert o.s., make an effort

esfuerzo etc [es'fwerθo] vb ver **esforzar ♦** nm effort

esfumarse [esfu'marse] vr (apoyo, esperanzas) to fade away

esgrima [es'rrima] nf fencing

esgrimir [esrri'mir] vt (arma) to brandish; (argumento) to use

esguince [es'xinθe] nm (MED) sprain

eslabón [esla'ßon] nm link

eslip [ez'lip] nm pants pl (BRIT), briefs pl

eslovaco, a [eslo'ßako, a] adj, nm/f Slovak, Slovakian ♦ nm (LING) Slovak, Slovakian

Eslovaquia [eslo'ßakja] nf Slovakia

esmaltar [esmal'tar] vt to enamel; **esmalte** nm enamel; **esmalte de uñas** nail varnish o polish

esmerado, a [esme'raðo, a] adj careful, neat

esmeralda [esme'ralda] nf emerald

esmerarse [esme'rarse] vr (aplicarse) to take great pains, exercise great care; (afanarse) to work hard

esmero [es'mero] nm (great) care

esnob [es'nob] (pl **~s**) adj (persona) snobbish ♦ nm/f snob; **~ismo** nm snobbery

eso ['eso] pron that, that thing o matter; **~ de su coche** that business about his car; **~ de ir al cine** all that about going to the cinema; **a ~ de las cinco** at about five o'clock; **en ~** thereupon, at that point; **~ es** that's it; **¡~ sí que es vida!** now that is really living!; **por ~ te lo dije** that's why I told you; **y ~ que llovía** in spite of the fact it was raining

esos ['esos] adj demos ver **ese**

ésos ['esos] pron ver **ése**

espabilar etc [espaßi'lar] = **despabilar** etc

espacial [espa'θjal] adj (del espacio) space cpd

espaciar [espa'θjar] vt to space (out)

espacio [es'paθjo] nm space; (MUS) interval; (RADIO, TV) programme (BRIT), program (US); **el ~** space; **~so, a** adj spacious, roomy

espada [es'paða] nf sword; **~s** nfpl (NAIPES) spades

espaguetis [espa'ɣetis] nmpl spaghetti sg

espalda [es'palda] nf (gen) back; **~s** nfpl (hombros) shoulders; **a ~s de uno** behind sb's back; **tenderse de ~s** to lie (down) on one's back; **volver la ~ a alguien** to cold-shoulder sb

espantajo [espan'taxo] nm = **espantapájaros**

espantapájaros [espanta'paxaros] nm inv scarecrow

espantar [espan'tar] vt (asustar) to frighten, scare; (ahuyentar) to frighten off; (asombrar) to horrify, appal; **~se** vr to get frightened o scared; to be appalled

espanto [es'panto] nm (susto) fright; (terror) terror; (asombro) astonishment; **~so, a** adj frightening; terrifying; astonishing

España [es'paɲa] nf Spain; **español, a** adj Spanish ♦ nm/f Spaniard ♦ nm (LING) Spanish

esparadrapo [espara'ðrapo] nm (sticking) plaster (BRIT), adhesive tape (US)

esparcimiento [esparθi'mjento] nm (dispersión) spreading; (diseminación) scattering; (fig) cheerfulness

esparcir [espar'θir] vt to spread; (diseminar) to scatter; **~se** vr to spread (out); to scatter; (divertirse) to enjoy o.s.

espárrago [es'parraxo] nm asparagus

esparto [es'parto] nm esparto (grass)

espasmo [es'pasmo] nm spasm

espátula [es'patula] nf spatula

especia [es'peθja] nf spice

especial [espe'θjal] adj special; **~idad** nf speciality (BRIT), specialty (US)

especie [es'peθje] nf (BIO) species; (clase) kind, sort; **en ~** in kind

especificar [espeθifi'kar] vt to specify; **específico, a** adj specific

espécimen [es'peθimen] (pl **especímenes**) nm specimen

espectáculo [espek'takulo] nm (gen) spectacle; (TEATRO etc) show

espectador, a [espekta'ðor, a] nm/f spectator

espectro [es'pektro] nm ghost; (fig) spectre

especular [espeku'lar] vt, vi to speculate

espejismo [espe'xismo] nm mirage

espejo [es'pexo] nm mirror; **~ retrovisor** rear-view mirror

espeluznante [espeluθ'nante] adj horrifying, hair-raising

espera [es'pera] nf (pausa, intervalo) wait; (JUR: plazo) respite; **en ~ de** waiting for; (con expectativa) expecting

esperanza [espe'ranθa] nf (confianza) hope; (expectativa) expectation; **hay pocas ~s de que venga** there is little prospect of his coming

esperar [espe'rar] vt (aguardar) to wait for; (tener expectativa de) to expect; (desear) to hope for ♦ vi to wait; to expect; to hope

esperma [es'perma] nf sperm

espesar [espe'sar] vt to thicken; **~se** vr to thicken, get thicker

espeso, a [es'peso, a] adj thick; **espesor** nm thickness

espía [es'pia] nm/f spy; **espiar** vt (observar) to spy on

espiga [es'piɣa] nf (BOT: de trigo etc) ear

espigón [espi'ɣon] nm (BOT) ear; (NAUT) breakwater

espina [es'pina] nf thorn; (de pez) bone; **~ dorsal** (ANAT) spine

espinaca [espi'naka] nf spinach

espinazo [espi'naθo] nm spine, backbone

espinilla [espi'niʎa] nf (ANAT: tibia) shin(bone); (grano) blackhead

espinoso, a [espi'noso, a] adj (planta) thorny, prickly; (asunto) difficult

espionaje [espjo'naxe] nm spying, espionage

espiral [espi'ral] adj, nf spiral

espirar [espi'rar] vt to breathe out, exhale

espiritista [espiri'tista] adj, nm/f spiritualist

espíritu [es'piritu] nm spirit; **espiritual** adj spiritual

espita [es'pita] nf tap

espléndido, a [es'plendiðo, a] adj (magnífico) magnificent, splendid; (generoso) generous

esplendor [esplen'dor] nm splendour

espolear [espole'ar] vt to spur on

espoleta [espo'leta] nf (de bomba) fuse

espolón [espo'lon] nm sea wall

espolvorear [espolßore'ar] vt to dust, sprinkle

esponja [es'ponxa] nf sponge; (fig) sponger; **esponjoso, a** adj spongy

espontaneidad [espontanei'ðað] nf spontaneity; **espontáneo, a** adj spontaneous

esposa [es'posa] nf wife; **~s** nfpl handcuffs; **esposar** vt to handcuff

esposo [es'poso] nm husband

espray [es'prai] nm spray

espuela [es'pwela] nf spur

espuma [es'puma] nf foam; (de cerveza) froth, head; (de jabón) lather; **espumadera** nf (utensilio) skimmer; **espumoso, a** adj frothy, foamy; (vino) sparkling

esqueleto [eske'leto] nm skeleton

esquema [es'kema] nm (diagrama) diagram; (dibujo) plan; (FILOSOFÍA) schema

esquí [es'ki] (pl **~s**) nm (objeto) ski; (DEPORTE) skiing; **~ acuático** water-skiing; **esquiar** vi to ski

esquilar [eski'lar] vt to shear

esquimal [eski'mal] adj, nm/f Eskimo

esquina [es'kina] nf corner

esquinazo [eski'naθo] nm: **dar ~ a algn** to give sb the slip

esquirol [eski'rol] nm blackleg

esquivar [eski'ßar] vt to avoid

esquivo, a [es'kißo, a] adj evasive; (tímido) reserved; (huraño) unsociable

esta ['esta] adj demos ver **este²**

está vb ver **estar**

ésta ['esta] pron ver **éste**

estabilidad [estaßili'ðað] nf stability; **estable** adj stable

establecer [estaßle'θer] vt to establish; **~se** vr to establish o.s.; (echar raíces) to settle (down); **establecimiento** nm establishment

establo [es'taßlo] nm (AGR) stable

estaca [es'taka] nf stake, post; (de tienda de campaña) peg

estacada [esta'kaða] nf (cerca) fence, fencing; (palenque) stockade

estación [esta'θjon] nf station; (del año) season; **~ de autobuses** bus station; **~ balnearia** seaside resort; **~ de servicio** service station

estacionamiento [estaθjona'mjento] nm (AUTO) parking; (MIL) stationing

estacionar [estaθjo'nar] vt (AUTO) to park; (MIL) to station; **~io, a** adj stationary; (COM: mercado) slack

estadio [es'taðjo] nm (fase) stage, phase; (DEPORTE) stadium

estadista [esta'ðista] nm (POL) statesman; (ESTADÍSTICA) statistician

estadística [esta'ðistika] nf figure, statistic; (ciencia) statistics sg

estado [es'taðo] nm (POL: condición) state; **~ de ánimo** state of mind; **~ de cuenta** bank statement; **~ de sitio** state of siege; **~ civil** marital status; **~ mayor** staff; **estar en ~** to be pregnant; **(los) E~s Unidos** nmpl the United States (of America) sg

estadounidense [estaðouni'ðense] adj United States cpd, American ♦ nm/f American

estafa [es'tafa] nf swindle, trick; **estafar** vt to swindle, defraud

estafeta [esta'feta] nf (oficina de correos) post office; **~ diplomática** diplomatic bag

estáis vb ver **estar**

estallar [esta'ʎar] vi to burst; (bomba) to explode, go off; (epidemia, guerra, rebelión) to break out; **~ en llanto** to burst into tears; **estallido** nm explosion; (fig) outbreak

estampa [es'tampa] nf print, engraving

estampado, a [estam'paðo, a] adj printed ♦ nm (impresión: acción) printing; (: efecto) print; (marca) stamping

estampar [estam'par] vt (imprimir) to print; (marcar) to stamp; (metal) to engrave; (poner sello en) to stamp; (fig) to stamp, imprint

estampida [estam'piða] nf stampede

estampido [estam'piðo] nm bang, report

están vb ver **estar**

estancado, a [estan'kaðo, a] *adj* stagnant

estancar [estan'kar] *vt* (*aguas*) to hold up, hold back; (*COM*) to monopolize; (*fig*) to block, hold up; **~se** *vr* to stagnate

estancia [es'tanθja] *nf* (*permanencia*) stay; (*sala*) room; (*AM*) farm, ranch; **estanciero** (*AM*) *nm* farmer, rancher

estanco, a [es'tanko, a] *adj* watertight ♦ *nm* tobacconist's (shop), cigar store (*US*)

estándar [es'tandar] *adj*, *nm* standard; **estandarizar** *vt* to standardize

estandarte [estan'darte] *nm* banner, standard

estanque [es'tanke] *nm* (*lago*) pool, pond; (*AGR*) reservoir

estanquero, a [estan'kero, a] *nm/f* tobacconist

estante [es'tante] *nm* (*armario*) rack, stand; (*biblioteca*) bookcase; (*anaquel*) shelf; (*AM*) prop; **estantería** *nf* shelving, shelves *pl*

estaño [es'tano] *nm* tin

PALABRA CLAVE
---

estar [es'tar] *vi* **1** (*posición*) to be; **está en la plaza** it's in the square; **¿está Juan?** is Juan in?; **estamos a 30 km de Junín** we're 30 kms from Junín

2 (+ *adj: estado*) to be; **~ enfermo** to be ill; **está muy elegante** he's looking very smart; **¿cómo estás?** how are you keeping?

3 (+ *gerundio*) to be; **estoy leyendo** I'm reading

4 (*uso pasivo*): **está condenado a muerte** he's been condemned to death; **está envasado en ...** it's packed in ...

5 (*con fechas*): **¿a cuántos estamos?** what's the date today?; **estamos a 5 de mayo** it's the 5th of May

6 (*locuciones*): **¿estamos?** (*¿de acuerdo?*) okay?; (*¿listo?*) ready?; **¡ya está bien!** that's enough!

7: **~ de**: **~ de vacaciones/viaje** to be on holiday/away *o* on a trip; **está de camarero** he's working as a waiter

8: **~ para**: **está para salir** he's about to leave; **no estoy para bromas** I'm not in the mood for jokes

9: **~ por** (*propuesta etc*) to be in favour of; (*persona etc*) to support, side with; **está por limpiar** it still has to be cleaned

10: **~ sin**: **~ sin dinero** to have no money; **está sin terminar** it isn't finished yet

♦ **~se** *vr*: **se estuvo en la cama toda la tarde** he stayed in bed all afternoon

---

estas ['estas] *adj demos ver* **este²**

éstas ['estas] *pron ver* **éste**

estatal [esta'tal] *adj* state *cpd*

estático, a [es'tatiko, a] *adj* static

estatua [es'tatwa] *nf* statue

estatura [esta'tura] *nf* stature, height

estatuto [esta'tuto] *nm* (*JUR*) statute; (*de ciudad*) bye-law; (*de comité*) rule

este¹ ['este] *nm* east

este² ['este] (*f* **esta**, *pl* **estos, estas**) *adj demos* (*sg*) this; (*pl*) these

esté *etc vb ver* **estar**

éste ['este] (*f* **ésta**, *pl* **éstos, éstas**) *pron* (*sg*) this (one); (*pl*) these (ones); **ése ... ~ ...** the former ... the latter ....

estelar [este'lar] *adj* (*ASTRO*) stellar; (*actuación, reparto*) star (*atr*)

estén *etc vb ver* **estar**

estepa [es'tepa] *nf* (*GEO*) steppe

estera [es'tera] *nf* mat(ting)

estéreo [es'tereo] *adj inv, nm* stereo; **estereotipo** *nm* stereotype

estéril [es'teril] *adj* sterile, barren; (*fig*) vain, futile; **esterilizar** *vt* to sterilize

esterlina [ester'lina] *adj*: **libra ~** pound sterling

estés *etc vb ver* **estar**

estética [es'tetika] *nf* aesthetics *sg*

estético, a [es'tetiko, a] *adj* aesthetic

estibador [estißa'ðor] *nm* stevedore, docker

estiércol [es'tjerkol] *nm* dung, manure

estigma [es'tivma] *nm* stigma

estilarse [esti'larse] *vr* to be in fashion

estilo [es'tilo] *nm* style; (*TEC*) stylus; (*NATACIÓN*) stroke; **algo por el ~** something along those lines

estima [es'tima] *nf* esteem, respect

estimación [estima'θjon] *nf* (*evaluación*) estimation; (*aprecio, afecto*) esteem, regard

estimar [esti'mar] *vt* (*evaluar*) to estimate; (*valorar*) to value; (*apreciar*) to esteem, respect; (*pensar, considerar*) to think, reckon

estimulante [estimu'lante] *adj* stimulating ♦ *nm* stimulant

estimular [estimu'lar] *vt* to stimulate; (*excitar*) to excite

estímulo [es'timulo] *nm* stimulus; (*ánimo*) encouragement

estipulación [estipula'θjon] *nf* stipulation, condition

estipular [estipu'lar] *vt* to stipulate

estirado, a [esti'raðo, a] *adj* (*tenso*) (stretched *o* drawn) tight; (*fig: persona*) stiff, pompous

estirar [esti'rar] *vt* to stretch; (*dinero, suma etc*) to stretch out; **~se** *vr* to stretch

estirón [esti'ron] *nm* pull, tug; (*crecimiento*) spurt, sudden growth; **dar un ~** (*niño*) to shoot up

estirpe [es'tirpe] *nf* stock, lineage

estival [esti'ßal] *adj* summer *cpd*

esto ['esto] *pron* this, this thing *o* matter; **~ de la boda** this business about the wedding

Estocolmo [esto'kolmo] *nm* Stockholm

estofado [esto'faðo] *nm* stew

estofar [esto'far] *vt* to stew

estómago [es'tomaɣo] *nm* stomach; **tener ~** to be thick-skinned

estorbar [estor'βar] *vt* to hinder, obstruct; (*molestar*) to bother, disturb ♦ *vi* to be in the way; **estorbo** *nm* (*molestia*) bother, nuisance; (*obstáculo*) hindrance, obstacle

estornudar [estornu'ðar] *vi* to sneeze

estos ['estos] *adj demos ver* **este²**

éstos ['estos] *pron ver* **éste**

estoy *vb ver* **estar**

estrado [es'traðo] *nm* platform

estrafalario, a [estrafa'larjo, a] *adj* odd, eccentric

estrago [es'traɣo] *nm* ruin, destruction; **hacer ~s en** to wreak havoc among

estragón [estra'ɣon] *nm* tarragon

estrambótico, a [estram'botiko, a] *adj* (*persona*) eccentric; (*peinado, ropa*) outlandish

estrangulador, a [estrangula'ðor, a] *nm/f* strangler ♦ *nm* (*TEC*) throttle; (*AUTO*) choke

estrangular [estrangu'lar] *vt* (*persona*) to strangle; (*MED*) to strangulate

estratagema [estrata'xema] *nf* (*MIL*) stratagem; (*astucia*) cunning

estrategia [estra'texja] *nf* strategy; **estratégico, a** *adj* strategic

estrato [es'trato] *nm* stratum, layer

estrechamente [es'tretʃamente] *adv* (*íntimamente*) closely, intimately; (*pobremente*: *vivir*) poorly

estrechar [estre'tʃar] *vt* (*reducir*) to narrow; (*COSTURA*) to take in; (*abrazar*) to hug, embrace; **~se** *vr* (*reducirse*) to narrow, grow narrow; (*abrazarse*) to embrace; **~ la mano** to shake hands

estrechez [estre'tʃeθ] *nf* narrowness; (*de ropa*) tightness; **estrecheces** *nfpl* (*dificultades económicas*) financial difficulties

estrecho, a [es'tretʃo, a] *adj* narrow; (*apretado*) tight; (*íntimo*) close, intimate; (*miserable*) mean ♦ *nm* strait; **~ de miras** narrow-minded

estrella [es'treʎa] *nf* star; **~ de mar** (*ZOOL*) starfish; **~ fugaz** shooting star; **estrellado, a** *adj* (*forma*) star-shaped; (*cielo*) starry

estrellar [estre'ʎar] *vt* (*hacer añicos*) to smash (to pieces); (*huevos*) to fry; **~se** *vr* to smash; (*chocarse*) to crash; (*fracasar*) to fail

estremecer [estreme'θer] *vt* to shake; **~se** *vr* to shake, tremble; **estremecimiento** *nm* (*temblor*) trembling, shaking

estrenar [estre'nar] *vt* (*vestido*) to wear for the first time; (*casa*) to move into; (*película, obra de teatro*) to première; **~se** *vr* (*persona*) to make one's début; **estreno** *nm* (*CINE etc*) première

estreñido, a [estre'ɲiðo, a] *adj* constipated

estreñimiento [estreɲi'mjento] *nm* constipation

estrépito [es'trepito] *nm* noise, racket; (*fig*) fuss; **estrepitoso, a** *adj* noisy; (*fiesta*) rowdy

estría [es'tria] *nf* groove

estribación [estriβa'θjon] *nf* (*GEO*) spur, foothill

estribar [estri'βar] *vi*: **~ en** to lie on

estribillo [estri'βiʎo] *nm* (*LITERATURA*) refrain; (*MUS*) chorus

estribo [es'triβo] *nm* (*de jinete*) stirrup; (*de coche, tren*) step; (*de puente*) support; (*GEO*) spur; **perder los ~s** to fly off the handle

estribor [estri'βor] *nm* (*NAUT*) starboard

estricto, a [es'trikto, a] *adj* (*riguroso*) strict; (*severo*) severe

estridente [estri'ðente] *adj* (*color*) loud; (*voz*) raucous

estropajo [estro'paxo] *nm* scourer

estropear [estrope'ar] *vt* to spoil; (*dañar*) to damage; **~se** *vr* (*objeto*) to get damaged; (*persona*: *la piel etc*) to be ruined

estructura [estruk'tura] *nf* structure

estruendo [es'trwendo] *nm* (*ruido*) racket, din; (*fig*: *alboroto*) uproar, turmoil

estrujar [estru'xar] *vt* (*apretar*) to squeeze; (*aplastar*) to crush; (*fig*) to drain, bleed

estuario [es'twarjo] *nm* estuary

estuche [es'tutʃe] *nm* box, case

estudiante [estu'ðjante] *nm/f* student; **estudiantil** *adj* student *cpd*

estudiar [estu'ðjar] *vt* to study

estudio [es'tuðjo] *nm* study; (*CINE, ARTE, RADIO*) studio; **~s** *nmpl* studies; (*erudición*) learning *sg*; **~so, a** *adj* studious

estufa [es'tufa] *nf* heater, fire

estupefaciente [estupefa'θjente] *nm* drug, narcotic

estupefacto, a [estupe'fakto, a] *adj* speechless, thunderstruck

estupendo, a [estu'pendo, a] *adj* wonderful, terrific; (*fam*) great; ¡~! that's great!, fantastic!

estupidez [estupi'ðeθ] *nf* (*torpeza*) stupidity; (*acto*) stupid thing (to do)

estúpido, a [es'tupiðo, a] *adj* stupid, silly

estupor [estu'por] *nm* stupor; (*fig*) astonishment, amazement

estuve *etc vb ver* **estar**

esvástica [es'βastika] *nf* swastika

ETA ['eta] (*ESP*) *nf abr* (= *Euskadi ta Askatasuna*) ETA

etapa [e'tapa] *nf* (*de viaje*) stage; (*DEPORTE*) leg; (*parada*) stopping place; (*fase*) stage, phase

etarra [e'tarra] *nm/f* member of ETA

etc. *abr* (= *etcétera*) etc

etcétera |et'θetera| adv etcetera

eternidad |eterni'ðaθ| nf eternity; **eterno, a** adj eternal, everlasting

ética |'etika| nf ethics pl

ético, a |'etiko, a| adj ethical

etiqueta |eti'keta| nf (modales) etiquette; (rótulo) label, tag

Eucaristía |eukaris'tia| nf Eucharist

eufemismo |eufe'mismo| nm euphemism

euforia |eu'forja| nf euphoria

euro |'euro| sm (moneda) euro

eurodiputado, a |eurodipu'taðo, a| nm/f Euro MP, MEP

Europa |eu'ropa| nf Europe; **europeo, a** adj, nm/f European

Euskadi |eus'kaði| nm the Basque Country o Provinces pl

euskera |eus'kera| nm (LING) Basque

evacuación |eßakwa'θjon| nf evacuation

evacuar |eßa'kwar| vt to evacuate

evadir |eßa'ðir| vt to evade, avoid; **~se** vr to escape

evaluar |eßa'lwar| vt to evaluate

evangelio |eßan'xeljo| nm gospel

evaporar |eßapo'rar| vt to evaporate; **~se** vr to vanish

evasión |eßa'sjon| nf escape, flight; (fig) evasion; **~ de capitales** flight of capital

evasiva |eßa'sißa| nf (pretexto) excuse

evasivo, a |eßa'sißo, a| adj evasive, non-committal

evento |e'ßento| nm event

eventual |eßen'twal| adj possible, conditional (upon circumstances); (trabajador) casual, temporary

evidencia |eßi'ðenθja| nf evidence, proof; **evidenciar** vt (hacer patente) to make evident; (probar) to prove, show; **evidenciarse** vr to be evident

evidente |eßi'ðente| adj obvious, clear, evident

evitar |eßi'tar| vt (evadir) to avoid; (impedir) to prevent

evocar |eßo'kar| vt to evoke, call forth

evolución |eßolu'θjon| nf (desarrollo) evolution, development; (cambio) change; (MIL) manoeuvre; **evolucionar** vi to evolve; to manoeuvre

ex |eks| adj ex-; **el ~ ministro** the former minister, the ex-minister

exacerbar |eksaθer'ßar| vt to irritate, annoy

exactamente |eksakta'mente| adv exactly

exactitud |eksakti'tuð| nf exactness; (precisión) accuracy; (puntualidad) punctuality; **exacto, a** adj exact; accurate; punctual; **¡exacto!** exactly!

exageración |eksaxera'θjon| nf exaggeration

exagerar |eksaxe'rar| vt, vi to exaggerate

exaltado, a |eksal'taðo, a| adj (apasionado) over-excited, worked-up; (POL) extreme

exaltar |eksal'tar| vt to exalt, glorify; **~se** vr (excitarse) to get excited o worked-up

examen |ek'samen| nm examination

examinar |eksami'nar| vt to examine; **~se** vr to be examined, take an examination

exasperar |eksaspe'rar| vt to exasperate; **~se** vr to get exasperated, lose patience

Exca. abr = **Excelencia**

excavadora |ekskaßa'ðora| nf excavator

excavar |ekska'ßar| vt to excavate

excedencia |eksθe'ðenθja| nf: **estar en ~** to be on leave; **pedir o solicitar la ~** to ask for leave

excedente |eksθe'ðente| adj, nm excess, surplus

exceder |eksθe'ðer| vt to exceed, surpass; **~se** vr (extralimitarse) to go too far

excelencia |eksθe'lenθja| nf excellence; **E~** Excellency; **excelente** adj excellent

excentricidad |eksθentriθi'ðaθ| nf eccentricity; **excéntrico, a** adj, nm/f eccentric

excepción |eksθep'θjon| nf exception; **excepcional** adj exceptional

excepto |eks'θepto| adv excepting, except (for)

exceptuar |eksθep'twar| vt to except, exclude

excesivo, a |eksθe'sißo, a| adj excessive

exceso |eks'θeso| nm (gen) excess; (COM) surplus; **~ de equipaje/peso** excess luggage/weight

excitación |eksθita'θjon| nf (sensación) excitement; (acción) excitation

excitado, a |eksθi'taðo, a| adj excited; (emociones) aroused

excitar |eksθi'tar| vt to excite; (incitar) to urge; **~se** vr to get excited

exclamación |eksklama'θjon| nf exclamation

exclamar |ekskla'mar| vi to exclaim

excluir |eksklu'ir| vt to exclude; (dejar fuera) to shut out; (descartar) to reject; **exclusión** nf exclusion

exclusiva |eksklu'sißa| nf (PRENSA) exclusive, scoop; (COM) sole right

exclusivo, a |eksklu'sißo, a| adj exclusive; **derecho ~** sole o exclusive right

Excmo. abr = **excelentísimo**

excomulgar |ekskomul'var| vt (REL) to excommunicate

excomunión |ekskomu'njon| nf excommunication

excursión |ekskur'sjon| nf excursion, outing; **excursionista** nm/f (turista) sightseer

excusa |eks'kusa| nf excuse; (disculpa) apology

excusar [eksku'sar] vt to excuse; **~se** vr (disculparse) to apologize

exhalar [eksa'lar] vt to exhale, breathe out; (olor etc) to give off; (suspiro) to breathe, heave

exhaustivo, a [eksaus'tiβo, a] adj (análisis) thorough; (estudio) exhaustive

exhausto, a [ek'sausto, a] adj exhausted

exhibición [eksiβi'θjon] nf exhibition, display, show

exhibir [eksi'βir] vt to exhibit, display, show

exhortar [eksor'tar] vt: **~ a** to exhort to

exigencia [eksi'xenθja] nf demand, requirement; **exigente** adj demanding

exigir [eksi'xir] vt (gen) to demand, require; **~ el pago** to demand payment

exiliado, a [eksi'ljaðo, a] adj exiled ♦ nm/f exile

exilio [ek'siljo] nm exile

eximir [eksi'mir] vt to exempt

existencia [eksis'tenθja] nf existence; **~s** nfpl stock(s) (pl)

existir [eksis'tir] vi to exist, be

éxito ['eksito] nm (triunfo) success; (MUS etc) hit; **tener ~** to be successful

exonerar [eksone'rar] vt to exonerate; **~ de una obligación** to free from an obligation

exorbitante [eksorβi'tante] adj (precio) exorbitant; (cantidad) excessive

exorcizar [eksorθi'θar] vt to exorcize

exótico, a [ek'sotiko, a] adj exotic

expandir [ekspan'dir] vt to expand

expansión [ekspan'sjon] nf expansion

expansivo, a [ekspan'siβo, a] adj: **onda ~a** shock wave

expatriarse [ekspa'trjarse] vr to emigrate; (POL) to go into exile

expectativa [ekspekta'tiβa] nf (espera) expectation; (perspectiva) prospect

expedición [ekspeði'θjon] nf (excursión) expedition

expediente [ekspe'ðjente] nm expedient; (JUR: procedimento) action, proceedings pl; (: papeles) dossier, file, record

expedir [ekspe'ðir] vt (despachar) to send, forward; (pasaporte) to issue

expendedor, a [ekspende'ðor, a] nm/f (vendedor) dealer

expensas [eks'pensas] nfpl: **a ~ de** at the expense of

experiencia [ekspe'rjenθja] nf experience

experimentado, a [eksperimen'taðo, a] adj experienced

experimentar [eksperimen'tar] vt (en laboratorio) to experiment with; (probar) to test, try out; (notar, observar) to experience; (deterioro, pérdida) to suffer; **experimento** nm experiment

experto, a [eks'perto, a] adj expert, skilled ♦ nm/f expert

expiar [ekspi'ar] vt to atone for

expirar [ekspi'rar] vi to expire

explanada [eskpla'naða] nf (llano) plain

explayarse [ekspla'jarse] vr (en discurso) to speak at length; **~ con uno** to confide in sb

explicación [eksplika'θjon] nf explanation

explicar [ekspli'kar] vt to explain; **~se** vr to explain (o.s.)

explícito, a [eks'pliθito, a] adj explicit

explique etc vb ver **explicar**

explorador, a [eksplora'ðor, a] nm/f (pionero) explorer; (MIL) scout ♦ nm (MED) probe; (TEC) (radar) scanner

explorar [eksplo'rar] vt to explore; (MED) to probe; (radar) to scan

explosión [eksplo'sjon] nf explosion; **explosivo, a** adj explosive

explotación [eksplota'θjon] nf exploitation; (de planta etc) running

explotar [eksplo'tar] vt to exploit; to run, operate ♦ vi to explode

exponer [ekspo'ner] vt to expose; (cuadro) to display; (vida) to risk; (idea) to explain; **~se** vr: **~se a (hacer)** algo to run the risk of (doing) sth

exportación [eksporta'θjon] nf (acción) export; (mercancías) exports pl

exportar [ekspor'tar] vt to export

exposición [eksposi'θjon] nf (gen) exposure; (de arte) show, exhibition; (explicación) explanation; (declaración) account, statement

expresamente [ekspresa'mente] adv (decir) clearly; (a propósito) expressly

expresar [ekspre'sar] vt to express; **expresión** nf expression

expresivo, a [ekspre'siβo, a] adj (persona, gesto, palabras) expressive; (cariñoso) affectionate

expreso, a [eks'preso, a] pp de **expresar** ♦ adj (explícito) express; (claro) specific, clear; (tren) fast ♦ adv: **mandar ~** to send by express (delivery)

express [eks'pres] (AM) adv: **enviar algo ~** to send sth special delivery

exprimidor [eksprimi'ðor] nm squeezer

exprimir [ekspri'mir] vt (fruta) to squeeze; (zumo) to squeeze out

expropiar [ekspro'pjar] vt to expropriate

expuesto, a [eks'pwesto, a] pp de **exponer** ♦ adj exposed; (cuadro etc) on show, on display

expulsar [ekspul'sar] vt (echar) to eject, throw out; (alumno) to expel; (despedir) to sack, fire; (DEPORTE) to send off; **expulsión** nf expulsion; sending-off

exquisito, a [ekski'sito, a] adj exquisite; (comida) delicious

éxtasis ['ekstasis] nm ecstasy

extender [eksten'der] vt to extend; (*los brazos*) to stretch out, hold out; (*mapa, tela*) to spread (out), open (out); (*mantequilla*) to spread; (*certificado*) to issue; (*cheque, recibo*) to make out; (*documento*) to draw up; **~se** vr (*gen*) to extend; (*persona: en el suelo*) to stretch out; (*epidemia*) to spread;

extendido, a adj (*abierto*) spread out, open, (*brazos*) outstretched; (*costumbre*) widespread

extensión [eksten'sjon] nf (*de terreno, mar*) expanse, stretch; (*de tiempo*) length, duration; (*TEL*) extension; **en toda la ~ de la palabra** in every sense of the word

extenso, a [eks'tenso, a] adj extensive

extenuar [ekste'nwar] vt (*debilitar*) to weaken

exterior [ekste'rjor] adj (*de fuera*) external; (*afuera*) outside, exterior; (*apariencia*) outward; (*deuda, relaciones*) foreign ♦ nm (*gen*) exterior, outside; (*aspecto*) outward appearance; (*DEPORTE*) wing(er); (*países extranjeros*) abroad; **en el ~** abroad; **al ~** outwardly, on the surface

exterminar [ekstermi'nar] vt to exterminate; **exterminio** nm extermination

externo, a [eks'terno, a] adj (*exterior*) external, outside; (*superficial*) outward ♦ nm/f day pupil

extinguir [ekstin'gir] vt (*fuego*) to extinguish, put out; (*raza, población*) to wipe out; **~se** vr (*fuego*) to go out; (*BIO*) to die out, become extinct

extinto, a [eks'tinto, a] adj extinct

extintor [ekstin'tor] nm (fire) extinguisher

extirpar [ekstir'par] vt (*MED*) to remove (surgically)

extorsión [ekstor'sjon] nf extorsion

extra ['ekstra] adj inv (*tiempo*) extra; (*chocolate, vino*) good-quality ♦ nm/f extra ♦ nm extra; (*bono*) bonus

extracción [ekstrak'θjon] nf extraction; (*en lotería*) draw

extracto [eks'trakto] nm extract

extradición [ekstradi'θjon] nf extradition

extraer [ekstra'er] vt to extract, take out

extraescolar [ekstraesko'lar] adj: **actividad ~** extracurricular activity

extralimitarse [ekstralimi'tarse] vr to go too far

extranjero, a [ekstran'xero, a] adj foreign ♦ nm/f foreigner ♦ nm foreign countries pl; **en el ~** abroad

extrañar [ekstra'ɲar] vt (*sorprender*) to find strange o odd; (*echar de menos*) to miss; **~se** vr (*sorprenderse*) to be amazed, be surprised

extrañeza [ekstra'ɲeθa] nf (*rareza*) strangeness, oddness; (*asombro*) amazement,

surprise

extraño, a [eks'traɲo, a] adj (*extranjero*) foreign; (*raro, sorprendente*) strange, odd

extraordinario, a [ekstraorði'narjo, a] adj extraordinary; (*edición, número*) special ♦ nm (*de periódico*) special edition; **horas extraordinarias** overtime sg

extrarradio [ekstra'rraðjo] nm suburbs

extravagancia [ekstraβa'ɣanθja] nf oddness; outlandishness; **extravagante** adj (*excéntrico*) eccentric; (*estrafalario*) outlandish

extraviado, a [ekstra'βjaðo, a] adj lost, missing

extraviar [ekstra'βjar] vt (*persona: desorientar*) to mislead, misdirect; (*perder*) to lose, misplace; **~se** vr to lose one's way, get lost; **extravío** nm loss; (*fig*) deviation

extremar [ekstre'mar] vt to carry to extremes; **~se** vr to do one's utmost, make every effort

extremaunción [ekstremaun'θjon] nf extreme unction

extremidad [ekstremi'ðað] nf (*punta*) extremity; **~es** nfpl (*ANAT*) extremities

extremo, a [eks'tremo, a] adj extreme; (*último*) last ♦ nm end; (*límite, grado sumo*) extreme; **en último ~** as a last resort

extrovertido, a [ekstroβer'tiðo, a] adj, nm/f extrovert

exuberancia [eksuβe'ranθja] nf exuberance; **exuberante** adj exuberant; (*fig*) luxuriant, lush

eyacular [ejaku'lar] vt, vi to ejaculate

F, f

f.a.b. abr (= *franco a bordo*) f.o.b.

fabada [fa'βaða] nf bean and sausage stew

fábrica ['faβrika] nf factory; **marca de ~** trademark; **precio de ~** factory price

fabricación [faβrika'θjon] nf (*manufactura*) manufacture; (*producción*) production; **de ~ casera** home-made; **~ en serie** mass production

fabricante [faβri'kante] nm/f manufacturer

fabricar [faβri'kar] vt (*manufacturar*) to manufacture, make; (*construir*) to build; (*cuento*) to fabricate, devise

fábula ['faβula] nf (*cuento*) fable; (*chisme*) rumour; (*mentira*) fib

fabuloso, a [faβu'loso, a] adj (*oportunidad, tiempo*) fabulous, great

facción [fak'θjon] nf (*POL*) faction; **facciones** nfpl (*del rostro*) features

faceta [fa'θeta] nf facet

facha ['fatʃa] (*fam*) nf (*aspecto*) look; (*cara*) face

fachada [fa'tʃaða] nf (*ARQ*) façade, front

fácil ['faθil] *adj* (*simple*) easy; (*probable*) likely
facilidad [faθili'ðað] *nf* (*capacidad*) ease; (*sencillez*) simplicity; (*de palabra*) fluency; **~es** *nfpl* facilities
facilitar [faθili'tar] *vt* (*hacer fácil*) to make easy; (*proporcionar*) to provide
fácilmente ['faθilmente] *adv* easily
facsímil [fak'simil] *nm* facsimile, fax
factible [fak'tiβle] *adj* feasible
factor [fak'tor] *nm* factor
factura [fak'tura] *nf* (*cuenta*) bill;
facturación *nf* (*de equipaje*) check-in;
facturar *vt* (*COM*) to invoice, charge for; (*equipaje*) to check in
facultad [fakul'tað] *nf* (*aptitud, ESCOL etc*) faculty; (*poder*) power
faena [fa'ena] *nf* (*trabajo*) work; (*quehacer*) task, job
faisán [fai'san] *nm* pheasant
faja ['faxa] *nf* (*para la cintura*) sash; (*de mujer*) corset; (*de tierra*) strip
fajo ['faxo] *nm* (*de papeles*) bundle; (*de billetes*) wad
falacia [fa'laθja] *nf* fallacy
falda ['falda] *nf* (*prenda de vestir*) skirt
falla ['faʎa] *nf* (*defecto*) fault, flaw
fallar [fa'ʎar] *vt* (*JUR*) to pronounce sentence on ♦ *vi* (*memoria*) to fail; (*motor*) to miss
fallecer [faʎe'θer] *vi* to pass away, die;
fallecimiento *nm* decease, demise
fallido, a [fa'ʎiðo, a] *adj* (*gen*) frustrated, unsuccessful
fallo ['faʎo] *nm* (*JUR*) verdict, ruling; (*fracaso*) failure; **~ cardíaco** heart failure
falsedad [false'ðað] *nf* falseness; (*hipocresía*) hypocrisy; (*mentira*) falsehood
falsificar [falsifi'kar] *vt* (*firma etc*) to forge; (*moneda*) to counterfeit
falso, a ['falso, a] *adj* false; (*documento, moneda etc*) fake; **en ~** falsely
falta ['falta] *nf* (*defecto*) fault, flaw; (*privación*) lack, want; (*ausencia*) absence; (*carencia*) shortage; (*equivocación*) mistake; (*DEPORTE*) foul; **echar en ~** to miss; **hacer ~ hacer algo** to be necessary to do sth; **me hace ~ una pluma** I need a pen; **~ de educación** bad manners *pl*
faltar [fal'tar] *vi* (*escasear*) to be lacking, be wanting; (*ausentarse*) to be absent, be missing; **faltan 2 horas para llegar** there are 2 hours to go till arrival; **~ al respeto a uno** to be disrespectful to sb; **¡no faltaba más!** (*no hay de qué*) don't mention it!
fama ['fama] *nf* (*renombre*) fame; (*reputación*) reputation
famélico, a [fa'meliko, a] *adj* starving
familia [fa'milja] *nf* family; **~ política** in-laws *pl*
familiar [fami'ljar] *adj* (*relativo a la familia*) family *cpd*; (*conocido, informal*) familiar ♦ *nm*

relative, relation; **~idad** *nf* (*gen*) familiarity; (*informalidad*) homeliness; **~izarse** *vr*:
~izarse con to familiarize o.s. with
famoso, a [fa'moso, a] *adj* (*renombrado*) famous
fanático, a [fa'natiko, a] *adj* fanatical ♦ *nm/f* fanatic; (*CINE, DEPORTE*) fan; **fanatismo** *nm* fanaticism
fanfarrón, ona [fanfa'rron, ona] *adj* boastful
fango ['fango] *nm* mud; **~so, a** *adj* muddy
fantasía [fanta'sia] *nf* fantasy, imagination; **joyas de ~** imitation jewellery *sg*
fantasma [fan'tasma] *nm* (*espectro*) ghost, apparition; (*fanfarrón*) show-off
fantástico, a [fan'tastiko, a] *adj* fantastic
farmacéutico, a [farma'θeutiko, a] *adj* pharmaceutical ♦ *nm/f* chemist (*BRIT*), pharmacist
farmacia [far'maθja] *nf* chemist's (shop) (*BRIT*), pharmacy; **~ de turno** duty chemist; **~ de guardia** all-night chemist
fármaco ['farmako] *nm* drug
faro ['faro] *nm* (*NAUT: torre*) lighthouse; (*AUTO*) headlamp; **~s antiniebla** fog lamps; **~s delanteros/traseros** headlights/rear lights
farol [fa'rol] *nm* lantern, lamp
farola [fa'rola] *nf* street lamp (*BRIT*) o light (*US*)
farsa ['farsa] *nf* (*gen*) farce
farsante [far'sante] *nm/f* fraud, fake
fascículo [fas'θikulo] *nm* (*de revista*) part, instalment
fascinar [fasθi'nar] *vt* (*gen*) to fascinate
fascismo [fas'θismo] *nm* fascism; **fascista** *adj, nm/f* fascist
fase ['fase] *nf* phase
fastidiar [fasti'ðjar] *vt* (*molestar*) to annoy, bother; (*estropear*) to spoil; **~se** *vr*: **¡que se fastidie!** (*fam*) he'll just have to put up with it!
fastidio [fas'tiðjo] *nm* (*molestia*) annoyance; **~so, a** *adj* (*molesto*) annoying
fastuoso, a [fas'twoso, a] *adj* (*banquete, boda*) lavish; (*acto*) pompous
fatal [fa'tal] *adj* (*gen*) fatal; (*desgraciado*) ill-fated; (*fam: malo, pésimo*) awful; **~idad** *nf* (*destino*) fate; (*mala suerte*) misfortune
fatiga [fa'tiɣa] *nf* (*cansancio*) fatigue, weariness
fatigar [fati'ɣar] *vt* to tire, weary; **~se** *vr* to get tired
fatigoso, a [fati'ɣoso, a] *adj* (*cansador*) tiring
fatuo, a ['fatwo, a] *adj* (*vano*) fatuous; (*presuntuoso*) conceited
favor [fa'βor] *nm* favour; **estar a ~ de** to be in favour of; **haga el ~ de...** would you be so good as to..., kindly...; **por ~** please; **~able** *adj* favourable

favorecer [faßoɾe'θeɾ] vt to favour; (*vestido etc*) to become, flatter; **este peinado le favorece** this hairstyle suits him

favorito, a [faßo'ɾito, a] adj, nm/f favourite

fax [faks] nm inv fax; **mandar por ~ to** fax

faz [faθ] nf face; **la ~ de la tierra** the face of the earth

fe [fe] nf (*REL*) faith; (*documento*) certificate; **prestar ~** a to believe, credit; **actuar con buena/mala ~** to act in good/bad faith; **dar ~ de** to bear witness to

fealdad [feal'dað] nf ugliness

febrero [fe'ßɾeɾo] nm February

febril [fe'ßɾil] adj (*fig: actividad*) hectic; (*mente, mirada*) feverish

fecha ['fetʃa] nf date; **~ de caducidad** (*de producto alimenticio*) sell-by date; (*de contrato etc*) expiry date; **con ~ adelantada** postdated; **en ~ próxima** soon; **hasta la ~** to date, so far; **poner ~ to** date; **fechar** vt to date

fecundar [fekun'daɾ] vt (*generar*) to fertilize, make fertile; **fecundo, a** adj (*fértil*) fertile; (*fig*) prolific; (*productivo*) productive

federación [feðeɾa'θjon] nf federation

felicidad [feliθi'ðað] nf happiness; **~es** nfpl (*felicitaciones*) best wishes, congratulations

felicitación [feliθita'θjon] nf: **¡felicitaciones!** congratulations!

felicitar [feliθi'taɾ] vt to congratulate

feligrés, esa [feli'ɣɾes, esa] nm/f parishioner

feliz [fe'liθ] adj happy

felpudo [fel'puðo] nm doormat

femenino, a [feme'nino, a] adj, nm feminine

feminista [femi'nista] adj, nm/f feminist

fenómeno [fe'nomeno] nm phenomenon; (*fig*) freak, accident ♦ adj great ♦ excl great!, marvellous!; **fenomenal** adj = **fenómeno**

feo, a ['feo, a] adj (*gen*) ugly; (*desagradable*) bad, nasty

féretro ['feɾetɾo] nm (*ataúd*) coffin; (*sarcófago*) bier

feria ['feɾja] nf (*gen*) fair; (*descanso*) holiday, rest day; (*AM: mercado*) village market; (: *cambio*) loose o small change

fermentar [feɾmen'taɾ] vi to ferment

ferocidad [feɾoθi'ðað] nf fierceness, ferocity

feroz [fe'roθ] adj (*cruel*) cruel; (*salvaje*) fierce

férreo, a ['feɾeo, a] adj iron

ferretería [feɾete'ɾja] nf (*tienda*) ironmonger's (shop) (*BRIT*), hardware store

ferrocarril [feɾoka'ril] nm railway

ferroviario, a [feɾo'ßjaɾjo, a] adj rail cpd

fértil ['feɾtil] adj (*productivo*) fertile; (*rico*) rich; **fertilidad** nf (*gen*) fertility; (*productividad*) fruitfulness

ferviente [feɾ'ßjente] adj fervent

fervor [feɾ'ßoɾ] nm fervour; **~oso, a** adj fervent

festejar [feste'xaɾ] vt (*celebrar*) to celebrate

festejo [fes'texo] nm celebration; **festejos** nmpl (*fiestas*) festivals

festín [fes'tin] nm feast, banquet

festival [festi'ßal] nm festival

festividad [festißi'ðað] nf festivity

festivo, a [fes'tißo, a] adj (*de fiesta*) festive; (*CINE, LITERATURA*) humorous; **día ~** holiday

fétido, a ['fetiðo, a] adj foul-smelling

feto ['feto] nm foetus

fiable ['fjaßle] adj (*persona*) trustworthy; (*máquina*) reliable

fiador, a [fja'ðoɾ, a] nm/f (*JUR*) surety, guarantor; (*COM*) backer; **salir ~ por uno** to stand bail for sb

fiambre ['fjambɾe] nm cold meat

fianza ['fjanθa] nf surety; (*JUR*): **libertad bajo ~** release on bail

fiar [fi'aɾ] vt (*salir garante de*) to guarantee; (*vender a crédito*) to sell on credit; (*secreto*): **~ a** to confide (to) ♦ vi to trust; **~se** vr to trust (in), rely on; **~se de uno** to rely on sb

fibra ['fißɾa] nf fibre; **~ óptica** optical fibre

ficción [fik'θjon] nf fiction

ficha ['fitʃa] nf (*TEL*) token; (*en juegos*) counter, marker; (*tarjeta*) (index) card; **fichar** vt (*archivar*) to file, index; (*DEPORTE*) to sign; **estar fichado** to have a record; **fichero** nm box file; (*INFORM*) file

ficticio, a [fik'tiθjo, a] adj (*imaginario*) fictitious; (*falso*) fabricated

fidelidad [fiðeli'ðað] nf (*lealtad*) fidelity, loyalty; **alta ~** high fidelity, hi-fi

fideos [fi'ðeos] nmpl noodles

fiebre ['fjeßɾe] nf (*MED*) fever; (*fig*) fever, excitement; **~ amarilla/del heno** yellow/hay fever; **~ palúdica** malaria; **tener ~** to have a temperature

fiel [fjel] adj (*leal*) faithful, loyal; (*fiable*) reliable; (*exacto*) accurate, faithful ♦ nm: **los ~es** the faithful

fieltro ['fjeltɾo] nm felt

fiera ['fjeɾa] nf (*animal feroz*) wild animal o beast; (*fig*) dragon; *ver tb* **fiero**

fiero, a ['fjeɾo, a] adj (*cruel*) cruel; (*feroz*) fierce; (*duro*) harsh

fiesta ['fjesta] nf party; (*de pueblo*) festival; (*vacaciones, tb:* **~s**) holiday sg; (*REL*): **~ de guardar** day of obligation

figura [fi'ɣuɾa] nf (*gen*) figure; (*forma, imagen*) shape, form; (*NAIPES*) face card

figurar [fiɣu'ɾaɾ] vt (*representar*) to represent; (*fingir*) to figure ♦ vi to figure; **~se** vr (*imaginarse*) to imagine; (*suponer*) to suppose

fijador [fixa'ðoɾ] nm (*FOTO etc*) fixative; (*de pelo*) gel

fijar [fi'xaɾ] vt (*gen*) to fix; (*estampilla*) to affix, stick (on); **~se** vr: **~se en** to notice

fijo, a ['fixo, a] adj (*gen*) fixed; (*firme*) firm;

(*permanente*) permanent ♦ *adv*: **mirar ~ to stare**

fila ['fila] *nf* row; (*MIL*) rank; **ponerse en ~ to line up, get into line**

filántropo, a [fi'lantropo, a] *nm/f* philanthropist

filatelia [fila'telja] *nf* philately, stamp collecting

filete [fi'lete] *nm* (*carne*) fillet steak; (*pescado*) fillet

filiación [filja'θjon] *nf* (*POL*) affiliation

filial [fi'ljal] *adj* filial ♦ *nf* subsidiary

Filipinas [fili'pinas] *nfpl*: **las ~** the Philippines; **filipino, a** *adj, nm/f* Philippine

filmar [fil'mar] *vt* to film, shoot

filo ['filo] *nm* (*gen*) edge; **sacar ~ a** to sharpen; **al ~ del mediodía** at about midday; **de doble ~** double-edged

filón [fi'lon] *nm* (*MINERÍA*) vein, lode; (*fig*) goldmine

filosofía [filoso'fia] *nf* philosophy; **filósofo, a** *nm/f* philosopher

filtrar [fil'trar] *vt, vi* to filter, strain; **~se** *vr* to filter; **filtro** *nm* (*TEC, utensilio*) filter

fin [fin] *nm* end; (*objetivo*) aim, purpose; **al ~ y al cabo** when all's said and done; **a ~ de** in order to; **por ~** finally; **en ~** in short; **~ de semana** weekend

final [fi'nal] *adj* final ♦ *nm* end, conclusion ♦ *nf* final; **~idad** *nf* (*propósito*) purpose, intention; **~ista** *nm/f* finalist; **~izar** *vt* to end, finish; (*INFORM*) to log out o off ♦ *vi* to end, come to an end

financiar [finan'θjar] *vt* to finance; **financiero, a** *adj* financial ♦ *nm/f* financier

finca ['finka] *nf* (*bien inmueble*) property, land; (*casa de campo*) country house; (*AM*) farm

fingir [fin'xir] *vt* (*simular*) to simulate, feign ♦ *vi* (*aparentar*) to pretend

finlandés, esa [finlan'des, esa] *adj* Finnish ♦ *nm/f* Finn ♦ *nm* (*LING*) Finnish

Finlandia [fin'landja] *nf* Finland

fino, a ['fino, a] *adj* fine; (*delgado*) slender; (*de buenas maneras*) polite, refined; (*jerez*) fino, dry

firma ['firma] *nf* signature; (*COM*) firm, company

firmamento [firma'mento] *nm* firmament

firmar [fir'mar] *vt* to sign

firme ['firme] *adj* firm; (*estable*) stable; (*sólido*) solid; (*constante*) steady; (*decidido*) resolute ♦ *nm* road (surface); **~mente** *adv* firmly; **~za** *nf* firmness; (*constancia*) steadiness; (*solidez*) solidity

fiscal [fis'kal] *adj* fiscal ♦ *nm/f* public prosecutor; **año ~** tax o fiscal year

fisco ['fisko] *nm* (*hacienda*) treasury, exchequer (*BRIT*)

fisgar [fis'ʁar] *vt* to pry into

fisgonear [fisʁone'ar] *vt* to poke one's nose into ♦ *vi* to pry, spy

física ['fisika] *nf* physics *sg*; *ver tb* **físico**

físico, a ['fisiko, a] *adj* physical ♦ *nm* physique ♦ *nm/f* physicist

fisura [fi'sura] *nf* crack; (*MED*) fracture

flác(c)ido, a ['fla(k)θiðo, a] *adj* flabby

flaco, a ['flako, a] *adj* (*muy delgado*) skinny, thin; (*débil*) weak, feeble

flagrante [fla'ʁrante] *adj* flagrant

flamante [fla'mante] (*fam*) *adj* brilliant; (*nuevo*) brand-new

flamenco, a [fla'menko, a] *adj* (*de Flandes*) Flemish; (*baile, música*) flamenco ♦ *nm* (*baile, música*) flamenco

flan [flan] *nm* creme caramel

flaqueza [fla'keθa] *nf* (*delgadez*) thinness, leanness; (*fig*) weakness

flash [flaʃ] (*pl* **~s** o **~es**) *nm* (*FOTO*) flash

flauta ['flauta] *nf* (*MUS*) flute

flecha ['fletʃa] *nf* arrow

flechazo [fle'tʃaθo] *nm* love at first sight

fleco ['fleko] *nm* fringe

flema ['flema] *nm* phlegm

flequillo [fle'kiʎo] *nm* (*pelo*) fringe

flexible [flek'sißle] *adj* flexible

flexión [flek'sjon] *nf* press-up

flexo ['flekso] *nm* adjustable table-lamp

flojera [flo'xera] (*AM: fam*) *nf*: **me da ~** I can't be bothered

flojo, a ['floxo, a] *adj* (*gen*) loose; (*sin fuerzas*) limp; (*débil*) weak

flor [flor] *nf* flower; **a ~ de** on the surface of; **~ecer** *vi* (*BOT*) to flower, bloom; (*fig*) to flourish; **~eciente** *adj* (*BOT*) in flower, flowering; (*fig*) thriving; **~ero** *nm* vase; **~istería** *nf* florist's (shop)

flota ['flota] *nf* fleet

flotador [flota'ðor] *nm* (*gen*) float; (*para nadar*) rubber ring

flotar [flo'tar] *vi* (*gen*) to float; **flote** *nm*: **a flote** afloat; **salir a flote** (*fig*) to get back on one's feet

fluctuar [fluk'twar] *vi* (*oscilar*) to fluctuate

fluidez [flui'ðeθ] *nf* fluidity; (*fig*) fluency

flúido, a [fluiðo, a] *adj, nm* fluid

fluir [flu'ir] *vi* to flow

flujo ['fluxo] *nm* flow; **~ y reflujo** ebb and flow

flúor ['fluor] *nm* fluoride

fluvial [flußi'al] *adj* (*navegación, cuenca*) fluvial, river *cpd*

foca ['foka] *nf* seal

foco ['foko] *nm* focus; (*ELEC*) floodlight; (*AM*) (light) bulb

fofo, a ['fofo, a] *adj* soft, spongy; (*carnes*) flabby

fogata [fo'ʁata] *nf* bonfire

fogón [fo'ɣon] *nm* (*de cocina*) ring, burner

fogoso, a [fo'ɣoso, a] *adj* spirited

folio ['foljo] *nm* folio, page

follaje [fo'ʎaxe] *nm* foliage

folletín [foʎe'tin] *nm* newspaper serial

folleto [fo'ʎeto] *nm* (POL) pamphlet

follón [fo'ʎon] (*fam*) *nm* (*lío*) mess; (*conmoción*) fuss; **armar un ~** to kick up a row

fomentar [fomen'tar] *vt* (MED) to foment; **fomento** *nm* (*promoción*) promotion

fonda ['fonda] *nf* inn

fondo ['fondo] *nm* (*de mar*) bottom; (*de coche, sala*) back; (ARTE etc) background; (*reserva*) fund; **~s** *nmpl* (COM) funds, resources; **una investigación a ~** a thorough investigation; **en el ~** at bottom, deep down

fonobuzón [fonoßu'θon] *nm* voice mail

fontanería [fontane'ria] *nf* plumbing; **fontanero, a** *nm/f* plumber

footing ['futin] *nm* jogging; **hacer ~** to jog, go jogging

forastero, a [foras'tero, a] *nm/f* stranger

forcejear [forθexe'ar] *vi* (*luchar*) to struggle

forense [fo'rense] *nm/f* pathologist

forjar [for'xar] *vt* to forge

forma ['forma] *nf* (*figura*) form, shape; (MED) fitness; (*método*) way, means; **las ~s** the conventions; **estar en ~** to be fit

formación [forma'θjon] *nf* (*gen*) formation; (*educación*) education; **~ profesional** vocational training

formal [for'mal] *adj* (*gen*) formal; (*fig: serio*) serious; (: *de fiar*) reliable; **~idad** *nf* formality; seriousness; **~izar** *vt* (JUR) to formalize; (*situación*) to put in order, regularize; **~izarse** *vr* (*situación*) to be put in order, be regularized

formar [for'mar] *vt* (*componer*) to form, shape; (*constituir*) to make up, constitute; (ESCOL) to train, educate; **~se** *vr* (ESCOL) to be trained, educated; (*cobrar forma*) to form, take form; (*desarrollarse*) to develop

formatear [formate'ar] *vt* to format

formativo, a [forma'tiβo, a] *adj* (*lecturas, años*) formative

formato [for'mato] *nm* format

formidable [formi'ðaßle] *adj* (*temible*) formidable; (*estupendo*) tremendous

fórmula ['formula] *nf* formula

formular [formu'lar] *vt* (*queja*) to make, lodge; (*petición*) to draw up; (*pregunta*) to pose

formulario [formu'larjo] *nm* form

fornido, a [for'niðo, a] *adj* well-built

forrar [fo'rrar] *vt* (*abrigo*) to line; (*libro*) to cover; **forro** *nm* (*de cuaderno*) cover; (COSTURA) lining; (*de sillón*) upholstery

fortalecer [fortale'θer] *vt* to strengthen

fortaleza [forta'leθa] *nf* (MIL) fortress, stronghold; (*fuerza*) strength; (*determinación*) resolution

fortuito, a [for'twito, a] *adj* accidental

fortuna [for'tuna] *nf* (*suerte*) fortune, (good) luck; (*riqueza*) fortune, wealth

forzar [for'θar] *vt* (*puerta*) to force (open); (*compeler*) to compel

forzoso, a [for'θoso, a] *adj* necessary

fosa ['fosa] *nf* (*sepultura*) grave; (*en tierra*) pit; **~s nasales** nostrils

fósforo ['fosforo] *nm* (QUIM) phosphorus; (*cerilla*) match

foso ['foso] *nm* ditch; (TEATRO) pit; (AUTO etc) **~ de reconocimiento** inspection pit

foto ['foto] *nf* photo, snap(shot); **sacar una ~** to take a photo o picture

fotocopia [foto'kopja] *nf* photocopy; **fotocopiadora** *nf* photocopier; **fotocopiar** *vt* to photocopy

fotografía [fotoɣra'fia] *nf* (ARTE) photography; (*una ~*) photograph; **fotografiar** *vt* to photograph

fotógrafo, a [fo'toɣrafo, a] *nm/f* photographer

fracasar [fraka'sar] *vi* (*gen*) to fail

fracaso [fra'kaso] *nm* failure

fracción [frak'θjon] *nf* fraction; **fraccionamiento** (AM) *nm* housing estate

fractura [frak'tura] *nf* fracture, break

fragancia [fra'ɣanθja] *nf* (*olor*) fragrance, perfume

frágil ['fraxil] *adj* (*débil*) fragile; (COM) breakable

fragmento [fraɣ'mento] *nm* (*pedazo*) fragment

fragua ['fraɣwa] *nf* forge; **fraguar** *vt* to forge; (*fig*) to concoct ♦ *vi* to harden

fraile ['fraile] *nm* (REL) friar; (: *monje*) monk

frambuesa [fram'bwesa] *nf* raspberry

francamente *adv* (*hablar, decir*) frankly; (*realmente*) really

francés, esa [fran'θes, esa] *adj* French ♦ *nm/f* Frenchman/woman ♦ *nm* (LING) French

Francia ['franθja] *nf* France

franco, a ['franko, a] *adj* (*cándido*) frank, open; (COM: *exento*) free ♦ *nm* (*moneda*) franc

francotirador, a [frankotira'ðor, a] *nm/f* sniper

franela [fra'nela] *nf* flannel

franja ['franxa] *nf* fringe

franquear [franke'ar] *vt* (*camino*) to clear; (*carta, paquete postal*) to frank, stamp; (*obstáculo*) to overcome

franqueo [fran'keo] *nm* postage

franqueza [fran'keθa] *nf* (*candor*) frankness

frasco ['frasko] *nm* bottle, flask; **~ al vacío** (vacuum) flask

frase ['frase] nf sentence; ~ **hecha** set phrase; (pey) stock phrase

fraterno, a [fra'terno, a] adj brotherly, fraternal

fraude ['frauðe] nm (cualidad) dishonesty; (acto) fraud; **fraudulento, a** adj fraudulent

frazada [fra'saða] (AM) nf blanket

frecuencia [fre'kwenθja] nf frequency; **con ~** frequently, often

frecuentar [frekwen'tar] vt to frequent

fregadero [freɣa'ðero] nm (kitchen) sink

fregar [fre'ɣar] vt (frotar) to scrub; (platos) to wash (up); (AM) to annoy

fregona [fre'ɣona] nf mop

freír [fre'ir] vt to fry

frenar [fre'nar] vt to brake; (fig) to check

frenazo [fre'naθo] nm: **dar un ~** to brake sharply

frenesí [frene'si] nm frenzy; **frenético, a** adj frantic

freno ['freno] nm (TEC, AUTO) brake; (de cabalgadura) bit; (fig) check

frente ['frente] nm (ARQ, POL) front; (de objeto) front part ♦ nf forehead, brow; ~ **a** in front of; (en situación opuesta de) opposite; **al ~ de** (fig) at the head of; **chocar de ~** to crash head-on; **hacer ~ a** to face up to

fresa ['fresa] (ESP) nf strawberry

fresco, a ['fresko, a] adj (nuevo) fresh; (frío) cool; (descarado) cheeky ♦ nm (aire) fresh air; (ARTE) fresco; (AM: jugo) fruit drink ♦ nm/f (fam): **ser un ~** to have a nerve; **tomar el ~** to get some fresh air; **frescura** nf freshness; (descaro) cheek, nerve

frialdad [frial'daθ] nf (gen) coldness; (indiferencia) indifference

fricción [frik'θjon] nf (gen) friction; (acto) rub(bing); (MED) massage

frigidez [frixi'ðeθ] nf frigidity

frigorífico [friɣo'rifiko] nm refrigerator

frijol [fri'xol] nm kidney bean

frío, a etc ['frio, a] vb ver **freír** ♦ adj cold; (indiferente) indifferent ♦ nm cold; indifference; **hace ~** it's cold; **tener ~** to be cold

frito, a ['frito, a] adj fried; **me trae ~ ese hombre** I'm sick and tired of that man; **fritos** nmpl fried food

frívolo, a ['friβolo, a] adj frivolous

frontal [fron'tal] adj frontal; **choque ~** head-on collision

frontera [fron'tera] nf frontier; **fronterizo, a** adj frontier cpd; (contiguo) bordering

frontón [fron'ton] nm (DEPORTE: cancha) pelota court; (: juego) pelota

frotar [fro'tar] vt to rub; **~se** vr: **~se las manos** to rub one's hands

fructífero, a [fruk'tifero, a] adj fruitful

fruncir [frun'θir] vt to pucker; (COSTURA) to pleat; ~ **el ceño** to knit one's brow

frustrar [frus'trar] vt to frustrate

fruta ['fruta] nf fruit; **frutería** nf fruit shop; **frutero, a** adj fruit cpd ♦ nm/f fruiterer ♦ nm fruit bowl

frutilla [fru'tiʎa] (AM) nf strawberry

fruto ['fruto] nm fruit; (fig: resultado) result; (: beneficio) benefit; ~**s secos** nuts; (pasas etc) dried fruit sg

fue vb ver **ser; ir**

fuego ['fweɣo] nm (gen) fire; **a ~ lento** on a low heat; ¿**tienes ~?** have you (got) a light?; ~**s artificiales** o **de artificio** fireworks

fuente ['fwente] nf fountain; (manantial, fig) spring; (origen) source; (plato) large dish

fuera etc ['fwera] vb ver **ser, ir** ♦ adv out(side); (en otra parte) away; (excepto, salvo) except, save ♦ prep: ~ **de** outside; (fig) besides; ~ **de sí** beside o.s.; **por ~** (on the) outside

fuera-borda [fwera'βorða] nm speedboat

fuerte ['fwerte] adj strong; (golpe) hard; (ruido) loud; (comida) rich; (lluvia) heavy; (dolor) intense ♦ adv strongly; hard; loud(ly)

fuerza etc ['fwerθa] vb ver **forzar** ♦ nf (fortaleza) strength; (TEC, ELEC) power; (coacción) force; (MIL: tb: ~s) forces pl; **a ~ de** by dint of; **cobrar ~s** to recover one's strength; **tener ~s para** to have the strength to; **a la ~** forcibly, by force; **por ~** of necessity; ~ **de voluntad** willpower

fuga ['fuɣa] nf (huida) flight, escape; (de gas etc) leak

fugarse [fu'ɣarse] vr to flee, escape

fugaz [fu'ɣaθ] adj fleeting

fugitivo, a [fuxi'tiβo, a] adj, nm/f fugitive

fui vb ver **ser; ir**

fulano, a [fu'lano, a] nm/f so-and-so, what's-his-name/what's-her-name

fulminante [fulmi'nante] adj (fig: mirada) fierce; (MED: enfermedad, ataque) sudden; (fam: éxito, golpe) sudden

fumador, a [fuma'ðor, a] nm/f smoker

fumar [fu'mar] vt, vi to smoke; ~ **en pipa** to smoke a pipe

función [fun'θjon] nf function; (en trabajo) duties pl; (espectáculo) show; **entrar en funciones** to take up one's duties

funcionar [funθjo'nar] vi (gen) to function; (máquina) to work; "**no funciona**" "out of order"

funcionario, a [funθjo'narjo, a] nm/f civil servant

funda ['funda] nf (gen) cover; (de almohada) pillowcase

fundación [funda'θjon] nf foundation

fundamental [fundamen'tal] adj fundamental, basic

fundamentar [fundamen'tar] vt (poner

base) to lay the foundations of; (*establecer*) to found; (*fig*) to base; **fundamento** *nm* (*base*) foundation

fundar [fun'dar] *vt* to found; **~se** *vr*: **~se en** to be founded on

fundición [fundi'θjon] *nf* fusing; (*fábrica*) foundry

fundir [fun'dir] *vt* (*gen*) to fuse; (*metal*) to smelt, melt down; (*nieve etc*) to melt; (*COM*) to merge; (*estatua*) to cast; **~se** *vr* (*colores etc*) to merge, blend; (*unirse*) to fuse together; (*ELEC: fusible, lámpara etc*) to fuse, blow; (*nieve etc*) to melt

fúnebre ['funeβre] *adj* funeral *cpd*, funereal

funeral [fune'ral] *nm* funeral; **funeraria** *nf* undertaker's

funesto, a [fu'nesto, a] *adj* (*día*) ill-fated; (*decisión*) fatal

furgón [fur'ɣon] *nm* wagon; **furgoneta** *nf* (*AUTO, COM*) (transit) van (*BRIT*), pick-up (truck) (*US*)

furia ['furja] *nf* (*ira*) fury; (*violencia*) violence; **furibundo, a** *adj* furious; **furioso, a** *adj* (*iracundo*) furious; (*violento*) violent; **furor** *nm* (*cólera*) rage

furtivo, a [fur'tiβo, a] *adj* furtive ♦ *nm* poacher

fusible [fu'siβle] *nm* fuse

fusil [fu'sil] *nm* rifle; **~ar** *vt* to shoot

fusión [fu'sjon] *nf* (*gen*) melting; (*unión*) fusion; (*COM*) merger

fútbol ['futβol] *nm* football; **futbolín** *nm* table football; **futbolista** *nm* footballer

futuro, a [fu'turo, a] *adj, nm* future

G, g

gabardina [gaβar'ðina] *nf* raincoat, gabardine

gabinete [gaβi'nete] *nm* (*POL*) cabinet; (*estudio*) study; (*de abogados etc*) office

gaceta [ga'θeta] *nf* gazette

gachas ['gatʃas] *nfpl* porridge *sg*

gafas ['gafas] *nfpl* glasses; **~ de sol** sunglasses

gafe ['gafe] *nm* jinx

gaita ['gaita] *nf* bagpipes *pl*

gajes ['gaxes] *nmpl*: **los ~ del oficio** occupational hazards

gajo ['gaxo] *nm* (*de naranja*) segment

gala ['gala] *nf* (*traje de etiqueta*) full dress; **~s** *nfpl* (*ropa*) finery *sg*; **estar de ~** to be in one's best clothes; **hacer ~ de** to display

galante [ga'lante] *adj* gallant; **galantería** *nf* (*caballerosidad*) gallantry; (*cumplido*) politeness; (*comentario*) compliment

galápago [ga'lapaɣo] *nm* (*ZOOL*) turtle

galardón [galar'ðon] *nm* award, prize

galaxia [ga'laksja] *nf* galaxy

galera [ga'lera] *nf* (*nave*) galley; (*carro*) wagon; (*IMPRENTA*) galley

galería [gale'ria] *nf* (*gen*) gallery; (*balcón*) veranda(h); (*pasillo*) corridor

Gales ['gales] *nm* (*tb: País de ~*) Wales; **galés, esa** *adj* Welsh ♦ *nm/f* Welshman/ woman ♦ *nm* (*LING*) Welsh

galgo, a ['galɣo, a] *nm/f* greyhound

galimatías [galima'tias] *nmpl* (*lenguaje*) gibberish *sg*, nonsense *sg*

gallardía [gaʎar'ðia] *nf* (*valor*) bravery

gallego, a [ga'ʎeɣo, a] *adj, nm/f* Galician

galleta [ga'ʎeta] *nf* biscuit (*BRIT*), cookie (*US*)

gallina [ga'ʎina] *nf* hen ♦ *nm/f* (*fam: cobarde*) chicken; **gallinero** *nm* henhouse; (*TEATRO*) top gallery

gallo ['gaʎo] *nm* cock, rooster

galón [ga'lon] *nm* (*MIL*) stripe; (*COSTURA*) braid; (*medida*) gallon

galopar [galo'par] *vi* to gallop

gama ['gama] *nf* (*fig*) range

gamba ['gamba] *nf* prawn (*BRIT*), shrimp (*US*)

gamberro, a [gam'berro, a] *nm/f* hooligan, lout

gamuza [ga'muθa] *nf* chamois

gana ['gana] *nf* (*deseo*) desire, wish; (*apetito*) appetite; (*voluntad*) will; (*añoranza*) longing; **de buena ~** willingly; **de mala ~** reluctantly; **me da ~s de** I feel like, I want to; **no me da la ~** I don't feel like it; **tener ~s de** to feel like

ganadería [ganaðe'ria] *nf* (*ganado*) livestock; (*ganado vacuno*) cattle *pl*; (*cría, comercio*) cattle raising

ganado [ga'naðo] *nm* livestock; **~ lanar** sheep *pl*; **~ mayor** cattle *pl*; **~ porcino** pigs *pl*

ganador, a [gana'ðor, a] *adj* winning ♦ *nm/f* winner

ganancia [ga'nanθja] *nf* (*lo ganado*) gain; (*aumento*) increase; (*beneficio*) profit; **~s** *nfpl* (*ingresos*) earnings; (*beneficios*) profit *sg*, winnings

ganar [ga'nar] *vt* (*obtener*) to get, obtain; (*sacar ventaja*) to gain; (*salario etc*) to earn; (*DEPORTE, premio*) to win; (*derrotar a*) to beat; (*alcanzar*) to reach ♦ *vi* (*DEPORTE*) to win; **~se** *vr*: **~se la vida** to earn one's living

ganchillo [gan'tʃiʎo] *nm* crochet

gancho ['gantʃo] *nm* (*gen*) hook; (*colgador*) hanger

gandul, a [gan'dul, a] *adj, nm/f* good-for-nothing, layabout

ganga ['ganga] *nf* bargain

gangrena [gan'grena] *nf* gangrene

ganso, a ['ganso, a] *nm/f* (*ZOOL*) goose; (*fam*) idiot

ganzúa [gan'θua] *nf* skeleton key

garabatear [garaβate'ar] *vi, vt* (*al escribir*) to scribble, scrawl

garabato [gara'βato] *nm* (*escritura*) scrawl,

scribble
garaje [ga'raxe] *nm* garage
garante [ga'rante] *adj* responsible ♦ *nm/f* guarantor
garantía [garan'tia] *nf* guarantee
garantizar [garanti'θar] *vt* to guarantee
garbanzo [gar'ßanθo] *nm* chickpea (*BRIT*), garbanzo (*US*)
garbo [garßo] *nm* grace, elegance
garfio ['garfjo] *nm* grappling iron
garganta [gar'xanta] *nf* (*ANAT*) throat; (*de botella*) neck; **gargantilla** *nf* necklace
gárgaras ['garvaras] *nfpl:* hacer ~ to gargle
garita [ga'rita] *nf* cabin, hut; (*MIL*) sentry box
garra ['garra] *nf* (*de gato, TEC*) claw; (*de ave*) talon; (*fam: mano*) hand, paw
garrafa [ga'rrafa] *nf* carafe, decanter
garrapata [garra'pata] *nf* tick
garrote [ga'rrote] *nm* (*palo*) stick; (*porra*) cudgel; (*suplicio*) garrotte
garza ['garθa] *nf* heron
gas [gas] *nm* gas
gasa ['gasa] *nf* gauze
gaseosa [gase'osa] *nf* lemonade
gaseoso, a [gase'oso, a] *adj* gassy, fizzy
gasoil [ga'soil] *nm* diesel (oil)
gasóleo [ga'soleo] *nm* = gasoil
gasolina [gaso'lina] *nf* petrol, gas(oline) (*US*); **gasolinera** *nf* petrol (*BRIT*) o gas (*US*) station
gastado, a [gas'taðo, a] *adj* (*dinero*) spent; (*ropa*) worn out; (*usado: frase etc*) trite
gastar [gas'tar] *vt* (*dinero, tiempo*) to spend; (*fuerzas*) to use up; (*desperdiciar*) to waste; (*llevar*) to wear; **~se** *vr* to wear out; (*estropearse*) to waste; ~ **en** to spend on; ~ **bromas** to crack jokes; ¿**qué número gastas?** what size (shoe) do you take?
gasto ['gasto] *nm* (*desembolso*) expenditure, spending; (*consumo, uso*) use; **~s** *nmpl* (*desembolsos*) expenses; (*cargos*) charges, costs
gastronomía [gastrono'mia] *nf* gastronomy
gatear [gate'ar] *vi* (*andar a gatas*) to go on all fours
gatillo [ga'tiλo] *nm* (*de arma de fuego*) trigger; (*de dentista*) forceps
gato, a ['gato, a] *nm/f* cat ♦ *nm* (*TEC*) jack; **andar a gatas** to go on all fours
gaviota [ga'ßjota] *nf* seagull
gay [ge] *adj inv, nm* gay, homosexual
gazpacho [gaθ'patʃo] *nm* gazpacho
gel [xel] *nm* (*tb:* ~ **de baño/ducha**) gel
gelatina [xela'tina] *nf* jelly; (*polvos etc*) gelatine
gema ['xema] *nf* gem
gemelo, a [xe'melo, a] *adj, nm/f* twin; **~s** *nmpl* (*de camisa*) cufflinks; (*prismáticos*) field glasses, binoculars

gemido [xe'miðo] *nm* (*quejido*) moan, groan; (*aullido*) howl
Géminis ['xeminis] *nm* Gemini
gemir [xe'mir] *vi* (*quejarse*) to moan, groan; (*aullar*) to howl
generación [xenera'θjon] *nf* generation
general [xene'ral] *adj* general ♦ *nm* general; **por lo** o **en ~** in general; **G~itat** *nf* Catalan parliament; **~izar** *vt* to generalize; **~izarse** *vr* to become generalized, spread; **~mente** *adv* generally
generar [xene'rar] *vt* to generate
género ['xenero] *nm* (*clase*) kind, sort; (*tipo*) type; (*BIO*) genus; (*LING*) gender; (*COM*) material; ~ **humano** human race
generosidad [xenerosi'ðað] *nf* generosity; **generoso, a** *adj* generous
genial [xe'njal] *adj* inspired; (*idea*) brilliant; (*afable*) genial
genio ['xenjo] *nm* (*carácter*) nature, disposition; (*humor*) temper; (*facultad creadora*) genius; **de mal ~** bad-tempered
genital [xeni'tal] *adj* genital; **genitales** *nmpl* genitals
gente ['xente] *nf* (*personas*) people *pl*; (*parientes*) relatives *pl*
gentil [xen'til] *adj* (*elegante*) graceful; (*encantador*) charming; **~eza** *nf* grace; charm; (*cortesía*) courtesy
gentío [xen'tio] *nm* crowd, throng
genuino, a [xe'nwino, a] *adj* genuine
geografía [xeoɣra'fia] *nf* geography
geología [xeolo'xia] *nf* geology
geometría [xeome'tria] *nf* geometry
gerencia [xe'renθja] *nf* management; **gerente** *nm/f* (*supervisor*) manager; (*jefe*) director
geriatría [xeria'tria] *nf* (*MED*) geriatrics *sg*
germen ['xermen] *nm* germ
germinar [xermi'nar] *vi* to germinate
gesticular [xestiku'lar] *vi* to gesticulate; (*hacer muecas*) to grimace; **gesticulación** *nf* gesticulation; (*mueca*) grimace
gestión [xes'tjon] *nf* management; (*diligencia, acción*) negotiation; **gestionar** *vt* (*lograr*) to try to arrange; (*dirigir*) to manage
gesto ['xesto] *nm* (*mueca*) grimace; (*ademán*) gesture
Gibraltar [xißral'tar] *nm* Gibraltar; **gibraltareño, a** *adj, nm/f* Gibraltarian
gigante [xi'ßante] *adj, nm/f* giant; **gigantesco, a** *adj* gigantic
gilipollas [xili'poλas] (*fam*) *adj inv* daft ♦ *nm/f inv* wally
gimnasia [xim'nasja] *nf* gymnastics *pl*; **gimnasio** *nm* gymnasium; **gimnasta** *nm/f* gymnast
gimotear [ximote'ar] *vi* to whine, whimper
ginebra [xi'neßra] *nf* gin

ginecólogo, a [xine'koloɣo, a] *nm/f* gynaecologist

gira ['xira] *nf* tour, trip

girar [xi'rar] *vt (dar la vuelta)* to turn (around); *(: rápidamente)* to spin; *(COM: giro postal)* to draw; *(: letra de cambio)* to issue ♦ *vi* to turn (round); *(rápido)* to spin

girasol [xira'sol] *nm* sunflower

giratorio, a [xira'torjo, a] *adj* revolving

giro ['xiro] *nm (movimiento)* turn, revolution; *(LING)* expression; *(COM)* draft; **~ bancario/postal** bank giro/postal order

gis [xis] *(AM) nm* chalk

gitano, a [xi'tano, a] *adj, nm/f* gypsy

glacial [gla'θjal] *adj* icy, freezing

glaciar [gla'θjar] *nm* glacier

glándula ['glandula] *nf* gland

global [glo'ßal] *adj* global

globo ['gloßo] *nm (esfera)* globe, sphere; *(aerostato, juguete)* balloon

glóbulo ['gloßulo] *nm* globule; *(ANAT)* corpuscle

gloria ['glorja] *nf* glory

glorieta [glo'rjeta] *nf (de jardín)* bower, arbour; *(plazoleta)* roundabout *(BRIT)*, traffic circle *(US)*

glorificar [glorifi'kar] *vt (enaltecer)* to glorify, praise

glorioso, a [glo'rjoso, a] *adj* glorious

glotón, ona [glo'ton, ona] *adj* gluttonous, greedy ♦ *nm/f* glutton

glucosa [glu'kosa] *nf* glucose

gobernador, a [goßerna'ðor, a] *adj* governing ♦ *nm/f* governor; **gobernante** *adj* governing

gobernar [goßer'nar] *vt (dirigir)* to guide, direct; *(POL)* to rule, govern ♦ *vi* to govern; *(NAUT)* to steer

gobierno *etc* [go'ßjerno] *vb ver* **gobernar** ♦ *nm (POL)* government; *(dirección)* guidance, direction; *(NAUT)* steering

goce *etc* ['goθe] *vb ver* **gozar** ♦ *nm* enjoyment

gol [gol] *nm* goal

golf [golf] *nm* golf

golfa ['golfa] *(fam!) nf (mujer)* slut, whore

golfo, a ['golfo, a] *nm (GEO)* gulf ♦ *nm/f (fam: niño)* urchin; *(gamberro)* lout

golondrina [golon'drina] *nf* swallow

golosina [golo'sina] *nf (dulce)* sweet; **goloso, a** *adj* sweet-toothed

golpe ['golpe] *nm* blow; *(de puño)* punch; *(de mano)* smack; *(de remo)* stroke; *(fig: choque)* clash; **no dar ~** to be bone idle; **de un ~** with one blow; **de ~** suddenly; **~ (de estado)** coup (d'état); **golpear** *vt, vi* to strike, knock; *(asestar)* to beat; *(de puño)* to punch; *(golpetear)* to tap

goma ['goma] *nf (caucho)* rubber; *(elástico)* elastic; *(una ~)* elastic band; **~ espuma** foam rubber; **~ de pegar** gum, glue; **~ de borrar** eraser, rubber *(BRIT)*

gomina [go'mina] *nf* hair gel

gordo, a ['gorðo, a] *adj (gen)* fat; *(fam)* enormous; **el (premio) ~** *(en lotería)* first prize; **gordura** *nf* fat; *(corpulencia)* fatness, stoutness

gorila [go'rila] *nm* gorilla

gorjear [gorxe'ar] *vi* to twitter, chirp

gorra ['gorra] *nf* cap; *(de niño)* bonnet; *(militar)* bearskin; **entrar de ~** *(fam)* to gatecrash; **ir de ~** to sponge

gorrión [go'rrjon] *nm* sparrow

gorro ['gorro] *nm (gen)* cap; *(de niño, mujer)* bonnet

gorrón, ona [go'rron, ona] *nm/f* scrounger; **gorronear** *(fam) vi* to scrounge

gota ['gota] *nf (gen)* drop; *(de sudor)* bead; *(MED)* gout; **gotear** *vi* to drip; *(lloviznar)* to drizzle; **gotera** *nf* leak

gozar [go'θar] *vi* to enjoy o.s.; **~ de** *(disfrutar)* to enjoy; *(poseer)* to possess

gozne ['goθne] *nm* hinge

gozo ['goθo] *nm (alegría)* joy; *(placer)* pleasure

gr. *abr (= gramo, gramos)* g

grabación [graßa'θjon] *nf* recording

grabado [gra'ßaðo] *nm* print, engraving

grabadora [graßa'ðora] *nf* tape-recorder

grabar [gra'ßar] *vt* to engrave; *(discos, cintas)* to record

gracia ['graθja] *nf (encanto)* grace, gracefulness; *(humor)* humour, wit; **¡(muchas) ~s!** thanks (very much)!; **~s a** thanks to; **tener ~** *(chiste etc)* to be funny; **no me hace ~** I am not keen; **gracioso, a** *adj (divertido)* funny, amusing; *(cómico)* comical ♦ *nm/f (TEATRO)* comic character

grada ['graða] *nf (de escalera)* step; *(de anfiteatro)* tier, row; **~s** *nfpl (DEPORTE: de estadio)* terraces

gradería [graðe'ria] *nf (gradas)* (flight of) steps *pl*; *(de anfiteatro)* tiers *pl*, rows *pl*; *(DEPORTE: de estadio)* terraces *pl*; **~ cubierta** covered stand

grado ['graðo] *nm* degree; *(de aceite, vino)* grade; *(grada)* step; *(MIL)* rank; **de buen ~** willingly

graduación [graðwa'θjon] *nf (del alcohol)* proof, strength; *(ESCOL)* graduation; *(MIL)* rank

gradual [gra'ðwal] *adj* gradual

graduar [gra'ðwar] *vt (gen)* to graduate; *(MIL)* to commission; **~se** *vr* to graduate; **~se la vista** to have one's eyes tested

gráfica ['grafika] *nf* graph

gráfico, a ['grafiko, a] *adj* graphic ♦ *nm* diagram; **~s** *nmpl (INFORM)* graphics

grajo ['graxo] *nm* rook

Gral abr (= *General*) Gen.

gramática [gra'matika] nf grammar

gramo ['gramo] nm gramme (*BRIT*), gram (*US*)

gran [gran] adj ver **grande**

grana ['grana] nf (*color, tela*) scarlet

granada [gra'naða] nf pomegranate; (*MIL*) grenade

granate [gra'nate] adj deep red

Gran Bretaña [-bre'taɲa] nf Great Britain

grande ['grande] (*antes de nmsg*: **gran**) adj (*de tamaño*) big, large; (*alto*) tall; (*distinguido*) great; (*impresionante*) grand ♦ nm grandee; **grandeza** nf greatness

grandioso, a [gran'djoso, a] adj magnificent, grand

granel [gra'nel]: **a ~** adv (*COM*) in bulk

granero [gra'nero] nm granary, barn

granito [gra'nito] nm (*AGR*) small grain; (*roca*) granite

granizado [grani'θaðo] nm iced drink

granizar [grani'θar] vi to hail; **granizo** nm hail

granja ['granxa] nf (*gen*) farm; **granjear** vt to win, gain; **granjearse** vr to win, gain; **granjero, a** nm/f farmer

grano ['grano] nm grain; (*semilla*) seed; (*de café*) bean; (*MED*) pimple, spot

granuja [gra'nuxa] nm/f rogue; (*golfillo*) urchin

grapa ['grapa] nf staple; (*TEC*) clamp; **grapadora** nf stapler

grasa ['grasa] nf (*gen*) grease; (*de cocinar*) fat, lard; (*sebo*) suet; (*mugre*) filth; **grasiento, a** adj greasy; (*de aceite*) oily; **graso, a** adj (*leche, queso, carne*) fatty; (*pelo, piel*) greasy

gratificación [gratifika'θjon] nf (*bono*) bonus; (*recompensa*) reward

gratificar [gratifi'kar] vt to reward

gratinar [grati'nar] vt to cook au gratin

gratis ['gratis] adv free

gratitud [grati'tuð] nf gratitude

grato, a ['grato, a] adj (*agradable*) pleasant, agreeable

gratuito, a [gra'twito, a] adj (*gratis*) free; (*sin razón*) gratuitous

gravamen [gra'ßamen] nm (*impuesto*) tax

gravar [gra'ßar] vt to tax

grave ['graße] adj heavy; (*serio*) grave, serious; **~dad** nf gravity

gravilla [gra'ßiʎa] nf gravel

gravitar [graßi'tar] vi to gravitate; **~ sobre** to rest on

graznar [graθ'nar] vi (*cuervo*) to squawk; (*pato*) to quack; (*hablar ronco*) to croak

Grecia ['greθja] nf Greece

gremio ['gremjo] nm trade, industry

greña ['greɲa] nf (*cabellos*) shock of hair

gresca ['greska] nf uproar

griego, a ['grjeʝo, a] adj, nm/f Greek

grieta ['grjeta] nf crack

grifo ['grifo] nm tap; (*AM: AUTO*) petrol (*BRIT*) o gas (*US*) station

grilletes [gri'ʎetes] nmpl fetters

grillo ['griʎo] nm (*ZOOL*) cricket

gripe ['gripe] nf flu, influenza

gris [gris] adj (*color*) grey

gritar [gri'tar] vt, vi to shout, yell; **grito** nm shout, yell; (*de horror*) scream

grosella [gro'seʎa] nf (red)currant; **~ negra** blackcurrant

grosería [grose'ria] nf (*actitud*) rudeness; (*comentario*) vulgar comment; **grosero, a** adj (*poco cortés*) rude, bad-mannered; (*ordinario*) vulgar, crude

grosor [gro'sor] nm thickness

grotesco, a [gro'tesko, a] adj grotesque

grúa ['grua] nf (*TEC*) crane; (*de petróleo*) derrick

grueso, a ['grweso, a] adj thick; (*persona*) stout ♦ nm bulk; **el ~ de** the bulk of

grulla ['gruʎa] nf crane

grumo ['grumo] nm clot, lump

gruñido [gru'ɲiðo] nm grunt; (*de persona*) grumble

gruñir [gru'ɲir] vi (*animal*) to growl; (*persona*) to grumble

grupa ['grupa] nf (*ZOOL*) rump

grupo ['grupo] nm group; (*TEC*) unit, set

gruta ['gruta] nf grotto

guadaña [gwa'ðaɲa] nf scythe

guagua [gwa'xwa] (*AM*) nf (*niño*) baby; (*bus*) bus

guante ['gwante] nm glove; **~ra** nf glove compartment

guapo, a ['gwapo, a] adj good-looking, attractive; (*elegante*) smart

guarda ['gwarða] nm/f (*persona*) guard, keeper ♦ nf (*acto*) guarding; (*custodia*) custody; **~bosques** nm inv gamekeeper; **~costas** nm inv coastguard vessel ♦ nm/f guardian, protector; **~espaldas** nm/f inv bodyguard; **~meta** nm/f goalkeeper; **guardar** vt (*gen*) to keep; (*vigilar*) to guard, watch over; (*dinero: ahorrar*) to save; **guardarse** vr (*preservarse*) to protect o.s.; (*evitar*) to avoid; **guardar cama** to stay in bed; **~rropa** nm (*armario*) wardrobe; (*en establecimiento público*) cloakroom

guardería [gwarðe'ria] nf nursery

guardia ['gwarðja] nf (*MIL*) guard; (*cuidado*) care, custody ♦ nm/f guard; (*policía*) policeman/woman; **estar de ~** to be on guard; **montar ~** to mount guard; **G~ Civil** Civil Guard; **G~ Nacional** National Guard

guardián, ana [gwar'ðjan, ana] nm/f (*gen*) guardian, keeper

guarecer [gware'θer] vt (*proteger*) to protect;

(*abrigar*) to shelter; **~se** *vr* to take refuge
guarida [gwa'riða] *nf* (*de animal*) den, lair; (*refugio*) refuge
guarnecer [gwarne'θer] *vt* (*equipar*) to provide; (*adornar*) to adorn; (*TEC*) to reinforce; **guarnición** *nf* (*de vestimenta*) trimming; (*de piedra*) mount; (*CULIN*) garnish; (*arneses*) harness; (*MIL*) garrison
guarro, a ['gwarro, a] *nm/f* pig
guasa ['gwasa] *nf* joke; **guasón, ona** *adj* (*bromista*) joking ♦ *nm/f* wit; joker
Guatemala [gwate'mala] *nf* Guatemala
guay [gwai] (*fam*) *adj* super, great
gubernativo, a [gußerna'tißo, a] *adj* governmental
guerra ['gerra] *nf* war; **~ civil** civil war; **~ fría** cold war; **dar ~** to annoy; **guerrear** *vi* to wage war; **guerrero, a** *adj* fighting; (*carácter*) warlike ♦ *nm/f* warrior
guerrilla [ge'rriʎa] *nf* guerrilla warfare; (*tropas*) guerrilla band o group
guía *etc* ['gia] *vb ver* **guiar** ♦ *nm/f* (*persona*) guide ♦ *nf* (*libro*) guidebook; **~ de ferrocarriles** railway timetable; **~ telefónica** telephone directory
guiar [gi'ar] *vt* to guide, direct; (*AUTO*) to steer; **~se** *vr*: **~se por** to be guided by
guijarro [gi'xarro] *nm* pebble
guillotina [giʎo'tina] *nf* guillotine
guinda ['ginda] *nf* morello cherry
guindilla [gin'diʎa] *nf* chilli pepper
guiñapo [gi'ɲapo] *nm* (*harapo*) rag; (*persona*) reprobate, rogue
guiñar [gi'ɲar] *vt* to wink
guión [gi'on] *nm* (*LING*) hyphen, dash; (*CINE*) script; **guionista** *nm/f* scriptwriter
guiri ['giri] (*fam*: *pey*) *nm/f* foreigner
guirnalda [gir'nalda] *nf* garland
guisado [gi'saðo] *nm* stew
guisante [gi'sante] *nm* pea
guisar [gi'sar] *vt, vi* to cook; **guiso** *nm* cooked dish
guitarra [gi'tarra] *nf* guitar
gula ['gula] *nf* gluttony, greed
gusano [gu'sano] *nm* worm; (*lombriz*) earthworm
gustar [gus'tar] *vt* to taste, sample ♦ *vi* to please, be pleasing; **~ de algo** to like o enjoy sth; **me gustan las uvas** I like grapes; **le gusta nadar** she likes o enjoys swimming
gusto ['gusto] *nm* (*sentido, sabor*) taste; (*placer*) pleasure; **tiene ~ a menta** it tastes of mint; **tener buen ~** to have good taste; **sentirse a ~** to feel at ease; **mucho ~ (en conocerle)** pleased to meet you; **el ~ es mío** the pleasure is mine; **con ~** willingly, gladly; **~so, a** *adj* (*sabroso*) tasty; (*agradable*) pleasant

H, h

ha *vb ver* **haber**
haba ['aßa] *nf* bean
Habana [a'ßana] *nf*: **la ~** Havana
habano [a'ßano] *nm* Havana cigar
habéis *vb ver* **haber**

PALABRA CLAVE
---

haber [a'ßer] *vb aux* **1** (*tiempos compuestos*) to have; **había comido** I had eaten; **antes/después de ~lo visto** before seeing/after seeing o having seen it
2: **¡~lo dicho antes!** you should have said so before!
3: **~ de: he de hacerlo** I have to do it; **ha de llegar mañana** it should arrive tomorrow
♦ *vb impers* **1** (*existencia*: *sg*) there is; (: *pl*) there are; **hay un hermano/dos hermanos** there is one brother/there are two brothers; **¿cuánto hay de aquí a Sucre?** how far is it from here to Sucre?
2 (*obligación*): **hay que hacer algo** something must be done; **hay que apuntarlo para acordarse** you have to write it down to remember
3: **¡hay que ver!** well I never!
4: **¡no hay de o por (*AM*) qué!** don't mention it!, not at all!
5: **¿qué hay?** (*¿qué pasa?*) what's up?, what's the matter?; (*¿qué tal?*) how's it going?
♦ **~se** *vr*: **habérselas con uno** to have it out with sb
♦ *vt*: **he aquí unas sugerencias** here are some suggestions; **no hay cintas blancas pero sí las hay rojas** there aren't any white ribbons but there are some red ones
♦ *nm* (*en cuenta*) credit side; **~es** *nmpl* assets; **¿cuánto tengo en el ~?** how much do I have in my account?; **tiene varias novelas en su ~** he has several novels to his credit

---

habichuela [aßi'tʃwela] *nf* kidney bean
hábil ['aßil] *adj* (*listo*) clever, smart; (*capaz*) fit, capable; (*experto*) expert; **día ~** working day; **habilidad** *nf* skill, ability
habilitar [aßili'tar] *vt* (*capacitar*) to enable; (*dar instrumentos*) to equip; (*financiar*) to finance
hábilmente [aßil'mente] *adv* skilfully, expertly
habitación [aßita'θjon] *nf* (*cuarto*) room; (*BIO*: *morada*) habitat; **~ sencilla** o **individual** single room; **~ doble** o **de matrimonio** double room
habitante [aßi'tante] *nm/f* inhabitant
habitar [aßi'tar] *vt* (*residir en*) to inhabit;

(*ocupar*) to occupy ♦ *vi* to live

hábito [ˈaßito] *nm* habit

habitual [aßiˈtwal] *adj* usual

habituar [aßiˈtwar] *vt* to accustom; **~se** *vr*: **~se a** to get used to

habla [ˈaßla] *nf* (*capacidad de hablar*) speech; (*idioma*) language; (*dialecto*) dialect; **perder el ~** to become speechless; **de ~ francesa** French-speaking; **estar al ~** to be in contact; (*TEL*) to be on the line; **¡González al ~!** (*TEL*) González speaking!

hablador, a [aßlaˈðor, a] *adj* talkative ♦ *nm/f* chatterbox

habladuría [aßlaðuˈria] *nf* rumour; **~s** *nfpl* gossip *sg*

hablante [aˈßlante] *adj* speaking ♦ *nm/f* speaker

hablar [aˈßlar] *vt* to speak, talk ♦ *vi* to speak; **~se** *vr* to speak to each other; **~ con** to speak to; **~ de** to speak *o* about; **"se habla inglés"** "English spoken here"; **¡ni ~!** it's out of the question!

habré *etc vb ver* **haber**

hacendoso, a [aθenˈdoso, a] *adj* industrious

PALABRA CLAVE
---

hacer [aˈθer] *vt* **1** (*fabricar, producir*) to make; (*construir*) to build; **~ una película** *etc* to make a film/noise; **el guisado lo hice yo** I made *o* cooked the stew

2 (*ejecutar: trabajo etc*) to do; **~ la colada** to do the washing; **~ la comida** to do the cooking; **¿qué haces?** what are you doing?; **~ el malo** *o* **el papel del malo** (*TEATRO*) to play the villain

3 (*estudios, algunos deportes*) to do; **~ español/económicas** to do *o* study Spanish/economics; **~ yoga/gimnasia** to do yoga/go to gym

4 (*transformar, incidir en*): **esto lo hará más difícil** this will make it more difficult; **salir te hará sentir mejor** going out will make you feel better

5 (*cálculo*): **2 y 2 hacen 4** 2 and 2 make 4; **éste hace 100** this one makes 100

6 (+ *sub*): **esto hará que ganemos** this will make us win; **harás que no quiera venir** you'll stop him wanting to come

7 (*como sustituto de vb*) to do; **él bebió y yo hice lo mismo** he drank and I did likewise

8: no hace más que criticar all he does is criticize

♦ *vb semi-aux*: **hacer** + *infin* **1** (*directo*): **les hice venir** I made *o* had them come;

~ trabajar a los demás to get others to work

2 (*por intermedio de otros*): **~ reparar algo** to get sth repaired

♦ *vi* **1**: **haz como que no lo sabes** act as if you don't know

2 (*ser apropiado*): **si os hace** if it's alright with you

3: **~ de**: **~ de madre para uno** to be like a mother to sb; (*TEATRO*): **~ de Otelo** to play Othello

♦ *vb impers* **1**: **hace calor/frío** it's hot/cold; *ver tb* **bueno; sol; tiempo**

2 (*tiempo*): **hace 3 años** 3 years ago; **hace un mes que voy/no voy** I've been going/I haven't been for a month

3: **¿cómo has hecho para llegar tan rápido?** how did you manage to get here so quickly?

♦ **~se** *vr* **1** (*volverse*) to become; **se hicieron amigos** they became friends

2 (*acostumbrarse*): **~se a** to get used to

3: se hace con huevos y leche it's made out of eggs and milk; **eso no se hace** that's not done

4 (*obtener*): **~se de** *o* **con algo** to get hold of sth

5 (*fingirse*): **~se el sueco** to turn a deaf ear

hacha [ˈatʃa] *nf* axe; (*antorcha*) torch

hachís [aˈtʃis] *nm* hashish

hacia [ˈaθja] *prep* (*en dirección de*) towards; (*cerca de*) near; (*actitud*) towards; **~ arriba/abajo** up(wards)/down(wards); **~ mediodía** about noon

hacienda [aˈθjenda] *nf* (*propiedad*) property; (*finca*) farm; (*AM*) ranch; **~ pública** public finance; **(Ministerio de) H~** Exchequer (*BRIT*), Treasury Department (*US*)

hada [ˈaða] *nf* fairy

hago *etc vb ver* **hacer**

Haití [aiˈti] *nm* Haiti

halagar [alaˈɣar] *vt* to flatter

halago [aˈlaɣo] *nm* flattery; **halagüeño, a** *adj* flattering

halcón [alˈkon] *nm* falcon, hawk

hallar [aˈʎar] *vt* (*gen*) to find; (*descubrir*) to discover; (*toparse con*) to run into; **~se** *vr* to be (situated); **hallazgo** *nm* discovery; (*cosa*) find

halterofilia [alteroˈfilja] *nf* weightlifting

hamaca [aˈmaka] *nf* hammock

hambre [ˈambre] *nf* hunger; (*plaga*) famine; (*deseo*) longing; **tener ~** to be hungry; **hambriento, a** *adj* hungry, starving

hamburguesa [amburˈɣesa] *nf* hamburger; **hamburguesería** *nf* burger bar

han *vb ver* **haber**

harapiento, a [araˈpjento, a] *adj* tattered, in rags

harapos [aˈrapos] *nmpl* rags

haré *etc vb ver* **hacer**

harina [aˈrina] *nf* flour

hartar [arˈtar] *vt* to satiate, glut; (*fig*) to tire, sicken; **~se** *vr* (*de comida*) to fill o.s., gorge o.s.; (*cansarse*) to get fed up (*de* with);

hartazgo *nm* surfeit, glut; **harto, a** *adj*
(*lleno*) full; (*cansado*) fed up ♦ *adv* (*bastante*)
enough; (*muy*) very; **estar harto de** to be fed
up with

has *vb ver* **haber**

hasta ['asta] *adv* even ♦ *prep* (*alcanzando a*)
as far as; up to; down to; (*de tiempo: a tal
hora*) till, until; (*antes de*) before ♦ *conj*:
~ **que** until; ~ **luego/el sábado** see you soon/
on Saturday

hastiar [as'tjar] *vt* (*gen*) to weary; (*aburrir*)
to bore; ~**se** *vr*: ~**se de** to get fed up with;
hastío *nm* weariness; boredom

hatillo [a'tiʎo] *nm* belongings *pl*, kit;
(*montón*) bundle, heap

hay *vb ver* **haber**

Haya ['aja] *nf*: **la** ~ The Hague

haya *etc* ['aja] *vb ver* **haber** ♦ *nf* beech tree

haz [aθ] *vb ver* **hacer** ♦ *nm* (*de luz*) beam

hazaña [a'θaɲa] *nf* feat, exploit

hazmerreír [aθmerre'ir] *nm inv* laughing
stock

he *vb ver* **haber**

hebilla [e'ßiʎa] *nf* buckle, clasp

hebra ['eßra] *nf* thread; (*BOT: fibra*) fibre,
grain

hebreo, a [e'ßreo, a] *adj, nm/f* Hebrew ♦ *nm*
(*LING*) Hebrew

hechizar [etʃi'θar] *vt* to cast a spell on,
bewitch

hechizo [e'tʃiθo] *nm* witchcraft, magic; (*acto
de magia*) spell, charm

hecho, a ['etʃo, a] *pp de* **hacer** ♦ *adj* (*carne*)
done; (*COSTURA*) ready-to-wear ♦ *nm* deed,
act; (*dato*) fact; (*cuestión*) matter; (*suceso*)
event ♦ *excl* agreed!, done!; **¡bien ~!** well
done!; **de** ~ in fact, as a matter of fact

hechura [e'tʃura] *nf* (*forma*) form, shape;
(*de persona*) build

hectárea [ek'tarea] *nf* hectare

heder [e'ðer] *vi* to stink, smell

hediondo, a [e'ðjondo, a] *adj* stinking

hedor [e'ðor] *nm* stench

helada [e'laða] *nf* frost

heladera [ela'ðera] (*AM*) *nf* (*refrigerador*)
refrigerator

helado, a [e'laðo, a] *adj* frozen; (*glacial*) icy;
(*fig*) chilly, cold ♦ *nm* ice cream

helar [e'lar] *vt* to freeze, ice (up); (*dejar
atónito*) to amaze; (*desalentar*) to discourage
♦ *vi* to freeze; ~**se** *vr* to freeze

helecho [e'letʃo] *nm* fern

hélice ['eliθe] *nf* (*TEC*) propeller

helicóptero [eli'koptero] *nm* helicopter

hembra ['embra] *nf* (*BOT, ZOOL*) female;
(*mujer*) woman; (*TEC*) nut

hemorragia [emo'rraxja] *nf* haemorrhage

hemorroides [emo'rroiðes] *nfpl*
haemorrhoids, piles

hemos *vb ver* **haber**

hendidura [endi'ðura] *nf* crack, split

heno ['eno] *nm* hay

herbicida [erßi'θiða] *nm* weedkiller

heredad [ere'ðað] *nf* landed property;
(*granja*) farm

heredar [ere'ðar] *vt* to inherit; **heredero, a**
nm/f heir(ess)

hereje [e'rexe] *nm/f* heretic

herencia [e'renθja] *nf* inheritance

herida [e'riða] *nf* wound, injury; *ver tb* **herido**

herido, a [e'riðo, a] *adj* injured, wounded
♦ *nm/f* casualty

herir [e'rir] *vt* to wound, injure; (*fig*) to offend

hermanastro, a [erma'nastro, a] *nm/f*
stepbrother/sister

hermandad [erman'dað] *nf* brotherhood

hermano, a [er'mano, a] *nm/f* brother/sister;
~ **gemelo** twin brother; **hermana gemela** twin
sister; ~ **político** brother-in-law; **hermana
política** sister-in-law

hermético, a [er'metiko, a] *adj* hermetic;
(*fig*) watertight

hermoso, a [er'moso, a] *adj* beautiful,
lovely; (*estupendo*) splendid; (*guapo*)
handsome; **hermosura** *nf* beauty

hernia ['ernja] *nf* hernia

héroe ['eroe] *nm* hero

heroína [ero'ina] *nf* (*mujer*) heroine; (*droga*)
heroin

heroísmo [ero'ismo] *nm* heroism

herradura [erra'ðura] *nf* horseshoe

herramienta [erra'mjenta] *nf* tool

herrero [e'rrero] *nm* blacksmith

herrumbre [e'rrumbre] *nf* rust

hervidero [erßi'ðero] *nm* (*fig*) swarm; (*POL
etc*) hotbed

hervir [er'ßir] *vi* to boil; (*burbujear*) to
bubble; (*fig*): ~ **de** to teem with; ~ **a fuego
lento** to simmer; **hervor** *nm* boiling; (*fig*)
ardour, fervour

heterosexual [eterosek'swal] *adj*
heterosexual

hice *etc vb ver* **hacer**

hidratante [iðra'tante] *adj*: **crema** ~
moisturizing cream, moisturizer; **hidratar** *vt*
(*piel*) to moisturize; **hidrato** *nm*: **hidratos de
carbono** carbohydrates

hidráulica [i'ðraulika] *nf* hydraulics *sg*

hidráulico, a [i'ðrauliko, a] *adj* hydraulic

hidro... [iðro] *prefijo* hydro..., water-...;
~**eléctrico, a** *adj* hydroelectric; ~**fobia** *nf*
hydrophobia, rabies; **hidrógeno** *nm*
hydrogen

hiedra ['jeðra] *nf* ivy

hiel [jel] *nf* gall, bile; (*fig*) bitterness

hiela *etc vb ver* **helar**

hielo ['jelo] *nm* (*gen*) ice; (*escarcha*) frost;
(*fig*) coldness, reserve

hiena ['jena] nf hyena

hierba ['jerßa] nf (*pasto*) grass; (*CULIN, MED: planta*) herb; **mala ~** weed; (*fig*) evil influence; **~buena** nf mint

hierro ['jerro] nm (*metal*) iron; (*objeto*) iron object

hígado ['ɣaðo] nm liver

higiene [i'xjene] nf hygiene; **higiénico, a** adj hygienic

higo ['iɣo] nm fig; **higuera** nf fig tree

hijastro, a [i'xastro, a] nm/f stepson/ daughter

hijo, a [i'ixo, a] nm/f son/daughter, child; **~s** nmpl children, sons and daughters; **~ de papá/mamá** daddy's/mummy's boy; **~ de puta** (*fam!*) bastard (!), son of a bitch (!)

hilar [i'lar] vt to spin; **~ fino** to split hairs

hilera [i'lera] nf row, file

hilo ['ilo] nm thread; (*BOT*) fibre; (*metal*) wire; (*de agua*) trickle, thin stream

hilvanar [ilßa'nar] vt (*COSTURA*) to tack (*BRIT*), baste (*US*); (*fig*) to do hurriedly

himno ['imno] nm hymn; **~ nacional** national anthem

hincapié [inka'pje] nm: **hacer ~ en** to emphasize

hincar [in'kar] vt to drive (in), thrust (in); **~se** vr: **~se de rodillas** to kneel down

hincha ['intʃa] (*fam*) nm/f fan

hinchado, a [in'tʃaðo, a] adj (*gen*) swollen; (*persona*) pompous

hinchar [in'tʃar] vt (*gen*) to swell; (*inflar*) to blow up, inflate; (*fig*) to exaggerate; **~se** vr (*inflarse*) to swell up; (*fam: de comer*) to stuff o.s.; **hinchazón** nf (*MED*) swelling; (*altivez*) arrogance

hinojo [i'noxo] nm fennel

hipermercado [ipermer'kaðo] nm hypermarket, superstore

hípico, a ['ipiko, a] adj horse cpd

hipnotismo [ipno'tismo] nm hypnotism; **hipnotizar** vt to hypnotize

hipo ['ipo] nm hiccups pl

hipocresía [ipokre'sia] nf hypocrisy; **hipócrita** adj hypocritical ♦ nm/f hypocrite

hipódromo [i'poðromo] nm racetrack

hipopótamo [ipo'potamo] nm hippopotamus

hipoteca [ipo'teka] nf mortgage

hipótesis [i'potesis] nf inv hypothesis

hiriente [i'rjente] adj offensive, wounding

hispánico, a [is'paniko, a] adj Hispanic

hispano, a [is'pano, a] adj Hispanic, Spanish, Hispano- ♦ nm/f Spaniard; **H~américa** nf Latin America; **~americano, a** adj, nm/f Latin American

histeria [is'terja] nf hysteria

historia [is'torja] nf history; (*cuento*) story, tale; **~s** nfpl (*chismes*) gossip sg; **dejarse de ~s**

to come to the point; **pasar a la ~** to go down in history; **~dor, a** nm/f historian; **historial** nm (*profesional*) curriculum vitae, C.V.; (*MED*) case history; **histórico, a** adj historical; (*memorable*) historic

historieta [isto'rjeta] nf tale, anecdote; (*dibujos*) comic strip

hito ['ito] nm (*fig*) landmark

hizo vb ver **hacer**

Hnos abr (= *Hermanos*) Bros.

hocico [o'θiko] nm snout

hockey ['xoki] nm hockey; **~ sobre hielo** ice hockey

hogar [o'ɣar] nm fireplace, hearth; (*casa*) home; (*vida familiar*) home life; **~eño, a** adj home cpd; (*persona*) home-loving

hoguera [o'ɣera] nf (*gen*) bonfire

hoja ['oxa] nf (*gen*) leaf; (*de flor*) petal; (*de papel*) sheet; (*página*) page; **~ de afeitar** razor blade

hojalata [oxa'lata] nf tin(plate)

hojaldre [o'xaldre] nm (*CULIN*) puff pastry

hojear [oxe'ar] vt to leaf through, turn the pages of

hola ['ola] excl hello!

Holanda [o'landa] nf Holland; **holandés, esa** adj Dutch ♦ nm/f Dutchman/woman ♦ nm (*LING*) Dutch

holgado, a [ol'ɣaðo, a] adj (*ropa*) loose, baggy; (*rico*) comfortable

holgar [ol'ɣar] vi (*descansar*) to rest; (*sobrar*) to be superfluous; **huelga decir que** it goes without saying that

holgazán, ana [olɣa'θan, ana] adj idle, lazy ♦ nm/f loafer

holgura [ol'ɣura] nf looseness, bagginess; (*TEC*) play, free movement; (*vida*) comfortable living

hollín [o'ʎin] nm soot

hombre ['ombre] nm (*gen*) man; (*raza humana*): **el ~** man(kind) ♦ excl: **¡sí ~!** (*claro*) of course!; (*para énfasis*) man, old boy; **~ de negocios** businessman; **~ de pro** honest man; **~-rana** frogman

hombrera [om'brera] nf shoulder strap

hombro ['ombro] nm shoulder

hombruno, a [om'bruno, a] adj mannish

homenaje [ome'naxe] nm (*gen*) homage; (*tributo*) tribute

homicida [omi'θiða] adj homicidal ♦ nm/f murderer; **homicidio** nm murder, homicide

homologar [omolo'ðar] vt (*COM: productos, tamaños*) to standardize; **homólogo, a** nm/ f: **su** etc **homólogo** his etc counterpart o opposite number

homosexual [omosek'swal] adj, nm/f homosexual

hondo, a [ondo, a] adj deep; **lo ~** the depth(s) (pl), the bottom; **~nada** nf hollow, depression; (*cañón*) ravine

Honduras [on'duras] *nf* Honduras

hondureño, a [ondu'reɲo, a] *adj, nm/f* Honduran

honestidad [onesti'ðað] *nf* purity, chastity; (*decencia*) decency; **honesto, a** *adj* chaste; decent, honest; (*justo*) just

hongo ['ongo] *nm* (BOT: *gen*) fungus; (: *comestible*) mushroom; (: *venenoso*) toadstool

honor [o'nor] *nm* (*gen*) honour; **en ~ a la verdad** to be fair; **~able** *adj* honourable

honorario, a [ono'rarjo, a] *adj* honorary; **~s** *nmpl* fees

honra ['onra] *nf* (*gen*) honour; (*renombre*) good name; **~dez** *nf* honesty; (*de persona*) integrity; **~do, a** *adj* honest, upright

honrar [on'rar] *vt* to honour; **~se** *vr*: **~se con algo/de hacer algo** to be honoured by sth/to do sth

honroso, a [on'roso, a] *adj* (*honrado*) honourable; (*respetado*) respectable

hora ['ora] *nf* (*una ~*) hour; (*tiempo*) time; **¿qué ~ es?** what time is it?; **¿a qué ~?** at what time?; **media ~** half an hour; **a la ~ de recreo** at playtime; **a primera ~** first thing (in the morning); **a última ~** at the last moment; **a altas ~s** in the small hours; **¡a buena ~!** about time, too!; **dar la ~** to strike the hour; **~s de oficina/de trabajo** office/working hours; **~s de visita** visiting times; **~s extras** o **extraordinarias** overtime *sg*; **~s punta** rush hours

horadar [ora'ðar] *vt* to drill, bore

horario, a [o'rarjo, a] *adj* hourly, hour *cpd* ♦ *nm* timetable; **~ comercial** business hours *pl*

horca ['orka] *nf* gallows *sg*

horcajadas [orka'xaðas]: **a ~** *adv* astride

horchata [or'tʃata] *nf* cold drink made from tiger nuts and water, tiger nut milk

horizontal [oriθon'tal] *adj* horizontal

horizonte [ori'θonte] *nm* horizon

horma ['orma] *nf* mould

hormiga [or'miɣa] *nf* ant; **~s** *nfpl* (MED) pins and needles

hormigón [ormi'ɣon] *nm* concrete; **~ armado/pretensado** reinforced/prestressed concrete

hormigueo [ormi'ɣeo] *nm* (*comezón*) itch

hormona [or'mona] *nf* hormone

hornada [or'naða] *nf* batch (of loaves *etc*)

hornillo [or'niʎo] *nm* (*cocina*) portable stove

horno ['orno] *nm* (CULIN) oven; (TEC) furnace; **alto ~** blast furnace

horóscopo [o'roskopo] *nm* horoscope

horquilla [or'kiʎa] *nf* hairpin; (AGR) pitchfork

horrendo, a [o'rrendo, a] *adj* horrendous, frightful

horrible [o'rriβle] *adj* horrible, dreadful

horripilante [orripi'lante] *adj* hair-raising, horrifying

horror [o'rror] *nm* horror, dread; (*atrocidad*) atrocity; **¡qué ~!** (*fam*) how awful!; **~izar** *vt* to horrify, frighten; **~izarse** *vr* to be horrified; **~oso, a** *adj* horrifying, ghastly

hortaliza [orta'liθa] *nf* vegetable

hortelano, a [orte'lano, a] *nm/f* (market) gardener

hortera [or'tera] (*fam*) *adj* tacky

hosco, a ['osko, a] *adj* sullen, gloomy

hospedar [ospe'ðar] *vt* to put up; **~se** *vr* to stay, lodge

hospital [ospi'tal] *nm* hospital

hospitalario, a [ospita'larjo, a] *adj* (*acogedor*) hospitable; **hospitalidad** *nf* hospitality

hostal [os'tal] *nm* small hotel

hostelería [ostele'ria] *nf* hotel business o trade

hostia ['ostja] *nf* (REL) host, consecrated wafer; (*fam!: golpe*) whack, punch ♦ *excl* (*fam!*): **¡~(s)!** damn!

hostigar [osti'ɣar] *vt* to whip; (*fig*) to harass, pester

hostil [os'til] *adj* hostile; **~idad** *nf* hostility

hotel [o'tel] *nm* hotel; **~ero, a** *adj* hotel *cpd* ♦ *nm/f* hotelier

hoy [oi] *adv* (*este día*) today; (*la actualidad*) now(adays) ♦ *nm* present time; **~ (en) día** now(adays)

hoyo ['ojo] *nm* hole, pit; **hoyuelo** *nm* dimple

hoz [oθ] *nf* sickle

hube *etc vb ver* **haber**

hucha ['utʃa] *nf* money box

hueco, a ['weko, a] *adj* (*vacío*) hollow, empty; (*resonante*) booming ♦ *nm* hollow, cavity

huelga *etc* ['welɣa] *vb ver* **holgar** ♦ *nf* strike; **declararse en ~** to go on strike, come out on strike; **~ de hambre** hunger strike

huelguista [wel'ɣista] *nm/f* striker

huella ['weʎa] *nf* (*pisada*) tread; (*marca del paso*) footprint, footstep; (: *de animal, máquina*) track; **~ digital** fingerprint

huelo *etc vb ver* **oler**

huérfano, a ['werfano, a] *adj* orphan(ed) ♦ *nm/f* orphan

huerta ['werta] *nf* market garden; (*en Murcia y Valencia*) irrigated region

huerto ['werto] *nm* kitchen garden; (*de árboles frutales*) orchard

hueso ['weso] *nm* (ANAT) bone; (*de fruta*) stone

huésped, a ['wespeð, a] *nm/f* guest

huesudo, a [we'suðo, a] *adj* bony, big-boned

hueva ['weβa] *nf* roe

huevera [we'βera] *nf* eggcup

huevo ['weβo] *nm* egg; **~ duro/escalfado/frito**

(*ESP*) o **estrellado** (*AM*)/**pasado por agua** hard-boiled/poached/fried/soft-boiled egg; **~s revueltos** scrambled eggs

huida [u'iða] *nf* escape, flight

huidizo, a [ui'ðiθo, a] *adj* shy

huir [u'ir] *vi* (*escapar*) to flee, escape; (*evitar*) to avoid; **~se** *vr* (*escaparse*) to escape

hule ['ule] *nm* oilskin

humanidad [umani'ðað] *nf* (*género humano*) man(kind); (*cualidad*) humanity

humanitario, a [umani'tarjo, a] *adj* humanitarian

humano, a [u'mano, a] *adj* (*gen*) human; (*humanitario*) humane ♦ *nm* human; **ser ~ human** being

humareda [uma'reða] *nf* cloud of smoke

humedad [ume'ðað] *nf* (*del clima*) humidity; (*de pared etc*) dampness; **a prueba de ~** damp-proof; **humedecer** *vt* to moisten, wet; **humedecerse** *vr* to get wet

húmedo, a ['umeðo, a] *adj* (*mojado*) damp, wet; (*tiempo etc*) humid

humildad [umil'dað] *nf* humility, humbleness; **humilde** *adj* humble, modest

humillación [umiʎa'θjon] *nf* humiliation; **humillante** *adj* humiliating

humillar [umi'ʎar] *vt* to humiliate; **~se** *vr* to humble o.s., grovel

humo ['umo] *nm* (*de fuego*) smoke; (*gas nocivo*) fumes *pl*; (*vapor*) steam, vapour; **~s** *nmpl* (*fig*) conceit *sg*

humor [u'mor] *nm* (*disposición*) mood, temper; (*lo que divierte*) humour; **de buen/ mal ~** in a good/bad mood; **~ista** *nm/f* comic; **~ístico, a** *adj* funny, humorous

hundimiento [undi'mjento] *nm* (*gen*) sinking; (*colapso*) collapse

hundir [un'dir] *vt* to sink; (*edificio, plan*) to ruin, destroy; **~se** *vr* to sink, collapse

húngaro, a ['ungaro, a] *adj, nm/f* Hungarian

Hungría [un'gria] *nf* Hungary

huracán [ura'kan] *nm* hurricane

huraño, a [u'raɲo, a] *adj* (*antisocial*) unsociable

hurgar [ur'ɣar] *vt* to poke, jab; (*remover*) to stir (up); **~se** *vr*: **~se (las narices)** to pick one's nose

hurón, ona [u'ron, ona] *nm* (*ZOOL*) ferret

hurtadillas [urta'ðiʎas]: **a ~** *adv* stealthily, on the sly

hurtar [ur'tar] *vt* to steal; **hurto** *nm* theft, stealing

husmear [usme'ar] *vt* (*oler*) to sniff out, scent; (*fam*) to pry into

huyo *etc vb ver* **huir**

I, i

iba *etc vb ver* **ir**

ibérico, a [i'ßeriko, a] *adj* Iberian

iberoamericano, a [ißeroameri'kano, a] *adj, nm/f* Latin American

Ibiza [i'ßiθa] *nf* Ibiza

iceberg [iße'ßer] *nm* iceberg

icono [i'kono] *nm* ikon, icon

iconoclasta [ikono'klasta] *adj* iconoclastic ♦ *nm/f* iconoclast

ictericia [ikte'riθja] *nf* jaundice

I + D *abr* (= *Investigación y Desarrollo*) R & D

ida ['iða] *nf* going, departure; **~ y vuelta** round trip, return

idea [i'ðea] *nf* idea; **no tengo la menor ~** I haven't a clue

ideal [iðe'al] *adj, nm* ideal; **~ista** *nm/f* idealist; **~izar** *vt* to idealize

idear [iðe'ar] *vt* to think up; (*aparato*) to invent; (*viaje*) to plan

idem ['iðem] *pron* ditto

idéntico, a [i'ðentiko, a] *adj* identical

identidad [iðenti'ðað] *nf* identity

identificación [iðentifika'θjon] *nf* identification

identificar [iðentifi'kar] *vt* to identify; **~se** *vr*: **~se con** to identify with

ideología [iðeolo'xia] *nf* ideology

idilio [i'ðiljo] *nm* love-affair

idioma [i'ðjoma] *nm* (*gen*) language

idiota [i'ðjota] *adj* idiotic ♦ *nm/f* idiot; **idiotez** *nf* idiocy

ídolo ['iðolo] *nm* (*tb: fig*) idol

idóneo, a [i'ðoneo, a] *adj* suitable

iglesia [i'ɣlesja] *nf* church

ignorancia [iɣno'ranθja] *nf* ignorance; **ignorante** *adj* ignorant, uninformed ♦ *nm/f* ignoramus

ignorar [iɣno'rar] *vt* not to know, be ignorant of; (*no hacer caso a*) to ignore

igual [i'ɣwal] *adj* (*gen*) equal; (*similar*) like, similar; (*mismo*) (the) same; (*constante*) constant; (*temperatura*) even ♦ *nm/f* equal; **~ que** like, the same as; **me da o es ~** I don't care; **son ~es** they're the same; **al ~ que** *prep, conj* like, just like

igualada [iɣwa'laða] *nf* equaliser

igualar [iɣwa'lar] *vt* (*gen*) to equalize, make equal; (*allanar, nivelar*) to level (off), even (out); **~se** *vr* (*platos de balanza*) to balance out

igualdad [iɣwal'dað] *nf* equality; (*similaridad*) sameness; (*uniformidad*) uniformity

igualmente [iɣwal'mente] *adv* equally; (*también*) also, likewise ♦ *excl* the same to

you!
ikurriña [iku'rriɲa] *nf* Basque flag
ilegal [ile'val] *adj* illegal
ilegítimo, a [ile'xitimo, a] *adj* illegitimate
ileso, a [i'leso, a] *adj* unhurt
ilícito, a [i'liθito] *adj* illicit
ilimitado, a [ilimi'taðo, a] *adj* unlimited
ilógico, a [i'loxiko, a] *adj* illogical
iluminación [ilumina'θjon] *nf* illumination; (*alumbrado*) lighting
iluminar [ilumi'nar] *vt* to illuminate, light (up); (*fig*) to enlighten
ilusión [ilu'sjon] *nf* illusion; (*quimera*) delusion; (*esperanza*) hope; **hacerse ilusiones** to build up one's hopes; **ilusionado, a** *adj* excited; **ilusionar** *vi*: **le ilusiona ir de vacaciones** he's looking forward to going on holiday; **ilusionarse** *vr*: **ilusionarse (con)** to get excited (about)
ilusionista [ilusjo'nista] *nm/f* conjurer
iluso, a [i'luso, a] *adj* easily deceived ♦ *nm/f* dreamer
ilusorio, a [ilu'sorjo, a] *adj* (*de ilusión*) illusory, deceptive; (*esperanza*) vain
ilustración [ilustra'θjon] *nf* illustration; (*saber*) learning, erudition; **la I~** the Enlightenment; **ilustrado, a** *adj* illustrated; learned
ilustrar [ilus'trar] *vt* to illustrate; (*instruir*) to instruct; (*explicar*) to explain, make clear; **~se** *vr* to acquire knowledge
ilustre [i'lustre] *adj* famous, illustrious
imagen [i'maxen] *nf* (*gen*) image; (*dibujo*) picture
imaginación [imaxina'θjon] *nf* imagination
imaginar [imaxi'nar] *vt* (*gen*) to imagine; (*idear*) to think up; (*suponer*) to suppose; **~se** *vr* to imagine; **~io, a** *adj* imaginary; **imaginativo, a** *adj* imaginative
imán [i'man] *nm* magnet
imbécil [im'beθil] *nm/f* imbecile, idiot
imitación [imita'θjon] *nf* imitation
imitar [imi'tar] *vt* to imitate; (*parodiar, remedar*) to mimic, ape
impaciencia [impa'θjenθja] *nf* impatience; **impaciente** *adj* impatient; (*nervioso*) anxious
impacto [im'pakto] *nm* impact
impar [im'par] *adj* odd
imparcial [impar'θjal] *adj* impartial, fair
impartir [impar'tir] *vt* to impart, give
impasible [impa'sißle] *adj* impassive
impecable [impe'kaßle] *adj* impeccable
impedimento [impeði'mento] *nm* impediment, obstacle
impedir [impe'ðir] *vt* (*obstruir*) to impede, obstruct; (*estorbar*) to prevent
impenetrable [impene'traßle] *adj* impenetrable; (*fig*) incomprehensible

imperar [impe'rar] *vi* (*reinar*) to rule, reign; (*fig*) to prevail, reign; (*precio*) to be current
imperativo, a [impera'tißo, a] *adj* (*urgente, LING*) imperative
imperceptible [imperθep'tißle] *adj* imperceptible
imperdible [imper'ðißle] *nm* safety pin
imperdonable [imperðo'naßle] *adj* unforgivable, inexcusable
imperfección [imperfek'θjon] *nf* imperfection
imperfecto, a [imper'fekto, a] *adj* imperfect
imperial [impe'rjal] *adj* imperial; **~ismo** *nm* imperialism
imperio [im'perjo] *nm* empire; (*autoridad*) rule, authority; (*fig*) pride, haughtiness; **~so, a** *adj* imperious; (*urgente*) urgent; (*imperativo*) imperative
impermeable [imperme'aßle] *adj* waterproof ♦ *nm* raincoat, mac (*BRIT*)
impersonal [imperso'nal] *adj* impersonal
impertinencia [imperti'nenθja] *nf* impertinence; **impertinente** *adj* impertinent
imperturbable [impertur'ßaßle] *adj* imperturbable
ímpetu ['impetu] *nm* (*impulso*) impetus, impulse; (*impetuosidad*) impetuosity; (*violencia*) violence
impetuoso, a [impe'twoso, a] *adj* impetuous; (*río*) rushing; (*acto*) hasty
impío, a [im'pio, a] *adj* impious, ungodly
implacable [impla'kaßle] *adj* implacable
implantar [implan'tar] *vt* to introduce
implicar [impli'kar] *vt* to involve; (*entrañar*) to imply
implícito, a [im'pliθito, a] *adj* (*tácito*) implicit; (*sobreentendido*) implied
implorar [implo'rar] *vt* to beg, implore
imponente [impo'nente] *adj* (*impresionante*) impressive, imposing; (*solemne*) grand
imponer [impo'ner] *vt* (*gen*) to impose; (*exigir*) to exact; **~se** *vr* to assert o.s.; (*prevalecer*) to prevail; **imponible** *adj* (*COM*) taxable
impopular [impopu'lar] *adj* unpopular
importación [importa'θjon] *nf* (*acto*) importing; (*mercancías*) imports *pl*
importancia [impor'tanθja] *nf* importance; (*valor*) value, significance; (*extensión*) size, magnitude; **importante** *adj* important; valuable, significant
importar [impor'tar] *vt* (*del extranjero*) to import; (*costar*) to amount to ♦ *vi* to be important, matter; **me importa un rábano** I couldn't care less; **no importa** it doesn't matter; **¿le importa que fume?** do you mind if I smoke?
importe [im'porte] *nm* (*total*) amount; (*valor*) value

importunar [importu'nar] *vt* to bother, pester

imposibilidad [imposiβili'ðað] *nf* impossibility; **imposibilitar** *vt* to make impossible, prevent

imposible [impo'siβle] *adj* (*gen*) impossible; (*insoportable*) unbearable, intolerable

imposición [imposi'θjon] *nf* imposition; (COM: *impuesto*) tax; (: *inversión*) deposit

impostor, a [impos'tor, a] *nm/f* impostor

impotencia [impo'tenθja] *nf* impotence; **impotente** *adj* impotent

impracticable [imprakti'kaβle] *adj* (*irrealizable*) impracticable; (*intransitable*) impassable

impreciso, a [impre'θiso, a] *adj* imprecise, vague

impregnar [impreɣ'nar] *vt* to impregnate; **~se** *vr* to become impregnated

imprenta [im'prenta] *nf* (*acto*) printing; (*aparato*) press; (*casa*) printer's; (*letra*) print

imprescindible [impresθin'diβle] *adj* essential, vital

impresión [impre'sjon] *nf* (*gen*) impression; (IMPRENTA) printing; (*edición*) edition; (FOTO) print; (*marca*) imprint; **~ digital** fingerprint

impresionable [impresjo'naβle] *adj* (*sensible*) impressionable

impresionante [impresjo'nante] *adj* impressive; (*tremendo*) tremendous; (*maravilloso*) great, marvellous

impresionar [impresjo'nar] *vt* (*conmover*) to move; (*afectar*) to impress, strike; (*película fotográfica*) to expose; **~se** *vr* to be impressed; (*conmoverse*) to be moved

impreso, a [im'preso, a] *pp de* **imprimir** ♦ *adj* printed; **~s** *nmpl* printed matter; **impresora** *nf* printer

imprevisto, a [impre'βisto, a] *adj* (*gen*) unforeseen; (*inesperado*) unexpected

imprimir [impri'mir] *vt* to imprint, impress, stamp; (*textos*) to print; (INFORM) to output, print out

improbable [impro'βaβle] *adj* improbable; (*inverosímil*) unlikely

improcedente [improθe'ðente] *adj* inappropriate

improductivo, a [improðuk'tiβo, a] *adj* unproductive

improperio [impro'perjo] *nm* insult

impropio, a [im'propjo, a] *adj* improper

improvisado, a [improβi'saðo, a] *adj* improvised

improvisar [improβi'sar] *vt* to improvise

improviso, a [impro'βiso, a] *adj*: **de ~** unexpectedly, suddenly

imprudencia [impru'ðenθja] *nf* imprudence; (*indiscreción*) indiscretion; (*descuido*) carelessness; **imprudente** *adj*

unwise, imprudent; (*indiscreto*) indiscreet

impúdico, a [im'puðiko, a] *adj* shameless; (*lujurioso*) lecherous

impuesto, a [im'pwesto, a] *adj* imposed ♦ *nm* tax; **~ sobre el valor añadido** value added tax

impugnar [impuɣ'nar] *vt* to oppose, contest; (*refutar*) to refute, impugn

impulsar [impul'sar] *vt* to drive; (*promover*) to promote, stimulate

impulsivo, a [impul'siβo, a] *adj* impulsive; **impulso** *nm* impulse; (*fuerza, empuje*) thrust, drive; (*fig: sentimiento*) urge, impulse

impune [im'pune] *adj* unpunished

impureza [impu'reθa] *nf* impurity; **impuro, a** *adj* impure

imputar [impu'tar] *vt* to attribute

inacabable [inaka'βaβle] *adj* (*infinito*) endless; (*interminable*) interminable

inaccesible [inakθe'siβle] *adj* inaccessible

inacción [inak'θjon] *nf* inactivity

inaceptable [inaθep'taβle] *adj* unacceptable

inactividad [inaktiβi'ðað] *nf* inactivity; (COM) dullness; **inactivo, a** *adj* inactive

inadecuado, a [inaðe'kwaðo, a] *adj* (*insuficiente*) inadequate; (*inapto*) unsuitable

inadmisible [inaðmi'siβle] *adj* inadmissible

inadvertido, a [inaðβer'tiðo, a] *adj* (*no visto*) unnoticed

inagotable [inaɣo'taβle] *adj* inexhaustible

inaguantable [inaɣwan'taβle] *adj* unbearable

inalterable [inalte'raβle] *adj* immutable, unchangeable

inanición [inani'θjon] *nf* starvation

inanimado, a [inani'maðo, a] *adj* inanimate

inapreciable [inapre'θjaβle] *adj* (*cantidad, diferencia*) imperceptible; (*ayuda, servicio*) invaluable

inaudito, a [inau'ðito, a] *adj* unheard-of

inauguración [inauɣura'θjon] *nf* inauguration; opening

inaugurar [inauɣu'rar] *vt* to inaugurate; (*exposición*) to open

inca ['inka] *nm/f* Inca

incalculable [inkalku'laβle] *adj* incalculable

incandescente [inkandes'θente] *adj* incandescent

incansable [inkan'saβle] *adj* tireless, untiring

incapacidad [inkapaθi'ðað] *nf* incapacity; (*incompetencia*) incompetence; **~ física/mental** physical/mental disability

incapacitar [inkapaθi'tar] *vt* (*inhabilitar*) to incapacitate, render unfit; (*descalificar*) to disqualify

incapaz [inka'paθ] *adj* incapable

incautación [inkauta'θjon] *nf* confiscation

incautarse [inkau'tarse] *vr*: **~ de** to seize, confiscate

incauto, a [in'kauto, a] *adj* (*imprudente*) incautious, unwary

incendiar [inθen'djar] *vt* to set fire to; (*fig*) to inflame; **~se** *vr* to catch fire; **~io, a** *adj* incendiary

incendio [in'θendjo] *nm* fire

incentivo [inθen'tiβo] *nm* incentive

incertidumbre [inθerti'ðumbre] *nf* (*inseguridad*) uncertainty; (*duda*) doubt

incesante [inθe'sante] *adj* incessant

incesto [in'θesto] *nm* incest

incidencia [inθi'ðenθja] *nf* (MAT) incidence

incidente [inθi'ðente] *nm* incident

incidir [inθi'ðir] *vi* (*influir*) to influence; (*afectar*) to affect; **~ en un error** to fall into error

incienso [in'θjenso] *nm* incense

incierto, a [in'θjerto, a] *adj* uncertain

incineración [inθinera'θjon] *nf* incineration; (*de cadáveres*) cremation

incinerar [inθine'rar] *vt* to burn; (*cadáveres*) to cremate

incipiente [inθi'pjente] *adj* incipient

incisión [inθi'sjon] *nf* incision

incisivo, a [inθi'siβo, a] *adj* sharp, cutting; (*fig*) incisive

incitar [inθi'tar] *vt* to incite, rouse

inclemencia [inkle'menθja] *nf* (*severidad*) harshness, severity; (*del tiempo*) inclemency

inclinación [inklina'θjon] *nf* (*gen*) inclination; (*de tierras*) slope, incline; (*de cabeza*) nod, bow; (*fig*) leaning, bent

inclinar [inkli'nar] *vt* to incline; (*cabeza*) to nod, bow ♦ *vi* to lean, slope; **~se** *vr* to bow; (*encorvarse*) to stoop; **~se a** (*parecerse a*) to take after, resemble; **~se ante** to bow down to; **me inclino a pensar que** I'm inclined to think that

incluir [inklu'ir] *vt* to include; (*incorporar*) to incorporate; (*meter*) to enclose

inclusive [inklu'siβe] *adv* inclusive ♦ *prep* including

incluso [in'kluso] *adv* even

incógnita [in'koɣnita] *nf* (MAT) unknown quantity

incógnito [in'koɣnito] *nm*: **de ~** incognito

incoherente [inkoe'rente] *adj* incoherent

incoloro, a [inko'loro, a] *adj* colourless

incólume [in'kolume] *adj* unhurt, unharmed

incomodar [inkomo'ðar] *vt* to inconvenience; (*molestar*) to bother, trouble; (*fastidiar*) to annoy; **~se** *vr* to put o.s. out; (*fastidiarse*) to get annoyed

incomodidad [inkomoði'ðað] *nf* inconvenience; (*fastidio, enojo*) annoyance; (*de vivienda*) discomfort

incómodo, a [in'komoðo, a] *adj* (*inconfortable*) uncomfortable; (*molesto*) annoying; (*inconveniente*) inconvenient

incomparable [inkompa'raβle] *adj* incomparable

incompatible [inkompa'tiβle] *adj* incompatible

incompetencia [inkompe'tenθja] *nf* incompetence; **incompetente** *adj* incompetent

incompleto, a [inkom'pleto, a] *adj* incomplete, unfinished

incomprensible [inkompren'siβle] *adj* incomprehensible

incomunicado, a [inkomuni'kaðo, a] *adj* (*aislado*) cut off, isolated; (*confinado*) in solitary confinement

inconcebible [inkonθe'βiβle] *adj* inconceivable

incondicional [inkondiθjo'nal] *adj* unconditional; (*apoyo*) wholehearted; (*partidario*) staunch

inconexo, a [inko'nekso, a] *adj* (*gen*) unconnected; (*desunido*) disconnected

inconfundible [inkonfun'diβle] *adj* unmistakable

incongruente [inkon'grwente] *adj* incongruous

inconsciencia [inkons'θjenθja] *nf* unconsciousness; (*fig*) thoughtlessness; **inconsciente** *adj* unconscious; thoughtless

inconsecuente [inkonse'kwente] *adj* inconsistent

inconsiderado, a [inkonsiðe'raðo, a] *adj* inconsiderate

inconsistente [inkonsis'tente] *adj* weak; (*tela*) flimsy

inconstancia [inkon'stanθja] *nf* inconstancy; (*inestabilidad*) unsteadiness; **inconstante** *adj* inconstant

incontable [inkon'taβle] *adj* countless, innumerable

incontestable [inkontes'taβle] *adj* unanswerable; (*innegable*) undeniable

incontinencia [inkonti'nenθja] *nf* incontinence

inconveniencia [inkombe'njenθja] *nf* unsuitability, inappropriateness; (*descortesía*) impoliteness; **inconveniente** *adj* unsuitable; impolite ♦ *nm* obstacle; (*desventaja*) disadvantage; **el inconveniente es que ...** the trouble is that ...

incordiar [inkor'ðjar] (*fam*) *vt* to bug, annoy

incorporación [inkorpora'θjon] *nf* incorporation

incorporar [inkorpo'rar] *vt* to incorporate; **~se** *vr* to sit up

incorrección [inkorrek'θjon] *nf* (*gen*) incorrectness, inaccuracy; (*descortesía*) bad-mannered behaviour; **incorrecto, a** *adj* (*gen*) incorrect, wrong; (*comportamiento*) bad-mannered

incorregible [inkorre'xiβle] *adj* incorrigible
incredulidad [inkreðuli'ðað] *nf* incredulity; (*escepticismo*) scepticism; **incrédulo, a** *adj* incredulous, unbelieving; sceptical
increíble [inkre'iβle] *adj* incredible
incremento [inkre'mento] *nm* increment; (*aumento*) rise, increase
increpar [inkre'par] *vt* to reprimand
incruento, a [in'krwento, a] *adj* bloodless
incrustar [inkrus'tar] *vt* to incrust; (*piedras: en joya*) to inlay
incubar [inku'βar] *vt* to incubate
inculcar [inkul'kar] *vt* to inculcate
inculpar [inkul'par] *vt* (*acusar*) to accuse; (*achacar, atribuir*) to charge, blame
inculto, a [in'kulto, a] *adj* (*persona*) uneducated; (*grosero*) uncouth ♦ *nm/f* ignoramus
incumplimiento [inkumpli'mjento] *nm* non-fulfilment; ~ **de contrato** breach of contract
incurrir [inku'rrir] *vi*: ~ **en** to incur; (*crimen*) to commit; ~ **en un error** to make a mistake
indagación [indaɣa'θjon] *nf* investigation; (*búsqueda*) search; (*JUR*) inquest
indagar [inda'ɣar] *vt* to investigate; to search; (*averiguar*) to ascertain
indecente [inde'θente] *adj* indecent, improper; (*lascivo*) obscene
indecible [inde'θiβle] *adj* unspeakable; (*indescriptible*) indescribable
indeciso, a [inde'θiso, a] *adj* (*por decidir*) undecided; (*vacilante*) hesitant
indefenso, a [inde'fenso, a] *adj* defenceless
indefinido, a [indefi'niðo, a] *adj* indefinite; (*vago*) vague, undefined
indeleble [inde'leβle] *adj* indelible
indemne [in'demne] *adj* (*objeto*) undamaged; (*persona*) unharmed, unhurt
indemnizar [indemni'θar] *vt* to indemnify; (*compensar*) to compensate
independencia [indepen'denθja] *nf* independence
independiente [indepen'djente] *adj* (*libre*) independent; (*autónomo*) self-sufficient
indeterminado, a [indetermi'naðo, a] *adj* indefinite; (*desconocido*) indeterminate
India ['indja] *nf*: **la ~** India
indicación [indika'θjon] *nf* indication; (*señal*) sign; (*sugerencia*) suggestion, hint
indicado, a [indi'kaðo, a] *adj* (*momento, método*) right; (*tratamiento*) appropriate; (*solución*) likely
indicador [indika'ðor] *nm* indicator; (*TEC*) gauge, meter
indicar [indi'kar] *vt* (*mostrar*) to indicate, show; (*termómetro etc*) to read, register; (*señalar*) to point to
índice ['indiθe] *nm* index; (*catálogo*)

catalogue; (*ANAT*) index finger, forefinger
indicio [in'diθjo] *nm* indication, sign; (*en pesquisa etc*) clue
indiferencia [indife'renθja] *nf* indifference; (*apatía*) apathy; **indiferente** *adj* indifferent
indígena [in'dixena] *adj* indigenous, native ♦ *nm/f* native
indigencia [indi'xenθja] *nf* poverty, need
indigestión [indixes'tjon] *nf* indigestion
indigesto, a [indi'xesto, a] *adj* (*alimento*) indigestible; (*fig*) turgid
indignación [indiɣna'θjon] *nf* indignation
indignar [indiɣ'nar] *vt* to anger, make indignant; ~**se** *vr*: ~**se por** to get indignant about
indigno, a [in'diɣno, a] *adj* (*despreciable*) low, contemptible; (*inmerecido*) unworthy
indio, a ['indjo, a] *adj, nm/f* Indian
indirecta [indi'rekta] *nf* insinuation, innuendo; (*sugerencia*) hint
indirecto, a [indi'rekto, a] *adj* indirect
indiscreción [indiskre'θjon] *nf* (*imprudencia*) indiscretion; (*irreflexión*) tactlessness; (*acto*) gaffe, faux pas
indiscreto, a [indis'kreto, a] *adj* indiscreet
indiscriminado, a [indiskrimi'naðo, a] *adj* indiscriminate
indiscutible [indisku'tiβle] *adj* indisputable, unquestionable
indispensable [indispen'saβle] *adj* indispensable, essential
indisponer [indispo'ner] *vt* to spoil, upset; (*salud*) to make ill; ~**se** *vr* to fall ill; ~**se con uno** to fall out with sb
indisposición [indisposi'θjon] *nf* indisposition
indispuesto, a [indis'pwesto, a] *adj* (*enfermo*) unwell, indisposed
indistinto, a [indis'tinto, a] *adj* indistinct; (*vago*) vague
individual [indiβi'ðwal] *adj* individual; (*habitación*) single ♦ *nm* (*DEPORTE*) singles *sg*
individuo, a [indi'βiðwo, a] *adj, nm* individual
índole ['indole] *nf* (*naturaleza*) nature; (*clase*) sort, kind
indómito, a [in'domito, a] *adj* indomitable
inducir [indu'θir] *vt* to induce; (*inferir*) to infer; (*persuadir*) to persuade
indudable [indu'ðaβle] *adj* undoubted; (*incuestionable*) unquestionable
indulgencia [indul'xenθja] *nf* indulgence
indultar [indul'tar] *vt* (*perdonar*) to pardon, reprieve; (*librar de pago*) to exempt; **indulto** *nm* pardon; exemption
industria [in'dustrja] *nf* industry; (*habilidad*) skill; **industrial** *adj* industrial ♦ *nm* industrialist
inédito, a [in'eðito, a] *adj* (*texto*)

unpublished; (*nuevo*) new
inefable [ine'faβle] *adj* ineffable,
indescribable
ineficaz [inefi'kaθ] *adj* (*inútil*) ineffective;
(*ineficiente*) inefficient
ineludible [inelu'ðiβle] *adj* inescapable,
unavoidable
ineptitud [inepti'tuð] *nf* ineptitude,
Incompetence; **inepto, a** *adj* inept,
incompetent
inequívoco, a [ine'kiβoko, a] *adj*
unequivocal; (*inconfundible*) unmistakable
inercia [in'erθja] *nf* inertia; (*pasividad*)
passivity
inerme [in'erme] *adj* (*sin armas*) unarmed;
(*indefenso*) defenceless
inerte [in'erte] *adj* inert; (*inmóvil*) motionless
inesperado, a [inespe'raðo, a] *adj*
unexpected, unforeseen
inestable [ines'taβle] *adj* unstable
inevitable [ineβi'taβle] *adj* inevitable
inexactitud [ineksakti'tuð] *nf* inaccuracy;
inexacto, a *adj* inaccurate; (*falso*) untrue
inexperto, a [inek'sperto, a] *adj* (*novato*)
inexperienced
infalible [infa'liβle] *adj* infallible; (*plan*)
foolproof
infame [in'fame] *adj* infamous; (*horrible*)
dreadful; **infamia** *nf* infamy; (*deshonra*)
disgrace
infancia [in'fanθja] *nf* infancy, childhood
infantería [infante'ria] *nf* infantry
infantil [infan'til] *adj* (*pueril, aniñado*)
infantile; (*cándido*) childlike; (*literatura, ropa
etc*) children's
infarto [in'farto] *nm* (*tb:* ~ de miocardio)
heart attack
infatigable [infati'xaβle] *adj* tireless, untiring
infección [infek'θjon] *nf* infection;
infeccioso, a *adj* infectious
infectar [infek'tar] *vt* to infect; ~**se** *vr* to
become infected
infeliz [infe'liθ] *adj* unhappy, wretched
♦ *nm/f* wretch
inferior [infe'rjor] *adj* inferior; (*situación*)
lower ♦ *nm/f* inferior, subordinate
inferir [infe'rir] *vt* (*deducir*) to infer, deduce;
(*causar*) to cause
infestar [infes'tar] *vt* to infest
infidelidad [infiðeli'ðað] *nf* (*gen*) infidelity,
unfaithfulness
infiel [in'fjel] *adj* unfaithful, disloyal; (*erróneo*)
inaccurate ♦ *nm/f* infidel, unbeliever
infierno [in'fjerno] *nm* hell
infiltrarse [infil'trarse] *vr:* ~ en to infiltrate
in(to); (*persona*) to work one's way in(to)
ínfimo, a [a ['infimo, a] *adj* (*más bajo*) lowest;
(*despreciable*) vile, mean
infinidad [infini'ðað] *nf* infinity;

(*abundancia*) great quantity
infinito, a [infi'nito, a] *adj, nm* infinite
inflación [infla'θjon] *nf* (*hinchazón*) swelling;
(*monetaria*) inflation; (*fig*) conceit;
inflacionario, a *adj* inflationary
inflamar [infla'mar] *vt* (MED, *fig*) to inflame;
~**se** *vr* to catch fire; to become inflamed
inflar [in'flar] *vt* (*hinchar*) to inflate, blow up;
(*fig*) to exaggerate; ~**se** *vr* to swell (up); (*fig*)
to get conceited
inflexible [inflek'siβle] *adj* inflexible; (*fig*)
unbending
infligir [infli'xir] *vt* to inflict
influencia [influ'enθja] *nf* influence;
influenciar *vt* to influence
influir [influ'ir] *vt* to influence
influjo [in'fluxo] *nm* influence
influya *etc vb ver* **influir**
influyente [influ'jente] *adj* influential
información [informa'θjon] *nf* information;
(*noticias*) news *sg*; (JUR) inquiry; I~ (*oficina*)
Information Office; (*mostrador*) Information
Desk; (TEL) Directory Enquiries
informal [infor'mal] *adj* (*gen*) informal
informar [infor'mar] *vt* (*gen*) to inform;
(*revelar*) to reveal, make known ♦ *vi* (JUR) to
plead; (*denunciar*) to inform; (*dar cuenta de*)
to report on; ~**se** *vr* to find out; ~**se de** to
inquire into
informática [infor'matika] *nf* computer
science, information technology
informe [in'forme] *adj* shapeless ♦ *nm* report
infortunio [infor'tunjo] *nm* misfortune
infracción [infrak'θjon] *nf* infraction,
infringement
infranqueable [infranke'aβle] *adj*
impassable; (*fig*) insurmountable
infravalorar [infrabalo'rar] *vt* to undervalue,
underestimate
infringir [infrin'xir] *vt* to infringe, contravene
infructuoso, a [infruk'twoso, a] *adj*
fruitless, unsuccessful
infundado, a [infun'daðo, a] *adj*
groundless, unfounded
infundir [infun'dir] *vt* to infuse, instil
infusión [infu'sjon] *nf* infusion; ~ de
manzanilla camomile tea
ingeniar [inxe'njar] *vt* to think up, devise;
~**se** *vr:* ~**se para** to manage to
ingeniería [inxenje'ria] *nf* engineering;
~ genética genetic engineering; **ingeniero, a**
nm/f engineer; **ingeniero de caminos/de
sonido** civil engineer/sound engineer
ingenio [in'xenjo] *nm* (*talento*) talent;
(*agudeza*) wit; (*habilidad*) ingenuity,
inventiveness; ~ azucarero (AM) sugar refinery
ingenioso, a [inxe'njoso, a] *adj* ingenious,
clever; (*divertido*) witty
ingenuidad [inxenwi'ðað] *nf* ingenuousness;

(*sencillez*) simplicity; **ingenuo, a** *adj* ingenuous

ingerir [inxe'rir] *vt* to ingest; (*tragar*) to swallow; (*consumir*) to consume

Inglaterra [ingla'terra] *nf* England

ingle ['ingle] *nf* groin

inglés, esa [in'gles, esa] *adj* English ♦ *nm/f* Englishman/woman ♦ *nm* (*LING*) English

ingratitud [ingrati'tuð] *nf* ingratitude; **ingrato, a** *adj* (*gen*) ungrateful

ingrediente [ingre'ðjente] *nm* ingredient

ingresar [ingre'sar] *vt* (*dinero*) to deposit ♦ *vi* to come in; ~ **en un club** to join a club; ~ **en el hospital** to go into hospital

ingreso [in'greso] *nm* (*entrada*) entry; (: *en hospital etc*) admission; ~**s** *nmpl* (*dinero*) income *sg*; (: *COM*) takings *pl*

inhabitable [inaßi'taßle] *adj* uninhabitable

inhalar [ina'lar] *vt* to inhale

inherente [ine'rente] *adj* inherent

inhibir [ini'ßir] *vt* to inhibit

inhóspito, a [i'nospito, a] *adj* (*región, paisaje*) inhospitable

inhumano, a [inu'mano, a] *adj* inhuman

inicial [ini'θjal] *adj, nf* initial

iniciar [ini'θjar] *vt* (*persona*) to initiate; (*empezar*) to begin, commence; (*conversación*) to start up

iniciativa [iniθja'tißa] *nf* initiative; **la ~ privada** private enterprise

ininterrumpido, a [ininterrum'piðo, a] *adj* uninterrupted

injerencia [inxe'renθja] *nf* interference

injertar [inxer'tar] *vt* to graft; **injerto** *nm* graft

injuria [in'xurja] *nf* (*agravio, ofensa*) offence; (*insulto*) insult; **injuriar** *vt* to insult; **injurioso, a** *adj* offensive; insulting

injusticia [inxus'tiθja] *nf* injustice

injusto, a [in'xusto, a] *adj* unjust, unfair

inmadurez [inmaðu'reθ] *nf* immaturity

inmediaciones [inmeðja'θjones] *nfpl* neighbourhood *sg*, environs

inmediato, a [inme'ðjato, a] *adj* immediate; (*contiguo*) adjoining; (*rápido*) prompt; (*próximo*) neighbouring, next; **de ~** immediately

inmejorable [inmexo'raßle] *adj* unsurpassable; (*precio*) unbeatable

inmenso, a [in'menso, a] *adj* immense, huge

inmerecido, a [inmere'θiðo, a] *adj* undeserved

inmigración [inmivra'θjon] *nf* immigration

inmiscuirse [inmisku'irse] *vr* to interfere, meddle

inmobiliaria [inmoßi'ljarja] *nf* estate agency

inmobiliario, a [inmoßi'ljarjo, a] *adj* real-estate *cpd*, property *cpd*

inmolar [inmo'lar] *vt* to immolate, sacrifice

inmoral [inmo'ral] *adj* immoral

inmortal [inmor'tal] *adj* immortal; ~**izar** *vt* to immortalize

inmóvil [in'moßil] *adj* immobile

inmueble [in'mweßle] *adj*: **bienes ~s** real estate, landed property ♦ *nm* property

inmundicia [inmun'diθja] *nf* filth; **inmundo, a** *adj* filthy

inmune [in'mune] *adj*: ~ **(a)** (*MED*) immune (to)

inmunidad [inmuni'ðað] *nf* immunity

inmutarse [inmu'tarse] *vr* to turn pale; **no se inmutó** he didn't turn a hair

innato, a [in'nato, a] *adj* innate

innecesario, a [inneθe'sarjo, a] *adj* unnecessary

innoble [in'noßle] *adj* ignoble

innovación [innoßa'θjon] *nf* innovation

innovar [inno'ßar] *vt* to introduce

inocencia [ino'θenθja] *nf* innocence

inocentada [inoθen'taða] *nf* practical joke

inocente [ino'θente] *adj* (*ingenuo*) naive, innocent; (*inculpable*) innocent; (*sin malicia*) harmless ♦ *nm/f* simpleton

inodoro [ino'ðoro] *nm* toilet, lavatory (*BRIT*)

inofensivo, a [inofen'sißo, a] *adj* inoffensive, harmless

inolvidable [inolßi'ðaßle] *adj* unforgettable

inopinado, a [inopi'naðo, a] *adj* unexpected

inoportuno, a [inopor'tuno, a] *adj* untimely; (*molesto*) inconvenient

inoxidable [inoksi'ðaßle] *adj*: **acero ~** stainless steel

inquebrantable [inkeßran'taßle] *adj* unbreakable

inquietar [inkje'tar] *vt* to worry, trouble; ~**se** *vr* to worry, get upset; **inquieto, a** *adj* anxious, worried; **inquietud** *nf* anxiety, worry

inquilino, a [inki'lino, a] *nm/f* tenant

inquirir [inki'rir] *vt* to enquire into, investigate

insaciable [insa'θjaßle] *adj* insatiable

insalubre [insa'lußre] *adj* unhealthy

inscribir [inskri'ßir] *vt* to inscribe; ~ **a uno en** (*lista*) to put sb on; (*censo*) to register sb on

inscripción [inskrip'θjon] *nf* inscription; (*ESCOL etc*) enrolment; (*censo*) registration

insecticida [insekti'θiða] *nm* insecticide

insecto [in'sekto] *nm* insect

inseguridad [insevuri'ðað] *nf* insecurity

inseguro, a [inse'yuro, a] *adj* insecure; (*inconstante*) unsteady; (*incierto*) uncertain

insensato, a [insen'sato, a] *adj* foolish, stupid

insensibilidad [insensißili'ðað] *nf* (*gen*) insensitivity; (*dureza de corazón*) callousness

insensible [insen'sißle] *adj (gen)* insensitive; (*movimiento*) imperceptible; (*sin sentido*) numb

insertar [inser'tar] *vt* to insert

inservible [inser'ßißle] *adj* useless

insidioso, a [insi'ðjoso, a] *adj* insidious

insignia [in'siɣnja] *nf (señal distintiva)* badge; (*estandarte*) flaq

insignificante [insiɣnifi'kante] *adj* insignificant

insinuar [insi'nwar] *vt* to insinuate, imply

insípido, a [in'sipiðo, a] *adj* insipid

insistencia [insis'tenθja] *nf* insistence

insistir [insis'tir] *vi* to insist; ~ **en algo** to insist on sth; (*enfatizar*) to stress sth

insolación [insola'θjon] *nf (MED)* sunstroke

insolencia [inso'lenθja] *nf* insolence; **insolente** *adj* insolent

insólito, a [in'solito, a] *adj* unusual

insoluble [inso'lußle] *adj* insoluble

insolvencia [insol'ßenθja] *nf* insolvency

insomnio [in'somnjo] *nm* insomnia

insondable [inson'daßle] *adj* bottomless; (*fig*) impenetrable

insonorizado, a [insonori'θaðo, a] *adj* (*cuarto etc*) soundproof

insoportable [insopor'taßle] *adj* unbearable

insospechado, a [insospe'tʃaðo, a] *adj* (*inesperado*) unexpected

inspección [inspek'θjon] *nf* inspection, check; **inspeccionar** *vt (examinar)* to inspect, examine; (*controlar*) to check

inspector, a [inspek'tor, a] *nm/f* inspector

inspiración [inspira'θjon] *nf* inspiration

inspirar [inspi'rar] *vt* to inspire; (*MED*) to inhale; ~**se** *vr*: ~**se en** to be inspired by

instalación [instala'θjon] *nf (equipo)* fittings *pl*, equipment; ~ **eléctrica** wiring

instalar [insta'lar] *vt (establecer)* to instal; (*erguir*) to set up, erect; ~**se** *vr* to establish o.s.; (*en una vivienda*) to move into

instancia [ins'tanθja] *nf (JUR)* petition; (*ruego*) request; **en última** ~ as a last resort

instantánea [instan'tanea] *nf* snap(shot)

instantáneo, a [instan'taneo, a] *adj* instantaneous; **café** ~ instant coffee

instante [ins'tante] *nm* instant, moment

instar [ins'tar] *vt* to press, urge

instaurar [instau'rar] *vt (costumbre)* to establish; (*normas, sistema*) to bring in, introduce; (*gobierno*) to instal

instigar [insti'ɣar] *vt* to instigate

instinto [ins'tinto] *nm* instinct; **por** ~ instinctively

institución [institu'θjon] *nf* institution, establishment

instituir [institu'ir] *vt* to establish; (*fundar*) to found; **instituto** *nm (gen)* institute; (*ESP: ESCOL*) ≈ comprehensive (*BRIT*) o high (*US*) school

institutriz [institu'triθ] *nf* governess

instrucción [instruk'θjon] *nf* instruction

instructivo, a [instruk'tißo, a] *adj* instructive

instruir [instru'ir] *vt (gen)* to instruct; (*enseñar*) to teach, educate

instrumento [instru'mento] *nm (gen)* instrument; (*herramienta*) tool, implement

insubordinarse [insußorði'narse] *vr* to rebel

insuficiencia [insufi'θjenθja] *nf (carencia)* lack; (*inadecuación*) inadequacy; **insuficiente** *adj (gen)* insufficient; (*ESCOL: calificación*) unsatisfactory

insufrible [insu'frißle] *adj* insufferable

insular [insu'lar] *adj* insular

insultar [insul'tar] *vt* to insult; **insulto** *nm* insult

insumiso, a [insu'miso, a] *nm/f (POL)* person who refuses to do military service or its substitute, community service

insuperable [insupe'raßle] *adj (excelente)* unsurpassable; (*problema etc*) insurmountable

insurgente [insur'xente] *adj, nm/f* insurgent

insurrección [insurrek'θjon] *nf* insurrection, rebellion

intachable [inta'tʃaßle] *adj* irreproachable

intacto, a [in'takto, a] *adj* intact

integral [inte'ɣral] *adj* integral; (*completo*) complete; **pan** ~ wholemeal (*BRIT*) o wholewheat (*US*) bread

integrar [inte'ɣrar] *vt* to make up, compose; (*MAT, fig*) to integrate

integridad [inteɣri'ðað] *nf* wholeness; (*carácter*) integrity; **íntegro, a** *adj* whole, entire; (*honrado*) honest

intelectual [intelek'twal] *adj, nm/f* intellectual

inteligencia [inteli'xenθja] *nf* intelligence; (*ingenio*) ability; **inteligente** *adj* intelligent

inteligible [inteli'xißle] *adj* intelligible

intemperie [intem'perje] *nf*: **a la** ~ out in the open, exposed to the elements

intempestivo, a [intempes'tißo, a] *adj* untimely

intención [inten'θjon] *nf (gen)* intention, purpose; **con segundas intenciones** maliciously; **con** ~ deliberately

intencionado, a [intenθjo'naðo, a] *adj* deliberate; **bien** ~ well-meaning; **mal** ~ ill-disposed, hostile

intensidad [intensi'ðað] *nf (gen)* intensity; (*ELEC, TEC*) strength; **llover con** ~ to rain hard

intenso, a [in'tenso, a] *adj* intense; (*sentimiento*) profound, deep

intentar [inten'tar] *vt (tratar)* to try, attempt; **intento** *nm* attempt

interactivo, a [interak'tißo, a] *adj (INFORM)*

interactive

intercalar [interka'lar] *vt* to insert

intercambio [inter'kambjo] *nm* exchange, swap

interceder [interθe'ðer] *vi* to intercede

interceptar [interθep'tar] *vt* to intercept

intercesión [interθe'sjon] *nf* intercession

interés [inte'res] *nm* (*gen*) interest; (*parte*) share, part; (*pey*) self-interest; **intereses creados** vested interests

interesado, a [intere'saðo, a] *adj* interested; (*prejuiciado*) prejudiced; (*pey*) mercenary, self-seeking

interesante [intere'sante] *adj* interesting

interesar [intere'sar] *vt, vi* to interest, be of interest to; **~se** *vr*: **~se en o por** to take an interest in

interferir [interfe'rir] *vt* to interfere with; (*TEL*) to jam ♦ *vi* to interfere

interfono [inter'fono] *nm* intercom

interino, a [inte'rino, a] *adj* temporary ♦ *nm/f* temporary holder of a post; (*MED*) locum; (*ESCOL*) supply teacher

interior [inte'rjor] *adj* inner, inside; (*COM*) domestic, internal ♦ *nm* interior, inside; (*fig*) soul, mind; **Ministerio del I~** ≈ Home Office (*BRIT*), ≈ Department of the Interior (*US*)

interjección [interxek'θjon] *nf* interjection

interlocutor, a [interloku'tor, a] *nm/f* speaker

intermediario, a [interme'ðjarjo, a] *nm/f* intermediary

intermedio, a [inter'meðjo, a] *adj* intermediate ♦ *nm* interval

interminable [intermi'naßle] *adj* endless

intermitente [intermi'tente] *adj* intermittent ♦ *nm* (*AUTO*) indicator

internacional [internaθjo'nal] *adj* international

internado [inter'naðo] *nm* boarding school

internar [inter'nar] *vt* to intern; (*en un manicomio*) to commit; **~se** *vr* (*penetrar*) to penetrate

Internet [inter'net] *nm o nf* Internet

interno, a [in'terno, a] *adj* internal, interior; (*POL etc*) domestic ♦ *nm/f* (*alumno*) boarder

interponer [interpo'ner] *vt* to interpose, put in; **~se** *vr* to intervene

interpretación [interpreta'θjon] *nf* interpretation

interpretar [interpre'tar] *vt* to interpret; (*TEATRO, MUS*) to perform, play; **intérprete** *nm/f* (*LING*) interpreter, translator; (*MUS, TEATRO*) performer, artist(e)

interrogación [interroɣa'θjon] *nf* interrogation; (*LING: tb: signo de ~*) question mark

interrogar [interro'ɣar] *vt* to interrogate, question

interrumpir [interrum'pir] *vt* to interrupt

interrupción [interrup'θjon] *nf* interruption

interruptor [interrup'tor] *nm* (*ELEC*) switch

intersección [intersek'θjon] *nf* intersection

interurbano, a [interur'ßano, a] *adj*: **llamada interurbana** long-distance call

intervalo [inter'ßalo] *nm* interval; (*descanso*) break; **a ~s** at intervals, every now and then

intervenir [interße'nir] *vt* (*controlar*) to control, supervise; (*MED*) to operate on ♦ *vi* (*participar*) to take part, participate; (*mediar*) to intervene

interventor, a [interßen'tor, a] *nm/f* inspector; (*COM*) auditor

intestino [intes'tino] *nm* intestine

intimar [inti'mar] *vi* to become friendly

intimidad [intimi'ðað] *nf* intimacy; (*familiaridad*) familiarity; (*vida privada*) private life; (*JUR*) privacy

íntimo, a ['intimo, a] *adj* intimate

intolerable [intole'raßle] *adj* intolerable, unbearable

intoxicación [intoksika'θjon] *nf* poisoning

intranet [intra'net] *nf* intranet

intranquilizarse [intrankili'θarse] *vr* to get worried o anxious; **intranquilo, a** *adj* worried

intransigente [intransi'xente] *adj* intransigent

intransitable [intransi'taßle] *adj* impassable

intrépido, a [in'trepiðo, a] *adj* intrepid

intriga [in'triɣa] *nf* intrigue; (*plan*) plot; **intrigar** *vt, vi* to intrigue

intrincado, a [intrin'kaðo, a] *adj* intricate

intrínseco, a [in'trinseko, a] *adj* intrinsic

introducción [introðuk'θjon] *nf* introduction

introducir [introðu'θir] *vt* (*gen*) to introduce; (*moneda etc*) to insert; (*INFORM*) to input, enter

intromisión [intromi'sjon] *nf* interference, meddling

introvertido, a [introßer'tiðo, a] *adj, nm/f* introvert

intruso, a [in'truso, a] *adj* intrusive ♦ *nm/f* intruder

intuición [intwi'θjon] *nf* intuition

inundación [inunda'θjon] *nf* flood(ing); **inundar** *vt* to flood; (*fig*) to swamp, inundate

inusitado, a [inusi'taðo, a] *adj* unusual, rare

inútil [in'util] *adj* useless; (*esfuerzo*) vain, fruitless; **inutilidad** *nf* uselessness

inutilizar [inutili'θar] *vt* to make o render useless; **~se** *vr* to become useless

invadir [imba'ðir] *vt* to invade

inválido, a [im'baliðo, a] *adj* invalid ♦ *nm/f* invalid

invariable [imba'rjaßle] *adj* invariable

invasión [imba'sjon] nf invasion
invasor, a [imba'sor, a] adj invading ♦ nm/f invader
invención [imben'θjon] nf invention
inventar [imben'tar] vt to invent
inventario [imben'tarjo] nm inventory
inventiva [imben'tiβa] nf inventiveness
invento [im'bento] nm invention
inventor, a [imben'tor, a] nm/f inventor
invernadero [imberna'δero] nm greenhouse
inverosímil [imbero'simil] adj implausible
inversión [imber'sjon] nf (COM) investment
inverso, a [im'berso, a] adj inverse, opposite; **en el orden** ~ in reverse order; **a la inversa** inversely, the other way round
inversor, a [imber'sor, a] nm/f (COM) investor
invertir [imber'tir] vt (COM) to invest; (volcar) to turn upside down; (tiempo etc) to spend
investigación [imbestiɣa'θjon] nf investigation; (ESCOL) research; ~ **de mercado** market research
investigar [imbesti'ɣar] vt to investigate; (ESCOL) to do research into
invierno [im'bjerno] nm winter
invisible [imbi'siβle] adj invisible
invitado, a [imbi'taδo, a] nm/f guest
invitar [imbi'tar] vt to invite; (incitar) to entice; (pagar) to buy, pay for
invocar [imbo'kar] vt to invoke, call on
involucrar [imbolu'krar] vt: ~ **en** to involve in; ~**se** vr: ~ **en** to get mixed up in
involuntario, a [imbolun'tarjo, a] adj (movimiento, gesto) involuntary; (error) unintentional
inyección [injek'θjon] nf injection
inyectar [injek'tar] vt to inject

PALABRA CLAVE

---

ir [ir] vi **1** to go; (a pie) to walk; (viajar) to travel; ~ **caminando** to walk; **fui en tren** I went o travelled by train; **¡(ahora) voy!** (I'm just) coming!
2: ~ **(a) por**: ~ **(a) por el médico** to fetch the doctor
3 (progresar: persona, cosa) to go; **el trabajo va muy bien** work is going very well; **¿cómo te va?** how are things going?; **me va muy bien** I'm getting on very well; **le fue fatal** it went awfully badly for him
4 (funcionar): **el coche no va muy bien** the car isn't running very well
5: **te va estupendamente ese color** that colour suits you fantastically well
6 (locuciones): **¿vino? – ¡que va!** did he come? – of course not!; **vamos, no llores** come on, don't cry; **¡vaya coche!** what a car!, that's some car!

7: **no vaya a ser: tienes que correr, no vaya a ser que pierdas el tren** you'll have to run so as not to miss the train
8 (+ pp): **iba vestido muy bien** he was very well dressed
9: **no me** etc **va ni me viene** I etc don't care
♦ vb aux **1**: ~ **a: voy/iba a hacerlo hoy** I am/was going to do it today
2 (+ gerundio): **iba anocheciendo** it was getting dark; **todo se me iba aclarando** everything was gradually becoming clearer to me
3 (+ pp = pasivo): **van vendidos 300 ejemplares** 300 copies have been sold so far
♦ ~**se** vr **1**: **¿por dónde se va al zoológico?** which is the way to the zoo?
2 (marcharse) to leave; **ya se habrán ido** they must already have left o gone

---

ira ['ira] nf anger, rage
Irak [i'rak] nm = **Iraq**
Irán [i'ran] nm Iran; **iraní** adj, nm/f Iranian
Iraq [i'rak] nm Iraq; **iraquí** adj, nm/f Iraqui
iris ['iris] nm inv (tb: **arco** ~) rainbow; (ANAT) iris
Irlanda [ir'landa] nf Ireland; **irlandés, esa** adj Irish ♦ nm/f Irishman/woman; **los irlandeses** the Irish
ironía [iro'nia] nf irony; **irónico, a** adj ironic(al)
IRPF ['i 'erre 'pe 'efe] n abr (= Impuesto sobre la Renta de las Personas Físicas) (personal) income tax
irreal [irre'al] adj unreal
irrecuperable [irrekupe'raβle] adj irrecoverable, irretrievable
irreflexión [irreflek'sjon] nf thoughtlessness
irregular [irreɣu'lar] adj (gen) irregular; (situación) abnormal
irremediable [irreme'δjaβle] adj irremediable; (vicio) incurable
irreparable [irrepa'raβle] adj (daños) irreparable; (pérdida) irrecoverable
irresoluto, a [irreso'luto, a] adj irresolute, hesitant
irrespetuoso, a [irrespe'twoso, a] adj disrespectful
irresponsable [irrespon'saβle] adj irresponsible
irreversible [irreβer'siβle] adj irreversible
irrigar [irri'ɣar] vt to irrigate
irrisorio, a [irri'sorjo, a] adj derisory, ridiculous
irritar [irri'tar] vt to irritate, annoy
irrupción [irrup'θjon] nf irruption; (invasión) invasion
isla ['isla] nf island
islandés, esa [islan'des, esa] adj Icelandic ♦ nm/f Icelander

Islandia [is'landja] *nf* Iceland
isleño, a [is'leɲo, a] *adj* island *cpd* ♦ *nm/f* islander
Israel [isra'el] *nm* Israel; **israelí** *adj, nm/f* Israeli
istmo ['istmo] *nm* isthmus
Italia [i'talja] *nf* Italy; **italiano, a** *adj, nm/f* Italian
itinerario [itine'rarjo] *nm* itinerary, route
IVA ['iβa] *nm abr* (= *impuesto sobre el valor añadido*) VAT
izar [i'θar] *vt* to hoist
izdo, a *abr* (= *izquierdo, a*) l.
izquierda [iθ'kjerda] *nf* left; (POL) left (wing); **a la ~** (*estar*) on the left; (*torcer etc*) (to the) left
izquierdista [iθkjer'ðista] *nm/f* left-winger, leftist
izquierdo, a [iθ'kjerðo, a] *adj* left

J, j

jabalí [xaβa'li] *nm* wild boar
jabalina [xaβa'lina] *nf* javelin
jabón [xa'βon] *nm* soap; **jabonar** *vt* to soap
jaca ['xaka] *nf* pony
jacinto [xa'θinto] *nm* hyacinth
jactarse [xak'tarse] *vr* to boast, brag
jadear [xaðe'ar] *vi* to pant, gasp for breath; **jadeo** *nm* panting, gasping
jaguar [xa'xwar] *nm* jaguar
jalea [xa'lea] *nf* jelly
jaleo [xa'leo] *nm* racket, uproar; **armar un ~** to kick up a racket
jalón [xa'lon] (AM) *nm* tug
jamás [xa'mas] *adv* never
jamón [xa'mon] *nm* ham; **~ dulce**, **~ de York** cooked ham; **~ serrano** cured ham
Japón [xa'pon] *nm*: **el ~** Japan; **japonés, esa** *adj, nm/f* Japanese ♦ *nm* (LING) Japanese
jaque ['xake] *nm*: **~ mate** checkmate
jaqueca [xa'keka] *nf* (very bad) headache, migraine
jarabe [xa'raβe] *nm* syrup
jarcia ['xarθja] *nf* (NAUT) ropes *pl*, rigging
jardín [xar'ðin] *nm* garden; **~ de infancia** (ESP) o **de niños** (AM) nursery (school); **jardinería** *nf* gardening; **jardinero, a** *nm/f* gardener
jarra ['xarra] *nf* jar; (*jarro*) jug
jarro ['xarro] *nm* jug
jarrón [xa'rron] *nm* vase
jaula ['xaula] *nf* cage
jauría [xau'ria] *nf* pack of hounds
jazmín [xaθ'min] *nm* jasmine
J. C. *abr* (= *Jesucristo*) J.C.
jefa ['xefa] *nf ver* **jefe**
jefatura [xefa'tura] *nf*: **~ de policía** police headquarters *sg*

jefe, a ['xefe, a] *nm/f* (gen) chief, head; (*patrón*) boss; **~ de cocina** chef; **~ de estación** stationmaster; **~ de estado** head of state
jengibre [xen'xiβre] *nm* ginger
jeque ['xeke] *nm* sheik
jerarquía [xerar'kia] *nf* (*orden*) hierarchy; (*rango*) rank; **jerárquico, a** *adj* hierarchic(al)
jerez [xe'reθ] *nm* sherry
jerga ['xerɣa] *nf* jargon
jeringa [xe'ringa] *nf* syringe; (AM) annoyance, bother; **~ de engrase** grease gun; **jeringar** *vt* (fam) to annoy, bother; **jeringuilla** *nf* syringe
jeroglífico [xero'ɣlifiko] *nm* hieroglyphic
jersey [xer'sei] (*pl* **~s**) *nm* jersey, pullover, jumper
Jerusalén [xerusa'len] *n* Jerusalem
Jesucristo [xesu'kristo] *nm* Jesus Christ
jesuita [xe'swita] *adj, nm* Jesuit
Jesús [xe'sus] *nm* Jesus; **¡~!** good heavens!; (*al estornudar*) bless you!
jinete, a [xi'nete, a] *nm/f* horseman/woman, rider
jipijapa [xipi'xapa] (AM) *nm* straw hat
jirafa [xi'rafa] *nf* giraffe
jirón [xi'ron] *nm* rag, shred
jocoso, a [xo'koso, a] *adj* humorous, jocular
joder [xo'ðer] (fam!) *vt, vi* to fuck(!)
jofaina [xo'faina] *nf* washbasin
jornada [xor'naða] *nf* (*viaje de un día*) day's journey; (*camino o viaje entero*) journey; (*día de trabajo*) working day
jornal [xor'nal] *nm* (day's) wage; **~ero** *nm* (day) labourer
joroba [xo'roβa] *nf* hump, hunched back; **~do, a** *adj* hunchbacked ♦ *nm/f* hunchback
jota ['xota] *nf* (the letter) J; (*danza*) Aragonese dance; **no saber ni ~** to have no idea
joven ['xoβen] (*pl* **jóvenes**) *adj* young ♦ *nm* young man, youth ♦ *nf* young woman, girl
jovial [xo'βjal] *adj* cheerful, jolly
joya ['xoja] *nf* jewel, gem; (fig: persona) gem; **joyería** *nf* (joyas) jewellery; (tienda) jeweller's (shop); **joyero** *nm* (persona) jeweller; (caja) jewel case
juanete [xwa'nete] *nm* (del pie) bunion
jubilación [xuβila'θjon] *nf* (retiro) retirement
jubilado, a [xuβi'laðo, a] *adj* retired ♦ *nm/f* pensioner (BRIT), senior citizen
jubilar [xuβi'lar] *vt* to pension off, retire; (fam) to discard; **~se** *vr* to retire
júbilo ['xuβilo] *nm* joy, rejoicing; **jubiloso, a** *adj* jubilant
judía [xu'ðia] *nf* (CULIN) bean; **~ verde** French bean; *ver tb* **judío**
judicial [xuði'θjal] *adj* judicial
judío, a [xu'ðio, a] *adj* Jewish ♦ *nm/f* Jew(ess)
judo ['xuðo] *nm* judo

juego etc ['xweɣo] vb ver **jugar** ♦ nm (gen) play; (pasatiempo, partido) game; (en casino) gambling; (conjunto) set; **fuera de ~** (DEPORTE: persona) offside; (: pelota) out of play; **J~s Olímpicos** Olympic Games

juerga ['xwerɣa] nf binge; (fiesta) party; **ir de ~** to go out on a binge

jueves ['xweßes] nm inv Thursday

juez [xweθ] nm/f judge; **~ de línea** linesman; **~ de salida** starter

jugada [xu'ɣaða] nf play; **buena ~** good move/shot/stroke etc

jugador, a [xuɣa'ðor, a] nm/f player; (en casino) gambler

jugar [xu'ɣar] vt, vi to play; (en casino) to gamble; (apostar) to bet; **~ al fútbol** to play football

juglar [xu'ɣlar] nm minstrel

jugo ['xuɣo] nm (BOT) juice; (fig) essence, substance; **~ de fruta** (AM) fruit juice; **~so, a** adj juicy; (fig) substantial, important

juguete [xu'ɣete] nm toy; **~ar** vi to play; **~ría** nf toyshop

juguetón, ona [xuɣe'ton, ona] adj playful

juicio ['xwiθjo] nm judgement; (razón) sanity, reason; (opinión) opinion; **~so, a** adj wise, sensible

julio ['xuljo] nm July

junco ['xunko] nm rush, reed

jungla ['xungla] nf jungle

junio ['xunjo] nm June

junta ['xunta] nf (asamblea) meeting, assembly; (comité, consejo) board, council, committee; (TEC) joint

juntar [xun'tar] vt to join, unite; (maquinaria) to assemble, put together; (dinero) to collect; **~se** vr to join, meet; (reunirse: personas) to meet, assemble; (arrimarse) to approach, draw closer; **~se con uno** to join sb

junto, a ['xunto, a] adj joined; (unido) united; (anexo) near, close; (contiguo, próximo) next, adjacent ♦ adv: **todo ~** all at once; **~s together**; **~ a** near (to), next to

jurado [xu'raðo] nm (JUR: individuo) juror; (: grupo) jury; (de concurso: grupo) panel (of judges); (: individuo) member of a panel

juramento [xura'mento] nm oath; (maldición) oath, curse; **prestar ~** to take the oath; **tomar ~ a** to swear in, administer the oath to

jurar [xu'rar] vt, vi to swear; **~ en falso** to commit perjury; **jurárselas a uno** to have it in for sb

jurídico, a [xu'riðiko, a] adj legal

jurisdicción [xurisðik'θjon] nf (poder, autoridad) jurisdiction; (territorio) district

jurisprudencia [xurispru'ðenθja] nf jurisprudence

jurista [xu'rista] nm/f jurist

justamente [xusta'mente] adv justly, fairly; (precisamente) just, exactly

justicia [xus'tiθja] nf justice; (equidad) fairness, justice; **justiciero, a** adj just, righteous

justificación [xustifika'θjon] nf justification; **justificar** vt to justify

justo, a ['xusto, a] adj (equitativo) just, fair, right; (preciso) exact, correct; (ajustado) tight ♦ adv (precisamente) exactly, precisely; (AM: apenas a tiempo) just in time

juvenil [xuße'nil] adj youthful

juventud [xußen'tuð] nf (adolescencia) youth; (jóvenes) young people pl

juzgado [xuθ'ɣaðo] nm tribunal; (JUR) court

juzgar [xuθ'ɣar] vt to judge; **a ~ por ...** to judge by ..., judging by ...

K, k

kg abr (= kilogramo) kg

kilo ['kilo] nm kilo ♦ pref: **~gramo** nm kilogramme; **~metraje** nm distance in kilometres, ≈ mileage; **kilómetro** nm kilometre; **~vatio** nm kilowatt

kiosco ['kjosko] nm = **quiosco**

km abr (= kilómetro) km

Kosovo [ko'sovo] nm Kosovo

kv abr (= kilovatio) kw

L, l

l abr (= litro) l

la [la] art def the ♦ pron her; (Ud.) you; (cosa) it ♦ nm (MUS) la; **~ del sombrero rojo** the girl in the red hat; tb ver **el**

laberinto [laße'rinto] nm labyrinth

labia ['laßja] nf fluency; (pey) glib tongue

labio ['laßjo] nm lip

labor [la'ßor] nf labour; (AGR) farm work; (tarea) job, task; (COSTURA) needlework; **~able** adj (AGR) workable; **día ~able** working day; **~al** adj (accidente) at work; (jornada) working

laboratorio [laßora'torjo] nm laboratory

laborioso, a [laßo'rjoso, a] adj (persona) hard-working; (trabajo) tough

laborista [laßo'rista] adj: **Partido L~** Labour Party

labrado, a [la'ßraðo, a] adj worked; (madera) carved; (metal) wrought

labrador, a [laßra'ðor, a] adj farming cpd ♦ nm/f farmer

labranza [la'ßranθa] nf (AGR) cultivation

labrar [la'ßrar] vt (gen) to work; (madera etc) to carve; (fig) to cause, bring about

labriego, a [la'ßrjeɣo, a] nm/f peasant

laca ['laka] *nf* lacquer
lacayo [la'kajo] *nm* lackey
lacio, a [la'laθjo, a] *adj* (*pelo*) lank, straight
lacón [la'kon] *nm* shoulder of pork
lacónico, a [la'koniko, a] *adj* laconic
lacra ['lakra] *nf* (*fig*) blot; **lacrar** *vt* (*cerrar*) to seal (with sealing wax); **lacre** *nm* sealing wax
lactancia [lak'tanθja] *nf* lactation
lactar [lak'tar] *vt, vi* to suckle
lácteo, a ['lakteo, a] *adj*: **productos ~s** dairy products
ladear [laðe'ar] *vt* to tip, tilt ♦ *vi* to tilt; **~se** *vr* to lean
ladera [la'ðera] *nf* slope
lado ['laðo] *nm* (*gen*) side; (*fig*) protection; (*MIL*) flank; **al ~ de** beside; **poner de ~** to put on its side; **poner a un ~** to put aside; **por todos ~s** on all sides, all round (*BRIT*)
ladrar [la'ðrar] *vi* to bark; **ladrido** *nm* bark, barking
ladrillo [la'ðriʎo] *nm* (*gen*) brick; (*azulejo*) tile
ladrón, ona [la'ðron, ona] *nm/f* thief
lagartija [laxar'tixa] *nf* (*ZOOL*) (small) lizard
lagarto [la'xarto] *nm* (*ZOOL*) lizard
lago ['laxo] *nm* lake
lágrima ['laxrima] *nf* tear
laguna [la'xuna] *nf* (*lago*) lagoon; (*hueco*) gap
laico, a ['laiko, a] *adj* lay
lamentable [lamen'taβle] *adj* lamentable, regrettable; (*miserable*) pitiful
lamentar [lamen'tar] *vt* (*sentir*) to regret; (*deplorar*) to lament; **lo lamento mucho** I'm very sorry; **~se** *vr* to lament; **lamento** *nm* lament
lamer [la'mer] *vt* to lick
lámina ['lamina] *nf* (*plancha delgada*) sheet; (*para estampar, estampa*) plate
lámpara ['lampara] *nf* lamp; **~ de alcohol/gas** spirit/gas lamp; **~ de pie** standard lamp
lamparón [lampa'ron] *nm* grease spot
lana ['lana] *nf* wool
lancha ['lantʃa] *nf* launch; **~ de pesca** fishing boat; **~ salvavidas/torpedera** lifeboat/torpedo boat
langosta [lan'gosta] *nf* (*crustáceo*) lobster; (: *de río*) crayfish; **langostino** *nm* Dublin Bay prawn
languidecer [langiðe'θer] *vi* to languish; **languidez** *nf* langour; **lánguido, a** *adj* (*gen*) languid; (*sin energía*) listless
lanilla [la'niʎa] *nf* nap
lanza ['lanθa] *nf* (*arma*) lance, spear
lanzamiento [lanθa'mjento] *nm* (*gen*) throwing; (*NAUT, COM*) launch, launching; **~ de peso** putting the shot
lanzar [lan'θar] *vt* (*gen*) to throw; (*DEPORTE:*

pelota) to bowl; (*NAUT, COM*) to launch; (*JUR*) to evict; **~se** *vr* to throw o.s.
lapa ['lapa] *nf* limpet
lapicero [lapi'θero] *nm* pencil; (*AM: bolígrafo*) Biro ®
lápida ['lapiða] *nf* stone; **~ mortuoria** headstone; **~ conmemorativa** memorial stone; **lapidario, a** *adj, nm* lapidary
lápiz ['lapiθ] *nm* pencil; **~ de color** coloured pencil; **~ de labios** lipstick
lapón, ona [la'pon, ona] *nm/f* Laplander, Lapp
lapso ['lapso] *nm* (*de tiempo*) interval; (*error*) error
lapsus ['lapsus] *nm inv* error, mistake
largar [lar'xar] *vt* (*soltar*) to release; (*aflojar*) ~to loosen; (*lanzar*) to launch; (*fam*) to let fly; (*velas*) to unfurl; (*AM*) to~throw; **~se** *vr* (*fam*) to beat it; **~se a** (*AM*) to start to
largo, a ['larxo, a] *adj* (*longitud*) long; (*tiempo*) lengthy; (*fig*) generous ♦ *nm* length; (*MUS*) largo; **dos años ~s** two long years; **tiene 9 metros de ~** it is 9 metres long; **a lo ~ de** along; (*tiempo*) all through, throughout; **~metraje** *nm* feature film
laringe [la'rinxe] *nf* larynx; **laringitis** *nf* laryngitis
larva ['larβa] *nf* larva
las [las] *art def* the ♦ *pron* them; **~ que cantan** the ones/women/girls who sing; *tb ver* **el**
lascivo, a [las'θiβo, a] *adj* lewd
láser ['laser] *nm* laser
lástima ['lastima] *nf* (*pena*) pity; **dar ~** to be pitiful; **es una ~ que** it's a pity that; **¡qué ~!** what a pity!; **ella está hecha una ~** she looks pitiful
lastimar [lasti'mar] *vt* (*herir*) to wound; (*ofender*) to offend; **~se** *vr* to hurt o.s.; **lastimero, a** *adj* pitiful, pathetic
lastre ['lastre] *nm* (*TEC, NAUT*) ballast; (*fig*) dead weight
lata ['lata] *nf* (*metal*) tin; (*caja*) tin (*BRIT*), can; (*fam*) nuisance; **en ~** tinned (*BRIT*), canned; **dar (la) ~** to be a nuisance
latente [la'tente] *adj* latent
lateral [late'ral] *adj* side *cpd*, lateral ♦ *nm* (*TEATRO*) wings
latido [la'tiðo] *nm* (*del corazón*) beat
latifundio [lati'fundjo] *nm* large estate; **latifundista** *nm/f* owner of a large estate
latigazo [lati'xaθo] *nm* (*golpe*) lash; (*sonido*) crack
látigo ['latixo] *nm* whip
latín [la'tin] *nm* Latin
latino, a [la'tino, a] *adj* Latin; **~americano, a** *adj, nm/f* Latin-American
latir [la'tir] *vi* (*corazón, pulso*) to beat
latitud [lati'tuð] *nf* (*GEO*) latitude
latón [la'ton] *nm* brass

latoso, a [la'toso, a] *adj* (*molesto*) annoying; (*aburrido*) boring

laúd [la'uð] *nm* lute

laurel [lau'rel] *nm* (*BOT*) laurel; (*CULIN*) bay

lava ['laßa] *nf* lava

lavabo ['la'ßaßo] *nm* (*pila*) washbasin; (*tb:* ~*s*) toilet

lavado [la'ßaðo] *nm* washing; (*de ropa*) laundry; (*ARTE*) wash; ~ **de cerebro** brainwashing; ~ **en seco** dry-cleaning

lavadora [laßa'ðora] *nf* washing machine

lavanda [la'ßanda] *nf* lavender

lavandería [laßande'ria] *nf* laundry; (*automática*) launderette

lavaplatos [laßa'platos] *nm inv* dishwasher

lavar [la'ßar] *vt* to wash; (*borrar*) to wipe away; ~**se** *vr* to wash o.s.; ~**se las manos** to wash one's hands; ~**se los dientes** to brush one's teeth; ~ **y marcar** (*pelo*) to shampoo and set; ~ **en seco** to dry-clean; ~ **los platos** to wash the dishes

lavavajillas [laßaßa'xiʎas] *nm inv* dishwasher

laxante [lak'sante] *nm* laxative

lazada [la'θaða] *nf* bow

lazarillo [laθa'riʎo] *nm*: **perro** ~ guide dog

lazo ['laθo] *nm* knot; (*lazada*) bow; (*para animales*) lasso; (*trampa*) snare; (*vínculo*) tie

le [le] *pron* (*directo*) him (o her); (: *usted*) you; (*indirecto*) to him (o her o it); (: *usted*) to you

leal [le'al] *adj* loyal; ~**tad** *nf* loyalty

lección [lek'θjon] *nf* lesson

leche ['letʃe] *nf* milk; **tiene mala** ~ (*fam!*) he's a swine (*!*); ~ **condensada/en polvo** condensed/powdered milk; ~ **desnatada** skimmed milk; ~**ra** *nf* (*vendedora*) milkmaid; (*recipiente*) (milk) churn; (*AM*) cow; ~**ro, a** *adj* dairy

lecho ['letʃo] *nm* (*cama, de río*) bed; (*GEO*) layer

lechón [le'tʃon] *nm* sucking (*BRIT*) o suckling (*US*) pig

lechoso, a [le'tʃoso, a] *adj* milky

lechuga [le'tʃuɣa] *nf* lettuce

lechuza [le'tʃuθa] *nf* owl

lector, a [lek'tor, a] *nm/f* reader ♦ *nm*: ~ **de discos compactos** CD player

lectura [lek'tura] *nf* reading

leer [le'er] *vt* to read

legado [le'ɣaðo] *nm* (*don*) bequest; (*herencia*) legacy; (*enviado*) legate

legajo [le'xaxo] *nm* file

legal [le'ɣal] *adj* (*gen*) legal; (*persona*) trustworthy; ~**idad** *nf* legality

legalizar [leɣali'θar] *vt* to legalize; (*documento*) to authenticate

legaña [le'ɣaɲa] *nf* sleep (*in eyes*)

legar [le'ɣar] *vt* to bequeath, leave

legendario, a [lexen'darjo, a] *adj* legendary

legión [le'xjon] *nf* legion; **legionario, a** *adj* legionary ♦ *nm* legionnaire

legislación [lexisla'θjon] *nf* legislation

legislar [lexis'lar] *vi* to legislate

legislatura [lexisla'tura] *nf* (*POL*) period of office

legitimar [lexiti'mar] *vt* to legitimize; **legítimo, a** *adj* (*genuino*) authentic; (*legal*) legitimate

lego, a ['leɣo, a] *adj* (*REL*) secular; (*ignorante*) ignorant ♦ *nm* layman

legua ['leɣwa] *nf* league

legumbres [le'ɣumbres] *nfpl* pulses

leído, a [le'iðo, a] *adj* well-read

lejanía [lexa'nia] *nf* distance; **lejano, a** *adj* far-off; (*en el tiempo*) distant; (*fig*) remote

lejía [le'xia] *nf* bleach

lejos ['lexos] *adv* far, far away; **a lo** ~ in the distance; **de** o **desde** ~ from afar; ~ **de** far from

lelo, a ['lelo, a] *adj* silly ♦ *nm/f* idiot

lema ['lema] *nm* motto; (*POL*) slogan

lencería [lenθe'ria] *nf* linen, drapery

lengua ['lengwa] *nf* tongue; (*LING*) language; **morderse la** ~ to hold one's tongue

lenguado [len'gwaðo] *nm* sole

lenguaje [len'gwaxe] *nm* language

lengüeta [len'gweta] *nf* (*ANAT*) epiglottis; (*zapatos*) tongue, (*MUS*) reed

lente ['lente] *nf* lens; (*lupa*) magnifying glass; ~**s** *nfpl* (*gafas*) glasses; ~**s de contacto** contact lenses

lenteja [len'texa] *nf* lentil; **lentejuela** *nf* sequin

lentilla [len'tiʎa] *nf* contact lens

lentitud [lenti'tuð] *nf* slowness; **con** ~ slowly

lento, a ['lento, a] *adj* slow

leña ['leɲa] *nf* firewood; ~**dor, a** *nm/f* woodcutter

leño ['leɲo] *nm* (*trozo de árbol*) log; (*madera*) timber; (*fig*) blockhead

Leo ['leo] *nm* Leo

león [le'on] *nm* lion; ~ **marino** sea lion

leopardo [leo'parðo] *nm* leopard

leotardos [leo'tarðos] *nmpl* tights

lepra ['lepra] *nf* leprosy; **leproso, a** *nm/f* leper

lerdo, a ['lerðo, a] *adj* (*lento*) slow; (*patoso*) clumsy

les [les] *pron* (*directo*) them; (: *ustedes*) you; (*indirecto*) to them; (: *ustedes*) to you

lesbiana [les'ßjana] *adj, nf* lesbian

lesión [le'sjon] *nf* wound, lesion; (*DEPORTE*) injury; **lesionado, a** *adj* injured ♦ *nm/f* injured person

letal [le'tal] *adj* lethal

letanía [leta'nia] *nf* litany

letargo [le'tarɣo] *nm* lethargy

letra ['letra] *nf* letter; (*escritura*) handwriting;

(*MUS*) lyrics *pl*; ~ **de cambio** bill of exchange; ~ **de imprenta** print; **~do, a** *adj* learned ♦ *nm/f* lawyer; **letrero** *nm* (*cartel*) sign; (*etiqueta*) label

letrina [le'trina] *nf* latrine

leucemia [leu'θemja] *nf* leukaemia

levadizo [leβa'ðiθo] *adj*: **puente ~** drawbridge

levadura [leβa'ðura] *nf* (*para el pan*) yeast; (*de la cerveza*) brewer's yeast

levantamiento [leβanta'mjento] *nm* raising, lifting; (*rebelión*) revolt, uprising; ~ **de pesos** weight-lifting

levantar [leβan'tar] *vt* (*gen*) to raise; (*del suelo*) to pick up; (*hacia arriba*) to lift (up); (*plan*) to make, draw up; (*mesa*) to clear; (*campamento*) to strike; (*fig*) to cheer up, hearten; **~se** *vr* to get up; (*enderezarse*) to straighten up; (*rebelarse*) to rebel; ~ **el ánimo** to cheer up

levante [le'βante] *nm* east coast; **el L~** *region of Spain extending from Castellón to Murcia*

levar [le'βar] *vt* to weigh

leve [le'βe] *adj* light; (*fig*) trivial; **~dad** *nf* lightness

levita [le'βita] *nf* frock coat

léxico ['leksiko] *nm* (*vocabulario*) vocabulary

ley [lei] *nf* (*gen*) law; (*metal*) standard

leyenda [le'jenda] *nf* legend

leyó *etc vb ver* **leer**

liar [li'ar] *vt* to tie (up); (*unir*) to bind; (*envolver*) to wrap (up); (*enredar*) to confuse; (*cigarrillo*) to roll; **~se** *vr* (*fam*) to get involved; **~se a palos** to get involved in a fight

Líbano ['liβano] *nm*: **el ~** (the) Lebanon

libelo [li'βelo] *nm* satire, lampoon

libélula [li'βelula] *nf* dragonfly

liberación [liβera'θjon] *nf* liberation; (*de la cárcel*) release

liberal [liβe'ral] *adj, nm/f* liberal; **~idad** *nf* liberality, generosity

liberar [liβe'rar] *vt* to liberate

libertad [liβer'tað] *nf* liberty, freedom; ~ **de culto/de prensa/de comercio** freedom of worship/of the press/of trade; ~ **condicional** probation; ~ **bajo palabra** parole; ~ **bajo fianza** bail

libertar [liβer'tar] *vt* (*preso*) to set free; (*de una obligación*) to release; (*eximir*) to exempt

libertino, a [liβer'tino, a] *adj* permissive ♦ *nm/f* permissive person

libra ['liβra] *nf* pound; (*ASTROLOGÍA*): **L~** Libra; ~ **esterlina** pound sterling

librar [li'βrar] *vt* (*de peligro*) to save; (*batalla*) to wage, fight; (*de impuestos*) to exempt; (*cheque*) to make out; (*JUR*) to exempt; **~se** *vr*: **~se de** to escape from, free o.s. from

libre ['liβre] *adj* free; (*lugar*) unoccupied;

(*asiento*) vacant; (*de deudas*) free of debts; ~ **de impuestos** free of tax; **tiro ~** free kick; **los 100 metros ~** the 100 metres free-style (race); **al aire ~** in the open air

librería [liβre'ria] *nf* (*tienda*) bookshop; **librero, a** *nm/f* bookseller

libreta [li'βreta] *nf* notebook; ~ **de ahorros** savings book

libro ['liβro] *nm* book; ~ **de bolsillo** paperback; ~ **de caja** cashbook; ~ **de cheques** chequebook (*BRIT*), checkbook (*US*); ~ **de texto** textbook

Lic. *abr* = **licenciado, a**

licencia [li'θenθja] *nf* (*gen*) licence; (*permiso*) permission; ~ **por enfermedad** sick leave; ~ **de caza** game licence; **~do, a** *adj* licensed ♦ *nm/f* graduate; **licenciar** *vt* (*empleado*) to dismiss; (*permitir*) to permit, allow; (*soldado*) to discharge; (*estudiante*) to confer a degree upon; **licenciarse** *vr*: **licenciarse en letras** to graduate in arts

licencioso, a [liθen'θjoso, a] *adj* licentious

licitar [liθi'tar] *vt* to bid for; (*AM*) to sell by auction

lícito, a ['liθito, a] *adj* (*legal*) lawful; (*justo*) fair, just; (*permisible*) permissible

licor [li'kor] *nm* spirits *pl* (*BRIT*), liquor (*US*); (*de frutas etc*) liqueur

licuadora [likwa'ðora] *nf* blender

licuar [li'kwar] *vt* to liquidize

líder ['liðer] *nm/f* leader; **liderato** *nm* leadership; **liderazgo** *nm* leadership

lidia ['liðja] *nf* bullfighting; (*una ~*) bullfight; **toros de ~** fighting bulls; **lidiar** *vt, vi* to fight

liebre ['ljeβre] *nf* hare

lienzo ['ljenθo] *nm* linen; (*ARTE*) canvas; (*ARQ*) wall

liga ['liɣa] *nf* (*de medias*) garter, suspender; (*AM: gomita*) rubber band; (*confederación*) league

ligadura [liɣa'ðura] *nf* bond, tie; (*MED, MUS*) ligature

ligamento [liɣa'mento] *nm* ligament

ligar [li'ɣar] *vt* (*atar*) to tie; (*unir*) to join; (*MED*) to bind up; (*MUS*) to slur ♦ *vi* to mix, blend; (*fam*) (*él*) **liga mucho** he pulls a lot of women; **~se** *vr* to commit o.s.

ligereza [lixe'reθa] *nf* lightness; (*rapidez*) swiftness; (*agilidad*) agility; (*superficialidad*) flippancy

ligero, a [li'xero, a] *adj* (*de peso*) light; (*tela*) thin; (*rápido*) swift, quick; (*ágil*) agile, nimble; (*de importancia*) slight; (*de carácter*) flippant, superficial ♦ *adv*: **a la ligera** superficially

liguero [li'ɣero] *nm* suspender (*BRIT*) o garter (*US*) belt

lija ['lixa] *nf* (*ZOOL*) dogfish; (*tb: papel de ~*) sandpaper

lila ['lila] *nf* lilac

lima ['lima] *nf* file; (*BOT*) lime; ~ **de uñas** nailfile; **limar** *vt* to file

limitación [limita'θjon] *nf* limitation, limit; ~ **de velocidad** speed limit

limitar [limi'tar] *vt* to limit; (*reducir*) to reduce, cut down ♦ *vi*: ~ **con** to border on; ~**se** *vr*: ~**se a** to limit o.s. to

límite ['limite] *nm* (*gen*) limit; (*fin*) end; (*frontera*) border; ~ **de velocidad** speed limit

limítrofe [li'mitrofe] *adj* neighbouring

limón [li'mon] *nm* lemon ♦ *adj*: **amarillo** ~ lemon-yellow; **limonada** *nf* lemonade

limosna [li'mosna] *nf* alms *pl*; **vivir de** ~ to live on charity

limpiaparabrisas [limpjapara'ßrisas] *nm inv* windscreen (*BRIT*) *o* windshield (*US*) wiper

limpiar [lim'pjar] *vt* to clean; (*con trapo*) to wipe; (*quitar*) to wipe away; (*zapatos*) to shine, polish; (*fig*) to clean up

limpieza [lim'pjeθa] *nf* (*estado*) cleanliness; (*acto*) cleaning; (: *de las calles*) cleansing; (: *de zapatos*) polishing; (*habilidad*) skill; (*fig: POLICÍA*) clean-up; (*pureza*) purity; (*MIL*): **operación de** ~ mopping-up operation; ~ **en seco** dry cleaning

limpio, a ['limpjo, a] *adj* clean; (*moralmente*) pure; (*COM*) clear, net; (*fam*) honest ♦ *adv*: **jugar** ~ to play fair; **pasar a** (*ESP*) *o* **en** (*AM*) ~ to make a clean copy

linaje [li'naxe] *nm* lineage, family

lince ['linθe] *nm* lynx

linchar [lin'tʃar] *vt* to lynch

lindar [lin'dar] *vi* to adjoin; ~ **con** to border on; **linde** *nm o f* boundary; **lindero, a** *adj* adjoining ♦ *nm* boundary

lindo, a ['lindo, a] *adj* pretty, lovely ♦ *adv*: **nos divertimos de lo** ~ we had a marvellous time; **canta muy** ~ (*AM*) he sings beautifully

línea ['linea] *nf* (*gen*) line; **en** ~ (*INFORM*) on line; ~ **aérea** airline; ~ **de meta** goal line; (*de carrera*) finishing line; ~ **recta** straight line

lingote [lin'gote] *nm* ingot

lingüista [lin'gwista] *nm/f* linguist; **lingüística** *nf* linguistics *sg*

lino ['lino] *nm* linen; (*BOT*) flax

linóleo [li'noleo] *nm* lino, linoleum

linterna [lin'terna] *nf* torch (*BRIT*), flashlight (*US*)

lío ['lio] *nm* bundle; (*fam*) fuss; (*desorden*) muddle, mess; **armar un** ~ to make a fuss

liquen ['liken] *nm* lichen

liquidación [likiða'θjon] *nf* liquidation; **venta de** ~ clearance sale

liquidar [liki'ðar] *vt* (*mercancías*) to liquidate; (*deudas*) to pay off; (*empresa*) to wind up

líquido, a ['likiðo, a] *adj* liquid; (*ganancia*) net ♦ *nm* liquid; ~ **imponible** net taxable income

lira ['lira] *nf* (*MUS*) lyre; (*moneda*) lira

lírico, a ['liriko, a] *adj* lyrical

lirio ['lirjo] *nm* (*BOT*) iris

lirón [li'ron] *nm* (*ZOOL*) dormouse; (*fig*) sleepyhead

Lisboa [lis'ßoa] *n* Lisbon

lisiado, a [li'sjaðo, a] *adj* injured ♦ *nm/f* cripple

lisiar [li'sjar] *vt* to maim; ~**se** *vr* to injure o.s.

liso, a ['liso, a] *adj* (*terreno*) flat; (*cabello*) straight; (*superficie*) even; (*tela*) plain

lisonja [li'sonxa] *nf* flattery

lista ['lista] *nf* list; (*de alumnos*) school register; (*de libros*) catalogue; (*de platos*) menu; (*de precios*) price list; **pasar** ~ to call the roll; ~ **de correos** poste restante; ~ **de espera** waiting list; **tela de** ~**s** striped material; **listín** *nm*: ~ (**telefónico**) telephone directory

listo, a ['listo, a] *adj* (*perspicaz*) smart, clever; (*preparado*) ready

listón [lis'ton] *nm* (*de madera, metal*) strip

litera [li'tera] *nf* (*en barco, tren*) berth; (*en dormitorio*) bunk, bunk bed

literal [lite'ral] *adj* literal

literario, a [lite'rarjo, a] *adj* literary

literato, a [lite'rato, a] *adj* literary ♦ *nm/f* writer

literatura [litera'tura] *nf* literature

litigar [liti'var] *vt* to fight ♦ *vi* (*JUR*) to go to law; (*fig*) to dispute, argue

litigio [li'tixjo] *nm* (*JUR*) lawsuit; (*fig*): **en** ~ **con** in dispute with

litografía [litovra'fia] *nf* lithography; (*una* ~) lithograph

litoral [lito'ral] *adj* coastal ♦ *nm* coast, seaboard

litro ['litro] *nm* litre

liviano, a [li'ßjano, a] *adj* (*cosa, objeto*) trivial

lívido, a ['lißiðo, a] *adj* livid

llaga ['ʎava] *nf* wound

llama ['ʎama] *nf* flame; (*ZOOL*) llama

llamada [ʎa'maða] *nf* call; ~ **al orden** call to order; ~ **a pie de página** reference note

llamamiento [ʎama'mjento] *nm* call

llamar [ʎa'mar] *vt* to call; (*atención*) to attract ♦ *vi* (*por teléfono*) to telephone; (*a la puerta*) to knock (*o* ring); (*por señas*) to beckon; (*MIL*) to call up; ~**se** *vr* to be called, be named; **¿cómo se llama usted?** what's your name?

llamarada [ʎama'raða] *nf* (*llamas*) blaze; (*rubor*) flush

llamativo, a [ʎama'tißo, a] *adj* showy; (*color*) loud

llano, a ['ʎano, a] *adj* (*superficie*) flat; (*persona*) straightforward; (*estilo*) clear ♦ *nm* plain, flat ground

llanta ['ʎanta] *nf* (*wheel*) rim; (*AM*): ~ (**de**

goma) tyre; (: *cámara*) inner (tube)
llanto [ˈʎanto] *nm* weeping
llanura [ʎaˈnura] *nf* plain
llave [ˈʎaβe] *nf* key; (*del agua*) tap;
(*MECÁNICA*) spanner; (*de la luz*) switch; (*MUS*)
key; ~ **inglesa** monkey wrench; ~ **maestra**
master key; ~ **de contacto** (*AUTO*) ignition
key; ~ **de paso** stopcock; **echar la ~ a** to lock
up; **~ro** *nm* keyring
llegada [ʎeˈɣaða] *nf* arrival
llegar [ʎeˈɣar] *vi* to arrive; (*alcanzar*) to
reach; (*bastar*) to be enough; **~se** *vr*: **~se a** to
approach; **~ a** to manage to, succeed in; **~ a
saber** to find out; **~ a ser** to become; **~ a las
manos de** to come into the hands of
llenar [ʎeˈnar] *vt* to fill; (*espacio*) to cover;
(*formulario*) to fill in o up; (*fig*) to heap
lleno, a [ˈʎeno, a] *adj* full, filled; (*repleto*) full
up ♦ *nm* (*TEATRO*) full house; **dar de ~ contra
un muro** to hit a wall head-on
llevadero, a [ʎeβaˈðero, a] *adj* bearable,
tolerable
llevar [ʎeˈβar] *vt* to take; (*ropa*) to wear;
(*cargar*) to carry; (*quitar*) to take away; (*en
coche*) to drive; (*transportar*) to transport;
(*traer: dinero*) to carry; (*conducir*) to lead;
(*MAT*) to carry ♦ *vi* (*suj: camino etc*): **~ a** to
lead to; **~se** *vr* to carry off, take away;
llevamos dos días aquí we have been here for
two days; **él me lleva 2 años** he's 2 years
older than me; (*COM*): **~ los libros** to keep
the books; **~se bien** to get on well (together)
llorar [ʎoˈrar] *vt, vi* to cry, weep; **~ de risa** to
cry with laughter
lloriquear [ʎorikeˈar] *vi* to snivel, whimper
lloro [ˈʎoro] *nm* crying, weeping; **llorón, ona**
adj tearful ♦ *nm/f* cry-baby; **~so, a** *adj* (*gen*)
weeping, tearful; (*triste*) sad, sorrowful
llover [ʎoˈβer] *vi* to rain
llovizna [ʎoˈβiθna] *nf* drizzle; **lloviznar** *vi* to
drizzle
llueve *etc vb ver* **llover**
lluvia [ˈʎuβja] *nf* rain; **~ radioactiva**
(*radioactive*) fallout; **lluvioso, a** *adj* rainy
lo [lo] *art def*: **~ bello** the beautiful, what is
beautiful, that which is beautiful ♦ *pron*
(*persona*) him; (*cosa*) it; *tb ver* **el**
loable [loˈaβle] *adj* praiseworthy; **loar** *vt* to
praise
lobo [ˈloβo] *nm* wolf; **~ de mar** (*fig*) sea dog;
~ marino seal
lóbrego, a [ˈloβreɣo, a] *adj* dark; (*fig*)
gloomy
lóbulo [ˈloβulo] *nm* lobe
local [loˈkal] *adj* local ♦ *nm* place, site;
(*oficinas*) premises *pl*; **~idad** *nf* (*barrio*)
locality; (*lugar*) location; (*TEATRO*) seat, ticket;
~izar *vt* (*ubicar*) to locate, find; (*restringir*) to
localize; (*situar*) to place

loción [loˈθjon] *nf* lotion
loco, a [ˈloko, a] *adj* mad ♦ *nm/f* lunatic, mad
person
locomotora [lokomoˈtora] *nf* engine,
locomotive
locuaz [loˈkwaθ] *adj* loquacious
locución [lokuˈθjon] *nf* expression
locura [loˈkura] *nf* madness; (*acto*) crazy act
locutor, a [lokuˈtor, a] *nm/f* (*RADIO*)
announcer; (*comentarista*) commentator; (*TV*)
newsreader
locutorio [lokuˈtorjo] *nm* (*en telefónica*)
telephone booth
lodo [ˈloðo] *nm* mud
lógica [ˈloxika] *nf* logic
lógico, a [ˈloxiko, a] *adj* logical
logística [loˈxistika] *nf* logistics *sg*
logotipo [loðoˈtipo] *nm* logo
logrado, a [loˈðraðo, a] *adj* (*interpretación,
reproducción*) polished, excellent
lograr [loˈɣrar] *vt* to achieve; (*obtener*) to get,
obtain; **~ hacer** to manage to do; **~ que uno
venga** to manage to get sb to come
logro [ˈloɣro] *nm* achievement, success
loma [ˈloma] *nf* hillock (*BRIT*), small hill
lombriz [lomˈbriθ] *nf* worm
lomo [ˈlomo] *nm* (*de animal*) back; (*CULIN: de
cerdo*) pork loin; (: *de vaca*) rib steak; (*de
libro*) spine
lona [ˈlona] *nf* canvas
loncha [ˈlontʃa] *nf* = **lonja**
lonche [ˈlontʃe] (*AM*) *nm* lunch; **~ría** (*AM*) *nf*
snack bar, diner (*US*)
Londres [ˈlondres] *n* London
longaniza [longaˈniθa] *nf* pork sausage
longitud [lonxiˈtuð] *nf* length; (*GEO*)
longitude; **tener 3 metros de ~** to be 3 metres
long; **~ de onda** wavelength
lonja [ˈlonxa] *nf* slice; (*de tocino*) rasher; **~ de
pescado** fish market
loro [ˈloro] *nm* parrot
los [los] *art def* the ♦ *pron* them; (*ustedes*)
you; **mis libros y ~ tuyos** my books and
yours; *tb ver* **el**
losa [ˈlosa] *nf* stone; **~ sepulcral** gravestone
lote [ˈlote] *nm* portion; (*COM*) lot
lotería [loteˈria] *nf* lottery; (*juego*) lotto
loza [ˈloθa] *nf* crockery
lubina [luˈβina] *nf* sea bass
lubricante [luβriˈkante] *nm* lubricant
lubricar [luβriˈkar] *vt* to lubricate
lucha [ˈlutʃa] *nf* fight, struggle; **~ de clases**
class struggle; **~ libre** wrestling; **luchar** *vi* to
fight
lucidez [luθiˈðeθ] *nf* lucidity
lúcido, a [ˈluθiðo, a] *adj* (*persona*) lucid;
(*mente*) logical; (*idea*) crystal-clear
luciérnaga [luˈθjernaɣa] *nf* glow-worm
lucir [luˈθir] *vt* to illuminate, light (up);

(ostentar) to show off ♦ vi (brillar) to shine;
~se vr (irónico) to make a fool of o.s.
lucro ['lukro] nm profit, gain
lúdico, a ['ludiko, a] adj (aspecto, actividad)
play cpd
luego ['lwe o] adv (después) next; (más
tarde) later, afterwards
lugar [lu'ɣar] nm place; (sitio) spot; **en ~ de**
instead of; **hacer ~** to make room; **fuera de ~**
out of place; **tener ~** to take place; **~ común**
commonplace
lugareño, a [luɣa'reɲo, a] adj village cpd
♦ nm/f villager
lugarteniente [luɣarte'njente] nm deputy
lúgubre ['luɣuβre] adj mournful
lujo ['luxo] nm luxury; (fig) profusion,
abundance; **~so, a** adj luxurious
lujuria [lu'xurja] nf lust
lumbre ['lumbre] nf fire; (para cigarrillo) light
lumbrera [lum'brera] nf luminary
luminoso, a [lumi'noso, a] adj luminous,
shining
luna ['luna] nf moon; (de un espejo) glass; (de
gafas) lens; (fig) crescent; **~ llena/nueva** full/
new moon; **estar en la ~** to have one's head
in the clouds; **~ de miel** honeymoon
lunar [lu'nar] adj lunar ♦ nm (ANAT) mole;
tela de ~es spotted material
lunes ['lunes] nm inv Monday
lupa ['lupa] nf magnifying glass
lustrar [lus'trar] vt (mueble) to polish;
(zapatos) to shine; **lustre** nm polish; (fig)
lustre; **dar lustre a** to polish; **lustroso, a** adj
shining
luto ['luto] nm mourning; **llevar el o vestirse
de ~** to be in mourning
Luxemburgo [luksem'burɣo] nm Luxembourg
luz [luθ] (pl luces) nf light; **dar a ~ un niño** to
give birth to a child; **sacar a la ~** to bring to
light; **dar o encender** (ESP) **o prender** (AM)/
apagar la ~ to switch the light on/off; **a todas
luces** by any reckoning; **tener pocas luces** to
be dim o stupid; **~ roja/verde** red/green light;
~ de freno brake light; **luces de tráfico** traffic
lights; **traje de luces** bullfighter's costume

M, m

m abr (= metro) m; (= minuto) m
macarrones [maka'rrones] nmpl macaroni
sg
macedonia [maθe'ðonja] nf: **~ de frutas**
fruit salad
macerar [maθe'rar] vt to macerate
maceta [ma'θeta] nf (de flores) pot of
flowers; (para plantas) flowerpot
machacar [matʃa'kar] vt to crush, pound

♦ vi (insistir) to go on, keep on
machete [ma'tʃete] (AM) nm machete,
(large) knife
machismo [ma'tʃismo] nm male
chauvinism; **machista** adj, nm sexist
macho ['matʃo] adj male; (fig) virile ♦ nm
male; (fig) he-man
macizo, a [ma'θiθo, a] adj (grande) massive;
(fuerte, sólido) solid ♦ nm mass, chunk
madeja [ma'ðexa] nf (de lana) skein, hank;
(de pelo) mass, mop
madera [ma'ðera] nf wood; (fig) nature,
character; **una ~** a piece of wood
madero [ma'ðero] nm beam
madrastra [ma'ðrastra] nf stepmother
madre ['maðre] adj mother cpd; (AM)
tremendous ♦ nf mother; (de vino etc) dregs
pl; **~ política/soltera** mother-in-law/unmarried
mother
Madrid [ma'ðrið] n Madrid
madriguera [maðri'ɣera] nf burrow
madrileño, a [maðri'leɲo, a] adj of o from
Madrid ♦ nm/f native of Madrid
madrina [ma'ðrina] nf godmother; (ARQ)
prop, shore; (TEC) brace; (de boda)
bridesmaid
madrugada [maðru'ɣaða] nf early morning;
(alba) dawn, daybreak
madrugador, a [maðruɣa'ðor, a] adj early-
rising
madrugar [maðru'ɣar] vi to get up early;
(fig) to get ahead
madurar [maðu'rar] vt, vi (fruta) to ripen;
(fig) to mature; **madurez** nf ripeness;
maturity; **maduro, a** adj ripe; mature
maestra [ma'estra] nf ver **maestro**
maestría [maes'tria] nf mastery; (habilidad)
skill, expertise
maestro, a [ma'estro, a] adj masterly;
(principal) main ♦ nm/f master/mistress;
(profesor) teacher ♦ nm (autoridad) authority;
(MUS) maestro; (AM) skilled workman;
~ albañil master mason
magdalena [maɣða'lena] nf fairy cake
magia ['maxja] nf magic; **mágico, a** adj
magic(al) ♦ nm/f magician
magisterio [maxis'terjo] nm (enseñanza)
teaching; (profesión) teaching profession;
(maestros) teachers pl
magistrado [maxis'traðo] nm magistrate
magistral [maxis'tral] adj magisterial; (fig)
masterly
magnánimo, a [maɣ'nanimo, a] adj
magnanimous
magnate [maɣ'nate] nm magnate, tycoon
magnético, a [maɣ'netiko, a] adj magnetic;
magnetizar vt to magnetize
magnetofón [maɣneto'fon] nm tape
recorder; **magnetofónico, a** adj: **cinta**

magnetofónica recording tape
magnetófono [maɣne'tofono] *nm* = **magnetofón**
magnífico, a [maɣ'nifiko, a] *adj* splendid, magnificent
magnitud [maɣni'tuð] *nf* magnitude
mago, a ['maɣo, a] *nm/f* magician; **los Reyes M~s** the Magi, the Three Wise Men
magro, a ['maɣro, a] *adj* (*carne*) lean
maguey [ma'ɣei] *nm* agave
magullar [maɣu'ʎar] *vt* (*amoratar*) to bruise; (*dañar*) to damage
mahometano, a [maome'tano, a] *adj* Mohammedan
mahonesa [mao'nesa] *nf* mayonnaise
maíz [ma'iθ] *nm* maize (*BRIT*), corn (*US*); sweet corn
majadero, a [maxa'ðero, a] *adj* silly, stupid
majestad [maxes'taθ] *nf* majesty; **majestuoso, a** *adj* majestic
majo, a ['maxo, a] *adj* nice; (*guapo*) attractive, good-looking; (*elegante*) smart
mal [mal] *adv* badly; (*equivocadamente*) wrongly ♦ *adj* = **malo** ♦ *nm* evil; (*desgracia*) misfortune; (*daño*) harm, damage; (*MED*) illness; **~ que bien** rightly or wrongly; **ir de ~ en peor** to get worse and worse
malabarismo [malaßa'rismo] *nm* juggling; **malabarista** *nm/f* juggler
malaria [ma'larja] *nf* malaria
malcriado, a [mal'krjaðo, a] *adj* spoiled
maldad [mal'daθ] *nf* evil, wickedness
maldecir [malde'θir] *vt* to curse ♦ *vi*: **~ de** to speak ill of
maldición [maldi'θjon] *nf* curse
maldito, a [mal'dito, a] *adj* (*condenado*) damned; (*perverso*) wicked; **¡~ sea!** damn it!
maleante [male'ante] *nm/f* criminal, crook
maledicencia [maleði'θenθja] *nf* slander, scandal
maleducado, a [maleðu'kaðo, a] *adj* bad-mannered, rude
malentendido [malenten'diðo] *nm* misunderstanding
malestar [males'tar] *nm* (*gen*) discomfort; (*fig: inquietud*) uneasiness; (*POL*) unrest
maleta [ma'leta] *nf* case, suitcase; (*AUTO*) boot (*BRIT*), trunk (*US*); **hacer las ~s** to pack; **maletera** (*AM*) *nf*, **maletero** *nm* (*AUTO*) boot (*BRIT*), trunk (*US*); **maletín** *nm* small case, bag
malévolo, a [ma'leßolo, a] *adj* malicious, spiteful
maleza [ma'leθa] *nf* (*hierbas malas*) weeds *pl*; (*arbustos*) thicket
malgastar [malɣas'tar] *vt* (*tiempo, dinero*) to waste; (*salud*) to ruin
malhechor, a [male'tʃor, a] *nm/f* delinquent
malhumorado, a [malumo'raðo, a] *adj* bad-tempered

malicia [ma'liθja] *nf* (*maldad*) wickedness; (*astucia*) slyness, guile; (*mala intención*) malice, spite; (*carácter travieso*) mischievousness; **malicioso, a** *adj* wicked, evil; sly, crafty; malicious, spiteful; mischievous
maligno, a [ma'liɣno, a] *adj* evil; (*malévolo*) malicious; (*MED*) malignant
malla ['maʎa] *nf* mesh; (*de baño*) swimsuit; (*de ballet, gimnasia*) leotard; **~s** *nfpl* tights; **~ de alambre** wire mesh
Mallorca [ma'ʎorka] *nf* Majorca
malo, a ['malo, a] *adj* bad; (*falso*) false ♦ *nm/f* villain; **estar ~** to be ill
malograr [malo'ɣrar] *vt* to spoil; (*plan*) to upset; (*ocasión*) to waste; **~se** *vr* (*plan etc*) to fail, come to grief; (*persona*) to die before one's time
malparado, a [malpa'raðo, a] *adj*: **salir ~** to come off badly
malpensado, a [malpen'saðo, a] *adj* nasty
malsano, a [mal'sano, a] *adj* unhealthy
malteada [malte'aða] (*AM*) *nf* milk shake
maltratar [maltra'tar] *vt* to ill-treat, mistreat
maltrecho, a [mal'tretʃo, a] *adj* battered, damaged
malvado, a [mal'ßaðo, a] *adj* evil, villainous
malversar [malßer'sar] *vt* to embezzle, misappropriate
Malvinas [mal'ßinas]: **Islas ~** *nfpl* Falkland Islands
malvivir [malßi'ßir] *vi* to live poorly
mama ['mama] *nf* (*de animal*) teat; (*de mujer*) breast
mamá [ma'ma] (*pl* **~s**) (*fam*) *nf* mum, mummy
mamar [ma'mar] *vt, vi* to suck
mamarracho [mama'rratʃo] *nm* sight, mess
mamífero [ma'mifero] *nm* mammal
mampara [mam'para] *nf* (*entre habitaciones*) partition; (*biombo*) screen
mampostería [mamposte'ria] *nf* masonry
manada [ma'naða] *nf* (*ZOOL*) herd; (: *de leones*) pride; (: *de lobos*) pack
manantial [manan'tjal] *nm* spring
manar [ma'nar] *vi* to run, flow
mancha ['mantʃa] *nf* stain, mark; (*ZOOL*) patch; **manchar** *vt* (*gen*) to stain, mark; (*ensuciar*) to soil, dirty
manchego, a [man'tʃeɣo, a] *adj* of o from La Mancha
manco, a ['manko, a] *adj* (*de un brazo*) one-armed; (*de una mano*) one-handed; (*fig*) defective, faulty
mancomunar [mankomu'nar] *vt* to unite, bring together; (*recursos*) to pool; (*JUR*) to make jointly responsible; **mancomunidad** *nf* union, association; (*comunidad*) community;

(JUR) joint responsibility

mandamiento [manda'mjento] *nm (orden)* order, command; *(REL)* commandment; ~ **judicial** warrant

mandar [man'dar] *vt (ordenar)* to order; *(dirigir)* to lead, command; *(enviar)* to send; *(pedir)* to order, ask for ♦ *vi* to be in charge; *(pey)* to be bossy; **¿mande?** pardon?, excuse me?; ~ **hacer un traje** to have a suit made

mandarina [manda'rina] *nf* tangerine, mandarin (orange)

mandato [man'dato] *nm (orden)* order; *(POL: período)* term of office; *(: territorio)* mandate; ~ **judicial** (search) warrant

mandíbula [man'diβula] *nf* jaw

mandil [man'dil] *nm* apron

mando ['mando] *nm (MIL)* command; *(de país)* rule; *(el primer lugar)* lead; *(POL)* term of office; *(TEC)* control; ~ **a la izquierda** left-hand drive

mandón, ona [man'don, ona] *adj* bossy, domineering

manejable [mane'xaβle] *adj* manageable

manejar [mane'xar] *vt* to manage; *(máquina)* to work, operate; *(caballo etc)* to handle; *(casa)* to run, manage; *(AM: AUTO)* to drive; **~se** *vr (comportarse)* to act, behave; *(arreglárselas)* to manage; **manejo** *nm* management; handling; running; driving; *(facilidad de trato)* ease, confidence; **manejos** *nmpl (intrigas)* intrigues

manera [ma'nera] *nf* way, manner, fashion; **~s** *nfpl (modales)* manners; **su ~ de ser** the way he is; *(aire)* his manner; **de ninguna ~** no way, by no means; **de otra ~** otherwise; **de todas ~s** at any rate; **no hay ~ de persuadirle** there's no way of convincing him

manga ['manga] *nf (de camisa)* sleeve; *(de riego)* hose

mangar [man'gar] *(fam) vt* to pinch, nick

mango ['mango] *nm* handle; *(BOT)* mango

mangonear [mangone'ar] *vi (meterse)* to meddle, interfere; *(ser mandón)* to boss people about

manguera [man'gera] *nf* hose

manía [ma'nia] *nf (MED)* mania; *(fig: moda)* rage, craze; *(disgusto)* dislike; *(malicia)* spite; **maníaco, a** *adj* maniac(al) ♦ *nm/f* maniac

maniatar [manja'tar] *vt* to tie the hands of

maniático, a [ma'njatiko, a] *adj* maniac(al) ♦ *nm/f* maniac

manicomio [mani'komjo] *nm* mental hospital *(BRIT)*, insane asylum *(US)*

manifestación [manifesta'θjon] *nf (declaración)* statement, declaration; *(de emoción)* show, display; *(POL: desfile)* demonstration; *(: concentración)* mass meeting

manifestar [manifes'tar] *vt* to show,

manifest; *(declarar)* to state, declare; **manifiesto, a** *adj* clear, manifest ♦ *nm* manifesto

manillar [mani'ʎar] *nm* handlebars *pl*

maniobra [ma'njoβra] *nf* manœuvre; **~s** *nfpl (MIL)* manœuvres; **maniobrar** *vt* to manœuvre

manipulación [manipula'θjon] *nf* manipulation

manipular [manipu'lar] *vt* to manipulate; *(manejar)* to handle

maniquí [mani'ki] *nm* dummy ♦ *nm/f* model

manirroto, a [mani'rroto, a] *adj* lavish, extravagant ♦ *nm/f* spendthrift

manivela [mani'βela] *nf* crank

manjar [man'xar] *nm (tasty)* dish

mano ['mano] *nf* hand; *(ZOOL)* foot, paw; *(de pintura)* coat; *(serie)* lot, series; **a ~** by hand; **a ~ derecha/izquierda** on the right(-hand side)/left(-hand side); **de primera ~** (at) first hand; **de segunda ~** (at) second hand; **robo a ~ armada** armed robbery; **~ de obra** labour, manpower; **estrechar la ~ a uno** to shake sb's hand

manojo [ma'noxo] *nm* handful, bunch; ~ **de llaves** bunch of keys

manopla [ma'nopla] *nf* mitten

manoseado, a [manose'aðo, a] *adj* well-worn

manosear [manose'ar] *vt (tocar)* to handle, touch; *(desordenar)* to mess up, rumple; *(insistir en)* to overwork; *(AM)* to caress, fondle

manotazo [mano'taθo] *nm* slap, smack

mansalva [man'salβa]: **a ~** *adv* indiscriminately

mansedumbre [manse'ðumbre] *nf* gentleness, meekness

mansión [man'sjon] *nf* mansion

manso, a ['manso, a] *adj* gentle, mild; *(animal)* tame

manta ['manta] *nf* blanket; *(AM: poncho)* poncho

manteca [man'teka] *nf* fat; *(AM)* butter; ~ **de cacahuete/cacao** peanut/cocoa butter; ~ **de cerdo** lard

mantecado [mante'kaðo] *(AM) nm* ice cream

mantel [man'tel] *nm* tablecloth

mantendré *etc vb ver* **mantener**

mantener [mante'ner] *vt* to support, maintain; *(alimentar)* to sustain; *(conservar)* to keep; *(TEC)* to maintain, service; **~se** *vr (seguir de pie)* to be still standing; *(no ceder)* to hold one's ground; *(subsistir)* to sustain o.s., keep going; **mantenimiento** *nm* maintenance; sustenance; *(sustento)* support

mantequilla [mante'kiʎa] *nf* butter

mantilla [man'tiʎa] *nf* mantilla; **~s** *nfpl (de*

bebé) baby clothes

manto ['manto] *nm* (*capa*) cloak; (*de ceremonia*) robe, gown

mantuve *etc vb ver* **mantener**

manual [ma'nwal] *adj* manual ♦ *nm* manual, handbook

manufactura [manufak'tura] *nf* manufacture; (*fábrica*) factory; **manufacturado, a** *adj* (*producto*) manufactured

manuscrito, a [manus'krito, a] *adj* handwritten ♦ *nm* manuscript

manutención [manuten'θjon] *nf* maintenance; (*sustento*) support

manzana [man'θana] *nf* apple; (*ARQ*) block (of houses)

manzanilla [manθa'niʎa] *nf* (*planta*) camomile; (*infusión*) camomile tea

manzano [man'θano] *nm* apple tree

maña ['maɲa] *nf* (*gen*) skill, dexterity; (*pey*) guile; (*destreza*) trick, knack

mañana [ma'ɲana] *adv* tomorrow ♦ *nm* future ♦ *nf* morning; **de** o **por la** ~ in the morning; ¡**hasta** ~! see you tomorrow!; ~ **por la** ~ tomorrow morning

mañoso, a [ma'ɲoso, a] *adj* (*hábil*) skilful; (*astuto*) smart, clever

mapa ['mapa] *nm* map

maqueta [ma'keta] *nf* (*scale*) model

maquillaje [maki'ʎaxe] *nm* make-up; (*acto*) making up

maquillar [maki'ʎar] *vt* to make up; ~**se** *vr* to put on (some) make-up

máquina ['makina] *nf* machine; (*de tren*) locomotive, engine; (*FOTO*) camera; (*AM: coche*) car; (*fig*) machinery; **escrito a** ~ typewritten; ~ **de escribir** typewriter; ~ **de coser/lavar** sewing/washing machine

maquinación [makina'θjon] *nf* machination, plot

maquinal [maki'nal] *adj* (*fig*) mechanical, automatic

maquinaria [maki'narja] *nf* (*máquinas*) machinery; (*mecanismo*) mechanism, works *pl*

maquinilla [maki'niʎa] *nf*: ~ **de afeitar** razor

maquinista [maki'nista] *nm/f* (*de tren*) engine driver; (*TEC*) operator; (*NAUT*) engineer

mar [mar] *nm* o *f* sea; ~ **adentro** o **afuera** out at sea; **en alta** ~ on the high seas; **la** ~ **de** (*fam*) lots of; **el M~ Negro/Báltico** the Black/Baltic Sea

maraña [ma'raɲa] *nf* (*maleza*) thicket; (*confusión*) tangle

maravilla [mara'βiʎa] *nf* marvel, wonder; (*BOT*) marigold; **maravillar** *vt* to astonish, amaze; **maravillarse** *vr* to be astonished, be amazed; **maravilloso, a** *adj* wonderful, marvellous

marca ['marka] *nf* (*gen*) mark; (*sello*) stamp; (*COM*) make, brand; **de** ~ excellent, outstanding; ~ **de fábrica** trademark; ~ **registrada** registered trademark

marcado, a [mar'kaðo, a] *adj* marked, strong

marcador [marka'ðor] *nm* (*DEPORTE*) scoreboard; (*: persona*) scorer

marcapasos [marka'pasos] *nm inv* pacemaker

marcar [mar'kar] *vt* (*gen*) to mark; (*número de teléfono*) to dial; (*gol*) to score; (*números*) to record, keep a tally of; (*pelo*) to set ♦ *vi* (*DEPORTE*) to score; (*TEL*) to dial

marcha ['martʃa] *nf* march; (*TEC*) running, working; (*AUTO*) gear; (*velocidad*) speed; (*fig*) progress; (*dirección*) course; **poner en** ~ to put into gear; (*fig*) to set in motion, get going; **dar** ~ **atrás** to reverse, put into reverse; **estar en** ~ to be under way, be in motion

marchar [mar'tʃar] *vi* (*ir*) to go; (*funcionar*) to work, go; ~**se** *vr* to go (away), leave

marchitar [martʃi'tar] *vt* to wither, dry up; ~**se** *vr* (*BOT*) to wither; (*fig*) to fade away; **marchito, a** *adj* withered, faded; (*fig*) in decline

marcial [mar'θjal] *adj* martial, military

marciano, a [mar'θjano, a] *adj, nm/f* Martian

marco ['marko] *nm* frame; (*moneda*) mark; (*fig*) framework

marea [ma'rea] *nf* tide

marear [mare'ar] *vt* (*fig*) to annoy, upset; (*MED*): ~ **a uno** to make sb feel sick; ~**se** *vr* (*tener náuseas*) to feel sick; (*desvanecerse*) to feel faint; (*aturdirse*) to feel dizzy; (*fam: emborracharse*) to get tipsy

maremoto [mare'moto] *nm* tidal wave

mareo [ma'reo] *nm* (*náusea*) sick feeling; (*en viaje*) travel sickness; (*aturdimiento*) dizziness; (*fam: lata*) nuisance

marfil [mar'fil] *nm* ivory

margarina [marɣa'rina] *nf* margarine

margarita [marɣa'rita] *nf* (*BOT*) daisy; (**rueda**) ~ daisywheel

margen ['marxen] *nm* (*borde*) edge, border; (*fig*) margin, space ♦ *nf* (*de río etc*) bank; **dar** ~ **para** to give an opportunity for; **mantenerse al** ~ to keep out (of things)

marginar [marxi'nar] *vt* (*socialmente*) to marginalize, ostracize

marica [ma'rika] (*fam*) *nm* sissy

maricón [mari'kon] (*fam*) *nm* queer

marido [ma'riðo] *nm* husband

marihuana [mari'wana] *nf* marijuana, cannabis

marina [ma'rina] *nf* navy; ~ **mercante** merchant navy

marinero, a [mari'nero, a] *adj* sea *cpd* ♦ *nm* sailor, seaman

marino, a [ma'rino, a] *adj* sea *cpd*, marine ♦ *nm* sailor

marioneta [marjo'neta] *nf* puppet

mariposa [mari'posa] *nf* butterfly

mariquita [mari'kita] *nf* ladybird (*BRIT*), ladybug (*US*)

mariscos [ma'riskos] *nmpl* shellfish *inv*, seafood(s)

marítimo, a [ma'ritimo, a] *adj* sea *cpd*, maritime

mármol ['marmol] *nm* marble

marqués, esa [mar'kes, esa] *nm/f* marquis/ marchioness

marrón [ma'rron] *adj* brown

marroquí [marro'ki] *adj, nm/f* Moroccan ♦ *nm* Morocco (leather)

Marruecos [ma'rrwekos] *nm* Morocco

martes ['martes] *nm inv* Tuesday

martillo [mar'tiʎo] *nm* hammer; **~ neumático** pneumatic drill (*BRIT*), jackhammer

mártir ['martir] *nm/f* martyr; **martirio** *nm* martyrdom; (*fig*) torture, torment

marxismo [mark'sismo] *nm* Marxism; **marxista** *adj, nm/f* Marxist

marzo ['marθo] *nm* March

PALABRA CLAVE

más [mas] *adj, adv* 1: **~ (que, de)** (*compar*) more (than), ... + er (than); **~ grande/ inteligente** bigger/more intelligent; **trabaja ~ (que yo)** he works more (than me); *ver tb* **cada**

2 (*superl*): **el ~** the most, ... + est; **el ~ grande/inteligente (de)** the biggest/most intelligent (in)

3 (*negativo*): **no tengo ~ dinero** I haven't got any more money; **no viene ~ por aquí** he doesn't come round here any more

4 (*adicional*): **no le veo ~ solución que ...** I see no other solution than to ...; **¿quién ~?** anybody else?

5 (+ *adj: valor intensivo*): **¡qué perro ~ sucio!** what a filthy dog!; **¡es ~ tonto!** he's so stupid!

6 (*locuciones*): **~ o menos** more or less; **los ~** most people; **es ~** furthermore; **~ bien** rather; **¡qué ~ da!** what does it matter!; *ver tb* **no**

7: **por ~: por ~ que te esfuerces** no matter how hard you try; **por ~ que quisiera** ... much as I should like to ...

8: **de ~: veo que aquí estoy de ~** I can see I'm not needed here; **tenemos uno de ~** we've got one extra

♦ *prep*: **2 ~ 2 son 4** 2 and 2 or plus 2 are 4

♦ *nm inv*: **este trabajo tiene sus ~ y sus menos** this job's got its good points and its bad points

---

mas [mas] *conj* but

masa ['masa] *nf* (*mezcla*) dough; (*volumen*) volume, mass; (*FÍSICA*) mass; **en ~** en masse; **las ~s** (*POL*) the masses

masacre [ma'sakre] *nf* massacre

masaje [ma'saxe] *nm* massage

máscara ['maskara] *nf* mask; **mascarilla** *nf* (*de belleza, MED*) mask

masculino, a [masku'lino, a] *adj* masculine; (*BIO*) male

masía [ma'sia] *nf* farmhouse

masificación [masifika'θjon] *nf* overcrowding

masivo, a [ma'siβo, a] *adj* mass *cpd*

masón [ma'son] *nm* (free)mason

masoquista [maso'kista] *nm/f* masochist

masticar [masti'kar] *vt* to chew

mástil ['mastil] *nm* (*de navío*) mast; (*de guitarra*) neck

mastín [mas'tin] *nm* mastiff

masturbación [masturβa'θjon] *nf* masturbation

masturbarse [mastur'βarse] *vr* to masturbate

mata ['mata] *nf* (*arbusto*) bush, shrub; (*de hierba*) tuft

matadero [mata'ðero] *nm* slaughterhouse, abattoir

matador, a [mata'ðor, a] *adj* killing ♦ *nm/f* killer ♦ *nm* (*TAUR*) matador, bullfighter

matamoscas [mata'moskas] *nm inv* (*palo*) fly swat

matanza [ma'tanθa] *nf* slaughter

matar [ma'tar] *vt, vi* to kill; **~se** *vr* (*suicidarse*) to kill o.s., commit suicide; (*morir*) to be o get killed; **~ el hambre** to stave off hunger

matasellos [mata'seʎos] *nm inv* postmark

mate ['mate] *adj* matt ♦ *nm* (*en ajedrez*) (check)mate; (*AM: hierba*) maté; (: *vasija*) gourd

matemáticas [mate'matikas] *nfpl* mathematics; **matemático, a** *adj* mathematical ♦ *nm/f* mathematician

materia [ma'terja] *nf* (*gen*) matter; (*TEC*) material; (*ESCOL*) subject; **en ~ de** on the subject of; **~ prima** raw material; **material** *adj* material ♦ *nm* material; (*TEC*) equipment; **materialismo** *nm* materialism; **materialista** *adj* materialist(ic); **materialmente** *adv* materially; (*fig*) absolutely

maternal [mater'nal] *adj* motherly, maternal

maternidad [materni'ðað] *nf* motherhood, maternity; **materno, a** *adj* maternal; (*lengua*) mother *cpd*

matinal [mati'nal] *adj* morning *cpd*

matiz [ma'tiθ] *nm* shade; **~ar** *vt* (*variar*) to vary; (*ARTE*) to blend; **~ar de** to tinge with

matón [ma'ton] *nm* bully

matorral [mato'rral] *nm* thicket

matraca [ma'traka] *nf* rattle

matrícula [ma'trikula] *nf* (*registro*) register; (*AUTO*) registration number; (: *placa*) number plate; **matricular** *vt* to register, enrol

matrimonial [matrimo'njal] *adj* matrimonial

matrimonio [matri'monjo] *nm* (*pareja*) (married) couple; (*unión*) marriage

matriz [ma'triθ] *nf* (*ANAT*) womb; (*TEC*) mould; **casa ~** (*COM*) head office

matrona [ma'trona] *nf* (*persona de edad*) matron; (*comadrona*) midwife

maullar [mau'ʎar] *vi* to mew, miaow

maxilar [maksi'lar] *nm* jaw(bone)

máxima ['maksima] *nf* maxim

máxime ['maksime] *adv* especially

máximo, a ['maksimo, a] *adj* maximum; (*más alto*) highest; (*más grande*) greatest ♦ *nm* maximum

mayo ['majo] *nm* May

mayonesa [majo'nesa] *nf* mayonnaise

mayor [ma'jor] *adj* main, chief; (*adulto*) adult; (*de edad avanzada*) elderly; (*MUS*) major; (*compar: de tamaño*) bigger; (: *de edad*) older; (*superl: de tamaño*) biggest; (: *de edad*) oldest ♦ *nm* (*adulto*) adult; **al por ~** wholesale; **~ de edad** adult; **~es** *nmpl* (*antepasados*) ancestors

mayoral [majo'ral] *nm* foreman

mayordomo [major'ðomo] *nm* butler

mayoría [majo'ria] *nf* majority, greater part

mayorista [majo'rista] *nm/f* wholesaler

mayoritario, a [majori'tarjo, a] *adj* majority *cpd*

mayúscula [ma'juskula] *nf* capital letter

mayúsculo, a [ma'juskulo, a] *adj* (*fig*) big, tremendous

mazapán [maθa'pan] *nm* marzipan

mazo ['maθo] *nm* (*martillo*) mallet; (*de flores*) bunch; (*DEPORTE*) bat

me [me] *pron* (*directo*) me; (*indirecto*) (to) me; (*reflexivo*) (to) myself; ¡**dámelo!** give it to me!

mear [me'ar] (*fam*) *vi* to pee, piss (!)

mecánica [me'kanika] *nf* (*ESCOL*) mechanics *sg*; (*mecanismo*) mechanism; *ver tb* **mecánico**

mecánico, a [me'kaniko, a] *adj* mechanical ♦ *nm/f* mechanic

mecanismo [meka'nismo] *nm* mechanism; (*marcha*) gear

mecanografía [mekanoɣra'fia] *nf* typewriting; **mecanógrafo, a** *nm/f* typist

mecate [me'kate] (*AM*) *nm* rope

mecedora [meθe'ðora] *nf* rocking chair

mecer [me'θer] *vt* (*cuna*) to rock; **~se** *vr* to rock; (*ramo*) to sway

mecha ['metʃa] *nf* (*de vela*) wick; (*de bomba*) fuse

mechero [me'tʃero] *nm* (*cigarette*) lighter

mechón [me'tʃon] *nm* (*gen*) tuft; (*de pelo*) lock

medalla [me'ðaʎa] *nf* medal

media ['meðja] *nf* (*ESP*) stocking; (*AM*) sock; (*promedio*) average

mediado, a [me'ðjaðo, a] *adj* half-full; (*trabajo*) half-completed; **a ~s de** in the middle of, halfway through

mediano, a [me'ðjano, a] *adj* (*regular*) medium, average; (*mediocre*) mediocre

medianoche [meðja'notʃe] *nf* midnight

mediante [me'ðjante] *adv* by (means of), through

mediar [me'ðjar] *vi* (*interceder*) to mediate, intervene

medicación [meðika'θjon] *nf* medication, treatment

medicamento [meðika'mento] *nm* medicine, drug

medicina [meði'θina] *nf* medicine

medición [meði'θjon] *nf* measurement

médico, a ['meðiko, a] *adj* medical ♦ *nm/f* doctor

medida [me'ðiða] *nf* measure; (*medición*) measurement; (*prudencia*) moderation, prudence; **en cierta/gran ~** up to a point/to a great extent; **un traje a la ~** made-to-measure suit; **~ de cuello** collar size; **a ~ de** in proportion to; (*de acuerdo con*) in keeping with; **a ~ que** (*conforme*) as

medio, a ['meðjo, a] *adj* half (*a*); (*punto*) mid, middle; (*promedio*) average ♦ *adv* half ♦ *nm* (*centro*) middle, centre; (*promedio*) average; (*método*) means, way; (*ambiente*) environment; **~s** *nmpl* means, resources; **~ litro** half a litre; **las tres y media** half past three; **medio ambiente** environment; **M~ Oriente** Middle East; **a ~ terminar** half finished; **pagar a medias** to share the cost; **~ambiental** *adj* (*política, efectos*) environmental

mediocre [me'ðjokre] *adj* mediocre

mediodía [meðjo'ðia] *nm* midday, noon

medir [me'ðir] *vt, vi* (*gen*) to measure

meditar [meði'tar] *vt* to ponder, think over, meditate on; (*planear*) to think out

mediterráneo, a [meðite'rraneo, a] *adj* Mediterranean ♦ *nm*: **el M~** the Mediterranean (Sea)

médula ['meðula] *nf* (*ANAT*) marrow; **~ espinal** spinal cord

medusa [me'ðusa] (*ESP*) *nf* jellyfish

megafonía [meɣafo'nia] *nf* public address system, PA system; **megáfono** *nm* megaphone

megalómano, a [meɣa'lomano, a] *nm/f* megalomaniac

mejicano, a [mexi'kano, a] *adj*, *nm/f* Mexican

Méjico ['mexiko] *nm* Mexico

mejilla [me'xiʎa] *nf* cheek

mejillón [mexi'ʎon] *nm* mussel

mejor [me'xor] *adj, adv (compar)* better; *(superl)* best; **a lo ~** probably; *(quizá)* maybe; **~ dicho** rather; **tanto ~** so much the better

mejora [me'xora] *nf* improvement; **mejorar** *vt* to improve, make better ♦ *vi* to improve, get better; **mejorarse** *vr* to improve, get better

melancólico, a [melaŋ'koliko, a] *adj (triste)* sad, melancholy; *(soñador)* dreamy

melena [me'lena] *nf (de persona)* long hair; *(ZOOL)* mane

mellizo, a [me'ʎiθo, a] *adj, nm/f* twin; **~s** *nmpl (AM)* cufflinks

melocotón [meloko'ton] *(ESP) nm* peach

melodía [melo'ðia] *nf* melody, tune

melodrama [melo'ðrama] *nm* melodrama; **melodramático, a** *adj* melodramatic

melón [me'lon] *nm* melon

membrete [mem'brete] *nm* letterhead

membrillo [mem'briʎo] *nm* quince; **carne de ~** quince jelly

memorable [memo'raβle] *adj* memorable

memoria [me'morja] *nf (gen)* memory; **~s** *nfpl (de autor)* memoirs; **memorizar** *vt* to memorize

menaje [me'naxe] *nm:* **~ de cocina** kitchenware

mencionar [menθjo'nar] *vt* to mention

mendigar [mendi'var] *vt* to beg (for)

mendigo, a [men'diɣo, a] *nm/f* beggar

mendrugo [men'druɣo] *nm* crust

menear [mene'ar] *vt* to move; **~se** *vr* to shake; *(balancearse)* to sway; *(moverse)* to move; *(fig)* to get a move on

menestra [me'nestra] *nf:* **~ de verduras** vegetable stew

menguante [meŋ'gwante] *adj* decreasing, diminishing

menguar [meŋ'gwar] *vt* to lessen, diminish ♦ *vi* to diminish, decrease

menopausia [meno'pausja] *nf* menopause

menor [me'nor] *adj (más pequeño: compar)* smaller; *(: superl)* smallest; *(más joven: compar)* younger; *(: superl)* youngest; *(MUS)* minor ♦ *nm/f (joven)* young person, juvenile; **no tengo la ~ idea** I haven't the faintest idea; **al por ~** retail; **~ de edad** person under age

Menorca [me'norka] *nf* Minorca

PALABRA CLAVE
---

menos [menos] *adj* 1: **~ (que, de)** *(compar: cantidad)* less (than); *(: número)* fewer (than); **con ~ entusiasmo** with less enthusiasm; **~ gente** fewer people; *ver tb* **cada**

2 *(superl):* **es el que ~ culpa tiene** he is the least to blame

♦ *adv* 1 *(compar):* **~ (que, de)** less (than); **me gusta ~ que el otro** I like it less than the other one

2 *(superl):* **es el ~ listo (de su clase)** he's the least bright in his class; **de todas ellas es la que ~ me agrada** out of all of them she's the one I like least; **(por) lo ~** at (the very) least

3 *(locuciones):* **no quiero verle y ~ visitarle** I don't want to see him let alone visit him; **tenemos 7 de ~** we're seven short

♦ *prep* except; *(cifras)* minus; **todos ~ él** everyone except (for) him; **5 ~ 2** 5 minus 2

♦ *conj:* **a ~ que: a ~ que venga mañana** unless he comes tomorrow

---

menospreciar [menospre'θjar] *vt* to underrate, undervalue; *(despreciar)* to scorn, despise

mensaje [men'saxe] *nm* message; **~ro, a** *nm/f* messenger

menstruación [menstrua'θjon] *nf* menstruation

menstruar [mens'trwar] *vi* to menstruate

mensual [men'swal] *adj* monthly; **1000 ptas ~es** 1000 ptas a month; **~idad** *nf (salario)* monthly salary; *(COM)* monthly payment, monthly instalment

menta ['menta] *nf* mint

mental [men'tal] *adj* mental; **~idad** *nf* mentality; **~izar** *vt (sensibilizar)* to make aware; *(convencer)* to convince; *(padres)* to prepare (mentally); **~izarse** *vr (concienciarse)* to become aware; **~izarse (de)** to get used to the idea (of); **~izarse de que ...** *(convencerse)* to get it into one's head that ...

mentar [men'tar] *vt* to mention, name

mente ['mente] *nf* mind

mentir [men'tir] *vi* to lie

mentira [men'tira] *nf (una ~)* lie; *(acto)* lying; *(invención)* fiction; **parece ~ que ...** it seems incredible that ..., I can't believe that ...

mentiroso, a [menti'roso, a] *adj* lying ♦ *nm/f* liar

menú [me'nu] *(pl ~s) nm* menu; *(AM)* set meal; **~ del día** set menu

menudo, a [me'nuðo, a] *adj (pequeño)* small, tiny; *(sin importancia)* petty, insignificant; **¡~ negocio!** *(fam)* some deal!; **a ~** often, frequently

meñique [me'ɲike] *nm* little finger

meollo [me'oʎo] *nm (fig)* core

mercado [mer'kaðo] *nm* market

mercancía [merkan'θia] *nf* commodity; **~s** *nfpl* goods, merchandise *sg*

mercantil [merkan'til] *adj* mercantile, commercial

mercenario, a [merθe'narjo, a] *adj, nm*

mercenary

mercería [merθe'ria] *nf* haberdashery (*BRIT*), notions (*US*); (*tienda*) haberdasher's (*BRIT*), notions store (*US*); (*AM*) drapery

mercurio [mer'kurjo] *nm* mercury

merecer [mere'θer] *vt* to deserve, merit ♦ *vi* to be deserving, be worthy; **merece la pena** it's worthwhile; **merecido, a** *adj* (well) deserved; **llevar su merecido** to get one's deserts

merendar [meren'dar] *vt* to have for tea ♦ *vi* to have tea; (*en el campo*) to have a picnic; **merendero** *nm* open-air cafe

merengue [me'renge] *nm* meringue

meridiano [meri'ðjano] *nm* (*GEO*) meridian

merienda [me'rjenda] *nf* (*light*) tea, afternoon snack; (*de campo*) picnic

mérito ['merito] *nm* merit; (*valor*) worth, value

merluza [mer'luθa] *nf* hake

merma ['merma] *nf* decrease; (*pérdida*) wastage; **mermar** *vt* to reduce, lessen ♦ *vi* to decrease, dwindle

mermelada [merme'laða] *nf* jam

mero, a ['mero, a] *adj* mere; (*AM: fam*) very

merodear [meroðe'ar] *vi*: ~ **por** to prowl about

mes [mes] *nm* month

mesa ['mesa] *nf* table; (*de trabajo*) desk; (*GEO*) plateau; ~ **directiva** board; ~ **redonda** (*reunión*) round table; **poner/quitar la** ~ to lay/clear the table; **mesero, a** (*AM*) *nm/f* waiter/waitress

meseta [me'seta] *nf* (*GEO*) meseta, tableland

mesilla [me'siʎa] *nf*: ~ (**de noche**) bedside table

mesón [me'son] *nm* inn

mestizo, a [mes'tiθo, a] *adj* half-caste, of mixed race ♦ *nm/f* half-caste

mesura [me'sura] *nf* moderation, restraint

meta ['meta] *nf* goal; (*de carrera*) finish

metabolismo [metaβo'lismo] *nm* metabolism

metáfora [me'tafora] *nf* metaphor

metal [me'tal] *nm* (*materia*) metal; (*MUS*) brass; **metálico, a** *adj* metallic; (*de metal*) metal ♦ *nm* (*dinero contante*) cash

metalurgia [meta'lurxja] *nf* metallurgy

meteoro [mete'oro] *nm* meteor; ~**logía** *nf* meteorology

meter [me'ter] *vt* (*colocar*) to put, place; (*introducir*) to put in, insert; (*involucrar*) to involve; (*causar*) to make, cause; ~**se** *vr*: ~**se en** to go into, enter; (*fig*) to interfere in, meddle in; ~**se a** to start; ~**se a escritor** to become a writer; ~**se con uno** to provoke sb, pick a quarrel with sb

meticuloso, a [metiku'loso, a] *adj* meticulous, thorough

metódico, a [me'toðiko, a] *adj* methodical

método ['metoðo] *nm* method

metralleta [metra'ʎeta] *nf* sub-machine-gun

métrico, a ['metriko, a] *adj* metric

metro ['metro] *nm* metre; (*tren*) underground (*BRIT*), subway (*US*)

México ['mexiko] *nm* Mexico; **Ciudad de ~** Mexico City

mezcla ['meθkla] *nf* mixture; **mezclar** *vt* to mix (up); **mezclarse** *vr* to mix, mingle; **mezclarse en** to get mixed up in, get involved in

mezquino, a [meθ'kino, a] *adj* mean

mezquita [meθ'kita] *nf* mosque

mg. *abr* (= *miligramo*) mg

mi [mi] *adj pos* my ♦ *nm* (*MUS*) E

mí [mi] *pron* me; myself

mía ['mia] *pron ver* **mío**

miaja ['mjaxa] *nf* crumb

michelín [mitʃe'lin] (*fam*) *nm* (*de grasa*) spare tyre

micro ['mikro] (*AM*) *nm* minibus

microbio [mi'kroβjo] *nm* microbe

micrófono [mi'krofono] *nm* microphone

microondas [mikro'ondas] *nm inv* (*tb*: *horno* ~) microwave (oven)

microscopio [mikro'skopjo] *nm* microscope

miedo ['mjeðo] *nm* fear; (*nerviosismo*) apprehension, nervousness; **tener** ~ to be afraid; **de** ~ wonderful, marvellous; **hace un frío de** ~ (*fam*) it's terribly cold; ~**so, a** *adj* fearful, timid

miel [mjel] *nf* honey

miembro ['mjembro] *nm* limb; (*socio*) member; ~ **viril** penis

mientras ['mjentras] *conj* while; (*duración*) as long as ♦ *adv* meanwhile; ~ **tanto** meanwhile; ~ **más tiene, más quiere** the more he has, the more he wants

miércoles ['mjerkoles] *nm inv* Wednesday

mierda ['mjerða] (*fam!*) *nf* shit (*!*)

miga ['miʏa] *nf* crumb; (*fig: meollo*) essence; **hacer buenas ~s** (*fam*) to get on well

migración [miʏra'θjon] *nf* migration

mil [mil] *num* thousand; **dos ~ libras** two thousand pounds

milagro [mi'laʏro] *nm* miracle; ~**so, a** *adj* miraculous

milésima [mi'lesima] *nf* (*de segundo*) thousandth

mili ['mili] (*fam*) *nf*: **hacer la** ~ to do one's military service

milicia [mi'liθja] *nf* militia; (*servicio militar*) military service

milímetro [mi'limetro] *nm* millimetre

militante [mili'tante] *adj* militant

militar [mili'tar] *adj* military ♦ *nm/f* soldier ♦ *vi* (*MIL*) to serve; (*en un partido*) to be a member

milla ['miʎa] *nf* mile
millar [mi'ʎar] *nm* thousand
millón [mi'ʎon] *num* million; **millonario, a** *nm/f* millionaire
mimar [mi'mar] *vt* to spoil, pamper
mimbre ['mimbre] *nm* wicker
mímica ['mimika] *nf* (*para comunicarse*) sign language; (*imitación*) mimicry
mimo ['mimo] *nm* (*caricia*) caress; (*de niño*) spoiling; (*TEATRO*) mime; (: *actor*) mime artist
mina ['mina] *nf* mine; **minar** *vt* to mine; (*fig*) to undermine
mineral [mine'ral] *adj* mineral ♦ *nm* (*GEO*) mineral; (*mena*) ore
minero, a [mi'nero, a] *adj* mining *cpd* ♦ *nm/f* miner
miniatura [minja'tura] *adj inv, nf* miniature
MiniDisc ® [mini'ðisk] *nm* MiniDisc®
minifalda [mini'falda] *nf* miniskirt
mínimo, a ['minimo, a] *adj, nm* minimum
minino, a [mi'nino, a] (*fam*) *nm/f* puss, pussy
ministerio [minis'terjo] *nm* Ministry; **M~ de Hacienda/de Asuntos Exteriores** Treasury (*BRIT*), Treasury Department (*US*)/Foreign Office (*BRIT*), State Department (*US*)
ministro, a [mi'nistro, a] *nm/f* minister
minoría [mino'ria] *nf* minority
minucioso, a [minu'θjoso, a] *adj* thorough, meticulous; (*prolijo*) very detailed
minúscula [mi'nuskula] *nf* small letter
minúsculo, a [mi'nuskulo, a] *adj* tiny, minute
minusválido, a [minus'βaliðo, a] *adj* (physically) handicapped ♦ *nm/f* (physically) handicapped person
minuta [mi'nuta] *nf* (*de comida*) menu
minutero [minu'tero] *nm* minute hand
minuto [mi'nuto] *nm* minute
mío, a ['mio, a] *pron*: **el ~/la mía** mine; **un amigo ~** a friend of mine; **lo ~** what is mine
miope [mi'ope] *adj* short-sighted
mira ['mira] *nf* (*de arma*) sight(s) (*pl*); (*fig*) aim, intention
mirada [mi'raða] *nf* look, glance; (*expresión*) look, expression; **clavar la ~ en** to stare at; **echar una ~ a** to glance at
mirado, a [mi'raðo, a] *adj* (*sensato*) sensible; (*considerado*) considerate; **bien/mal ~** well/not well thought of; **bien ~** all things considered
mirador [mira'ðor] *nm* viewpoint, vantage point
mirar [mi'rar] *vt* to look at; (*observar*) to watch; (*considerar*) to consider, think over; (*vigilar, cuidar*) to watch, look after ♦ *vi* to look; (*ARQ*) to face; **~se** *vr* (*dos personas*) to look at each other; **~ bien/mal** to think highly of/have a poor opinion of; **~se al espejo** to look at o.s. in the mirror
mirilla [mi'riʎa] *nf* spyhole, peephole
mirlo ['mirlo] *nm* blackbird
misa ['misa] *nf* mass
miserable [mise'raβle] *adj* (*avaro*) mean, stingy; (*nimio*) miserable, paltry; (*lugar*) squalid; (*fam*) vile, despicable ♦ *nm/f* (*malvado*) rogue
miseria [mi'serja] *nf* (*pobreza*) poverty; (*tacañería*) meanness, stinginess; (*condiciones*) squalor; **una ~** a pittance
misericordia [miseri'korðja] *nf* (*compasión*) compassion, pity; (*piedad*) mercy
misil [mi'sil] *nm* missile
misión [mi'sjon] *nf* mission; **misionero, a** *nm/f* missionary
mismo, a ['mismo, a] *adj* (*semejante*) same; (*después de pron*) -self; (*para énfasis*) very ♦ *adv*: **aquí/hoy ~** right here/this very day; **ahora ~** right now ♦ *conj*: **lo ~ que** just like, just as; **el ~ traje** the same suit; **en ese ~ momento** at that very moment; **vino el ~ Ministro** the minister himself came; **yo ~ lo vi** I saw it myself; **lo ~** the same (thing); **da lo ~** it's all the same; **quedamos en las mismas** we're no further forward; **por lo ~** for the same reason
misterio [mis'terjo] *nm* mystery; **~so, a** *adj* mysterious
mitad [mi'tað] *nf* (*medio*) half; (*centro*) middle; **a ~ de precio** (at) half-price; **en o a ~ del camino** halfway along the road; **cortar por la ~** to cut through the middle
mitigar [miti'var] *vt* to mitigate; (*dolor*) to ease; (*sed*) to quench
mitin ['mitin] (*pl* **mítines**) *nm* meeting
mito ['mito] *nm* myth
mixto, a ['miksto, a] *adj* mixed
ml. *abr* (= *mililitro*) ml
mm. *abr* (= *milímetro*) mm
mobiliario [moβi'ljarjo] *nm* furniture
mochila [mo'tʃila] *nf* rucksack (*BRIT*), backpack
moción [mo'θjon] *nf* motion
moco ['moko] *nm* mucus; **~s** *nmpl* (*fam*) snot; **limpiarse los ~s de la nariz** (*fam*) to wipe one's nose
moda ['moða] *nf* fashion; (*estilo*) style; **a la o de ~** in fashion, fashionable; **pasado de ~** out of fashion
modales [mo'ðales] *nmpl* manners
modalidad [moðali'ðað] *nf* kind, variety
modelar [moðe'lar] *vt* to model
modelo [mo'ðelo] *adj inv, nm, nm/f* model
módem ['moðem] *nm* (*INFORM*) modem
moderado, a [moðe'raðo, a] *adj* moderate
moderar [moðe'rar] *vt* to moderate; (*violencia*) to restrain, control; (*velocidad*) to reduce; **~se** *vr* to restrain o.s., control o.s.

modernizar [moðerni'θar] vt to modernize

moderno, a [mo'ðerno, a] adj modern; (actual) present-day

modestia [mo'ðestja] nf modesty; **modesto, a** adj modest

módico, a ['moðiko, a] adj moderate, reasonable

modificar [moðifi'kar] vt to modify

modisto, a [mo'ðisto, a] nm/f (diseñador) couturier, designer; (que confecciona) dressmaker

modo ['moðo] nm way, manner; (MUS) mode; **~s** nmpl manners; **de ningún ~** in no way; **de todos ~s** at any rate; **~ de empleo** directions pl (for use)

modorra [mo'ðorra] nf drowsiness

mofa ['mofa] nf: **hacer ~ de** to mock; **mofarse** vr: **mofarse de** to mock, scoff at

mogollón [moʁo'ʎon] (fam) adv a hell of a lot

moho ['moo] nm mould, mildew; (en metal) rust; **~so, a** adj mouldy; rusty

mojar [mo'xar] vt to wet; (humedecer) to damp(en), moisten; (calar) to soak; **~se** vr to get wet

mojón [mo'xon] nm boundary stone

molde ['molde] nm mould; (COSTURA) pattern; (fig) model; **~ado** nm soft perm; **~ar** vt to mould

mole ['mole] nf mass, bulk; (edificio) pile

moler [mo'ler] vt to grind, crush

molestar [moles'tar] vt to bother; (fastidiar) to annoy; (incomodar) to inconvenience, put out ♦ vi to be a nuisance; **~se** vr to bother; (incomodarse) to go to trouble; (ofenderse) to take offence; **¿(no) te molesta si ...?** do you mind if ...?

molestia [mo'lestja] nf bother, trouble; (incomodidad) inconvenience; (MED) discomfort; **es una ~** it's a nuisance; **molesto, a** adj (que fastidia) annoying; (incómodo) inconvenient; (inquieto) uncomfortable, ill at ease; (enfadado) annoyed

molido, a [mo'liðo, a] adj: **estar ~** (fig) to be exhausted o dead beat

molinillo [moli'niʎo] nm: **~ de carne/café** mincer/coffee grinder

molino [mo'lino] nm (edificio) mill; (máquina) grinder

momentáneo, a [momen'taneo, a] adj momentary

momento [mo'mento] nm moment; **de ~** at the moment, for the moment

momia ['momja] nf mummy

monarca [mo'narka] nm/f monarch, ruler; **monarquía** nf monarchy; **monárquico, a** nm/f royalist, monarchist

monasterio [monas'terjo] nm monastery

mondar [mon'dar] vt to peel; **~se** vr: **~se de risa** (fam) to split one's sides laughing

moneda [mo'neða] nf (tipo de dinero) currency, money; (pieza) coin; **una ~ de 5 pesetas** a 5 peseta piece; **monedero** nm purse; **monetario, a** adj monetary, financial

monitor, a [moni'tor, a] nm/f instructor, coach ♦ nm (TV) set; (INFORM) monitor

monja ['monxa] nf nun

monje ['monxe] nm monk

mono, a ['mono, a] adj (bonito) lovely, pretty; (gracioso) nice, charming ♦ nm/f monkey, ape ♦ nm dungarees pl; (overoles) overalls pl

monopatín [monopa'tin] nm skateboard

monopolio [mono'poljo] nm monopoly; **monopolizar** vt to monopolize

monotonía [monoto'nia] nf (sonido) monotone; (fig) monotony

monótono, a [mo'notono, a] adj monotonous

monstruo ['monstrwo] nm monster ♦ adj inv fantastic; **~so, a** adj monstrous

montaje [mon'taxe] nm assembly; (TEATRO) décor; (CINE) montage

montaña [mon'taɲa] nf (monte) mountain; (sierra) mountains pl, mountainous area; (AM: selva) forest; **~ rusa** roller coaster; **montañero, a** nm/f mountaineer; **montañés, esa** nm/f highlander; **montañismo** nm mountaineering

montar [mon'tar] vt (subir a) to mount, get on; (TEC) to assemble, put together; (negocio) to set up; (arma) to cock; (colocar) to lift on to; (CULIN) to beat ♦ vi to mount, get on; (sobresalir) to overlap; **~ en cólera** to get angry; **~ a caballo** to ride, go horseriding

monte ['monte] nm (montaña) mountain; (bosque) woodland; (área sin cultivar) wild area, wild country; **M~ de Piedad** pawnshop

montón [mon'ton] nm heap, pile; (fig): **un ~ de** heaps of, lots of

monumento [monu'mento] nm monument

monzón [mon'θon] nm monsoon

moño ['moɲo] nm bun

moqueta [mo'keta] nf fitted carpet

mora ['mora] nf blackberry; ver tb **moro**

morada [mo'raða] nf (casa) dwelling, abode

morado, a [mo'raðo, a] adj purple, violet ♦ nm bruise

moral [mo'ral] adj moral ♦ nf (ética) ethics pl; (moralidad) morals pl, morality; (ánimo) morale

moraleja [mora'lexa] nf moral

moralidad [morali'ðað] nf morals pl, morality

morboso, a [mor'ßoso, a] adj morbid

morcilla [mor'θiʎa] nf blood sausage, ≈ black pudding (BRIT)

mordaz [mor'ðaθ] *adj* (*crítica*) biting, scathing

mordaza [mor'ðaθa] *nf* (*para la boca*) gag; (*TEC*) clamp

morder [mor'ðer] *vt* to bite; (*fig: consumir*) to eat away, eat into; **mordisco** *nm* bite

moreno, a [mo'reno, a] *adj* (*color*) (dark) brown; (*de tez*) dark; (*de pelo ~*) dark-haired; (*negro*) black

morfina [mor'fina] *nf* morphine

moribundo, a [mori'ßundo, a] *adj* dying

morir [mo'rir] *vi* to die; (*fuego*) to die down; (*luz*) to go out; **~se** *vr* to die; (*fig*) to be dying; **murió en un accidente** he was killed in an accident; **~se por algo** to be dying for sth

moro, a [moro, a] *adj* Moorish ♦ *nm/f* Moor

moroso, a [mo'roso, a] *nm/f* bad debtor, defaulter

morral [mo'rral] *nm* haversack

morro [morro] *nm* (*ZOOL*) snout, nose; (*AUTO, AVIAT*) nose

morsa ['morsa] *nf* walrus

mortadela [morta'ðela] *nf* mortadella

mortaja [mor'taxa] *nf* shroud

mortal [mor'tal] *adj* mortal; (*golpe*) deadly; **~idad** *nf* mortality

mortero [mor'tero] *nm* mortar

mortífero, a [mor'tifero, a] *adj* deadly, lethal

mortificar [mortifi'kar] *vt* to mortify

mosca ['moska] *nf* fly

Moscú [mos'ku] *n* Moscow

mosquearse [moske'arse] (*fam*) *vr* (*enojarse*) to get cross; (*ofenderse*) to take offence

mosquitero [moski'tero] *nm* mosquito net

mosquito [mos'kito] *nm* mosquito

mostaza [mos'taθa] *nf* mustard

mosto ['mosto] *nm* (unfermented) grape juice

mostrador [mostra'ðor] *nm* (*de tienda*) counter; (*de café*) bar

mostrar [mos'trar] *vt* to show; (*exhibir*) to display, exhibit; (*explicar*) to explain; **~se** *vr*: **~se amable** to be kind; to prove to be kind; **no se muestra muy inteligente** he doesn't seem (to be) very intelligent

mota ['mota] *nf* speck, tiny piece; (*en diseño*) dot

mote ['mote] *nm* nickname

motín [mo'tin] *nm* (*del pueblo*) revolt, rising; (*del ejército*) mutiny

motivar [moti'ßar] *vt* (*causar*) to cause, motivate; (*explicar*) to explain, justify; **motivo** *nm* motive, reason

moto ['moto] (*fam*) *nf* = **motocicleta**

motocicleta [motoθi'kleta] *nf* motorbike (*BRIT*), motorcycle

motor [mo'tor] *nm* motor, engine; **~ a chorro** o **de reacción/de explosión** jet engine/internal combustion engine

motora [mo'tora] *nf* motorboat

movedizo, a [moße'ðiθo, a] *adj ver* **arena**

mover [mo'ßer] *vt* to move; (*cabeza*) to shake; (*accionar*) to drive; (*fig*) to cause, provoke; **~se** *vr* to move; (*fig*) to get a move on

móvil ['moßil] *adj* mobile; (*pieza de máquina*) moving; (*mueble*) movable ♦ *nm* motive; **movilidad** *nf* mobility; **movilizar** *vt* to mobilize

movimiento [moßi'mjento] *nm* movement; (*TEC*) motion; (*actividad*) activity

mozo, a ['moθo, a] *adj* (*joven*) young ♦ *nm/f* youth, young man/girl

muchacho, a [mu'tʃatʃo, a] *nm/f* (*niño*) boy/girl; (*criado*) servant; (*criada*) maid

muchedumbre [mutʃe'ðumbre] *nf* crowd

PALABRA CLAVE

---

mucho, a [mutʃo, a] *adj* **1** (*cantidad*) a lot of, much; (*número*) lots of, a lot of, many; **~ dinero** a lot of money; **hace ~ calor** it's very hot; **muchas amigas** lots o a lot of friends
2 (*sg: grande*): **ésta es mucha casa para él** this house is much too big for him
♦ *pron*: **tengo ~ que hacer** I've got a lot to do; **~s dicen que ...** a lot of people say that ...; *ver tb* **tener**
♦ *adv* **1**: **me gusta ~** I like it a lot; **lo siento ~** I'm very sorry; **come ~** he eats a lot; **¿te vas a quedar ~?** are you going to be staying long?
2 (*respuesta*) very; **¿estás cansado? – ¡~!** are you tired? – very!
3 (*locuciones*): **como ~** at (the) most; **con ~: el mejor con ~** by far the best; **ni ~ menos: no es rico ni ~ menos** he's far from being rich
4: **por o que: por ~ que le creas** no matter how o however much you believe her

---

muda ['muða] *nf* change of clothes

mudanza [mu'ðanθa] *nf* (*de casa*) move

mudar [mu'ðar] *vt* to change; (*ZOOL*) to shed ♦ *vi* to change; **~se** *vr* (*la ropa*) to change; **~se de casa** to move house

mudo, a ['muðo, a] *adj* dumb; (*callado, CINE*) silent

mueble ['mweßle] *nm* piece of furniture; **~s** *nmpl* furniture *sg*

mueca ['mweka] *nf* face, grimace; **hacer ~s a** to make faces at

muela ['mwela] *nf* (*back*) tooth

muelle ['mweʎe] *nm* spring; (*NAUT*) wharf; (*malecón*) pier

muero *etc vb ver* **morir**

muerte ['mwerte] *nf* death; (*homicidio*) murder; **dar ~ a** to kill

muerto, a ['mwerto, a] *pp de* **morir** ♦ *adj*

dead ♦ nm/f dead man/woman; (difunto) deceased; (cadáver) corpse; estar ~ de cansancio to be dead tired

muestra ['mwestra] nf (señal) indication, sign; (demostración) demonstration; (prueba) proof; (estadística) sample; (modelo) model, pattern; (testimonio) token

muestreo [mwes'treo] nm sample, sampling

muestro etc vb ver **mostrar**

muevo etc vb ver **mover**

mugir [mu'xir] vi (vaca) to moo

mugre ['muxre] nf dirt, filth; **mugriento, a** adj dirty, filthy

mujer [mu'xer] nf woman; (esposa) wife; **~iego** nm womanizer

mula ['mula] nf mule

muleta [mu'leta] nf (para andar) crutch; (TAUR) stick with red cape attached

mullido, a [mu'ʎiðo, a] adj (cama) soft; (hierba) soft, springy

multa ['multa] nf fine; **poner una ~ a** to fine; **multar** vt to fine

multicines [multi'θines] nmpl multiscreen cinema

multinacional [multinaθjo'nal] nf multinational

múltiple ['multiple] adj multiple; (pl) many, numerous

multiplicar [multipli'kar] vt (MAT) to multiply; (fig) to increase; **~se** vr (BIO) to multiply; (fig) to be everywhere at once

multitud [multi'tuð] nf (muchedumbre) crowd; **~ de** lots of

mundano, a [mun'dano, a] adj worldly

mundial [mun'djal] adj world-wide, universal; (guerra, récord) world cpd

mundo ['mundo] nm world; **todo el ~** everybody; **tener ~** to be experienced, know one's way around

munición [muni'θjon] nf ammunition

municipal [muniθi'pal] adj municipal, local

municipio [muni'θipjo] nm (ayuntamiento) town council, corporation; (territorio administrativo) town, municipality

muñeca [mu'ɲeka] nf (ANAT) wrist; (juguete) doll

muñeco [mu'ɲeko] nm (figura) figure; (marioneta) puppet; (fig) puppet, pawn

mural [mu'ral] adj mural, wall cpd ♦ nm mural

muralla [mu'raʎa] nf (city) wall(s) (pl)

murciélago [mur'θjelaxo] nm bat

murmullo [mur'muʎo] nm murmur(ing); (cuchicheo) whispering

murmuración [murmura'θjon] nf gossip; **murmurar** vi to murmur, whisper; (cotillear) to gossip

muro ['muro] nm wall

muscular [musku'lar] adj muscular

músculo ['muskulo] nm muscle

museo [mu'seo] nm museum; **~ de arte** art gallery

musgo ['musxo] nm moss

música ['musika] nf music; ver tb **músico**

músico, a ['musiko, a] adj musical ♦ nm/f musician

muslo ['muslo] nm thigh

mustio, a ['mustjo, a] adj (persona) depressed, gloomy; (planta) faded, withered

musulmán, ana [musul'man, ana] nm/f Moslem

mutación [muta'θjon] nf (BIO) mutation; (cambio) (sudden) change

mutilar [muti'lar] vt to mutilate; (a una persona) to maim

mutismo [mu'tismo] nm (de persona) uncommunicativeness; (de autoridades) silence

mutuamente [mutwa'mente] adv mutually

mutuo, a ['mutwo, a] adj mutual

muy [mwi] adv very; (demasiado) too; **M~ Señor mío** Dear Sir; **~ de noche** very late at night; **eso es ~ de él** that's just like him

N, n

N abr (= norte) N

nabo ['naßo] nm turnip

nácar ['nakar] nm mother-of-pearl

nacer [na'θer] vi to be born; (de huevo) to hatch; (vegetal) to sprout; (río) to rise; **nací en Barcelona** I was born in Barcelona; **nació una sospecha en su mente** a suspicion formed in her mind; **nacido, a** adj born; **recién nacido** newborn; **naciente** adj new, emerging; (sol) rising; **nacimiento** nm birth; (de Navidad) Nativity; (de río) source

nación [na'θjon] nf nation; **nacional** adj national; **nacionalismo** nm nationalism; **nacionalista** nm/f nationalist; **nacionalizar** vt to nationalize; **nacionalizarse** vr (persona) to become naturalized

nada ['naða] pron nothing ♦ adv not at all, in no way; **no decir ~** to say nothing, not to say anything; **~ más** nothing else; **de ~** don't mention it

nadador, a [naða'ðor, a] nm/f swimmer

nadar [na'ðar] vi to swim

nadie ['naðje] pron nobody, no-one; **~ habló** nobody spoke; **no había ~** there was nobody there, there wasn't anybody there

nado ['naðo]: **a ~** adv: **pasar a ~** to swim across

nafta ['nafta] (AM) nf petrol (BRIT), gas (US)

naipe ['naipe] nm (playing) card; **~s** nmpl cards

nalgas ['nalxas] nfpl buttocks

nana ['nana] nf lullaby

naranja [na'ranxa] adj inv, nf orange; **media ~** (fam) better half; **naranjada** nf orangeade; **naranjo** nm orange tree

narciso [nar'θiso] nm narcissus

narcótico, a [nar'kotiko, a] adj, nm narcotic; **narcotizar** vt to drug; **narcotráfico** nm drug trafficking o running

nardo ['narðo] nm lily

narigudo, a [narı'ɣuðo, a] adj big-nosed

nariz [na'riθ] nf nose

narración [narra'θjon] nf narration; **narrador, a** nm/f narrator

narrar [na'rrar] vt to narrate, recount; **narrativa** nf narrative

nata ['nata] nf cream

natación [nata'θjon] nf swimming

natal [na'tal] adj: **ciudad ~** home town; **~idad** nf birth rate

natillas [na'tiʎas] nfpl custard sg

nativo, a [na'tiβo, a] adj, nm/f native

nato, a ['nato, a] adj born; **un músico ~** a born musician

natural [natu'ral] adj natural; (fruta etc) fresh ♦ nm/f native ♦ nm (disposición) nature

naturaleza [natura'leθa] nf nature; (género) nature, kind; **~ muerta** still life

naturalidad [naturali'ðað] nf naturalness

naturalmente [natural'mente] adv (de modo natural) in a natural way; **¡~!** of course!

naufragar [naufra'ɣar] vi to sink; **naufragio** nm shipwreck; **náufrago, a** nm/f castaway, shipwrecked person

nauseabundo, a [nausea'ßundo, a] adj nauseating, sickening

náuseas ['nauseas] nfpl nausea sg; **me da ~** it makes me feel sick

náutico, a ['nautiko, a] adj nautical

navaja [na'βaxa] nf knife; (de barbero, peluquero) razor

naval [na'ßal] adj naval

Navarra [na'ßarra] n Navarre

nave ['naße] nf (barco) ship, vessel; (ARQ) nave; **~ espacial** spaceship

navegación [naßeva'θjon] nf navigation; (viaje) sea journey; **~ aérea** air traffic; **~ costera** coastal shipping; **navegador** nm (INFORM) browser; **navegante** nm/f navigator; **navegar** vi (barco) to sail; (avión) to fly

navidad [naßi'ðað] nf Christmas; **~es** nfpl Christmas time; **Feliz N~** Merry Christmas; **navideño, a** adj Christmas cpd

navío [na'ßio] nm ship

nazca etc vb ver **nacer**

nazi ['naθi] adj, nm/f Nazi

NE abr (= nor(d)este) NE

neblina [ne'ßlina] nf mist

nebulosa [neßu'losa] nf nebula

necesario, a [neθe'sarjo, a] adj necessary

neceser [neθe'ser] nm toilet bag; (bolsa grande) holdall

necesidad [neθesi'ðað] nf necessity; (lo inevitable) necessity; (miseria) poverty, need; **en caso de ~** in case of need o emergency; **hacer sus ~es** to relieve o.s.

necesitado, a [neθesi'taðo, a] adj needy, poor; **~ de** in need of

necesitar [neθesi'tar] vt to need, require

necio, a ['neθjo, a] adj foolish

necrópolis [ne'kropolis] nf inv cemetery

nectarina [nekta'rina] nf nectarine

nefasto, a [ne'fasto, a] adj ill-fated, unlucky

negación [neɣa'θjon] nf negation; (rechazo) refusal, denial

negar [ne'ɣar] vt (renegar, rechazar) to refuse; (prohibir) to refuse, deny; (desmentir) to deny; **~se** vr: **~se a** to refuse to

negativa [neɣa'tißa] nf negative; (rechazo) refusal, denial

negativo, a [neɣa'tißo, a] adj, nm negative

negligencia [neɣli'xenθja] nf negligence; **negligente** adj negligent

negociado [neɣo'θjaðo] nm department, section

negociante [neɣo'θjante] nm/f businessman/woman

negociar [neɣo'θjar] vt, vi to negotiate; **~ en** to deal in, trade in

negocio [ne'ɣoθjo] nm (COM) business; (asunto) affair, business; (operación comercial) deal, transaction; (AM) firm; (lugar) place of business; **los ~s** business sg; **hacer ~** to do business

negra ['neɣra] nf (MUS) crotchet; ver tb **negro**

negro, a ['neɣro, a] adj black; (suerte) awful ♦ nm black ♦ nm/f black man/woman

nene, a ['nene, a] nm/f baby, small child

nenúfar [ne'nufar] nm water lily

neologismo [neolo'xismo] nm neologism

neón [ne'on] nm: **luces/lámpara de ~** neon lights/lamp

neoyorquino, a [neojor'kino, a] adj (of) New York

nervio ['nerßjo] nm nerve; **nerviosismo** nm nervousness, nerves pl; **~so, a** adj nervous

neto, a ['neto, a] adj net

neumático, a [neu'matiko, a] adj pneumatic ♦ nm (ESP) tyre (BRIT), tire (US); **~ de recambio** spare tyre

neurasténico, a [neuras'teniko, a] adj (fig) hysterical

neurólogo, a [neu'roloɣo, a] nm/f neurologist

neurona [neu'rona] nf nerve cell

neutral [neu'tral] adj neutral; **~izar** vt to neutralize; (contrarrestar) to counteract

neutro, a ['neutro, a] adj (BIO, LING) neuter

neutrón [neu'tron] *nm* neutron

nevada [ne'βaða] *nf* snowstorm; (*caída de nieve*) snowfall

nevar [ne'βar] *vi* to snow

nevera [ne'βera] (*ESP*) *nf* refrigerator (*BRIT*), icebox (*US*)

nevería [neβe'ria] (*AM*) *nf* ice-cream parlour

nexo ['nekso] *nm* link, connection

ni [ni] *conj* nor, neither; (*tb:* ~ **siquiera**) not ... even; ~ **aunque que** not even if; ~ **blanco** ~ **negro** neither white nor black

Nicaragua [nika'raɣwa] *nf* Nicaragua; **nicaragüense** *adj, nm/f* Nicaraguan

nicho ['nitʃo] *nm* niche

nicotina [niko'tina] *nf* nicotine

nido ['niðo] *nm* nest

niebla ['njeβla] *nf* fog; (*neblina*) mist

niego *etc vb ver* **negar**

nieto, a ['njeto, a] *nm/f* grandson/daughter; ~**s** *nmpl* grandchildren

nieve *etc* ['njeβe] *vb ver* **nevar ♦** *nf* snow; (*AM*) icecream

N.I.F. *nm abr* (= *Número de Identificación Fiscal*) *personal identification number used for financial and tax purposes*

nimiedad [nimje'ðað] *nf* triviality

nimio, a ['nimjo, a] *adj* trivial, insignificant

ninfa ['ninfa] *nf* nymph

ningún [nin'gun] *adj ver* **ninguno**

ninguno, a [nin'guno, a] (*delante de nm*: **ningún**) *adj* no **♦** *pron* (*nadie*) nobody; (*ni uno*) none, not one; (*ni uno ni otro*) neither; **de ninguna manera** by no means, not at all

niña ['nina] *nf* (*ANAT*) pupil; *ver tb* **niño**

niñera [ni'nera] *nf* nursemaid, nanny; **niñería** *nf* childish act

niñez [ni'neθ] *nf* childhood; (*infancia*) infancy

niño, a ['nino, a] *adj* (*joven*) young; (*inmaduro*) immature **♦** *nm/f* child, boy/girl

nipón, ona [ni'pon, ona] *adj, nm/f* Japanese

níquel ['nikel] *nm* nickel; **niquelar** *vt* (*TEC*) to nickel-plate

níspero ['nispero] *nm* medlar

nitidez [niti'ðeθ] *nf* (*claridad*) clarity; (: *de imagen*) sharpness; **nítido, a** *adj* clear; sharp

nitrato [ni'trato] *nm* nitrate

nitrógeno [ni'troxeno] *nm* nitrogen

nivel [ni'βel] *nm* (*GEO*) level; (*norma*) level, standard; (*altura*) height; ~ **de aceite** oil level; ~ **de aire** spirit level; ~ **de vida** standard of living; ~**ar** *vt* to level out; (*fig*) to even up; (*COM*) to balance

NN. UU. *nfpl abr* (= *Naciones Unidas*) UN *sg*

no [no] *adv* no; not; (*con verbo*) not **♦** *excl* no!; ~ **tengo nada** I don't have anything, I have nothing; ~ **es el mío** it's not mine; **ahora** ~ not now; *¿*~ **lo sabes?** don't you know?; ~ **mucho** not much; ~ **bien termine, lo entregaré** as soon as I finish I'll hand it

over; ~ **más: ayer** ~ **más** just yesterday; **¡pase** ~ **más!** come in!; **¡a que** ~ **lo sabes!** I bet you don't know!; **¡cómo** ~! of course!; **los países** ~ **alineados** the non-aligned countries; **la** ~ **intervención** non-intervention

noble ['noβle] *adj, nm/f* noble; ~**za** *nf* nobility

noche ['notʃe] *nf* night, night-time; (*la tarde*) evening; **de** ~, **por la** ~ at night; **es de** ~ it's dark

nochebuena [notʃe'βwena] *nf* Christmas Eve

nochevieja [notʃe'βjexa] *nf* New Year's Eve

noción [no'θjon] *nf* notion

nocivo, a [no'θiβo, a] *adj* harmful

noctámbulo, a [nok'tambulo, a] *nm/f* sleepwalker

nocturno, a [nok'turno, a] *adj* (*de la noche*) nocturnal, night *cpd*; (*de la tarde*) evening *cpd* **♦** *nm* nocturne

nodriza [no'ðriθa] *nf* wet nurse; **buque** o **nave** ~ supply ship

nogal [no'ɣal] *nm* walnut tree

nómada ['nomaða] *adj* nomadic **♦** *nm/f* nomad

nombramiento [nombra'mjento] *nm* naming; (*a un empleo*) appointment

nombrar [nom'brar] *vt* (*designar*) to name; (*mencionar*) to mention; (*dar puesto a*) to appoint

nombre ['nombre] *nm* name; (*sustantivo*) noun; ~ **y apellidos** name in full; ~ **común/ propio** common/proper noun; ~ **de pila/de soltera** Christian/maiden name; **poner** ~ **a** to call, name

nómina ['nomina] *nf* (*lista*) payroll; (*hoja*) payslip

nominal [nomi'nal] *adj* nominal

nominar [nomi'nar] *vt* to nominate

nominativo, a [nomina'tiβo, a] *adj* (*COM*): **cheque** ~ **a X** cheque made out to X

nono, a ['nono, a] *adj* ninth

nordeste [nor'ðeste] *adj* north-east, north-eastern, north-easterly **♦** *nm* north-east

nórdico, a ['norðiko, a] *adj* Nordic

noreste [no'reste] *adj, nm* = **nordeste**

noria ['norja] *nf* (*AGR*) waterwheel; (*de carnaval*) big (*BRIT*) o Ferris (*US*) wheel

norma ['norma] *nf* rule (of thumb)

normal [nor'mal] *adj* (*corriente*) normal; (*habitual*) usual, natural; ~**idad** *nf* normality; **restablecer la** ~**idad** to restore order; ~**izar** *vt* (*reglamentar*) to normalize; (*TEC*) to standardize; ~**izarse** *vr* to return to normal; ~**mente** *adv* normally

normando, a [nor'mando, a] *adj, nm/f* Norman

normativa [norma'tiβa] *nf* (*set of*) rules *pl*, regulations *pl*

noroeste [noro'este] *adj* north-west, north-

western, north-westerly ♦ *nm* north-west
norte ['norte] *adj* north, northern, northerly ♦ *nm* north; (*fig*) guide
norteamericano, a [norteameri'kano, a] *adj, nm/f* (North) American
Noruega [no'rweɣa] *nf* Norway
noruego, a [no'rweɣo, a] *adj, nm/f* Norwegian
nos [nos] *pron* (*directo*) us; (*indirecto*) us; to us; for us; from us; (*reflexivo*) (to) ourselves; (*recíproco*) (to) each other; **~ levantamos a las 7** we get up at 7
nosotros, as [no'sotros, as] *pron* (*sujeto*) we; (*después de prep*) us
nostalgia [nos'talxja] *nf* nostalgia
nota ['nota] *nf* note; (*ESCOL*) mark
notable [no'taβle] *adj* notable; (*ESCOL*) outstanding
notar [no'tar] *vt* to notice, note; **~se** *vr* to be obvious; **se nota que** ... one observes that ...
notarial [nota'rjal] *adj*: **acta ~** affidavit
notario [no'tarjo] *nm* notary
noticia [no'tiθja] *nf* (*información*) piece of news; **las ~s** the news *sg*; **tener ~s de alguien** to hear from sb
noticiero [noti'θjero] (*AM*) *nm* news bulletin
notificación [notifika'θjon] *nf* notification; **notificar** *vt* to notify, inform
notoriedad [notorje'ðað] *nf* fame, renown; **notorio, a** *adj* (*público*) well-known; (*evidente*) obvious
novato, a [no'βato, a] *adj* inexperienced ♦ *nm/f* beginner, novice
novecientos, as [noβe'θjentos, as] *num* nine hundred
novedad [noβe'ðað] *nf* (*calidad de nuevo*) newness; (*noticia*) piece of news; (*cambio*) change, (new) development
novel [no'βel] *adj* new; (*inexperto*) inexperienced, ♦ *nm/f* beginner
novela [no'βela] *nf* novel
noveno, a [no'βeno, a] *adj* ninth
noventa [no'βenta] *num* ninety
novia ['noβja] *nf ver* novio
noviazgo [no'βjaθɣo] *nm* engagement
novicio, a [no'βiθjo, a] *nm/f* novice
noviembre [no'βjembre] *nm* November
novillada [noβi'ʎaða] *nf* (*TAUR*) bullfight with young bulls; **novillero** *nm* novice bullfighter; **novillo** *nm* young bull, bullock; **hacer novillos** (*fam*) to play truant
novio, a ['noβjo, a] *nm/f* boyfriend/girlfriend; (*prometido*) fiancé/fiancée; (*recién casado*) bridegroom/bride; **los ~s** the newly-weds
nubarrón [nuβa'rron] *nm* storm cloud
nube ['nuβe] *nf* cloud
nublado, a [nu'βlaðo, a] *adj* cloudy; **nublarse** *vr* to grow dark
nubosidad [nuβosi'ðað] *nf* cloudiness; **había**

mucha **~** it was very cloudy
nuca ['nuka] *nf* nape of the neck
nuclear [nukle'ar] *adj* nuclear
núcleo ['nukleo] *nm* (*centro*) core; (*FÍSICA*) nucleus
nudillo [nu'ðiʎo] *nm* knuckle
nudista [nu'ðista] *adj* nudist
nudo ['nuðo] *nm* knot; **~so, a** *adj* knotty
nuera ['nwera] *nf* daughter-in-law
nuestro, a ['nwestro, a] *adj pos* our ♦ *pron* ours; **~ padre** our father; **un amigo ~** a friend of ours; **es el ~** it's ours
nueva ['nweβa] *nf* piece of news
nuevamente [nweβa'mente] *adv* (*otra vez*) again; (*de nuevo*) anew
Nueva York [-'jɔrk] *n* New York
Nueva Zelanda [-θe'landa] *nf* New Zealand
nueve ['nweβe] *num* nine
nuevo, a ['nweβo, a] *adj* (*gen*) new; **de ~** again
nuez [nweθ] *nf* walnut; **~ de Adán** Adam's apple; **~ moscada** nutmeg
nulidad [nuli'ðað] *nf* (*incapacidad*) incompetence; (*abolición*) nullity
nulo, a ['nulo, a] *adj* (*inepto, torpe*) useless; (*inválido*) (null and) void; (*DEPORTE*) drawn, tied
núm. *abr* (= número) no
numeración [numera'θjon] *nf* (*cifras*) numbers *pl*; (*arábiga, romana etc*) numerals *pl*
numeral [nume'ral] *nm* numeral
numerar [nume'rar] *vt* to number
número ['numero] *nm* (*gen*) number; (*tamaño: de zapato*) size; (*ejemplar: de diario*) number, issue; **sin ~** numberless, unnumbered; **~ de matrícula/de teléfono** registration/telephone number; **~ atrasado** back number
numeroso, a [nume'roso, a] *adj* numerous
nunca ['nunka] *adv* (*jamás*) never; **~ lo pensé** I never thought it; **no viene ~** he never comes; **~ más** never again; **más que ~** more than ever
nupcias ['nupθjas] *nfpl* wedding *sg*, nuptials
nutria ['nutrja] *nf* otter
nutrición [nutri'θjon] *nf* nutrition
nutrido, a [nu'triðo, a] *adj* (*alimentado*) nourished; (*fig: grande*) large; (*abundante*) abundant
nutrir [nu'trir] *vt* (*alimentar*) to nourish; (*dar de comer*) to feed; (*fig*) to strengthen; **nutritivo, a** *adj* nourishing, nutritious
nylon [ni'lon] *nm* nylon

Ñ

ñato, a ['ɲato, a] (AM) adj snub-nosed
ñoñería [ɲoɲe'ria] nf insipidness
ñoño, a ['ɲoɲo, a] adj (AM: tonto) silly, stupid; (soso) insipid; (persona) spineless

O, o

O abr (= oeste) W
o [o] conj or
o/ abr (= orden) o.
oasis [o'asis] nm inv oasis
obcecarse [oßθe'karse] vr to get o become stubborn
obedecer [oßeðe'θer] vt to obey; **obediencia** nf obedience; **obediente** adj obedient
obertura [oßer'tura] nf overture
obesidad [oßesi'ðað] nf obesity; **obeso, a** adj obese
obispo [o'ßispo] nm bishop
objeción [oßxe'θjon] nf objection; **poner objeciones** to raise objections
objetar [oßxe'tar] vt, vi to object
objetivo, a [oßxe'tißo, a] adj, nm objective
objeto [oß'xeto] nm (cosa) object; (fin) aim
objetor, a [oßxe'tor, a] nm/f objector
oblicuo, a [o'ßlikwo, a] adj oblique; (mirada) sidelong
obligación [oßliɣa'θjon] nf obligation; (COM) bond
obligar [oßli'ɣar] vt to force; ~**se** vr to bind o.s.; **obligatorio, a** adj compulsory, obligatory
oboe [o'ßoe] nm oboe
obra ['oßra] nf work; (ARQ) construction, building; (TEATRO) play; ~ **maestra** masterpiece; ~**s públicas** public works; **por** ~ **de** thanks to (the efforts of); **obrar** vt to work; (tener efecto) to have an effect on ♦ vi to act, behave; (tener efecto) to have an effect; **la carta obra en su poder** the letter is in his/her possession
obrero, a [o'ßrero, a] adj (clase) working; (movimiento) labour cpd ♦ nm/f (gen) worker; (sin oficio) labourer
obscenidad [oßsθeni'ðað] nf obscenity; **obsceno, a** adj obscene
obscu... = **oscu...**
obsequiar [oßse'kjar] vt (ofrecer) to present with; (agasajar) to make a fuss of, lavish attention on; **obsequio** nm (regalo) gift; (cortesía) courtesy, attention
observación [oßserßa'θjon] nf observation; (reflexión) remark
observador, a [oßserßa'ðor, a] nm/f observer
observar [oßser'ßar] vt to observe; (anotar) to notice; ~**se** vr to keep to, observe
obsesión [oßse'sjon] nf obsession; **obsesivo, a** adj obsessive
obsoleto, a [oßso'leto, a] adj obsolete
obstáculo [oßs'takulo] nm obstacle; (impedimento) hindrance, drawback
obstante [oßs'tante]: **no** ~ adv nevertheless
obstinado, a [oßsti'naðo, a] adj obstinate, stubborn
obstinarse [oßsti'narse] vr to be obstinate; ~ **en** to persist in
obstrucción [oßstruk'θjon] nf obstruction; **obstruir** vt to obstruct
obtener [oßte'ner] vt (gen) to obtain; (premio) to win
obturador [oßtura'ðor] nm (FOTO) shutter
obvio, a ['oßßjo, a] adj obvious
oca ['oka] nf (animal) goose; (juego) ≈ snakes and ladders
ocasión [oka'sjon] nf (oportunidad) opportunity, chance; (momento) occasion, time; (causa) cause; **de** ~ secondhand; **ocasionar** vt to cause
ocaso [o'kaso] nm (fig) decline
occidente [okθi'ðente] nm west
OCDE nf abr (= Organización de Cooperación y Desarrollo Económico) OECD
océano [o'θeano] nm ocean; **el** ~ **Índico** the Indian Ocean
ochenta [o'tʃenta] num eighty
ocho ['otʃo] num eight; ~ **días** a week
ocio [o'θjo] nm (tiempo) leisure; (pey) idleness; ~**so, a** adj (inactivo) idle; (inútil) useless
octavilla [okta'viʎa] nf leaflet, pamphlet
octavo, a [ok'taßo, a] adj eighth
octubre [ok'tußre] nm October
ocular [oku'lar] adj ocular, eye cpd; **testigo** ~ eyewitness
oculista [oku'lista] nm/f oculist
ocultar [okul'tar] vt (esconder) to hide; (callar) to conceal; **oculto, a** adj hidden; (fig) secret
ocupación [okupa'θjon] nf occupation
ocupado, a [oku'paðo, a] adj (persona) busy; (plaza) occupied, taken; (teléfono) engaged; **ocupar** vt (gen) to occupy; **ocuparse** vr: **ocuparse de o en** (gen) to concern o.s. with; (cuidar) to look after
ocurrencia [oku'rrenθja] nf (idea) bright idea
ocurrir [oku'rrir] vi to happen; ~**se** vr: **se me ocurrió que** ... it occurred to me that ...
odiar [o'ðjar] vt to hate; **odio** nm hate, hatred; **odioso, a** adj (gen) hateful; (malo)

nasty

odontólogo, a [oðon'toloɣo, a] *nm/f* dentist, dental surgeon

OEA *nf abr* (= *Organización de Estados Americanos*) OAS

oeste [o'este] *nm* west; **una película del ~** a western

ofender [ofen'der] *vt* (*agraviar*) to offend; (*insultar*) to insult; **~se** *vr* to take offence; **ofensa** *nf* offence; **ofensiva** *nf* offensive; **ofensivo, a** *adj* offensive

oferta [o'ferta] *nf* offer; (*propuesta*) proposal; **la ~ y la demanda** supply and demand; **artículos en ~** goods on offer

oficial [ofi'θjal] *adj* official ♦ *nm* (MIL) officer

oficina [ofi'θina] *nf* office; **~ de correos** post office; **~ de turismo** tourist office; **oficinista** *nm/f* clerk

oficio [o'fiθjo] *nm* (*profesión*) profession; (*puesto*) post; (REL) service; **ser del ~** to be an old hand; **tener mucho ~** to have a lot of experience; **~ de difuntos** funeral service

oficioso, a [ofi'θjoso, a] *adj* (pey) officious; (*no oficial*) unofficial, informal

ofimática [ofi'matika] *nf* office automation

ofrecer [ofre'θer] *vt* (*dar*) to offer; (*proponer*) to propose; **~se** *vr* (*persona*) to offer o.s., volunteer; (*situación*) to present itself; **¿qué se le ofrece?, ¿se le ofrece algo?** what can I do for you?, can I get you anything?

ofrecimiento [ofreθi'mjento] *nm* offer

oftalmólogo, a [oftal'moloɣo, a] *nm/f* ophthalmologist

ofuscar [ofus'kar] *vt* (*por pasión*) to blind; (*por luz*) to dazzle

oída [o'iða] *nf*: **de ~s** by hearsay

oído [o'iðo] *nm* (ANAT) ear; (*sentido*) hearing

oigo *etc vb ver* **oír**

oír [o'ir] *vt* (*gen*) to hear; (*atender a*) to listen to; **¡oiga!** listen!; **~ misa** to attend mass

OIT *nf abr* (= *Organización Internacional del Trabajo*) ILO

ojal [o'xal] *nm* buttonhole

ojalá [oxa'la] *excl* if only (it were so)!, some hope! ♦ *conj* if only ...!, would that ...!; **~ (que) venga hoy** I hope he comes today

ojeada [oxe'aða] *nf* glance

ojera [o'xera] *nf*: **tener ~s** to have bags under one's eyes

ojeriza [oxe'riθa] *nf* ill-will

ojeroso, a [oxe'roso, a] *adj* haggard

ojo [o'xo] *nm* eye; (*de puente*) span; (*de cerradura*) keyhole ♦ *excl* careful!; **tener ~ para** to have an eye for; **~ de buey** porthole

okupa [o'kupa] (fam) *nm/f* squatter

ola [o'la] *nf* wave

olé [o'le] *excl* bravo!, olé!

oleada [ole'aða] *nf* big wave, swell; (fig) wave

oleaje [ole'axe] *nm* swell

óleo ['oleo] *nm* oil; **oleoducto** *nm* (oil) pipeline

oler [o'ler] *vt* (*gen*) to smell; (*inquirir*) to pry into; (fig: *sospechar*) to sniff out ♦ *vi* to smell; **~ a** to smell of

olfatear [olfate'ar] *vt* to smell; (*inquirir*) to pry into; **olfato** *nm* sense of smell

oligarquía [oliɣar'kia] *nf* oligarchy

olimpíada [olim'piaða] *nf*: **las O~s** the Olympics; **olímpico, a** [o'limpiko, a] *adj* Olympic

oliva [o'liβa] *nf* (*aceituna*) olive; **aceite de ~** olive oil; **olivo** *nm* olive tree

olla ['oʎa] *nf* pan; (*comida*) stew; **~ a presión** o **exprés** pressure cooker; **~ podrida** *type of Spanish stew*

olmo ['olmo] *nm* elm (tree)

olor [o'lor] *nm* smell; **~oso, a** *adj* scented

olvidar [olβi'ðar] *vt* to forget; (*omitir*) to omit; **~se** *vr* (fig) to forget o.s.; **se me olvidó** I forgot

olvido [ol'βiðo] *nm* oblivion; (*despiste*) forgetfulness

ombligo [om'bliɣo] *nm* navel

omisión [omi'sjon] *nf* (*abstención*) omission; (*descuido*) neglect

omiso, a [o'miso, a] *adj*: **hacer caso ~ de** to ignore, pass over

omitir [omi'tir] *vt* to omit

omnipotente [omnipo'tente] *adj* omnipotent

omóplato [o'moplato] *nm* shoulder blade

OMG *nm abr* (= *Organismo Modificado Genéticamente*) GMO

OMS *nf abr* (= *Organización Mundial de la Salud*) WHO

once ['onθe] *num* eleven; **~s** (AM) *nfpl* tea break

onda ['onda] *nf* wave; **~ corta/larga/media** short/long/medium wave; **ondear** *vt*, *vi* to wave; (*tener ondas*) to be wavy; (*agua*) to ripple; **ondearse** *vr* to swing, sway

ondulación [ondula'θjon] *nf* undulation; **ondulado, a** *adj* wavy

ondular [ondu'lar] *vt* (*el pelo*) to wave ♦ *vi* to undulate; **~se** *vr* to undulate

ONG *nf abr* (= *organización no gubernamental*) NGO

ONU ['onu] *nf abr* (= *Organización de las Naciones Unidas*) UNO

opaco, a [o'pako, a] *adj* opaque

opción [op'θjon] *nf* (*gen*) option; (*derecho*) right, option

OPEP ['opep] *nf abr* (= *Organización de Países Exportadores de Petróleo*) OPEC

ópera ['opera] *nf* opera; **~ bufa** o **cómica** comic opera

operación [opera'θjon] *nf* (*gen*) operation;

(COM) transaction, deal

operador, a [opera'ðor, a] nm/f operator;
(CINE: proyección) projectionist; (: rodaje)
cameraman

operar [ope'rar] vt (producir) to produce,
bring about; (MED) to operate on ♦ vi (COM)
to operate, deal; ~**se** vr to occur; (MED) to
have an operation

opereta [ope'reta] nf operetta

opinar [opi'nar] vt to think ♦ vi to give one's
opinion; **opinión** nf (creencia) belief;
(criterio) opinion

opio ['opjo] nm opium

oponente [opo'nente] nm/f opponent

oponer [opo'ner] vt (resistencia) to put up,
offer; ~**se** vr (objetar) to object; (estar frente a
frente) to be opposed; (dos personas) to
oppose each other; ~ **A a B** to set A against
B; **me opongo a pensar que ...** I refuse to
believe o think that ...

oportunidad [oportuni'ðað] nf (ocasión)
opportunity; (posibilidad) chance

oportuno, a [opor'tuno, a] adj (en su
tiempo) opportune, timely; (respuesta)
suitable; **en el momento ~** at the right
moment

oposición [oposi'θjon] nf opposition;
oposiciones nfpl (ESCOL) public examinations

opositor, a [oposi'tor, a] nm/f (adversario)
opponent; (candidato): ~ **(a)** candidate (for)

opresión [opre'sjon] nf oppression;

opresivo, a adj oppressive; **opresor, a**
nm/f oppressor

oprimir [opri'mir] vt to squeeze; (fig) to
oppress

optar [op'tar] vi (elegir) to choose; ~ **por** to
opt for; **optativo, a** adj optional

óptico, a ['optiko, a] adj optic(al) ♦ nm/f
optician; **óptica** nf optician's (shop); **desde
esta óptica** from this point of view

optimismo [opti'mismo] nm optimism;
optimista nm/f optimist

óptimo, a ['optimo, a] adj (el mejor) very
best

opuesto, a [o'pwesto, a] adj (contrario)
opposite; (antagónico) opposing

opulencia [opu'lenθja] nf opulence;
opulento, a adj opulent

oración [ora'θjon] nf (REL) prayer; (LING)
sentence

orador, a [ora'ðor, a] nm/f (conferenciante)
speaker, orator

oral [o'ral] adj oral

orangután [orangu'tan] nm orangutan

orar [o'rar] vi to pray

oratoria [ora'torja] nf oratory

órbita ['orβita] nf orbit

orden ['orðen] nm (gen) order ♦ nf (gen)
order; (INFORM) command; ~ **del día** agenda;

de primer ~ first-rate; **en ~ de prioridad** in
order of priority

ordenado, a [orðe'naðo, a] adj (metódico)
methodical; (arreglado) orderly

ordenador [orðena'ðor] nm computer;
~ **central** mainframe computer

ordenanza [orðe'nanθa] nf ordinance

ordenar [orðe'nar] vt (mandar) to order;
(poner orden) to put in order, arrange; ~**se** vr
(REL) to be ordained

ordeñar [orðe'nar] vt to milk

ordinario, a [orði'narjo, a] adj (común)
ordinary, usual; (vulgar) vulgar, common

orégano [o'reχano] nm oregano

oreja [o'reχa] nf ear; (MECÁNICA) lug, flange

orfanato [orfa'nato] nm orphanage

orfandad [orfan'dað] nf orphanhood

orfebrería [orfeβre'ria] nf gold/silver work

orgánico, a [or'βaniko, a] adj organic

organigrama [orβani'βrama] nm flow chart

organismo [orβa'nismo] nm (BIO) organism;
(POL) organization

organización [orβaniθa'θjon] nf
organization; **organizar** vt to organize

órgano ['orβano] nm organ

orgasmo [or'βasmo] nm orgasm

orgía [or'χia] nf orgy

orgullo [or'βuʎo] nm pride; **orgulloso, a** adj
(gen) proud; (altanero) haughty

orientación [orjenta'θjon] nf (posición)
position; (dirección) direction

oriental [orjen'tal] adj eastern; (del Lejano
Oriente) oriental

orientar [orjen'tar] vt (situar) to orientate;
(señalar) to point; (dirigir) to direct; (guiar)
to guide; ~**se** vr to get one's bearings

oriente [o'rjente] nm east; **Cercano/
Medio/Lejano O~** Near/Middle/Far East

origen [o'rixen] nm origin

original [orixi'nal] adj (nuevo) original;
(extraño) odd, strange; ~**idad** nf originality

originar [orixi'nar] vt to start, cause; ~**se** vr
to originate; ~**io, a** adj original; ~**io de** native
of

orilla [o'riʎa] nf (borde) border; (de río) bank;
(de bosque, tela) edge; (de mar) shore

orina [o'rina] nf urine; **orinal** nm (chamber)
pot; **orinar** vi to urinate; **orinarse** vr to wet
o.s.; **orines** nmpl urine

oriundo, a [o'rjundo, a] adj: ~ **de** native of

ornitología [ornitolo'χia] nf ornithology,
bird-watching

oro ['oro] nm gold; ~**s** nmpl (NAIPES) hearts

oropel [oro'pel] nm tinsel

orquesta [or'kesta] nf orchestra; ~ **de
cámara/sinfónica** chamber/symphony
orchestra

orquídea [or'kiðea] nf orchid

ortiga [or'tiβa] nf nettle

ortodoxo, a [orto'ðokso, a] *adj* orthodox
ortografía [ortoɣra'fia] *nf* spelling
ortopedia [orto'peðja] *nf* orthopaedics *sg*;
  ortopédico, a *adj* orthopaedic
oruga [o'ruɣa] *nf* caterpillar
orzuelo [or'θwelo] *nm* stye
os [os] *pron* (*gen*) you; (*a vosotros*) to you
osa ['osa] *nf* (she-)bear; **O~ Mayor/Menor**
  Great/Little Bear
osadía [osa'ðia] *nf* daring
osar [o'sar] *vi* to dare
oscilación [osθila'θjon] *nf* (*movimiento*)
  oscillation; (*fluctuación*) fluctuation
oscilar [osθi'lar] *vi* to oscillate; to fluctuate
oscurecer [oskure'θer] *vt* to darken ♦ *vi* to
  grow dark; **~se** *vr* to grow o get dark
oscuridad [oskuri'ðað] *nf* obscurity;
  (*tinieblas*) darkness
oscuro, a [os'kuro, a] *adj* dark; (*fig*) obscure;
  a oscuras in the dark
óseo, a ['oseo, a] *adj* bone *cpd*
oso ['oso] *nm* bear; **~ de peluche** teddy bear;
  ~ hormiguero anteater
ostentación [ostenta'θjon] *nf* (*gen*)
  ostentation; (*acto*) display
ostentar [osten'tar] *vt* (*gen*) to show;
  (*pey*) to flaunt, show off; (*poseer*) to have,
  possess
ostra ['ostra] *nf* oyster
OTAN ['otan] *nf abr* (= *Organización del
  Tratado del Atlántico Norte*) NATO
otear [ote'ar] *vt* to observe; (*fig*) to look into
otitis [o'titis] *nf* earache
otoñal [oto'ɲal] *adj* autumnal
otoño [o'toɲo] *nm* autumn
otorgar [otor'ɣar] *vt* (*conceder*) to concede;
  (*dar*) to grant
otorrinolaringólogo, a [oto'rrino, a], **otorrinolaringólogo, a** [otorrinolarin'goloɣo, a] *nm/f* ear,
  nose and throat specialist

PALABRA CLAVE

---

otro, a ['otro, a] *adj* **1** (*distinto: sg*) another;
  (: *pl*) other; **con ~s amigos** with other o
  different friends
  2 (*adicional*): **tráigame ~ café (más), por
  favor** can I have another coffee please; **~s 10
  días más** another ten days
  ♦ *pron* **1**: **el ~** the other one; **(los) ~s** (the)
  others; **de ~** somebody else's; **que lo haga ~**
  let somebody else do it
  2 (*recíproco*): **se odian (la) una a (la) otra**
  they hate one another o each other
  3: **~ tanto: comer ~ tanto** to eat the same o
  as much again; **recibió una decena de
  telegramas y otras tantas llamadas** he got
  about ten telegrams and as many calls

ovación [oβa'θjon] *nf* ovation

oval [o'βal] *adj* oval; **~ado, a** *adj* oval; **óvalo**
  nm oval
ovario [o'βarjo] *nm* ovary
oveja [o'βexa] *nf* sheep
overol [oβe'rol] (*AM*) *nm* overalls *pl*
ovillo [o'βiʎo] *nm* (*de lana*) ball of wool;
  hacerse un ~ to curl up
OVNI ['oβni] *nm abr* (= *objeto volante no
  identificado*) UFO
ovulación [oβula'θjon] *nf* ovulation; **óvulo**
  nm ovum
oxidación [oksiða'θjon] *nf* rusting
oxidar [oksi'ðar] *vt* to rust; **~se** *vr* to go rusty
óxido ['oksiðo] *nm* oxide
oxigenado, a [oksixe'naðo, a] *adj* (*QUÍM*)
  oxygenated; (*pelo*) bleached
oxígeno [ok'sixeno] *nm* oxygen
oyente [o'jente] *nm/f* listener, hearer
oyes *etc vb ver* **oír**
ozono [o'θono] *nm* ozone

P, p

P *abr* (= *padre*) Fr.
pabellón [paβe'ʎon] *nm* bell tent; (*ARQ*)
  pavilion; (*de hospital etc*) block, section;
  (*bandera*) flag
pacer [pa'θer] *vi* to graze
paciencia [pa'θjenθja] *nf* patience
paciente [pa'θjente] *adj, nm/f* patient
pacificación [paθifika'θjon] *nf* pacification
pacificar [paθifi'kar] *vt* to pacify;
  (*tranquilizar*) to calm
pacífico, a [pa'θifiko, a] *adj* (*persona*)
  peaceable; (*existencia*) peaceful; **el (océano)
  P~** the Pacific (Ocean)
pacifismo [paθi'fismo] *nm* pacifism;
  pacifista *nm/f* pacifist
pacotilla [pako'tiʎa] *nf*: **de ~** (*actor, escritor*)
  third-rate; (*mueble etc*) cheap
pactar [pak'tar] *vt* to agree to o on ♦ *vi* to
  come to an agreement
pacto ['pakto] *nm* (*tratado*) pact; (*acuerdo*)
  agreement
padecer [paðe'θer] *vt* (*sufrir*) to suffer;
  (*soportar*) to endure, put up with;
  padecimiento *nm* suffering
padrastro [pa'ðrastro] *nm* stepfather
padre ['paðre] *nm* father ♦ *adj* (*fam*): **un
  éxito ~** a tremendous success; **~s** *nmpl*
  parents
padrino [pa'ðrino] *nm* (*REL*) godfather; (*tb:
  ~ de boda*) best man; (*fig*) sponsor, patron;
  ~s *nmpl* godparents
padrón [pa'ðron] *nm* (*censo*) census, roll
paella [pa'eʎa] *nf* paella, *dish of rice with
  meat, shellfish etc*

paga ['paɣa] nf (pago) payment; (sueldo) pay, wages pl

pagano, a [pa'ɣano, a] adj, nm/f pagan, heathen

pagar [pa'ɣar] vt to pay; (las compras, crimen) to pay for; (fig: favor) to repay ♦ vi to pay; **~ al contado/a plazos** to pay (in) cash/in instalments

pagaré [paɣa're] nm I.O.U.

página ['paxina] nf page; **~ de inicio** (INFORM) home page

pago ['paɣo] nm (dinero) payment; **~ anticipado/a cuenta/contra reembolso/en especie** advance payment/payment on account/cash on delivery/payment in kind; **en ~ de** in return for

pág(s). abr (= página(s)) p(p).

pague etc vb ver **pagar**

país [pa'is] nm (gen) country; (región) land; **los P~es Bajos** the Low Countries; **el P~ Vasco** the Basque Country

paisaje [pai'saxe] nm landscape, scenery

paisano, a [pai'sano, a] adj of the same country ♦ nm/f (compatriota) fellow countryman/woman; **vestir de ~** (soldado) to be in civvies; (guardia) to be in plain clothes

paja ['paxa] nf straw; (fig) rubbish (BRIT), trash (US)

pajarita [paxa'rita] nf (corbata) bow tie

pájaro ['paxaro] nm bird; **~ carpintero** woodpecker

pajita [pa'xita] nf (drinking) straw

pala ['pala] nf spade, shovel; (raqueta etc) bat; (: de tenis) racquet; (CULIN) slice; **~ matamoscas** fly swat

palabra [pa'laβra] nf word; (facultad) (power of) speech; (derecho de hablar) right to speak; **tomar la ~** (en mitin) to take the floor

palabrota [pala'βrota] nf swearword

palacio [pa'laθjo] nm palace; (mansión) mansion, large house; **~ de justicia** courthouse; **~ municipal** town/city hall

paladar [pala'ðar] nm palate; **paladear** vt to taste

palanca [pa'lanka] nf lever; (fig) pull, influence

palangana [palan'gana] nf washbasin

palco ['palko] nm box

Palestina [pales'tina] nf Palestine; **palestino, a** nm/f Palestinian

paleta [pa'leta] nf (de pintor) palette; (de albañil) trowel; (de ping-pong) bat; (AM) ice lolly

paleto, a [pa'leto, a] (fam, pey) nm/f yokel

paliar [pa'ljar] vt (mitigar) to mitigate, alleviate; **paliativo** nm palliative

palidecer [paliðe'θer] vi to turn pale; **palidez** nf paleness; **pálido, a** adj pale

palillo [pa'liʎo] nm (mondadientes) toothpick; (para comer) chopstick

paliza [pa'liθa] nf beating, thrashing

palma ['palma] nf (ANAT) palm; (árbol) palm tree; **batir** o **dar ~s** to clap, applaud; **~da** nf slap; **~das** nfpl clapping sg, applause sg

palmar [pal'mar] (fam) vi (tb: ~la) to die, kick the bucket

palmear [palme'ar] vi to clap

palmera [pal'mera] nf (BOT) palm tree

palmo ['palmo] nm (medida) span; (fig) small amount; **~ a ~** inch by inch

palo ['palo] nm stick; (poste) post; (de tienda de campaña) pole; (mango) handle, shaft; (golpe) blow, hit; (de golf) club; (de béisbol) bat; (NAUT) mast; (NAIPES) suit

paloma [pa'loma] nf dove, pigeon

palomitas [palo'mitas] nfpl popcorn sg

palpar [pal'par] vt to touch, feel

palpitación [palpita'θjon] nf palpitation

palpitante [palpi'tante] adj palpitating; (fig) burning

palpitar [palpi'tar] vi to palpitate; (latir) to beat

palta ['palta] (AM) nf avocado (pear)

paludismo [palu'ðismo] nm malaria

pamela [pa'mela] nf picture hat, sun hat

pampa ['pampa] (AM) nf pampas, prairie

pan [pan] nm bread; (una barra) loaf; **~ integral** wholemeal (BRIT) o wholewheat (US) bread; **~ rallado** breadcrumbs pl

pana ['pana] nf corduroy

panadería [panaðe'ria] nf baker's (shop); **panadero, a** nm/f baker

Panamá [pana'ma] nm Panama; **panameño, a** adj Panamanian

pancarta [pan'karta] nf placard, banner

panda ['panda] nm (ZOOL) panda

pandereta [pande'reta] nf tambourine

pandilla [pan'diʎa] nf set, group; (de criminales) gang; (pey: camarilla) clique

panecillo [pane'θiʎo] nm (bread) roll

panel [pa'nel] nm panel; **~ solar** solar panel

panfleto [pan'fleto] nm pamphlet

pánico ['paniko] nm panic

panorama [pano'rama] nm panorama; (vista) view

pantalla [pan'taʎa] nf (de cine) screen; (de lámpara) lampshade

pantalón [panta'lon] nm trousers; **pantalones** nmpl trousers

pantano [pan'tano] nm (ciénaga) marsh, swamp; (depósito: de agua) reservoir; (fig) jam, difficulty

panteón [pante'on] nm: **~ familiar** family tomb

pantera [pan'tera] nf panther

panti(e)s ['pantis] nmpl tights

pantomima [panto'mima] nf pantomime

pantorrilla [panto'rriʎa] nf calf (of the leg)

pantufla [pan'tufla] *nf* slipper
panty(s) ['panti(s)] *nm(pl)* tights
panza ['panθa] *nf* belly, paunch
pañal [pa'ɲal] *nm* nappy (*BRIT*), diaper (*US*); **~es** *nmpl* (*fig*) early stages, infancy *sg*
paño ['paɲo] *nm* (*tela*) cloth; (*pedazo de tela*) (piece of) cloth; (*trapo*) duster, rag; **~ higiénico** sanitary towel; **~s menores** underclothes
pañuelo [pa'ɲwelo] *nm* handkerchief, hanky (*fam*); (*para la cabeza*) (head)scarf
papa ['papa] *nm*: **el P~** the Pope ♦ *nf* (*AM*) potato
papá [pa'pa] (*pl* **~s**) (*fam*) *nm* dad(dy), pa (*US*)
papada [pa'paða] *nf* double chin
papagayo [papa'vajo] *nm* parrot
papanatas [papa'natas] (*fam*) *nm inv* simpleton
paparrucha [papa'rrutʃa] *nf* piece of nonsense
papaya [pa'paja] *nf* papaya
papear [pape'ar] (*fam*) *vt, vi* to scoff
papel [pa'pel] *nm* paper; (*hoja de ~*) sheet of paper; (*TEATRO, fig*) role; **~ de calco/carbón/de cartas** tracing paper/carbon paper/stationery; **~ de envolver/pintado** wrapping paper/wallpaper; **~ de aluminio/higiénico** aluminium (*BRIT*) o aluminum (*US*) foil/toilet paper; **~ de estaño** o **plata** tinfoil; **~ de lija** sandpaper; **~ moneda** paper money; **~ secante** blotting paper
papeleo [pape'leo] *nm* red tape
papelera [pape'lera] *nf* wastepaper basket; (*en la calle*) litter bin
papelería [papele'ria] *nf* stationer's (shop)
papeleta [pape'leta] *nf* (*POL*) ballot paper; (*ESCOL*) report
paperas [pa'peras] *nfpl* mumps *sg*
papilla [pa'piʎa] *nf* (*para niños*) baby food
paquete [pa'kete] *nm* (*de cigarrillos etc*) packet; (*CORREOS etc*) parcel; (*AM*) package tour; (: *fam*) nuisance
par [par] *adj* (*igual*) like, equal; (*MAT*) even ♦ *nm* equal; (*de guantes*) pair; (*de veces*) couple; (*POL*) peer; (*GOLF, COM*) par; **abrir a ~ en ~** to open wide
para ['para] *prep* for; **no es ~ comer** it's not for eating; **decir ~ sí** to say to o.s.; **¿~ qué lo quieres?** what do you want it for?; **se casaron ~ separarse otra vez** they married only to separate again; **lo tendré ~ mañana** I'll have it (for) tomorrow; **ir ~ casa** to go home, head for home; **~ profesor es muy estúpido** he's very stupid for a teacher; **¿quién es usted ~ gritar así?** who are you to shout like that?; **tengo bastante ~ vivir** I have enough to live on; *ver tb* **con**
parabién [para'ßjen] *nm* congratulations *pl*

parábola [pa'raßola] *nf* parable; (*MAT*) parabola; **parabólica** *nf* (*tb*: **antena ~**) satellite dish
parabrisas [para'ßrisas] *nm inv* windscreen (*BRIT*), windshield (*US*)
paracaídas [paraka'iðas] *nm inv* parachute; **paracaidista** *nm/f* parachutist; (*MIL*) paratrooper
parachoques [para'tʃokes] *nm inv* (*AUTO*) bumper; (*MECÁNICA etc*) shock absorber
parada [pa'raða] *nf* stop; (*acto*) stopping; (*de industria*) shutdown, stoppage; (*lugar*) stopping place; **~ de autobús** bus stop
paradero [para'ðero] *nm* stopping-place; (*situación*) whereabouts
parado, a [pa'raðo, a] *adj* (*persona*) motionless, standing still; (*fábrica*) closed, at a standstill; (*coche*) stopped; (*AM*) standing (up); (*sin empleo*) unemployed, idle
paradoja [para'ðoxa] *nf* paradox
parador [para'ðor] *nm* parador, state-run hotel
paráfrasis [pa'rafrasis] *nf inv* paraphrase
paraguas [pa'raɣwas] *nm inv* umbrella
Paraguay [para'ɣwai] *nm*: **el ~** Paraguay; **paraguayo, a** *adj, nm/f* Paraguayan
paraíso [para'iso] *nm* paradise, heaven
paraje [pa'raxe] *nm* place, spot
paralelo, a [para'lelo, a] *adj* parallel
parálisis [pa'ralisis] *nf inv* paralysis; **paralítico, a** *adj, nm/f* paralytic
paralizar [parali'θar] *vt* to paralyse; **~se** *vr* to become paralysed; (*fig*) to come to a standstill
paramilitar [paramili'tar] *adj* paramilitary
páramo ['paramo] *nm* bleak plateau
parangón [paran'gon] *nm*: **sin ~** incomparable
paranoico, a [para'noiko, a] *nm/f* paranoiac
parapente [para'pente] *nm* (*deporte*) paragliding; (*aparato*) paraglider
parapléjico, a [para'plexiko, a] *adj, nm/f* paraplegic
parar [pa'rar] *vt* to stop; (*golpe*) to ward off ♦ *vi* to stop; **~se** *vr* to stop; (*AM*) to stand up; **ha parado de llover** it has stopped raining; **van a ir a ~ a comisaría** they're going to end up in the police station; **~se en** to pay attention to
pararrayos [para'rrajos] *nm inv* lightning conductor
parásito, a [pa'rasito, a] *nm/f* parasite
parcela [par'θela] *nf* plot, piece of ground
parche ['partʃe] *nm* (*gen*) patch
parchís [par'tʃis] *nm* ludo
parcial [par'θjal] *adj* (*pago*) part-; (*eclipse*) partial; (*JUR*) prejudiced, biased; (*POL*) partisan; **~idad** *nf* prejudice, bias
pardillo, a [par'ðiʎo, a] (*pey*) *adj* yokel

parecer [pare'θer] *nm* (*opinión*) opinion, view; (*aspecto*) looks *pl* ♦ *vi* (*tener apariencia*) to seem, look; (*asemejarse*) to look *o* seem like; (*aparecer, llegar*) to appear; **~se** *vr* to look alike, resemble each other; **~se a** to look like, resemble; **según parece** evidently, apparently; **me parece que** I think (that), it seems to me that

parecido, a [pare'θiðo, a] *adj* similar ♦ *nm* similarity, likeness, resemblance; **bien ~** good-looking, nice-looking

pared [pa'reð] *nf* wall

pareja [pa'rexa] *nf* (*par*) pair; (*dos personas*) couple; (*otro: de un par*) other one (of a pair); (*persona*) partner

parentela [paren'tela] *nf* relations *pl*

parentesco [paren'tesko] *nm* relationship

paréntesis [pa'rentesis] *nm inv* parenthesis; (*en escrito*) bracket

parezco *etc vb ver* **parecer**

pariente, a [pa'rjente, a] *nm/f* relative, relation

parir [pa'rir] *vt* to give birth to ♦ *vi* (*mujer*) to give birth, have a baby

París [pa'ris] *n* Paris

parking ['parkin] *nm* car park (*BRIT*), parking lot (*US*)

parlamentar [parlamen'tar] *vi* to parley

parlamentario, a [parlamen'tarjo, a] *adj* parliamentary ♦ *nm/f* member of parliament

parlamento [parla'mento] *nm* parliament

parlanchín, ina [parlan'tʃin, ina] *adj* indiscreet ♦ *nm/f* chatterbox

parlar [par'lar] *vi* to chatter (away)

paro ['paro] *nm* (*huelga*) stoppage (of work), strike; (*desempleo*) unemployment; **subsidio de ~** unemployment benefit

parodia [pa'roðja] *nf* parody; **parodiar** *vt* to parody

parpadear [parpaðe'ar] *vi* (*ojos*) to blink; (*luz*) to flicker

párpado ['parpaðo] *nm* eyelid

parque ['parke] *nm* (*lugar verde*) park; **~ de atracciones/infantil/zoológico** fairground/playground/zoo

parqué [par'ke] *nm* parquet (flooring)

parquímetro [par'kimetro] *nm* parking meter

parra ['parra] *nf* (grape)vine

párrafo ['parrafo] *nm* paragraph; **echar un ~** (*fam*) to have a chat

parranda [pa'rranda] (*fam*) *nf* spree, binge

parrilla [pa'rriʎa] *nf* (*CULIN*) grill; (*de coche*) grille; (**carne a la**) **~** barbecue; **~da** *nf* barbecue

párroco ['parroko] *nm* parish priest

parroquia [pa'rrokja] *nf* parish; (*iglesia*) parish church; (*COM*) clientele, customers *pl*; **~no, a** *nm/f* parishioner; client, customer

parsimonia [parsi'monja] *nf* calmness, level-headedness

parte ['parte] *nm* message; (*informe*) report ♦ *nf* part; (*lado, cara*) side; (*de reparto*) share; (*JUR*) party; **en alguna ~ de Europa** somewhere in Europe; **en/por todas ~s** everywhere; **en gran ~** to a large extent; **la mayor ~ de los españoles** most Spaniards; **de un tiempo a esta ~** for some time past; **de ~ de alguien** on sb's behalf; **¿de ~ de quién?** (*TEL*) who is speaking?; **por ~** on the part of; **yo por mi ~** I for my part; **por otra ~** on the other hand; **dar ~** to inform; **tomar ~** to take part

partición [parti'θjon] *nf* division, sharing-out; (*POL*) partition

participación [partiθipa'θjon] *nf* (*acto*) participation, taking part; (*parte, COM*) share; (*de lotería*) shared prize; (*aviso*) notice, notification

participante [partiθi'pante] *nm/f* participant

participar [partiθi'par] *vt* to notify, inform ♦ *vi* to take part

partícipe [par'tiθipe] *nm/f* participant

particular [partiku'lar] *adj* (*especial*) particular, special; (*individual, personal*) private, personal ♦ *nm* (*punto, asunto*) particular, point; (*individuo*) individual; **tiene coche ~** he has a car of his own

partida [par'tiða] *nf* (*salida*) departure; (*COM*) entry, item; (*juego*) game; (*grupo de personas*) band, group; **mala ~** dirty trick; **~ de nacimiento/matrimonio/defunción** birth/marriage/death certificate

partidario, a [parti'ðarjo, a] *adj* partisan ♦ *nm/f* supporter, follower

partido [par'tiðo] *nm* (*POL*) party; (*DEPORTE*) game, match; **sacar ~ de** to profit *o* benefit from; **tomar ~** to take sides

partir [par'tir] *vt* (*dividir*) to split, divide; (*compartir, distribuir*) to share (out), distribute; (*romper*) to break open, split open; (*rebanada*) to cut (off) ♦ *vi* (*ponerse en camino*) to set off *o* out; (*comenzar*) to start (off *o* out); **~se** *vr* to crack *o* split *o* break (in two *etc*); **a ~ de** (starting) from

partitura [parti'tura] *nf* (*MUS*) score

parto ['parto] *nm* birth; (*fig*) product, creation; **estar de ~** to be in labour

pasa ['pasa] *nf* raisin; **~ de Corinto/de Esmirna** currant/sultana

pasada [pa'saða] *nf* passing, passage; **de ~** in passing, incidentally; **una mala ~** a dirty trick

pasadizo [pasa'ðiθo] *nm* (*pasillo*) passage, corridor; (*callejuela*) alley

pasado, a [pa'saðo, a] *adj* past; (*malo: comida, fruta*) bad; (*muy cocido*) overdone; (*anticuado*) out of date ♦ *nm* past; **~ mañana** the day after tomorrow; **el mes ~** last month

pasador [pasa'ðor] nm (cerrojo) bolt; (de pelo) hair slide; (horquilla) grip

pasaje [pa'saxe] nm passage; (pago de viaje) fare; (los pasajeros) passengers pl; (pasillo) passageway

pasajero, a [pasa'xero, a] adj passing; (situación, estado) temporary; (amor, enfermedad) brief ♦ nm/f passenger

pasamontañas [pasamon'taɲas] nm inv balaclava helmet

pasaporte [pasa'porte] nm passport

pasar [pa'sar] vt to pass; (tiempo) to spend; (desgracias) to suffer, endure; (noticia) to give, pass on; (río) to cross; (barrera) to pass through; (falta) to overlook, tolerate; (contrincante) to surpass, do better than; (coche) to overtake; (CINE) to show; (enfermedad) to give, infect with ♦ vi (gen) to pass; (terminarse) to be over; (ocurrir) to happen; ~se vr (flores) to fade; (comida) to go bad o off; (fig) to overdo it, go too far; ~ de to go beyond, exceed; ~ por (AM) to fetch; ~lo bien/mal to have a good/bad time; ¡pase! come in!; hacer ~ to show in; ~se al enemigo to go over to the enemy; se me pasó I forgot; no se le pasa nada he misses nothing; pase lo que pase come what may; ¿qué pasa? what's going on?, what's up?; ¿qué te pasa? what's wrong?

pasarela [pasa'rela] nf footbridge; (en barco) gangway

pasatiempo [pasa'tjempo] nm pastime, hobby

Pascua ['paskwa] nf: ~ (de Resurrección) Easter; ~ de Navidad Christmas; ~s nfpl Christmas (time); ¡felices ~s! Merry Christmas!

pase ['pase] nm pass; (CINE) performance, showing

pasear [pase'ar] vt to take for a walk; (exhibir) to parade, show off ♦ vi to walk, go for a walk; ~se vr to walk, go for a walk; ~ en coche to go for a drive; paseo nm (avenida) avenue; (distancia corta) walk, stroll; dar un o ir de paseo to go for a walk

pasillo [pa'siʎo] nm passage, corridor

pasión [pa'sjon] nf passion

pasivo, a [pa'siβo, a] adj passive; (inactivo) inactive ♦ nm (COM) liabilities pl, debts pl

pasmar [pas'mar] vt (asombrar) to amaze, astonish; **pasmo** nm amazement, astonishment; (resfriado) chill; (fig) wonder, marvel; **pasmoso, a** adj amazing, astonishing

paso, a ['paso, a] adj dried ♦ nm step; (modo de andar) walk; (huella) footprint; (rapidez) speed, pace, rate; (camino accesible) way through, passage; (cruce) crossing; (pasaje) passing, passage; (GEO) pass; (estrecho) strait;

~ a nivel (FERRO) level-crossing; ~ de peatones pedestrian crossing; a ese ~ (fig) at that rate; salir al ~ de o a to waylay; estar de ~ to be passing through; ~ elevado flyover; prohibido el ~ no entry; ceda el ~ give way

pasota [pa'sota] (fam) adj, nm/f ≈ dropout; ser un (tipo) ~ to be a bit of a dropout; (ser indiferente) not to care about anything

pasta ['pasta] nf paste; (CULIN: masa) dough; (: de bizcochos etc) pastry; (fam) dough; ~s nfpl (bizcochos) pastries, small cakes; (fideos, espaguetis etc) pasta; ~ de dientes o dentífrica toothpaste

pastar [pas'tar] vt, vi to graze

pastel [pas'tel] nm (dulce) cake; (ARTE) pastel; ~ de carne meat pie; ~ería nf cake shop

pasteurizado, a [pasteuri'θaðo, a] adj pasteurized

pastilla [pas'tiʎa] nf (de jabón, chocolate) bar; (píldora) tablet, pill

pasto ['pasto] nm (hierba) grass; (lugar) pasture, field

pastor, a [pas'tor, a] nm/f shepherd/ess ♦ nm (REL) clergyman, pastor; ~ alemán Alsatian

pata ['pata] nf (pierna) leg; (pie) foot; (de muebles) leg; ~s arriba upside down; metedura de ~ (fam) gaffe; meter la ~ (fam) to put one's foot in it; (TEC): ~ de cabra crowbar; tener buena/mala ~ to be lucky/ unlucky; ~da nf kick; (en el suelo) stamp

patalear [patale'ar] vi (en el suelo) to stamp one's feet

patata [pa'tata] nf potato; ~s fritas chips, French fries; (de bolsa) crisps

paté [pa'te] nm pâté

patear [pate'ar] vt (pisar) to stamp on, trample (on); (pegar con el pie) to kick ♦ vi to stamp (with rage), stamp one's feet

patentar [paten'tar] vt to patent

patente [pa'tente] adj obvious, evident; (COM) patent ♦ nf patent

paternal [pater'nal] adj fatherly, paternal; **paterno, a** adj paternal

patético, a [pa'tetiko, a] adj pathetic, moving

patilla [pa'tiʎa] nf (de gafas) side(piece); ~s nfpl sideburns

patín [pa'tin] nm skate; (de trineo) runner; **patinaje** nm skating; **patinar** vi to skate; (resbalarse) to skid, slip; (fam) to slip up, blunder

patio ['patjo] nm (de casa) patio, courtyard; ~ de recreo playground

pato ['pato] nm duck; pagar el ~ (fam) to take the blame, carry the can

patológico, a [pato'loxiko, a] adj pathological

patoso, a [pa'toso, a] (fam) adj clumsy

patraña [pa'traɲa] *nf* story, fib

patria ['patrja] *nf* native land, mother country

patrimonio [patri'monjo] *nm* inheritance; (*fig*) heritage

patriota [pa'trjota] *nm/f* patriot; **patriotismo** *nm* patriotism

patrocinar [patroθi'nar] *vt* to sponsor; **patrocinio** *nm* sponsorship

patrón, ona [pa'tron, ona] *nm/f* (*jefe*) boss, chief, master/mistress; (*propietario*) landlord/lady; (*REL*) patron saint ♦ *nm* (*TEC, COSTURA*) pattern

patronal [patro'nal] *adj:* **la clase ~** management

patronato [patro'nato] *nm* sponsorship; (*acto*) patronage; (*fundación benéfica*) trust, foundation

patrulla [pa'truʎa] *nf* patrol

pausa ['pausa] *nf* pause, break

pausado, a [pau'saðo, a] *adj* slow, deliberate

pauta ['pauta] *nf* line, guide line

pavimento [paβi'mento] *nm* (*con losas*) pavement, paving

pavo ['paβo] *nm* turkey; **~ real** peacock

pavor [pa'βor] *nm* dread, terror

payaso, a [pa'jaso, a] *nm/f* clown

payo, a ['pajo, a] *nm/f* non-gipsy

paz [paθ] *nf* peace; (*tranquilidad*) peacefulness, tranquillity; **hacer las paces** to make peace; (*fig*) to make up

pazo ['paθo] *nm* country house

P.D. *abr* (= *posdata*) P.S., p.s.

peaje [pe'axe] *nm* toll

peatón [pea'ton] *nm* pedestrian

peca ['peka] *nf* freckle

pecado [pe'kaðo] *nm* sin; **pecador, a** *adj* sinful ♦ *nm/f* sinner

pecaminoso, a [pekami'noso, a] *adj* sinful

pecar [pe'kar] *vi* (*REL*) to sin; **peca de generoso** he is generous to a fault

pecera [pe'θera] *nf* fish tank; (*redondo*) goldfish bowl

pecho ['petʃo] *nm* (*ANAT*) chest; (*de mujer*) breast; **dar el ~ a** to breast-feed; **tomar algo a ~** to take sth to heart

pechuga [pe'tʃuxa] *nf* breast

peculiar [peku'ljar] *adj* special, peculiar; (*característico*) typical, characteristic; **~idad** *nf* peculiarity; special feature, characteristic

pedal [pe'ðal] *nm* pedal; **~ear** *vi* to pedal

pedante [pe'ðante] *adj* pedantic ♦ *nm/f* pedant; **~ría** *nf* pedantry

pedazo [pe'ðaθo] *nm* piece, bit; **hacerse ~s** to smash, shatter

pedernal [peðer'nal] *nm* flint

pediatra [pe'ðjatra] *nm/f* paediatrician

pedido [pe'ðiðo] *nm* (*COM*) order; (*petición*) request

pedir [pe'ðir] *vt* to ask for, request; (*comida,*

COM: mandar) to order; (*necesitar*) to need, demand, require ♦ *vi* to ask; **me pidió que cerrara la puerta** he asked me to shut the door; **¿cuánto piden por el coche?** how much are they asking for the car?

pedo ['peðo] (*fam!*) *nm* fart

pega ['peɣa] *nf* snag; **poner ~s (a)** to complain (about)

pegadizo, a [peɣa'ðiθo, a] *adj* (*MUS*) catchy

pegajoso, a [peɣa'xoso, a] *adj* sticky, adhesive

pegamento [peɣa'mento] *nm* gum, glue

pegar [pe'ɣar] *vt* (*papel, sellos*) to stick (on); (*cartel*) to stick up; (*coser*) to sew (on); (*unir: partes*) to join, fix together; (*MED*) to give, infect with; (*dar: golpe*) to give, deal ♦ *vi* (*adherirse*) to stick, adhere; (*ir juntos: colores*) to match, go together; (*golpear*) to hit; (*quemar: el sol*) to strike hot, burn (*fig*); **~se** *vr* (*gen*) to stick; (*dos personas*) to hit each other, fight; (*fam*): **~ un grito** to let out a yell; **~ un salto** to jump (with fright); **~ en** to touch; **~se un tiro** to shoot o.s.

pegatina [peɣa'tina] *nf* sticker

pegote [pe'ɣote] (*fam*) *nm* eyesore, sight

peinado [pei'naðo] *nm* hairstyle

peinar [pei'nar] *vt* to comb; (*hacer estilo*) to style; **~se** *vr* to comb one's hair

peine ['peine] *nm* comb; **~ta** *nf* ornamental comb

p.ej. *abr* (= *por ejemplo*) e.g.

Pekín [pe'kin] *n* Pekin(g)

pelado, a [pe'laðo, a] *adj* (*fruta, patata etc*) peeled; (*cabeza*) shorn; (*campo, fig*) bare; (*fam: sin dinero*) broke

pelaje [pe'laxe] *nm* (*ZOOL*) fur, coat; (*fig*) appearance

pelar [pe'lar] *vt* (*fruta, patatas etc*) to peel; (*cortar el pelo a*) to cut the hair of; (*quitar la piel: animal*) to skin; **~se** *vr* (*la piel*) to peel off; **voy a ~me** I'm going to get my hair cut

peldaño [pel'daɲo] *nm* step

pelea [pe'lea] *nf* (*lucha*) fight; (*discusión*) quarrel, row

peleado, a [pele'aðo, a] *adj:* **estar ~ (con uno)** to have fallen out (with sb)

pelear [pele'ar] *vi* to fight; **~se** *vr* to fight; (*reñirse*) to fall out, quarrel

peletería [pelete'ria] *nf* furrier's, fur shop

pelícano [pe'likano] *nm* pelican

película [pe'likula] *nf* film; (*cobertura ligera*) thin covering; (*FOTO: rollo*) roll o reel of film

peligro [pe'liɣro] *nm* danger; (*riesgo*) risk; **correr ~ de** to run the risk of; **~so, a** *adj* dangerous; risky

pelirrojo, a [peli'rroxo, a] *adj* red-haired, red-headed ♦ *nm/f* redhead

pellejo [pe'ʎexo] *nm* (*de animal*) skin, hide

pellizcar [peʎiθ'kar] *vt* to pinch, nip

pelma ['pelma] (*fam*) *nm/f* pain (in the neck)

pelmazo [pel'maθo] (*fam*) *nm* = **pelma**

pelo ['pelo] *nm* (*cabellos*) hair; (*de barba, bigote*) whisker; (*de animal: pellejo*) hair, fur, coat; **al ~** just right; **venir al ~** to be exactly what one needs; **un hombre de ~ en pecho** a brave man; **por los ~s** by the skin of one's teeth; **no tener ~s en la lengua** to be outspoken, not mince words; **tomar el ~ a uno** to pull sb's leg

pelota [pe'lota] *nf* ball; **en ~** stark naked; **hacer la ~ (a uno)** (*fam*) to creep (to sb); **~ vasca** pelota

pelotari [pelo'tari] *nm* pelota player

pelotón [pelo'ton] *nm* (*MIL*) squad, detachment

peluca [pe'luka] *nf* wig

peluche [pe'lutʃe] *nm*: **oso/muñeco de ~** teddy bear/soft toy

peludo, a [pe'luðo, a] *adj* hairy, shaggy

peluquería [peluke'ria] *nf* hairdresser's; **peluquero, a** *nm/f* hairdresser

pelusa [pe'lusa] *nf* (*BOT*) down; (*en tela*) fluff

pena ['pena] *nf* (*congoja*) grief, sadness; (*remordimiento*) regret; (*dificultad*) trouble; (*dolor*) pain; (*JUR*) sentence; **merecer o valer la ~** to be worthwhile; **a duras ~s** with great difficulty; **~ de muerte** death penalty; **~ pecuniaria** fine; **¡qué ~!** what a shame!

penal [pe'nal] *adj* penal ♦ *nm* (*cárcel*) prison

penalidad [penali'ðað] *nf* (*problema, dificultad*) trouble, hardship; (*JUR*) penalty, punishment; **~es** *nfpl* trouble, hardship

penalti, penalty [pe'nalti] (*pl* **~s** o **~es**) *nm* penalty (kick)

pendiente [pen'djente] *adj* pending, unsettled ♦ *nm* earring ♦ *nf* hill, slope

pene ['pene] *nm* penis

penetración [penetra'θjon] *nf* (*acto*) penetration; (*agudeza*) sharpness, insight

penetrante [pene'trante] *adj* (*herida*) deep; (*persona, arma*) sharp; (*sonido*) penetrating, piercing; (*mirada*) searching; (*viento, ironía*) biting

penetrar [pene'trar] *vt* to penetrate, pierce; (*entender*) to grasp ♦ *vi* to penetrate, go in; (*entrar*) to enter, go in; (*líquido*) to soak in; (*fig*) to pierce

penicilina [peniθi'lina] *nf* penicillin

península [pe'ninsula] *nf* peninsula; **peninsular** *adj* peninsular

penique [pe'nike] *nm* penny

penitencia [peni'tenθja] *nf* penance

penoso, a [pe'noso, a] *adj* (*lamentable*) distressing; (*difícil*) arduous, difficult

pensador, a [pensa'ðor, a] *nm/f* thinker

pensamiento [pensa'mjento] *nm* thought; (*mente*) mind; (*idea*) idea

pensar [pen'sar] *vt* to think; (*considerar*) to

think over, think out; (*proponerse*) to intend, plan; (*imaginarse*) to think up, invent ♦ *vi* to think; **~ en** to aim at, aspire to; **pensativo, a** *adj* thoughtful, pensive

pensión [pen'sjon] *nf* (*casa*) boarding o guest house; (*dinero*) pension; (*cama y comida*) board and lodging, **~ completa** full board; **media ~** half-board; **pensionista** *nm/f* (*jubilado*) (old-age) pensioner; (*huésped*) lodger

penúltimo, a [pe'nultimo, a] *adj* penultimate, last but one

penumbra [pe'numbra] *nf* half-light

penuria [pe'nurja] *nf* shortage, want

peña ['peɲa] *nf* (*roca*) rock; (*cuesta*) cliff, crag; (*grupo*) group, circle; (*AM: club*) folk club

peñasco [pe'ɲasko] *nm* large rock, boulder

peñón [pe'ɲon] *nm* wall of rock; **el P~** the Rock (of Gibraltar)

peón [pe'on] *nm* labourer; (*AM*) farm labourer, farmhand; (*AJEDREZ*) pawn

peonza [pe'onθa] *nf* spinning top

peor [pe'or] *adj* (*comparativo*) worse; (*superlativo*) worst ♦ *adv* worse; worst; **de mal en ~** from bad to worse

pepinillo [pepi'niʎo] *nm* gherkin

pepino [pe'pino] *nm* cucumber; **(no) me importa un ~** I don't care one bit

pepita [pe'pita] *nf* (*BOT*) pip; (*MINERÍA*) nugget

pepito [pe'pito] *nm*: **~ (de ternera)** steak sandwich

pequeñez [peke'ɲeθ] *nf* smallness, littleness; (*trivialidad*) trifle, triviality

pequeño, a [pe'keɲo, a] *adj* small, little

pera ['pera] *nf* pear; **peral** *nm* pear tree

percance [per'kanθe] *nm* setback, misfortune

percatarse [perka'tarse] *vr*: **~ de** to notice, take note of

percebe [per'θeβe] *nm* barnacle

percepción [perθep'θjon] *nf* (*vista*) perception; (*idea*) notion, idea

percha ['pertʃa] *nf* (*coat*)hanger; (*ganchos*) coat hooks *pl*; (*de ave*) perch

percibir [perθi'βir] *vt* to perceive, notice; (*COM*) to earn, get

percusión [perku'sjon] *nf* percussion

perdedor, a [perðe'ðor, a] *adj* losing ♦ *nm/f* loser

perder [per'ðer] *vt* to lose; (*tiempo, palabras*) to waste; (*oportunidad*) to lose, miss; (*tren*) to miss ♦ *vi* to lose; **~se** *vr* (*extraviarse*) to get lost; (*desaparecer*) to disappear, be lost to view; (*arruinarse*) to be ruined; **echar a ~** (*comida*) to spoil, ruin; (*oportunidad*) to waste

perdición [perði'θjon] *nf* perdition, ruin

pérdida ['perðiða] *nf* loss; (*de tiempo*) waste;

~s *nfpl* (*COM*) losses

perdido, a [per'ðiðo, a] *adj* lost

perdiz [per'ðiθ] *nf* partridge

perdón [per'ðon] *nm* (*disculpa*) pardon, forgiveness; (*clemencia*) mercy; ¡~! sorry!, I beg your pardon!; **perdonar** *vt* to pardon, forgive; (*la vida*) to spare; (*excusar*) to exempt, excuse; ¡perdone (usted)! sorry!, I beg your pardon!

perdurar [perðu'rar] *vi* (*resistir*) to last, endure; (*seguir existiendo*) to stand, still exist

perecedero, a [pereθe'ðero, a] *adj* perishable

perecer [pere'θer] *vi* to perish, die

peregrinación [pereɣrina'θjon] *nf* (*REL*) pilgrimage

peregrino, a [pere'ɣrino, a] *adj* (*idea*) strange, absurd ♦ *nm/f* pilgrim

perejil [pere'xil] *nm* parsley

perenne [pe'renne] *adj* everlasting, perennial

pereza [pe'reθa] *nf* laziness, idleness; **perezoso, a** *adj* lazy, idle

perfección [perfek'θjon] *nf* perfection; **perfeccionar** *vt* to perfect; (*mejorar*) to improve; (*acabar*) to complete, finish

perfectamente [perfekta'mente] *adv* perfectly

perfecto, a [per'fekto, a] *adj* perfect; (*total*) complete

perfil [per'fil] *nm* profile; (*contorno*) silhouette, outline; (*ARQ*) (cross) section; **~es** *nmpl* features; **~ar** *vt* (*trazar*) to outline; (*fig*) to shape, give character to

perforación [perfora'θjon] *nf* perforation; (*con taladro*) drilling; **perforadora** *nf* punch

perforar [perfo'rar] *vt* to perforate; (*agujero*) to drill, bore; (*papel*) to punch a hole in ♦ *vi* to drill, bore

perfume [per'fume] *nm* perfume, scent

pericia [pe'riθja] *nf* skill, expertise

periferia [peri'ferja] *nf* periphery; (*de ciudad*) outskirts *pl*

periférico [peri'feriko] (*AM*) *nm* ring road (*BRIT*), beltway (*US*)

perímetro [pe'rimetro] *nm* perimeter

periódico, a [pe'rjoðiko, a] *adj* periodic(al) ♦ *nm* newspaper

periodismo [perjo'ðismo] *nm* journalism; **periodista** *nm/f* journalist

periodo [pe'rjoðo] *nm* period

período [pe'rioðo] *nm* = **periodo**

periquito [peri'kito] *nm* budgerigar, budgie

perito, a [pe'rito, a] *adj* (*experto*) expert; (*diestro*) skilled, skilful ♦ *nm/f* expert; skilled worker; (*técnico*) technician

perjudicar [perxuði'kar] *vt* (*gen*) to damage, harm; **perjudicial** *adj* damaging, harmful; (*en detrimento*) detrimental; **perjuicio** *nm* damage, harm

perjurar [perxu'rar] *vi* to commit perjury

perla ['perla] *nf* pearl; **me viene de ~s** it suits me fine

permanecer [permane'θer] *vi* (*quedarse*) to stay, remain; (*seguir*) to continue to be

permanencia [perma'nenθja] *nf* permanence; (*estancia*) stay

permanente [perma'nente] *adj* permanent, constant ♦ *nf* perm

permiso [per'miso] *nm* permission; (*licencia*) permit, licence; **con ~** excuse me; **estar de ~** (*MIL*) to be on leave; **~ de conducir** driving licence (*BRIT*), driver's license (*US*)

permitir [permi'tir] *vt* to permit, allow

pernera [per'nera] *nf* trouser leg

pernicioso, a [perni'θjoso, a] *adj* pernicious

pero ['pero] *conj* but; (*aún*) yet ♦ *nm* (*defecto*) flaw, defect; (*reparo*) objection

perpendicular [perpendiku'lar] *adj* perpendicular

perpetrar [perpe'trar] *vt* to perpetrate

perpetuar [perpe'twar] *vt* to perpetuate; **perpetuo, a** *adj* perpetual

perplejo, a [per'plexo, a] *adj* perplexed, bewildered

perra ['perra] *nf* (*ZOOL*) bitch; **estar sin una ~** to be flat broke

perrera [pe'rrera] *nf* kennel

perrito [pe'rrito] *nm*: **~ caliente** hot dog

perro ['perro] *nm* dog

persa ['persa] *adj*, *nm/f* Persian

persecución [perseku'θjon] *nf* pursuit, chase; (*REL, POL*) persecution

perseguir [perse'ɣir] *vt* to pursue, hunt; (*cortejar*) to chase after; (*molestar*) to pester, annoy; (*REL, POL*) to persecute

perseverante [perseße'rante] *adj* persevering, persistent

perseverar [perseße'rar] *vi* to persevere, persist

persiana [per'sjana] *nf* (Venetian) blind

persignarse [persiɣ'narse] *vr* to cross o.s.

persistente [persis'tente] *adj* persistent

persistir [persis'tir] *vi* to persist

persona [per'sona] *nf* person; **~ mayor** elderly person

personaje [perso'naxe] *nm* important person, celebrity; (*TEATRO etc*) character

personal [perso'nal] *adj* (*particular*) personal; (*para una persona*) single, for one person ♦ *nm* personnel, staff; **~idad** *nf* personality

personarse [perso'narse] *vr* to appear in person

personificar [personifi'kar] *vt* to personify

perspectiva [perspek'tißa] *nf* perspective; (*vista, panorama*) view, panorama; (*posibilidad futura*) outlook, prospect

perspicacia [perspi'kaθja] *nf* discernment, perspicacity

perspicaz [perspi'kaθ] *adj* shrewd
persuadir [perswa'ðir] *vt (gen)* to persuade; *(convencer)* to convince; **~se** *vr* to become convinced; **persuasión** *nf* persuasion; **persuasivo, a** *adj* persuasive; convincing
pertenecer [pertene'θer] *vi* to belong; *(fig)* to concern; **perteneciente** *adj*: **perteneciente a** belonging to; **pertenencia** *nf* ownership; **pertenencias** *nfpl (bienes)* possessions, property *sg*
pertenezca *etc vb ver* **pertenecer**
pértiga ['pertiɣa] *nf*: **salto de ~** pole vault
pertinente [perti'nente] *adj* relevant, pertinent; *(apropiado)* appropriate; **~ a** concerning, relevant to
perturbación [perturßa'θjon] *nf (POL)* disturbance; *(MED)* upset, disturbance
perturbado, a [pertur'ßaðo, a] *adj* mentally unbalanced
perturbar [pertur'ßar] *vt (el orden)* to disturb; *(MED)* to upset, disturb; *(mentalmente)* to perturb
Perú [pe'ru] *nm*: **el ~** Peru; **peruano, a** *adj, nm/f* Peruvian
perversión [perßer'sjon] *nf* perversion; **perverso, a** *adj* perverse; *(depravado)* depraved
pervertido, a [perßer'tiðo, a] *adj* perverted ♦ *nm/f* pervert
pervertir [perßer'tir] *vt* to pervert, corrupt
pesa ['pesa] *nf* weight; *(DEPORTE)* shot
pesadez [pesa'ðeθ] *nf (peso)* heaviness; *(lentitud)* slowness; *(aburrimiento)* tediousness
pesadilla [pesa'ðiʎa] *nf* nightmare, bad dream
pesado, a [pe'saðo, a] *adj* heavy; *(lento)* slow; *(difícil, duro)* tough, hard; *(aburrido)* boring, tedious; *(tiempo)* sultry
pésame ['pesame] *nm* expression of condolence, message of sympathy; **dar el ~** to express one's condolences
pesar [pe'sar] *vt* to weigh ♦ *vi* to weigh; *(ser pesado)* to weigh a lot, be heavy; *(fig: opinión)* to carry weight; **no pesa mucho** it is not very heavy ♦ *nm (arrepentimiento)* regret; *(pena)* grief, sorrow; **a ~ de** o **pese a (que)** in spite of, despite
pesca ['peska] *nf (acto)* fishing; *(lo pescado)* catch; **ir de ~** to go fishing
pescadería [peskaðe'ria] *nf* fish shop, fishmonger's *(BRIT)*
pescadilla [peska'ðiʎa] *nf* whiting
pescado [pes'kaðo] *nm* fish
pescador, a [peska'ðor, a] *nm/f* fisherman/woman
pescar [pes'kar] *vt (tomar)* to catch; *(intentar tomar)* to fish for; *(conseguir: trabajo)* to manage to get ♦ *vi* to fish, go fishing

pescuezo [pes'kweθo] *nm* neck
pesebre [pe'seßre] *nm* manger
peseta [pe'seta] *nf* peseta
pesimista [pesi'mista] *adj* pessimistic ♦ *nm/f* pessimist
pésimo, a ['pesimo, a] *adj* awful, dreadful
peso ['peso] *nm* weight; *(balanza)* scales *pl*; *(moneda)* peso; **~ bruto/neto** gross/net weight; **vender al ~** to sell by weight
pesquero, a [pes'kero, a] *adj* fishing *cpd*
pesquisa [pes'kisa] *nf* inquiry, investigation
pestaña [pes'taɲa] *nf (ANAT)* eyelash; *(borde)* rim; **pestañear** *vi* to blink
peste ['peste] *nf* plague; *(mal olor)* stink, stench
pesticida [pesti'θiða] *nm* pesticide
pestillo [pes'tiʎo] *nm (cerrojo)* bolt; *(picaporte)* doorhandle
petaca [pe'taka] *nf (de cigarros)* cigarette case; *(de pipa)* tobacco pouch; *(AM: maleta)* suitcase
pétalo ['petalo] *nm* petal
petardo [pe'tardo] *nm* firework, firecracker
petición [peti'θjon] *nf (pedido)* request, plea; *(memorial)* petition; *(JUR)* plea
petrificar [petrifi'kar] *vt* to petrify
petróleo [pe'troleo] *nm* oil, petroleum; **petrolero, a** *adj* petroleum *cpd* ♦ *nm* (oil) tanker
peyorativo, a [pejora'tißo, a] *adj* pejorative
pez [peθ] *nm* fish
pezón [pe'θon] *nm* teat, nipple
pezuña [pe'θuɲa] *nf* hoof
piadoso, a [pja'ðoso, a] *adj (devoto)* pious, devout; *(misericordioso)* kind, merciful
pianista [pja'nista] *nm/f* pianist
piano ['pjano] *nm* piano
piar [pjar] *vi* to cheep
pibe, a ['piße, a] *(AM) nm/f* boy/girl
picadero [pika'ðero] *nm* riding school
picadillo [pika'ðiʎo] *nm* mince, minced meat
picado, a [pi'kaðo, a] *adj* pricked, punctured; *(CULIN)* minced, chopped; *(mar)* choppy; *(diente)* bad; *(tabaco)* cut; *(enfadado)* cross
picador [pika'ðor] *nm (TAUR)* picador; *(minero)* faceworker
picadura [pika'ðura] *nf (pinchazo)* puncture; *(de abeja)* sting; *(de mosquito)* bite; *(tabaco picado)* cut tobacco
picante [pi'kante] *adj* hot; *(comentario)* racy, spicy
picaporte [pika'porte] *nm (manija)* doorhandle; *(pestillo)* latch
picar [pi'kar] *vt (agujerear, perforar)* to prick, puncture; *(abeja)* to sting; *(mosquito, serpiente)* to bite; *(CULIN)* to mince, chop; *(incitar)* to incite, goad; *(dañar, irritar)* to annoy, bother; *(quemar: lengua)* to burn,

sting ♦ vi (pez) to bite, take the bait; (sol) to burn, scorch; (abeja, MED) to sting; (mosquito) to bite; **~se** vr (agriarse) to turn sour, go off; (ofenderse) to take offence

picardía [pikar'ðia] nf villainy; (astucia) slyness, craftiness; (una ~) dirty trick; (palabra) rude/bad word o expression

pícaro, a ['pikaro, a] adj (malicioso) villainous; (travieso) mischievous ♦ nm (astuto) crafty sort; (sinvergüenza) rascal, scoundrel

pichón [pi'tʃon] nm young pigeon

pico ['piko] nm (de ave) beak; (punta) sharp point; (TEC) pick, pickaxe; (GEO) peak, summit; **y ~** and a bit

picor [pi'kor] nm itch

picotear [pikote'ar] vt to peck ♦ vi to nibble, pick

picudo, a [pi'kuðo, a] adj pointed, with a point

pidió etc vb ver **pedir**

pido etc vb ver **pedir**

pie [pje] (pl **~s**) nm foot; (fig: motivo) motive, basis; (: fundamento) foothold; **ir a ~** to go on foot, walk; **estar de ~** to be standing (up); **ponerse de ~** to stand up; **de ~s a cabeza** from top to bottom; **al ~ de la letra** (citar) literally, verbatim; (copiar) exactly, word for word; **en ~ de guerra** on a war footing; **dar ~ a** to give cause for; **hacer ~** (en el agua) to touch (the) bottom

piedad [pje'ðað] nf (lástima) pity, compassion; (clemencia) mercy; (devoción) piety, devotion

piedra ['pjeðra] nf stone; (roca) rock; (de mechero) flint; (METEOROLOGÍA) hailstone

piel [pjel] nf (ANAT) skin; (ZOOL) skin, hide, fur; (cuero) leather; (BOT) skin, peel

pienso etc vb ver **pensar**

pierdo etc vb ver **perder**

pierna ['pjerna] nf leg

pieza ['pjeθa] nf piece; (habitación) room; **~ de recambio** o **repuesto** spare (part)

pigmeo, a [piɣ'meo, a] adj, nm/f pigmy

pijama [pi'xama] nm pyjamas pl

pila ['pila] nf (ELEC) battery; (montón) heap, pile; (lavabo) sink

píldora ['pildora] nf pill; **la ~ (anticonceptiva)** the (contraceptive) pill

pileta [pi'leta] nf basin, bowl; (AM) swimming pool

pillaje [pi'ʎaxe] nm pillage, plunder

pillar [pi'ʎar] vt (saquear) to pillage, plunder; (fam: coger) to catch; (: agarrar) to grasp, seize; (: entender) to grasp, catch on to; **~se** vr: **~se un dedo con la puerta** to catch one's finger in the door

pillo, a ['piʎo, a] adj villainous; (astuto) sly, crafty ♦ nm/f rascal, rogue, scoundrel

piloto [pi'loto] nm pilot; (de aparato) (pilot) light; (AUTO: luz) tail o rear light; (: conductor) driver

pimentón [pimen'ton] nm paprika

pimienta [pi'mjenta] nf pepper

pimiento [pi'mjento] nm pepper, pimiento

pin [pin] (pl **pins**) nm badge

pinacoteca [pinako'teka] nf art gallery

pinar [pi'nar] nm pine forest (BRIT), pine grove (US)

pincel [pin'θel] nm paintbrush

pinchadiscos [pintʃa'ðiskos] nm/f inv disc-jockey, DJ

pinchar [pin'tʃar] vt (perforar) to prick, pierce; (neumático) to puncture; (fig) to prod

pinchazo [pin'tʃaθo] nm (perforación) prick; (de neumático) puncture; (fig) prod

pincho ['pintʃo] nm savoury (snack); **~ moruno** shish kebab; **~ de tortilla** small slice of omelette

ping-pong ['pin'pon] nm table tennis

pingüino [pin'gwino] nm penguin

pino ['pino] nm pine (tree)

pinta ['pinta] nf spot; (de líquidos) spot, drop; (aspecto) appearance, look(s) (pl); **~do, a** adj spotted; (de colores) colourful; **~das** nfpl graffiti sg

pintar [pin'tar] vt to paint ♦ vi to paint; (fam) to count, be important; **~se** vr to put on make-up

pintor, a [pin'tor, a] nm/f painter

pintoresco, a [pinto'resko, a] adj picturesque

pintura [pin'tura] nf painting; **~ a la acuarela** watercolour; **~ al óleo** oil painting

pinza ['pinθa] nf (ZOOL) claw; (para colgar ropa) clothes peg; (TEC) pincers pl; **~s** nfpl (para depilar etc) tweezers pl

piña ['piɲa] nf (fruto del pino) pine cone; (fruta) pineapple; (fig) group

piñón [pi'ɲon] nm (fruto) pine nut; (TEC) pinion

pío, a ['pio, a] adj (devoto) pious, devout; (misericordioso) merciful

piojo ['pjoxo] nm louse

pionero, a [pjo'nero, a] adj pioneering ♦ nm/f pioneer

pipa ['pipa] nf pipe; **~s** nfpl (BOT) (edible) sunflower seeds

pipí [pi'pi] (fam) nm: **hacer ~** to have a wee(-wee) (BRIT), have to go (wee-wee) (US)

pique ['pike] nm (resentimiento) pique, resentment; (rivalidad) rivalry, competition; **irse a ~** to sink; (esperanza, familia) to be ruined

piqueta [pi'keta] nf pick(axe)

piquete [pi'kete] nm (MIL) squad, party; (de obreros) picket

pirado, a [pi'raðo, a] (fam) adj round the

bend ♦ nm/f nutter

piragua [pi'raɣwa] nf canoe; **piragüismo** nm canoeing

pirámide [pi'ramiðe] nf pyramid

pirata [pi'rata] adj, nm pirate ♦ nm/f: **~ informático/a** hacker

Pirineo(s) [piri'neo(s)] nm(pl) Pyrenees pl

pirómano, a [pi'romano, a] nm/f (MED, JUR) arsonist

piropo [pi'ropo] nm compliment, (piece of) flattery

pirueta [pi'rweta] nf pirouette

pis [pis] (fam) nm pee, piss; **hacer ~** to have a pee; (para niños) to wee-wee

pisada [pi'saða] nf (paso) footstep; (huella) footprint

pisar [pi'sar] vt (caminar sobre) to walk on, tread on; (apretar con el pie) to press; (fig) to trample on, walk all over ♦ vi to tread, step, walk

piscina [pis'θina] nf swimming pool

Piscis ['pisθis] nm Pisces

piso ['piso] nm (suelo, planta) floor; (apartamento) flat, apartment; **primer ~** (ESP) first floor; (AM) ground floor

pisotear [pisote'ar] vt to trample (on o underfoot)

pista ['pista] nf track, trail; (indicio) clue; **~ de aterrizaje** runway; **~ de baile** dance floor; **~ de hielo** ice rink; **~ de tenis** tennis court

pistola [pis'tola] nf pistol; (TEC) spray-gun; **pistolero, a** nm/f gunman/woman, gangster

pistón [pis'ton] nm (TEC) piston; (MUS) key

pitar [pi'tar] vt (silbato) to blow; (rechiflar) to whistle at, boo ♦ vi to whistle; (AUTO) to sound o toot one's horn; (AM) to smoke

pitillo [pi'tiʎo] nm cigarette

pito ['pito] nm whistle; (de coche) horn

pitón [pi'ton] nm (ZOOL) python

pitonisa [pito'nisa] nf fortune-teller

pitorreo [pito'rreo] nm joke; **estar de ~** to be joking

pizarra [pi'θarra] nf (piedra) slate; (encerado) blackboard

pizca ['piθka] nf pinch, spot; (fig) spot, speck; **ni ~** not a bit

placa ['plaka] nf plate; (distintivo) badge, insignia; **~ de matrícula** number plate

placentero, a [plaθen'tero, a] adj pleasant, agreeable

placer [pla'θer] nm pleasure ♦ vt to please

plácido, a ['plaθiðo, a] adj placid

plaga ['plaɣa] nf pest; (MED) plague; (abundancia) abundance; **plagar** vt to infest, plague; (llenar) to fill

plagio ['plaxjo] nm plagiarism

plan [plan] nm (esquema, proyecto) plan; (idea, intento) idea, intention; **tener ~** (fam) to have a date; **tener un ~** (fam) to have an

affair; **en ~ económico** (fam) on the cheap; **vamos en ~ de turismo** we're going as tourists; **si te pones en ese ~** ... if that's your attitude ...

plana ['plana] nf sheet (of paper), page; (TEC) trowel; **en primera ~** on the front page; **~ mayor** staff

plancha ['plantʃa] nf (para planchar) iron, (rótulo) plate, sheet; (NAUT) gangway; **a la ~** (CULIN) grilled; **~do** nm ironing; **planchar** vt to iron ♦ vi to do the ironing

planeador [planea'ðor] nm glider

planear [plane'ar] vt to plan ♦ vi to glide

planeta [pla'neta] nm planet

planicie [pla'niθje] nf plain

planificación [planifika'θjon] nf planning; **~ familiar** family planning

plano, a ['plano, a] adj flat, level, even ♦ nm (MAT, TEC) plane; (FOTO) shot; (ARQ) plan; (GEO) map; (de ciudad) map, street plan; **primer ~** close-up; **caer de ~** to fall flat

planta ['planta] nf (BOT, TEC) plant; (ANAT) sole of the foot, foot; (piso) floor; (AM: personal) staff; **~ baja** ground floor

plantación [planta'θjon] nf (AGR) plantation; (acto) planting

plantar [plan'tar] vt (BOT) to plant; (levantar) to erect, set up; **~se** vr to stand firm; **~ a uno en la calle** to throw sb out; **dejar plantado a uno** (fam) to stand sb up

plantear [plante'ar] vt (problema) to pose; (dificultad) to raise

plantilla [plan'tiʎa] nf (de zapato) insole; (personal) personnel; **ser de ~** to be on the staff

plantón [plan'ton] nm (MIL) guard, sentry; (fam) long wait; **dar (un) ~ a uno** to stand sb up

plasmar [plas'mar] vt (dar forma) to mould, shape; (representar) to represent; **~se** vr: **~se en** to take the form of

plasta ['plasta] (fam) adj inv boring ♦ nm/f bore

plástico, a ['plastiko, a] adj plastic ♦ nm plastic

Plastilina ® [plasti'lina] nf Plasticine ®

plata ['plata] nf (metal) silver; (cosas hechas de ~) silverware; (AM) cash, dough; **hablar en ~** to speak bluntly o frankly

plataforma [plata'forma] nf platform; **~ de lanzamiento/perforación** launch(ing) pad/ drilling rig

plátano ['platano] nm (fruta) banana; (árbol) plane tree; banana tree

platea [pla'tea] nf (TEATRO) pit

plateado, a [plate'aðo, a] adj silver; (TEC) silver-plated

plática ['platika] nf talk, chat; **platicar** vi to talk, chat

platillo [pla'tiʎo] nm saucer; **~s** nmpl (MUS) cymbals; **~ volador** o **volante** flying saucer
platino [pla'tino] nm platinum; **~s** nmpl (AUTO) contact points
plato ['plato] nm plate, dish; (parte de comida) course; (comida) dish; **~ combinado** set main course (served on one plate); **~ fuerte** main course; **primer ~** first course
playa ['plaja] nf beach; (costa) seaside; **~ de estacionamiento** (AM) car park
playera [pla'jera] nf (AM: camiseta) T-shirt; **~s** nfpl (zapatos) canvas shoes
plaza ['plaθa] nf square; (mercado) market(place); (sitio) room, space; (en vehículo) seat, place; (colocación) post, job; **~ de toros** bullring
plazo ['plaθo] nm (lapso de tiempo) time, period; (fecha de vencimiento) expiry date; (pago parcial) instalment; **a corto/largo ~** short-/long-term; **comprar algo a ~s** to buy sth on hire purchase (BRIT) o on time (US)
plazoleta [plaθo'leta] nf small square
pleamar [plea'mar] nf high tide
plebe ['pleβe] nf: **la ~** the common people pl, the masses pl; (pey) the plebs pl; **~yo, a** adj plebeian; (pey) coarse, common
plebiscito [pleβis'θito] nm plebiscite
plegable [ple'vaβle] adj collapsible; (silla) folding
plegar [ple'var] vt (doblar) to fold, bend; (COSTURA) to pleat; **~se** vr to yield, submit
pleito ['pleito] nm (JUR) lawsuit, case; (fig) dispute, feud
plenilunio [pleni'lunjo] nm full moon
plenitud [pleni'tuð] nf plenitude, fullness; (abundancia) abundance
pleno, a ['pleno, a] adj full; (completo) complete ♦ nm plenum; **en ~ día** in broad daylight; **en ~ verano** at the height of summer; **en plena cara** full in the face
pliego etc ['pljexo] vb ver **plegar** ♦ nm (hoja) sheet (of paper); (carta) sealed letter/ document; **~ de condiciones** details pl, specifications pl
pliegue etc ['pljexe] vb ver **plegar** ♦ nm fold, crease; (de vestido) pleat
plomero [plo'mero] nm (AM) plumber
plomo ['plomo] nm (metal) lead; (ELEC) fuse; **sin ~** unleaded
pluma ['pluma] nf feather; (para escribir): **~ (estilográfica)** ink pen; **~ fuente** (AM) fountain pen
plumero [plu'mero] nm (para el polvo) feather duster
plumón [plu'mon] nm (de ave) down; (AM: fino) felt-tip pen; (: ancho) marker
plural [plu'ral] adj plural; **~idad** nf plurality
pluriempleo [pluriem'pleo] nm having more than one job

plus [plus] nm bonus; **~valía** nf (COM) appreciation
población [poβla'θjon] nf population; (pueblo, ciudad) town, city
poblado, a [po'βlaðo, a] adj inhabited ♦ nm (aldea) village; (pueblo) (small) town; **densamente ~** densely populated
poblador, a [poβla'ðor, a] nm/f settler, colonist
poblar [po'βlar] vt (colonizar) to colonize; (fundar) to found; (habitar) to inhabit
pobre ['poβre] adj poor ♦ nm/f poor person; **~za** nf poverty
pocilga [po'θilxa] nf pigsty
pócima ['poθima] nf = **poción**

PALABRA CLAVE
---

poco, a ['poko, a] adj **1** (sg) little, not much; **~ tiempo** little o not much time; **de ~ interés** of little interest, not very interesting; **poca cosa** not much
2 (pl) few, not many; **unos ~s** a few, some; **~s niños comen lo que les conviene** few children eat what they should
♦ adv **1** little, not much; **cuesta ~** it doesn't cost much
2 (+ adj: = negativo, antónimo): **~ amable/ inteligente** not very nice/intelligent
3: **por ~ me caigo** I almost fell
4: **a ~: a ~ de haberse casado** shortly after getting married
5: **~ a ~** little by little
♦ nm a little, a bit; **un ~ triste/de dinero** a little sad/money

---

podar [po'ðar] vt to prune

PALABRA CLAVE
---

poder [po'ðer] vi **1** (capacidad) can, be able to; **no puedo hacerlo** I can't do it, I'm unable to do it
2 (permiso) can, may, be allowed to; **¿se puede?** may I (o we)?; **puedes irte ahora** you may go now; **no se puede fumar en este hospital** smoking is not allowed in this hospital
3 (posibilidad) may, might, could; **puede llegar mañana** he may o might arrive tomorrow; **pudiste haberte hecho daño** you might o could have hurt yourself; **¡podías habérmelo dicho antes!** you might have told me before!
4: **puede ser: puede ser** perhaps; **puede ser que lo sepa Tomás** Tomás may o might know
5: **¡no puedo más!** I've had enough!; **no pude menos que dejarlo** I couldn't help but leave it; **es tonto a más no ~** he's as stupid as they come
6: **~ con: no puedo con este crío** this kid's too

much for me
♦ nm power; ~ **adquisitivo** purchasing
power; **detentar** o **ocupar** o **estar en el ~** to be
in power

poderoso, a [poðeˈroso, a] adj (político, país)
powerful
podio [ˈpoðjo] nm (DEPORTE) podium
podium [ˈpoðjum] = **podio**
podrido, a [poˈðriðo, a] adj rotten, bad;
(fig) rotten, corrupt
podrir [poˈðrir] = **pudrir**
poema [poˈema] nm poem
poesía [poeˈsia] nf poetry
poeta [poˈeta] nm/f poet; **poético, a** adj
poetic(al)
poetisa [poeˈtisa] nf (woman) poet
póker [ˈpoker] nm poker
polaco, a [poˈlako, a] adj Polish ♦ nm/f
Pole
polar [poˈlar] adj polar; **~idad** nf polarity;
~izarse vr to polarize
polea [poˈlea] nf pulley
polémica [poˈlemika] nf polemics sg; (una ~)
controversy, polemic
polen [ˈpolen] nm pollen
policía [poliˈθia] nm/f policeman/woman
♦ nf police; **~co, a** adj police cpd; **novela
policíaca** detective story; **policial** adj police
cpd
polideportivo [poliðeporˈtiβo] nm sports
centre o complex
poligamia [poliˈɣamja] nf polygamy
polígono [poˈliɣono] nm (MAT) polygon;
~ industrial industrial estate
polilla [poˈliʎa] nf moth
polio [ˈpoljo] nf polio
política [poˈlitika] nf politics sg; (económica,
agraria etc) policy; ver tb **político**
político, a [poˈlitiko, a] adj political;
(discreto) tactful; (de familia) -in-law ♦ nm/f
politician; **padre ~** father-in-law
póliza [ˈpoliθa] nf certificate, voucher;
(impuesto) tax stamp; **~ de seguros** insurance
policy
polizón [poliˈθon] nm stowaway
pollera [poˈʎera] nf (AM) skirt
pollería [poʎeˈria] nf poulterer's (shop)
pollo [ˈpoʎo] nm chicken
polo [ˈpolo] nm (GEO, ELEC) pole; (helado) ice
lolly; (DEPORTE) polo; (suéter) polo-neck;
~ Norte/Sur North/South Pole
Polonia [poˈlonja] nf Poland
poltrona [polˈtrona] nf easy chair
polución [poluˈθjon] nf pollution
polvera [polˈβera] nf powder compact
polvo [ˈpolβo] nm dust; (QUÍM, CULIN, MED)
powder; **~s** nmpl (maquillaje) powder sg;
quitar el ~ to dust; **~ de talco** talcum powder;

estar hecho ~ (fam) to be worn out o
exhausted
pólvora [ˈpolβora] nf gunpowder; (fuegos
artificiales) fireworks pl
polvoriento, a [polβoˈrjento, a] adj
(superficie) dusty; (sustancia) powdery
pomada [poˈmaða] nf cream, ointment
pomelo [poˈmelo] nm grapefruit
pómez [ˈpomeθ] nf: **piedra ~** pumice stone
pomo [ˈpomo] nm doorknob
pompa [ˈpompa] nf (burbuja) bubble;
(bomba) pump; (esplendor) pomp,
splendour; **pomposo, a** adj splendid,
magnificent; (pey) pompous
pómulo [ˈpomulo] nm cheekbone
pon [pon] vb ver **poner**
ponche [ˈpontʃe] nm punch
poncho [ˈpontʃo] nm poncho
ponderar [pondeˈrar] vt (considerar) to
weigh up, consider; (elogiar) to praise highly,
speak in praise of
pondré etc vb ver **poner**

╔══════════════════════╗
║ **PALABRA CLAVE** ║
╚══════════════════════╝

poner [poˈner] vt 1 (colocar) to put;
(telegrama) to send; (obra de teatro) to put
on; (película) to show; **ponlo más fuerte** turn
it up; **¿qué ponen en el Excelsior?** what's on
at the Excelsior?
2 (tienda) to open; (instalar: gas etc) to put
in; (radio, TV) to switch o turn on
3 (suponer): **pongamos que ...** let's suppose
that ...
4 (contribuir): **el gobierno ha puesto otro
millón** the government has contributed
another million
5 (TELEC): **póngame con el Sr. López** can you
put me through to Mr. López?
6 : **~ a uno de: le han puesto de director general**
they've appointed him general manager
7 (+ adj) to make; **me estás poniendo
nerviosa** you're making me nervous
8 (dar nombre): **al hijo le pusieron Diego** they
called their son Diego
♦ vi (gallina) to lay
♦ **~se** vr 1 (colocarse): **se puso a mi lado** he
came and stood beside me; **tú ponte en esa
silla** you go and sit on that chair
2 (vestido, cosméticos) to put on; **¿por qué no
te pones el vestido nuevo?** why don't you put
on o wear your new dress?
3 (+ adj) to turn; to get, become; **se puso
muy serio** he got very serious; **después de
lavarla la tela se puso azul** after washing it
the material turned blue
4 : **~se a: se puso a llorar** he started to cry;
tienes que ~te a estudiar you must get down
to studying
5 : **~se a bien con uno** to make it up with sb;

~se a mal con uno to get on the wrong side of sb

pongo etc vb ver **poner**

poniente [po'njente] nm (occidente) west; (viento) west wind

pontífice [pon'tifiθe] nm pope, pontiff

popa ['popa] nf stern

popular [popu'lar] adj popular; (cultura) of the people, folk cpd; **~idad** nf popularity; **~izarse** vr to become popular

---

PALABRA CLAVE

por [por] prep 1 (objetivo) for; **luchar ~ la patria** to fight for one's country

2 (+ infin): **~ no llegar tarde** so as not to arrive late; **~ citar unos ejemplos** to give a few examples

3 (causa) out of, because of; **~ escasez de fondos** through o for lack of funds

4 (tiempo): **~ la mañana/noche** in the morning/at night; **se queda ~ una semana** she's staying (for) a week

5 (lugar): **pasar ~ Madrid** to pass through Madrid; **ir a Guayaquil ~ Quito** to go to Guayaquil via Quito; **caminar ~ la calle** to walk along the street; ver tb **todo**

6 (cambio, precio): **te doy uno nuevo ~ el que tienes** I'll give you a new one (in return) for the one you've got

7 (valor distributivo): **550 pesetas ~ hora/cabeza** 550 pesetas an o per hour/a o per head

8 (modo, medio) by; **~ correo/avión** by post/air; **día ~ día** day by day; **entrar ~ la entrada principal** to go in through the main entrance

9: **10 ~ 10 son 100** 10 times 10 is 100

10 (en lugar de): **vino él ~ su jefe** he came instead of his boss

11: **~ mí que revienten** as far as I'm concerned they can drop dead

12: **¿~ qué?** why?; **¿~ qué no?** why not?

---

porcelana [porθe'lana] nf porcelain; (china) china

porcentaje [porθen'taxe] nm percentage

porción [por'θjon] nf (parte) portion, share; (cantidad) quantity, amount

pordiosero, a [pordjo'sero, a] nm/f beggar

porfiar [por'fjar] vi to persist, insist; (disputar) to argue stubbornly

pormenor [porme'nor] nm detail, particular

pornografía [pornoxra'fia] nf pornography

poro ['poro] nm pore; **~so, a** adj porous

porque ['porke] conj (a causa de) because; (ya que) since; (con el fin de) so that, in order that

porqué [por'ke] nm reason, cause

porquería [porke'ria] nf (suciedad) filth, dirt;

(acción) dirty trick; (objeto) small thing, trifle; (fig) rubbish

porra ['porra] nf (arma) stick, club

porrazo [po'rraθo] nm blow, bump

porro ['porro] (fam) nm (droga) joint (fam)

porrón [po'rron] nm glass wine jar with a long spout

portaaviones [porta'(a)βjones] nm inv aircraft carrier

portada [por'taða] nf (de revista) cover

portador, a [porta'ðor, a] nm/f carrier, bearer; (COM) bearer, payee

portaequipajes [portaeki'paxes] nm inv (AUTO: maletero) boot; (: baca) luggage rack

portal [por'tal] nm (entrada) vestibule, hall; (portada) porch, doorway; (puerta de entrada) main door

portamaletas [portama'letas] nm inv (AUTO: maletero) boot; (: baca) roof rack

portarse [por'tarse] vr to behave, conduct o.s.

portátil [por'tatil] adj portable

portavoz [porta'βoθ] nm/f spokesman/woman

portazo [por'taθo] nm: **dar un ~** to slam the door

porte ['porte] nm (COM) transport; (precio) transport charges pl

portento [por'tento] nm marvel, wonder; **~so, a** adj marvellous, extraordinary

porteño, a [por'teno, a] adj of o from Buenos Aires

portería [porte'ria] nf (oficina) porter's office; (DEPORTE) goal

portero, a [por'tero, a] nm/f porter; (conserje) caretaker; (ujier) doorman; (DEPORTE) goalkeeper; **~ automático** intercom

pórtico ['portiko] nm (patio) portico, porch; (fig) gateway; (arcada) arcade

portorriqueño, a [portorri'keno, a] adj Puerto Rican

Portugal [portu'yal] nm Portugal; **portugués, esa** adj, nm/f Portuguese ♦ nm (LING) Portuguese

porvenir [porβe'nir] nm future

pos [pos] prep: **en ~ de** after, in pursuit of

posada [po'saða] nf (refugio) shelter, lodging; (mesón) guest house; **dar ~ a** to give shelter to, take in

posaderas [posa'ðeras] nfpl backside sg, buttocks

posar [po'sar] vt (en el suelo) to lay down, put down; (la mano) to place, put gently ♦ vi (modelo) to sit, pose; **~se** vr to settle; (pájaro) to perch; (avión) to land, come down

posavasos [posa'βasos] nm inv coaster; (para cerveza) beermat

posdata [pos'ðata] nf postscript

pose ['pose] nf pose

poseedor, a [posee'ðor, a] nm/f owner,

possessor; (*de récord, puesto*) holder

poseer [poseˈer] *vt* to possess, own; (*ventaja*) to enjoy; (*récord, puesto*) to hold

posesión [poseˈsjon] *nf* possession; **posesionarse** *vr*: **posesionarse de** to take possession of, take over

posesivo, a [poseˈsiβo, a] *adj* possessive

posgrado [posˈɣraðo] *nm*: **curso de ~** postgraduate course

posibilidad [posiβiliˈðað] *nf* possibility; (*oportunidad*) chance; **posibilitar** *vt* to make possible; (*hacer realizable*) to make feasible

posible [poˈsiβle] *adj* possible; (*realizable*) feasible; **de ser ~** if possible; **en lo ~** as far as possible

posición [posiˈθjon] *nf* position; (*rango social*) status

positivo, a [posiˈtiβo, a] *adj* positive

poso [ˈposo] *nm* sediment; (*heces*) dregs *pl*

posponer [pospoˈner] *vt* (*relegar*) to put behind/below; (*aplazar*) to postpone

posta [ˈposta] *nf*: **a ~** deliberately, on purpose

postal [posˈtal] *adj* postal ♦ *nf* postcard

poste [ˈposte] *nm* (*de telégrafos etc*) post, pole; (*columna*) pillar

póster [ˈposter] (*pl* **pósteres, pósters**) *nm* poster

postergar [posterˈɣar] *vt* to postpone, delay

posteridad [posteriˈðað] *nf* posterity

posterior [posteˈrjor] *adj* back, rear; (*siguiente*) following, subsequent; (*más tarde*) later; **~idad** *nf*: **con ~idad** later, subsequently

postgrado [postˈɣraðo] *nm* = **posgrado**

postizo, a [posˈtiθo, a] *adj* false, artificial ♦ *nm* hairpiece

postor, a [posˈtor, a] *nm/f* bidder

postre [ˈpostre] *nm* sweet, dessert

postrero, a [posˈtrero, a] (*delante de nmsg*: **postrer**) *adj* (*último*) last; (*que viene detrás*) rear

postulado [postuˈlaðo] *nm* postulate

póstumo, a [ˈpostumo, a] *adj* posthumous

postura [posˈtura] *nf* (*del cuerpo*) posture, position; (*fig*) attitude, position

potable [poˈtaβle] *adj* drinkable; **agua ~** drinking water

potaje [poˈtaxe] *nm* thick vegetable soup

pote [ˈpote] *nm* pot, jar

potencia [poˈtenθja] *nf* power; **~l** [potenˈθjal] *adj, nm* potential; **~r** *vt* to boost

potente [poˈtente] *adj* powerful

potro, a [ˈpotro, a] *nm/f* (*ZOOL*) colt/filly ♦ *nm* (*de gimnasia*) vaulting horse

pozo [ˈpoθo] *nm* well; (*de río*) deep pool; (*de mina*) shaft

P.P. *abr* (= *porte pagado*) CP

práctica [ˈpraktika] *nf* practice; (*método*) method; (*arte, capacidad*) skill; **en la ~** in practice

practicable [praktiˈkaβle] *adj* practicable; (*camino*) passable

practicante [praktiˈkante] *nm/f* (*MED*: *ayudante de doctor*) medical assistant; (: *enfermero*) nurse; (*quien practica algo*) practitioner ♦ *adj* practising

practicar [praktiˈkar] *vt* to practise; (*DEPORTE*) to play; (*realizar*) to carry out, perform

práctico, a [ˈpraktiko, a] *adj* practical; (*instruido: persona*) skilled, expert

practique *etc vb ver* **practicar**

pradera [praˈðera] *nf* meadow; (*US etc*) prairie

prado [ˈpraðo] *nm* (*campo*) meadow, field; (*pastizal*) pasture

Praga [ˈpraɣa] *n* Prague

pragmático, a [praɣˈmatiko, a] *adj* pragmatic

preámbulo [preˈambulo] *nm* preamble, introduction

precario, a [preˈkarjo, a] *adj* precarious

precaución [prekauˈθjon] *nf* (*medida preventiva*) preventive measure, precaution; (*prudencia*) caution, wariness

precaver [prekaˈβer] *vt* to guard against; (*impedir*) to forestall; **~se** *vr*: **~se de** o **contra algo** to (be on one's) guard against sth; **precavido, a** *adj* cautious, wary

precedente [preθeˈðente] *adj* preceding; (*anterior*) former ♦ *nm* precedent

preceder [preθeˈðer] *vt, vi* to precede, go before, come before

precepto [preˈθepto] *nm* precept

preciado, a [preˈθjaðo, a] *adj* (*estimado*) esteemed, valuable

preciarse [preˈθjarse] *vr* to boast; **~se de** to pride o.s. on, boast of being

precinto [preˈθinto] *nm* (*tb*: **~ de garantía**) seal

precio [ˈpreθjo] *nm* price; (*costo*) cost; (*valor*) value, worth; (*de viaje*) fare; **~ al contado/de coste/de oportunidad** cash/cost/bargain price; **~ al detalle** o **al por menor** retail price; **~ tope** top price

preciosidad [preθjosiˈðað] *nf* (*valor*) (high) value, (great) worth; (*encanto*) charm; (*cosa bonita*) beautiful thing; **es una ~** it's lovely, it's really beautiful

precioso, a [preˈθjoso, a] *adj* precious; (*de mucho valor*) valuable; (*fam*) lovely, beautiful

precipicio [preθiˈpiθjo] *nm* cliff, precipice; (*fig*) abyss

precipitación [preθipitaˈθjon] *nf* haste; (*lluvia*) rainfall

precipitado, a [preθipiˈtaðo, a] *adj* (*conducta*) hasty, rash; (*salida*) hasty, sudden

precipitar [preθipiˈtar] *vt* (*arrojar*) to hurl down, throw; (*apresurar*) to hasten; (*acelerar*) to speed up, accelerate; **~se** *vr* to throw o.s.; (*apresurarse*) to rush; (*actuar sin pensar*) to act rashly

precisamente [preθisaˈmente] *adv* precisely; (*exactamente*) precisely, exactly

precisar [preθiˈsar] *vt* (*necesitar*) to need, require; (*fijar*) to determine exactly, fix; (*especificar*) to specify

precisión [preθiˈsjon] *nf* (*exactitud*) precision

preciso, a [preˈθiso, a] *adj* (*exacto*) precise; (*necesario*) necessary, essential

preconcebido, a [prekonθeˈβiðo, a] *adj* preconceived

precoz [preˈkoθ] *adj* (*persona*) precocious; (*calvicie etc*) premature

precursor, a [prekurˈsor, a] *nm/f* predecessor, forerunner

predecir [preðeˈθir] *vt* to predict, forecast

predestinado, a [preðestiˈnaðo, a] *adj* predestined

predicar [preðiˈkar] *vt, vi* to preach

predicción [preðikˈθjon] *nf* prediction

predilecto, a [preðiˈlekto, a] *adj* favourite

predisponer [preðispoˈner] *vt* to predispose; (*pey*) to prejudice; **predisposición** *nf* inclination; prejudice, bias

predominante [preðomiˈnante] *adj* predominant

predominar [preðomiˈnar] *vt* to dominate ♦ *vi* to predominate; (*prevalecer*) to prevail; **predominio** *nm* predominance; prevalence

preescolar [pre(e)skoˈlar] *adj* preschool

prefabricado, a [prefaβriˈkaðo, a] *adj* prefabricated

prefacio [preˈfaθjo] *nm* preface

preferencia [prefeˈrenθja] *nf* preference; **de ~** preferably, for preference

preferible [prefeˈriβle] *adj* preferable

preferir [prefeˈrir] *vt* to prefer

prefiero *etc vb ver* **preferir**

prefijo [preˈfixo] *nm* (*TELEC*) (dialling) code

pregonar [preɣoˈnar] *vt* to proclaim, announce

pregunta [preˈɣunta] *nf* question; **hacer una ~** to ask a question

preguntar [preɣunˈtar] *vt* to ask; (*cuestionar*) to question ♦ *vi* to ask; **~se** *vr* to wonder; **~ por alguien** to ask for sb

preguntón, ona [preɣunˈton, ona] *adj* inquisitive

prehistórico, a [preisˈtoriko, a] *adj* prehistoric

prejuicio [preˈxwiθjo] *nm* (*acto*) prejudgement; (*idea preconcebida*) preconception; (*parcialidad*) prejudice, bias

preliminar [prelimiˈnar] *adj* preliminary

preludio [preˈluðjo] *nm* prelude

prematuro, a [premaˈturo, a] *adj* premature

premeditación [premeðitaˈθjon] *nf* premeditation

premeditar [premeðiˈtar] *vt* to premeditate

premiar [preˈmjar] *vt* to reward; (*en un concurso*) to give a prize to

premio [ˈpremjo] *nm* reward; prize; (*COM*) premium

premonición [premoniˈθjon] *nf* premonition

prenatal [prenaˈtal] *adj* antenatal, prenatal

prenda [ˈprenda] *nf* (*ropa*) garment, article of clothing; (*garantía*) pledge; **~s** *nfpl* (*talentos*) talents, gifts

prendedor [prendeˈðor] *nm* brooch

prender [prenˈder] *vt* (*captar*) to catch, capture; (*detener*) to arrest; (*COSTURA*) to pin, attach; (*sujetar*) to fasten ♦ *vi* to catch; (*arraigar*) to take root; **~se** *vr* (*encenderse*) to catch fire

prendido, a [prenˈdiðo, a] (*AM*) *adj* (*luz etc*) on

prensa [ˈprensa] *nf* press; **la ~** the press; **prensar** *vt* to press

preñado, a [preˈɲaðo, a] *adj* pregnant; **~ de** pregnant with, full of

preocupación [preokupaˈθjon] *nf* worry, concern; (*ansiedad*) anxiety

preocupado, a [preokuˈpaðo, a] *adj* worried, concerned; (*ansioso*) anxious

preocupar [preokuˈpar] *vt* to worry; **~se** *vr* to worry; **~se de algo** (*hacerse cargo*) to take care of sth

preparación [preparaˈθjon] *nf* (*acto*) preparation; (*estado*) readiness; (*entrenamiento*) training

preparado, a [prepaˈraðo, a] *adj* (*dispuesto*) prepared; (*CULIN*) ready (to serve) ♦ *nm* preparation

preparar [prepaˈrar] *vt* (*disponer*) to prepare, get ready; (*TEC: tratar*) to prepare, process; (*entrenar*) to teach, train; **~se** *vr*: **~se a o para** to prepare to o for, get ready to o for;

preparativo, a *adj* preparatory, preliminary; **preparativos** *nmpl* preparations;

preparatoria (*AM*) *nf* sixth-form college (*BRIT*), senior high school (*US*)

prerrogativa [prerroɣaˈtiβa] *nf* prerogative, privilege

presa [ˈpresa] *nf* (*cosa apresada*) catch; (*víctima*) victim; (*de animal*) prey; (*de agua*) dam

presagiar [presaˈxjar] *vt* to presage, forebode; **presagio** *nm* omen

prescindir [presθinˈdir] *vi*: **~ de** (*privarse de*) to do without, go without; (*descartar*) to dispense with

prescribir [preskriˈβir] *vt* to prescribe; **prescripción** *nf* prescription

presencia [preˈsenθja] *nf* presence; **presencial** *adj*: **testigo presencial** eyewitness; **presenciar** *vt* to be present at;

(*asistir a*) to attend; (*ver*) to see, witness
presentación [presenta'θjon] *nf*
presentation; (*introducción*) introduction
presentador, a [presenta'ðor, a] *nm/f*
presenter, compère
presentar [presen'tar] *vt* to present; (*ofrecer*)
to offer; (*mostrar*) to show, display; (*a una
persona*) to introduce; **~se** *vr* (*llegar
inesperadamente*) to appear, turn up;
(*ofrecerse como candidato*) to run, stand;
(*aparecer*) to show, appear; (*solicitar empleo*)
to apply
presente [pre'sente] *adj* present ♦ *nm*
present; **hacer ~** to state, declare; **tener ~** to
remember, bear in mind
presentimiento [presenti'mjento] *nm*
premonition, presentiment
presentir [presen'tir] *vt* to have a
premonition of .
preservación [preserßa'θjon] *nf* protection,
preservation
preservar [preser'ßar] *vt* to protect,
preserve; **preservativo** *nm* sheath, condom
presidencia [presi'ðenθja] *nf* presidency;
(*de comité*) chairmanship
presidente [presi'ðente] *nm/f* president; (*de
comité*) chairman/woman
presidiario [presi'ðjarjo] *nm* convict
presidio [pre'sidjo] *nm* prison, penitentiary
presidir [presi'ðir] *vt* (*dirigir*) to preside at,
preside over; (: *comité*) to take the chair at;
(*dominar*) to dominate, rule ♦ *vi* to preside;
to take the chair
presión [pre'sjon] *nf* pressure; **presionar** *vt*
to press; (*fig*) to press, put pressure on ♦ *vi*:
presionar para to press for
preso, a ['preso, a] *nm/f* prisoner; **tomar** *o*
llevar ~ a uno to arrest sb, take sb prisoner
prestación [presta'θjon] *nf* service;
(*subsidio*) benefit; **prestaciones** *nfpl* (*TEC,
AUT*) performance features
prestado, a [pres'taðo, a] *adj* on loan; **pedir
~** to borrow
prestamista [presta'mista] *nm/f*
moneylender
préstamo ['prestamo] *nm* loan; **~ hipotecario**
mortgage
prestar [pres'tar] *vt* to lend, loan; (*atención*)
to pay; (*ayuda*) to give
presteza [pres'teθa] *nf* speed, promptness
prestigio [pres'tixjo] *nm* prestige; **~so, a** *adj*
(*honorable*) prestigious; (*famoso, renombrado*)
renowned, famous
presumido, a [presu'miðo, a] *adj* (*persona*)
vain
presumir [presu'mir] *vt* to presume ♦ *vi*
(*tener aires*) to be conceited; **según cabe ~** as
may be presumed, presumably; **presunción**
nf presumption; **presunto, a** *adj* (*supuesto*)

supposed, presumed; (*así llamado*) so-called;
presuntuoso, a *adj* conceited,
presumptuous
presuponer [presupo'ner] *vt* to presuppose
presupuesto [presu'pwesto] *pp de*
presuponer ♦ *nm* (*FINANZAS*) budget;
(*estimación: de costo*) estimate
pretencioso, a [preten'θjoso, a] *adj*
pretentious
pretender [preten'der] *vt* (*intentar*) to try to,
seek to; (*reivindicar*) to claim; (*buscar*) to
seek, try for; (*cortejar*) to woo, court; **~ que**
to expect that; **pretendiente** *nm/f* (*amante*)
suitor; (*al trono*) pretender; **pretensión** *nf*
(*aspiración*) aspiration; (*reivindicación*) claim;
(*orgullo*) pretension
pretexto [pre'teksto] *nm* pretext; (*excusa*)
excuse
prevalecer [preßale'θer] *vi* to prevail
prevención [preßen'θjon] *nf* prevention;
(*precaución*) precaution
prevenido, a [preße'niðo, a] *adj* prepared,
ready; (*cauteloso*) cautious
prevenir [preße'nir] *vt* (*impedir*) to prevent;
(*predisponer*) to prejudice, bias; (*avisar*) to
warn; (*preparar*) to prepare, get ready; **~se** *vr*
to get ready, prepare; **~se contra** to take
precautions against; **preventivo, a** *adj*
preventive, precautionary
prever [pre'ßer] *vt* to foresee
previo, a ['preßjo, a] *adj* (*anterior*) previous;
(*preliminar*) preliminary ♦ *prep*: **~ acuerdo de
los otros** subject to the agreement of the
others
previsión [preßi'sjon] *nf* (*perspicacia*)
foresight; (*predicción*) forecast; **previsto, a**
adj anticipated, forecast
prima ['prima] *nf* (*COM*) bonus; **~ de seguro**
insurance premium; *ver tb* **primo**
primacía [prima'θia] *nf* primacy
primario, a [pri'marjo, a] *adj* primary
primavera [prima'ßera] *nf* spring(-time)
primera [pri'mera] *nf* (*AUTO*) first gear;
(*FERRO: tb*: **~ clase**) first class; **de ~** (*fam*)
first-class, first-rate
primero, a [pri'mero, a] (*delante de nmsg*:
primer) *adj* first; (*principal*) prime ♦ *adv* first;
(*más bien*) sooner, rather; **primera plana** front
page
primicia [pri'miθja] *nf* (*tb*: **~ informativa**)
scoop
primitivo, a [primi'tißo, a] *adj* primitive;
(*original*) original
primo, a ['primo, a] *adj* prime ♦ *nm/f* cousin;
(*fam*) fool, idiot; **~ hermano** first cousin;
materias primas raw materials
primogénito, a [primo'xenito, a] *adj* first-
born
primordial [primor'ðjal] *adj* basic,

fundamental

primoroso, a [primo'roso, a] *adj* exquisite, delicate

princesa [prin'θesa] *nf* princess

principal [prinθi'pal] *adj* principal, main ♦ *nm* (*jefe*) chief, principal

príncipe ['prinθipe] *nm* prince

principiante [prinθi'pjante] *nm/f* beginner

principio [prin'θipjo] *nm* (*comienzo*) beginning, start; (*origen*) origin; (*primera etapa*) rudiment, basic idea; (*moral*) principle; a **~s de** at the beginning of

pringoso, a [prin'yoso, a] *adj* (*grasiento*) greasy; (*pegajoso*) sticky

pringue ['pringe] *nm* (*grasa*) grease, fat, dripping

prioridad [priori'ðað] *nf* priority

prisa ['prisa] *nf* (*apresuramiento*) hurry, haste; (*rapidez*) speed; (*urgencia*) (sense of) urgency; **a** o **de ~** quickly; **correr ~** to be urgent; **darse ~** to hurry up; **estar de** o **tener ~** to be in a hurry

prisión [pri'sjon] *nf* (*cárcel*) prison; (*período de cárcel*) imprisonment; **prisionero, a** *nm/f* prisoner

prismáticos [pris'matikos] *nmpl* binoculars

privación [priβa'θjon] *nf* deprivation; (*falta*) want, privation

privado, a [pri'βaðo, a] *adj* private

privar [pri'βar] *vt* to deprive; **privativo, a** *adj* exclusive

privilegiado, a [priβile'xjaðo, a] *adj* privileged; (*memoria*) very good

privilegiar [priβile'xjar] *vt* to grant a privilege to; (*favorecer*) to favour

privilegio [priβi'lexjo] *nm* privilege; (*concesión*) concession

pro [pro] *nm* o *f* profit, advantage ♦ *prep*: **asociación ~ ciegos** association for the blind ♦ *prefijo*: **~ soviético/americano** pro-Soviet/American; **en ~ de** on behalf of, for; **los ~s y los contras** the pros and cons

proa ['proa] *nf* bow, prow; **de ~** bow *cpd*, fore

probabilidad [proβaβili'ðað] *nf* probability, likelihood; (*oportunidad, posibilidad*) chance, prospect; **probable** *adj* probable, likely

probador [proβa'ðor] *nm* (*en tienda*) fitting room

probar [pro'βar] *vt* (*demostrar*) to prove; (*someter a prueba*) to test, try out; (*ropa*) to try on; (*comida*) to taste ♦ *vi* to try; **~se un traje** to try on a suit

probeta [pro'βeta] *nf* test tube

problema [pro'βlema] *nm* problem

procedente [proθe'ðente] *adj* (*razonable*) reasonable; (*conforme a derecho*) proper, fitting; **~ de** coming from, originating in

proceder [proθe'ðer] *vi* (*avanzar*) to proceed; (*actuar*) to act; (*ser correcto*) to be right (and proper), be fitting ♦ *nm* (*comportamiento*) behaviour, conduct; **~ de** to come from, originate in; **procedimiento** *nm* procedure; (*proceso*) process; (*método*) means *pl*, method

procesado, a [proθe'saðo, a] *nm/f* accused

procesador [proθesa'ðor] *nm*: **~ de textos** word processor

procesar [proθe'sar] *vt* to try, put on trial

procesión [proθe'sjon] *nf* procession

proceso [pro'θeso] *nm* process; (*JUR*) trial

proclamar [prokla'mar] *vt* to proclaim

procreación [prokrea'θjon] *nf* procreation

procrear [prokre'ar] *vt, vi* to procreate

procurador, a [prokura'ðor, a] *nm/f* attorney

procurar [proku'rar] *vt* (*intentar*) to try, endeavour; (*conseguir*) to get, obtain; (*asegurar*) to secure; (*producir*) to produce

prodigio [pro'ðixjo] *nm* prodigy; (*milagro*) wonder, marvel; **~so, a** *adj* prodigious, marvellous

pródigo, a ['proðiyo, a] *adj*: **hijo ~** prodigal son

producción [proðuk'θjon] *nf* (*gen*) production; (*producto*) output; **~ en serie** mass production

producir [proðu'θir] *vt* to produce; (*causar*) to cause, bring about; **~se** *vr* (*cambio*) to come about; (*accidente*) to take place; (*problema etc*) to arise; (*hacerse*) to be produced, be made; (*estallar*) to break out

productividad [proðuktiβi'ðað] *nf* productivity; **productivo, a** *adj* productive; (*provechoso*) profitable

producto [pro'ðukto] *nm* product

productor, a [proðuk'tor, a] *adj* productive, producing ♦ *nm/f* producer

proeza [pro'eθa] *nf* exploit, feat

profanar [profa'nar] *vt* to desecrate, profane; **profano, a** *adj* profane ♦ *nm/f* layman/woman

profecía [profe'θia] *nf* prophecy

proferir [profe'rir] *vt* (*palabra, sonido*) to utter; (*injuria*) to hurl, let fly

profesión [profe'sjon] *nf* profession; **profesional** *adj* professional

profesor, a [profe'sor, a] *nm/f* teacher; **~ado** *nm* teaching profession

profeta [pro'feta] *nm/f* prophet; **profetizar** *vt, vi* to prophesy

prófugo, a ['profuyo, a] *nm/f* fugitive; (*MIL*: *desertor*) deserter

profundidad [profundi'ðað] *nf* depth; **profundizar** *vi*: **profundizar en** to go deeply into; **profundo, a** *adj* deep; (*misterio, pensador*) profound

progenitor [proxeni'tor] *nm* ancestor; **~es** *nmpl* (*padres*) parents

programa [pro'vrama] nm programme
(BRIT), program (US); **~ción** nf programming;
~dor, a nm/f programmer; **programar** vt to
program

progresar [provre'sar] vi to progress, make
progress; **progresista** adj, nm/f progressive;
progresivo, a adj progressive; (gradual)
gradual; (continuo) continuous; **progreso**
nm progress

prohibición [proißi'θjon] nf prohibition, ban

prohibir [proi'ßir] vt to prohibit, ban, forbid;
se prohibe fumar, prohibido fumar no
smoking; **"prohibido el paso"** "no entry"

prójimo, a ['proximo, a] nm/f fellow man;
(vecino) neighbour

proletariado [proleta'rjaðo] nm proletariat

proletario, a [prole'tarjo, a] adj, nm/f
proletarian

proliferación [prolifera'θjon] nf proliferation

proliferar [prolife'rar] vi to proliferate;
prolífico, a adj prolific

prólogo ['prolovo] nm prologue

prolongación [prolonga'θjon] nf extension;
prolongado, a adj (largo) long; (alargado)
lengthy

prolongar [prolon'var] vt to extend;
(reunión etc) to prolong; (calle, tubo) to
extend

promedio [pro'meðjo] nm average; (de
distancia) middle, mid-point

promesa [pro'mesa] nf promise

prometer [prome'ter] vt to promise ♦ vi to
show promise; **~se** vr (novios) to get
engaged; **prometido, a** adj promised;
engaged ♦ nm/f fiancé/fiancée

prominente [promi'nente] adj prominent

promiscuo, a [pro'miskwo, a] adj
promiscuous

promoción [promo'θjon] nf promotion

promotor [promo'tor] nm promoter;
(instigador) instigator

promover [promo'ßer] vt to promote;
(causar) to cause; (instigar) to instigate, stir
up

promulgar [promul'var] vt to promulgate;
(anunciar) to proclaim

pronombre [pro'nombre] nm pronoun

pronosticar [pronosti'kar] vt to predict,
foretell, forecast; **pronóstico** nm prediction,
forecast; **pronóstico del tiempo** weather
forecast

pronto, a ['pronto, a] adj (rápido) prompt,
quick; (preparado) ready ♦ adv quickly,
promptly; (en seguida) at once, right away;
(dentro de poco) soon; (temprano) early
♦ nm: **tener ~s de enojo** to be quick-
tempered; **de ~** suddenly; **por lo ~**
meanwhile, for the present

pronunciación [pronunθja'θjon] nf
pronunciation

pronunciar [pronun'θjar] vt to pronounce;
(discurso) to make, deliver; **~se** vr to revolt,
rebel; (declararse) to declare o.s.

propagación [propava'θjon] nf propagation

propaganda [propa'vanda] nf (política)
propaganda; (comercial) advertising

propagar [propa'var] vt to propagate

propensión [propen'sjon] nf inclination,
propensity; **propenso, a** adj inclined to; **ser
propenso a** to be inclined to, have a tendency
to

propicio, a [pro'piθjo, a] adj favourable,
propitious

propiedad [propje'ðað] nf property;
(posesión) possession, ownership; **~ particular**
private property

propietario, a [propje'tarjo, a] nm/f owner,
proprietor

propina [pro'pina] nf tip

propio, a ['propjo, a] adj own, of one's own;
(característico) characteristic, typical; (debido)
proper; (mismo) selfsame, very; **el ~ ministro**
the minister himself; **¿tienes casa propia?**
have you a house of your own?

proponer [propo'ner] vt to propose, put
forward; (problema) to pose; **~se** vr to
propose, intend

proporción [propor'θjon] nf proportion;
(MAT) ratio; **proporciones** nfpl (dimensiones)
dimensions; (fig) size sg; **proporcionado, a**
adj proportionate; (regular) medium,
middling; (justo) just right; **proporcionar** vt
(dar) to give, supply, provide

proposición [proposi'θjon] nf proposition;
(propuesta) proposal

propósito [pro'posito] nm purpose; (intento)
aim, intention ♦ adv: **a ~** by the way,
incidentally; (a posta) on purpose,
deliberately; **a ~ de** about, with regard to

propuesta [pro'pwesta] vb ver **proponer** ♦ nf
proposal

propulsar [propul'sar] vt to drive, propel;
(fig) to promote, encourage; **propulsión** nf
propulsion; **propulsión a chorro o por reacción**
jet propulsion

prórroga ['prorrova] nf extension; (JUR) stay;
(COM) deferment; (DEPORTE) extra time;
prorrogar vt (período) to extend; (decisión)
to defer, postpone

prorrumpir [prorrum'pir] vi to burst forth,
break out

prosa ['prosa] nf prose

proscrito, a [pro'skrito, a] adj banned

proseguir [prose'xir] vt to continue, carry on
♦ vi to continue, go on

prospección [prospek'θjon] nf exploration;
(del oro) prospecting

prospecto [pros'pekto] nm prospectus

prosperar [prospe'rar] vi to prosper, thrive, flourish; **prosperidad** nf prosperity; (*éxito*) success; **próspero, a** adj prosperous, flourishing; (*que tiene éxito*) successful

prostíbulo [pros'tiβulo] nm brothel (*BRIT*), house of prostitution (*US*)

prostitución [prostitu'θjon] nf prostitution

prostituir [prosti'twir] vt to prostitute; **~se** vr to prostitute o.s., become a prostitute

prostituta [prosti'tuta] nf prostitute

protagonista [protaɣo'nista] nm/f protagonist

protagonizar [protaɣoni'θar] vt to take the chief rôle in

protección [protek'θjon] nf protection

protector, a [protek'tor, a] adj protective, protecting ♦ nm/f protector

proteger [prote'xer] vt to protect; **protegido, a** nm/f protégé/protégée

proteína [prote'ina] nf protein

protesta [pro'testa] nf protest; (*declaración*) protestation

protestante [protes'tante] adj Protestant

protestar [protes'tar] vt to protest, declare ♦ vi to protest

protocolo [proto'kolo] nm protocol

prototipo [proto'tipo] nm prototype

prov. abr (= *provincia*) prov

provecho [pro'βetʃo] nm advantage, benefit; (*FINANZAS*) profit; ¡**buen ~!** bon appétit!; **en ~ de** to the benefit of; **sacar ~ de** to benefit from, profit by

proveer [proβe'er] vt to provide, supply ♦ vi: **~ a** to provide for

provenir [proβe'nir] vi: **~ de** to come from, stem from

proverbio [pro'βerβjo] nm proverb

providencia [proβi'ðenθja] nf providence

provincia [pro'βinθja] nf province; **~no, a** adj provincial; (*del campo*) country cpd

provisión [proβi'sjon] nf provision; (*abastecimiento*) provision, supply; (*medida*) measure, step

provisional [proβisjo'nal] adj provisional

provocación [proβoka'θjon] nf provocation

provocar [proβo'kar] vt to provoke; (*alentar*) to tempt, invite; (*causar*) to bring about, lead to; (*promover*) to promote; (*estimular*) to rouse, stimulate; ¿**te provoca un café?** (*AM*) would you like a coffee?; **provocativo, a** adj provocative

próximamente [proksima'mente] adv shortly, soon

proximidad [proksimi'ðað] nf closeness, proximity; **próximo, a** adj near, close; (*vecino*) neighbouring; (*siguiente*) next

proyectar [projek'tar] vt (*objeto*) to hurl, throw; (*luz*) to cast, shed; (*CINE*) to screen, show; (*planear*) to plan

proyectil [projek'til] nm projectile, missile

proyecto [pro'jekto] nm plan; (*estimación de costo*) detailed estimate

proyector [projek'tor] nm (*CINE*) projector

prudencia [pru'ðenθja] nf (*sabiduría*) wisdom; (*cuidado*) care; **prudente** adj sensible, wise; (*conductor*) careful

prueba etc ['prweβa] vb ver **probar** ♦ nf proof; (*ensayo*) test, trial; (*degustación*) tasting, sampling; (*de ropa*) fitting; **a ~** on trial; **a ~ de** proof against; **a ~ de agua/fuego** waterproof/fireproof; **someter a ~** to put to the test

prurito [pru'rito] nm itch; (*de bebé*) nappy (*BRIT*) o diaper (*US*) rash

psico... [siko] *prefijo* psycho...; **~análisis** nm inv psychoanalysis; **~logía** nf psychology; **~lógico, a** adj psychological; **psicólogo, a** nm/f psychologist; **psicópata** nm/f psychopath; **~sis** nf inv psychosis

psiquiatra [si'kjatra] nm/f psychiatrist; **psiquiátrico, a** adj psychiatric

psíquico, a ['sikiko, a] adj psychic(al)

PSOE [pe'soe] nm abr = **Partido Socialista Obrero Español**

pta(s) abr = **peseta(s)**

pts abr = **pesetas**

púa ['pua] nf (*BOT, ZOOL*) prickle, spine; (*para guitarra*) plectrum (*BRIT*), pick (*US*); **alambre de ~** barbed wire

pubertad [puβer'tað] nf puberty

publicación [puβlika'θjon] nf publication

publicar [puβli'kar] vt (*editar*) to publish; (*hacer público*) to publicize; (*divulgar*) to make public, divulge

publicidad [puβliθi'ðað] nf publicity; (*COM: propaganda*) advertising; **publicitario, a** adj publicity cpd; advertising cpd

público, a ['puβliko, a] adj public ♦ nm public; (*TEATRO etc*) audience

puchero [pu'tʃero] nm (*CULIN: guiso*) stew; (: *olla*) cooking pot; **hacer ~s** to pout

pude etc vb ver **poder**

púdico, a ['puðiko, a] adj modest

pudiente [pu'ðjente] adj (*rico*) wealthy, well-to-do

pudiera etc vb ver **poder**

pudor [pu'ðor] nm modesty

pudrir [pu'ðrir] vt to rot; **~se** vr to rot, decay

pueblo ['pweβlo] nm people; (*nación*) nation; (*aldea*) village

puedo etc vb ver **poder**

puente ['pwente] nm bridge; **hacer ~** (*inf*) to take extra days off work between 2 public holidays; to take a long weekend; **~ aéreo** shuttle service; **~ colgante** suspension bridge

puerco, a ['pwerko, a] nm/f pig/sow ♦ adj (*sucio*) dirty, filthy; (*obsceno*) disgusting; **~ de mar** porpoise; **~ marino** dolphin

pueril [pwe'ril] *adj* childish

puerro ['pwerro] *nm* leek

puerta ['pwerta] *nf* door; (*de jardín*) gate; (*portal*) doorway; (*fig*) gateway; (*portería*) goal; **a la ~** at the door; **a ~ cerrada** behind closed doors; **~ giratoria** revolving door

puerto ['pwerto] *nm* port; (*paso*) pass; (*fig*) haven, refuge

Puerto Rico [pwerto'riko] *nm* Puerto Rico; **puertorriqueño, a** *adj, nm/f* Puerto Rican

pues [pwes] *adv* (*entonces*) then; (*bueno*) well, well then; (*así que*) so ♦ *conj* (*ya que*) since; **¡~!** (*sí*) yes!, certainly!

puesta ['pwesta] *nf* (*apuesta*) bet, stake; **~ en marcha** starting; **~ del sol** sunset

puesto, a ['pwesto, a] *pp de* **poner** ♦ *adj*: **tener algo ~** to have sth on, be wearing sth ♦ *nm* (*lugar, posición*) place; (*trabajo*) post, job; (*COM*) stall ♦ *conj*: **~ que** since, as

púgil ['puxil] *nm* boxer

pugna ['puɣna] *nf* battle, conflict; **pugnar** *vi* (*luchar*) to struggle, fight; (*pelear*) to fight

pujar [pu'xar] *vi* (*en subasta*) to bid; (*esforzarse*) to struggle, strain

pulcro, a ['pulkro, a] *adj* neat, tidy

pulga ['pulɣa] *nf* flea

pulgada [pul'ɣaða] *nf* inch

pulgar [pul'ɣar] *nm* thumb

pulir [pu'lir] *vt* to polish; (*alisar*) to smooth; (*fig*) to polish up, touch up

pulla ['puʎa] *nf* cutting remark

pulmón [pul'mon] *nm* lung; **pulmonía** *nf* pneumonia

pulpa ['pulpa] *nf* pulp; (*de fruta*) flesh, soft part

pulpería [pulpe'ria] (*AM*) *nf* (*tienda*) small grocery store

púlpito ['pulpito] *nm* pulpit

pulpo ['pulpo] *nm* octopus

pulsación [pulsa'θjon] *nf* beat; **pulsaciones** pulse rate

pulsar [pul'sar] *vt* (*tecla*) to touch, tap; (*MUS*) to play; (*botón*) to press, push ♦ *vi* to pulsate; (*latir*) to beat, throb; (*MED*): **~ a uno** to take sb's pulse

pulsera [pul'sera] *nf* bracelet

pulso ['pulso] *nm* (*ANAT*) pulse; (*fuerza*) strength; (*firmeza*) steadiness, steady hand

pulverizador [pulßeriθa'ðor] *nm* spray, spray gun

pulverizar [pulßeri'θar] *vt* to pulverize; (*líquido*) to spray

puna ['puna] (*AM*) *nf* mountain sickness

punitivo, a [puni'tißo, a] *adj* punitive

punta ['punta] *nf* point, tip; (*extremidad*) end; (*fig*) touch, trace; **horas ~s** peak hours, rush hours; **sacar ~ a** to sharpen

puntada [pun'taða] *nf* (*COSTURA*) stitch

puntal [pun'tal] *nm* prop, support

puntapié [punta'pje] *nm* kick

puntear [punte'ar] *vt* to tick, mark

puntería [punte'ria] *nf* (*de arma*) aim, aiming; (*destreza*) marksmanship

puntero, a [pun'tero, a] *adj* leading ♦ *nm* (*palo*) pointer

puntiagudo, a [puntja'ɣuðo, a] *adj* sharp, pointed

puntilla [pun'tiʎa] *nf* (*encaje*) lace edging o trim; (**andar**) **de ~s** (to walk) on tiptoe

punto ['punto] *nm* (*gen*) point; (*señal diminuta*) spot, dot; (*COSTURA, MED*) stitch; (*lugar*) spot, place; (*momento*) point, moment; **a ~** ready; **estar a ~ de** to be on the point of o about to; **en ~** on the dot; **~ muerto** dead centre; (*AUTO*) neutral (gear); **~ final** full stop (*BRIT*), period (*US*); **~ y coma** semicolon; **~ de interrogación** question mark; **~ de vista** point of view, viewpoint; **hacer ~** (*tejer*) to knit

puntuación [puntwa'θjon] *nf* punctuation; (*puntos: en examen*) mark(s) (*pl*); (: *DEPORTE*) score

puntual [pun'twal] *adj* (*a tiempo*) punctual; (*exacto*) exact, accurate; **~idad** *nf* punctuality; exactness, accuracy; **~izar** *vt* to fix, specify

puntuar [pun'twar] *vi* (*DEPORTE*) to score, count

punzada [pun'θaða] *nf* (*de dolor*) twinge

punzante [pun'θante] *adj* (*dolor*) shooting, sharp; (*herramienta*) sharp; **punzar** *vt* to prick, pierce ♦ *vi* to shoot, stab

puñado [pu'ɲaðo] *nm* handful

puñal [pu'ɲal] *nm* dagger; **~ada** *nf* stab

puñetazo [puɲe'taθo] *nm* punch

puño ['puɲo] *nm* (*ANAT*) fist; (*cantidad*) fistful, handful; (*COSTURA*) cuff; (*de herramienta*) handle

pupila [pu'pila] *nf* pupil

pupitre [pu'pitre] *nm* desk

puré [pu're] *nm* puree; (*sopa*) (thick) soup; **~ de patatas** mashed potatoes

pureza [pu'reθa] *nf* purity

purga ['purɣa] *nf* purge; **purgante** *adj, nm* purgative; **purgar** *vt* to purge

purgatorio [purɣa'torjo] *nm* purgatory

purificar [purifi'kar] *vt* to purify; (*refinar*) to refine

puritano, a [puri'tano, a] *adj* (*actitud*) puritanical; (*iglesia, tradición*) puritan ♦ *nm/f* puritan

puro, a ['puro, a] *adj* pure; (*verdad*) simple, plain ♦ *adv*: **de ~ cansado** out of sheer tiredness ♦ *nm* cigar

púrpura ['purpura] *nf* purple; **purpúreo, a** *adj* purple

pus [pus] *nm* pus

puse *etc vb ver* **poner**

pusiera etc vb ver **poner**
pústula ['pustula] nf pimple, sore
puta ['puta] (fam!) nf whore, prostitute
putrefacción [putrefak'θjon] nf rotting, putrefaction
PVP abr (ESP: = precio venta al público) RRP
pyme, PYME ['pime] nf abr (= Pequeña y Mediana Empresa) SME

Q, q

que [ke] conj 1 (con oración subordinada: muchas veces no se traduce) that; **dijo ~ vendría** he said (that) he would come; **espero ~ lo encuentres** I hope (that) you find it; ver tb **el**
2 (en oración independiente): **¡~ entre!** send him in; **¡~ se mejore tu padre!** I hope your father gets better
3 (enfático): **¿me quieres? – ¡~ sí!** do you love me? – of course!
4 (consecutivo: muchas veces no se traduce) that; **es tan grande ~ no lo puedo levantar** it's so big (that) I can't lift it
5 (comparaciones) than; **yo ~ tú/él** if I were you/him; ver tb **más; menos; mismo**
6 (valor disyuntivo): **~ le guste o no** whether he likes it or not; **~ venga o ~ no venga** whether he comes or not
7 (porque): **no puedo, ~ tengo ~ quedarme en casa** I can't, I've got to stay in
♦ pron 1 (cosa) that, which; (+ prep) which; **el sombrero ~ te compraste** the hat (that o which) you bought; **la cama en ~ dormí** the bed (that o which) I slept in
2 (persona: suj) that, who; (: objeto) that, whom; **el amigo ~ me acompañó al museo** the friend that o who went to the museum with me: **la chica ~ invité** the girl (that o whom) I invited

qué [ke] adj what?, which? ♦ pron what?; **¡~ divertido!** how funny!; **¿~ edad tienes?** how old are you?; **¿de ~ me hablas?** what are you saying to me?; **¿~ tal?** how are you?, how are things?; **¿~ hay (de nuevo)?** what's new?
quebradizo, a [keßra'ðiθo, a] adj fragile; (persona) frail
quebrado, a [ke'ßraðo, a] adj (roto) broken ♦ nm/f bankrupt ♦ nm (MAT) fraction
quebrantar [keßran'tar] vt (infringir) to violate, transgress; **~se** vr (persona) to fail in health
quebranto [ke'ßranto] nm damage, harm; (dolor) grief, pain

quebrar [ke'ßrar] vt to break, smash ♦ vi to go bankrupt; **~se** vr to break, get broken; (MED) to be ruptured
quedar [ke'ðar] vi to stay, remain; (encontrarse: sitio) to be; (haber aún) to remain, be left; **~se** vr to remain, stay (behind); **~se (con) algo** to keep sth; **~ en** (acordar) to agree on/to; **~ en nada** to come to nothing; **~ por hacer** to be still to be done; **~ ciego/mudo** to be left blind/dumb; **no te queda bien ese vestido** that dress doesn't suit you; **eso queda muy lejos** that's a long way (away); **quedamos a las seis** we agreed to meet at six
quedo, a ['keðo, a] adj still ♦ adv softly, gently
quehacer [kea'θer] nm task, job; **~es (domésticos)** nmpl household chores
queja ['kexa] nf complaint; **quejarse** vr (enfermo) to moan, groan; (protestar) to complain; **quejarse de que** to complain (about the fact) that; **quejido** nm moan
quemado, a [ke'maðo, a] adj burnt
quemadura [kema'ðura] nf burn, scald
quemar [ke'mar] vt to burn; (fig: malgastar) to burn up, squander ♦ vi to be burning hot; **~se** vr (consumirse) to burn (up); (del sol) to get sunburnt
quemarropa [kema'rropa]: **a ~** adv point-blank
quepo etc vb ver **caber**
querella [ke'reʎa] nf (JUR) charge; (disputa) dispute; **~rse** vr (JUR) to file a complaint

querer [ke'rer] vt 1 (desear) to want; **quiero más dinero** I want more money; **quisiera** o **querría un té** I'd like a tea; **sin ~** unintentionally; **quiero ayudar/que vayas** I want to help/you to go
2 (preguntas: para pedir algo): **¿quiere abrir la ventana?** could you open the window?; **¿quieres echarme una mano?** can you give me a hand?
3 (amar) to love; (tener cariño a) to be fond of; **quiere mucho a sus hijos** he's very fond of his children
4 (requerir): **esta planta quiere más luz** this plant needs more light
5: **le pedí que me dejara ir pero no quiso** I asked him to let me go but he refused

querido, a [ke'riðo, a] adj dear ♦ nm/f darling; (amante) lover
queso ['keso] nm cheese
quicio ['kiθjo] nm hinge; **sacar a uno de ~** to get on sb's nerves
quiebra ['kjeßra] nf break, split; (COM) bankruptcy; (ECON) slump

quiebro ['kjeβro] nm (*del cuerpo*) swerve

quien [kjen] *pron* who; **hay ~ piensa que** there are those who think that; **no hay ~ lo haga** no-one will do it

quién [kjen] *pron* who, whom; **¿~ es?** who's there?

quienquiera [kjen'kjera] (*pl* **quienesquiera**) *pron* whoever

quiero *etc vb ver* **querer**

quieto, a ['kjeto, a] *adj* still; (*carácter*) placid; **quietud** *nf* stillness

quilate [ki'late] nm carat

quilla ['kiʎa] *nf* keel

quimera [ki'mera] *nf* chimera; **quimérico, a** *adj* fantastic

químico, a ['kimiko, a] *adj* chemical ♦ nm/f chemist ♦ nf chemistry

quincalla [kin'kaʎa] *nf* hardware, ironmongery (*BRIT*)

quince ['kinθe] *num* fifteen; **~ días** a fortnight; **~añero, a** nm/f teenager; **~na** nf fortnight; (*pago*) fortnightly pay; **~nal** *adj* fortnightly

quiniela [ki'njela] *nf* football pools *pl*; **~s** *nfpl* (*impreso*) pools coupon *sg*

quinientos, as [ki'njentos, as] *adj, num* five hundred

quinina [ki'nina] *nf* quinine

quinto, a ['kinto, a] *adj* fifth ♦ nf country house; (*MIL*) call-up, draft

quiosco ['kjosko] nm (*de música*) bandstand; (*de periódicos*) news stand

quirófano [ki'rofano] nm operating theatre

quirúrgico, a [ki'rurxiko, a] *adj* surgical

quise *etc vb ver* **querer**

quisiera *etc vb ver* **querer**

quisquilloso, a [kiski'ʎoso, a] *adj* (*susceptible*) touchy; (*meticuloso*) pernickety

quiste ['kiste] nm cyst

quitaesmalte [kitaes'malte] nm nail-polish remover

quitamanchas [kita'mantʃas] nm *inv* stain remover

quitanieves [kita'njeßes] nm *inv* snowplough (*BRIT*), snowplow (*US*)

quitar [ki'tar] *vt* to remove, take away; (*ropa*) to take off; (*dolor*) to relieve; **¡quita de ahí!** get away!; **~se** *vr* to withdraw; (*ropa*) to take off; **se quitó el sombrero** he took off his hat

quite ['kite] nm (*esgrima*) parry; (*evasión*) dodge

Quito ['kito] n Quito

quizá(s) [ki'θa(s)] *adv* perhaps, maybe

R, r

rábano ['raßano] nm radish; **me importa un ~** I don't give a damn

rabia ['raßja] *nf* (*MED*) rabies *sg*; (*ira*) fury, rage; **rabiar** *vi* to have rabies; to rage, be furious; **rabiar por algo** to long for sth

rabieta [ra'ßjeta] *nf* tantrum, fit of temper

rabino [ra'ßino] nm rabbi

rabioso, a [ra'ßjoso, a] *adj* rabid; (*fig*) furious

rabo ['raßo] nm tail

racha ['ratʃa] *nf* gust of wind: **buena/mala ~** spell of good/bad luck

racial [ra'θjal] *adj* racial, race *cpd*

racimo [ra'θimo] nm bunch

raciocinio [raθjo'θinjo] nm reason

ración [ra'θjon] *nf* portion; **raciones** *nfpl* rations

racional [raθjo'nal] *adj* (*razonable*) reasonable; (*lógico*) rational; **~izar** *vt* to rationalize

racionar [raθjo'nar] *vt* to ration (out)

racismo [ra'θismo] nm racism; **racista** *adj, nm/f* racist

radar [ra'ðar] nm radar

radiactivo, a [raðjak'tiβo, a] *adj* = **radioactivo**

radiador [raðja'ðor] nm radiator

radiante [ra'ðjante] *adj* radiant

radical [raði'kal] *adj, nm/f* radical

radicar [raði'kar] *vi*: **~ en** (*dificultad, problema*) to lie in; (*solución*) to consist in; **~se** *vr* to establish o.s., put down (one's) roots

radio ['raðjo] *nf* radio; (*aparato*) radio (set) ♦ nm (*MAT*) radius; (*QUÍM*) radium; **~actividad** *nf* radioactivity; **~activo, a** *adj* radioactive; **~difusión** *nf* broadcasting; **~emisora** *nf* transmitter, radio station; **~escucha** nm/f listener; **~grafía** *nf* X-ray; **~grafiar** *vt* to X-ray; **~terapia** *nf* radiotherapy; **~yente** nm/f listener

ráfaga ['rafaxa] *nf* gust; (*de luz*) flash; (*de tiros*) burst

raído, a [ra'iðo, a] *adj* (*ropa*) threadbare

raigambre [rai'sambre] *nf* (*BOT*) roots *pl*; (*fig*) tradition

raíz [ra'iθ] *nf* root; **~ cuadrada** square root; **a ~ de** as a result of

raja ['raxa] *nf* (*de melón etc*) slice; (*grieta*) crack; **rajar** *vt* to split; (*fam*) to slash; **rajarse** *vr* to split, crack; **rajarse de** to back out of

rajatabla [raxa'taßla]: **a ~** *adv* (*estrictamente*) strictly, to the letter

rallador [raʎa'ðor] nm grater

rallar [ra'ʎar] *vt* to grate

rama ['rama] *nf* branch; **~je** nm branches *pl*, foliage; **ramal** nm (*de cuerda*) strand; (*FERRO*) branch line (*BRIT*); (*AUTO*) branch (road) (*BRIT*)

rambla ['rambla] *nf* (*avenida*) avenue

ramificación [ramifika'θjon] *nf* ramification

ramificarse [ramifi'karse] *vr* to branch out
ramillete [rami'ʎete] *nm* bouquet
ramo ['ramo] *nm* branch; (*sección*) department, section
rampa ['rampa] *nf* ramp
ramplón, ona [ram'plon, ona] *adj* uncouth, coarse
rana ['rana] *nf* frog; **salto de ~** leapfrog
ranchero [ran'tʃero] *nm* (AM) rancher; smallholder
rancho ['rantʃo] *nm* (*grande*) ranch; (*pequeño*) small farm
rancio, a ['ranθjo, a] *adj* (*comestibles*) rancid; (*vino*) aged, mellow; (*fig*) ancient
rango ['rango] *nm* rank, standing
ranura [ra'nura] *nf* groove; (*de teléfono etc*) slot
rapar [ra'par] *vt* to shave; (*los cabellos*) to crop
rapaz [ra'paθ] (*nf*: **rapaza**) *nm/f* young boy/ girl ♦ *adj* (ZOOL) predatory
rape ['rape] *nm* (*pez*) monkfish; **al ~** cropped
rapé [ra'pe] *nm* snuff
rapidez [rapi'ðeθ] *nf* speed, rapidity; **rápido, a** *adj* fast, quick ♦ *adv* quickly ♦ *nm* (FERRO) express; **rápidos** *nmpl* rapids
rapiña [ra'piɲa] *nm* robbery; **ave de ~** bird of prey
raptar [rap'tar] *vt* to kidnap; **rapto** *nm* kidnapping; (*impulso*) sudden impulse; (*éxtasis*) ecstasy, rapture
raqueta [ra'keta] *nf* racquet
raquítico, a [ra'kitiko, a] *adj* stunted; (*fig*) poor, inadequate; **raquitismo** *nm* rickets *sg*
rareza [ra'reθa] *nf* rarity; (*fig*) eccentricity
raro, a ['raro, a] *adj* (*poco común*) rare; (*extraño*) odd, strange; (*excepcional*) remarkable
ras [ras] *nm*: **a ~ de** level with; **a ~ de tierra** at ground level
rasar [ra'sar] *vt* (*igualar*) to level
rascacielos [raska'θjelos] *nm inv* skyscraper
rascar [ras'kar] *vt* (*con las uñas etc*) to scratch; (*raspar*) to scrape; **~se** *vr* to scratch (o.s.)
rasgar [ras'var] *vt* to tear, rip (up)
rasgo ['rasvo] *nm* (*con pluma*) stroke; **~s** *nmpl* (*facciones*) features, characteristics; **a grandes ~s** in outline, broadly
rasguñar [rasvu'par] *vt* to scratch; **rasguño** *nm* scratch
raso, a ['raso, a] *adj* (*liso*) flat, level; (*a baja altura*) very low ♦ *nm* satin; **cielo ~** clear sky
raspadura [raspa'ðura] *nf* (*acto*) scrape, scraping; (*marca*) scratch; **~s** *nfpl* (*de papel etc*) scrapings
raspar [ras'par] *vt* to scrape; (*arañar*) to scratch; (*limar*) to file
rastra ['rastra] *nf* (AGR) rake; **a ~s** by

dragging; (*fig*) unwillingly
rastreador [rastrea'ðor] *nm* tracker; **~ de minas** minesweeper
rastrear [rastre'ar] *vt* (*seguir*) to track
rastrero, a [ras'trero, a] *adj* (BOT, ZOOL) creeping; (*fig*) despicable, mean
rastrillo [ras'triʎo] *nm* rake
rastro ['rastro] *nm* (AGR) rake; (*pista*) track, trail; (*vestigio*) trace; **el R~** the Madrid fleamarket
rastrojo [ras'troxo] *nm* stubble
rasurador [rasura'ðor] (AM) *nm* electric shaver
rasuradora [rasura'ðora] (AM) *nf* = **rasurador**
rasurarse [rasu'rarse] *vr* to shave
rata ['rata] *nf* rat
ratear [rate'ar] *vt* (*robar*) to steal
ratero, a [ra'tero, a] *adj* light-fingered ♦ *nm/f* (*carterista*) pickpocket; (AM: *de casas*) burglar
ratificar [ratifi'kar] *vt* to ratify
rato ['rato] *nm* while, short time; **a ~s** from time to time; **hay para ~** there's still a long way to go; **al poco ~** soon afterwards; **pasar el ~** to kill time; **pasar un buen/mal ~** to have a good/rough time; **en mis ~s libres** in my spare time
ratón [ra'ton] *nm* mouse; **ratonera** *nf* mousetrap
raudal [rau'ðal] *nm* torrent; **a ~es** in abundance
raya ['raja] *nf* line; (*marca*) scratch; (*en tela*) stripe; (*de pelo*) parting; (*límite*) boundary; (*pez*) ray; (*puntuación*) dash; **a ~s** striped; **pasarse de la ~** to go too far: **tener a ~** to keep in check; **rayar** *vt* to line; to scratch; (*subrayar*) to underline ♦ *vi*: **rayar en** o **con** to border on
rayo ['rajo] *nm* (*del sol*) ray, beam; (*de luz*) shaft; (*en una tormenta*) (flash of) lightning; **~s X** X-rays
raza ['raθa] *nf* race; **~ humana** human race
razón [ra'θon] *nf* reason; (*justicia*) right, justice; (*razonamiento*) reasoning; (*motivo*) reason, motive; (MAT) ratio; **a ~ de 10 cada día** at the rate of 10 a day; **"~: ..."** "inquiries to ..."; **en ~ de** with regard to; **dar ~ a uno** to agree that sb is right; **tener ~** to be right; **~ directa/inversa** direct/inverse proportion; **~ de ser** raison d'être; **razonable** *adj* reasonable; (*justo, moderado*) fair; **razonamiento** *nm* (*juicio*) judg(e)ment; (*argumento*) reasoning; **razonar** *vt, vi* to reason, argue
reacción [reak'θjon] *nf* reaction; **avión a ~** jet plane; **~ en cadena** chain reaction; **reaccionar** *vi* to react; **reaccionario, a** *adj* reactionary
reacio, a [re'aθjo, a] *adj* stubborn

reactivar [reakti'ßar] vt to revitalize
reactor [reak'tor] nm reactor
readaptación [reaðapta'θjon] nf:
~ **profesional** industrial retraining
reajuste [rea'xuste] nm readjustment
real [re'al] adj real; (del rey, fig) royal
realce [re'alθe] nm (lustre, fig) splendour;
poner de ~ to emphasize
realidad [reali'ðað] nf reality, fact; (verdad)
truth
realista [rea'lista] nm/f realist
realización [realiθa'θjon] nf fulfilment
realizador, a [realiθa'ðor, a] nm/f film-
maker
realizar [reali'θar] vt (objetivo) to achieve;
(plan) to carry out; (viaje) to make,
undertake; ~**se** vr to come about, come
true
realmente [real'mente] adv really, actually
realquilar [realki'lar] vt to sublet
realzar [real'θar] vt to enhance; (acentuar) to
highlight
reanimar [reani'mar] vt to revive; (alentar)
to encourage; ~**se** vr to revive
reanudar [reanu'ðar] vt (renovar) to renew;
(historia, viaje) to resume
reaparición [reapari'θjon] nf reappearance
rearme [re'arme] nm rearmament
rebaja [re'ßaxa] nf (COM) reduction; (: descuento) discount; ~**s** nfpl (COM) sale; **rebajar**
vt (bajar) to lower; (reducir) to reduce;
(disminuir) to lessen; (humillar) to humble
rebanada [reßa'naða] nf slice
rebañar [reßa'ɲar] vt (comida) to scrape up;
(plato) to scrape clean
rebaño [re'ßaɲo] nm herd; (de ovejas) flock
rebasar [reßa'sar] vt (tb: ~ **de**) to exceed
rebatir [reßa'tir] vt to refute
rebeca [re'ßeka] nf cardigan
rebelarse [reße'larse] vr to rebel, revolt
rebelde [re'ßelde] adj rebellious; (niño)
unruly ♦ nm/f rebel; **rebeldía** nf
rebelliousness; (desobediencia) disobedience
rebelión [reße'ljon] nf rebellion
reblandecer [reßlande'θer] vt to soften
rebobinar [reßoßi'nar] vt (cinta, película de
video) to rewind
rebosante [reßo'sante] adj overflowing
rebosar [reßo'sar] vi (líquido, recipiente) to
overflow; (abundar) to abound, be plentiful
rebotar [reßo'tar] vt to bounce; (rechazar) to
repel ♦ vi (pelota) to bounce; (bala) to
ricochet; **rebote** nm rebound; **de rebote** on
the rebound
rebozado, a [reßo'θaðo, a] adj fried in
batter o breadcrumbs
rebozar [reßo'θar] vt to wrap up; (CULIN) to
fry in batter o breadcrumbs
rebuscado, a [reßus'kaðo, a] adj

(amanerado) affected; (palabra) recherché;
(idea) far-fetched
rebuscar [reßus'kar] vi: ~ **(en/por)** to search
carefully (in/for)
rebuznar [reßuθ'nar] vi to bray
recado [re'kaðo] nm (mensaje) message;
(encargo) errand; **tomar un ~** (TEL) to take a
message
recaer [reka'er] vi to relapse; ~ **en** to fall to o
on; (criminal etc) to fall back into, relapse
into; **recaída** nf relapse
recalcar [rekal'kar] vt (fig) to stress,
emphasize
recalcitrante [rekalθi'trante] adj recalcitrant
recalentar [rekalen'tar] vt (volver a calentar)
to reheat; (calentar demasiado) to overheat
recámara [re'kamara] (AM) nf bedroom
recambio [re'kambjo] nm spare; (de pluma)
refill
recapacitar [rekapaθi'tar] vi to reflect
recargado, a [rekar'γaðo, a] adj overloaded
recargar [rekar'γar] vt to overload; (batería)
to recharge; **recargo** nm surcharge;
(aumento) increase
recatado, a [reka'taðo, a] adj (modesto)
modest, demure; (prudente) cautious
recato [re'kato] nm (modestia) modesty,
demureness; (cautela) caution
recaudación [rekauða'θjon] nf (acción)
collection; (cantidad) takings pl; (en deporte)
gate; **recaudador, a** nm/f tax collector
recelar [reθe'lar] vt: ~ **que** (sospechar) to
suspect that; (temer) to fear that ♦ vi: ~ **de** to
distrust; **recelo** nm distrust, suspicion;
receloso, a adj distrustful, suspicious
recepción [reθep'θjon] nf reception;
recepcionista nm/f receptionist
receptáculo [reθep'takulo] nm receptacle
receptivo, a [reθep'tißo, a] adj receptive
receptor, a [reθep'tor, a] nm/f recipient
♦ nm (TEL) receiver
recesión [reθe'sjon] nf (COM) recession
receta [re'θeta] nf (CULIN) recipe; (MED)
prescription
rechazar [retʃa'θar] vt to reject; (oferta) to
turn down; (ataque) to repel
rechazo [re'tʃaθo] nm rejection
rechifla [re'tʃifla] nf hissing, booing; (fig)
derision
rechinar [retʃi'nar] vi to creak; (dientes) to
grind
rechistar [retʃis'tar] vi: **sin ~** without a
murmur
rechoncho, a [re'tʃontʃo, a] (fam) adj
thickset (BRIT), heavy-set (US)
rechupete [retʃu'pete]: **de ~** (comida)
delicious, scrumptious
recibidor, a [reθißi'ðor, a] nm entrance hall
recibimiento [reθißi'mjento] nm reception,

welcome
recibir [reθi'ßir] vt to receive; (*dar la
bienvenida*) to welcome ♦ vi to entertain; **~se**
vr: **~se de** to qualify as; **recibo** nm receipt
reciclar [reθi'klar] vt to recycle
recién [re'θjen] adv recently, newly; **los
~ casados** the newly-weds; **el ~ llegado** the
newcomer; **el ~ nacido** the newborn child
reciente [re'θjente] adj recent; (*fresco*) fresh;
~mente adv recently
recinto [re'θinto] nm enclosure; (*área*) area,
place
recio, a ['reθjo, a] adj strong, tough; (*voz*)
loud ♦ adv hard; loud(ly)
recipiente [reθi'pjente] nm receptacle
reciprocidad [reθiproβi'ðað] nf reciprocity;
recíproco, a adj reciprocal
recital [reθi'tal] nm (MUS) recital; (LITERATURA)
reading
recitar [reθi'tar] vt to recite
reclamación [reklama'θjon] nf claim,
demand; (*queja*) complaint
reclamar [rekla'mar] vt to claim, demand
♦ vi: **~ contra** to complain about; **~ a uno en
justicia** to take sb to court; **reclamo** nm
(*anuncio*) advertisement; (*tentación*)
attraction
reclinar [rekli'nar] vt to recline, lean; **~se** vr
to lean back
recluir [reklu'ir] vt to intern, confine
reclusión [reklu'sjon] nf (*prisión*) prison;
(*refugio*) seclusion; **~ perpetua** life
imprisonment
recluta [re'kluta] nm/f recruit ♦ nf
recruitment; **reclutar** vt (*datos*) to collect;
(*dinero*) to collect up; **~miento**
[rekluta'mjento] nm recruitment
recobrar [reko'ßrar] vt (*salud*) to recover;
(*rescatar*) to get back; **~se** vr to recover
recodo [re'koðo] nm (*de río, camino*) bend
recogedor [rekoxe'ðor] nm dustpan
recoger [reko'xer] vt to collect; (AGR) to
harvest; (*levantar*) to pick up; (*juntar*) to
gather; (*pasar a buscar*) to come for, get;
(*dar asilo*) to give shelter to; (*faldas*) to
gather up; (*pelo*) to put up; **~se** vr (*retirarse*)
to retire; **recogido, a** adj (*lugar*) quiet,
secluded; (*pequeño*) small ♦ nf (CORREOS)
collection; (AGR) harvest
recolección [rekolek'θjon] nf (AGR)
harvesting; (*colecta*) collection
recomendación [rekomenda'θjon] nf
(*sugerencia*) suggestion, recommendation;
(*referencia*) reference
recomendar [rekomen'dar] vt to suggest,
recommend; (*confiar*) to entrust
recompensa [rekom'pensa] nf reward,
recompense; **recompensar** vt to reward,
recompense

recomponer [rekompo'ner] vt to mend
reconciliación [rekonθilja'θjon] nf
reconciliation
reconciliar [rekonθi'ljar] vt to reconcile;
~se vr to become reconciled
recóndito, a [re'kondito, a] adj (*lugar*)
hidden, secret
reconfortar [rekonfor'tar] vt to comfort
reconocer [rekono'θer] vt to recognize;
(*registrar*) to search; (MED) to examine;
reconocido, a adj recognized; (*agradecido*)
grateful; **reconocimiento** nm recognition;
search; examination; gratitude; (*confesión*)
admission
reconquista [rekon'kista] nf reconquest; **la
R~** the Reconquest (of Spain)
reconstituyente [rekonstitu'jente] nm
tonic
reconstruir [rekonstru'ir] vt to reconstruct
reconversión [rekonßer'sjon] nf:
~ industrial industrial rationalization
recopilación [rekopila'θjon] nf (*resumen*)
summary; (*compilación*) compilation;
recopilar vt to compile
récord ['rekorð] (*pl* **~s**) adj inv, nm record
recordar [rekor'ðar] vt (*acordarse de*) to
remember; (*acordar a otro*) to remind ♦ vi to
remember
recorrer [reko'rrer] vt (*país*) to cross, travel
through; (*distancia*) to cover; (*registrar*) to
search; (*repasar*) to look over; **recorrido** nm
run, journey; **tren de largo recorrido** main-line
train
recortado, a [rekor'taðo, a] adj uneven,
irregular
recortar [rekor'tar] vt to cut out; **recorte** nm
(*acción, de prensa*) cutting; (*de telas, chapas*)
trimming; **recorte presupuestario** budget cut
recostado, a [rekos'taðo, a] adj leaning;
estar ~ to be lying down
recostar [rekos'tar] vt to lean; **~se** vr to lie
down
recoveco [reko'ßeko] nm (*de camino, río etc*)
bend; (*en casa*) cubby hole
recreación [rekrea'θjon] nf recreation
recrear [rekre'ar] vt (*entretener*) to entertain;
(*volver a crear*) to recreate; **recreativo, a** adj
recreational; **recreo** nm recreation; (ESCOL)
break, playtime
recriminar [rekrimi'nar] vt to reproach ♦ vi
to recriminate; **~se** vr to reproach each other
recrudecer [rekruðe'θer] vt, vi to worsen;
~se vr to worsen
recrudecimiento [rekruðeθi'mjento] nm
upsurge
recta ['rekta] nf straight line
rectángulo, a [rek'tangulo, a] adj
rectangular ♦ nm rectangle
rectificar [rektifi'kar] vt to rectify; (*volverse*

recto) to straighten ♦ vi to correct o.s.

rectitud [rekti'tuð] nf straightness; (fig) rectitude

recto, a ['rekto, a] adj straight; (persona) honest, upright ♦ nm rectum

rector, a [rek'tor, a] adj governing

recuadro [re'kwaðro] nm box; (TIPOGRAFÍA) inset

recubrir [rcku'ßrir] vt: ~ (con) (pintura, crema) to cover (with)

recuento [re'kwento] nm inventory; **hacer el ~ de** to count o reckon up

recuerdo [re'kwerðo] nm souvenir; **~s** nmpl (memorias) memories; **¡~s a tu madre!** give my regards to your mother!

recular [reku'lar] vi to back down

recuperable [rekupe'raßle] adj recoverable

recuperación [rekupera'θjon] nf recovery

recuperar [rekupe'rar] vt to recover; (tiempo) to make up; **~se** vr to recuperate

recurrir [reku'rrir] vi (JUR) to appeal; **~ a** to resort to; (persona) to turn to; **recurso** nm resort; (medios) means pl, resources pl; (JUR) appeal

recusar [reku'sar] vt to reject, refuse

red [reð] nf net, mesh; (FERRO etc) network; (trampa) trap; **la R~** (Internet) the Net

redacción [reðak'θjon] nf (acción) editing; (personal) editorial staff; (ESCOL) essay, composition

redactar [reðak'tar] vt to draw up, draft; (periódico) to edit

redactor, a [reðak'tor, a] nm/f editor

redada [re'ðaða] nf: **~ policial** police raid, round-up

rededor [reðe'ðor] nm: **al o en ~** around, round about

redención [reðen'θjon] nf redemption

redicho, a [re'ðitʃo, a] adj affected

redil [re'ðil] nm sheepfold

redimir [reði'mir] vt to redeem

rédito ['reðito] nm interest, yield

redoblar [reðo'ßlar] vt to redouble ♦ vi (tambor) to roll

redomado, a [reðo'maðo, a] adj (astuto) sly, crafty; (perfecto) utter

redonda [re'ðonda] nf: **a la ~** around, round about

redondear [reðonde'ar] vt to round, round off

redondel [reðon'del] nm (círculo) circle; (TAUR) bullring, arena

redondo, a [re'ðondo, a] adj (circular) round; (completo) complete

reducción [reðuk'θjon] nf reduction

reducido, a [reðu'θiðo, a] adj reduced; (limitado) limited; (pequeño) small

reducir [reðu'θir] vt to reduce; to limit; **~se** vr to diminish

redundancia [reðun'danθja] nf redundancy

reembolsar [re(e)mbol'sar] vt (persona) to reimburse; (dinero) to repay, pay back; (depósito) to refund; **reembolso** nm reimbursement; refund

reemplazar [re(e)mpla'θar] vt to replace; **reemplazo** nm replacement; **de reemplazo** (MIL) reserve

reencuentro [re(e)n'kwentro] nm reunion

referencia [refe'renθja] nf reference; **con ~ a** with reference to

referéndum [refe'rendum] (pl **~s**) nm referendum

referente [refe'rente] adj: **~ a** concerning, relating to

referir [refe'rir] vt (contar) to tell, recount; (relacionar) to refer, relate; **~se** vr: **~se a** to refer to

refilón [refi'lon]: **de ~** adv obliquely

refinado, a [refi'naðo, a] adj refined

refinamiento [refina'mjento] nm refinement

refinar [refi'nar] vt to refine; **refinería** nf refinery

reflejar [refle'xar] vt to reflect; **reflejo, a** adj reflected; (movimiento) reflex ♦ nm reflection; (ANAT) reflex

reflexión [reflek'sjon] nf reflection; **reflexionar** vt to reflect on ♦ vi to reflect; (detenerse) to pause (to think)

reflexivo, a [reflek'sißo, a] adj thoughtful; (LING) reflexive

reflujo [re'fluxo] nm ebb

reforma [re'forma] nf reform; (ARQ etc) repair; **~ agraria** agrarian reform

reformar [refor'mar] vt to reform; (modificar) to change, alter; (ARQ) to repair; **~se** vr to mend one's ways

reformatorio [reforma'torjo] nm reformatory

reforzar [refor'θar] vt to strengthen; (ARQ) to reinforce; (fig) to encourage

refractario, a [refrak'tarjo, a] adj (TEC) heat-resistant

refrán [re'fran] nm proverb, saying

refregar [refre'ɣar] vt to scrub

refrenar [refre'nar] vt to check, restrain

refrendar [refren'dar] vt (firma) to endorse, countersign; (ley) to approve

refrescante [refres'kante] adj refreshing, cooling

refrescar [refres'kar] vt to refresh ♦ vi to cool down; **~se** vr to get cooler; (tomar aire fresco) to go out for a breath of fresh air; (beber) to have a drink

refresco [re'fresko] nm soft drink, cool drink; **"~s"** "refreshments"

refriega [re'frjeɣa] nf scuffle, brawl

refrigeración [refrixera'θjon] nf

refrigeration; (*de sala*) air-conditioning

refrigerador [refrixera'ðor] *nm* refrigerator (*BRIT*), icebox (*US*)

refrigerar [refrixe'rar] *vt* to refrigerate; (*sala*) to air-condition

refuerzo [re'fwerθo] *nm* reinforcement; (*TEC*) support

refugiado, a [refu'xjaðo, a] *nm/f* refugee

refugiarse [refu'xjarse] *vr* to take refuge, shelter

refugio [re'fuxjo] *nm* refuge; (*protección*) shelter

refunfuñar [refunfu'ɲar] *vi* to grunt, growl; (*quejarse*) to grumble

refutar [refu'tar] *vt* to refute

regadera [reɣa'ðera] *nf* watering can

regadío [reɣa'ðio] *nm* irrigated land

regalado, a [reɣa'laðo, a] *adj* comfortable, luxurious; (*gratis*) free, for nothing

regalar [reɣa'lar] *vt* (*dar*) to give (as a present); (*entregar*) to give away; (*mimar*) to pamper, make a fuss of

regaliz [reɣa'liθ] *nm* liquorice

regalo [re'ɣalo] *nm* (*obsequio*) gift, present; (*gusto*) pleasure

regañadientes [reɣaɲa'ðjentes]: **a ~** *adv* reluctantly

regañar [reɣa'ɲar] *vt* to scold ♦ *vi* to grumble; **regañón, ona** *adj* nagging

regar [re'ɣar] *vt* to water, irrigate; (*fig*) to scatter, sprinkle

regatear [reɣate'ar] *vt* (*COM*) to bargain over; (*escatimar*) to be mean with ♦ *vi* to bargain, haggle; (*DEPORTE*) to dribble; **regateo** *nm* bargaining; dribbling; (*del cuerpo*) swerve, dodge

regazo [re'ɣaθo] *nm* lap

regeneración [rexenera'θjon] *nf* regeneration

regenerar [rexene'rar] *vt* to regenerate

regentar [rexen'tar] *vt* to direct, manage; **regente** (*COM*) manager; (*POL*) regent

régimen ['reximen] (*pl* **regímenes**) *nm* regime; (*MED*) diet

regimiento [rexi'mjento] *nm* regiment

regio, a ['rexjo, a] *adj* royal, regal; (*fig: suntuoso*) splendid; (*AM: fam*) great, terrific

región [re'xjon] *nf* region

regir [re'xir] *vt* to govern, rule; (*dirigir*) to manage, run ♦ *vi* to apply, be in force

registrar [rexis'trar] *vt* (*buscar*) to search; (: *en cajón*) to look through; (*inspeccionar*) to inspect; (*anotar*) to register, record; (*INFORM*) to log; **~se** *vr* to register; (*ocurrir*) to happen

registro [re'xistro] *nm* (*acto*) registration; (*MUS, libro*) register; (*inspección*) inspection, search; **~ civil** registry office

regla ['reɣla] *nf* (*ley*) rule, regulation; (*de medir*) ruler, rule; (*MED: período*) period

reglamentación [reɣlamenta'θjon] *nf* (*acto*) regulation; (*lista*) rules *pl*

reglamentar [reɣlamen'tar] *vt* to regulate; **reglamentario, a** *adj* statutory; **reglamento** *nm* rules *pl*, regulations *pl*

regocijarse [reɣoθi'xarse] *vr*: **~ de** to rejoice at, be happy about; **regocijo** *nm* joy, happiness

regodearse [reɣoðe'arse] *vr* to be glad, be delighted; **regodeo** *nm* delight

regresar [reɣre'sar] *vi* to come back, go back, return; **regresivo, a** *adj* backward; (*fig*) regressive; **regreso** *nm* return

reguero [re'ɣero] *nm* (*de sangre etc*) trickle; (*de humo*) trail

regulador [reɣula'ðor] *nm* regulator; (*de radio etc*) knob, control

regular [reɣu'lar] *adj* regular; (*normal*) normal, usual; (*común*) ordinary; (*organizado*) regular, orderly; (*mediano*) average; (*fam*) not bad, so-so ♦ *adv* so-so, alright ♦ *vt* (*controlar*) to control, regulate; (*TEC*) to adjust; **por lo ~** as a rule; **~idad** *nf* regularity; **~izar** *vt* to regularize

regusto [re'ɣusto] *nm* aftertaste

rehabilitación [reaβilita'θjon] *nf* rehabilitation; (*ARQ*) restoration

rehabilitar [reaβili'tar] *vt* to rehabilitate; (*ARQ*) to restore; (*reintegrar*) to reinstate

rehacer [rea'θer] *vt* (*reparar*) to mend, repair; (*volver a hacer*) to redo, repeat; **~se** *vr* (*MED*) to recover

rehén [re'en] *nm* hostage

rehuir [reu'ir] *vt* to avoid, shun

rehusar [reu'sar] *vt*, *vi* to refuse

reina ['reina] *nf* queen; **~do** *nm* reign

reinante [rei'nante] *adj* (*fig*) prevailing

reinar [rei'nar] *vi* to reign

reincidir [reinθi'ðir] *vi* to relapse

reincorporarse [reinkorpo'rarse] *vr*: **~ a** to rejoin

reino ['reino] *nm* kingdom; **el R~ Unido** the United Kingdom

reintegrar [reinte'ɣrar] *vt* (*reconstituir*) to reconstruct; (*persona*) to reinstate; (*dinero*) to refund, pay back; **~se** *vr*: **~se a** to return to

reír [re'ir] *vi* to laugh; **~se** *vr* to laugh; **~se de** to laugh at

reiterar [reite'rar] *vt* to reiterate

reivindicación [reiβindika'θjon] *nf* (*demanda*) claim, demand; (*justificación*) vindication

reivindicar [reiβindi'kar] *vt* to claim

reja ['rexa] *nf* (*de ventana*) grille, bars *pl*; (*en la calle*) grating

rejilla [re'xiʎa] *nf* grating, grille; (*muebles*) wickerwork; (*de ventilación*) vent; (*de coche etc*) luggage rack

rejoneador [rexonea'ðor] *nm* mounted

bullfighter

rejuvenecer [rexußene'θer] vt, vi to rejuvenate

relación [rela'θjon] nf relation, relationship; (MAT) ratio; (narración) report; **relaciones públicas** public relations; **con ~ a, en ~ con** in relation to; **relacionar** vt to relate, connect; **relacionarse** vr to be connected, be linked

relajación [relaxa'θjon] nf relaxation

relajado, a [rela'xaðo, a] adj (disoluto) loose; (cómodo) relaxed; (MED) ruptured

relajar [rela'xar] vt to relax; **~se** vr to relax

relamerse [rela'merse] vr to lick one's lips

relamido, a [rela'miðo, a] adj (pulcro) overdressed; (afectado) affected

relámpago [re'lampaxo] nm flash of lightning; **visita/huelga ~** lightning visit/strike; **relampaguear** vi to flash

relatar [rela'tar] vt to tell, relate

relativo, a [rela'tiβo, a] adj relative; **en lo ~ a** concerning

relato [re'lato] nm (narración) story, tale

relegar [rele'xar] vt to relegate

relevante [rele'ßante] adj eminent, outstanding

relevar [rele'ßar] vt (sustituir) to relieve; **~se** vr to relay; **~ a uno de un cargo** to relieve sb of his post

relevo [re'leßo] nm relief; **carrera de ~s** relay race

relieve [re'ljeße] nm (ARTE, TEC) relief; (fig) prominence, importance; **bajo ~** bas-relief

religión [reli'xjon] nf religion; **religioso, a** adj religious ♦ nm/f monk/nun

relinchar [relin'tʃar] vi to neigh; **relincho** nm neigh; (acto) neighing

reliquia [re'likja] nf relic; **~ de familia** heirloom

rellano [re'ʎano] nm (ARQ) landing

rellenar [reʎe'nar] vt (llenar) to fill up; (CULIN) to stuff; (COSTURA) to pad; **relleno, a** adj full up; stuffed ♦ nm stuffing; (de tapicería) padding

reloj [re'lo(x)] nm clock; **~ (de pulsera)** wristwatch; **~ despertador** alarm (clock); **poner el ~** to set one's watch (o the clock); **~ero, a** nm/f clockmaker; watchmaker

reluciente [relu'θjente] adj brilliant, shining

relucir [relu'θir] vi to shine; (fig) to excel

relumbrar [relum'brar] vi to dazzle, shine brilliantly

remachar [rema'tʃar] vt to rivet; (fig) to hammer home, drive home; **remache** nm rivet

remanente [rema'nente] nm remainder; (COM) balance; (de producto) surplus

remangar [reman'gar] vt to roll up

remanso [re'manso] nm pool

remar [re'mar] vi to row

rematado, a [rema'taðo, a] adj complete, utter

rematar [rema'tar] vt to finish off; (COM) to sell off cheap ♦ vi to end, finish off; (DEPORTE) to shoot

remate [re'mate] nm end, finish; (punta) tip; (DEPORTE) shot; (ARQ) top; **de o para ~** to crown it all (BRIT), to top it off

remedar [reme'ðar] vt to imitate

remediar [reme'ðjar] vt to remedy; (subsanar) to make good, repair; (evitar) to avoid

remedio [re'meðjo] nm remedy; (alivio) relief, help; (JUR) recourse, remedy; **poner ~ a** to correct, stop; **no tener más ~** to have no alternative; **¡qué ~!** there's no choice!; **sin ~** hopeless

remedo [re'meðo] nm imitation; (pey) parody

remendar [remen'dar] vt to repair; (con parche) to patch

remesa [re'mesa] nf remittance; (COM) shipment

remiendo [re'mjendo] nm mend; (con parche) patch; (cosido) darn

remilgado, a [remil'xaðo, a] adj prim; (afectado) affected

remilgo [re'milxo] nm primness; (afectación) affectation

reminiscencia [reminis'θenθja] nf reminiscence

remiso, a [re'miso, a] adj slack, slow

remite [re'mite] nm (en sobre) name and address of sender

remitir [remi'tir] vt to remit, send ♦ vi to slacken; (en carta): **remite: X** sender: X; **remitente** nm/f sender

remo ['remo] nm (de barco) oar; (DEPORTE) rowing

remojar [remo'xar] vt to steep, soak; (galleta etc) to dip, dunk

remojo [re'moxo] nm: **dejar la ropa en ~** to leave clothes to soak

remolacha [remo'latʃa] nf beet, beetroot

remolcador [remolka'ðor] nm (NAUT) tug; (AUTO) breakdown lorry

remolcar [remol'kar] vt to tow

remolino [remo'lino] nm eddy; (de agua) whirlpool; (de viento) whirlwind; (de gente) crowd

remolque [re'molke] nm tow, towing; (cuerda) towrope; **llevar a ~** to tow

remontar [remon'tar] vt to mend; **~se** vr to soar; **~se a** (COM) to amount to; **~ el vuelo** to soar

remorder [remor'ðer] vt to distress, disturb; **~le la conciencia a uno** to have a guilty conscience; **remordimiento** nm remorse

remoto, a [re'moto, a] adj remote

remover [remo'ßer] *vt* to stir; (*tierra*) to turn over; (*objetos*) to move round

remozar [remo'θar] *vt* (*ARQ*) to refurbish

remuneración [remunera'θjon] *nf* remuneration

remunerar [remune'rar] *vt* to remunerate; (*premiar*) to reward

renacer [rena'θer] *vi* to be reborn; (*fig*) to revive; **renacimiento** *nm* rebirth; **el Renacimiento** the Renaissance

renacuajo [rena'kwaxo] *nm* (*ZOOL*) tadpole

renal [re'nal] *adj* renal, kidney *cpd*

rencilla [ren'θiʎa] *nf* quarrel

rencor [ren'kor] *nm* rancour, bitterness; **~oso, a** *adj* spiteful

rendición [rendi'θjon] *nf* surrender

rendido, a [ren'diðo, a] *adj* (*sumiso*) submissive; (*cansado*) worn-out, exhausted

rendija [ren'dixa] *nf* (*hendedura*) crack, cleft

rendimiento [rendi'mjento] *nm* (*producción*) output; (*TEC, COM*) efficiency

rendir [ren'dir] *vt* (*vencer*) to defeat; (*producir*) to produce; (*dar beneficio*) to yield; (*agotar*) to exhaust ♦ *vi* to pay; **~se** *vr* (*someterse*) to surrender; (*cansarse*) to wear o.s. out; **~ homenaje** o **culto a** to pay homage to

renegar [rene'var] *vi* (*renunciar*) to renounce; (*blasfemar*) to blaspheme; (*quejarse*) to complain

RENFE ['renfe] *nf abr* (= *Red Nacional de los Ferrocarriles Españoles*) ≈ BR (*BRIT*)

renglón [ren'glon] *nm* (*línea*) line; (*COM*) item, article; **a ~ seguido** immediately after

renombrado, a [renom'braðo, a] *adj* renowned

renombre [re'nombre] *nm* renown

renovación [renoßa'θjon] *nf* (*de contrato*) renewal; (*ARQ*) renovation

renovar [reno'ßar] *vt* to renew; (*ARQ*) to renovate

renta ['renta] *nf* (*ingresos*) income; (*beneficio*) profit; (*alquiler*) rent; **~ vitalicia** annuity; **rentable** *adj* profitable; **rentar** *vt* to produce, yield

renuncia [re'nunθja] *nf* resignation

renunciar [renun'θjar] *vt* to renounce; (*tabaco, alcohol etc*): **~ a** to give up; (*oferta, oportunidad*) to turn down; (*puesto*) to resign ♦ *vi* to resign

reñido, a [re'niðo, a] *adj* (*batalla*) bitter, hard-fought; **estar ~ con uno** to be on bad terms with sb

reñir [re'nir] *vt* (*regañar*) to scold ♦ *vi* (*estar peleado*) to quarrel, fall out; (*combatir*) to fight

reo ['reo] *nm/f* culprit, offender; **~ de muerte** prisoner condemned to death

reojo [re'oxo]: **de ~** *adv* out of the corner of one's eye

reparación [repara'θjon] *nf* (*acto*) mending, repairing; (*TEC*) repair; (*fig*) amends, reparation

reparar [repa'rar] *vt* to repair; (*fig*) to make amends for; (*observar*) to observe ♦ *vi*: **~ en** (*darse cuenta de*) to notice; (*prestar atención a*) to pay attention to

reparo [re'paro] *nm* (*advertencia*) observation; (*duda*) doubt; (*dificultad*) difficulty; **poner ~s (a)** to raise objections (to)

repartición [reparti'θjon] *nf* distribution; (*división*) division; **repartidor, a** *nm/f* distributor

repartir [repar'tir] *vt* to distribute, share out; (*CORREOS*) to deliver; **reparto** *nm* distribution; delivery; (*TEATRO, CINE*) cast; (*AM: urbanización*) housing estate (*BRIT*), real estate development (*US*)

repasar [repa'sar] *vt* (*ESCOL*) to revise; (*MECÁNICA*) to check, overhaul; (*COSTURA*) to mend; **repaso** *nm* revision; overhaul, checkup; mending

repatriar [repa'trjar] *vt* to repatriate

repecho [re'petʃo] *nm* steep incline

repelente [repe'lente] *adj* repellent, repulsive

repeler [repe'ler] *vt* to repel

repensar [repen'sar] *vt* to reconsider

repente [re'pente] *nm*: **de ~** suddenly; **~ de ira** fit of anger

repentino, a [repen'tino, a] *adj* sudden

repercusión [reperku'sjon] *nf* repercussion

repercutir [reperku'tir] *vi* (*objeto*) to rebound; (*sonido*) to echo; **~ en** (*fig*) to have repercussions on

repertorio [reper'torjo] *nm* list; (*TEATRO*) repertoire

repetición [repeti'θjon] *nf* repetition

repetir [repe'tir] *vt* to repeat; (*plato*) to have a second helping of ♦ *vi* to repeat; (*sabor*) to come back; **~se** *vr* (*volver sobre un tema*) to repeat o.s.

repetitivo, a [repeti'tißo, a] *adj* repetitive, repetitious

repicar [repi'kar] *vt* (*campanas*) to ring

repique [re'pike] *nm* pealing, ringing; **~teo** *nm* pealing; (*de tambor*) drumming

repisa [re'pisa] *nf* ledge, shelf; (*de ventana*) windowsill; **~ de chimenea** mantelpiece

repito *etc vb ver* **repetir**

replantearse [replante'arse] *vr*: **~ un problema** to reconsider a problem

replegarse [reple'varse] *vr* to fall back, retreat

repleto, a [re'pleto, a] *adj* replete, full up

réplica ['replika] *nf* answer; (*ARTE*) replica

replicar [repli'kar] *vi* to answer; (*objetar*) to argue, answer back

repliegue [re'pljeve] *nm* (*MIL*) withdrawal

repoblación [repoβla'θjon] *nf* repopulation; (*de río*) restocking; ~ **forestal** reafforestation

repoblar [repo'βlar] *vt* to repopulate; (*con árboles*) to reafforest

repollo [re'poʎo] *nm* cabbage

reponer [repo'ner] *vt* to replace, put back; (*TEATRO*) to revive; ~**se** *vr* to recover; ~ **que** to reply that

reportaje [repor'taxe] *nm* report, article

reportero, a [repor'tero, a] *nm/f* reporter

reposacabezas [reposaka'βeθas] *nm inv* headrest

reposado, a [repo'saðo, a] *adj* (*descansado*) restful; (*tranquilo*) calm

reposar [repo'sar] *vi* to rest, repose

reposición [reposi'θjon] *nf* replacement; (*CINE*) remake

reposo [re'poso] *nm* rest

repostar [repos'tar] *vt* to replenish; (*AUTO*) to fill up (with petrol (*BRIT*) o gasoline (*US*))

repostería [reposte'ria] *nf* confectioner's (shop); **repostero, a** *nm/f* confectioner

reprender [repren'der] *vt* to reprimand

represa [re'presa] *nf* dam; (*lago artificial*) lake, pool

represalia [repre'salja] *nf* reprisal

representación [representa'θjon] *nf* representation; (*TEATRO*) performance; **representante** *nm/f* representative; performer

representar [represen'tar] *vt* to represent; (*TEATRO*) to perform; (*edad*) to look; ~**se** *vr* to imagine; **representativo, a** *adj* representative

represión [repre'sjon] *nf* repression

reprimenda [repri'menda] *nf* reprimand, rebuke

reprimir [repri'mir] *vt* to repress

reprobar [repro'βar] *vt* to censure, reprove

reprochar [repro'tʃar] *vt* to reproach; **reproche** *nm* reproach

reproducción [reproðuk'θjon] *nf* reproduction

reproducir [reproðu'θir] *vt* to reproduce; ~**se** *vr* to breed; (*situación*) to recur

reproductor, a [reproðuk'tor, a] *adj* reproductive

reptil [rep'til] *nm* reptile

república [re'puβlika] *nf* republic; **R~ Dominicana** Dominican Republic; **republicano, a** *adj, nm/f* republican

repudiar [repu'ðjar] *vt* to repudiate; (*fe*) to renounce

repuesto [re'pwesto] *nm* (*pieza de recambio*) spare (part); (*abastecimiento*) supply; **rueda de ~** spare wheel

repugnancia [repuɣ'nanθja] *nf* repugnance; **repugnante** *adj* repugnant, repulsive

repugnar [repuɣ'nar] *vt* to disgust

repulsa [re'pulsa] *nf* rebuff

repulsión [repul'sjon] *nf* repulsion, aversion; **repulsivo, a** *adj* repulsive

reputación [reputa'θjon] *nf* reputation

requemado, a [reke'maðo, a] *adj* (*quemado*) scorched; (*bronceado*) tanned

requerimiento [rekeri'mjento] *nm* request; (*JUR*) summons

requerir [reke'rir] *vt* (*pedir*) to ask, request; (*exigir*) to require; (*llamar*) to send for, summon

requesón [reke'son] *nm* cottage cheese

requete... [re'kete] *prefijo* extremely

réquiem ['rekjem] (*pl ~s*) *nm* requiem

requisito [reki'sito] *nm* requirement, requisite

res [res] *nf* beast, animal

resaca [re'saka] *nf* (*en el mar*) undertow, undercurrent; (*fam*) hangover

resaltar [resal'tar] *vi* to project, stick out; (*fig*) to stand out

resarcir [resar'θir] *vt* to compensate; ~**se** *vr* to make up for

resbaladizo, a [resβala'ðiθo, a] *adj* slippery

resbalar [resβa'lar] *vi* to slip, slide; (*fig*) to slip (up); ~**se** *vr* to slip, slide; to slip (up); **resbalón** *nm* (*acción*) slip

rescatar [reska'tar] *vt* (*salvar*) to save, rescue; (*objeto*) to get back, recover; (*cautivos*) to ransom

rescate [res'kate] *nm* rescue; (*de objeto*) recovery; **pagar un ~** to pay a ransom

rescindir [resθin'dir] *vt* to rescind

rescisión [resθi'sjon] *nf* cancellation

rescoldo [res'koldo] *nm* embers *pl*

resecar [rese'kar] *vt* to dry thoroughly; (*MED*) to cut out, remove; ~**se** *vr* to dry up

reseco, a [re'seko, a] *adj* very dry; (*fig*) skinny

resentido, a [resen'tiðo, a] *adj* resentful

resentimiento [resenti'mjento] *nm* resentment, bitterness

resentirse [resen'tirse] *vr* (*debilitarse: persona*) to suffer; ~ **de** (*consecuencias*) to feel the effects of; ~ **de** (*o por*) **algo** to resent sth, be bitter about sth

reseña [re'seɲa] *nf* (*cuenta*) account; (*informe*) report; (*LITERATURA*) review

reseñar [rese'ɲar] *vt* to describe; (*LITERATURA*) to review

reserva [re'serβa] *nf* reserve; (*reservación*) reservation; **a ~ de que ... unless ...; con toda ~** in strictest confidence

reservado, a [reser'βaðo, a] *adj* reserved; (*retraído*) cold, distant ♦ *nm* private room

reservar [reser'βar] *vt* (*guardar*) to keep; (*habitación, entrada*) to reserve; ~**se** *vr* to save o.s.; (*callar*) to keep to o.s.

resfriado [resfri'aðo] *nm* cold; **resfriarse** *vr*

to cool; (MED) to catch (a) cold

resguardar [resɣwar'ðar] vt to protect, shield; **~se** vr: **~se de** to guard against; **resguardo** nm defence; (vale) voucher; (recibo) receipt, slip

residencia [resi'ðenθja] nf residence; **~l** nf (urbanización) housing estate

residente [resi'ðente] adj, nm/f resident

residir [resi'ðir] vi to reside, live; **~ en** to reside in, lie in

residuo [re'siðwo] nm residue

resignación [resiɣna'θjon] nf resignation; **resignarse** vr: **resignarse a** o **con** to resign o.s. to, be resigned to

resina [re'sina] nf resin

resistencia [resis'tenθja] nf (dureza) endurance, strength; (oposición, ELEC) resistance; **resistente** adj strong, hardy; resistant

resistir [resis'tir] vt (soportar) to bear; (oponerse a) to resist, oppose; (aguantar) to put up with ♦ vi to resist; (aguantar) to last, endure; **~se** vr: **~se a** to refuse to, resist

resolución [resolu'θjon] nf resolution; (decisión) decision; **resoluto, a** adj resolute

resolver [resol'ßer] vt to resolve; (solucionar) to solve, resolve; (decidir) to decide, settle; **~se** vr to make up one's mind

resonancia [reso'nanθja] nf (del sonido) resonance; (repercusión) repercussion

resonar [reso'nar] vi to ring, echo

resoplar [reso'plar] vi to snort; **resoplido** nm heavy breathing

resorte [re'sorte] nm spring; (fig) lever

respaldar [respal'dar] vt to back (up), support; **~se** vr to lean back; **~se con** o **en** (fig) to take one's stand on; **respaldo** nm (de sillón) back; (fig) support, backing

respectivo, a [respek'tißo, a] adj respective; **en lo ~ a** with regard to

respecto [res'pekto] nm: **al ~** on this matter; **con ~ a, ~ de** with regard to, in relation to

respetable [respe'taßle] adj respectable

respetar [respe'tar] vt to respect; **respeto** nm respect; (acatamiento) deference; **respetos** nmpl respects; **respetuoso, a** adj respectful

respingo [res'pingo] nm start, jump

respiración [respira'θjon] nf breathing; (MED) respiration; (ventilación) ventilation

respirar [respi'rar] vi to breathe; **respiratorio, a** adj respiratory; **respiro** nm breathing; (fig: descanso) respite

resplandecer [resplande'θer] vi to shine; **resplandeciente** adj resplendent, shining; **resplandor** nm brilliance, brightness; (de luz, fuego) blaze

responder [respon'der] vt to answer ♦ vi to answer; (fig) to respond; (pey) to answer

back; **~ de** o **por** to answer for; **respondón, ona** adj cheeky

responsabilidad [responsaßili'ðað] nf responsibility

responsabilizarse [responsaßili'θarse] vr to make o.s. responsible, take charge

responsable [respon'saßle] adj responsible

respuesta [res'pwesta] nf answer, reply

resquebrajar [reskeßra'xar] vt to crack, split; **~se** vr to crack, split

resquemor [reske'mor] nm resentment

resquicio [res'kiθjo] nm chink; (hendedura) crack

resta ['resta] nf (MAT) remainder

restablecer [restaßle'θer] vt to re-establish, restore; **~se** vr to recover

restallar [resta'ʎar] vi to crack

restante [res'tante] adj remaining; **lo ~** the remainder

restar [res'tar] vt (MAT) to subtract; (fig) to take away ♦ vi to remain, be left

restauración [restaura'θjon] nf restoration

restaurante [restau'rante] nm restaurant

restaurar [restau'rar] vt to restore

restitución [restitu'θjon] nf return, restitution

restituir [restitu'ir] vt (devolver) to return, give back; (rehabilitar) to restore

resto ['resto] nm (resto) rest, remainder; (apuesta) stake; **~s** nmpl remains

restregar [restre'ɣar] vt to scrub, rub

restricción [restrik'θjon] nf restriction

restrictivo, a [restrik'tißo, a] adj restrictive

restringir [restrin'xir] vt to restrict, limit

resucitar [resuθi'tar] vt, vi to resuscitate, revive

resuello [re'sweʎo] nm (aliento) breath; **estar sin ~** to be breathless

resuelto, a [re'swelto, a] pp de **resolver** ♦ adj resolute, determined

resultado [resul'taðo] nm result; (conclusión) outcome; **resultante** adj resulting, resultant

resultar [resul'tar] vi (ser) to be; (llegar a ser) to turn out to be; (salir bien) to turn out well; (COM) to amount to; **~ de** to stem from; **me resulta difícil hacerlo** it's difficult for me to do it

resumen [re'sumen] nm (pl **resúmenes**) summary, résumé; **en ~** in short

resumir [resu'mir] vt to sum up; (cortar) to abridge, cut down; (condensar) to summarize

resurgir [resur'xir] vi (reaparecer) to reappear

resurrección [resurre(k)'θjon] nf resurrection

retablo [re'taßlo] nm altarpiece

retaguardia [reta'ɣwarðja] nf rearguard

retahíla [reta'ila] nf series, string

retal [re'tal] nm remnant

retar [re'tar] vt to challenge; (desafiar) to

defy, dare

retardar [retar'ðar] vt (demorar) to delay; (hacer más lento) to slow down; (retener) to hold back

retazo [re'taθo] nm snippet (BRIT), fragment

retener [rete'ner] vt (intereses) to withhold

reticente [reti'θente] adj (tono) insinuating; (postura) reluctant; **ser ~ a hacer algo** to be reluctant o unwilling to do sth

retina [re'tina] nf retina

retintín [retin'tin] nm jangle, jingle

retirada [reti'raða] nf (MIL, refugio) retreat; (de dinero) withdrawal; (de embajador) recall; **retirado, a** adj (lugar) remote; (vida) quiet; (jubilado) retired

retirar [reti'rar] vt to withdraw; (quitar) to remove; (jubilar) to retire, pension off; **~se** vr to retreat, withdraw; to retire; (acostarse) to retire, go to bed; **retiro** nm retreat; retirement; (pago) pension

reto ['reto] nm dare, challenge

retocar [reto'kar] vt (fotografía) to touch up, retouch

retoño [re'toɲo] nm sprout, shoot; (fig) offspring, child

retoque [re'toke] nm retouching

retorcer [retor'θer] vt to twist; (manos, lavado) to wring; **~se** vr to become twisted; (mover el cuerpo) to writhe

retorcido, a [retor'θiðo, a] adj (persona) devious

retórica [re'torika] nf rhetoric; (pey) affectedness; **retórico, a** adj rhetorical

retornar [retor'nar] vt to return, give back ♦ vi to return, go/come back; **retorno** nm return

retortijón [retorti'xon] nm twist, twisting

retozar [reto'θar] vi (juguetear) to frolic, romp; (saltar) to gambol; **retozón, ona** adj playful

retracción [retrak'θjon] nf retraction

retractarse [retrak'tarse] vr to retract; **me retracto** I take that back

retraerse [retra'erse] vr to retreat, withdraw; **retraído, a** adj shy, retiring; **retraimiento** nm retirement; (timidez) shyness

retransmisión [retransmi'sjon] nf repeat (broadcast)

retransmitir [retransmi'tir] vt (mensaje) to relay; (TV etc) to repeat, retransmit; (: en vivo) to broadcast live

retrasado, a [retra'saðo, a] adj late; (MED) mentally retarded; (país etc) backward, underdeveloped

retrasar [retra'sar] vt (demorar) to postpone, put off; (retardar) to slow down ♦ vi (atrasarse) to be late; (reloj) to be slow; (producción) to fall (off); (quedarse atrás) to lag behind; **~se** vr to be late; to be slow; to

fall (off); to lag behind

retraso [re'traso] nm (demora) delay; (lentitud) slowness; (tardanza) lateness; (atraso) backwardness; **~s** (FINANZAS) nmpl arrears; **llegar con ~** to arrive late; **~ mental** mental deficiency

retratar [retra'tar] vt (ARTE) to paint the portrait of; (fotografiar) to photograph; (fig) to depict, describe; **~se** vr to have one's portrait painted; to have one's photograph taken; **retrato** nm portrait; (fig) likeness; **retrato-robot** nm Identikit ® picture

retreta [re'treta] nf retreat

retrete [re'trete] nm toilet

retribución [retriβu'θjon] nf (recompensa) reward; (pago) pay, payment

retribuir [retri'βwir] vt (recompensar) to reward; (pagar) to pay

retro... ['retro] prefijo retro...

retroactivo, a [retroak'tiβo, a] adj retroactive, retrospective

retroceder [retroθe'ðer] vi (echarse atrás) to move back(wards); (fig) to back down

retroceso [retro'θeso] nm backward movement; (MED) relapse; (fig) backing down

retrógrado, a [re'troɣraðo, a] adj retrograde, retrogressive; (POL) reactionary

retrospectivo, a [retrospek'tiβo, a] adj retrospective

retrovisor [retroβi'sor] nm (tb: espejo ~) rear-view mirror

retumbar [retum'bar] vi to echo, resound

reúma [re'uma], **reuma** ['reuma] nm rheumatism

reumatismo [reuma'tismo] nm = **reúma**

reunificar [reunifi'kar] vt to reunify

reunión [reu'njon] nf (asamblea) meeting; (fiesta) party

reunir [reu'nir] vt (juntar) to reunite, join (together); (recoger) to gather (together); (personas) to get together; (cualidades) to combine; **~se** vr (personas: en asamblea) to meet, gather

revalidar [reβali'ðar] vt (ratificar) to confirm, ratify

revalorizar [reβalori'θar] vt to revalue, reassess

revancha [re'βantʃa] nf revenge

revelación [reβela'θjon] nf revelation

revelado [reβe'laðo] nm developing

revelar [reβe'lar] vt to reveal; (FOTO) to develop

reventa [re'βenta] nf (de entradas: para concierto) touting

reventar [reβen'tar] vt to burst, explode

reventón [reβen'ton] nm (AUTO) blow-out (BRIT), flat (US)

reverencia [reβe'renθja] nf reverence;

reverenciar vt to revere

reverendo, a [reβe'rendo, a] adj reverend

reverente [reβe'rente] adj reverent

reversible [reβer'siβle] adj (prenda) reversible

reverso [re'βerso] nm back, other side; (de moneda) reverse

revertir [reβer'tir] vi to revert

revés [re'βes] nm back, wrong side; (fig) reverse, setback; (DEPORTE) backhand; **al ~** the wrong way round; (de arriba abajo) upside down; (ropa) inside out; **volver algo del ~** to turn sth round; (ropa) to turn sth inside out

revestir [reβes'tir] vt (cubrir) to cover, coat

revisar [reβi'sar] vt (examinar) to check; (texto etc) to revise; **revisión** nf revision

revisor, a [reβi'sor, a] nm/f inspector; (FERRO) ticket collector

revista [re'βista] nf magazine, review; (TEATRO) revue; (inspección) inspection; **pasar ~ a** to review, inspect

revivir [reβi'βir] vi to revive

revocación [reβoka'θjon] nf repeal

revocar [reβo'kar] vt to revoke

revolcarse [reβol'karse] vr to roll about

revolotear [reβolote'ar] vi to flutter

revoltijo [reβol'tixo] nm mess, jumble

revoltoso, a [reβol'toso, a] adj (travieso) naughty, unruly

revolución [reβolu'θjon] nf revolution; **revolucionar** vt to revolutionize; **revolucionario, a** adj, nm/f revolutionary

revolver [reβol'βer] vt (desordenar) to disturb, mess up; (mover) to move about ♦ vi: **~ en** to go through, rummage (about) in; **~se** vr (volver contra) to turn on o against

revólver [re'βolβer] nm revolver

revuelo [re'βwelo] nm fluttering; (fig) commotion

revuelta [re'βwelta] nf (motín) revolt; (agitación) commotion

revuelto, a [re'βwelto, a] pp de **revolver** ♦ adj (mezclado) mixed-up, in disorder

rey [rei] nm king; **Día de R~es** Twelfth Night

reyerta [re'jerta] nf quarrel, brawl

rezagado, a [reθa'γaðo, a] nm/f straggler

rezagar [reθa'γar] vt (dejar atrás) to leave behind; (retrasar) to delay, postpone

rezar [re'θar] vi to pray; **~ con** (fam) to concern, have to do with; **rezo** nm prayer

rezongar [reθon'gar] vi to grumble

rezumar [reθu'mar] vt to ooze

ría ['ria] nf estuary

riada [ri'aða] nf flood

ribera [ri'βera] nf (de río) bank; (: área) riverside

ribete [ri'βete] nm (de vestido) border; (fig) addition; **~ar** vt to edge, border

ricino [ri'θino] nm: **aceite de ~** castor oil

rico, a ['riko, a] adj rich; (adinerado) wealthy, rich; (lujoso) luxurious; (comida) delicious; (niño) lovely, cute ♦ nm/f rich person

rictus ['riktus] nm (mueca) sneer, grin

ridiculez [riðiku'leθ] nf absurdity

ridiculizar [riðikuli'θar] vt to ridicule

ridículo, a [ri'ðikulo, a] adj ridiculous; **hacer el ~** to make a fool of o.s.; **poner a uno en ~** to make a fool of sb

riego ['rjeγo] nm (aspersión) watering; (irrigación) irrigation

riel [rjel] nm rail

rienda ['rjenda] nf rein; **dar ~ suelta a** to give free rein to

riesgo ['rjesγo] nm risk; **correr el ~ de** to run the risk of

rifa ['rifa] nf (lotería) raffle; **rifar** vt to raffle

rifle ['rifle] nm rifle

rigidez [rixi'ðeθ] nf rigidity, stiffness; (fig) strictness; **rígido, a** adj rigid, stiff; strict, inflexible

rigor [ri'γor] nm strictness, rigour; (inclemencia) harshness; **de ~** de rigueur, essential; **riguroso, a** adj rigorous; harsh; (severo) severe

rimar [ri'mar] vi to rhyme

rimbombante [rimbom'bante] adj pompous

rímel ['rimel] nm mascara

rímmel ['rimel] nm = **rímel**

rincón [rin'kon] nm corner (inside)

rinoceronte [rinoθe'ronte] nm rhinoceros

riña ['riɲa] nf (disputa) argument; (pelea) brawl

riñón [ri'ɲon] nm kidney

río etc ['rio] vb ver **reir** ♦ nm river; (fig) torrent, stream; **~ abajo/arriba** downstream/ upstream; **~ de la Plata** River Plate

rioja [ri'oxa] nm (vino) rioja (wine)

rioplatense [riopla'tense] adj of o from the River Plate region

riqueza [ri'keθa] nf wealth, riches pl; (cualidad) richness

risa ['risa] nf laughter; (una ~) laugh; **¡qué ~!** what a laugh!

risco ['risko] nm crag, cliff

risible [ri'siβle] adj ludicrous, laughable

risotada [riso'taða] nf guffaw, loud laugh

ristra ['ristra] nf string

risueño, a [ri'sweɲo, a] adj (sonriente) smiling; (contento) cheerful

ritmo ['ritmo] nm rhythm; **a ~ lento** slowly; **trabajar a ~ lento** to go slow

rito ['rito] nm rite

ritual [ri'twal] adj, nm ritual

rival [ri'βal] adj, nm/f rival; **~idad** nf rivalry; **~izar** vi: **~izar con** to rival, vie with

rizado, a [ri'θaðo, a] adj curly ♦ nm curls pl

rizar [ri'θar] vt to curl; **~se** vr (pelo) to curl;

(*agua*) to ripple; **rizo** *nm* curl; ripple

RNE *nf abr* = **Radio Nacional de España**

robar [ro'βar] *vt* to rob; (*objeto*) to steal; (*casa etc*) to break into; (*NAIPES*) to draw

roble ['roβle] *nm* oak; **~dal** *nm* oakwood

robo ['roβo] *nm* robbery, theft

robot [ro'βot] *nm* robot; **~ (de cocina)** food processor

robustecer [roβuste'θer] *vt* to strengthen

robusto, a [ro'βusto, a] *adj* robust, strong

roca ['roka] *nf* rock

roce ['roθe] *nm* (*caricia*) brush; (*TEC*) friction; (*en la piel*) graze; **tener ~ con** to be in close contact with

rociar [ro'θjar] *vt* to spray

rocín [ro'θin] *nm* nag, hack

rocío [ro'θio] *nm* dew

rocoso, a [ro'koso, a] *adj* rocky

rodaballo [roða'baʎo] *nm* turbot

rodado, a [ro'ðaðo, a] *adj* (*con ruedas*) wheeled

rodaja [ro'ðaxa] *nf* slice

rodaje [ro'ðaxe] *nm* (*CINE*) shooting, filming; (*AUTO*): **en ~** running in

rodar [ro'ðar] *vt* (*vehículo*) to wheel (along); (*escalera*) to roll down; (*viajar por*) to travel (over) ♦ *vi* to roll; (*coche*) to go, run; (*CINE*) to shoot, film

rodear [roðe'ar] *vt* to surround ♦ *vi* to go round; **~se** *vr*: **~se de amigos** to surround o.s. with friends

rodeo [ro'ðeo] *nm* (*ruta indirecta*) detour; (*evasión*) evasion; (*AM*) rodeo; **hablar sin ~s** to come to the point, speak plainly

rodilla [ro'ðiʎa] *nf* knee; **de ~s** kneeling; **ponerse de ~s** to kneel (down)

rodillo [ro'ðiʎo] *nm* roller; (*CULIN*) rolling-pin

roedor, a [roe'ðor, a] *adj* gnawing ♦ *nm* rodent

roer [ro'er] *vt* (*masticar*) to gnaw; (*corroer, fig*) to corrode

rogar [ro'ɣar] *vt*, *vi* (*pedir*) to ask for; (*suplicar*) to beg, plead; **se ruega no fumar** please do not smoke

rojizo, a [ro'xiθo, a] *adj* reddish

rojo, a ['roxo, a] *adj, nm* red; **al ~ vivo** red-hot

rol [rol] *nm* list, roll; (*papel*) role

rollito [ro'ʎito] *nm*: **~ de primavera** spring roll

rollizo, a [ro'ʎiθo, a] *adj* (*objeto*) cylindrical; (*persona*) plump

rollo ['roʎo] *nm* roll; (*de cuerda*) coil; (*madera*) log; (*fam*) bore; **¡qué ~!** what a carry-on!

Roma ['roma] *n* Rome

romance [ro'manθe] *nm* (*amoroso*) romance; (*LITERATURA*) ballad

romano, a [ro'mano, a] *adj, nm/f* Roman; **a la romana** in batter

romanticismo [romanti'θismo] *nm* romanticism

romántico, a [ro'mantiko, a] *adj* romantic

rombo ['rombo] *nm* (*GEOM*) rhombus

romería [rome'ria] *nf* (*REL*) pilgrimage; (*excursión*) trip, outing

romero, a [ro'mero, a] *nm/f* pilgrim ♦ *nm* rosemary

romo, a ['romo, a] *adj* blunt; (*fig*) dull

rompecabezas [rompeka'βeθas] *nm inv* riddle, puzzle; (*juego*) jigsaw (puzzle)

rompeolas [rompe'olas] *nm inv* breakwater

romper [rom'per] *vt* to break; (*hacer pedazos*) to smash; (*papel, tela etc*) to tear, rip ♦ *vi* (*olas*) to break; (*sol, diente*) to break through; **~ un contrato** to break a contract; **~ a** (*empezar a*) to start (suddenly) to; **~ a llorar** to burst into tears; **~ con uno** to fall out with sb

ron [ron] *nm* rum

roncar [ron'kar] *vi* to snore

ronco, a ['ronko, a] *adj* (*afónico*) hoarse; (*áspero*) raucous

ronda ['ronda] *nf* (*gen*) round; (*patrulla*) patrol; **rondar** *vt* to patrol ♦ *vi* to patrol; (*fig*) to prowl round

ronquido [ron'kiðo] *nm* snore, snoring

ronronear [ronrone'ar] *vi* to purr; **ronroneo** *nm* purr

roña ['roɲa] *nf* (*VETERINARIA*) mange; (*mugre*) dirt, grime; (*óxido*) rust

roñoso, a [ro'ɲoso, a] *adj* (*mugriento*) filthy; (*tacaño*) mean

ropa ['ropa] *nf* clothes *pl*, clothing; **~ blanca** linen; **~ de cama** bed linen; **~ interior** underwear; **~ para lavar** washing; **~je** *nm* gown, robes *pl*

ropero [ro'pero] *nm* linen cupboard; (*guardarropa*) wardrobe

rosa ['rosa] *adj* pink ♦ *nf* rose; **~ de los vientos** the compass

rosado, a [ro'saðo, a] *adj* pink ♦ *nm* rosé

rosal [ro'sal] *nm* rosebush

rosario [ro'sarjo] *nm* (*REL*) rosary; **rezar el ~** to say the rosary

rosca ['roska] *nf* (*de tornillo*) thread; (*de humo*) coil, spiral; (*pan, postre*) ring-shaped roll/pastry

rosetón [rose'ton] *nm* rosette; (*ARQ*) rose window

rosquilla [ros'kiʎa] *nf* doughnut-shaped fritter

rostro ['rostro] *nm* (*cara*) face

rotación [rota'θjon] *nf* rotation; **~ de cultivos** crop rotation

rotativo, a [rota'tiβo, a] *adj* rotary

roto, a ['roto, a] *pp de* **romper** ♦ *adj* broken

rotonda [ro'tonda] *nf* roundabout

rótula ['rotula] *nf* kneecap; (*TEC*) ball-and-socket joint

rotulador [rotula'ðor] *nm* felt-tip pen

rotular [rotu'lar] *vt* (*carta, documento*) to head, entitle; (*objeto*) to label; **rótulo** *nm* heading, title; label; (*letrero*) sign

rotundamente [rotunda'mente] *adv* (*negar*) flatly; (*responder, afirmar*) emphatically; **rotundo, a** *adj* round; (*enfático*) emphatic

rotura [ro'tura] *nf* (*acto*) breaking; (*MED*) fracture

roturar [rotu'rar] *vt* to plough

rozadura [roθa'ðura] *nf* abrasion, graze

rozar [ro'θar] *vt* (*frotar*) to rub; (*arañar*) to scratch; (*tocar ligeramente*) to shave, touch lightly; **~se** *vr* to rub (together); **~se con** (*fam*) to rub shoulders with

rte. *abr* (= *remite, remitente*) sender

RTVE *nf abr* = **Radiotelevisión Española**

rubí [ru'ßi] *nm* ruby; (*de reloj*) jewel

rubio, a ['rußjo, a] *adj* fair-haired, blond(e) ♦ *nm/f* blond/blonde; **tabaco ~** Virginia tobacco

rubor [ru'ßor] *nm* (*sonrojo*) blush; (*timidez*) bashfulness; **~izarse** *vr* to blush

rúbrica [ru'ßrika] *nf* (*de la firma*) flourish; **rubricar** *vt* (*firmar*) to sign with a flourish; (*concluir*) to sign and seal

rudimentario, a [ruðimen'tarjo, a] *adj* rudimentary; **rudimento** *nm* rudiment

rudo, a ['ruðo, a] *adj* (*sin pulir*) unpolished; (*grosero*) coarse; (*violento*) violent; (*sencillo*) simple

rueda ['rweða] *nf* wheel; (*círculo*) ring, circle; (*rodaja*) slice, round; **~ delantera/trasera/de repuesto** front/back/spare wheel; **~ de prensa** press conference

ruedo ['rweðo] *nm* (*círculo*) circle; (*TAUR*) arena, bullring

ruego *etc* ['rweɣo] *vb ver* **rogar** ♦ *nm* request

rufián [ru'fjan] *nm* scoundrel

rugby ['ruɣßi] *nm* rugby

rugido [ru'xiðo] *nm* roar

rugir [ru'xir] *vi* to roar

rugoso, a [ru'ɣoso, a] *adj* (*arrugado*) wrinkled; (*áspero*) rough; (*desigual*) ridged

ruido ['rwiðo] *nm* noise; (*sonido*) sound; (*alboroto*) racket, row; (*escándalo*) commotion, rumpus; **~so, a** *adj* noisy, loud; (*fig*) sensational

ruin [rwin] *adj* contemptible, mean

ruina ['rwina] *nf* ruin; (*colapso*) collapse; (*de persona*) ruin, downfall

ruindad [rwin'dað] *nf* lowness, meanness; (*acto*) low o mean act

ruinoso, a [rwi'noso, a] *adj* ruinous; (*destartalado*) dilapidated, tumbledown; (*COM*) disastrous

ruiseñor [rwise'ɲor] *nm* nightingale

ruleta [ru'leta] *nf* roulette

rulo ['rulo] *nm* (*para el pelo*) curler

Rumanía [ruma'nia] *nf* Rumania

rumba ['rumba] *nf* rumba

rumbo ['rumbo] *nm* (*ruta*) route, direction; (*ángulo de dirección*) course, bearing; (*fig*) course of events; **ir con ~ a** to be heading for

rumboso, a [rum'boso, a] *adj* generous

rumiante [ru'mjante] *nm* ruminant

rumiar [ru'mjar] *vt* to chew; (*fig*) to chew over ♦ *vi* to chew the cud

rumor [ru'mor] *nm* (*ruido sordo*) low sound; (*murmuración*) murmur, buzz

rumorearse *vr*: **se rumorea que** it is rumoured that

runrún [run'run] *nm* (*voces*) murmur, sound of voices; (*fig*) rumour

rupestre [ru'pestre] *adj* rock *cpd*

ruptura [rup'tura] *nf* rupture

rural [ru'ral] *adj* rural

Rusia ['rusja] *nf* Russia; **ruso, a** *adj, nm/f* Russian

rústica ['rustika] *nf*: **libro en ~** paperback (book); *ver tb* **rústico**

rústico, a ['rustiko, a] *adj* rustic; (*ordinario*) coarse, uncouth ♦ *nm/f* yokel

ruta ['ruta] *nf* route

rutina [ru'tina] *nf* routine; **~rio, a** *adj* routine

S, s

S *abr* (= *santo, a*) St; (= *sur*) S

s. *abr* (= *siglo*) C.; (= *siguiente*) foll

S.A. *abr* (= *Sociedad Anónima*) Ltd. (*BRIT*), Inc. (*US*)

sábado ['saßaðo] *nm* Saturday

sábana ['saßana] *nf* sheet

sabandija [saßan'dixa] *nf* bug, insect

sabañón [saßa'ɲon] *nm* chilblain

saber [sa'ßer] *vt* to know; (*llegar a conocer*) to find out, learn; (*tener capacidad de*) to know how to ♦ *vi*: **~ a** to taste of, taste like ♦ *nm* knowledge, learning; **~ a** namely; **¿sabes conducir/nadar?** can you drive/swim?; **¿sabes francés?** do you speak French?; **~ de memoria** to know by heart; **hacer ~ algo a uno** to inform sb of sth, let sb know sth

sabiduría [saßiðu'ria] *nf* (*conocimientos*) wisdom; (*instrucción*) learning

sabiendas [sa'ßjendas]: **a ~** *adv* knowingly

sabio, a ['saßjo, a] *adj* (*docto*) learned; (*prudente*) wise, sensible

sabor [sa'ßor] *nm* taste, flavour; **~ear** *vt* to taste, savour; (*fig*) to relish

sabotaje [saßo'taxe] *nm* sabotage

saboteador, a [saßotea'ðor, a] *nm/f* saboteur

sabotear [saßote'ar] *vt* to sabotage

sabré *etc vb ver* **saber**
sabroso, a [sa'ßroso, a] *adj* tasty; (*fig: fam*) racy, salty
sacacorchos [saka'kortʃos] *nm inv* corkscrew
sacapuntas [saka'puntas] *nm inv* pencil sharpener
sacar [sa'kar] *vt* to take out; (*fig: extraer*) to get (out); (*quitar*) to remove, get out; (*hacer salir*) to bring out; (*conclusión*) to draw; (*novela etc*) to publish, bring out; (*ropa*) to take off; (*obra*) to make; (*premio*) to receive; (*entradas*) to get; (*TENIS*) to serve; ~ **adelante** (*niño*) to bring up; (*negocio*) to carry on, go on with; ~ **a uno a bailar** to get sb up to dance; ~ **una foto** to take a photo; ~ **la lengua** to stick out one's tongue; ~ **buenas/ malas notas** to get good/bad marks
sacarina [saka'rina] *nf* saccharin(e)
sacerdote [saθer'ðote] *nm* priest
saciar [sa'θjar] *vt* (*hambre, sed*) to satisfy; ~**se** *vr* (*de comida*) to get full up; **comer hasta** ~**se** to eat one's fill
saco ['sako] *nm* bag; (*grande*) sack; (*su contenido*) bagful; (*AM*) jacket; ~ **de dormir** sleeping bag
sacramento [sakra'mento] *nm* sacrament
sacrificar [sakrifi'kar] *vt* to sacrifice; **sacrificio** *nm* sacrifice
sacrilegio [sakri'lexjo] *nm* sacrilege; **sacrílego, a** *adj* sacrilegious
sacristía [sakris'tia] *nf* sacristy
sacro, a ['sakro, a] *adj* sacred
sacudida [saku'ðiða] *nf* (*agitación*) shake, shaking; (*sacudimiento*) jolt, bump; ~ **eléctrica** electric shock
sacudir [saku'ðir] *vt* to shake; (*golpear*) to hit
sádico, a ['saðiko, a] *adj* sadistic ♦ *nm/f* sadist; **sadismo** *nm* sadism
saeta [sa'eta] *nf* (*flecha*) arrow
sagacidad [saɣaθi'ðað] *nf* shrewdness, cleverness; **sagaz** *adj* shrewd, clever
sagitario [saxi'tarjo] *nm* Sagittarius
sagrado, a [sa'ɣraðo, a] *adj* sacred, holy
Sáhara ['saara] *nm*: **el** ~ the Sahara (desert)
sal [sal] *vb ver* **salir** ♦ *nf* salt
sala ['sala] *nf* room; (~ **de estar**) living room; (*TEATRO*) house, auditorium; (*de hospital*) ward; ~ **de apelación** court; ~ **de espera** waiting room; ~ **de estar** living room; ~ **de fiestas** dance hall
salado, a [sa'laðo, a] *adj* salty; (*fig*) witty, amusing; **agua salada** salt water
salar [sa'lar] *vt* to salt, add salt to
salarial [sala'rjal] *adj* (*aumento, revisión*) wage *cpd*, salary *cpd*
salario [sa'larjo] *nm* wage, pay
salchicha [sal'tʃitʃa] *nf* (pork) sausage; **salchichón** *nm* (salami-type) sausage

saldar [sal'dar] *vt* to pay; (*vender*) to sell off; (*fig*) to settle, resolve; **saldo** *nm* (*pago*) settlement; (*de una cuenta*) balance; (*lo restante*) remnant(s) (*pl*), remainder; **saldos** *nmpl* (*en tienda*) sale
saldré *etc vb ver* **salir**
salero [sa'lero] *nm* salt cellar
salgo *etc vb ver* **salir**
salida [sa'liða] *nf* (*puerta etc*) exit, way out; (*acto*) leaving, going out; (*de tren, AVIAT*) departure; (*TEC*) output, production; (*fig*) way out; (*COM*) opening; (*GEO, válvula*) outlet; (*de gas*) leak; **calle sin** ~ cul-de-sac; ~ **de incendios** fire escape
saliente [sa'ljente] *adj* (*ARQ*) projecting; (*sol*) rising; (*fig*) outstanding

salir [sa'lir] *vi* **1** (*partir: tb:* ~ **de**) to leave; **Juan ha salido** Juan is out; **salió de la cocina** he came out of the kitchen
2 (*aparecer*) to appear; (*disco, libro*) to come out; **anoche salió en la tele** she appeared o was on TV last night; **salió en todos los periódicos** it was in all the papers
3 (*resultar*): **la muchacha nos salió muy trabajadora** the girl turned out to be a very hard worker; **la comida le ha salido exquisita** the food was delicious; **sale muy caro** it's very expensive
4: ~**le a uno algo**: **la entrevista que hice me salió bien/mal** the interview I did went o turned out well/badly
5: ~ **adelante**: **no sé como haré para** ~ **adelante** I don't know how I'll get by
♦ ~**se** *vr* (*líquido*) to spill; (*animal*) to escape

salmo ['salmo] *nm* psalm
salmón [sal'mon] *nm* salmon
salmonete [salmo'nete] *nm* red mullet
salmuera [sal'mwera] *nf* pickle, brine
salón [sa'lon] *nm* (*de casa*) living room, lounge; (*muebles*) lounge suite; ~ **de belleza** beauty parlour; ~ **de baile** dance hall
salpicadero [salpika'ðero] *nm* (*AUTO*) dashboard
salpicar [salpi'kar] *vt* (*rociar*) to sprinkle, spatter; (*esparcir*) to scatter
salpicón [salpi'kon] *nm*: ~ **de mariscos** seafood salad
salsa ['salsa] *nf* sauce; (*con carne asada*) gravy; (*fig*) spice
saltamontes [salta'montes] *nm inv* grasshopper
saltar [sal'tar] *vt* to jump (over), leap (over); (*dejar de lado*) to skip, miss out ♦ *vi* to jump, leap; (*pelota*) to bounce; (*al aire*) to fly up; (*quebrarse*) to break; (*al agua*) to dive; (*fig*) to explode, blow up

salto ['salto] nm jump, leap; (al agua) dive; ~ **de agua** waterfall; ~ **de altura** high jump

saltón, ona [sal'ton, ona] adj (ojos) bulging, popping; (dientes) protruding

salud [sa'luð] nf health; ¡(a su) ~! cheers!, good health!; ~**able** adj (de buena ~) healthy; (provechoso) good, beneficial

saludar [salu'ðar] vt to greet; (MIL) to salute; **saludo** nm greeting; "**saludos**" (en carta) "best wishes", "regards"

salva ['salßa] nf: ~ **de aplausos** ovation

salvación [salßa'θjon] nf salvation; (rescate) rescue

salvado [sal'ßaðo] nm bran

salvaguardar [salßaɣwar'ðar] vt to safeguard

salvajada [salßa'xaða] nf atrocity

salvaje [sal'ßaxe] adj wild; (tribu) savage; **salvajismo** nm savagery

salvamento [salßa'mento] nm rescue

salvar [sal'ßar] vt (rescatar) to save, rescue; (resolver) to overcome, resolve; (cubrir distancias) to cover, travel; (hacer excepción) to except, exclude; (barco) to salvage

salvavidas [salßa'ßiðas] adj inv: **bote/chaleco/cinturón** ~ lifeboat/life jacket/life belt

salvo, a ['salßo, a] adj safe ♦ adv except (for), save; **a** ~ out of danger; ~ **que** unless; ~**conducto** nm safe-conduct

san [san] adj saint; **S**~ **Juan** St John

sanar [sa'nar] vt (herida) to heal; (persona) to cure ♦ vi (persona) to get well, recover; (herida) to heal

sanatorio [sana'torjo] nm sanatorium

sanción [san'θjon] nf sanction; **sancionar** vt to sanction

sandalia [san'dalja] nf sandal

sandez [san'deθ] nf foolishness

sandía [san'dia] nf watermelon

sandwich ['sandwitʃ] (pl ~**s**, ~**es**) nm sandwich

saneamiento [sanea'mjento] nm sanitation

sanear [sane'ar] vt to clean up; (terreno) to drain

sangrar [san'grar] vt, vi to bleed; **sangre** nf blood

sangría [san'gria] nf sangria, sweetened drink of red wine with fruit

sangriento, a [san'grjento, a] adj bloody

sanguijuela [sangi'xwela] nf (ZOOL, fig) leech

sanguinario, a [sangi'narjo, a] adj bloodthirsty

sanguíneo, a [san'gineo, a] adj blood cpd

sanidad [sani'ðaθ] nf: ~ (**pública**) public health

sanitario, a [sani'tarjo, a] adj health cpd; ~**s** nmpl toilets (BRIT), washroom (US)

sano, a ['sano, a] adj healthy; (sin daños)

sound; (comida) wholesome; (entero) whole, intact; ~ **y salvo** safe and sound

Santiago [san'tjaɣo] nm: ~ (**de Chile**) Santiago

santiamén [santja'men] nm: **en un** ~ in no time at all

santidad [santi'ðaθ] nf holiness, sanctity

santiguarse [santi'ɣwarse] vr to make the sign of the cross

santo, a ['santo, a] adj holy; (fig) wonderful, miraculous ♦ nm/f saint ♦ nm saint's day; ~ **y seña** password

santuario [san'twarjo] nm sanctuary, shrine

saña ['sana] nf rage, fury

sapo ['sapo] nm toad

saque ['sake] nm (TENIS) service, serve; (FÚTBOL) throw-in; ~ **de esquina** corner (kick)

saquear [sake'ar] vt (MIL) to sack; (robar) to loot, plunder; (fig) to ransack; **saqueo** nm sacking; looting, plundering; ransacking

sarampión [saram'pjon] nm measles sg

sarcasmo [sar'kasmo] nm sarcasm; **sarcástico, a** adj sarcastic

sardina [sar'ðina] nf sardine

sargento [sar'xento] nm sergeant

sarmiento [sar'mjento] nm (BOT) vine shoot

sarna ['sarna] nf itch; (MED) scabies

sarpullido [sarpu'ʎiðo] nm (MED) rash

sarro ['sarro] nm (en dientes) tartar, plaque

sartén [sar'ten] nf frying pan

sastre ['sastre] nm tailor; ~**ría** nf (arte) tailoring; (tienda) tailor's (shop)

Satanás [sata'nas] nm Satan

satélite [sa'telite] nm satellite

sátira ['satira] nf satire

satisfacción [satisfak'θjon] nf satisfaction

satisfacer [satisfa'θer] vt to satisfy; (gastos) to meet; (pérdida) to make good; ~**se** vr to satisfy o.s., be satisfied; (vengarse) to take revenge; **satisfecho, a** adj satisfied; (contento) content(ed), happy; (tb: satisfecho de sí mismo) self-satisfied, smug

saturar [satu'rar] vt to saturate; ~**se** vr (mercado, aeropuerto) to reach saturation point

sauce ['sauθe] nm willow; ~ **llorón** weeping willow

sauna ['sauna] nf sauna

savia ['saßja] nf sap

saxofón [sakso'fon] nm saxophone

sazonar [saθo'nar] vt to ripen; (CULIN) to flavour, season

SE abr (= sudeste) SE

PALABRA CLAVE

---

se [se] pron **1** (reflexivo: sg: m) himself; (: f) herself; (: pl) themselves; (: cosa) itself; (: de Vd) yourself; (: de Vds) yourselves; ~ **está preparando** she's preparing herself; **para usos**

léxicos del pron ver el vb en cuestión, p.ej. **arrepentirse**

2 (*con complemento indirecto*) to him; to her; to them; to it; to you; **a usted ~ lo dije ayer** I told you yesterday; **~ compró un sombrero** he bought himself a hat; **~ rompió la pierna** he broke his leg

3 (*uso recíproco*) each other, one another; **~ miraron (el uno al otro)** they looked at each other o one another

4 (*en oraciones pasivas*): **se han vendido muchos libros** a lot of books have been sold

5 (*impers*): **~ dice que** people say that, it is said that; **allí ~ come muy bien** the food there is very good, you can eat very well there

---

sé *vb ver* **saber; ser**
sea *etc vb ver* **ser**
sebo ['seβo] *nm* fat, grease
secador [seka'ðor] *nm*: **~ de pelo** hair-dryer
secadora [seka'ðora] *nf* tumble dryer
secar [se'kar] *vt* to dry; **~se** *vr* to dry (off); (*río, planta*) to dry up
sección [sek'θjon] *nf* section
seco, a ['seko, a] *adj* dry; (*carácter*) cold; (*respuesta*) sharp, curt; **habrá pan a secas** there will be just bread; **decir algo a secas** to say sth curtly; **parar en ~** to stop dead
secretaría [sekreta'ria] *nf* secretariat
secretario, a [sekre'tarjo, a] *nm/f* secretary
secreto, a [se'kreto, a] *adj* secret; (*persona*) secretive ♦ *nm* secret; (*calidad*) secrecy
secta ['sekta] *nf* sect; **~rio, a** *adj* sectarian
sector [sek'tor] *nm* sector
secuela [se'kwela] *nf* consequence
secuencia [se'kwenθja] *nf* sequence
secuestrar [sekwes'trar] *vt* to kidnap; (*bienes*) to seize, confiscate; **secuestro** *nm* kidnapping; seizure, confiscation
secular [seku'lar] *adj* secular
secundar [sekun'dar] *vt* to second, support
secundario, a [sekun'darjo, a] *adj* secondary
sed [seð] *nf* thirst; **tener ~** to be thirsty
seda ['seða] *nf* silk
sedal [se'ðal] *nm* fishing line
sedante [se'ðante] *nm* sedative
sede ['seðe] *nf* (*de gobierno*) seat; (*de compañía*) headquarters *pl*; **Santa S~** Holy See
sedentario, a [seðen'tarjo, a] *adj* sedentary
sediento, a [se'ðjento, a] *adj* thirsty
sedimento [seði'mento] *nm* sediment
sedoso, a [se'ðoso, a] *adj* silky, silken
seducción [seðuk'θjon] *nf* seduction
seducir [seðu'θir] *vt* to seduce; (*cautivar*) to charm, fascinate; (*atraer*) to attract; **seductor, a** *adj* seductive; charming, fascinating; attractive ♦ *nm/f* seducer

segar [se'ɣar] *vt* (*mies*) to reap, cut; (*hierba*) to mow, cut
seglar [se'ɣlar] *adj* secular, lay
segregación [seɣreɣa'θjon] *nf* segregation. **~ racial** racial segregation
segregar [seɣre'ɣar] *vt* to segregate, separate
seguida [se'ɣiða] *nf*: **en ~** at once, right away
seguido, a [se'ɣiðo, a] *adj* (*continuo*) continuous, unbroken; (*recto*) straight ♦ *adv* (*directo*) straight (on); (*después*) after; (*AM: a menudo*) often; **~s** consecutive, successive; **5 días ~s** 5 days running, 5 days in a row
seguimiento [seɣi'mjento] *nm* chase, pursuit; (*continuación*) continuation
seguir [se'ɣir] *vt* to follow; (*venir después*) to follow on, come after; (*proseguir*) to continue; (*perseguir*) to chase, pursue ♦ *vi* (*gen*) to follow; (*continuar*) to continue, carry o go on; **~se** *vr* to follow; **sigo sin comprender** I still don't understand; **sigue lloviendo** it's still raining
según [se'ɣun] *prep* according to ♦ *adv*: **¿irás? — ~** are you going? — it all depends ♦ *conj* as; **~ caminamos** while we walk
segundo, a [se'ɣundo, a] *adj* second ♦ *nm* second ♦ *nf* second meaning; **de segunda mano** second-hand; **segunda (clase)** second class; **segunda enseñanza** secondary education; **segunda (marcha)** (*AUT*) second (gear)
seguramente [seɣura'mente] *adv* surely; (*con certeza*) for sure, with certainty
seguridad [seɣuri'ðað] *nf* safety; (*del estado, de casa etc*) security; (*certidumbre*) certainty; (*confianza*) confidence; (*estabilidad*) stability; **~ social** social security
seguro, a [se'ɣuro, a] *adj* (*cierto*) sure, certain; (*fiel*) trustworthy; (*libre de peligro*) safe; (*bien defendido, firme*) secure ♦ *adv* for sure, certainly ♦ *nm* (*COM*) insurance; **~ contra terceros/a todo riesgo** third party/ comprehensive insurance; **~s sociales** social security *sg*
seis [seis] *num* six
seísmo [se'ismo] *nm* tremor, earthquake
selección [selek'θjon] *nf* selection; **seleccionar** *vt* to pick, choose, select
selectividad [selektiβi'ðað] (*ESP*) *nf* university entrance examination
selecto, a [se'lekto, a] *adj* select, choice; (*escogido*) selected
sellar [se'ʎar] *vt* (*documento oficial*) to seal; (*pasaporte, visado*) to stamp
sello ['seʎo] *nm* stamp; (*precinto*) seal
selva ['selβa] *nf* (*bosque*) forest, woods *pl*; (*jungla*) jungle
semáforo [se'maforo] *nm* (*AUTO*) traffic lights *pl*; (*FERRO*) signal
semana [se'mana] *nf* week; **entre ~** during

the week; **S~ Santa** Holy Week; **semanal** *adj* weekly; **~rio** *nm* weekly magazine

semblante [sem'blante] *nm* face; *(fig)* look

sembrar [sem'brar] *vt* to sow; *(objetos)* to sprinkle, scatter about; *(noticias etc)* to spread

semejante [seme'xante] *adj (parecido)* similar ♦ *nm* fellow man, fellow creature; **~s** alike, similar; **nunca hizo cosa ~** he never did any such thing; **semejanza** *nf* similarity, resemblance

semejar [seme'xar] *vi* to seem like, resemble; **~se** *vr* to look alike, be similar

semen ['semen] *nm* semen

semestral [semes'tral] *adj* half-yearly, bi-annual

semicírculo [semi'θirkulo] *nm* semicircle

semidesnatado, a [semiðesna'taðo, a] *adj* semi-skimmed

semifinal [semifi'nal] *nf* semifinal

semilla [se'miʎa] *nf* seed

seminario [semi'narjo] *nm (REL)* seminary; *(ESCOL)* seminar

sémola ['semola] *nf* semolina

Sena ['sena] *nm*: **el ~** the (river) Seine

senado [se'naðo] *nm* senate; **senador, a** *nm/f* senator

sencillez [senθi'ʎeθ] *nf* simplicity; *(de persona)* naturalness; **sencillo, a** *adj* simple, natural, unaffected

senda ['senda] *nf* path, track

senderismo [sende'rismo] *nm* hiking

sendero [sen'dero] *nm* path, track

sendos, as ['sendos, as] *adj pl*: **les dio ~ golpes** he hit both of them

senil [se'nil] *adj* senile

seno ['seno] *nm (ANAT)* bosom, bust; *(fig)* bosom; **~s** breasts

sensación [sensa'θjon] *nf* sensation; *(sentido)* sense; *(sentimiento)* feeling; **sensacional** *adj* sensational

sensato, a [sen'sato, a] *adj* sensible

sensible [sen'sible] *adj* sensitive; *(apreciable)* perceptible, appreciable; *(pérdida)* considerable; **~ro, a** *adj* sentimental

sensitivo, a [sensi'tiβo, a] *adj* sense *cpd*

sensorial [senso'rjal] *adj* sensory

sensual [sen'swal] *adj* sensual

sentada [sen'taða] *nf* sitting; *(protesta)* sit-in

sentado, a [sen'taðo, a] *adj*: **estar ~** to sit, be sitting (down); **dar por ~** to take for granted, assume

sentar [sen'tar] *vt* to sit, seat; *(fig)* to establish ♦ *vi (vestido)* to suit; *(alimento)*: **~ bien/mal a** to agree/disagree with; **~se** *vr (persona)* to sit, sit down; *(los depósitos)* to settle

sentencia [sen'tenθja] *nf (máxima)* maxim, saying; *(JUR)* sentence; **sentenciar** *vt* to sentence

sentido, a [sen'tiðo, a] *adj (pérdida)* regrettable; *(carácter)* sensitive ♦ *nm* sense; *(sentimiento)* feeling; *(significado)* sense, meaning; *(dirección)* direction; **mi más ~ pésame** my deepest sympathy; **~ del humor** sense of humour; **~ único** one-way (street); **tener ~** to make sense

sentimental [sentimen'tal] *adj* sentimental; **vida ~** love life

sentimiento [senti'mjento] *nm* feeling

sentir [sen'tir] *vt* to feel; *(percibir)* to perceive, sense; *(lamentar)* to regret, be sorry for ♦ *vi (tener la sensación)* to feel; *(lamentarse)* to feel sorry ♦ *nm* opinion, judgement; **~se bien/mal** to feel well/ill; **lo siento** I'm sorry

seña ['seɲa] *nf* sign; *(MIL)* password; **~s** *nfpl (dirección)* address *sg*; **~s personales** personal description *sg*

señal [se'ɲal] *nf* sign; *(síntoma)* symptom; *(FERRO, TELEC)* signal; *(marca)* mark; *(COM)* deposit; **en ~ de** as a token of, as a sign of; **~ar** *vt* to mark; *(indicar)* to point out, indicate

señor [se'ɲor] *nm (hombre)* man; *(caballero)* gentleman; *(dueño)* owner, master; *(trato: antes de nombre propio)* Mr; (: *hablando directamente)* sir; **muy ~ mío** Dear Sir; **el ~ alcalde/presidente** the mayor/president

señora [se'ɲora] *nf (dama)* lady; *(trato: antes de nombre propio)* Mrs; (: *hablando directamente)* madam; *(esposa)* wife; **Nuestra S~** Our Lady

señorita [seɲo'rita] *nf (con nombre y/o apellido)* Miss; *(mujer joven)* young lady

señorito [seɲo'rito] *nm* young gentleman; *(pey)* rich kid

señuelo [se'ɲwelo] *nm* decoy

sepa *etc vb ver* **saber**

separación [separa'θjon] *nf* separation; *(división)* division; *(hueco)* gap

separar [sepa'rar] *vt* to separate; *(dividir)* to divide; **~se** *vr (parte)* to come away; *(partes)* to come apart; *(persona)* to leave, go away; *(matrimonio)* to separate; **separatismo** *nm* separatism

sepia ['sepja] *nf* cuttlefish

septentrional [septentrjo'nal] *adj* northern

septiembre [sep'tjembre] *nm* September

séptimo, a ['septimo, a] *adj, nm* seventh

sepulcral [sepul'kral] *adj (fig: silencio, atmósfera)* deadly; **sepulcro** *nm* tomb, grave

sepultar [sepul'tar] *vt* to bury; **sepultura** *nf (acto)* burial; *(tumba)* grave, tomb

sequedad [seke'ðað] *nf* dryness; *(fig)* brusqueness, curtness

sequía [se'kia] *nf* drought

séquito ['sekito] *nm (de rey etc)* retinue; *(seguidores)* followers *pl*

PALABRA CLAVE

ser [ser] vi **1** (*descripción*) to be; **es médica/
muy alta** she's a doctor/very tall; **la familia es
de Cuzco** his (o her *etc*) family is from Cuzco;
soy Ana (*TELEC*) Ana speaking o here
2 (*propiedad*): **es de Joaquín** it's Joaquín's, it
belongs to Joaquín
3 (*horas, fechas, números*): **es la una** it's one
o'clock; **son las seis y media** it's half-past six;
es el 1 de junio it's the first of June; **somos/
son seis** there are six of us/them
4 (*en oraciones pasivas*): **ha sido descubierto
ya** it's already been discovered
5: **es de esperar que** ... it is to be hoped o I
etc hope that ...
6 (*locuciones con sub*): **o sea** that is to say;
sea él sea su hermana either him or his sister
7: **a no ~ por él** ... but for him ...
8: **a no ~ que**: **a no ~ que tenga uno ya** unless
he's got one already
♦ *nm* being; **~ humano** human being

serenarse [sere'narse] *vr* to calm down
sereno, a [se'reno, a] *adj* (*persona*) calm,
unruffled; (*el tiempo*) fine, settled; (*ambiente*)
calm, peaceful ♦ *nm* night watchman
serial [ser'jal] *nm* serial
serie [serje] *nf* series; (*cadena*) sequence,
succession; **fuera de ~** out of order; (*fig*)
special, out of the ordinary; **fabricación en ~**
mass production
seriedad [serje'ðað] *nf* seriousness;
(*formalidad*) reliability; **serio, a** *adj* serious;
reliable, dependable; grave, serious; **en serio**
adv seriously
serigrafía [seriɣra'fia] *nf* silk-screen printing
sermón [ser'mon] *nm* (*REL*) sermon
seropositivo, a [seroposi'tiβo] *adj* HIV
positive
serpentear [serpente'ar] *vi* to wriggle;
(*camino, río*) to wind, snake
serpentina [serpen'tina] *nf* streamer
serpiente [ser'pjente] *nf* snake; **~ de
cascabel** rattlesnake
serranía [serra'nia] *nf* mountainous area
serrar [se'rrar] *vt* = **aserrar**
serrín [se'rrin] *nm* = **aserrín**
serrucho [se'rrutʃo] *nm* saw
servicio [ser'βiθjo] *nm* service; **~s** *nmpl*
toilet(s); **~ incluido** service charge included;
~ militar military service
servidumbre [serβi'ðumbre] *nf* (*sujeción*)
servitude; (*criados*) servants *pl*, staff
servil [ser'βil] *adj* servile
servilleta [serβi'ʎeta] *nf* serviette, napkin
servir [ser'βir] *vt* to serve ♦ *vi* to serve; (*tener
utilidad*) to be of use, be useful; **~se** *vr* to
serve o help o.s.; **~se de algo** to make use of

sth, use sth; **sírvase pasar** please come in
sesenta [se'senta] *num* sixty
sesgo [sesɣo] *nm* slant, twist; (*fig*) slant, twist
sesión [se'sjon] *nf* (*POL*) session, sitting;
(*CINE*) showing
seso ['seso] *nm* brain; **sesudo, a** *adj* sensible,
wise
seta ['seta] *nf* mushroom; **~ venenosa**
toadstool
setecientos, as [sete'θjentos, as] *adj, num*
seven hundred
setenta [se'tenta] *num* seventy
seto ['seto] *nm* hedge
seudónimo [seu'ðonimo] *nm* pseudonym
severidad [seβeri'ðað] *nf* severity; **severo, a**
adj severe
Sevilla [se'βiʎa] *n* Seville; **sevillano, a** *adj* of
o from Seville ♦ *nm/f* native o inhabitant of
Seville
sexo ['sekso] *nm* sex
sexto, a ['seksto, a] *adj, num* sixth
sexual [sek'swal] *adj* sexual; **vida ~** sex life
si [si] *conj* if; **me pregunto ~** ... I wonder if o
whether ...
sí [si] *adv* yes ♦ *nm* consent ♦ *pron* (*uso
impersonal*) oneself; (*sg: m*) himself; (*: f*)
herself; (*: de cosa*) itself; (*de usted*) yourself;
(*pl*) themselves; (*de ustedes*) yourselves;
(*recíproco*) each other; **él no quiere pero yo ~**
he doesn't want to but I do; **ella ~ vendrá** she
will certainly come, she is sure to come; **claro
que ~** of course; **creo que ~** I think so
siamés, esa [sja'mes, esa] *adj, nm/f* Siamese
SIDA ['siða] *nm abr* (= *Síndrome de
Inmunodeficiencia Adquirida*) AIDS
siderúrgico, a [siðe'rurxico, a] *adj* iron and
steel *cpd*
sidra ['siðra] *nf* cider
siembra ['sjembra] *nf* sowing
siempre ['sjempre] *adv* always; **~ que** (*cada vez*)
whenever; (*dado que*) provided that; **como ~**
as usual; **para ~** for ever
sien [sjen] *nf* temple
siento *etc vb ver* **sentar**; **sentir**
sierra ['sjerra] *nf* (*TEC*) saw; (*cadena de
montañas*) mountain range
siervo, a ['sjerβo, a] *nm/f* slave
siesta ['sjesta] *nf* siesta, nap; **echar la ~ to**
have an afternoon nap o a siesta
siete ['sjete] *num* seven
sífilis ['sifilis] *nf* syphilis
sifón [si'fon] *nm* syphon; **whisky con ~** whisky
and soda
sigla ['siɣla] *nf* abbreviation; acronym
siglo ['siɣlo] *nm* century; (*fig*) age
significación [siɣnifika'θjon] *nf* significance
significado [siɣnifi'kaðo] *nm* (*de palabra
etc*) meaning

significar [siɣnifi'kar] *vt* to mean, signify; (*notificar*) to make known, express; **significativo, a** *adj* significant

signo ['siɣno] *nm* sign; **~ de admiración** *o* **exclamación** exclamation mark; **~ de interrogación** question mark

sigo *etc vb ver* **seguir**

siguiente [si'ɣjente] *adj* next, following

siguió *etc vb ver* **seguir**

sílaba ['silaβa] *nf* syllable

silbar [sil'ßar] *vt, vi* to whistle; **silbato** *nm* whistle; **silbido** *nm* whistle, whistling

silenciador [silenθja'ðor] *nm* silencer

silenciar [silen'θjar] *vt* (*persona*) to silence; (*escándalo*) to hush up; **silencio** *nm* silence, quiet; **silencioso, a** *adj* silent, quiet

silla ['siʎa] *nf* (*asiento*) chair; (*tb: ~ de montar*) saddle; **~ de ruedas** wheelchair

sillón [si'ʎon] *nm* armchair, easy chair

silueta [si'lweta] *nf* silhouette; (*de edificio*) outline; (*figura*) figure

silvestre [sil'ßestre] *adj* wild

simbólico, a [sim'boliko, a] *adj* symbolic(al)

simbolizar [simboli'θar] *vt* to symbolize

símbolo ['simbolo] *nm* symbol

simetría [sime'tria] *nf* symmetry

simiente [si'mjente] *nf* seed

similar [simi'lar] *adj* similar

simio ['simjo] *nm* ape

simpatía [simpa'tia] *nf* liking; (*afecto*) affection; (*amabilidad*) kindness; **simpático, a** *adj* nice, pleasant; kind

simpatizante [simpati'θante] *nm/f* sympathizer

simpatizar [simpati'θar] *vi*: **~ con** to get on well with

simple ['simple] *adj* simple; (*elemental*) simple, easy; (*mero*) mere; (*puro*) pure, sheer ♦ *nm/f* simpleton; **~za** *nf* simpleness; (*necedad*) silly thing; **simplificar** *vt* to simplify

simposio [sim'posjo] *nm* symposium

simular [simu'lar] *vt* to simulate

simultáneo, a [simul'taneo, a] *adj* simultaneous

sin [sin] *prep* without; **la ropa está ~ lavar** the clothes are unwashed; **~ que** without; **~ embargo** however, still

sinagoga [sina'ɣoɣa] *nf* synagogue

sinceridad [sinθeri'ðað] *nf* sincerity; **sincero, a** *adj* sincere

sincronizar [sinkroni'θar] *vt* to synchronize

sindical [sindi'kal] *adj* union *cpd*, trade-union *cpd*; **~ista** *adj, nm/f* trade unionist

sindicato [sindi'kato] *nm* (*de trabajadores*) trade(s) union; (*de negociantes*) syndicate

síndrome ['sindrome] *nm* (MED) syndrome; **~ de abstinencia** (MED) withdrawal symptoms

sinfín [sin'fin] *nm*: **un ~ de** a great many, no end of

sinfonía [sinfo'nia] *nf* symphony

singular [singu'lar] *adj* singular; (*fig*) outstanding, exceptional; (*raro*) peculiar, odd; **~idad** *nf* singularity, peculiarity; **~izarse** *vr* to distinguish o.s., stand out

siniestro, a [si'njestro, a] *adj* sinister ♦ *nm* (*accidente*) accident

sinnúmero [sin'numero] *nm* = **sinfín**

sino ['sino] *nm* fate, destiny ♦ *conj* (*pero*) but; (*salvo*) except, save

sinónimo, a [si'nonimo, a] *adj* synonymous ♦ *nm* synonym

síntesis ['sintesis] *nf* synthesis; **sintético, a** *adj* synthetic

sintetizar [sinteti'θar] *vt* to synthesize

sintió *vb ver* **sentir**

síntoma ['sintoma] *nm* symptom

sintonía [sinto'nia] *nf* (RADIO, MUS: *de programa*) tuning; **sintonizar** *vt* (RADIO: *emisora*) to tune in

sinvergüenza [simber'xwenθa] *nm/f* rogue, scoundrel; **¡es un ~!** he's got a nerve!

siquiera [si'kjera] *conj* even if, even though ♦ *adv* at least; **ni ~** not even

sirena [si'rena] *nf* siren

Siria ['sirja] *nf* Syria

sirviente, a [sir'ßjente, a] *nm/f* servant

sirvo *etc vb ver* **servir**

sisear [sise'ar] *vt, vi* to hiss

sistema [sis'tema] *nm* system; (*método*) method; **sistemático, a** *adj* systematic

sitiar [si'tjar] *vt* to besiege, lay siege to

sitio ['sitjo] *nm* (*lugar*) place; (*espacio*) room, space; (MIL) siege; **~ Web** (INFORM) website

situación [sitwa'θjon] *nf* situation, position; (*estatus*) position, standing

situado, a [situ'aðo] *adj* situated, placed

situar [si'twar] *vt* to place, put; (*edificio*) to locate, situate

slip [slip] *nm* pants *pl*, briefs *pl*

smoking ['smokin, es'mokin] (*pl* **~s**) *nm* dinner jacket (BRIT), tuxedo (US)

snob [es'nob] = **esnob**

SO *abr* (= *suroeste*) SW

sobaco [so'ßako] *nm* armpit

sobar [so'ßar] *vt* (*ropa*) to rumple; (*comida*) to play around with

soberanía [soßera'nia] *nf* sovereignty; **soberano, a** *adj* sovereign; (*fig*) supreme ♦ *nm/f* sovereign

soberbia [so'ßerßja] *nf* pride; haughtiness, arrogance; magnificence

soberbio, a [so'ßerßjo, a] *adj* (*orgulloso*) proud; (*altivo*) haughty, arrogant; (*estupendo*) magnificent, superb

sobornar [soßor'nar] *vt* to bribe; **soborno** *nm* bribe

sobra ['soßra] *nf* excess, surplus; **~s** *nfpl* left-

overs, scraps; **de ~** surplus, extra; **tengo de ~**
I've more than enough; **~do, a** adj (más que
suficiente) more than enough; (superfluo)
excessive; **sobrante** adj remaining, extra
♦ nm surplus, remainder

sobrar [so'βrar] vt to exceed, surpass ♦ vi
(tener de más) to be more than enough;
(quedar) to remain, be left (over)

sobrasada [soβra'saða] nf pork sausage
spread

sobre ['soβre] prep (gen) on; (encima) on
(top of); (por encima de, arriba de) over,
above; (más que) more than; (además) in
addition to, besides; (alrededor de) about
♦ nm envelope; **~ todo** above all

sobrecama [soβre'kama] nf bedspread

sobrecargar [soβrekar'γar] vt (camión) to
overload; (COM) to surcharge

sobredosis [soβre'ðosis] nf inv overdose

sobreentender [soβre(e)nten'der] vt to
deduce, infer; **~se** vr: **se sobreentiende que ...**
it is implied that ...

sobrehumano, a [soβreu'mano, a] adj
superhuman

sobrellevar [soβreʎe'βar] vt to bear, endure

sobremesa [soβre'mesa] nf: **durante la ~**
after dinner; **ordenador de ~** desktop
computer

sobrenatural [soβrenatu'ral] adj
supernatural

sobrenombre [soβre'nombre] nm nickname

sobrepasar [soβrepa'sar] vt to exceed,
surpass

sobreponerse [soβrepo'nerse] vr: **~ a** to
overcome

sobresaliente [soβresa'ljente] adj
outstanding, excellent

sobresalir [soβresa'lir] vi to project, jut out;
(fig) to stand out, excel

sobresaltar [soβresal'tar] vt (asustar) to
scare, frighten; (sobrecoger) to startle;
sobresalto nm (movimiento) start; (susto)
scare; (turbación) sudden shock

sobretodo [soβre'toðo] nm overcoat

sobrevenir [soβreβe'nir] vi (ocurrir) to
happen (unexpectedly); (resultar) to follow,
ensue

sobreviviente [soβreβi'βjente] adj surviving
♦ nm/f survivor

sobrevivir [soβreβi'βir] vi to survive

sobrevolar [soβreβo'lar] vt to fly over

sobriedad [soβrje'ðað] nf sobriety,
soberness; (moderación) moderation, restraint

sobrino, a [so'βrino, a] nm/f nephew/niece

sobrio, a ['soβrjo, a] adj sober; (moderado)
moderate, restrained

socarrón, ona [soka'rron, ona] adj
(sarcástico) sarcastic, ironic(al)

socavar [soka'βar] vt (tb fig) to undermine

socavón [soka'βon] nm (hoyo) hole

sociable [so'θjaβle] adj (persona) sociable,
friendly; (animal) social

social [so'θjal] adj social; (COM) company cpd

socialdemócrata [soθjalde'mokrata] nm/f
social democrat

socialista [soθja'lista] adj, nm/f socialist

socializar [soθjali'θar] vt to socialize

sociedad [soθje'ðað] nf society; (COM)
company; **~ anónima** limited company; **~ de
consumo** consumer society

socio, a ['soθjo, a] nm/f (miembro) member;
(COM) partner

sociología [soθjolo'xia] nf sociology;
sociólogo, a nm/f sociologist

socorrer [soko'rrer] vt to help; **socorrista**
nm/f first aider; (en piscina, playa) lifeguard;
socorro nm (ayuda) help, aid; (MIL) relief;
¡socorro! help!

soda ['soða] nf (sosa) soda; (bebida) soda
(water)

sofá [so'fa] (pl **~s**) nm sofa, settee; **~-cama**
nm studio couch; sofa bed

sofisticación [sofistika'θjon] nf
sophistication

sofocar [sofo'kar] vt to suffocate; (apagar) to
smother, put out; **~se** vr to suffocate; (fig) to
blush, feel embarrassed; **sofoco** nm
suffocation; embarrassment

sofreír [sofre'ir] vt (CULIN) to fry lightly

soga ['soxa] nf rope

sois vb ver **ser**

soja ['soxa] nf soya

sol [sol] nm sun; (luz) sunshine, sunlight; **hace
~** it is sunny

solamente [sola'mente] adv only, just

solapa [so'lapa] nf (de chaqueta) lapel; (de
libro) jacket

solapado, a [sola'paðo, a] adj (intenciones)
underhand; (gestos, movimiento) sly

solar [so'lar] adj solar, sun cpd

solaz [so'laθ] nm recreation, relaxation; **~ar** vt
(divertir) to amuse

soldado [sol'daðo] nm soldier; **~ raso** private

soldador [solda'ðor] nm soldering iron;
(persona) welder

soldar [sol'dar] vt to solder, weld

soleado, a [sole'aðo, a] adj sunny

soledad [sole'ðað] nf solitude; (estado infeliz)
loneliness

solemne [so'lemne] adj solemn;
solemnidad nf solemnity

soler [so'ler] vi to be in the habit of, be
accustomed to; **suele salir a las ocho** she
usually goes out at 8 o'clock

solfeo [sol'feo] nm solfa

solicitar [soliθi'tar] vt (permiso) to ask for,
seek; (puesto) to apply for; (votos) to canvass
for; (atención) to attract

solícito, a [so'liθito, a] *adj* (*diligente*)
diligent; (*cuidadoso*) careful; **solicitud** *nf*
(*calidad*) great care; (*petición*) request; (*a un*
puesto) application

solidaridad [soliðari'ðað] *nf* solidarity;
solidario, a *adj* (*participación*) joint,
common; (*compromiso*) mutually binding

solidez [soli'ðeθ] *nf* solidity; **sólido, a** *adj*
solid

soliloquio [soli'lokjo] *nm* soliloquy

solista [so'lista] *nm/f* soloist

solitario, a [soli'tarjo, a] *adj* (*persona*)
lonely, solitary; (*lugar*) lonely, desolate
♦ *nm* (*reclusa*) recluse; (*en la sociedad*)
loner ♦ *nm* solitaire

sollozar [soʎo'θar] *vi* to sob; **sollozo** *nm* sob

solo, a ['solo, a] *adj* (*único*) single, sole; (*sin*
compañía) alone; (*solitario*) lonely; **hay una**
sola dificultad there is just one difficulty; **a**
solas alone, by oneself

sólo ['solo] *adv* only, just

solomillo [solo'miʎo] *nm* sirloin

soltar [sol'tar] *vt* (*dejar ir*) to let go of;
(*desprender*) to unfasten, loosen; (*librar*) to
release, set free; (*risa etc*) to let out

soltero, a [sol'tero, a] *adj* single, unmarried
♦ *nm/f* bachelor/single woman; **solterón,**
ona *nm/f* old bachelor/spinster

soltura [sol'tura] *nf* looseness, slackness; (*de*
los miembros) agility, ease of movement; (*en*
el hablar) fluency, ease

soluble [so'luβle] *adj* (QUÍM) soluble;
(*problema*) solvable; **~ en agua** soluble in
water

solución [solu'θjon] *nf* solution; **solucionar**
vt (*problema*) to solve; (*asunto*) to settle,
resolve

solventar [solβen'tar] *vt* (*pagar*) to settle,
pay; (*resolver*) to resolve; **solvente** *adj*
(ECON: *empresa, persona*) solvent

sombra ['sombra] *nf* shadow; (*como*
protección) shade; **~s** *nfpl* (*oscuridad*)
darkness *sg*, shadows; **tener buena/mala ~** to
be lucky/unlucky

sombrero [som'brero] *nm* hat

sombrilla [som'briʎa] *nf* parasol, sunshade

sombrío, a [som'brio, a] *adj* (*oscuro*) dark;
(*triste*) sombre, sad; (*persona*) gloomy

somero, a [so'mero, a] *adj* superficial

someter [some'ter] *vt* (*país*) to conquer;
(*persona*) to subject to one's will; (*informe*) to
present, submit; **~se** *vr* to give in, yield,
submit; **~ a** to subject to

somier [so'mjer] (*pl* **somiers**) *n* spring
mattress

somnífero [som'nifero] *nm* sleeping pill

somnolencia [somno'lenθja] *nf* sleepiness,
drowsiness

somos *vb ver* **ser**

son [son] *vb ver* **ser** ♦ *nm* sound; **en ~ de**
broma as a joke

sonajero [sona'xero] *nm* (baby's) rattle

sonambulismo [sonambu'lismo] *nm*
sleepwalking; **sonámbulo, a** *nm/f*
sleepwalker

sonar [so'nar] *vt* to ring ♦ *vi* to sound; (*hacer*
ruido) to make a noise; (*pronunciarse*) to be
sounded, be pronounced; (*ser conocido*) to
sound familiar; (*campana*) to ring; (*reloj*) to
strike, chime; **~se** *vr*: **~se (las narices)** to blow
one's nose; **me suena ese nombre** that name
rings a bell

sonda ['sonda] *nf* (NAUT) sounding; (TEC)
bore, drill; (MED) probe

sondear [sonde'ar] *vt* to sound; to bore
(into), drill; to probe, sound; (*fig*) to sound
out; **sondeo** *nm* sounding; boring, drilling;
(*fig*) poll, enquiry

sonido [so'niðo] *nm* sound

sonoro, a [so'noro, a] *adj* sonorous;
(*resonante*) loud, resonant

sonreír [sonre'ir] *vi* to smile; **~se** *vr* to smile;
sonriente *adj* smiling; **sonrisa** *nf* smile

sonrojarse [sonro'xarse] *vr* to blush, go red;
sonrojo *nm* blush

soñador, a [soɲa'ðor, a] *nm/f* dreamer

soñar [so'ɲar] *vt, vi* to dream; **~ con** to dream
about o of

soñoliento, a [soɲo'ljento, a] *adj* sleepy,
drowsy

sopa ['sopa] *nf* soup

sopesar [sope'sar] *vt* to consider, weigh up

soplar [so'plar] *vt* (*polvo*) to blow away, blow
off; (*inflar*) to blow up; (*vela*) to blow out
♦ *vi* to blow; **soplo** *nm* blow, puff; (*de*
viento) puff, gust

soplón, ona [so'plon, ona] (*fam*), *nm/f*
(*niño*) telltale; (*de policía*) grass (*fam*)

sopor [so'por] *nm* drowsiness

soporífero [sopo'rifero] *nm* sleeping pill

soportable [sopor'taβle] *adj* bearable

soportar [sopor'tar] *vt* to bear, carry; (*fig*) to
bear, put up with; **soporte** *nm* support; (*fig*)
pillar, support

soprano [so'prano] *nf* soprano

sorber [sor'βer] *vt* (*chupar*) to sip; (*absorber*)
to soak up, absorb

sorbete [sor'βete] *nm* iced fruit drink

sorbo ['sorβo] *nm* (*trago: grande*) gulp,
swallow; (: *pequeño*) sip

sordera [sor'ðera] *nf* deafness

sórdido, a ['sorðiðo, a] *adj* dirty, squalid

sordo, a ['sorðo, a] *adj* (*persona*) deaf ♦ *nm/f*
deaf person; **~mudo, a** *adj* deaf and dumb

sorna ['sorna] *nf* sarcastic tone

soroche [so'rotʃe] (AM) *nm* mountain sickness

sorprendente [sorpren'dente] *adj* surprising

sorprender [sorpren'der] *vt* to surprise;

sorpresa nf surprise

sortear [sorte'ar] vt to draw lots for; (rifar) to raffle; (dificultad) to avoid; **sorteo** nm (en lotería) draw; (rifa) raffle

sortija [sor'tixa] nf ring; (rizo) ringlet, curl

sosegado, a [sose'βaðo, a] adj quiet, calm

sosegar [sose'var] vt to quieten, calm; (el ánimo) to reassure ♦ vi to rest; **sosiego** nm quiet(ness), calm(ness)

soslayo [sos'lajo]: **de ~** adv obliquely, sideways

soso, a ['soso, a] adj (CULIN) tasteless; (aburrido) dull, uninteresting

sospecha [sos'petʃa] nf suspicion; **sospechar** vt to suspect; **sospechoso, a** adj suspicious; (testimonio, opinión) suspect ♦ nm/f suspect

sostén [sos'ten] nm (apoyo) support; (sujetador) bra; (alimentación) sustenance, food

sostener [soste'ner] vt to support; (mantener) to keep up, maintain; (alimentar) to sustain, keep going; **~se** vr to support o.s.; (seguir) to continue, remain; **sostenido, a** adj continuous, sustained; (prolongado) prolonged

sotana [so'tana] nf (REL) cassock

sótano ['sotano] nm basement

soviético, a [so'βjetiko, a] adj Soviet; **los ~s** the Soviets

soy vb ver **ser**

Sr. abr (= Señor) Mr

Sra. abr (= Señora) Mrs

S.R.C. abr (= se ruega contestación) R.S.V.P.

Sres. abr (= Señores) Messrs

Srta. abr (= Señorita) Miss

Sta. abr (= Santa) St

status ['status, e'status] nm inv status

Sto. abr (= Santo) St

su [su] pron (de él) his; (de ella) her; (de una cosa) its; (de ellos, ellas) their; (de usted, ustedes) your

suave ['swaβe] adj gentle; (superficie) smooth; (trabajo) easy; (música, voz) soft, sweet; **suavidad** nf gentleness; smoothness; softness, sweetness; **suavizante** nm (de ropa) softener; (del pelo) conditioner; **suavizar** vt to soften; (quitar la aspereza) to smooth (out)

subalimentado, a [suβalimen'taðo, a] adj undernourished

subasta [su'βasta] nf auction; **subastar** vt to auction (off)

subcampeón, ona [suβkampe'on, ona] nm/f runner-up

subconsciente [suβkon'sθjente] adj, nm subconscious

subdesarrollado, a [suβðesarro'λaðo, a] adj underdeveloped

subdesarrollo [suβðesa'rroλo] nm underdevelopment

subdirector, a [suβðirek'tor, a] nm/f assistant director

súbdito, a [suβðito, a] nm/f subject

subestimar [suβesti'mar] vt to underestimate, underrate

subida [su'βiða] nf (de montaña etc) ascent, climb; (de precio) rise, increase; (pendiente) slope, hill

subir [su'βir] vt (objeto) to raise, lift up; (cuesta, calle) to go up; (colina, montaña) to climb; (precio) to raise, put up ♦ vi to go up, come up; (a un coche) to get in; (a un autobús, tren o avión) to get on, board; (precio) to rise, go up; (río, marea) to rise; **~se** vr to get up, climb

súbito, a ['suβito, a] adj (repentino) sudden; (imprevisto) unexpected

subjetivo, a [suβxe'tiβo, a] adj subjective

sublevación [suβleβa'θjon] nf revolt, rising

sublevar [suβle'βar] vt to rouse to revolt; **~se** vr to revolt, rise

sublime [su'βlime] adj sublime

submarinismo [suβmari'nismo] nm scuba diving

submarino, a [suβma'rino, a] adj underwater ♦ nm submarine

subnormal [suβnor'mal] adj subnormal ♦ nm/f subnormal person

subordinado, a [suβorði'naðo, a] adj, nm/f subordinate

subrayar [suβra'jar] vt to underline

subsanar [suβsa'nar] vt to recitfy

subscribir [suβskri'βir] vt = **suscribir**

subsidio [suβ'siðjo] nm (ayuda) aid, financial help; (subvención) subsidy, grant; (de enfermedad, paro etc) benefit, allowance

subsistencia [suβsis'tenθja] nf subsistence

subsistir [suβsis'tir] vi to subsist; (sobrevivir) to survive, endure

subterráneo, a [suβte'rraneo, a] adj underground, subterranean ♦ nm underpass, underground passage

subtítulo [suβ'titulo] nm (CINE) subtitle

suburbano, a [suβur'βano, a] adj suburban

suburbio [su'βurβjo] nm (barrio) slum quarter

subvención [suββen'θjon] nf (ECON) subsidy, grant; **subvencionar** vt to subsidize

subversión [suββer'sjon] nf subversion; **subversivo, a** adj subversive

subyugar [suββju'var] vt (país) to subjugate, subdue; (enemigo) to overpower; (voluntad) to dominate

sucedáneo, a [suθe'ðaneo, a] adj substitute ♦ nm substitute (food)

suceder [suθe'ðer] vt, vi to happen; (seguir) to succeed, follow; **lo que sucede es que** ...

the fact is that ...; **sucesión** nf succession; (serie) sequence, series

sucesivamente [suθesiβa'mente] adv: **y así ~** and so on

sucesivo, a [suθe'siβo, a] adj successive, following; **en lo ~** in future, from now on

suceso [su'θeso] nm (hecho) event, happening; (incidente) incident

suciedad [suθje'ðað] nf (estado) dirtiness; (mugre) dirt, filth

sucinto, a [su'θinto, a] adj (conciso) succinct, concise

sucio, a ['suθjo, a] adj dirty

suculento, a [suku'lento, a] adj succulent

sucumbir [sukum'bir] vi to succumb

sucursal [sukur'sal] nf branch (office)

sudadera [suða'ðera] nf sweatshirt

Sudáfrica [su'ð'afrika] nf South Africa

Sudamérica [suða'merika] nf South America; **sudamericano, a** adj, nm/f South American

sudar [su'ðar] vt, vi to sweat

sudeste [su'ðeste] nm south-east

sudoeste [suðo'este] nm south-west

sudor [su'ðor] nm sweat; **~oso, a** adj sweaty, sweating

Suecia ['sweθja] nf Sweden; **sueco, a** adj Swedish ♦ nm/f Swede

suegro, a ['swevro, a] nm/f father-/mother-in-law

suela ['swela] nf sole

sueldo ['sweldo] nm pay, wage(s) (pl)

suele etc vb ver **soler**

suelo ['swelo] nm (tierra) ground; (de casa) floor

suelto, a ['swelto, a] adj loose; (libre) free; (separado) detached; (ágil) quick, agile ♦ nm (loose) change, small change

sueño etc ['sweno] vb ver **soñar** ♦ nm sleep; (somnolencia) sleepiness, drowsiness; (lo soñado, fig) dream; **tener ~** to be sleepy

suero ['swero] nm (MED) serum; (de leche) whey

suerte ['swerte] nf (fortuna) luck; (azar) chance; (destino) fate, destiny; (especie) sort, kind; **tener ~** to be lucky; **de otra ~** otherwise, if not; **de ~ que** so that, in such a way that

suéter ['sweter] nm sweater

suficiente [sufi'θjente] adj enough, sufficient ♦ nm (ESCOL) pass

sufragio [su'fraxjo] nm (voto) vote; (derecho de voto) suffrage

sufrido, a [su'friðo, a] adj (persona) tough; (paciente) long-suffering, patient

sufrimiento [sufri'mjento] nm (dolor) suffering

sufrir [su'frir] vt (padecer) to suffer; (soportar) to bear, put up with; (apoyar) to hold up, support ♦ vi to suffer

sugerencia [suxe'renθja] nf suggestion

sugerir [suxe'rir] vt to suggest; (sutilmente) to hint

sugestión [suxes'tjon] nf suggestion; (sutil) hint; **sugestionar** vt to influence

sugestivo, a [suxes'tiβo, a] adj stimulating; (fascinante) fascinating

suicida [sui'θiða] adj suicidal ♦ nm/f suicidal person; (muerto) suicide, person who has committed suicide; **suicidarse** vr to commit suicide, kill o.s.; **suicidio** nm suicide

Suiza ['swiθa] nf Switzerland; **suizo, a** adj, nm/f Swiss

sujeción [suxe'θjon] nf subjection

sujetador [suxeta'ðor] nm (sostén) bra

sujetar [suxe'tar] vt (fijar) to fasten; (detener) to hold down; **~se** vr to subject o.s.; **sujeto, a** adj fastened, secure ♦ nm subject; (individuo) individual; **sujeto a** subject to

suma ['suma] nf (cantidad) total, sum; (de dinero) sum; (acto) adding (up), addition; **en ~** in short

sumamente [suma'mente] adv extremely, exceedingly

sumar [su'mar] vt to add (up) ♦ vi to add up

sumario, a [su'marjo, a] adj brief, concise ♦ nm summary

sumergir [sumer'xir] vt to submerge; (hundir) to sink

suministrar [sumini'strar] vt to supply, provide; **suministro** nm supply; (acto) supplying, providing

sumir [su'mir] vt to sink, submerge; (fig) to plunge

sumisión [sumi'sjon] nf (acto) submission; (calidad) submissiveness, docility; **sumiso, a** adj submissive, docile

sumo, a ['sumo, a] adj great, extreme; (autoridad) highest, supreme

suntuoso, a [sun'twoso, a] adj sumptuous, magnificent

supe etc vb ver **saber**

supeditar [supeði'tar] vt: **~ algo a algo** to subordinate sth to sth

super... [super] prefijo super..., over...;
~bueno adj great, fantastic

súper ['super] nf (gasolina) three-star (petrol)

superar [supe'rar] vt (sobreponerse a) to overcome; (rebasar) to surpass, do better than; (pasar) to go beyond; **~se** vr to excel o.s.

superávit [supe'raβit] nm inv surplus

superficial [superfi'θjal] adj superficial; (medida) surface cpd, of the surface

superficie [super'fiθje] nf surface; (área) area

superfluo, a [su'perflwo, a] adj superfluous

superior [supe'rjor] adj (piso, clase) upper; (temperatura, número, nivel) higher; (mejor:

calidad, producto) superior, better ♦ *nm/f* superior; **~idad** *nf* superiority

supermercado [supermer'kaðo] *nm* supermarket

superponer [superpo'ner] *vt* to superimpose

supersónico, a [super'soniko, a] *adj* supersonic

superstición [supersti'θjon] *nf* superstition; **supersticioso, a** *adj* superstitious

supervisar [superβi'sar] *vt* to supervise

supervivencia [superβi'βenθja] *nf* survival

superviviente [superβi'βjente] *adj* surviving

supiera *etc vb ver* **saber**

suplantar [suplan'tar] *vt* to supplant

suplemento [suple'mento] *nm* supplement

suplente [su'plente] *adj, nm/f* substitute

supletorio, a [suple'torjo, a] *adj* supplementary ♦ *nm* supplement; **teléfono ~** extension

súplica ['suplika] *nf* request; (*JUR*) petition

suplicar [supli'kar] *vt* (*cosa*) to beg (for), plead for; (*persona*) to beg, plead with

suplicio [su'pliθjo] *nm* torture

suplir [su'plir] *vt* (*compensar*) to make good, make up for; (*reemplazar*) to replace, substitute ♦ *vi*: **~ a** to take the place of, substitute for

supo *etc vb ver* **saber**

suponer [supo'ner] *vt* to suppose; **suposición** *nf* supposition

supremacía [suprema'θia] *nf* supremacy

supremo, a [su'premo, a] *adj* supreme

supresión [supre'sjon] *nf* suppression; (*de derecho*) abolition; (*de palabra etc*) deletion; (*de restricción*) cancellation, lifting

suprimir [supri'mir] *vt* to suppress; (*derecho, costumbre*) to abolish; (*palabra etc*) to delete; (*restricción*) to cancel, lift

supuesto, a [su'pwesto, a] *pp de* **suponer** ♦ *adj* (*hipotético*) supposed ♦ *nm* assumption, hypothesis; **~ que** since; **por ~** of course

sur [sur] *nm* south

surcar [sur'kar] *vt* to plough; **surco** *nm* (*en metal, disco*) groove; (*AGR*) furrow

surgir [sur'xir] *vi* to arise, emerge; (*dificultad*) to come up, crop up

suroeste [suro'este] *nm* south-west

surtido, a [sur'tiðo, a] *adj* mixed, assorted ♦ *nm* (*selección*) selection, assortment; (*abastecimiento*) supply, stock; **~r** *nm* (*also*: **~r de gasolina**) petrol pump (*BRIT*), gas pump (*US*)

surtir [sur'tir] *vt* to supply, provide ♦ *vi* to spout, spurt

susceptible [susθep'tiβle] *adj* susceptible; (*sensible*) sensitive; **~ de** capable of

suscitar [susθi'tar] *vt* to cause, provoke; (*interés, sospechas*) to arouse

suscribir [suskri'βir] *vt* (*firmar*) to sign; (*respaldar*) to subscribe to, endorse; **~se** *vr* to subscribe; **suscripción** *nf* subscription

susodicho, a [suso'ðitʃo, a] *adj* above-mentioned

suspender [suspen'der] *vt* (*objeto*) to hang (up), suspend; (*trabajo*) to stop, suspend; (*ESCOL*) to fail; (*interrumpir*) to adjourn; (*atrasar*) to postpone; **suspensión** *nf* suspension; (*fig*) stoppage, suspension

suspenso, a [sus'penso, a] *adj* hanging, suspended; (*ESCOL*) failed ♦ *nm* (*ESCOL*) fail; **quedar** *o* **estar en ~** to be pending

suspicacia [suspi'kaθja] *nf* suspicion, mistrust; **suspicaz** *adj* suspicious, distrustful

suspirar [suspi'rar] *vi* to sigh; **suspiro** *nm* sigh

sustancia [sus'tanθja] *nf* substance

sustentar [susten'tar] *vt* (*alimentar*) to sustain, nourish; (*objeto*) to hold up, support; (*idea, teoría*) to maintain, uphold; (*fig*) to sustain, keep going; **sustento** *nm* support; (*alimento*) sustenance, food

sustituir [sustitu'ir] *vt* to substitute, replace; **sustituto, a** *nm/f* substitute, replacement

susto ['susto] *nm* fright, scare

sustraer [sustra'er] *vt* to remove, take away; (*MAT*) to subtract

susurrar [susu'rrar] *vi* to whisper; **susurro** *nm* whisper

sutil [su'til] *adj* (*aroma, diferencia*) subtle; (*tenue*) thin; (*inteligencia, persona*) sharp; **~eza** *nf* subtlety; thinness

suyo, a ['sujo, a] (*con artículo o después del verbo* **ser**) *adj* (*de él*) his; (*de ella*) hers; (*de ellos, ellas*) theirs; (*de Ud, Uds*) yours; **un amigo ~** a friend of his (*o* hers *o* theirs *o* yours)

T, t

tabacalera [taβaka'lera] *nf*: **T~** Spanish state tobacco monopoly

tabaco [ta'βako] *nm* tobacco; (*fam*) cigarettes *pl*

taberna [ta'βerna] *nf* bar, pub (*BRIT*)

tabique [ta'βike] *nm* partition (wall)

tabla ['taβla] *nf* (*de madera*) plank; (*estante*) shelf; (*de vestido*) pleat; (*ARTE*) panel; **~s** *nfpl*: **estar** *o* **quedar en ~s** to draw; **~do** *nm* (*plataforma*) platform; (*TEATRO*) stage

tablao [ta'βlao] *nm* (*tb*: **~ flamenco**) flamenco show

tablero [ta'βlero] *nm* (*de madera*) plank, board; (*de ajedrez, damas*) board; **~ de anuncios** notice (*BRIT*) *o* bulletin (*US*) board

tableta [ta'βleta] *nf* (*MED*) tablet; (*de chocolate*) bar

tablón [ta'ßlon] nm (de suelo) plank; (de techo) beam; ~ **de anuncios** notice board (BRIT), bulletin board (US)

tabú [ta'ßu] nm taboo

tabular [taßu'lar] vt to tabulate

taburete [taßu'rete] nm stool

tacaño, a [ta'kaɲo, a] adj mean

tacha ['tatʃa] nf flaw; (TEC) stud; **tachar** vt (borrar) to cross out; **tachar de** to accuse of

tácito, a ['taθito, a] adj tacit

taciturno, a [taθi'turno, a] adj silent

taco ['tako] nm (BILLAR) cue; (libro de billetes) book; (AM: de zapato) heel; (tarugo) peg; (palabrota) swear word

tacón [ta'kon] nm heel; **de ~ alto** high heeled; **taconeo** nm (heel) stamping

táctica ['taktika] nf tactics pl

táctico, a ['taktiko, a] adj tactical

tacto ['takto] nm touch; (fig) tact

taimado, a [tai'maðo, a] adj (astuto) sly

tajada [ta'xaða] nf slice

tajante [ta'xante] adj sharp

tajo ['taxo] nm (corte) cut; (GEO) cleft

tal [tal] adj such; ~ **vez** perhaps ♦ pron (persona) someone, such a one; (cosa) something, such a thing; ~ **como** such as; ~ **para cual** (dos iguales) two of a kind ♦ adv: ~ **como** (igual) just as; ~ **cual** (como es) just as it is; **¿qué ~?** how are things?; **¿qué ~ te gusta?** how do you like it? ♦ conj: **con ~ de que** provided that

taladrar [tala'ðrar] vt to drill; **taladro** nm drill

talante [ta'lante] nm (humor) mood; (voluntad) will, willingness

talar [ta'lar] vt to fell, cut down; (devastar) to devastate

talco ['talko] nm (polvos) talcum powder

talego [ta'leɣo] nm sack

talento [ta'lento] nm talent; (capacidad) ability

TALGO ['talɣo] (ESP) nm abr (= tren articulado ligero Goicoechea-Oriol) ≈ HST (BRIT)

talismán [talis'man] nm talisman

talla ['taʎa] nf (estatura, fig, MED) height, stature; (palo) measuring rod; (ARTE) carving; (medida) size

tallado, a [ta'ʎaðo, a] adj carved ♦ nm carving

tallar [ta'ʎar] vt (madera) to carve; (metal etc) to engrave; (medir) to measure

tallarines [taʎa'rines] nmpl noodles

talle ['taʎe] nm (ANAT) waist; (fig) appearance

taller [ta'ʎer] nm (TEC) workshop; (de artista) studio

tallo ['taʎo] nm (de planta) stem; (de hierba) blade; (brote) shoot

talón [ta'lon] nm (ANAT) heel; (COM) counterfoil; (cheque) cheque (BRIT), check (US)

talonario [talo'narjo] nm (de cheques) chequebook (BRIT), checkbook (US); (de recibos) receipt book

tamaño, a [ta'maɲo, a] adj (tan grande) such a big; (tan pequeño) such a small ♦ nm size; **de ~ natural** full-size

tamarindo [tama'rindo] nm tamarind

tambalearse [tambale'arse] vr (persona) to stagger; (vehículo) to sway

también [tam'bjen] adv (igualmente) also, too, as well; (además) besides

tambor [tam'bor] nm drum; (ANAT) eardrum; ~ **del freno** brake drum

tamiz [ta'miθ] nm sieve; **~ar** vt to sieve

tampoco [tam'poko] adv nor, neither; **yo ~ lo compré** I didn't buy it either

tampón [tam'pon] nm tampon

tan [tan] adv so; ~ **es así que ...** so much so that ....

tanda ['tanda] nf (gen) series; (turno) shift

tangente [tan'xente] nf tangent

Tánger ['tanxer] n Tangier(s)

tangible [tan'xißle] adj tangible

tanque ['tanke] nm (cisterna, MIL) tank; (AUTO) tanker

tantear [tante'ar] vt (calcular) to reckon (up); (medir) to take the measure of; (probar) to test, try out; (tomar la medida: persona) to take the measurements of; (situación) to weigh up; (persona: opinión) to sound out ♦ vi (DEPORTE) to score; **tanteo** nm (cálculo) (rough) calculation; (prueba) test, trial; (DEPORTE) scoring

tanto, a ['tanto, a] adj (cantidad) so much, as much; **~s** so many, as many; **20 y ~s** 20-odd ♦ adv (cantidad) so much, as much; (tiempo) so long, as long ♦ conj: **en ~ que** while; **hasta ~ (que)** until such time as ♦ nm (suma) certain amount; (proporción) so much; (punto) point; (gol) goal; **un ~ perezoso** somewhat lazy ♦ pron: **cada uno paga ~** each one pays so much; ~ **tú como yo** both you and I; ~ **como eso** as much as that; ~ **más ... cuanto que** all the more ... because; ~ **mejor/peor** so much the better/the worse; ~ **si viene como si va** whether he comes or whether he goes; ~ **es así que** so much so that; **por o por lo ~** therefore; **me he vuelto ronco de o con ~ hablar** I have become hoarse with so much talking; **a ~s de agosto** on such and such a day in August

tapa ['tapa] nf (de caja, olla) lid; (de botella) top; (de libro) cover; (comida) snack

tapadera [tapa'ðera] nf lid, cover

tapar [ta'par] vt (cubrir) to cover; (envolver) to wrap o cover up; (la vista) to obstruct; (persona, falta) to conceal; (AM) to fill; **~se** vr to wrap o.s. up

taparrabo [tapa'rraβo] *nm* loincloth

tapete [ta'pete] *nm* table cover

tapia ['tapja] *nf* (*garden*) wall; **tapiar** *vt* to wall in

tapicería [tapiθe'ria] *nf* tapestry; (*para muebles*) upholstery; (*tienda*) upholsterer's (*shop*)

tapiz [ta'piθ] *nm* (*alfombra*) carpet; (*tela tejida*) tapestry; **~ar** *vt* (*muebles*) to upholster

tapón [ta'pon] *nm* (*de botella*) top; (*de lavabo*) plug; **~ de rosca** screw-top

taquigrafía [takiɣra'fia] *nf* shorthand; **taquígrafo, a** *nm/f* shorthand writer, stenographer

taquilla [ta'kiʎa] *nf* (*donde se compra*) booking office; (*suma recogida*) takings *pl*; **taquillero, a** *adj*: **función taquillera** box office success ♦ *nm/f* ticket clerk

tara ['tara] *nf* (*defecto*) defect; (COM) tare

tarántula [ta'rantula] *nf* tarantula

tararear [tarare'ar] *vi* to hum

tardar [tar'ðar] *vi* (*tomar tiempo*) to take a long time; (*llegar tarde*) to be late; (*demorar*) to delay; **¿tarda mucho el tren?** does the train take (very) long?; **a más ~** at the latest; **no tardes en venir** come soon

tarde ['tarðe] *adv* late ♦ *nf* (*de día*) afternoon; (*al anochecer*) evening; **de ~ en ~** from time to time; **¡buenas ~s!** good afternoon!; **a o por la ~** in the afternoon; in the evening

tardío, a [tar'ðio, a] *adj* (*retrasado*) late; (*lento*) slow (to arrive)

tarea [ta'rea] *nf* task; (*faena*) chore; (ESCOL) homework

tarifa [ta'rifa] *nf* (*lista de precios*) price list; (*precio*) tariff

tarima [ta'rima] *nf* (*plataforma*) platform

tarjeta [tar'xeta] *nf* card; **~ postal/de crédito/de Navidad** postcard/credit card/Christmas card; **~ cliente** loyalty card

tarro ['tarro] *nm* jar, pot

tarta ['tarta] *nf* (*pastel*) cake; (*de base dura*) tart

tartamudear [tartamuðe'ar] *vi* to stammer; **tartamudo, a** *adj* stammering ♦ *nm/f* stammerer

tártaro, a ['tartaro, a] *adj*: **salsa tártara** tartar(e) sauce

tasa ['tasa] *nf* (*precio*) (fixed) price, rate; (*valoración*) valuation; (*medida, norma*) measure, standard; **~ de cambio/interés** exchange/interest rate; **~s universitarias** university fees; **~s de aeropuerto** airport tax; **~ción** *nf* valuation; **~dor, a** *nm/f* valuer

tasar [ta'sar] *vt* (*arreglar el precio*) to fix a price for; (*valorar*) to value, assess

tasca ['taska] (*fam*) *nf* pub

tatarabuelo, a [tatara'βwelo, a] *nm/f* great-

great-grandfather/mother

tatuaje [ta'twaxe] *nm* (*dibujo*) tattoo; (*acto*) tattooing

tatuar [ta'twar] *vt* to tattoo

taurino, a [tau'rino, a] *adj* bullfighting *cpd*

Tauro ['tauro] *nm* Taurus

tauromaquia [tauro'makja] *nf* tauromachy, (art of) bullfighting

taxi ['taksi] *nm* taxi

taxista [tak'sista] *nm/f* taxi driver

taza ['taθa] *nf* cup; (*de retrete*) bowl; **~ para café** coffee cup; **tazón** *nm* (*taza grande*) mug, large cup; (*de fuente*) basin

te [te] *pron* (*complemento de objeto*) you; (*complemento indirecto*) (to) you; (*reflexivo*) (to) yourself; **¿~ duele mucho el brazo?** does your arm hurt a lot?; **~ equivocas** you're wrong; **¡cálma~!** calm down!

té [te] *nm* tea

tea ['tea] *nf* torch

teatral [tea'tral] *adj* theatre *cpd*; (*fig*) theatrical

teatro [te'atro] *nm* theatre; (LITERATURA) plays *pl*, drama

tebeo [te'βeo] *nm* comic

techo ['tetʃo] *nm* (*externo*) roof; (*interno*) ceiling; **~ corredizo** sunroof

tecla ['tekla] *nf* key; **~do** *nm* keyboard; **teclear** *vi* (MUS) to strum; (*con los dedos*) to tap ♦ *vt* (INFORM) to key in

técnica ['teknika] *nf* technique; (*tecnología*) technology; *ver tb* **técnico**

técnico, a ['tekniko, a] *adj* technical ♦ *nm/f* technician; (*experto*) expert

tecnología [teknolo'xia] *nf* technology; **tecnológico, a** *adj* technological

tedio ['teðjo] *nm* boredom, tedium; **~so, a** *adj* boring, tedious

teja ['texa] *nf* tile; (BOT) lime (tree); **~do** *nm* (tiled) roof

tejemaneje [texema'nexe] *nm* (*lío*) fuss; (*intriga*) intrigue

tejer [te'xer] *vt* to weave; (*hacer punto*) to knit; (*fig*) to fabricate; **tejido** *nm* (*tela*) material, fabric; (*telaraña*) web; (ANAT) tissue

tel [tel] *abr* (= *teléfono*) tel

tela ['tela] *nf* (*tejido*) material; (*telaraña*) web; (*en líquido*) skin; **telar** *nm* (*máquina*) loom

telaraña [tela'raɲa] *nf* cobweb

tele ['tele] (*fam*) *nf* telly (BRIT), tube (US)

tele... ['tele] *pref* tele...; **~comunicación** *nf* telecommunication; **~control** *nm* remote control; **~diario** *nm* television news; **~difusión** *nf* (television) broadcast; **~dirigido, a** *adj* remote-controlled

teléf *abr* (= *teléfono*) tel

teleférico [tele'feriko] *nm* (*de esquí*) ski-lift

telefonear [telefone'ar] *vi* to telephone

telefónico, a [tele'foniko, a] *adj* telephone

cpd

telefonillo [telefo'niʎo] *nm* (*de puerta*) intercom

telefonista [telefo'nista] *nm/f* telephonist

teléfono [te'lefono] *nm* (tele)phone; **estar hablando al ~** to be on the phone; **llamar a uno por ~** to ring sb (up) o phone sb (up); **~ móvil** car phone; **~ portátil** mobile phone

telegrafía [teleɣra'fia] *nf* telegraphy

telégrafo [te'leɣrafo] *nm* telegraph

telegrama [tele'ɣrama] *nm* telegram

tele: **~impresor** *nm* teleprinter (*BRIT*), teletype (*US*); **~novela** *nf* soap (opera); **~objetivo** *nm* telephoto lens; **~patía** *nf* telepathy; **~pático, a** *adj* telepathic; **~scópico, a** *adj* telescopic; **~scopio** *nm* telescope; **~silla** *nm* chairlift; **~spectador, a** *nm/f* viewer; **~squí** *nm* ski-lift; **~tarjeta** *nf* phonecard; **~tipo** *nm* teletype; **~ventas** *nfpl* telesales

televidente [teleßi'ðente] *nm/f* viewer

televisar [teleßi'sar] *vt* to televise

televisión [teleßi'sjon] *nf* television; **~ en colores** colour television; **~ digital** digital television

televisor [teleßi'sor] *nm* television set

télex ['teleks] *nm inv* telex

telón [te'lon] *nm* curtain; **~ de acero** (*POL*) iron curtain; **~ de fondo** backcloth, background

tema ['tema] *nm* (*asunto*) subject, topic; (*MUS*) theme; **temática** *nf* (*social, histórica, artística*) range of topics; **temático, a** *adj* thematic

temblar [tem'blar] *vi* to shake, tremble; (*de frío*) to shiver; **temblón, ona** *adj* shaking; **temblor** *nm* trembling; (*de tierra*) earthquake; **tembloroso, a** *adj* trembling

temer [te'mer] *vt* to fear ♦ *vi* to be afraid; **temo que llegue tarde** I am afraid he may be late

temerario, a [teme'rarjo, a] *adj* (*descuidado*) reckless; (*irreflexivo*) hasty; **temeridad** *nf* (*imprudencia*) rashness; (*audacia*) boldness

temeroso, a [teme'roso, a] *adj* (*miedoso*) fearful; (*que inspira temor*) frightful

temible [te'mißle] *adj* fearsome

temor [te'mor] *nm* (*miedo*) fear; (*duda*) suspicion

témpano ['tempano] *nm:* **~ de hielo** ice-floe

temperamento [tempera'mento] *nm* temperament

temperatura [tempera'tura] *nf* temperature

tempestad [tempes'tað] *nf* storm; **tempestuoso, a** *adj* stormy

templado, a [tem'plaðo, a] *adj* (*moderado*) moderate; (*frugal*) frugal; (*agua*) lukewarm; (*clima*) mild; (*MUS*) well-tuned; **templanza** *nf* moderation; mildness

templar [tem'plar] *vt* (*moderar*) to moderate; (*furia*) to restrain; (*calor*) to reduce; (*afinar*) to tune (up); (*acero*) to temper; (*tuerca*) to tighten up; **temple** *nm* (*ajuste*) tempering; (*afinación*) tuning; (*pintura*) tempera

templo ['templo] *nm* (*iglesia*) church; (*pagano etc*) temple

temporada [tempo'raða] *nf* time, period; (*estación*) season

temporal [tempo'ral] *adj* (*no permanente*) temporary; (*REL*) temporal ♦ *nm* storm

tempranero, a [tempra'nero, a] *adj* (*BOT*) early; (*persona*) early-rising

temprano, a [tem'prano, a] *adj* early; (*demasiado pronto*) too soon, too early

ten *vb ver* **tener**

tenaces [te'naθes] *adj pl ver* **tenaz**

tenacidad [tenaθi'ðað] *nf* tenacity; (*dureza*) toughness; (*terquedad*) stubbornness

tenacillas [tena'θiʎas] *nfpl* tongs; (*para el pelo*) curling tongs (*BRIT*) o iron *sg* (*US*); (*MED*) forceps

tenaz [te'naθ] *adj* (*material*) tough; (*persona*) tenacious; (*creencia, resistencia*) stubborn

tenaza(s) [te'naθa(s)] *nf(pl)* (*MED*) forceps; (*TEC*) pliers; (*ZOOL*) pincers

tendedero [tende'ðero] *nm* (*para ropa*) drying place; (*cuerda*) clothes line

tendencia [ten'denθja] *nf* tendency; **tener ~ a** to tend to, have a tendency to; **tendencioso, a** *adj* tendentious

tender [ten'der] *vt* (*extender*) to spread out; (*colgar*) to hang out; (*vía férrea, cable*) to lay; (*estirar*) to stretch ♦ *vi:* **~ a** to tend to, have a tendency towards; **~se** *vr* to lie down; **~ la cama/la mesa** (*AM*) to make the bed/lay (*BRIT*) o set (*US*) the table

tenderete [tende'rete] *nm* (*puesto*) stall; (*exposición*) display of goods

tendero, a [ten'dero, a] *nm/f* shopkeeper

tendido, a [ten'diðo, a] *adj* (*acostado*) lying down, flat; (*colgado*) hanging ♦ *nm* (*TAUR*) front rows of seats; **a galope ~** flat out

tendón [ten'don] *nm* tendon

tendré *etc vb ver* **tener**

tenebroso, a [tene'ßroso, a] *adj* (*oscuro*) dark; (*fig*) gloomy

tenedor [tene'ðor] *nm* (*CULIN*) fork; **~ de libros** book-keeper

tenencia [te'nenθja] *nf* (*de casa*) tenancy; (*de oficio*) tenure; (*de propiedad*) possession

---
PALABRA CLAVE
---

tener [te'ner] *vt* **1** (*poseer, gen*) to have; (*en la mano*) to hold; **¿tienes un boli?** have you got a pen?; **va a ~ un niño** she's going to have a baby; **¡ten** (*o* **tenga**)!, **¡aquí tienes** (*o* **tiene**)!** here you are!

2 (*edad, medidas*) to be; **tiene 7 años** she's 7

(years old); **tiene 15 cm de largo** it's 15 cm
long; *ver* **calor; hambre** *etc*
3 (*considerar*): **lo tengo por brillante** I
consider him to be brilliant; **~ en mucho a
uno** to think very highly of sb
4 (+ *pp*: = *pretérito*): **tengo terminada ya la
mitad del trabajo** I've done half the work
already
5: **~ que hacer algo** to have to do sth; **tengo
que acabar este trabajo hoy** I have to finish
this job today
6: ¿qué tienes, estás enfermo? what's the
matter with you, are you ill?
♦ **~se** *vr* **1: ~se en pie** to stand up
2: ~se por to think o.s.; **se tiene por muy listo**
he thinks himself very clever

tengo *etc vb ver* **tener**
tenia ['tenja] *nf* tapeworm
teniente [te'njente] *nm* (*rango*) lieutenant;
(*ayudante*) deputy
tenis ['tenis] *nm* tennis; **~ de mesa** table
tennis; **~ta** *nm/f* tennis player
tenor [te'nor] *nm* (*sentido*) meaning; (*MUS*)
tenor; **a ~ de** on the lines of
tensar [ten'sar] *vt* to tighten; (*arco*) to draw
tensión [ten'sjon] *nf* tension; (*TEC*) stress;
(*MED*): **~ arterial** blood pressure; **tener la
~ alta** to have high blood pressure
tenso, a ['tenso, a] *adj* tense
tentación [tenta'θjon] *nf* temptation
tentáculo [ten'takulo] *nm* tentacle
tentador, a [tenta'ðor, a] *adj* tempting
tentar [ten'tar] *vt* (*seducir*) to tempt; (*atraer*)
to attract; **tentativa** *nf* attempt; **tentativa de
asesinato** attempted murder
tentempié [tentem'pje] *nm* snack
tenue ['tenwe] *adj* (*delgado*) thin, slender;
(*neblina*) light; (*lazo, vínculo*) slight
teñir [te'nir] *vt* to dye; (*fig*) to tinge; **~se** *vr*
to dye; **~se el pelo** to dye one's hair
teología [teolo'xia] *nf* theology
teoría [teo'ria] *nf* theory; **en ~** in theory;
teóricamente *adv* theoretically; **teórico,
a** *adj* theoretic(al) ♦ *nm/f* theoretician,
theorist; **teorizar** *vi* to theorize
terapéutico, a [tera'peutiko, a] *adj*
therapeutic
terapia [te'rapja] *nf* therapy
tercer [ter'θer] *adj ver* **tercero**
tercermundista [terθermun'dista] *adj* Third
World *cpd*
tercero, a [ter'θero, a] *adj* (*delante de nmsg:*
tercer) third ♦ *nm* (*JUR*) third party
terceto [ter'θeto] *nm* trio
terciar [ter'θjar] *vi* (*participar*) to take part;
(*hacer de árbitro*) to mediate; **~se** *vr* to come
up; **~io, a** *adj* tertiary
tercio ['terθjo] *nm* third

terciopelo [terθjo'pelo] *nm* velvet
terco, a ['terko, a] *adj* obstinate
tergal ® [ter'val] *nm* type of polyester
tergiversar [terxiβer'sar] *vt* to distort
termal [ter'mal] *adj* thermal
termas ['termas] *nfpl* hot springs
térmico, a ['termiko, a] *adj* thermal
terminación [termina'θjon] *nf* (*final*) end;
(*conclusión*) conclusion, ending
terminal [termi'nal] *adj, nm, nf* terminal
terminante [termi'nante] *adj* (*final*) final,
definitive; (*tajante*) categorical; **~mente** *adv*:
~mente prohibido strictly forbidden
terminar [termi'nar] *vt* (*completar*) to
complete, finish; (*concluir*) to end ♦ *vi* (*llegar
a su fin*) to end; (*parar*) to stop; (*acabar*) to
finish; **~se** *vr* to come to an end; **~ por hacer
algo** to end up (by) doing sth
término ['termino] *nm* end, conclusion;
(*parada*) terminus; (*límite*) boundary;
~ medio average; (*fig*) middle way; **en último
~** (*a fin de cuentas*) in the last analysis; (*como
último recurso*) as a last resort
terminología [terminolo'xia] *nf*
terminology
termodinámico, a [termoði'namiko, a] *adj*
thermodynamic
termómetro [ter'mometro] *nm* thermometer
termonuclear [termonukle'ar] *adj*
thermonuclear
termo(s) ® ['termo(s)] *nm* Thermos ®
(flask)
termostato [termo'stato] *nm* thermostat
ternero, a [ter'nero, a] *nm/f* (*animal*) calf
♦ *nf* (*carne*) veal
ternura [ter'nura] *nf* (*trato*) tenderness;
(*palabra*) endearment; (*cariño*) fondness
terquedad [terke'ðað] *nf* obstinacy
terrado [te'rraðo] *nm* terrace
terraplén [terra'plen] *nm* embankment
terrateniente [terrate'njente] *nm/f*
landowner
terraza [te'rraθa] *nf* (*balcón*) balcony;
(*tejado*) (flat) roof; (*AGR*) terrace
terremoto [terre'moto] *nm* earthquake
terrenal [terre'nal] *adj* earthly
terreno [te'rreno] *nm* (*tierra*) land; (*parcela*)
plot; (*suelo*) soil; (*fig*) field; **un ~** a piece of
land
terrestre [te'rrestre] *adj* terrestrial; (*ruta*)
land *cpd*
terrible [te'rriβle] *adj* terrible, awful
territorio [terri'torjo] *nm* territory
terrón [te'rron] *nm* (*de azúcar*) lump; (*de
tierra*) clod, lump
terror [te'rror] *nm* terror; **~ífico, a** *adj*
terrifying; **~ista** *adj, nm/f* terrorist
terso, a ['terso, a] *adj* (*liso*) smooth; (*pulido*)

polished; **tersura** nf smoothness
tertulia [ter'tulja] nf (reunión informal) social gathering; (grupo) group, circle
tesis ['tesis] nf inv thesis
tesón [te'son] nm (firmeza) firmness; (tenacidad) tenacity
tesorero, a [teso'rero, a] nm/f treasurer
tesoro [te'soro] nm treasure; (COM, POL) treasury
testaferro [testa'ferro] nm figurehead
testamentario, a [testamen'tarjo, a] adj testamentary ♦ nm/f executor/executrix
testamento [testa'mento] nm will
testar [tes'tar] vi to make a will
testarudo, a [testa'ruðo, a] adj stubborn
testículo [tes'tikulo] nm testicle
testificar [testifi'kar] vt to testify; (fig) to attest ♦ vi to give evidence
testigo [tes'tiɣo] nm/f witness; ~ de cargo/descargo witness for the prosecution/defence; ~ ocular eye witness
testimoniar [testimo'njar] vt to testify to; (fig) to show; **testimonio** nm testimony
teta ['teta] nf (de biberón) teat; (ANAT: fam) breast
tétanos ['tetanos] nm tetanus
tetera [te'tera] nf teapot
tétrico, a ['tetriko, a] adj gloomy, dismal
textil [teks'til] adj textile
texto ['teksto] nm text; **textual** adj textual
textura [teks'tura] nf (de tejido) texture
tez [teθ] nf (cutis) complexion
ti [ti] pron you; (reflexivo) yourself
tía ['tia] nf (pariente) aunt; (fam) chick, bird
tibieza [ti'βjeθa] nf (temperatura) tepidness; (actitud) coolness; **tibio, a** adj lukewarm
tiburón [tiβu'ron] nm shark
tic [tik] nm (ruido) click; (de reloj) tick; (MED): ~ nervioso nervous tic
tictac [tik'tak] nm (de reloj) tick tock
tiempo ['tjempo] nm time; (época, período) age, period; (METEOROLOGÍA) weather; (LING) tense; (DEPORTE) half; a ~ in time; a un o al mismo ~ at the same time; al poco ~ very soon (after); se quedó poco ~ he didn't stay very long; hace poco ~ not long ago; mucho ~ a long time; de ~ en ~ from time to time; hace buen/mal ~ the weather is fine/bad; estar a ~ to be in time; hace ~ some time ago; hacer ~ to while away the time; motor de 2 ~s two-stroke engine; primer ~ first half
tienda ['tjenda] nf shop, store; ~ (de campaña) tent; ~ de alimentación o comestibles grocer's (BRIT), grocery store (US)
tienes etc vb ver **tener**
tienta ['tjenta] nf ver **tentar** ♦ nf: andar a ~s to grope one's way along
tiento ['tjento] vb ver **tentar** ♦ nm (tacto) touch; (precaución) wariness

tierno, a ['tjerno, a] adj (blando) tender; (fresco) fresh; (amable) sweet
tierra ['tjerra] nf earth; (suelo) soil; (mundo) earth, world; (país) country, land; ~ adentro inland
tieso, a ['tjeso, a] adj (rígido) rigid; (duro) stiff; (fam: orgulloso) conceited
tiesto ['tjesto] nm flowerpot
tifoidea [tifoi'ðea] nf typhoid
tifón [ti'fon] nm typhoon
tifus ['tifus] nm typhus
tigre ['tiɣre] nm tiger
tijera [ti'xera] nf scissors pl; (ZOOL) claw; ~s nfpl scissors; (para plantas) shears
tijeretear [tixerete'ar] vt to snip
tila ['tila] nf lime blossom tea
tildar [til'dar] vt: ~ de to brand as
tilde ['tilde] nf (TIP) tilde
tilín [ti'lin] nm tinkle
tilo ['tilo] nm lime tree
timar [ti'mar] vt (estafar) to swindle
timbal [tim'bal] nm small drum
timbrar [tim'brar] vt to stamp
timbre ['timbre] nm (sello) stamp; (campanilla) bell; (tono) timbre; (COM) stamp duty
timidez [timi'ðeθ] nf shyness; **tímido, a** adj shy
timo ['timo] nm swindle
timón [ti'mon] nm helm, rudder; **timonel** nm helmsman
tímpano ['timpano] nm (ANAT) eardrum; (MUS) small drum
tina ['tina] nf tub; (baño) bath(tub); **tinaja** nf large jar
tinglado [tin'ɡlaðo] nm (cobertizo) shed; (fig: truco) trick; (intriga) intrigue
tinieblas [ti'njeβlas] nfpl darkness sg; (sombras) shadows
tino ['tino] nm (habilidad) skill; (juicio) insight
tinta ['tinta] nf ink; (TEC) dye; (ARTE) colour
tinte ['tinte] nm dye
tintero [tin'tero] nm inkwell
tintinear [tintine'ar] vt to tinkle
tinto ['tinto] nm red wine
tintorería [tintore'ria] nf dry cleaner's
tintura [tin'tura] nf (QUÍM) dye; (farmacéutico) tincture
tío ['tio] nm (pariente) uncle; (fam: individuo) bloke (BRIT), guy
tiovivo [tio'βiβo] nm merry-go-round
típico, a ['tipiko, a] adj typical
tipo ['tipo] nm (clase) type, kind; (hombre) fellow; (ANAT: de hombre) build; (: de mujer) figure; (IMPRENTA) type; ~ bancario/de descuento/de interés/de cambio bank/discount/interest/exchange rate
tipografía [tipoɣra'fia] nf printing cpd; **tipográfico, a** adj printing cpd

tíquet ['tiket] (*pl* ~s) *nm* ticket; (*en tienda*) cash slip

tiquismiquis [tikis'mikis] *nm inv* fussy person ♦ *nmpl* (*querellas*) squabbling *sg*; (*escrúpulos*) silly scruples

tira ['tira] *nf* strip; (*fig*) abundance; ~ **y afloja** give and take

tirabuzón [tiraβu'θon] *nm* (*rizo*) curl

tirachinas [tira'tʃinas] *nm inv* catapult

tirada [ti'raða] *nf* (*acto*) cast, throw; (*serie*) series; (*TIP*) printing, edition; **de una** ~ at one go

tirado, a [ti'raðo, a] *adj* (*barato*) dirt-cheap; (*fam: fácil*) very easy

tirador [tira'ðor] *nm* (*mango*) handle

tiranía [tira'nia] *nf* tyranny; **tirano, a** *adj* tyrannical ♦ *nm/f* tyrant

tirante [ti'rante] *adj* (*cuerda etc*) tight, taut; (*relaciones*) strained ♦ *nm* (*ARQ*) stay; (*TEC*) ~s *nmpl* (*de pantalón*) braces (*BRIT*), suspenders (*US*); **tirantez** *nf* tightness; (*fig*) tension

tirar [ti'rar] *vt* to throw; (*dejar caer*) to drop; (*volcar*) to upset; (*derribar*) to knock down o over; (*desechar*) to throw out o away; (*dinero*) to squander; (*imprimir*) to print ♦ *vi* (*disparar*) to shoot; (*de la puerta etc*) to pull; (*fam: andar*) to go; (*tender a, buscar realizar*) to tend to; (*DEPORTE*) to shoot; ~se *vr* to throw o.s.; ~ **abajo** to bring down, destroy; **tira más a su padre** he takes more after his father; **ir tirando** to manage; **a todo** ~ at the most

tirita [ti'rita] *nf* (sticking) plaster (*BRIT*), bandaid (*US*)

tiritar [tiri'tar] *vi* to shiver

tiro ['tiro] *nm* (*lanzamiento*) throw; (*disparo*) shot; (*DEPORTE*) shot; (*GOLF, TENIS*) drive; (*alcance*) range; ~ **al blanco** target practice; **caballo de** ~ cart-horse; **andar de** ~s **largos** to be all dressed up; **al** ~ (*AM*) at once

tirón [ti'ron] *nm* (*sacudida*) pull, tug; **de un** ~ in one go, all at once

tiroteo [tiro'teo] *nm* exchange of shots, shooting

tísico, a ['tisiko, a] *adj* consumptive

tisis ['tisis] *nf inv* consumption, tuberculosis

títere ['titere] *nm* puppet

titiritero, a [titiri'tero, a] *nm/f* puppeteer

titubeante [tituβe'ante] *adj* (*al andar*) shaky, tottering; (*al hablar*) stammering; (*dudoso*) hesitant

titubear [tituβe'ar] *vi* to stagger; to stammer; (*fig*) to hesitate; **titubeo** *nm* staggering; stammering; hesitation

titulado, a [titu'laðo, a] *adj* (*libro*) entitled; (*persona*) titled

titular [titu'lar] *adj* titular ♦ *nm/f* holder ♦ *nm* headline ♦ *vt* to title; ~se *vr* to be entitled

título *nm* title; (*de diario*) headline; (*certificado*) professional qualification; (*universitario*) (university) degree; **a título de** in the capacity of

tiza ['tiθa] *nf* chalk

tiznar [tiθ'nar] *vt* to blacken

tizón [ti'θon] *nm* brand

toalla [to'aʎa] *nf* towel

tobillo [to'βiʎo] *nm* ankle

tobogán [toβo'ɣan] *nm* (*montaña rusa*) roller-coaster; (*de niños*) chute, slide

tocadiscos [toka'ðiskos] *nm inv* record player

tocado, a [to'kaðo, a] *adj* (*fam*) touched ♦ *nm* headdress

tocador [toka'ðor] *nm* (*mueble*) dressing table; (*cuarto*) boudoir; (*fam*) ladies' toilet (*BRIT*) o room (*US*)

tocante [to'kante]: ~ **a** *prep* with regard to

tocar [to'kar] *vt* to touch; (*MUS*) to play; (*referirse a*) to allude to; (*timbre*) to ring ♦ *vi* (*a la puerta*) to knock (on o at the door); (*ser de turno*) to fall to, be the turn of; (*ser hora*) to be due; ~se *vr* (*cubrirse la cabeza*) to cover one's head; (*tener contacto*) to touch (each other); **por lo que a mí me toca** as far as I am concerned; **te toca a ti** it's your turn

tocayo, a [to'kajo, a] *nm/f* namesake

tocino [to'θino] *nm* bacon

todavía [toða'βia] *adv* (*aun*) even; (*aún*) still, yet; ~ **más** yet more; ~ **no** not yet

PALABRA CLAVE

todo, a ['toðo, a] *adj* **1** (*con artículo sg*) all; **toda la carne** all the meat; **toda la noche** all night, the whole night; ~ **el libro** the whole book; **toda una botella** a whole bottle; ~ **lo contrario** quite the opposite; **está toda sucia** she's all dirty; **por** ~ **el país** throughout the whole country

2 (*con artículo pl*) all; every; ~s **los libros** all the books; **todas las noches** every night; ~s **los que quieran salir** all those who want to leave

♦ *pron* **1** everything, all; ~s everyone, everybody; **lo sabemos** ~ we know everything; ~s **querían más tiempo** everybody o everyone wanted more time; **nos marchamos** ~s all of us left

2: **con** ~: **con** ~ **él me sigue gustando** even so I still like him

♦ *adv* all; **vaya** ~ **seguido** keep straight on o ahead

♦ *nm*: **como un** ~ as a whole; **del** ~: **no me agrada del** ~ I don't entirely like it

todopoderoso, a [toðopoðe'roso, a] *adj* all powerful; (*REL*) almighty

toga ['toɣa] *nf* toga; (*ESCOL*) gown

Tokio ['tokjo] n Tokyo

toldo ['toldo] nm (para el sol) sunshade (BRIT), parasol; (tienda) marquee

tolerancia [tole'ranθja] nf tolerance; **tolerante** adj (sociedad) liberal; (persona) open-minded

tolerar [tole'rar] vt to tolerate; (resistir) to endure

toma ['toma] nf (acto) taking; (MED) dose; ~ **(de corriente)** socket

tomar [to'mar] vt to take; (aspecto) to take on; (beber) to drink ♦ vi to take; (AM) to drink; ~**se** vr to take; ~**se por** to consider o.s. to be; ~ **a bien/a mal** to take well/badly; ~ **en serio** to take seriously; ~ **el pelo a alguien** to pull sb's leg; ~**la con uno** to pick a quarrel with sb; **¡tome!** here you are!; ~ **el sol** to sunbathe

tomate [to'mate] nm tomato

tomillo [to'miʎo] nm thyme

tomo ['tomo] nm (libro) volume

ton [ton] abr = **tonelada** ♦ nm: **sin ~ ni son** without rhyme or reason

tonada [to'naða] nf tune

tonalidad [tonali'ðað] nf tone

tonel [to'nel] nm barrel

tonelada [tone'laða] nf ton; **tonelaje** nm tonnage

tónica ['tonika] nf (MUS) tonic; (fig) keynote

tónico, a ['toniko, a] adj tonic ♦ nm (MED) tonic

tonificar [tonifi'kar] vt to tone up

tono ['tono] nm tone; **fuera de ~** inappropriate; **darse ~** to put on airs

tontería [tonte'ria] nf (estupidez) foolishness; (cosa) stupid thing; (acto) foolish act; ~**s** nfpl (disparates) rubbish sg, nonsense sg

tonto, a ['tonto, a] adj stupid, silly ♦ nm/f fool

topar [to'par] vi: ~ **contra** o **en** to run into; ~ **con** to run up against

tope ['tope] adj maximum ♦ nm (fin) end; (límite) limit; (FERRO) buffer; (AUTO) bumper; **al ~** end to end

tópico, a ['topiko, a] adj topical ♦ nm platitude

topo ['topo] nm (ZOOL) mole; (fig) blunderer

topografía [topoɣra'fia] nf topography; **topógrafo, a** nm/f topographer

toque etc ['toke] vb ver **tocar** ♦ nm touch; (MUS) beat; (de campana) peal; **dar un ~ a** to warn; ~ **de queda** curfew

toqué vb ver **tocar**

toquetear [tokete'ar] vt to finger

toquilla [to'kiʎa] nf (pañuelo) headscarf; (chal) shawl

tórax ['toraks] nm thorax

torbellino [torbe'ʎino] nm whirlwind; (fig) whirl

torcedura [torθe'ðura] nf twist; (MED) sprain

torcer [tor'θer] vt to twist; (la esquina) to turn; (MED) to sprain ♦ vi (desviar) to turn off; ~**se** vr (ladearse) to bend; (desviarse) to go astray; (fracasar) to go wrong; **torcido, a** adj twisted; (fig) crooked ♦ nm curl

tordo, a ['torðo, a] adj dappled ♦ nm thrush

torear [tore'ar] vt (fig: evadir) to avoid; (jugar con) to tease ♦ vi to fight bulls; **toreo** nm bullfighting; **torero, a** nm/f bullfighter

tormenta [tor'menta] nf storm; (fig: confusión) turmoil

tormento [tor'mento] nm torture; (fig) anguish

tornar [tor'nar] vt (devolver) to return, give back; (transformar) to transform ♦ vi to go back; ~**se** vr (ponerse) to become

tornasolado, a [tornaso'laðo, a] adj (brillante) iridescent; (reluciente) shimmering

torneo [tor'neo] nm tournament

tornillo [tor'niʎo] nm screw

torniquete [torni'kete] nm (MED) tourniquet

torno ['torno] nm (TEC) winch; (tambor) drum; **en ~ (a)** round, about

toro ['toro] nm bull; (fam) he-man; **los ~s** bullfighting

toronja [to'ronxa] nf grapefruit

torpe ['torpe] adj (poco hábil) clumsy, awkward; (necio) dim; (lento) slow

torpedo [tor'peðo] nm torpedo

torpeza [tor'peθa] nf (falta de agilidad) clumsiness; (lentitud) slowness; (error) mistake

torre ['torre] nf tower; (de petróleo) derrick

torrefacto, a [torre'fakto, a] adj roasted

torrente [to'rrente] nm torrent

tórrido, a ['torriðo, a] adj torrid

torrija [to'rrixa] nf French toast

torsión [tor'sjon] nf twisting

torso ['torso] nm torso

torta ['torta] nf cake; (fam) slap

tortícolis [tor'tikolis] nm inv stiff neck

tortilla [tor'tiʎa] nf omelette; (AM) maize pancake; ~ **francesa/española** plain/potato omelette

tórtola ['tortola] nf turtledove

tortuga [tor'tuɣa] nf tortoise

tortuoso, a [tor'twoso, a] adj winding

tortura [tor'tura] nf torture; **torturar** vt to torture

tos [tos] nf cough; ~ **ferina** whooping cough

tosco, a ['tosko, a] adj coarse

toser [to'ser] vi to cough

tostada [tos'taða] nf piece of toast; **tostado, a** adj toasted; (por el sol) dark brown; (piel) tanned

tostador [tosta'ðor] nm toaster

tostar [tos'tar] vt to toast; (café) to roast; (persona) to tan; ~**se** vr to get brown

total [to'tal] *adj* total ♦ *adv* in short; (*al fin y al cabo*) when all is said and done ♦ *nm* total; **~ que** to cut (*BRIT*) o make (*US*) a long story short

totalidad [totali'ðað] *nf* whole

totalitario, a [totali'tarjo, a] *adj* totalitarian

tóxico, a ['toksiko, a] *adj* toxic ♦ *nm* poison; **toxicómano, a** *nm/f* drug addict

toxina [to'ksina] *nf* toxin

tozudo, a [to'θuðo, a] *adj* obstinate

traba ['traßa] *nf* bond, tie; (*cadena*) shackle

trabajador, a [traßaxa'ðor, a] *adj* hard-working ♦ *nm/f* worker

trabajar [traßa'xar] *vt* to work; (*AGR*) to till; (*empeñarse en*) to work at; (*convencer*) to persuade ♦ *vi* to work; (*esforzarse*) to strive; **trabajo** *nm* work; (*tarea*) task; (*POL*) labour; (*fig*) effort; **tomarse el trabajo de** to take the trouble to; **trabajo por turno/a destajo** shift work/piecework; **trabajoso, a** *adj* hard

trabalenguas [traßa'lengwas] *nm inv* tongue twister

trabar [tra'ßar] *vt* (*juntar*) to join, unite; (*atar*) to tie down, fetter; (*agarrar*) to seize; (*amistad*) to strike up; **~se** *vr* to become entangled; **trabársele a uno la lengua** to be tongue-tied

tracción [trak'θjon] *nf* traction; **~ delantera/ trasera** front-wheel/rear-wheel drive

tractor [trak'tor] *nm* tractor

tradición [traði'θjon] *nf* tradition; **tradicional** *adj* traditional

traducción [traðuk'θjon] *nf* translation

traducir [traðu'θir] *vt* to translate; **traductor, a** *nm/f* translator

traer [tra'er] *vt* to bring; (*llevar*) to carry; (*llevar puesto*) to wear; (*incluir*) to carry; (*causar*) to cause; **~se** *vr*: **~se algo** to be up to sth

traficar [trafi'kar] *vi* to trade

tráfico ['trafiko] *nm* (*COM*) trade; (*AUTO*) traffic

tragaluz [traɣa'luθ] *nm* skylight

tragaperras [traɣa'perras] *nm o f inv* slot machine

tragar [tra'ɣar] *vt* to swallow; (*devorar*) to devour, bolt down; **~se** *vr* to swallow

tragedia [tra'xeðja] *nf* tragedy; **trágico, a** *adj* tragic

trago ['traɣo] *nm* (*líquido*) drink; (*bocado*) gulp; (*fam: de bebida*) swig; (*desgracia*) blow

traición [trai'θjon] *nf* treachery; (*JUR*) treason; (*una ~*) act of treachery; **traicionar** *vt* to betray

traicionero, a [traiθjo'nero, a] *adj* treacherous

traidor, a [trai'ðor, a] *adj* treacherous ♦ *nm/f* traitor

traigo *etc vb ver* **traer**

traje ['traxe] *vb ver* **traer** ♦ *nm* (*de hombre*) suit; (*de mujer*) dress; (*vestido típico*) costume; **~ de baño** swimsuit; **~ de luces** bullfighter's costume

trajera *etc vb ver* **traer**

trajín [tra'xin] *nm* (*fam: movimiento*) bustle; **trajinar** *vi* (*moverse*) to bustle about

trama ['trama] *nf* (*intriga*) plot; (*de tejido*) weft (*BRIT*), woof (*US*); **tramar** *vt* to plot; (*TEC*) to weave

tramitar [trami'tar] *vt* (*asunto*) to transact; (*negociar*) to negotiate

trámite ['tramite] *nm* (*paso*) step; (*JUR*) transaction; **~s** *nmpl* (*burocracia*) procedure *sg*; (*JUR*) proceedings

tramo ['tramo] *nm* (*de tierra*) plot; (*de escalera*) flight; (*de vía*) section

tramoya [tra'moja] *nf* (*TEATRO*) piece of stage machinery; **tramoyista** *nm/f* scene shifter; (*fig*) trickster

trampa ['trampa] *nf* trap; (*en el suelo*) trapdoor; (*truco*) trick; (*engaño*) fiddle; **trampear** *vt, vi* to cheat

trampolín [trampo'lin] *nm* (*de piscina etc*) diving board

tramposo, a [tram'poso, a] *adj* crooked, cheating ♦ *nm/f* crook, cheat

tranca ['tranka] *nf* (*palo*) stick; (*de puerta, ventana*) bar; **trancar** *vt* to bar

trance ['tranθe] *nm* (*momento difícil*) difficult moment o juncture; (*estado hipnotizado*) trance

tranquilidad [trankili'ðað] *nf* (*calma*) calmness, stillness; (*paz*) peacefulness

tranquilizar [trankili'θar] *vt* (*calmar*) to calm (down); (*asegurar*) to reassure; **~se** *vr* to calm down; **tranquilo, a** *adj* (*calmado*) calm; (*apacible*) peaceful; (*mar*) calm; (*mente*) untroubled

transacción [transak'θjon] *nf* transaction

transbordador [transßorða'ðor] *nm* ferry

transbordar [transßor'ðar] *vt* to transfer; **transbordo** *nm* transfer; **hacer transbordo** to change (trains *etc*)

transcurrir [transku'rrir] *vi* (*tiempo*) to pass; (*hecho*) to take place

transcurso [trans'kurso] *nm*: **~ del tiempo** lapse (of time)

transeúnte [transe'unte] *nm/f* passer-by

transferencia [transfe'renθja] *nf* transference; (*COM*) transfer

transferir [transfe'rir] *vt* to transfer

transformador [transforma'ðor] *nm* (*ELEC*) transformer

transformar [transfor'mar] *vt* to transform; (*convertir*) to convert

tránsfuga ['transfuɣa] *nm/f* (*MIL*) deserter; (*POL*) turncoat

transfusión [transfu'sjon] *nf* transfusion

transgénico, a [trans'xeniko, a] *adj* genetically modified, GM

transición [transi'θjon] *nf* transition

transigir [transi'xir] *vi* to compromise, make concessions

transistor [transis'tor] *nm* transistor

transitar [transi'tar] *vi* to go (from place to place); **tránsito** *nm* transit; (*AUTO*) traffic; **transitorio, a** *adj* transitory

transmisión [transmi'sjon] *nf* (*TEC*) transmission; (*transferencia*) transfer; ~ **en directo/exterior** live/outside broadcast

transmitir [transmi'tir] *vt* to transmit; (*RADIO, TV*) to broadcast

transparencia [transpa'renθja] *nf* transparency; (*claridad*) clearness, clarity; (*foto*) slide

transparentar [transparen'tar] *vt* to reveal ♦ *vi* to be transparent; **transparente** *adj* transparent; (*claro*) clear

transpirar [transpi'rar] *vi* to perspire

transportar [transpor'tar] *vt* to transport; (*llevar*) to carry; **transporte** *nm* transport; (*COM*) haulage

transversal [transßer'sal] *adj* transverse, cross

tranvía [tram'bia] *nm* tram

trapecio [tra'peθjo] *nm* trapeze; **trapecista** *nmf* trapeze artist

trapero, a [tra'pero, a] *nm/f* ragman

trapicheo [trapi'tʃeo] (*fam*) *nm* scheme, fiddle

trapo ['trapo] *nm* (*tela*) rag; (*de cocina*) cloth

tráquea ['trakea] *nf* windpipe

traqueteo [trake'teo] *nm* rattling

tras [tras] *prep* (*detrás*) behind; (*después*) after

trasatlántico [trasat'lantiko] *nm* (*barco*) (cabin) cruiser

trascendencia [trasθen'denθja] *nf* (*importancia*) importance; (*FILOSOFÍA*) transcendence

trascendental [trasθenden'tal] *adj* important; (*FILOSOFÍA*) transcendental

trascender [trasθen'der] *vi* (*noticias*) to come out; (*suceso*) to have a wide effect

trasero, a [tra'sero, a] *adj* back, rear ♦ *nm* (*ANAT*) bottom

trasfondo [tras'fondo] *nm* background

trasgredir [trasɣre'ðir] *vt* to contravene

trashumante [trasu'mante] *adj* (*animales*) migrating

trasladar [trasla'ðar] *vt* to move; (*persona*) to transfer; (*postergar*) to postpone; (*copiar*) to copy; **~se** *vr* (*mudarse*) to move; **traslado** *nm* move; (*mudanza*) move, removal

traslucir [traslu'θir] *vt* to show; **~se** *vr* to be translucent; (*fig*) to be revealed

trasluz [tras'luθ] *nm* reflected light; **al ~** against *o* up to the light

trasnochador, a [trasnotʃa'ðor, a] *nm/f* night owl

trasnochar [trasno'tʃar] *vi* (*acostarse tarde*) to stay up late

traspapelar [traspape'lar] *vt* (*document, carta*) to mislay, misplace

traspasar [traspa'sar] *vt* (*suj: bala etc*) to pierce, go through; (*propiedad*) to sell, transfer; (*calle*) to cross over; (*límites*) to go beyond; (*ley*) to break; **traspaso** *nm* (*venta*) transfer, sale

traspié [tras'pje] *nm* (*tropezón*) trip; (*error*) blunder

trasplantar [trasplan'tar] *vt* to transplant

traste ['traste] *nm* (*MUS*) fret; **dar al ~ con algo** to ruin sth

trastero [tras'tero] *nm* storage room

trastienda [tras'tjenda] *nf* back of shop

trasto ['trasto] (*pey*) *nm* (*cosa*) piece of junk; (*persona*) dead loss

trastornado, a [trastor'naðo, a] *adj* (*loco*) mad, crazy

trastornar [trastor'nar] *vt* (*fig: planes*) to disrupt; (*: nervios*) to shatter; (*: persona*) to drive crazy; **~se** *vr* (*volverse loco*) to go mad *o* crazy; **trastorno** *nm* (*acto*) overturning; (*confusión*) confusion

tratable [tra'taßle] *adj* friendly

tratado [tra'taðo] *nm* (*POL*) treaty; (*COM*) agreement

tratamiento [trata'mjento] *nm* treatment; ~ **de textos** (*INFORM*) word processing *cpd*

tratar [tra'tar] *vt* (*ocuparse de*) to treat; (*manejar, TEC*) to handle; (*MED*) to treat; (*dirigirse a: persona*) to address ♦ *vi*: ~ **de** (*hablar sobre*) to deal with, be about; (*intentar*) to try to; **~se** *vr* to treat each other; ~ **con** (*COM*) to trade in; (*negociar*) to negotiate with; (*tener contactos*) to have dealings with; **¿de qué se trata?** what's it about?; **trato** *nm* dealings *pl*; (*relaciones*) relationship; (*comportamiento*) manner; (*COM*) agreement

trauma ['trauma] *nm* trauma

través [tra'ßes] *nm* (*fig*) reverse; **al ~** across, crossways; **a ~ de** across; (*sobre*) over; (*por*) through

travesaño [traße'saɲo] *nm* (*ARQ*) crossbeam; (*DEPORTE*) crossbar

travesía [traße'sia] *nf* (*calle*) cross-street; (*NAUT*) crossing

travesura [traße'sura] *nf* (*broma*) prank; (*ingenio*) wit

traviesa [tra'ßjesa] *nf* (*ARQ*) crossbeam

travieso, a [tra'ßjeso, a] *adj* (*niño*) naughty

trayecto [tra'jekto] *nm* (*ruta*) road, way; (*viaje*) journey; (*tramo*) stretch; **~ria** *nf* trajectory; (*fig*) path

traza ['traθa] *nf* (*aspecto*) looks *pl*; (*señal*)

sign; **~do, a** adj: **bien ~do** shapely, well-formed ♦ nm (ARQ) plan, design; (fig) outline

trazar [tra'θar] vt (ARQ) to plan; (ARTE) to sketch; (fig) to trace; (plan) to draw up; **trazo** nm (línea) line; (bosquejo) sketch

trébol ['treβol] nm (BOT) clover

trece ['treθe] num thirteen

trecho ['tretʃo] nm (distancia) distance; (de tiempo) while; **de ~ en ~** at intervals

tregua ['treɣwa] nf (MIL) truce; (fig) respite

treinta ['treinta] num thirty

tremendo, a [tre'mendo, a] adj (terrible) terrible; (imponente: cosa) imposing; (fam: fabuloso) tremendous

trémulo, a ['tremulo, a] adj quivering

tren [tren] nm train; **~ de aterrizaje** undercarriage

trenca ['trenka] nf duffel coat

trenza ['trenθa] nf (de pelo) plait (BRIT), braid (US); **trenzar** vt (pelo) to plait, braid; **trenzarse** vr (AM) to become involved

trepadora [trepa'ðora] nf (BOT) climber

trepar [tre'par] vt, vi to climb

trepidante [trepi'ðante] adj (acción) fast; (ritmo) hectic

tres [tres] num three

tresillo [tre'siʎo] nm three-piece suite; (MUS) triplet

treta ['treta] nf trick

triángulo ['trjangulo] nm triangle

tribu ['triβu] nf tribe

tribuna [tri'βuna] nf (plataforma) platform; (DEPORTE) (grand)stand

tribunal [triβu'nal] nm (JUR) court; (comisión, fig) tribunal

tributar [triβu'tar] vt (gen) to pay; **tributo** nm (COM) tax

tricotar [triko'tar] vi to knit

trigal [tri'ɣal] nm wheat field

trigo ['triɣo] nm wheat

trigueño, a [tri'ɣeɲo, a] adj (pelo) corn-coloured

trillado, a [tri'ʎaðo, a] adj threshed; (asunto) trite, hackneyed; **trilladora** nf threshing machine

trillar [tri'ʎar] vt (AGR) to thresh

trimestral [trimes'tral] adj quarterly; (ESCOL) termly

trimestre [tri'mestre] nm (ESCOL) term

trinar [tri'nar] vi (pájaros) to sing; (rabiar) to fume, be angry

trinchar [trin'tʃar] vt to carve

trinchera [trin'tʃera] nf (fosa) trench

trineo [tri'neo] nm sledge

trinidad [trini'ðað] nf trio; (REL): **la T~** the Trinity

trino ['trino] nm trill

tripa ['tripa] nf (ANAT) intestine; (fam: tb: ~s) insides pl

triple ['triple] adj triple

triplicado, a [tripli'kaðo, a] adj: **por ~** in triplicate

tripulación [tripula'θjon] nf crew

tripulante [tripu'lante] nm/f crewman/woman

tripular [tripu'lar] vt (barco) to man; (AUTO) to drive

triquiñuela [triki'ɲwela] nf trick

tris [tris] nm inv crack; **en un ~** in an instant

triste ['triste] adj sad; (lamentable) sorry, miserable; **~za** nf (aflicción) sadness; (melancolía) melancholy

triturar [tritu'rar] vt (moler) to grind; (mascar) to chew

triunfar [trjun'far] vi (tener éxito) to triumph; (ganar) to win; **triunfo** nm triumph

trivial [tri'βjal] adj trivial; **~izar** vt to minimize, play down

triza ['triθa] nf: **hacer ~s** to smash to bits; (papel) to tear to shreds

trocar [tro'kar] vt to exchange

trocear [troθe'ar] vt (carne, manzana) to cut up, cut into pieces

trocha ['trotʃa] nf short cut

troche ['trotʃe]: **a ~ y moche** adv helter-skelter, pell-mell

trofeo [tro'feo] nm (premio) trophy; (éxito) success

tromba ['tromba] nf downpour

trombón [trom'bon] nm trombone

trombosis [trom'bosis] nf inv thrombosis

trompa ['trompa] nf horn; (trompo) humming top; (hocico) snout; (fam): **cogerse una ~** to get tight

trompazo [trom'paθo] nm bump, bang

trompeta [trom'peta] nf trumpet; (clarín) bugle

trompicón [trompi'kon]: **a ~es** adv in fits and starts

trompo ['trompo] nm spinning top

trompón [trom'pon] nm bump

tronar [tro'nar] vt (AM) to shoot ♦ vi to thunder; (fig) to rage

tronchar [tron'tʃar] vt (árbol) to chop down; (fig: vida) to cut short; (: esperanza) to shatter; (persona) to tire out; **~se** vr to fall down

tronco ['tronko] nm (de árbol, ANAT) trunk

trono ['trono] nm throne

tropa ['tropa] nf (MIL) troop; (soldados) soldiers pl

tropel [tro'pel] nm (muchedumbre) crowd

tropezar [trope'θar] vi to trip, stumble; (error) to slip up; **~ con** to run into; (topar con) to bump into; **tropezón** nm trip; (fig) blunder

tropical [tropi'kal] adj tropical

trópico ['tropiko] nm tropic

tropiezo [tro'pjeθo] *vb ver* **tropezar** ♦ *nm* (*error*) slip, blunder; (*desgracia*) misfortune; (*obstáculo*) snag

trotamundos [trota'mundos] *nm inv* globetrotter

trotar [tro'tar] *vi* to trot; **trote** *nm* trot; (*fam*) travelling; **de mucho trote** hard-wearing

trozo ['troθo] *nm* bit, piece

trucha ['trutʃa] *nf* trout

truco ['truko] *nm* (*habilidad*) knack; (*engaño*) trick

trueno ['trweno] *nm* thunder; (*estampido*) bang

trueque *etc* ['trweke] *vb ver* **trocar** ♦ *nm* exchange; (*COM*) barter

trufa ['trufa] *nf* (*BOT*) truffle

truhán, ana [tru'an, ana] *nm/f* rogue

truncar [trun'kar] *vt* (*cortar*) to truncate; (*fig: la vida etc*) to cut short; (: *el desarrollo*) to stunt

tu [tu] *adj* your

tú [tu] *pron* you

tubérculo [tu'βerkulo] *nm* (*BOT*) tuber

tuberculosis [tußerku'losis] *nf inv* tuberculosis

tubería [tuße'ria] *nf* pipes *pl*; (*conducto*) pipeline

tubo ['tußo] *nm* tube, pipe; ~ **de ensayo** test tube; ~ **de escape** exhaust (pipe)

tuerca ['twerka] *nf* nut

tuerto, a ['twerto, a] *adj* blind in one eye ♦ *nm/f* one-eyed person

tuerza *etc vb ver* **torcer**

tuétano ['twetano] *nm* marrow; (*BOT*) pith

tufo ['tufo] *nm* (*hedor*) stench

tul [tul] *nm* tulle

tulipán [tuli'pan] *nm* tulip

tullido, a [tu'λiðo, a] *adj* crippled

tumba ['tumba] *nf* (*sepultura*) tomb

tumbar [tum'bar] *vt* to knock down; **~se** *vr* (*echarse*) to lie down; (*extenderse*) to stretch out

tumbo ['tumbo] *nm*: **dar ~s** to stagger

tumbona [tum'bona] *nf* (*butaca*) easy chair; (*de playa*) deckchair (*BRIT*), beach chair (*US*)

tumor [tu'mor] *nm* tumour

tumulto [tu'multo] *nm* turmoil

tuna ['tuna] *nf* (*MUS*) student music group; *ver tb* **tuno**

tunante [tu'nante] *nm/f* rascal

tunda ['tunda] *nf* (*golpeo*) beating

túnel ['tunel] *nm* tunnel

Túnez ['tuneθ] *nm* Tunisia; (*ciudad*) Tunis

tuno, a ['tuno, a] *nm/f* (*fam*) rogue ♦ *nm* member of student music group

tupido, a [tu'piðo, a] *adj* (*denso*) dense; (*tela*) close-woven

turba ['turßa] *nf* crowd

turbante [tur'ßante] *nm* turban

turbar [tur'ßar] *vt* (*molestar*) to disturb; (*incomodar*) to upset; **~se** *vr* to be disturbed

turbina [tur'ßina] *nf* turbine

turbio, a ['turßjo, a] *adj* cloudy; (*tema etc*) confused

turbulencia [turßu'lenθja] *nf* turbulence; (*fig*) restlessness; **turbulento, a** *adj* turbulent; (*fig: intranquilo*) restless; (: *ruidoso*) noisy

turco, a ['turko, a] *adj* Turkish ♦ *nm/f* Turk

turismo [tu'rismo] *nm* tourism; (*coche*) car; **turista** *nm/f* tourist; **turístico, a** *adj* tourist *cpd*

turnar [tur'nar] *vi* to take (it in) turns; **~se** *vr* to take (it in) turns; **turno** *nm* (*de trabajo*) shift; (*juegos etc*) turn

turquesa [tur'kesa] *nf* turquoise

Turquía [tur'kia] *nf* Turkey

turrón [tu'rron] *nm* (*dulce*) nougat

tutear [tute'ar] *vt* to address as familiar "tú"; **~se** *vr* to be on familiar terms

tutela [tu'tela] *nf* (*legal*) guardianship; **tutelar** *adj* tutelary ♦ *vt* to protect

tutor, a [tu'tor, a] *nm/f* (*legal*) guardian; (*ESCOL*) tutor

tuve *etc vb ver* **tener**

tuviera *etc vb ver* **tener**

tuyo, a ['tujo, a] *adj* yours, of yours ♦ *pron* yours; **un amigo ~** a friend of yours; **los ~s** (*fam*) your relations, your family

TV ['te'ße] *nf abr* (= *televisión*) TV

TVE *nf abr* = **Televisión Española**

U, u

u [u] *conj* or

ubicar [ußi'kar] *vt* to place, situate; (*AM: encontrar*) to find; **~se** *vr* to lie, be located

ubre ['ußre] *nf* udder

UCI *nf abr* (= *Unidad de Cuidados Intensivos*) ICU

Ud(s) *abr* = **usted(es)**

UE *nf abr* (= *Unión Europea*) EU

ufanarse [ufa'narse] *vr* to boast; ~ **de** to pride o.s. on; **ufano, a** *adj* (*arrogante*) arrogant; (*presumido*) conceited

UGT *nf abr* = **Unión General de Trabajadores**

ujier [u'xjer] *nm* usher; (*portero*) doorkeeper

úlcera ['ulθera] *nf* ulcer

ulcerar [ulθe'rar] *vt* to make sore; **~se** *vr* to ulcerate

ulterior [ulte'rjor] *adj* (*más allá*) farther, further; (*subsecuente, siguiente*) subsequent

últimamente ['ultimamente] *adv* (*recientemente*) lately, recently

ultimar [ulti'mar] *vt* to finish; (*finalizar*) to finalize; (*AM: rematar*) to finish off

ultimátum [ulti'matum] (*pl* **~s**) *nm* ultimatum

último, a ['ultimo, a] *adj* last; (*más reciente*) latest, most recent; (*más bajo*) bottom; (*más alto*) top; **en las últimas** on one's last legs; **por ~** finally

ultra ['ultra] *adj* ultra ♦ *nm/f* extreme right-winger

ultrajar [ultra'xar] *vt* (*ofender*) to outrage; (*insultar*) to insult, abuse; **ultraje** *nm* outrage; insult

ultramar [ultra'mar] *nm*: **de o en ~** abroad, overseas

ultramarinos [ultrama'rinos] *nmpl* groceries; **tienda de ~** grocer's (shop)

ultranza [ul'tranθa]: **a ~** *adv* (*a todo trance*) at all costs; (*completo*) outright

ultratumba [ultra'tumba] *nf*: **la vida de ~** the next life

umbral [um'bral] *nm* (*gen*) threshold

umbrío, a [um'brio, a] *adj* shady

un, una [un, 'una] *art indef* a; (*antes de vocal*) an; **una mujer/naranja** a woman/an orange
♦ *adj*: **unos** (o **unas**): **hay unos regalos para ti** there are some presents for you; **hay unas cervezas en la nevera** there are some beers in the fridge

unánime [u'nanime] *adj* unanimous; **unanimidad** *nf* unanimity

undécimo, a [un'deθimo, a] *adj* eleventh

ungir [un'xir] *vt* to anoint

ungüento [un'gwento] *nm* ointment

únicamente ['unikamente] *adv* solely, only

único, a ['uniko, a] *adj* only, sole; (*sin par*) unique

unidad [uni'ðað] *nf* unity; (*COM, TEC etc*) unit

unido, a [u'niðo, a] *adj* joined, linked; (*fig*) united

unificar [unifi'kar] *vt* to unite, unify

uniformar [unifor'mar] *vt* to make uniform, level up; (*persona*) to put into uniform

uniforme [uni'forme] *adj* uniform, equal; (*superficie*) even ♦ *nm* uniform; **uniformidad** *nf* uniformity; (*de terreno*) levelness, evenness

unilateral [unilate'ral] *adj* unilateral

unión [u'njon] *nf* union; (*acto*) uniting, joining; (*unidad*) unity; (*TEC*) joint; **la U~ Europea** the European Union; **la U~ Soviética** the Soviet Union

unir [u'nir] *vt* (*juntar*) to join, unite; (*atar*) to tie, fasten; (*combinar*) to combine; **~se** *vr* to join together, unite; (*empresas*) to merge

unísono [u'nisono] *nm*: **al ~ in** unison

universal [unißer'sal] *adj* universal; (*mundial*) world *cpd*

universidad [unißersi'ðað] *nf* university

universitario, a [unißersi'tarjo, a] *adj* university *cpd* ♦ *nm/f* (*profesor*) lecturer; (*estudiante*) (university) student; (*graduado*) graduate

universo [uni'ßerso] *nm* universe

uno, a ['uno, a] *adj* one; **es todo ~** it's all one and the same; **~s pocos** a few; **~s cien** about a hundred
♦ *pron* **1** one; **quiero sólo ~** I only want one; **~ de ellos** one of them
2 (*alguien*) somebody, someone; **conozco a ~ que se te parece** I know somebody o someone who looks like you; **~ mismo** oneself; **~s querían quedarse** some (people) wanted to stay
3: (**los**) **~s ... (los) otros** ... some ... others; **una y otra son muy agradables** they're both very nice
♦ *nf* one; **es la una** it's one o'clock
♦ *nm* (number) one

untar [un'tar] *vt* (*mantequilla*) to spread; (*engrasar*) to grease, oil

uña ['uɲa] *nf* (*ANAT*) nail; (*garra*) claw; (*casco*) hoof; (*arrancaclavos*) claw

uranio [u'ranjo] *nm* uranium

urbanidad [urßani'ðað] *nf* courtesy, politeness

urbanismo [urßa'nismo] *nm* town planning

urbanización [urßaniθa'θjon] *nf* (*barrio, colonia*) housing estate

urbanizar [urßani'θar] *vt* (*zona*) to develop, urbanize

urbano, a [ur'ßano, a] *adj* (*de ciudad*) urban; (*cortés*) courteous, polite

urbe ['urße] *nf* large city

urdimbre [ur'ðimbre] *nf* (*de tejido*) warp; (*intriga*) intrigue

urdir [ur'ðir] *vt* to warp; (*complot*) to plot, contrive

urgencia [ur'xenθja] *nf* urgency; (*prisa*) haste, rush; (*emergencia*) emergency; **servicios de ~** emergency services; **"Urgencias"** "Casualty"; **urgente** *adj* urgent

urgir [ur'xir] *vi* to be urgent; **me urge** I'm in a hurry for it

urinario, a [uri'narjo, a] *adj* urinary ♦ *nm* urinal

urna ['urna] *nf* urn; (*POL*) ballot box

urraca [u'rraka] *nf* magpie

URSS *nf*: **la ~** the USSR

Uruguay [uru'ɣwai] *nm*: **el ~** Uruguay; **uruguayo, a** *adj, nm/f* Uruguayan

usado, a [u'saðo, a] *adj* used; (*de segunda mano*) secondhand

usar [u'sar] *vt* to use; (*ropa*) to wear; (*tener costumbre*) to be in the habit of; **~se** *vr* to be used; **uso** *nm* use; wear; (*costumbre*) usage, custom; (*moda*) fashion; **al uso** in keeping with custom; **al uso de** in the style of

usted [us'teð] *pron* (*sg*) you *sg*; (*pl*): ~**es** you *pl*

usual [u'swal] *adj* usual

usuario, a [usu'arjo, a] *nm/f* user

usura [u'sura] *nf* usury; **usurero, a** *nm/f* usurer

usurpar [usur'par] *vt* to usurp

utensilio [uten'siljo] *nm* tool; (*CULIN*) utensil

útero ['utero] *nm* uterus, womb

útil ['util] *adj* useful ♦ *nm* tool; **utilidad** *nf* usefulness; (*COM*) profit; **utilizar** *vt* to use, utilize

utopía [uto'pia] *nf* Utopia; **utópico, a** *adj* Utopian

uva ['uβa] *nf* grape

V, v

v *abr* (= *voltio*) v

va *vb ver* ir

vaca ['baka] *nf* (*animal*) cow; **carne de ~** beef

vacaciones [baka'θjones] *nfpl* holidays

vacante [ba'kante] *adj* vacant, empty ♦ *nf* vacancy

vaciar [ba'θjar] *vt* to empty out; (*ahuecar*) to hollow out; (*moldear*) to cast; ~**se** *vr* to empty

vacilante [baθi'lante] *adj* unsteady; (*habla*) faltering; (*dudoso*) hesitant

vacilar [baθi'lar] *vi* to be unsteady; (*al hablar*) to falter; (*dudar*) to hesitate, waver; (*memoria*) to fail

vacío, a [ba'θio, a] *adj* empty; (*puesto*) vacant; (*desocupado*) idle; (*vano*) vain ♦ *nm* emptiness; (*FÍSICA*) vacuum; (*un ~*) (empty) space

vacuna [ba'kuna] *nf* vaccine; **vacunar** *vt* to vaccinate

vacuno, a [ba'kuno, a] *adj* cow *cpd*; **ganado ~** cattle

vacuo, a ['bakwo, a] *adj* empty

vadear [baðe'ar] *vt* (*río*) to ford; **vado** *nm* ford

vagabundo, a [baɣa'βundo, a] *adj* wandering ♦ *nm* tramp

vagamente [baɣa'mente] *adv* vaguely

vagancia [ba'ɣanθja] *nf* (*pereza*) idleness, laziness

vagar [ba'ɣar] *vi* to wander; (*no hacer nada*) to idle

vagina [ba'xina] *nf* vagina

vago, a ['baɣo, a] *adj* vague; (*perezoso*) lazy ♦ *nm/f* (*vagabundo*) tramp; (*flojo*) lazybones *sg*, idler

vagón [ba'ɣon] *nm* (*FERRO: de pasajeros*)

carriage; (: *de mercancías*) wagon

vaguedad [baɣe'ðað] *nf* vagueness

vaho ['bao] *nm* (*vapor*) vapour, steam; (*respiración*) breath

vaina ['baina] *nf* sheath

vainilla [bai'niʎa] *nf* vanilla

vainita [bai'nita] (*AM*) *nf* green o French bean

vais *vb ver* ir

vaivén [bai'ßen] *nm* to-and-fro movement; (*de tránsito*) coming and going; **vaivenes** *nmpl* (*fig*) ups and downs

vajilla [ba'xiʎa] *nf* crockery, dishes *pl*; **lavar la ~** to do the washing-up (*BRIT*), wash the dishes (*US*)

valdré *etc vb ver* valer

vale ['bale] *nm* voucher; (*recibo*) receipt; (*pagaré*) IOU

valedero, a [bale'ðero, a] *adj* valid

valenciano, a [balen'θjano, a] *adj* Valencian

valentía [balen'tia] *nf* courage, bravery

valer [ba'ler] *vt* to be worth; (*MAT*) to equal; (*costar*) to cost ♦ *vi* (*ser útil*) to be useful; (*ser válido*) to be valid; ~**se** *vr* to take care of oneself; ~**se de** to make use of, take advantage of; **~ la pena** to be worthwhile; **¿vale?** (*ESP*) OK?

valeroso, a [bale'roso, a] *adj* brave, valiant

valgo *etc vb ver* valer

valía [ba'lia] *nf* worth, value

validar [bali'ðar] *vt* to validate; **validez** *nf* validity; **válido, a** *adj* valid

valiente [ba'ljente] *adj* brave, valiant ♦ *nm* hero

valioso, a [ba'ljoso, a] *adj* valuable

valla ['baʎa] *nf* fence; (*DEPORTE*) hurdle; **~ publicitaria** hoarding; **vallar** *vt* to fence in

valle ['baʎe] *nm* valley

valor [ba'lor] *nm* value, worth; (*precio*) price; (*valentía*) valour, courage; (*importancia*) importance; **~es** *nmpl* (*COM*) securities; **~ar** *vt* to value

vals [bals] *nm inv* waltz

válvula ['balßula] *nf* valve

vamos *vb ver* ir

vampiro, resa [bam'piro, 'resa] *nm/f* vampire

van *vb ver* ir

vanagloriarse [banaɣlo'rjarse] *vr* to boast

vandalismo [banda'lismo] *nm* vandalism; **vándalo, a** *nm/f* vandal

vanguardia [ban'gwardja] *nf* vanguard; (*ARTE etc*) avant-garde

vanidad [bani'ðað] *nf* vanity; **vanidoso, a** *adj* vain, conceited

vano, a ['bano, a] *adj* vain

vapor [ba'por] *nm* vapour; (*vaho*) steam; **al ~** (*CULIN*) steamed; **~izador** *nm* atomizer; **~izar** *vt* to vaporize; **~oso, a** *adj* vaporous

vapulear [bapule'ar] *vt* to beat, thrash

vaquero, a [ba'kero, a] *adj* cattle *cpd* ♦ *nm* cowboy; **~s** *nmpl* (*pantalones*) jeans

vaquilla [ba'kiʎa] *nf* (*ZOOL*) heifer

vara ['bara] *nf* stick; (*TEC*) rod; **~ mágica** magic wand

variable [ba'rjaßle] *adj, nf* variable

variación [baria'θjon] *nf* variation

variar [bar'jar] *vt* to vary; (*modificar*) to modify; (*cambiar de posición*) to switch around ♦ *vi* to vary

varicela [bari'θela] *nf* chickenpox

varices [ba'riθes] *nfpl* varicose veins

variedad [barje'ðað] *nf* variety

varilla [ba'riʎa] *nf* stick; (*BOT*) twig; (*TEC*) rod; (*de rueda*) spoke

vario, a ['barjo, a] *adj* varied; **~s** various, several

varita [ba'rita] *nf*: **~ mágica** magic wand

varón [ba'ron] *nm* male, man; **varonil** *adj* manly, virile

Varsovia [bar'soßja] *n* Warsaw

vas *vb ver* **ir**

vasco, a ['basko, a] *adj, nm/f* Basque

vascongado, a [baskon'gaðo, a] *adj* Basque; **las Vascongadas** the Basque Country

vascuence [bas'kwenθe] *adj* = **vascongado**

vaselina [base'lina] *nf* Vaseline ®

vasija [ba'sixa] *nf* container, vessel

vaso ['baso] *nm* glass, tumbler; (*ANAT*) vessel

vástago ['bastaxo] *nm* (*BOT*) shoot; (*TEC*) rod; (*fig*) offspring

vasto, a ['basto, a] *adj* vast, huge

Vaticano [bati'kano] *nm*: **el ~** the Vatican

vatio ['batjo] *nm* (*ELEC*) watt

vaya *etc vb ver* **ir**

Vd(s) *abr* = **usted(es)**

ve *vb ver* **ir**; **ver**

vecindad [beθin'dað] *nf* neighbourhood; (*habitantes*) residents *pl*

vecindario [beθin'darjo] *nm* neighbourhood; residents *pl*

vecino, a [be'θino, a] *adj* neighbouring ♦ *nm/f* neighbour; (*residente*) resident

veda ['beða] *nf* prohibition

vedar [be'ðar] *vt* (*prohibir*) to ban, prohibit; (*impedir*) to stop, prevent

vegetación [bexeta'θjon] *nf* vegetation

vegetal [bexe'tal] *adj, nm* vegetable

vegetariano, a [bexeta'rjano, a] *adj, nm/f* vegetarian

vehemencia [be(e)'menθja] *nf* vehemence; **vehemente** *adj* vehement

vehículo [be'ikulo] *nm* vehicle; (*MED*) carrier

veía *etc vb ver* **ver**

veinte ['beinte] *num* twenty

vejación [bexa'θjon] *nf* vexation; (*humillación*) humiliation

vejar [be'xar] *vt* (*irritar*) to annoy, vex; (*humillar*) to humiliate

vejez [be'xeθ] *nf* old age

vejiga [be'xixa] *nf* (*ANAT*) bladder

vela ['bela] *nf* (*de cera*) candle; (*NAUT*) sail; (*insomnio*) sleeplessness; (*vigilia*) vigil; (*MIL*) sentry duty; **estar a dos ~s** (*fam: sin dinero*) to be skint

velado, a [be'laðo, a] *adj* veiled; (*sonido*) muffled; (*FOTO*) blurred ♦ *nf* soirée

velar [be'lar] *vt* (*vigilar*) to keep watch over ♦ *vi* to stay awake; **~ por** to watch over, look after

velatorio [bela'torjo] *nm* (*funeral*) wake

veleidad [belei'ðað] *nf* (*ligereza*) fickleness; (*capricho*) whim

velero [be'lero] *nm* (*NAUT*) sailing ship; (*AVIAT*) glider

veleta [be'leta] *nf* weather vane

veliz [be'lis] (*AM*) *nm* suitcase

vello ['beʎo] *nm* down, fuzz

velo ['belo] *nm* veil

velocidad [beloθi'ðað] *nf* speed; (*TEC, AUTO*) gear

velocímetro [belo'θimetro] *nm* speedometer

veloz [be'loθ] *adj* fast

ven *vb ver* **venir**

vena ['bena] *nf* vein

venado [be'naðo] *nm* deer

vencedor, a [benße'ðor, a] *adj* victorious ♦ *nm/f* victor, winner

vencer [ben'θer] *vt* (*dominar*) to defeat, beat; (*derrotar*) to vanquish; (*superar, controlar*) to overcome, master ♦ *vi* (*triunfar*) to win (through), triumph; (*plazo*) to expire; **vencido, a** *adj* (*derrotado*) defeated, beaten; (*COM*) due ♦ *adv*: **pagar vencido** to pay in arrears; **vencimiento** *nm* (*COM*) maturity

venda ['benda] *nf* bandage; **vendaje** *nm* bandage, dressing; **vendar** *vt* to bandage; **vendar los ojos** to blindfold

vendaval [benda'ßal] *nm* (*viento*) gale

vendedor, a [bende'ðor, a] *nm/f* seller

vender [ben'der] *vt* to sell; **~ al contado/al por mayor/al por menor** to sell for cash/ wholesale/retail

vendimia [ben'dimja] *nf* grape harvest

vendré *etc vb ver* **venir**

veneno [be'neno] *nm* poison; (*de serpiente*) venom; **~so, a** *adj* poisonous; venomous

venerable [bene'raßle] *adj* venerable; **venerar** *vt* (*respetar*) to revere; (*adorar*) to worship

venéreo, a [be'nereo, a] *adj*: **enfermedad venérea** venereal disease

venezolano, a [beneθo'lano, a] *adj* Venezuelan

Venezuela [bene'θwela] *nf* Venezuela

venganza [ben'ganθa] *nf* vengeance, revenge; **vengar** *vt* to avenge; **vengarse** *vr* to take revenge; **vengativo, a** adj (persona) vindictive

vengo etc vb ver **venir**

venia ['benja] nf (perdón) pardon; (permiso) consent

venial [be'njal] adj venial

venida [be'niða] nf (llegada) arrival; (regreso) return

venidero, a [beni'ðero, a] adj coming, future

venir [be'nir] vi to come; (llegar) to arrive; (ocurrir) to happen; (fig): ~ **de** to stem from; ~ **bien/mal** to be suitable/unsuitable; **el año que viene** next year; ~**se abajo** to collapse

venta ['benta] nf (COM) sale; ~ **a plazos** hire purchase; ~ **al contado/al por mayor/al por menor** o **al detalle** cash sale/wholesale/retail; ~ **con derecho a retorno** sale or return; "**en ~**" "for sale"

ventaja [ben'taxa] nf advantage; **ventajoso, a** adj advantageous

ventana [ben'tana] nf window; **ventanilla** nf (de taquilla) window (of booking office etc)

ventilación [bentila'θjon] nf ventilation; (corriente) draught

ventilador [bentila'ðor] nm fan

ventilar [benti'lar] vt to ventilate; (para secar) to put out to dry; (asunto) to air, discuss

ventisca [ben'tiska] nf blizzard

ventrílocuo, a [ben'trilokwo, a] nm/f ventriloquist

ventura [ben'tura] nf (felicidad) happiness; (buena suerte) luck; (destino) fortune; **a la (buena)** ~ at random; **venturoso, a** adj happy; (afortunado) lucky, fortunate

veo etc vb ver **ver**

ver [ber] vt to see; (mirar) to look at, watch; (entender) to understand; (investigar) to look into; ♦ vi to see; to understand; ~**se** vr (encontrarse) to meet; (dejarse ~) to be seen; (hallarse: en un apuro) to find o.s., be; **a** ~ let's see; **no tener nada que** ~ **con** to have nothing to do with; **a mi modo de** ~ as I see it

vera ['bera] nf edge, verge; (de río) bank

veracidad [beraθi'ðað] nf truthfulness

veranear [berane'ar] vi to spend the summer; **veraneo** nm summer holiday; **veraniego, a** adj summer cpd

verano [be'rano] nm summer

veras ['beras] nfpl truth sg; **de** ~ really, truly

veraz [be'raθ] adj truthful

verbal [ber'βal] adj verbal

verbena [ber'βena] nf (baile) open-air dance

verbo ['berβo] nm verb; ~**so, a** adj verbose

verdad [ber'ðað] nf truth; (fiabilidad) reliability; **de** ~ real, proper; **a decir** ~ to tell the truth; ~**ero, a** adj (veraz) true, truthful; (fiable) reliable; (fig) real

verde ['berðe] adj green; (chiste) blue, dirty

♦ nm green; **viejo** ~ dirty old man; ~**ar** vi to turn green; **verdor** nm greenness

verdugo [ber'ðuxo] nm executioner

verdulero, a [berðu'lero, a] nm/f greengrocer

verduras [ber'ðuras] nfpl (CULIN) greens

vereda [be'reða] nf path; (AM) pavement (BRIT), sidewalk (US)

veredicto [bere'ðikto] nm verdict

vergonzoso, a [berɣon'θoso, a] adj shameful; (tímido) timid, bashful

vergüenza [ber'ɣwenθa] nf shame, sense of shame; (timidez) bashfulness; (pudor) modesty; **me da** ~ I'm ashamed

verídico, a [be'riðiko, a] adj true, truthful

verificar [berifi'kar] vt to check; (corroborar) to verify; (llevar a cabo) to carry out; ~**se** vr (predicción) to prove to be true

verja ['berxa] nf (cancela) iron gate; (valla) iron railings pl; (de ventana) grille

vermut [ber'mut] (pl ~s) nm vermouth

verosímil [bero'simil] adj likely, probable; (relato) credible

verruga [be'rruxa] nf wart

versado, a [ber'saðo, a] adj: ~ **en** versed in

versátil [ber'satil] adj versatile

versión [ber'sjon] nf version

verso ['berso] nm verse; **un** ~ a line of poetry

vértebra ['berteβra] nf vertebra

verter [ber'ter] vt (líquido: adrede) to empty, pour (out); (: sin querer) to spill; (basura) to dump ♦ vi to flow

vertical [berti'kal] adj vertical

vértice ['bertiθe] nm vertex, apex

vertidos [ber'tiðos] nmpl waste sg

vertiente [ber'tjente] nf slope; (fig) aspect

vertiginoso, a [bertixi'noso, a] adj giddy, dizzy

vértigo ['bertixo] nm vertigo; (mareo) dizziness

vesícula [be'sikula] nf blister

vespino ® [bes'pino] nm o nf moped

vestíbulo [bes'tiβulo] nm hall; (de teatro) foyer

vestido [bes'tiðo] pp de **vestir**; ~ **de azul/ marinero** dressed in blue/as a sailor ♦ nm (ropa) clothes pl, clothing; (de mujer) dress, frock

vestigio [bes'tixjo] nm (huella) trace; ~**s** nmpl (restos) remains

vestimenta [besti'menta] nf clothing

vestir [bes'tir] vt (poner: ropa) to put on; (llevar: ropa) to wear; (proveer de ropa a) to clothe; (suj: sastre) to make clothes for ♦ vi to dress; (verse bien) to look good; ~**se** vr to get dressed, dress o.s.

vestuario [bes'twarjo] nm clothes pl, wardrobe; (TEATRO: cuarto) dressing room; (DEPORTE) changing room

veta ['beta] *nf* (*vena*) vein, seam; (*en carne*) streak; (*de madera*) grain

vetar [be'tar] *vt* to veto

veterano, a [bete'rano, a] *adj, nm* veteran

veterinaria [beteri'narja] *nf* veterinary science; *ver tb* **veterinario**

veterinario, a [beteri'narjo, a] *nm/f* vet(erinary surgeon)

veto ['beto] *nm* veto

vez [beθ] *nf* time; (*turno*) turn; **a la ~ que** at the same time as; **a su ~** in its turn; **otra ~** again; **una ~** once; **de una ~** in one go; **de una ~ para siempre** once and for all; **en ~ de** instead of; **a o algunas veces** sometimes; **una y otra ~** repeatedly; **de ~ en cuando** from time to time; **7 veces 9** 7 times 9; **hacer las veces de** to stand in for; **tal ~** perhaps

vía ['bia] *nf* track, route; (*FERRO*) line; (*fig*) way; (*ANAT*) passage, tube ♦ *prep* via, by way of; **por ~ judicial** by legal means; **por ~ oficial** through official channels; **en ~s de** in the process of; **~ aérea** airway; **V~ Láctea** Milky Way; **~ pública** public road o thoroughfare

viable ['bjaβle] *adj* (*solución, plan, alternativa*) feasible

viaducto [bja'ðukto] *nm* viaduct

viajante [bja'xante] *nm* commercial traveller

viajar [bja'xar] *vi* to travel; **viaje** *nm* journey; (*gira*) tour; (*NAUT*) voyage; **estar de viaje** to be on a trip; **viaje de ida y vuelta** round trip; **viaje de novios** honeymoon; **viajero, a** *adj* travelling; (*ZOOL*) migratory ♦ *nm/f* (*quien viaja*) traveller; (*pasajero*) passenger

vial [bjal] *adj* road *cpd*, traffic *cpd*

víbora ['biβora] *nf* viper; (*AM*) poisonous snake

vibración [biβra'θjon] *nf* vibration

vibrar [bi'βrar] *vt, vi* to vibrate

vicario [bi'karjo] *nm* curate

vicepresidente [biθepresi'ðente] *nm/f* vice-president

viceversa [biθe'βersa] *adv* vice versa

viciado, a [bi'θjaðo, a] *adj* (*corrompido*) corrupt; (*contaminado*) foul, contaminated; **viciar** *vt* (*pervertir*) to pervert; (*JUR*) to nullify; (*estropear*) to spoil; **viciarse** *vr* to become corrupted

vicio ['biθjo] *nm* vice; (*mala costumbre*) bad habit; **~so, a** *adj* (*muy malo*) vicious; (*corrompido*) depraved ♦ *nm/f* depraved person

vicisitud [biθisi'tuð] *nf* vicissitude

víctima ['biktima] *nf* victim

victoria [bik'torja] *nf* victory; **victorioso, a** *adj* victorious

vid [bið] *nf* vine

vida ['biða] *nf* (*gen*) life; (*duración*) lifetime; **de por ~** for life; **en la/mi ~** never; **estar con ~** to be still alive; **ganarse la ~** to earn one's living

vídeo ['biðeo] *nm* video ♦ *adj inv*: **película ~** video film; **~cámara** *nf* camcorder; **~casete** *nm* video cassette, videotape; **~club** *nm* video club; **~juego** *nm* video game

vidriero, a [bi'ðrjero, a] *nm/f* glazier ♦ *nf* (*ventana*) stained-glass window; (*AM*: *de tienda*) shop window; (*puerta*) glass door

vidrio ['biðrjo] *nm* glass

vieira ['bjeira] *nf* scallop

viejo, a ['bjexo, a] *adj* old ♦ *nm/f* old man/ woman; **hacerse ~** to get old

Viena ['bjena] *n* Vienna

vienes *etc vb ver* **venir**

vienés, esa [bje'nes, esa] *adj* Viennese

viento ['bjento] *nm* wind; **hacer ~** to be windy

vientre ['bjentre] *nm* belly; (*matriz*) womb

viernes ['bjernes] *nm inv* Friday; **V~ Santo** Good Friday

Vietnam [bjet'nam] *nm*: **el ~** Vietnam; **vietnamita** *adj* Vietnamese

viga ['biɣa] *nf* beam, rafter; (*de metal*) girder

vigencia [bi'xenθja] *nf* validity; **estar en ~** to be in force; **vigente** *adj* valid, in force; (*imperante*) prevailing

vigésimo, a [bi'xesimo, a] *adj* twentieth

vigía [bi'xia] *nm* look-out

vigilancia [bixi'lanθja] *nf*: **tener a uno bajo ~** to keep watch on sb

vigilar [bixi'lar] *vt* to watch over ♦ *vi* (*gen*) to be vigilant; (*hacer guardia*) to keep watch; **~ por** to take care of

vigilia [vi'xilja] *nf* wakefulness, being awake; (*REL*) fast

vigor [bi'xor] *nm* vigour, vitality; **en ~** in force; **entrar/poner en ~** to come/put into effect; **~oso, a** *adj* vigorous

VIH *nm abr* (= *virus de la inmunodeficiencia humana*) HIV; **~ positivo/negativo** HIV-positive/-negative

vil [bil] *adj* vile, low; **~eza** *nf* vileness; (*acto*) base deed

vilipendiar [bilipen'djar] *vt* to vilify, revile

villa ['biʎa] *nf* (*casa*) villa; (*pueblo*) small town; (*municipalidad*) municipality; **~ miseria** (*AM*) shantytown

villancico [biʎan'θiko] *nm* (Christmas) carol

villorrio [bi'ʎorrjo] *nm* shantytown

vilo ['bilo]: **en ~** *adv* in the air, suspended; (*fig*) on tenterhooks, in suspense

vinagre [bi'naɣre] *nm* vinegar

vinagreta [bina'xreta] *nf* vinaigrette, French dressing

vinculación [binkula'θjon] *nf* (*lazo*) link, bond; (*acción*) linking

vincular [binku'lar] *vt* to link, bind; **vínculo** *nm* link, bond

vine *etc vb ver* **venir**

vinicultura [binikul'tura] *nf* wine growing
viniera *etc vb ver* **venir**
vino ['bino] *vb ver* **venir** ♦ *nm* wine;
~ **blanco/tinto** white/red wine
viña ['biɲa] *nf* vineyard; **viñedo** *nm* vineyard
viola ['bjola] *nf* viola
violación [bjola'θjon] *nf* violation; ~ **(sexual)** rape
violar [bjo'lar] *vt* to violate; (*sexualmente*) to rape
violencia [bjo'lenθja] *nf* violence, force;
(*incomodidad*) embarrassment; (*acto injusto*)
unjust act; **violentar** *vt* to force; (*casa*) to
break into; (*agredir*) to assault; (*violar*) to
violate; **violento, a** *adj* violent; (*furioso*)
furious; (*situación*) embarrassing; (*acto*)
forced, unnatural
violeta [bjo'leta] *nf* violet
violín [bjo'lin] *nm* violin
violón [bjo'lon] *nm* double bass
viraje [bi'raxe] *nm* turn; (*de vehículo*) swerve;
(*fig*) change of direction; **virar** *vi* to change
direction
virgen ['birxen] *adj, nf* virgin
Virgo ['birxo] *nm* Virgo
viril [bi'ril] *adj* virile; ~**idad** *nf* virility
virtud [bir'tuð] *nf* virtue; **en** ~ **de** by virtue of;
virtuoso, a *adj* virtuous ♦ *nm/f* virtuoso
viruela [bi'rwela] *nf* smallpox
virulento, a [biru'lento, a] *adj* virulent
virus ['birus] *nm inv* virus
visa ['bisa] (*AM*) *nf* = **visado**
visado [bi'saðo] *nm* visa
víscera [bisθera] *nf* (*ANAT, ZOOL*) gut, bowel;
~**s** *nfpl* entrails
visceral [bisθe'ral] *adj* (*odio*) intense;
reacción ~ gut reaction
viscoso, a [bis'koso, a] *adj* viscous
visera [bi'sera] *nf* visor
visibilidad [bisiβili'ðað] *nf* visibility; **visible**
adj visible; (*fig*) obvious
visillos [bi'siʎos] *nmpl* lace curtains
visión [bi'sjon] *nf* (*ANAT*) vision, (eye)sight;
(*fantasía*) vision, fantasy
visita [bi'sita] *nf* call, visit; (*persona*) visitor;
hacer una ~ to pay a visit
visitar [bisi'tar] *vt* to visit, call on
vislumbrar [bislum'brar] *vt* to glimpse,
catch a glimpse of
viso ['biso] *nm* (*del metal*) glint, gleam; (*de
tela*) sheen; (*aspecto*) appearance
visón [bi'son] *nm* mink
visor [bi'sor] *nm* (*FOTO*) viewfinder
víspera ['bispera] *nf*: **la** ~ **de** ... the day
before ...
vista ['bista] *nf* sight, vision; (*capacidad de
ver*) (eye)sight; (*mirada*) look(s) (*pl*); **a
primera** ~ at first glance; **hacer la** ~ **gorda** to
turn a blind eye; **volver la** ~ to look back;

está a la ~ **que** it's obvious that; **en** ~ **de** in
view of; **en** ~ **de que** in view of the fact that;
¡**hasta la** ~! so long!, see you!; **con** ~**s a** with a
view to; ~**zo** *nm* glance; **dar** *o* **echar un** ~**zo a**
to glance at
visto, a ['bisto, a] *pp de* **ver** ♦ *vb ver tb* **vestir**
♦ *adj* seen; (*considerado*) considered ♦ *nm*:
~ **bueno** approval; "~ **bueno**" "approved";
por lo ~ apparently; **está** ~ **que** it's clear that;
está bien/mal ~ it's acceptable/unacceptable;
~ **que** since, considering that
vistoso, a [bis'toso, a] *adj* colourful
visual [bi'swal] *adj* visual
vital [bi'tal] *adj* life *cpd*, living *cpd*; (*fig*) vital;
(*persona*) lively, vivacious; ~**icio, a** *adj* for
life; ~**idad** *nf* (*de persona, negocio*) energy;
(*de ciudad*) liveliness
vitamina [bita'mina] *nf* vitamin
viticultor, a [bitikul'tor, a] *nm/f* wine
grower; **viticultura** *nf* wine growing
vitorear [bitore'ar] *vt* to cheer, acclaim
vitrina [bi'trina] *nf* show case; (*AM*) shop
window
viudez *nf* widowhood
viudo, a ['bjuðo, a] *nm/f* widower/widow
viva ['biβa] *excl* hurrah!: ¡~ **el rey!** long live
the king!
vivacidad [biβaθi'ðað] *nf* (*vigor*) vigour;
(*vida*) liveliness
vivaracho, a [biβa'ratʃo, a] *adj* jaunty, lively;
(*ojos*) bright, twinkling
vivaz [bi'βaθ] *adj* lively
víveres ['biβeres] *nmpl* provisions
vivero [bi'βero] *nm* (*para plantas*) nursery;
(*para peces*) fish farm; (*fig*) hotbed
viveza [bi'βeθa] *nf* liveliness; (*agudeza:
mental*) sharpness
vivienda [bi'βjenda] *nf* housing; (*una* ~)
house; (*piso*) flat (*BRIT*), apartment (*US*)
viviente [bi'βjente] *adj* living
vivir [bi'βir] *vt, vi* to live ♦ *nm* life, living
vivo, a ['biβo, a] *adj* living, alive; (*fig:
descripción*) vivid; (*persona: astuto*) smart,
clever; **en** ~ (*transmisión etc*) live
vocablo [bo'kaβlo] *nm* (*palabra*) word;
(*término*) term
vocabulario [bokaβu'larjo] *nm* vocabulary
vocación [boka'θjon] *nf* vocation;
vocacional (*AM*) *nf* ≈ technical college
vocal [bo'kal] *adj* vocal ♦ *nf* vowel; ~**izar** *vt*
to vocalize
vocear [boθe'ar] *vt* (*para vender*) to cry;
(*aclamar*) to acclaim; (*fig*) to proclaim ♦ *vi* to
yell; **vocerío** *nm* shouting
vocero [bo'θero] *nm/f* spokesman/woman
voces ['boθes] *pl de* **voz**
vociferar [boθife'rar] *vt* to shout ♦ *vi* to yell
vodka ['boðka] *nm o f* vodka
vol *abr* = **volumen**

volador, a [bola'ðor, a] *adj* flying

volandas [bo'landas]: **en ~** *adv* in the air

volante [bo'lante] *adj* flying ♦ *nm* (*de coche*) steering wheel; (*de reloj*) balance

volar [bo'lar] *vt* (*edificio*) to blow up ♦ *vi* to fly

volátil [bo'latil] *adj* volatile

volcán [bol'kan] *nm* volcano; **~ico, a** *adj* volcanic

volcar [bol'kar] *vt* to upset, overturn; (*tumbar, derribar*) to knock over; (*vaciar*) to empty out ♦ *vi* to overturn; **~se** *vr* to tip over

voleibol [bolei'βol] *nm* volleyball

volqué etc *vb ver* **volcar**

voltaje [bol'taxe] *nm* voltage

voltear [bolte'ar] *vt* to turn over; (*volcar*) to turn upside down

voltereta [bolte'reta] *nf* somersault

voltio ['boltjo] *nm* volt

voluble [bo'lußle] *adj* fickle

volumen [bo'lumen] (*pl* **volúmenes**) *nm* volume; **voluminoso, a** *adj* voluminous; (*enorme*) massive

voluntad [bolun'tað] *nf* will; (*resolución*) willpower; (*deseo*) desire, wish

voluntario, a [bolun'tarjo, a] *adj* voluntary ♦ *nm/f* volunteer

voluntarioso, a [bolunta'rjoso, a] *adj* headstrong

voluptuoso, a [bolup'twoso, a] *adj* voluptuous

volver [bol'ßer] *vt* (*gen*) to turn; (*dar vuelta a*) to turn (over); (*voltear*) to turn round, turn upside down; (*poner al revés*) to turn inside out; (*devolver*) to return ♦ *vi* to return, go back, come back; **~se** *vr* to turn round; **~ la espalda** to turn one's back; **~ triste** *etc* **a uno** to make sb sad *etc*; **~ a hacer** to do again; **~ en sí** to come to; **~se insoportable/ muy caro** to get *o* become unbearable/very expensive; **~se loco** to go mad

vomitar [bomi'tar] *vt, vi* to vomit; **vómito** *nm* vomit

voraz [bo'raθ] *adj* voracious

vos [bos] (*AM*) *pron* you

vosotros, as [bo'sotros, as] *pron* you; (*reflexivo*): **entre/para ~** among/for yourselves

votación [bota'θjon] *nf* (*acto*) voting; (*voto*) vote

votar [bo'tar] *vi* to vote; **voto** *nm* vote; (*promesa*) vow; **votos** (good) wishes

voy *vb ver* **ir**

voz [boθ] *nf* voice; (*grito*) shout; (*rumor*) rumour; (*LING*) word; **dar voces** to shout, yell; **a media ~** in a low voice; **a ~ en cuello** *o* **en grito** at the top of one's voice; **de viva ~** verbally; **en ~ alta** aloud; **~ de mando** command

vuelco ['bwelko] *vb ver* **volcar** ♦ *nm* spill, overturning

vuelo ['bwelo] *vb ver* **volar** ♦ *nm* flight; (*encaje*) lace, frill; **coger al ~** to catch in flight; **~ charter/regular** charter/scheduled flight; **~ libre** (*DEPORTE*) hang-gliding

vuelque etc *vb ver* **volcar**

vuelta ['bwelta] *nf* (*gen*) turn; (*curva*) bend, curve; (*regreso*) return; (*revolución*) revolution; (*de circuito*) lap; (*de papel, tela*) reverse; (*cambio*) change; **a la ~** on one's return; **a ~ de correo** by return of post; **dar ~s** (*suj: cabeza*) to spin; **dar ~s a una idea** to turn over an idea (in one's head); **estar de ~** to be back; **dar una ~** to go for a walk; (*en coche*) to go for a drive; **~ ciclista** (*DEPORTE*) (cycle) tour

vuelto *pp de* **volver**

vuelvo etc *vb ver* **volver**

vuestro, a ['bwestro, a] *adj* your; **un amigo ~** a friend of yours ♦ *pron*: **el ~/la vuestra, los ~s/las vuestras** yours

vulgar [bul'var] *adj* (*ordinario*) vulgar; (*común*) common; **~idad** *nf* commonness; (*acto*) vulgarity; (*expresión*) coarse expression; **~izar** *vt* to popularize

vulgo ['bulvo] *nm* common people

vulnerable [bulne'raßle] *adj* vulnerable

vulnerar [bulne'rar] *vt* (*ley, acuerdo*) to violate, breach; (*derechos, intimidad*) to violate; (*reputación*) to damage

W, w

Walkman ® [wak'man] *nm* Walkman ®

wáter ['bater] *nm* toilet

whisky ['wiski] *nm* whisky, whiskey

WWW *nm o nf abr* (*INFORM*: = World Wide Web*) WWW

X, x

xenofobia [kseno'foßja] *nf* xenophobia

xilófono [ksi'lofono] *nm* xylophone

Y, y

y [i] *conj* and

ya [ja] *adv* (*gen*) already; (*ahora*) now; (*en seguida*) at once; (*pronto*) soon ♦ *excl* all right! ♦ *conj* (*ahora que*) now that; **~ lo sé** I know; **~ que** since

yacer [ja'θer] *vi* to lie

yacimiento [jaθi'mjento] *nm* (*de mineral*) deposit; (*arqueológico*) site

yanqui ['janki] *adj, nm/f* Yankee

yate ['jate] *nm* yacht

yazco etc vb ver **yacer**

yedra ['jeðra] nf ivy

yegua ['jeɣwa] nf mare

yema ['jema] nf (del huevo) yolk; (BOT) leaf bud; (fig) best part; **~ del dedo** fingertip

yergo etc vb ver **erguir**

yermo, a ['jermo, a] adj (estéril, fig) barren ♦ nm wasteland

yerno ['jerno] nm son-in-law

yerro etc vb ver **errar**

yeso ['jeso] nm plaster

yo [jo] pron I; **soy ~** it's me, it is I

yodo ['joðo] nm iodine

yoga ['joɣa] nm yoga

yogur(t) [jo'ɣur(t)] nm yoghurt

yugo ['juɣo] nm yoke

Yugoslavia [juɣos'laßja] nf Yugoslavia

yugular [juɣu'lar] adj jugular

yunque ['junke] nm anvil

yunta ['junta] nf yoke

yuxtaponer [jukstapo'ner] vt to juxtapose; **yuxtaposición** nf juxtaposition

Z, z

zafar [θa'far] vt (soltar) to untie; (superficie) to clear; **~se** vr (escaparse) to escape; (TEC) to slip off

zafio, a ['θafjo, a] adj coarse

zafiro [θa'firo] nm sapphire

zaga ['θaɣa] nf: **a la ~** behind, in the rear

zaguán [θa'ɣwan] nm hallway

zaherir [θae'rir] vt (criticar) to criticize

zaino, a ['θaino, a] adj (caballo) chestnut

zalamería [θalame'ria] nf flattery; **zalamero, a** adj flattering; (cobista) suave

zamarra [θa'marra] nf (chaqueta) sheepskin jacket

zambullirse [θambu'ʎirse] vr to dive

zampar [θam'par] vt to gobble down

zanahoria [θana'orja] nf carrot

zancada [θan'kaða] nf stride

zancadilla [θanka'ðiʎa] nf trip

zanco ['θanko] nm stilt

zancudo, a [θan'kuðo, a] adj long-legged ♦ nm (AM) mosquito

zángano ['θangano] nm drone

zanja ['θanxa] nf ditch; **zanjar** vt (resolver) to resolve

zapata [θa'pata] nf (MECÁNICA) shoe

zapatear [θapate'ar] vi to tap with one's feet

zapatería [θapate'ria] nf (oficio) shoemaking; (tienda) shoe shop; (fábrica) shoe factory; **zapatero, a** nm/f shoemaker

zapatilla [θapa'tiʎa] nf slipper; **~ de deporte** training shoe

zapato [θa'pato] nm shoe

zapping ['θapin] nm channel-hopping; **hacer ~** to flick through the channels

zar [θar] nm tsar, czar

zarandear [θarande'ar] (fam) vt to shake vigorously

zarpa ['θarpa] nf (garra) claw

zarpar [θar'par] vi to weigh anchor

zarza ['θarθa] nf (BOT) bramble; **zarzal** nm (matorral) bramble patch

zarzamora [θarθa'mora] nf blackberry

zarzuela [θar'θwela] nf Spanish light opera

zigzag ['θiɣ'θaɣ] nm zigzag; **zigzaguear** vi to zigzag

zinc [θink] nm zinc

zócalo ['θokalo] nm (ARQ) plinth, base

zodíaco [θo'ðiako] nm (ASTRO) zodiac

zona ['θona] nf (zone; **~ fronteriza** border area

zoo ['θoo] nm zoo

zoología [θoolo'xia] nf zoology; **zoológico, a** adj zoological ♦ nm (tb: parque ~) zoo; **zoólogo, a** nm/f zoologist

zoom [θum] nm zoom lens

zopilote [θopi'lote] (AM) nm buzzard

zoquete [θo'kete] nm (fam) blockhead

zorro, a ['θorro, a] adj crafty ♦ nm/f fox/ vixen

zozobra [θo'θoßra] nf (fig) anxiety; **zozobrar** vi (hundirse) to capsize; (fig) to fail

zueco ['θweko] nm clog

zumbar [θum'bar] vt (golpear) to hit ♦ vi to buzz; **zumbido** nm buzzing

zumo ['θumo] nm juice

zurcir [θur'θir] vt (coser) to darn

zurdo, a ['θurðo, a] adj (persona) left-handed

zurrar [θu'rrar] (fam) vt to wallop

ENGLISH – SPANISH

INGLÉS – ESPAÑOL

A, a

A [eɪ] n (MUS) la m

> **KEYWORD**

a [ə] indef art (before vowel or silent h: an)
1 un(a); ~ **book** un libro; **an apple** una manzana; **she's** ~ **doctor** (ella) es médica
2 (instead of the number "one") un(a); ~ **year ago** hace un año; ~ **hundred/thousand** etc **pounds** cien/mil etc libras
3 (in expressing ratios, prices etc): **3** ~ **day/week** 3 al día/a la semana; **10 km an hour** 10 km por hora; **£5** ~ **person** £5 por persona; **30p** ~ **kilo** 30p el kilo

A.A. n abbr (= Automobile Association: BRIT) ≈ RACE m (SP); (= Alcoholics Anonymous) Alcohólicos Anónimos
A.A.A. (US) n abbr (= American Automobile Association) ≈ RACE m (SP)
aback [ə'bæk] adv: **to be taken** ~ quedar desconcertado
abandon [ə'bændən] vt abandonar; (give up) renunciar a
abate [ə'beɪt] vi (storm) amainar; (anger) aplacarse; (terror) disminuir
abattoir ['æbətwɑ:*] (BRIT) n matadero
abbey ['æbɪ] n abadía
abbot ['æbət] n abad m
abbreviation [əbri:vɪ'eɪʃən] n (short form) abreviatura
abdicate ['æbdɪkeɪt] vt renunciar a ♦ vi abdicar
abdomen ['æbdəmən] n abdomen m
abduct [æb'dʌkt] vt raptar, secuestrar
abeyance [ə'beɪəns] n: **in** ~ (law) en desuso; (matter) en suspenso
abide [ə'baɪd] vt: **I can't** ~ **it/him** no lo/le puedo ver; ~ **by** vt fus atenerse a
ability [ə'bɪlɪtɪ] n habilidad f, capacidad f; (talent) talento
abject ['æbdʒɛkt] adj (poverty) miserable; (apology) rastrero
ablaze [ə'bleɪz] adj en llamas, ardiendo
able ['eɪbl] adj capaz; (skilled) hábil; **to be** ~ **to do sth** poder hacer algo; ~-**bodied** adj sano; **ably** adv hábilmente
abnormal [æb'nɔ:məl] adj anormal
aboard [ə'bɔ:d] adv a bordo ♦ prep a bordo de
abode [ə'bəud] n: **of no fixed** ~ sin domicilio

fijo
abolish [ə'bɔlɪʃ] vt suprimir, abolir
aborigine [æbə'rɪdʒɪnɪ] n aborigen m/f
abort [ə'bɔ:t] vt, vi abortar; ~**ion** [ə'bɔ:ʃən] n aborto; **to have an** ~**ion** abortar, hacerse abortar; ~**ive** adj malogrado

> **KEYWORD**

about [ə'baut] adv **1** (approximately) más o menos, aproximadamente; ~ **a hundred/thousand** etc unos(unas) cien/mil etc; **it takes** ~ **10 hours** se tarda unas or más o menos 10 horas; **at** ~ **2 o'clock** sobre las dos; **I've just** ~ **finished** casi he terminado
2 (referring to place) por todas partes; **to leave things lying** ~ dejar las cosas (tiradas) por ahí; **to run** ~ correr por todas partes; **to walk** ~ pasearse, ir y venir
3: to be ~ **to do sth** estar a punto de hacer algo
♦ prep **1** (relating to) de, sobre, acerca de; **a book** ~ **London** un libro sobre or acerca de Londres; **what is it** ~? ¿de qué se trata?, ¿qué pasa?; **we talked** ~ **it** hablamos de eso or ello; **what** or **how** ~ **doing this?** ¿qué tal si hacemos esto?
2 (referring to place) por; **to walk** ~ **the town** caminar por la ciudad

above [ə'bʌv] adv encima, por encima, arriba
♦ prep encima de; (greater than: in number) más de; (: in rank) superior a; **mentioned** ~ susodicho; ~ **all** sobre todo; ~ **board** adj legítimo
abrasive [ə'breɪzɪv] adj abrasivo; (manner) brusco
abreast [ə'brɛst] adv de frente; **to keep** ~ **of** (fig) mantenerse al corriente de
abroad [ə'brɔ:d] adv (to be) en el extranjero; (to go) al extranjero
abrupt [ə'brʌpt] adj (sudden) brusco; (curt) áspero
abruptly [ə'brʌptlɪ] adv (leave) repentinamente; (speak) bruscamente
abscess ['æbsɪs] n absceso
abscond [əb'skɔnd] vi (thief): **to** ~ **with** fugarse con; (prisoner): **to** ~ (**from**) escaparse (de)
absence ['æbsəns] n ausencia
absent ['æbsənt] adj ausente; ~**ee** [-'ti:] n

ausente *m/f*; **~-minded** *adj* distraído
absolute ['æbsəluːt] *adj* absoluto; **~ly**
[-'luːtlɪ] *adv* (*totally*) totalmente; (*certainly!*)
¡por supuesto (que sí)!
absolve [əb'zɔlv] *vt*: **to ~ sb (from)** absolver
a alguien (de)
absorb [əb'zɔːb] *vt* absorber; **to be ~ed in a
book** estar absorto en un libro; **~ent cotton**
(*US*) *n* algodón *m* hidrófilo; **~ing** *adj*
absorbente
absorption [əb'zɔːpʃən] *n* absorción *f*
abstain [əb'steɪn] *vi*: **to ~ (from)** abstenerse
(de)
abstinence ['æbstɪnəns] *n* abstinencia
abstract ['æbstrækt] *adj* abstracto
absurd [əb'sɜːd] *adj* absurdo
abundance [ə'bʌndəns] *n* abundancia
abuse [*n* ə'bjuːs, *vb* ə'bjuːz] *n* (*insults*) insultos
mpl, injurias *fpl*; (*ill-treatment*) malos tratos
mpl; (*misuse*) abuso ♦ *vt* insultar; maltratar;
abusar de; **abusive** *adj* ofensivo
abysmal [ə'bɪzməl] *adj* pésimo; (*failure*)
garrafal; (*ignorance*) supino
abyss [ə'bɪs] *n* abismo
AC *abbr* (= *alternating current*) corriente *f*
alterna
academic [ækə'dɛmɪk] *adj* académico,
universitario; (*pej: issue*) puramente teórico
♦ *n* estudioso/a; profesor(a) *m/f*
universitario/a
academy [ə'kædəmɪ] *n* (*learned body*)
academia; (*school*) instituto, colegio; **~ of
music** conservatorio
accelerate [æk'sɛləreɪt] *vt, vi* acelerar;
accelerator (*BRIT*) *n* acelerador *m*
accent ['æksɛnt] *n* acento; (*fig*) énfasis *m*
accept [ək'sɛpt] *vt* aceptar; (*responsibility,
blame*) admitir; **~able** *adj* aceptable; **~ance**
n aceptación *f*
access ['æksɛs] *n* acceso; **to have ~ to** tener
libre acceso a; **~ible** [-'sɛsəbl] *adj* (*place,
person*) accesible; (*knowledge etc*) asequible
accessory [æk'sɛsərɪ] *n* accesorio; (*LAW*):
~ to cómplice de
accident ['æksɪdənt] *n* accidente *m*; (*chance
event*) casualidad *f*; **by ~** (*unintentionally*) sin
querer; (*by chance*) por casualidad; **~al**
[-'dɛntl] *adj* accidental, fortuito; **~ally**
[-'dɛntəlɪ] *adv* sin querer; por casualidad;
~ insurance *n* seguro contra accidentes;
~-prone *adj* propenso a los accidentes
acclaim [ə'kleɪm] *vt* aclamar, aplaudir ♦ *n*
aclamación *f*, aplausos *mpl*
acclimatize [ə'klaɪmətaɪz] (*US*: **acclimate**) *vt*:
to become ~d aclimatarse
accommodate [ə'kɔmədeɪt] *vt* (*subj:
person*) alojar, hospedar; (: *car, hotel etc*)
tener cabida para; (*oblige, help*) complacer;
accommodating *adj* servicial, complaciente

accommodation [əkɔmə'deɪʃən] *n* (*US*
accommodations *npl*) alojamiento
accompany [ə'kʌmpənɪ] *vt* acompañar
accomplice [ə'kʌmplɪs] *n* cómplice *m/f*
accomplish [ə'kʌmplɪʃ] *vt* (*finish*) concluir;
(*achieve*) lograr; **~ed** *adj* experto, hábil;
~ment *n* (*skill: gen pl*) talento; (*completion*)
realización *f*
accord [ə'kɔːd] *n* acuerdo ♦ *vt* conceder; **of
his own ~** espontáneamente; **~ance** *n*: **in
~ance with** de acuerdo con; **~ing**: **~ing to**
prep según; (*in accordance with*) conforme a;
~ingly *adv* (*appropriately*) de acuerdo con
esto; (*as a result*) en consecuencia
accordion [ə'kɔːdɪən] *n* acordeón *m*
accost [ə'kɔst] *vt* abordar, dirigirse a
account [ə'kaunt] *n* (*COMM*) cuenta; (*report*)
informe *m*; **~s** *npl* (*COMM*) cuentas *fpl*; **of no ~**
de ninguna importancia; **on ~** a cuenta; **on
no ~** bajo ningún concepto; **on ~ of** a causa
de, por motivo de; **to take into ~, take ~ of**
tener en cuenta; **~ for** *vt fus* (*explain*)
explicar; (*represent*) representar; **~able** *adj*:
~able to responsable (ante); **~ancy** *n*
contabilidad *f*; **~ant** *n* contable *m/f*,
contador(a) *m/f*; **~ number** *n* (*at bank etc*)
número de cuenta
accrued interest [ə'kruːd-] *n* interés *m*
acumulado
accumulate [ə'kjuːmjuleɪt] *vt* acumular ♦ *vi*
acumularse
accuracy ['ækjurəsɪ] *n* (*of total*) exactitud *f*;
(*of description etc*) precisión *f*
accurate ['ækjurɪt] *adj* (*total*) exacto;
(*description*) preciso; (*person*) cuidadoso;
(*device*) de precisión; **~ly** *adv* con precisión
accusation [ækju'zeɪʃən] *n* acusación *f*
accuse [ə'kjuːz] *vt*: **to ~ sb (of sth)** acusar a
uno (de algo); **~d** *n* (*LAW*) acusado/a
accustom [ə'kʌstəm] *vt* acostumbrar; **~ed**
adj: **~ed to** acostumbrado a
ace [eɪs] *n* as *m*
ache [eɪk] *n* dolor *m* ♦ *vi* doler; **my head ~s**
me duele la cabeza
achieve [ə'tʃiːv] *vt* (*aim, result*) alcanzar;
(*success*) lograr, conseguir; **~ment** *n*
(*completion*) realización *f*; (*success*) éxito
acid ['æsɪd] *adj* ácido; (*taste*) agrio ♦ *n* (*CHEM,
inf: LSD*) ácido; **~ rain** *n* lluvia ácida
acknowledge [ək'nɔlɪdʒ] *vt* (*letter: also*:
~ receipt of) acusar recibo de; (*fact, situation,
person*) reconocer; **~ment** *n* acuse *m* de
recibo
acne ['æknɪ] *n* acné *m*
acorn ['eɪkɔːn] *n* bellota
acoustic [ə'kuːstɪk] *adj* acústico; **~s** *n, npl*
acústica *sg*
acquaint [ə'kweɪnt] *vt*: **to ~ sb with sth**
(*inform*) poner a uno al corriente de algo; **to**

be ~ed with conocer; ~ance n (person)
conocido/a; (with person, subject)
conocimiento

acquire [əˈkwaɪə*] vt adquirir; **acquisition**
[ækwɪˈzɪʃən] n adquisición f

acquit [əˈkwɪt] vt absolver, exculpar; **to ~ o.s.
well** salir con éxito

acre [ˈeɪkə*] n acre m

acrid [ˈækrɪd] adj acre

acrobat [ˈækrəbæt] n acróbata m/f

across [əˈkrɒs] prep (on the other side of) al
otro lado de, del otro lado de; (crosswise) a
través de ♦ adv de un lado a otro, de una
parte a otra; a través, al través;
(measurement): **the road is 10m ~** la carretera
tiene 10m de ancho; **to run/swim ~** atravesar
corriendo/nadando; **~ from** enfrente de

acrylic [əˈkrɪlɪk] adj acrílico ♦ n acrílica f

act [ækt] n acto, acción f; (of play) acto; (in
music hall etc) número; (LAW) decreto, ley f
♦ vi (behave) comportarse; (have effect: drug,
chemical) hacer efecto; (THEATRE) actuar;
(pretend) fingir; (take action) obrar ♦ vt
(part) hacer el papel de; **in the ~ of: to catch
sb in the ~ of ...** pillar a uno en el momento
en que ...; **to ~ as** actuar or hacer de; **~ing**
adj suplente ♦ n (activity) actuación f;
(profession) profesión f de actor

action [ˈækʃən] n acción f, acto; (MIL) acción
f, batalla; (LAW) proceso, demanda; **out of ~**
(person) fuera de combate; (thing)
estropeado; **to take ~** tomar medidas;
~ replay n (TV) repetición f

activate [ˈæktɪveɪt] vt activar

active [ˈæktɪv] adj activo, enérgico; (volcano)
en actividad; **~ly** adv (participate)
activamente; (discourage, dislike)
enérgicamente; **activity** [-ˈtɪvɪtɪ] n actividad
f; **activity holiday** n vacaciones fpl con
actividades organizadas

actor [ˈæktə*] n actor m

actress [ˈæktrɪs] n actriz f

actual [ˈæktjuəl] adj verdadero, real;
(emphatic use) propiamente dicho; **~ly** adv
realmente, en realidad; (even) incluso

acumen [ˈækjumən] n perspicacia

acute [əˈkjuːt] adj agudo

ad [æd] n abbr = **advertisement**

A.D. adv abbr (= anno Domini) A.C.

adamant [ˈædəmənt] adj firme, inflexible

adapt [əˈdæpt] vt adaptar ♦ vi: **to ~ (to)**
adaptarse a, ajustarse (a); **~able** adj
adaptable; **~er, ~or** n (ELEC) adaptador m

add [æd] vt añadir, agregar; (figures: also:
~ up) sumar ♦ vi: **to ~ to** (increase)
aumentar, acrecentar; **it doesn't ~ up** (fig) no
tiene sentido

adder [ˈædə*] n víbora

addict [ˈædɪkt] n adicto/a; (enthusiast)
entusiasta m/f; **~ed** [əˈdɪktɪd] adj: **to be ~ed
to** ser adicto a; (football etc) ser fanático de;
~ion [əˈdɪkʃən] n (to drugs etc) adicción f;
~ive [əˈdɪktɪv] adj que causa adicción

addition [əˈdɪʃən] n (adding up) adición f;
(thing added) añadidura, añadido; **in ~**
además, por añadidura; **in ~ to** además de;
~al adj adicional

additive [ˈædɪtɪv] n aditivo

address [əˈdrɛs] n dirección f, señas fpl;
(speech) discurso ♦ vt (letter) dirigir; (speak
to) dirigirse a, dirigir la palabra a; (problem)
tratar

adept [ˈædɛpt] adj: **~ at** experto or hábil en

adequate [ˈædɪkwɪt] adj (satisfactory)
adecuado; (enough) suficiente

adhere [ədˈhɪə*] vi: **to ~ to** (stick to) pegarse
a; (fig: abide by) observar; (: belief etc) ser
partidario de

adhesive [ədˈhiːzɪv] n adhesivo; **~ tape** n
(BRIT) cinta adhesiva; (US: MED) esparadrapo

ad hoc [ædˈhɒk] adj ad hoc

adjacent [əˈdʒeɪsənt] adj: **~ to** contiguo a,
inmediato a

adjective [ˈædʒɛktɪv] n adjetivo

adjoining [əˈdʒɔɪnɪŋ] adj contiguo, vecino

adjourn [əˈdʒɜːn] vt aplazar ♦ vi suspenderse

adjudicate [əˈdʒuːdɪkeɪt] vi sentenciar

adjust [əˈdʒʌst] vt (change) modificar;
(clothing) arreglar; (machine) ajustar ♦ vi: **to
~ (to)** adaptarse a; **~able** adj ajustable;
~ment n adaptación f; (to machine, prices)
ajuste m

ad-lib [ædˈlɪb] vt, vi improvisar; **ad lib** adv de
forma improvisada

administer [ədˈmɪnɪstə*] vt administrar;
administration [-ˈtreɪʃən] n (management)
administración f; (government) gobierno;
administrative [-trətɪv] adj administrativo

admiral [ˈædmərəl] n almirante m; **A~ty**
(BRIT) n Ministerio de Marina, Almirantazgo

admiration [ædməˈreɪʃən] n admiración f

admire [ədˈmaɪə*] vt admirar; **~r** n (fan)
admirador(a) m/f

admission [ədˈmɪʃən] n (to university, club)
ingreso; (entry fee) entrada; (confession)
confesión f

admit [ədˈmɪt] vt (confess) confesar; (permit
to enter) dejar entrar, dar entrada a; (to club,
organization) admitir; (accept: defeat)
reconocer; **to be ~ted to hospital** ingresar en
el hospital; **~ to** vt fus confesarse culpable
de; **~tance** n entrada; **~tedly** adv es cierto
or verdad que

admonish [ədˈmɒnɪʃ] vt amonestar

ad nauseam [ædˈnɔːsɪæm] adv hasta el
cansancio

ado [əˈduː] n: **without (any) more ~** sin más
(ni más)

adolescent [ædəu'lɛsnt] *adj, n* adolescente *m/f*
adopt [ə'dɔpt] *vt* adoptar; **~ed** *adj* adoptivo; **~ion** [ə'dɔpʃən] *n* adopción *f*
adore [ə'dɔ:*] *vt* adorar
Adriatic [eɪdrɪ'ætɪk] *n*: **the ~ (Sea)** el (Mar) Adriático
adrift [ə'drɪft] *adv* a la deriva
adult ['ædʌlt] *n* adulto/a ♦ *adj* (*grown-up*) adulto; (*for adults*) para adultos
adultery [ə'dʌltərɪ] *n* adulterio
advance [əd'vɑ:ns] *n* (*progress*) adelanto, progreso; (*money*) anticipo, préstamo; (*MIL*) avance *m* ♦ *adj*: **~ booking** venta anticipada; **~ notice, ~ warning** previo aviso ♦ *vt* (*money*) anticipar; (*theory, idea*) proponer (para la discusión) ♦ *vi* avanzar, adelantarse; **to make ~s (to sb)** hacer proposiciones (a alguien); **in ~** por adelantado; **~d** *adj* avanzado; (*SCOL*: *studies*) adelantado
advantage [əd'vɑ:ntɪdʒ] *n* (*also TENNIS*) ventaja; **to take ~ of** (*person*) aprovecharse de; (*opportunity*) aprovechar
Advent ['ædvənt] *n* (*REL*) Adviento
adventure [əd'vɛntʃə*] *n* aventura; **adventurous** [-tʃərəs] *adj* atrevido; aventurero
adverb ['ædvə:b] *n* adverbio
adverse ['ædvə:s] *adj* adverso, contrario
adversity [əd'və:sɪtɪ] *n* infortunio
advert ['ædvə:t] (*BRIT*) *n abbr* = **advertisement**
advertise ['ædvətaɪz] *vi* (*in newspaper etc*) anunciar, hacer publicidad; **to ~ for** (*staff, accommodation etc*) buscar por medio de anuncios ♦ *vt* anunciar; **~ment** [əd'və:tɪsmənt] *n* (*COMM*) anuncio; **~r** *n* anunciante *m/f*; **advertising** *n* publicidad *f*, anuncios *mpl*; (*industry*) industria publicitaria
advice [əd'vaɪs] *n* consejo, consejos *mpl*; (*notification*) aviso; **a piece of ~** un consejo; **to take legal ~** consultar con un abogado
advisable [əd'vaɪzəbl] *adj* aconsejable, conveniente
advise [əd'vaɪz] *vt* aconsejar; (*inform*): **to ~ sb of sth** informar a uno de algo; **to ~ sb against sth/doing sth** desaconsejar algo a uno/aconsejar a uno que no haga algo; **~dly** [əd'vaɪzɪdlɪ] *adv* (*deliberately*) deliberadamente; **~r** *n* = **advisor**; **advisor** *n* consejero/a; (*consultant*) asesor(a) *m/f*; **advisory** *adj* consultivo
advocate ['ædvəkeɪt] *vt* abogar por ♦ *n* [-kɪt] (*lawyer*) abogado/a; (*supporter*): **~ of** defensor(a) *m/f* de
Aegean [i:'dʒi:ən] *n*: **the ~ (Sea)** el (Mar) Egeo
aerial ['ɛərɪəl] *n* antena ♦ *adj* aéreo
aerobics [ɛə'rəubɪks] *n* aerobic *m*
aeroplane ['ɛərəpleɪn] (*BRIT*) *n* avión *m*
aerosol ['ɛərəsɔl] *n* aerosol *m*
aesthetic [i:s'θɛtɪk] *adj* estético
afar [ə'fɑ:*] *adv*: **from ~** desde lejos
affair [ə'fɛə*] *n* asunto; (*also*: *love ~*) aventura (amorosa)
affect [ə'fɛkt] *vt* (*influence*) afectar, influir en; (*afflict, concern*) afectar; (*move*) conmover; **~ed** *adj* afectado
affection [ə'fɛkʃən] *n* afecto, cariño; **~ate** *adj* afectuoso, cariñoso
affinity [ə'fɪnɪtɪ] *n* (*bond, rapport*): **to feel an ~ with** sentirse identificado con; (*resemblance*) afinidad *f*
afflict [ə'flɪkt] *vt* afligir
affluence ['æfluəns] *n* opulencia, riqueza
affluent ['æfluənt] *adj* (*wealthy*) acomodado; **the ~ society** la sociedad opulenta
afford [ə'fɔ:d] *vt* (*provide*) proporcionar; **can we ~ (to buy) it?** ¿tenemos bastante dinero para comprarlo?
Afghanistan [æf'gænɪstæn] *n* Afganistán *m*
afield [ə'fi:ld] *adv*: **far ~** muy lejos
afloat [ə'fləut] *adv* (*floating*) a flote
afoot [ə'fut] *adv*: **there is something ~** algo se está tramando
afraid [ə'freɪd] *adj*: **to be ~ of** (*person*) tener miedo a; (*thing*) tener miedo de; **to be ~ to** tener miedo de, temer; **I am ~ that** me temo que; **I am ~ not/so** lo siento, pero no/es así
afresh [ə'frɛʃ] *adv* de nuevo, otra vez
Africa ['æfrɪkə] *n* África; **~n** *adj, n* africano/a *m/f*
after ['ɑ:ftə*] *prep* (*time*) después de; (*place, order*) detrás de, tras ♦ *adv* después ♦ *conj* después (de) que; **what/who are you ~?** ¿qué/a quién busca usted?; **~ having done/he left** después de haber hecho/después de que se marchó; **to name sb ~ sb** llamar a uno por uno; **it's twenty ~ eight** (*US*) son las ocho y veinte; **to ask ~ sb** preguntar por alguien; **~ all** después de todo, al fin y al cabo; **~ you!** ¡pase usted!; **~-effects** *npl* consecuencias *fpl*, efectos *mpl*; **~math** *n* consecuencias *fpl*, resultados *mpl*; **~noon** *n* tarde *f*; **~s** (*inf*) *n* (*dessert*) postre *m*; **~-sales service** (*BRIT*) *n* servicio de asistencia pos-venta; **~-shave (lotion)** *n* aftershave *m*; **~sun (lotion/cream)** *n* loción *f*/crema para después del sol, aftersun *m*; **~thought** *n* ocurrencia (tardía); **~wards** (*US* **~ward**) *adv* después, más tarde
again [ə'gɛn] *adv* otra vez, de nuevo; **to do sth ~** volver a hacer algo; **~ and ~** una y otra vez
against [ə'gɛnst] *prep* (*in opposition to*) en contra de; (*leaning on, touching*) contra, junto a
age [eɪdʒ] *n* edad *f*; (*period*) época ♦ *vi*

envejecer(se) ♦ vt envejecer; **she is 20 years of ~** tiene 20 años; **to come of ~** llegar a la mayoría de edad; **it's been ~s since I saw you** hace siglos que no te veo; **~d 10** de 10 años de edad; **the ~d** ['eɪdʒɪd] npl los ancianos; **~ group** n: **to be in the same ~ group** tener la misma edad; **~ limit** n edad f mínima (or máxima)

agency ['eɪdʒənsɪ] n agencia

agenda [ə'dʒɛndə] n orden m del día

agent ['eɪdʒənt] n agente m/f; (COMM: holding concession) representante m/f, delegado/a; (CHEM, fig) agente m

aggravate ['ægrəveɪt] vt (situation) agravar; (person) irritar

aggregate ['ægrɪgɪt] n conjunto

aggressive [ə'grɛsɪv] adj (belligerent) agresivo; (assertive) enérgico

aggrieved [ə'griːvd] adj ofendido, agraviado

aghast [ə'gɑːst] adj horrorizado

agile ['ædʒaɪl] adj ágil

agitate ['ædʒɪteɪt] vt (trouble) inquietar ♦ vi: **to ~ for/against** hacer campaña pro or en favor de/en contra de

AGM n abbr (= annual general meeting) asamblea anual

ago [ə'gəu] adv: **2 days ~** hace 2 días; **not long ~** hace poco; **how long ~?** ¿hace cuánto tiempo?

agog [ə'gɔg] adj (eager) ansioso; (excited) emocionado

agonizing ['ægənaɪzɪŋ] adj (pain) atroz; (decision, wait) angustioso

agony ['ægənɪ] n (pain) dolor m agudo; (distress) angustia; **to be in ~** retorcerse de dolor

agree [ə'griː] vt (price, date) acordar, quedar en ♦ vi (have same opinion): **to ~ (with/that)** estar de acuerdo (con/que); (correspond) coincidir, concordar; (consent) acceder; **to ~ with** (subj: person) estar de acuerdo con, ponerse de acuerdo con; (: food) sentar bien a; (LING) concordar con; **to ~ to sth/to do sth** consentir en algo/aceptar hacer algo; **to ~ that** (admit) estar de acuerdo en que; **~able** adj (sensation) agradable; (person) simpático; (willing) de acuerdo, conforme; **~d** adj (time, place) convenido; **~ment** n acuerdo; (contract) contrato; **in ~ment** de acuerdo, conforme

agricultural [ægrɪ'kʌltʃərəl] adj agrícola

agriculture ['ægrɪkʌltʃə*] n agricultura

aground [ə'graund] adv: **to run ~** (NAUT) encallar, embarrancar

ahead [ə'hɛd] adv (in front) delante; (into the future): **she had no time to think ~** no tenía tiempo de hacer planes para el futuro; **~ of** delante de; (in advance of) antes de; **~ of time** antes de la hora; **go right** or **straight ~**

(direction) siga adelante; (permission) hazlo (or hágalo)

aid [eɪd] n ayuda, auxilio; (device) aparato ♦ vt ayudar, auxiliar; **in ~ of** a beneficio de

aide [eɪd] n (person, also: MIL) ayudante m/f

AIDS [eɪdz] n abbr (= acquired immune deficiency syndrome) SIDA m

ailment ['eɪlmənt] n enfermedad f, achaque m

aim [eɪm] vt (gun, camera) apuntar; (missile, remark) dirigir; (blow) asestar ♦ vi (also: take ~) apuntar ♦ n (in shooting: skill) puntería; (objective) propósito, meta; **to ~ at** (with weapon) apuntar a; (objective) aspirar a, pretender; **to ~ to do** tener la intención de hacer; **~less** adj sin propósito, sin objeto

ain't [eɪnt] (inf) = **am not**; **aren't**; **isn't**

air [ɛə*] n aire m; (appearance) aspecto ♦ vt (room) ventilar; (clothes, ideas) airear ♦ cpd aéreo; **to throw sth into the ~** (ball etc) lanzar algo al aire; **by ~** (travel) en avión; **to be on the ~** (RADIO, TV) estar en antena; **~bed** (BRIT) n colchón m neumático; **~-conditioned** adj climatizado; **~ conditioning** n aire acondicionado; **~craft** n inv avión m; **~craft carrier** n porta(a)viones m inv; **~field** n campo de aviación; **A~ Force** n fuerzas fpl aéreas, aviación f; **~ freshener** n ambientador m; **~gun** n escopeta de aire comprimido; **~ hostess** (BRIT) n azafata; **~ letter** (BRIT) n carta aérea; **~lift** n puente m aéreo; **~line** n línea aérea; **~liner** n avión m de pasajeros; **~mail** n: **by ~mail** por avión; **~plane** (US) n avión m; **~port** n aeropuerto; **~ raid** n ataque m aéreo; **~sick** adj: **to be ~sick** marearse (en avión); **~space** n espacio aéreo; **~tight** adj hermético; **~-traffic controller** n controlador(a) m/f aéreo/a; **~y** adj (room) bien ventilado; (fig: manner) desenfadado

aisle [aɪl] n (of church) nave f; (of theatre, supermarket) pasillo; **~ seat** n (on plane) asiento de pasillo

ajar [ə'dʒɑː*] adj entreabierto

alarm [ə'lɑːm] n (in shop, bank) alarma; (anxiety) inquietud f ♦ vt asustar, inquietar; **~ call** n (in hotel etc) alarma; **~ clock** n despertador m

alas [ə'læs] adv desgraciadamente

albeit [ɔːl'biːɪt] conj aunque

album ['ælbəm] n álbum m; (L.P.) elepé m

alcohol ['ælkəhɔl] n alcohol m; **~ic** [-'hɔlɪk] adj, n alcohólico/a m/f

ale [eɪl] n cerveza

alert [ə'ləːt] adj (attentive) atento; (to danger, opportunity) alerta ♦ n alarma ♦ vt poner sobre aviso; **to be on the ~** (also MIL) estar alerta or sobre aviso

algebra ['ældʒɪbrə] n álgebra

Algeria [æl'dʒɪərɪə] n Argelia
alias ['eɪlɪəs] adv alias, conocido por ♦ n (of criminal) apodo; (of writer) seudónimo
alibi ['ælɪbaɪ] n coartada
alien ['eɪlɪən] n (foreigner) extranjero/a; (extraterrestrial) extraterrestre m/f ♦ adj: ~ to ajeno a; ~**ate** vt enajenar, alejar
alight [ə'laɪt] adj ardiendo; (eyes) brillante ♦ vi (person) apearse, bajar; (bird) posarse
align [ə'laɪn] vt alinear
alike [ə'laɪk] adj semejantes, iguales ♦ adv igualmente, del mismo modo; **to look ~** parecerse
alimony ['ælɪmənɪ] n manutención f
alive [ə'laɪv] adj vivo; (lively) alegre

KEYWORD

all [ɔːl] adj (sg) todo/a; (pl) todos/as; ~ **day** todo el día; ~ **night** toda la noche; ~ **men** todos los hombres; ~ **five came** vinieron los cinco; ~ **the books** todos los libros; ~ **his life** toda su vida
♦ pron 1 todo; **I ate it** ~, **I ate** ~ **of it** me lo comí todo; ~ **of us went** fuimos todos; ~ **the boys went** fueron todos los chicos; **is that** ~? ¿eso es todo?, ¿algo más?; (in shop) ¿algo más?, ¿alguna cosa más?
2 (in phrases): **above** ~ sobre todo; por encima de todo; **after** ~ después de todo; **at** ~: **not at** ~ (in answer to question) en absoluto; (in answer to thanks) ¡de nada!, ¡no hay de qué!; **I'm not at** ~ **tired** no estoy nada cansado/a; **anything at** ~ **will do** cualquier cosa viene bien; ~ **in** ~ a fin de cuentas
♦ adv: ~ **alone** completamente solo/a; **it's not as hard as** ~ **that** no es tan difícil como lo pintas; ~ **the more/the better** tanto más/mejor; ~ **but** casi; **the score is 2** ~ están empatados a 2

all clear n (after attack etc) fin m de la alerta; (fig) luz f verde
allege [ə'ledʒ] vt pretender; ~**dly** [ə'ledʒɪdlɪ] adv supuestamente, según se afirma
allegiance [ə'liːdʒəns] n lealtad f
allergy ['ælədʒɪ] n alergia
alleviate [ə'liːvɪeɪt] vt aliviar
alley ['ælɪ] n callejuela
alliance [ə'laɪəns] n alianza
allied ['ælaɪd] adj aliado
alligator ['ælɪgeɪtə*] n (ZOOL) caimán m
all-in (BRIT) adj, adv (charge) todo incluido
all-night adj (café, shop) abierto toda la noche; (party) que dura toda la noche
allocate ['æləkeɪt] vt (money etc) asignar
allot [ə'lɒt] vt asignar; ~**ment** n ración f; (garden) parcela
all-out adj (effort etc) supremo; **all out** adv con todas las fuerzas

allow [ə'lau] vt permitir, dejar; (a claim) admitir; (sum, time etc) dar, conceder; (concede): **to ~ that** reconocer que; **to ~ sb to do** permitir a alguien hacer; **he is ~ed to ...** se le permite ...; ~ **for** vt fus tener en cuenta; ~**ance** n subvención f; (welfare payment) subsidio, pensión f; (pocket money) dinero de bolsillo; (tax ~ance) desgravación f; **to make** ~**ances for** (person) disculpar a; (thing) tener en cuenta
alloy ['ælɔɪ] n mezcla
all: ~ **right** adv bien; (as answer) ¡conforme!, ¡está bien!; ~**rounder** n: **he's a good** ~**rounder** se le da bien todo; ~**time** adj (record) de todos los tiempos
alluring [ə'ljuərɪŋ] adj atractivo, tentador(a)
ally ['ælaɪ] n aliado/a ♦ vt: **to ~ o.s. with** aliarse con
almighty [ɔːl'maɪtɪ] adj todopoderoso; (row etc) imponente
almond ['ɑːmənd] n almendra
almost ['ɔːlməust] adv casi
alone [ə'ləun] adj, adv solo; **to leave sb** ~ dejar a uno en paz; **to leave sth** ~ no tocar algo, dejar algo sin tocar; **let** ~ ... y mucho menos ...
along [ə'lɒŋ] prep a lo largo de, por ♦ adv: **is he coming** ~ **with us?** ¿viene con nosotros?; **he was limping** ~ iba cojeando; ~ **with** junto con; **all** ~ (all the time) desde el principio; ~**side** prep al lado de ♦ adv al lado
aloof [ə'luːf] adj reservado ♦ adv: **to stand** ~ mantenerse apartado
aloud [ə'laud] adv en voz alta
alphabet ['ælfəbet] n alfabeto
Alps [ælps] npl: **the** ~ los Alpes
already [ɔːl'redɪ] adv ya
alright ['ɔːl'raɪt] (BRIT) adv = **all right**
Alsatian [æl'seɪʃən] n (dog) pastor m alemán
also ['ɔːlsəu] adv también, además
altar ['ɔːltə*] n altar m
alter ['ɔːltə*] vt cambiar, modificar ♦ vi cambiar; ~**ation** [ɔːltə'reɪʃən] n cambio; (to clothes) arreglo; (to building) arreglos mpl
alternate [adj ɔl'tɜːnɪt, vb 'ɔːltəneɪt] adj (actions etc) alternativo; (events) alterno; (US) = **alternative** ♦ vi: **to ~ (with)** alternar (con); **on ~ days** un día sí y otro no; **alternating current** [-neɪtɪŋ] n corriente f alterna
alternative [ɔl'tɜːnətɪv] adj alternativo ♦ n alternativa; ~ **medicine** medicina alternativa; ~**ly** adv: ~**ly one could ...** por otra parte uno podría ...
although [ɔːl'ðəu] conj aunque
altitude ['æltɪtjuːd] n altura
alto ['æltəu] n (female) contralto f; (male) alto
altogether [ɔːltə'geðə*] adv completamente, del todo; (on the whole) en total, en conjunto
aluminium [ælju'mɪnɪəm] (BRIT), **alumi-**

num [ə'lu:mɪnəm] (US) n aluminio
always ['ɔ:lweɪz] adv siempre
Alzheimer's (disease) ['æltshaɪməz-] n
enfermedad f de Alzheimer
AM n abbr (= Assembly Member)
parlamentario/a m/f
am [æm] vb see **be**
a.m. adv abbr (= ante meridiem) de la mañana
amalgamate [ə'mælgəmeɪt] vi amalgamarse
♦ vt amalgamar, unir
amateur ['æmətə*] n aficionado/a, amateur
m/f; **~ish** adj inexperto, superficial
amaze [ə'meɪz] vt asombrar, pasmar; **to be
~d (at)** quedar pasmado (de); **~ment** n
asombro, sorpresa; **amazing** adj
extraordinario; (fantastic) increíble
Amazon ['æməzən] n (GEO) Amazonas m
ambassador [æm'bæsədə*] n embajador(a)
m/f
amber ['æmbə*] n ámbar m; **at ~** (BRIT: AUT)
en el amarillo
ambiguous [æm'bɪgjuəs] adj ambiguo
ambition [æm'bɪʃən] n ambición f;
ambitious [-ʃəs] adj ambicioso
ambulance ['æmbjuləns] n ambulancia
ambush ['æmbuʃ] n emboscada ♦ vt tender
una emboscada a
amenable [ə'mi:nəbl] adj: **to be ~ to** dejarse
influir por
amend [ə'mend] vt enmendar; **to make ~s**
dar cumplida satisfacción
amenities [ə'mi:nɪtɪz] npl comodidades fpl
America [ə'merɪkə] n (USA) Estados mpl
Unidos; **~n** adj, n norteamericano/a m/f;
estadounidense m/f
amiable ['eɪmɪəbl] adj amable, simpático
amicable ['æmɪkəbl] adj amistoso, amigable
amid(st) [ə'mɪd(st)] prep entre, en medio de
amiss [ə'mɪs] adv: **to take sth ~** tomar algo a
mal; **there's something ~** pasa algo
ammonia [ə'məunɪə] n amoníaco
ammunition [æmju'nɪʃən] n municiones fpl
amnesty ['æmnɪstɪ] n amnistía
amok [ə'mɔk] adv: **to run ~** enloquecerse,
desbocarse
among(st) [ə'mʌŋ(st)] prep entre, en medio
de
amorous ['æmərəs] adj amoroso
amount [ə'maunt] n (gen) cantidad f; (of bill
etc) suma, importe m ♦ vi: **to ~ to** sumar; (be
same as) equivaler a, significar
amp(ère) ['æmp(ɛə*)] n amperio
ample ['æmpl] adj (large) grande; (abundant)
abundante; (enough) bastante, suficiente
amplifier ['æmplɪfaɪə*] n amplificador m
amuse [ə'mju:z] vt divertir; (distract) distraer,
entretener; **~ment** n diversión f; (pastime)
pasatiempo; (laughter) risa; **~ment arcade** n
salón m de juegos; **~ment park** n parque m de

atracciones
an [æn] indef art see **a**
anaemic [ə'ni:mɪk] (US **anemic**) adj anémico;
(fig) soso, insípido
anaesthetic [ænɪs'θetɪk] n (US **anesthetic**)
anestesia
analog(ue) ['ænəlɔg] adj (computer, watch)
analógico
analyse ['ænəlaɪz] (US **analyze**) vt analizar;
analysis [ə'næləsɪs] (pl **analyses**) n análisis m
inv; **analyst** [-lɪst] n (political analyst,
psychoanalyst) analista m/f
analyze ['ænəlaɪz] (US) vt = **analyse**
anarchist ['ænəkɪst] n anarquista m/f
anatomy [ə'nætəmɪ] n anatomía
ancestor ['ænsɪstə*] n antepasado
anchor ['æŋkə*] n ancla, áncora ♦ vi (also: **to
drop ~**) anclar ♦ vt anclar; **to weigh ~** levar
anclas
anchovy ['æntʃəvɪ] n anchoa
ancient ['eɪnʃənt] adj antiguo
ancillary [æn'sɪlərɪ] adj auxiliar
and [ænd] conj y; (before i-, hi- + consonant)
e; **men ~ women** hombres y mujeres; **father
~ son** padre e hijo; **trees ~ grass** árboles y
hierba; **~ so on** etcétera, y así sucesivamente;
try ~ come procura venir; **he talked ~ talked**
habló sin parar; **better ~ better** cada vez mejor
Andes ['ændi:z] npl: **the ~** los Andes
anemic etc [ə'ni:mɪk] (US) = **anaemic** etc
anesthetic etc [ænɪs'θetɪk] (US) =
anaesthetic etc
anew [ə'nju:] adv de nuevo, otra vez
angel ['eɪndʒəl] n ángel m
anger ['æŋgə*] n cólera
angina [æn'dʒaɪnə] n angina (del pecho)
angle ['æŋgl] n ángulo; **from their ~** desde su
punto de vista
angler ['æŋglə*] n pescador(a) m/f (de caña)
Anglican ['æŋglɪkən] adj, n anglicano/a m/f
angling ['æŋglɪŋ] n pesca con caña
Anglo... ['æŋgləu] prefix anglo...
angrily ['æŋgrɪlɪ] adv coléricamente,
airadamente
angry ['æŋgrɪ] adj enfadado, airado; (wound)
inflamado; **to be ~ with sb/at sth** estar
enfadado con alguien/por algo; **to get ~**
enfadarse, enojarse
anguish ['æŋgwɪʃ] n (physical) tormentos
mpl; (mental) angustia
animal ['ænɪməl] n animal m; (pej: person)
bestia ♦ adj animal
animate ['ænɪmɪt] adj vivo; **~d** [-meɪtɪd] adj
animado
aniseed ['ænɪsi:d] n anís m
ankle ['æŋkl] n tobillo m; **~ sock** n calcetín
m corto
annex [n 'æneks, vb æ'neks] n (also: BRIT:
annexe) (building) edificio anexo ♦ vt

(*territory*) anexionar

annihilate [əˈnaɪəleɪt] *vt* aniquilar

anniversary [ænɪˈvɜːsərɪ] *n* aniversario

announce [əˈnauns] *vt* anunciar; **~ment** *n* anuncio; (*official*) declaración *f*; **~r** *n* (RADIO) locutor(a) *m/f*; (*TV*) presentador(a) *m/f*

annoy [əˈnɔɪ] *vt* molestar, fastidiar; **don't get ~ed!** ¡no se enfade!; **~ance** *n* enojo; **~ing** *adj* molesto, fastidioso; (*person*) pesado

annual [ˈænjuəl] *adj* anual ♦ *n* (BOT) anual *m*; (*book*) anuario; **~ly** *adv* anualmente, cada año

annul [əˈnʌl] *vt* anular

annum [ˈænəm] *n see* per

anonymous [əˈnɒnɪməs] *adj* anónimo

anorak [ˈænəræk] *n* anorak *m*

anorexia [ænəˈrɛksɪə] *n* (MED: also: **~ nervosa**) anorexia

another [əˈnʌðə*] *adj* (*one more, a different one*) otro ♦ *pron* otro; *see* **one**

answer [ˈɑːnsə*] *n* contestación *f*, respuesta; (*to problem*) solución *f* ♦ *vi* contestar, responder ♦ *vt* (*reply to*) contestar a, responder a; (*problem*) resolver; (*prayer*) escuchar; **in ~ to your letter** contestando or en contestación a su carta; **to ~ the phone** contestar or coger el teléfono; **to ~ the bell** *or* **the door** acudir a la puerta; **~ back** *vi* replicar, ser respondón/ona; **~ for** *vt fus* responder de or por; **~ to** *vt fus* (*description*) corresponder a; **~able** *adj*: **~able to sb for sth** responsable ante uno de algo; **~ing machine** *n* contestador *m* automático

ant [ænt] *n* hormiga

antagonism [ænˈtægənɪzm] *n* antagonismo, hostilidad *f*

antagonize [ænˈtægənaɪz] *vt* provocar la enemistad de

Antarctic [æntˈɑːktɪk] *n*: **the ~** el Antártico

antelope [ˈæntɪləup] *n* antílope *m*

antenatal [ˈæntɪˈneɪtl] *adj* antenatal, prenatal; **~ clinic** *n* clínica prenatal

anthem [ˈænθəm] *n*: **national ~** himno nacional

anthropology [ænθrəˈpɔlədʒɪ] *n* antropología

anti... [ænti] *prefix* anti...; **~-aircraft** [-ˈɛəkrɑːft] *adj* antiaéreo; **~biotic** [-baɪˈɔtɪk] *n* antibiótico; **~body** [ˈæntɪbɔdɪ] *n* anticuerpo

anticipate [ænˈtɪsɪpeɪt] *vt* prever; (*expect*) esperar, contar con; (*look forward to*) esperar con ilusión; (*do first*) anticiparse a, adelantarse a; **anticipation** [-ˈpeɪʃən] *n* (*expectation*) previsión *f*; (*eagerness*) ilusión *f*, expectación *f*

anticlimax [æntɪˈklaɪmæks] *n* decepción *f*

anticlockwise [æntɪˈklɔkwaɪz] (BRIT) *adv* en dirección contraria a la de las agujas del reloj

antics [ˈæntɪks] *npl* gracias *fpl*

anticyclone [æntɪˈsaɪkləun] *n* anticiclón *m*

antidepressant [ˈæntɪdɪˈprɛsnt] *n* antidepresivo

antidote [ˈæntɪdəut] *n* antídoto

antifreeze [ˈæntɪfriːz] *n* anticongelante *m*

antihistamine [æntɪˈhɪstəmiːn] *n* antihistamínico

antiquated [ˈæntɪkweɪtɪd] *adj* anticuado

antique [ænˈtiːk] *n* antigüedad *f* ♦ *adj* antiguo; **~ dealer** *n* anticuario/a; **~ shop** *n* tienda de antigüedades

antiquity [ænˈtɪkwɪtɪ] *n* antigüedad *f*

antiseptic [æntɪˈsɛptɪk] *adj, n* antiséptico

antlers [ˈæntləz] *npl* cuernas *fpl*, cornamenta *sg*

anus [ˈeɪnəs] *n* ano

anvil [ˈænvɪl] *n* yunque *m*

anxiety [æŋˈzaɪətɪ] *n* inquietud *f*; (MED) ansiedad *f*; **~ to do** deseo de hacer

anxious [ˈæŋkʃəs] *adj* inquieto, preocupado; (*worrying*) preocupante; (*keen*): **to be ~ to do** tener muchas ganas de hacer

---

KEYWORD

any [ˈɛnɪ] *adj* **1** (*in questions etc*) algún/ alguna; **have you ~ butter/children?** ¿tienes mantequilla/hijos?; **if there are ~ tickets left** si quedan billetes, si queda algún billete

2 (*with negative*): **I haven't ~ money/books** no tengo dinero/libros

3 (*no matter which*) cualquier; **~ excuse will do** valdrá or servirá cualquier excusa; **choose ~ book you like** escoge el libro que quieras; **~ teacher you ask will tell you** cualquier profesor al que preguntes te lo dirá

4 (*in phrases*): **in ~ case** de todas formas, en cualquier caso; **~ day now** cualquier día (de estos); **at ~ moment** en cualquier momento, de un momento a otro; **at ~ rate** en todo caso; **~ time: come (at) ~ time** ven cuando quieras; **he might come (at) ~ time** podría llegar de un momento a otro

♦ *pron* **1** (*in questions etc*): **have you got ~?** ¿tienes alguno(s)/a(s)?; **can ~ of you sing?** ¿sabe cantar alguno de vosotros/ustedes?

2 (*with negative*): **I haven't ~ (of them)** no tengo ninguno

3 (*no matter which one(s)*): **take ~ of those books (you like)** toma el libro que quieras de ésos

♦ *adv* **1** (*in questions etc*): **do you want ~ more soup/sandwiches?** ¿quieres más sopa/bocadillos?; **are you feeling ~ better?** ¿te sientes algo mejor?

2 (*with negative*): **I can't hear him ~ more** ya no le oigo; **don't wait ~ longer** no esperes más

---

anybody [ˈɛnɪbɔdɪ] *pron* cualquiera; (*in*

interrogative sentences) alguien; (*in negative sentences*): **I don't see ~** no veo a nadie; **if ~ should phone ...** si llama alguien ...

anyhow ['enɪhaʊ] *adv* (*at any rate*) de todos modos, de todas formas; (*haphazard*): **do it ~ you like** hazlo como quieras; **she leaves things just ~** deja las cosas como quiera o de cualquier modo; **I shall go ~** de todos modos iré

anyone ['enɪwʌn] *pron* = **anybody**

anything ['enɪθɪŋ] *pron* (*in questions etc*) algo, alguna cosa; (*with negative*) nada; **can you see ~?** ¿ves algo?; **if ~ happens to me ...** si algo me ocurre ...; (*no matter what*): **you can say ~ you like** puedes decir lo que quieras; **~ will do** vale todo *o* cualquier cosa; **he'll eat ~** come de todo *o* lo que sea

anyway ['enɪweɪ] *adv* (*at any rate*) de todos modos, de todas formas; **I shall go ~** iré de todos modos; (*besides*): **~, I couldn't come even if I wanted to** además, no podría venir aunque quisiera; **why are you phoning, ~?** ¿entonces, por qué llamas?, ¿por qué llamas, pues?

anywhere ['enɪweə*] *adv* (*in questions etc*): **can you see him ~?** ¿le ves por algún lado?; **are you going ~?** ¿vas a algún sitio?; (*with negative*): **I can't see him ~** no le veo por ninguna parte; **~ in the world** (*no matter where*) en cualquier parte (del mundo); **put the books down ~** deja los libros donde quieras

apart [ə'pɑːt] *adv* (*aside*) aparte; (*situation*): **~ (from)** separado (de); (*movement*): **to pull ~** separar; **10 miles ~** separados por 10 millas; **to take ~** desmontar; **~ from** *prep* aparte de

apartheid [ə'pɑːteɪt] *n* apartheid *m*

apartment [ə'pɑːtmənt] *n* (*US*) piso (*SP*), departamento (*AM*), apartamento; (*room*) cuarto; **~ building** (*US*) *n* edificio de apartamentos

apathetic [æpə'θetɪk] *adj* apático, indiferente

ape [eɪp] *n* mono ♦ *vt* imitar, remedar

aperitif [ə'perɪtiːf] *n* aperitivo

aperture ['æpətjʊə*] *n* rendija, resquicio; (*PHOT*) abertura

APEX ['eɪpeks] *n abbr* (= *Advanced Purchase Excursion Fare*) tarifa APEX *f*

apex *n* ápice *m*; (*fig*) cumbre *f*

apiece [ə'piːs] *adv* cada uno

aplomb [ə'plɒm] *n* aplomo

apologetic [əpɒlə'dʒetɪk] *adj* de disculpa; (*person*) arrepentido

apologize [ə'pɒlədʒaɪz] *vi*: **to ~ (for sth to sb)** disculparse (con alguien de algo)

apology [ə'pɒlədʒɪ] *n* disculpa, excusa

apostrophe [ə'pɒstrəfɪ] *n* apóstrofo *m*

appal [ə'pɔːl] *vt* horrorizar, espantar; **~ling** *adj* espantoso; (*awful*) pésimo

apparatus [æpə'reɪtəs] *n* (*equipment*) equipo; (*organization*) aparato; (*in gymnasium*) aparatos *mpl*

apparel [ə'pærəl] (*US*) *n* ropa

apparent [ə'pærənt] *adj* aparente; (*obvious*) evidente; **~ly** *adv* por lo visto, al parecer

appeal [ə'piːl] *vi* (*LAW*) apelar ♦ *n* (*LAW*) apelación *f*; (*request*) llamamiento; (*plea*) petición *f*; (*charm*) atractivo; **to ~ for** reclamar; **to ~ to** (*be attractive to*) atraer; **it doesn't ~ to me** no me atrae, no me llama la atención; **~ing** *adj* (*attractive*) atractivo

appear [ə'pɪə*] *vi* aparecer, presentarse; (*LAW*) comparecer; (*publication*) salir (a luz), publicarse; (*seem*) parecer; **to ~ on TV/in "Hamlet"** salir por la tele/hacer un papel en "Hamlet"; **it would ~ that** parecería que; **~ance** *n* aparición *f*; (*look*) apariencia, aspecto

appease [ə'piːz] *vt* (*pacify*) apaciguar; (*satisfy*) satisfacer

appendices [ə'pendɪsiːz] *npl* of **appendix**

appendicitis [əpendɪ'saɪtɪs] *n* apendicitis *f*

appendix [ə'pendɪks] (*pl* **appendices**) *n* apéndice *m*

appetite ['æpɪtaɪt] *n* apetito; (*fig*) deseo, anhelo

appetizer ['æpɪtaɪzə*] *n* (*drink*) aperitivo; (*food*) tapas *fpl* (*SP*)

applaud [ə'plɔːd] *vt, vi* aplaudir

applause [ə'plɔːz] *n* aplausos *mpl*

apple ['æpl] *n* manzana; **~ tree** *n* manzano

appliance [ə'plaɪəns] *n* aparato

applicable [ə'plɪkəbl] *adj* (*relevant*): **to be ~ (to)** referirse (a)

applicant ['æplɪkənt] *n* candidato/a; solicitante *m/f*

application [æplɪ'keɪʃən] *n* aplicación *f*; (*for a job etc*) solicitud *f*, petición *f*; **~ form** *n* solicitud *f*

applied [ə'plaɪd] *adj* aplicado

apply [ə'plaɪ] *vt* (*paint etc*) poner; (*law etc*: *put into practice*) poner en vigor ♦ *vi*: **to ~ to** (*ask*) dirigirse a; (*be applicable*) ser aplicable a; **to ~ for** (*permit, grant, job*) solicitar; **to ~ o.s. to** aplicarse a, dedicarse a

appoint [ə'pɔɪnt] *vt* (*to post*) nombrar; **~ed** *adj*: **at the ~ed time** a la hora señalada; **~ment** *n* (*with client*) cita; (*act*) nombramiento; (*post*) puesto; (*at hairdresser etc*): **to have an ~ment** tener hora; **to make an ~ment (with sb)** citarse (con uno)

appraisal [ə'preɪzl] *n* valoración *f*

appreciate [ə'priːʃɪeɪt] *vt* apreciar, tener en mucho; (*be grateful for*) agradecer; (*be aware of*) comprender ♦ *vi* (*COMM*) aumentar(se) en valor; **appreciation** [-'eɪʃən] *n* apreciación *f*; (*gratitude*) reconocimiento, agradecimiento; (*COMM*) aumento en valor

appreciative [əˈpriːʃɪətɪv] *adj* apreciativo; (*comment*) agradecido

apprehensive [æprɪˈhensɪv] *adj* aprensivo

apprentice [əˈprentɪs] *n* aprendiz/a *m/f*; **~ship** *n* aprendizaje *m*

approach [əˈprəʊtʃ] *vi* acercarse ♦ *vt* acercarse a; (*ask, apply to*) dirigirse a; (*situation, problem*) abordar ♦ *n* acercamiento; (*access*) acceso; (*to problem, situation*): **~ (to)** actitud *f* (ante); **~able** *adj* (*person*) abordable; (*place*) accesible

appropriate [*adj* əˈprəʊprɪɪt, *vb* əˈprəʊprɪeɪt] *adj* apropiado, conveniente ♦ *vt* (*take*) apropiarse de

approval [əˈpruːvəl] *n* aprobación *f*, visto bueno; (*permission*) consentimiento; **on ~** (*COMM*) a prueba

approve [əˈpruːv] *vt* aprobar; **~ of** *vt fus* (*thing*) aprobar; (*person*): **they don't ~ of her** (ella) no les parece bien

approximate [əˈprɒksɪmɪt] *adj* aproximado; **~ly** *adv* aproximadamente, más o menos

apricot [ˈeɪprɪkɒt] *n* albaricoque *m* (*SP*), damasco (*AM*)

April [ˈeɪprəl] *n* abril *m*; **~ Fools' Day** *n* el primero de abril; ≈ día *m* de los Inocentes (*28 December*)

apron [ˈeɪprən] *n* delantal *m*

apt [æpt] *adj* acertado, apropiado; (*likely*): **~ to do** propenso a hacer

aquarium [əˈkweərɪəm] *n* acuario

Aquarius [əˈkweərɪəs] *n* Acuario

Arab [ˈærəb] *adj, n* árabe *m/f*

Arabian [əˈreɪbɪən] *adj* árabe

Arabic [ˈærəbɪk] *adj* árabe; (*numerals*) arábigo ♦ *n* árabe *m*

arable [ˈærəbl] *adj* cultivable

Aragon [ˈærəɡən] *n* Aragón *m*

arbitrary [ˈɑːbɪtrərɪ] *adj* arbitrario

arbitration [ɑːbɪˈtreɪʃən] *n* arbitraje *m*

arcade [ɑːˈkeɪd] *n* (*round a square*) soportales *mpl*; (*shopping mall*) galería comercial

arch [ɑːtʃ] *n* arco; (*of foot*) arco del pie ♦ *vt* arquear

archaeologist [ɑːkɪˈɒlədʒɪst] (*US* **archeologist**) *n* arqueólogo/a

archaeology [ɑːkɪˈɒlədʒɪ] (*US* **archeology**) *n* arqueología

archbishop [ɑːtʃˈbɪʃəp] *n* arzobispo

archeology *etc* [ɑːkɪˈɒlədʒɪ] (*US*) = **archaeology** *etc*

archery [ˈɑːtʃərɪ] *n* tiro al arco

architect [ˈɑːkɪtekt] *n* arquitecto/a; **~ure** *n* arquitectura

archives [ˈɑːkaɪvz] *npl* archivo

Arctic [ˈɑːktɪk] *adj* ártico ♦ *n*: **the ~** el Ártico

ardent [ˈɑːdənt] *adj* ardiente, apasionado

arduous [ˈɑːdjuəs] *adj* (*task*) arduo; (*journey*) agotador(a)

are [ɑː*] *vb see* **be**

area [ˈeərɪə] *n* área, región *f*; (*part of place*) zona; (*MATH etc*) área, superficie *f*; (*in room: e.g. dining ~*) parte *f*; (*of knowledge, experience*) campo

arena [əˈriːnə] *n* estadio; (*of circus*) pista

aren't [ɑːnt] = **are not**

Argentina [ɑːdʒənˈtiːnə] *n* Argentina; **Argentinian** [-ˈtɪnɪən] *adj, n* argentino/a *m/f*

arguably [ˈɑːɡjuəblɪ] *adv* posiblemente

argue [ˈɑːɡjuː] *vi* (*quarrel*) discutir, pelearse; (*reason*) razonar, argumentar; **to ~ that** sostener que

argument [ˈɑːɡjumənt] *n* discusión *f*, pelea; (*reasons*) argumento; **~ative** [-ˈmentətɪv] *adj* discutidor(a)

Aries [ˈeərɪz] *n* Aries *m*

arise [əˈraɪz] (*pt* **arose**, *pp* **arisen**) *vi* surgir, presentarse

arisen [əˈrɪzn] *pp of* **arise**

aristocrat [ˈærɪstəkræt] *n* aristócrata *m/f*

arithmetic [əˈrɪθmətɪk] *n* aritmética

ark [ɑːk] *n*: **Noah's A~** el Arca *f* de Noé

arm [ɑːm] *n* brazo ♦ *vt* armar; **~s** *npl* armas *fpl*; **~ in ~** cogidos del brazo

armaments [ˈɑːməmənts] *npl* armamento

armchair [ˈɑːmtʃeə*] *n* sillón *m*, butaca

armed [ɑːmd] *adj* armado; **~ robbery** *n* robo a mano armada

armour [ˈɑːmə*] (*US* **armor**) *n* armadura; (*MIL: tanks*) blindaje *m*; **~ed car** *n* coche *m* (*SP*) or carro (*AM*) blindado

armpit [ˈɑːmpɪt] *n* sobaco, axila

armrest [ˈɑːmrest] *n* apoyabrazos *m inv*

army [ˈɑːmɪ] *n* ejército; (*fig*) multitud *f*

aroma [əˈrəʊmə] *n* aroma *m*, fragancia; **~therapy** *n* aromaterapia

arose [əˈrəʊz] *pt of* **arise**

around [əˈraʊnd] *adv* alrededor; (*in the area*): **there is no one else ~** no hay nadie más por aquí ♦ *prep* alrededor de

arouse [əˈraʊz] *vt* despertar; (*anger*) provocar

arrange [əˈreɪndʒ] *vt* arreglar, ordenar; (*organize*) organizar; **to ~ to do sth** quedar en hacer algo; **~ment** *n* arreglo; (*agreement*) acuerdo; **~ments** *npl* (*preparations*) preparativos *mpl*

array [əˈreɪ] *n*: **~ of** (*things*) serie *f* de; (*people*) conjunto de

arrears [əˈrɪəz] *npl* atrasos *mpl*; **to be in ~ with one's rent** estar retrasado en el pago del alquiler

arrest [əˈrest] *vt* detener; (*sb's attention*) llamar ♦ *n* detención *f*; **under ~** detenido

arrival [əˈraɪvl] *n* llegada; **new ~** recién llegado/a; (*baby*) recién nacido

arrive [əˈraɪv] *vi* llegar; (*baby*) nacer

arrogant [ˈærəɡənt] *adj* arrogante

arrow [ˈærəʊ] *n* flecha

arse [ɑːs] (BRIT: infl) n culo, trasero

arson ['ɑːsn] n incendio premeditado

art [ɑːt] n arte m; (skill) destreza; **A~s** npl (SCOL) Letras fpl

artery ['ɑːtəri] n arteria

art gallery n pinacoteca; (saleroom) galería de arte

arthritis [ɑː'θraɪtɪs] n artritis f

artichoke ['ɑːtɪtʃəʊk] n alcachofa; **Jerusalem ~** aguaturma

article ['ɑːtɪkl] n artículo; (BRIT: LAW: training): **~s** npl contrato de aprendizaje; **~ of clothing** prenda de vestir

articulate [adj ɑː'tɪkjʊlɪt, vb ɑː'tɪkjʊleɪt] adj claro, bien expresado ♦ vt expresar; **~d lorry** (BRIT) n trailer m

artificial [ɑːtɪ'fɪʃəl] adj artificial; (affected) afectado

artillery [ɑː'tɪləri] n artillería

artisan [ɑː'tɪzæn] n artesano

artist ['ɑːtɪst] n artista m/f; (MUS) intérprete m/f; **~ic** [ɑː'tɪstɪk] adj artístico; **~ry** n arte m, habilidad f (artística)

art school n escuela de bellas artes

KEYWORD

as [æz] conj **1** (referring to time) cuando, mientras; a medida que; **~ the years went by** con el paso de los años; **he came in ~ I was leaving** entró cuando me marchaba; **~ from tomorrow** desde or a partir de mañana

2 (in comparisons): **~ big ~** tan grande como; **twice ~ big ~** el doble de grande que; **~ much money/many books ~** tanto dinero/ tantos libros como; **~ soon ~** en cuanto

3 (since, because) como, ya que; **he left early ~ he had to be home by 10** se fue temprano ya que tenía que estar en casa a las 10

4 (referring to manner, way): **do ~ you wish** haz lo que quieras; **~ she said** como dijo; **he gave it to me ~ a present** me lo dio de regalo

5 (in the capacity of): **he works ~ a barman** trabaja de barman; **~ chairman of the company, he ...** como presidente de la compañía, ...

6 (concerning): **~ for or to that** por or en lo que respecta a eso

7: **~ if or though** como si; **he looked ~ if he was ill** parecía como si estuviera enfermo, tenía aspecto de enfermo; see also **long; such; well**

a.s.a.p. abbr (= as soon as possible) cuanto antes

asbestos [æz'bestəs] n asbesto, amianto

ascend [ə'send] vt subir; (throne) ascender or subir a

ascent [ə'sent] n subida; (slope) cuesta, pendiente f

ascertain [æsə'teɪn] vt averiguar

ash [æʃ] n ceniza; (tree) fresno

ashamed [ə'ʃeɪmd] adj avergonzado, apenado (AM); **to be ~ of** avergonzarse de

ashore [ə'ʃɔː*] adv en tierra; (swim etc) a tierra

ashtray ['æʃtreɪ] n cenicero

Ash Wednesday n miércoles m de Ceniza

Asia ['eɪʃə] n Asia; **~n** adj, n asiático/a m/f

aside [ə'saɪd] adv a un lado ♦ n aparte m

ask [ɑːsk] vt (question) preguntar; (invite) invitar; **to ~ sb sth/to do sth** preguntar algo a alguien/pedir a alguien que haga algo; **to ~ sb about sth** preguntar algo a alguien; **to ~ (sb) a question** hacer una pregunta (a alguien); **to ~ sb out to dinner** invitar a cenar a uno; **~ after** vt fus preguntar por; **~ for** vt fus pedir; (trouble) buscar

asking price n precio inicial

asleep [ə'sliːp] adj dormido; **to fall ~** dormirse, quedarse dormido

asparagus [əs'pærəgəs] n (plant) espárrago; (food) espárragos mpl

aspect ['æspekt] n aspecto, apariencia; (direction in which a building etc faces) orientación f

aspersions [əs'pɜːʃənz] npl: **to cast ~ on** difamar a, calumniar a

asphyxiation [æsfɪksɪ'eɪʃən] n asfixia

aspire [əs'paɪə*] vi: **to ~ to** aspirar a, ambicionar

aspirin ['æsprɪn] n aspirina

ass [æs] n asno, burro; (inf: idiot) imbécil m/f; (US: infl) culo, trasero

assailant [ə'seɪlənt] n asaltador(a) m/f, agresor(a) m/f

assassinate [ə'sæsɪneɪt] vt asesinar; **assassination** [əsæsɪ'neɪʃən] n asesinato

assault [ə'sɔːlt] n asalto; (LAW) agresión f ♦ vt asaltar, atacar; (sexually) violar

assemble [ə'sembl] vt reunir, juntar; (TECH) montar ♦ vi reunirse, juntarse

assembly [ə'semblɪ] n reunión f, asamblea; (parliament) parlamento; (construction) montaje m; **~ line** n cadena de montaje

assent [ə'sent] n asentimiento, aprobación f

assert [ə'sɜːt] vt afirmar; (authority) hacer valer; **~ion** [-ʃən] n afirmación f

assess [ə'ses] vt valorar, calcular; (tax, damages) fijar; (for tax) gravar; **~ment** n valoración f; (for tax) gravamen m; **~or** n asesor(a) m/f

asset ['æset] n ventaja; **~s** npl (COMM) activo; (property, funds) fondos mpl

assign [ə'saɪn] vt: **to ~ (to)** (date) fijar (para); (task) asignar (a); (resources) destinar (a); **~ment** n tarea

assist [ə'sɪst] vt ayudar; **~ance** n ayuda, auxilio; **~ant** n ayudante m/f; (BRIT: also:

shop ~ant) dependiente/a *m/f*

associate [*adj, n* ə'səuʃɪɪt, *vb* ə'səuʃɪeɪt] *adj* asociado ♦ *n* (*at work*) colega *m/f* ♦ *vt* asociar; (*ideas*) relacionar ♦ *vi*: **to ~ with sb** tratar con alguien

association [əsəusɪ'eɪʃən] *n* asociación *f*

assorted [ə'sɔːtɪd] *adj* surtido, variado

assortment [ə'sɔːtmənt] *n* (*of shapes, colours*) surtido; (*of books*) colección *f*; (*of people*) mezcla

assume [ə'sjuːm] *vt* suponer; (*responsibilities*) asumir; (*attitude*) adoptar, tomar

assumption [ə'sʌmpʃən] *n* suposición *f*, presunción *f*; (*of power etc*) toma

assurance [ə'ʃuərəns] *n* garantía, promesa; (*confidence*) confianza, aplomo; (*insurance*) seguro

assure [ə'ʃuə*] *vt* asegurar

asthma ['æsmə] *n* asma

astonish [ə'stɔnɪʃ] *vt* asombrar, pasmar; **~ment** *n* asombro, sorpresa

astound [ə'staund] *vt* asombrar, pasmar

astray [ə'streɪ] *adv*: **to go ~** extraviarse; **to lead ~** (*morally*) llevar por mal camino

astride [ə'straɪd] *prep* a caballo *or* horcajadas sobre

astrology [æs'trɔlədʒɪ] *n* astrología

astronaut ['æstrənɔːt] *n* astronauta *m/f*

astronomy [æs'trɔnəmɪ] *n* astronomía

asylum [ə'saɪləm] *n* (*refuge*) asilo; (*mental hospital*) manicomio

---

KEYWORD

---

at [æt] *prep* **1** (*referring to position*) en; (*direction*) a; **~ the top** en lo alto; **~ home/ school** en casa/la escuela; **to look ~ sth/sb** mirar algo/a uno

2 (*referring to time*): **~ 4 o'clock** a las 4; **~ night** por la noche; **~ Christmas** en Navidad; **~ times** a veces

3 (*referring to rates, speed etc*): **~ £1 a kilo** a una libra el kilo; **two ~ a time** de dos en dos; **~ 50 km/h** a 50 km/h

4 (*referring to manner*): **~ a stroke** de un golpe; **~ peace** en paz

5 (*referring to activity*): **to be ~ work** estar trabajando; (*in the office etc*) estar en el trabajo; **to play ~ cowboys** jugar a los vaqueros; **to be good ~ sth** ser bueno en algo

6 (*referring to cause*): **shocked/surprised/ annoyed ~ sth** asombrado/sorprendido/ fastidiado por algo; **I went ~ his suggestion** fui a instancias suyas

---

ate [eɪt] *pt of* eat

atheist ['eɪθɪɪst] *n* ateo/a

Athens ['æθɪnz] *n* Atenas

athlete ['æθliːt] *n* atleta *m/f*

athletic [æθ'lɛtɪk] *adj* atlético; **~s** *n* atletismo

Atlantic [ət'læntɪk] *adj* atlántico ♦ *n*: **the ~ (Ocean)** el (Océano) Atlántico

atlas ['ætləs] *n* atlas *m*

A.T.M. *n abbr* (= *automated telling machine*) cajero automático

atmosphere ['ætməsfɪə*] *n* atmósfera; (*of place*) ambiente *m*

atom ['ætəm] *n* átomo; **~ic** [ə'tɔmɪk] *adj* atómico; **~(ic) bomb** *n* bomba atómica; **~izer** ['ætəmaɪzə*] *n* atomizador *m*

atone [ə'təun] *vi*: **to ~ for** expiar

atrocious [ə'trəuʃəs] *adj* atroz

attach [ə'tætʃ] *vt* (*fasten*) atar; (*join*) unir, sujetar; (*document, letter*) adjuntar; (*importance etc*) dar, conceder; **to be ~ed to sb/sth** (*to like*) tener cariño a alguien/algo

attaché case [ə'tæʃeɪ-] *n* maletín *m*

attachment [ə'tætʃmənt] *n* (*tool*) accesorio; (*love*): **~ (to)** apego (a)

attack [ə'tæk] *vt* (*MIL*) atacar; (*subj: criminal*) agredir, asaltar; (*criticize*) criticar; (*task*) emprender ♦ *n* ataque *m*, asalto; (*on sb's life*) atentado; (*fig: criticism*) crítica; (*of illness*) ataque *m*; **heart ~** infarto (de miocardio); **~er** *n* agresor/a *m/f*, asaltante *m/f*

attain [ə'teɪn] *vt* (*also*: **~ to**) alcanzar; (*achieve*) lograr, conseguir

attempt [ə'tɛmpt] *n* tentativa, intento; (*attack*) atentado ♦ *vt* intentar; **~ed** *adj*: **~ed burglary/murder/suicide** tentativa *or* intento de robo/asesinato/suicidio

attend [ə'tɛnd] *vt* asistir a; (*patient*) atender; **~ to** *vt fus* ocuparse de; (*customer, patient*) atender a; **~ance** *n* asistencia, presencia; (*people present*) concurrencia; **~ant** *n* ayudante *m/f*; (*in garage etc*) encargado/a ♦ *adj* (*dangers*) concomitante

attention [ə'tɛnʃən] *n* atención *f*; (*care*) atenciones *fpl* ♦ *excl* (*MIL*) ¡firme(s)!; **for the ~ of ...** (*ADMIN*) atención ...

attentive [ə'tɛntɪv] *adj* atento

attic ['ætɪk] *n* desván *m*

attitude ['ætɪtjuːd] *n* actitud *f*; (*disposition*) disposición *f*

attorney [ə'təːnɪ] *n* (*lawyer*) abogado/a; **A~ General** *n* (*BRIT*) ≈ Presidente *m* del Consejo del Poder Judicial (*SP*); (*US*) ≈ ministro de justicia

attract [ə'trækt] *vt* atraer; (*sb's attention*) llamar; **~ion** [ə'trækʃən] *n* encanto; (*gen pl: amusements*) diversiones *fpl*; (*PHYSICS*) atracción *f*; (*fig: towards sb, sth*) atractivo; **~ive** *adj* guapo; (*interesting*) atrayente

attribute [*n* 'ætrɪbjuːt, *vb* ə'trɪbjuːt] *n* atributo ♦ *vt*: **to ~ sth to** atribuir algo a

attrition [ə'trɪʃən] *n*: **war of ~** guerra de agotamiento

aubergine ['əubəʒiːn] (*BRIT*) *n* berenjena; (*colour*) morado

auburn ['ɔ:bən] *adj* color castaño rojizo

auction ['ɔ:kʃən] *n* (*also: sale by ~*) subasta ♦ *vt* subastar; **~eer** [-'nɪə*] *n* subastador(a) *m/f*

audible ['ɔ:dɪbl] *adj* audible, que se puede oír

audience ['ɔ:dɪəns] *n* público; (*RADIO*) radioescuchas *mpl*; (*TV*) telespectadores *mpl*; (*interview*) audiencia

audio-visual [ɔ:dɪəʊ'vɪzjuəl] *adj* audiovisual; **~ aid** *n* ayuda audiovisual

audit ['ɔ:dɪt] *vt* revisar, intervenir

audition [ɔ:'dɪʃən] *n* audición *f*

auditor ['ɔ:dɪtə*] *n* interventor(a) *m/f*, censor(a) *m/f* de cuentas

augment [ɔ:g'ment] *vt* aumentar

augur ['ɔ:gə*] *vi*: **it ~s well** es un buen augurio

August ['ɔ:gəst] *n* agosto

aunt [ɑ:nt] *n* tía; **~ie** *n diminutive of* **aunt**; **~y** *n diminutive of* **aunt**

au pair ['əʊ'peə*] *n* (*also: ~ girl*) (chica) au pair *f*

auspicious [ɔ:s'pɪʃəs] *adj* propicio, de buen augurio

Australia [ɒs'treɪlɪə] *n* Australia; **~n** *adj, n* australiano/a *m/f*

Austria ['ɒstrɪə] *n* Austria; **~n** *adj, n* austríaco/a *m/f*

authentic [ɔ:'θentɪk] *adj* auténtico

author ['ɔ:θə] *n* autor(a) *m/f*

authoritarian [ɔ:θɔrɪ'teərɪən] *adj* autoritario

authoritative [ɔ:'θɔrɪtətɪv] *adj* autorizado; (*manner*) autoritario

authority [ɔ:'θɔrɪtɪ] *n* autoridad *f*; (*official permission*) autorización *f*; **the authorities** *npl* las autoridades

authorize ['ɔ:θəraɪz] *vt* autorizar

auto ['ɔ:təʊ] (*US*) *n* coche *m* (*SP*), carro (*AM*), automóvil *m*

auto: **~biography** [ɔ:təbaɪ'ɔgrəfɪ] *n* autobiografía; **~graph** ['ɔ:təgrɑ:f] *n* autógrafo ♦ *vt* (*photo etc*) dedicar; (*programme*) firmar; **~mated** ['ɔ:təmeɪtɪd] *adj* automatizado; **~matic** [ɔ:tə'mætɪk] *adj* automático ♦ *n* (*gun*) pistola automática; (*car*) coche *m* automático; **~matically** *adv* automáticamente; **~mation** [ɔ:tə'meɪʃən] *n* reconversión *f*; **~mobile** ['ɔ:təməbi:l] (*US*) *n* coche *m* (*SP*), carro (*AM*), automóvil *m*; **~nomy** [ɔ:'tɔnəmɪ] *n* autonomía

autumn ['ɔ:təm] *n* otoño

auxiliary [ɔ:g'zɪlɪərɪ] *adj, n* auxiliar *m/f*

avail [ə'veɪl] *vt*: **to ~ o.s. of** aprovechar(se) de ♦ *n*: **to no ~** en vano, sin resultado

available [ə'veɪləbl] *adj* disponible; (*unoccupied*) libre; (*person: unattached*) soltero y sin compromiso

avalanche ['ævəlɑ:nʃ] *n* alud *m*, avalancha

avant-garde ['ævɑ̃'gɑ:d] *adj* de vanguardia

Ave. *abbr* = **avenue**

avenge [ə'vendʒ] *vt* vengar

avenue ['ævənju:] *n* avenida; (*fig*) camino

average ['ævərɪdʒ] *n* promedio, término medio ♦ *adj* medio, de término medio; (*ordinary*) regular, corriente ♦ *vt* sacar un promedio de; **on ~** por regla general; **~ out** *vi*: **to ~ out at** salir en un promedio de

averse [ə'vɜ:s] *adj*: **to be ~ to sth/doing** sentir aversión *or* antipatía por algo/por hacer

avert [ə'vɜ:t] *vt* prevenir; (*blow*) desviar; (*one's eyes*) apartar

aviary ['eɪvɪərɪ] *n* pajarera, avería

avocado [ævə'kɑ:dəʊ] *n* (*also: BRIT: ~ pear*) aguacate *m* (*SP*), palta (*AM*)

avoid [ə'vɔɪd] *vt* evitar, eludir

await [ə'weɪt] *vt* esperar, aguardar

awake [ə'weɪk] (*pt* awoke, *pp* awoken *or* awaked) *adj* despierto ♦ *vt* despertar ♦ *vi* despertarse; **to be ~** estar despierto; **~ning** *n* el despertar

award [ə'wɔ:d] *n* premio; (*LAW: damages*) indemnización *f* ♦ *vt* otorgar, conceder; (*LAW: damages*) adjudicar

aware [ə'weə*] *adj*: **(of)** consciente (de); **to become ~ of/that** (*realize*) darse cuenta de/de que; (*learn*) enterarse de/de que; **~ness** *n* conciencia; (*knowledge*) conocimiento

away [ə'weɪ] *adv* fuera; (*movement*): **she went ~** se marchó; (*far ~*) lejos; **two kilometres ~** a dos kilómetros de distancia; **two hours ~ by car** a dos horas en coche; **the holiday was two weeks ~** faltaban dos semanas para las vacaciones; **he's ~ for a week** estará ausente una semana; **to take ~ (from)** quitar (a); (*subtract*) substraer (de); **to work/pedal ~** seguir trabajando/ pedaleando; **to fade ~** (*colour*) desvanecerse; (*sound*) apagarse; **~ game** *n* (*SPORT*) partido de fuera

awe [ɔ:] *n* admiración *f* respetuosa; **~-inspiring** *adj* imponente

awful ['ɔ:fəl] *adj* horroroso; (*quantity*): **an ~ lot (of)** cantidad (de); **~ly** *adv* (*very*) terriblemente

awkward ['ɔ:kwəd] *adj* desmañado, torpe; (*shape*) incómodo; (*embarrassing*) delicado, difícil

awning ['ɔ:nɪŋ] *n* (*of tent, caravan, shop*) toldo

awoke [ə'wəʊk] *pt of* **awake**

awoken [ə'wəʊkən] *pp of* **awake**

awry [ə'raɪ] *adv*: **to be ~** estar descolocado *or* mal puesto

axe [æks] (*US* ax) *n* hacha ♦ *vt* (*project*) cortar; (*jobs*) reducir

axes ['æksi:z] *npl of* **axis**

axis ['æksɪs] (*pl* axes) *n* eje *m*

axle ['æksl] *n* eje *m*, árbol *m*

ay(e) [aɪ] *excl* sí

B, b

B [biː] *n* (MUS) si *m*
B.A. *abbr* = Bachelor of Arts
baby ['beɪbɪ] *n* bebé *m/f*; (US: *inf*: *darling*) mi amor; **~ carriage** (US) *n* cochecito; **~-sit** *vi* hacer de canguro; **~-sitter** *n* canguro/a; **~ wipe** *n* toallita húmeda (*para bebés*)
bachelor ['bætʃələ*] *n* soltero; **B~ of Arts/ Science** licenciado/a en Filosofía y Letras/ Ciencias
back [bæk] *n* (of *person*) espalda; (of *animal*) lomo; (of *hand*) dorso; (*as opposed to front*) parte *f* de atrás; (of *chair*) respaldo; (of *page*) reverso; (of *book*) final *m*; (FOOTBALL) defensa *m*; (of *crowd*): **the ones at the ~** los del fondo ♦ *vt* (*candidate: also*: **~ up**) respaldar, apoyar; (*horse: at races*) apostar a; (*car*) dar marcha atrás a o con ♦ *vi* (*car etc*) ir (*or salir or entrar*) marcha atrás ♦ *adj* (*payment, rent*) atrasado; (*seats, wheels*) de atrás ♦ *adv* (*not forward*) (hacia) atrás; (*returned*): **he's ~** está de vuelta, ha vuelto; **he ran ~** volvió corriendo; (*restitution*): **throw the ball ~** devuelve la pelota; **can I have it ~?** ¿me lo devuelve?; (*again*): **he called ~** llamó de nuevo; **~ down** *vi* echarse atrás; **~ out** *vi* (of *promise*) volverse atrás; **~ up** *vt* (*person*) apoyar, respaldar; (*theory*) defender; (COMPUT) hacer una copia preventiva *or* de reserva; **~bencher** (BRIT) *n* miembro del parlamento sin cargo relevante; **~bone** *n* columna vertebral; **~date** *vt* (*pay rise*) dar efecto retroactivo a; (*letter*) poner fecha atrasada a; **~drop** *n* telón *m* de fondo; **~fire** *vi* (AUT) petardear; (*plans*) fallar, salir mal; **~ground** *n* fondo; (of *events*) antecedentes *mpl*; (*basic knowledge*) bases *fpl*; (*experience*) conocimientos *mpl*, educación *f*; **family ~ground** origen *m*, antecedentes *mpl*; **~hand** *n* (TENNIS: *also*: **~hand stroke**) revés *m*; **~hander** (BRIT) *n* (*bribe*) soborno; **~ing** *n* (*fig*) apoyo, respaldo; **~lash** *n* reacción *f*; **~log** *n*: **~log of work** trabajo atrasado; **~ number** *n* (of *magazine etc*) número atrasado; **~pack** *n* mochila; **~packer** *n* mochilero(a); **~ pay** *n* pago atrasado; **~side** (*inf*) *n* trasero, culo; **~stage** *adv* entre bastidores; **~stroke** *n* espalda; **~up** *adj* suplementario; (COMPUT) de reserva ♦ *n* (*support*) apoyo; (*also*: **~-up file**) copia preventiva *or* de reserva; **~ward** *adj* (*person, country*) atrasado; **~wards** *adv* hacia atrás; (*read a list*) al revés; (*fall*) de espaldas; **~yard** *n* traspatio
bacon ['beɪkən] *n* tocino, beicon *m*

bad [bæd] *adj* malo; (*mistake, accident*) grave; (*food*) podrido, pasado; **his ~ leg** su pierna lisiada; **to go ~** (*food*) pasarse
badge [bædʒ] *n* insignia; (*policeman's*) chapa, placa
badger ['bædʒə*] *n* tejón *m*
badly ['bædlɪ] *adv* mal; **to reflect ~ on sb** influir negativamente en la reputación de uno; **~ wounded** gravemente herido; **he needs it ~** le hace gran falta; **to be ~ off (for money)** andar mal de dinero
badminton ['bædmɪntən] *n* bádminton *m*
bad-tempered *adj* de mal genio *or* carácter; (*temporarily*) de mal humor
bag [bæg] *n* bolsa; (*handbag*) bolso; (*satchel*) mochila; (*case*) maleta; **~s of** (*inf*) un montón de; **~gage** *n* equipaje *m*; **~gage allowance** *n* límite *m* de equipaje; **~gage reclaim** *n* recogida de equipajes; **~gy** *adj* amplio; **~pipes** *npl* gaita
Bahamas [bə'hɑːməz] *npl*: **the ~** las Islas Bahamas
bail [beɪl] *n* fianza ♦ *vt* (*prisoner: gen: grant ~ to*) poner en libertad bajo fianza; (*boat: also*: **~ out**) achicar; **on ~** (*prisoner*) bajo fianza; **to ~ sb out** obtener la libertad de uno bajo fianza; *see also* **bale**
bailiff ['beɪlɪf] *n* alguacil *m*
bait [beɪt] *n* cebo ♦ *vt* poner cebo en; (*tease*) tomar el pelo a
bake [beɪk] *vt* cocer (al horno) ♦ *vi* cocerse; **~d beans** *npl* judías *fpl* en salsa de tomate; **~d potato** *n* patata al horno; **~r** *n* panadero; **~ry** *n* panadería; (*for cakes*) pastelería; **baking** *n* (*act*) amasar *m*; (*batch*) hornada; **baking powder** *n* levadura (en polvo)
balance ['bæləns] *n* equilibrio; (COMM: *sum*) balance *m*; (*remainder*) resto; (*scales*) balanza ♦ *vt* equilibrar; (*budget*) nivelar; (*account*) saldar; (*make equal*) equilibrar; **~ of trade/ payments** balanza de comercio/pagos; **~d** *adj* (*personality, diet*) equilibrado; (*report*) objetivo; **~ sheet** *n* balance *m*
balcony ['bælkənɪ] *n* (*open*) balcón *m*; (*closed*) galería; (*in theatre*) anfiteatro
bald [bɔːld] *adj* calvo; (*tyre*) liso
bale [beɪl] *n* (AGR) paca, fardo; (of *papers etc*) fajo; **~ out** *vi* lanzarse en paracaídas
Balearics [bælɪ'ærɪks] *npl*: **the ~** las Baleares
ball [bɔːl] *n* pelota; (*football*) balón *m*; (of *wool, string*) ovillo; (*dance*) baile *m*; **to play ~** (*fig*) cooperar
ballast ['bæləst] *n* lastre *m*
ball bearings *npl* cojinetes *mpl* de bolas
ballerina [bælə'riːnə] *n* bailarina
ballet ['bæleɪ] *n* ballet *m*; **~ dancer** *n* bailarín/ina *m/f*
balloon [bə'luːn] *n* globo

ballot ['bælət] *n* votación *f*; **~ paper** *n* papeleta (para votar)

ballpoint (pen) ['bɔːlpɔɪnt-] *n* bolígrafo

ballroom ['bɔːlrʊm] *n* salón *m* de baile

Baltic ['bɔːltɪk] *n*: **the ~ (Sea)** el (Mar) Báltico

ban [bæn] *n* prohibición *f*, proscripción *f* ♦ *vt* prohibir, proscribir

banal [bə'nɑːl] *adj* banal, vulgar

banana [bə'nɑːnə] *n* plátano (*SP*), banana (*AM*)

band [bænd] *n* grupo; (*strip*) faja, tira; (*stripe*) lista; (*MUS: jazz*) orquesta; (: *rock*) grupo; (: *MIL*) banda; **~ together** *vi* juntarse, asociarse

bandage ['bændɪdʒ] *n* venda, vendaje *m* ♦ *vt* vendar

Bandaid ® ['bændeɪd] (*US*) *n* tirita

bandit ['bændɪt] *n* bandido

bandy-legged ['bændɪ'legd] *adj* estevado

bang [bæŋ] *n* (*of gun, exhaust*) estallido, detonación *f*; (*of door*) portazo; (*blow*) golpe *m* ♦ *vt* (*door*) cerrar de golpe; (*one's head*) golpear ♦ *vi* estallar; (*door*) cerrar de golpe

Bangladesh [bæŋglə'deʃ] *n* Bangladesh *m*

bangs [bæŋz] (*US*) *npl* flequillo

banish ['bænɪʃ] *vt* desterrar

banister(s) ['bænɪstə(z)] *n(pl)* barandilla, pasamanos *m inv*

bank [bæŋk] *n* (*COMM*) banco; (*of river, lake*) ribera, orilla; (*of earth*) terraplén *m* ♦ *vi* (*AVIAT*) ladearse; **~ on** *vt fus* contar con; **~ account** *n* cuenta de banco; **~ card** *n* tarjeta bancaria; **~er** *n* banquero; **~er's card** (*BRIT*) *n* = **~ card**; **B~ holiday** (*BRIT*) *n* día *m* festivo; **~ing** *n* banca; **~note** *n* billete *m* de banco; **~ rate** *n* tipo de interés bancario

bankrupt ['bæŋkrʌpt] *adj* quebrado, insolvente; **to go ~** hacer bancarrota; **to be ~** estar en quiebra; **~cy** *n* quiebra

bank statement *n* balance *m* or detalle *m* de cuenta

banner ['bænə*] *n* pancarta

bannister(s) ['bænɪstə(z)] *n(pl)* = **banister(s)**

baptism ['bæptɪzəm] *n* bautismo; (*act*) bautizo

bar [bɑː*] *n* (*pub*) bar *m*; (*counter*) mostrador *m*; (*rod*) barra; (*of window, cage*) reja; (*of soap*) pastilla; (*of chocolate*) tableta; (*fig: hindrance*) obstáculo; (*prohibition*) proscripción *f*; (*MUS*) barra ♦ *vt* (*road*) obstruir; (*person*) excluir; (*activity*) prohibir; **the B~** (*LAW*) la abogacía; **behind ~s** entre rejas; **~ none** sin excepción

barbaric [bɑː'bærɪk] *adj* bárbaro

barbecue ['bɑːbɪkjuː] *n* barbacoa

barbed wire ['bɑːbd-] *n* alambre *m* de púas

barber ['bɑːbə*] *n* peluquero, barbero

bar code *n* código de barras

bare [beə*] *adj* desnudo; (*trees*) sin hojas; (*necessities etc*) básico ♦ *vt* desnudar; (*teeth*) enseñar; **~back** *adv* a pelo, sin silla; **~faced** *adj* descarado; **~foot** *adj*, *adv* descalzo; **~ly** *adv* apenas

bargain ['bɑːgɪn] *n* pacto, negocio; (*good buy*) ganga ♦ *vi* negociar; (*haggle*) regatear; **into the ~** además, por añadidura; **~ for** *vt fus*: **he got more than he ~ed for** le resultó peor de lo que esperaba

barge [bɑːdʒ] *n* barcaza; **~ in** *vi* irrumpir; (*interrupt: conversation*) interrumpir

bark [bɑːk] *n* (*of tree*) corteza; (*of dog*) ladrido ♦ *vi* ladrar

barley ['bɑːlɪ] *n* cebada

barmaid ['bɑːmeɪd] *n* camarera

barman ['bɑːmən] *n* camarero, barman *m*

barn [bɑːn] *n* granero

barometer [bə'rɒmɪtə*] *n* barómetro

baron ['bærən] *n* barón *m*; (*press ~ etc*) magnate *m*; **~ess** *n* baronesa

barracks ['bærəks] *npl* cuartel *m*

barrage ['bærɑːʒ] *n* (*MIL*) descarga, bombardeo; (*dam*) presa; (*of criticism*) lluvia, aluvión *m*

barrel ['bærəl] *n* barril *m*; (*of gun*) cañón *m*

barren ['bærən] *adj* estéril

barricade [bærɪ'keɪd] *n* barricada

barrier ['bærɪə*] *n* barrera

barring ['bɑːrɪŋ] *prep* excepto, salvo

barrister ['bærɪstə*] (*BRIT*) *n* abogado/a

barrow ['bærəʊ] *n* (*cart*) carretilla (de mano)

bartender ['bɑːtɛndə*] (*US*) *n* camarero, barman *m*

barter ['bɑːtə*] *vt*: **to ~ sth for sth** trocar algo por algo

base [beɪs] *n* base *f* ♦ *vt*: **to ~ sth on** basar or fundar algo en ♦ *adj* bajo, infame

baseball ['beɪsbɔːl] *n* béisbol *m*

basement ['beɪsmənt] *n* sótano

bases¹ ['beɪsiːz] *npl* of **basis**

bases² ['beɪsɪz] *npl* of **base**

bash [bæʃ] (*inf*) *vt* golpear

bashful ['bæʃfʊl] *adj* tímido, vergonzoso

basic ['beɪsɪk] *adj* básico; **~ally** *adv* fundamentalmente, en el fondo; (*simply*) sencillamente; **~s** *npl*: **the ~s** los fundamentos

basil ['bæzl] *n* albahaca

basin ['beɪsn] *n* cuenco, tazón *m*; (*GEO*) cuenca; (*also*: **wash~**) lavabo

basis ['beɪsɪs] (*pl* **bases**) *n* base *f*; **on a part-time/trial ~** a tiempo parcial/a prueba

bask [bɑːsk] *vi*: **to ~ in the sun** tomar el sol

basket ['bɑːskɪt] *n* cesta, cesto; canasta; **~ball** *n* baloncesto

Basque [bæsk] *adj*, *n* vasco/a *m/f*; **~ Country** *n* Euskadi *m*, País *m* Vasco

bass [beɪs] *n* (*MUS: instrument*) bajo; (*double ~*) contrabajo; (*singer*) bajo

bassoon [bə'su:n] *n* fagot *m*

bastard ['bɑːstəd] *n* bastardo; (*infl*) hijo de puta (!)

bat [bæt] *n* (*ZOOL*) murciélago; (*for ball games*) palo; (*BRIT: for table tennis*) pala ♦ *vt*: **he didn't ~ an eyelid** ni pestañeó

batch [bætʃ] *n* (*of bread*) hornada; (*of letters etc*) lote *m*

bated ['beɪtɪd] *adj*: **with ~ breath** sin respirar

bath [bɑːθ, *pl* bɑːðz] *n* (*action*) baño; (*~tub*) baño (*SP*), bañera (*SP*), tina (*AM*) ♦ *vt* bañar; **to have a ~** bañarse, tomar un baño; *see also* **baths**

bathe [beɪð] *vi* bañarse ♦ *vt* (*wound*) lavar; **~r** *n* bañista *m/f*

bathing ['beɪðɪŋ] *n* el bañarse; **~ costume** (*US* **~ suit**) *n* traje *m* de baño

bath: **~robe** *n* (*man's*) batín *m*; (*woman's*) bata; **~room** *n* (cuarto de) baño; **~s** [bɑːðz] *npl* (*also: swimming ~s*) piscina; **~ towel** *n* toalla de baño

baton ['bætən] *n* (*MUS*) batuta; (*ATHLETICS*) testigo; (*weapon*) porra

batter ['bætə*] *vt* maltratar; (*subj: rain etc*) azotar ♦ *n* masa (para rebozar); **~ed** *adj* (*hat, pan*) estropeado

battery ['bætərɪ] *n* (*AUT*) batería; (*of torch*) pila

battle ['bætl] *n* batalla; (*fig*) lucha ♦ *vi* luchar; **~ship** *n* acorazado

bawl [bɔːl] *vi* chillar, gritar; (*child*) berrear

bay [beɪ] *n* (*GEO*) bahía; **B~ of Biscay** ≈ mar Cantábrico; **to hold sb at ~** mantener a alguien a raya; **~ leaf** *n* hoja de laurel

bay window *n* ventana salediza

bazaar [bə'zɑː*] *n* bazar *m*; (*fete*) venta con fines benéficos

B. & B. *n abbr* (= *bed and breakfast*) cama y desayuno

BBC *n abbr* (= *British Broadcasting Corporation*) cadena de radio y televisión estatal británica

B.C. *adv abbr* (= *before Christ*) a. de C.

KEYWORD

be [biː] (*pt* **was, were,** *pp* **been**) *aux vb* **1** (*with present participle: forming continuous tenses*): **what are you doing?** ¿qué estás haciendo?, ¿qué haces?; **they're coming tomorrow** vienen mañana; **I've been waiting for you for hours** llevo horas esperándote

2 (*with pp: forming passives*) ser (*but often replaced by active or reflective constructions*); **to ~ murdered** ser asesinado; **the box had been opened** habían abierto la caja; **the thief was nowhere to ~ seen** no se veía al ladrón por ninguna parte

3 (*in tag questions*): **it was fun, wasn't it?** fue divertido, ¿no? *or* ¿verdad?; **he's good-**

looking, isn't he? es guapo, ¿no te parece?; **she's back again, is she?** entonces, ¿ha vuelto?

4 (+ *to* + *infin*): **the house is to ~ sold** (*necessity*) hay que vender la casa; (*future*) van a vender la casa; **he's not to open it** no tiene que abrirlo

♦ *vb* + *complement* **1** (*with n or num complement, but see also 3, 4, 5 and impers vb below*) ser; **he's a doctor** es médico; **2 and 2 are 4** 2 y 2 son 4

2 (*with adj complement: expressing permanent or inherent quality*) ser; (: *expressing state seen as temporary or reversible*) estar; **I'm English** soy inglés/esa; **she's tall/pretty** es alta/bonita; **he's young** es joven; **~ careful/good/quiet** ten cuidado/pórtate bien/cállate; **I'm tired** estoy cansado/a; **it's dirty** está sucio/a

3 (*of health*) estar; **how are you?** ¿cómo estás?; **he's very ill** está muy enfermo; **I'm better now** ya estoy mejor

4 (*of age*) tener; **how old are you?** ¿cuántos años tienes?; **I'm sixteen (years old)** tengo dieciséis años

5 (*cost*) costar; ser; **how much was the meal?** ¿cuánto fue *or* costó la comida?; **that'll ~ £5.75, please** son £5.75, por favor; **this shirt is £17** esta camisa cuesta £17

♦ *vi* **1** (*exist, occur etc*) existir, haber; **the best singer that ever was** el mejor cantante que existió jamás; **is there a God?** ¿hay un Dios?, ¿existe Dios?; **~ that as it may** sea como sea; **so ~ it** así sea

2 (*referring to place*) estar; **I won't ~ here tomorrow** no estaré aquí mañana

3 (*referring to movement*): **where have you been?** ¿dónde has estado?

♦ *impers vb* **1** (*referring to time*): **it's 5 o'clock** son las 5; **it's the 28th of April** estamos a 28 de abril

2 (*referring to distance*): **it's 10 km to the village** el pueblo está a 10 km

3 (*referring to the weather*): **it's too hot/cold** hace demasiado calor/frío; **it's windy today** hace viento hoy

4 (*emphatic*): **it's me** soy yo; **it was Maria who paid the bill** fue María la que pagó la cuenta

---

beach [biːtʃ] *n* playa ♦ *vt* varar

beacon ['biːkən] *n* (*lighthouse*) faro; (*marker*) guía

bead [biːd] *n* cuenta; (*of sweat etc*) gota

beak [biːk] *n* pico

beaker ['biːkə*] *n* vaso de plástico

beam [biːm] *n* (*ARCH*) viga, travesaño; (*of light*) rayo, haz *m* de luz ♦ *vi* brillar; (*smile*) sonreír

bean [biːn] *n* judía; **runner/broad ~**

habichuela/haba; **coffee** ~ grano de café;
~**sprouts** *npl* brotes *mpl* de soja
bear [bɛə*] (*pt* bore, *pp* borne) *n* oso ♦ *vt*
(*weight etc*) llevar; (*cost*) pagar;
(*responsibility*) tener; (*endure*) soportar,
aguantar; (*children*) parir, tener; (*fruit*) dar
♦ *vi*: **to ~ right/left** torcer a la derecha/
izquierda; ~ **out** *vt* (*suspicions*) corroborar,
confirmar; (*person*) dar la razón a; ~ **up** *vi*
(*remain cheerful*) mantenerse animado
beard [bɪəd] *n* barba; ~**ed** *adj* con barba,
barbudo
bearer ['bɛərə*] *n* portador(a) *m/f*
bearing ['bɛərɪŋ] *n* porte *m*,
comportamiento; (*connection*) relación *f*; ~**s**
npl (*also*: **ball ~s**) cojinetes *mpl* a bolas; **to
take a ~** tomar marcaciones; **to find one's ~s**
orientarse
beast [biːst] *n* bestia; (*inf*) bruto, salvaje *m*;
~**ly** (*inf*) *adj* horrible
beat [biːt] (*pt* beat, *pp* beaten) *n* (*of heart*)
latido; (*MUS*) ritmo, compás *m*; (*of
policeman*) ronda ♦ *vt* pegar, golpear; (*eggs*)
batir; (*defeat*: *opponent*) vencer, derrotar;
(*: record*) sobrepasar ♦ *vi* (*heart*) latir; (*drum*)
redoblar; (*rain, wind*) azotar; **off the ~en
track** aislado; **to ~ it** (*inf*) largarse; ~ **off** *vt*
rechazar; ~ **up** *vt* (*attack*) dar una paliza a;
~**ing** *n* paliza
beautiful ['bjuːtɪful] *adj* precioso, hermoso,
bello; ~**ly** *adv* maravillosamente
beauty ['bjuːtɪ] *n* belleza; ~ **salon** *n* salón *m*
de belleza; ~ **spot** *n* (*TOURISM*) lugar *m*
pintoresco
beaver ['biːvə*] *n* castor *m*
became [bɪ'keɪm] *pt of* become
because [bɪ'kɔz] *conj* porque; ~ **of** debido a,
a causa de
beckon ['bɛkən] *vt* (*also*: ~ **to**) llamar con
señas
become [bɪ'kʌm] (*irreg*: *like* come) *vt* (*suit*)
favorecer, sentar bien a ♦ *vi* (+ *n*) hacerse,
llegar a ser; (+ *adj*) ponerse, volverse; **to
~ fat** engordar
becoming [bɪ'kʌmɪŋ] *adj* (*behaviour*)
decoroso; (*clothes*) favorecedor
bed [bɛd] *n* cama; (*of flowers*) macizo; (*of
coal, clay*) capa; (*of river*) lecho; (*of sea*)
fondo; **to go to ~** acostarse; ~ **and
breakfast** *n* (*place*) pensión *f*; (*terms*) cama
y desayuno; ~**clothes** *npl* ropa de cama;
~**ding** *n* ropa de cama
bedraggled [bɪ'drægld] *adj* (*untidy*: *person*)
desastrado; (*clothes, hair*) desordenado
bed: ~**ridden** *adj* postrado en cama;
~**room** *n* dormitorio; ~**side** *n*: **at the ~side
of** a la cabecera de; ~**sit(ter)** (*BRIT*) *n* estudio
(*SP*), suite *m* (*AM*); ~**spread** *n* cubrecama *m*,
colcha; ~**time** *n* hora de acostarse

bee [biː] *n* abeja
beech [biːtʃ] *n* haya
beef [biːf] *n* carne *f* de vaca; **roast ~** rosbif *m*;
~**burger** *n* hamburguesa; **B~eater** *n*
alabardero de la Torre de Londres
beehive ['biːhaɪv] *n* colmena
beeline ['biːlaɪn] *n*: **to make a ~ for** ir
derecho a
been [biːn] *pp of* be
beer [bɪə*] *n* cerveza
beet [biːt] (*US*) *n* (*also*: **red ~**) remolacha
beetle ['biːtl] *n* escarabajo
beetroot ['biːtruːt] (*BRIT*) *n* remolacha
before [bɪ'fɔː*] *prep* (*of time*) antes de; (*of
space*) delante de ♦ *conj* antes (de) que
♦ *adv* antes, anteriormente; delante,
adelante; ~ **going** antes de marcharse; ~ **she
goes** antes de que se vaya; **the week ~** la
semana anterior; **I've never seen it ~** no lo he
visto nunca; ~**hand** *adv* de antemano, con
anticipación
beg [bɛg] *vi* pedir limosna ♦ *vt* pedir, rogar;
(*entreat*) suplicar; **to ~ sb to do sth** rogar a
uno que haga algo; *see also* **pardon**
began [bɪ'gæn] *pt of* begin
beggar ['bɛgə*] *n* mendigo/a
begin [bɪ'gɪn] (*pt* began, *pp* begun) *vt, vi*
empezar, comenzar; **to ~ doing** *or* **to do sth**
empezar a hacer algo; ~**ner** *n* principiante
m/f; ~**ning** *n* principio, comienzo
begun [bɪ'gʌn] *pp of* begin
behalf [bɪ'hɑːf] *n*: **on ~ of** en nombre de, por;
(*for benefit of*) en beneficio de; **on my/his ~**
por mí/él
behave [bɪ'heɪv] *vi* (*person*) portarse,
comportarse; (*well*: *also*: ~ **o.s.**) portarse
bien; **behaviour** (*US* behavior) *n*
comportamiento, conducta
behind [bɪ'haɪnd] *prep* detrás de;
(*supporting*): **to be ~ sb** apoyar a alguien
♦ *adv* detrás, por detrás, atrás ♦ *n* trasero; **to
be ~ (schedule)** ir retrasado; ~ **the scenes**
(*fig*) entre bastidores
behold [bɪ'həuld] (*irreg*: *like* hold) *vt*
contemplar
beige [beɪʒ] *adj* color beige
Beijing ['beɪ'dʒɪŋ] *n* Pekín *m*
being ['biːɪŋ] *n* ser *m*; (*existence*): **in ~**
existente; **to come into ~** aparecer
Beirut [beɪ'ruːt] *n* Beirut *m*
Belarus [bɛlə'ruːs] *n* Bielorrusia
belated [bɪ'leɪtɪd] *adj* atrasado, tardío
belch [bɛltʃ] *vi* eructar ♦ *vt* (*gen*: ~ **out**: *smoke
etc*) arrojar
Belgian ['bɛldʒən] *adj, n* belga *m/f*
Belgium ['bɛldʒəm] *n* Bélgica
belief [bɪ'liːf] *n* opinión *f*; (*faith*) fe *f*
believe [bɪ'liːv] *vt, vi* creer; **to ~ in** creer en;
~**r** *n* partidario/a; (*REL*) creyente *m/f*, fiel *m/f*

belittle [bɪˈlɪtl] vt quitar importancia a

bell [bel] n campana; (*small*) campanilla; (*on door*) timbre m

belligerent [bɪˈlɪdʒərənt] adj agresivo

bellow [ˈbeləu] vi bramar; (*person*) rugir

belly [ˈbelɪ] n barriga, panza

belong [bɪˈlɔŋ] vi: **to ~ to** pertenecer a; (*club etc*) ser socio de; **this book ~s here** este libro va aquí; **~ings** npl pertenencias fpl

beloved [bɪˈlʌvɪd] adj querido/a

below [bɪˈləu] prep bajo, debajo de; (*less than*) inferior a ♦ adv abajo, (por) debajo; **see ~** véase más abajo

belt [belt] n cinturón m; (*TECH*) correa, cinta ♦ vt (*thrash*) pegar con correa; **~way** (*US*) n (*AUT*) carretera de circunvalación

bench [bentʃ] n banco; (*BRIT: POL*): **the Government/Opposition ~es** (los asientos de) los miembros del Gobierno/de la Oposición; **the B~** (*LAW: judges*) magistratura

bend [bend] (*pt, pp* bent) vt doblar ♦ vi inclinarse ♦ n (*BRIT: in road, river*) curva; (*in pipe*) codo; **~ down** vi inclinarse, doblarse; **~ over** vi inclinarse

beneath [bɪˈniːθ] prep bajo, debajo de; (*unworthy of*) indigno de ♦ adv abajo, (por) debajo

benefactor [ˈbenɪfæktə*] n bienhechor m

beneficial [benɪˈfɪʃəl] adj beneficioso

benefit [ˈbenɪfɪt] n beneficio; (*allowance of money*) subsidio ♦ vt beneficiar ♦ vi: **he'll ~ from it** le sacará provecho

benevolent [bɪˈnevələnt] adj (*person*) benévolo

benign [bɪˈnaɪn] adj benigno; (*smile*) afable

bent [bent] pt, pp of **bend** ♦ n inclinación f ♦ adj: **to be ~ on** estar empeñado en

bequest [bɪˈkwest] n legado

bereaved [bɪˈriːvd] npl: **the ~** los íntimos de una persona afligidos por su muerte

beret [ˈbereɪ] n boina

Berlin [bəːˈlɪn] n Berlín

berm [bəːm] (*US*) n (*AUT*) arcén m

Bermuda [bəːˈmjuːdə] n las Bermudas

berry [ˈberɪ] n baya

berserk [bəˈsəːk] adj: **to go ~** perder los estribos

berth [bəːθ] n (*bed*) litera; (*cabin*) camarote m; (*for ship*) amarradero ♦ vi atracar, amarrar

beseech [bɪˈsiːtʃ] (*pt, pp* besought) vt suplicar

beset [bɪˈset] (*pt, pp* beset) vt (*person*) acosar

beside [bɪˈsaɪd] prep junto a, al lado de; **to be ~ o.s. with anger** estar fuera de sí; **that's ~ the point** eso no tiene nada que ver; **~s** adv además ♦ prep además de

besiege [bɪˈsiːdʒ] vt sitiar; (*fig*) asediar

best [best] adj (el/la) mejor ♦ adv (lo) mejor; **the ~ part of** (*quantity*) la mayor parte de; **at ~ en el mejor de los casos**; **to make the ~ of sth** sacar el mejor partido de algo; **to do one's ~** hacer lo posible; **to the ~ of my knowledge** que yo sepa; **to the ~ of my ability** como mejor puedo; **~-before date** n fecha de consumo preferente; **~ man** n padrino de boda

bestow [bɪˈstəu] vt (*title*) otorgar

bestseller [ˈbestˈselə*] n éxito de librería, bestseller m

bet [bet] (*pt, pp* bet *or* betted) n apuesta ♦ vt: **to ~ money on** apostar dinero por; **to ~ sb sth** apostar algo a uno ♦ vi apostar

betray [bɪˈtreɪ] vt traicionar; (*trust*) faltar a; **~al** n traición f

better [ˈbetə*] adj, adv mejor ♦ vt superar ♦ n: **to get the ~ of sb** quedar por encima de alguien; **you had ~ do it** más vale que lo hagas; **he thought ~ of it** cambió de parecer; **to get ~** (*MED*) mejorar(se); **~ off** adj mejor; (*wealthier*) más acomodado

betting [ˈbetɪŋ] n juego, el apostar; **~ shop** (*BRIT*) n agencia de apuestas

between [bɪˈtwiːn] prep entre ♦ adv (*time*) mientras tanto; (*place*) en medio

beverage [ˈbevərɪdʒ] n bebida

beware [bɪˈweə*] vi: **to ~ (of)** tener cuidado (con); **"~ of the dog"** "perro peligroso"

bewildered [bɪˈwɪldəd] adj aturdido, perplejo

beyond [bɪˈjɔnd] prep más allá de; (*past: understanding*) fuera de; (*after: date*) después de, más allá de; (*above*) superior a ♦ adv (*in space*) más allá; (*in time*) posteriormente; **~ doubt** fuera de toda duda; **~ repair** irreparable

bias [ˈbaɪəs] n (*prejudice*) prejuicio, pasión f; (*preference*) predisposición f; **~(s)ed** adj parcial

bib [bɪb] n babero

Bible [ˈbaɪbl] n Biblia

bicarbonate of soda [baɪˈkɑːbənɪt-] n bicarbonato sódico

bicker [ˈbɪkə*] vi pelearse

bicycle [ˈbaɪsɪkl] n bicicleta

bid [bɪd] (*pt* bade *or* bid, *pp* bidden *or* bid) n oferta, postura; (*in tender*) licitación f; (*attempt*) tentativa, conato ♦ vi hacer una oferta ♦ vt (*offer*) ofrecer; **to ~ sb good day** dar a uno los buenos días; **~der** n: **the highest ~der** el mejor postor; **~ding** n (*at auction*) ofertas fpl

bide [baɪd] vt: **to ~ one's time** esperar el momento adecuado

bifocals [baɪˈfəuklz] npl gafas fpl (*SP*) or anteojos mpl (*AM*) bifocales

big [bɪg] adj grande; (*brother, sister*) mayor

bigheaded [ˈbɪgˈhedɪd] adj engreído

bigot [ˈbɪgət] n fanático/a, intolerante m/f;

~ed adj fanático, intolerante; **~ry** n fanatismo, intolerancia
big top n (at circus) carpa
bike [baɪk] n bici f
bikini [bɪˈkiːnɪ] n bikini m
bilingual [barˈlɪŋgwəl] adj bilingüe
bill [bɪl] n cuenta; (invoice) factura; (POL) proyecto de ley; (US: banknote) billete m; (of bird) pico; (of show) programa m; **"post no ~s"** "prohibido fijar carteles"; **to fit** or **fill the ~** (fig) cumplir con los requisitos; **~board** (US) n cartelera
billet [ˈbɪlɪt] n alojamiento
billfold [ˈbɪlfəuld] (US) n cartera
billiards [ˈbɪljədz] n billar m
billion [ˈbɪljən] n (BRIT) billón m (millón de millones); (US) mil millones mpl
bimbo [ˈbɪmbəu] (inf) n tía buena sin seso
bin [bɪn] n (for rubbish) cubo (SP) or bote m (AM) de la basura; (container) recipiente m
bind [baɪnd] (pt, pp bound) vt atar; (book) encuadernar; (oblige) obligar ♦ n (inf: nuisance) lata; **~ing** adj (contract) obligatorio
binge [bɪndʒ] (inf) n: **to go on a ~** ir de juerga
bingo [ˈbɪngəu] n bingo m
binoculars [bɪˈnɔkjuləz] npl prismáticos mpl
bio... [baɪə] prefix: **~chemistry** n bioquímica; **~degradable** [baɪəudɪˈgreɪdəbl] adj (biodegradable); **~graphy** [baɪˈɔgrəfɪ] n biografía; **~logical** adj biológico; **~logy** [baɪˈɔlədʒɪ] n biología
birch [bəːtʃ] n (tree) abedul m
bird [bəːd] n ave f, pájaro; (BRIT: inf: girl) chica; **~'s eye view** n (aerial view) vista de pájaro; (overview) visión f de conjunto; **~ watcher** n ornitólogo/a
Biro ® [ˈbaɪrəu] n bolígrafo
birth [bəːθ] n nacimiento; **to give ~ to** parir, dar a luz; **~ certificate** n partida de nacimiento; **~ control** n (policy) control m de natalidad; (methods) métodos mpl anticonceptivos; **~day** n cumpleaños m inv ♦ cpd (cake, card etc) de cumpleaños; **~place** n lugar m de nacimiento; **~ rate** n (tasa de) natalidad f
biscuit [ˈbɪskɪt] (BRIT) n galleta, bizcocho (AM)
bisect [baɪˈsekt] vt bisecar
bishop [ˈbɪʃəp] n obispo; (CHESS) alfil m
bit [bɪt] pt of **bite** ♦ n trozo, pedazo, pedacito; (COMPUT) bit m, bitio; (for horse) freno, bocado; **a ~ of** una poco de; **a ~ mad** un poco loco; **~ by ~** poco a poco
bitch [bɪtʃ] n perra; (inf!: woman) zorra (!)
bite [baɪt] (pt bit, pp bitten) vt, vi morder; (insect etc) picar ♦ n (insect ~) picadura; (mouthful) bocado; **to ~ one's nails** comerse las uñas; **let's have a ~ (to eat)** (inf) vamos a comer algo

bitter [ˈbɪtə*] adj amargo; (wind) cortante, penetrante; (battle) encarnizado ♦ n (BRIT: beer) cerveza típica británica a base de lúpulos; **~ness** n lo amargo, amargura; (anger) rencor m
bizarre [bɪˈzɑː*] adj raro, extraño
black [blæk] adj negro; (tea, coffee) solo ♦ n color m negro; (person): **B~** negro/a ♦ vt (BRIT: INDUSTRY) boicotear; **to give sb a ~ eye** ponerle a uno el ojo morado; **~ and blue** (bruised) amoratado; **to be in the ~** (bank account) estar en números negros; **~berry** n zarzamora; **~bird** n mirlo; **~board** n pizarra; **~ coffee** n café m solo; **~currant** n grosella negra; **~en** vt (fig) desacreditar; **~ ice** n hielo invisible en la carretera; **~leg** (BRIT) n esquirol m, rompehuelgas m inv; **~list** n lista negra; **~mail** n chantaje m ♦ vt chantajear; **~ market** n mercado negro; **~out** n (MIL) oscurecimiento; (power cut) apagón m; (TV, RADIO) interrupción f de programas; (fainting) desvanecimiento; **B~ Sea** n: **the B~ Sea** el Mar Negro; **~ sheep** n (fig) oveja negra; **~smith** n herrero; **~ spot** n (AUT) lugar m peligroso; (for unemployment etc) punto negro
bladder [ˈblædə*] n vejiga
blade [bleɪd] n hoja; (of propeller) paleta; **a ~ of grass** una brizna de hierba
blame [bleɪm] n culpa ♦ vt: **to ~ sb for sth** echar a uno la culpa de algo; **to be to ~** tener la culpa de
bland [blænd] adj (music, taste) soso
blank [blæŋk] adj en blanco; (look) sin expresión ♦ n (of memory): **my mind is a ~** no puedo recordar nada; (on form) blanco, espacio en blanco; (cartridge) cartucho sin bala or de fogueo; **~ cheque** n cheque m en blanco
blanket [ˈblæŋkɪt] n manta (SP), cobija (AM); (of snow) capa; (of fog) manto
blare [blɛə*] vi sonar estrepitosamente
blasé [ˈblɑːzeɪ] adj hastiado
blast [blɑːst] n (of wind) ráfaga, soplo; (of explosive) explosión f ♦ vt (blow up) volar; **~-off** n (SPACE) lanzamiento
blatant [ˈbleɪtənt] adj descarado
blaze [bleɪz] n (fire) fuego; (fig: of colour) despliegue m; (: of glory) esplendor m ♦ vi arder en llamas; (fig) brillar ♦ vt: **to ~ a trail** (fig) abrir (un) camino; **in a ~ of publicity** con gran publicidad
blazer [ˈbleɪzə*] n chaqueta de uniforme de colegial o de socio de club
bleach [bliːtʃ] n (also: household ~) lejía ♦ vt blanquear; **~ed** adj (hair) teñido (de rubio); **~ers** (US) npl (SPORT) gradas fpl al sol
bleak [bliːk] adj (countryside) desierto; (prospect) poco prometedor(a); (weather)

crudo; (*smile*) triste

bleat [bli:t] *vi* balar

bleed [bli:d] (*pt, pp* **bled**) *vt, vi* sangrar; **my nose is ~ing** me está sangrando la nariz

bleeper ['bli:pə*] *n* busca *m*

blemish ['blemiʃ] *n* marca, mancha; (*on reputation*) tacha

blend [blend] *n* mezcla ♦ *vt* mezclar; (*colours etc*) combinar, mezclar ♦ *vi* (*colours etc: also: ~ in*) combinarse, mezclarse

bless [bles] (*pt, pp* **blessed** *or* **blest**) *vt* bendecir; **~ you!** (*after sneeze*) ¡Jesús!; **~ing** *n* (*approval*) aprobación *f*; (*godsend*) don *m* del cielo, bendición *f*; (*advantage*) beneficio, ventaja

blew [blu:] *pt of* **blow**

blind [blaınd] *adj* ciego, (*fig*): **~ (to)** ciego (a) ♦ *n* (*for window*) persiana ♦ *vt* cegar; (*dazzle*) deslumbrar; (*deceive*): **to ~ sb to ...** cegar a uno a ...; **the ~** *npl* los ciegos; **~ alley** *n* callejón *m* sin salida; **~ corner** (*BRIT*) *n* esquina escondida; **~fold** *n* venda ♦ *adv* con los ojos vendados ♦ *vt* vendar los ojos a; **~ly** *adv* a ciegas, ciegamente; **~ness** *n* ceguera; **~ spot** *n* (*AUT*) ángulo ciego

blink [blıŋk] *vi* parpadear, pestañear; (*light*) oscilar; **~ers** *npl* anteojeras *fpl*

bliss [blıs] *n* felicidad *f*

blister ['blıstə*] *n* ampolla ♦ *vi* (*paint*) ampollarse

blizzard ['blızəd] *n* ventisca

bloated ['bləutıd] *adj* hinchado; (*person: full*) ahíto

blob [blɔb] *n* (*drop*) gota; (*indistinct object*) bulto

bloc [blɔk] *n* (*POL*) bloque *m*

block [blɔk] *n* bloque *m*; (*in pipes*) obstáculo; (*of buildings*) manzana (*SP*), cuadra (*AM*) ♦ *vt* obstruir, cerrar; (*progress*) estorbar; **~ of flats** (*BRIT*) bloque *m* de pisos; **mental ~** bloqueo mental; **~ade** [-'keıd] *n* bloqueo ♦ *vt* bloquear; **~age** *n* estorbo, obstrucción *f*; **~buster** *n* (*book*) bestseller *m*; (*film*) éxito de público; **~ letters** *npl* letras *fpl* de molde

bloke [bləuk] (*BRIT: inf*) *n* tipo, tío

blond(e) [blɔnd] *adj, n* rubio/a *m/f*

blood [blʌd] *n* sangre *f*; **~ donor** *n* donante *m/f* de sangre; **~ group** *n* grupo sanguíneo; **~hound** *n* sabueso; **~ poisoning** *n* envenenamiento de la sangre; **~ pressure** *n* presión *f* sanguínea; **~shed** *n* derramamiento de sangre; **~shot** *adj* inyectado en sangre; **~stream** *n* corriente *f* sanguínea; **~ test** *n* análisis *m inv* de sangre; **~thirsty** *adj* sanguinario; **~ vessel** *n* vaso sanguíneo; **~y** *adj* sangriento; (*nose etc*) lleno de sangre; (*BRIT: inf!*): **this ~y...** este condenado *o* puñetero ... (!) ♦ *adv*: **~y strong/good** (*BRIT: inf!*) terriblemente fuerte/bueno; **~y-minded**

(*BRIT: inf*) *adj* puñetero (!)

bloom [blu:m] *n* flor *f* ♦ *vi* florecer

blossom ['blɔsəm] *n* flor *f* ♦ *vi* (*also fig*) florecer

blot [blɔt] *n* borrón *m*; (*fig*) mancha ♦ *vt* (*stain*) manchar; **~ out** *vt* (*view*) tapar

blotchy ['blɔtʃı] *adj* (*complexion*) lleno de manchas

blotting paper ['blɔtıŋ-] *n* papel *m* secante

blouse [blauz] *n* blusa

blow [bləu] (*pt* **blew**, *pp* **blown**) *n* golpe *m*; (*with sword*) espadazo ♦ *vi* soplar; (*dust, sand etc*) volar; (*fuse*) fundirse ♦ *vt* (*subj: wind*) llevarse; (*fuse*) quemar; (*instrument*) tocar; **to ~ one's nose** sonarse; **~ away** *vt* llevarse, arrancar; **~ down** *vt* derribar; **~ off** *vt* arrebatar; **~ out** *vi* apagarse; **~ over** *vi* amainar; **~ up** *vi* estallar ♦ *vt* volar; (*tyre*) inflar; (*PHOT*) ampliar; **~-dry** *n* moldeado (con secador); **~lamp** (*BRIT*) *n* soplete *m*, lámpara de soldar; **~-out** *n* (*of tyre*) pinchazo; **~torch** *n* = **~lamp**

blue [blu:] *adj* azul; (*depressed*) deprimido; **~ film/joke** película/chiste *m* verde; **out of the ~** (*fig*) de repente; **~bell** *n* campanilla, campánula azul; **~bottle** *n* moscarda, mosca azul; **~print** *n* (*fig*) anteproyecto

bluff [blʌf] *vi* tirarse un farol, farolear ♦ *n* farol *m*; **to call sb's ~** coger a uno la palabra

blunder ['blʌndə*] *n* patinazo, metedura de pata ♦ *vi* cometer un error, meter la pata

blunt [blʌnt] *adj* (*pencil*) despuntado; (*knife*) desafilado, romo; (*person*) franco, directo

blur [blə:*] *n* (*shape*): **to become a ~** hacerse borroso ♦ *vt* (*vision*) enturbiar; (*distinction*) borrar

blush [blʌʃ] *vi* ruborizarse, ponerse colorado ♦ *n* rubor *m*

blustery ['blʌstərı] *adj* (*weather*) tempestuoso, tormentoso

boar [bɔ:*] *n* verraco, cerdo

board [bɔ:d] *n* (*card~*) cartón *m*; (*wooden*) tabla, tablero; (*on wall*) tablón *m*; (*for chess etc*) tablero; (*committee*) junta, consejo; (*in firm*) mesa *or* junta directiva; (*NAUT, AVIAT*): **on ~** a bordo ♦ *vt* (*ship*) embarcarse en; (*train*) subir a; **full ~** (*BRIT*) pensión completa; **half ~** (*BRIT*) media pensión; **to go by the ~** (*fig*) ser abandonado *or* olvidado; **~ up** *vt* (*door*) tapiar; **~ and lodging** *n* casa y comida; **~er** *n* (*SCOL*) interno/a; **~ing card** (*BRIT*) *n* tarjeta de embarque; **~ing house** *n* casa de huéspedes; **~ing pass** (*US*) *n* = **~ing card**; **~ing school** *n* internado; **~ room** *n* sala de juntas

boast [bəust] *vi*: **to ~ (about** *or* **of)** alardear (de)

boat [bəut] *n* barco, buque *m*; (*small*) barca, bote *m*

bob [bɔb] vi (also: ~ up and down) menearse, balancearse; ~ **up** vi (re)aparecer de repente

bobby ['bɔbɪ] n (BRIT: inf) n poli m

bobsleigh ['bɔbsleɪ] n bob m

bode [bəud] vi: **to ~ well/ill (for)** ser prometedor/poco prometedor (para)

bodily ['bɔdɪlɪ] adj corporal ♦ adv (move: person) en peso

body ['bɔdɪ] n cuerpo; (corpse) cadáver m; (of car) caja, carrocería; (fig: group) grupo; (: organization) organismo; **~-building** n culturismo; **~guard** n guardaespaldas m inv; **~work** n carrocería

bog [bɔg] n pantano, ciénaga ♦ vt: **to get ~ged down** (fig) empantanarse, atascarse

bogus ['bəugəs] adj falso, fraudulento

boil [bɔɪl] vt (water) hervir; (eggs) pasar por agua, cocer ♦ vi hervir; (fig: with anger) estar furioso; (: with heat) asfixiarse ♦ n (MED) furúnculo, divieso; **to come to the ~, to come to a ~** (US) comenzar a hervir; **to ~ down to** (fig) reducirse a; **~ over** vi salirse, rebosar; (anger etc) llegar al colmo; **~ed egg** n huevo cocido (SP) or pasado (AM); **~ed potatoes** npl patatas fpl (SP) or papas fpl (AM) hervidas; **~er** n caldera; **~er suit** (BRIT) n mono; **~ing point** n punto de ebullición

boisterous ['bɔɪstərəs] adj (noisy) bullicioso; (excitable) exuberante; (crowd) tumultuoso

bold [bəuld] adj valiente, audaz; (pej) descarado; (colour) llamativo

Bolivia [bə'lɪvɪə] n Bolivia; **~n** adj, n boliviano/a m/f

bollard ['bɔləd] (BRIT) n (AUT) poste m

bolt [bəult] n (lock) cerrojo; (with nut) perno, tornillo ♦ adv: ~ **upright** rígido, erguido ♦ vt (door) echar el cerrojo a; (also: ~ together) sujetar con tornillos; (food) engullir ♦ vi fugarse; (horse) desbocarse

bomb [bɔm] n bomba ♦ vt bombardear; ~ **disposal** n desmontaje m de explosivos; **~er** n (AVIAT) bombardero; **~shell** n (fig) bomba

bond [bɔnd] n (promise) fianza; (FINANCE) bono; (link) vínculo, lazo; (COMM): **in ~** en depósito bajo fianza

bondage ['bɔndɪdʒ] n esclavitud f

bone [bəun] n hueso; (of fish) espina ♦ vt deshuesar; quitar las espinas a; ~ **idle** adj gandul; ~ **marrow** n médula

bonfire ['bɔnfaɪə*] n hoguera, fogata

bonnet ['bɔnɪt] n gorra; (BRIT: of car) capó m

bonus ['bəunəs] n (payment) paga extraordinaria, plus m; (fig) bendición f

bony ['bəunɪ] adj (arm, face) huesudo; (MED: tissue) óseo; (meat) lleno de huesos; (fish) lleno de espinas

boo [bu:] excl ¡uh! ♦ vt abuchear, rechiflar

booby trap ['bu:bɪ-] n trampa explosiva

book [buk] n libro; (of tickets) taco; (of stamps etc) librito ♦ vt (ticket) sacar; (seat, room) reservar; **~s** npl (COMM) cuentas fpl, contabilidad f; **~case** n librería, estante m para libros; **~ing office** n (BRIT: RAIL) despacho de billetes (SP) or boletos (AM); (THEATRE) taquilla (SP), boletería (AM); **~keeping** n contabilidad f; **~let** n folleto; **~maker** n corredor m de apuestas; **~seller** n librero; **~shop, ~ store** n librería

boom [bu:m] n (noise) trueno, estampido; (in prices etc) alza rápida; (ECON, in population) boom m ♦ vi (cannon) hacer gran estruendo, retumbar; (ECON) estar en alza

boon [bu:n] n favor m, beneficio

boost [bu:st] n estímulo, empuje m ♦ vt estimular, empujar; **~er** n (MED) reinyección f

boot [bu:t] n bota; (BRIT: of car) maleta, maletero ♦ vt (COMPUT) arrancar; **to ~** (in addition) además, por añadidura

booth [bu:ð] n (telephone ~, voting ~) cabina

booze [bu:z] (inf) n bebida

border ['bɔ:də*] n borde m, margen m; (of a country) frontera; (for flowers) arriate m ♦ vt (road) bordear; (another country: also: ~ **on**) lindar con; **B~s** n: **the B~s** región fronteriza entre Escocia e Inglaterra; ~ **on** vt fus (insanity etc) rayar en; **~line** n: **on the ~line** en el límite; **~line case** n caso dudoso

bore [bɔ:*] pt of bear ♦ vt (hole) hacer un agujero en; (well) perforar; (person) aburrir ♦ n (person) pelmazo, pesado; (of gun) calibre m; **to be ~d** estar aburrido; **~dom** n aburrimiento

boring ['bɔ:rɪŋ] adj aburrido

born [bɔ:n] adj: **to be ~** nacer; **I was ~ in 1960** nací en 1960

borne [bɔ:n] pp of bear

borough ['bʌrə] n municipio

borrow ['bɔrəu] vt: **to ~ sth (from sb)** tomar algo prestado (a alguien)

Bosnia(-Herzegovina) ['bɔːsnɪə(herzə'gəuvɪːnə)] n Bosnia (-Herzegovina)

bosom ['buzəm] n pecho

boss [bɔs] n jefe m ♦ vt (also: ~ **about** or **around**) mangonear; **~y** adj mandón/ona

bosun ['bəusn] n contramaestre m

botany ['bɔtənɪ] n botánica

botch [bɔtʃ] vt (also: ~ **up**) arruinar, estropear

both [bəuθ] adj, pron ambos/as, los/las dos; ~ **of us went, we ~ went** fuimos los dos, ambos fuimos ♦ adv: ~ **A and B** tanto A como B

bother ['bɔðə*] vt (worry) preocupar; (disturb) molestar, fastidiar ♦ vi (also: ~ o.s.) molestarse ♦ n (trouble) dificultad f; (nuisance) molestia, lata; **to ~ doing** tomarse la molestia de hacer

bottle ['bɒtl] n botella; (small) frasco; (baby's) biberón m ♦ vt embotellar; ~ **up** suprimir; ~ **bank** n contenedor de vidrio; **~neck** n (AUT) embotellamiento; (in supply) obstáculo; **~-opener** n abrebotellas m inv

bottom ['bɒtəm] n (of box, sea) fondo; (buttocks) trasero, culo; (of page) pie m; (of list) final m; (of class) último/a ♦ adj (lowest) más bajo; (last) último

bough [bau] n rama

bought [bɔːt] pt, pp of **buy**

boulder ['bəuldə*] n canto rodado

bounce [bauns] vi (ball) (re)botar; (cheque) ser rechazado ♦ vt hacer (re)botar ♦ n (rebound) (re)bote m; **~r** (inf) n gorila m (que echa a los alborotadores de un bar, club etc)

bound [baund] pt, pp of **bind** ♦ n (leap) salto; (gen pl: limit) límite m ♦ vi (leap) saltar ♦ vt (border) rodear ♦ adj: ~ **by** rodeado de; **to be ~ to do sth** (obliged) tener el deber de hacer algo; **he's ~ to come** es seguro que vendrá; **out of ~s** prohibido el paso; ~ **for** con destino a

boundary ['baundrɪ] n límite m

bouquet ['bukeɪ] n (of flowers) ramo

bourgeois ['buəʒwɑː] adj burgués/esa m/f

bout [baut] n (of malaria etc) ataque m; (of activity) período; (BOXING etc) combate m, encuentro

bow¹ [bau] n (knot) lazo; (weapon, MUS) arco

bow² [bau] n (of the head) reverencia; (NAUT: also: ~s) proa ♦ vi inclinarse, hacer una reverencia; (yield): **to ~ to** or **before** ceder ante, someterse a

bowels [bauəlz] npl intestinos mpl, vientre m; (fig) entrañas fpl

bowl [bəul] n tazón m, cuenco; (ball) bola ♦ vi (CRICKET) arrojar la pelota; see also **bowls**

bow-legged ['bəu'legɪd] adj estevado

bowler ['bəulə*] n (CRICKET) lanzador m (de la pelota); (BRIT: also: ~ **hat**) hongo, bombín m

bowling ['bəulɪŋ] n (game) bochas fpl, bolos mpl; ~ **alley** n bolera; ~ **green** n pista para bochas

bowls [bəulz] n juego de las bochas, bolos mpl

bow tie ['bəu-] n corbata de lazo, pajarita

box [bɒks] n (also: **cardboard** ~) caja, cajón m; (THEATRE) palco ♦ vt encajonar ♦ vi (SPORT) boxear; **~er** ['bɒksə*] n (person) boxeador m; **~ing** ['bɒksɪŋ] n (SPORT) boxeo; **B~ing Day** (BRIT) n día en que se dan los aguinaldos, 26 de diciembre; **~ing gloves** npl guantes mpl de boxeo; **~ing ring** n ring m, cuadrilátero; ~ **office** n taquilla (SP), boletería (AM); **~room** n trastero

boy [bɔɪ] n (young) niño; (older) muchacho, chico; (son) hijo

boycott ['bɔɪkɒt] n boicot m ♦ vt boicotear

boyfriend ['bɔɪfrɛnd] n novio

boyish ['bɔɪɪʃ] adj juvenil; (girl) con aspecto de muchacho

B.R. n abbr (formerly = British Rail) ≈ RENFE f (SP)

bra [brɑː] n sostén m, sujetador m

brace [breɪs] n (BRIT: also: ~s: on teeth) corrector m, aparato; (tool) berbiquí m ♦ vt (knees, shoulders) tensionar; **~s** npl (BRIT) tirantes mpl; **to ~ o.s.** (fig) prepararse

bracelet ['breɪslɪt] n pulsera, brazalete m

bracing ['breɪsɪŋ] adj vigorizante, tónico

bracket ['brækɪt] n (TECH) soporte m, puntal m; (group) clase f, categoría; (also: **brace** ~) soporte m, abrazadera; (also: **round** ~) paréntesis m inv; (also: **square** ~) corchete m ♦ vt (word etc) poner entre paréntesis

brag [bræg] vi jactarse

braid [breɪd] n (trimming) galón m; (of hair) trenza

brain [breɪn] n cerebro; **~s** npl sesos mpl; **she's got ~s** es muy lista; **~wash** vt lavar el cerebro; **~wave** n idea luminosa; **~y** adj muy inteligente

braise [breɪz] vt cocer a fuego lento

brake [breɪk] n (on vehicle) freno ♦ vi frenar; ~ **light** n luz f de frenado

bran [bræn] n salvado

branch [brɑːntʃ] n rama; (COMM) sucursal f; ~ **out** vi (fig) extenderse

brand [brænd] n marca; (fig: type) tipo ♦ vt (cattle) marcar con hierro candente; **~-new** adj flamante, completamente nuevo

brandy ['brændɪ] n coñac m

brash [bræʃ] adj (forward) descarado

brass [brɑːs] n latón m; **the ~** (MUS) los cobres; ~ **band** n banda de metal

brat [bræt] (pej) n mocoso/a

brave [breɪv] adj valiente, valeroso ♦ vt (face up to) desafiar; **~ry** n valor m, valentía

brawl [brɔːl] n pelea, reyerta

brazen ['breɪzn] adj descarado, cínico ♦ vt: **to ~ it out** echarle cara

Brazil [brə'zɪl] n (el) Brasil; **~ian** adj, n brasileño/a m/f

breach [briːtʃ] vt abrir brecha en ♦ n (gap) brecha; (breaking): ~ **of contract** infracción f de contrato; ~ **of the peace** perturbación f del órden público

bread [brɛd] n pan m; ~ **and butter** n pan con mantequilla; (fig) pan (de cada día); **~bin** n panera; **~crumbs** npl migajas fpl; (CULIN) pan rallado; **~line** n: **on the ~line** en la miseria

breadth [brɛtθ] n anchura; (fig) amplitud f

breadwinner ['brɛdwɪnə*] n sustento m de la familia

break [breɪk] (pt **broke**, pp **broken**) vt romper;

(*promise*) faltar a; (*law*) violar, infringir; (*record*) batir ♦ *vi* romperse, quebrarse; (*storm*) estallar; (*weather*) cambiar; (*dawn*) despuntar; (*news etc*) darse a conocer ♦ *n* (*gap*) abertura; (*fracture*) fractura; (*time*) intervalo; (: *at school*) período de recreo; (*chance*) oportunidad *f*; **to ~ the news to sb** comunicar la noticia a uno; **~ down** *vt* (*figures, data*) analizar, descomponer ♦ *vi* (*machine*) estropearse; (*AUT*) averiarse; (*person*) romper a llorar; (*talks*) fracasar; **~ even** *vi* cubrir los gastos; **~ free** or **loose** *vi* escaparse; **~ in** *vt* (*horse etc*) domar ♦ *vi* (*burglar*) forzar una entrada; (*interrupt*) interrumpir; **~ into** *vt fus* (*house*) forzar; **~ off** *vi* (*speaker*) pararse, detenerse; (*branch*) partir; **~ open** *vt* (*door etc*) abrir por la fuerza, forzar; **~ out** *vi* estallar; (*prisoner*) escaparse; **to ~ out in spots** salirle a uno granos; **~ up** *vi* (*ship*) hacerse pedazos; (*crowd, meeting*) disolverse; (*marriage*) deshacerse; (*SCOL*) terminar (el curso) ♦ *vt* (*rocks etc*) partir; (*journey*) partir; (*fight etc*) acabar con; **~age** *n* rotura; **~down** *n* (*AUT*) avería; (*in communications*) interrupción *f*; (*MED: also: nervous ~down*) colapso, crisis *f* nerviosa; (*of marriage, talks*) fracaso; (*of statistics*) análisis *m inv*; **~down van** (*BRIT*) *n* (camión *m*) grúa; **~er** *n* (ola) rompiente *f*

breakfast ['brɛkfəst] *n* desayuno

break: **~-in** *n* robo con allanamiento de morada; **~ing and entering** *n* (*LAW*) violación *f* de domicilio, allanamiento de morada; **~through** *n* (*also fig*) avance *m*; **~water** *n* rompeolas *m inv*

breast [brɛst] *n* (*of woman*) pecho, seno; (*chest*) pecho; (*of bird*) pechuga; **~-feed** (*irreg: like* **feed**) *vt, vi* amamantar, criar a los pechos; **~-stroke** *n* braza de pecho

breath [brɛθ] *n* aliento, respiración *f*; **to take a deep ~** respirar hondo; **out of ~** sin aliento, sofocado

Breathalyser ® ['brɛθəlaɪzə*] (*BRIT*) *n* alcoholímetro *m*

breathe [briːð] *vt, vi* respirar; **~ in** *vt, vi* aspirar; **~ out** *vt, vi* espirar; **~r** *n* respiro; **breathing** *n* respiración *f*

breath: **~less** *adj* sin aliento, jadeante; **~taking** *adj* imponente, pasmoso

breed [briːd] (*pt, pp* **bred**) *vt* criar ♦ *vi* reproducirse, procrear ♦ *n* (*ZOOL*) raza, casta; (*type*) tipo; **~ing** *n* (*of person*) educación *f*

breeze [briːz] *n* brisa

breezy ['briːzɪ] *adj* de mucho viento, ventoso; (*person*) despreocupado

brevity ['brɛvɪtɪ] *n* brevedad *f*

brew [bruː] *vt* (*tea*) hacer; (*beer*) elaborar ♦ *vi* (*fig: trouble*) prepararse; (*storm*) amenazar; **~ery** *n* fábrica de cerveza,

cervecería

bribe [braɪb] *n* soborno ♦ *vt* sobornar, cohechar; **~ry** *n* soborno, cohecho

bric-a-brac ['brɪkəbræk] *n inv* baratijas *fpl*

brick [brɪk] *n* ladrillo; **~layer** *n* albañil *m*

bridal ['braɪdl] *adj* nupcial

bride [braɪd] *n* novia; **~groom** *n* novio; **~smaid** *n* dama de honor

bridge [brɪdʒ] *n* puente *m*; (*NAUT*) puente *m* de mando; (*of nose*) caballete *m*; (*CARDS*) bridge *m* ♦ *vt* (*fig*): **to ~ a gap** llenar un vacío

bridle ['braɪdl] *n* brida, freno; **~ path** *n* camino de herradura

brief [briːf] *adj* breve, corto ♦ *n* (*LAW*) escrito; (*task*) cometido, encargo ♦ *vt* informar; **~s** *npl* (*for men*) calzoncillos *mpl*; (*for women*) bragas *fpl*; **~case** *n* cartera (*SP*), portafolio (*AM*); **~ing** *n* (*PRESS*) informe *m*; **~ly** *adv* (*glance*) fugazmente; (*say*) en pocas palabras

brigadier [brɪgə'dɪə*] *n* general *m* de brigada

bright [braɪt] *adj* brillante; (*room*) luminoso; (*day*) de sol; (*person: clever*) listo, inteligente; (: *lively*) alegre; (*colour*) vivo; (*future*) prometedor(a); **~en** (*also: ~en up*) *vt* (*room*) hacer más alegre; (*event*) alegrar ♦ *vi* (*weather*) despejarse; (*person*) animarse, alegrarse; (*prospects*) mejorar

brilliance ['brɪljəns] *n* brillo, brillantez *f*; (*of talent etc*) brillantez

brilliant ['brɪljənt] *adj* brillante; (*inf*) fenomenal

brim [brɪm] *n* borde *m*; (*of hat*) ala

brine [braɪn] *n* (*CULIN*) salmuera

bring [brɪŋ] (*pt, pp* **brought**) *vt* (*thing, person: with you*) traer; (: *to sb*) llevar, conducir; (*trouble, satisfaction*) causar; **~ about** *vt* ocasionar, producir; **~ back** *vt* volver a traer; (*return*) devolver; **~ down** *vt* (*government, plane*) derribar; (*price*) rebajar; **~ forward** *vt* adelantar; **~ off** *vt* (*task, plan*) lograr, conseguir; **~ out** *vt* sacar; (*book etc*) publicar; (*meaning*) subrayar; **~ round** *vt* (*unconscious person*) hacer volver en sí; **~ up** *vt* subir; (*person*) educar, criar; (*question*) sacar a colación; (*food: vomit*) devolver, vomitar

brink [brɪŋk] *n* borde *m*

brisk [brɪsk] *adj* (*abrupt: tone*) brusco; (*person*) enérgico, vigoroso; (*pace*) rápido; (*trade*) activo

bristle ['brɪsl] *n* cerda ♦ *vi*: **to ~ in anger** temblar de rabia

Britain ['brɪtən] *n* (*also: Great ~*) Gran Bretaña

British ['brɪtɪʃ] *adj* británico ♦ *npl*: **the ~** los británicos; **~ Isles** *npl*: **the ~ Isles** las Islas Británicas; **~ Rail** *n* ≈ RENFE *f* (*SP*)

Briton ['brɪtən] *n* británico/a

brittle ['brɪtl] *adj* quebradizo, frágil

broach [brəʊtʃ] vt (subject) abordar

broad [brɔːd] adj ancho; (range) amplio; (smile) abierto; (general: outlines etc) general; (accent) cerrado; **in ~ daylight** en pleno día; **~cast** (irreg: like **cast**) n emisión f ♦ vt (RADIO) emitir; (TV) transmitir ♦ vi emitir; transmitir; **~en** vt ampliar ♦ vi ensancharse; **to ~en one's mind** hacer más tolerante a uno; **~ly** adv en general; **~-minded** adj tolerante, liberal

broccoli ['brɒkəlɪ] n brécol m

brochure ['brəʊʃjʊə*] n folleto

broil [brɔɪl] vt (CULIN) asar a la parrilla

broke [brəʊk] pt of **break** ♦ adj (inf) pelado, sin blanca

broken ['brəʊkən] pp of **break** ♦ adj roto; (machine: also: ~ **down**) averiado; **~ leg** pierna rota; **in ~ English** en un inglés imperfecto; **~-hearted** adj con el corazón partido

broker ['brəʊkə*] n agente m/f, bolsista m/f; (insurance ~) agente de seguros

brolly ['brɒlɪ] (BRIT: inf) n paraguas m inv

bronchitis [brɒŋ'kaɪtɪs] n bronquitis f

bronze [brɒnz] n bronce m

brooch [brəʊtʃ] n prendedor m, broche m

brood [bruːd] n camada, cría ♦ vi (person) dejarse obsesionar

broom [brum] n escoba; (BOT) retama

Bros. abbr (= Brothers) Hnos

broth [brɒθ] n caldo

brothel ['brɒθl] n burdel m

brother ['brʌðə*] n hermano; **~-in-law** n cuñado

brought [brɔːt] pt, pp of **bring**

brow [brau] n (forehead) frente m; (eye~) ceja; (of hill) cumbre f

brown [braun] adj (colour) marrón; (hair) castaño; (tanned) bronceado, moreno ♦ n (colour) color m marrón or pardo ♦ vt (CULIN) dorar; **~ bread** n pan integral

Brownie ['braunɪ] n niña exploradora; **b~** (US: cake) pastel de chocolate con nueces

brown paper n papel m de estraza

brown sugar n azúcar m terciado

browse [brauz] vi (through book) hojear; (in shop) mirar; **~r** n (COMPUT) navegador m

bruise [bruːz] n cardenal m (SP), moretón m (AM) ♦ vt magullar

brunch [brʌntʃ] n desayuno-almuerzo

brunette [bruː'net] n morena

brunt [brʌnt] n: **to bear the ~ of** llevar el peso de

brush [brʌʃ] n cepillo; (for painting, shaving etc) brocha; (artist's) pincel m; (with police etc) roce m ♦ vt (sweep) barrer; (groom) cepillar; (also: ~ **against**) rozar al pasar; **~ aside** vt rechazar, no hacer caso a; **~ up**

vt (knowledge) repasar, refrescar; **~wood** n (sticks) leña

Brussels ['brʌslz] n Bruselas; **~ sprout** n col f de Bruselas

brute [bruːt] n bruto; (person) bestia ♦ adj: **by ~ force** a fuerza bruta

B.Sc. abbr (= Bachelor of Science) licenciado en Ciencias

BSE n abbr (= bovine spongiform encephalopathy) encefalopatía espongiforme bovina

bubble ['bʌbl] n burbuja ♦ vi burbujear, borbotar; **~ bath** n espuma para el baño; **~ gum** n chicle m de globo

buck [bʌk] n (rabbit) conejo macho; (deer) gamo; (US: inf) dólar m ♦ vi corcovear; **to pass the ~ (to sb)** echar (a uno) el muerto; **~ up** vi (cheer up) animarse, cobrar ánimo

bucket ['bʌkɪt] n cubo, balde m

buckle ['bʌkl] n hebilla ♦ vt abrochar con hebilla ♦ vi combarse

bud [bʌd] n (of plant) brote m, yema; (of flower) capullo ♦ vi brotar, echar brotes

Buddhism ['bʊdɪzm] n Budismo

budding ['bʌdɪŋ] adj en ciernes, en embrión

buddy ['bʌdɪ] (US) n compañero, compinche m

budge [bʌdʒ] vt mover; (fig) hacer ceder ♦ vi moverse, ceder

budgerigar ['bʌdʒərɪgɑː*] n periquito

budget ['bʌdʒɪt] n presupuesto ♦ vi: **to ~ for sth** presupuestar algo

budgie ['bʌdʒɪ] n = **budgerigar**

buff [bʌf] adj (colour) color de ante ♦ n (inf: enthusiast) entusiasta m/f

buffalo ['bʌfələu] (pl ~ or ~es) n (BRIT) búfalo; (US: bison) bisonte m

buffer ['bʌfə*] n (COMPUT) memoria intermedia; (RAIL) tope m

buffet[1] ['bufeɪ] n (BRIT: in station) bar m, cafetería; (food) buffet m; **~ car** (BRIT) n (RAIL) coche-comedor m

buffet[2] ['bʌfɪt] vt golpear

bug [bʌg] n (esp US: insect) bicho, sabandija; (COMPUT) error m; (germ) microbio, bacilo; (spy device) micrófono oculto ♦ vt (inf: annoy) fastidiar; (room) poner micrófono oculto en

buggy ['bʌgɪ] n cochecito de niño

bugle ['bjuːgl] n corneta, clarín m

build [bɪld] (pt, pp **built**) n (of person) tipo ♦ vt construir, edificar; **~ up** vt (morale, forces, production) acrecentar; (stocks) acumular; **~er** n (contractor) contratista m/f; **~ing** n construcción f; (structure) edificio; **~ing society** (BRIT) n sociedad f inmobiliaria

built [bɪlt] pt, pp of **build** ♦ adj: **~-in** (wardrobe etc) empotrado; **~-up area** n zona urbanizada

233

bulb [bʌlb] n (BOT) bulbo; (ELEC) bombilla (SP), foco (AM)

Bulgaria [bʌl'geərɪə] n Bulgaria; **~n** adj, n búlgaro/a m/f

bulge [bʌldʒ] n bulto, protuberancia ♦ vi bombearse, pandearse; (pocket etc): **to ~ (with)** rebosar (de)

bulk [bʌlk] n masa, mole f; **in ~** (COMM) a granel; **the ~ of** la mayor parte de; **~y** adj voluminoso, abultado

bull [bul] n toro; (male elephant, whale) macho; **~dog** n dogo

bulldozer ['buldəuzə*] n bulldozer m

bullet ['bulɪt] n bala

bulletin ['bulɪtɪn] n anuncio, parte m; (journal) boletín m; **~ board** n (US) tablón m de anuncios; (COMPUT) tablero de noticias

bulletproof ['bulɪtpruːf] adj a prueba de balas

bullfight ['bulfaɪt] n corrida de toros; **~er** n torero; **~ing** n los toros, el toreo

bullion ['buljən] n oro (or plata) en barras

bullock ['bulək] n novillo

bullring ['bulrɪŋ] n plaza de toros

bull's-eye n centro del blanco

bully ['bulɪ] n valentón m, matón m ♦ vt intimidar, tiranizar

bum [bʌm] n (inf: backside) culo; (esp US: tramp) vagabundo

bumblebee ['bʌmblbiː] n abejorro

bump [bʌmp] n (blow) tope m, choque m; (jolt) sacudida; (on road etc) bache m; (on head etc) chichón m ♦ vt (strike) chocar contra; **~ into** vt fus chocar contra, tropezar con; (person) topar con; **~er** n (AUT) parachoques m inv ♦ adj: **~er crop/harvest** cosecha abundante; **~er cars** npl coches mpl de choque; **~y** adj (road) lleno de baches

bun [bʌn] n (BRIT: cake) pastel m; (US: bread) bollo; (of hair) moño

bunch [bʌntʃ] n (of flowers) ramo; (of keys) manojo; (of bananas) piña; (of people) grupo; (pej) pandilla; **~es** npl (in hair) coletas fpl

bundle ['bʌndl] n bulto, fardo; (of sticks) haz m; (of papers) legajo ♦ vt (also: **~ up**) atar, envolver; **to ~ sth/sb into** meter algo/a alguien precipitadamente en

bungalow ['bʌŋgələu] n bungalow m, chalé m

bungle ['bʌŋgl] vt hacer mal

bunion ['bʌnjən] n juanete m

bunk [bʌŋk] n litera; **~ beds** npl literas fpl

bunker ['bʌŋkə*] n (coal store) carbonera; (MIL) refugio; (GOLF) bunker m

bunny ['bʌnɪ] n (also: **~ rabbit**) conejito

buoy [bɔɪ] n boya; **~ant** adj (ship) capaz de flotar; (economy) boyante; (person) optimista

burden ['bɔːdn] n carga ♦ vt cargar

bureau [bjuə'rəu] (pl **bureaux**) n (BRIT: writing desk) escritorio, buró m; (US: chest of drawers) cómoda; (office) oficina, agencia

bureaucracy [bjuə'rɔkrəsɪ] n burocracia

burglar ['bɜːglə*] n ladrón/ona m/f; **~ alarm** n alarma f antirrobo; **~y** n robo con allanamiento, robo de una casa

burial ['berɪəl] n entierro

burly ['bɜːlɪ] adj fornido, membrudo

Burma ['bɜːmə] n Birmania

burn [bɜːn] (pt, pp **burned** or **burnt**) vt quemar; (house) incendiar ♦ vi quemarse, arder; incendiarse; (sting) escocer ♦ n quemadura; **~ down** vt incendiar; **~er** n (on cooker etc) quemador m; **~ing** adj (building etc) en llamas; (hot: sand etc) abrasador(a); (ambition) ardiente

burrow ['bʌrəu] n madriguera ♦ vi hacer una madriguera; (rummage) hurgar

bursary ['bɜːsərɪ] (BRIT) n beca

burst [bɜːst] (pt, pp **burst**) vt reventar; (subj: river: banks etc) romper ♦ vi reventarse; (tyre) pincharse ♦ n (of gunfire) ráfaga; (also: **~ pipe**) reventón m; **a ~ of energy/speed/enthusiasm** una explosión de energía/un ímpetu de velocidad/un arranque de entusiasmo; **to ~ into flames** estallar en llamas; **to ~ into tears** deshacerse en lágrimas; **to ~ out laughing** soltar la carcajada; **to ~ open** abrirse de golpe; **to be ~ing with** (subj: container) estar lleno a rebosar de; (person) reventar por or de; **~ into** vt fus (room etc) irrumpir en

bury ['berɪ] vt enterrar; (body) enterrar, sepultar

bus [bʌs] (pl **~es**) n autobús m

bush [buʃ] n arbusto; (scrub land) monte m; **to beat about the ~** andar(se) con rodeos

bushy [buʃɪ] adj (thick) espeso, poblado

busily ['bɪzɪlɪ] adv afanosamente

business ['bɪznɪs] n (matter) asunto; (trading) comercio, negocios mpl; (firm) empresa, casa; (occupation) oficio; **to be away on ~** estar en viaje de negocios; **it's my ~ to ...** me toca or corresponde ...; **it's none of my ~** yo no tengo nada que ver; **he means ~** habla en serio; **~like** adj eficiente; **~man** hombre m de negocios; **~ trip** n viaje m de negocios; **~woman** n mujer f de negocios

busker ['bʌskə*] (BRIT) n músico/a ambulante

bus: ~ shelter n parada cubierta; **~ station** n estación f de autobuses; **~-stop** n parada de autobús

bust [bʌst] n (ANAT) pecho; (sculpture) busto ♦ adj (inf: broken) roto, estropeado; **to go ~** quebrar

bustle ['bʌsl] n bullicio, movimiento ♦ vi menearse, apresurarse; **bustling** adj (town) animado, bullicioso

busy ['bɪzɪ] *adj* ocupado, atareado; (*shop, street*) concurrido, animado; (*TEL: line*) comunicando ♦ *vt:* **to ~ o.s. with** ocuparse en; **~body** *n* entrometido/a; **~ signal** (*US*) *n* (*TEL*) señal *f* de comunicando

KEYWORD

but [bʌt] *conj* **1** pero; **he's not very bright, ~ he's hard-working** no es muy inteligente, pero es trabajador

2 (*in direct contradiction*) sino; **he's not English ~ French** no es inglés sino francés; **he didn't sing ~ he shouted** no cantó sino que gritó **3** (*showing disagreement, surprise etc*): **~ that's far too expensive!** ¡pero eso es carísimo!; **~ it does work!** ¡(pero) sí que funciona!

♦ *prep* (*apart from, except*) menos, salvo; **we've had nothing ~ trouble** no hemos tenido más que problemas; **no-one ~ him can do it** nadie más que él puede hacerlo; **who ~ a lunatic would do such a thing?** ¿sólo un loco haría una cosa así?; **~ for you/your help** si no fuera por ti/tu ayuda; **anything ~ that** cualquier cosa menos eso

♦ *adv* (*just, only*): **she's ~ a child** no es más que una niña; **had I ~ known** si lo hubiera sabido; **I can ~ try** al menos lo puedo intentar; **it's all ~ finished** está casi acabado

butcher ['bʊtʃə*] *n* carnicero ♦ *vt* hacer una carnicería con; (*cattle etc*) matar; **~'s (shop)** *n* carnicería

butler ['bʌtlə*] *n* mayordomo

butt [bʌt] *n* (*barrel*) tonel *m*; (*of gun*) culata; (*of cigarette*) colilla; (*BRIT: fig: target*) blanco ♦ *vt* dar cabezadas contra, top(et)ar; **~ in** *vi* (*interrupt*) interrumpir

butter ['bʌtə*] *n* mantequilla ♦ *vt* untar con mantequilla; **~cup** *n* botón *m* de oro

butterfly ['bʌtəflaɪ] *n* mariposa; (*SWIMMING: also: ~ stroke*) braza de mariposa

buttocks ['bʌtəks] *npl* nalgas *fpl*

button ['bʌtn] *n* botón *m*; (*US*) placa, chapa ♦ *vt* (*also: ~ up*) abotonar, abrochar ♦ *vi* abrocharse

buttress ['bʌtrɪs] *n* contrafuerte *m*

buy [baɪ] (*pt, pp bought*) *vt* comprar ♦ *n* compra; **to ~ sb sth/sth from sb** comprarle algo a alguien; **to ~ sb a drink** invitar a alguien a tomar algo; **~er** *n* comprador(a) *m/f*

buzz [bʌz] *n* zumbido; (*inf: phone call*) llamada (por teléfono) ♦ *vi* zumbar; **~er** *n* timbre *m*; **~ word** *n* palabra que está de moda

KEYWORD

by [baɪ] *prep* **1** (*referring to cause, agent*) por; de; **killed ~ lightning** muerto por un relámpago; **a painting ~ Picasso** un cuadro de Picasso

2 (*referring to method, manner, means*): **~ bus/car/train** en autobús/coche/tren; **to pay ~ cheque** pagar con un cheque; **~ moonlight/candlelight** a la luz de la luna/ una vela; **~ saving hard, he ...** ahorrando, ...

3 (*via, through*) por; **we came ~ Dover** vinimos por Dover

4 (*close to, past*): **the house ~ the river** la casa junto al río; **she rushed ~ me** pasó a mi lado como una exhalación; **I go ~ the post office every day** paso por delante de Correos todos los días

5 (*time: not later than*) para; (: *during*): **~ daylight** de día; **~ 4 o'clock** para las cuatro; **~ this time tomorrow** mañana a estas horas; **~ the time I got here it was too late** cuando llegué ya era demasiado tarde

6 (*amount*): **~ the metre/kilo** por metro/kilo; **paid ~ the hour** pagado por hora

7 (*MATH, measure*): **to divide/multiply ~ 3** dividir/multiplicar por 3; **a room 3 metres ~ 4** una habitación de 3 metros por 4; **it's broader ~ a metre** es un metro más ancho

8 (*according to*) según, de acuerdo con; **it's 3 o'clock ~ my watch** según mi reloj, son las tres; **it's all right ~ me** por mí, está bien

9: (*all*) **~ oneself** *etc* todo solo; **he did it (all) ~ himself** lo hizo él solo; **he was standing (all) ~ himself in a corner** estaba de pie solo en un rincón

10: **~ the way** a propósito, por cierto; **this wasn't my idea, ~ the way** pues, no fue idea mía

♦ *adv* **1** *see* **go; pass** *etc*

2: **~ and ~** finalmente; **they'll come back ~ and ~** acabarán volviendo; **~ and large** en líneas generales, en general

bye(-bye) ['baɪ('baɪ)] *excl* adiós, hasta luego

by(e)-law *n* ordenanza municipal

by-: ~election (*BRIT*) *n* elección *f* parcial; **~gone** ['baɪɡɔn] *adj* pasado, del pasado ♦ *n*: **let ~gones be ~gones** lo pasado, pasado está; **~pass** ['baɪpɑːs] *n* carretera de circunvalación; (*MED*) (operación *f* de) by-pass *m* ♦ *vt* evitar; **~product** *n* subproducto, derivado; (*of situation*) consecuencia; **~stander** ['baɪstændə*] *n* espectador(a) *m/f*

byte [baɪt] *n* (*COMPUT*) byte *m*, octeto

byword ['baɪwəːd] *n*: **to be a ~ for** ser conocidísimo por

C, c

C [siː] *n* (MUS) do *m*

C. *abbr* (= *centigrade*) C.

C.A. *abbr* = **chartered accountant**

cab [kæb] *n* taxi *m*; (*of truck*) cabina

cabbage [ˈkæbɪdʒ] *n* col *f*, berza

cabin [ˈkæbɪn] *n* cabaña; (*on ship*) camarote *m*; (*on plane*) cabina; ~ **crew** *n* tripulación *f* de cabina; ~ **cruiser** *n* yate *m* de motor

cabinet [ˈkæbɪnɪt] *n* (POL) consejo de ministros; (*furniture*) armario; (*also: display* ~) vitrina

cable [ˈkeɪbl] *n* cable *m* ♦ *vt* cablegrafiar; ~-**car** *n* teleférico; ~ **television** *n* televisión *f* por cable

cache [kæʃ] *n* (*of arms, drugs etc*) alijo

cackle [ˈkækl] *vi* lanzar risotadas; (*hen*) cacarear

cactus [ˈkæktəs] (*pl* **cacti**) *n* cacto

cadge [kædʒ] (*inf*) *vt* gorronear

Caesarean [siːˈzɛərɪən] *adj*: ~ (**section**) cesárea

café [ˈkæfeɪ] *n* café *m*

cafeteria [kæfɪˈtɪərɪə] *n* cafetería

cage [keɪdʒ] *n* jaula

cagey [ˈkeɪdʒɪ] (*inf*) *adj* cauteloso, reservado

cagoule [kəˈɡuːl] *n* chubasquero

cajole [kəˈdʒəul] *vt* engatusar

cake [keɪk] *n* (CULIN: *large*) tarta; (: *small*) pastel *m*; (*of soap*) pastilla; ~**d** *adj*: ~**d with** cubierto de

calculate [ˈkælkjuleɪt] *vt* calcular; **calculation** [-ˈleɪʃən] *n* cálculo, cómputo; **calculator** *n* calculadora

calendar [ˈkæləndə*] *n* calendario; ~ **month/year** *n* mes *m*/año civil

calf [kɑːf] (*pl* **calves**) *n* (*of cow*) ternero, becerro; (*of other animals*) cría; (*also:* ~skin) piel *f* de becerro; (ANAT) pantorrilla

calibre [ˈkælɪbə*] (US **caliber**) *n* calibre *m*

call [kɔːl] *vt* llamar; (*meeting*) convocar ♦ *vi* (*shout*) llamar; (TEL) llamar (por teléfono), telefonear (*esp* AM); (*visit: also:* ~ **in**, ~ **round**) hacer una visita ♦ *n* llamada; (*of bird*) canto; **to be ~ed** llamarse; **on** ~ (*on duty*) de guardia; ~ **back** *vi* (*return*) volver; (TEL) volver a llamar; ~ **for** *vt fus* (*demand*) pedir, exigir; (*fetch*) venir por (SP), pasar por (AM); ~ **off** *vt* (*cancel: meeting, race*) cancelar; (: *deal*) anular; (: *strike*) desconvocar; ~ **on** *vt fus* (*visit*) visitar; (*turn to*) acudir a; ~ **out** *vi* gritar; ~ **up** *vt* (MIL) llamar al servicio militar; (TEL) llamar; ~**box** (BRIT) *n* cabina telefónica; ~ **centre** *n* (BRIT) centro de llamadas; ~**er** *n* visita; (TEL) usuario/a; ~ **girl** *n* prostituta; ~-**in** (US) *n*

(*programa m*) coloquio (por teléfono); ~**ing** *n* vocación *f*; (*occupation*) profesión *f*; ~**ing card** (US) *n* tarjeta de visita

callous [ˈkæləs] *adj* insensible, cruel

calm [kɑːm] *adj* tranquilo; (*sea*) liso, en calma ♦ *n* calma, tranquilidad *f* ♦ *vt* calmar, tranquilizar; ~ **down** *vi* calmarse, tranquilizarse ♦ *vt* calmar, tranquilizar

Calor gas ® [ˈkælə*-] *n* butano

calorie [ˈkælərɪ] *n* caloría

calves [kɑːvz] *npl of* **calf**

Cambodia [kæmˈbəudjə] *n* Camboya

camcorder [ˈkæmkɔːdə*] *n* videocámara

came [keɪm] *pt of* **come**

camel [ˈkæməl] *n* camello

camera [ˈkæmərə] *n* máquina fotográfica; (CINEMA, TV) cámara; **in** ~ (LAW) a puerta cerrada; ~**man** *n* cámara *m*

camouflage [ˈkæməflɑːʒ] *n* camuflaje *m* ♦ *vt* camuflar

camp [kæmp] *n* campamento, camping *m*; (MIL) campamento; (*for prisoners*) campo; (*fig: faction*) bando ♦ *vi* acampar ♦ *adj* afectado, afeminado

campaign [kæmˈpeɪn] *n* (MIL, POL *etc*) campaña ♦ *vi* hacer campaña

camp: ~**bed** (BRIT) *n* cama de campaña; ~**er** *n* campista *m/f*; (*vehicle*) caravana; ~**ing** *n* camping *m*; **to go** ~**ing** hacer camping; ~**site** *n* camping *m*

campus [ˈkæmpəs] *n* ciudad *f* universitaria

can¹ [kæn] *n* (*of oil, water*) bidón *m*; (*tin*) lata, bote *m* ♦ *vt* enlatar

KEYWORD

can² [kæn] (*negative* **cannot, can't**; *conditional and pt* **could**) *aux vb* **1** (*be able to*) poder; **you ~ do it if you try** puedes hacerlo si lo intentas; **I ~'t see you** no te veo

2 (*know how to*) saber; **I ~ swim/play tennis/ drive** sé nadar/jugar al tenis/conducir; ~ **you speak French?** ¿hablas *or* sabes hablar francés?

3 (*may*) poder; ~ **I use your phone?** ¿me dejas *or* puedo usar tu teléfono?

4 (*expressing disbelief, puzzlement etc*): **it ~'t be true!** ¡no puede ser (verdad)!; **what** CAN **he want?** ¿qué querrá?

5 (*expressing possibility, suggestion etc*): **he could be in the library** podría estar en la biblioteca; **she could have been delayed** pudo haberse retrasado

Canada [ˈkænədə] *n* (el) Canadá; **Canadian** [kəˈneɪdɪən] *adj*, *n* canadiense *m/f*

canal [kəˈnæl] *n* canal *m*

canary [kəˈnɛərɪ] *n* canario; **the C~ Islands** *npl* las (Islas) Canarias

cancel [ˈkænsəl] *vt* cancelar; (*train*) suprimir;

(cross out) tachar, borrar; **~lation** |-'leɪʃən] n cancelación f; supresión f

cancer ['kænsə*] n cáncer m; **C~** (ASTROLOGY) Cáncer m

candid ['kændɪd] adj franco, abierto

candidate ['kændɪdeɪt] n candidato/a

candle ['kændl] n vela; (in church) cirio; **~light** n: **by ~light** a la luz de una vela; **~stick** n (single) candelero; (low) palmatoria; (bigger, ornate) candelabro

candour ['kændə*] (US candor) n franqueza

candy ['kændɪ] n azúcar m cande; (US) caramelo; **~floss** (BRIT) n algodón m (azucarado)

cane [keɪn] n (BOT) caña; (stick) vara, palmeta; (for furniture) mimbre f ♦ (BRIT) vt (SCOL) castigar (con vara)

canister ['kænɪstə*] n bote m, lata, de lata bombona

cannabis ['kænəbɪs] n marijuana

canned [kænd] adj en lata, de lata

cannon ['kænən] (pl ~ or ~s) n cañón m

cannot ['kænɔt] = **can not**

canoe [kə'nu:] n canoa; (SPORT) piragua; **~ing** n piragüismo

canon ['kænən] n (clergyman) canónigo; (standard) canon m

can-opener n abrelatas m inv

canopy ['kænəpɪ] n dosel m; toldo

can't [kænt] = **can not**

canteen [kæn'ti:n] n (eating place) cantina; (BRIT: of cutlery) juego

canter ['kæntə*] vi ir a medio galope

canvas ['kænvəs] n (material) lona; (painting) lienzo, (NAUT) velas fpl

canvass ['kænvəs] vi (POL): **to ~ for** solicitar votos por ♦ vt (COMM) sondear

canyon ['kænjən] n cañón m

cap [kæp] n (hat) gorra; (of pen) capuchón m; (of bottle) tapa, tapón m; (contraceptive) diafragma m; (for toy gun) cápsula ♦ vt (outdo) superar; (limit) recortar

capability [keɪpə'bɪlɪtɪ] n capacidad f

capable ['keɪpəbl] adj capaz

capacity [kə'pæsɪtɪ] n capacidad f; (position) calidad f

cape [keɪp] n capa; (GEO) cabo

caper ['keɪpə*] n (CULIN: gen: ~s) alcaparra; (prank) broma

capital ['kæpɪtl] n (also: ~ city) capital f; (money) capital m; (also: ~ letter) mayúscula; **~ gains tax** n impuesto sobre las ganancias de capital; **~ism** n capitalismo; **~ist** adj, n capitalista m/f; **~ize on** vt fus aprovechar; **~ punishment** n pena de muerte

Capricorn ['kæprɪkɔ:n] n (ASTROLOGY) Capricornio

capsize [kæp'saɪz] vt volcar, hacer zozobrar ♦ vi volcarse, zozobrar

capsule ['kæpsju:l] n cápsula

captain ['kæptɪn] n capitán m

caption ['kæpʃən] n (heading) título; (to picture) leyenda

captive ['kæptɪv] adj, n cautivo/a m/f

capture ['kæptʃə*] vt prender, apresar; (animal, COMPUT) capturar; (place) tomar; (attention) captar, llamar ♦ n apresamiento; captura; toma; (data ~) formulación f de datos

car [kɑ:*] n coche m, carro (AM), automóvil m; (US: RAIL) vagón m

carafe [kə'ræf] n jarra

carat ['kærət] n quilate m

caravan ['kærəvæn] n (BRIT) caravana, ruló f; (in desert) caravana; **~ning** n: **to go ~ning** ir de vacaciones en caravana, viajar en caravana; **~ site** (BRIT) n camping m para caravanas

carbohydrate [kɑ:bəu'haɪdreɪt] n hidrato de carbono; (food) fécula

carbon ['kɑ:bən] n carbono; **~ paper** n papel m carbón

car boot sale n mercadillo organizado en un aparcamiento, en el que se exponen las mercancías en el maletero del coche

carburettor [kɑ:bju'retə*] (US carburetor) n carburador m

card [kɑ:d] n (material) cartulina; (index ~ etc) ficha; (playing ~) carta, naipe m; (visiting ~, greetings ~ etc) tarjeta; **~board** n cartón m

cardiac ['kɑ:dɪæk] adj cardíaco

cardigan ['kɑ:dɪgən] n rebeca

cardinal ['kɑ:dɪnl] adj cardinal; (importance, principal) esencial ♦ n cardenal m

card index n fichero

care [keə*] n cuidado; (worry) inquietud f; (charge) cargo, custodia ♦ vi: **to ~ about** (person, animal, thing, idea) preocuparse por; **~ of** en casa de, al cuidado de; **in sb's ~** a cargo de uno; **to take ~** to cuidarse de, tener cuidado de; **to take ~ of** cuidar; (problem etc) ocuparse de; **I don't ~** no me importa; **I couldn't ~ less** eso me trae sin cuidado; **~ for** vt fus cuidar a; (like) querer

career [kə'rɪə*] n profesión f; (in work, school) carrera ♦ vi (also: ~ along) correr a toda velocidad; **~ woman** n mujer f dedicada a su profesión

care: ~free adj despreocupado; **~ful** adj cuidadoso; (cautious) cauteloso; **(be) ~ful!** ¡tenga cuidado!; **~fully** adv con cuidado, cuidadosamente; con cautela; **~less** adj descuidado; (heedless) poco atento; **~lessness** n descuido; falta de atención; **~r** ['keərə*] n enfermero/a m/f (official); (unpaid) persona que cuida a un pariente o vecino

caress [kə'rɛs] n caricia ♦ vt acariciar

caretaker ['kɛəteɪkə*] n portero/a, conserje m/f

car-ferry n transbordador m para coches

cargo ['kɑ:gəu] (pl ~es) n cargamento, carga

car hire n alquiler m de automóviles

Caribbean [kærɪ'bi:ən] n: **the ~ (Sea)** el (Mar) Caribe

caring ['kɛərɪŋ] adj humanitario; (behaviour) afectuoso

carnation [kɑ:'neɪʃən] n clavel m

carnival ['kɑ:nɪvəl] n carnaval m; (US: funfair) parque m de atracciones

carol ['kærəl] n: **(Christmas) ~** villancico

carp [kɑ:p] n (fish) carpa

car park (BRIT) n aparcamiento, parking m

carpenter ['kɑ:pɪntə*] n carpintero/a

carpet ['kɑ:pɪt] n alfombra; (fitted) moqueta ♦ vt alfombrar

car phone n teléfono movil

car rental (US) n alquiler m de coches

carriage ['kærɪdʒ] n (BRIT: RAIL) vagón m; (horse-drawn) coche m; (of goods) transporte m; (: cost) porte m, flete m; **~way** (BRIT) n (part of road) calzada

carrier ['kærɪə*] n (transport company) transportista, empresa de transportes; (MED) portador m; **~ bag** (BRIT) n bolsa de papel or plástico

carrot ['kærət] n zanahoria

carry ['kærɪ] vt (subj: person) llevar; (transport) transportar; (involve: responsibilities etc) entrañar, implicar; (MED) ser portador de ♦ vi (sound) oírse; **to get carried away** (fig) entusiasmarse; **~ on** vi (continue) seguir (adelante), continuar ♦ vt proseguir, continuar; **~ out** vt (orders) cumplir; (investigation) llevar a cabo, realizar; **~ cot** (BRIT) n cuna portátil; **~-on** (inf) n (fuss) lío

cart [kɑ:t] n carro, carreta ♦ vt (inf: transport) acarrear

carton ['kɑ:tən] n (box) caja (de cartón); (of milk etc) bote m; (of yogurt) tarrina

cartoon [kɑ:'tu:n] n (PRESS) caricatura; (comic strip) tira cómica; (film) dibujos mpl animados

cartridge ['kɑ:trɪdʒ] n cartucho; (of pen) recambio; (of record player) cápsula

carve [kɑ:v] vt (meat) trinchar; (wood, stone) cincelar, esculpir; (initials etc) grabar; **~ up** vt dividir, repartir; **carving** n (object) escultura; (design) talla; (art) tallado; **carving knife** n trinchante m

car wash n lavado de coches

case [keɪs] n (container) caja; (MED) caso; (for jewels etc) estuche m; (LAW) causa, proceso; (BRIT: also: suit~) maleta; **in ~ of** en caso de;

in any ~ en todo caso; **just in ~** por si acaso

cash [kæʃ] n dinero en efectivo, dinero contante ♦ vt cobrar, hacer efectivo; **to pay (in) ~** pagar al contado; **~ on delivery** cóbrese al entregar; **~book** n libro de caja; **~ card** n tarjeta f dinero; **~ desk** (BRIT) n caja; **~ dispenser** n cajero automático

cashew [kæ'fu:] n (also: **~ nut**) anacardo

cash flow n flujo de fondos, cash-flow m

cashier [kæ'fɪə*] n cajero/a

cashmere ['kæʃmɪə*] n cachemira

cash register n caja

casing ['keɪsɪŋ] n revestimiento

casino [kə'si:nəu] n casino

casket ['kɑ:skɪt] n cofre m, estuche m; (US: coffin) ataúd m

casserole ['kæsərəul] n (food, pot) cazuela

cassette [kæ'sɛt] n cassette f; **~ player/recorder** n tocacassettes m inv, cassette m

cast [kɑ:st] (pt, pp cast) vt (throw) echar, arrojar, lanzar; (glance, eyes) dirigir; (THEATRE): **to ~ sb as Othello** dar a uno el papel de Otelo ♦ vi (FISHING) lanzar ♦ n (THEATRE) reparto; (also: plaster ~) vaciado; **to ~ one's vote** votar; **to ~ doubt on** suscitar dudas acerca de; **~ off** vi (NAUT) desamarrar; (KNITTING) cerrar (los puntos); **~ on** vi (KNITTING) poner los puntos

castanets [kæstə'nɛts] npl castañuelas fpl

castaway ['kɑ:stəweɪ] n náufrago/a

caster sugar ['kɑ:stə*-] (BRIT) n azúcar m extrafino

Castile [kæs'ti:l] n Castilla; **Castilian** adj, n castellano/a m/f

casting vote ['kɑ:stɪŋ-] (BRIT) n voto decisivo

cast iron n hierro fundido

castle ['kɑ:sl] n castillo; (CHESS) torre f

castor oil ['kɑ:stə*-] n aceite m de ricino

casual ['kæʒjul] adj fortuito; (irregular: work etc) eventual, temporero; (unconcerned) despreocupado; (clothes) de sport; **~ly** adv de manera despreocupada; (dress) de sport

casualty ['kæʒjultɪ] n víctima, herido; (dead) muerto; (MED: department) urgencias fpl

cat [kæt] n gato; (big ~) felino

Catalan ['kætəlæn] adj, n catalán/ana m/f

catalogue ['kætələg] (US catalog) n catálogo ♦ vt catalogar

Catalonia [kætə'ləunɪə] n Cataluña

catalyst ['kætəlɪst] n catalizador m

catalytic convertor [kætə'lɪtɪk kən'vɜ:tə*] n catalizador m

catapult ['kætəpʌlt] n tirachinas m inv

catarrh [kə'tɑ:*] n catarro

catastrophe [kə'tæstrəfɪ] n catástrofe f

catch [kætʃ] (pt, pp caught) vt coger (SP), agarrar (AM); (arrest) detener; (grasp) asir; (breath) contener; (surprise: person)

sorprender; (attract: attention) captar; (hear)
oír; (MED) contagiarse de, coger; (also: ~ up)
alcanzar ♦ vi (fire) encenderse; (in branches
etc) enredarse ♦ n (fish etc) pesca; (act of
catching) cogida; (hidden problem) dificultad
f; (game) pilla-pilla; (of lock) pestillo,
cerradura; **to ~ fire** encenderse; **to ~ sight of**
divisar; **~ on** vi (understand) caer en la
cuenta; (grow popular) hacerse popular; **~
up** vi (fig) ponerse al día; **~ing** ['kætʃɪŋ] adj
(MED) contagioso; **~ment area** ['kætʃmənt-]
(BRIT) n zona de captación; **~phrase**
['kætʃfreɪz] n lema, eslogan m; **~y** ['kætʃɪ]
adj (tune) pegadizo

category ['kætɪɡərɪ] n categoría, clase f

cater ['keɪtə*] vi: **to ~ for** (BRIT) abastecer a;
(needs) atender a; (COMM: parties etc)
proveer comida a; **~er** n abastecedor(a) m/f,
proveedor(a) m/f; **~ing** n (trade) hostelería

caterpillar ['kætəpɪlə*] n oruga, gusano

cathedral [kə'θiːdrəl] n catedral f

catholic ['kæθəlɪk] adj (tastes etc) amplio;
C~ adj, n (REL) católico/a m/f

CAT scan [kæt-] n TAC f, tomografía

Cat'seye ® ['kæts'aɪ] (BRIT) n (AUT) catafoto

cattle ['kætl] npl ganado

catty ['kætɪ] adj malicioso, rencoroso

caucus ['kɔːkəs] n (POL) camarilla política;
(: US: to elect candidates) comité m electoral

caught [kɔːt] pt, pp of **catch**

cauliflower ['kɔlɪflauə*] n coliflor f

cause [kɔːz] n causa, motivo, razón f;
(principle: also: POL) causa ♦ vt causar

caution ['kɔːʃən] n cautela, prudencia;
(warning) advertencia, amonestación f ♦ vt
amonestar; **cautious** adj cauteloso,
prudente, precavido

cavalry ['kævəlrɪ] n caballería

cave [keɪv] n cueva, caverna; **~ in** vi (roof etc)
derrumbarse, hundirse

caviar(e) ['kævɪɑː*] n caviar m

CB n abbr (= Citizens' Band (Radio)) banda
ciudadana

CBI n abbr (= Confederation of British Industry)
≈ C.E.O.E. f (SP)

cc abbr = cubic centimetres; = carbon
copy

CD n abbr (= compact disc) DC m; (player)
(reproductor m de) disco compacto;
~ player n lector m de discos compactos;
~-ROM [siːdiːˈrɔm] n abbr CD-ROM m

cease [siːs] vt, vi cesar; **~fire** n alto m el
fuego; **~less** adj incesante

cedar ['siːdə*] n cedro

ceiling ['siːlɪŋ] n techo; (fig) límite m

celebrate ['selɪbreɪt] vt celebrar ♦ vi
divertirse; **~d** adj célebre; **celebration**
[-'breɪʃən] n fiesta, celebración f

celery ['selərɪ] n apio

cell [sel] n celda; (BIOL) célula; (ELEC) elemento

cellar ['selə*] n sótano; (for wine) bodega

cello ['tʃelau] n violoncelo

Cellophane ® ['seləfeɪn] n celofán m

cellphone ['selfəun] n teléfono celular

Celt [kelt, selt] adj, n celta m/f; **~ic** adj celta

cement [sə'ment] n cemento; **~ mixer** n
hormigonera

cemetery ['semɪtrɪ] n cementerio

censor ['sensə*] n censor m ♦ vt (cut)
censurar; **~ship** n censura

censure ['senʃə*] vt censurar

census ['sensəs] n censo

cent [sent] n (unit of dollar) centavo, céntimo;
(unit of euro) céntimo; see also **per**

centenary [sen'tiːnərɪ] n centenario

center ['sentə*] (US) = **centre**

centi... [sentɪ] prefix: **~grade** adj centígrado;
~litre (US **~liter**) n centilitro; **~metre** (US
~meter) n centímetro

centipede ['sentɪpiːd] n ciempiés m inv

central ['sentrəl] adj central; (of house etc)
céntrico; **C~ America** n Centroamérica;
~ heating n calefacción f central; **~ize** vt
centralizar

centre ['sentə*] (US **center**) n centro; (fig)
núcleo ♦ vt centrar; **~-forward** n (SPORT)
delantero centro; **~-half** n (SPORT) medio
centro

century ['sentjurɪ] n siglo; **20th ~** siglo veinte

ceramic [sɪ'ræmɪk] adj cerámico; **~s** n
cerámica

cereal ['siːrɪəl] n cereal m

ceremony ['serɪmənɪ] n ceremonia; **to stand
on ~** hacer ceremonias, estar de cumplido

certain ['səːtən] adj seguro; (person): **a ~ Mr
Smith** un tal Sr Smith; (particular, some)
cierto; **for ~** a ciencia cierta; **~ly** adv
(undoubtedly) ciertamente; (of course) desde
luego, por supuesto; **~ty** n certeza,
certidumbre f, seguridad f; (inevitability)
certeza

certificate [sə'tɪfɪkɪt] n certificado

certified ['səːtɪfaɪd]: **~ mail** (US) n correo
certificado; **~ public accountant** (US) n
contable m/f diplomado/a

certify ['səːtɪfaɪ] vt certificar; (award diploma
to) conceder un diploma a; (declare insane)
declarar loco

cervical ['səːvɪkl] adj cervical

cervix ['səːvɪks] n cuello del útero

cf. abbr (= compare) cfr

CFC n abbr (= chlorofluorocarbon) CFC m

ch. abbr (= chapter) cap

chain [tʃeɪn] n cadena; (of mountains)
cordillera; (of events) sucesión f ♦ vt (also:
~ up) encadenar; **~ reaction** n reacción f en
cadena; **~-smoke** vi fumar un cigarrillo tras
otro; **~ store** n tienda de una cadena, ≈

gran almacén
chair [tʃeə*] *n* silla; (*armchair*) sillón *m*,
butaca; (*of university*) cátedra; (*of meeting
etc*) presidencia ♦ *vt* (*meeting*) presidir; **~lift**
n telesilla; **~man** *n* presidente *m*
chalk [tʃɔ:k] *n* (*GEO*) creta; (*for writing*) tiza
(*SP*), gis *m* (*AM*)
challenge [ˈtʃælɪndʒ] *n* desafío, reto ♦ *vt*
desafiar, retar; (*statement, right*) poner en
duda; **to ~ sb to do sth** retar a uno a que
haga algo; **challenging** *adj* exigente; (*tone*)
de desafío
chamber [ˈtʃeɪmbə*] *n* cámara, sala; (*POL*)
cámara; (*BRIT: LAW: gen pl*) despacho; **~ of
commerce** cámara de comercio; **~maid** *n*
camarera; **~ music** *n* música de cámara
chamois [ˈʃæmwɑ:] *n* gamuza
champagne [ʃæmˈpeɪn] *n* champaña *m*,
champán *m*
champion [ˈtʃæmpɪən] *n* campeón/ona *m/f*;
(*of cause*) defensor(a) *m/f*; **~ship** *n*
campeonato
chance [tʃɑ:ns] *n* (*opportunity*) ocasión *f*,
oportunidad *f*; (*likelihood*) posibilidad *f*; (*risk*)
riesgo ♦ *vt* arriesgar, probar ♦ *adj* fortuito,
casual; **to ~ it** arriesgarse, intentarlo; **to take a
~** arriesgarse; **by ~** por casualidad
chancellor [ˈtʃɑ:nsələ*] *n* canciller *m*; **C~ of
the Exchequer** (*BRIT*) *n* Ministro de
Hacienda
chandelier [ʃændəˈlɪə*] *n* araña (de luces)
change [tʃeɪndʒ] *vt* cambiar; (*replace*)
cambiar, reemplazar; (*gear, clothes, job*)
cambiar de; (*transform*) transformar ♦ *vi*
cambiar(se); (*trains*) hacer transbordo;
(*traffic lights*) cambiar de color; (*be
transformed*): **to ~ into** transformarse en ♦ *n*
cambio; (*alteration*) modificación *f*,
transformación *f*; (*of clothes*) muda; (*coins*)
suelto, sencillo; (*money returned*) vuelta; **to
~ gear** (*AUT*) cambiar de marcha; **to ~ one's
mind** cambiar de opinión or idea; **for a ~** para
variar; **~able** *adj* (*weather*) cambiable;
~ machine *n* máquina de cambio; **~over** *n*
(*to new system*) cambio; **changing** *adj*
cambiante; **changing room** (*BRIT*) *n*
vestuario
channel [ˈtʃænl] *n* (*TV*) canal *m*; (*of river*)
cauce *m*; (*groove*) conducto; (*fig: medium*)
medio ♦ *vt* (*river etc*) encauzar; **the (English)
C~** el Canal (de la Mancha); **the C~ Islands**
las Islas Normandas; **the C~ Tunnel** el túnel
del Canal de la Mancha, el Eurotúnel; **~-
hopping** *n* (*TV*) zapping *m*
chant [tʃɑ:nt] *n* (*of crowd*) gritos *mpl*; (*REL*)
canto ♦ *vt* (*slogan, word*) repetir a gritos
chaos [ˈkeɪɒs] *n* caos *m*
chap [tʃæp] (*BRIT: inf*) *n* (*man*) tío, tipo
chapel [ˈtʃæpəl] *n* capilla

chaperone [ˈʃæpərəun] *n* carabina
chaplain [ˈtʃæplɪn] *n* capellán *m*
chapped [tʃæpt] *adj* agrietado
chapter [ˈtʃæptə*] *n* capítulo
char [tʃɑ:*] *vt* (*burn*) carbonizar, chamuscar
character [ˈkærɪktə*] *n* carácter *m*,
naturaleza, índole *f*; (*moral strength,
personality*) carácter; (*in novel, film*) personaje
m; **~istic** [-ˈrɪstɪk] *adj* característico ♦ *n*
característica
charcoal [ˈtʃɑ:kəul] *n* carbón *m* vegetal;
(*ART*) carboncillo
charge [tʃɑ:dʒ] *n* (*LAW*) cargo, acusación *f*;
(*cost*) precio, coste *m*; (*responsibility*) cargo
♦ *vt* (*LAW*): **to ~ (with)** acusar (de); (*battery*)
cargar; (*price*) pedir; (*customer*) cobrar ♦ *vi*
precipitarse; (*MIL*) cargar, atacar; **~s** *npl*: **to
reverse the ~s** (*BRIT: TEL*) revertir el cobro; **to
take ~ of** hacerse cargo de, encargarse de; **to
be in ~ of** estar encargado de; (*business*)
mandar; **how much do you ~?** ¿cuánto cobra
usted?; **to ~ an expense (up) to sb's account**
cargar algo a cuenta de alguien; **~ card** *n*
tarjeta de cuenta
charity [ˈtʃærɪtɪ] *n* caridad *f*; (*organization*)
sociedad *f* benéfica; (*money, gifts*) limosnas
fpl
charm [tʃɑ:m] *n* encanto, atractivo;
(*talisman*) hechizo; (*on bracelet*) dije *m* ♦ *vt*
encantar; **~ing** *adj* encantador(a)
chart [tʃɑ:t] *n* (*diagram*) cuadro; (*graph*)
gráfica; (*map*) carta de navegación ♦ *vt*
(*course*) trazar; (*progress*) seguir; **~s** *npl* (*Top
40*): **the ~s** ≈ los 40 principales (*SP*)
charter [ˈtʃɑ:tə*] *vt* (*plane*) alquilar; (*ship*)
fletar ♦ *n* (*document*) carta; (*of university,
company*) estatutos *mpl*; **~ed accountant**
(*BRIT*) *n* contable *m/f* diplomado/a; **~ flight** *n*
vuelo chárter
chase [tʃeɪs] *vt* (*pursue*) perseguir; (*also:
~ away*) ahuyentar ♦ *n* persecución *f*
chasm [ˈkæzəm] *n* sima
chassis [ˈʃæsɪ] *n* chasis *m*
chat [tʃæt] *vi* (*also: have a ~*) charlar ♦ *n*
charla; **~ show** (*BRIT*) *n* programa *m* de
entrevistas
chatter [ˈtʃætə*] *vi* (*person*) charlar; (*teeth*)
castañetear ♦ *n* (*of birds*) parloteo; (*of
people*) charla, cháchara; **~box** (*inf*) *n*
parlanchín/ina *m/f*
chatty [ˈtʃætɪ] *adj* (*style*) informal; (*person*)
hablador(a)
chauffeur [ˈʃəufə*] *n* chófer *m*
chauvinist [ˈʃəuvɪnɪst] *n* (*male ~*) machista
m; (*nationalist*) chovinista *m/f*
cheap [tʃi:p] *adj* barato; (*joke*) de mal gusto;
(*poor quality*) de mala calidad ♦ *adv* barato;
~ day return *n* billete *m* de ida y vuelta el
mismo día; **~er** *adj* más barato; **~ly** *adv*

barato, a bajo precio
cheat [tʃi:t] vi hacer trampa ♦ vt: **to ~ sb (out of sth)** estafar (algo) a uno ♦ n (person) tramposo/a
check [tʃɛk] vt (examine) controlar; (facts) comprobar; (halt) parar, detener; (restrain) refrenar, restringir ♦ n (inspection) control m, inspección f; (curb) freno; (US: bill) nota, cuenta; (US) = **cheque**; (pattern: gen pl) cuadro ♦ adj (also: ~ed: pattern, cloth) a cuadros; **~ in** vi (at hotel) firmar el registro; (at airport) facturar el equipaje ♦ vt (luggage) facturar; **~ out** vi (of hotel) marcharse; **~ up** vi: **to ~ up on sth** comprobar algo; **to ~ up on sb** investigar a alguien; **~ered** (US) adj = **check; chequered; ~ers** (US) n juego de damas; **~-in (desk)** n mostrador m de facturación; **~ing account** (US) n cuenta corriente; **~mate** n jaque m mate; **~out** n caja; **~point** n (punto de) control m; **~room** (US) n consigna; **~up** n (MED) reconocimiento general
cheek [tʃi:k] n mejilla; (impudence) descaro; **what a ~!** ¡qué caral; **~bone** n pómulo; **~y** adj fresco, descarado
cheep [tʃi:p] vi piar
cheer [tʃiə*] vt vitorear, aplaudir; (gladden) alegrar, animar ♦ vi dar vivas ♦ n viva m; **~s** npl aplausos mpl; **~s!** ¡salud!; **~ up** vi animarse ♦ vt alegrar, animar; **~ful** adj alegre
cheerio [tʃiəri'əu] (BRIT) excl ¡hasta luego!
cheese [tʃi:z] n queso; **~board** n tabla de quesos
cheetah ['tʃi:tə] n leopardo cazador
chef [ʃɛf] n jefe/a m/f de cocina
chemical ['kɛmɪkəl] adj químico ♦ n producto químico
chemist ['kɛmɪst] n (BRIT: pharmacist) farmacéutico/a; (scientist) químico/a; **~ry** n química; **~'s (shop)** (BRIT) n farmacia
cheque [tʃɛk] (US check) n cheque m; **~book** n talonario de cheques (SP), chequera (AM); **~ card** n tarjeta de cheque
chequered ['tʃɛkəd] (US checkered) adj (fig) accidentado
cherish ['tʃɛrɪʃ] vt (love) querer, apreciar; (protect) cuidar; (hope etc) abrigar
cherry ['tʃɛri] n cereza; (also: ~ tree) cerezo
chess [tʃɛs] n ajedrez m; **~board** n tablero (de ajedrez)
chest [tʃɛst] n (ANAT) pecho; (box) cofre m, cajón m; **~ of drawers** n cómoda
chestnut ['tʃɛsnʌt] n castaña; **~ (tree)** n castaño
chew [tʃu:] vt mascar, masticar; **~ing gum** n chicle m
chic [ʃi:k] adj elegante
chick [tʃɪk] n pollito, polluelo; (inf: girl) chica
chicken ['tʃɪkɪn] n gallina, pollo; (food) pollo;

(inf: coward) gallina m/f; **~ out** (inf) vi rajarse; **~pox** n varicela
chicory ['tʃɪkəri] n (for coffee) achicoria; (salad) escarola
chief [tʃi:f] n jefe/a m/f ♦ adj principal; **~ executive** n director(a) m/f general; **~ly** adv principalmente
chilblain ['tʃɪlblein] n sabañón m
child [tʃaild] (pl children) n niño/a; (offspring) hijo/a; **~birth** n parto; **~hood** n niñez f, infancia; **~ish** adj pueril, aniñado; **~like** adj de niño; **~ minder** (BRIT) n madre f de día; **~ren** ['tʃɪldrən] npl of **child**
Chile ['tʃɪli] n Chile m; **~an** adj, n chileno/a m/f
chill [tʃɪl] n frío; (MED) resfriado ♦ vt enfriar; (CULIN) congelar
chil(l)i ['tʃɪli] (BRIT) n chile m (SP), ají m (AM)
chilly ['tʃɪli] adj frío
chime [tʃaim] n repique m, (of clock) campanada ♦ vi repicar; sonar
chimney ['tʃɪmni] n chimenea; **~ sweep** n deshollinador m
chimpanzee [tʃɪmpæn'zi:] n chimpancé m
chin [tʃɪn] n mentón m, barbilla
china ['tʃainə] n porcelana; (crockery) loza
China ['tʃainə] n China; **Chinese** [tʃai'ni:z] adj chino ♦ n inv chino/a; (LING) chino
chink [tʃɪŋk] n (opening) grieta, hendedura; (noise) tintineo
chip [tʃɪp] n (gen pl: CULIN: BRIT) patata (SP) or papa (AM) frita; (: US: also: potato ~) patata or papa frita; (of wood) astilla; (of glass, stone) lasca; (at poker) ficha; (COMPUT) chip m ♦ vt (cup, plate) desconchar
chiropodist [kɪ'rɔpədɪst] (BRIT) n pedicuro/a, callista m/f
chirp [tʃə:p] vi (bird) gorjear, piar
chisel ['tʃɪzl] n (for wood) escoplo; (for stone) cincel m
chit [tʃɪt] n nota
chitchat ['tʃɪttʃæt] n chismes mpl, habladurías fpl
chivalry ['ʃivəlri] n caballerosidad f
chives [tʃaivz] npl cebollinos mpl
chlorine ['klɔ:ri:n] n cloro
chock-a-block ['tʃɔkə'blɔk] adj atestado
chock-full ['tʃɔk'ful] adj atestado
chocolate ['tʃɔklɪt] n chocolate m; (sweet) bombón m
choice [tʃɔis] n elección f, selección f; (option) opción f; (preference) preferencia ♦ adj escogido
choir ['kwaiə*] n coro; **~boy** n niño de coro
choke [tʃəuk] vi ahogarse; (on food) atragantarse ♦ vt estrangular, ahogar; (block): **to be ~d with** estar atascado de ♦ n (AUT) estárter m
cholesterol [kə'lɛstərɔl] n colesterol m

choose [tʃuːz] (pt **chose**, pp **chosen**) vt escoger, elegir; (team) seleccionar; **to ~ to do sth** optar por hacer algo

choosy ['tʃuːzɪ] adj delicado

chop [tʃɔp] vt (wood) cortar, tajar; (CULIN: also: ~ up) picar ♦ n (CULIN) chuleta; **~s** npl (jaws) boca, labios mpl

chopper ['tʃɔpə*] n (helicopter) helicóptero

choppy ['tʃɔpɪ] adj (sea) picado, agitado

chopsticks ['tʃɔpstɪks] npl palillos mpl

chord [kɔːd] n (MUS) acorde m

chore [tʃɔː*] n faena, tarea; (routine task) trabajo rutinario

chorus ['kɔːrəs] n coro; (repeated part of song) estribillo

chose [tʃəuz] pt of **choose**

chosen ['tʃəuzn] pp of **choose**

chowder ['tʃaudə*] n (esp US) sopa de pescado

Christ [kraɪst] n Cristo

christen ['krɪsn] vt bautizar

Christian ['krɪstɪən] adj, n cristiano/a m/f; **~ity** [-'ænɪtɪ] n cristianismo; **~ name** n nombre m de pila

Christmas ['krɪsməs] n Navidad f; **Merry ~!** ¡Felices Pascuas!; **~ card** n crismas m inv, tarjeta de Navidad; **~ Day** n día m de Navidad; **~ Eve** n Nochebuena; **~ tree** n árbol m de Navidad

chrome [krəum] n cromo

chronic ['krɔnɪk] adj crónico

chronological [krɔnə'lɔdʒɪkəl] adj cronológico

chubby ['tʃʌbɪ] adj regordete

chuck [tʃʌk] (inf) vt lanzar, arrojar; (BRIT: also: ~ up) abandonar; **~ out** vt (person) echar (fuera); (rubbish etc) tirar

chuckle ['tʃʌkl] vi reírse entre dientes

chug [tʃʌg] vi resoplar; (car, boat: also: ~ along) avanzar traqueteando

chum [tʃʌm] n compañero/a

chunk [tʃʌŋk] n pedazo, trozo

church [tʃəːtʃ] n iglesia; **~yard** n cementerio

churn [tʃəːn] n (for butter) mantequera; (for milk) lechera; **~ out** vt producir en serie

chute [ʃuːt] n (also: rubbish ~) vertedero; (for coal etc) rampa de caída

chutney ['tʃʌtnɪ] n condimento a base de frutas de la India

CIA (US) n abbr (= Central Intelligence Agency) CIA f

CID (BRIT) n abbr (= Criminal Investigation Department) ≈ B.I.C. f (SP)

cider ['saɪdə*] n sidra

cigar [sɪ'gɑː*] n puro

cigarette [sɪgə'rɛt] n cigarrillo (SP), cigarro (AM); pitillo; **~ case** n pitillera; **~ end** n colilla

Cinderella [sɪndə'rɛlə] n Cenicienta

cinders ['sɪndəz] npl cenizas fpl

cine camera ['sɪnɪ-] (BRIT) n cámara cinematográfica

cinema ['sɪnəmə] n cine m

cinnamon ['sɪnəmən] n canela

circle ['səːkl] n círculo; (in theatre) anfiteatro ♦ vi dar vueltas ♦ vt (surround) rodear, cercar; (move round) dar la vuelta a

circuit ['səːkɪt] n circuito; (tour) gira; (track) pista; (lap) vuelta; **~ous** [səː'kjuːɪtəs] adj indirecto

circular ['səːkjulə*] adj circular ♦ n circular f

circulate ['səːkjuleɪt] vi circular; (person: at party etc) hablar con los invitados ♦ vt poner en circulación; **circulation** [-'leɪʃən] n circulación f; (of newspaper) tirada

circumstances ['səːkəmstənsɪz] npl circunstancias fpl; (financial condition) situación f económica

circus ['səːkəs] n circo

CIS n abbr (= Commonwealth of Independent States) CEI f

cistern ['sɪstən] n tanque m, depósito; (in toilet) cisterna

citizen ['sɪtɪzn] n (POL) ciudadano/a; (of city) vecino/a, habitante m/f; **~ship** n ciudadanía

citrus fruits ['sɪtrəs-] npl agrios mpl

city ['sɪtɪ] n ciudad f; **the C~** centro financiero de Londres

civic ['sɪvɪk] adj cívico; (authorities) municipal; **~ centre** (BRIT) n centro público

civil ['sɪvɪl] adj civil; (polite) atento, cortés; **~ engineer** n ingeniero de caminos(, canales y puertos); **~ian** [sɪ'vɪlɪən] adj civil (no militar) ♦ n civil m/f, paisano/a

civilization [sɪvɪlaɪ'zeɪʃən] n civilización f

civilized ['sɪvɪlaɪzd] adj civilizado

civil: ~ law n derecho civil; **~ servant** n funcionario/a del Estado; **C~ Service** n administración f pública; **~ war** n guerra civil

claim [kleɪm] vt exigir, reclamar; (rights etc) reivindicar; (assert) pretender ♦ vi (for insurance) reclamar ♦ n reclamación f; pretensión f; **~ant** n demandante m/f

clairvoyant [klɛə'vɔɪənt] n clarividente m/f

clam [klæm] n almeja

clamber ['klæmbə*] vi trepar

clammy ['klæmɪ] adj frío y húmedo

clamour ['klæmə*] (US **clamor**) vi: **to ~ for** clamar por, pedir a voces

clamp [klæmp] n abrazadera, grapa ♦ vt (2 things together) cerrar fuertemente; (one thing on another) afianzar (con abrazadera); (AUT: wheel) poner el cepo a; **~ down on** vt fus (subj: government, police) reforzar la lucha contra

clang [klæŋ] vi sonar, hacer estruendo

clap [klæp] vi aplaudir; **~ping** n aplausos mpl

claret ['klærət] n burdeos m inv

clarify ['klærɪfaɪ] vt aclarar

clarinet [klærɪ'net] n clarinete m

clash [klæʃ] n enfrentamiento; choque m;
desacuerdo; estruendo ♦ vi (fight)
enfrentarse; (beliefs) chocar; (disagree) estar
en desacuerdo; (colours) desentonar; (two
events) coincidir

clasp [klɑːsp] n (hold) apretón m; (of
necklace, bag) cierre m ♦ vt apretar; abrazar

class [klɑːs] n clase f ♦ vt clasificar

classic ['klæsɪk] adj, n clásico; **~al** adj clásico

classified ['klæsɪfaɪd] adj (information)
reservado; **~ advertisement** n anuncio por
palabras

classmate ['klɑːsmeɪt] n compañero/a de
clase

classroom ['klɑːsrum] n aula

clatter ['klætə*] n estrépito ♦ vi hacer ruido or
estrépito

clause [klɔːz] n cláusula; (LING) oración f

claw [klɔː] n (of cat) uña; (of bird of prey)
garra; (of lobster) pinza

clay [kleɪ] n arcilla

clean [kliːn] adj limpio; (record, reputation)
bueno, intachable; (joke) decente ♦ vt
limpiar; (hands etc) lavar; **~ out** vt limpiar;
~ up vt limpiar, asear; **~-cut** adj (person)
bien parecido; **~er** n (person) asistenta;
(substance) producto para la limpieza; **~er's**
n tintorería; **~ing** n limpieza; **~liness**
['klenlɪnɪs] n limpieza

cleanse [klenz] vt limpiar; **~r** n (for face)
crema limpiadora

clean-shaven adj sin barba, afeitado

cleansing department (BRIT) n
departamento de limpieza

clear [klɪə*] adj claro; (road, way) libre;
(conscience) limpio, tranquilo; (skin) terso;
(sky) despejado ♦ vt (space) despejar,
limpiar; (LAW: suspect) absolver; (obstacle)
salvar, saltar por encima de; (cheque) aceptar
♦ vi (fog etc) despejarse ♦ adv: **~ of** a
distancia de; **to ~ the table** recoger or
levantar la mesa; **~ up** vt limpiar; (mystery)
aclarar, resolver; **~ance** n (removal) despeje
m; (permission) acreditación f; **~-cut** adj bien
definido, nítido; **~ing** n (in wood) claro;
~ing bank (BRIT) n cámara de compensación; **~ly** adv claramente; (evidently) sin
duda; **~way** (BRIT) n carretera donde no se
puede parar

clef [klef] n (MUS) clave f

cleft [kleft] n (in rock) grieta, hendedura

clench [klentʃ] vt apretar, cerrar

clergy ['klɜːdʒɪ] n clero; **~man** n clérigo

clerical ['klerɪkəl] adj de oficina; (REL) clerical

clerk [klɑːk, (US) klɜːrk] n (BRIT) oficinista m/f;
(US) dependiente/a m/f

clever ['klevə*] adj (intelligent) inteligente,

listo; (skilful) hábil; (device, arrangement)
ingenioso

click [klɪk] vt (tongue) chasquear; (heels)
taconear ♦ vi (COMPUT) hacer clic

client ['klaɪənt] n cliente m/f

cliff [klɪf] n acantilado

climate ['klaɪmɪt] n clima m

climax ['klaɪmæks] n (of battle, career)
apogeo; (of film, book) punto culminante;
(sexual) orgasmo

climb [klaɪm] vi subir; (plant) trepar; (move
with effort): **to ~ over a wall/into a car** trepar
a una tapia/subir a un coche ♦ vt (stairs)
subir; (tree) trepar a; (mountain) escalar ♦ n
subida; **~-down** n vuelta atrás; **~er** n
alpinista m/f (SP), andinista m/f (AM); **~ing** n
alpinismo (SP), andinismo (AM)

clinch [klɪntʃ] vt (deal) cerrar; (argument)
remachar

cling [klɪŋ] (pt, pp clung) vi: **to ~ to** agarrarse
a; (clothes) pegarse a

clinic ['klɪnɪk] n clínica; **~al** adj clínico; (fig)
frío

clink [klɪŋk] vi tintinar

clip [klɪp] n (for hair) horquilla; (also: paper ~)
sujetapapeles m inv, clip m; (TV, CINEMA)
fragmento ♦ vt (cut) cortar; (also:
~ together) unir; **~pers** npl (for gardening)
tijeras fpl; **~ping** n (newspaper) recorte m

clique [kliːk] n camarilla

cloak [kləuk] n capa, manto ♦ vt (fig)
encubrir, disimular; **~room** n guardarropa;
(BRIT: WC) lavabo (SP), aseos mpl (SP), baño
(AM)

clock [klɔk] n reloj m; **~ in** or **on** vi fichar,
picar; **~ off** or **out** vi fichar or picar la salida;
~wise adv en el sentido de las agujas del
reloj; **~work** n aparato de relojería ♦ adj
(toy) de cuerda

clog [klɔg] n zueco, chanclo ♦ vt atascar ♦ vi
(also: ~ up) atascarse

cloister ['klɔɪstə*] n claustro

close¹ [kləus] adj (near): **~ (to)** cerca (de);
(friend) íntimo; (connection) estrecho;
(examination) detallado, minucioso; (weather)
bochornoso; **to have a ~ shave** (fig) escaparse
por un pelo ♦ adv cerca; **~ by**, **~ at hand** muy
cerca; **~ to** prep cerca de

close² [kləuz] vt (shut) cerrar; (end) concluir,
terminar ♦ vi (shop etc) cerrarse; (end)
concluirse, terminarse ♦ vi (end) fin m, final
m, conclusión f; **~ down** vi cerrarse
definitivamente; **~d** adj (shop etc) cerrado;
~d shop n taller m gremial

close-knit [kləus'nɪt] adj (fig) muy unido

closely ['kləuslɪ] adv (study) con detalle;
(watch) de cerca; (resemble) estrechamente

closet ['klɔzɪt] n armario

close-up ['kləusʌp] n primer plano

closure ['kləʊʒə*] n cierre m
clot [klɔt] n (gen: blood ~) coágulo; (inf: idiot) imbécil m/f ♦ vi (blood) coagularse
cloth [klɔθ] n (material) tela, paño; (rag) trapo
clothe [kləʊð] vt vestir; **~s** npl ropa; **~s brush** n cepillo (para la ropa); **~s line** n cuerda (para tender la ropa); **~s peg** (US **~s pin**) n pinza
clothing ['kləʊðɪŋ] n = **clothes**
cloud [klaʊd] n nube f; **~burst** n aguacero; **~y** adj nublado, nubloso; (liquid) turbio
clout [klaʊt] vt dar un tortazo a
clove [kləʊv] n clavo; **~ of garlic** diente m de ajo
clover ['kləʊvə*] n trébol m
clown [klaʊn] n payaso ♦ vi (also: ~ about, ~ around) hacer el payaso
cloying ['klɔɪŋ] adj empalagoso
club [klʌb] n (society) club m; (weapon) porra, cachiporra; (also: golf ~) palo ♦ vt aporrear ♦ vi: **to ~ together** (for gift) comprar entre todos; **~s** npl (CARDS) tréboles mpl; **~ class** n (AVIAT) clase f preferente; **~house** n local social, sobre todo en clubs deportivos
cluck [klʌk] vi cloquear
clue [kluː] n pista; (in crosswords) indicación f; **I haven't a ~** no tengo ni idea
clump [klʌmp] n (of trees) grupo
clumsy ['klʌmzɪ] adj (person) torpe, desmañado; (tool) difícil de manejar; (movement) desgarbado
clung [klʌŋ] pt, pp of **cling**
cluster ['klʌstə*] n grupo ♦ vi agruparse, apiñarse
clutch [klʌtʃ] n (AUT) embrague m; (grasp): **~es** garras fpl ♦ vt asir; agarrar
clutter ['klʌtə*] vt atestar
cm abbr (= centimetre) cm
CND n abbr (= Campaign for Nuclear Disarmament) plataforma pro desarme nuclear
Co. abbr = county; company
c/o abbr (= care of) c/a, a/c
coach [kəʊtʃ] n autocar m (SP), coche m de línea; (horse-drawn) coche m; (of train) vagón m, coche m; (SPORT) entrenador(a) m/f, instructor(a) m/f; (tutor) profesor(a) m/f particular ♦ vt (SPORT) entrenar; (student) preparar, enseñar; **~ trip** n excursión f en autocar
coal [kəʊl] n carbón m; **~ face** n frente m de carbón; **~field** n yacimiento de carbón
coalition [kəʊə'lɪʃən] n coalición f
coalman ['kəʊlmən] (irreg) n carbonero
coalmine ['kəʊlmaɪn] n mina de carbón
coarse [kɔːs] adj basto, burdo; (vulgar) grosero, ordinario
coast [kəʊst] n costa, litoral m ♦ vi (AUT) ir en punto muerto; **~al** adj costero, costanero;

~guard n guardacostas m inv; **~line** n litoral m
coat [kəʊt] n abrigo; (of animal) pelaje m, lana; (of paint) mano f, capa ♦ vt cubrir, revestir; **~ of arms** n escudo de armas; **~ hanger** n percha (SP), gancho (AM); **~ing** n capa, baño
coax [kəʊks] vt engatusar
cobbler ['kɔblə] n zapatero (remendón)
cobbles ['kɔblz] npl, **cobblestones** ['kɔblstəunz] npl adoquines mpl
cobweb ['kɔbweb] n telaraña
cocaine [kə'keɪn] n cocaína
cock [kɔk] n (rooster) gallo; (male bird) macho ♦ vt (gun) amartillar; **~erel** n gallito
cockle ['kɔkl] n berberecho
cockney ['kɔknɪ] n habitante de ciertos barrios de Londres
cockpit ['kɔkpɪt] n cabina
cockroach ['kɔkrəutʃ] n cucaracha
cocktail ['kɔkteɪl] n coctel m, cóctel m; **~ cabinet** n mueble-bar m; **~ party** n coctel m, cóctel m
cocoa ['kəʊkəʊ] n cacao; (drink) chocolate m
coconut ['kəʊkənʌt] n coco
cod [kɔd] n bacalao
C.O.D. abbr (= cash on delivery) C.A.E.
code [kəʊd] n código; (cipher) clave f; (dialling ~) prefijo; (post ~) código postal
cod-liver oil ['kɔdlɪvər-] n aceite m de hígado de bacalao
coercion [kəʊ'əːʃən] n coacción f
coffee ['kɔfɪ] n café m; **~ bar** (BRIT) n cafetería; **~ bean** n grano de café; **~ break** n descanso (para tomar café); **~pot** n cafetera; **~ table** n mesita (para servir el café)
coffin ['kɔfɪn] n ataúd m
cog [kɔg] n (wheel) rueda dentada; (tooth) diente m
cogent ['kəʊdʒənt] adj convincente
cognac ['kɔnjæk] n coñac m
coil [kɔɪl] n rollo; (ELEC) bobina, carrete m; (contraceptive) espiral f ♦ vt enrollar
coin [kɔɪn] n moneda ♦ vt (word) inventar, idear; **~age** n moneda; **~-box** (BRIT) n cabina telefónica
coincide [kəʊɪn'saɪd] vi coincidir; (agree) estar de acuerdo; **coincidence** [kəʊ'ɪn-sɪdəns] n casualidad f
Coke ® [kəʊk] n Coca-Cola ®
coke [kəʊk] n (coal) coque m
colander ['kɔləndə*] n colador m, escurridor m
cold [kəʊld] adj frío ♦ n frío; (MED) resfriado; **it's ~** hace frío; **to be ~** (person) tener frío; **to catch ~** enfriarse; **to catch a ~** resfriarse, acatarrarse; **in ~ blood** a sangre fría; **~-shoulder** vt dar or volver la espalda a;

~ sore n herpes mpl or fpl

coleslaw ['kəulslɔ:] n especie de ensalada de col

colic ['kɔlɪk] n cólico

collapse [kə'læps] vi hundirse, derrumbarse; (MED) sufrir un colapso ♦ n hundimiento, derrumbamiento; (MED) colapso; **collapsible** adj plegable

collar ['kɔlə*] n (of coat, shirt) cuello; (of dog etc) collar; **~bone** n clavícula

collateral [kɔ'lætərəl] n garantía colateral

colleague ['kɔli:g] n colega m/f; (at work) compañero, a

collect [kə'lekt] vt (litter, mail etc) recoger; (as a hobby) coleccionar; (BRIT: call and pick up) recoger; (debts, subscriptions etc) recaudar ♦ vi reunirse; (dust) acumularse; to call ~ (US: TEL) llamar a cobro revertido; **~ion** [kə'lekʃən] n colección f; (of mail, for charity) recogida; **~or** n coleccionista m/f

college ['kɔlɪdʒ] n colegio mayor; (of agriculture, technology) escuela universitaria

collide [kə'laɪd] vi chocar

colliery ['kɔlɪərɪ] (BRIT) n mina de carbón

collision [kə'lɪʒən] n choque m

colloquial [kə'ləukwɪəl] adj familiar, coloquial

Colombia [kə'lɔmbɪə] n Colombia; **~n** adj, n colombiano/a

colon ['kəulən] n (sign) dos puntos; (MED) colon m

colonel ['kə:nl] n coronel m

colonial [kə'ləunɪəl] adj colonial

colony ['kɔlənɪ] n colonia

colour ['kʌlə*] (US **color**) n color m ♦ vt color(e)ar; (dye) teñir; (fig: account) adornar; (: judgement) distorsionar ♦ vi (blush) sonrojarse; **~s** npl (of party, club) colores mpl; **in ~** en color; **~ in** vt colorear; **~ bar** n segregación f racial; **~-blind** adj daltónico; **~ed** adj de color; (photo) en color; **~ film** n película en color; **~ful** adj lleno de color; (story) fantástico; (person) excéntrico; **~ing** n (complexion) tez f; (in food) colorante m; **~ scheme** n combinación f de colores; **~ television** n televisión f en color

colt [kəult] n potro

column ['kɔləm] n columna; **~ist** ['kɔləmnɪst] n columnista m/f

coma ['kəumə] n coma m

comb [kəum] n peine m; (ornamental) peineta ♦ vt (hair) peinar; (area) registrar a fondo

combat ['kɔmbæt] n combate m ♦ vt combatir

combination [kɔmbɪ'neɪʃən] n combinación f

combine [vb kəm'baɪn, n 'kɔmbaɪn] vt combinar; (qualities) reunir ♦ vi combinarse

♦ n (ECON) cartel m; **~ (harvester)** n cosechadora

KEYWORD

---

come [kʌm] (pt **came**, pp **come**) vi **1** (movement towards) venir; **to ~ running** venir corriendo

2 (arrive) llegar; **he's ~ here to work** ha venido aquí para trabajar; **to ~ home** volver a casa

3 (reach): **to ~ to** llegar a; **the bill came to £40** la cuenta ascendía a cuarenta libras

4 (occur): **an idea came to me** se me ocurrió una idea

5 (be, become): **to ~ loose/undone** etc aflojarse/desabrocharse, desatarse etc; **I've ~ to like him** por fin ha llegado a gustarme

come about vi suceder, ocurrir

come across vt fus (person) topar con; (thing) dar con

come away vi (leave) marcharse; (become detached) desprenderse

come back vi (return) volver

come by vt fus (acquire) conseguir

come down vi (price) bajar; (tree, building) ser derribado

come forward vi presentarse

come from vt fus (place, source) ser de

come in vi (visitor) entrar; (train, report) llegar; (fashion) ponerse de moda; (on deal etc) entrar

come in for vt fus (criticism etc) recibir

come into vt fus (money) heredar; (be involved) tener que ver con; **to ~ into fashion** ponerse de moda

come off vi (button) soltarse, desprenderse; (attempt) salir bien

come on vi (pupil) progresar; (work, project) desarrollarse; (lights) encenderse; (electricity) volver; **~ on!** ¡vamos!

come out vi (fact) salir a la luz; (book, sun) salir; (stain) quitarse

come round vi (after faint, operation) volver en sí

come to vi (wake) volver en sí

come up vi (sun) salir; (problem) surgir; (event) aproximarse; (in conversation) mencionarse

come up against vt fus (resistance etc) tropezar con

come up with vt fus (idea) sugerir; (money) conseguir

come upon vt fus (find) dar con

---

comeback ['kʌmbæk] n: **to make a ~** (THEATRE) volver a las tablas

comedian [kə'mi:dɪən] n cómico; **comedienne** [-'ɛn] n cómica

comedy ['kɔmɪdɪ] n comedia; (humour)

comicidad f

comet ['kɔmɪt] n cometa m

comeuppance [kʌm'ʌpəns] n: **to get one's ~** llevar su merecido

comfort ['kʌmfət] n bienestar m; (relief) alivio ♦ vt consolar; **~s** npl (of home etc) comodidades fpl; **~able** adj cómodo; (financially) acomodado; (easy) fácil; **~ably** adv (sit) cómodamente; (live) holgadamente; **~ station** n (US) n servicios mpl

comic ['kɔmɪk] adj (also: ~al) cómico ♦ n (comedian) cómico; (BRIT: for children) tebeo; (BRIT: for adults) comic m; **~ strip** n tira cómica

coming ['kʌmɪŋ] n venida, llegada ♦ adj que viene; **~(s) and going(s)** n(pl) ir y venir m, ajetreo

comma ['kɔmə] n coma

command [kə'mɑːnd] n orden f, mandato; (MIL: authority) mando; (mastery) dominio ♦ vt (troops) mandar; (give orders to): **to ~ sb to do** mandar or ordenar a uno hacer; **~eer** [kɔmən'dɪə*] vt requisar; **~er** n (MIL) comandante m/f, jefe/a m/f

commemorate [kə'meməreɪt] vt conmemorar

commence [kə'mens] vt, vi comenzar, empezar

commend [kə'mend] vt elogiar, alabar; (recommend) recomendar

commensurate [kə'menʃərɪt] adj: **~ with** en proporción a, que corresponde a

comment ['kɔment] n comentario ♦ vi: **to ~ on** hacer comentarios sobre; **"no ~"** (written) "sin comentarios"; (spoken) "no tengo nada que decir"; **~ary** ['kɔməntəri] n comentario; **~ator** ['kɔmənteɪtə*] n comentarista m/f

commerce ['kɔməːs] n comercio

commercial [kə'məːʃəl] adj comercial ♦ n (TV, RADIO) anuncio

commiserate [kə'mɪzəreɪt] vi: **to ~ with** compadecerse de, condolerse de

commission [kə'mɪʃən] n (committee, fee) comisión f ♦ vt (work of art) encargar; **out of ~** fuera de servicio; **~aire** [kəmɪʃə'neə*] n (BRIT) n portero; **~er** n (POLICE) comisario de policía

commit [kə'mɪt] vt (act) cometer; (resources) dedicar; (to sb's care) entregar; **to ~ o.s. (to do)** comprometerse (a hacer); **to ~ suicide** suicidarse; **~ment** n compromiso; (to ideology etc) entrega

committee [kə'mɪti] n comité m

commodity [kə'mɔdɪti] n mercancía

common ['kɔmən] adj común; (pej) ordinario ♦ n campo común; **the C~s** npl (BRIT) (la Cámara de) los Comunes mpl; **in ~** en común; **~er** n plebeyo; **~ law** n ley f consuetudinaria; **~ly** adv comúnmente;

C~ Market n Mercado Común; **~place** adj de lo más común; **~room** n sala común; **~ sense** n sentido común; **the C~wealth** n la Commonwealth

commotion [kə'məuʃən] n tumulto, confusión f

commune [n 'kɔmjuːn, vb kə'mjuːn] n (group) comuna ♦ vi: **to ~ with** comulgar or conversar con

communicate [kə'mjuːnɪkeɪt] vt comunicar ♦ vi: **to ~ (with)** comunicarse (con); (in writing) estar en contacto (con)

communication [kəmjuːnɪ'keɪʃən] n comunicación f; **~ cord** (BRIT) n timbre m de alarma

communion [kə'mjuːnɪən] n (also: Holy C~) comunión f

communiqué [kə'mjuːnɪkeɪ] n comunicado, parte f

communism ['kɔmjunɪzəm] n comunismo; **communist** adj, n comunista m/f

community [kə'mjuːnɪti] n comunidad f; (large group) colectividad f; **~ centre** n centro social; **~ chest** (US) n arca comunitaria, fondo común

commutation ticket [kɔmju'teɪʃən-] (US) n billete m de abono

commute [kə'mjuːt] vi viajar a diario de la casa al trabajo ♦ vt conmutar; **~r** n persona (que viaja ... see vi)

compact [adj kəm'pækt, n 'kɔmpækt] adj compacto ♦ n (also: powder ~) polvera; **~ disc** n compact disc m; **~ disc player** n reproductor m de disco compacto, compact disc m

companion [kəm'pænɪən] n compañero/a; **~ship** n compañerismo

company ['kʌmpəni] n compañía; (COMM) sociedad f, compañía; **to keep sb ~** acompañar a uno; **~ secretary** (BRIT) n secretario/a de compañía

comparative [kəm'pærətɪv] adj relativo; (study) comparativo; **~ly** adv (relatively) relativamente

compare [kəm'peə*] vt: **to ~ sth/sb with/to** comparar algo/a uno con ♦ vi: **to ~ (with)** compararse (con); **comparison** [-'pærɪsn] n comparación f

compartment [kəm'pɑːtmənt] n (also: RAIL) compartim(i)ento

compass ['kʌmpəs] n brújula; **~es** npl (MATH) compás m

compassion [kəm'pæʃən] n compasión f; **~ate** adj compasivo

compatible [kəm'pætɪbl] adj compatible

compel [kəm'pel] vt obligar

compensate ['kɔmpenseɪt] vt compensar ♦ vi: **to ~ for** compensar; **compensation** [-'seɪʃən] n (for loss) indemnización f

compère ['kɔmpeə*] n presentador m
compete [kəm'pi:t] vi (take part) tomar parte, concurrir; (vie with): **to ~ with** competir con, hacer competencia a
competent ['kɔmpɪtənt] adj competente, capaz
competition [kɔmpɪ'tɪʃən] n (contest) concurso; (rivalry) competencia
competitive [kəm'petɪtɪv] adj (ECON, SPORT) competitivo
competitor [kəm'petɪtə*] n (rival) competidor(a) m/f; (participant) concursante m/f
complacency [kəm'pleɪsnsɪ] n autosatisfacción f
complacent [kəm'pleɪsənt] adj autocomplaciente
complain [kəm'pleɪn] vi quejarse; (COMM) reclamar; **~t** n queja; reclamación f; (MED) enfermedad f
complement [n 'kɔmplɪmənt, vb 'kɔmplɪment] n complemento; (esp of ship's crew) dotación f ♦ vt (enhance) complementar; **~ary** [kɔmplɪ'mentərɪ] adj complementario
complete [kəm'pli:t] adj (full) completo; (finished) acabado ♦ vt (fulfil) completar; (finish) acabar; (a form) llenar; **~ly** adv completamente; **completion** [-'pli:ʃən] n terminación f; (of contract) realización f
complex ['kɔmpleks] adj, n complejo
complexion [kəm'plekʃən] n (of face) tez f, cutis m
compliance [kəm'plaɪəns] n (submission) sumisión f; (agreement) conformidad f; **in ~ with** de acuerdo con
complicate ['kɔmplɪkeɪt] vt complicar; **~d** adj complicado; **complication** [-'keɪʃən] n complicación f
compliment ['kɔmplɪmənt] n (formal) cumplido ♦ vt felicitar; **~s** npl (regards) saludos mpl; **to pay sb a ~** hacer cumplidos a uno; **~ary** [-'mentərɪ] adj lisonjero; (free) de favor
comply [kəm'plaɪ] vi: **to ~ with** cumplir con
component [kəm'pəunənt] adj componente ♦ n (TECH) pieza
compose [kəm'pəuz] vt: **to be ~d of** componerse de; (music etc) componer; **to ~ o.s.** tranquilizarse; **~d** adj sosegado; **~r** n (MUS) compositor(a) m/f; **composition** [kɔmpə'zɪʃən] n composición f
compost ['kɔmpɔst] n abono (vegetal)
composure [kəm'pəuʒə*] n serenidad f, calma
compound ['kɔmpaund] n (CHEM) compuesto; (LING) palabra compuesta; (enclosure) recinto ♦ adj compuesto; (fracture) complicado

comprehend [kɔmprɪ'hend] vt comprender; **comprehension** [-'henʃən] n comprensión f
comprehensive [kɔmprɪ'hensɪv] adj exhaustivo; (INSURANCE) contra todo riesgo; **~ (school)** n centro estatal de enseñanza secundaria; ≈ Instituto Nacional de Bachillerato (SP)
compress [vb kəm'pres, n 'kɔmpres] vt comprimir; (information) condensar ♦ n (MED) compresa
comprise [kəm'praɪz] vt (also: **be ~d of**) comprender, constar de; (constitute) constituir
compromise ['kɔmprəmaɪz] n (agreement) arreglo ♦ vt comprometer ♦ vi transigir
compulsion [kəm'pʌlʃən] n compulsión f; (force) obligación f
compulsive [kəm'pʌlsɪv] adj compulsivo; (viewing, reading) obligado
compulsory [kəm'pʌlsərɪ] adj obligatorio
computer [kəm'pju:tə*] n ordenador m, computador m, computadora; **~ game** n juego para ordenador; **~-generated** adj realizado por ordenador, creado por ordenador; **~ize** vt (data) computerizar; (system) informatizar; **~ programmer** n programador(a) m/f; **~ programming** n programación f; **~ science** n informática; **computing** [kəm'pju:tɪŋ] n (activity, science) informática
comrade ['kɔmrɪd] n (POL, MIL) camarada; (friend) compañero/a; **~ship** n camaradería, compañerismo
con [kɔn] vt (deceive) engañar; (cheat) estafar ♦ n estafa
conceal [kən'si:l] vt ocultar
conceit [kən'si:t] n presunción f; **~ed** adj presumido
conceive [kən'si:v] vt, vi concebir
concentrate ['kɔnsəntreɪt] vi concentrarse ♦ vt concentrar
concentration [kɔnsən'treɪʃən] n concentración f
concept ['kɔnsept] n concepto
concern [kən'sɜ:n] n (matter) asunto; (COMM) empresa; (anxiety) preocupación f ♦ vt (worry) preocupar; (involve) afectar; (relate to) tener que ver con; **to be ~ed (about)** interesarse (por), preocuparse (por); **~ing** prep sobre, acerca de
concert ['kɔnsət] n concierto; **~ed** [kən'sɜ:tɪd] adj (efforts etc) concertado; **~ hall** n sala de conciertos
concerto [kən'tʃɜ:təu] n concierto
concession [kən'seʃən] n concesión f; **tax ~** privilegio fiscal
conclude [kən'klu:d] vt concluir; (treaty etc) firmar; (agreement) llegar a; (decide) llegar a la conclusión de; **conclusion** [-'klu:ʒən] n

conclusión f; firma; **conclusive** [-'kluːsɪv] adj decisivo, concluyente

concoct [kən'kɒkt] vt confeccionar; (plot) tramar; **~ion** [-'kɒkʃən] n mezcla

concourse ['kɒŋkɔːs] n vestíbulo

concrete ['kɒŋkriːt] n hormigón m ♦ adj de hormigón; (fig) concreto

concur [kən'kəː*] vi estar de acuerdo, asentir

concurrently [kən'kʌrntlɪ] adv al mismo tiempo

concussion [kən'kʌʃən] n conmoción f cerebral

condemn [kən'dɛm] vt condenar; (building) declarar en ruina

condense [kən'dɛns] vi condensarse ♦ vt condensar, abreviar; **~d milk** n leche f condensada

condition [kən'dɪʃən] n condición f, estado; (requirement) condición f ♦ vt condicionar; **on ~ that** a condición (de) que; **~er** n suavizante

condolences [kən'dəulənsɪz] npl pésame m

condom ['kɒndəm] n condón m

condone [kən'dəun] vt condonar

conducive [kən'djuːsɪv] adj: **~ to** conducente a

conduct [n 'kɒndʌkt, vb kən'dʌkt] n conducta, comportamiento ♦ vt (lead) conducir; (manage) llevar a cabo, dirigir; (MUS) dirigir; **to ~ o.s.** comportarse; **~ed tour** (BRIT) n visita acompañada; **~or** n (of orchestra) director m; (US: on train) revisor(a) m/f; (on bus) cobrador m; (ELEC) conductor m; **~ress** n (on bus) cobradora

cone [kəun] n cono; (pine ~) piña; (on road) pivote m; (for ice-cream) cucurucho

confectioner [kən'fɛkʃənə*] n repostero/a; **~'s (shop)** n confitería; **~y** n dulces mpl

confer [kən'fəː*] vt: **to ~ sth on** otorgar algo a ♦ vi conferenciar

conference ['kɒnfərns] n (meeting) reunión f; (convention) congreso

confess [kən'fɛs] vt confesar ♦ vi admitir; **~ion** [-'fɛʃən] n confesión f

confetti [kən'fɛtɪ] n confeti m

confide [kən'faɪd] vi: **to ~ in** confiar en

confidence ['kɒnfɪdns] n (also: self-~) confianza; (secret) confidencia; **in ~** (speak, write) en confianza; **~ trick** n timo; **confident** adj seguro de sí mismo; (certain) seguro; **confidential** [kɒnfɪ'dɛnʃəl] adj confidencial

confine [kən'faɪn] vt (limit) limitar; (shut up) encerrar; **~d** adj (space) reducido; **~ment** n (prison) prisión f; **~s** ['kɒnfaɪnz] npl confines mpl

confirm [kən'fəːm] vt confirmar; **~ation** [kɒnfə'meɪʃən] n confirmación f; **~ed** adj empedernido

confiscate ['kɒnfɪskeɪt] vt confiscar

conflict [n 'kɒnflɪkt, vb kən'flɪkt] n conflicto ♦ vi (opinions) chocar; **~ing** adj contradictorio

conform [kən'fɔːm] vi conformarse; **to ~ to** ajustarse a

confound [kən'faund] vt confundir

confront [kən'frʌnt] vt (problems) hacer frente a; (enemy, danger) enfrentarse con; **~ation** [kɒnfrən'teɪʃən] n enfrentamiento

confuse [kən'fjuːz] vt (perplex) aturdir, desconcertar; (mix up) confundir; (complicate) complicar; **~d** adj confuso; (person) perplejo; **confusing** adj confuso; **confusion** [-'fjuːʒən] n confusión f

congeal [kən'dʒiːl] vi (blood) coagularse; (sauce etc) cuajarse

congested [kən'dʒɛstɪd] adj congestionado; **congestion** n congestión f

congratulate [kən'grætjuleɪt] vt: **to ~ sb (on)** felicitar a uno (por); **congratulations** [-'leɪʃənz] npl felicitaciones fpl; **congratulations!** ¡enhorabuena!

congregate ['kɒŋɡrɪɡeɪt] vi congregarse; **congregation** [-'ɡeɪʃən] n (of a church) feligreses mpl

congress ['kɒŋɡrɛs] n congreso; (US): **C~** Congreso; **C~man** (irreg) (US) n miembro del Congreso

conifer ['kɒnɪfə*] n conífera

conjunctivitis [kəndʒʌŋktɪ'vaɪtɪs] n conjuntivitis f

conjure ['kʌndʒə*] vi hacer juegos de manos; **~ up** vt (ghost, spirit) hacer aparecer; (memories) evocar; **~r** n ilusionista m/f

con man ['kɒn-] n estafador m

connect [kə'nɛkt] vt juntar, unir; (ELEC) conectar; (TEL: subscriber) poner; (: caller) poner al habla; (fig) relacionar, asociar ♦ vi: **to ~ with** (train) enlazar con; **to be ~ed with** (associated) estar relacionado con; **~ion** [-ʃən] n juntura, unión f; (ELEC) conexión f; (RAIL) enlace m; (TEL) comunicación f; (fig) relación f

connive [kə'naɪv] vi: **to ~ at** hacer la vista gorda a

connoisseur [kɒnɪ'səə*] n experto/a, entendido/a

conquer ['kɒŋkə*] vt (territory) conquistar; (enemy, feelings) vencer; **~or** n conquistador m

conquest ['kɒŋkwest] n conquista

cons [kɒnz] npl see **convenience**; **pro**

conscience ['kɒnʃəns] n conciencia

conscientious [kɒnʃɪ'ɛnʃəs] adj concienzudo; (objection) de conciencia

conscious ['kɒnʃəs] adj (deliberate) deliberado; (awake, aware) consciente; **~ness** n conciencia; (MED) conocimiento

conscript ['kɒnskrɪpt] n recluta m; **~ion** [kən'skrɪpʃən] n servicio militar (obligatorio)

consensus [kən'sɛnsəs] n consenso

consent [kən'sɛnt] n consentimiento ♦ vi: **to ~ (to)** consentir (en)

consequence ['kɒnsɪkwəns] n consecuencia; (significance) importancia

consequently ['kɒnsɪkwəntlɪ] adv por consiguiente

conservation [kɒnsə'veɪʃən] n conservación f

conservative [kən'sɔːvətɪv] adj conservador(a); (estimate etc) cauteloso; **C~** (BRIT) adj, n (POL) conservador(a) m/f

conservatory [kən'sɔːvətrɪ] n invernadero; (MUS) conservatorio

conserve [kən'sɔːv] vt conservar ♦ n conserva

consider [kən'sɪdə*] vt considerar; (take into account) tener en cuenta; (study) estudiar, examinar; **to ~ doing sth** pensar en (la posibilidad de) hacer algo; **~able** adj considerable; **~ably** adv notablemente; **~ate** adj considerado; **consideration** [-'reɪʃən] n consideración f; (factor) factor m; **to give sth further consideration** estudiar algo más a fondo; **~ing** prep teniendo en cuenta

consign [kən'saɪn] vt: **to ~ to** (sth unwanted) relegar a; (person) destinar a; **~ment** n envío

consist [kən'sɪst] vi: **to ~ of** consistir en

consistency [kən'sɪstənsɪ] n (of argument etc) coherencia; consecuencia; (thickness) consistencia

consistent [kən'sɪstənt] adj (person) consecuente; (argument etc) coherente

consolation [kɒnsə'leɪʃən] n consuelo

console¹ [kən'səʊl] vt consolar

console² [kən'səʊl] n consola

consonant ['kɒnsənənt] n consonante f

consortium [kən'sɔːtɪəm] n consorcio

conspicuous [kən'spɪkjuəs] adj (visible) visible

conspiracy [kən'spɪrəsɪ] n conjura, complot m

constable ['kʌnstəbl] (BRIT) n policía m/f; **chief ~** ≈ jefe m de policía

constabulary [kən'stæbjulərɪ] n ≈ policía

constant ['kɒnstənt] adj constante; **~ly** adv constantemente

constipated ['kɒnstɪpeɪtɪd] adj estreñido; **constipation** [kɒnstɪ'peɪʃən] n estreñimiento

constituency [kən'stɪtjuənsɪ] n (POL: area) distrito electoral; (: electors) electorado;

constituent [-ənt] n (POL) elector(a) m/f; (part) componente m

constitution [kɒnstɪ'tjuːʃən] n constitución f; **~al** adj constitucional

constraint [kən'streɪnt] n obligación f; (limit) restricción f

construct [kən'strʌkt] vt construir; **~ion** [-ʃən] n construcción f; **~ive** adj constructivo

consul ['kɒnsl] n cónsul m/f; **~ate** ['kɒnsjulɪt] n consulado

consult [kən'sʌlt] vt consultar; **~ant** n (BRIT: MED) especialista m/f; (other specialist) asesor(a) m/f; **~ation** [kɒnsəl'teɪʃən] n consulta; **~ing room** (BRIT) n consultorio

consume [kən'sjuːm] vt (eat) comerse; (drink) beberse; (fire etc, COMM) consumir; **~r** n consumidor(a) m/f; **~r goods** npl bienes mpl de consumo

consummate ['kɒnsʌmeɪt] vt consumar

consumption [kən'sʌmpʃən] n consumo

cont. abbr (= continued) sigue

contact ['kɒntækt] n contacto; (person) contacto; (: pej) enchufe m ♦ vt ponerse en contacto con; **~ lenses** npl lentes fpl de contacto

contagious [kən'teɪdʒəs] adj contagioso

contain [kən'teɪn] vt contener; **to ~ o.s.** contenerse; **~er** n recipiente m; (for shipping etc) contenedor m

contaminate [kən'tæmɪneɪt] vt contaminar

cont'd abbr (= continued) sigue

contemplate ['kɒntəmpleɪt] vt contemplar; (reflect upon) considerar

contemporary [kən'tɛmpərərɪ] adj, n contemporáneo/a m/f

contempt [kən'tɛmpt] n desprecio; **~ of court** (LAW) desacato a (los tribunales); **~ible** adj despreciable; **~uous** adj desdeñoso

contend [kən'tɛnd] vt (argue) afirmar ♦ vi: **to ~ with/for** luchar contra/por; **~er** n (SPORT) contendiente m/f

content [adj, vb kən'tɛnt, n 'kɒntɛnt] adj (happy) contento; (satisfied) satisfecho ♦ vt contentar; satisfacer ♦ n contenido; **~s** npl contenido; (table of) **~s** índice m de materias; **~ed** adj contento; satisfecho

contention [kən'tɛnʃən] n (assertion) aseveración f; (disagreement) discusión f

contest [n 'kɒntɛst, vb kən'tɛst] n lucha; (competition) concurso ♦ vt (dispute) impugnar; (POL) presentarse como candidato/a en; **~ant** n concursante m/f; (in fight) contendiente m/f

context ['kɒntɛkst] n contexto

continent ['kɒntɪnənt] n continente m; **the C~** (BRIT) el continente europeo; **~al** [-'nɛntl] adj continental; **~al breakfast** n desayuno estilo europeo; **~al quilt** (BRIT) n edredón m

contingency [kən'tɪndʒənsɪ] n contingencia

continual [kən'tɪnjuəl] adj continuo; **~ly** adv constantemente

continuation [kəntɪnju'eɪʃən] n prolongación f; (after interruption) reanudación f

continue [kən'tɪnjuː] vi, vt seguir, continuar

continuous [kən'tɪnjuəs] adj continuo

contort [kən'tɔ:t] vt retorcer

contour ['kɒntuə*] n contorno; (also: ~ line) curva de nivel

contraband ['kɒntrəbænd] n contrabando

contraceptive [kɒntrə'septɪv] adj, n anticonceptivo

contract [n 'kɒntrækt, vb kən'trækt] n contrato ♦ vi (COMM): **to ~ to do sth** comprometerse por contrato a hacer algo; (become smaller) contraerse, encogerse ♦ vt contraer; ~**ion** [kən'trækʃən] n contracción f; ~**or** n contratista m/f

contradict [kɒntrə'dɪkt] vt contradecir; ~**ion** [-ʃən] n contradicción f

contraption [kən'træpʃən] (pej) n artilugio m

contrary[1] ['kɒntrərɪ] adj contrario ♦ n lo contrario; **on the ~** al contrario; **unless you hear to the ~** a no ser que le digan lo contrario

contrary[2] [kən'trɛərɪ] adj (perverse) terco

contrast [n 'kɒntrɑ:st, vt kən'trɑ:st] n contraste m ♦ vt comparar; **in ~ to** en contraste con

contravene [kɒntrə'vi:n] vt infringir

contribute [kən'trɪbju:t] vi contribuir ♦ vt: **to ~ £10/an article to** contribuir con 10 libras/un artículo a; **to ~ to** (charity) donar a; (newspaper) escribir para; (discussion) intervenir en; **contribution** [kɒntrɪ'bju:ʃən] n (donation) donativo; (BRIT: for social security) cotización f; (to debate) intervención f; (to journal) colaboración f; **contributor** n contribuyente m/f; (to newspaper) colaborador(a) m/f

contrive [kən'traɪv] vt (invent) idear ♦ vi: **to ~ to do** lograr hacer

control [kən'trəul] vt controlar; (process etc) dirigir; (machinery) manejar; (temper) dominar; (disease) contener ♦ n control m; ~**s** npl (of vehicle) instrumentos mpl de mando; (of radio) controles mpl; (governmental) medidas fpl de control; **under** ~ bajo control; **to be in** ~ **of** tener el mando de; **the car went out of** ~ se perdió el control del coche; ~**led substance** n sustancia controlada; ~ **panel** n tablero de instrumentos; ~ **room** n sala de mando; ~ **tower** n (AVIAT) torre f de control

controversial [kɒntrə'vɜ:ʃl] adj polémico

controversy ['kɒntrəvɜ:sɪ] n polémica

convalesce [kɒnvə'les] vi convalecer

convector [kən'vektə*] n calentador m de aire

convene [kən'vi:n] vt convocar ♦ vi reunirse

convenience [kən'vi:nɪəns] n (easiness) comodidad f; (suitability) idoneidad f; (advantage) ventaja; **at your** ~ cuando le sea conveniente; **all modern ~s, all mod cons** (BRIT) todo confort

convenient [kən'vi:nɪənt] adj (useful) útil; (place, time) conveniente

convent ['kɒnvənt] n convento

convention [kən'venʃən] n convención f; (meeting) asamblea; (agreement) convenio; ~**al** adj convencional

converge [kən'vɜ:dʒ] vi convergir; (people): **to ~ on** dirigirse todos a

conversant [kən'vɜ:snt] adj: **to be ~ with** estar al tanto de

conversation [kɒnvə'seɪʃən] n conversación f; ~**al** adj familiar; ~**al skill** facilidad f de palabra

converse [n 'kɒnvɜ:s, vb kən'vɜ:s] n inversa ♦ vi conversar; ~**ly** [-'vɜ:slɪ] adv a la inversa

conversion [kən'vɜ:ʃən] n conversión f

convert [vb kən'vɜ:t, n 'kɒnvɜ:t] vt (REL, COMM) convertir; (alter): **to ~ sth into/to** transformar algo en/convertir algo a ♦ n converso/a; ~**ible** adj convertible ♦ n descapotable m

convey [kən'veɪ] vt llevar; (thanks) comunicar; (idea) expresar; ~**or belt** n cinta transportadora

convict [vb kən'vɪkt, n 'kɒnvɪkt] vt (find guilty) declarar culpable a ♦ n presidiario/a; ~**ion** [-ʃən] n condena; (belief, certainty) convicción f

convince [kən'vɪns] vt convencer; ~**d** adj: ~**d of/that** convencido de/de que; **convincing** adj convincente

convoluted ['kɒnvəlu:tɪd] adj (argument etc) enrevesado

convoy ['kɒnvɔɪ] n convoy m

convulse [kən'vʌls] vt: **to be** ~**d with laughter** desternillarse de risa; **convulsion** [-'vʌlʃən] n convulsión f

cook [kuk] vt (stew etc) guisar; (meal) preparar ♦ vi cocer; (person) cocinar ♦ n cocinero/a; ~ **book** n libro de cocina; ~**er** n cocina; ~**ery** n cocina; ~**ery book** (BRIT) n = ~ **book**; ~**ie** (US) n galleta; ~**ing** n cocina

cool [ku:l] adj fresco; (not afraid) tranquilo; (unfriendly) frío ♦ vt enfriar ♦ vi enfriarse; ~**ness** n frescura; tranquilidad f; (indifference) falta de entusiasmo

coop [ku:p] n gallinero ♦ vt: **to ~ up** (fig) encerrar

cooperate [kəu'ɒpəreɪt] vi cooperar, colaborar; **cooperation** [-'reɪʃən] n cooperación f, colaboración f; **cooperative** [-rətɪv] adj (business) cooperativo; (person) servicial ♦ n cooperativa

coordinate [vb kəu'ɔ:dɪneɪt, n kəu'ɔ:dɪnət] vt coordinar ♦ n (MATH) coordenada; ~**s** npl (clothes) coordinados mpl; **coordination** [-'neɪʃən] n coordinación f

co-ownership [kəu'əunəʃip] n co-propiedad f

cop [kɔp] (inf) n poli m (SP), tira m (AM)

cope [kəup] vi: to ~ with (problem) hacer frente a

copper ['kɔpə*] n (metal) cobre m; (BRIT: inf) poli m; ~s npl (money) calderilla (SP), centavos mpl (AM)

copulate ['kɔpjuleit] vi copularse

copy ['kɔpi] n copia; (of book etc) ejemplar m ♦ vt copiar; ~right n derechos mpl de autor

coral ['kɔrəl] n coral m

cord [kɔ:d] n cuerda; (ELEC) cable m; (fabric) pana

cordial ['kɔ:diəl] adj cordial ♦ n cordial m

cordon ['kɔ:dn] n cordón m; ~ off vt acordonar

corduroy ['kɔ:dərɔi] n pana

core [kɔ:*] n centro, núcleo; (of fruit) corazón m; (of problem) meollo ♦ vt quitar el corazón de

coriander [kɔri'ændə*] n culantro

cork [kɔ:k] n corcho; (tree) alcornoque m; ~screw n sacacorchos m inv

corn [kɔ:n] n (BRIT: cereal crop) trigo; (US: maize) maíz m; (on foot) callo; ~ on the cob (CULIN) maíz m en la mazorca (SP), choclo (AM)

corned beef ['kɔ:nd-] n carne f acecinada (en lata)

corner ['kɔ:nə*] n (outside) esquina; (inside) rincón m; (in road) curva; (FOOTBALL) córner m; (BOXING) esquina ♦ vt (trap) arrinconar; (COMM) acaparar ♦ vi (in car) tomar las curvas; ~stone n (also fig) piedra angular

cornet ['kɔ:nit] n (MUS) corneta; (BRIT: of ice-cream) cucurucho

cornflakes ['kɔ:nfleiks] npl copos mpl de maíz, cornflakes mpl

cornflour ['kɔ:nflauə*] (BRIT), **cornstarch** ['kɔ:nsta:tʃ] (US) n harina de maíz

Cornwall ['kɔ:nwəl] n Cornualles m

corny ['kɔ:ni] (inf) adj gastado

coronary ['kɔrənəri] n (also: ~ thrombosis) infarto

coronation [kɔrə'neiʃən] n coronación f

coroner ['kɔrənə*] n juez m (de instrucción)

corporal ['kɔ:pərl] n cabo ♦ adj: ~ punishment castigo corporal

corporate ['kɔ:pərit] adj (action, ownership) colectivo; (finance, image) corporativo

corporation [kɔ:pə'reiʃən] n (of town) ayuntamiento; (COMM) corporación f

corps [kɔ:*, pl kɔ:z] n inv cuerpo; **diplomatic** ~ cuerpo diplomático; **press** ~ gabinete m de prensa

corpse [kɔ:ps] n cadáver m

correct [kə'rekt] adj justo, exacto; (proper) correcto ♦ vt corregir; (exam) corregir, calificar; ~ion [-ʃən] n (act) corrección f; (instance) rectificación f

correspond [kɔris'pɔnd] vi (write): to ~ (with) escribirse (con); (be equivalent to): to ~ (to) corresponder (a); (be in accordance): to ~ (with) corresponder (con); ~ence n correspondencia; ~ence course n curso por correspondencia; ~ent n corresponsal m/f

corridor ['kɔridɔ:*] n pasillo

corrode [kə'rəud] vt corroer ♦ vi corroerse

corrugated ['kɔrəgeitid] adj ondulado; ~ iron n chapa ondulada

corrupt [kə'rʌpt] adj (person) corrupto; (COMPUT) corrompido ♦ vt corromper; (COMPUT) degradar

Corsica ['kɔ:sikə] n Córcega

cosmetic [kɔz'metik] adj, n cosmético

cosmopolitan [kɔzmə'pɔlitn] adj cosmopolita

cost [kɔst] (pt, pp cost) n (price) precio; ~s npl (COMM) costes mpl; (LAW) costas fpl ♦ vi costar, valer ♦ vt preparar el presupuesto de; **how much does it ~?** ¿cuánto cuesta?; **to ~ sb time/effort** costarle a uno tiempo/esfuerzo; **it ~ him his life** le costó la vida; **at all ~s** cueste lo que cueste

co-star ['kəusta:*] n coprotagonista m/f

Costa Rica ['kɔstə'ri:kə] n Costa Rica; ~**n** adj, n costarriqueño/a m/f

cost-effective [kɔsti'fektiv] adj rentable

costly ['kɔstli] adj costoso

cost-of-living [kɔstəv'liviŋ] adj: ~ **allowance** plus m de carestía de vida; ~ **index** índice m del costo de vida

cost price (BRIT) n precio de coste

costume ['kɔstju:m] n traje m; (BRIT: also: swimming ~) traje de baño; ~ **jewellery** n bisutería

cosy ['kəuzi] (US **cozy**) adj (person) cómodo; (room) acogedor(a)

cot [kɔt] n (BRIT: child's) cuna; (US: campbed) cama de campaña

cottage ['kɔtidʒ] n casita de campo; (rustic) barraca; ~ **cheese** n requesón m

cotton ['kɔtn] n algodón m; (thread) hilo; ~ **on to** (inf) vt fus caer en la cuenta de; ~ **candy** (US) n algodón m (azucarado); ~ **wool** (BRIT) n algodón m (hidrófilo)

couch [kautʃ] n sofá m; (doctor's etc) diván m

couchette [ku:'ʃet] n litera

cough [kɔf] vi toser ♦ n tos f; ~ **drop** n pastilla para la tos

could [kud] pt of **can²**; ~**n't** = **could not**

council ['kaunsl] n consejo; **city** or **town** ~ consejo municipal; ~ **estate** (BRIT) n urbanización f de viviendas municipales de alquiler; ~ **house** (BRIT) n vivienda municipal de alquiler; ~**lor** n concejal(a) m/f

counsel ['kaunsl] n (advice) consejo; (lawyer)

abogado/a ♦ vt aconsejar; **~lor** n consejero/
a; **~or** (US) n abogado/a
count [kaunt] vt contar; (include) incluir ♦ vi
contar ♦ n cuenta; (of votes) escrutinio;
(level) nivel m; (nobleman) conde m; **~ on** vt
fus contar con; **~down** n cuenta atrás
countenance ['kauntınəns] n semblante m,
rostro ♦ vt (tolerate) aprobar, tolerar
counter ['kauntə*] n (in shop) mostrador m;
(in games) ficha ♦ vt contrarrestar ♦ adv: to
run **~ to** ser contrario a, ir en contra de; **~act**
vt contrarrestar
counterfeit ['kauntəfıt] n falsificación f,
simulación f ♦ vt falsificar ♦ adj falso,
falsificado
counterfoil ['kauntəfoıl] n talón m
counterpart ['kauntəpɑːt] n homólogo/a
counter-productive [kauntəprə'dʌktıv]
adj contraproducente
countersign ['kauntəsaın] vt refrendar
countess ['kauntıs] n condesa
countless ['kauntlıs] adj innumerable
country ['kʌntrı] n país m; (native land)
patria; (as opposed to town) campo; (region)
región f, tierra; **~ dancing** (BRIT) n baile m
regional; **~ house** n casa de campo; **~man**
n (irreg) (compatriot) compatriota m; (rural)
campesino, paisano; **~side** n campo
county ['kauntı] n condado
coup [kuː] (pl **~s**) n (also: **~ d'état**) golpe m
(de estado); (achievement) éxito
couple ['kʌpl] n (of things) par m; (of people)
pareja; (married **~**) matrimonio; **a ~** of un par
de
coupon ['kuːpɔn] n cupón m; (voucher) valé
m
courage ['kʌrıdʒ] n valor m, valentía; **~ous**
[kə'reıdʒəs] adj valiente
courgette [kuə'ʒɛt] (BRIT) n calabacín m (SP),
calabacita (AM)
courier ['kurıə*] n mensajero/a; (for tourists)
guía m/f (de turismo)
course [kɔːs] n (direction) dirección f; (of
river, SCOL) curso; (process) transcurso; (MED):
~ of treatment tratamiento; (of ship) rumbo;
(part of meal) plato; (GOLF) campo; **of ~**
desde luego, naturalmente; **of ~!** ¡claro!
court [kɔːt] n (royal) corte f; (LAW) tribunal m,
juzgado; (TENNIS etc) pista, cancha ♦ vt
(woman) cortejar a; **to take to ~** demandar
courteous ['kɜːtıəs] adj cortés
courtesy ['kɜːtəsı] n cortesía; **(by) ~ of** por
cortesía de; **~ bus**, **~ coach** n autobús m
gratuito
court-house ['kɔːthaus] (US) n palacio de
justicia
courtier ['kɔːtıə*] n cortesano
court-martial (pl **courts-martial**) n consejo
de guerra

courtroom ['kɔːtrum] n sala de justicia
courtyard ['kɔːtjɑːd] n patio
cousin ['kʌzn] n primo/a; **first ~** primo/a
carnal, primo/a hermano/a
cove [kəuv] n cala, ensenada
covenant ['kʌvənənt] n pacto
cover ['kʌvə*] vt cubrir; (feelings, mistake)
ocultar; (with lid) tapar; (book etc) forrar;
(distance) recorrer; (include) abarcar;
(protect: also: INSURANCE) cubrir; (PRESS)
investigar; (discuss) tratar ♦ n cubierta; (lid)
tapa; (for chair etc) funda; (envelope) sobre
m; (for book) forro; (of magazine) portada;
(shelter) abrigo; (INSURANCE) cobertura; (of
spy) cobertura; **~s** npl (on bed) sábanas;
mantas; **to take ~** (shelter) protegerse,
resguardarse; **under ~** (indoors) bajo techo;
under ~ of darkness al amparo de la
oscuridad; **under separate ~** (COMM) por
separado; **~ up** vi: **to ~ up for sb** encubrir a
uno; **~age** n (TV, PRESS) cobertura; **~alls** (US)
npl mono; **~ charge** n precio del cubierto;
~ing n capa; **~ing letter** (US **~ letter**) n
carta de explicación; **~ note** n (INSURANCE)
póliza provisional
covert ['kʌuvət] adj secreto, encubierto
cover-up n encubrimiento
cow [kau] n vaca; (infl: woman) bruja ♦ vt
intimidar
coward ['kauəd] n cobarde m/f; **~ice** [-ıs] n
cobardía; **~ly** adj cobarde
cowboy ['kaubɔı] n vaquero
cower ['kauə*] vi encogerse (de miedo)
coy [kɔı] adj tímido
cozy ['kəuzı] (US) adj = **cosy**
CPA (US) n abbr = **certified public accountant**
crab [kræb] n cangrejo; **~ apple** n manzana
silvestre
crack [kræk] n grieta; (noise) crujido; (drug)
crack m ♦ vt agrietar, romper; (nut) cascar;
(solve: problem) resolver; (: code) descifrar;
(whip etc) chasquear; (knuckles) crujir; (joke)
contar ♦ adj (expert) de primera; **~ down
on** vt fus adoptar fuertes medidas contra;
~ up vi (MED) sufrir una crisis nerviosa; **~er** n
(biscuit) cráquer m; (Christmas **~er**) petardo
sorpresa
crackle ['krækl] vi crepitar
cradle ['kreıdl] n cuna
craft [krɑːft] n (skill) arte m; (trade) oficio;
(cunning) astucia; (boat: pl inv) barco;
(plane: pl inv) avión m
craftsman ['krɑːftsmən] n artesano; **~ship** n
(quality) destreza
crafty ['krɑːftı] adj astuto
crag [kræg] n peñasco
cram [kræm] vt (fill): **to ~ sth with** llenar algo
(a reventar) de; (put): **to ~ sth into** meter
algo a la fuerza en ♦ vi (for exams) empollar

cramp [kræmp] *n* (*MED*) calambre *m*; **~ed**
adj apretado, estrecho
cranberry ['krænbərı] *n* arándano agrio
crane [kreɪn] *n* (*TECH*) grúa; (*bird*) grulla
crank [kræŋk] *n* manivela; (*person*) chiflado
cranny ['krænɪ] *n see* **nook**
crash [kræʃ] *n* (*noise*) estrépito; (*of cars etc*)
choque *m*; (*of plane*) accidente *m* de
aviación; (*COMM*) quiebra ♦ *vt* (*car, plane*)
estrellar ♦ *vi* (*car, plane*) estrellarse; (*two
cars*) chocar; (*COMM*) quebrar; **~ course** *n*
curso acelerado; **~ helmet** *n* casco
(protector); **~ landing** *n* aterrizaje *m* forzado
crass [kræs] *adj* grosero, maleducado
crate [kreɪt] *n* cajón *m* de embalaje; (*for
bottles*) caja
cravat(e) [krə'væt] *n* pañuelo
crave [kreɪv] *vt, vi*: **to ~ (for)** ansiar, anhelar
crawl [krɔːl] *vi* (*drag o.s.*) arrastrarse; (*child*)
andar a gatas, gatear; (*vehicle*) avanzar
(lentamente) ♦ *n* (*SWIMMING*) crol *m*
crayfish ['kreɪfɪʃ] *n inv* (*freshwater*) cangrejo
de río; (*saltwater*) cigala
crayon ['kreɪən] *n* lápiz *m* de color
craze [kreɪz] *n* (*fashion*) moda
crazy ['kreɪzɪ] *adj* (*person*) loco; (*idea*)
disparatado; (*inf: keen*): **~ about sb/sth** loco
por uno/algo
creak [kriːk] *vi* (*floorboard*) crujir; (*hinge etc*)
chirriar, rechinar
cream [kriːm] *n* (*of milk*) nata, crema; (*lotion*)
crema; (*fig*) flor *f* y nata ♦ *adj* (*colour*) color
crema; **~ cake** *n* pastel *m* de nata;
~ cheese *n* queso blanco; **~y** *adj* cremoso;
(*colour*) color crema
crease [kriːs] *n* (*fold*) pliegue *m*; (*in trousers*)
raya; (*wrinkle*) arruga ♦ *vt* (*wrinkle*) arrugar
♦ *vi* (*wrinkle up*) arrugarse
create [kriː'eɪt] *vt* crear; **creation** [-ʃən] *n*
creación *f*; **creative** *adj* creativo; **creator** *n*
creador(a) *m/f*
creature ['kriːtʃə*] *n* (*animal*) animal *m*,
bicho; (*person*) criatura
crèche [kreʃ] *n* guardería (infantil)
credence ['kriːdəns] *n*: **to lend** *or* **give ~ to**
creer en, dar crédito a
credentials [krɪ'denʃlz] *npl* (*references*)
referencias *fpl*; (*identity papers*) documentos
mpl de identidad
credible ['kredɪbl] *adj* creíble; (*trustworthy*)
digno de confianza
credit ['kredɪt] *n* crédito; (*merit*) honor *m*,
mérito ♦ *vt* (*COMM*) abonar; (*believe: also*:
give ~ to) creer, prestar fe a ♦ *adj* crediticio;
~s *npl* (*CINEMA*) fichas *fpl* técnicas; **to be in ~**
(*person*) tener saldo a favor; **to ~ sb with** (*fig*)
reconocer a uno el mérito de; **~ card** *n*
tarjeta de crédito; **~or** *n* acreedor(a) *m/f*
creed [kriːd] *n* credo

creek [kriːk] *n* cala, ensenada; (*US*) riachuelo
creep [kriːp] (*pt, pp* **crept**) *vi* arrastrarse; **~er**
n enredadera; **~y** *adj* (*frightening*)
horripilante
cremate [krɪ'meɪt] *vt* incinerar
crematorium [kremə'tɔːrɪəm] (*pl
crematoria*) *n* crematorio
crêpe [kreɪp] *n* (*fabric*) crespón *m*; (*also*:
~ rubber) crepé *m*; **~ bandage** (*BRIT*) *n*
venda de crepé
crept [krept] *pt, pp of* **creep**
crescent ['kresnt] *n* media luna; (*street*) calle
f (*en forma de semicírculo*)
cress [kres] *n* berro
crest [krest] *n* (*of bird*) cresta; (*of hill*) cima,
cumbre *f*; (*of coat of arms*) blasón *m*; **~fallen**
adj alicaído
crevice ['krevɪs] *n* grieta, hendedura
crew [kruː] *n* (*of ship etc*) tripulación *f*; (*TV,
CINEMA*) equipo; **~-cut** *n* corte *m* al rape; **~-
neck** *n* cuello a la caja
crib [krɪb] *n* cuna ♦ *vt* (*inf*) plagiar
crick [krɪk] *n* (*in neck*) tortícolis *f*
cricket ['krɪkɪt] *n* (*insect*) grillo; (*game*)
críquet *m*
crime [kraɪm] *n* (*no pl: illegal activities*)
crimen *m*; (*illegal action*) delito; **criminal**
['krɪmɪnl] *n* criminal *m/f*, delincuente *m/f*
♦ *adj* criminal; (*illegal*) delictivo; (*law*) penal
crimson ['krɪmzn] *adj* carmesí
cringe [krɪndʒ] *vi* agacharse, encogerse
crinkle ['krɪŋkl] *vt* arrugar
cripple ['krɪpl] *n* lisiado/a, cojo/a ♦ *vt* lisiar,
mutilar
crisis ['kraɪsɪs] (*pl crises*) *n* crisis *f inv*
crisp [krɪsp] *adj* fresco; (*vegetables etc*)
crujiente; (*manner*) seco; **~s** (*BRIT*) *npl*
patatas *fpl* (*SP*) or papas *fpl* (*AM*) fritas
crisscross ['krɪskrɔs] *adj* entrelazado
criterion [kraɪ'tɪərɪən] (*pl criteria*) *n* criterio
critic ['krɪtɪk] *n* crítico/a; **~al** *adj* crítico;
(*illness*) grave; **~ally** *adv* (*speak etc*) en tono
crítico; (*ill*) gravemente; **~ism** ['krɪtɪsɪzm] *n*
crítica; **~ize** ['krɪtɪsaɪz] *vt* criticar
croak [krəuk] *vi* (*frog*) croar; (*raven*) graznar;
(*person*) gruñir
Croatia [krəu'eɪʃə] *n* Croacia
crochet ['krəuʃeɪ] *n* ganchillo
crockery ['krɔkərɪ] *n* loza, vajilla
crocodile ['krɔkədaɪl] *n* cocodrilo
crocus ['krəukəs] *n* croco, crocus *m*
croft [krɔft] *n* granja pequeña
crony ['krəunɪ] (*inf: pej*) *n* compinche *m/f*
crook [kruk] *n* ladrón/ona *m/f*; (*of shepherd*)
cayado; **~ed** ['krukɪd] *adj* torcido; (*dishonest*)
nada honrado
crop [krɔp] *n* (*produce*) cultivo; (*amount
produced*) cosecha; (*riding ~*) látigo de
montar ♦ *vt* cortar, recortar; **~ up** *vi* surgir,

presentarse

cross [krɔs] n cruz f; (hybrid) cruce m ♦ vt (street etc) cruzar, atravesar ♦ adj de mal humor, enojado; **~ out** vt tachar; **~ over** vi cruzar; **~bar** n travesaño; **~country (race)** n carrera a campo traviesa, cross m; **~examine** vt interrogar; **~-eyed** adj bizco; **~fire** n fuego cruzado; **~ing** n (sea passage) travesía; (also: pedestrian ~ing) paso para peatones; **~ing guard** (US) n persona encargada de ayudar a los niños a cruzar la calle; **~ purposes** npl: to be at ~ purposes no comprenderse uno a otro; **~reference** n referencia, llamada; **~roads** n cruce m, encrucijada; **~ section** n corte m transversal; (of population) muestra (representativa); **~walk** (US) n paso de peatones; **~wind** n viento de costado; **~word** n crucigrama m

crotch [krɔtʃ] n (ANAT, of garment) entrepierna

crotchet ['krɔtʃɪt] n (MUS) negra

crouch [krautʃ] vi agacharse, acurrucarse

crow [krəu] n (bird) cuervo; (of cock) canto, cacareo ♦ vi (cock) cantar

crowbar ['krəubɑ:ʳ] n palanca

crowd [kraud] n muchedumbre f, multitud f ♦ vt (fill) llenar ♦ vi (gather): to ~ round reunirse en torno a; (cram): to ~ in entrar en tropel; **~ed** adj (full) atestado; (densely populated) superpoblado

crown [kraun] n corona; (of head) coronilla; (for tooth) funda; (of hill) cumbre f ♦ vt coronar; (fig) completar, rematar; **~ jewels** npl joyas fpl reales; **~ prince** n príncipe m heredero

crow's feet npl patas fpl de gallo

crucial ['kru:ʃl] adj decisivo

crucifix ['kru:sɪfɪks] n crucifijo; **~ion** [-'fɪkʃən] n crucifixión f

crude [kru:d] adj (materials) bruto; (fig: basic) tosco; (: vulgar) ordinario; **~ (oil)** n (petróleo) crudo

cruel ['kruəl] adj cruel; **~ty** n crueldad f

cruise [kru:z] n crucero ♦ vi (ship) hacer un crucero; (car) ir a velocidad de crucero; **~r** n (motorboat) yate m de motor; (warship) crucero

crumb [krʌm] n miga, migaja

crumble ['krʌmbl] vt desmenuzar ♦ vi (building, also fig) desmoronarse; **crumbly** adj que se desmigaja fácilmente

crumpet ['krʌmpɪt] n ≈ bollo para tostar

crumple ['krʌmpl] vt (paper) estrujar; (material) arrugar

crunch [krʌntʃ] vt (with teeth) mascar; (underfoot) hacer crujir ♦ n (fig) hora o momento de la verdad; **~y** adj crujiente

crusade [kru:'seɪd] n cruzada

crush [krʌʃ] n (crowd) aglomeración f; (infatuation): to have a ~ on sb estar loco por uno; (drink): lemon ~ limonada ♦ vt aplastar; (paper) estrujar; (cloth) arrugar; (fruit) exprimir; (opposition) aplastar; (hopes) destruir

crust [krʌst] n corteza; (of snow, ice) costra

crutch [krʌtʃ] n muleta

crux [krʌks] n: the ~ of lo esencial de, el quid de

cry [kraɪ] vi llorar; (shout: also: ~ out) gritar ♦ n (shriek) chillido; (shout) grito; **~ off** vi echarse atrás

cryptic ['krɪptɪk] adj enigmático, secreto

crystal ['krɪstl] n cristal m; **~-clear** adj claro como el agua

cub [kʌb] n cachorro; (also: ~ scout) niño explorador

Cuba ['kju:bə] n Cuba; **~n** adj, n cubano/a m/f

cube [kju:b] n cubo ♦ vt (MATH) cubicar; **cubic** adj cúbico

cubicle ['kju:bɪkl] n (at pool) caseta; (for bed) cubículo

cuckoo ['kuku:] n cuco; **~ clock** n reloj m de cucú

cucumber ['kju:kʌmbəʳ] n pepino

cuddle ['kʌdl] vt abrazar ♦ vi abrazarse

cue [kju:] n (snooker ~) taco; (THEATRE etc) señal f

cuff [kʌf] n (of sleeve) puño; (US: of trousers) vuelta; (blow) bofetada; **off the ~** adv de improviso; **~links** npl gemelos mpl

cuisine [kwɪ'zi:n] n cocina

cul-de-sac ['kʌldəsæk] n callejón m sin salida

cull [kʌl] vt (idea) sacar ♦ n (of animals) matanza selectiva

culminate ['kʌlmɪneɪt] vi: to ~ in terminar en; **culmination** [-'neɪʃən] n culminación f, colmo

culottes [ku:'lɔts] npl falda pantalón f

culprit ['kʌlprɪt] n culpable m/f

cult [kʌlt] n culto

cultivate ['kʌltɪveɪt] vt (also fig) cultivar; **~d** adj culto; **cultivation** [-'veɪʃən] n cultivo

cultural ['kʌltʃərəl] adj cultural

culture ['kʌltʃəʳ] n (also fig) cultura; (BIO) cultivo; **~d** adj culto

cumbersome ['kʌmbəsəm] adj de mucho bulto, voluminoso; (process) enrevesado

cunning ['kʌnɪŋ] n astucia ♦ adj astuto

cup [kʌp] n taza; (as prize) copa

cupboard ['kʌbəd] n armario; (kitchen) alacena

cup tie (BRIT) n partido de copa

curate ['kjuərɪt] n cura m

curator [kjuə'reɪtəʳ] n director(a) m/f

curb [kə:b] vt refrenar; (person) reprimir ♦ n freno; (US) bordillo

curdle ['kə:dl] vi cuajarse

cure [kjuə*] vt curar ♦ n cura, curación f; (fig: solution) remedio

curfew ['kə:fju:] n toque m de queda

curiosity [kjuərɪ'ɔsɪtɪ] n curiosidad f

curious ['kjuərɪəs] adj curioso; (person: interested): **to be ~** sentir curiosidad

curl [kə:l] n rizo ♦ vt (hair) rizar ♦ vi rizarse; **~ up** vi (person) hacerse un ovillo; **~er** n rulo; **~y** adj rizado

currant ['kʌrnt] n pasa (de Corinto); (black~, red~) grosella

currency ['kʌrnsɪ] n moneda; **to gain ~** (fig) difundirse

current ['kʌrnt] n corriente f ♦ adj (accepted) corriente; (present) actual; **~ account** (BRIT) n cuenta corriente; **~ affairs** npl noticias fpl de actualidad; **~ly** adv actualmente

curriculum [kə'rɪkjuləm] (pl **~s** or **curricula**) n plan m de estudios; **~ vitae** n currículum m

curry ['kʌrɪ] n curry m ♦ vt: **to ~ favour with** buscar favores con; **~ powder** n curry m en polvo

curse [kə:s] vi soltar tacos ♦ vt maldecir ♦ n maldición f; (swearword) palabrota, taco

cursor ['kə:sə*] n (COMPUT) cursor m

cursory ['kə:sərɪ] adj rápido, superficial

curt [kə:t] adj corto, seco

curtail [kə:'teɪl] vt (visit etc) acortar; (freedom) restringir; (expenses etc) reducir

curtain ['kə:tn] n cortina; (THEATRE) telón m

curts(e)y ['kə:tsɪ] vi hacer una reverencia

curve [kə:v] n curva ♦ vi (road) hacer una curva; (line etc) curvarse

cushion ['kuʃən] n cojín m; (of air) colchón m ♦ vt (shock) amortiguar

custard ['kʌstəd] n natillas fpl

custody ['kʌstədɪ] n custodia; **to take into ~** detener

custom ['kʌstəm] n costumbre f; (COMM) clientela; **~ary** adj acostumbrado

customer ['kʌstəmə*] n cliente m/f

customized ['kʌstəmaɪzd] adj (car etc) hecho a encargo

custom-made adj hecho a la medida

customs ['kʌstəmz] npl aduana; **~ officer** n aduanero/a

cut [kʌt] (pt, pp **cut**) vt cortar; (price) rebajar; (text, programme) acortar; (reduce) reducir ♦ vi cortar ♦ n (of garment) corte m; (in skin) cortadura; (in salary etc) rebaja; (in spending) reducción f, recorte m; (slice of meat) tajada; **to ~ a tooth** echar un diente; **~ down** vt (tree) derribar; (reduce) reducir; **~ off** vt cortar; (person, place) aislar; (TEL) desconectar; **~ out** vt (shape) recortar; (stop: activity etc) dejar; (remove) quitar; **~ up** vt cortar (en pedazos); **~back** n reducción f

cute [kju:t] adj mono

cuticle ['kju:tɪkl] n cutícula

cutlery ['kʌtlərɪ] n cubiertos mpl

cutlet ['kʌtlɪt] n chuleta; (nut etc ~) plato vegetariano hecho con nueces y verdura en forma de chuleta

cut: **~out** n (switch) dispositivo de seguridad, disyuntor m; (cardboard ~out) recortable m; **~-price** (US **~rate**) adj a precio reducido; **~throat** n asesino/a ♦ adj feroz

cutting ['kʌtɪŋ] adj (remark) mordaz ♦ n (BRIT: from newspaper) recorte m; (from plant) esqueje m

CV n abbr = **curriculum vitae**

cwt abbr = **hundredweight(s)**

cyanide ['saɪənaɪd] n cianuro

cybercafé ['saɪbəkæfeɪ] n cibercafé m

cycle ['saɪkl] n ciclo; (bicycle) bicicleta ♦ vi ir en bicicleta; **~ lane** n carril-bici m; **~ path** n carril-bici m; **cycling** n ciclismo; **cyclist** n ciclista m/f

cyclone ['saɪkləun] n ciclón m

cygnet ['sɪgnɪt] n pollo de cisne

cylinder ['sɪlɪndə*] n cilindro; (of gas) bombona; **~-head gasket** n junta de culata

cymbals ['sɪmblz] npl platillos mpl

cynic ['sɪnɪk] n cínico/a; **~al** adj cínico; **~ism** ['sɪnɪsɪzəm] n cinismo

Cyprus ['saɪprəs] n Chipre f

cyst [sɪst] n quiste m; **~itis** [-'taɪtɪs] n cistitis f

czar [za:*] n zar m

Czech [tʃek] adj, n checo/a m/f; **~ Republic** n la República Checa

D, d

D [di:] n (MUS) re m

dab [dæb] vt (eyes, wound) tocar (ligeramente); (paint, cream) poner un poco de

dabble ['dæbl] vi: **to ~ in** ser algo aficionado a

dad [dæd] n = **daddy**

daddy ['dædɪ] n papá m

daffodil ['dæfədɪl] n narciso

daft [dɑ:ft] adj tonto

dagger ['dægə*] n puñal m, daga

daily ['deɪlɪ] adj diario, cotidiano ♦ adv todos los días, cada día

dainty ['deɪntɪ] adj delicado

dairy ['deərɪ] n (shop) lechería; (on farm) vaquería; **~ farm** n granja; **~ products** npl productos mpl lácteos; **~ store** (US) n lechería

daisy ['deɪzɪ] n margarita

dale [deɪl] n valle m

dam [dæm] n presa ♦ vt construir una presa sobre, represar

damage ['dæmɪdʒ] n lesión f; daño; (dents etc) desperfectos mpl; (fig) perjuicio ♦ vt dañar, perjudicar; (*spoil, break*) estropear; **~s** *npl* (*LAW*) daños *mpl* y perjuicios

damn [dæm] *vt* condenar; (*curse*) maldecir ♦ *n* (*inf*): **I don't give a ~** me importa un pito ♦ *adj* (*inf: also:* ~ed) maldito; **~ (it)!** ¡maldito sea!; **~ing** *adj* (*evidence*) irrecusable

damp [dæmp] *adj* húmedo, mojado ♦ *n* humedad *f* ♦ *vt* (*also:* ~en: *cloth, rag*) mojar; (*: enthusiasm*) enfriar

damson ['dæmzən] *n* ciruela damascena

dance [dɑːns] *n* baile *m* ♦ *vi* bailar; **~ hall** *n* salón *m* de baile; **~r** *n* bailador(a) *m/f*; (*professional*) bailarín/ina *m/f*; **dancing** *n* baile *m*

dandelion ['dændɪlaɪən] *n* diente *m* de león

dandruff ['dændrəf] *n* caspa

Dane [deɪn] *n* danés/esa *m/f*

danger ['deɪndʒə*] *n* peligro; (*risk*) riesgo; **~!** (*on sign*) ¡peligro de muerte!; **to be in ~ of** correr riesgo de; **~ous** *adj* peligroso; **~ously** *adv* peligrosamente

dangle ['dæŋgl] *vt* colgar ♦ *vi* pender, colgar

Danish ['deɪnɪʃ] *adj* danés/esa ♦ *n* (*LING*) danés *m*

dare [dɛə*] *vt*: **to ~ sb to do** desafiar a uno a hacer ♦ *vi*: **to ~ (to) do sth** atreverse a hacer algo; **I ~ say** (*I suppose*) puede ser (que); **daring** *adj* atrevido, osado ♦ *n* atrevimiento, osadía

dark [dɑːk] *adj* oscuro; (*hair, complexion*) moreno ♦ *n*: **in the ~** a oscuras; **to be in the ~ about** (*fig*) no saber nada de; **after ~** después del anochecer; **~en** *vt* (*colour*) hacer más oscuro ♦ *vi* oscurecerse; **~ glasses** *npl* gafas *fpl* (*SP*), anteojos *mpl* negros (*AM*); **~ness** *n* oscuridad *f*; **~room** *n* cuarto oscuro

darling ['dɑːlɪŋ] *adj, n* querido/a *m/f*

darn [dɑːn] *vt* zurcir

dart [dɑːt] *n* dardo; (*in sewing*) sisa ♦ *vi* precipitarse; **~ away/along** *vi* salir/marchar disparado; **~board** *n* diana; **~s** *n* dardos *mpl*

dash [dæʃ] *n* (*small quantity: of liquid*) gota, chorrito; (*: of solid*) pizca; (*sign*) raya ♦ *vt* (*throw*) tirar; (*hopes*) defraudar ♦ *vi* precipitarse, ir de prisa; **~ away** or **off** *vi* marcharse apresuradamente

dashboard ['dæʃbɔːd] *n* (*AUT*) salpicadero

dashing ['dæʃɪŋ] *adj* gallardo

data ['deɪtə] *npl* datos *mpl*; **~base** *n* base *f* de datos; **~ processing** *n* proceso de datos

date [deɪt] *n* (*day*) fecha; (*with friend*) cita; (*fruit*) dátil *m* ♦ *vt* fechar; (*person*) salir con; **~ of birth** fecha de nacimiento; **to ~** *adv* hasta la fecha; **~d** *adj* anticuado; **~ rape** *n* violación ocurrida durante una cita con un conocido

daub [dɔːb] *vt* embadurnar

daughter ['dɔːtə*] *n* hija; **~-in-law** *n* nuera,

hija política

daunting ['dɔːntɪŋ] *adj* desalentador(a)

dawdle ['dɔːdl] *vi* (*go slowly*) andar muy despacio

dawn [dɔːn] *n* alba, amanecer *m*; (*fig*) nacimiento ♦ *vi* (*day*) amanecer; (*fig*): **it ~ed on him that ...** cayó en la cuenta de que ...

day [deɪ] *n* día *m*; (*working ~*) jornada; (*hey~*) tiempos *mpl*, días *mpl*; **the ~ before/after** el día anterior/siguiente; **the ~ after tomorrow** pasado mañana; **the ~ before yesterday** anteayer; **the following ~** el día siguiente; **by ~** de día; **~break** *n* amanecer *m*; **~dream** *vi* soñar despierto; **~light** *n* luz *f* (del día); **~ return** (*BRIT*) *n* billete *m* de ida y vuelta (en un día); **~time** *n* día *m*; **~-to-~** *adj* cotidiano

daze [deɪz] *vt* (*stun*) aturdir ♦ *n*: **in a ~** aturdido

dazzle ['dæzl] *vt* deslumbrar

DC *abbr* (= *direct current*) corriente *f* continua

dead [dɛd] *adj* muerto; (*limb*) dormido; (*telephone*) cortado; (*battery*) agotado ♦ *adv* (*completely*) totalmente; (*exactly*) exactamente; **to shoot sb ~** matar a uno a tiros; **~ tired** muerto (de cansancio); **to stop ~** parar en seco; **the ~** *npl* los muertos; **to be a ~ loss** (*inf: person*) ser un inútil; **~en** *vt* (*blow, sound*) amortiguar; (*pain etc*) aliviar; **~ end** *n* callejón *m* sin salida; **~ heat** *n* (*SPORT*) empate *m*; **~line** *n* fecha (or hora) tope; **~lock** *n*: **to reach ~lock** llegar a un punto muerto; **~ly** *adj* mortal, fatal; **~pan** *adj* sin expresión; **the D~ Sea** *n* el Mar Muerto

deaf [dɛf] *adj* sordo; **~en** *vt* ensordecer; **~ness** *n* sordera

deal [diːl] (*pt, pp* dealt) *n* (*agreement*) pacto, convenio; (*business ~*) trato ♦ *vt* dar; (*card*) repartir; **a great ~ (of)** bastante, mucho; **~ in** *vt fus* tratar en, comerciar en; **~ with** *vt fus* (*people*) tratar con; (*problem*) ocuparse de; (*subject*) tratar de; **~ings** *npl* (*COMM*) transacciones *fpl*; (*relations*) relaciones *fpl*

dealt [dɛlt] *pt, pp* of **deal**

dean [diːn] *n* (*REL*) deán *m*; (*SCOL: BRIT*) decano; (*: US*) decano; rector *m*

dear [dɪə*] *adj* querido; (*expensive*) caro ♦ *adj*: **my ~** mi querido/a ♦ *excl*: **~ me!** ¡Dios mío!; **D~ Sir/Madam** (*in letter*) Muy Señor Mío, Estimado Señor/Estimada Señora; **D~ Mr/Mrs X** Estimado/a Señor(a) X; **~ly** *adv* (*love*) mucho; (*pay*) caro

death [dɛθ] *n* muerte *f*; **~ certificate** *n* partida de defunción; **~ly** *adj* (*white*) como un muerto; (*silence*) sepulcral; **~ penalty** *n* pena de muerte; **~ rate** *n* mortalidad *f*; **~ toll** *n* número de víctimas

debacle [deɪ'bɑːkl] *n* desastre *m*

debase [dɪ'beɪs] vt degradar
debatable [dɪ'beɪtəbl] adj discutible
debate [dɪ'beɪt] n debate m ♦ vt discutir
debit ['debɪt] n debe m ♦ vt: **to ~ a sum to sb**
or **to sb's account** cargar una suma en cuenta
a alguien
debris ['debriː] n escombros mpl
debt [det] n deuda; **to be in ~** tener deudas;
~or n deudor(a) m/f
début ['deɪbjuː] n presentación f
decade ['dekeɪd] n decenio, década
decadence ['dekədəns] n decadencia
decaff ['diːkæf] (inf) n descafeinado
decaffeinated [dɪ'kæfɪneɪtɪd] adj
descafeinado
decanter [dɪ'kæntə*] n garrafa
decay [dɪ'keɪ] n (of building)
desmoronamiento; (of tooth) caries f inv ♦ vi
(rot) pudrirse
deceased [dɪ'siːst] n: **the ~** el/la difunto/a
deceit [dɪ'siːt] n engaño; **~ful** adj engañoso;
deceive [dɪ'siːv] vt engañar
December [dɪ'sembə*] n diciembre m
decent ['diːsənt] adj (proper) decente;
(person: kind) amable, bueno
deception [dɪ'sepʃən] n engaño
deceptive [dɪ'septɪv] adj engañoso
decibel ['desɪbel] n decibel(io) m
decide [dɪ'saɪd] vt (person: decide; (question,
argument) resolver ♦ vi decidir; **to ~ to do/
that** decidir hacer/que; **to ~ on sth** decidirse
por algo; **~d** adj (resolute) decidido; (clear,
definite) indudable; **~dly** [-dɪdlɪ] adv
decididamente; (emphatically) con resolución
deciduous [dɪ'sɪdjuəs] adj de hoja caduca
decimal ['desɪməl] adj decimal ♦ n decimal
m; **~ point** n coma decimal
decipher [dɪ'saɪfə*] vt descifrar
decision [dɪ'sɪʒən] n decisión f
decisive [dɪ'saɪsɪv] adj decisivo; (person)
decidido
deck [dek] n (NAUT) cubierta; (of bus) piso;
(record ~) platina; (of cards) baraja; **~chair** n
tumbona
declaration [deklə'reɪʃən] n declaración f
declare [dɪ'kleə*] vt declarar
decline [dɪ'klaɪn] n disminución f, descenso
♦ vt rehusar ♦ vi (person, business) decaer;
(strength) disminuir
decoder [diː'kəudə*] n (TV) decodificador m
décor ['deɪkɔ:*] n decoración f; (THEATRE)
decorado
decorate ['dekəreɪt] vt (adorn): **to ~ (with)**
adornar (de), decorar (de); (paint) pintar;
(paper) empapelar; **decoration** [-'reɪʃən] n
adorno; (act) decoración f; (medal)
condecoración f; **decorator** n (workman)
pintor m (decorador)
decorum [dɪ'kɔːrəm] n decoro

decoy ['diːkɔɪ] n señuelo
decrease [n 'diːkriːs, vb dɪ'kriːs] n: **~ (in)**
disminución f (de) ♦ vt disminuir, reducir ♦ vi
reducirse
decree [dɪ'kriː] n decreto; **~ nisi** n sentencia
provisional de divorcio
dedicate ['dedɪkeɪt] vt dedicar; **dedication**
[-'keɪʃən] n (devotion) dedicación f; (in book)
dedicatoria
deduce [dɪ'djuːs] vt deducir
deduct [dɪ'dʌkt] vt restar; descontar; **~ion**
[dɪ'dʌkʃən] n (amount deducted) descuento;
(conclusion) deducción f, conclusión f
deed [diːd] n hecho, acto; (feat) hazaña;
(LAW) escritura
deep [diːp] adj profundo; (expressing
measurements) de profundidad; (voice) bajo;
(breath) profundo; (colour) intenso ♦ adv:
the spectators stood 20 ~ los espectadores se
formaron de 20 en fondo; **to be 4 metres ~**
tener 4 metros de profundidad; **~en** vt
ahondar, profundizar ♦ vi aumentar, crecer;
~-freeze n congelador m; **~-fry** vt freír en
aceite abundante; **~ly** adv (breathe) a pleno
pulmón; (interested, moved, grateful)
profundamente, hondamente; **~-sea diving**
n buceo de altura; **~-seated** adj (beliefs)
(profundamente) arraigado
deer [dɪə*] n inv ciervo
deface [dɪ'feɪs] vt (wall, surface) estropear,
pintarrajear
default [dɪ'fɔːlt] n: **by ~** (win) por
incomparecencia ♦ adj (COMPUT) por defecto
defeat [dɪ'fiːt] n derrota ♦ vt derrotar, vencer;
~ist adj, n derrotista m/f
defect [n 'diːfekt, vb dɪ'fekt] n defecto ♦ vi: **to
~ to the enemy** pasarse al enemigo; **~ive**
[dɪ'fektɪv] adj defectuoso
defence [dɪ'fens] (US **defense**) n defensa;
~less adj indefenso
defend [dɪ'fend] vt defender; **~ant** n
acusado/a; (in civil case) demandado/a; **~er**
n defensor(a) m/f; (SPORT) defensa m/f
defense [dɪ'fens] (US) n = **defence**
defensive [dɪ'fensɪv] adj defensivo ♦ n: **on
the ~** a la defensiva
defer [dɪ'fə:*] vt aplazar
defiance [dɪ'faɪəns] n desafío; **in ~ of** en
contra de; **defiant** [dɪ'faɪənt] adj
(challenging) desafiante, retador(a)
deficiency [dɪ'fɪʃənsɪ] n (lack) falta; (defect)
defecto; **deficient** [dɪ'fɪʃənt] adj deficiente
deficit ['defɪsɪt] n déficit m
define [dɪ'faɪn] vt (word etc) definir; (limits
etc) determinar
definite ['defɪnɪt] adj (fixed) determinado;
(obvious) claro; (certain) indudable; **he was
~ about it** no dejó lugar a dudas (sobre ello);
~ly adv desde luego, por supuesto

definition [defɪ'nɪʃən] *n* definición *f*; (*clearness*) nitidez *f*

deflate [di:'fleɪt] *vt* desinflar

deflect [dɪ'flekt] *vt* desviar

defraud [dɪ'frɔːd] *vt*: **to ~ sb of sth** estafar algo a uno

defrost [di:'frɔst] *vt* descongelar; **~er** (*US*) *n* (*demister*) eliminador *m* de vaho

deft [deft] *adj* diestro, hábil

defunct [dɪ'fʌŋkt] *adj* difunto; (*organization etc*) ya que no existe

defuse [di:'fjuːz] *vt* desactivar; (*situation*) calmar

defy [dɪ'faɪ] *vt* (*resist*) oponerse a; (*challenge*) desafiar; (*fig*): **it defies description** resulta imposible describirlo

degenerate [*vb* dɪ'dʒenəreɪt, *adj* dɪ'dʒenərɪt] *vi* degenerar ♦ *adj* degenerado

degree [dɪ'griː] *n* grado; (*SCOL*) título; **to have a ~ in maths** tener una licenciatura en matemáticas; **by ~s** (*gradually*) poco a poco, por etapas; **to some ~** hasta cierto punto

dehydrated [di:haɪ'dreɪtɪd] *adj* deshidratado; (*milk*) en polvo

de-ice [di:'aɪs] *vt* deshelar

deign [deɪn] *vi*: **to ~ to do** dignarse hacer

dejected [dɪ'dʒektɪd] *adj* abatido, desanimado

delay [dɪ'leɪ] *vt* demorar, aplazar; (*person*) entretener; (*train*) retrasar ♦ *vi* tardar ♦ *n* demora, retraso; **to be ~ed** retrasarse; **without ~** en seguida, sin tardar

delectable [dɪ'lektəbl] *adj* (*person*) encantador(a); (*food*) delicioso

delegate [*n* 'delɪgɪt, *vb* 'delɪgeɪt] *n* delegado/a ♦ *vt* (*person*) delegar en; (*task*) delegar

delete [dɪ'liːt] *vt* suprimir, tachar

deliberate [*adj* dɪ'lɪbərɪt, *vb* dɪ'lɪbəreɪt] *adj* (*intentional*) intencionado; (*slow*) pausado, lento ♦ *vi* deliberar; **~ly** *adv* (*on purpose*) a propósito

delicacy ['delɪkəsɪ] *n* delicadeza; (*choice food*) manjar *m*

delicate ['delɪkɪt] *adj* delicado; (*fragile*) frágil

delicatessen [delɪkə'tesn] *n* ultramarinos *mpl* finos

delicious [dɪ'lɪʃəs] *adj* delicioso

delight [dɪ'laɪt] *n* (*feeling*) placer *m*, deleite *m*; (*person, experience etc*) encanto, delicia ♦ *vt* encantar, deleitar; **to take ~ in** deleitarse en; **~ed** *adj*: **~ed (at or with/to do)** encantado (con/de hacer); **~ful** *adj* encantador(a), delicioso

delinquent [dɪ'lɪŋkwənt] *adj, n* delincuente *m/f*

delirious [dɪ'lɪrɪəs] *adj*: **to be ~** delirar, desvariar; **to be ~ with** estar loco de

deliver [dɪ'lɪvə*] *vt* (*distribute*) repartir; (*hand over*) entregar; (*message*) comunicar;

(*speech*) pronunciar; (*MED*) asistir al parto de; **~y** *n* reparto; entrega; (*of speaker*) modo de expresarse; (*MED*) parto, alumbramiento; **to take ~y of** recibir

delude [dɪ'luːd] *vt* engañar

deluge ['deljuːdʒ] *n* diluvio

delusion [dɪ'luːʒən] *n* ilusión *f*, engaño

de luxe [də'lʌks] *adj* de lujo

demand [dɪ'mɑːnd] *vt* (*gen*) exigir; (*rights*) reclamar ♦ *n* exigencia; (*claim*) reclamación *f*; (*ECON*) demanda; **to be in ~** ser muy solicitado; **on ~** a solicitud; **~ing** *adj* (*boss*) exigente; (*work*) absorbente

demean [dɪ'miːn] *vt*: **to ~ o.s.** rebajarse

demeanour [dɪ'miːnə*] (*US* **demeanor**) *n* porte *m*, conducta

demented [dɪ'mentɪd] *adj* demente

demise [dɪ'maɪz] *n* (*death*) fallecimiento

demister [di:'mɪstə*] *n* (*AUT*) eliminador *m* de vaho

demo ['deməu] (*inf*) *n abbr* (= *demonstration*) manifestación *f*

democracy [dɪ'mɔkrəsɪ] *n* democracia; **democrat** ['deməkræt] *n* demócrata *m/f*; **democratic** [demə'krætɪk] *adj* democrático; (*US*) demócrata

demolish [dɪ'mɔlɪʃ] *vt* derribar, demoler; (*fig: argument*) destruir

demon ['diːmən] *n* (*evil spirit*) demonio

demonstrate ['demənstreɪt] *vt* demostrar; (*skill, appliance*) mostrar ♦ *vi* manifestarse; **demonstration** [-'streɪʃən] *n* (*POL*) manifestación *f*; (*proof, exhibition*) demostración *f*; **demonstrator** *n* (*POL*) manifestante *m/f*; (*COMM*) demostrador(a) *m/f*; vendedor(a) *m/f*

demote [dɪ'məut] *vt* degradar

demure [dɪ'mjuə*] *adj* recatado

den [den] *n* (*of animal*) guarida; (*room*) habitación *f*

denial [dɪ'naɪəl] *n* (*refusal*) negativa; (*of report etc*) negación *f*

denim ['denɪm] *n* tela vaquera; **~s** *npl* vaqueros *mpl*

Denmark ['denmɑːk] *n* Dinamarca

denomination [dɪnɔmɪ'neɪʃən] *n* valor *m*; (*REL*) confesión *f*

denounce [dɪ'nauns] *vt* denunciar

dense [dens] *adj* (*crowd*) denso; (*thick*) espeso; (: *foliage etc*) tupido; (*inf: stupid*) torpe; **~ly** *adv*: **~ly populated** con una alta densidad de población

density ['densɪtɪ] *n* densidad *f*; **single/ double-~ disk** *n* (*COMPUT*) disco de densidad sencilla/doble densidad

dent [dent] *n* abolladura ♦ *vt* (*also*: **make a ~ in**) abollar

dental ['dentl] *adj* dental; **~ surgeon** *n* odontólogo/a

dentist ['dentɪst] n dentista m/f
dentures ['dentʃəz] npl dentadura (postiza)
deny [dɪ'naɪ] vt negar; (charge) rechazar
deodorant [di:'əudərənt] n desodorante m
depart [dɪ'pɑ:t] vi irse, marcharse; (train) salir; to ~ from (fig: differ from) apartarse de
department [dɪ'pɑ:tmənt] n (COMM) sección f; (SCOL) departamento; (POL) ministerio; ~ store n gran almacén m
departure [dɪ'pɑ:tʃə*] n partida, ida; (of train) salida; (of employee) marcha; a new ~ un nuevo rumbo; ~ lounge n (at airport) sala de embarque
depend [dɪ'pend] vi: to ~ on depender de; (rely on) contar con; it ~s depende, según; ~ing on the result según el resultado; ~able adj (person) formal, serio; (watch) exacto; (car) seguro; ~ant n dependiente m/f; ~ent adj: to be ~ent on depender de ♦ n = dependant
depict [dɪ'pɪkt] vt (in picture) pintar; (describe) representar
depleted [dɪ'pli:tɪd] adj reducido
deploy [dɪ'plɔɪ] vt desplegar
deport [dɪ'pɔ:t] vt deportar
deposit [dɪ'pɔzɪt] n depósito; (CHEM) sedimento; (of ore, oil) yacimiento ♦ vt (gen) depositar; ~ account n (BRIT) cuenta de ahorros
depot ['depəu] n (storehouse) depósito; (for vehicles) parque m; (US) estación f
depreciate [dɪ'pri:ʃɪeɪt] vi depreciarse, perder valor
depress [dɪ'pres] vt deprimir; (wages etc) hacer bajar; (press down) apretar; ~ed adj deprimido; ~ing adj deprimente; ~ion [dɪ'preʃən] n depresión f
deprivation [deprɪ'veɪʃən] n privación f
deprive [dɪ'praɪv] vt: to ~ sb of privar a uno de; ~d adj necesitado
depth [depθ] n profundidad f; (of cupboard) fondo; to be in the ~s of despair sentir la mayor desesperación; to be out of one's ~ (in water) no hacer pie; (fig) sentirse totalmente perdido
deputize ['depjutaɪz] vi: to ~ for sb suplir a uno
deputy ['depjuti] adj: ~ head subdirector(a) m/f ♦ n sustituto/a, suplente m/f; (US: POL) diputado/a; (US: also: ~ sheriff) agente m (del sheriff)
derail [dɪ'reɪl] vt: to be ~ed descarrilarse
deranged [dɪ'reɪndʒd] adj trastornado
derby ['da:bɪ] (US) n (hat) hongo
derelict ['derɪlɪkt] adj abandonado
derisory [dɪ'raɪzərɪ] adj (sum) irrisorio
derive [dɪ'raɪv] vt (benefit etc) obtener ♦ vi: to ~ from derivarse de
derogatory [dɪ'rɔgətərɪ] adj despectivo

descend [dɪ'send] vt, vi descender, bajar; to ~ from descender de; to ~ to rebajarse a; ~ant n descendiente m/f
descent [dɪ'sent] n descenso; (origin) descendencia
describe [dɪs'kraɪb] vt describir; **description** [-'krɪpʃən] n descripción f; (sort) clase f, género
desecrate ['desɪkreɪt] vt profanar
desert [n 'dezət, vb dɪ'zə:t] n desierto ♦ vt abandonar ♦ vi (MIL) desertar; ~er [dɪ'zə:tə*] n desertor(a) m/f; ~ion [dɪ'zə:ʃən] n deserción f; (LAW) abandono; ~ island n isla desierta; ~s [dɪ'zə:ts] npl: to get one's just ~s llevar su merecido
deserve [dɪ'zə:v] vt merecer, ser digno de; **deserving** adj (person) digno; (action, cause) meritorio
design [dɪ'zaɪn] n (sketch) bosquejo; (layout, shape) diseño; (pattern) dibujo; (intention) intención f ♦ vt diseñar
designate [vb 'dezɪgneɪt, adj 'dezɪgnɪt] vt (appoint) nombrar; (destine) designar ♦ adj designado
designer [dɪ'zaɪnə*] n diseñador(a) m/f; (fashion ~) modisto/a, diseñador(a) m/f de moda
desirable [dɪ'zaɪərəbl] adj (proper) deseable; (attractive) atractivo
desire [dɪ'zaɪə*] n deseo ♦ vt desear
desk [desk] n (in office) escritorio; (for pupil) pupitre m; (in hotel, at airport) recepción f; (BRIT: in shop, restaurant) caja
desk-top publishing ['desktɔp-] n autoedición f
desolate ['desəlɪt] adj (place) desierto; (person) afligido
despair [dɪs'peə*] n desesperación f ♦ vi: to ~ of perder la esperanza de
despatch [dɪs'pætʃ] n, vt = dispatch
desperate ['despərɪt] adj desesperado; (fugitive) peligroso; to be ~ for sth/to do necesitar urgentemente algo/hacer; ~ly adv desesperadamente; (very) terriblemente, gravemente
desperation [despə'reɪʃən] n desesperación f; in (sheer) ~ (absolutamente) desesperado
despicable [dɪs'pɪkəbl] adj vil, despreciable
despise [dɪs'paɪz] vt despreciar
despite [dɪs'paɪt] prep a pesar de, pese a
despondent [dɪs'pɔndənt] adj deprimido, abatido
dessert [dɪ'zə:t] n postre m; ~spoon n cuchara (de postre)
destination [destɪ'neɪʃən] n destino
destiny ['destɪnɪ] n destino
destitute ['destɪtju:t] adj desamparado, indigente
destroy [dɪs'trɔɪ] vt destruir; (animal)

sacrificar; **~er** n (NAUT) destructor m

destruction [dɪs'trʌkʃən] n destrucción f

detach [dɪ'tætʃ] vt separar; (unstick) despegar; **~ed** adj (attitude) objetivo, imparcial; **~ed house** n ≈ chalé m, ≈ chalet m; **~ment** n (aloofness) frialdad f; (MIL) destacamento

detail ['di:teɪl] n detalle m; (no pl: in picture etc) detalles mpl; (trifle) pequeñez f ♦ vt detallar; (MIL) destacar; **in ~** detalladamente; **~ed** adj detallado

detain [dɪ'teɪn] vt retener; (in captivity) detener

detect [dɪ'tɛkt] vt descubrir; (MED, POLICE) identificar; (MIL, RADAR, TECH) detectar; **~ion** [dɪ'tɛkʃən] n descubrimiento; identificación f; **~ive** n detective m/f; **~ive story** n novela policíaca; **~or** n detector m

detention [dɪ'tɛnʃən] n detención f, arresto; (SCOL) castigo

deter [dɪ'tə:*] vt (dissuade) disuadir

detergent [dɪ'tə:dʒənt] n detergente m

deteriorate [dɪ'tɪərɪəreɪt] vi deteriorarse; **deterioration** [-'reɪʃən] n deterioro

determination [dɪtə:mɪ'neɪʃən] n resolución f

determine [dɪ'tə:mɪn] vt determinar; **~d** adj (person) resuelto, decidido; **~d to do** resuelto a hacer

deterrent [dɪ'tɛrənt] n (MIL) fuerza de disuasión

detest [dɪ'tɛst] vt aborrecer

detonate ['dɛtəneɪt] vi estallar ♦ vt hacer detonar

detour ['di:tuə*] n (gen, US: AUT) desviación f

detract [dɪ'trækt] vt: **to ~ from** quitar mérito a, desvirtuar

detriment ['dɛtrɪmənt] n: **to the ~ of** en perjuicio de; **~al** [dɛtrɪ'mɛntl] adj: **~al (to)** perjudicial (a)

devaluation [di:vælju'eɪʃən] n devaluación f

devalue [di:'vælju:] vt (currency) devaluar; (fig) quitar mérito a

devastate ['dɛvəsteɪt] vt devastar; (fig): **to be ~d by** quedar destrozado por; **devastating** adj devastador(a); (fig) arrollador(a)

develop [dɪ'vɛləp] vt desarrollar; (PHOT) revelar; (disease) coger; (habit) adquirir; (fault) empezar a tener ♦ vi desarrollarse; (advance) progresar; (facts, symptoms) aparecer; **~er** n promotor m; **~ing country** n país m en (vías de) desarrollo; **~ment** n desarrollo; (advance) progreso; (of affair, case) desenvolvimiento; (of land) urbanización f

deviation [di:vɪ'eɪʃən] n desviación f

device [dɪ'vaɪs] n (apparatus) aparato, mecanismo

devil ['dɛvl] n diablo, demonio

devious ['di:vɪəs] adj taimado

devise [dɪ'vaɪz] vt idear, inventar

devoid [dɪ'vɔɪd] adj: **~ of** desprovisto de

devolution [di:və'lu:ʃən] n (POL) descentralización f

devote [dɪ'vəut] vt: **to ~ sth to** dedicar algo a; **~d** adj (loyal) leal, fiel; **to be ~d to sb** querer con devoción a alguien; **the book is ~d to politics** el libro trata de la política; **~e** [dɛvəu'ti:] n entusiasta m/f; (REL) devoto/a; **devotion** n dedicación f; (REL) devoción f

devour [dɪ'vauə*] vt devorar

devout [dɪ'vaut] adj devoto

dew [dju:] n rocío

diabetes [daɪə'bi:tiz] n diabetes f; **diabetic** [-'bɛtɪk] adj, n diabético/a m/f

diabolical [daɪə'bɔlɪkəl] (inf) adj (weather, behaviour) pésimo

diagnosis [daɪəg'nəusɪs] (pl -ses) n diagnóstico

diagonal [daɪ'ægənl] adj, n diagonal f

diagram ['daɪəgræm] n diagrama m, esquema m

dial ['daɪəl] n esfera, cuadrante m, cara (AM); (on radio etc) selector m; (of phone) disco ♦ vt (number) marcar

dialling ['daɪəlɪŋ]: **~ code** n prefijo; **~ tone** (US **dial tone**) n (BRIT) señal f or tono de marcar

dialogue ['daɪəlɔg] (US **dialog**) n diálogo

diameter [daɪ'æmɪtə*] n diámetro

diamond ['daɪəmənd] n diamante m; (shape) rombo; **~s** npl (CARDS) diamantes mpl

diaper ['daɪəpə*] (US) n pañal m

diaphragm ['daɪəfræm] n diafragma m

diarrhoea [daɪə'ri:ə] (US **diarrhea**) n diarrea

diary ['daɪərɪ] n (daily account) diario; (book) agenda

dice [daɪs] n inv dados mpl ♦ vt (CULIN) cortar en cuadritos

Dictaphone ® ['dɪktəfəun] n dictáfono ®

dictate [dɪk'teɪt] vt dictar; (conditions) imponer; **dictation** [-'teɪʃən] n dictado; (giving of orders) órdenes fpl

dictator [dɪk'teɪtə*] n dictador m; **~ship** n dictadura

dictionary ['dɪkʃənrɪ] n diccionario

did [dɪd] pt of **do**

didn't ['dɪdənt] = **did not**

die [daɪ] vi morir; (fig: fade) desvanecerse, desaparecer; **to be dying for sth/to do sth** morirse por algo/de ganas de hacer algo; **~ away** vi (sound, light) perderse; **~ down** vi apagarse; (wind) amainar; **~ out** vi desaparecer

diesel ['di:zəl] n vehículo con motor Diesel; **~ engine** n motor m Diesel; **~ (oil)** n gasoil m

diet ['daɪət] n dieta; (*restricted food*) régimen m ♦ vi (*also*: be on a ~) estar a dieta, hacer régimen

differ ['dɪfə*] vi: to ~ (from) (*be different*) ser distinto (a), diferenciarse (de); (*disagree*) discrepar (de); ~**ence** n diferencia; (*disagreement*) desacuerdo; ~**ent** adj diferente, distinto; ~**entiate** [-'renʃɪeɪt] vi: to ~**entiate (between)** distinguir (entre); ~**ently** adv de otro modo, en forma distinta

difficult ['dɪfɪkəlt] adj difícil; ~**y** n dificultad f

diffident ['dɪfɪdənt] adj tímido

dig [dɪg] (*pt, pp dug*) vt (*hole, ground*) cavar ♦ n (*prod*) empujón m; (*archaeological*) excavación f; (*remark*) indirecta; to ~ **one's nails into** clavar las uñas en; ~ **into** vt fus (*savings*) consumir; ~ **up** vt (*information*) desenterrar; (*plant*) desarraigar

digest [vb daɪ'dʒest, n 'daɪdʒest] vt (*food*) digerir; (*facts*) asimilar ♦ n resumen m; ~**ion** [dɪ'dʒestʃən] n digestión f

digit ['dɪdʒɪt] n (*number*) dígito; (*finger*) dedo; ~**al** adj digital; ~**al TV** n televisión f digital

dignified ['dɪgnɪfaɪd] adj grave, solemne

dignity ['dɪgnɪtɪ] n dignidad f

digress [daɪ'gres] vi: to ~ **from** apartarse de

digs [dɪgz] (*BRIT: inf*) npl pensión f, alojamiento

dilapidated [dɪ'læpɪdeɪtɪd] adj desmoronado, ruinoso

dilemma [daɪ'lemə] n dilema m

diligent ['dɪlɪdʒənt] adj diligente

dilute [daɪ'luːt] vt diluir

dim [dɪm] adj (*light*) débil; (*outline*) indistinto; (*room*) oscuro; (*inf: stupid*) lerdo ♦ vt (*light*) bajar

dime [daɪm] (*US*) n moneda de diez centavos

dimension [dɪ'menʃən] n dimensión f

diminish [dɪ'mɪnɪʃ] vt, vi disminuir

diminutive [dɪ'mɪnjutɪv] adj diminuto ♦ n (*LING*) diminutivo

dimmers ['dɪməz] (*US*) npl (*AUT: dipped headlights*) luces fpl cortas; (: *parking lights*) luces fpl de posición

dimple ['dɪmpl] n hoyuelo

din [dɪn] n estruendo, estrépito

dine [daɪn] vi cenar; ~**r** n (*person*) comensal m/f; (*US*) restaurante m económico

dinghy ['dɪŋgɪ] n bote m; (*also*: rubber ~) lancha (neumática)

dingy ['dɪndʒɪ] adj (*room*) sombrío; (*colour*) sucio

dining car ['daɪnɪŋ-] (*BRIT*) n (*RAIL*) coche-comedor m

dining room n comedor m

dinner ['dɪnə*] n (*evening meal*) cena; (*lunch*) comida; (*public*) cena, banquete m; ~ **jacket** n smoking m; ~ **party** n cena; ~ **time** n

(*evening*) hora de cenar; (*midday*) hora de comer

dinosaur ['daɪnəsɔː*] n dinosaurio

diocese ['daɪəsɪs] n diócesis f inv

dip [dɪp] n (*slope*) pendiente m; (*in sea*) baño; (*CULIN*) salsa ♦ vt (*in water*) mojar; (*ladle etc*) meter; (*BRIT: AUT*): to ~ **one's lights** poner luces de cruce ♦ vi (*road etc*) descender, bajar

diploma [dɪ'pləumə] n diploma m

diplomacy [dɪ'pləuməsɪ] n diplomacia

diplomat ['dɪpləmæt] n diplomático/a; ~**ic** [dɪplə'mætɪk] adj diplomático

diprod ['dɪprɒd] (*US*) n = **dipstick**

dipstick ['dɪpstɪk] (*BRIT*) n (*AUT*) varilla de nivel (del aceite)

dipswitch ['dɪpswɪtʃ] (*BRIT*) n (*AUT*) interruptor m

dire [daɪə*] adj calamitoso

direct [daɪ'rekt] adj directo; (*challenge*) claro; (*person*) franco ♦ vt dirigir; (*order*): to ~ **sb to do sth** mandar a uno hacer algo ♦ adv derecho; **can you ~ me to...?** ¿puede indicarme dónde está...?; ~ **debit** (*BRIT*) n domiciliación f bancaria de recibos

direction [dɪ'rekʃən] n dirección f; **sense of ~** sentido de la dirección; ~**s** npl (*instructions*) instrucciones fpl; ~**s for use** modo de empleo

directly [dɪ'rektlɪ] adv (*in straight line*) directamente; (*at once*) en seguida

director [dɪ'rektə*] n director(a) m/f

directory [dɪ'rektərɪ] n (*TEL*) guía (telefónica); (*COMPUT*) directorio; ~ **enquiries**, ~ **assistance** (*US*) n (servicio de) información f

dirt [dɜːt] n suciedad f; (*earth*) tierra; ~-**cheap** adj baratísimo; ~**y** adj sucio; (*joke*) verde (*SP*), colorado (*AM*) ♦ vt ensuciar; (*stain*) manchar; ~**y trick** n juego sucio

disability [dɪsə'bɪlɪtɪ] n incapacidad f

disabled [dɪs'eɪbld] adj: to be physically ~ ser minusválido/a; to be mentally ~ ser deficiente mental

disadvantage [dɪsəd'vɑːntɪdʒ] n desventaja, inconveniente m

disagree [dɪsə'griː] vi (*differ*) discrepar; to ~ **(with)** no estar de acuerdo (con); ~**able** adj desagradable; (*person*) antipático; ~**ment** n desacuerdo

disallow [dɪsə'lau] vt (*goal*) anular; (*claim*) rechazar

disappear [dɪsə'pɪə*] vi desaparecer; ~**ance** n desaparición f

disappoint [dɪsə'pɔɪnt] vt decepcionar, defraudar; ~**ed** adj decepcionado; ~**ing** adj decepcionante; ~**ment** n decepción f

disapproval [dɪsə'pruːvəl] n desaprobación f

disapprove [dɪsə'pruːv] vi: to ~ **of** ver mal

disarmament [dɪs'ɑːməmənt] n desarme m

disarray [dɪsə'reɪ] n: in ~ (*army, organization*)

desorganizado; (*hair, clothes*) desarreglado

disaster [dɪ'zɑːstə*] *n* desastre *m*

disband [dɪs'bænd] *vt* disolver ♦ *vi* desbandarse

disbelief [dɪsbə'liːf] *n* incredulidad *f*

disc [dɪsk] *n* disco; (*COMPUT*) = **disk**

discard [dɪs'kɑːd] *vt* (*old things*) tirar; (*fig*) descartar

discern [dɪ'sɜːn] *vt* percibir, discernir; (*understand*) comprender; **~ing** *adj* perspicaz

discharge [*vb* dɪs'tʃɑːdʒ, *n* 'dɪstʃɑːdʒ] *vt* (*task, duty*) cumplir; (*waste*) verter; (*patient*) dar de alta; (*employee*) despedir; (*soldier*) licenciar; (*defendant*) poner en libertad ♦ *n* (*ELEC*) descarga; (*MED*) supuración *f*; (*dismissal*) despedida; (*of duty*) desempeño; (*of debt*) pago, descargo

discipline ['dɪsɪplɪn] *n* disciplina ♦ *vt* disciplinar; (*punish*) castigar

disc jockey *n* pinchadiscos *m/f inv*

disclaim [dɪs'kleɪm] *vt* negar

disclose [dɪs'kləʊz] *vt* revelar; **disclosure** [-'kləʊʒə*] *n* revelación *f*

disco ['dɪskəʊ] *n abbr* = **discothèque**

discomfort [dɪs'kʌmfət] *n* incomodidad *f*; (*unease*) inquietud *f*; (*physical*) malestar *m*

disconcert [dɪskən'sɜːt] *vt* desconcertar

disconnect [dɪskə'nekt] *vt* separar; (*ELEC etc*) desconectar

discontent [dɪskən'tent] *n* descontento; **~ed** *adj* descontento

discontinue [dɪskən'tɪnjuː] *vt* interrumpir; (*payments*) suspender; "**~d**" (*COMM*) "ya no se fabrica"

discord ['dɪskɔːd] *n* discordia; (*MUS*) disonancia

discothèque ['dɪskəʊtek] *n* discoteca

discount [*n* 'dɪskaʊnt, *vb* dɪs'kaʊnt] *n* descuento ♦ *vt* descontar

discourage [dɪs'kʌrɪdʒ] *vt* desalentar; (*advise against*): **to ~ sb from doing** disuadir a uno de hacer

discover [dɪs'kʌvə*] *vt* descubrir; (*error*) darse cuenta de; **~y** *n* descubrimiento

discredit [dɪs'kredɪt] *vt* desacreditar

discreet [dɪs'kriːt] *adj* (*tactful*) discreto; (*careful*) circunspecto, prudente

discrepancy [dɪs'krepənsɪ] *n* diferencia

discretion [dɪs'kreʃən] *n* (*tact*) discreción *f*; **at the ~ of** a criterio de

discriminate [dɪs'krɪmɪneɪt] *vi*: **to ~ between** distinguir entre; **to ~ against** discriminar contra; **discriminating** *adj* entendido; **discrimination** [-'neɪʃən] *n* (*discernment*) perspicacia; (*bias*) discriminación *f*

discuss [dɪs'kʌs] *vt* discutir; (*a theme*) tratar; **~ion** [dɪs'kʌʃən] *n* discusión *f*

disdain [dɪs'deɪn] *n* desdén *m*

disease [dɪ'ziːz] *n* enfermedad *f*

disembark [dɪsɪm'bɑːk] *vt, vi* desembarcar

disentangle [dɪsɪn'tæŋɡl] *vt* soltar; (*wire, thread*) desenredar

disfigure [dɪs'fɪɡə*] *vt* (*person*) desfigurar; (*object*) afear

disgrace [dɪs'ɡreɪs] *n* ignominia; (*shame*) vergüenza, escándalo ♦ *vt* deshonrar; **~ful** *adj* vergonzoso

disgruntled [dɪs'ɡrʌntld] *adj* disgustado, descontento

disguise [dɪs'ɡaɪz] *n* disfraz *m* ♦ *vt* disfrazar; **in ~** disfrazado

disgust [dɪs'ɡʌst] *n* repugnancia ♦ *vt* repugnar, dar asco a; **~ing** *adj* repugnante, asqueroso; (*behaviour etc*) vergonzoso

dish [dɪʃ] *n* (*gen*) plato; **to do** or **wash the ~es** fregar los platos; **~ out** *vt* repartir; **~ up** *vt* servir; **~cloth** *n* estropajo

dishearten [dɪs'hɑːtn] *vt* desalentar

dishevelled [dɪ'ʃevəld] (*US* **disheveled**) *adj* (*hair*) despeinado; (*appearance*) desarreglado

dishonest [dɪs'ɒnɪst] *adj* (*person*) poco honrado, tramposo; (*means*) fraudulento; **~y** *n* falta de honradez

dishonour [dɪs'ɒnə*] (*US* **dishonor**) *n* deshonra; **~able** *adj* deshonroso

dishtowel ['dɪʃtaʊəl] (*US*) *n* estropajo

dishwasher ['dɪʃwɒʃə*] *n* lavaplatos *m inv*

disillusion [dɪsɪ'luːʒən] *vt* desilusionar

disinfect [dɪsɪn'fekt] *vt* desinfectar; **~ant** *n* desinfectante *m*

disintegrate [dɪs'ɪntɪɡreɪt] *vi* disgregarse, desintegrarse

disinterested [dɪs'ɪntrəstɪd] *adj* desinteresado

disjointed [dɪs'dʒɔɪntɪd] *adj* inconexo

disk [dɪsk] *n* (*esp US*) = **disc**; (*COMPUT*) disco, disquete *m*; **single-/double-sided ~** disco de una cara/dos caras; **~ drive** *n* disc drive *m*; **~ette** *n* = **disk**

dislike [dɪs'laɪk] *n* antipatía, aversión *f* ♦ *vt* tener antipatía a

dislocate ['dɪsləkeɪt] *vt* dislocar

dislodge [dɪs'lɒdʒ] *vt* sacar

disloyal [dɪs'lɔɪəl] *adj* desleal

dismal ['dɪzml] *adj* (*gloomy*) deprimente, triste; (*very bad*) malísimo, fatal

dismantle [dɪs'mæntl] *vt* desmontar, desarmar

dismay [dɪs'meɪ] *n* consternación *f* ♦ *vt* consternar

dismiss [dɪs'mɪs] *vt* (*worker*) despedir; (*pupils*) dejar marchar; (*soldiers*) dar permiso para irse; (*idea, LAW*) rechazar; (*possibility*) descartar; **~al** *n* despido

dismount [dɪs'maʊnt] *vi* apearse

disobedient [dɪsə'biːdɪənt] *adj* desobediente

disobey [dɪsə'beɪ] *vt* desobedecer

disorder [dɪsˈɔːdə*] n desorden m; (rioting) disturbios mpl; (MED) trastorno; **~ly** adj desordenado; (meeting) alborotado; (conduct) escandaloso

disorientated [dɪsˈɔːrɪenteɪtəd] adj desorientado

disown [dɪsˈəun] vt (action) renegar de; (person) negar cualquier tipo de relación con

disparaging [dɪsˈpærɪdʒɪŋ] adj despreciativo

dispassionate [dɪsˈpæʃənɪt] adj (unbiased) imparcial

dispatch [dɪsˈpætʃ] vt enviar ♦ n (sending) envío; (PRESS) informe m; (MIL) parte m

dispel [dɪsˈpel] vt disipar

dispense [dɪsˈpens] vt (medicines) preparar; **~ with** vt fus prescindir de; **~r** n (container) distribuidor m automático; **dispensing chemist** (BRIT) n farmacia

disperse [dɪsˈpəːs] vt dispersar ♦ vi dispersarse

dispirited [dɪˈspɪrɪtɪd] adj desanimado, desalentado

displace [dɪsˈpleɪs] vt desplazar, reemplazar; **~d person** n (POL) desplazado/a

display [dɪsˈpleɪ] n (in shop window) escaparate m; (exhibition) exposición f; (COMPUT) visualización f; (of feeling) manifestación f ♦ vt exponer; manifestar; (ostentatiously) lucir

displease [dɪsˈpliːz] vt (offend) ofender; (annoy) fastidiar; **~d** adj: **~d with** disgustado con; **displeasure** [-ˈpleʒə*] n disgusto

disposable [dɪsˈpəuzəbl] adj desechable; (income) disponible; **~ nappy** n pañal m desechable

disposal [dɪsˈpəuzl] n (of rubbish) destrucción f; **at one's ~** a su disposición

dispose [dɪsˈpəuz] vi: **to ~ of** (unwanted goods) deshacerse de; (problem etc) resolver; **~d** adj: **~d to do** dispuesto a hacer; **to be well-~d towards sb** estar bien dispuesto hacia uno; **disposition** [dɪspəˈzɪʃən] n (nature) temperamento; (inclination) propensión f

disprove [dɪsˈpruːv] vt refutar

dispute [dɪsˈpjuːt] n disputa; (also: industrial ~) conflicto (laboral) ♦ vt (argue) disputar, discutir; (question) cuestionar

disqualify [dɪsˈkwɔlɪfaɪ] vt (SPORT) desclasificar; **to ~ sb for sth/from doing sth** incapacitar a alguien para algo/hacer algo

disquiet [dɪsˈkwaɪət] n preocupación f, inquietud f

disregard [dɪsrɪˈgɑːd] vt (ignore) no hacer caso de

disrepair [dɪsrɪˈpeə*] n: **to fall into ~** (building) desmoronarse

disreputable [dɪsˈrepjutəbl] adj (person) de mala fama; (behaviour) vergonzoso

disrespectful [dɪsrɪˈspektful] adj irrespetuoso

disrupt [dɪsˈrʌpt] vt (plans) desbaratar, trastornar; (conversation) interrumpir

dissatisfaction [dɪssætɪsˈfækʃən] n disgusto, descontento

dissect [dɪˈsekt] vt disecar

dissent [dɪˈsent] n disensión f

dissertation [dɪsəˈteɪʃən] n tesina

disservice [dɪsˈsəːvɪs] n: **to do sb a ~** perjudicar a alguien

dissimilar [dɪˈsɪmɪlə*] adj distinto

dissipate [ˈdɪsɪpeɪt] vt disipar; (waste) desperdiciar

dissolve [dɪˈzɔlv] vt disolver ♦ vi disolverse; **to ~ in(to) tears** deshacerse en lágrimas

dissuade [dɪˈsweɪd] vt: **to ~ sb (from)** disuadir a uno (de)

distance [ˈdɪstəns] n distancia; **in the ~** a lo lejos

distant [ˈdɪstənt] adj lejano; (manner) reservado, frío

distaste [dɪsˈteɪst] n repugnancia; **~ful** adj repugnante, desagradable

distended [dɪˈstendɪd] adj (stomach) hinchado

distil [dɪsˈtɪl] (US **distill**) vt destilar; **~lery** n destilería

distinct [dɪsˈtɪŋkt] adj (different) distinto; (clear) claro; (unmistakeable) inequívoco; **as ~ from** a diferencia de; **~ion** [dɪsˈtɪŋkʃən] n distinción f; (honour) honor m; (in exam) sobresaliente m; **~ive** adj distintivo

distinguish [dɪsˈtɪŋgwɪʃ] vt distinguir; **to ~ o.s.** destacarse; **~ed** adj (eminent) distinguido; **~ing** adj (feature) distintivo

distort [dɪsˈtɔːt] vt distorsionar; (shape, image) deformar; **~ion** [dɪsˈtɔːʃən] n distorsión f; deformación f

distract [dɪsˈtrækt] vt distraer; **~ed** adj distraído; **~ion** [dɪsˈtrækʃən] n distracción f; (confusion) aturdimiento

distraught [dɪsˈtrɔːt] adj loco de inquietud

distress [dɪsˈtres] n (anguish) angustia, aflicción f ♦ vt afligir; **~ing** adj angustioso; doloroso; **~ signal** n señal f de socorro

distribute [dɪsˈtrɪbjuːt] vt distribuir; (share out) repartir; **distribution** [-ˈbjuːʃən] n distribución f, reparto; **distributor** n (AUT) distribuidor m; (COMM) distribuidora

district [ˈdɪstrɪkt] n (of country) zona, región f; (of town) barrio; (ADMIN) distrito; **~ attorney** (US) n fiscal m/f; **~ nurse** (BRIT) n enfermera que atiende a pacientes a domicilio

distrust [dɪsˈtrʌst] n desconfianza ♦ vt desconfiar de

disturb [dɪsˈtəːb] vt (person: bother, interrupt) molestar; (: upset) perturbar, inquietar; (disorganize) alterar; **~ance** n (upheaval) perturbación f; (political etc: gen pl) disturbio; (of mind) trastorno; **~ed** adj (worried, upset) preocupado, angustiado; **emotionally ~ed** trastornado; (childhood) inseguro; **~ing** adj inquietante, perturbador(a)

disuse [dɪs'juːs] n: **to fall into ~** caer en desuso

disused [dɪs'juːzd] adj abandonado

ditch [dɪtʃ] n zanja; (irrigation ~) acequia ♦ vt (inf: partner) deshacerse de; (: plan, car etc) abandonar

dither ['dɪðə*] (pej) vi vacilar

ditto ['dɪtəu] adv ídem, lo mismo

divan [dɪ'væn] n (also: ~ bed) cama turca

dive [daɪv] n (from board) salto; (underwater) buceo; (of submarine) sumersión f ♦ vi (swimmer: into water) saltar; (: under water) zambullirse, bucear; (fish, submarine) sumergirse; (bird) lanzarse en picado; **to ~ into** (bag etc) meter la mano en; (place) meterse de prisa en; **~r** n (underwater) buzo

diverse [daɪ'vɜːs] adj diversos/as, varios/as

diversion [daɪ'vɜːʃən] n (BRIT: AUT) desviación f; (distraction, MIL) diversión f; (of funds) distracción f

divert [daɪ'vɜːt] vt (turn aside) desviar

divide [dɪ'vaɪd] vt dividir; (separate) separar ♦ vi dividirse; (road) bifurcarse; **~d highway** (US) n carretera de doble calzada

dividend ['dɪvɪdɛnd] n dividendo; (fig): **to pay ~s** proporcionar beneficios

divine [dɪ'vaɪn] adj (also fig) divino

diving ['daɪvɪŋ] n (SPORT) salto; (underwater) buceo; **~ board** n trampolín m

divinity [dɪ'vɪnɪtɪ] n divinidad f; (SCOL) teología

division [dɪ'vɪʒən] n división f; (sharing out) reparto; (disagreement) diferencias fpl; (COMM) sección f

divorce [dɪ'vɔːs] n divorcio ♦ vt divorciarse de; **~d** adj divorciado; **~e** [-'siː] n divorciado/a

divulge [daɪ'vʌldʒ] vt divulgar, revelar

D.I.Y. (BRIT) adj, n abbr = **do-it-yourself**

dizzy ['dɪzɪ] adj (spell) de mareo; **to feel ~** marearse

DJ n abbr = **disc jockey**

KEYWORD

---

do [duː] (pt **did**, pp **done**) n (inf: party etc): **we're having a little ~ on Saturday** damos una fiestecita el sábado; **it was rather a grand ~** fue un acontecimiento a lo grande

♦ aux vb **1** (in negative constructions: not translated) **I don't understand** no entiendo

2 (to form questions: not translated) **didn't you know?** ¿no lo sabías?; **what ~ you think?** ¿qué opinas?

3 (for emphasis, in polite expressions): **people**

~ make mistakes sometimes sí que se cometen errores a veces; **she does seem rather late** a mí también me parece que se ha retrasado; **~ sit down/help yourself** siéntate/ sírvete por favor; **~ take care!** ¡ten cuidado (, te pido)!

4 (used to avoid repeating vb): **she sings better than I ~** canta mejor que yo; **~ you agree? — yes, I ~/no, I don't** ¿estás de acuerdo? — sí (lo estoy)/no (lo estoy); **she lives in Glasgow — so ~ I** vive en Glasgow — yo también; **he didn't like it and neither did we** no le gustó y a nosotros tampoco; **who made this mess? — I did** ¿quién hizo esta chapuza? — yo; **he asked me to help him and I did** me pidió que le ayudara y lo hice

5 (in question tags): **you like him, don't you?** te gusta, ¿verdad? or ¿no?; **I don't know him, ~ I?** creo que no le conozco

♦ vt **1** (gen, carry out, perform etc): **what are you ~ing tonight?** ¿qué haces esta noche?; **what can I ~ for you?** ¿en qué puedo servirle?; **to ~ the washing-up/cooking** fregar los platos/cocinar; **to ~ one's teeth/nails** lavarse los dientes/arreglarse el pelo/arreglarse las uñas

2 (AUT etc): **the car was ~ing 100** el coche iba a 100; **we've done 200 km already** ya hemos hecho 200 km; **he can ~ 100 in that car** puede ir a 100 en ese coche

♦ vi **1** (act, behave) hacer; **~ as I ~** haz como yo

2 (get on, fare): **he's ~ing well/badly at school** va bien/mal en la escuela; **the firm is ~ing well** la empresa anda or va bien; **how ~ you ~?** mucho gusto; (less formal) ¿qué tal?

3 (suit): **will it ~?** ¿sirve?, ¿está or va bien?

4 (be sufficient) bastar; **will £10 ~?** ¿será bastante con £10?; **that'll ~** así está bien; **that'll ~!** (in annoyance) ¡ya está bien!, ¡basta ya!; **to make ~ (with)** arreglárselas (con)

do away with vt fus (kill, disease) eliminar; (abolish: law etc) abolir; (withdraw) retirar

do up vt (laces) atar; (zip, dress, shirt) abrochar; (renovate: room, house) renovar

do with vt fus (need): **I could ~ with a drink/some help** no me vendría mal un trago/un poco de ayuda; (be connected) tener que ver con; **what has it got to ~ with you?** ¿qué tiene que ver contigo?

do without vi pasar sin; **if you're late for tea then you'll ~ without** si llegas tarde tendrás que quedarte sin cenar ♦ vt fus pasar sin; **I can ~ without a car** puedo pasar sin coche

---

dock [dɒk] n (NAUT) muelle m; (LAW) banquillo (de los acusados); **~s** npl (NAUT) muelles mpl, puerto sg ♦ vi (enter ~) atracar (la) muelle; (SPACE) acoplarse; **~er** n trabajador m portuario, estibador m; **~yard** n astillero

doctor ['dɔktə*] n médico/a; (*Ph.D. etc*) doctor(a) m/f ♦ vt (*drink etc*) adulterar; **D~ of Philosophy** n Doctor en Filosofía y Letras

document ['dɔkjumənt] n documento; **~ary** [-'mɛntərɪ] adj documental ♦ n documental m

dodge [dɔdʒ] n (*fig*) truco ♦ vt evadir; (*blow*) esquivar

dodgems ['dɔdʒəmz] (*BRIT*) npl coches mpl de choque

doe [dəu] n (*deer*) cierva, gama; (*rabbit*) coneja

does [dʌz] vb see do; **~n't** = **does not**

dog [dɔg] n perro ♦ vt seguir los pasos de; (*subj: bad luck*) perseguir; **~ collar** n collar m de perro; (*of clergyman*) alzacuellos m inv; **~eared** adj sobado

dogged ['dɔgɪd] adj tenaz, obstinado

dogsbody ['dɔgzbɔdɪ] (*BRIT: inf*) n burro de carga

doings ['duːɪŋz] npl (*activities*) actividades fpl

do-it-yourself n bricolaje m

doldrums ['dɔldrəmz] npl: **to be in the ~** (*person*) estar abatido; (*business*) estar estancado

dole [dəul] (*BRIT*) n (*payment*) subsidio de paro; **on the ~** parado; **~ out** vt repartir

doll [dɔl] n muñeca; (*US: inf: woman*) muñeca, gachí f

dollar ['dɔlə*] n dólar m

dolled up (*inf*) adj arreglado

dolphin ['dɔlfɪn] n delfín m

domain [də'meɪn] n (*fig*) campo, competencia; (*land*) dominios mpl

dome [dəum] n (*ARCH*) cúpula

domestic [də'mɛstɪk] adj (*animal, duty*) doméstico; (*flight, policy*) nacional; **~ated** adj domesticado; (*home-loving*) casero, hogareño

dominate ['dɔmɪneɪt] vt dominar

domineering [dɔmɪ'nɪərɪŋ] adj dominante

dominion [də'mɪnɪən] n dominio

domino ['dɔmɪnəu] (*pl* **~es**) n ficha de dominó; **~es** n (*game*) dominó

don [dɔn] (*BRIT*) n profesor(a) m/f universitario/a

donate [də'neɪt] vt donar; **donation** [də'neɪʃən] n donativo

done [dʌn] pp of **do**

donkey ['dɔŋkɪ] n burro

donor ['dəunə*] n donante m/f; **~ card** n carnet m de donante de órganos

don't [dəunt] = **do not**

donut ['dəunʌt] (*US*) n = **doughnut**

doodle ['duːdl] vi hacer dibujitos or garabatos

doom [duːm] n (*fate*) suerte f ♦ vt: **to be ~ed to failure** estar condenado al fracaso

door [dɔː*] n puerta; **~bell** n timbre m;

~ handle n tirador m; (*of car*) manija; **~man** (*irreg*) n (*in hotel*) portero; **~mat** n felpudo, estera; **~step** n peldaño; **~-to-~** adj de puerta en puerta; **~way** n entrada, puerta

dope [dəup] n (*inf: illegal drug*) droga; (: *person*) imbécil m/f ♦ vt (*horse etc*) drogar

dormant ['dɔːmənt] adj inactivo

dormitory ['dɔːmɪtrɪ] n (*BRIT*) dormitorio; (*US*) colegio mayor

dormouse ['dɔːmaus] (*pl* **-mice**) n lirón m

DOS n abbr (= disk operating system) DOS m

dosage ['dəusɪdʒ] n dosis f inv

dose [dəus] n dósis f inv

doss house ['dɔss-] (*BRIT*) n pensión f de mala muerte

dossier ['dɔsɪeɪ] n expediente m, dosier m

dot [dɔt] n punto ♦ vi: **~ted with** salpicado de; **on the ~** en punto

double ['dʌbl] adj doble ♦ adv (*twice*): **to cost ~** costar el doble ♦ n doble m ♦ vt doblar ♦ vi doblarse; **on the ~, at the ~** (*BRIT*) corriendo; **~ bass** n contrabajo; **~ bed** n cama de matrimonio; **~ bend** (*BRIT*) n doble curva; **~-breasted** adj cruzado; **~-click** vi (*COMPUT*) hacer doble clic; **~cross** vt (*trick*) engañar; (*betray*) traicionar; **~-decker** n autobús m de dos pisos; **~ glazing** (*BRIT*) n doble acristalamiento; **~ room** n habitación f doble; **~s** n (*TENNIS*) juego de dobles; **doubly** adv doblemente

doubt [daut] n duda ♦ vt dudar; (*suspect*) dudar de; **to ~ that** dudar que; **~ful** adj dudoso; (*person*): **to be ~ful about sth** tener dudas sobre algo; **~less** adv sin duda

dough [dəu] n masa, pasta; **~nut** (*US* **donut**) n ≈ rosquilla

dove [dʌv] n paloma

dovetail ['dʌvteɪl] vi (*fig*) encajar

dowdy ['daudɪ] adj (*person*) mal vestido; (*clothes*) pasado de moda

down [daun] n (*feathers*) plumón m, flojel m ♦ adv (*~wards*) abajo, hacia abajo; (*on the ground*) por o en tierra ♦ prep abajo ♦ vt (*inf: drink*) beberse; **~ with X!** ¡abajo X!; **~and-out** n vagabundo/a; **~-at-heel** adj venido a menos; (*appearance*) desaliñado; **~cast** adj abatido; **~fall** n caída, ruina; **~hearted** adj desanimado; **~hill** adv: **to go ~hill** (*also fig*) ir cuesta abajo; **~ payment** n entrada, pago al contado; **~pour** n aguacero; **~right** adj (*nonsense, lie*) manifiesto; (*refusal*) terminante; **~size** vi (*ECON: company*) reducir la plantilla de

Down's syndrome ['daunz-] n síndrome m de Down

down: ~stairs adv (*below*) (en la casa de) abajo; (*~wards*) escaleras abajo; **~stream** adv aguas or río abajo; **~-to-earth** adj práctico; **~town** adv en el centro de la ciudad; **~ under** adv en Australia (or Nueva Zelanda); **~ward** [-wəd] adj, adv hacia abajo; **~wards** [-wədz] adv hacia abajo

dowry ['dauri] n dote f

doz. abbr = **dozen**

doze [dəuz] vi dormitar; **~ off** vi quedarse medio dormido

dozen ['dʌzn] n docena; **a ~ books** una docena de libros; **~s of** cantidad de

Dr. abbr = doctor; drive

drab [dræb] adj gris, monótono

draft [drɑːft] n (first copy) borrador m; (POL: of bill) anteproyecto; (US: call-up) quinta ♦ vt (plan) preparar; (write roughly) hacer un borrador de; see also **draught**

draftsman ['drɑːftsmən] (US) n = **draughts-man**

drag [dræg] vt arrastrar; (river) dragar, rastrear ♦ vi (time) pasar despacio; (play, film etc) hacerse pesado ♦ n (inf) lata; (women's clothing): **in ~** vestido de travesti; **~ on** vi ser interminable; **~ and drop** vt (COMPUT) arrastrar y soltar

dragon ['drægən] n dragón m

dragonfly ['drægənflaɪ] n libélula

drain [dreɪn] n desaguadero; (in street) sumidero; (source of loss): **to be a ~ on** consumir, agotar ♦ vt (land, marshes) desaguar; (reservoir) desecar; (vegetables) escurrir ♦ vi escurrirse; **~age** n (act) desagüe m; (MED, AGR) drenaje m; (sewage) alcantarillado; **~ing board** (US **~board**) n escurridera, escurridor m; **~pipe** n tubo de desagüe

drama ['drɑːmə] n (art) teatro; (play) drama m; (excitement) emoción f; **~tic** [drə'mætɪk] adj dramático; (sudden, marked) espectacular; **~tist** ['dræmətɪst] n dramaturgo/a; **~tize** ['dræmətaɪz] vt (events) dramatizar

drank [dræŋk] pt of **drink**

drape [dreɪp] vt (cloth) colocar; (flag) colgar; **~s** (US) npl cortinas fpl

drastic ['dræstɪk] adj (measure) severo; (change) radical, drástico

draught [drɑːft] (US **draft**) n (of air) corriente f de aire; (NAUT) calado; **on ~** (of beer) de barril; **~ beer** n cerveza de barril; **~board** (BRIT) n tablero de damas; **~s** (BRIT) n (game) juego de damas

draughtsman ['drɑːftsmən] (US **draftsman**) (irreg) n delineante m

draw [drɔː] (pt drew, pp drawn) vt (picture) dibujar; (cart) tirar de; (curtain) correr; (take out) sacar; (attract) atraer; (money) retirar; (wages) cobrar ♦ n (SPORT) empatar ♦ n (SPORT) empate m; (lottery) sorteo; **~ near** vi acercarse; **~ out** vi (lengthen) alargarse ♦ vt sacar; **~ up** vi (stop) pararse ♦ vt (chair)

acercar; (document) redactar; **~back** n inconveniente m, desventaja; **~bridge** n puente m levadizo

drawer [drɔː•] n cajón m

drawing ['drɔːɪŋ] n dibujo; **~ board** n tablero (de dibujante); **~ pin** (BRIT) n chincheta; **~ room** n salón m

drawl [drɔːl] n habla lenta y cansina

drawn [drɔːn] pp of **draw**

dread [dred] n pavor m, terror m ♦ vt temer, tener miedo or pavor a; **~ful** adj horroroso

dream [driːm] (pt, pp **dreamed** or **dreamt**) n sueño ♦ vt, vi soñar; **~y** adj (distracted) soñador(a), distraído; (music) suave

dreary ['drɪərɪ] adj monótono

dredge [dredʒ] vt dragar

dregs [dregz] npl posos mpl; (of humanity) hez f

drench [drentʃ] vt empapar

dress [dres] n vestido; (clothing) ropa ♦ vt vestir; (wound) vendar ♦ vi vestirse; **to get ~ed** vestirse; **~ up** vi vestirse de etiqueta; (in fancy dress) disfrazarse; **~ circle** (BRIT) n principal m; **~er** n (furniture) aparador m; (: US) cómoda (con espejo); **~ing** n (MED) vendaje m; (CULIN) aliño; **~ing gown** (BRIT) n bata; **~ing room** n (THEATRE) camarín m; (SPORT) vestuario; **~ing table** n tocador m; **~maker** n modista, costurera; **~ rehearsal** n ensayo general

drew [druː] pt of **draw**

dribble ['drɪbl] vi (baby) babear ♦ vt (ball) regatear

dried [draɪd] adj (fruit) seco; (milk) en polvo

drier ['draɪə•] n = **dryer**

drift [drɪft] n (of current etc) flujo; (of snow) ventisquero; (meaning) significado ♦ vi (boat) ir a la deriva; (sand, snow) amontonarse; **~wood** n madera de deriva

drill [drɪl] n (~ bit) broca; (tool for DIY etc) taladro; (of dentist) fresa; (for mining etc) perforadora, barrena; (MIL) instrucción f ♦ vt perforar, taladrar; (troops) enseñar la instrucción a ♦ vi (for oil) perforar

drink [drɪŋk] (pt drank, pp drunk) n bebida; (sip) trago ♦ vt, vi beber; **to have a ~** tomar algo; tomar una copa or un trago; **a ~ of water** un trago de agua; **~er** n bebedor(a) m/f; **~ing water** n agua potable

drip [drɪp] n (act) goteo; (one ~) gota; (MED) gota a gota m ♦ vi gotear; **~-dry** adj (shirt) inarrugable; **~ping** n (animal fat) pringue m

drive [draɪv] (pt drove, pp driven) n (journey) viaje m (en coche); (also: **~way**) entrada; (energy) energía, vigor m; (COMPUT: also: disk ~) drive m ♦ vt (car) conducir (SP), manejar (AM); (nail) clavar; (push) empujar; (TECH: motor) impulsar ♦ vi (AUT: at controls) conducir; (: travel) pasearse en coche; **left-/**

right-hand ~ conducción f a la izquierda/derecha; **to ~ sb mad** volverle loco a uno

drivel ['drɪvl] (inf) n tonterías fpl

driven ['drɪvn] pp of **drive**

driver ['draɪvə*] n conductor(a) m/f (SP), chofer m (AM); (of taxi, bus) chofer; **~'s license** (US) n carnet m de conducir

driveway ['draɪvweɪ] n entrada

driving ['draɪvɪŋ] n el conducir (SP), el manejar (AM); **~ instructor** n instructor(a) m/f de conducción or manejo; **~ lesson** n clase f de conducción or manejo; **~ licence** (BRIT) n permiso de conducir; **~ school** n autoescuela; **~ test** n examen m de conducción or manejo

drizzle ['drɪzl] n llovizna

drool [dru:l] vi babear

droop [dru:p] vi (flower) marchitarse; (shoulders) encorvarse; (head) inclinarse

drop [drɔp] n (of water) gota; (lessening) baja; (fall) caída ♦ vt dejar caer; (voice, eyes, price) bajar; (passenger) dejar; (omit) omitir ♦ vi (object) caer; (wind) amainar; **~s** npl (MED) gotas fpl; **~ off** vi (sleep) dormirse ♦ vt (passenger) dejar; **~ out** vi (withdraw) retirarse; **~-out** n marginado/a; (SCOL) estudiante que abandona los estudios; **~per** n cuentagotas m inv; **~pings** npl excremento

drought [draut] n sequía

drove [drəuv] pt of **drive**

drown [draun] vt ahogar ♦ vi ahogarse

drowsy ['drauzɪ] adj soñoliento; **to be ~** tener sueño

drug [drʌg] n medicamento; (narcotic) droga ♦ vt drogar; **to be on ~s** drogarse; **~ addict** n drogadicto/a; **~gist** (US) n farmacéutico; **~store** (US) n farmacia

drum [drʌm] n tambor m; (for oil, petrol) bidón m; **~s** npl batería; **~mer** n tambor m

drunk [drʌŋk] pp of **drink** ♦ adj borracho ♦ n (also: **~ard**) borracho/a; **~en** adj borracho; (laughter, party) de borrachos

dry [draɪ] adj seco; (day) sin lluvia; (climate) árido, seco ♦ vt secar; (tears) enjugarse ♦ vi secarse; **~ up** vi (river) secarse; **~-cleaner's** n tintorería; **~-cleaning** n lavado en seco; **~er** n (for hair) secador m; (US: for clothes) secadora; **~ rot** n putrefacción f fungoide

DSS n abbr = **Department of Social Security**

DTP n abbr (= desk-top publishing) autoedición f

dual ['djuəl] adj doble; **~ carriageway** (BRIT) n carretera de doble calzada; **~-purpose** adj de doble uso

dubbed [dʌbd] adj (CINEMA) doblado

dubious ['dju:bɪəs] adj indeciso; (reputation, company) sospechoso

duchess ['dʌtʃɪs] n duquesa

duck [dʌk] n pato ♦ vi agacharse; **~ling** n patito

duct [dʌkt] n conducto, canal m

dud [dʌd] n (object, tool) engaño, engañifa ♦ adj: **~ cheque** (BRIT) cheque m sin fondos

due [dju:] adj (owed): **he is ~ £10** se le deben 10 libras; (expected: event): **the meeting is ~ on Wednesday** la reunión tendrá lugar el miércoles; (: arrival) **the train is ~ at 8am** el tren tiene su llegada para las 8; (proper) debido ♦ n: **to give sb his (or her) ~** ser justo con alguien ♦ adv: **~ north** derecho al norte; **~s** npl (for club, union) cuota; (in harbour) derechos mpl; **in ~ course** a su debido tiempo; **~ to** debido a; **to be ~ to** deberse a

duet [dju:'et] n dúo

duffel bag ['dʌfl] n bolsa de lona

duffel coat n trenca, abrigo de tres cuartos

dug [dʌg] pt, pp of **dig**

duke [dju:k] n duque m

dull [dʌl] adj (light) débil; (stupid) torpe; (boring) pesado; (sound, pain) sordo; (weather, day) gris ♦ vt (pain, grief) aliviar; (mind, senses) entorpecer

duly ['dju:lɪ] adv debidamente; (on time) a su debido tiempo

dumb [dʌm] adj mudo; (pej: stupid) estúpido; **~founded** [dʌm'faundɪd] adj pasmado

dummy ['dʌmɪ] n (tailor's ~) maniquí m; (mock-up) maqueta; (BRIT: for baby) chupete m ♦ adj falso, postizo

dump [dʌmp] n (also: rubbish ~) basurero, vertedero; (inf: place) cuchitril m ♦ vt (put down) dejar; (get rid of) deshacerse de; (COMPUT: data) transferir

dumpling ['dʌmplɪŋ] n bola de masa hervida

dumpy ['dʌmpɪ] adj regordete/a

dunce [dʌns] n zopenco

dung [dʌŋ] n estiércol m

dungarees [dʌŋgə'ri:z] npl mono

dungeon ['dʌndʒən] n calabozo

duplex ['dju:pleks] n dúplex m

duplicate [n 'dju:plɪkət, vb 'dju:plɪkeɪt] n duplicado ♦ vt duplicar; (photocopy) fotocopiar; (repeat) repetir; **in ~** por duplicado

durable ['djuərəbl] adj duradero

duration [djuə'reɪʃən] n duración f

during ['djuərɪŋ] prep durante

dusk [dʌsk] n crepúsculo, anochecer m

dust [dʌst] n polvo ♦ vt quitar el polvo a, desempolvar; (cake etc): **to ~ with** espolvorear de; **~bin** (BRIT) n cubo de la basura (SP), balde m (AM); **~er** n paño, trapo; **~man** (BRIT irreg) n basurero; **~y** adj polvoriento

Dutch [dʌtʃ] adj holandés/esa ♦ n (LING) holandés m; **the ~** npl los holandeses; **to go ~** (inf) pagar cada uno lo suyo; **~man/**

woman (*irreg*) *n* holandés/esa *m/f*

duty ['dju:tɪ] *n* deber *m*; (*tax*) derechos *mpl* de aduana; **on ~** de servicio; (*at night etc*) de guardia; **off ~** libre (de servicio); **~-free** *adj* libre de impuestos

duvet ['du:veɪ] (*BRIT*) *n* edredón *m*

DVD *n abbr* (= *digital versatile or video disc*) DVD *m*

dwarf [dwɔːf] (*pl* **dwarves**) *n* enano/a ♦ *vt* empequeñecer

dwell [dwɛl] (*pt, pp* **dwelt**) *vi* morar; **~ on** *vt fus* explayarse en

dwindle ['dwɪndl] *vi* menguar, disminuir

dye [daɪ] *n* tinte *m* ♦ *vt* teñir

dying ['daɪɪŋ] *adj* moribundo, agonizante

dyke [daɪk] (*BRIT*) *n* dique *m*

dynamic [daɪ'næmɪk] *adj* dinámico

dynamite ['daɪnəmaɪt] *n* dinamita

dynamo ['daɪnəməu] *n* dínamo *f*

dynasty ['dɪnəstɪ] *n* dinastía

E, e

E [i:] *n* (*MUS*) mi *m*

each [i:tʃ] *adj* cada *inv* ♦ *pron* cada uno; **~ other** el uno al otro; **they hate ~ other** se odian (entre ellos *or* mutuamente); **they have 2 books ~** tienen 2 libros por persona

eager ['i:gə*] *adj* (*keen*) entusiasmado; **to be ~ to do sth** tener muchas ganas de hacer algo, impacientarse por hacer algo; **to be ~ for** tener muchas ganas de

eagle ['i:gl] *n* águila

ear [ɪə*] *n* oreja; oído; (*of corn*) espiga; **~ache** *n* dolor *m* de oídos; **~drum** *n* tímpano

earl [ə:l] *n* conde *m*

earlier ['ə:lɪə*] *adj* anterior ♦ *adv* antes

early ['ə:lɪ] *adv* temprano; (*before time*) con tiempo, con anticipación ♦ *adj* temprano; (*settlers etc*) primitivo; (*death, departure*) prematuro; (*reply*) pronto; **to have an ~ night** acostarse temprano; **in the ~ or ~ in the spring/19th century** a principios de primavera/del siglo diecinueve; **~ retirement** *n* jubilación *f* anticipada

earmark ['ɪəmɑːk] *vt*: **to ~ (for)** reservar (para), destinar (a)

earn [ə:n] *vt* (*salary*) percibir; (*interest*) devengar; (*praise*) merecerse

earnest ['ə:nɪst] *adj* (*wish*) fervoroso; (*person*) serio, formal; **in ~** en serio

earnings ['ə:nɪŋz] *npl* (*personal*) sueldo, ingresos *mpl*; (*company*) ganancias *fpl*

ear: **~phones** *npl* auriculares *mpl*; **~ring** *n* pendiente *m*, arete *m*; **~shot** *n*: **within ~shot** al alcance del oído

earth [ə:θ] *n* tierra; (*BRIT: ELEC*) cable *m* de toma de tierra ♦ *vt* (*BRIT: ELEC*) conectar a

tierra; **~enware** *n* loza (de barro); **~quake** *n* terremoto; **~y** *adj* (*fig: vulgar*) grosero

ease [i:z] *n* facilidad *f*; (*comfort*) comodidad *f* ♦ *vt* (*lessen: problem*) mitigar; (: *pain*) aliviar; (: *tension*) reducir; **to ~ sth in/out** meter/sacar algo con cuidado; **at ~!** (*MIL*) ¡descansen!; **~ off** *or* **up** *vi* (*wind, rain*) amainar; (*slow down*) aflojar la marcha

easel ['i:zl] *n* caballete *m*

easily ['i:zɪlɪ] *adv* fácilmente

east [i:st] *n* este *m* ♦ *adj* del este, oriental; (*wind*) este ♦ *adv* al este, hacia el este; **the E~** el Oriente; (*POL*) los países del Este

Easter ['i:stə*] *n* Pascua (de Resurrección); **~ egg** *n* huevo de Pascua

east: **~erly** ['i:stəlɪ] *adj* (*to the east*) al este; (*from the east*) del este; **~ern** ['i:stən] *adj* del este, oriental; (*oriental*) oriental; (*communist*) del este; **~ward(s)** ['i:stwəd(z)] *adv* hacia el este

easy ['i:zɪ] *adj* fácil; (*simple*) sencillo; (*comfortable*) holgado, cómodo; (*relaxed*) tranquilo ♦ *adv*: **to take it** *or* **things ~** (*not worry*) tomarlo con calma; (*rest*) descansar; **~ chair** *n* sillón *m*; **~-going** *adj* acomodadizo

eat [i:t] (*pt* **ate**, *pp* **eaten**) *vt* comer; **~ away at** *vt fus* corroer; mermar; **~ into** *vt fus* corroer; (*savings*) mermar

eaves [i:vz] *npl* alero

eavesdrop ['i:vzdrɔp] *vi*: **to ~ (on)** escuchar a escondidas

ebb [ɛb] *n* reflujo ♦ *vi* bajar; (*fig: also*: **~ away**) decaer

ebony ['ɛbənɪ] *n* ébano

EC *n abbr* (= *European Community*) CE *f*

ECB *n abbr* (= *European Central Bank*) BCE *m*

eccentric [ɪk'sɛntrɪk] *adj, n* excéntrico/a *m/f*

echo ['ɛkəu] (*pl* **~es**) *n* eco *m* ♦ *vt* (*sound*) repetir ♦ *vi* resonar, hacer eco

éclair [ɪ'klɛə*] *n* pastelillo relleno de crema y con chocolate por encima

eclipse [ɪ'klɪps] *n* eclipse *m*

ecology [ɪ'kɔlədʒɪ] *n* ecología

e-commerce *n abbr* (= *electronic commerce*) comercio electrónico

economic [i:kə'nɔmɪk] *adj* económico; (*business etc*) rentable; **~al** *adj* económico; **~s** *n* (*SCOL*) economía ♦ *npl* (*of project etc*) rentabilidad *f*

economize [ɪ'kɔnəmaɪz] *vi* economizar, ahorrar

economy [ɪ'kɔnəmɪ] *n* economía; **~ class** *n* (*AVIAT*) clase *f* económica; **~ size** *n* tamaño económico

ecstasy ['ɛkstəsɪ] *n* éxtasis *m inv*; (*drug*) éxtasis *m inv*; **ecstatic** [ɛks'tætɪk] *adj* extático

ECU ['eɪkju:] *n* (= *European Currency Unit*) ECU *m*

Ecuador ['ekwədɔ:r] *n* Ecuador *m*; **~ian** *adj, n* ecuatoriano/a *m/f*

eczema ['eksɪmə] n eczema m

edge [edʒ] n (of knife) filo; (of object) borde m; (of lake) orilla ♦ vt (SEWING) ribetear; **on ~** (fig) = edgy; **to ~ away from** alejarse poco a poco de; **~ways** adv: **he couldn't get a word in ~ways** no pudo meter ni baza

edgy ['edʒɪ] adj nervioso, inquieto

edible ['edɪbl] adj comestible

Edinburgh ['edɪnbərə] n Edimburgo

edit ['edɪt] vt (be editor of) dirigir; (text, report) corregir, preparar; **~ion** [ɪ'dɪʃən] n edición f; **~or** n (of newspaper) director(a) m/f; (of column): **foreign/political ~or** encargado de la sección de extranjero/política; (of book) redactor(a) m/f; **~orial** [-'tɔːrɪəl] adj editorial ♦ n editorial m

educate ['edjʊkeɪt] vt (gen) educar; (instruct) instruir

education [edjʊ'keɪʃən] n educación f; (schooling) enseñanza; (SCOL) pedagogía; **~al** adj (policy etc) educacional; (experience) docente; (toy) educativo

EEC n abbr (= European Economic Community) CEE f

eel [iːl] n anguila

eerie ['ɪərɪ] adj misterioso

effect [ɪ'fekt] n efecto ♦ vt efectuar, llevar a cabo; **to take ~** (law) entrar en vigor or vigencia; (drug) surtir efecto; **in ~** en realidad; **~ive** adj eficaz; (actual) verdadero; **~ively** adv eficazmente; (in reality) efectivamente; **~iveness** n eficacia

effeminate [ɪ'femɪnɪt] adj afeminado

efficiency [ɪ'fɪʃənsɪ] n eficiencia; rendimiento

efficient [ɪ'fɪʃənt] adj eficiente; (machine) de buen rendimiento

effort ['efət] n esfuerzo; **~less** adj sin ningún esfuerzo; (style) natural

effusive [ɪ'fjuːsɪv] adj efusivo

e.g. adv abbr (= exempli gratia) p. ej.

egg [eg] n huevo; **hard-boiled/soft-boiled ~** huevo duro/pasado por agua; **~ on** vt incitar; **~cup** n huevera; **~ plant** (esp US) n berenjena; **~shell** n cáscara de huevo

ego ['iːgəʊ] n ego; **~tism** n egoísmo; **~tist** n egoísta m/f

Egypt ['iːdʒɪpt] n Egipto; **~ian** [ɪ'dʒɪpʃən] adj, n egipcio/a m/f

eiderdown ['aɪdədaʊn] n edredón m

eight [eɪt] num ocho; **~een** num diez y ocho, dieciocho; **eighth** [eɪtθ] num octavo; **~y** num ochenta

Eire ['eərə] n Eire m

either ['aɪðə*] adj cualquiera de los dos; (both, each) cada ♦ pron: **~ (of them)** cualquiera (de los dos) ♦ adv tampoco; **on ~ side** en ambos lados; **I don't like ~** no me gusta ninguno/a de los/las dos; **no, I don't ~** no, yo tampoco ♦ conj: **~ yes or no** o sí o no

eject [ɪ'dʒekt] vt echar, expulsar; (tenant) desahuciar; **~or seat** n asiento proyectable

elaborate [adj ɪ'læbərɪt, vb ɪ'læbəreɪt] adj (complex) complejo ♦ vt (expand) ampliar; (refine) refinar ♦ vi explicar con más detalles

elastic [ɪ'læstɪk] n elástico ♦ adj elástico; (fig) flexible; **~ band** (BRIT) n gomita

elated [ɪ'leɪtɪd] adj: **to be ~** regocijarse

elbow ['elbəʊ] n codo

elder ['eldə*] adj mayor ♦ n (tree) saúco; (person) mayor; **~ly** adj de edad, mayor ♦ npl: **the ~ly** los mayores

eldest ['eldɪst] adj, n el/la mayor

elect [ɪ'lekt] vt elegir ♦ adj: **the president** el presidente electo; **to ~** to do optar por hacer; **~ion** [ɪ'lekʃən] n elección f; **~ioneering** [ɪlekʃə'nɪərɪŋ] n campaña electoral; **~or** n elector(a) m/f; **~oral** adj electoral; **~orate** n electorado

electric [ɪ'lektrɪk] adj eléctrico; **~al** adj eléctrico; **~ blanket** n manta eléctrica; **~ fire** n estufa eléctrica; **~ian** [ɪlek'trɪʃən] n electricista m/f; **~ity** [ɪlek'trɪsɪtɪ] n electricidad f; **electrify** [ɪ'lektrɪfaɪ] vt (RAIL) electrificar; (fig: audience) electrizar

electronic [ɪlek'trɒnɪk] adj electrónico; **~ mail** n correo electrónico; **~s** n electrónica

elegant ['elɪgənt] adj elegante

element ['elɪmənt] n elemento; (of kettle etc) resistencia; **~ary** [-'mentərɪ] adj elemental; (primitive) rudimentario; (school) primario

elephant ['elɪfənt] n elefante m

elevation [elɪ'veɪʃən] n elevación f; (height) altura

elevator ['elɪveɪtə*] n (US) ascensor m; (in warehouse etc) montacargas m inv

eleven [ɪ'levn] num once; **~ses** (BRIT) npl café m de las once; **~th** num undécimo

elicit [ɪ'lɪsɪt] vt: **to ~ (from)** sacar (de)

eligible ['elɪdʒəbl] adj: **an ~ young man/woman** un buen partido; **to be ~ for sth** llenar los requisitos para algo

elm [elm] n olmo

elongated ['iːlɒŋgeɪtɪd] adj alargado

elope [ɪ'ləʊp] vi fugarse (para casarse)

eloquent ['eləkwənt] adj elocuente

else [els] adv: **something ~** otra cosa; **somewhere ~** en otra parte; **everywhere ~** en todas partes menos aquí; **where ~?** ¿dónde más?, ¿en qué otra parte?; **there was little ~ to do** apenas quedaba otra cosa que hacer; **nobody ~ spoke** no habló nadie más; **~where** adv (be) en otra parte; (go) a otra parte

elude [ɪ'luːd] vt (subj: idea etc) escaparse a; (capture) esquivar

elusive [ɪ'luːsɪv] adj esquivo; (quality) difícil de encontrar

emaciated [ɪ'meɪsɪeɪtɪd] adj demacrado

E-mail, e-mail ['iːmeɪl] n abbr (= electronic mail) correo electrónico, e-mail m

emancipate [ɪˈmænsɪpeɪt] *vt* emancipar
embankment [ɪmˈbæŋkmənt] *n* terraplén *m*
embark [ɪmˈbɑːk] *vi* embarcarse ♦ *vt* embarcar; **to ~ on** (*journey*) emprender; (*course of action*) lanzarse a; **~ation** [ɛmbɑːˈkeɪʃən] *n* (*people*) embarco; (*goods*) embarque *m*
embarrass [ɪmˈbærəs] *vt* avergonzar; (*government etc*) dejar en mal lugar; **~ed** *adj* (*laugh, silence*) embarazoso; **~ing** (*situation*) violento; (*question*) embarazoso; **~ment** *n* (*shame*) vergüenza; (*problem*): **to be an ~ment for sb** poner en un aprieto a uno
embassy [ˈembəsɪ] *n* embajada
embedded [ɪmˈbedɪd] *adj* (*object*) empotrado; (*thorn etc*) clavado
embellish [ɪmˈbelɪʃ] *vt* embellecer; (*story*) adornar
embers [ˈembəz] *npl* rescoldo, ascua
embezzle [ɪmˈbezl] *vt* desfalcar, malversar
embitter [ɪmˈbɪtə*] *vt* (*fig: sour*) amargar
embody [ɪmˈbɔdɪ] *vt* (*spirit*) encarnar; (*include*) incorporar
embossed [ɪmˈbɔst] *adj* realzado
embrace [ɪmˈbreɪs] *vt* abrazar, dar un abrazo a; (*include*) abarcar ♦ *vi* abrazarse ♦ *n* abrazo
embroider [ɪmˈbrɔɪdə*] *vt* bordar; **~y** *n* bordado
embryo [ˈembrɪəu] *n* embrión *m*
emerald [ˈemərəld] *n* esmeralda
emerge [ɪˈmɜːdʒ] *vi* salir; (*arise*) surgir
emergency [ɪˈmɜːdʒənsɪ] *n* crisis *f inv*; **in an ~** en caso de urgencia; **state of ~** estado de emergencia; **~ cord** (*US*) *n* timbre *m* de alarma; **~ exit** *n* salida de emergencia; **~ landing** *n* aterrizaje *m* forzoso; **~ services** *npl* (*fire, police, ambulance*) servicios *mpl* de urgencia *or* emergencia
emery board [ˈemərɪ-] *n* lima de uñas
emigrate [ˈemɪgreɪt] *vi* emigrar
emissions [ɪˈmɪʃənz] *npl* emisión *f*
emit [ɪˈmɪt] *vt* emitir; (*smoke*) arrojar; (*smell*) despedir; (*sound*) producir
emotion [ɪˈməuʃən] *n* emoción *f*; **~al** *adj* (*needs*) emocional; (*person*) sentimental; (*scene*) conmovedor(a), emocionante; (*speech*) emocionado
emperor [ˈempərə*] *n* emperador *m*
emphasis [ˈemfəsɪs] (*pl* **-ses**) *n* énfasis *m inv*
emphasize [ˈemfəsaɪz] *vt* (*word, point*) subrayar, recalcar; (*feature*) hacer resaltar
emphatic [emˈfætɪk] *adj* (*reply*) categórico; (*person*) insistente
empire [ˈempaɪə*] *n* (*also fig*) imperio
employ [ɪmˈplɔɪ] *vt* emplear; **~ee** [-ˈiː] *n* empleado/a; **~er** *n* patrón/ona *m/f*; empresario; **~ment** *n* (*work*) trabajo; **~ment agency** *n* agencia de colocaciones
empower [ɪmˈpauə*] *vt*: **to ~ sb to do sth** autorizar a uno para hacer algo
empress [ˈempris] *n* emperatriz *f*
emptiness [ˈemptinɪs] *n* vacío; (*of life etc*) vaciedad *f*
empty [ˈemptɪ] *adj* vacío; (*place*) desierto; (*house*) desocupado; (*threat*) vano ♦ *vt* vaciar; (*place*) dejar vacío ♦ *vi* vaciarse; (*house etc*) quedar desocupado; **~-handed** *adj* con las manos vacías
EMU *n abbr* (= *European Monetary Union*) UME *f*
emulate [ˈemjuleɪt] *vt* emular
emulsion [ɪˈmʌlʃən] *n* emulsión *f*; (*also: ~ paint*) pintura emulsión
enable [ɪˈneɪbl] *vt*: **to ~ sb to do sth** permitir a uno hacer algo
enamel [ɪˈnæməl] *n* esmalte *m*; (*also: ~ paint*) pintura esmaltada
enchant [ɪnˈtʃɑːnt] *vt* encantar; **~ing** *adj* encantador(a)
encl. *abbr* (= *enclosed*) adj
enclose [ɪnˈkləuz] *vt* (*land*) cercar; (*letter etc*) adjuntar; **please find ~d** te mandamos adjunto
enclosure [ɪnˈkləuʒə*] *n* cercado, recinto
encompass [ɪnˈkʌmpəs] *vt* abarcar
encore [ɔŋˈkɔː*] *excl* ¡otra!, ¡bis! ♦ *n* bis *m*
encounter [ɪnˈkauntə*] *n* encuentro ♦ *vt* encontrar, encontrarse con; (*difficulty*) tropezar con
encourage [ɪnˈkʌrɪdʒ] *vt* alentar, animar; (*activity*) fomentar; (*growth*) estimular; **~ment** *n* estímulo; (*of industry*) fomento
encroach [ɪnˈkrəutʃ] *vi*: **to ~ (up)on** invadir; (*rights*) usurpar; (*time*) adueñarse de
encyclop(a)edia [ɛnsaɪkləuˈpiːdɪə] *n* enciclopedia
end [end] *n* (*gen, also aim*) fin *m*; (*of table*) extremo; (*of street*) final *m*; (*SPORT*) lado ♦ *vt* terminar, acabar; (*also: bring to an ~, put an ~ to*) acabar con ♦ *vi* terminar, acabar; **in the ~** al fin; **on ~** (*object*) de punta, de cabeza; **to stand on ~** (*hair*) erizarse; **for hours on ~** hora tras hora; **~ up** *vi*: **to ~ up in** terminar en; (*place*) ir a parar en
endanger [ɪnˈdeɪndʒə*] *vt* poner en peligro; **an ~ed species** una especie en peligro de extinción
endearing [ɪnˈdɪərɪŋ] *adj* simpático, atractivo
endeavour [ɪnˈdevə*] (*US* **endeavor**) *n* esfuerzo; (*attempt*) tentativa ♦ *vi*: **to ~ to do** esforzarse por hacer; (*try*) procurar hacer
ending [ˈendɪŋ] *n* (*of book*) desenlace *m*; (*LING*) terminación *f*
endive [ˈendaɪv] *n* (*chicory*) endibia; (*curly*) escarola
endless [ˈendlɪs] *adj* interminable, inacabable
endorse [ɪnˈdɔːs] *vt* (*cheque*) endosar; (*approve*) aprobar; **~ment** *n* (*on driving licence*) nota de inhabilitación

endure [ɪn'djuə*] vt (bear) aguantar, soportar ♦ vi (last) durar

enemy ['enəmɪ] adj, n enemigo/a m/f

energetic [ɛnə'dʒɛtɪk] adj enérgico

energy ['enədʒɪ] n energía

enforce [ɪn'fɔːs] vt (LAW) hacer cumplir

engage [ɪn'geɪdʒ] vt (attention) llamar; (interest) ocupar; (in conversation) abordar; (worker) contratar; (AUT): **to ~ the clutch** embragar ♦ vi (TECH) engranar; **to ~ in** dedicarse a, ocuparse en; **~d** adj (BRIT: busy, in use) ocupado; (betrothed) prometido; **to get ~d** prometerse; **~d tone** (BRIT) n (TEL) señal f de comunicando; **~ment** n (appointment) compromiso, cita; (booking) contratación f; (to marry) compromiso; (period) noviazgo; **~ment ring** n anillo de prometida

engaging [ɪn'geɪdʒɪŋ] adj atractivo

engine ['endʒɪn] n (AUT) motor m; (RAIL) locomotora; **~ driver** n maquinista m/f

engineer [endʒɪ'nɪə*] n ingeniero; (BRIT: for repairs) mecánico; (on ship, US: RAIL) maquinista m; **~ing** n ingeniería

England ['ɪŋglənd] n Inglaterra

English ['ɪŋglɪʃ] adj inglés/esa ♦ n (LING) inglés m; **the ~** npl los ingleses mpl; **the ~ Channel** n (el Canal de) la Mancha; **~man/woman** (irreg) n inglés/esa m/f

engraving [ɪn'greɪvɪŋ] n grabado

engrossed [ɪn'grəust] adj: **~ in** absorto en

engulf [ɪn'gʌlf] vt (subj: water) sumergir, hundir; (: fire) prender; (: fear) apoderarse de

enhance [ɪn'hɑːns] vt (gen) aumentar; (beauty) realzar

enjoy [ɪn'dʒɔɪ] vt (health, fortune) disfrutar de, gozar de; (like) gustarle a uno; **to ~ o.s.** divertirse; **~able** adj agradable; (amusing) divertido; **~ment** n (joy) placer m; (activity) diversión f

enlarge [ɪn'lɑːdʒ] vt aumentar; (broaden) extender; (PHOT) ampliar ♦ vi: **to ~ on** (subject) tratar con más detalles; **~ment** n (PHOT) ampliación f

enlighten [ɪn'laɪtn] vt (inform) informar; **~ed** adj comprensivo; **the E~ment** n (HISTORY) ≈ la Ilustración, ≈ el Siglo de las Luces

enlist [ɪn'lɪst] vt alistar; (support) conseguir ♦ vi alistarse

enmity ['enmɪtɪ] n enemistad f

enormous [ɪ'nɔːməs] adj enorme

enough [ɪ'nʌf] adj: **~ time/books** bastante tiempo/bastantes libros ♦ pron bastante(s) ♦ adv: **big ~** bastante grande; **he has not worked ~** no ha trabajado bastante; **have you got ~?** ¿tiene usted bastante(s)?; **~ to eat** (lo) suficiente or (lo) bastante para comer; **~!** ¡basta ya!; **that's ~, thanks** con eso basta,

gracias; **I've had ~ of him** estoy harto de él; **... which, funnily or oddly ~ ...** ... lo que, por extraño que parezca ...

enquire [ɪn'kwaɪə*] vt, vi = **inquire**

enrage [ɪn'reɪdʒ] vt enfurecer

enrol [ɪn'rəul] (US **enroll**) vt (members) inscribir; (SCOL) matricular ♦ vi inscribirse; matricularse; **~ment** (US **enrollment**) n inscripción f; matriculación f

en route [ɔn'ruːt] adv durante el viaje

en suite [ɔn'swiːt] adj: **with ~ bathroom** con baño

ensure [ɪn'ʃuə*] vt asegurar

entail [ɪn'teɪl] vt suponer

entangled [ɪn'tæŋgld] adj: **to become ~ (in)** quedarse enredado (en) or enmarañado (en)

enter ['entə*] vt (room) entrar en; (club) hacerse socio de; (army) alistarse en; (sb for a competition) inscribir; (write down) apuntar; (COMPUT) meter ♦ vi entrar; **~ for** vt fus presentarse para; **~ into** vt fus (discussion etc) entablar; (agreement) llegar a, firmar

enterprise ['entəpraɪz] n empresa; (spirit) iniciativa; **free ~** la libre empresa; **private ~** la iniciativa privada; **enterprising** adj emprendedor/a

entertain [entə'teɪn] vt (amuse) divertir; (invite: guest) invitar (a casa); (idea) abrigar; **~er** n artista m/f; **~ing** adj divertido, entretenido; **~ment** n (amusement) diversión f; (show) espectáculo

enthralled [ɪn'θrɔːld] adj encantado

enthusiasm [ɪn'θuːzɪæzəm] n entusiasmo

enthusiast [ɪn'θuːzɪæst] n entusiasta m/f; **~ic** [-'æstɪk] adj entusiasta; **to be ~ic about** entusiasmarse por

entire [ɪn'taɪə*] adj entero; **~ly** adv totalmente; **~ty** [ɪn'taɪərətɪ] n: **in its ~ty** en su totalidad

entitle [ɪn'taɪtl] vt: **to ~ sb to sth** dar a uno derecho a algo; **~d** adj (book) titulado; **to be ~d to do** tener derecho a hacer

entrance [n 'entrəns, vb ɪn'trɑːns] n entrada ♦ vt encantar, hechizar; **to gain ~ to** (university etc) ingresar en; **~ examination** n examen m de ingreso; **~ fee** n cuota; **~ ramp** (US) n (AUT) rampa de acceso

entrant ['entrənt] n (in race, competition) participante m/f; (in examination) candidato/a

entrenched [en'trentʃd] adj inamovible

entrepreneur [ɔntrəprə'nə:] n empresario

entrust [ɪn'trʌst] vt: **to ~ sth to sb** confiar algo a uno

entry ['entrɪ] n entrada; (in competition) participación f; (in register) apunte m; (in account) partida; (in reference book) artículo; **"no ~"** "prohibido el paso"; (AUT) "dirección prohibida"; **~ form** n hoja de inscripción; **~ phone** n portero automático

envelop [ɪn'vɛləp] vt envolver
envelope ['ɛnvələup] n sobre m
envious ['ɛnvɪəs] adj envidioso; (look) de envidia
environment [ɪn'vaɪərnmənt] n (surroundings) entorno; (natural world): **the ~** el medio ambiente; **~al** [-'mɛntl] adj ambiental; medioambiental; **~-friendly** adj no perjudicial para el medio ambiente
envisage [ɪn'vɪzɪdʒ] vt prever
envoy ['ɛnvɔɪ] n enviado
envy ['ɛnvɪ] n envidia ♦ vt tener envidia a; to **~ sb sth** envidiar algo a uno
epic ['ɛpɪk] n épica ♦ adj épico
epidemic [ɛpɪ'dɛmɪk] n epidemia
epilepsy ['ɛpɪlɛpsɪ] n epilepsia
episode ['ɛpɪsəud] n episodio
epitomize [ɪ'pɪtəmaɪz] vt epitomar, resumir
equal ['i:kwl] adj igual; (treatment) equitativo ♦ n igual m/f ♦ vt ser igual a; (fig) igualar; to **be ~ to** (task) estar a la altura de; **~ity** [i:'kwɔlɪtɪ] n igualdad f; **~ize** vi (SPORT) empatar; **~ly** adv igualmente; (share etc) a partes iguales
equate [ɪ'kweɪt] vt: to **~ sth with** equiparar algo con; **equation** [ɪ'kweɪʒən] n (MATH) ecuación f
equator [ɪ'kweɪtə*] n ecuador m
equilibrium [i:kwɪ'lɪbrɪəm] n equilibrio
equip [ɪ'kwɪp] vt equipar; (person) proveer; to **be well ~ped** estar bien equipado; **~ment** n equipo; (tools) avíos mpl
equities ['ɛkwɪtɪz] (BRIT) npl (COMM) derechos mpl sobre or en el activo
equivalent [ɪ'kwɪvələnt] adj: **~ (to)** equivalente (a) ♦ n equivalente m
era ['ɪərə] n era, época
eradicate [ɪ'rædɪkeɪt] vt erradicar
erase [ɪ'reɪz] vt borrar; **~r** n goma de borrar
erect [ɪ'rɛkt] adj erguido ♦ vt erigir, levantar; (assemble) montar; **~ion** [-ʃən] n construcción f; (assembly) montaje m; (PHYSIOL) erección f
ERM n abbr (= Exchange Rate Mechanism) tipo de cambio europeo
erode [ɪ'rəud] vt (GEO) erosionar; (metal) corroer, desgastar; (fig) desgastar
erotic [ɪ'rɔtɪk] adj erótico
errand ['ɛrnd] n recado (SP), mandado (AM)
erratic [ɪ'rætɪk] adj desigual, poco uniforme
error ['ɛrə*] n error m, equivocación f
erupt [ɪ'rʌpt] vi entrar en erupción; (fig) estallar; **~ion** [ɪ'rʌpʃən] n erupción f; (of war) estallido
escalate ['ɛskəleɪt] vi extenderse, intensificarse
escalator ['ɛskəleɪtə*] n escalera móvil
escapade [ɛskə'peɪd] n travesura
escape [ɪ'skeɪp] n fuga ♦ vi escaparse; (flee) huir, evadirse; (leak) fugarse ♦ vt (respon-

sibility etc) evitar, eludir; (consequences) escapar a; (elude): **his name ~s me** no me sale su nombre; to **~ from** (place) escaparse de; (person) escaparse a
escort [n 'ɛskɔːt, vb ɪ'skɔːt] n acompañante m/f; (MIL) escolta ♦ vt acompañar
Eskimo ['ɛskɪməu] n esquimal m/f
especially [ɪ'spɛʃlɪ] adv (above all) sobre todo; (particularly) en particular, especialmente
espionage ['ɛspɪənɑːʒ] n espionaje m
esplanade [ɛsplə'neɪd] n (by sea) paseo marítimo
Esquire [ɪ'skwaɪə] (abbr **Esq.**) n: **J. Brown, ~** Sr. D. J. Brown
essay ['ɛseɪ] n (LITERATURE) ensayo; (SCOL: short) redacción f; (: long) trabajo
essence ['ɛsns] n esencia
essential [ɪ'sɛnʃl] adj (necessary) imprescindible; (basic) esencial; **~s** npl lo imprescindible, lo esencial; **~ly** adv esencialmente
establish [ɪ'stæblɪʃ] vt establecer; (prove) demostrar; (relations) entablar; (reputation) ganarse; **~ed** adj (business) conocido; (practice) arraigado; **~ment** n establecimiento; **the E-ment** la clase dirigente
estate [ɪ'steɪt] n (land) finca, hacienda; (inheritance) herencia; (BRIT: also: housing ~) urbanización f; **~ agent** n agente m/f inmobiliario/a; **~ car** (BRIT) n furgoneta
esteem [ɪ'stiːm] n: to **hold sb in high ~** estimar en mucho a uno
esthetic [ɪs'θɛtɪk] (US) adj = **aesthetic**
estimate [n 'ɛstɪmət, vb 'ɛstɪmeɪt] n estimación f, apreciación f; (assessment) tasa, cálculo; (COMM) presupuesto ♦ vt estimar, tasar; calcular; **estimation** [-'meɪʃən] n opinión f, juicio; cálculo
estranged [ɪ'streɪndʒd] adj separado
estuary ['ɛstjuərɪ] n estuario, ría
etc abbr (= et cetera) etc
eternal [ɪ'təːnl] adj eterno
eternity [ɪ'təːnɪtɪ] n eternidad f
ethical ['ɛθɪkl] adj ético; **ethics** ['ɛθɪks] n ética ♦ npl moralidad f
Ethiopia [i:θɪ'əupɪə] n Etiopia
ethnic ['ɛθnɪk] adj étnico; **~ minority** n minoría étnica
ethos ['i:θɔs] n genio, carácter m
etiquette ['ɛtɪkɛt] n etiqueta
EU n abbr (= European Union) UE f
euro n euro
Eurocheque ['juərəutʃɛk] n Eurocheque m
Euroland ['juərəulænd] n Eurolandia
Europe ['juərəp] n Europa; **~an** [-'pi:ən] adj, n europeo/a m/f; **~an Community** n Comunidad f Europea; **~an Union** n Unión f Europea

evacuate |ɪ'vækjueɪt| vt (people) evacuar; (place) desocupar

evade |ɪ'veɪd| vt evadir, eludir

evaporate |ɪ'væpəreɪt| vi evaporarse; (fig) desvanecerse; **~d milk** n leche f evaporada

evasion |ɪ'veɪʒən| n evasión f

eve |i:v| n: **on the ~ of** en vísperas de

even |'i:vn| adj (level) llano; (smooth) liso; (speed, temperature) uniforme; (number) par ♦ adv hasta, incluso; (introducing a comparison) aún, todavía; **~ if, ~ though** aunque + sub; **~ more** aun más; **~ so** aun así; **not ~** ni siquiera; **~ he was there** hasta él estuvo allí; **~ on Sundays** incluso los domingos; **to get ~ with sb** ajustar cuentas con uno

evening |'i:vnɪŋ| n tarde f; (late) noche f; **in the ~** por la tarde; **~ class** n clase f nocturna; **~ dress** n (no pl: formal clothes) traje m de etiqueta; (woman's) traje m de noche

event |ɪ'vent| n suceso, acontecimiento; (SPORT) prueba; **in the ~ of** en caso de; **~ful** adj (life) activo; (day) ajetreado

eventual |ɪ'ventʃuəl| adj final; **~ity** |-'ælɪtɪ| n eventualidad f; **~ly** adv (finally) finalmente; (in time) con el tiempo

ever |'evə*| adv (at any time) nunca, jamás; (at all times) siempre; (in question): **why ~ not?** ¿y por qué no?; **the best ~** lo nunca visto; **have you ~ seen it?** ¿lo ha visto usted alguna vez?; **better than ~** mejor que nunca; **~ since** adv desde entonces ♦ conj después de que; **~green** n árbol m de hoja perenne; **~lasting** adj eterno, perpetuo

---KEYWORD---

every |'evrɪ| adj **1** (each) cada; **~ one of them** (persons) todos ellos/as; (objects) cada uno de ellos/as; **~ shop in the town was closed** todas las tiendas de la ciudad estaban cerradas

2 (all possible) todo/a; **I gave you ~ assistance** te di toda la ayuda posible; **I have ~ confidence in him** tiene toda mi confianza; **we wish you ~ success** te deseamos toda suerte de éxitos

3 (showing recurrence) todo/a; **~ day/week** todos los días/todas las semanas; **~ other car had been broken into** habían forzado uno de cada dos coches; **she visits me ~ other/third day** me visita cada dos/tres días; **~ now and then** de vez en cuando

every: ~body pron = everyone; **~day** adj (daily) cotidiano, de todos los días; (usual) acostumbrado; **~one** pron todos/as, todo el mundo; **~thing** pron todo; **this shop sells ~thing** esta tienda vende de todo; **~where** adv: **I've been looking for you ~where** te he estado buscando por todas partes; **~where you go you meet ...** en todas partes encuentras ...

evict |ɪ'vɪkt| vt desahuciar; **~ion** |ɪ'vɪkʃən| n desahucio

evidence |'evɪdəns| n (proof) prueba; (of witness) testimonio; (sign) indicios mpl; **to give ~** prestar declaración, dar testimonio

evident |'evɪdənt| adj evidente, manifiesto; **~ly** adv por lo visto

evil |'i:vl| adj malo; (influence) funesto ♦ n mal m

evoke |ɪ'vəuk| vt evocar

evolution |i:və'lu:ʃən| n evolución f

evolve |ɪ'vɔlv| vt desarrollar ♦ vi evolucionar, desarrollarse

ewe |ju:| n oveja

ex- |eks| prefix ex

exact |ɪg'zækt| adj exacto; (person) meticuloso ♦ vt: **to ~ sth (from)** exigir algo (de); **~ing** adj exigente; (conditions) arduo; **~ly** adv exactamente; (indicating agreement) exacto

exaggerate |ɪg'zædʒəreɪt| vt, vi exagerar; **exaggeration** |-'reɪʃən| n exageración f

exalted |ɪg'zɔ:ltɪd| adj eminente

exam |ɪg'zæm| n abbr (SCOL) = **examination**

examination |ɪgzæmɪ'neɪʃən| n examen m; (MED) reconocimiento

examine |ɪg'zæmɪn| vt examinar; (inspect) inspeccionar, escudriñar; (MED) reconocer; **~r** n examinador(a) m/f

example |ɪg'zɑ:mpl| n ejemplo; **for ~** por ejemplo

exasperate |ɪg'zɑ:spəreɪt| vt exasperar, irritar; **exasperation** |-'ʃən| n exasperación f, irritación f

excavate |'ekskəveɪt| vt excavar

exceed |ɪk'si:d| vt (amount) exceder; (number) pasar de; (speed limit) sobrepasar; (powers) excederse en; (hopes) superar; **~ingly** adv sumamente, sobremanera

excellent |'eksələnt| adj excelente

except |ɪk'sept| prep (also: ~ for, ~ing) excepto, salvo ♦ vt exceptuar, excluir; **~ if/when** excepto si/cuando; **~ that** salvo que; **~ion** |ɪk'sepʃən| n excepción f; **to take ~ion to** ofenderse por; **~ional** |ɪk'sepʃənl| adj excepcional

excerpt |'eksə:pt| n extracto

excess |ɪk'ses| n exceso; **~es** npl (of cruelty etc) atrocidades fpl; **~ baggage** n exceso de equipaje; **~ fare** n suplemento; **~ive** adj excesivo

exchange |ɪks'tʃeɪndʒ| n intercambio; (conversation) diálogo; (also: telephone ~) central f (telefónica) ♦ vt: **to ~ (for)** cambiar (por); **~ rate** n tipo de cambio

exchequer |ɪks'tʃekə*| (BRIT) n: **the E~** la

Hacienda del Fisco
excise ['ɛksaɪz] n impuestos mpl sobre el alcohol y el tabaco
excite [ɪk'saɪt] vt (stimulate) estimular; (arouse) excitar; **~d** adj: **to get ~d** emocionarse; **~ment** n (agitation) excitación f; (exhilaration) emoción f; **exciting** adj emocionante
exclaim [ɪk'skleɪm] vi exclamar; **exclamation** [ɛksklə'meɪʃən] n exclamación f; **exclamation mark** n punto de admiración
exclude [ɪk'sklu:d] vt excluir; exceptuar
exclusive [ɪk'sklu:sɪv] adj exclusivo; (club, district) selecto; **~ of tax** excluyendo impuestos; **~ly** adv únicamente
excruciating [ɪk'skru:ʃɪeɪtɪŋ] adj (pain) agudísimo, atroz; (noise, embarrassment) horrible
excursion [ɪk'skə:ʃən] n (tourist ~) excursión f
excuse [n ɪk'skju:s, vb ɪk'skju:z] n disculpa, excusa; (pretext) pretexto ♦ vt (justify) justificar; (forgive) disculpar, perdonar; **to ~ sb from doing sth** dispensar a uno de hacer algo; **~ me!** (attracting attention) ¡por favor!; (apologizing) ¡perdón!; **if you will ~ me** con su permiso
ex-directory ['ɛksdɪ'rɛktərɪ] (BRIT) adj que no consta en la guía
execute ['ɛksɪkju:t] vt (plan) realizar; (order) cumplir; (person) ajusticiar, ejecutar; **execution** [-'kju:ʃən] n realización f; cumplimiento; ejecución f
executive [ɪg'zɛkjutɪv] n (person, committee) ejecutivo; (POL: committee) poder m ejecutivo ♦ adj ejecutivo
exemplify [ɪg'zɛmplɪfaɪ] vt ejemplificar; (illustrate) ilustrar
exempt [ɪg'zɛmpt] adj: **~ from** exento de ♦ vt: **to ~ sb from** eximir a uno de; **~ion** [-ʃən] n exención f
exercise ['ɛksəsaɪz] n ejercicio ♦ vt (patience) usar de; (right) valerse de; (dog) llevar de paseo; (mind) preocupar ♦ vi (also: **to take ~**) hacer ejercicio(s); **~ bike** n ciclostát m, bicicleta estática; **~ book** n cuaderno
exert [ɪg'zə:t] vt ejercer; **to ~ o.s.** esforzarse; **~ion** [-ʃən] n esfuerzo
exhale [ɛks'heɪl] vt despedir ♦ vi exhalar
exhaust [ɪg'zɔ:st] n (AUT: also: ~ pipe) escape m; (: fumes) gases mpl de escape ♦ vt agotar; **~ed** adj agotado; **~ion** [ɪg'zɔ:stʃən] n agotamiento; **nervous ~ion** postración f nerviosa; **~ive** adj exhaustivo
exhibit [ɪg'zɪbɪt] n (ART) obra expuesta; (LAW) objeto expuesto ♦ vt (show: emotions) manifestar; (: courage, skill) demostrar; (paintings) exponer; **~ion** [ɛksɪ'bɪʃən] n

exposición f; (of talent etc) demostración f
exhilarating [ɪg'zɪləreɪtɪŋ] adj estimulante, tónico
exile ['ɛksaɪl] n exilio; (person) exiliado/a ♦ vt desterrar, exiliar
exist [ɪg'zɪst] vi existir; (live) vivir; **~ence** n existencia; **~ing** adj existente, actual
exit ['ɛksɪt] n salida ♦ vi (THEATRE) hacer mutis; (COMPUT) salir (al sistema); **~ poll** n encuesta a la salida de los colegios electorales; **~ ramp** (US) n (AUT) vía de acceso
exodus ['ɛksədəs] n éxodo
exonerate [ɪg'zɔnəreɪt] vt: **to ~ from** exculpar de
exotic [ɪg'zɔtɪk] adj exótico
expand [ɪk'spænd] vt ampliar; (number) aumentar ♦ vi (population) aumentar; (trade etc) expandirse; (gas, metal) dilatarse
expanse [ɪk'spæns] n extensión f
expansion [ɪk'spænʃən] n (of population) aumento; (of trade) expansión f
expect [ɪk'spɛkt] vt esperar; (require) contar con; (suppose) suponer ♦ vi: **to be ~ing** (pregnant woman) estar embarazada; **~ancy** n (anticipation) esperanza; **life ~ancy** esperanza de vida; **~ant mother** n futura madre f; **~ation** [ɛkspɛk'teɪʃən] n (hope) esperanza; (belief) expectativa
expedient [ɪk'spi:dɪənt] adj conveniente, oportuno ♦ n recurso, expediente m
expedition [ɛkspə'dɪʃən] n expedición f
expel [ɪk'spɛl] vt arrojar; (from place) expulsar
expend [ɪk'spɛnd] vt (money) gastar; (time, energy) consumir; **~iture** n gastos mpl, desembolso; consumo
expense [ɪk'spɛns] n gasto, gastos mpl; (high cost) costa; **~s** npl (COMM) gastos mpl; **at the ~ of** a costa de; **~ account** n cuenta de gastos
expensive [ɪk'spɛnsɪv] adj caro, costoso
experience [ɪk'spɪərɪəns] n experiencia ♦ vt experimentar; (suffer) sufrir; **~d** adj experimentado
experiment [ɪk'spɛrɪmənt] n experimento ♦ vi hacer experimentos
expert ['ɛkspə:t] adj experto, perito ♦ n experto/a, perito/a; (specialist) especialista m/f; **~ise** [-'ti:z] n pericia
expire [ɪk'spaɪə*] vi caducar, vencer; **expiry** n vencimiento
explain [ɪk'spleɪn] vt explicar; **explanation** [ɛksplə'neɪʃən] n explicación f; **explanatory** [ɪk'splænətrɪ] adj explicativo; aclaratorio
explicit [ɪk'splɪsɪt] adj explícito
explode [ɪk'spləʊd] vi estallar, explotar; (population) crecer rápidamente; (with anger) reventar
exploit [n 'ɛksplɔɪt, vb ɪk'splɔɪt] n hazaña ♦ vt explotar; **~ation** [-'teɪʃən] n explotación f

exploratory [ɪkˈsplɔːrətrɪ] adj de exploración; (fig: talks) exploratorio, preliminar

explore [ɪkˈsplɔː*] vt explorar; (fig) examinar; investigar; **~r** n explorador(a) m/f

explosion [ɪkˈspləʊʒən] n (also fig) explosión f; **explosive** [ɪksˈpləʊsɪv] adj, n explosivo

exponent [ɪkˈspəʊnənt] n (of theory etc) partidario/a; (of skill etc) exponente m/f

export [vb ekˈspɔːt, n ˈekspɔːt] vt exportar ♦ n (process) exportación f; (product) producto de exportación ♦ cpd de exportación; **~er** n exportador m

expose [ɪkˈspəʊz] vt exponer; (unmask) desenmascarar; **~d** adj expuesto

exposure [ɪkˈspəʊʒə*] n exposición f; (publicity) publicidad f; (PHOT: speed) velocidad f de obturación; (: shot) fotografía; **to die from ~** (MED) morir de frío; **~ meter** n fotómetro

express [ɪkˈspres] adj (definite) expreso, explícito; (BRIT: letter etc) urgente ♦ n (train) rápido ♦ vt expresar; **~ion** [ɪkˈspreʃən] n expresión f; (of actor etc) sentimiento; **~ly** adv expresamente; **~way** (US) n (urban motorway) autopista

exquisite [ekˈskwɪzɪt] adj exquisito

extend [ɪkˈstend] vt (visit, street) prolongar; (building) ampliar; (invitation) ofrecer ♦ vi (land) extenderse; (period of time) prolongarse

extension [ɪkˈstenʃən] n extensión f; (building) ampliación f; (of time) prolongación f; (TEL: in private house) línea derivada; (: in office) extensión f

extensive [ɪkˈstensɪv] adj extenso; (damage) importante; (knowledge) amplio; **~ly** adv: **he's travelled ~ly** ha viajado por muchos países

extent [ɪkˈstent] n (breadth) extensión f; (scope) alcance m; **to some ~** hasta cierto punto; **to the ~ of...** hasta el punto de...; **to such an ~ that...** hasta tal punto que...; **to what ~?** ¿hasta qué punto?

extenuating [ɪkˈstenjʊeɪtɪŋ] adj: **~ circumstances** fpl atenuantes

exterior [ekˈstɪərɪə*] adj exterior, externo ♦ n exterior m

external [ekˈstɜːnl] adj externo

extinct [ɪkˈstɪŋkt] adj (volcano) extinguido; (race) extinto

extinguish [ɪkˈstɪŋgwɪʃ] vt extinguir, apagar; **~er** n extintor m

extort [ɪkˈstɔːt] vt obtener por fuerza; **~ionate** adj excesivo, exorbitante

extra [ˈekstrə] adj adicional ♦ adv (in addition) de más ♦ n (luxury, addition) extra m; (CINEMA, THEATRE) extra m/f, comparsa m/f

extra... [ˈekstrə] prefix extra...

extract [vb ɪkˈstrækt, n ˈekstrækt] vt sacar;

(tooth) extraer; (money, promise) obtener ♦ n extracto

extracurricular [ekstrəkəˈrɪkjʊlə*] adj extraescolar, extra-académico

extradite [ˈekstrədaɪt] vt extraditar

extra: ~marital adj extramatrimonial; **~mural** [ekstrəˈmjuərl] adj extraescolar; **~ordinary** [ɪkˈstrɔːdnrɪ] adj extraordinario; (odd) raro

extravagance [ɪkˈstrævəgəns] n derroche m, despilfarro; (thing bought) extravagancia

extravagant [ɪkˈstrævəgənt] adj (lavish: person) pródigo; (: gift) (demasiado) caro; (wasteful) despilfarrador(a)

extreme [ɪkˈstriːm] adj extremo, extremado ♦ n extremo; **~ly** adv sumamente, extremadamente

extricate [ˈekstrɪkeɪt] vt: **to ~ sth/sb from** librar algo/a uno de

extrovert [ˈekstrəvɜːt] n extrovertido/a

eye [aɪ] n ojo ♦ vt mirar de soslayo, ojear; **to keep an ~ on** vigilar; **~bath** n ojera; **~brow** n ceja; **~drops** npl gotas fpl para los ojos, colino; **~lash** n pestaña; **~lid** n párpado; **~liner** n lápiz m de ojos; **~-opener** n revelación f, gran sorpresa; **~shadow** n sombreador m de ojos; **~sight** n vista; **~sore** n monstruosidad f; **~ witness** n testigo m/f presencial

F, f

F [ef] n (MUS) fa m

F. abbr = **Fahrenheit**

fable [ˈfeɪbl] n fábula

fabric [ˈfæbrɪk] n tejido, tela

fabulous [ˈfæbjuləs] adj fabuloso

façade [fəˈsɑːd] n fachada

face [feɪs] n (ANAT) cara, rostro; (of clock) esfera (SP), cara (AM); (of mountain) cara, ladera; (of building) fachada ♦ vt (direction) estar de cara a; (situation) hacer frente a; (facts) aceptar; **~ down** (person, card) boca abajo; **to lose ~** desprestigiarse; **to make** or **pull a ~** hacer muecas; **in the ~ of** (difficulties etc) ante; **on the ~ of it** a primera vista; **~ to ~ cara a cara; ~ up to** vt fus hacer frente a, arrostrar; **~ cloth** (BRIT) n manopla; **~ cream** n crema (de belleza); **~ lift** n estirado facial; (of building) renovación f; **~ powder** n polvos mpl; **~-saving** adj para salvar las apariencias; **~ value** n (of stamp) valor m nominal; **to take sth at ~ value** (fig) tomar algo en sentido literal

facilities [fəˈsɪlɪtɪz] npl (buildings) instalaciones fpl; (equipment) servicios mpl; **credit ~** facilidades fpl de crédito

facing [ˈfeɪsɪŋ] prep frente a

facsimile [fæk'sɪmɪlɪ] n (replica) facsímil(e) m; (machine) telefax m; (fax) fax m

fact [fækt] n hecho; **in ~** en realidad

factor ['fæktə*] n factor m

factory ['fæktərɪ] n fábrica

factual ['fæktjuəl] adj basado en los hechos

faculty ['fækəltɪ] n facultad f; (US: teaching staff) personal m docente

fad [fæd] n novedad f, moda

fade [feɪd] vi desteñirse; (sound, smile) desvanecerse; (light) apagarse; (flower) marchitarse; (hope, memory) perderse

fag [fæg] (BRIT: inf) n (cigarette) pitillo (SP), cigarro

fail [feɪl] vt (candidate) suspender; (exam) no aprobar (SP), reprobar (AM); (subj: memory etc) fallar a ♦ vi suspender; (be unsuccessful) fracasar; (strength, brakes) fallar; (light) acabarse; **to ~ to do sth** (neglect) dejar de hacer algo; (be unable) no poder hacer algo; **without ~** sin falta; **~ing** n falta, defecto ♦ prep a falta de; **~ure** ['feɪljə*] n fracaso; (person) fracasado/a; (mechanical etc) fallo

faint [feɪnt] adj débil; (recollection) vago; (mark) apenas visible ♦ n desmayo ♦ vi desmayarse; **to feel ~** estar mareado, marearse

fair [feə*] adj justo; (hair, person) rubio; (weather) bueno; (good enough) regular; (considerable) considerable ♦ adv (play) limpio ♦ n feria; (BRIT: funfair) parque m de atracciones; **~ly** adv (justly) con justicia; (quite) bastante; **~ness** n justicia, imparcialidad f; **~ play** n juego limpio

fairy ['feərɪ] n hada; **~ tale** n cuento de hadas

faith [feɪθ] n fe f; (trust) confianza; (sect) religión f; **~ful** adj (loyal: troops etc) leal; (spouse) fiel; (account) exacto; **~fully** adv fielmente; **yours ~fully** (BRIT: in letters) le saluda atentamente

fake [feɪk] n (painting etc) falsificación f; (person) impostor/a m/f ♦ adj falso ♦ vt fingir; (painting etc) falsificar

falcon ['fɔːlkən] n halcón m

fall [fɔːl] (pt fell, pp fallen) n caída; (in price etc) descenso; (US) otoño ♦ vi caer(se); (price) bajar, descender; **~s** npl (water~) cascada, salto de agua; **to ~ flat** (on one's face) caerse (boca abajo); (plan) fracasar; (joke, story) no hacer gracia; **~ back** vi retroceder; **~ back on** vt fus (remedy etc) recurrir a; **~ behind** vi quedarse atrás; **~ down** vi (person) caerse; (building, hopes) derrumbarse; **~ for** vt fus (trick) dejarse engañar por; (person) enamorarse de; **~ in** vi (roof) hundirse; (MIL) alinearse; **~ off** vi caerse; (diminish) disminuir; **~ out** vi (friends etc) reñir; (hair, teeth) caerse; **~ through** vi (plan, project) fracasar

fallacy ['fæləsɪ] n error m

fallen ['fɔːlən] pp of **fall**

fallout ['fɔːlaʊt] n lluvia radioactiva

fallow ['fæləʊ] adj en barbecho

false [fɔːls] adj falso; **under ~ pretences** con engaños; **~ alarm** n falsa alarma; **~ teeth** (BRIT) npl dentadura postiza

falter ['fɔːltə*] vi vacilar; (engine) fallar

fame [feɪm] n fama

familiar [fə'mɪlɪə*] adj conocido, familiar; (tone) de confianza; **to be ~ with** (subject) conocer (bien)

family ['fæmɪlɪ] n familia; **~ business** n negocio familiar; **~ doctor** n médico/a de cabecera

famine ['fæmɪn] n hambre f, hambruna

famished ['fæmɪʃt] adj hambriento

famous ['feɪməs] adj famoso, célebre; **~ly** adv (get on) estupendamente

fan [fæn] n abanico; (ELEC) ventilador m; (of pop star) fan m/f; (SPORT) hincha m/f ♦ vt abanicar; (fire, quarrel) atizar

fanatic [fə'nætɪk] n fanático/a

fan belt n correa del ventilador

fanciful ['fænsɪful] adj (design, name) fantástico

fancy ['fænsɪ] n (whim) capricho, antojo; (imagination) imaginación f ♦ adj (luxury) lujoso, de lujo ♦ vt (feel like, want) tener ganas de; (imagine) imaginarse; (think) creer; **to take a ~ to sb** tomar cariño a uno; **he fancies her** (inf) le gusta (ella) mucho; **~ dress** n disfraz m; **~-dress ball** n baile m de disfraces

fanfare ['fænfeə*] n fanfarria (de trompeta)

fang [fæŋ] n colmillo

fantastic [fæn'tæstɪk] adj (enormous) enorme; (strange, wonderful) fantástico

fantasy ['fæntəzɪ] n (dream) sueño; (unreality) fantasía

far [fɑː*] adj (distant) lejano ♦ adv lejos; (much, greatly) mucho; **~ away, ~ off** (a lo) lejos; **~ better** mucho mejor; **~ from** lejos de; **by ~** con mucho; **go as ~ as the farm** vaya hasta la granja; **as ~ as I know** que yo sepa; **how ~?** ¿hasta dónde?; (fig) ¿hasta qué punto?; **~away** adj remoto; (look) distraído

farce [fɑːs] n farsa

fare [feə*] n (on trains, buses) precio (del billete); (in taxi: cost) tarifa; (food) comida; **half ~** medio pasaje m; **full ~** pasaje completo

Far East n: **the ~** el Extremo Oriente

farewell [feə'wel] excl, n adiós m

farm [fɑːm] n granja (SP), finca (AM), estancia (AM) ♦ vt cultivar; **~er** n granjero (SP), estanciero (AM); **~hand** n peón m; **~house** n granja, casa de hacienda (AM); **~ing** n agricultura; (of crops) cultivo; (of animals) cría; **~land** n tierra de cultivo; **~ worker** n

= ~**hand**; ~**yard** n corral m

far-reaching [fɑː'riːtʃɪŋ] adj (reform, effect) de gran alcance

fart [fɑːt] (inf!) vi tirarse un pedo (!)

farther ['fɑːðə*] adv más lejos, más allá ♦ adj más lejano

farthest ['fɑːðɪst] superlative of **far**

fascinate ['fæsɪneɪt] vt fascinar; **fascination** [-'neɪʃən] n fascinación f

fascism ['fæʃɪzəm] n fascismo

fashion ['fæʃən] n moda; (~ industry) industria de la moda; (manner) manera ♦ vt formar; **in** ~ a la moda; **out of** ~ pasado de moda; ~**able** adj de moda; ~ **show** n desfile m de modelos

fast [fɑːst] adj rápido; (dye, colour) resistente; (clock): **to be** ~ estar adelantado ♦ adv rápidamente, de prisa; (stuck, held) firmemente ♦ n ayuno ♦ vi ayunar; ~ **asleep** profundamente dormido

fasten ['fɑːsn] vt atar, sujetar; (coat, belt) abrochar ♦ vi atarse; abrocharse; ~**er**, ~**ing** n cierre m; (of door etc) cerrojo

fast food n comida rápida, platos mpl preparados

fastidious [fæs'tɪdɪəs] adj (fussy) quisquilloso

fat [fæt] adj gordo; (book) grueso; (profit) grande, pingüe ♦ n grasa; (on person) carnes fpl; (lard) manteca

fatal ['feɪtl] adj (mistake) fatal; (injury) mortal; ~**ity** [fə'tælɪtɪ] n (road death etc) víctima; ~**ly** adv fatalmente; mortalmente

fate [feɪt] n destino; (of person) suerte f; ~**ful** adj fatídico

father ['fɑːðə*] n padre m; ~-**in-law** n suegro; ~**ly** adj paternal

fathom ['fæðəm] n braza ♦ vt (mystery) desentrañar; (understand) lograr comprender

fatigue [fə'tiːg] n fatiga, cansancio

fatten ['fætn] vt, vi engordar

fatty ['fætɪ] adj (food) graso ♦ n (inf) gordito/a, gordinflón/ona m/f

fatuous ['fætjuəs] adj fatuo, necio

faucet ['fɔːsɪt] (US) n grifo (SP), llave f (AM)

fault [fɔːlt] n (blame) culpa; (defect: in person, machine) defecto; (GEO) falla ♦ vt criticar; **it's my** ~ es culpa mía; **to find** ~ **with** criticar, poner peros a; **at** ~ culpable; ~**y** adj defectuoso

fauna ['fɔːnə] n fauna

favour ['feɪvə*] (US **favor**) n favor m; (approval) aprobación f ♦ vt (proposition) estar a favor de, aprobar; (assist) ser propicio a; **to do sb a** ~ hacer un favor a uno; **to find** ~ **with sb** caer en gracia a uno; **in** ~ **of** a favor de; ~**able** adj favorable; ~**ite** ['feɪvrɪt] adj, n favorito, preferido

fawn [fɔːn] n cervato ♦ adj (also: ~-coloured) color de cervato, leonado ♦ vi: **to** ~ **(up)on** adular

fax [fæks] n (document) fax m; (machine) telefax m ♦ vt mandar por telefax

FBI (US) n abbr (= Federal Bureau of Investigation) ≈ BIC f (SP)

fear [fɪə*] n miedo, temor m ♦ vt tener miedo de, temer; **for** ~ **of** por si; ~**ful** adj temeroso, miedoso; (awful) terrible; ~**less** adj audaz

feasible ['fiːzəbl] adj factible

feast [fiːst] n banquete m; (REL: also: ~ **day**) fiesta ♦ vi festejar

feat [fiːt] n hazaña

feather ['feðə*] n pluma

feature ['fiːtʃə*] n característica; (article) artículo de fondo ♦ vt (subj: film) presentar ♦ vi: **to** ~ **in** tener un papel destacado en; ~**s** npl (of face) facciones fpl; ~ **film** n largometraje m

February ['februərɪ] n febrero

fed [fed] pt, pp of **feed**

federal ['fedərəl] adj federal

fed up [fed'ʌp] adj: **to be** ~ **(with)** estar harto (de)

fee [fiː] n pago; (professional) derechos mpl, honorarios mpl; (of club) cuota; **school** ~**s** matrícula

feeble ['fiːbl] adj débil; (joke) flojo

feed [fiːd] (pt, pp **fed**) n comida; (of animal) pienso; (on printer) dispositivo de alimentación ♦ vt alimentar; (BRIT: baby: breast~) dar el pecho a; (animal) dar de comer a; (data, information): **to** ~ **into** meter en; ~ **on** vt fus alimentarse de; ~**back** n reacción f, feedback m

feel [fiːl] (pt, pp **felt**) n (sensation) sensación f; (sense of touch) tacto; (impression): **to have the** ~ **of** parecerse a ♦ vt tocar; (pain etc) sentir; (think, believe) creer; **to** ~ **hungry/cold** tener hambre/frío; **to** ~ **lonely/better** sentirse solo/mejor; **I don't** ~ **well** no me siento bien; **it** ~**s soft** es suave al tacto; **to** ~ **like** (want) tener ganas de; ~ **about** or **around** vi tantear; ~**er** n (of insect) antena; ~**ing** n (physical) sensación f; (foreboding) presentimiento; (emotion) sentimiento

feet [fiːt] npl of **foot**

feign [feɪn] vt fingir

fell [fel] pt of **fall** ♦ vt (tree) talar

fellow ['feləu] n tipo, tío (SP); (comrade) compañero; (of learned society) socio/a ♦ cpd: ~ **citizen** n conciudadano/a; ~ **countryman** (irreg) n compatriota m; ~ **men** npl semejantes mpl; ~**ship** n compañerismo; (grant) beca

felony ['felənɪ] n crimen m

felt [felt] pt, pp of **feel** ♦ n fieltro; ~-**tip pen** n rotulador m

female ['fiːmeɪl] n (pej: woman) mujer f, tía; (ZOOL) hembra ♦ adj femenino; hembra

feminine ['feminin] *adj* femenino
feminist ['feminist] *n* feminista
fence [fens] *n* valla, cerca ♦ *vt* (*also:* ~ *in*) cercar ♦ *vi* (*SPORT*) hacer esgrima; **fencing** *n* esgrima
fend [fend] *vi:* **to ~ for o.s.** valerse por sí mismo; ~ **off** *vt* (*attack*) rechazar; (*questions*) evadir
fender ['fendə*] *n* guardafuego; (*US: AUT*) parachoques *m inv*
ferment [*vb* fə'ment, *n* 'fəment] *vi* fermentar ♦ *n* (*fig*) agitación *f*
fern [fə:n] *n* helecho
ferocious [fə'rəuʃəs] *adj* feroz
ferret ['ferit] *n* hurón *m*
ferry ['feri] *n* (*small*) barca (de pasaje), balsa; (*large: also:* ~*boat*) transbordador *m* (*SP*), embarcadero (*AM*) ♦ *vt* transportar
fertile ['fə:tail] *adj* fértil; (*BIOL*) fecundo; **fertilize** ['fə:tilaiz] *vt* (*BIOL*) fecundar; (*AGR*) abonar; **fertilizer** *n* abono
fester ['festə*] *vi* ulcerarse
festival ['festivəl] *n* (*REL*) fiesta; (*ART, MUS*) festival *m*
festive ['festiv] *adj* festivo; **the ~ season** (*BRIT: Christmas*) las Navidades
festivities [fes'tivitiz] *npl* fiestas *fpl*
festoon [fes'tu:n] *vt:* **to ~ with** engalanar con
fetch [fetʃ] *vt* ir a buscar; (*sell for*) venderse por
fête [feit] *n* fiesta
fetus ['fi:təs] (*US*) *n* = **foetus**
feud [fju:d] *n* (*hostility*) enemistad *f*; (*quarrel*) disputa
fever ['fi:və*] *n* fiebre *f*; **~ish** *adj* febril
few [fju:] *adj* (*not many*) pocos ♦ *pron* pocos; algunos; **a ~** *adj* unos pocos, algunos; **~er** *adj* menos; **~est** *adj* los/las menos
fiancé [fi'ã:ŋsei] *n* novio, prometido; **~e** *n* novia, prometida
fib [fib] *n* mentirilla
fibre ['faibə*] (*US* **fiber**) *n* fibra; **~glass** (**Fiberglass** ® *US*) *n* fibra de vidrio
fickle ['fikl] *adj* inconstante
fiction ['fikʃən] *n* ficción *f*; **~al** *adj* novelesco; **fictitious** [fik'tiʃəs] *adj* ficticio
fiddle ['fidl] *n* (*MUS*) violín *m*; (*cheating*) trampa ♦ *vt* (*BRIT: accounts*) falsificar; ~ **with** *vt fus* juguetear con
fidget ['fidʒit] *vi* enredar; **stop ~ing!** ¡estate quieto!
field [fi:ld] *n* campo; (*fig*) campo, esfera; (*SPORT*) campo, cancha (*AM*); ~ **marshal** *n* mariscal *m*; **~work** *n* trabajo de campo
fiend [fi:nd] *n* demonio
fierce [fiəs] *adj* feroz; (*wind, heat*) fuerte; (*fighting, enemy*) encarnizado
fiery ['faiəri] *adj* (*burning*) ardiente; (*temperament*) apasionado

fifteen [fif'ti:n] *num* quince
fifth [fifθ] *num* quinto
fifty ['fifti] *num* cincuenta; **~-~** *adj* (*deal, split*) a medias ♦ *adv* a medias, mitad por mitad
fig [fig] *n* higo
fight [fait] (*pt, pp* **fought**) *n* (*gen*) pelea; (*MIL*) combate *m*; (*struggle*) lucha ♦ *vt* luchar contra; (*cancer, alcoholism*) combatir; (*election*) intentar ganar; (*emotion*) resistir ♦ *vi* pelear, luchar; **~er** *n* combatiente *m/f*; (*plane*) caza *m*; **~ing** *n* combate *m*, pelea
figment ['figmənt] *n:* **a ~ of the imagination** una quimera
figurative ['figjurativ] *adj* (*meaning*) figurado; (*style*) figurativo
figure ['figə*] *n* (*DRAWING, GEOM*) figura, dibujo; (*number, cipher*) cifra; (*body, outline*) tipo; (*personality*) figura ♦ *vt* (*esp US*) imaginar ♦ *vi* (*appear*) figurar; ~ **out** *vt* (*work out*) resolver; **~head** *n* (*NAUT*) mascarón *m* de proa; (*pej: leader*) figura decorativa; ~ **of speech** *n* figura retórica
file [fail] *n* (*tool*) lima; (*dossier*) expediente *m*; (*folder*) carpeta; (*COMPUT*) fichero; (*row*) fila ♦ *vt* limar; (*LAW: claim*) presentar; (*store*) archivar; ~ **in/out** *vi* entrar/salir en fila; **filing cabinet** *n* fichero, archivador *m*
fill [fil] *vt* (*space*): **to ~ (with)** llenar (de); (*vacancy, need*): cubrir ♦ *n:* **to eat one's ~** llenarse; ~ **in** *vt* rellenar; ~ **up** *vt* llenar (hasta el borde) ♦ *vi* (*AUT*) poner gasolina
fillet ['filit] *n* filete *m*; ~ **steak** *n* filete *m* de ternera
filling ['filiŋ] *n* (*CULIN*) relleno; (*for tooth*) empaste *m*; ~ **station** *n* estación *f* de servicio
film [film] *n* película ♦ *vt* (*scene*) filmar ♦ *vt* rodar (una película); ~ **star** *n* astro, estrella de cine
filter ['filtə*] *n* filtro ♦ *vt* filtrar; ~ **lane** (*BRIT*) *n* carril *m* de selección; **~-tipped** *adj* con filtro
filth [filθ] *n* suciedad *f*; **~y** *adj* sucio; (*language*) obsceno
fin [fin] *n* (*gen*) aleta
final ['fainl] *adj* (*last*) final, último; (*definitive*) definitivo, terminante ♦ *n* (*BRIT: SPORT*) final *f*; **~s** *npl* (*SCOL*) examen *m* final; (*US: SPORT*) final *f*
finale [fi'nɑ:li] *n* final *m*
final: **~ist** *n* (*SPORT*) finalista *m/f*; **~ize** *vt* concluir, completar; **~ly** *adv* (*lastly*) por último, finalmente; (*eventually*) por fin
finance [fai'næns] *n* (*money*) fondos *mpl*; **~s** *npl* finanzas *fpl*; (*personal ~s*) situación *f* económica ♦ *vt* financiar; **financial** [-'nænʃəl] *adj* financiero
find [faind] (*pt, pp* **found**) *vt* encontrar, hallar; (*come upon*) descubrir ♦ *n* hallazgo;

descubrimiento; **to ~ sb guilty** (*LAW*) declarar culpable a uno; **~ out** *vt* averiguar; (*truth, secret*) descubrir; **to ~ out about** (*subject*) informarse sobre; (*by chance*) enterarse de; **~ings** *npl* (*LAW*) veredicto, fallo; (*of report*) recomendaciones *fpl*

fine [faɪn] *adj* excelente; (*thin*) fino ♦ *adv* (*well*) bien ♦ *n* (*LAW*) multa ♦ *vt* (*LAW*) multar; **to be ~** (*person*) estar bien; (*weather*) hacer buen tiempo; **~ arts** *npl* bellas artes *fpl*

finery [ˈfaɪnərɪ] *n* adornos *mpl*

finger [ˈfɪŋgə*] *n* dedo ♦ *vt* (*touch*) manosear; **little/index ~** (dedo) meñique *m/* índice *m*; **~nail** *n* uña; **~print** *n* huella dactilar; **~tip** *n* yema del dedo

finish [ˈfɪnɪʃ] *n* (*end*) fin *m*; (*SPORT*) meta; (*polish etc*) acabado ♦ *vt, vi* terminar; **to ~ doing sth** acabar de hacer algo; **to ~ third** llegar el tercero; **~ off** *vt* acabar, terminar; (*kill*) acabar con; **~ up** *vt* acabar, terminar ♦ *vi* ir a parar, terminar; **~ing line** *n* línea de llegada *or* meta

finite [ˈfaɪnaɪt] *adj* finito; (*verb*) conjugado

Finland [ˈfɪnlənd] *n* Finlandia

Finn [fɪn] *n* finlandés/esa *m/f*; **~ish** *adj* finlandés/esa ♦ *n* (*LING*) finlandés *m*

fir [fə:*] *n* abeto

fire [ˈfaɪə*] *n* fuego; (*in hearth*) lumbre *f*; (*accidental*) incendio; (*heater*) estufa ♦ *vt* (*gun*) disparar; (*interest*) despertar; (*dismiss*) despedir ♦ *vi* (*shoot*) disparar; **on ~** ardiendo, en llamas; **~ alarm** *n* alarma de incendios; **~arm** *n* arma de fuego; **~ brigade** (*US* **~ department**) *n* (cuerpo de) bomberos *mpl*; **~ engine** *n* coche *m* de bomberos; **~ escape** *n* escalera de incendios; **~ extinguisher** *n* extintor *m* (de incendios); **~guard** *n* rejilla de protección; **~man** (*irreg*) *n* bombero; **~place** *n* chimenea; **~side** *n*: **by the ~side** al lado de la chimenea; **~ station** *n* parque *m* de bomberos; **~wood** *n* leña; **~works** *npl* fuegos *mpl* artificiales

firing squad [ˈfaɪrɪŋ-] *n* pelotón *m* de ejecución

firm [fə:m] *adj* firme; (*look, voice*) resuelto ♦ *n* firma, empresa; **~ly** *adv* firmemente; resueltamente

first [fə:st] *adj* primero ♦ *adv* (*before others*) primero; (*when listing reasons etc*) en primer lugar, primeramente ♦ *n* (*person: in race*) primero/a; (*AUT*) primera; (*BRIT: SCOL*) título de licenciado con calificación de sobresaliente; **at ~** al principio; **~ of all** ante todo; **~ aid** *n* primera ayuda, primeros auxilios *mpl*; **~ aid kit** *n* botiquín *m*; **~-class** *adj* (*excellent*) de primera (categoría); (*ticket etc*) de primera clase; **~-hand** *adj* de primera mano; **F~ Lady** (*esp US*) *n* primera dama; **~ly** *adv*

en primer lugar; **~ name** *n* nombre *m* (de pila); **~-rate** *adj* estupendo

fish [fɪʃ] *n inv* pez *m*; (*food*) pescado ♦ *vt, vi* pescar; **to go ~ing** ir de pesca; **~erman** (*irreg*) *n* pescador *m*; **~ farm** *n* criadero de peces; **~ fingers** (*BRIT*) *npl* croquetas *fpl* de pescado; **~ing boat** *n* barca de pesca; **~ing line** *n* sedal *m*; **~ing rod** *n* caña (de pescar); **~monger's (shop)** (*BRIT*) *n* pescadería; **~ sticks** (*US*) *npl* = **~ fingers**; **~y** (*inf*) *adj* sospechoso

fist [fɪst] *n* puño

fit [fɪt] *adj* (*healthy*) en (buena) forma; (*proper*) adecuado, apropiado ♦ *vt* (*subj: clothes*) estar *or* sentar bien a; (*instal*) poner; (*equip*) proveer, dotar; (*facts*) cuadrar *or* corresponder con ♦ *vi* (*clothes*) sentar bien; (*in space, gap*) caber; (*facts*) coincidir ♦ *n* (*MED*) ataque *m*; **~ to** (*ready*) a punto de; **~ for** apropiado para; **a ~ of anger/pride** un arranque de cólera/orgullo; **this dress is a good ~** este vestido me sienta bien; **by ~s and starts** a rachas; **~ in** *vi* (*fig: person*) llevarse bien (con todos); **~ful** *adj* espasmódico, intermitente; **~ment** *n* módulo adosable; **~ness** *n* (*MED*) salud *f*; **~ted carpet** *n* moqueta; **~ted kitchen** *n* cocina amueblada; **~ter** *n* ajustador *m*; **~ting** *adj* apropiado ♦ *n* (*of dress*) prueba; (*of piece of equipment*) instalación *f*; **~ting room** *n* probador *m*; **~tings** *npl* instalaciones *fpl*

five [faɪv] *num* cinco; **~r** (*inf*) *n* (*BRIT*) billete *m* de cinco libras; (*US*) billete *m* de cinco dólares

fix [fɪks] *vt* (*secure*) fijar, asegurar; (*mend*) arreglar; (*prepare*) preparar ♦ *n*: **to be in a ~** estar en un aprieto; **~ up** *vt* (*meeting*) arreglar; **to ~ sb up with sth** proveer a uno de algo; **~ation** [fɪkˈseɪʃən] *n* obsesión *f*; **~ed** *adj* (*prices etc*) fijo; **~ture** *n* (*SPORT*) encuentro; **~tures** *npl* (*cupboards etc*) instalaciones *fpl* fijas

fizzy [ˈfɪzɪ] *adj* (*drink*) gaseoso

fjord [fjɔːd] *n* fiordo

flabbergasted [ˈflæbəgɑːstɪd] *adj* pasmado, alucinado

flabby [ˈflæbɪ] *adj* gordo

flag [flæg] *n* bandera; (*stone*) losa ♦ *vi* decaer; **to ~ sb down** hacer señas a uno para que se pare; **~pole** *n* asta de bandera; **~ship** *n* buque *m* insignia, (*fig*) bandera

flair [flɛə*] *n* aptitud *f* especial

flak [flæk] *n* (*MIL*) fuego antiaéreo; (*inf: criticism*) lluvia de críticas

flake [fleɪk] *n* (*of rust, paint*) escama; (*of snow, soap powder*) copo ♦ *vi* (*also: ~ off*) desconcharse

flamboyant [flæmˈbɔɪənt] *adj* (*dress*) vistoso; (*person*) extravagante

flame [fleɪm] n llama
flamingo [fləˈmɪŋgəu] n flamenco
flammable [ˈflæməbl] adj inflamable
flan [flæn] (BRIT) n tarta
flank [flæŋk] n (of animal) ijar m; (of army) flanco ♦ vt flanquear
flannel [ˈflænl] n (BRIT: also: face ~) manopla; (fabric) franela
flap [flæp] n (of pocket, envelope) solapa ♦ vt (wings, arms) agitar ♦ vi (sail, flag) ondear
flare [flɛə*] n llamarada; (MIL) bengala; (in skirt etc) vuelo; ~ **up** vi encenderse; (fig: person) encolerizarse; (: revolt) estallar
flash [flæʃ] n relámpago; (also: news ~) noticias fpl de última hora; (PHOT) flash m ♦ vt (light, headlights) lanzar un destello con; (news, message) transmitir; (smile) lanzar ♦ vi brillar; (hazard light etc) lanzar destellos; **in a ~ en un instante; he ~ed by or past** pasó como un rayo; **~back** n (CINEMA) flashback m; **~bulb** n bombilla fusible; **~ cube** n cubo de flash; **~light** n linterna
flashy [ˈflæʃɪ] (pej) adj ostentoso
flask [flɑːsk] n frasco; (also: vacuum ~) termo
flat [flæt] adj llano; (smooth) liso; (tyre) desinflado; (battery) descargado; (beer) muerto; (refusal etc) rotundo; (MUS) desafinado; (rate) fijo ♦ n (BRIT: apartment) piso (SP), departamento (AM), apartamento; (AUT) pinchazo; (MUS) bemol m; **to work ~ out** trabajar a toda mecha; **~ly** adv terminantemente, de plano; **~ten** vt (also: ~ten out) allanar; (smooth out) alisar; (building, plants) arrasar
flatter [ˈflætə*] vt adular, halagar; **~ing** adj halagüeño; (dress) que favorece; **~y** n adulación f
flaunt [flɔːnt] vt ostentar, lucir
flavour [ˈfleɪvə*] (US flavor) n sabor m, gusto ♦ vt sazonar, condimentar; **strawberry-~ed** con sabor a fresa; **~ing** n (in product) aromatizante m
flaw [flɔː] n defecto; **~less** adj impecable
flax [flæks] n lino
flea [fliː] n pulga
fleck [flɛk] n (mark) mota
flee [fliː] (pt, pp fled) vt huir de ♦ vi huir, fugarse
fleece [fliːs] n vellón m; (wool) lana ♦ vt (inf) desplumar
fleet [fliːt] n flota; (of lorries etc) escuadra
fleeting [ˈfliːtɪŋ] adj fugaz
Flemish [ˈflɛmɪʃ] adj flamenco
flesh [flɛʃ] n carne f; (skin) piel f; (of fruit) pulpa; **~ wound** n herida superficial
flew [fluː] pt of **fly**
flex [flɛks] n cordón m ♦ vt (muscles) tensar; **~ible** adj flexible
flick [flɪk] n capirotazo; chasquido ♦ vt (with

hand) dar un capirotazo a; (whip etc) chasquear; (switch) accionar; ~ **through** vt fus hojear
flicker [ˈflɪkə*] vi (light) parpadear; (flame) vacilar
flier [ˈflaɪə*] n aviador(a) m/f
flight [flaɪt] n vuelo; (escape) huida, fuga; (also: ~ of steps) tramo (de escaleras); ~ **attendant** (US) n camarero/azafata; ~ **deck** n (AVIAT) cabina de mandos; (NAUT) cubierta de aterrizaje
flimsy [ˈflɪmzɪ] adj (thin) muy ligero; (building) endeble; (excuse) flojo
flinch [flɪntʃ] vi encogerse; **to ~ from** retroceder ante
fling [flɪŋ] (pt, pp flung) vt arrojar
flint [flɪnt] n pedernal m; (in lighter) piedra
flip [flɪp] vt dar la vuelta a; (switch: turn on) encender; (: turn off) apagar; (coin) echar a cara o cruz
flippant [ˈflɪpənt] adj poco serio
flipper [ˈflɪpə*] n aleta
flirt [flɜːt] vi coquetear, flirtear ♦ n coqueta
float [fləut] n flotador m; (in procession) carroza; (money) reserva ♦ vi flotar; (swimmer) hacer la plancha
flock [flɔk] n (of sheep) rebaño; (of birds) bandada ♦ vi: **to ~ to** acudir en tropel a
flog [flɔg] vt azotar
flood [flʌd] n inundación f; (of letters, imports etc) avalancha ♦ vt inundar ♦ vi (place) inundarse; (people): **to ~ into** inundar; **~ing** n inundaciones fpl; **~light** n foco
floor [flɔː*] n suelo; (storey) piso; (of sea) fondo ♦ vt (subj: question) dejar sin respuesta; (: blow) derribar; **ground ~, first ~** (US) planta baja; **first ~, second ~** (US) primer piso; **~board** n tabla; **~ show** n cabaret m
flop [flɔp] n fracaso ♦ vi (fail) fracasar; (fall) derrumbarse; **~py** adj flojo ♦ n (COMPUT: also: ~py disk) floppy m
flora [ˈflɔːrə] n flora
floral [ˈflɔːrl] adj (pattern) floreado
florid [ˈflɔrɪd] adj florido; (complexion) rubicundo
florist [ˈflɔrɪst] n florista m/f; **~'s (shop)** n florería
flounder [ˈflaundə*] vi (swimmer) patalear; (fig: economy) estar en dificultades ♦ n (ZOOL) platija
flour [ˈflauə*] n harina
flourish [ˈflʌrɪʃ] vi florecer ♦ n ademán m, movimiento (ostentoso)
flout [flaut] vt burlarse de
flow [fləu] n (movement) flujo; (of traffic) circulación f; (tide) corriente f ♦ vi (river, blood) fluir; (traffic) circular; ~ **chart** n organigrama m
flower [ˈflauə*] n flor f ♦ vi florecer; ~ **bed** n

macizo; **~pot** n tiesto; **~y** adj (fragrance) floral; (pattern) floreado; (speech) florido

flown [fləun] pp of **fly**

flu [flu:] n: **to have ~** tener la gripe

fluctuate ['flʌktjʊeɪt] vi fluctuar

fluent ['flu:ənt] adj (linguist) que habla perfectamente; (speech) elocuente; **he speaks ~ French, he's ~ in French** domina el francés; **~ly** adv con fluidez

fluff [flʌf] n pelusa; **~y** adj de pelo suave

fluid ['flu:ɪd] adj (movement) fluido, líquido; (situation) inestable ♦ n fluido, líquido

fluke [flu:k] (inf) n chiripa

flung [flʌŋ] pt, pp of **fling**

fluoride ['fluəraɪd] n fluoruro

flurry ['flʌrɪ] n (of snow) temporal m; **~ of activity** frenesí m de actividad

flush [flʌʃ] n rubor m; (fig: of youth etc) resplandor m ♦ vt limpiar con agua ♦ vi ruborizarse ♦ adj: **~ with** a ras de; **to ~ the toilet** hacer funcionar la cisterna; **~ed** adj ruborizado

flustered ['flʌstəd] adj aturdido

flute [flu:t] n flauta

flutter ['flʌtə*] n (of wings) revoloteo, aleteo; **a ~ of panic/excitement** una oleada de pánico/excitación ♦ vi revolotear

flux [flʌks] n: **to be in a state of ~** estar continuamente cambiando

fly [flaɪ] (pt **flew**, pp **flown**) n mosca; (on trousers: also: flies) bragueta ♦ vt (plane) pilot(e)ar; (cargo) transportar (en avión); (distances) recorrer (en avión) ♦ vi volar; (passengers) ir en avión; (escape) evadirse; (flag) ondear; **~ away** or **off** vi emprender el vuelo; **~-drive** n: **~-drive holiday** vacaciones que incluyen vuelo y alquiler de coche; **~ing** n (activity) (el) volar; (action) vuelo ♦ adj: **~ing visit** visita relámpago; **with ~ing colours** con lucimiento; **~ing saucer** n platillo volante; **~ing start** n: **to get off to a ~ing start** empezar con buen pie; **~over** (BRIT) n paso a desnivel or superior; **~sheet** n (for tent) doble techo

foal [fəul] n potro

foam [fəum] n espuma ♦ vi hacer espuma; **~ rubber** n goma espuma

fob [fɔb] vt: **to ~ sb off with sth** despachar a uno con algo

focal point ['fəukl-] n (fig) centro de atención

focus ['fəukəs] (pl **~es**) n foco; (centre) centro ♦ vt (field glasses etc) enfocar ♦ vi: **to ~ (on)** enfocar (a); (issue etc) centrarse en; **in/out of ~** enfocado/desenfocado

fodder ['fɔdə*] n pienso

foetus ['fi:təs] (US **fetus**) n feto

fog [fɔg] n niebla; **~gy** adj: **it's ~gy** hay niebla, está brumoso; **~ lamp** (US **~ light**) n (AUT)

faro de niebla

foil [fɔɪl] vt frustrar ♦ n hoja; (kitchen ~) papel m (de) aluminio; (complement) complemento; (FENCING) florete m

fold [fəuld] n (bend, crease) pliegue m; (AGR) redil m ♦ vt doblar; (arms) cruzar; **~ up** vi plegarse, doblarse; (business) quebrar ♦ vt (map etc) plegar; **~er** n (for papers) carpeta; (COMPUT) directorio; **~ing** adj (chair, bed) plegable

foliage ['fəulɪdʒ] n follaje m

folk [fəuk] npl gente f ♦ adj popular, folklórico; **~s** npl (family) familia sg, parientes mpl; **~lore** ['fəuklɔ:*] n folklore m; **~ song** n canción f popular or folklórica

follow ['fɔləu] vt seguir ♦ vi seguir; (result) resultar; **to ~ suit** hacer lo mismo; **~ up** vt (letter, offer) responder a; (case) investigar; **~er** n (of person, belief) partidario/a; **~ing** adj siguiente ♦ n afición f, partidarios mpl

folly ['fɔlɪ] n locura

fond [fɔnd] adj (memory, smile etc) cariñoso; (hopes) ilusorio; **to be ~ of** tener cariño a; (pastime, food) ser aficionado a

fondle ['fɔndl] vt acariciar

font [fɔnt] n pila bautismal; (TYP) fundición f

food [fu:d] n comida; **~ mixer** n batidora; **~ poisoning** n intoxicación f alimenticia; **~ processor** n robot m de cocina; **~stuffs** npl comestibles mpl

fool [fu:l] n tonto/a; (CULIN) puré m de frutas con nata ♦ vt engañar ♦ vi (gen: ~ around) bromear; **~hardy** adj temerario; **~ish** adj tonto; (careless) imprudente; **~proof** adj (plan etc) infalible

foot [fut] (pl **feet**) n pie m; (measure) pie m (= 304 mm); (of animal) pata ♦ vt (bill) pagar; **on ~** a pie; **~age** n (CINEMA) imágenes fpl; **~ball** n balón m; (game: BRIT) fútbol m; (: US) fútbol m americano; **~ball player** n (BRIT: also: **~baller**) futbolista m; (US) jugador m de fútbol americano; **~brake** n freno de pie; **~bridge** n puente m para peatones; **~hills** npl estribaciones fpl; **~hold** n pie m firme; **~ing** n (fig) posición f; **to lose one's ~ing** perder el pie; **~lights** npl candilejas fpl; **~note** n nota (al pie de la página); **~path** n sendero; **~print** n huella, pisada; **~step** n paso; **~wear** n calzado

---
KEYWORD
---

for [fɔ:] prep 1 (indicating destination, intention) para; **the train ~ London** el tren con destino a or de Londres; **he left ~ Rome** marchó para Roma; **he went ~ the paper** fue por el periódico; **is this ~ me?** ¿es esto para mí?; **it's time ~ lunch** es la hora de comer 2 (indicating purpose) para; **what's it ~?** ¿para qué (es)?; **to pray ~ peace** rezar por la paz

3 (*on behalf of, representing*): **the MP ~ Hove** el diputado por Hove; **he works ~ the government/a local firm** trabaja para el gobierno/en una empresa local; **I'll ask him ~ you** se lo pediré por ti; **G ~ George** G de Gerona

4 (*because of*) por esta razón; **~ fear of being criticized** por temor a ser criticado

5 (*with regard to*) para; **it's cold ~ July** hace frío para julio; **he has a gift ~ languages** tiene don de lenguas

6 (*in exchange for*) por; **I sold it ~ £5** lo vendí por £5; **to pay 50 pence ~ a ticket** pagar 50 peniques por un billete

7 (*in favour of*): **are you ~ or against us?** ¿estás con nosotros o contra nosotros?; **I'm all ~ it** estoy totalmente a favor; **vote ~ X** vote (a) X

8 (*referring to distance*): **there are roadworks ~ 5 km** hay obras en 5 km; **we walked ~ miles** caminamos kilómetros y kilómetros

9 (*referring to time*): **he was away ~ 2 years** estuvo fuera (durante) dos años; **it hasn't rained ~ 3 weeks** no ha llovido durante *or* en 3 semanas; **I have known her ~ years** la conozco desde hace años; **can you do it ~ tomorrow?** ¿lo podrás hacer para mañana?

10 (*with infinitive clauses*): **it is not ~ me to decide** la decisión no es cosa mía; **it would be best ~ you to leave** sería mejor que te fueras; **there is still time ~ you to do it** todavía te queda tiempo para hacerlo; **~ this to be possible ...** para que esto sea posible ...

11 (*in spite of*) a pesar de; **~ all his complaints** a pesar de sus quejas

♦ *conj* (*since, as: rather formal*) puesto que

forage ['fɒrɪdʒ] *vi* (*animal*) forrajear; (*person*): **to ~ for** hurgar en busca de

foray ['fɒreɪ] *n* incursión *f*

forbid [fə'bɪd] (*pt* forbad(e), *pp* forbidden) *vt* prohibir; **to ~ sb to do sth** prohibir a uno hacer algo; **~ding** *adj* amenazador(a)

force [fɔ:s] *n* fuerza ♦ *vt* forzar; (*push*) meter a la fuerza; **to ~ o.s. to do** hacer un esfuerzo por hacer; **the F~s** *npl* (*BRIT*) las Fuerzas Armadas; **in ~** en vigor; **~d** [fɔ:st] *adj* forzado; **~-feed** *vt* alimentar a la fuerza; **~ful** *adj* enérgico

forcibly ['fɔ:səblɪ] *adv* a la fuerza; (*speak*) enérgicamente

ford [fɔ:d] *n* vado

fore [fɔ:*] *n*: **to come to the ~** empezar a destacar

fore: ~arm *n* antebrazo; **~boding** *n* presentimiento; **~cast** *n* pronóstico ♦ *vt* (*irreg: like cast*) pronosticar; **~court** *n* patio; **~finger** *n* (dedo) índice *m*; **~front** *n*: **in the ~front of** en la vanguardia de

forego *vt* = **forgo**

foregone ['fɔ:gɒn] *pp* of **forego** ♦ *adj*: **it's a ~ conclusion** es una conclusión evidente

foreground ['fɔ:graʊnd] *n* primer plano

forehead ['fɒrɪd] *n* frente *f*

foreign ['fɒrɪn] *adj* extranjero; (*trade*) exterior; (*object*) extraño; **~er** *n* extranjero/a; **~ exchange** *n* divisas *fpl*; **F~ Office** (*BRIT*) *n* Ministerio de Asuntos Exteriores; **F~ Secretary** (*BRIT*) *n* Ministro de Asuntos Exteriores

fore: ~leg *n* pata delantera; **~man** (*irreg*) *n* capataz *m*; (*in construction*) maestro de obras; **~most** *adj* principal ♦ *adv*: **first and ~most** ante todo

forensic [fə'rensɪk] *adj* forense

fore: ~runner *n* precursor(a) *m/f*; **~see** (*pt* foresaw, *pp* foreseen) *vt* prever; **~seeable** *adj* previsible; **~shadow** *vt* prefigurar, anunciar; **~sight** *n* previsión *f*

forest ['fɒrɪst] *n* bosque *m*

forestry ['fɒrɪstrɪ] *n* silvicultura

foretaste ['fɔ:teɪst] *n* muestra

foretell [fɔ:'tel] (*pt, pp* foretold) *vt* predecir, pronosticar

forever [fə'revə*] *adv* para siempre; (*endlessly*) constantemente

foreword ['fɔ:wə:d] *n* prefacio

forfeit ['fɔ:fɪt] *vt* perder

forgave [fə'geɪv] *pt* of **forgive**

forge [fɔ:dʒ] *n* herrería ♦ *vt* (*signature, money*) falsificar; (*metal*) forjar; **~ ahead** *vi* avanzar mucho; **~ry** *n* falsificación *f*

forget [fə'get] (*pt* forgot, *pp* forgotten) *vt* olvidar ♦ *vi* olvidarse; **~ful** *adj* despistado; **~-me-not** *n* nomeolvides *f inv*

forgive [fə'gɪv] (*pt* forgave, *pp* forgiven) *vt* perdonar; **to ~ sb for sth** perdonar algo a uno; **~ness** *n* perdón *m*

forgo [fɔ:'gəʊ] (*pt* forwent, *pp* forgone) *vt* (*give up*) renunciar a; (*go without*) privarse de

forgot [fə'gɒt] *pt* of **forget**

forgotten [fə'gɒtn] *pp* of **forget**

fork [fɔ:k] *n* (*for eating*) tenedor *m*; (*for gardening*) horca; (*of roads*) bifurcación *f* ♦ *vi* (*road*) bifurcarse; **~ out** (*inf*) *vt* (*pay*) desembolsar; **~-lift truck** *n* máquina elevadora

forlorn [fə'lɔ:n] *adj* (*person*) triste, melancólico; (*place*) abandonado; (*attempt, hope*) desesperado

form [fɔ:m] *n* forma; (*BRIT: SCOL*) clase *f*; (*document*) formulario ♦ *vt* formar; (*idea*) concebir; (*habit*) adquirir; **in top ~** en plena forma; **to ~ a queue** hacer cola

formal ['fɔ:məl] *adj* (*offer, receipt*) por escrito; (*person etc*) correcto; (*occasion, dinner*) de etiqueta; (*dress*) correcto; (*garden*) (de estilo) clásico; **~ity** [-'mælɪtɪ] *n* (*procedure*) trámite m; corrección f; etiqueta; **~ly** adv oficialmente

format ['fɔ:mæt] n formato ♦ vt (COMPUT) formatear

formative ['fɔ:mətɪv] adj (years) de formación; (influence) formativo

former ['fɔ:mə*] adj anterior; (earlier) antiguo; (ex) ex; the **~ ... the latter** ... aquél ... éste ...; **~ly** adv antes

formula ['fɔ:mjulə] n fórmula

forsake [fə'seɪk] (pt forsook, pp forsaken) vt (gen) abandonar; (plan) renunciar a

fort [fɔ:t] n fuerte m

forte ['fɔ:tɪ] n fuerte m

forth [fɔ:θ] adv: **back and ~** de acá para allá; **and so ~** y así sucesivamente; **~coming** adj próximo, venidero; (help, information) disponible; (character) comunicativo; **~right** adj franco; **~with** adv en el acto

fortify ['fɔ:tɪfaɪ] vt (city) fortificar; (person) fortalecer

fortitude ['fɔ:tɪtju:d] n fortaleza

fortnight ['fɔ:tnaɪt] (BRIT) n quince días mpl; quincena; **~ly** adj de cada quince días, quincenal ♦ adv cada quince días, quincenalmente

fortress ['fɔ:trɪs] n fortaleza

fortunate ['fɔ:tʃənɪt] adj afortunado; **it is ~ that** ... (es una) suerte que ...; **~ly** adv afortunadamente

fortune ['fɔ:tʃən] n suerte f; (wealth) fortuna; **~-teller** n adivino/a

forty ['fɔ:tɪ] num cuarenta

forum ['fɔ:rəm] n foro

forward ['fɔ:wəd] adj (movement, position) avanzado; (front) delantero; (in time) adelantado; (not shy) atrevido ♦ n (SPORT) delantero ♦ vt (letter) remitir; (career) promocionar; **to move ~** avanzar; **~(s)** adv (hacia) adelante

fossil ['fɔsl] n fósil m

foster ['fɔstə*] vt (child) acoger en una familia; fomentar; **~ child** n hijo/a adoptivo/a

fought [fɔ:t] pt, pp of **fight**

foul [faul] adj sucio, puerco; (weather, smell etc) asqueroso; (language) grosero; (temper) malísimo ♦ n (SPORT) falta ♦ vt (dirty) ensuciar; **~ play** n (LAW) muerte f violenta

found [faund] pt, pp of **find** ♦ vt fundar; **~ation** [-'deɪʃən] n (act) fundación f; (basis) base f; (also: **~ation cream**) crema base; **~ations** npl (of building) cimientos mpl

founder ['faundə*] n fundador(a) m/f ♦ vi hundirse

foundry ['faundrɪ] n fundición f

fountain ['fauntɪn] n fuente f; **~ pen** n pluma (estilográfica) (SP), pluma-fuente f (AM)

four [fɔ:*] num cuatro; **on all ~s** a gatas; **~-poster (bed)** n cama de dosel; **~teen** num catorce; **~th** num cuarto

fowl [faul] n ave f (de corral)

fox [fɔks] n zorro ♦ vt confundir

foyer ['fɔɪeɪ] n vestíbulo

fraction ['frækʃən] n fracción f

fracture ['fræktʃə*] n fractura

fragile ['frædʒaɪl] adj frágil

fragment ['frægmənt] n fragmento

fragrant ['freɪgrənt] adj fragante, oloroso

frail [freɪl] adj frágil; (person) débil

frame [freɪm] n (TECH) armazón m; (of person) cuerpo; (of picture, door etc) marco; (of spectacles: also: **~s**) montura ♦ vt enmarcar; **~ of mind** n estado de ánimo; **~work** n marco

France [frɑ:ns] n Francia

franchise ['fræntʃaɪz] n (POL) derecho de votar, sufragio; (COMM) licencia, concesión f

frank [fræŋk] adj franco ♦ vt (letter) franquear; **~ly** adv francamente

frantic ['fræntɪk] adj (distraught) desesperado; (hectic) frenético

fraternity [frə'tɜ:nɪtɪ] n (feeling) fraternidad f; (group of people) círculos mpl

fraud [frɔ:d] n fraude m; (person) impostor(a) m/f

fraught [frɔ:t] adj: **~ with** lleno de

fray [freɪ] vi deshilacharse

freak [fri:k] n (person) fenómeno; (event) suceso anormal

freckle ['frekl] n peca

free [fri:] adj libre; (gratis) gratuito ♦ vt (prisoner etc) poner en libertad; (jammed object) soltar; **~ (of charge), for ~** gratis; **~dom** ['fri:dəm] n libertad f; **F~fone** ® ['fri:fəun] n número gratuito; **~-for-all** n riña general; **~ gift** n prima; **~hold** n propiedad f vitalicia; **~ kick** n tiro libre; **~lance** adj independiente ♦ adv por cuenta propia; **~ly** adv libremente; (liberally) generosamente; **F~mason** n francmasón m; **F~post** ® n porte m pagado; **~-range** adj (hen, eggs) de granja; **~ trade** n libre comercio; **~way** (US) n autopista; **~ will** n libre albedrío; **of one's own ~ will** por su propia voluntad

freeze [fri:z] (pt froze, pp frozen) vi (weather) helar; (liquid, pipe, person) helarse, congelarse ♦ vt helar; (food, prices, salaries) congelar ♦ n helada; (on arms, wages) congelación f; **~-dried** adj liofilizado; **~r** n congelador m (SP), congeladora (AM)

freezing ['fri:zɪŋ] adj helado; **3 degrees below ~** tres grados bajo cero; **~ point** n punto de congelación

freight [freɪt] n (goods) carga; (money charged) flete m; **~ train** n (US) n tren m de mercancías

French [frentʃ] adj francés/esa ♦ n (LING)
francés m; **the ~** npl los franceses; **~ bean** n
judía verde; **~ fried potatoes** npl patatas fpl
(SP) or papas fpl (AM) fritas; **~ fries** (US) np!
= **~ fried potatoes**; **~man/woman** (irreg) n
francés/esa m/f; **~ window** n puerta de
cristal

frenzy ['frenzi] n frenesí m

frequent [adj 'fri:kwənt, vb frɪ'kwent] adj
frecuente ♦ vt frecuentar; **~ly** [-əntlɪ] adv
frecuentemente, a menudo

fresh [freʃ] adj fresco; (bread) tierno; (new)
nuevo; **~en** vi (wind, air) soplar más recio;
~en up vi (person) arreglarse, lavarse; **~er**
(BRIT: inf) n (UNIV) estudiante m/f de primer
año; **~ly** adv (made, painted etc) recién;
~man (US irreg) n = **~er**; **~ness** n frescura;
~water adj (fish) de agua dulce

fret [fret] vi inquietarse

friar ['fraɪə*] n fraile m; (before name) fray m

friction ['frɪkʃən] n fricción f

Friday ['fraɪdɪ] n viernes m inv

fridge [frɪdʒ] (BRIT) n nevera (SP),
refrigeradora (AM)

fried [fraɪd] adj frito

friend [frend] n amigo/a; **~ly** adj simpático;
(government) amigo; (place) acogedor(a);
(match) amistoso; **~ly fire** fuego amigo,
disparos mpl del propio bando; **~ship** n
amistad f

frieze [fri:z] n friso

fright [fraɪt] n (terror) terror m; (scare) susto;
to take ~ asustarse; **~en** vt asustar; **~ened**
adj asustado; **~ening** adj espantoso; **~ful** adj
espantoso, horrible

frill [frɪl] n volante m

fringe [frɪndʒ] n (BRIT: of hair) flequillo; (on
lampshade etc) flecos mpl; (of forest etc)
borde m, margen m; **~ benefits** npl
beneficios mpl marginales

frisk [frɪsk] vt cachear, registrar

frisky ['frɪskɪ] adj juguetón/ona

fritter ['frɪtə*] n buñuelo; **~ away** vt
desperdiciar

frivolous ['frɪvələs] adj frívolo

frizzy ['frɪzɪ] adj rizado

fro [frəʊ] see to

frock [frɔk] n vestido

frog [frɔg] n rana; **~man** n hombre-rana m

frolic ['frɔlɪk] vi juguetear

KEYWORD

from [frɔm] prep **1** (indicating starting place)
de, desde; **where do you come ~?** ¿de dónde
eres?; **~ London to Glasgow** de Londres a
Glasgow; **to escape ~ sth/sb** escaparse de
algo/alguien

2 (indicating origin etc) de; **a letter/telephone
call ~ my sister** una carta/llamada de mi

hermana; **tell him ~ me that ...** dígale de mi
parte que ...

3 (indicating time): **~ one o'clock to** or **until** or
till two de(sde) la una a or hasta las dos;
~ January (on) a partir de enero

4 (indicating distance) de; **the hotel is 1 km
~ the beach** el hotel está a 1 km de la playa

5 (indicating price, number etc) de; **prices
range ~ £10 to £50** los precios van desde £10
a or hasta £50; **the interest rate was
increased ~ 9% to 10%** el tipo de interés fue
incrementado de un 9% a un 10%

6 (indicating difference) de; **he can't tell red
~ green** no sabe distinguir el rojo del verde;
to be different ~ sb/sth ser diferente a algo/
alguien

7 (because of, on the basis of): **~ what he
says** por lo que dice; **weak ~ hunger**
debilitado por el hambre

front [frʌnt] n (foremost part) parte f
delantera; (of house) fachada; (of dress)
delantero; (promenade: also: sea ~) paseo
marítimo; (MIL, POL, METEOROLOGY) frente m;
(fig: appearances) apariencias fpl ♦ adj
(wheel, leg) delantero; (row, line) primero; **in
~ (of)** delante (de); **~ door** n puerta
principal; **~ier** ['frʌntɪə*] n frontera; **~ page**
n primera plana; **~ room** (BRIT) n salón m,
sala; **~-wheel drive** n tracción f delantera

frost [frɔst] n helada; (also: hoar~) escarcha;
~bite n congelación f; **~ed** adj (glass)
deslustrado; **~y** adj (weather) de helada;
(welcome etc) glacial

froth [frɔθ] n espuma

frown [fraʊn] vi fruncir el ceño

froze [frəʊz] pt of freeze

frozen ['frəʊzn] pp of freeze

fruit [fru:t] n inv fruta; fruto; (fig) fruto;
resultados mpl; **~erer** n frutero/a; **~erer's
(shop)** n frutería; **~ful** adj provechoso; **~ion**
[fru:'ɪʃən] n: **to come to ~ion** realizarse;
~ juice n zumo (SP) or jugo (AM) de fruta;
~ machine (BRIT) n máquina f tragaperras;
~ salad n macedonia (SP) or ensalada (AM)
de frutas

frustrate [frʌs'treɪt] vt frustrar

fry [fraɪ] (pt, pp fried) vt freír; **small ~** gente f
menuda; **~ing pan** n sartén f

ft. abbr = **foot**; **feet**

fudge [fʌdʒ] n (CULIN) caramelo blando

fuel [fjuəl] n (for heating) combustible m;
(coal) carbón m; (wood) leña; (for engine)
carburante m; **~ oil** n fuel oil m; **~ tank** n
depósito (de combustible)

fugitive ['fju:dʒɪtɪv] n fugitivo/a

fulfil [ful'fɪl] vt (function) cumplir con;
(condition) satisfacer; (wish, desire) realizar;
~ment (US **fulfillment**) n satisfacción f; (of

promise, desire) realización f
full [ful] *adj* lleno; (*fig*) pleno; (*complete*)
completo; (*maximum*) máximo; (*information*)
detallado; (*price*) íntegro; (*skirt*) amplio
♦ *adv*: **to know ~ well that** saber
perfectamente que; **I'm ~ (up)** no puedo
más; **~ employment** pleno empleo; **a ~ two
hours** dos horas completas; **at ~ speed** a
máxima velocidad; **in ~** (*reproduce, quote*)
íntegramente; **~-length** *adj* (*novel etc*)
entero; (*coat*) largo; (*portrait*) de cuerpo
entero; **~ moon** *n* luna llena; **~-scale** *adj*
(*attack, war*) en gran escala; (*model*) de
tamaño natural; **~ stop** *n* punto; **~-time** *adj*
(*work*) de tiempo completo ♦ *adv*: **to work
~-time** trabajar a tiempo completo; **~y** *adv*
completamente; (*at least*) por lo menos; **~y-
fledged** *adj* (*teacher, barrister*) diplomado
fumble ['fʌmbl] *vi*: **to ~ with** manejar
torpemente
fume [fjuːm] *vi* (*rage*) estar furioso; **~s** *npl*
humo, gases *mpl*
fun [fʌn] *n* (*amusement*) diversión f; **to have ~**
divertirse; **for ~** en broma; **to make ~ of**
burlarse de
function ['fʌŋkʃən] *n* función f ♦ *vi*
funcionar; **~al** *adj* (*operational*) en buen
estado; (*practical*) funcional
fund [fʌnd] *n* fondo; (*reserve*) reserva; **~s** *npl*
(*money*) fondos *mpl*
fundamental [fʌndə'mentl] *adj*
fundamental
funeral ['fjuːnərəl] *n* (*burial*) entierro;
(*ceremony*) funerales *mpl*; **~ parlour** (*BRIT*) *n*
funeraria; **~ service** *n* misa de difuntos,
funeral *m*
funfair ['fʌnfeə*] (*BRIT*) *n* parque *m* de
atracciones
fungus ['fʌŋgəs] (*pl* fungi) *n* hongo; (*mould*)
moho
funnel ['fʌnl] *n* embudo; (*of ship*) chimenea
funny ['fʌnɪ] *adj* gracioso, divertido; (*strange*)
curioso, raro
fur [fəː*] *n* piel f; (*BRIT: in kettle etc*) sarro; **~
coat** *n* abrigo de pieles
furious ['fjʊərɪəs] *adj* furioso; (*effort*) violento
furlong ['fəːlɒŋ] *n* octava parte de una milla,
= 201.17 m
furnace ['fəːnɪs] *n* horno
furnish ['fəːnɪʃ] *vt* amueblar; (*supply*)
suministrar; (*information*) facilitar; **~ings** *npl*
muebles *mpl*
furniture ['fəːnɪtʃə*] *n* muebles *mpl*; **piece of
~** mueble *m*
furrow ['fʌrəʊ] *n* surco
furry ['fəːrɪ] *adj* peludo
further ['fəːðə*] *adj* (*new*) nuevo, adicional
♦ *adv* más lejos; (*more*) más; (*moreover*)
además ♦ *vt* promover, adelantar;

~ education *n* educación f superior; **~more**
[fəːðə'mɔː:*] *adv* además
furthest ['fəːðɪst] *superlative of* **far**
fury ['fjʊərɪ] *n* furia
fuse [fjuːz] (*US* fuze) *n* fusible *m*; (*for bomb
etc*) mecha ♦ *vt* (*metal*) fundir; (*fig*) fusionar
♦ *vi* fundirse; fusionarse; (*BRIT: ELEC*): **to ~ the
lights** fundir los plomos; **~ box** *n* caja de
fusibles
fuss [fʌs] *n* (*excitement*) conmoción f;
(*trouble*) alboroto; **to make a ~** armar un lío
or jaleo; **to make a ~ of sb** mimar a uno; **~y**
adj (*person*) exigente; (*too ornate*) recargado
futile ['fjuːtaɪl] *adj* vano
future ['fjuːtʃə*] *adj* futuro; (*coming*) venidero
♦ *n* futuro; (*prospects*) porvenir; **in ~** de
ahora en adelante
fuze [fjuːz] (*US*) = **fuse**
fuzzy ['fʌzɪ] *adj* (*PHOT*) borroso; (*hair*) muy
rizado

G, g

G [dʒiː] *n* (*MUS*) sol *m*
g. *abbr* (= gram(s)) gr.
G8 *abbr* (= Group of Eight) el grupo de los 8
gabble ['gæbl] *vi* hablar atropelladamente
gable ['geɪbl] *n* aguilón *m*
gadget ['gædʒɪt] *n* aparato
Gaelic ['geɪlɪk] *adj, n* (*LING*) gaélico
gag [gæg] *n* (*on mouth*) mordaza; (*joke*) chiste
m ♦ *vt* amordazar
gaiety ['geɪtɪ] *n* alegría
gaily ['geɪlɪ] *adv* alegremente
gain [geɪn] *n*: **~ (in)** aumento (de); (*profit*)
ganancia ♦ *vt* ganar ♦ *vi* (*watch*) adelantarse;
to ~ from/by sth sacar provecho de algo; **to
~ on sb** ganar terreno a uno; **to ~ 3 lbs (in
weight)** engordar 3 libras
gal. *abbr* = **gallon**
gala ['gɑːlə] *n* fiesta
gale [geɪl] *n* (*wind*) vendaval *m*
gallant ['gælənt] *adj* valiente; (*towards ladies*)
atento
gall bladder ['gɔːl-] *n* vesícula biliar
gallery ['gælərɪ] *n* (*also: art ~: public*)
pinacoteca; (*: private*) galería de arte; (*for
spectators*) tribuna
gallon ['gælən] *n* galón *m* (*BRIT* = 4,546 *litros,
US* = 3,785 *litros*)
gallop ['gæləp] *n* galope *m* ♦ *vi* galopar
gallows ['gæləʊz] *n* horca
gallstone ['gɔːlstəʊn] *n* cálculo biliario
galore [gə'lɔː:*] *adv* en cantidad, en
abundancia
gambit ['gæmbɪt] *n* (*fig*): **(opening) ~**
estrategia (inicial)
gamble ['gæmbl] *n* (*risk*) riesgo ♦ *vt* jugar,

apostar ♦ vi (*take a risk*) jugárselas; (*bet*) apostar; **to ~ on** apostar a; (*success etc*) contar con; **~r** n jugador(a) m/f; **gambling** n juego

game [geɪm] n juego; (*match*) partido; (*of cards*) partida; (*HUNTING*) caza ♦ adj (*willing*): **to be ~ for anything** atreverse a todo; **big ~** caza mayor; **~keeper** n guardabosques m inv

gammon ['ɡæmən] n (*bacon*) tocino ahumado; (*ham*) jamón m ahumado

gamut ['ɡæmət] n gama

gang [ɡæŋ] n (*of criminals*) pandilla; (*of friends etc*) grupo; (*of workmen*) brigada; **~ up** vi: **to ~ up on sb** aliarse contra uno

gangster ['ɡæŋstə*] n gángster m

gangway ['ɡæŋweɪ] n (*on ship*) pasarela; (*BRIT: in theatre, bus etc*) pasillo

gaol [dʒeɪl] (*BRIT*) n, vt = **jail**

gap [ɡæp] n vacío, hueco; (*AM*); (*in trees, traffic*) claro; (*in time*) (*AM*); (*difference*): **~ (between)** diferencia (entre)

gape [ɡeɪp] vi mirar boquiabierto; (*shirt etc*) abrirse (completamente); **gaping** adj (completamente) abierto

garage ['ɡærɑːʒ] n garaje m; (*for repairs*) taller m

garbage ['ɡɑːbɪdʒ] (*US*) n basura; (*inf: nonsense*) tonterías fpl; **~ can** n cubo (*SP*) or bote m (*AM*) de la basura

garbled ['ɡɑːbld] adj (*distorted*) falsificado, amañado

garden ['ɡɑːdn] n jardín m; **~s** npl (*park*) parque m; **~er** n jardinero/a; **~ing** n jardinería

gargle ['ɡɑːgl] vi hacer gárgaras, gargarear (*AM*)

garish ['ɡεərɪʃ] adj chillón/ona

garland ['ɡɑːlənd] n guirnalda

garlic ['ɡɑːlɪk] n ajo

garment ['ɡɑːmənt] n prenda (de vestir)

garnish ['ɡɑːnɪʃ] vt (*CULIN*) aderezar

garrison ['ɡærɪsn] n guarnición f

garter ['ɡɑːtə*] n (*for sock*) liga; (*US*) liguero

gas [ɡæs] n gas m; (*fuel*) combustible m; (*US: gasoline*) gasolina ♦ vt asfixiar con gas; **~ cooker** (*BRIT*) n cocina de gas; **~ cylinder** n bombona de gas; **~ fire** n estufa de gas

gash [ɡæʃ] n raja; (*wound*) cuchillada ♦ vt rajar; acuchillar

gasket ['ɡæskɪt] n (*AUT*) junta de culata

gas mask n careta antigás

gas meter n contador m de gas

gasoline ['ɡæsəliːn] (*US*) n gasolina

gasp [ɡɑːsp] n boqueada; (*of shock etc*) grito sofocado ♦ vi (*pant*) jadear

gas station (*US*) n gasolinera

gastric ['ɡæstrɪk] adj gástrico

gate [ɡeɪt] n puerta; (*iron ~*) verja; **~crash** (*BRIT*) vt colarse en; **~way** n (*also fig*) puerta

gather ['ɡæðə*] vt (*flowers, fruit*) coger (*SP*), recoger; (*assemble*) reunir; (*pick up*) recoger; (*SEWING*) fruncir; (*understand*) entender ♦ vi (*assemble*) reunirse; **to ~ speed** ganar velocidad; **~ing** n reunión f, asamblea

gaudy ['ɡɔːdɪ] adj chillón/ona

gauge [ɡeɪdʒ] n (*instrument*) indicador m ♦ vt medir; (*fig*) juzgar

gaunt [ɡɔːnt] adj (*haggard*) demacrado; (*stark*) desolado

gauntlet ['ɡɔːntlɪt] n (*fig*): **to run the ~ of** exponerse a; **to throw down the ~** arrojar el guante

gauze [ɡɔːz] n gasa

gave [ɡeɪv] pt of **give**

gay [ɡeɪ] adj (*homosexual*) gay; (*joyful*) alegre; (*colour*) vivo

gaze [ɡeɪz] n mirada fija ♦ vi: **to ~ at sth** mirar algo fijamente

gazelle [ɡə'zɛl] n gacela

gazumping [ɡə'zʌmpɪŋ] (*BRIT*) n la subida del precio de una casa una vez que ya ha sido apalabrado

GB abbr = **Great Britain**

GCE n abbr (*BRIT*) = *General Certificate of Education*

GCSE (*BRIT*) n abbr (= *General Certificate of Secondary Education*) examen de reválida que se hace a los 16 años

gear [ɡɪə*] n equipo, herramientas fpl; (*TECH*) engranaje m; (*AUT*) velocidad f, marcha ♦ vt (*fig: adapt*): **to ~ sth to** adaptar or ajustar algo a; **top or high** (*US*)/**low ~** cuarta/primera velocidad; **in ~** en marcha; **~ box** n caja de cambios; **~ lever** n palanca de cambio; **~ shift** (*US*) n = **~ lever**

geese [ɡiːs] npl of **goose**

gel [dʒɛl] n gel m

gem [dʒɛm] n piedra preciosa

Gemini ['dʒɛmɪnaɪ] n Géminis m, Gemelos mpl

gender ['dʒɛndə*] n género

gene [dʒiːn] n gen(e) m

general ['dʒɛnərl] n general m ♦ adj general; **in ~** en general; **~ delivery** (*US*) n lista de correos; **~ election** n elecciones fpl generales; **~ly** adv generalmente, en general; **~ practitioner** n médico general

generate ['dʒɛnəreɪt] vt (*ELEC*) generar; (*jobs, profits*) producir

generation [dʒɛnə'reɪʃən] n generación f

generator ['dʒɛnəreɪtə*] n generador m

generosity [dʒɛnə'rɒsɪtɪ] n generosidad f

generous ['dʒɛnərəs] adj generoso

genetic [dʒɪ'nɛtɪk] adj: **~ engineering** ingeniería genética; **~ fingerprinting** identificación f genética

Geneva [dʒɪ'niːvə] n Ginebra

genial ['dʒiːnɪəl] adj afable, simpático

genitals ['dʒɛnɪtlz] npl (órganos mpl) genitales mpl

genius ['dʒiːnɪəs] n genio

genteel [dʒɛn'tiːl] adj fino, elegante

gentle ['dʒɛntl] adj apacible, dulce; (animal) manso; (breeze, curve etc) suave

gentleman ['dʒɛntlmən] (irreg) n señor m; (well-bred man) caballero

gently ['dʒɛntlɪ] adv dulcemente; suavemente

gentry ['dʒɛntrɪ] n alta burguesía

gents [dʒɛnts] n aseos mpl (de caballeros)

genuine ['dʒɛnjuɪn] adj auténtico; (person) sincero

geography [dʒɪ'ɔgrəfɪ] n geografía

geology [dʒɪ'ɔlədʒɪ] n geología

geometric(al) [dʒɪə'mɛtrɪk(l)] adj geométrico

geranium [dʒɪ'reɪnjəm] n geranio

geriatric [dʒɛrɪ'ætrɪk] adj, n geriátrico/a m/f

germ [dʒɜːm] n (microbe) microbio, bacteria; (seed, fig) germen m

German ['dʒɜːmən] adj alemán/ana ♦ n alemán/ana m/f; (LING) alemán m; **~ measles** n rubéola

Germany ['dʒɜːmənɪ] n Alemania

gesture ['dʒɛstjəʳ] n gesto; (symbol) muestra

KEYWORD

---

get [gɛt] (pt, pp **got**, pp **gotten** (US)) vi
1 (become, be) ponerse, volverse; **to ~ old/ tired** envejecer/cansarse; **to ~ drunk** emborracharse; **to ~ dirty** ensuciarse; **to ~ married** casarse; **when do I ~ paid?** ¿cuándo me pagan o se me paga?; **it's ~ting late** se está haciendo tarde
2 (go): **to ~ to/from** llegar a/de; **to ~ home** llegar a casa
3 (begin) empezar a; **to ~ to know sb** (llegar a) conocer a uno; **I'm ~ting to like him** me está empezando a gustar; **let's ~ going** or **started** ¡vamos (a empezar)!
4 (modal aux vb): **you've got to do it** tienes que hacerlo
♦ vt 1: **to ~ sth done** (finish) terminar algo; (have done) mandar hacer algo; **to ~ one's hair cut** cortarse el pelo; **to ~ the car going** or **to go** arrancar el coche; **to ~ sb to do sth** conseguir or hacer que alguien haga algo; **to ~ sth/sb ready** preparar algo/a alguien
2 (obtain: money, permission, results) conseguir; (find: job, flat) encontrar; (fetch: person, doctor) buscar; (object) ir a buscar, traer; **to ~ sth for sb** conseguir algo para alguien; **~ me Mr Jones, please** (TEL) póngame o comuníqueme con el Sr. Jones, por favor; **can I ~ you a drink?** ¿quieres algo de beber?
3 (receive: present, letter) recibir; (acquire: reputation) alcanzar; (: prize) ganar; **what did**

you ~ for your birthday? ¿qué te regalaron por tu cumpleaños?; **how much did you ~ for the painting?** ¿cuánto sacaste por el cuadro?
4 (catch) coger (SP), agarrar (AM); (hit: target etc) dar en; **to ~ sb by the arm/throat** coger or agarrar a uno por el brazo/cuello; **~ him!** ¡cógelo! (SP), ¡atrápalo! (AM); **the bullet got him in the leg** la bala le dio en la pierna
5 (take, move) llevar; **to ~ sth to sb** hacer llegar algo a alguien; **do you think we'll ~ it through the door?** ¿crees que lo podremos meter por la puerta?
6 (catch, take: plane, bus etc) coger (SP), tomar (AM); **where do I ~ the train for Birmingham?** ¿dónde se coge or se toma el tren para Birmingham?
7 (understand) entender; (hear) oír; **I've got it!** ¡ya lo tengo!, ¡eureka!; **I don't ~ your meaning** no te entiendo; **I'm sorry, I didn't ~ your name** lo siento, no cogí tu nombre
8 (have, possess): **to have got** tener

get about vi salir mucho; (news) divulgarse
get along vi (agree) llevarse bien; (depart) marcharse; (manage) = **get by**
get at vt fus (attack) atacar; (reach) alcanzar
get away vi marcharse; (escape) escaparse
get away with vt fus hacer impunemente
get back vi (return) volver ♦ vt recobrar
get by vi (pass) lograr pasar; (manage) arreglárselas
get down vi bajarse ♦ vt fus bajar ♦ vt bajar; (depress) deprimir
get down to vt fus (work) ponerse a
get in vi entrar; (train) llegar; (arrive home) volver a casa, regresar
get into vt fus entrar en; (vehicle) subir a; **to ~ into a rage** enfadarse
get off vi (from train etc) bajar; (depart: person, car) marcharse ♦ vt (remove) quitar ♦ vt fus (train, bus) bajar de
get on vi (at exam etc): **how are you ~ting on?** ¿cómo te va?; (agree): **to ~ on (with)** llevarse bien (con) ♦ vt fus subir a
get out vi salir; (of vehicle) bajar ♦ vt sacar
get out of vt fus salir de; (duty etc) escaparse de
get over vt fus (illness) recobrarse de
get round vt fus rodear; (fig: person) engatusar a
get through to vi (TEL) lograr comunicar
get through to vt fus (TEL) comunicar con
get together vi reunirse ♦ vt reunir, juntar
get up vi (rise) levantarse ♦ vt fus subir
get up to vt fus (reach) llegar a; (prank) hacer

---

geyser ['giːzəʳ] n (water heater) calentador m de agua; (GEO) géiser m

ghastly ['gɑːstlɪ] adj horrible

gherkin ['gəːkɪn] n pepinillo
ghetto blaster ['getəublɑːstə*] n cassette m
  portátil de gran tamaño
ghost [gəust] n fantasma m
giant ['dʒaɪənt] n gigante m/f ♦ adj
  gigantesco, gigante
gibberish ['dʒɪbərɪʃ] n galimatías m
giblets ['dʒɪblɪts] npl menudillos mpl
Gibraltar [dʒɪ'brɔːltə*] n Gibraltar m
giddy ['gɪdɪ] adj mareado
gift [gɪft] n regalo; (ability) talento; **~ed** adj
  dotado; **~ token** or **voucher** n vale m
  canjeable por un regalo
gigantic [dʒaɪ'gæntɪk] adj gigantesco
giggle ['gɪgl] vi reírse tontamente
gill [dʒɪl] n (measure) = 0.25 pints (BRIT =
  0.148l, US = 0.118l)
gills [gɪlz] npl (of fish) branquias fpl, agallas fpl
gilt [gɪlt] adj, n dorado; **~-edged** adj (COMM)
  de máxima garantía
gimmick ['gɪmɪk] n truco
gin [dʒɪn] n ginebra
ginger ['dʒɪndʒə*] n jengibre m; **~ ale**
  = **~ beer**; **~ beer** (BRIT) n gaseosa de jengibre;
  ~bread n pan m (or galleta) de jengibre
gingerly ['dʒɪndʒəlɪ] adv con cautela
gipsy ['dʒɪpsɪ] n = **gypsy**
giraffe [dʒɪ'rɑːf] n jirafa
girder ['gəːdə*] n viga
girl [gəːl] n (small) niña; (young woman)
  chica, joven f, muchacha; (daughter) hija; **an
  English ~** una (chica) inglesa; **~friend** n (of
  girl) amiga; (of boy) novia; **~ish** adj de niña
giro ['dʒaɪrəu] n (BRIT: bank ~) giro bancario;
  (post office ~) giro postal; (state benefit)
  cheque quincenal del subsidio de desempleo
gist [dʒɪst] n lo esencial
give [gɪv] (pt **gave**, pp **given**) vt dar; (deliver)
  entregar; (as gift) regalar ♦ vi (break)
  romperse; (stretch: fabric) dar de sí; **to ~ sb
  sth, ~ sth to sb** dar algo a uno; **~ away** vt
  (give free) regalar; (betray) traicionar;
  (disclose) revelar; **~ back** vt devolver; **~ in**
  vi ceder ♦ vt entregar; **~ off** vt despedir; **~
  out** vt distribuir; **~ up** vi rendirse, darse por
  vencido ♦ vt renunciar a; **to ~ up smoking**
  dejar de fumar; **to ~ o.s. up** entregarse;
  ~ way vi ceder; (BRIT: AUT) ceder el paso
glacier ['glæsɪə*] n glaciar m
glad [glæd] adj contento
gladly ['glædlɪ] adv con mucho gusto
glamorous ['glæmərəs] adj encantador(a),
  atractivo; **glamour** ['glæmə*] n encanto,
  atractivo
glance [glɑːns] n ojeada, mirada ♦ vi: **to ~ at**
  echar una ojeada a; **glancing** adj (blow)
  oblicuo
gland [glænd] n glándula
glare [glɛə*] n (of anger) mirada feroz; (of

light) deslumbramiento, brillo; **to be in the
  ~ of publicity** ser el foco de la atención
  pública ♦ vi deslumbrar; **to ~ at** mirar con
  odio a; **glaring** adj (mistake) manifiesto
glass [glɑːs] n vidrio, cristal m; (for drinking)
  vaso; (: with stem) copa; **~es** npl (spectacles)
  gafas fpl; **~house** n invernadero; **~ware** n
  cristalería
glaze [gleɪz] vt (window) poner cristales a;
  (pottery) vidriar ♦ n vidriado; **glazier**
  ['gleɪzɪə*] n vidriero/a
gleam [gliːm] vi brillar
glean [gliːn] vt (information) recoger
glee [gliː] n alegría, regocijo
glen [glɛn] n cañada
glib [glɪb] adj de mucha labia; (promise,
  response) poco sincero
glide [glaɪd] vi deslizarse; (AVIAT, birds)
  planear; **~r** n (AVIAT) planeador m; **gliding** n
  (AVIAT) vuelo sin motor
glimmer ['glɪmə*] n luz f tenue; (of interest)
  muestra; (of hope) rayo
glimpse [glɪmps] n vislumbre m ♦ vt
  vislumbrar, entrever
glint [glɪnt] vi centellear
glisten ['glɪsn] vi relucir, brillar
glitter ['glɪtə*] vi relucir, brillar
gloat [gləut] vi: **to ~ over** recrearse en
global ['gləubl] adj mundial; **~ warming**
  (re)calentamiento global o de la tierra
globe [gləub] n globo; (model) globo terráqueo
gloom [gluːm] n tinieblas fpl, oscuridad f;
  (sadness) tristeza, melancolía; **~y** adj (dark)
  oscuro; (sad) triste; (pessimistic) pesimista
glorious ['glɔːrɪəs] adj glorioso; (weather etc)
  magnífico
glory ['glɔːrɪ] n gloria
gloss [glɔs] n (shine) brillo; (paint) pintura de
  aceite; **~ over** vt fus disimular
glossary ['glɔsərɪ] n glosario
glossy ['glɔsɪ] adj lustroso; (magazine) de lujo
glove [glʌv] n guante m; **~ compartment** n
  (AUT) guantera
glow [gləu] vi brillar
glower ['glauə*] vi: **to ~ at** mirar con ceño
glue [gluː] n goma (de pegar), cemento ♦ vt
  pegar
glum [glʌm] adj (person, tone) melancólico
glut [glʌt] n superabundancia
glutton ['glʌtn] n glotón/ona m/f; **a ~ for
  work** un(a) trabajador(a) incansable
GM adj abbr (= genetically modified) transgénico
gnat [næt] n mosquito
gnaw [nɔː] vt roer
gnome [nəum] n gnomo
go [gəu] (pt **went**, pp **gone**, pl **~es**) vi ir;
  (travel) viajar; (depart) irse, marcharse;
  (work) funcionar, marchar; (be sold)
  venderse; (time) pasar; (fit, suit): **to ~ with**

hacer juego con; (become) ponerse; (break etc) estropearse, romperse ♦ n: to have a ~ (at) probar suerte (con); to be on the ~ no parar; whose ~ is it? ¿a quién le toca?; he's going to do it va a hacerlo; to ~ for a walk ir de paseo; to ~ dancing ir a bailar; how did it ~? ¿qué tal salió or resultó?, ¿cómo ha ido?; to ~ round the back pasar por detrás; ~ about vi (rumour) propagarse ♦ vt fus: how do I ~ about this? ¿cómo me las arreglo para hacer esto?; ~ ahead vi seguir adelante; ~ along vi ir ♦ vt fus bordear; to ~ along with (agree) estar de acuerdo con; ~ away vi irse, marcharse; ~ back vi volver; ~ back on vt fus (promise) faltar a; ~ by vi (time) pasar ♦ vt fus guiarse por; ~ down vi bajar; (ship) hundirse; (sun) ponerse ♦ vt fus bajar; ~ for vt fus (fetch) ir por; (like) gustar; (attack) atacar; ~ in vi entrar; ~ in for vt fus (competition) presentarse a; ~ into vt fus entrar en; (investigate) investigar; (embark on) dedicarse a; ~ off vi irse, marcharse; (food) pasarse; (explode) estallar; (event) realizarse ♦ vt fus dejar de gustar; I'm going off him/the idea ya no me gusta tanto él/la idea; ~ on vi (continue) seguir, continuar; (happen) pasar, ocurrir; to ~ on doing sth seguir haciendo algo; ~ out vi salir; (fire, light) apagarse; ~ over vi (ship) zozobrar ♦ vt fus (check) revisar; ~ through vt fus (town etc) atravesar; ~ up vi, vt fus subir; ~ without vt fus pasarse sin

goad [gəʊd] vt aguijonear

go-ahead adj (person) dinámico; (firm) innovador(a) ♦ n luz f verde

goal [gəʊl] n meta; (score) gol m; **~keeper** n portero; **~-post** n poste m (de la portería)

goat [gəʊt] n cabra

gobble ['gɒbl] vt (also: ~ down, ~ up) tragarse, engullir

go-between n intermediario/a

god [gɒd] n dios m; **G~** n Dios m; **~child** n ahijado/a; **~daughter** n ahijada; **~dess** n diosa; **~father** n padrino; **~-forsaken** adj dejado de la mano de Dios; **~mother** n madrina; **~send** n don m del cielo; **~son** n ahijado

goggles ['gɒglz] npl gafas fpl

going ['gəʊɪŋ] n (conditions) estado del terreno ♦ adj: the ~ rate la tarifa corriente or en vigor

gold [gəʊld] n oro ♦ adj de oro; **~en** adj (made of ~) de oro; (~ in colour) dorado; **~fish** n pez m de colores; **~mine** n (also fig) mina de oro; **~-plated** adj chapado en oro; **~smith** n orfebre m/f

golf [gɒlf] n golf m; ~ **ball** n (for game) pelota de golf; (on typewriter) esfera; ~ **club** n club m de golf; (stick) palo (de golf);

~ **course** n campo de golf; **~er** n golfista m/f

gone [gɒn] pp of go

good [gʊd] adj bueno; (pleasant) agradable; (kind) bueno, amable; (well-behaved) educado ♦ n bien m, provecho; **~s** npl (COMM) mercancías fpl; **~!** ¡qué bien!; **to be ~ at** tener aptitud para; **to be ~ for** servir para; **it's ~ for you** te hace bien; **would you be ~ enough to ...?** ¿podría hacerme el favor de ...?, ¿sería tan amable de ...?; **a ~ deal (of)** mucho; **a ~ many** muchos; **to make ~** reparar; **it's no ~ complaining** no vale la pena (de) quejarse; **for ~** para siempre, definitivamente; ~ **morning/afternoon** ¡buenos días/buenas tardes!; ~ **evening!** ¡buenas noches!; ~ **night!** ¡buenas noches!; **~bye!** ¡adiós!; **to say ~bye** despedirse; **G~ Friday** n Viernes m Santo; **~-looking** adj guapo; **~-natured** adj amable, simpático; **~ness** n (of person) bondad f; **for ~ness sake!** ¡por Dios!; **~ness gracious!** ¡Dios mío!; **~s train** n (BRIT) n tren m de mercancías; **~will** n buena voluntad f

goose [guːs] (pl geese) n ganso, oca

gooseberry ['guːzbərɪ] n grosella espinosa; **to play ~** hacer de carabina

gooseflesh ['guːsfleʃ] n = **goose pimples**

goose pimples npl carne f de gallina

gore [gɔː*] vt cornear ♦ n sangre f

gorge [gɔːdʒ] n barranco ♦ vr: **to ~ o.s. (on)** atracarse (de)

gorgeous ['gɔːdʒəs] adj (thing) precioso; (weather) espléndido; (person) guapísimo

gorilla [gəˈrɪlə] n gorila m

gorse [gɔːs] n tojo

gory ['gɔːrɪ] adj sangriento

go-slow (BRIT) n huelga de manos caídas

gospel ['gɒspl] n evangelio

gossip ['gɒsɪp] n (scandal) cotilleo, chismes mpl; (chat) charla; (scandalmonger) cotilla m/f, chismoso/a ♦ vi cotillear

got [gɒt] pt, pp of get; **~ten** (US) pp of get

gout [gaʊt] n gota

govern ['gʌvən] vt gobernar; (influence) dominar; **~ess** n institutriz f; **~ment** n gobierno; **~or** n gobernador(a) m/f; (of school etc) miembro del consejo; (of jail) director(a) m/f

gown [gaʊn] n traje m; (of teacher, BRIT: of judge) toga

G.P. n abbr = **general practitioner**

grab [græb] vt coger (SP) or agarrar (AM), arrebatar ♦ vi: **to ~ at** intentar agarrar

grace [greɪs] n gracia ♦ vt honrar; (adorn) adornar; **5 days' ~** un plazo de 5 días; **~ful** adj grácil, ágil; (style, shape) elegante, gracioso; **gracious** ['greɪʃəs] adj amable

grade [greɪd] n (quality) clase f, calidad f; (in

hierarchy) grado; (*SCOL: mark*) nota; (*US: school class*) curso ♦ *vt* clasificar; **~ crossing** (*US*) *n* paso a nivel; **~ school** (*US*) *n* escuela primaria

gradient ['greɪdɪənt] *n* pendiente *f*

gradual ['grædjuəl] *adj* paulatino; **~ly** *adv* paulatinamente

graduate [*n* 'grædjuɪt, *vb* 'grædjueɪt] *n* (*US: of high school*) graduado/a; (*of university*) licenciado/a ♦ *vi* graduarse; licenciarse; **graduation** [-'eɪʃən] *n* (*ceremony*) entrega del título

graffiti [grə'fiːtɪ] *n* pintadas *fpl*

graft [grɑːft] *n* (*AGR, MED*) injerto; (*BRIT: inf*) trabajo duro; (*bribery*) corrupción *f* ♦ *vt* injertar

grain [greɪn] *n* (*single particle*) grano; (*corn*) granos *mpl*, cereales *mpl*; (*of wood*) fibra

gram [græm] *n* gramo

grammar ['græmə*] *n* gramática; **~ school** (*BRIT*) *n* ≈ instituto de segunda enseñanza, liceo (*SP*)

grammatical [grə'mætɪkl] *adj* gramatical

gramme [græm] *n* = **gram**

gramophone ['græməfəun] (*BRIT*) *n* tocadiscos *m inv*

grand [grænd] *adj* magnífico, imponente; (*wonderful*) estupendo; (*gesture etc*) grandioso; **~children** *npl* nietos *mpl*; **~dad** (*inf*) *n* yayo, abuelito; **~daughter** *n* nieta; **~eur** ['grændjə*] *n* magnificencia, lo grandioso; **~father** *n* abuelo; **~ma** (*inf*) *n* yaya, abuelita; **~mother** *n* abuela; **~pa** (*inf*) *n* = **~dad**; **~parents** *npl* abuelos *mpl*; **~ piano** *n* piano de cola; **~son** *n* nieto; **~stand** *n* (*SPORT*) tribuna

granite ['grænɪt] *n* granito

granny ['grænɪ] (*inf*) *n* abuelita, yaya

grant [grɑːnt] *vt* (*concede*) conceder; (*admit*) reconocer ♦ *n* (*SCOL*) beca; (*ADMIN*) subvención *f*; **to take sth/sb for ~ed** dar algo por sentado/no hacer ningún caso a uno

granulated sugar ['grænjuːleɪtɪd-] (*BRIT*) *n* azúcar *m* blanquilla

grape [greɪp] *n* uva

grapefruit ['greɪpfruːt] *n* pomelo (*SP*), toronja (*AM*)

graph [grɑːf] *n* gráfica; **~ic** ['græfɪk] *adj* gráfico; **~ics** *n* artes *fpl* gráficas ♦ *npl* (*drawings*) dibujos *mpl*

grapple ['græpl] *vi*: **to ~ with sth/sb** agarrar a algo/uno

grasp [grɑːsp] *vt* agarrar, asir; (*understand*) comprender ♦ *n* (*grip*) asimiento; (*understanding*) comprensión *f*; **~ing** *adj* (*mean*) avaro

grass [grɑːs] *n* hierba; (*lawn*) césped *m*; **~hopper** *n* saltamontes *m inv*; **~-roots** *adj* (*fig*) popular

grate [greɪt] *n* parrilla de chimenea ♦ *vi*: **to ~ (on)** chirriar (sobre) ♦ *vt* (*CULIN*) rallar

grateful ['greɪtful] *adj* agradecido

grater ['greɪtə*] *n* rallador *m*

gratifying ['grætɪfaɪɪŋ] *adj* grato

grating ['greɪtɪŋ] *n* (*iron bars*) reja ♦ *adj* (*noise*) áspero

gratitude ['grætɪtjuːd] *n* agradecimiento

gratuity [grə'tjuːɪtɪ] *n* gratificación *f*

grave [greɪv] *n* tumba ♦ *adj* serio, grave

gravel ['grævl] *n* grava

gravestone ['greɪvstəun] *n* lápida

graveyard ['greɪvjɑːd] *n* cementerio

gravity ['grævɪtɪ] *n* gravedad *f*

gravy ['greɪvɪ] *n* salsa de carne

gray [greɪ] *adj* = **grey**

graze [greɪz] *vi* pacer ♦ *vt* (*touch lightly*) rozar; (*scrape*) raspar ♦ *n* (*MED*) abrasión *f*

grease [griːs] *n* (*fat*) grasa; (*lubricant*) lubricante *m* ♦ *vt* engrasar; lubrificar; **~proof paper** (*BRIT*) *n* papel *m* apergaminado; **greasy** *adj* grasiento

great [greɪt] *adj* grande; (*inf*) magnífico, estupendo; **G~ Britain** *n* Gran Bretaña; **~-grandfather** *n* bisabuelo; **~-grandmother** *n* bisabuela; **~ly** *adv* muy; (*with verb*) mucho; **~ness** *n* grandeza

Greece [griːs] *n* Grecia

greed [griːd] *n* (*also: ~iness*) codicia, avaricia; (*for food*) gula; (*for power etc*) avidez *f*; **~y** *adj* avaro; (*for food*) glotón/ona

Greek [griːk] *adj* griego ♦ *n* griego/a; (*LING*) griego

green [griːn] *adj* (*also POL*) verde; (*inexperienced*) novato ♦ *n* verde *m*; (*stretch of grass*) césped *m*; (*GOLF*) green *m*; **~s** *npl* (*vegetables*) verduras *fpl*; **~ belt** *n* zona verde; **~ card** *n* (*AUT*) carta verde; (*US: work permit*) permiso de trabajo para los extranjeros en EE. UU.; **~ery** *n* verdura; **~grocer** (*BRIT*) *n* verdulero/a; **~house** *n* invernadero; **~house effect** *n* efecto invernadero; **~house gas** *n* gases *mpl* de invernadero; **~ish** *adj* verdoso

Greenland ['griːnlənd] *n* Groenlandia

greet [griːt] *vt* (*welcome*) dar la bienvenida a; (*receive: news*) recibir; **~ing** *n* (*welcome*) bienvenida; **~ing(s) card** *n* tarjeta de felicitación

grenade [grə'neɪd] *n* granada

grew [gruː] *pt* of **grow**

grey [greɪ] *adj* gris; (*weather*) sombrío; **~-haired** *adj* canoso; **~hound** *n* galgo

grid [grɪd] *n* reja; (*ELEC*) red *f*; **~lock** *n* (*traffic jam*) retención *f*

grief [griːf] *n* dolor *m*, pena

grievance ['griːvəns] *n* motivo de queja, agravio

grieve [griːv] *vi* afligirse, acongojarse ♦ *vt* dar pena a; **to ~ for** llorar por

grievous ['griːvəs] adj: ~ **bodily harm** (LAW) daños mpl corporales graves

grill [grɪl] n (on cooker) parrilla; (also: mixed ~) parrillada ♦ vt (BRIT) asar a la parrilla; (inf: question) interrogar

grille [grɪl] n reja; (AUT) rejilla

grim [grɪm] adj (place) sombrío; (situation) triste; (person) ceñudo

grimace [grɪ'meɪs] n mueca ♦ vi hacer muecas

grime [graɪm] n mugre f, suciedad f

grin [grɪn] n sonrisa abierta ♦ vi sonreír abiertamente

grind [graɪnd] (pt, pp ground) vt (coffee, pepper etc) moler; (US: meat) picar; (make sharp) afilar ♦ n (work) rutina

grip [grɪp] n (hold) asimiento; (control) control m, dominio; (of tyre etc): **to have a good/bad ~** agarrarse bien/mal; (handle) asidero; (holdall) maletín m ♦ vt agarrar; (viewer, reader) fascinar; **to get to ~s with** enfrentarse con; ~**ping** adj absorbente

grisly ['grɪzlɪ] adj horripilante, horrible

gristle ['grɪsl] n ternilla

grit [grɪt] n gravilla; (courage) valor m ♦ vt (road) poner gravilla en; **to ~ one's teeth** apretar los dientes

groan [grəun] n gemido; quejido ♦ vi gemir; quejarse

grocer ['grəusə*] n tendero (de ultramarinos (SP)); ~**ies** npl comestibles mpl; ~**'s (shop)** n tienda de ultramarinos or de abarrotes (AM)

groin [grɔɪn] n ingle f

groom [gruːm] n mozo/a de cuadra; (also: bride~) novio ♦ vt (horse) almohazar; (fig): **to ~ sb for** preparar a uno para; **well-~ed** de buena presencia

groove [gruːv] n ranura, surco

grope [grəup] **to ~ for** vt fus buscar a tientas

gross [grəus] adj (neglect, injustice) grave; (vulgar: behaviour) grosero; (: appearance) de mal gusto; (COMM) bruto; ~**ly** adv (greatly) enormemente

grotto ['grɔtəu] n gruta

grotty ['grɔtɪ] (inf) adj horrible

ground [graund] pt, pp of **grind** ♦ n suelo, tierra, (SPORT) campo, terreno; (reason: gen pl) causa, razón f; (US: also: ~ wire) tierra ♦ vt (plane) mantener en tierra; (US: ELEC) conectar con tierra; ~**s** npl (of coffee etc) poso; (gardens etc) jardines mpl, parque m; **on the ~** en el suelo; **to the ~** al suelo; **to gain/lose ~** ganar/perder terreno; ~ **cloth** (US) n = ~**sheet**; ~**ing** n (in education) conocimientos mpl básicos; ~**less** adj infundado; ~**sheet** (BRIT) n tela impermeable; suelo; ~ **staff** n personal m de tierra; ~**work** n preparación f

group [gruːp] n grupo; (musical) conjunto

♦ vt (also: ~ together) agrupar ♦ vi (also: ~ together) agruparse

grouse [graus] n inv (bird) urogallo ♦ vi (complain) quejarse

grove [grəuv] n arboleda

grovel ['grɔvl] vi (fig): **to ~ before** humillarse ante

grow [grəu] (pt **grew**, pp **grown**) vi crecer; (increase) aumentar; (expand) desarrollarse; (become) volverse; **to ~ rich/weak** enriquecerse/debilitarse ♦ vt cultivar; (hair, beard) dejar crecer; ~ **up** vi crecer, hacerse hombre/mujer; ~**er** n cultivador(a) m/f, productor(a) m/f; ~**ing** adj creciente

growl [graul] vi gruñir

grown [grəun] pp of **grow**; ~-**up** n adulto, mayor m/f

growth [grəuθ] n crecimiento, desarrollo; (what has grown) brote m; (MED) tumor m

grub [grʌb] n larva, gusano; (inf: food) comida

grubby ['grʌbɪ] adj sucio, mugriento

grudge [grʌdʒ] n (motivo de) rencor m ♦ vt: **to ~ sb sth** dar algo a uno de mala gana; **to bear sb a ~** guardar rencor a uno

gruelling ['gruəlɪŋ] (US **grueling**) adj penoso, duro

gruesome ['gruːsəm] adj horrible

gruff [grʌf] adj (voice) ronco; (manner) brusco

grumble ['grʌmbl] vi refunfuñar, quejarse

grumpy ['grʌmpɪ] adj gruñón/ona

grunt [grʌnt] vi gruñir

G-string ['dʒiːstrɪŋ] n taparrabo

guarantee [gærən'tiː] n garantía ♦ vt garantizar

guard [gaːd] n (squad) guardia; (one man) guardia m; (BRIT: RAIL) jefe m de tren; (on machine) dispositivo de seguridad; (also: fire~) rejilla de protección ♦ vt guardar; (prisoner) vigilar; **to be on one's ~** estar alerta; ~ **against** vt fus (prevent) protegerse de; ~**ed** adj (fig) cauteloso; ~**ian** n guardián/ana m/f; (of minor) tutor(a) m/f; ~**'s van** n (BRIT: RAIL) furgón m

Guatemala [gwætɪ'maːlə] n Guatemala; ~**n** adj, n guatemalteco/a m/f

guerrilla [gə'rɪlə] n guerrillero/a

guess [ges] vi adivinar; (US) suponer ♦ vt adivinar; suponer ♦ n suposición f, conjetura; **to take** or **have a ~** tratar de adivinar; ~**work** n conjeturas fpl

guest [gest] n invitado/a; (in hotel) huésped(a) m/f; ~ **house** n casa de huéspedes, pensión f; ~ **room** n cuarto de huéspedes·

guffaw [gʌ'fɔː] vi reírse a carcajadas

guidance ['gaɪdəns] n (advice) consejos mpl

guide [gaɪd] n (person) guía m/f; (book, fig) guía ♦ vt (round museum etc) guiar; (lead)

conducir; (direct) orientar; **(girl)** ~ n
exploradora; **~book** n guía; **~ dog** n perro
m guía; **~lines** npl (advice) directrices fpl
guild [gɪld] n gremio
guilt [gɪlt] n culpabilidad f; **~y** adj culpable
guinea pig ['gɪnɪ-] n cobaya; (fig) conejillo
de Indias
guise [gaɪz] n: **in** or **under the ~ of** bajo
apariencia de
guitar [gɪ'tɑː*] n guitarra
gulf [gʌlf] n golfo; (abyss) abismo
gull [gʌl] n gaviota
gullible ['gʌlɪbl] adj crédulo
gully ['gʌlɪ] n barranco
gulp [gʌlp] vi tragar saliva ♦ vt (also: ~ down)
tragarse
gum [gʌm] n (ANAT) encía; (glue) goma,
cemento; (sweet) caramelo de goma; (also:
chewing-~) chicle m ♦ vt pegar con goma;
~boots (BRIT) npl botas fpl de goma
gun [gʌn] n (small) pistola, revólver m;
(shotgun) escopeta; (rifle) fusil m; (cannon)
cañón m; **~boat** n cañonero; **~fire** n
disparos mpl; **~man** n pistolero; **~point** n:
at ~point a mano armada; **~powder** n
pólvora; **~shot** n escopetazo
gurgle ['gəːgl] vi (baby) gorgotear; (water)
borbotear
gush [gʌʃ] vi salir a raudales; (person)
deshacerse en efusiones
gust [gʌst] n (of wind) ráfaga
gusto ['gʌstəu] n entusiasmo
gut [gʌt] n intestino; **~s** npl (ANAT) tripas fpl;
(courage) valor m
gutter ['gʌtə*] n (of roof) canalón m; (in
street) cuneta
guy [gaɪ] n (also: ~rope) cuerda; (inf: man) tío
(SP), tipo; (figure) monigote m
guzzle ['gʌzl] vi tragar ♦ vt engullir
gym [dʒɪm] n (also: gymnasium) gimnasio;
(also: gymnastics) gimnasia; **~nast** n
gimnasta m/f; **~ shoes** npl zapatillas fpl (de
deporte); **~ slip** (BRIT) n túnica de colegiala
gynaecologist [gaɪnɪ'kɔlədʒɪst] (US **gyne-
cologist**) n ginecólogo/a
gypsy ['dʒɪpsɪ] n gitano/a

H, h

haberdashery [hæbə'dæʃərɪ] (BRIT) n
mercería
habit ['hæbɪt] n hábito, costumbre f; (drug ~)
adicción f; (costume) hábito
habitual [hə'bɪtjuəl] adj acostumbrado,
habitual; (drinker, liar) empedernido
hack [hæk] vt (cut) cortar; (slice) tajar ♦ n
(pej: writer) escritor(a) m/f a sueldo; **~er** n
(COMPUT) pirata m/f informático/a

hackneyed ['hæknɪd] adj trillado
had [hæd] pt, pp of **have**
haddock ['hædək] (pl ~ or ~s) n especie de
merluza
hadn't ['hædnt] = **had not**
haemorrhage ['heməɪdʒ] (US **hemorrhage**)
n hemorragia
haemorrhoids ['hemərɔɪdz] (US **hemorrhoids**) npl hemorroides fpl
haggle ['hægl] vi regatear
Hague [heɪg] n: **The ~** La Haya
hail [heɪl] n granizo; (fig) lluvia ♦ vt saludar;
(taxi) llamar a; (acclaim) aclamar ♦ vi
granizar; **~stone** n (piedra de) granizo
hair [heə*] n pelo, cabellos mpl; (one ~) pelo,
cabello; (on legs etc) vello; **to do one's ~**
arreglarse el pelo; **to have grey ~** tener canas
fpl; **~brush** n cepillo (para el pelo); **~cut** n
corte m (de pelo); **~do** n peinado; **~dresser**
n peluquero/a; **~dresser's** n peluquería;
~ dryer n secador m de pelo; **~grip** n
horquilla; **~net** n redecilla; **~piece** n postizo;
~pin n horquilla; **~pin bend** (US **~pin curve**)
n curva de horquilla; **~raising** adj
espeluznante; **~ removing cream** n crema
depilatoria; **~ spray** n laca; **~style** n
peinado; **~y** adj peludo, velludo; (inf:
frightening) espeluznante
hake [heɪk] (pl inv or ~s) n merluza
half [hɑːf] (pl **halves**) n mitad f; (of beer) ≈
caña (SP), media pinta; (RAIL, BUS) billete m
de niño ♦ adj medio ♦ adv medio, a medias;
two and a ~ dos y media; **~ a dozen** media
docena; **~ a pound** media libra; **to cut sth in
~** cortar algo por la mitad; **~-caste**
['hɑːfkɑːst] n mestizo/a; **~-hearted** adj
indiferente, poco entusiasta; **~-hour** n media
hora; **~-mast** n: **at ~-mast** (flag) a media
asta; **~-price** adj, adv a mitad de precio;
~ term (BRIT) n (SCOL) vacaciones de
mediados del trimestre; **~-time** n descanso;
~way adv a medio camino; (in period of
time) a mitad de
hall [hɔːl] n (for concerts) sala; (entrance way)
hall m; vestíbulo; **~ of residence** (BRIT) n
residencia
hallmark ['hɔːlmɑːk] n sello
hallo [hə'ləu] excl = **hello**
Hallowe'en [hæləu'iːn] n víspera de Todos
los Santos
hallucination [həluːsɪ'neɪʃən] n alucinación
f
hallway ['hɔːlweɪ] n vestíbulo
halo ['heɪləu] n (of saint) halo, aureola
halt [hɔːlt] n (stop) alto, parada ♦ vt parar;
interrumpir ♦ vi pararse
halve [hɑːv] vt partir por la mitad
halves [hɑːvz] npl of **half**
ham [hæm] n jamón m (cocido)

hamburger ['hæmbɜ:gə*] n hamburguesa
hamlet ['hæmlɪt] n aldea
hammer ['hæmə*] n martillo ♦ vt (nail)
clavar; (force): **to ~ an idea into sb/a message
across** meter una idea en la cabeza a uno/
machacar una idea ♦ vi dar golpes
hammock ['hæmək] n hamaca
hamper ['hæmpə*] vt estorbar ♦ n cesto
hand [hænd] n mano f; (of clock) aguja;
(writing) letra; (worker) obrero ♦ vt dar,
pasar; **to give** or **lend sb a ~** echar una mano
a uno, ayudar a uno; **at ~** a mano; **in ~** (time)
libre; (job etc) entre manos; **on ~** (person,
services) a mano, al alcance; **to ~** (information
etc) a mano; **on the one ~ ...**, **on the other
~ ...** por una parte ... por otra (parte) ...; **~ in
vt** entregar; **~ out** vt distribuir; **~ over** vt
(deliver) entregar; **~bag** n bolso (SP), cartera
(AM); **~book** n manual m; **~brake** n freno
de mano; **~cuffs** npl esposas fpl; **~ful** n
puñado
handicap ['hændɪkæp] n minusvalía;
(disadvantage) desventaja; (SPORT) handicap
m ♦ vt estorbar; **mentally/physically ~ped**
deficiente m/f (mental)/minusválido/a
(físico/a)
handicraft ['hændɪkrɑːft] n artesanía;
(object) objeto de artesanía
handiwork ['hændɪwɜːk] n obra
handkerchief ['hæŋkətʃɪf] n pañuelo
handle ['hændl] n (of door etc) tirador m; (of
cup etc) asa; (of knife etc) mango; (for
winding) manivela ♦ vt (touch) tocar; (deal
with) encargarse de; (treat: people) manejar;
"~ with care" "(manéjese) con cuidado"; **to
fly off the ~** perder los estribos; **~bar(s)** n(pl)
manillar m
hand: ~ luggage n equipaje m de mano;
~made adj hecho a mano; **~out** n (money
etc) limosna; (leaflet) folleto; **~rail** n
pasamanos m inv; **~shake** n apretón m de
manos
handsome ['hænsəm] adj guapo; (building)
bello; (fig: profit) considerable
handwriting ['hændraɪtɪŋ] n letra
handy ['hændɪ] adj (close at hand) a la
mano; (tool etc) práctico; (skilful) hábil,
diestro
hang [hæŋ] (pt, pp hung) vt colgar; (criminal:
pt, pp hanged) ahorcar ♦ vi (painting, coat
etc) colgar; (hair, drapery) caer; **to get the
~ of sth** (inf) lograr dominar algo; **~ about**
or **around** vi haraganear; **~ on** vi (wait)
esperar; **~ up** vi (TEL) colgar ♦ vt colgar
hanger ['hæŋə*] n percha; **~on** n parásito
hang: ~gliding [-glaɪdɪŋ] n vuelo libre;
~over n (after drinking) resaca; **~up** n
complejo
hanker ['hæŋkə*] vi: **to ~ after** añorar

hankie ['hæŋkɪ], **hanky** ['hæŋkɪ] n abbr =
handkerchief
haphazard [hæp'hæzəd] adj fortuito
happen ['hæpən] vi suceder, ocurrir;
(chance): **he ~ed to hear/see** dió la casualidad
de que oyó/vió; **as it ~s** da la casualidad de
que; **~ing** n suceso, acontecimiento
happily ['hæpɪlɪ] adv (luckily) afortunadamente; (cheerfully) alegremente
happiness ['hæpɪnɪs] n felicidad f;
(cheerfulness) alegría
happy ['hæpɪ] adj feliz; (cheerful) alegre; **to
be ~ (with)** estar contento (con); **to be ~ to
do** estar encantado de hacer; **~ birthday!** ¡feliz
cumpleaños!; **~-go-lucky** adj despreocupado; **~ hour** n horas en las que la bebida es
más barata, happy hour f
harass ['hærəs] vt acosar, hostigar; **~ment** n
persecución f
harbour ['hɑːbə*] (US **harbor**) n puerto ♦ vt
(fugitive) dar abrigo a; (hope etc) abrigar
hard [hɑːd] adj duro; (difficult) difícil; (work)
arduo; (person) severo; (fact) innegable
♦ adv (work) mucho, duro; (think)
profundamente; **to look ~ at** clavar los ojos
en; **to try ~** esforzarse; **no ~ feelings!** ¡sin
rencor(es)!; **to be ~ of hearing** ser duro de
oído; **to be ~ done by** ser tratado
injustamente; **~back** n libro en cartoné;
~ cash n dinero contante; **~ disk** n
(COMPUT) disco duro o rígido; **~en** vt
endurecer; (fig) curtir ♦ vi endurecerse;
curtirse; **~-headed** adj realista; **~ labour** n
trabajos mpl forzados
hardly ['hɑːdlɪ] adv apenas; **~ ever** casi nunca
hard: ~ship n privación f; **~ shoulder** (BRIT)
n (AUT) arcén m; **~-up** (inf) adj sin un duro
(SP), sin plata (AM); **~ware** n ferretería;
(COMPUT) hardware m; (MIL) armamento;
~ware shop n ferretería; **~-wearing** adj
resistente, duradero; **~-working** adj
trabajador/a
hardy ['hɑːdɪ] adj fuerte; (plant) resistente
hare [heə*] n liebre f; **~-brained** adj
descabellado
harm [hɑːm] n daño, mal m ♦ vt (person)
hacer daño a; (health, interests) perjudicar;
(thing) dañar; **out of ~'s way** a salvo; **~ful** adj
dañino; **~less** adj (person) inofensivo; (joke
etc) inocente
harmony ['hɑːmənɪ] n armonía
harness ['hɑːnɪs] n arreos mpl; (for child)
arnés m; (safety ~) arneses mpl ♦ vt (horse)
enjaezar; (resources) aprovechar
harp [hɑːp] n arpa ♦ vi: **to ~ on (about)**
machacar (con)
harrowing ['hærəʊɪŋ] adj angustioso
harsh [hɑːʃ] adj (cruel) duro, cruel; (severe)
severo; (sound) áspero; (light)

deslumbrador(a)

harvest ['hɑ:vɪst] n (~ time) siega; (of cereals etc) cosecha; (of grapes) vendimia ♦ vt cosechar

has [hæz] vb see have

hash [hæʃ] n (CULIN) picadillo; (fig: mess) lío

hashish ['hæʃɪʃ] n hachís m

hasn't ['hæznt] = has not

hassle ['hæsl] (inf) n lata

haste [heɪst] n prisa; ~n ['heɪsn] vt acelerar ♦ vi darse prisa; **hastily** adv de prisa; precipitadamente; **hasty** adj apresurado; (rash) precipitado

hat [hæt] n sombrero

hatch [hætʃ] n (NAUT: also: ~way) escotilla; (also: service ~) ventanilla ♦ vi (bird) salir del cascarón ♦ vt incubar; (plot) tramar; 5 eggs have ~ed han salido 5 pollos

hatchback ['hætʃbæk] n (AUT) tres or cinco puertas m

hatchet ['hætʃɪt] n hacha

hate [heɪt] vt odiar, aborrecer ♦ n odio; ~**ful** adj odioso; **hatred** ['heɪtrɪd] n odio

haughty ['hɔ:tɪ] adj altanero

haul [hɔ:l] vt tirar ♦ n (of fish) redada; (of stolen goods etc) botín m; ~**age** (BRIT) n transporte m; (costs) gastos mpl de transporte; ~**ier** (US ~**er**) n transportista m/f

haunch [hɔ:ntʃ] n anca; (of meat) pierna

haunt [hɔ:nt] vt (subj: ghost) aparecerse en; (obsess) obsesionar ♦ n guarida

---

KEYWORD

have [hæv] (pt, pp **had**) aux vb **1** (gen) haber; to ~ arrived/eaten haber llegado/comido; **having finished** or **when he had finished**, he left cuando hubo acabado, se fue

2 (in tag questions): you've done it, ~n't you? lo has hecho, ¿verdad? or ¿no?

3 (in short answers and questions): I ~n't no; so I ~ pues, es verdad; we ~n't paid — yes we ~! no hemos pagado — ¡sí que hemos pagado!; **I've been there before, ~ you?** he estado allí antes, ¿y tú?

♦ modal aux vb (be obliged): to ~ (got) to do sth tener que hacer algo; you ~n't to tell her no hay que or no debes decírselo

♦ vt **1** (possess): he has (got) blue eyes/dark hair tiene los ojos azules/el pelo negro

2 (referring to meals etc): to ~ breakfast/lunch/dinner desayunar/comer/cenar; to ~ a drink/a cigarette tomar algo/fumar un cigarrillo

3 (receive) recibir; (obtain) obtener; may I ~ your address? ¿puedes darme tu dirección?; you can ~ it for £5 te lo puedes quedar por £5; I must ~ it by tomorrow lo necesito para mañana; to ~ a baby tener un niño or bebé

4 (maintain, allow): I won't ~ it/this

nonsense! ¡no lo permitiré!/¡no permitiré estas tonterías!; **we can't ~ that** no podemos permitir eso

5: to ~ sth done hacer or mandar hacer algo; to ~ one's hair cut cortarse el pelo; to ~ sb do sth hacer que alguien haga algo

6 (experience, suffer): to ~ a cold/flu tener un resfriado/la gripe; she had her bag stolen/her arm broken le robaron el bolso/se rompió un brazo; to ~ an operation operarse

7 (+ noun): to ~ a swim/walk/bath/rest nadar/dar un paseo/darse un baño/descansar; let's ~ a look vamos a ver; to ~ a meeting/party celebrar una reunión/una fiesta; let me ~ a try déjame intentarlo

have out vt: to ~ it out with sb (settle a problem etc) dejar las cosas en claro con alguien

---

haven ['heɪvn] n puerto; (fig) refugio

haven't ['hævnt] = have not

havoc ['hævək] n estragos mpl

hawk [hɔ:k] n halcón m

hay [heɪ] n heno; ~ **fever** n fiebre f del heno; ~**stack** n almiar m

haywire ['heɪwaɪə*] (inf) adj: **to go ~** (plan) embrollarse

hazard ['hæzəd] n peligro ♦ vt aventurar; ~**ous** adj peligroso; ~ **warning lights** npl (AUT) señales fpl de emergencia

haze [heɪz] n neblina

hazelnut ['heɪzlnʌt] n avellana

hazy ['heɪzɪ] adj brumoso; (idea) vago

he [hi:] pron él; ~ **who ...** él que ..., quien ...

head [hed] n cabeza; (leader) jefe/a m/f; (of school) director(a) m/f ♦ vt (list) encabezar; (group) capitanear; (company) dirigir; ~**s (or tails)** cara (o cruz); ~ **first** de cabeza; ~ **over heels** (in love) perdidamente; **to ~ the ball** cabecear (la pelota); ~ **for** vt fus dirigirse a; (disaster) ir camino de; ~**ache** n dolor m de cabeza; ~**dress** n tocado; ~**ing** n título; ~**lamp** (BRIT) n ~ **light**; ~**land** n promontorio; ~**light** n faro; ~**line** n titular m; ~**long** adv (fall) de cabeza; (rush) precipitadamente; ~**master/mistress** n director(a) m/f (de escuela); ~ **office** n oficina central, central f; ~**-on** adj (collision) de frente; ~**phones** npl auriculares mpl; ~**quarters** npl sede f central; (MIL) cuartel m general; ~**rest** n reposa-cabezas m inv; ~**room** n (in car) altura interior; (under bridge) (límite m de) altura; ~**scarf** n pañuelo; ~**strong** adj testarudo; ~ **waiter** n maître m; ~**way** n: **to make ~way** (fig) hacer progresos; ~**wind** n viento contrario; ~**y** adj (experience, period) apasionante; (wine) cabezón; (atmosphere) embriagador(a)

heal [hi:l] vt curar ♦ vi cicatrizarse

health [hɛlθ] n salud f; ~ **food** n alimentos mpl orgánicos; **the H~ Service** (BRIT) n el servicio de salud pública; ≈ el Insalud (SP); ~**y** adj sano, saludable

heap [hi:p] n montón m ♦ vt: **to ~ (up)** amontonar; **to ~ sth with** llenar algo hasta arriba de; ~**s of** un montón de

hear [hɪə*] (pt, pp **heard**) vt (also LAW) oír; (news) saber ♦ vi oír; **to ~ about** oír hablar de; **to ~ from sb** tener noticias de uno; ~**ing** n (sense) oído; (LAW) vista; ~**ing aid** n audífono; ~**say** n rumores mpl, habillas fpl

hearse [hɜ:s] n coche m fúnebre

heart [hɑ:t] n corazón m; (fig) valor m; (of lettuce) cogollo; ~**s** npl (CARDS) corazones mpl; **to lose/take ~** descorazonarse/cobrar ánimo; **at ~** en el fondo; **by ~** (learn, know) de memoria; ~ **attack** n infarto (de miocardio); ~**beat** n latido (del corazón); ~**breaking** adj desgarrador(a); ~**broken** adj: **she was ~broken about it** esto le partió el corazón; ~**burn** n acedía; ~ **failure** n fallo cardíaco; ~**felt** adj (deeply felt) más sentido

hearth [hɑ:θ] n (fireplace) chimenea

hearty ['hɑ:tɪ] adj (person) campechano; (laugh) sano; (dislike, support) absoluto

heat [hi:t] n calor m; (SPORT: also: **qualifying ~**) prueba eliminatoria ♦ vt calentar; ~ **up** vi calentarse ♦ vt calentar; ~**ed** adj caliente; (fig) acalorado; ~**er** n estufa; (in car) calefacción f

heath [hi:θ] (BRIT) n brezal m

heather ['hɛðə*] n brezo

heating ['hi:tɪŋ] n calefacción f

heatstroke ['hi:tstrəʊk] n insolación f

heatwave ['hi:tweɪv] n ola de calor

heave [hi:v] vt (pull) tirar; (push) empujar con esfuerzo; (lift) levantar (con esfuerzo) ♦ vi (chest) palpitar; (retch) tener náuseas ♦ n tirón m; empujón m; **to ~ a sigh** suspirar

heaven ['hɛvn] n cielo; (fig) una maravilla; ~**ly** adj celestial; (fig) maravilloso

heavily ['hɛvɪlɪ] adv pesadamente; (drink, smoke) con exceso; (sleep, sigh) profundamente; (depend) mucho

heavy ['hɛvɪ] adj pesado; (work, blow) duro; (sea, rain, meal) fuerte; (drinker, smoker) grande; (responsibility) grave; (schedule) ocupado; (weather) bochornoso; ~ **goods vehicle** n vehículo pesado; ~**weight** n (SPORT) peso pesado

Hebrew ['hi:bru:] adj, n (LING) hebreo

heckle ['hɛkl] vt interrumpir

hectic ['hɛktɪk] adj agitado

he'd [hi:d] = **he would; he had**

hedge [hɛdʒ] n seto ♦ vi contestar con evasivas; **to ~ one's bets** (fig) cubrirse

hedgehog ['hɛdʒhɔg] n erizo

heed [hi:d] vt (also: take ~ of) (pay attention to) hacer caso de; ~**less** adj: **to be ~less (of)** no hacer caso (de)

heel [hi:l] n talón m; (of shoe) tacón m ♦ vt (shoe) poner tacón a

hefty ['hɛftɪ] adj (person) fornido; (parcel, profit) gordo

heifer ['hɛfə*] n novilla, ternera

height [haɪt] n (of person) estatura; (of building) altura; (high ground) cerro; (altitude) altitud f; (fig: of season): **at the ~ of summer** en los días más calurosos del verano; (: of power etc) cúspide f; (: of stupidity etc) colmo; ~**en** vt elevar; (fig) aumentar

heir [ɛə*] n heredero; ~**ess** n heredera; ~**loom** n reliquia de familia

held [hɛld] pt, pp of **hold**

helicopter ['hɛlɪkɒptə*] n helicóptero

hell [hɛl] n infierno; ~! (inf) ¡demonios!

he'll [hi:l] = **he will; he shall**

hello [hə'ləʊ] excl ¡hola!; (to attract attention) ¡oiga!; (surprise) ¡caramba!

helm [hɛlm] n (NAUT) timón m

helmet ['hɛlmɪt] n casco

help [hɛlp] n ayuda; (cleaner etc) criada, asistenta ♦ vt ayudar; ~! ¡socorro!; ~ **yourself** sírvete; **he can't ~ it** no es culpa suya; ~**er** n ayudante m/f; ~**ful** adj útil; (person) servicial; (advice) útil; ~**ing** n ración f; ~**less** adj (incapable) incapaz; (defenceless) indefenso

hem [hɛm] n dobladillo ♦ vt poner o coser el dobladillo; ~ **in** vt cercar

hemorrhage ['hɛmərɪdʒ] (US) n = **haemorrhage**

hemorrhoids ['hɛmərɔɪdz] (US) npl = **haemorrhoids**

hen [hɛn] n gallina; (female bird) hembra

hence [hɛns] adv (therefore) por lo tanto; **2 years ~** de aquí a 2 años; ~**forth** adv de hoy en adelante

hepatitis [hɛpə'taɪtɪs] n hepatitis f

her [hɜ:*] pron (direct) la; (indirect) le; (stressed, after prep) ella ♦ adj su; see also **me; my**

herald ['hɛrəld] n heraldo ♦ vt anunciar; ~**ry** n heráldica

herb [hɜ:b] n hierba

herd [hɜ:d] n rebaño

here [hɪə*] adv aquí; (at this point) en este punto; ~! (present) ¡presente!; ~ **is/are** aquí está/están; ~ **she is** aquí está; ~**after** adv en el futuro; ~**by** adv (in letter) por la presente

heritage ['hɛrɪtɪdʒ] n patrimonio

hermit ['hɜ:mɪt] n ermitaño/a

hernia ['hɜ:nɪə] n hernia

hero ['hɪərəʊ] (pl ~**es**) n héroe m; (in book, film) protagonista m

heroin ['hɛrəʊɪn] n heroína

heroine ['hɛrəʊɪn] n heroína; (in book, film) protagonista

heron ['herən] n garza
herring ['herɪŋ] n arenque m
hers [hə:z] pron (el) suyo/(la) suya etc; see also mine[1]
herself [hə:'self] pron (reflexive) se; (emphatic) ella misma; (after prep) sí (misma); see also oneself
he's [hi:z] = he is; he has
hesitant ['hezɪtənt] adj vacilante
hesitate ['hezɪteɪt] vi vacilar; (in speech) titubear; (be unwilling) resistirse a; **hesitation** ['-teɪʃən] n indecisión f; titubeo; dudas fpl
heterosexual [hetərəu'seksjuəl] adj heterosexual
heyday ['heɪdeɪ] n: the ~ of el apogeo de
HGV n abbr = heavy goods vehicle
hi [haɪ] excl ¡hola!; (to attract attention) ¡oiga!
hiatus [haɪ'eɪtəs] n vacío
hibernate ['haɪbəneɪt] vi invernar
hiccough ['hɪkʌp] = hiccup
hiccup ['hɪkʌp] vi hipar; ~s npl hipo
hide [haɪd] (pt hid, pp hidden) n (skin) piel f ♦ vt esconder, ocultar ♦ vi: to ~ (from sb) esconderse or ocultarse (de uno); **~-and-seek** n escondite m
hideous ['hɪdɪəs] adj horrible
hiding ['haɪdɪŋ] n (beating) paliza; to be in ~ (concealed) estar escondido
hierarchy ['haɪərɑ:kɪ] n jerarquía
hi-fi ['haɪfaɪ] n estéreo, hifi m ♦ adj de alta fidelidad
high [haɪ] adj alto; (speed, number) grande; (price) elevado; (wind) fuerte; (voice) agudo ♦ adv alto, a gran altura; it is 20 m ~ tiene 20 m de altura; ~ in the air en las alturas; **~brow** adj intelectual; **~chair** n silla alta; **~er education** n educación f or enseñanza superior; **~-handed** adj despótico; **~-heeled** adj de tacón alto; ~ **jump** n (SPORT) salto de altura; the **H~lands** npl las tierras altas de Escocia; **~light** n (fig: of event) punto culminante; (in hair) reflejo ♦ vt subrayar; **~ly** adv (paid) muy bien; (critical, confidential) sumamente; (a lot): to speak/think **~ly** of hablar muy bien de/tener en mucho a; **~ly strung** adj hipertenso; **~ness** n altura; Her or His **H~ness** Su Alteza; **~-pitched** adj agudo; **~-rise block** n torre f de pisos; ~ **school** n ≈ Instituto Nacional de Bachillerato (SP); ~ **season** (BRIT) n temporada alta; ~ **street** (BRIT) n calle f mayor; **~way** n carretera; (US) carretera nacional; autopista; **H~way Code** (BRIT) n código de la circulación
hijack ['haɪdʒæk] vt secuestrar; **~er** n secuestrador(a) m/f
hike [haɪk] vi (go walking) ir de excursión (a pie) ♦ n caminata; **~r** n excursionista m/f;

hiking n senderismo
hilarious [hɪ'leərɪəs] adj divertidísimo
hill [hɪl] n colina; (high) montaña; (slope) cuesta; **~side** n ladera; ~ **walking** n senderismo (de montaña); **~y** adj montañoso
hilt [hɪlt] n (of sword) empuñadura; to the ~ (fig: support) incondicionalmente
him [hɪm] pron (direct) le, lo; (indirect) le; (stressed, after prep) él; see also me; **~self** pron (reflexive) se; (emphatic) él mismo; (after prep) sí (mismo); see also oneself
hinder ['hɪndə*] vt estorbar, impedir; **hindrance** ['hɪndrəns] n estorbo
hindsight ['haɪndsaɪt] n: with ~ en retrospectiva
Hindu ['hɪndu:] n hindú m/f
hinge [hɪndʒ] n bisagra, gozne m ♦ vi (fig): to ~ on depender de
hint [hɪnt] n indirecta; (advice) consejo; (sign) dejo ♦ vt: to ~ that insinuar que ♦ vi: to ~ at hacer alusión a
hip [hɪp] n cadera
hippopotamus [hɪpə'pɒtəməs] (pl ~es or hippopotami) n hipopótamo
hire ['haɪə*] vt (BRIT: car, equipment) alquilar; (worker) contratar ♦ n alquiler m; for ~ se alquila; (taxi) libre; **~(d) car** (BRIT) n coche m de alquiler; ~ **purchase** (BRIT) n compra a plazos
his [hɪz] pron (el) suyo/(la) suya etc ♦ adj su; see also mine[1]; my
Hispanic [hɪs'pænɪk] adj hispánico
hiss [hɪs] vi silbar
historian [hɪ'stɔ:rɪən] n historiador(a) m/f
historic(al) [hɪ'stɒrɪk(l)] adj histórico
history ['hɪstərɪ] n historia
hit [hɪt] (pt, pp hit) vt (strike) golpear, pegar; (reach: target) alcanzar; (collide with: car) chocar contra; (fig: affect) afectar ♦ n golpe m; (success) éxito; to ~ it off with sb llevarse bien con uno; **~-and-run driver** n conductor(a) que atropella y huye
hitch [hɪtʃ] vt (fasten) atar, amarrar; (also: ~ up) remangar ♦ n (difficulty) dificultad f; to ~ a lift hacer autostop
hitch-hike vi hacer autostop; **~hiking** n autostop m
hi-tech [haɪ'tek] adj de alta tecnología
hitherto ['hɪðə'tu:] adv hasta ahora
HIV n abbr (= human immunodeficiency virus) VIH m; **~-negative/positive** adj VIH negativo/positivo
hive [haɪv] n colmena
HMS abbr = His (Her) Majesty's Ship
hoard [hɔ:d] n (treasure) tesoro; (stockpile) provisión f ♦ vt acumular; (goods in short supply) acaparar; **~ing** n (for posters) cartelera
hoarse [hɔ:s] adj ronco

hoax [həʊks] n trampa

hob [hɔb] n quemador m

hobble ['hɔbl] vi cojear

hobby ['hɔbɪ] n pasatiempo, afición f

hobo ['həʊbəʊ] (US) n vagabundo

hockey ['hɔkɪ] n hockey m

hog [hɔg] n cerdo, puerco ♦ vt (fig) acaparar; **to go the whole ~** poner toda la carne en el asador

hoist [hɔɪst] n (crane) grúa ♦ vt levantar, alzar; (flag, sail) izar

hold [həʊld] (pt, pp **held**) vt sostener; (contain) contener; (have: power, qualification) tener; (keep back) retener; (believe) sostener; (consider) considerar; (keep in position): **to ~ one's head up** mantener la cabeza alta; (meeting) celebrar ♦ vi (withstand pressure) resistir; (be valid) valer ♦ n (grasp) asimiento; (fig) dominio; **~ the line!** (TEL) ¡no cuelgue!; **to ~ one's own** (fig) defenderse; **to catch** or **get (a) ~ of** agarrarse or asirse de; **~ back** vt retener; (secret) ocultar; **~ down** vt (person) sujetar; (job) mantener; **~ off** vt (enemy) rechazar; **~ on** vi agarrarse bien; (wait) esperar; **~ on!** (TEL) ¡(espere) un momento!; **~ on to** vt fus agarrarse a; (keep) guardar; **~ out** vt ofrecer ♦ vi (resist) resistir; **~ up** vt (raise) levantar; (support) apoyar; (delay) retrasar; (rob) asaltar; **~all** (BRIT) n bolsa; **~er** n (container) receptáculo; (of ticket, record) poseedor(a) m/f; (of office, title etc) titular m/f; **~ing** n (share) interés m; (farmland) parcela; **~up** n (robbery) atraco; (delay) retraso; (BRIT: in traffic) embotellamiento

hole [həʊl] n agujero

holiday ['hɔlədɪ] n vacaciones fpl; (public ~) (día m de) fiesta, día m feriado; **on ~** de vacaciones; **~ camp** n (BRIT: also: **~ centre**) centro de vacaciones; **~-maker** (BRIT) n turista m/f; **~ resort** n centro turístico

holiness ['həʊlɪnɪs] n santidad f

Holland ['hɔlənd] n Holanda

hollow ['hɔləʊ] adj hueco, vacío; (eyes) hundido; (sound) sordo ♦ n hueco; (in ground) hoyo ♦ vt: **to ~ out** excavar

holly ['hɔlɪ] n acebo

holocaust ['hɔləkɔːst] n holocausto

holy ['həʊlɪ] adj santo, sagrado; (water) bendito

homage ['hɔmɪdʒ] n homenaje m

home [həʊm] n casa; (country) patria; (institution) asilo ♦ cpd (domestic) casero, de casa; (ECON, POL) nacional ♦ adv (direction) a casa; (right in: nail etc) a fondo; **at ~** en casa; (in country) en el país; (fig) como pez en el agua; **to go/come ~** ir/volver a casa; **make yourself at ~** ¡estás en tu casa!; **~ address** n domicilio; **~land** n tierra natal; **~less** adj sin

hogar, sin casa; **~ly** adj (simple) sencillo; **~-made** adj casero; **H~ Office** (BRIT) n Ministerio del Interior; **~ page** n página de inicio; **~ rule** n autonomía; **H~ Secretary** (BRIT) n Ministro del Interior; **~sick** adj: **to be ~sick** tener morriña, sentir nostalgia; **~ town** n ciudad f natal; **~ward** ['həʊmwəd] adj (journey) hacia casa; **~work** n deberes mpl

homoeopathic [həʊmɪəʊ'pəθɪk] (US **homeopathic**) adj homeopático

homosexual [hɔməʊ'sɛksjuəl] adj, n homosexual m/f

Honduran [hɔn'djʊərən] adj, n hondureño/a m/f

Honduras [hɔn'djʊərəs] n Honduras f

honest ['ɔnɪst] adj honrado; (sincere) franco, sincero; **~ly** adv honradamente; francamente; **~y** n honradez f

honey ['hʌnɪ] n miel f; **~comb** n panal m; **~moon** n luna de miel; **~suckle** n madreselva

honk [hɔŋk] vi (AUT) tocar el pito, pitar

honorary ['ɔnərərɪ] adj (member, president) de honor; (title) honorífico; **~ degree** n doctorado honoris causa

honour ['ɔnə*] (US **honor**) vt honrar; (commitment, promise) cumplir con ♦ n honor m, honra; **~able** adj honorable; **~s degree** n (SCOL) título de licenciado con calificación alta

hood [hʊd] n capucha; (BRIT: AUT) capota; (US: AUT) capó m; (of cooker) campana de humos

hoof [huːf] (pl **hooves**) n pezuña

hook [hʊk] n gancho; (on dress) corchete m, broche m; (for fishing) anzuelo ♦ vt enganchar; (fish) pescar

hooligan ['huːlɪgən] n gamberro

hoop [huːp] n aro

hooray [huː'reɪ] excl = **hurray**

hoot [huːt] (BRIT) vi (AUT) tocar el pito, pitar; (siren) sonar la sirena; (owl) ulular; **~er** (BRIT) n (AUT) pito, claxon m; (NAUT) sirena

Hoover ® ['huːvə*] (BRIT) n aspiradora ♦ vt: **h~** pasar la aspiradora por

hooves [huːvz] npl of **hoof**

hop [hɔp] vi saltar, brincar; (on one foot) saltar con un pie

hope [həʊp] vt, vi esperar ♦ n esperanza; **I ~ so/not** espero que sí/no; **~ful** adj (person) optimista; (situation) prometedor(a); **~fully** adv con esperanza; (one hopes): **~fully he will recover** esperamos que se recupere; **~less** adj desesperado; (person): **to be ~less** ser un desastre

hops [hɔps] npl lúpulo

horizon [hə'raɪzn] n horizonte m; **~tal** [hɔrɪ'zɔntl] adj horizontal

hormone ['hɔːməʊn] n hormona

horn [hɔːn] n cuerno; (MUS: also: French ~) trompa; (AUT) pito, claxon m

hornet ['hɔːnɪt] n avispón m

horoscope ['hɔrəskəup] n horóscopo

horrible ['hɔrɪbl] adj horrible

horrid ['hɔrɪd] adj horrible, horroroso

horrify ['hɔrɪfaɪ] vt horrorizar

horror ['hɔrə*] n horror m; ~ **film** n película de horror

hors d'œuvre [ɔː'dəːvrə] n entremeses mpl

horse [hɔːs] n caballo; ~**back** n: on ~**back** a caballo; ~ **chestnut** n (tree) castaño de Indias; (nut) castaña de Indias; ~**man/woman** (irreg) n jinete/a m/f; ~**power** n caballo (de fuerza); ~-**racing** n carreras fpl de caballos; ~**radish** n rábano picante; ~**shoe** n herradura

hose [həuz] n (also: ~pipe) manguera

hospitable [hɔs'pɪtəbl] adj hospitalario

hospital ['hɔspɪtl] n hospital m

hospitality [hɔspɪ'tælɪtɪ] n hospitalidad f

host [həust] n anfitrión m; (TV, RADIO) presentador m; (REL) hostia; (large number): **a** ~ **of** multitud de

hostage ['hɔstɪdʒ] n rehén m

hostel ['hɔstl] n hostal m; (youth) ~ albergue m juvenil

hostess ['həustɪs] n anfitriona; (BRIT: air ~) azafata; (TV, RADIO) presentadora

hostile ['hɔstaɪl] adj hostil

hot [hɔt] adj caliente; (weather) caluroso, de calor; (as opposed to warm) muy caliente; (spicy) picante; **to be** ~ (person) tener calor; (object) estar caliente; (weather) hacer calor; ~**bed** n (fig) semillero; ~ **dog** n perro caliente

hotel [həu'tel] n hotel m

hot: ~**house** n invernadero; ~ **line** n (POL) teléfono rojo; ~**ly** adv con pasión, apasionadamente; ~-**water bottle** n bolsa de agua caliente

hound [haund] vt acosar ♦ n perro (de caza)

hour ['auə*] n hora; ~**ly** adj (de) cada hora

house [n haus, pl 'hauzɪz, vb hauz] n (gen, firm) casa; (POL) cámara; (THEATRE) sala ♦ vt (person) alojar; (collection) albergar; **on the** ~ (fig) la casa invita; ~ **arrest** n arresto domiciliario; ~**boat** n casa flotante; ~**bound** adj confinado en casa; ~**breaking** n allanamiento de morada; ~**hold** n familia; (home) casa; ~**keeper** n ama de llaves; ~**keeping** n (work) trabajos mpl domésticos; ~**keeping (money)** n dinero para gastos domésticos; ~-**warming party** n fiesta de estreno de una casa; ~**wife** (irreg) n ama de casa; ~**work** n faenas fpl (de la casa)

housing ['hauzɪŋ] n (act) alojamiento; (houses) viviendas fpl; ~ **development** n urbanización f; ~ **estate** (BRIT) n =

~ **development**

hovel ['hɔvl] n casucha

hover ['hɔvə*] vi flotar (en el aire); ~**craft** n aerodeslizador m

how [hau] adv (in what way) cómo; ~ **are you?** ¿cómo estás?; ~ **much milk/many people?** ¿cuánta leche/gente?; ~ **much does it cost?** ¿cuánto cuesta?; ~ **long have you been here?** ¿cuánto hace que estás aquí?; ~ **old are you?** ¿cuántos años tienes?; ~ **tall is he?** ¿cómo es de alto?; ~ **is school?** ¿cómo (te) va (en) la escuela?; ~ **was the film?** ¿qué tal la película?; ~ **lovely/awful!** ¡qué bonito/horror!

however [hau'evə*] adv: ~ **I do it** lo haga como lo haga; ~ **cold it is** por mucho frío que haga; ~ **fast he runs** por muy rápido que corra; ~ **did you do it?** ¿cómo lo hiciste? ♦ conj sin embargo, no obstante

howl [haul] n aullido ♦ vi aullar; (person) dar alaridos; (wind) ulular

H.P. n abbr = **hire purchase**

h.p. abbr = **horse power**

HQ n abbr = **headquarters**

hub [hʌb] n (of wheel) cubo; (fig) centro

hubcap ['hʌbkæp] n tapacubos m inv

huddle ['hʌdl] vi: **to** ~ **together** acurrucarse

hue [hjuː] n color m, matiz m

huff [hʌf] n: **in a** ~ enojado

hug [hʌg] vt abrazar; (thing) apretar con los brazos

huge [hjuːdʒ] adj enorme

hull [hʌl] n (of ship) casco

hullo [hə'ləu] excl = **hello**

hum [hʌm] vt tararear, canturrear ♦ vi tararear, canturrear; (insect) zumbar

human ['hjuːmən] adj, n humano; ~**e** [hjuː'meɪn] adj humano, humanitario; ~**itarian** [hjuːmænɪ'tɛərɪən] adj humanitario; ~**ity** [hjuː'mænɪtɪ] n humanidad f

humble ['hʌmbl] adj humilde

humdrum ['hʌmdrʌm] adj (boring) monótono, aburrido

humid ['hjuːmɪd] adj húmedo

humiliate [hjuː'mɪlɪeɪt] vt humillar

humorous ['hjuːmərəs] adj gracioso, divertido

humour ['hjuːmə*] (US humor) n humorismo, sentido del humor; (mood) humor m ♦ vt (person) complacer

hump [hʌmp] n (in ground) montículo; (camel's) giba

hunch [hʌntʃ] n (premonition) presentimiento; ~**back** n joroba m/f; ~**ed** adj jorobado

hundred ['hʌndrəd] num ciento; (before n) cien; ~**s of** centenares de; ~**weight** n (BRIT) = 50.8 kg; 112 lb; (US) = 45.3 kg; 100 lb

hung [hʌŋ] pt, pp of **hang**

Hungarian [hʌŋˈgeərɪən] *adj, n* húngaro/a *m/f*

Hungary [ˈhʌŋgərɪ] *n* Hungría

hunger [ˈhʌŋgə*] *n* hambre *f* ♦ *vi*: **to ~ for** (*fig*) tener hambre de, anhelar; **~ strike** *n* huelga de hambre

hungry [ˈhʌŋgrɪ] *adj*: **~ (for)** hambriento (de); **to be ~** tener hambre

hunk [hʌŋk] *n* (*of bread etc*) trozo, pedazo

hunt [hʌnt] *vt* (*seek*) buscar; (*SPORT*) cazar ♦ *vi* (*search*): **to ~ for** (*for*); (*SPORT*) cazar ♦ *n* búsqueda; caza, cacería; **~er** *n* cazador(a) *m/f*; **~ing** *n* caza

hurdle [ˈhɜːdl] *n* (*SPORT*) valla; (*fig*) obstáculo *m*

hurl [hɜːl] *vt* lanzar, arrojar

hurrah [huˈrɑː] *excl* = **hurray**

hurray [huˈreɪ] *excl* ¡viva!

hurricane [ˈhʌrɪkən] *n* huracán *m*

hurried [ˈhʌrɪd] *adj* (*rushed*) hecho de prisa; **~ly** *adv* con prisa, apresuradamente

hurry [ˈhʌrɪ] *n* prisa ♦ *vi* (*also: ~ up*) apresurarse, darse prisa ♦ *vt* (*also: ~ up: person*) dar prisa a; (: *work*) apresurar, hacer de prisa; **to be in a ~** tener prisa

hurt [hɜːt] (*pt, pp* **hurt**) *vt* hacer daño a ♦ *vi* doler ♦ *adj* lastimado; **~ful** *adj* (*remark etc*) hiriente

hurtle [ˈhɜːtl] *vi*: **to ~ past** pasar como un rayo; **to ~ down** ir a toda velocidad

husband [ˈhʌzbənd] *n* marido

hush [hʌʃ] *n* silencio ♦ *vt* hacer callar; **~!** ¡chitón!, ¡cállate!; **~ up** *vt* encubrir

husk [hʌsk] *n* (*of wheat*) cáscara

husky [ˈhʌskɪ] *adj* ronco ♦ *n* perro esquimal

hustle [ˈhʌsl] *vt* (*hurry*) dar prisa a ♦ *n*: **~ and bustle** ajetreo

hut [hʌt] *n* cabaña; (*shed*) cobertizo

hutch [hʌtʃ] *n* conejera

hyacinth [ˈhaɪəsɪnθ] *n* jacinto

hydrant [ˈhaɪdrənt] *n* (*also: fire ~*) boca de incendios

hydraulic [haɪˈdrɔːlɪk] *adj* hidráulico

hydroelectric [haɪdrəʊˈlektrɪk] *adj* hidroeléctrico

hydrofoil [ˈhaɪdrəfɔɪl] *n* aerodeslizador *m*

hydrogen [ˈhaɪdrədʒən] *n* hidrógeno

hygiene [ˈhaɪdʒiːn] *n* higiene *f*; **hygienic** [-ˈdʒiːnɪk] *adj* higiénico

hymn [hɪm] *n* himno

hype [haɪp] (*inf*) *n* bombardeo publicitario

hypermarket [ˈhaɪpəmɑːkɪt] *n* hipermercado

hyphen [ˈhaɪfn] *n* guión *m*

hypnotize [ˈhɪpnətaɪz] *vt* hipnotizar

hypocrisy [hɪˈpɔkrɪsɪ] *n* hipocresía; **hypocrite** [ˈhɪpəkrɪt] *n* hipócrita *m/f*; **hypocritical** [hɪpəˈkrɪtɪkl] *adj* hipócrita

hypothesis [haɪˈpɔθɪsɪs] *n* (*pl* **hypotheses**) *n* hipótesis *f inv*

hysteria [hɪˈstɪərɪə] *n* histeria; **hysterical** [-ˈsterɪkl] *adj* histérico; (*funny*) para morirse de risa; **hysterics** [-ˈsterɪks] *npl* histeria; **to be in hysterics** (*fig*) morirse de risa

I, i

I [aɪ] *pron* yo

ice [aɪs] *n* hielo; (*~ cream*) helado ♦ *vt* (*cake*) alcorzar ♦ *vi* (*also: ~ over, ~ up*) helarse; **~berg** *n* iceberg *m*; **~box** *n* (*BRIT*) congelador *m*; (*US*) nevera (*SP*), refrigeradora (*AM*); **~ cream** *n* helado; **~ cube** *n* cubito de hielo; **~d** *adj* (*cake*) escarchado; (*drink*) helado; **~ hockey** *n* hockey *m* sobre hielo

Iceland [ˈaɪslənd] *n* Islandia

ice: **~ lolly** (*BRIT*) *n* polo; **~ rink** *n* pista de hielo; **~ skating** *n* patinaje *m* sobre hielo

icicle [ˈaɪsɪkl] *n* carámbano

icing [ˈaɪsɪŋ] *n* (*CULIN*) alcorza; **~ sugar** (*BRIT*) *n* azúcar *m* glas(eado)

icy [ˈaɪsɪ] *adj* helado

I'd [aɪd] = **I would**; **I had**

idea [aɪˈdɪə] *n* idea

ideal [aɪˈdɪəl] *n* ideal *m* ♦ *adj* ideal

identical [aɪˈdentɪkl] *adj* idéntico

identification [aɪdentɪfɪˈkeɪʃən] *n* identificación *f*; (**means of**) **~** documentos *mpl* personales

identify [aɪˈdentɪfaɪ] *vt* identificar

Identikit ® [aɪˈdentɪkɪt] *n*: **~ (picture)** retrato-robot *m*

identity [aɪˈdentɪtɪ] *n* identidad *f*; **~ card** *n* carnet *m* de identidad

ideology [aɪdɪˈɔlədʒɪ] *n* ideología

idiom [ˈɪdɪəm] *n* modismo; (*style of speaking*) lenguaje *m*

idiosyncrasy [ɪdɪəˈsɪŋkrəsɪ] *n* idiosincrasia

idiot [ˈɪdɪət] *n* idiota *m/f*; **~ic** [-ˈɔtɪk] *adj* tonto

idle [ˈaɪdl] *adj* (*inactive*) ocioso; (*lazy*) holgazán/ana; (*unemployed*) parado, desocupado; (*machinery etc*) parado; (*talk etc*) frívolo ♦ *vi* (*machine*) marchar en vacío

idol [ˈaɪdl] *n* ídolo; **~ize** *vt* idolatrar

i.e. *abbr* (= *that is*) esto es

if [ɪf] *conj* si; **~ necessary** si fuera necesario, si hiciese falta; **~ I were you** yo en tu lugar; **~ so/not** de ser así/si no; **~ only I could!** ¡ojalá pudiera!; *see also* **as**; **even**

igloo [ˈɪgluː] *n* iglú *m*

ignite [ɪgˈnaɪt] *vt* (*set fire to*) encender ♦ *vi* encenderse

ignition [ɪgˈnɪʃən] *n* (*AUT: process*) ignición *f*; (: *mechanism*) encendido; **to switch on/off the ~** arrancar/apagar el motor; **~ key** *n* (*AUT*) llave *f* de contacto

ignorant [ˈɪgnərənt] *adj* ignorante; **to be ~ of** ignorar

ignore [ɪgˈnɔː*] vt (person, advice) no hacer caso de; (fact) pasar por alto

I'll [aɪl] = **I will; I shall**

ill [ɪl] adj enfermo, malo ♦ n mal m ♦ adv mal; **to be taken ~** ponerse enfermo; **~-advised** adj (decision) imprudente; **~-at-ease** adj incómodo

illegal [ɪˈliːgl] adj ilegal

illegible [ɪˈledʒɪbl] adj ilegible

illegitimate [ɪlɪˈdʒɪtɪmət] adj ilegítimo

ill-fated adj malogrado

ill feeling n rencor m

illicit [ɪˈlɪsɪt] adj ilícito

illiterate [ɪˈlɪtərət] adj analfabeto

ill: ~-mannered adj mal educado; **~ness** n enfermedad f; **~-treat** vt maltratar

illuminate [ɪˈluːmɪneɪt] vt (room, street) iluminar, alumbrar; **illumination** [-ˈneɪʃən] n alumbrado; **illuminations** npl (decorative lights) iluminaciones fpl, luces fpl

illusion [ɪˈluːʒən] n ilusión f; (trick) truco

illustrate [ˈɪləstreɪt] vt ilustrar

illustration [ɪləˈstreɪʃən] n (act of illustrating) ilustración f; (example) ejemplo, ilustración f; (in book) lámina

illustrious [ɪˈlʌstrɪəs] adj ilustre

I'm [aɪm] = **I am**

image [ˈɪmɪdʒ] n imagen f; **~ry** [-ərɪ] n imágenes fpl

imaginary [ɪˈmædʒɪnərɪ] adj imaginario

imagination [ɪmædʒɪˈneɪʃən] n imaginación f; (inventiveness) inventiva

imaginative [ɪˈmædʒɪnətɪv] adj imaginativo

imagine [ɪˈmædʒɪn] vt imaginarse

imbalance [ɪmˈbæləns] n desequilibrio

imitate [ˈɪmɪteɪt] vt imitar; **imitation** [ɪmɪˈteɪʃən] n imitación f; (copy) copia

immaculate [ɪˈmækjulət] adj inmaculado

immaterial [ɪməˈtɪərɪəl] adj (unimportant) sin importancia

immature [ɪməˈtjuə*] adj (person) inmaduro

immediate [ɪˈmiːdɪət] adj inmediato; (pressing) urgente, apremiante; (nearest: family) próximo; (: neighbourhood) inmediato; **~ly** adv (at once) en seguida; (directly) inmediatamente; **~ly next to** muy junto a

immense [ɪˈmens] adj inmenso, enorme; (importance) enorme

immerse [ɪˈmɜːs] vt (submerge) sumergir; **to be ~d in** (fig) estar absorto en

immersion heater [ɪˈmɜːʃən-] (BRIT) n calentador m de inmersión

immigrant [ˈɪmɪgrənt] n inmigrante m/f; **immigration** [ɪmɪˈgreɪʃən] n inmigración f

imminent [ˈɪmɪnənt] adj inminente

immobile [ɪˈməubaɪl] adj inmóvil

immoral [ɪˈmɒrl] adj inmoral

immortal [ɪˈmɔːtl] adj inmortal

immune [ɪˈmjuːn] adj: **~ (to)** inmune (a); **immunity** n (MED, of diplomat) inmunidad f

immunize [ˈɪmjunaɪz] vt inmunizar

impact [ˈɪmpækt] n impacto

impair [ɪmˈpeə*] vt perjudicar

impart [ɪmˈpɑːt] vt comunicar; (flavour) proporcionar

impartial [ɪmˈpɑːʃl] adj imparcial

impassable [ɪmˈpɑːsəbl] adj (barrier) infranqueable; (river, road) intransitable

impassive [ɪmˈpæsɪv] adj impasible

impatience [ɪmˈpeɪʃəns] n impaciencia

impatient [ɪmˈpeɪʃənt] adj impaciente; **to get or grow ~** impacientarse

impeccable [ɪmˈpekəbl] adj impecable

impede [ɪmˈpiːd] vt estorbar

impediment [ɪmˈpedɪmənt] n obstáculo, estorbo; (also: speech ~) defecto (del habla)

impending [ɪmˈpendɪŋ] adj inminente

imperative [ɪmˈperətɪv] adj (tone) imperioso; (need) imprescindible

imperfect [ɪmˈpɜːfɪkt] adj (goods etc) defectuoso ♦ n (LING: also: ~ tense) imperfecto

imperial [ɪmˈpɪərɪəl] adj imperial

impersonal [ɪmˈpɜːsənl] adj impersonal

impersonate [ɪmˈpɜːsəneɪt] vt hacerse pasar por; (THEATRE) imitar

impertinent [ɪmˈpɜːtɪnənt] adj impertinente, insolente

impervious [ɪmˈpɜːvɪəs] adj impermeable; (fig): **~ to** insensible a

impetuous [ɪmˈpetjuəs] adj impetuoso

impetus [ˈɪmpətəs] n ímpetu m; (fig) impulso

impinge [ɪmˈpɪndʒ]: **to ~ on** vt fus (affect) afectar a

implement [n ˈɪmplɪmənt, vb ˈɪmplɪment] n herramienta; (for cooking) utensilio ♦ vt (regulation) hacer efectivo; (plan) realizar

implicit [ɪmˈplɪsɪt] adj implícito; (belief, trust) absoluto

imply [ɪmˈplaɪ] vt (involve) suponer; (hint) dar a entender que

impolite [ɪmpəˈlaɪt] adj mal educado

import [vb ɪmˈpɔːt, n ˈɪmpɔːt] vt importar ♦ n (COMM) importación f; (: article) producto importado; (meaning) significado, sentido

importance [ɪmˈpɔːtəns] n importancia

important [ɪmˈpɔːtənt] adj importante; **it's not ~** no importa, no tiene importancia

importer [ɪmˈpɔːtə*] n importador(a) m/f

impose [ɪmˈpəuz] vt imponer ♦ vi: **to ~ on sb** abusar de uno; **imposing** adj imponente, impresionante

imposition [ɪmpəˈzɪʃn] n (of tax etc) imposición f; **to be an ~ on** (person) molestar a

impossible [ɪmˈpɒsɪbl] adj imposible; (person) insoportable

impotent ['ɪmpɔtənt] adj impotente
impound [ɪm'paund] vt embargar
impoverished [ɪm'pɔvərɪʃt] adj necesitado
impractical [ɪm'præktɪkl] adj (person, plan) poco práctico
imprecise [ɪmprɪ'saɪs] adj impreciso
impregnable [ɪm'pregnəbl] adj (castle) inexpugnable
impress [ɪm'pres] vt impresionar; (mark) estampar; **to ~ sth on sb** hacer entender algo a uno
impression [ɪm'preʃən] n impresión f; (imitation) imitación f; **to be under the ~ that** tener la impresión de que; **~ist** n impresionista m/f
impressive [ɪm'presɪv] adj impresionante
imprint ['ɪmprɪnt] n (outline) huella; (PUBLISHING) pie m de imprenta
imprison [ɪm'prɪzn] vt encarcelar; **~ment** n encarcelamiento; (term of ~ment) cárcel f
improbable [ɪm'prɔbəbl] adj improbable, inverosímil
improper [ɪm'prɔpə*] adj (unsuitable: conduct etc) incorrecto; (: activities) deshonesto
improve [ɪm'pruːv] vt mejorar; (foreign language) perfeccionar ♦ vi mejorarse; **~ment** n mejoramiento; perfección f; progreso
improvise ['ɪmprəvaɪz] vt, vi improvisar
impulse ['ɪmpʌls] n impulso; **to act on ~** obrar sin reflexión; **impulsive** [-'pʌlsɪv] adj irreflexivo
impure [ɪm'pjuə*] adj (adulterated) adulterado; (morally) impuro; **impurity** n impureza

---

KEYWORD

in [ɪn] prep 1 (indicating place, position, with place names) en; **~ the house/garden** en (la) casa/el jardín; **~ here/there** aquí/ahí or allí dentro; **~ London/England** en Londres/Inglaterra
2 (indicating time) en; **~ spring** en (la) primavera; **~ the afternoon** por la tarde; **at 4 o'clock ~ the afternoon** a las 4 de la tarde; **I did it ~ 3 hours/days** lo hice en 3 horas/días; **I'll see you ~ 2 weeks** or **~ 2 weeks' time** te veré dentro de 2 semanas
3 (indicating manner etc) en; **~ a loud/soft voice** en voz alta/baja; **~ pencil/ink** a lápiz/bolígrafo; **the boy ~ the blue shirt** el chico de la camisa azul
4 (indicating circumstances): **~ the sun/shade/rain** al sol/a la sombra/bajo la lluvia; **a change ~ policy** un cambio de política
5 (indicating mood, state): **~ tears** en lágrimas, llorando; **~ anger/despair** enfadado/desesperado; **to live ~ luxury** vivir lujosamente
6 (with ratios, numbers): **1 ~ 10 households, 1 household ~ 10** una de cada 10 familias; **20 pence ~ the pound** 20 peniques por libra; **they lined up ~ twos** se alinearon de dos en dos
7 (referring to people, works) en; entre; **the disease is common ~ children** la enfermedad es común entre los niños; **~ (the works of) Dickens** en (las obras de) Dickens
8 (indicating profession etc): **to be ~ teaching** estar en la enseñanza
9 (after superlative) de; **the best pupil ~ the class** el/la mejor alumno/a de la clase
10 (with present participle): **~ saying this** al decir esto
♦ adv: **to be ~** (person: at home) estar en casa; (work) estar; (train, ship, plane) haber llegado; (in fashion) estar de moda; **she'll be ~ later today** llegará más tarde hoy; **to ask sb ~** hacer pasar a uno; **to run/limp etc ~** entrar corriendo/cojeando etc
♦ n: **the ~s and outs** (of proposal, situation etc) los detalles

---

in. abbr = **inch**
inability [ɪnə'bɪlɪtɪ] n: **~ (to do)** incapacidad f (de hacer)
inaccurate [ɪn'ækjurət] adj inexacto, incorrecto
inadequate [ɪn'ædɪkwət] adj (income, reply etc) insuficiente; (person) incapaz
inadvertently [ɪnəd'vɜːtntlɪ] adv por descuido
inadvisable [ɪnəd'vaɪzəbl] adj poco aconsejable
inane [ɪ'neɪn] adj necio, fatuo
inanimate [ɪn'ænɪmət] adj inanimado
inappropriate [ɪnə'prəuprɪət] adj inadecuado; (improper) poco oportuno
inarticulate [ɪnɑː'tɪkjulət] adj (person) incapaz de expresarse; (speech) mal pronunciado
inasmuch as [ɪnəz'mʌtʃ-] conj puesto que, ya que
inauguration [ɪnɔːgju'reɪʃən] n ceremonia de apertura
inborn [ɪn'bɔːn] adj (quality) innato
inbred [ɪn'bred] adj innato; (family) engendrado por endogamia
Inc. abbr (US: = incorporated) S.A.
incapable [ɪn'keɪpəbl] adj incapaz
incapacitate [ɪnkə'pæsɪteɪt] vt: **to ~ sb** incapacitar a uno
incense [n 'ɪnsens, vb ɪn'sens] n incienso ♦ vt (anger) indignar, encolerizar
incentive [ɪn'sentɪv] n incentivo, estímulo
incessant [ɪn'sesnt] adj incesante, continuo; **~ly** adv constantemente

incest ['ɪnsɛst] n incesto

inch [ɪntʃ] n pulgada; **to be within an ~ of** estar a dos dedos de; **he didn't give an ~** no dio concesión alguna

incident ['ɪnsɪdnt] n incidente m

incidental [ɪnsɪ'dɛntl] adj accesorio; **~ to** relacionado con; **~ly** [-'dɛntəlɪ] adv (by the way) a propósito

incite [ɪn'saɪt] vt provocar

inclination [ɪnklɪ'neɪʃən] n (tendency) tendencia, inclinación f; (desire) deseo; (disposition) propensión f

incline [n 'ɪnklaɪn, vb ɪn'klaɪn] n pendiente m, cuesta ♦ vt (head) poner de lado ♦ vi inclinarse; **to be ~d to** (tend) ser propenso a

include [ɪn'kluːd] vt (incorporate) incluir; (in letter) adjuntar; **including** prep incluso, inclusive

inclusion [ɪn'kluːʒən] n inclusión f

inclusive [ɪn'kluːsɪv] adj inclusivo; **~ of tax** incluidos los impuestos

income ['ɪnkʌm] n (earned) ingresos mpl; (from property etc) renta; (from investment etc) rédito; **~ tax** n impuesto sobre la renta

incoming ['ɪnkʌmɪŋ] adj (flight, government etc) entrante

incomparable [ɪn'kɔmpərəbl] adj incomparable, sin par

incompatible [ɪnkəm'pætɪbl] adj incompatible

incompetent [ɪn'kɔmpɪtənt] adj incompetente

incomplete [ɪnkəm'pliːt] adj (partial: achievement etc) incompleto; (unfinished: painting etc) inacabado

incongruous [ɪn'kɔŋɡruəs] adj (strange) discordante; (inappropriate) incongruente

inconsiderate [ɪnkən'sɪdərət] adj desconsiderado

inconsistent [ɪnkən'sɪstənt] adj inconsecuente; (contradictory) incongruente; **~ with** (que) no concuerda con

inconspicuous [ɪnkən'spɪkjuəs] adj (colour, building etc) discreto; (person) que llama poco la atención

inconvenience [ɪnkən'viːnjəns] n inconvenientes mpl; (trouble) molestia, incomodidad f ♦ vt incomodar

inconvenient [ɪnkən'viːnjənt] adj incómodo, poco práctico; (time, place, visitor) inoportuno

incorporate [ɪn'kɔːpəreɪt] vt incorporar; (contain) comprender; (add) agregar; **~d** adj: **~d company** (US) ≈ sociedad f anónima

incorrect [ɪnkə'rɛkt] adj incorrecto

increase [n 'ɪnkriːs, vb ɪn'kriːs] n aumento ♦ vi aumentar; (grow) crecer; (price) subir ♦ vt aumentar; (price) subir; **increasing** adj creciente; **increasingly** adv cada vez más, más y más

incredible [ɪn'krɛdɪbl] adj increíble

incubator ['ɪnkjubeɪtə*] n incubadora

incumbent [ɪn'kʌmbənt] adj: **it is ~ on him to ... le incumbe ...**

incur [ɪn'kəː*] vt (expenditure) incurrir; (loss) sufrir; (anger, disapproval) provocar

indebted [ɪn'dɛtɪd] adj: **to be ~ to sb** estar agradecido a uno

indecent [ɪn'diːsnt] adj indecente; **~ assault** (BRIT) n atentado contra el pudor; **~ exposure** n exhibicionismo

indecisive [ɪndɪ'saɪsɪv] adj indeciso

indeed [ɪn'diːd] adv efectivamente, en realidad; (in fact) en efecto; (furthermore) es más; **yes ~!** ¡claro que sí!

indefinitely [ɪn'dɛfɪnɪtlɪ] adv (wait) indefinidamente

indemnity [ɪn'dɛmnɪtɪ] n (insurance) indemnidad f; (compensation) indemnización f

independence [ɪndɪ'pɛndns] n independencia

independent [ɪndɪ'pɛndənt] adj independiente

index ['ɪndɛks] (pl ~es) n (in book) índice m; (: in library etc) catálogo; (pl indices: ratio, sign) exponente m; **~ card** n ficha; **~ed** (US) adj = **~-linked**; **~ finger** n índice m; **~-linked** (BRIT) adj vinculado al índice del coste de la vida

India ['ɪndɪə] n la India; **~n** adj, n indio/a m/f; **Red ~n** piel roja m/f; **~n Ocean** Ocean el Océano Índico

indicate ['ɪndɪkeɪt] vt indicar; **indication** [-'keɪʃən] n indicio, señal f; **indicative** [ɪn'dɪkətɪv] adj: **to be indicative of** indicar; **indicator** n indicador m; (AUT) intermitente m

indices ['ɪndɪsiːz] npl of **index**

indictment [ɪn'daɪtmənt] n acusación f

indifferent [ɪn'dɪfrənt] adj indiferente; (mediocre) regular

indigenous [ɪn'dɪdʒɪnəs] adj indígena

indigestion [ɪndɪ'dʒɛstʃən] n indigestión f

indignant [ɪn'dɪɡnənt] adj: **to be ~ at sth/ with sb** indignarse por algo/con uno

indigo ['ɪndɪɡəʊ] adj de color añil ♦ n añil m

indirect [ɪndɪ'rɛkt] adj indirecto

indiscreet [ɪndɪ'skriːt] adj indiscreto, imprudente

indiscriminate [ɪndɪ'skrɪmɪnət] adj indiscriminado

indisputable [ɪndɪ'spjuːtəbl] adj incontestable

indistinct [ɪndɪ'stɪŋkt] adj (noise, memory etc) confuso

individual [ɪndɪ'vɪdjuəl] n individuo ♦ adj individual; (personal) personal; (particular)

particular; **~ly** adv (singly) individualmente

indoctrinate [m'dɒktrɪneɪt] vt adoctrinar

indoor ['ɪndɔ:*] adj (swimming pool) cubierto; (plant) de interior; (sport) bajo cubierta; **~s** [m'dɔ:z] adv dentro

induce [m'dju:s] vt inducir, persuadir; (bring about) producir; (birth) provocar; **~ment** n (incentive) incentivo; (pej: bribe) soborno

indulge [m'dʌldʒ] vt (whim) satisfacer; (person) complacer; (child) mimar ♦ vi: to **~ in** darse el gusto de; **~nce** n vicio; (leniency) indulgencia; **~nt** adj indulgente

industrial [m'dʌstrɪəl] adj industrial; **~ action** n huelga; **~ estate** (BRIT) n polígono (SP) or zona (AM) industrial; **~ist** n industrial m/f; **~ize** vt industrializar; **~ park** (US) n = **~ estate**

industrious [m'dʌstrɪəs] adj trabajador(a); (student) aplicado

industry ['ɪndəstrɪ] n industria; (diligence) aplicación f

inebriated [ɪ'ni:brɪeɪtɪd] adj borracho

inedible [m'edɪbl] adj incomible; (poisonous) no comestible

ineffective [ɪnɪ'fektɪv] adj ineficaz, inútil

ineffectual [ɪnɪ'fektjuəl] adj = **ineffective**

inefficient [ɪnɪ'fɪʃənt] adj ineficaz, ineficiente

inept [ɪ'nept] adj incompetente

inequality [ɪnɪ'kwɒlɪtɪ] n desigualdad f

inert [ɪ'nɜ:t] adj inerte, inactivo; (immobile) inmóvil

inescapable [ɪnɪ'skeɪpəbl] adj ineludible

inevitable [m'evɪtəbl] adj inevitable; **inevitably** adv inevitablemente

inexcusable [ɪnɪks'kju:zəbl] adj imperdonable

inexpensive [ɪnɪk'spensɪv] adj económico

inexperienced [ɪnɪk'spɪərɪənst] adj inexperto

infallible [m'fælɪbl] adj infalible

infamous ['ɪnfəməs] adj infame

infancy ['ɪnfənsɪ] n infancia

infant ['ɪnfənt] n niño/a; (baby) niño pequeño, bebé m; (pej) aniñado

infantry ['ɪnfəntrɪ] n infantería

infant school (BRIT) n parvulario

infatuated [m'fætjueɪtɪd] adj: **~ with** (in love) loco por

infatuation [ɪnfætu'eɪʃən] n enamoramiento, pasión f

infect [m'fekt] vt (wound) infectar; (food) contaminar; (person, animal) contagiar; **~ion** [m'fekʃən] n infección f; (fig) contagio; **~ious** [m'fekʃəs] adj (also fig) contagioso

infer [m'fɜ:*] vt deducir, inferir

inferior [m'fɪərɪə*] adj, n inferior m/f; **~ity** [-rɪ'ɒrətɪ] n inferioridad f

infertile [m'fɜ:taɪl] adj estéril; (person) infecundo

infested [m'festɪd] adj: **~ with** plagado de

in-fighting n (fig) lucha(s) f(pl) interna(s)

infinite ['ɪnfɪnɪt] adj infinito

infinitive [m'fɪnɪtɪv] n infinitivo

infinity [m'fɪnɪtɪ] n infinito; (an ~) infinidad f

infirmary [m'fɜ:mərɪ] n hospital m

inflamed [m'fleɪmd] adj: **to become ~** inflamarse

inflammable [m'flæməbl] adj inflamable

inflammation [ɪnfla'meɪʃən] n inflamación f

inflatable [m'fleɪtəbl] adj (ball, boat) inflable

inflate [m'fleɪt] vt (tyre, price etc) inflar; (fig) hinchar; **inflation** [m'fleɪʃən] n (ECON) inflación f

inflexible [m'fleksəbl] adj (rule) rígido; (person) inflexible

inflict [m'flɪkt] vt: **to ~ sth on sb** infligir algo en uno

influence ['ɪnfluəns] n influencia ♦ vt influir en, influenciar; **under the ~ of alcohol** en estado de embriaguez; **influential** [-'enfl] adj influyente

influenza [ɪnflu'enzə] n gripe f

influx ['ɪnflʌks] n afluencia

inform [m'fɔ:m] vt: **to ~ sb of sth** informar a uno sobre or de algo ♦ vi: **to ~ on sb** delatar a uno

informal [m'fɔ:məl] adj (manner, tone) familiar; (dress, interview, occasion) informal; (visit, meeting) extraoficial; **~ity** [-'mælɪtɪ] n informalidad f; sencillez f

informant [m'fɔ:mənt] n informante m/f

information [ɪnfə'meɪʃən] n información f; (knowledge) conocimientos mpl; **a piece of ~** un dato; **~ desk** n (mostrador m de) información f; **~ office** n oficina f

informative [m'fɔ:mətɪv] adj informativo

informer [m'fɔ:mə*] n (also: police ~) soplón/ona m/f

infra-red [ɪnfrə'red] adj infrarrojo

infrastructure ['ɪnfrəstrʌktʃə*] n (of system etc) infraestructura

infringe [m'frɪndʒ] vt infringir, violar ♦ vi: **to ~ on** abusar de; **~ment** n infracción f; (of rights) usurpación f

infuriating [m'fjuərɪeɪtɪŋ] adj (habit, noise) enloquecedor(a)

ingenious [m'dʒi:nɪəs] adj ingenioso; **ingenuity** [-dʒɪ'nju:ɪtɪ] n ingeniosidad f

ingenuous [m'dʒenjuəs] adj ingenuo

ingot ['ɪŋgət] n lingote m, barra

ingrained [m'greɪnd] adj arraigado

ingratiate [m'greɪʃɪeɪt] vt: **to ~ o.s. with** congraciarse con

ingredient [m'gri:dɪənt] n ingrediente m

inhabit [m'hæbɪt] vt vivir en; **~ant** n habitante m/f

inhale [m'heɪl] vt inhalar ♦ vi (breathe in) aspirar; (in smoking) tragar

inherent [ɪn'hɪərənt] *adj*: ~ **in** *or* **to** inherente a

inherit [ɪn'herɪt] *vt* heredar; **~ance** *n* herencia; (*fig*) patrimonio

inhibit [ɪn'hɪbɪt] *vt* inhibir, impedir; **~ed** *adj* (*PSYCH*) cohibido; **~ion** [-'bɪʃən] *n* cohibición f

inhospitable [ɪnhɔs'pɪtəbl] *adj* (*person*) inhospitalario; (*place*) inhóspito

inhuman [ɪn'hju:mən] *adj* inhumano

initial [ɪ'nɪʃl] *adj* primero ♦ *n* inicial f ♦ *vt* firmar con las iniciales; **~s** *npl* (*as signature*) iniciales *fpl*; (*abbreviation*) siglas *fpl*; **~ly** *adv* al principio

initiate [ɪ'nɪʃɪeɪt] *vt* iniciar; **to ~ proceedings against sb** (*LAW*) entablar proceso contra uno

initiative [ɪ'nɪʃɪətɪv] *n* iniciativa

inject [ɪn'dʒekt] *vt* inyectar; **to ~ sb with sth** inyectar algo a uno; **~ion** [ɪn'dʒekʃən] *n* inyección f

injunction [ɪn'dʒʌŋkʃən] *n* interdicto

injure ['ɪndʒə*] *vt* (*hurt*) herir, lastimar; (*fig: reputation etc*) perjudicar; **~d** *adj* (*person, arm*) herido, lastimado; **injury** *n* herida, lesión f; (*wrong*) perjuicio, daño; **injury time** *n* (*SPORT*) (tiempo de) descuento

injustice [ɪn'dʒʌstɪs] *n* injusticia

ink [ɪŋk] *n* tinta

inkling ['ɪŋklɪŋ] *n* sospecha; (*idea*) idea

inlaid ['ɪnleɪd] *adj* (*with wood, gems etc*) incrustado

inland [*adj* 'ɪnlənd, *adv* ɪn'lænd] *adj* (*waterway, port etc*) interior ♦ *adv* tierra adentro; **I~ Revenue** (*BRIT*) *n* departamento de impuestos; ≈ Hacienda (*SP*)

in-laws *npl* suegros *mpl*

inlet ['ɪnlet] *n* (*GEO*) ensenada, cala; (*TECH*) admisión f, entrada

inmate ['ɪnmeɪt] *n* (*in prison*) preso/a; presidiario/a; (*in asylum*) internado/a

inn [ɪn] *n* posada, mesón *m*

innate [ɪ'neɪt] *adj* innato

inner ['ɪnə*] *adj* (*courtyard, calm*) interior; (*feelings*) íntimo; **~ city** *n* barrios deprimidos del centro de una ciudad; **~ tube** *n* (*of tyre*) cámara (*SP*), llanta (*AM*)

innings ['ɪnɪŋz] *n* (*CRICKET*) entrada, turno

innocent ['ɪnəsnt] *adj* inocente

innocuous [ɪ'nɔkjuəs] *adj* inocuo

innovation [ɪnəu'veɪʃən] *n* novedad f

innuendo [ɪnju'endəu] (*pl* **~es**) *n* indirecta

inoculation [ɪnɔkju'leɪʃən] *n* inoculación f

in-patient *n* paciente *m/f* interno/a

input ['ɪnput] *n* entrada; (*of resources*) inversión f; (*COMPUT*) entrada de datos

inquest ['ɪnkwest] *n* (*coroner's*) encuesta judicial

inquire [ɪn'kwaɪə*] *vi* preguntar ♦ *vt*: **to ~ whether** preguntar si; **to ~ about** (*person*) preguntar por; (*fact*) informarse de; **~ into** *vt fus* investigar, indagar; **inquiry** *n* pregunta; (*investigation*) investigación f, pesquisa; **"Inquiries"** "Información"; **inquiry office** (*BRIT*) *n* oficina de información

inquisitive [ɪn'kwɪzɪtɪv] *adj* (*curious*) curioso

ins. *abbr* = **inches**

insane [ɪn'seɪn] *adj* loco; (*MED*) demente

insanity [ɪn'sænɪtɪ] *n* demencia, locura

inscription [ɪn'skrɪpʃən] *n* inscripción f; (*in book*) dedicatoria

inscrutable [ɪn'skru:təbl] *adj* inescrutable, insondable

insect ['ɪnsekt] *n* insecto; **~icide** [ɪn'sektɪsaɪd] *n* insecticida *m*; **~ repellent** *n* loción f contra insectos

insecure [ɪnsɪ'kjuə*] *adj* inseguro

insemination [ɪnsemɪ'neɪʃn] *n*: **artificial ~** inseminación f artificial

insensitive [ɪn'sensɪtɪv] *adj* insensible

insert [*vb* ɪn'sə:t, *n* 'ɪnsə:t] *vt* (*into sth*) introducir ♦ *n* encarte *m*; **~ion** [ɪn'sə:ʃən] *n* inserción f

in-service ['ɪnsə:vɪs] *adj* (*training, course*) a cargo de la empresa

inshore [ɪn'ʃɔ:*] *adj* de bajura ♦ *adv* (*be*) cerca de la orilla; (*move*) hacia la orilla

inside ['ɪn'saɪd] *n* interior *m* ♦ *adj* interior, interno ♦ *adv* (*be*) (por) dentro; (*go*) hacia dentro ♦ *prep* dentro de; (*of time*): **~ 10 minutes** en menos de 10 minutos; **~s** *npl* (*inf: stomach*) tripas *fpl*; **~ information** *n* información f confidencial; **~ lane** *n* (*AUT: in Britain*) carril *m* izquierdo; (: *in US, Europe etc*) carril *m* derecho; **~ out** *adv* (*turn*) al revés; (*know*) a fondo

insider dealing, insider trading *n* (*STOCK EXCHANGE*) abuso de información privilegiada

insight ['ɪnsaɪt] *n* perspicacia

insignificant [ɪnsɪg'nɪfɪknt] *adj* insignificante

insincere [ɪnsɪn'sɪə*] *adj* poco sincero

insinuate [ɪn'sɪnjueɪt] *vt* insinuar

insipid [ɪn'sɪpɪd] *adj* soso, insulso

insist [ɪn'sɪst] *vi* insistir; **to ~ on** insistir en; **to ~ that** insistir en que; (*claim*) exigir que; **~ent** *adj* insistente; (*noise, action*) persistente

insole ['ɪnsəul] *n* plantilla

insolent ['ɪnsələnt] *adj* insolente, descarado

insomnia [ɪn'sɔmnɪə] *n* insomnio

inspect [ɪn'spekt] *vt* inspeccionar, examinar; (*troops*) pasar revista a; **~ion** [ɪn'spekʃən] *n* inspección f, examen *m*; (*of troops*) revista; **~or** *n* inspector(a) *m/f*; (*BRIT: on buses, trains*) revisor(a) *m/f*

inspiration [ɪnspə'reɪʃən] *n* inspiración f; **inspire** [ɪn'spaɪə*] *vt* inspirar

instability [ɪnstə'bɪlɪtɪ] *n* inestabilidad f

install [ɪn'stɔ:l] *vt* instalar; (*official*) nombrar;

~ation [ɪnstəˈleɪʃən] n instalación f
instalment [ɪnˈstɔːlmənt] (US **installment**) n plazo; (of story) entrega; (of TV serial etc) capítulo; **in ~s** (pay, receive) a plazos
instance [ˈɪnstəns] n ejemplo, caso; **for ~** por ejemplo; **in the first ~** en primer lugar
instant [ˈɪnstənt] n instante m, momento ♦ adj inmediato; (coffee etc) instantáneo; **~ly** adv en seguida
instead [ɪnˈsted] adv en cambio; **~ of** en lugar de, en vez de
instep [ˈɪnstep] n empeine m
instil [ɪnˈstɪl] vt: **to ~ sth into** inculcar algo a
instinct [ˈɪnstɪŋkt] n instinto
institute [ˈɪnstɪtjuːt] n instituto; (professional body) colegio ♦ vt (begin) iniciar, empezar; (proceedings) entablar; (system, rule) establecer
institution [ɪnstɪˈtjuːʃən] n institución f; (MED: home) asilo; (: asylum) manicomio; (of system etc) establecimiento; (of custom) iniciación f
instruct [ɪnˈstrʌkt] vt: **to ~ sb in sth** instruir a uno en or sobre algo; **to ~ sb to do sth** dar instrucciones a uno de hacer algo; **~ion** [ɪnˈstrʌkʃən] n (teaching) instrucción f; **~ions** npl (orders) órdenes fpl; **~ions (for use)** modo de empleo; **~or** n instructor(a) m/f
instrument [ˈɪnstrəmənt] n instrumento; **~al** [-ˈmentl] adj (MUS) instrumental; **to be ~al in** ser (el) artífice de; **~ panel** n tablero (de instrumentos)
insufficient [ɪnsəˈfɪʃənt] adj insuficiente
insular [ˈɪnsjʊlə*] adj insular; (person) estrecho de miras
insulate [ˈɪnsjʊleɪt] vt aislar; **insulation** [-ˈleɪʃən] n aislamiento
insulin [ˈɪnsjʊlɪn] n insulina
insult [n ˈɪnsʌlt, vb ɪnˈsʌlt] n insulto ♦ vt insultar; **~ing** adj insultante
insurance [ɪnˈʃʊərəns] n seguro; **fire/life ~** seguro contra incendios/sobre la vida; **~ agent** n agente m/f de seguros; **~ policy** n póliza (de seguros)
insure [ɪnˈʃʊə*] vt asegurar
intact [ɪnˈtækt] adj íntegro; (unharmed) intacto
intake [ˈɪnteɪk] n (of food) ingestión f; (of air) consumo; (BRIT: SCOL): **an ~ of 200 a year** 200 matriculados al año
integral [ˈɪntɪɡrəl] adj (whole) íntegro; (part) integrante
integrate [ˈɪntɪɡreɪt] vt integrar ♦ vi integrarse
integrity [ɪnˈtegrɪtɪ] n honradez f, rectitud f
intellect [ˈɪntəlekt] n intelecto; **~ual** [-ˈlektjuəl] adj, n intelectual m/f
intelligence [ɪnˈtelɪdʒəns] n inteligencia
intelligent [ɪnˈtelɪdʒənt] adj inteligente

intelligible [ɪnˈtelɪdʒɪbl] adj inteligible, comprensible
intend [ɪnˈtend] vt (gift etc): **to ~ sth for** destinar algo a; **to ~ to do sth** tener intención de or pensar hacer algo
intense [ɪnˈtens] adj intenso; **~ly** adv (extremely) sumamente
intensify [ɪnˈtensɪfaɪ] vt intensificar; (increase) aumentar
intensive [ɪnˈtensɪv] adj intensivo; **~ care unit** n unidad f de vigilancia intensiva
intent [ɪnˈtent] n propósito; (LAW) premeditación f ♦ adj (absorbed) absorto; (attentive) atento; **to all ~s and purposes** prácticamente; **to be ~ on doing sth** estar resuelto a hacer algo
intention [ɪnˈtenʃən] n intención f, propósito; **~al** adj deliberado; **~ally** adv a propósito
intently [ɪnˈtentlɪ] adv atentamente, fijamente
interact [ɪntərˈækt] vi influirse mutuamente; **~ive** (COMPUT) interactivo
interchange [ˈɪntətʃeɪndʒ] n intercambio; (on motorway) intersección f; **~able** adj intercambiable
intercom [ˈɪntəkɔm] n interfono
intercourse [ˈɪntəkɔːs] n (sexual) relaciones fpl sexuales
interest [ˈɪntrɪst] n (also COMM) interés m ♦ vt interesar; **to be ~ed in** interesarse por; **~ing** adj interesante; **~ rate** n tipo or tasa de interés
interface [ˈɪntəfeɪs] n (COMPUT) junción f
interfere [ɪntəˈfɪə*] vi: **to ~ in** (quarrel, other people's business) entrometerse en; **to ~ with** (hinder) estorbar; (damage) estropear
interference [ɪntəˈfɪərəns] n intromisión f; (RADIO, TV) interferencia
interim [ˈɪntərɪm] n: **in the ~** en el ínterin ♦ adj provisional
interior [ɪnˈtɪərɪə*] n interior m ♦ adj interior; **~ designer** n interiorista m/f
interjection [ɪntəˈdʒekʃən] n interposición f; (LING) interjección f
interlock [ɪntəˈlɔk] vi entrelazarse
interlude [ˈɪntəluːd] n intervalo; (THEATRE) intermedio
intermediate [ɪntəˈmiːdɪət] adj intermedio
intermission [ɪntəˈmɪʃən] n intermisión f; (THEATRE) descanso
intern [vb ɪnˈtɜːn, n ˈɪntɜːn] vt internar ♦ n (US) interno/a
internal [ɪnˈtɜːnl] adj (layout, pipes, security) interior; (injury, structure, memo) internal; **~ly** adv: "**not to be taken ~ly**" "uso externo"; **I~ Revenue Service** (US) n departamento de impuestos; ≈ Hacienda (SP)
international [ɪntəˈnæʃənl] adj internacional

♦ n (BRIT: match) partido internacional

Internet ['ɪntənet] n: the ~ Internet m or f; ~ **café** n cibercafé m; ~ **Service Provider** n proveedor m de (acceso a) Internet

interplay ['ɪntəpleɪ] n interacción f

interpret [ɪn'tɜːprɪt] vt interpretar; (translate) traducir; (understand) entender ♦ vi hacer de intérprete; ~**er** n intérprete m/f

interrogate [ɪn'terəʊgeɪt] vt interrogar; **interrogation** [-'geɪʃən] n interrogatorio

interrupt [ɪntə'rʌpt] vt, vi interrumpir; ~**ion** [-'rʌpʃən] n interrupción f

intersect [ɪntə'sekt] vt (roads) cruzarse; ~**ion** [-'sekʃən] n (of roads) cruce m

intersperse [ɪntə'spɜːs] vt: to ~ with salpicar de

intertwine [ɪntə'twaɪn] vt entrelazarse

interval ['ɪntəvl] n intervalo; (BRIT: THEATRE, SPORT) descanso; (: SCOL) recreo; **at ~s** a ratos, de vez en cuando

intervene [ɪntə'viːn] vi intervenir; (event) interponerse; (time) transcurrir; **intervention** n intervención f

interview ['ɪntəvjuː] n entrevista ♦ vt entrevistarse con; ~**er** n entrevistador(a) m/f

intestine [ɪn'testɪn] n intestino

intimacy ['ɪntɪməsɪ] n intimidad f

intimate [adj 'ɪntɪmət, vb 'ɪntɪmeɪt] adj íntimo; (friendship) estrecho; (knowledge) profundo ♦ vt dar a entender

into ['ɪntuː] prep en; (towards) a; (inside) hacia el interior de; ~ **3 pieces/French** en 3 pedazos/al francés

intolerable [ɪn'tɔlərəbl] adj intolerable, insoportable

intolerant [ɪn'tɔlərənt] adj: ~ (of) intolerante (con o para)

intoxicated [ɪn'tɔksɪkeɪtɪd] adj embriagado

intractable [ɪn'træktəbl] adj (person) intratable; (problem) espinoso

intranet ['ɪntrənet] n intranet f

intransitive [ɪn'trænsɪtɪv] adj intransitivo

intravenous [ɪntrə'viːnəs] adj intravenoso

in-tray n bandeja de entrada

intricate ['ɪntrɪkət] adj (design, pattern) intrincado

intrigue [ɪn'triːg] n intriga ♦ vt fascinar; **intriguing** adj fascinante

intrinsic [ɪn'trɪnsɪk] adj intrínseco

introduce [ɪntrə'djuːs] vt introducir, meter; (speaker, TV show etc) presentar; **to ~ sb (to sb)** presentar uno (a otro); **to ~ sb to** (pastime, technique) introducir a uno a; **introduction** [-'dʌkʃən] n introducción f; (of person) presentación f; **introductory** [-'dʌktərɪ] adj introductorio; (lesson, offer) de introducción

introvert ['ɪntrəvɜːt] n introvertido/a ♦ adj (also: ~ed) introvertido

intrude [ɪn'truːd] vi (person) entrometerse; **to ~ on** estorbar; ~**r** n intruso/a; **intrusion** [-ʒən] n invasión f

intuition [ɪntjuː'ɪʃən] n intuición f

inundate ['ɪnʌndeɪt] vt: **to ~ with** inundar de

invade [ɪn'veɪd] vt invadir

invalid [n 'ɪnvəlɪd, adj ɪn'vælɪd] n (MED) minusválido/a ♦ adj (not valid) inválido, nulo

invaluable [ɪn'væljuəbl] adj inestimable

invariable [ɪn'veərɪəbl] adj invariable

invent [ɪn'vent] vt inventar; ~**ion** [ɪn'venʃən] n invento; (lie) ficción f, mentira; ~**ive** adj inventivo; ~**or** n inventor(a) m/f

inventory ['ɪnvəntrɪ] n inventario

invert [ɪn'vɜːt] vt invertir

inverted commas (BRIT) npl comillas fpl

invest [ɪn'vest] vt invertir ♦ vi: **to ~ in** (company etc) invertir dinero en; (fig: sth useful) comprar

investigate [ɪn'vestɪgeɪt] vt investigar; **investigation** [-'geɪʃən] n investigación f, pesquisa

investment [ɪn'vestmənt] n inversión f

investor [ɪn'vestə*] n inversionista m/f

invigilator [ɪn'vɪdʒɪleɪtə*] n persona que vigila en un examen

invigorating [ɪn'vɪgəreɪtɪŋ] adj vigorizante

invisible [ɪn'vɪzɪbl] adj invisible

invitation [ɪnvɪ'teɪʃən] n invitación f

invite [ɪn'vaɪt] vt invitar; (opinions etc) solicitar, pedir; **inviting** adj atractivo; (food) apetitoso

invoice ['ɪnvɔɪs] n factura ♦ vt facturar

involuntary [ɪn'vɔləntrɪ] adj involuntario

involve [ɪn'vɔlv] vt suponer, implicar; tener que ver con; (concern, affect) corresponder; **to ~ sb (in sth)** comprometer a uno (con algo); ~**d** adj complicado; **to be ~d in** (take part) tomar parte en; (be engrossed) estar muy metido en; ~**ment** n participación f; dedicación f

inward ['ɪnwəd] adj (movement) interior, interno; (thought, feeling) íntimo; ~(**s**) adv hacia dentro

I/O abbr (COMPUT = input/output) entrada/salida

iodine ['aɪəʊdiːn] n yodo

ion ['aɪən] n ion m; **ioniser** ['aɪənaɪzə*] n ionizador m

iota [aɪ'əʊtə] n jota, ápice m

IOU n abbr (= I owe you) pagaré m

IQ n abbr (= intelligence quotient) cociente m intelectual

IRA n abbr (= Irish Republican Army) IRA m

Iran [ɪ'rɑːn] n Irán m; ~**ian** [ɪ'reɪnɪən] adj, n iraní m/f

Iraq [ɪ'rɑːk] n Iraq; ~**i** adj, n iraquí m/f

irate [aɪ'reɪt] adj enojado, airado

Ireland ['aɪələnd] n Irlanda

iris ['aɪrɪs] (pl ~**es**) n (ANAT) iris m; (BOT) lirio

Irish ['aɪrɪʃ] adj irlandés/esa ♦ npl: **the ~** los irlandeses; **~man/woman** (irreg) n irlandés/esa m/f; **~ Sea** n: **the ~ Sea** el mar de Irlanda

iron ['aɪən] n hierro; (for clothes) plancha ♦ cpd de hierro ♦ vt (clothes) planchar; **~ out** vt (fig) allanar

ironic(al) [aɪ'rɔnɪk(l)] adj irónico

ironing ['aɪənɪŋ] n (activity) planchado; (clothes: ironed) ropa planchada; (: to be ironed) ropa por planchar; **~ board** n tabla de planchar

ironmonger's (shop) ['aɪənmʌŋgəz] (BRIT) n ferretería, quincallería

irony ['aɪrənɪ] n ironía

irrational [ɪ'ræʃənl] adj irracional

irreconcilable [ɪrekən'saɪləbl] adj (ideas) incompatible; (enemies) irreconciliable

irregular [ɪ'regjulə*] adj irregular; (surface) desigual; (action, event) anómalo; (behaviour) poco ortodoxo

irrelevant [ɪ'reləvənt] adj fuera de lugar, inoportuno

irresolute [ɪ'rezəluːt] adj indeciso

irrespective [ɪrɪ'spektɪv]: **~ of** prep sin tener en cuenta, no importa

irresponsible [ɪrɪ'spɔnsɪbl] adj (act) irresponsable; (person) poco serio

irrigate ['ɪrɪgeɪt] vt regar; **irrigation** [-'geɪʃən] n riego

irritable ['ɪrɪtəbl] adj (person) de mal humor

irritate ['ɪrɪteɪt] vt fastidiar; (MED) picar; **irritating** adj fastidioso; **irritation** [-'teɪʃən] n fastidio; irritación; picazón f, picor m

IRS (US) n abbr = Internal Revenue Service

is [ɪz] vb see be

Islam ['ɪzlɑːm] n Islam m; **~ic** [ɪz'læmɪk] adj islámico

island ['aɪlənd] n isla; **~er** n isleño/a

isle [aɪl] n isla

isn't ['ɪznt] = is not

isolate ['aɪsəleɪt] vt aislar; **~d** adj aislado; **isolation** [-'leɪʃən] n aislamiento

ISP n abbr = Internet Service Provider

Israel ['ɪzreɪl] n Israel m; **~i** [ɪz'reɪlɪ] adj, n israelí m/f

issue ['ɪsjuː] n (problem, subject, most important part) cuestión f; (outcome) resultado; (of banknotes etc) emisión f; (of newspaper etc) edición f ♦ vt (rations, equipment) distribuir, repartir; (orders) dar; (certificate, passport) expedir; (decree) promulgar; (magazine) publicar; (cheques) extender; (banknotes, stamps) emitir; **at ~** en cuestión; **to take ~ with sb (over)** estar en desacuerdo con uno (sobre); **to make an ~ of sth** hacer una cuestión de algo

Istanbul [ɪstæn'buːl] n Estambul m

---

it [ɪt] pron 1 (specific: subject: not generally translated) él/ella; (: direct object) lo, la; (: indirect object) le; (after prep) él/ella; (abstract concept) ello; **~'s on the table** está en la mesa; **I can't find ~** no lo (or la) encuentro; **give ~ to me** dámelo (or dámela); **I spoke to him about ~** le hablé del asunto; **what did you learn from ~?** ¿qué aprendiste de él (or ella)?; **did you go to ~?** (party, concert etc) ¿fuiste?

2 (impersonal): **~'s raining** llueve, está lloviendo; **~'s 6 o'clock/the 10th of August** son las 6/es el 10 de agosto; **how far is ~?** — **~'s 10 miles/2 hours on the train** ¿a qué distancia está? — a 10 millas/2 horas en tren; **who is ~?** — **~'s me** ¿quién es? — soy yo

Italian [ɪ'tæljən] adj italiano ♦ n italiano/a; (LING) italiano

italics [ɪ'tælɪks] npl cursiva

Italy ['ɪtəlɪ] n Italia

itch [ɪtʃ] n picazón f ♦ vi (part of body) picar; **to ~ to do sth** rabiar por hacer algo; **~y** adj: **my hand is ~y** me pica la mano

it'd ['ɪtd] = it would; it had

item ['aɪtəm] n artículo; (on agenda) asunto (a tratar); (also: news ~) noticia; **~ize** vt detallar

itinerary [aɪ'tɪnərərɪ] n itinerario

it'll ['ɪtl] = it will; it shall

its [ɪts] adj su; sus pl

it's [ɪts] = it is; it has

itself [ɪt'self] pron (reflexive) sí mismo/a; (emphatic) él mismo/ella misma

ITV n abbr (BRIT: = Independent Television) cadena de televisión comercial independiente del Estado

I.U.D. n abbr (= intra-uterine device) DIU m

I've [aɪv] = I have

ivory ['aɪvərɪ] n marfil m

ivy ['aɪvɪ] n (BOT) hiedra

J, j

jab [dʒæb] vt: **to ~ sth into sth** clavar algo en algo ♦ n (inf) (MED) pinchazo

jack [dʒæk] n (AUT) gato; (CARDS) sota; **~ up** vt (AUT) levantar con gato

jackal ['dʒækɔːl] n (ZOOL) chacal m

jacket ['dʒækɪt] n chaqueta, americana, saco (AM); (of book) sobrecubierta

jack: **~-knife** vi colear; **~ plug** n (ELEC) enchufe m de clavija; **~pot** n premio gordo

jaded ['dʒeɪdɪd] adj (tired) cansado; (fed-up) hastiado

jagged ['dʒægɪd] adj dentado

jail [dʒeɪl] n cárcel f ♦ vt encarcelar

jam [dʒæm] n mermelada; (also: traffic ~) embotellamiento; (inf: difficulty) apuro ♦ vt (passage etc) obstruir; (mechanism, drawer etc) atascar; (RADIO) interferir ♦ vi atascarse, trabarse; **to ~ sth into sth** meter algo a la fuerza en algo

Jamaica [dʒə'meɪkə] n Jamaica

jangle ['dʒæŋgl] vi entrechocar (ruidosamente)

janitor ['dʒænɪtə*] n (caretaker) portero, conserje m

January ['dʒænjuərɪ] n enero

Japan [dʒə'pæn] n (el) Japón; **~ese** [dʒæpə'niːz] adj japonés/esa ♦ n inv japonés/ esa m/f; (LING) japonés m

jar [dʒɑː*] n tarro, bote m ♦ vi (sound) chirriar; (colours) desentonar

jargon ['dʒɑːgən] n jerga

jasmine ['dʒæzmɪn] n jazmín m

jaundice ['dʒɔːndɪs] n ictericia

jaunt [dʒɔːnt] n excursión f

javelin ['dʒævlɪn] n jabalina

jaw [dʒɔː] n mandíbula

jay [dʒeɪ] n (ZOOL) arrendajo

jaywalker ['dʒeɪwɔːkə*] n peatón/ona m/f imprudente

jazz [dʒæz] n jazz m; **~ up** vt (liven up) animar, avivar

jealous ['dʒeləs] adj celoso; (envious) envidioso; **~y** n celos mpl; envidia

jeans [dʒiːnz] npl vaqueros mpl, tejanos mpl

Jeep ® [dʒiːp] n jeep m

jeer [dʒɪə*] vi: **to ~ (at)** (mock) mofarse (de)

jelly ['dʒelɪ] n (jam) jalea; (dessert etc) gelatina; **~fish** n inv medusa (SP), aguaviva (AM)

jeopardy ['dʒepədɪ] n: **to be in ~** estar en peligro

jerk [dʒɜːk] n (jolt) sacudida; (wrench) tirón m; (inf) imbécil m/f ♦ vt tirar bruscamente de ♦ vi (vehicle) traquetear

jersey ['dʒɜːzɪ] n jersey m; (fabric) (tejido de) punto

Jesus ['dʒiːzəs] n Jesús m

jet [dʒet] n (of gas, liquid) chorro; (AVIAT) avión m a reacción; **~-black** adj negro como el azabache; **~ engine** n motor m a reacción; **~ lag** n desorientación f después de un largo vuelo

jettison ['dʒetɪsn] vt desechar

jetty ['dʒetɪ] n muelle m, embarcadero

Jew [dʒuː] n judío

jewel ['dʒuːəl] n (lit) joya; (in watch) rubí m; **~ler** (US **~er**) n joyero/a; **~ler's (shop)** (US **~ry store**) n joyería; **~lery** (US **~ry**) n joyas fpl, alhajas fpl

Jewess ['dʒuːɪs] n judía

Jewish ['dʒuːɪʃ] adj judío

jibe [dʒaɪb] n mofa

jiffy ['dʒɪfɪ] (inf) n: **in a ~** en un santiamén

jigsaw ['dʒɪgsɔː] n (also: ~ puzzle) rompecabezas m inv, puzle m

jilt [dʒɪlt] vt dejar plantado a

jingle ['dʒɪŋgl] n musiquilla ♦ vi tintinear

jinx [dʒɪŋks] n: **there's a ~ on it** está gafado

jitters ['dʒɪtəz] (inf) npl: **to get the ~** ponerse nervioso

job [dʒɔb] n (task) tarea; (post) empleo; **it's not my ~** no me incumbe a mí; **it's a good ~ that** ... menos mal que ...; **just the ~!** ¡estupendo!; **~ centre** (BRIT) n oficina estatal de colocaciones; **~less** adj sin trabajo

jockey ['dʒɔkɪ] n jockey m/f ♦ vi: **to ~ for position** maniobrar para conseguir una posición

jog [dʒɔg] vt empujar (ligeramente) ♦ vi (run) hacer footing; **to ~ sb's memory** refrescar la memoria a uno; **~ along** vi (fig) ir tirando; **~ging** n footing m

join [dʒɔɪn] vt (things) juntar, unir; (club) hacerse socio de; (POL: party) afiliarse a; (queue) ponerse en; (meet: people) reunirse con ♦ vi (roads) juntarse; (rivers) confluir ♦ n juntura; **~ in** vi tomar parte, participar ♦ vt fus tomar parte or participar en; **~ up** vi reunirse; (MIL) alistarse

joiner ['dʒɔɪnə*] (BRIT) n carpintero/a; **~y** n carpintería

joint [dʒɔɪnt] n (TECH) junta, unión f; (ANAT) articulación f; (BRIT: CULIN) pieza de carne (para asar); (inf: place) tugurio; (: of cannabis) porro ♦ adj (common) común; (combined) combinado; **~ account** (with bank etc) cuenta común

joke [dʒəuk] n chiste m; (also: practical ~) broma ♦ vi bromear; **to play a ~ on** gastar una broma a; **~r** n (CARDS) comodín m

jolly ['dʒɔlɪ] adj (merry) alegre; (enjoyable) divertido ♦ adv (BRIT: inf) muy, terriblemente

jolt [dʒəult] n (jerk) sacudida; (shock) susto ♦ vt (physically) sacudir; (emotionally) asustar

jostle ['dʒɔsl] vt dar empellones a, codear

jot [dʒɔt] n: **not one ~** ni jota, ni pizca; **~ down** vt apuntar; **~ter** (BRIT) n bloc m

journal ['dʒɜːnl] n (magazine) revista; (diary) periódico, diario; **~ism** n periodismo; **~ist** n periodista m/f, reportero/a

journey ['dʒɜːnɪ] n viaje m; (distance covered) trayecto

jovial ['dʒəuvɪəl] adj risueño, jovial

joy [dʒɔɪ] n alegría; **~ful** adj alegre; **~ous** adj alegre; **~ ride** n (illegal) paseo en coche robado; **~rider** n gamberro que roba un coche para dar una vuelta y luego abandonarlo; **~ stick** n (AVIAT) palanca de mando; (COMPUT) palanca de control

JP n abbr = **Justice of the Peace**

Jr *abbr* = **junior**

jubilant ['dʒu:bɪlnt] *adj* jubiloso

judge [dʒʌdʒ] *n* juez *m/f*; (*fig: expert*) perito
♦ *vt* juzgar; (*consider*) considerar;
judg(e)ment *n* juicio

judiciary [dʒu:'dɪʃɪərɪ] *n* poder *m* judicial

judicious [dʒu:'dɪʃəs] *adj* juicioso

judo ['dʒu:dəu] *n* judo

jug [dʒʌg] *n* jarra

juggernaut ['dʒʌgənɔ:t] *n* (*BRIT*) (*huge truck*)
trailer *m*

juggle ['dʒʌgl] *vi* hacer juegos malabares; **~r**
n malabarista *m/f*

juice [dʒu:s] *n* zumo, jugo (*esp AM*); **juicy** *adj*
jugoso

jukebox ['dʒu:kbɔks] *n* máquina de discos

July [dʒu:'laɪ] *n* julio

jumble ['dʒʌmbl] *n* revoltijo ♦ *vt* (*also: ~ up*)
revolver; **~ sale** (*BRIT*) *n* venta de objetos
usados con fines benéficos

jumbo (jet) ['dʒʌmbəu-] *n* jumbo

jump [dʒʌmp] *vi* saltar, dar saltos; (*with fear
etc*) pegar un bote; (*increase*) aumentar ♦ *vt*
saltar ♦ *n* salto; aumento; **to ~ the queue**
(*BRIT*) colarse

jumper ['dʒʌmpə*] *n* (*BRIT: pullover*) suéter *m*,
jersey *m*; (*US: dress*) mandil *m*; **~ cables**
(*US*) *npl* = **jump leads**

jump leads (*BRIT*) *npl* cables *mpl* puente de
batería

jumpy ['dʒʌmpɪ] (*inf*) *adj* nervioso

Jun. *abbr* = **junior**

junction ['dʒʌŋkʃən] *n* (*BRIT: of roads*) cruce
m; (*RAIL*) empalme *m*

juncture ['dʒʌŋktʃə*] *n*: **at this ~** en este
momento, en esta coyuntura

June [dʒu:n] *n* junio

jungle ['dʒʌŋgl] *n* selva, jungla

junior ['dʒu:nɪə*] *adj* (*in age*) menor, más
joven; (*brother/sister etc*): **7 years her ~** siete
años menor que ella; (*position*) subalterno
♦ *n* menor *m/f*, joven *m/f*; **~ school** (*BRIT*) *n*
escuela primaria

junk [dʒʌŋk] *n* (*cheap goods*) baratijas *fpl*;
(*rubbish*) basura; **~ food** *n* alimentos
preparados y envasados de escaso valor
nutritivo

junkie ['dʒʌŋkɪ] (*inf*) *n* drogadicto/a, yonqui
m/f

junk mail *n* propaganda de buzón

junk shop *n* tienda de objetos usados

Junr *abbr* = **junior**

juror ['dʒuərə*] *n* jurado

jury ['dʒuərɪ] *n* jurado

just [dʒʌst] *adj* justo ♦ *adv* (*exactly*)
exactamente; (*only*) sólo, solamente; **he's
~ done it/left** acaba de hacerlo/irse; **~ right**
perfecto; **~ two o'clock** las dos en punto;
she's ~ as clever as you (ella) es tan lista

como tú; **~ as well that ...** menos mal que ...;
~ as he was leaving en el momento en que se
marchaba; **~ before/enough** justo antes/lo
suficiente; **~ here** aquí mismo; **he ~ missed**
ha fallado por poco; **~ listen to this** escucha
esto un momento

justice ['dʒʌstɪs] *n* justicia; (*US: judge*) juez *m*;
to do ~ to (*fig*) hacer justicia a; **J~ of the
Peace** *n* juez *m* de paz

justify ['dʒʌstɪfaɪ] *vt* justificar; (*text*) alinear

jut [dʒʌt] *vi* (*also: ~ out*) sobresalir

juvenile ['dʒu:vənaɪl] *adj* (*court*) de menores;
(*humour, mentality*) infantil ♦ *n* menor *m* de
edad

K, k

K *abbr* (= *one thousand*) mil; (= *kilobyte*)
kilobyte *m*, kiloocteto

kangaroo [kæŋgə'ru:] *n* canguro

karate [kə'rɑ:tɪ] *n* karate *m*

kebab [kə'bæb] *n* pincho moruno

keel [ki:l] *n* quilla; **on an even ~** (*fig*) en
equilibrio

keen [ki:n] *adj* (*interest, desire*) grande, vivo;
(*eye, intelligence*) agudo; (*competition*)
reñido; (*edge*) afilado; (*eager*) entusiasta; **to
be ~ to do** or **on doing sth** tener muchas
ganas de hacer algo; **to be ~ on sth/sb**
interesarse por algo/uno

keep [ki:p] (*pt, pp* **kept**) *vt* (*preserve, store*)
guardar; (*hold back*) quedarse con;
(*maintain*) mantener; (*detain*) detener;
(*shop*) ser propietario de; (*feed: family etc*)
mantener; (*promise*) cumplir; (*chickens, bees
etc*) criar; (*accounts*) llevar; (*diary*) escribir;
(*prevent*): **to ~ sb from doing sth** impedir a
uno hacer algo ♦ *vi* (*food*) conservarse;
(*remain*) seguir, continuar ♦ *n* (*of castle*)
torreón *m*; (*food etc*) comida, subsistencia;
(*inf*): **for ~s** para siempre; **to ~ doing sth**
seguir haciendo algo; **to ~ sb happy** tener a
uno contento; **to ~ a place tidy** mantener un
lugar limpio; **to ~ sth to o.s.** guardar algo
para sí mismo; **to ~ sth (back) from sb** ocultar
algo a uno; **to ~ time** (*clock*) mantener la
hora exacta; **~ on** *vi*: **to ~ on doing** seguir or
continuar haciendo; **to ~ on (about sth)** no
parar de hablar (de algo); **~ out** *vi* (*stay out*)
permanecer fuera; **"~ out"** "prohibida la
entrada"; **~ up** *vt* mantener, conservar ♦ *vi*
no retrasarse; **to ~ up with** (*pace*) ir al paso
de; (*level*) mantenerse a la altura de; **~er** *n*
guardián/ana *m/f*; **~-fit** *n* gimnasia (para
mantenerse en forma); **~ing** *n* (*care*)
cuidado; **in ~ing with** de acuerdo con; **~sake**
n recuerdo

kennel ['kɛnl] *n* perrera; **~s** *npl* residencia

canina

Kenya ['kɛnjə] n Kenia

kept [kɛpt] pt, pp of **keep**

kerb [kɜ:b] (BRIT) n bordillo

kernel ['kɜːnl] n (nut) almendra; (fig) meollo

ketchup ['kɛtʃəp] n salsa de tomate, catsup m

kettle ['kɛtl] n hervidor m de agua; **~ drum** n (MUS) timbal m

key [kiː] n llave f; (MUS) tono; (of piano, typewriter) tecla ♦ adj (issue etc) clave inv ♦ vt (also: ~ in) teclear; **~board** n teclado; **~ed up** adj (person) nervioso; **~hole** n ojo (de la cerradura); **~hole surgery** n cirugía cerrada, cirugía no invasiva; **~note** n (MUS) tónica; (of speech) punto principal or clave; **~ring** n llavero

khaki ['kɑːkɪ] n caqui

kick [kɪk] vt dar una patada or un puntapié a; (inf: habit) quitarse de ♦ vi (horse) dar coces ♦ n patada; puntapié m; (of animal) coz f; (thrill): **he does it for ~s** lo hace por pura diversión; **~ off** vi (SPORT) hacer el saque inicial

kid [kɪd] n (inf: child) chiquillo/a; (animal) cabrito; (leather) cabritilla ♦ vi (inf) bromear

kidnap ['kɪdnæp] vt secuestrar; **~per** n secuestrador(a) m/f; **~ping** n secuestro

kidney ['kɪdnɪ] n riñón m

kill [kɪl] vt matar; (murder) asesinar ♦ n matanza; **to ~ time** matar el tiempo; **~er** n asesino/a; **~ing** n (one) asesinato; (several) matanza; **to make a ~ing** (fig) hacer su agosto; **~joy** (BRIT) n aguafiestas m/f inv

kiln [kɪln] n horno

kilo ['kiːləu] n kilo; **~byte** n (COMPUT) kilobyte m, kilocteto; **~gram(me)** ['kɪləugræm] n kilo, kilogramo; **~metre** ['kɪləmiːtə*] (US **~meter**) n kilómetro; **~watt** ['kɪləuwɔt] n kilovatio

kilt [kɪlt] n falda escocesa

kin [kɪn] n see **next**

kind [kaɪnd] adj amable, atento ♦ n clase f, especie f; (species) género; **in ~** (COMM) en especie; **a ~ of** una especie de; **to be two of a ~** ser tal para cual

kindergarten ['kɪndəgɑːtn] n jardín m de la infancia

kind-hearted adj bondadoso, de buen corazón

kindle ['kɪndl] vt encender; (arouse) despertar

kindly ['kaɪndlɪ] adj bondadoso; cariñoso ♦ adv bondadosamente, amablemente; **will you ~ ...** sea usted tan amable de ...

kindness ['kaɪndnɪs] n (quality) bondad f, amabilidad f; (act) favor m

king [kɪŋ] n rey m; **~dom** n reino; **~fisher** n martín m pescador; **~-size** adj de tamaño extra

kiosk ['kiːɔsk] n quiosco; (BRIT: TEL) cabina

kipper ['kɪpə*] n arenque m ahumado

kiss [kɪs] n beso ♦ vt besar; **to ~ (each other)** besarse; **~ of life** n respiración f boca a boca

kit [kɪt] n (equipment) equipo; (tools etc) (caja de) herramientas fpl; (assembly ~) juego de armar

kitchen ['kɪtʃɪn] n cocina; **~ sink** n fregadero

kite [kaɪt] n (toy) cometa

kitten ['kɪtn] n gatito/a

kitty ['kɪtɪ] n (pool of money) fondo común

km abbr (= kilometre) km

knack [næk] n: **to have the ~ of doing sth** tener el don de hacer algo

knapsack ['næpsæk] n mochila

knead [niːd] vt amasar

knee [niː] n rodilla; **~cap** n rótula

kneel [niːl] (pt, pp **knelt**) vi (also: ~ down) arrodillarse

knew [njuː] pt of **know**

knickers ['nɪkəz] (BRIT) npl bragas fpl

knife [naɪf] (pl knives) n cuchillo ♦ vt acuchillar

knight [naɪt] n caballero; (CHESS) caballo; **~hood** (BRIT) n (title): **to receive a ~hood** recibir el título de Sir

knit [nɪt] vt tejer, tricotar ♦ vi hacer punto, tricotar; (bones) soldarse; **to ~ one's brows** fruncir el ceño; **~ting** n labor f de punto; **~ting machine** n máquina de tricotar; **~ting needle** n aguja de hacer punto; **~wear** n prendas fpl de punto

knives [naɪvz] npl of **knife**

knob [nɔb] n (of door) tirador m; (of stick) puño; (on radio, TV) botón m

knock [nɔk] vt (strike) golpear; (bump into) chocar contra; (inf) criticar ♦ vi (at door etc): **to ~ at/on** llamar a ♦ n golpe m; (on door) llamada; **~ down** vt atropellar; **~ off** (inf) vi (finish) salir del trabajo ♦ vt (from price) descontar; (inf: steal) birlar; **~ out** vt dejar sin sentido; (BOXING) poner fuera de combate, dejar K.O.; (in competition) eliminar; **~ over** vt (object) tirar; (person) atropellar; **~er** n (on door) aldabón m; **~out** n (BOXING) K.O. m, knockout m ♦ cpd (competition etc) eliminatorio

knot [nɔt] n nudo ♦ vt anudar

know [nəu] (pt knew, pp known) vt (facts) saber; (be acquainted with) conocer; (recognize) reconocer, conocer; **to ~ how to swim** saber nadar; **to ~ about or of sth/sb** saber de uno/algo; **~-all** n sabelotodo m/f; **~-how** n conocimientos mpl; **~ing** adj (look) de complicidad; **~ingly** adv (purposely) adrede; (smile, look) con complicidad

knowledge ['nɔlɪdʒ] n conocimiento; (learning) saber m, conocimientos mpl; **~able** adj entendido

knuckle ['nʌkl] n nudillo
Koran [kɔ'rɑːn] n Corán m
Korea [kə'rɪə] n Corea
kosher ['kəʊʃə*] adj autorizado por la ley judía
Kosovo ['kɒsəvəʊ] n Kosovo m

L, l

L (BRIT) abbr = **learner driver**
l. abbr (= litre) l
lab [læb] n abbr = **laboratory**
label ['leɪbl] n etiqueta ♦ vt poner etiqueta a
labor etc ['leɪbə*] (US) = **labour**
laboratory [lə'bɒrətərɪ] n laboratorio
laborious [lə'bɔːrɪəs] adj penoso
labour ['leɪbə*] (US **labor**) n (hard work) trabajo; (~ force) mano f de obra; (MED): **to be in ~** estar de parto ♦ vi: **to ~ (at sth)** trabajar (en algo) ♦ vt: **to ~ a point** insistir en un punto; **L~, the L~ party** (BRIT) el partido laborista, los laboristas mpl; **~ed** adj (breathing) fatigoso; **~er** n peón m; **farm ~er** peón m; (day ~er) jornalero
lace [leɪs] n encaje m; (of shoe etc) cordón m ♦ vt (shoes: also: ~ **up**) atarse (los zapatos)
lack [læk] n (absence) falta ♦ vt faltarle a uno, carecer de; **through** or **for ~ of** por falta de; **to be ~ing** faltar, no haber; **to be ~ing in sth** faltarle a uno algo
lacquer ['lækə*] n laca
lad [læd] n muchacho, chico
ladder ['lædə*] n escalera (de mano); (BRIT: in tights) carrera
laden ['leɪdn] adj: ~ **(with)** cargado (de)
ladle ['leɪdl] n cucharón m
lady ['leɪdɪ] n señora; (dignified, graceful) dama; "**ladies and gentlemen ...**" "señoras y caballeros ..."; **young ~** señorita; **the ladies' (room)** los servicios de señoras; **~bird** (US ~**bug**) n mariquita; **~like** adj fino; **L~ship** n: **your L~ship** su Señoría
lag [læg] n retraso ♦ vi (also: ~ **behind**) retrasarse, quedarse atrás ♦ vt (pipes) revestir
lager ['lɑːgə*] n cerveza (rubia)
lagoon [lə'guːn] n laguna
laid [leɪd] pt, pp of **lay**; ~ **back** (inf) adj relajado; ~ **up** adj: **to be ~ up (with)** tener que guardar cama (a causa de)
lain [leɪn] pp of **lie**
lake [leɪk] n lago
lamb [læm] n cordero; (meat) (carne f de) cordero; ~ **chop** n chuleta de cordero; **lambswool** n lana de cordero
lame [leɪm] adj cojo; (excuse) poco convincente
lament [lə'mɛnt] n quejo ♦ vt lamentarse de
laminated ['læmineɪtɪd] adj (metal)

laminado; (wood) contrachapado; (surface) plastificado
lamp [læmp] n lámpara; ~**post** (BRIT) n (poste m de) farol m; ~**shade** n pantalla
lance [lɑːns] vt (MED) abrir con lanceta
land [lænd] n tierra; (country) país m; (piece of ~) terreno; (estate) tierras fpl, finca ♦ vi (from ship) desembarcar; (AVIAT) aterrizar; (fig: fall) caer, terminar ♦ vt (passengers, goods) desembarcar; **to ~ sb with sth** (inf) hacer cargar a uno con algo; ~ **up** vi: **to ~ up in/at** ir a parar a/en; ~**fill site** ['lændfil-] n vertedero; ~**ing** n aterrizaje m; (of staircase) rellano; ~**ing gear** n (AVIAT) tren m de aterrizaje; ~**lady** n (of rented house, pub etc) dueña; ~**lord** n propietario; (of pub etc) patrón m; ~**mark** n lugar m conocido; **to be a ~mark** (fig) marcar un hito histórico; ~**owner** n terrateniente m/f; ~**scape** n paisaje m; ~**scape gardener** n arquitecto de jardines; ~**slide** n (GEO) corrimiento de tierras; (fig: POL) victoria arrolladora
lane [leɪn] n (in country) camino; (AUT) carril m; (in race) calle f
language ['læŋgwɪdʒ] n lenguaje m; (national tongue) idioma m, lengua; **bad ~** palabrotas fpl; ~ **laboratory** n laboratorio de idiomas
lank [læŋk] adj (hair) lacio
lanky ['læŋkɪ] adj larguirucho
lantern ['læntn] n linterna, farol m
lap [læp] n (of track) vuelta; (of body) regazo; **to sit on sb's ~** sentarse en las rodillas de uno ♦ vt (also: ~ **up**) beber a lengüetadas ♦ vi (waves) chapotear; ~ **up** vt (fig) tragarse
lapel [lə'pɛl] n solapa
Lapland ['læplænd] n Laponia
lapse [læps] n fallo; (moral) desliz m; (of time) intervalo ♦ vi (expire) caducar; (time) pasar, transcurrir; **to ~ into bad habits** caer en malos hábitos
laptop (computer) ['læptɒp-] n (ordenador m) portátil m
larch [lɑːtʃ] n alerce m
lard [lɑːd] n manteca (de cerdo)
larder ['lɑːdə*] n despensa
large [lɑːdʒ] adj grande; **at ~** (free) en libertad; (generally) en general; ~**ly** adv (mostly) en su mayor parte; (introducing reason) en gran parte; ~-**scale** adj (map) en gran escala; (fig) importante
lark [lɑːk] n (bird) alondra; (joke) broma
laryngitis [lærɪn'dʒaɪtɪs] n laringitis f
laser ['leɪzə*] n láser m; ~ **printer** n impresora (por) láser
lash [læʃ] n latigazo; (also: eye~) pestaña ♦ vt azotar; (tie): **to ~ to/together** atar a/atar; ~ **out** vi: **to ~ out (at sb)** (hit) arremeter (contra uno); **to ~ out against sb** lanzar invectivas contra uno

lass [læs] (BRIT) n chica
lasso [læ'su:] n lazo
last [lɑːst] adj último; (end: of series etc) final ♦ adv (most recently) la última vez; (finally) por último ♦ vi durar; (continue) continuar, seguir; ~ **night** anoche; ~ **week** la semana pasada; **at** ~ por fin; ~ **but one** penúltimo; **~-ditch** adj (attempt) último, desesperado; **~ing** adj duradero; **~ly** adv por último, finalmente; **~-minute** adj de última hora
latch [lætʃ] n pestillo
late [leɪt] adj (far on: in time, process etc) al final de; (not on time) tarde, atrasado; (dead) fallecido ♦ adv tarde; (behind time, schedule) con retraso; **of** ~ últimamente; ~ **at night** a última hora de la noche; **in** ~ **May** hacia fines de mayo; **the** ~ **Mr X** el difunto Sr X; **~comer** n recién llegado/a; **~ly** adv últimamente; ~**r** adj (date etc) posterior; (version etc) más reciente ♦ adv más tarde, después; **~st** ['leɪtɪst] adj último; **at the ~st** a más tardar
lathe [leɪð] n torno
lather ['lɑːðə*] n espuma (de jabón) ♦ vt enjabonar
Latin ['lætɪn] n latín m ♦ adj latino; ~ **America** n América latina; **~-American** adj, n latinoamericano/a
latitude ['lætɪtjuːd] n latitud f; (fig) libertad f
latter ['lætə*] adj último; (of two) segundo ♦ n: **the** ~ el último, éste; **~ly** adv últimamente
laudable ['lɔːdəbl] adj loable
laugh [lɑːf] n risa ♦ vi reír(se); (to do sth) for **a** ~ (hacer algo) en broma; ~ **at** vt fus reírse de; ~ **off** vt tomar algo a risa; **~able** adj ridículo; **~ing stock** n: **the ~ing stock of** el hazmerreír de; **~ter** n risa
launch [lɔːntʃ] n lanzamiento; (boat) lancha ♦ vt (ship) botar; (rocket etc) lanzar; (fig) comenzar; ~ **into** vt fus lanzarse a; **~(ing) pad** n plataforma de lanzamiento
launder ['lɔːndə*] vt lavar
Launderette ® [lɔːn'dret] (BRIT) n lavandería (automática)
Laundromat ® ['lɔːndrəmæt] (US) n = **Launderette**
laundry ['lɔːndrɪ] n (dirty) ropa sucia; (clean) colada; (room) lavadero
lavatory ['lævətərɪ] n wáter m
lavender ['lævəndə*] n lavanda
lavish ['lævɪʃ] adj (amount) abundante; (person): ~ **with** pródigo en ♦ vt: **to** ~ **sth on sb** colmar a uno de algo
law [lɔː] n ley f; (SCOL) derecho; (a rule) regla; (professions connected with ~) jurisprudencia; **~-abiding** adj respetuoso de la ley; ~ **and order** n orden m público; ~ **court** n tribunal m (de justicia); **~ful** adj legítimo, lícito;

~less adj (action) criminal
lawn [lɔːn] n césped m; **~mower** n cortacésped m; ~ **tennis** n tenis m sobre hierba
law school (US) n (SCOL) facultad f de derecho
lawsuit ['lɔːsuːt] n pleito
lawyer ['lɔːjə*] n abogado/a; (for sales, wills etc) notario/a
lax [læks] adj laxo
laxative ['læksətɪv] n laxante m
lay [leɪ] (pt, pp laid) pt of lie ♦ adj laico; (not expert) lego ♦ vt (place) colocar; (eggs, table) poner; (cable) tender; (carpet) extender; ~ **aside** or **by** vt dejar a un lado; ~ **down** vt (pen etc) dejar; (rules etc) establecer; **to** ~ **down the law** (pej) imponer las normas; ~ **off** vt (workers) despedir; ~ **on** vt (meal, facilities) proveer; ~ **out** vt (spread out) disponer, exponer; **~about** (inf) n vago/a; **~-by** n (BRIT: AUT) área de aparcamiento
layer ['leɪə*] n capa
layman ['leɪmən] (irreg) n lego
layout ['leɪaʊt] n (design) plan m, trazado; (PRESS) composición f
laze [leɪz] vi (also: ~ about) holgazanear
lazy ['leɪzɪ] adj perezoso, vago; (movement) lento
lb. abbr = **pound** (weight)
lead[1] [liːd] (pt, pp led) n (front position) delantera; (clue) pista; (ELEC) cable m; (for dog) correa; (THEATRE) papel m principal ♦ vt (walk etc in front of) ir a la cabeza de; (guide): **to** ~ **sb somewhere** conducir a uno a algún sitio; (be leader of) dirigir; (start, guide: activity) protagonizar ♦ vi (road, pipe etc) conducir a; (SPORT) ir primero; **to be in the** ~ (SPORT) llevar la delantera; (fig) ir a la cabeza; **to** ~ **the way** (also fig) llevar la delantera; ~ **away** vt llevar; ~ **back** vt (person, route) llevar de vuelta; ~ **on** vt (tease) engañar; ~ **to** vt fus producir, provocar; ~ **up to** vt fus (events) conducir a; (in conversation) preparar el terreno para
lead[2] [lɛd] n (metal) plomo; (in pencil) mina; **~ed petrol** n gasolina con plomo
leader ['liːdə*] n jefe/a m/f, líder m; (SPORT) líder m; **~ship** n dirección f; (position) mando; (quality) iniciativa
leading ['liːdɪŋ] adj (main) principal; (first) primero; (front) delantero; ~ **lady** n (THEATRE) primera actriz f; ~ **light** n (person) figura principal; ~ **man** (irreg) n (THEATRE) primer galán m
lead singer [liːd-] n cantante m/f
leaf [liːf] (pl leaves) n hoja ♦ vi: **to** ~ **through** hojear; **to turn over a new** ~ reformarse
leaflet ['liːflɪt] n folleto
league [liːg] n sociedad f; (FOOTBALL) liga; **to**

be in ~ with haberse confabulado con

leak [liːk] n (of liquid, gas) escape m, fuga; (in pipe) agujero; (in roof) gotera; (in security) filtración f ♦ vi (shoes, ship) hacer agua; (pipe) tener (un) escape; (roof) gotear; (liquid, gas) escaparse, fugarse; (fig) divulgarse ♦ vt (fig) filtrar

lean [liːn] (pt, pp leaned or leant) adj (thin) flaco; (meat) magro ♦ vt: to ~ sth on sth apoyar algo en algo ♦ vi (slope) inclinarse; to ~ against apoyarse contra; to ~ on apoyarse en; ~ **back/forward** vi inclinarse hacia atrás/adelante; ~ **out** vi asomarse; ~ **over** vi inclinarse; ~**ing** n: ~**ing (towards)** inclinación f (hacia); **leant** [lent] pt, pp of lean

leap [liːp] (pt, pp leaped or leapt) n salto ♦ vi saltar; ~**frog** n pídola; ~ **year** n año bisiesto

learn [ləːn] (pt, pp learned or learnt) vt aprender ♦ vi aprender; to ~ **about sth** enterarse de algo; to ~ **to do sth** aprender a hacer algo; ~**ed** [ˈləːnɪd] adj erudito; ~**er** n (BRIT: also: ~**er driver**) principiante m/f; ~**ing** n el saber m, conocimientos mpl

lease [liːs] n arriendo ♦ vt arrendar

leash [liːʃ] n correa

least [liːst] adj: **the** ~ (slightest) el menor, el más pequeño; (smallest amount of) mínimo ♦ adv (+ vb) menos; (+ adj): **the ~ expensive** el/la menos costoso/a; **the ~ possible effort** el menor esfuerzo posible; **at ~** por lo menos, al menos; **you could at ~ have written** por lo menos podías haber escrito; **not in the ~** en absoluto

leather [ˈlɛðə*] n cuero

leave [liːv] (pt, pp left) vt dejar; (go away from) abandonar; (place etc: permanently) salir de ♦ vi irse; (train etc) salir ♦ n permiso; to ~ **sth to sb** (money etc) legar algo a uno; (responsibility etc) encargar a uno de algo; to **be left** quedar, sobrar; **there's some milk left over** sobra or queda algo de leche; **on** ~ de permiso; ~ **behind** vt (on purpose) dejar; (accidentally) dejarse; ~ **out** vt omitir; ~ **of absence** n permiso de ausentarse

leaves [liːvz] npl of leaf

Lebanon [ˈlɛbənən] n: **the** ~ el Líbano

lecherous [ˈlɛtʃərəs] (pej) adj lascivo

lecture [ˈlɛktʃə*] n conferencia; (SCOL) clase f ♦ vi dar una clase ♦ vt (scold): to ~ **sb on** or **about sth** echar una reprimenda a uno por algo; **to give a** ~ **on** dar una conferencia sobre; ~**r** n conferenciante m/f; (BRIT: at university) profesor(a) m/f

led [led] pt, pp of lead

ledge [ledʒ] n (of window) repisa, alféizar m; (of mountain) saliente m

ledger [ˈlɛdʒə*] n libro mayor

leech [liːtʃ] n sanguijuela

leek [liːk] n puerro

leer [lɪə*] vi: to ~ **at sb** mirar de manera lasciva a uno

leeway [ˈliːweɪ] n (fig): **to have some** ~ tener cierta libertad de acción

left [left] pt, pp of leave ♦ adj izquierdo; (remaining): **there are 2** ~ quedan dos ♦ n izquierda ♦ adv a la izquierda; on or to the ~ a la izquierda; **the L~** (POL) la izquierda; ~**handed** adj zurdo; **the ~-hand side** n la izquierda; ~**luggage (office)** (BRIT) n consigna; ~**overs** npl sobras fpl; ~**wing** adj (POL) de izquierdas, izquierdista

leg [leg] n pierna, (of animal, chair) pata; (trouser ~) pernera; (CULIN: of lamb) pierna; (of chicken) pata; (of journey) etapa

legacy [ˈlɛgəsɪ] n herencia

legal [ˈliːgl] adj (permitted by law) lícito; (of law) legal; ~ **holiday** (US) n fiesta oficial; ~**ize** vt legalizar; ~**ly** adv legalmente; ~ **tender** n moneda de curso legal

legend [ˈlɛdʒənd] n (also fig: person) leyenda

legislation [lɛdʒɪsˈleɪʃən] n legislación f

legislature [ˈlɛdʒɪslətʃə*] n cuerpo legislativo

legitimate [lɪˈdʒɪtɪmət] adj legítimo

leg-room n espacio para las piernas

leisure [ˈlɛʒə*] n ocio, tiempo libre; **at** ~ con tranquilidad; ~ **centre** n centro de recreo; ~**ly** adv sin prisa; lento

lemon [ˈlɛmən] n limón m; ~**ade** n (fizzy) gaseosa; ~ **tea** n té m con limón

lend [lend] (pt, pp lent) vt: to ~ **sth to sb** prestar algo a alguien; ~**ing library** n biblioteca de préstamo

length [lɛŋθ] n (size) largo, longitud f; (distance): **the ~ of** todo lo largo de; (of swimming pool, cloth) largo; (of wood, string) trozo; (amount of time) duración f; **at** ~ (at last) por fin, finalmente; (lengthily) largamente; ~**en** vt alargar ♦ vi alargarse; ~**ways** adv a lo largo; ~**y** adj largo, extenso

lenient [ˈliːnɪənt] adj indulgente

lens [lenz] n (of spectacles) lente f; (of camera) objetivo

Lent [lent] n Cuaresma

lent [lent] pt, pp of lend

lentil [ˈlɛntl] n lenteja

Leo [ˈliːəu] n Leo

leotard [ˈliːətɑːd] n mallas fpl

leprosy [ˈlɛprəsɪ] n lepra

lesbian [ˈlɛzbɪən] n lesbiana

less [les] adj (in size, degree etc) menor; (in quality) menos ♦ pron, adv menos ♦ prep: ~ **tax/10% discount** menos impuestos/el 10 por ciento de descuento; ~ **than half** menos de la mitad; ~ **than ever** menos que nunca; ~ **and** ~ cada vez menos; **the** ~ **he works ...** cuanto menos trabaja ...; ~**en** vi disminuir, reducirse ♦ vt disminuir, reducir; ~**er** [ˈlɛsə*] adj menor; **to a ~er extent** en menor grado

lesson ['lɛsn] *n* clase *f*; (*warning*) lección *f*
let [lɛt] (*pt, pp* **let**) *vt* (*allow*) dejar, permitir; (*BRIT: lease*) alquilar; **to ~ sb do sth** dejar que uno haga algo; **to ~ sb know sth** comunicar algo a uno; **~'s go** ¡vamos!; **~ him come que venga**; **"to ~"** "se alquila"; **~ down** *vt* (*tyre*) desinflar; (*disappoint*) defraudar; **~ go** *vi, vt* soltar; **~ in** *vt* dejar entrar; (*visitor etc*) hacer pasar; **~ off** *vt* (*culprit*) dejar escapar; (*gun*) disparar; (*bomb*) accionar; (*firework*) hacer estallar; **~ on** (*inf*) *vi* divulgar; **~ out** *vt* dejar salir; (*sound*) soltar; **~ up** *vi* amainar, disminuir
lethal ['li:θl] *adj* (*weapon*) mortífero; (*poison, wound*) mortal
letter ['lɛtə*] *n* (*of alphabet*) letra; (*correspondence*) carta; **~ bomb** *n* carta-bomba; **~box** (*BRIT*) *n* buzón *m*; **~ing** *n* letras *fpl*
lettuce ['lɛtɪs] *n* lechuga
let-up *n* disminución *f*
leukaemia [lu:'ki:mɪə] (*US* **leukemia**) *n* leucemia
level ['lɛvl] *adj* (*flat*) llano ♦ *adv*: **to draw ~ with** llegar a la altura de ♦ *n* nivel *m*; (*height*) altura ♦ *vt* nivelar; allanar; (*destroy: building*) derribar; (: *forest*) arrasar; **to be ~ with** estar a nivel de; **"A" ~s** (*BRIT*) *npl* ≈ exámenes *mpl* de bachillerato superior, B.U.P.; **"O" ~s** (*BRIT*) *npl* ≈ exámenes *mpl* de octavo de básica; **on the ~** (*fig: honest*) serio; **~ off** *or* **out** *vi* (*prices etc*) estabilizarse; **~ crossing** (*BRIT*) *n* paso a nivel; **~-headed** *adj* sensato
lever ['li:və*] *n* (*also fig*) palanca ♦ *vt*: **to ~ up** levantar con palanca; **~age** *n* (*using bar etc*) apalancamiento; (*fig: influence*) influencia
levy ['lɛvɪ] *n* impuesto ♦ *vt* exigir, recaudar
lewd [lu:d] *adj* lascivo; (*joke*) obsceno, colorado (*AM*)
liability [laɪə'bɪlətɪ] *n* (*pej: person, thing*) estorbo, lastre *m*; (*JUR: responsibility*) responsabilidad *f*; **liabilities** *npl* (*COMM*) pasivo
liable ['laɪəbl] *adj* (*subject*): **~ to** sujeto a; (*responsible*): **~ for** responsable de; (*likely*): **~ to do** propenso a hacer
liaise [lɪ'eɪz] *vi*: **to ~ with** enlazar con; **liaison** [lɪ'eɪzɔn] *n* (*coordination*) enlace *m*; (*affair*) relaciones *fpl* amorosas
liar ['laɪə*] *n* mentiroso/a
libel ['laɪbl] *n* calumnia ♦ *vt* calumniar
liberal ['lɪbərəl] *adj* liberal; (*offer, amount etc*) generoso
liberate ['lɪbəreɪt] *vt* (*people: from poverty etc*) librar; (*prisoner*) libertar; (*country*) liberar
liberty ['lɪbətɪ] *n* libertad *f*; (*criminal*): **to be at ~** estar en libertad; **to be at ~ to do** estar libre para hacer; **to take the ~ of doing sth** tomarse la libertad de hacer algo

Libra ['li:brə] *n* Libra
librarian [laɪ'brɛərɪən] *n* bibliotecario/a
library ['laɪbrərɪ] *n* biblioteca
libretto [lɪ'brɛtəʊ] *n* libreto
Libya ['lɪbɪə] *n* Libia; **~n** *adj, n* libio/a *m/f*
lice [laɪs] *npl of* **louse**
licence ['laɪsəns] (*US* **license**) *n* licencia; (*permit*) permiso; (*also: driving ~*), (*US*) **driver's ~**) carnet *m* de conducir (*SP*), permiso (*AM*)
license ['laɪsəns] *n* (*US*) = **licence** ♦ *vt* autorizar, dar permiso a; **~d** *adj* (*for alcohol*) autorizado para vender bebidas alcohólicas; (*car*) matriculado; **~ plate** (*US*) *n* placa (de matrícula)
lick [lɪk] *vt* lamer; (*inf: defeat*) dar una paliza a; **to ~ one's lips** relamerse
licorice ['lɪkərɪs] (*US*) *n* = **liquorice**
lid [lɪd] *n* (*of box, case*) tapa; (*of pan*) tapadera
lido ['laɪdəʊ] *n* (*BRIT*) piscina
lie [laɪ] (*pt* **lay**, *pp* **lain**) *vi* (*rest*) estar echado, estar acostado; (*of object: be situated*) estar, encontrarse; (*tell lies: pt, pp* **lied**) mentir ♦ *n* mentira; **to ~ low** (*fig*) mantenerse a escondidas; **~ about** *or* **around** *vi* (*things*) estar tirado; (*BRIT: people*) estar tumbado; **~ down** (*BRIT*) *n*: **to have a ~down** echarse (una siesta); **~-in** (*BRIT*) *n*: **to have a ~-in** quedarse en la cama
lieu [lu:]: **in ~ of** *prep* en lugar de
lieutenant [lɛf'tɛnənt, (*US*) lu:'tɛnənt] *n* (*MIL*) teniente *m*
life [laɪf] (*pl* **lives**) *n* vida; **to come to ~** animarse; **~ assurance** (*BRIT*) *n* seguro de vida; **~belt** (*BRIT*) *n* salvavidas *m inv*; **~boat** *n* lancha de socorro; **~guard** *n* vigilante *m/f*, socorrista *m/f*; **~ insurance** *n* = **~ assurance**; **~ jacket** *n* chaleco salvavidas; **~less** *adj* sin vida; (*dull*) soso; **~like** *adj* (*model etc*) que parece vivo; (*realistic*) realista; **~long** *adj* de toda la vida; **~ preserver** (*US*) *n* cinturón *m*/chaleco salvavidas; **~ sentence** *n* cadena perpetua; **~-size** *adj* de tamaño natural; **~ span** *n* vida; **~style** *n* estilo de vida; **~ support system** *n* (*MED*) sistema *m* de respiración asistida; **~time** *n* (*of person*) vida; (*of thing*) período de vida
lift [lɪft] *vt* levantar; (*end: ban, rule*) levantar, suprimir ♦ *vi* (*fog*) disiparse ♦ *n* (*BRIT: machine*) ascensor *m*; **to give sb a ~** (*BRIT*) llevar a uno en el coche; **~-off** *n* despegue *m*
light [laɪt] (*pt, pp* **lighted** *or* **lit**) *n* luz *f*; (*lamp*) luz *f*, lámpara; (*AUT*) faro; (*for cigarette etc*): **have you got a ~?** ¿tienes fuego? ♦ *vt* (*candle, cigarette, fire*) encender (*SP*), prender (*AM*); (*room*) alumbrar ♦ *adj* (*colour*) claro; (*not heavy, also fig*) ligero; (*room*) con mucha luz; (*gentle, graceful*) ágil; **~s** *npl* (*traffic ~s*)

lightning → list

314

semáforos *mpl*; **to come to ~** salir a luz; **in the ~ of** (*new evidence etc*) a la luz de; **~ up** *vi* (*smoke*) encender un cigarrillo; (*face*) iluminarse ♦ *vt* (*illuminate*) iluminar, alumbrar; (*set fire to*) encender; **~ bulb** *n* bombilla (*SP*), foco (*AM*); **~en** *vt* (*make less heavy*) aligerar; **~er** *n* (*also: cigarette ~er*) encendedor *m*, mechero; **~-headed** *adj* (*dizzy*) mareado; (*excited*) exaltado; **~-hearted** *adj* (*person*) alegre; (*remark etc*) divertido; **~house** *n* faro; **~ing** (*system*) alumbrado; **~ly** *adv* ligeramente; (*not seriously*) con poca seriedad; **to get off ~ly** ser castigado con poca severidad; **~ness** *n* (*in weight*) ligereza

lightning ['laɪtnɪŋ] *n* relámpago, rayo; **~ conductor** (*US* **~ rod**) *n* pararrayos *m inv*

light: **~ pen** *n* lápiz *m* óptico; **~weight** *adj* (*suit*) ligero ♦ *n* (*BOXING*) peso ligero; **~ year** *n* año luz

like [laɪk] *vt* gustarle a uno ♦ *prep* como ♦ *adj* parecido, semejante ♦ *n*: **and the ~** y otros por el estilo; **his ~s and dislikes** sus gustos y aversiones; **I would ~**, **I'd ~** me gustaría; (*for purchase*) quisiera; **would you ~ a coffee?** ¿te apetece un café?; **I ~ swimming** me gusta nadar; **she ~s apples** le gustan las manzanas; **to be** *or* **look ~ sb/sth** parecerse a alguien/algo; **what does it look/taste/sound ~?** ¿cómo es/a qué sabe/cómo suena?; **that's just ~ him** es muy de él, es característico de él; **do it ~ this** hazlo así; **it is nothing ~ ...** no tiene parecido alguno con ...; **~able** *adj* simpático, agradable

likelihood ['laɪklɪhud] *n* probabilidad *f*

likely ['laɪklɪ] *adj* probable; **he's ~ to leave** is probable que se vaya; **not ~!** ¡ni hablar!

likeness ['laɪknɪs] *n* semejanza, parecido; **that's a good ~** se parece mucho

likewise ['laɪkwaɪz] *adv* igualmente; **to do ~** hacer lo mismo

liking ['laɪkɪŋ] *n*: **~ (for)** (*person*) cariño (a); (*thing*) afición (a); **to be to sb's ~** ser del gusto de uno

lilac ['laɪlək] *n* (*tree*) lilo; (*flower*) lila

lily ['lɪlɪ] *n* lirio, azucena; **~ of the valley** *n* lirio de los valles

limb [lɪm] *n* miembro

limber ['lɪmbə*] to: **~ up** *vi* (*SPORT*) hacer ejercicios de calentamiento

limbo ['lɪmbəu] *n*: **to be in ~** (*fig*) quedar a la expectativa

lime [laɪm] *n* (*tree*) limero; (*fruit*) lima; (*GEO*) cal *f*

limelight ['laɪmlaɪt] *n*: **to be in the ~** (*fig*) ser el centro de atención

limerick ['lɪmərɪk] *n especie de poema humorístico*

limestone ['laɪmstəun] *n* piedra caliza

limit ['lɪmɪt] *n* límite *m* ♦ *vt* limitar; **~ed** *adj* limitado; **to be ~ed to** limitarse a; **~ed (liability) company** (*BRIT*) *n* sociedad *f* anónima

limousine ['lɪməziːn] *n* limusina

limp [lɪmp] *n*: **to have a ~** tener cojera ♦ *vi* cojear ♦ *adj* flojo; (*material*) fláccido

limpet ['lɪmpɪt] *n* lapa

line [laɪn] *n* línea; (*rope*) cuerda; (*for fishing*) sedal *m*; (*wire*) hilo; (*row, series*) fila, hilera; (*of writing*) renglón *m*, línea; (*of song*) verso; (*on face*) arruga; (*RAIL*) vía ♦ *vt* (*road etc*) llenar; (*SEWING*) forrar; **to ~ the streets** llenar las aceras; **in ~ with** alineado con; (*according to*) de acuerdo con; **~ up** *vi* hacer cola ♦ *vt* alinear; (*prepare*) preparar; organizar

lined [laɪnd] *adj* (*face*) arrugado; (*paper*) rayado

linen ['lɪnɪn] *n* ropa blanca; (*cloth*) lino

liner ['laɪnə*] *n* vapor *m* de línea, transatlántico; (*for bin*) bolsa (de basura)

linesman ['laɪnzmən] *n* (*SPORT*) juez *m* de línea

line-up *n* (*US: queue*) cola; (*SPORT*) alineación *f*

linger ['lɪŋgə*] *vi* retrasarse, tardar en marcharse; (*smell, tradition*) persistir

lingerie ['lænʒəriː] *n* lencería

linguist ['lɪŋgwɪst] *n* lingüista *m/f*; **~ics** *n* lingüística

lining ['laɪnɪŋ] *n* forro; (*ANAT*) (membrana) mucosa

link [lɪŋk] *n* (*of a chain*) eslabón *m*; (*relationship*) relación *f*, vínculo ♦ *vt* vincular, unir; (*associate*): **to ~ with** *or* **to** relacionar con; **~s** *npl* (*GOLF*) campo de golf; **~ up** *vt* acoplar ♦ *vi* unirse

lino ['laɪnəu] *n* = **linoleum**

linoleum [lɪ'nəulɪəm] *n* linóleo

lion ['laɪən] *n* león *m*; **~ess** *n* leona

lip [lɪp] *n* labio

liposuction ['lɪpəusʌkʃən] *n* liposucción *f*

lip: **~read** *vi* leer los labios; **~ salve** *n* crema protectora para labios; **~ service** *n*: **to pay ~ service to sth** (*pej*) prometer algo de boquilla; **~stick** *n* lápiz *m* de labios, carmín *m*

liqueur [lɪ'kjuə*] *n* licor *m*

liquid ['lɪkwɪd] *adj, n* líquido; **~ize** [-aɪz] *vt* (*CULIN*) licuar; **~izer** [-aɪzə*] *n* licuadora

liquor ['lɪkə*] *n* licor *m*, bebidas *fpl* alcohólicas

liquorice ['lɪkərɪs] (*BRIT*) *n* regaliz *m*

liquor store (*US*) *n* bodega, tienda de vinos y bebidas alcohólicas

Lisbon ['lɪzbən] *n* Lisboa

lisp [lɪsp] *n* ceceo ♦ *vi* cecear

list [lɪst] *n* lista ♦ *vt* (*mention*) enumerar; (*put on a list*) poner en una lista; **~ed building** (*BRIT*) *n* monumento declarado de interés *histórico-artístico*

listen ['lɪsn] *vi* escuchar, oír; **to ~ to sb/sth** escuchar a uno/algo; **~er** *n* oyente *m/f*; (*RADIO*) radioyente *m/f*

listless ['lɪstlɪs] *adj* apático, indiferente

lit [lɪt] *pt, pp of* **light**

liter ['liːtə*] (*US*) *n* = **litre**

literacy ['lɪtərəsɪ] *n* capacidad *f* de leer y escribir

literal ['lɪtərl] *adj* literal

literary ['lɪtərərɪ] *adj* literario

literate ['lɪtərət] *adj* que sabe leer y escribir; (*educated*) culto

literature ['lɪtərɪtʃə*] *n* literatura *f*; (*brochures etc*) folletos *mpl*

lithe [laɪð] *adj* ágil

litigation [lɪtɪ'geɪʃən] *n* litigio

litre ['liːtə*] (*US* **liter**) *n* litro

litter ['lɪtə*] *n* (*rubbish*) basura; (*young animals*) camada, cría; **~ bin** (*BRIT*) *n* papelera; **~ed** *adj*: **~ed with** (*scattered*) lleno de

little ['lɪtl] *adj* (*small*) pequeño; (*not much*) poco ♦ *adv* poco; **a ~** un poco (de); **~ house/bird** casita/pajarito; **a ~ bit** un poquito; **~ by ~** poco a poco; **~ finger** *n* dedo meñique

live¹ [laɪv] *adj* (*animal*) vivo; (*wire*) conectado; (*broadcast*) en directo; (*shell*) cargado

live² [lɪv] *vi* vivir; **~ down** *vt* hacer olvidar; **~ on** *vt fus* (*food, salary*) vivir de; **~ together** *vi* vivir juntos; **~ up to** *vt fus* (*fulfil*) cumplir con

livelihood ['laɪvlɪhud] *n* sustento

lively ['laɪvlɪ] *adj* vivo; (*interesting: place, book etc*) animado

liven up ['laɪvn-] *vt* animar ♦ *vi* animarse

liver ['lɪvə*] *n* hígado

lives [laɪvz] *npl of* **life**

livestock ['laɪvstɔk] *n* ganado

livid ['lɪvɪd] *adj* lívido; (*furious*) furioso

living ['lɪvɪŋ] *adj* (*alive*) vivo ♦ *n*: **to earn** or **make a ~** ganarse la vida; **~ conditions** *npl* condiciones *fpl* de vida; **~ room** *n* sala (de estar); **~ standards** *npl* nivel *m* de vida; **~ wage** *n* jornal *m* suficiente para vivir

lizard ['lɪzəd] *n* lagarto; (*small*) lagartija

load [ləud] *n* carga; (*weight*) peso ♦ *vt* (*COMPUT*) cargar; (*also: ~ up*): **to ~ (with)** cargar (con or de); **a ~ of rubbish** (*inf*) tonterías *fpl*; **a ~ of, ~s of** (*fig*) (gran) cantidad f, montones de; **~ed** *adj* (*vehicle*): **to be ~ed with** estar cargado de; (*question*) intencionado; (*inf: rich*) forrado (de dinero)

loaf [ləuf] (*pl* **loaves**) *n* (barra de) pan *m*

loan [ləun] *n* préstamo ♦ *vt* prestar; **on ~** prestado

loath [ləuθ] *adj*: **to be ~ to do sth** estar poco

dispuesto a hacer algo

loathe [ləuð] *vt* aborrecer; (*person*) odiar; **loathing** *n* aversión *f*; odio

loaves [ləuvz] *npl of* **loaf**

lobby ['lɔbɪ] *n* vestíbulo, sala de espera; (*POL: pressure group*) grupo de presión ♦ *vt* presionar

lobster ['lɔbstə*] *n* langosta

local ['ləukl] *adj* local ♦ *n* (*pub*) bar *m*; **the ~s** los vecinos, los del lugar; **~ anaesthetic** *n* (*MED*) anestesia local; **~ authority** *n* municipio, ayuntamiento (*SP*); **~ call** *n* (*TEL*) llamada local; **~ government** *n* gobierno municipal; **~ity** [-'kælɪtɪ] *n* localidad *f*; **~ly** [-kəlɪ] *adv* en la vecindad; por aquí

locate [ləu'keɪt] *vt* (*find*) localizar; (*situate*): **to be ~d in** estar situado en

location [ləu'keɪʃən] *n* situación *f*; **on ~** (*CINEMA*) en exteriores

loch [lɔx] *n* lago

lock [lɔk] *n* (*of door, box*) cerradura; (*of canal*) esclusa; (*of hair*) mechón *m* ♦ *vt* (*with key*) cerrar (con llave) ♦ *vi* (*door etc*) cerrarse (con llave); (*wheels*) trabarse; **~ in** *vt* encerrar; **~ out** *vt* (*person*) cerrar la puerta a; **~ up** *vt* (*criminal*) meter en la cárcel; (*mental patient*) encerrar; (*house*) cerrar (con llave) ♦ *vi* echar la llave

locker ['lɔkə*] *n* casillero

locket ['lɔkɪt] *n* medallón *m*

locksmith ['lɔksmɪθ] *n* cerrajero/a

lockup ['lɔkʌp] *n* (*jail, cell*) cárcel *f*

locum ['ləukəm] *n* (*MED*) (médico/a) interino/a

locust ['ləukəst] *n* langosta

lodge [lɔdʒ] *n* casita (del guarda) ♦ *vi* (*person*): **to ~ (with)** alojarse (en casa de); (*bullet, bone*) incrustarse ♦ *vt* (*complaint*) presentar; **~r** *n* huésped(a) *m/f*

lodgings ['lɔdʒɪŋz] *npl* alojamiento

loft [lɔft] *n* desván *m*

lofty ['lɔftɪ] *adj* (*noble*) sublime; (*haughty*) altanero

log [lɔg] *n* (*of wood*) leño, tronco; (*written account*) diario ♦ *vt* anotar

logbook ['lɔgbuk] *n* (*NAUT*) diario de a bordo; (*AVIAT*) libro de vuelo; (*of car*) documentación *f* (del coche *SP*) or carro (*AM*)

loggerheads ['lɔgəhɛdz] *npl*: **to be at ~ (with)** estar en desacuerdo (con)

logic ['lɔdʒɪk] *n* lógica; **~al** *adj* lógico

logo ['ləugəu] *n* logotipo

loin [lɔɪn] *n* (*CULIN*) lomo, solomillo

loiter ['lɔɪtə*] *vi* (*linger*) entretenerse

loll [lɔl] *vi* (*also: ~ about*) repantigarse

lollipop ['lɔlɪpɔp] *n* chupa-chups ® *m inv*, pirulí *m*; **~ man/lady** (*BRIT irreg*) *n* persona encargada de ayudar a los niños a cruzar la *calle*

London ['lʌndən] n Londres; **~er** n londinense *m/f*

lone [ləun] *adj* solitario

loneliness ['ləunlinis] n soledad *f*; aislamiento

lonely ['ləunli] *adj* (*situation*) solitario; (*person*) solo; (*place*) aislado

long [lɔŋ] *adj* largo ♦ *adv* mucho tiempo, largamente ♦ *vi*: **to ~ for sth** anhelar algo; **so or as ~ as** mientras, con tal que; **don't be ~!** ¡no tardes!, ¡vuelve pronto!; **how ~ is the street?** ¿cuánto tiene la calle de largo?; **how ~ is the lesson?** ¿cuánto dura la clase?; **6 metres ~** que mide 6 metros, de 6 metros de largo; **6 months ~** que dura 6 meses, de 6 meses de duración; **all night ~** toda la noche; **he no ~er comes ya no viene; ~ before** mucho antes; **before ~** (+ *future*) dentro de poco; (+ *past*) poco tiempo después; **at ~ last** al fin, por fin; **~-distance** *adj* (*race*) de larga distancia; (*call*) interurbano; **~-haired** *adj* de pelo largo; **~hand** n escritura sin abreviaturas; **~ing** n anhelo, ansia; (*nostalgia*) nostalgia ♦ *adj* anhelante

longitude ['lɔŋgɪtjuːd] n longitud *f*

long: ~ jump n salto de longitud; **~-life** *adj* (*batteries*) de larga duración; (*milk*) uperizado; **~-lost** *adj* desaparecido hace mucho tiempo; **~-range** *adj* (*plan*) de gran alcance; (*missile*) de largo alcance; **~-sighted** (BRIT) *adj* présbita; **~-standing** *adj* de mucho tiempo; **~-suffering** *adj* sufrido; **~-term** *adj* a largo plazo; **~ wave** n onda larga; **~-winded** *adj* prolijo

loo [luː] (BRIT: *inf*) n wáter *m*

look [luk] *vi* mirar; (*seem*) parecer; (*building etc*): **to ~ south/on to the sea** dar al sur/al mar ♦ n (*gen*): **to have a ~** mirar; (*glance*) mirada; (*appearance*) aire *m*, aspecto; **~s** *npl* (*good ~s*) belleza; **~ (here)!** (*expressing annoyance etc*) ¡oye!; **~!** (*expressing surprise*) ¡mira!; **~ after** *vt fus* (*care for*) cuidar a; (*deal with*) encargarse de; **~ at** *vt fus* mirar; (*read quickly*) echar un vistazo a; **~ back** *vi* mirar hacia atrás; **~ down on** *vt fus* (*fig*) despreciar, mirar con desprecio; **~ for** *vt fus* buscar; **~ forward to** *vt fus* esperar con ilusión; (*in letters*): **we ~ forward to hearing from you** quedamos a la espera de sus gratas noticias; **~ into** *vt* investigar; **~ on** *vi* mirar (como espectador); **~ out** *vi* (*beware*): **to ~ out (for)** tener cuidado (de); **~ out for** *vt fus* (*seek*) buscar; (*await*) esperar; **~ round** *vi* volver la cabeza; **~ through** *vt fus* (*examine*) examinar; **~ to** *vt fus* (*rely on*) contar con; **~ up** *vi* mirar hacia arriba; (*improve*) mejorar ♦ *vt* (*word*) buscar; **~ up to** *vt fus* admirar; **~-out** n (*tower etc*) puesto de observación;

(*person*) vigía *m/f*; **to be on the ~-out for sth** estar al acecho de algo

loom [luːm] *vi*: **~ (up)** (*threaten*) surgir, amenazar; (*event: approach*) aproximarse

loony ['luːni] (*inf*) n, *adj* loco/a *m/f*

loop [luːp] n lazo ♦ *vt*: **to ~ sth round sth** pasar algo alrededor de algo; **~hole** n escapatoria

loose [luːs] *adj* suelto; (*clothes*) ancho; (*morals, discipline*) relajado; **to be on the ~** estar en libertad; **to be at a ~ end or at ~ ends** (US) no saber qué hacer; **~ change** n cambio; **~ chippings** *npl* (*on road*) gravilla suelta; **~ly** *adv* libremente, aproximadamente; **~n** *vt* aflojar

loot [luːt] n botín *m* ♦ *vt* saquear

lop off [lɔp-] *vt* (*branches*) podar

lop-sided *adj* torcido

lord [lɔːd] n señor *m*; **L~ Smith** Lord Smith; **the L~** el Señor; **my ~** (*to bishop*) Ilustrísima; (*to noble etc*) Señor; **good L~!** ¡Dios mío!; **the (House of) L~s** (BRIT) la Cámara de los Lores; **~ship** n: **your L~ship** su Señoría

lore [lɔː*] n tradiciones *fpl*

lorry ['lɔri] (BRIT) n camión *m*; **~ driver** n camionero/a

lose [luːz] (*pt, pp* **lost**) *vt* perder ♦ *vi* perder, ser vencido; **to ~ (time)** (*clock*) atrasarse; **~r** n perdedor(a) *m/f*

loss [lɔs] n pérdida; **heavy ~es** (MIL) grandes pérdidas; **to be at a ~** no saber qué hacer; **to make a ~** sufrir pérdidas

lost [lɔst] *pt, pp of* **lose** ♦ *adj* perdido; **~ property** (US **and found**) n objetos *mpl* perdidos

lot [lɔt] n (*group: of things*) grupo; (*at auctions*) lote *m*; **the ~** el todo, todos; **a ~** (*large number: of books etc*) muchos; (*a great deal*) mucho, bastante; **a ~ of, ~s of** mucho(s) (*pl*); **I read a ~** leo bastante; **to draw ~s (for sth)** echar suertes (para decidir algo)

lotion ['ləuʃən] n loción *f*

lottery ['lɔtəri] n lotería

loud [laud] *adj* (*voice, sound*) fuerte; (*laugh, shout*) estrepitoso; (*condemnation etc*) enérgico; (*gaudy*) chillón/ona ♦ *adv* (*speak etc*) fuerte; **out ~** en voz alta; **~hailer** (BRIT) n megáfono; **~ly** *adv* (*noisily*) fuerte; (*aloud*) en voz alta; **~speaker** n altavoz *m*

lounge [laundʒ] n salón *m*, sala (de estar); (*at airport etc*) sala; (BRIT: *also*: **~-bar**) salón-bar *m* ♦ *vi* (*also*: **~ about or around**) reposar, holgazanear

louse [laus] (*pl* **lice**) n piojo

lousy ['lauzi] (*inf*) *adj* (*bad quality*) malísimo, asqueroso; (*ill*) fatal

lout [laut] n gamberro/a

lovable ['lʌvəbl] *adj* amable, simpático

love [lʌv] n (romantic, sexual) amor m; (kind, caring) cariño ♦ vt amar, querer; (thing, activity) encantarle a uno; "~ from Anne" (on letter) "un abrazo (de) Anne"; **to ~ to do** encantarle a uno hacer; **to be/fall in ~ with** estar enamorado/enamorarse de; **to make ~** hacer el amor; **for the ~ of** por amor de; "**15 ~**" (TENNIS) "15 a cero"; **I ~ paella** me encanta la paella; **~ affair** n aventura sentimental; **~ letter** n carta de amor; **~ life** n vida sentimental

lovely ['lʌvlɪ] adj (delightful) encantador(a); (beautiful) precioso

lover ['lʌvə*] n amante m/f; (person in love) enamorado; (amateur): **a ~ of** un(a) aficionado/a or un(a) amante de

loving ['lʌvɪŋ] adj amoroso, cariñoso; (action) tierno

low [ləu] adj, ad bajo ♦ n (METEOROLOGY) área de baja presión; **to be ~ on** (supplies etc) andar mal de; **to feel ~** sentirse deprimido; **to turn (down) ~** bajar; **~-alcohol** adj de bajo contenido en alcohol; **~-calorie** adj bajo en calorías; **~-cut** adj (dress) escotado

lower ['ləuə*] adj más bajo; (less important) menos importante ♦ vt bajar; (reduce) reducir ♦ vr: **to ~ o.s. to** (fig) rebajarse a

low: **~-fat** adj (milk, yoghurt) desnatado; (diet) bajo en calorías; **~lands** npl (GEO) tierras fpl bajas; **~ly** adj humilde, inferior; **~ season** n la temporada baja

loyal ['lɔɪəl] adj leal; **~ty** n lealtad f; **~ty card** n tarjeta cliente

lozenge ['lɔzɪndʒ] n (MED) pastilla

L.P. n abbr (= long-playing record) elepé m

L-plates ['el-] (BRIT) npl placas fpl de aprendiz de conductor

Ltd abbr (= limited company) S.A.

lubricate ['lu:brɪkeɪt] vt lubricar, engrasar

luck [lʌk] n suerte f; **bad ~** mala suerte; **good ~!** ¡que tengas suerte!, ¡suerte!; **bad or hard or tough ~!** ¡qué pena!; **~ily** adv afortunadamente; **~y** adj afortunado; (at cards etc) con suerte; (object) que trae suerte

ludicrous ['lu:dɪkrəs] adj absurdo

lug [lʌg] vt (drag) arrastrar

luggage ['lʌgɪdʒ] n equipaje m; **~ rack** n (on car) baca, portaequipajes m inv

lukewarm ['lu:kwɔ:m] adj tibio

lull [lʌl] n tregua ♦ vt: **to ~ sb to sleep** arrullar a uno; **to ~ sb into a false sense of security** dar a alguien una falsa sensación de seguridad

lullaby ['lʌləbaɪ] n nana

lumbago [lʌm'beɪgəu] n lumbago

lumber ['lʌmbə*] n (junk) trastos mpl viejos; (wood) maderos mpl; **~ with** vt: **to be ~ed with** tener que cargar con algo; **~jack** n maderero

luminous ['lu:mɪnəs] adj luminoso

lump [lʌmp] n terrón m; (fragment) trozo; (swelling) bulto ♦ vt (also: ~ together) juntar; **~ sum** n suma global; **~y** adj (sauce) lleno de grumos; (mattress) lleno de bultos

lunatic ['lu:nətɪk] adj loco

lunch [lʌntʃ] n almuerzo, comida ♦ vi almorzar

luncheon ['lʌntʃən] n almuerzo; **~ voucher** (BRIT) n vale m de comida

lunch time n hora de comer

lung [lʌŋ] n pulmón m

lunge [lʌndʒ] vi (also: ~ forward) abalanzarse; **to ~ at** arremeter contra

lurch [lɜ:tʃ] vi dar sacudidas ♦ n sacudida; **to leave sb in the ~** dejar a uno plantado

lure [luə*] n (attraction) atracción f ♦ vt tentar

lurid ['luərɪd] adj (colour) chillón/ona; (account) espeluznante

lurk [lɜ:k] vi (person, animal) estar al acecho; (fig) acechar

luscious ['lʌʃəs] adj (attractive: person, thing) precioso; (food) delicioso

lush [lʌʃ] adj exuberante

lust [lʌst] n lujuria; (greed) codicia

lustre ['lʌstə*] (US luster) n lustre m, brillo

lusty ['lʌstɪ] adj robusto, fuerte

Luxembourg ['lʌksəmbəːg] n Luxemburgo

luxuriant [lʌg'zjuərɪənt] adj exuberante

luxurious [lʌg'zjuərɪəs] adj lujoso

luxury ['lʌkʃərɪ] n lujo ♦ cpd de lujo

lying ['laɪɪŋ] n mentiras fpl ♦ adj mentiroso

lyrical ['lɪrɪkl] adj lírico

lyrics ['lɪrɪks] npl (of song) letra

M, m

m. abbr = metre; mile; million

M.A. abbr = Master of Arts

mac [mæk] (BRIT) n impermeable m

macaroni [mækə'rəunɪ] n macarrones mpl

machine [mə'ʃi:n] n máquina ♦ vt (dress etc) coser a máquina; (TECH) hacer a máquina; **~ gun** n ametralladora; **~ language** n (COMPUT) lenguaje m máquina; **~ry** n maquinaria; (fig) mecanismo

macho ['mætʃəu] adj machista

mackerel ['mækrl] n inv caballa

mackintosh ['mækɪntɔʃ] (BRIT) n impermeable m

mad [mæd] adj loco; (idea) disparatado; (angry) furioso; (keen): **to be ~ about sth** volverle loco a uno algo

madam ['mædəm] n señora

madden ['mædn] vt volver loco

made [meɪd] pt, pp of make

Madeira [mə'dɪərə] n (GEO) Madera; (wine) vino de Madera

made-to-measure (BRIT) adj hecho a la

medida
madly ['mædlɪ] adv locamente
madman ['mædmən] (irreg) n loco
madness ['mædnɪs] n locura
Madrid [mə'drɪd] n Madrid
magazine [mægə'ziːn] n revista; (RADIO, TV)
programa m magazina
maggot ['mægət] n gusano
magic ['mædʒɪk] n magia ♦ adj mágico; **~ian**
[mə'dʒɪʃən] n mago/a; (conjurer) presti-
digitador(a) m/f
magistrate ['mædʒɪstreɪt] n juez m/f
(municipal)
magnet ['mægnɪt] n imán m; **~ic** [-'netɪk] adj
magnético; (personality) atrayente
magnificent [mæg'nɪfɪsənt] adj magnífico
magnify ['mægnɪfaɪ] vt (object) ampliar;
(sound) aumentar; **~ing glass** n lupa
magpie ['mægpaɪ] n urraca
mahogany [mə'hɒgənɪ] n caoba
maid [meɪd] n criada; **old ~** (pej) solterona
maiden ['meɪdn] n doncella ♦ adj (aunt etc)
solterona; (speech, voyage) inaugural;
~ name n nombre m de soltera
mail [meɪl] n correo; (letters) cartas fpl ♦ vt
echar al correo; **~box** (US) n buzón m; **~ing
list** n lista de direcciones; **~-order** n pedido
postal
maim [meɪm] vt mutilar, lisiar
main [meɪn] adj principal, mayor ♦ n (pipe)
cañería maestra; (US) red f eléctrica; **the ~s**
npl (BRIT: ELEC) la red eléctrica; **in the ~** en
general; **~frame** n (COMPUT) ordenador m
central; **~land** n tierra firme; **~ly** adv
principalmente; **~ road** n carretera; **~stay** n
(fig) pilar m; **~stream** n corriente f principal
maintain [meɪn'teɪn] vt mantener;
maintenance ['meɪntənəns] n mantenimiento; (LAW) manutención f
maize [meɪz] (BRIT) n maíz m (SP), choclo
(AM)
majestic [mə'dʒestɪk] adj majestuoso
majesty ['mædʒɪstɪ] n majestad f; (title):
Your M~ Su Majestad
major ['meɪdʒə*] n (MIL) comandante m ♦ adj
principal; (MUS) mayor
Majorca [mə'jɔːkə] n Mallorca
majority [mə'dʒɔrɪtɪ] n mayoría
make [meɪk] (pt, pp made) vt hacer;
(manufacture) fabricar; (mistake) cometer;
(speech) pronunciar; (cause to be): **to ~ sb
sad** poner triste a alguien; (force): **to ~ sb do
sth** obligar a alguien a hacer algo; (earn)
ganar; (equal): **2 and 2 ~ 4** 2 y 2 son 4 ♦ n
marca; **to ~ the bed** hacer la cama; **to ~ a
fool of sb** poner a alguien en ridículo; **to ~ a
profit/loss** obtener ganancias/sufrir pérdidas;
to ~ it (arrive) llegar; (achieve sth) tener
éxito; **what time do you ~ it?** ¿qué hora

tienes?; **to ~ do with** contentarse con; **~ for**
vt fus (place) dirigirse a; **~ out** vt (decipher)
descifrar; (understand) entender; (see)
distinguir; (cheque) extender; **~ up** vt
(invent) inventar; (prepare) hacer; (constitute)
constituir ♦ vi reconciliarse; (with cosmetics)
maquillarse; **~ up for** vt fus compensar; **~-
believe** n ficción f, invención f; **~r** n
fabricante m/f; (of film, programme) autor(a)
m/f; **~shift** adj improvisado; **~-up** n
maquillaje m; **~-up remover** n
desmaquillador m
making ['meɪkɪŋ] n (fig): **in the ~** en vías de
formación; **to have the ~s of** (person) tener
madera de
Malaysia [mə'leɪzɪə] n Malasia, Malaysia
male [meɪl] n (BIOL) macho ♦ adj (sex,
attitude) masculino; (child etc) varón
malfunction [mæl'fʌŋkʃən] n mal
funcionamiento
malice ['mælɪs] n malicia; **malicious**
[mə'lɪʃəs] adj malicioso; rencoroso
malignant [mə'lɪgnənt] adj (MED) maligno
mall [mɔːl] (US) n (also: shopping ~) centro
comercial
mallet ['mælɪt] n mazo
malnutrition [mælnjuː'trɪʃən] n desnutrición
f
malpractice [mæl'præktɪs] n negligencia
profesional
malt [mɔːlt] n malta; (whisky) whisky m de
malta
Malta ['mɔːltə] n Malta; **Maltese** [-'tiːz] adj,
n inv maltés/esa m/f
mammal ['mæml] n mamífero
mammoth ['mæməθ] n mamut m ♦ adj
gigantesco
man [mæn] (pl men) n hombre m; (~kind) el
hombre ♦ vt (NAUT) tripular; (MIL) guarnecer;
(operate: machine) manejar; **an old ~** un
viejo; **~ and wife** marido y mujer
manage ['mænɪdʒ] vi arreglárselas, ir tirando
♦ vt (be in charge of) dirigir; (control: person)
manejar; (: ship) gobernar; **~able** adj
manejable; **~ment** n dirección f; **~r** n
director(a) m/f; (of pop star) mánayer m/f;
(SPORT) entrenador(a) m/f; **~ress** n directora;
entrenadora; **~rial** [-ə'dʒɪərɪəl] adj directivo;
managing director n director(a) m/f
general
mandarin ['mændərɪn] n (also: ~ orange)
mandarina; (person) mandarín m
mandatory ['mændətərɪ] adj obligatorio
mane [meɪn] n (of horse) crin f; (of lion)
melena
maneuver [mə'nuːvə*] (US) = **manoeuvre**
manfully ['mænfəlɪ] adv valientemente
mangle ['mæŋgl] vt mutilar, destrozar
man: **~handle** vt maltratar; **~hole** n agujero

de acceso; **~hood** n edad f viril; (state)
virilidad f; **~~hour** n hora-hombre f; **~hunt** n
(POLICE) búsqueda y captura
mania ['meɪnɪə] n manía; **~c** ['meɪnɪæk] n
maníaco/a; (fig) maniático
manic ['mænɪk] adj frenético; **~-depressive**
n maníaco/a depresivo/a
manicure ['mænɪkjuə*] n manicura
manifest ['mænɪfest] vt manifestar, mostrar
♦ adj manifiesto
manifesto [mænɪ'festəu] n manifiesto
manipulate [mə'nɪpjuleɪt] vt manipular
man: **~kind** [mæn'kaɪnd] n humanidad f,
género humano; **~ly** adj varonil; **~-made** adj
artificial
manner ['mænə*] n manera, modo;
(behaviour) conducta, manera de ser; (type):
all ~ of things toda clase de cosas; **~s** npl
(behaviour) modales mpl; **bad ~s** mala
educación; **~ism** n peculiaridad f de lenguaje
(or de comportamiento)
manoeuvre [mə'nu:və*] n arce m (US **maneuver**) vt, vi
maniobrar ♦ n maniobra
manor ['mænə*] n (also: ~ **house**) casa
solariega
manpower ['mænpauə*] n mano f de obra
mansion ['mænʃən] n palacio, casa grande
manslaughter ['mænslɔ:tə*] n homicidio no
premeditado
mantelpiece ['mæntlpi:s] n repisa,
chimenea
manual ['mænjuəl] adj manual ♦ n manual
m
manufacture [mænju'fæktʃə*] vt fabricar
♦ n fabricación f; **~r** n fabricante m/f
manure [mə'njuə*] n estiércol m
manuscript ['mænjuskrɪpt] n manuscrito
many ['menɪ] adj, pron muchos/as; **a great ~**
muchísimos, un buen número de; **~ a time**
muchas veces
map [mæp] n mapa m; **to ~ out** vt proyectar
maple ['meɪpl] n arce m (SP), maple m (AM)
mar [mɑ:*] vt estropear
marathon ['mærəθən] n maratón m
marble ['mɑ:bl] n mármol m; (toy) canica
March [mɑ:tʃ] n marzo
march [mɑ:tʃ] vi (MIL) marchar; (demon-
strators) manifestarse ♦ n marcha; (demonstration) manifestación f
mare [meə*] n yegua
margarine [mɑ:dʒə'ri:n] n margarina
margin ['mɑ:dʒɪn] n margen m; (COMM:
profit ~) margen m de beneficios; **~al** adj
marginal; **~al seat** n (POL) escaño electoral
difícil de asegurar
marigold ['mærɪgəuld] n caléndula
marijuana [mærɪ'wɑ:nə] n marijuana
marina [mə'ri:nə] n puerto deportivo
marinate ['mærɪneɪt] vt marinar

marine [mə'ri:n] adj marino ♦ n soldado de
marina
marital ['mærɪtl] adj matrimonial; **~ status**
estado civil
marjoram ['mɑ:dʒərəm] n mejorana
mark [mɑ:k] n marca, señal f; (in snow, mud etc)
huella; (stain) mancha; (BRIT: SCOL) nota;
(currency) marco ♦ vt marcar; manchar; (damage: furniture) rayar; (indicate: place etc) señalar; (BRIT: SCOL) calificar, corregir; **to ~ time**
marcar el paso; (fig) marcar(se) un ritmo; **~ed**
adj (obvious) marcado, acusado; **~er** n (sign)
marcador m; (bookmark) señal f (de libro)
market ['mɑ:kɪt] n mercado ♦ vt (COMM)
comercializar; **~ garden** (BRIT) n huerto;
~ing n márketing m; **~place** n mercado;
~ research n análisis m inv de mercados
marksman ['mɑ:ksmən] n tirador m
marmalade ['mɑ:məleɪd] n mermelada de
naranja
maroon [mə'ru:n] vt: **to be ~ed** quedar
aislado; (fig) quedar abandonado
marquee [mɑ:'ki:] n entoldado
marriage ['mærɪdʒ] n (relationship,
institution) matrimonio; (wedding) boda;
(act) casamiento; **~ certificate** n partida de
casamiento
married ['mærɪd] adj casado; (life, love)
conyugal
marrow ['mærəu] n médula; (vegetable)
calabacín m
marry ['mærɪ] vt casarse con; (subj: father,
priest etc) casar ♦ vi (also: **get married**)
casarse
Mars [mɑ:z] n Marte m
marsh [mɑ:ʃ] n pantano; (salt ~) marisma
marshal ['mɑ:ʃl] n (MIL) mariscal m; (at
sports meeting etc) oficial m; (US: of police, fire
department) jefe/a m/f ♦ vt (thoughts etc)
ordenar; (soldiers) formar
marshy ['mɑ:ʃɪ] adj pantanoso
martial law ['mɑ:ʃl-] n ley f marcial
martyr ['mɑ:tə*] n mártir m/f; **~dom** n
martirio
marvel ['mɑ:vl] n maravilla, prodigio ♦ vi: **to
~ (at)** maravillarse (de); **~lous** (US **~ous**) adj
maravilloso
Marxist ['mɑ:ksɪst] adj, n marxista m/f
marzipan ['mɑ:zɪpæn] n mazapán m
mascara [mæs'kɑ:rə] n rímel m
masculine ['mæskjulɪn] adj masculino
mash [mæʃ] vt machacar; **~ed potatoes** npl
puré m de patatas (SP) or papas (AM)
mask [mɑ:sk] n máscara ♦ vt (cover): **to
~ one's face** ocultarse la cara; (hide: feelings)
esconder
mason ['meɪsn] n (also: stone~) albañil m;
(also: free~) masón m; **~ry** n (in building)
mampostería

masquerade [mæskə'reɪd] vi: **to ~ as** disfrazarse de, hacerse pasar por

mass [mæs] n (people) muchedumbre f; (of air, liquid etc) masa; (of detail, hair etc) gran cantidad f; (REL) misa ♦ cpd masivo ♦ vi reunirse; concentrarse; **the ~es** npl las masas; **~es of** (inf) montones de

massacre ['mæsəkə*] n masacre f

massage ['mæsɑːʒ] n masaje m ♦ vt dar masaje en

masseur [mæ'sə:*] n masajista m

masseuse [mæ'sə:z] n masajista f

massive ['mæsɪv] adj enorme; (support, changes) masivo

mass media npl medios mpl de comunicación

mass production n fabricación f en serie

mast [mɑːst] n (NAUT) mástil m; (RADIO etc) torre f

master ['mɑːstə*] n (of servant) amo; (of situation) dueño, maestro; (in primary school) maestro; (in secondary school) profesor m; (title for boys): **M~ X** Señorito X ♦ vt dominar; **M~ of Arts/Science** n licenciatura superior en Letras/Ciencias; **~ly** adj magistral; **~mind** n inteligencia superior ♦ vt dirigir, planear; **~piece** n obra maestra; **~y** n maestría

mat [mæt] n estera; (also: door~) felpudo; (also: table ~) salvamanteles m inv, posavasos m inv ♦ adj = matt

match [mætʃ] n cerilla, fósforo; (game) partido; (equal) igual m/f ♦ vt (go well with) hacer juego con; (equal) igualar; (correspond to) corresponderse con; (pair: also: ~ up) casar con ♦ vi hacer juego; **to be a good ~** hacer juego; **~box** n caja de cerillas; **~ing** adj que hace juego

mate [meɪt] n (work~) colega m/f; (inf: friend) amigo/a; (animal) macho m/hembra f; (in merchant navy) segundo de a bordo ♦ vi acoplarse, aparearse ♦ vt aparear

material [mə'tɪərɪəl] n (substance) materia; (information) material m; (cloth) tela, tejido ♦ adj material; (important) esencial; **~s** npl materiales mpl

maternal [mə'tə:nl] adj maternal

maternity [mə'tə:nɪtɪ] n maternidad f; **~ dress** n vestido premamá

math [mæθ] (US) n = **mathematics**

mathematical [mæθə'mætɪkl] adj matemático

mathematician [mæθəmə'tɪʃən] n matemático/a

mathematics [mæθə'mætɪks] n matemáticas fpl

maths [mæθs] (BRIT) n = **mathematics**

matinée ['mætɪneɪ] n sesión f de tarde

matrices ['meɪtrɪsiːz] npl of **matrix**

matriculation [mətrɪkju'leɪʃən] n (formalización f de) matrícula

matrimony ['mætrɪmənɪ] n matrimonio

matrix ['meɪtrɪks] (pl **matrices**) n matriz f

matron ['meɪtrən] n enfermera f jefe; (in school) ama de llaves

mat(t) [mæt] adj mate

matted ['mætɪd] adj enmarañado

matter ['mætə*] n cuestión f, asunto; (PHYSICS) sustancia, materia; (reading ~) material m; (MED: pus) pus m ♦ vi importar; **~s** npl (affairs) asuntos mpl, temas mpl; **it doesn't ~** no importa; **what's the ~?** ¿qué pasa?; **no ~ what** pase lo que pase; **as a ~ of course** por rutina; **as a ~ of fact** de hecho; **~-of-fact** adj prosaico, práctico

mattress ['mætrɪs] n colchón m

mature [mə'tjuə*] adj maduro ♦ vi madurar; **maturity** n madurez f

maul [mɔːl] vt magullar

mauve [məuv] adj de color malva (SP) or guinda (AM)

maximum ['mæksɪməm] (pl **maxima**) adj máximo ♦ n máximo

May [meɪ] n mayo

may [meɪ] (conditional: **might**) vi (indicating possibility): **he ~ come** puede que venga; (be allowed to): **~ I smoke?** ¿puedo fumar?; (wishes): **~ God bless you!** ¡que Dios te bendiga!; **you ~ as well go** bien puedes irte

maybe ['meɪbiː] adv quizá(s)

May Day n el primero de Mayo

mayhem ['meɪhem] n caos m total

mayonnaise [meɪə'neɪz] n mayonesa

mayor [mɛə*] n alcalde m; **~ess** n alcaldesa

maze [meɪz] n laberinto

M.D. abbr = **Doctor of Medicine**

me [miː] pron (direct) me; (stressed, after pron) mí; **can you hear ~?** ¿me oyes?; **he heard ME** me oyó a mí; **it's ~** soy yo; **give them to ~** dámelos/las; **with/without ~** conmigo/sin mí

meadow ['medəu] n prado, pradera

meagre ['miːgə*] (US **meager**) adj escaso, pobre

meal [miːl] n comida; (flour) harina; **~time** n hora de comer

mean [miːn] (pt, pp **meant**) adj (with money) tacaño; (unkind) mezquino, malo; (shabby) humilde; (average) medio ♦ vt (signify) querer decir, significar; (refer to) referirse a; (intend): **to ~ to do sth** pensar or pretender hacer algo ♦ n medio, término medio; **~s** npl (way) medio, manera; (money) recursos mpl, medios mpl; **by ~s of** mediante, por medio de; **by all ~s!** ¡naturalmente!, ¡claro que sí!; **do you ~ it?** ¿lo dices en serio?; **what do you ~?** ¿qué quiere decir?; **to be meant for sb/sth** ser para uno/algo

meander [mɪ'ændə*] vi (river) serpentear

meaning ['miːnɪŋ] n significado, sentido; (*purpose*) sentido, propósito; **~ful** adj significativo; **~less** adj sin sentido

meanness ['miːnnɪs] n (*with money*) tacañería; (*unkindness*) maldad f, mezquindad f; (*shabbiness*) humildad f

meant [mɛnt] pt, pp of **mean**

meantime ['miːntaɪm] adv (*also: in the ~*) mientras tanto

meanwhile ['miːnwaɪl] adv = **meantime**

measles ['miːzlz] n sarampión m

measure ['mɛʒə*] vt, vi medir ♦ n medida; (*ruler*) regla; **~ments** npl medidas fpl

meat [miːt] n carne f; **cold ~** fiambre m; **~ball** n albóndiga; **~ pie** n pastel m de carne

Mecca ['mɛkə] n La Meca

mechanic [mɪˈkænɪk] n mecánico/a; **~s** n mecánica ♦ npl mecanismo; **~al** adj mecánico

mechanism ['mɛkənɪzəm] n mecanismo

medal ['mɛdl] n medalla; **~lion** [mɪˈdælɪən] n medallón m; **~list** (US **~ist**) n (SPORT) medallista m/f

meddle ['mɛdl] vi: **to ~ in** entrometerse en; **to ~ with sth** manosear algo

media ['miːdɪə] npl medios mpl de comunicación ♦ npl of **medium**

mediaeval [mɛdɪˈiːvl] adj = **medieval**

mediate ['miːdɪeɪt] vi mediar; **mediator** n intermediario/a, mediador(a) m/f

Medicaid ® ['mɛdɪkeɪd] (US) n programa de ayuda médica para los pobres

medical ['mɛdɪkl] adj médico ♦ n reconocimiento médico

Medicare ® ['mɛdɪkɛə*] (US) n programa de ayuda médica para los ancianos

medication [mɛdɪˈkeɪʃən] n medicación f

medicine ['mɛdsɪn] n medicina; (*drug*) medicamento

medieval [mɛdɪˈiːvl] adj medieval

mediocre [miːdɪˈəʊkə*] adj mediocre

meditate ['mɛdɪteɪt] vi meditar

Mediterranean [mɛdɪtəˈreɪnɪən] adj mediterráneo; **the ~ (Sea)** el (Mar) Mediterráneo

medium ['miːdɪəm] (*pl* **media**) adj mediano, regular ♦ n (*means*) medio; (*pl* **mediums**: *person*) médium m/f; **~ wave** n onda media

meek [miːk] adj manso, sumiso

meet [miːt] (*pt, pp* **met**) vt encontrar; (*accidentally*) encontrarse con, tropezar con; (*by arrangement*) reunirse con; (*for the first time*) conocer; (*go and fetch*) ir a buscar; (*opponent*) enfrentarse con; (*obligations*) cumplir; (*encounter: problem*) hacer frente a; (*need*) satisfacer ♦ vi encontrarse; (*in session*) reunirse; (*join: objects*) unirse; (*for the first time*) conocerse; **~ with** vt fus (*difficulty*) tropezar con; **to ~ with success** tener éxito; **~ing** n

encuentro; (*arranged*) cita, compromiso; (*business ~ing*) reunión f; (*POL*) mitin m

megabyte ['mɛgəbaɪt] n (COMPUT) megabyte m, megaocteto

megaphone ['mɛgəfəʊn] n megáfono

melancholy ['mɛlənkəlɪ] n melancolía ♦ adj melancólico

mellow ['mɛləʊ] adj (*wine*) añejo; (*sound, colour*) suave ♦ vi (*person*) ablandar

melody ['mɛlədɪ] n melodía

melon ['mɛlən] n melón m

melt [mɛlt] vi (*metal*) fundirse; (*snow*) derretirse ♦ vt fundir; **~down** n (*in nuclear reactor*) fusión f de un reactor (nuclear); **~ing pot** n (*fig*) crisol m

member ['mɛmbə*] n (*gen, ANAT*) miembro; (*of club*) socio/a; **M~ of Parliament** (BRIT) diputado/a; **M~ of the European Parliament** (BRIT) eurodiputado/a; **M~ of the Scottish Parliament** (BRIT) diputado/a del Parlamento escocés; **~ship** n (*members*) número de miembros; (*state*) filiación f; **~ship card** n carnet m de socio

memento [məˈmɛntəʊ] n recuerdo

memo ['mɛməʊ] n apunte m, nota

memoirs ['mɛmwɑːz] npl memorias fpl

memorandum [mɛməˈrændəm] (*pl* **memoranda**) n apunte m, nota; (*official note*) acta

memorial [mɪˈmɔːrɪəl] n monumento conmemorativo ♦ adj conmemorativo

memorize ['mɛməraɪz] vt aprender de memoria

memory ['mɛmərɪ] n (*also: COMPUT*) memoria; (*instance*) recuerdo; (*of dead person*): **in ~ of** a la memoria de

men [mɛn] npl of **man**

menace ['mɛnəs] n amenaza ♦ vt amenazar; **menacing** adj amenazador(a)

mend [mɛnd] vt reparar, arreglar; (*darn*) zurcir ♦ vi reponerse ♦ n arreglo, reparación f; zurcido ♦ n: **to be on the ~** ir mejorando; **to ~ one's ways** enmendarse; **~ing** n reparación f; (*clothes*) ropa por remendar

meningitis [mɛnɪnˈdʒaɪtɪs] n meningitis f

menopause ['mɛnəʊpɔːz] n menopausia

menstruation [mɛnstruˈeɪʃən] n menstruación f

mental ['mɛntl] adj mental; **~ity** [-ˈtælɪtɪ] n mentalidad f

mention ['mɛnʃən] n mención f ♦ vt mencionar; (*speak of*) hablar de; **don't ~ it!** ¡de nada!

menu ['mɛnjuː] n (*set ~*) menú m; (*printed*) carta; (*COMPUT*) menú m

MEP n abbr = **Member of the European Parliament**

merchandise ['mɜːtʃəndaɪz] n mercancías fpl

merchant ['mɜːtʃənt] n comerciante m/f;

~ bank (BRIT) n banco comercial; **~ navy**
(US **~ marine**) n marina mercante
merciful ['mə:sɪful] adj compasivo;
(fortunate) afortunado
merciless ['mə:sɪlɪs] adj despiadado
mercury ['mə:kjurɪ] n mercurio
mercy ['mə:sɪ] n compasión f; (REL)
misericordia; **at the ~ of** a la merced de
merely ['mɪəlɪ] adv simplemente, sólo
merge [mə:dʒ] vt (join) unir ♦ vi unirse;
(COMM) fusionarse; (colours etc) fundirse; **~r**
n (COMM) fusión f
meringue [mə'ræŋ] n merengue m
merit ['merɪt] n mérito ♦ vt merecer
mermaid ['mə:meɪd] n sirena
merry ['merɪ] adj alegre; **M~ Christmas!**
¡Felices Pascuas!; **~-go-round** n tiovivo
mesh [meʃ] n malla
mesmerize ['mezməraɪz] vt hipnotizar
mess [mes] n (muddle: of situation) confusión
f; (: of room) desorden m; (dirt) porquería; (MIL)
comedor m; **~ about or around** (inf) vi
perder el tiempo; (pass the time)
entretenerse; **~ about or around with** (inf)
vt fus divertirse con; **~ up** vt (spoil)
estropear; (dirty) ensuciar
message ['mesɪdʒ] n recado, mensaje m
messenger ['mesɪndʒə*] n mensajero/a
Messrs abbr (on letters: = Messieurs) Sres
messy ['mesɪ] adj (dirty) sucio; (untidy)
desordenado
met [met] pt, pp of **meet**
metal ['metl] n metal m; **~lic** [-'tælɪk] adj
metálico
metaphor ['metəfə*] n metáfora
meteor ['mi:tɪə*] n meteoro; **~ite** [-aɪt] n
meteorito
meteorology [mi:tɪə'rɒlədʒɪ] n
meteorología
meter ['mi:tə*] n (instrument) contador m;
(US: unit) = **metre** ♦ vt (US: POST) franquear
method ['meθəd] n método
meths [meθs] (BRIT), **methylated spirit**
['meθɪleɪtɪd-] (BRIT) n alcohol m metilado or
desnaturalizado
metre ['mi:tə*] (US **meter**) n metro
metric ['metrɪk] adj métrico
metropolitan [metrə'pɒlɪtən] adj
metropolitano; **the M~ Police** (BRIT) la policía
londinense
mettle ['metl] n: **to be on one's ~** estar
dispuesto a mostrar todo lo que uno vale
mew [mju:] vi (cat) maullar
mews [mju:z] n: **~ flat** (BRIT) piso
acondicionado en antiguos establos o cocheras
Mexican ['meksɪkən] adj, n mejicano/a m/f,
mexicano/a m/f
Mexico ['meksɪkəʊ] n Méjico (SP), México
(AM); **~ City** n Ciudad f de Méjico or México

miaow [mi:'au] vi maullar
mice [maɪs] npl of **mouse**
micro... [maɪkrəʊ] prefix micro...; **~chip** n
microplaqueta; **~(computer)** n
microordenador m; **~phone** n micrófono;
~processor n microprocesador m; **~scope**
n microscopio; **~wave** n (also: **~wave oven**)
horno microondas
mid [mɪd] adj: **in ~ May** a mediados de mayo;
in ~ afternoon a media tarde; **in ~ air** en el
aire; **~day** n mediodía m
middle ['mɪdl] n centro; (half-way point)
medio; (waist) cintura ♦ adj de en medio;
(course, way) intermedio; **in the ~ of the night**
en plena noche; **~-aged** adj de mediana
edad; **the M~ Ages** npl la Edad Media; **~
class** adj de clase media; **the ~ class(es)**
n(pl) la clase media; **M~ East** n Oriente m
Medio; **~man** n intermediario; **~ name** n
segundo nombre; **~-of-the-road** adj
moderado; **~weight** n (BOXING) peso medio
middling ['mɪdlɪŋ] adj mediano
midge [mɪdʒ] n mosquito
midget ['mɪdʒɪt] n enano/a
Midlands ['mɪdləndz] npl: **the ~** la región
central de Inglaterra
midnight ['mɪdnaɪt] n medianoche f
midst [mɪdst] n: **in the ~ of** (crowd) en medio
de; (situation, action) en mitad de
midsummer [mɪd'sʌmə*] n: **in ~** en pleno
verano
midway [mɪd'weɪ] adj, adv: **~ (between)** a
medio camino (entre); **~ through** a la mitad
(de)
midweek [mɪd'wi:k] adv entre semana
midwife ['mɪdwaɪf] (pl **midwives**) n
comadrona, partera
might [maɪt] vb see **may** ♦ n fuerza, poder m;
~y adj fuerte, poderoso
migraine ['mi:greɪn] n jaqueca
migrant ['maɪgrənt] n adj (bird) migratorio;
(worker) emigrante
migrate [maɪ'greɪt] vi emigrar
mike [maɪk] n abbr (= microphone) micro
mild [maɪld] adj (person) apacible; (climate)
templado; (slight) ligero; (taste) suave;
(illness) leve; **~ly** adv ligeramente,
suavemente; **to put it ~ly** para no decir más
mile [maɪl] n milla; **~age** n número de millas,
≈ kilometraje m; **~ometer** [maɪ'lɒmɪtə*] n ≈
cuentakilómetros m inv; **~stone** n mojón m
militant ['mɪlɪtnt] adj, n militante m/f
military ['mɪlɪtərɪ] adj militar
militia [mɪ'lɪʃə] n milicia
milk [mɪlk] n leche f ♦ vt (cow) ordeñar; (fig)
chupar; **~ chocolate** n chocolate m con
leche; **~man** (irreg) n lechero; **~ shake** n
batido, malteada (AM); **~y** adj lechoso; **M~y
Way** n Vía Láctea

mill [mɪl] n (windmill etc) molino; (coffee ~) molinillo; (factory) fábrica ♦ vt moler ♦ vi (also: ~ about) arremolinarse

millennium [mɪ'lenɪəm] (pl ~s or millennia) n milenio, milenario; the ~ bug el (problema del) efecto 2000

miller ['mɪlə*] n molinero

milli... ['mɪlɪ] prefix: ~gram(me) n miligramo; ~metre (US ~meter) n milímetro

million ['mɪljən] n millón m; a ~ times un millón de veces; ~aire [-jə'nɛə*] n millonario/a

milometer [maɪ'lɒmɪtə*] (BRIT) n = mileometer

mime [maɪm] n mímica; (actor) mimo/a ♦ vt remedar ♦ vi actuar de mimo

mimic ['mɪmɪk] n imitador(a) m/f ♦ adj mímico ♦ vt remedar, imitar

min. abbr = minimum; minute(s)

mince [mɪns] vt picar ♦ n (BRIT: CULIN) carne f picada; ~meat n conserva de fruta picada; (US: meat) carne f picada; ~ pie n empanadilla rellena de fruta picada; ~r n picadora de carne

mind [maɪnd] n mente f; (intellect) intelecto; (contrasted with matter) espíritu m ♦ vt (attend to, look after) ocuparse de, cuidar; (be careful of) tener cuidado con; (object to): I don't ~ the noise no me molesta el ruido; it is on my ~ me preocupa; to bear sth in ~ tomar or tener algo en cuenta; to make up one's ~ decidirse; I don't ~ me es igual; ~ you, ... te advierto que ...; never ~! ¡es igual!, ¡no importa!; (don't worry) ¡no te preocupes!; "~ the step" "cuidado con el escalón"; ~er n guardaespaldas m inv; (child ~er) ≈ niñera; ~ful adj: ~ful of consciente de; ~less adj (crime) sin motivo; (work) de autómata

mine¹ [maɪn] pron el mío/la mía etc; a friend of ~ un(a) amigo/a mío/mía ♦ adj: this book is ~ este libro es mío

mine² [maɪn] n mina ♦ vt (coal) extraer; (bomb: beach etc) minar; ~field n campo de minas; miner n minero/a

mineral ['mɪnərəl] adj mineral ♦ n mineral m; ~s npl (BRIT: soft drinks) refrescos mpl; ~ water n agua mineral

mingle ['mɪŋɡl] vi: to ~ with mezclarse con

miniature ['mɪnətʃə*] adj (en) miniatura ♦ n miniatura

minibus ['mɪnɪbʌs] n microbús m

minimal ['mɪnɪml] adj mínimo

minimize ['mɪnɪmaɪz] vt minimizar; (play down) empequeñecer

minimum ['mɪnɪməm] (pl minima) n, adj mínimo

mining ['maɪnɪŋ] n explotación f minera

miniskirt ['mɪnɪskɜːt] n minifalda

minister ['mɪnɪstə*] n (BRIT: POL) ministro/a (SP), secretario/a (AM); (REL) pastor m ♦ vi: to ~ to atender a

ministry ['mɪnɪstrɪ] n (BRIT: POL) ministerio (SP), secretaría (AM); (REL) sacerdocio

mink [mɪŋk] n visón m

minnow ['mɪnəu] n pececillo (de agua dulce)

minor ['maɪnə*] adj (repairs, injuries) leve; (poet, planet) menor; (MUS) menor ♦ n (LAW) menor m de edad

Minorca [mɪ'nɔːkə] n Menorca

minority [maɪ'nɒrɪtɪ] n minoría

mint [mɪnt] n (plant) menta, hierbabuena; (sweet) caramelo de menta ♦ vt (coins) acuñar; the (Royal) M~, the (US) M~ la Casa de la Moneda; in ~ condition en perfecto estado

minus ['maɪnəs] n (also: ~ sign) signo de menos ♦ prep menos; 12 ~ 6 equals 6 12 menos 6 son 6; ~ 24°C menos 24 grados

minute¹ ['mɪnɪt] n minuto; (fig) momento; ~s npl (of meeting) actas fpl; at the last ~ a última hora

minute² [maɪ'njuːt] adj diminuto; (search) minucioso

miracle ['mɪrəkl] n milagro

mirage ['mɪrɑːʒ] n espejismo

mirror ['mɪrə*] n espejo; (in car) retrovisor m

mirth [mɜːθ] n alegría

misadventure [mɪsəd'ventʃə*] n desgracia

misapprehension [mɪsæprɪ'henʃən] n equivocación f

misappropriate [mɪsə'prəupnet] vt malversar

misbehave [mɪsbɪ'heɪv] vi portarse mal

miscalculate [mɪs'kælkjulet] vt calcular mal

miscarriage ['mɪskærɪdʒ] n (MED) aborto; ~ of justice error m judicial

miscellaneous [mɪsɪ'leɪnɪəs] adj varios/as, diversos/as

mischief ['mɪstʃɪf] n travesuras fpl, diabluras fpl; (maliciousness) malicia; mischievous [-tʃɪvəs] adj travieso

misconception [mɪskən'sepʃən] n idea equivocada; equivocación f

misconduct [mɪs'kɒndʌkt] n mala conducta; professional ~ falta profesional

misdemeanour [mɪsdɪ'miːnə*] (US misdemeanor) n delito, ofensa

miser ['maɪzə*] n avaro/a

miserable ['mɪzərəbl] adj (unhappy) triste, desgraciado; (unpleasant, contemptible) miserable

miserly ['maɪzəlɪ] adj avariento, tacaño

misery ['mɪzərɪ] n tristeza; (wretchedness) miseria, desdicha

misfire [mɪs'faɪə*] vi fallar

misfit ['mɪsfɪt] n inadaptado/a

misfortune [mɪs'fɔːtʃən] n desgracia

misgiving [mɪs'ɡɪvɪŋ] n (apprehension) presentimiento; to have ~s about sth tener dudas acerca de algo

misguided [mɪs'gaɪdɪd] adj equivocado

mishandle [mɪs'hændl] vt (mismanage) manejar mal

mishap ['mɪshæp] n desgracia, contratiempo

misinform [mɪsɪn'fɔːm] vt informar mal

misinterpret [mɪsɪn'tɜːprɪt] vt interpretar mal

misjudge [mɪs'dʒʌdʒ] vt juzgar mal

mislay [mɪs'leɪ] (irreg) vt extraviar, perder

mislead [mɪs'liːd] (irreg) vt llevar a conclusiones erróneas; **~ing** adj engañoso

mismanage [mɪs'mænɪdʒ] vt administrar mal

misplace [mɪs'pleɪs] vt extraviar

misprint ['mɪsprɪnt] n errata, error m de imprenta

Miss [mɪs] n Señorita

miss [mɪs] vt (train etc) perder; (fail to hit: target) errar; (regret the absence of): **I ~ him** (yo) le echo de menos or a faltar; (fail to see): **you can't ~ it** no tiene pérdida ♦ vi fallar ♦ n (shot) tiro fallido or perdido; **~ out** (BRIT) vt omitir

misshapen [mɪs'ʃeɪpən] adj deforme

missile ['mɪsaɪl] n (AVIAT) mísil m; (object thrown) proyectil m

missing ['mɪsɪŋ] adj (pupil) ausente; (thing) perdido; (MIL): **~ in action** desaparecido en combate

mission ['mɪʃən] n misión f; (official representation) delegación f; **~ary** n misionero/a

mist [mɪst] n (light) neblina; (heavy) niebla; (at sea) bruma ♦ vi (eyes: also: ~ over, ~ up) llenarse de lágrimas; (BRIT: windows: also: ~ over, ~ up) empañarse

mistake [mɪs'teɪk] (vt: irreg) n error m ♦ vt entender mal; **by ~** por equivocación; **to make a ~** equivocarse; **to ~ A for B** confundir A con B; **mistaken** pp of mistake ♦ adj equivocado; **to be mistaken** equivocarse, engañarse

mister ['mɪstə*] (inf) n señor m; see Mr

mistletoe ['mɪsltəʊ] n muérdago

mistook [mɪs'tʊk] pt of mistake

mistress ['mɪstrɪs] n (lover) amante f; (of house) señora (de la casa); (BRIT: in primary school) maestra; (in secondary school) profesora; (of situation) dueña

mistrust [mɪs'trʌst] vt desconfiar de

misty ['mɪstɪ] adj (day) de niebla; (glasses etc) empañado

misunderstand [mɪsʌndə'stænd] (irreg) vt, vi entender mal; **~ing** n malentendido

misuse [n mɪs'juːs, vb mɪs'juːz] n mal uso; (of power) abuso; (of funds) malversación f ♦ vt abusar de; malversar

mitt(en) ['mɪt(n)] n manopla

mix [mɪks] vt mezclar; (combine) unir ♦ vi mezclarse; (people) llevarse bien ♦ n mezcla; **~ up** vt mezclar; (confuse) confundir; **~ed** adj mixto; (feelings etc) encontrado; **~ed-up** adj (confused) confuso, revuelto; **~er** n (for food) licuadora; (for drinks) coctelera; (person): **he's a good ~er** tiene don de gentes; **~ture** n mezcla; (also: cough ~ture) jarabe m; **~-up** n confusión f

mm abbr (= millimetre) mm

moan [məʊn] n gemido ♦ vi gemir; (inf: complain): **to ~ (about)** quejarse (de)

moat [məʊt] n foso

mob [mɒb] n multitud f ♦ vt acosar

mobile ['məʊbaɪl] adj móvil ♦ n móvil m; **~ home** n caravana; **~ phone** n teléfono portátil

mock [mɒk] vt (ridicule) ridiculizar; (laugh at) burlarse de ♦ adj fingido; **~ exam** examen preparatorio antes de los exámenes oficiales; **~ery** n burla; **~-up** n maqueta

mod [mɒd] adj see convenience

mode [məʊd] n modo

model ['mɒdl] n modelo; (fashion ~, artist's ~) modelo m/f ♦ adj modelo ♦ vt (with clay etc) modelar (copy): **to ~ o.s. on** tomar como modelo a ♦ vi ser modelo; **to ~ clothes** pasar modelos, ser modelo; **~ railway** n ferrocarril m de juguete

modem ['məʊdəm] n modem m

moderate [adj 'mɒdərət, vb 'mɒdəreɪt] adj moderado/a ♦ vi moderarse, calmarse ♦ vt moderar

modern ['mɒdən] adj moderno; **~ize** vt modernizar

modest ['mɒdɪst] adj modesto; (small) módico; **~y** n modestia

modify ['mɒdɪfaɪ] vt modificar

mogul ['məʊgəl] n (fig) magnate m

mohair ['məʊheə*] n mohair m

moist [mɔɪst] adj húmedo; **~en** ['mɔɪsn] vt humedecer; **~ure** ['mɔɪstʃə*] n humedad f; **~urizer** ['mɔɪstʃəraɪzə*] n crema hidratante

molar ['məʊlə*] n muela

mold [məʊld] (US) n, vt = **mould**

mole [məʊl] n (animal, spy) topo; (spot) lunar m

molest [məʊ'lest] vt importunar; (assault sexually) abusar sexualmente de

mollycoddle ['mɒlɪkɒdl] vt mimar

molt [məʊlt] (US) vi = **moult**

molten ['məʊltən] adj fundido; (lava) líquido

mom [mɒm] (US) n = **mum**

moment ['məʊmənt] n momento; **at the ~** de momento, por ahora; **~ary** adj momentáneo; **~ous** [-'mentəs] adj trascendental, importante

momentum [məʊ'mentəm] n momento; (fig) ímpetu m; **to gather ~** cobrar velocidad;

(fig) ganar fuerza
mommy ['mɔmɪ] (US) n = **mummy**
Monaco ['mɔnəkəu] n Mónaco
monarch ['mɔnək] n monarca m/f; **~y** n
monarquía
monastery ['mɔnəstərɪ] n monasterio
Monday ['mʌndɪ] n lunes m inv
monetary ['mʌnɪtərɪ] adj monetario
money ['mʌnɪ] n dinero; (currency) moneda;
to make ~ ganar dinero; **~ order** n giro; **~-
spinner** (inf) n: **to be a ~-spinner** dar mucho
dinero
mongrel ['mʌŋgrəl] n (dog) perro mestizo
monitor ['mɔnɪtə*] n (SCOL) monitor m;
(also: television ~) receptor m de control; (of
computer) monitor m ♦ vt controlar
monk [mʌŋk] n monje m
monkey ['mʌŋkɪ] n mono; **~ nut** (BRIT) n
cacahuete m (SP), maní m (AM); **~ wrench**
n llave f inglesa
monopoly [mə'nɔpəlɪ] n monopolio
monotone ['mɔnətəun] n voz f (or tono)
monocorde
monotonous [mə'nɔtənəs] adj monótono
monsoon [mɔn'su:n] n monzón m
monster ['mɔnstə*] n monstruo
monstrous ['mɔnstrəs] adj (huge) enorme;
(atrocious, ugly) monstruoso
month [mʌnθ] n mes m; **~ly** adj mensual
♦ adv mensualmente
monument ['mɔnjumənt] n monumento
moo [mu:] vi mugir
mood [mu:d] n humor m; (of crowd, group)
clima m; **to be in a good/bad ~** estar de
buen/mal humor; **~y** adj (changeable) de
humor variable; (sullen) malhumorado
moon [mu:n] n luna; **~light** n luz f de la
luna; **~lighting** n pluriempleo; **~lit** adj: a
~lit night una noche de luna
Moor [muə*] n moro/a
moor [muə*] n páramo ♦ vt (ship) amarrar
♦ vi echar las amarras
Moorish ['muərɪʃ] adj moro; (architecture)
árabe, morisco
moorland ['muələnd] n páramo, brezal m
moose [mu:s] n inv alce m
mop [mɔp] n fregona; (of hair) greña, melena
♦ vt fregar; **~ up** vt limpiar
mope [məup] vi estar or andar deprimido
moped ['məuped] n ciclomotor m
moral ['mɔrl] adj moral ♦ n moraleja; **~s** npl
moralidad f, moral f
morale [mɔ'rɑ:l] n moral f
morality [mə'rælɪtɪ] n moralidad f
morass [mə'ræs] n pantano

<hr>

KEYWORD

more [mɔ:*] adj 1 (greater in number etc)
más; **~ people/work than before** más gente/

trabajo que antes
2 (additional) más; **do you want (some)
~ tea?** ¿quieres más té?; **is there any ~ wine?**
¿queda vino?; **it'll take a few ~ weeks** tardará
unas semanas más; **it's 2 kms ~ to the house**
faltan 2 kms para la casa; **~ time/letters than
we expected** más tiempo del que/más cartas
de las que esperábamos
♦ pron (greater amount, additional amount)
más; **~ than 10** más de 10; **it cost ~ than the
other one/than we expected** costó más que el
otro/más de lo que esperábamos; **is there any
~?** ¿hay más?; **many/much ~** muchos(as)/
mucho(a) más
♦ adv más; **~ dangerous/easily (than)** más
peligroso/fácilmente (que); **~ and
~ expensive** cada vez más caro; **~ or less** más
o menos; **~ than ever** más que nunca

<hr>

moreover [mɔ:'rəuvə*] adv además, por otra
parte
morning ['mɔ:nɪŋ] n mañana; (early ~)
madrugada ♦ cpd matutino, de la mañana; **in
the ~** por la mañana; **7 o'clock in the ~** las 7
de la mañana; **~ sickness** n náuseas fpl
matutinas
Morocco [mə'rɔkəu] n Marruecos m
moron ['mɔ:rɔn] (inf) n imbécil m/f
morphine ['mɔ:fi:n] n morfina
Morse [mɔ:s] n (also: ~ code) (código) Morse
morsel ['mɔ:sl] n (of food) bocado
mortar ['mɔ:tə*] n argamasa
mortgage ['mɔ:gɪdʒ] n hipoteca ♦ vt
hipotecar; **~ company** (US) n ≈ banco
hipotecario
mortuary ['mɔ:tjuərɪ] n depósito de
cadáveres
Moscow ['mɔskəu] n Moscú
Moslem ['mɔzləm] adj, n = **Muslim**
mosque [mɔsk] n mezquita
mosquito [mɔs'ki:təu] (pl ~es) n mosquito
(SP), zancudo (AM)
moss [mɔs] n musgo
most [məust] adj la mayor parte de, la
mayoría de ♦ pron la mayor parte, la mayoría
♦ adv el más; (very) muy; **the ~** (also: + adj)
el más; **~ of them** la mayor parte de ellos; **I
saw the ~** yo vi el que más; **at the (very) ~** a
lo sumo, todo lo más; **to make the ~ of**
aprovechar (al máximo); **a ~ interesting book**
un libro interesantísimo; **~ly** adv en su mayor
parte, principalmente
MOT (BRIT) n abbr (= Ministry of Transport):
the ~ (test) inspección (anual) obligatoria de
coches y camiones
motel [məu'tel] n motel m
moth [mɔθ] n mariposa nocturna; (clothes ~)
polilla
mother ['mʌðə*] n madre f ♦ adj materno

♦ vt (care for) cuidar (como una madre);
~**hood** n maternidad f; ~**in-law** n suegra;
~**ly** adj maternal; ~**-of-pearl** n nácar m; ~
to-be n futura madre f; ~ **tongue** n lengua
materna

motion ['məuʃən] n movimiento m; (gesture)
ademán m, señal f; (at meeting) moción f
♦ vt, vi: **to** ~ **(to) sb to do sth** hacer señas a
uno para que haga algo; ~**less** adj inmóvil;
~ **picture** n película

motivated ['məutɪveɪtɪd] adj motivado

motive ['məutɪv] n motivo

motley ['mɔtlɪ] adj variado

motor ['məutə*] n motor m; (BRIT: inf:
vehicle) coche m (SP), carro (AM), automóvil
m ♦ adj motor (f: motora or motriz); ~**bike** n
moto f; ~**boat** n lancha motora; ~**car** (BRIT)
n coche m, carro, automóvil m; ~**cycle** n
motocicleta; ~**cycle racing** n motociclismo;
~**cyclist** n motociclista m/f; ~**ing** (BRIT) n
automovilismo; ~**ist** n conductor(a) m/f,
automovilista m/f; ~ **racing** (BRIT) n carreras
fpl de coches, automovilismo; ~ **vehicle** n
automóvil m; ~**way** (BRIT) n autopista

mottled ['mɔtld] adj abigarrado, multicolor

motto ['mɔtəu] (pl ~**es**) n lema m;
(watchword) consigna

mould [məuld] (US **mold**) n molde m;
(mildew) moho ♦ vt moldear; (fig) formar;
~**y** adj enmohecido

moult [məult] (US **molt**) vi mudar la piel (or
las plumas)

mound [maund] n montón m, montículo

mount [maunt] n monte m ♦ vt montar,
subir a; (jewel) engarzar; (picture) enmarcar;
(exhibition etc) organizar ♦ vi (increase)
aumentar; ~ **up** vi aumentar

mountain ['mauntɪn] n montaña ♦ cpd de
montaña; ~ **bike** n bicicleta de montaña;
~**eer** [-'nɪə*] n montañero/a (SP), andinista
m/f (AM); ~**eering** [-'nɪərɪŋ] n montañismo,
andinismo; ~**ous** adj montañoso; ~ **rescue
team** n equipo de rescate de montaña;
~**side** n ladera de la montaña

mourn [mɔːn] vt llorar, lamentar ♦ vi: **to** ~ **for**
llorar la muerte de; ~**er** n doliente m/f;
dolorido/a; ~**ing** n luto; **in** ~**ing** de luto

mouse [maus] (pl **mice**) n (ZOOL, COMPUT)
ratón m; ~ **mat** n (COMPUT) alfombrilla;
~**trap** n ratonera

mousse [muːs] n (CULIN) crema batida; (for
hair) espuma (moldeadora)

moustache [məs'taːʃ] (US **mustache**) n
bigote m

mousy ['mausɪ] adj (hair) pardusco

mouth [mauθ, pl mauðz] n boca; (of river)
desembocadura; ~**ful** n bocado; ~ **organ** n
armónica; ~**piece** n (of musical instrument)
boquilla; (spokesman) portavoz m/f; ~**wash**

n enjuague m; ~**watering** adj apetitoso

movable ['muːvəbl] adj movible

move [muːv] n (movement) movimiento m; (in
game) jugada; (: turn to play) turno;
(change: of house) mudanza; (: of job)
cambio de trabajo ♦ vt mover; (emotionally)
conmover; (POL: resolution etc) proponer ♦ vi
moverse; (traffic) circular; (also: ~ house)
trasladarse, mudarse; **to** ~ **sb to do sth** mover
a uno a hacer algo; **to get a** ~ **on** darse prisa;
~ **about** or **around** vi moverse; (travel)
viajar; ~ **along** vi avanzar, adelantarse;
~ **away** vi alejarse; ~ **back** vi retroceder;
~ **forward** vi avanzar; ~ **in** vi (to a house)
instalarse; (police, soldiers) intervenir; ~ **on** vi
ponerse en camino; ~ **out** vi (of house)
mudarse; ~ **over** vi apartarse, hacer sitio;
~ **up** vi (employee) ser ascendido

moveable ['muːvəbl] adj = **movable**

movement ['muːvmənt] n movimiento

movie ['muːvɪ] n película; **to go to the** ~**s** ir al
cine

moving ['muːvɪŋ] adj (emotional)
conmovedor(a); (that moves) móvil

mow [məu] (pt mowed, pp mowed or mown)
vt (grass, corn) cortar, segar; ~ **down** vt
(shoot) acribillar; ~**er** n (also: lawn~er)
cortacéspedes m inv, segadora

MP n abbr = **Member of Parliament**

m.p.h. abbr = miles per hour (60 m.p.h. = 96
k.p.h.)

Mr ['mɪstə*] (US **Mr.**) n: ~ **Smith** (el) Sr. Smith

Mrs ['mɪsɪz] (US **Mrs.**) n: ~ **Smith** (la) Sra. Smith

Ms [mɪz] (US **Ms.**) n (= Miss or Mrs): ~ **Smith**
(la) Sr(t)a. Smith

M.Sc. abbr = **Master of Science**

MSP n abbr = **Member of the Scottish
Parliament**

much [mʌtʃ] adj mucho ♦ adv mucho;
(before pp) muy ♦ n or pron mucho; **how** ~ **is
it?** ¿cuánto es?, ¿cuánto cuesta?; **too** ~
demasiado; **it's not** ~ no es mucho; **as** ~ **as**
tanto como; **however** ~ **he tries** por mucho
que se esfuerce

muck [mʌk] n suciedad f; ~ **about** or
around (inf) vi perder el tiempo; (enjoy o.s.)
entretenerse; ~ **up** (inf) vt arruinar, estropear

mud [mʌd] n barro, lodo

muddle ['mʌdl] n desorden m, confusión f;
(mix-up) embrollo, lío ♦ vt (also: ~ up) embrollar, confundir; ~ **through** vi salir del paso

muddy ['mʌdɪ] adj fangoso, cubierto de lodo

mudguard ['mʌdgɑːd] n guardabarros m inv

muffin ['mʌfɪn] n panecillo dulce

muffle ['mʌfl] vt (sound) amortiguar; (against
cold) embozar; ~**d** adj (noise etc) amortiguado,
apagado; ~**r** (US) n (AUT) silenciador m

mug [mʌg] n taza grande (sin platillo); (for
beer) jarra; (inf: face) jeta; (: fool) bobo ♦ vt

(assault) asaltar; **~ging** n asalto
muggy ['mʌgɪ] adj bochornoso
mule [mjuːl] n mula
multi... [mʌltɪ] prefix multi...
multi-level [mʌltɪ'levl] (US) adj = **multi-storey**
multiple ['mʌltɪpl] adj múltiple ♦ n múltiplo; **~ sclerosis** n esclerosis f múltiple
multiplex cinema ['mʌltɪpleks-] n multicines mpl
multiplication [mʌltɪplɪ'keɪʃən] n multiplicación f
multiply ['mʌltɪplaɪ] vt multiplicar ♦ vi multiplicarse
multistorey [mʌltɪ'stɔːrɪ] (BRIT) adj de muchos pisos
multitude ['mʌltɪtjuːd] n multitud f
mum [mʌm] (BRIT: inf) n mamá ♦ adj: **to keep ~** mantener la boca cerrada
mumble ['mʌmbl] vt, vi hablar entre dientes, refunfuñar
mummy ['mʌmɪ] n (BRIT: mother) mamá; (embalmed) momia
mumps [mʌmps] n paperas fpl
munch [mʌntʃ] vt, vi mascar
mundane [mʌn'deɪn] adj trivial
municipal [mjuː'nɪsɪpl] adj municipal
murder ['mɜːdə*] n asesinato; (in law) homicidio ♦ vt asesinar, matar; **~er/ess** n asesino/a; **~ous** adj homicida
murky ['mɜːkɪ] adj (water) turbio; (street, night) lóbrego
murmur ['mɜːmə*] n murmullo ♦ vt, vi murmurar
muscle ['mʌsl] n músculo; (fig: strength) garra, fuerza; **~ in** vi entrometerse; **muscular** ['mʌskjulə*] adj muscular; (person) musculoso
muse [mjuːz] vi meditar ♦ n musa
museum [mjuː'zɪəm] n museo
mushroom ['mʌʃrum] n seta, hongo; (CULIN) champiñón m ♦ vi crecer de la noche a la mañana
music ['mjuːzɪk] n música; **~al** adj musical; (sound) melodioso; (person) con talento musical ♦ n (show) comedia musical; **~al instrument** n instrumento musical; **~ hall** n teatro de variedades; **~ian** [-'zɪʃən] n músico/a
Muslim ['mʌzlɪm] adj, n musulmán/ana m/f
muslin ['mʌzlɪn] n muselina
mussel ['mʌsl] n mejillón m
must [mʌst] aux vb (obligation): **I ~ do it** debo hacerlo, tengo que hacerlo; (probability): **he ~ be there by now** ya debe (de) estar allí ♦ n: **it's a ~** es imprescindible
mustache ['mʌstæʃ] (US) n = **moustache**
mustard ['mʌstəd] n mostaza
muster ['mʌstə*] vt juntar, reunir

mustn't ['mʌsnt] = **must not**
mute [mjuːt] adj, n mudo/a m/f
muted ['mjuːtɪd] adj callado; (colour) apagado
mutiny ['mjuːtɪnɪ] n motín m ♦ vi amotinarse
mutter ['mʌtə*] vt, vi murmurar
mutton ['mʌtn] n carne f de cordero
mutual ['mjuːtʃuəl] adj mutuo; (interest) común; **~ly** adv mutuamente
muzzle ['mʌzl] n hocico; (for dog) bozal m; (of gun) boca ♦ vt (dog) poner un bozal a
my [maɪ] adj mi(s); **~ house/brother/sisters** mi casa/mi hermano/mis hermanas; **I've washed ~ hair/cut ~ finger** me he lavado el pelo/cortado un dedo; **is this ~ pen or yours?** ¿es este bolígrafo mío o tuyo?
myself [maɪ'self] pron (reflexive) me; (emphatic) yo mismo; (after prep) mí (mismo); see also **oneself**
mysterious [mɪs'tɪərɪəs] adj misterioso
mystery ['mɪstərɪ] n misterio
mystify ['mɪstɪfaɪ] vt (perplex) dejar perplejo
myth [mɪθ] n mito

N, n

n/a abbr (= not applicable) no interesa
nag [næg] vt (scold) regañar; **~ging** adj (doubt) persistente; (pain) continuo
nail [neɪl] n (human) uña; (metal) clavo ♦ vt clavar; **to ~ sth to sth** clavar algo en algo; **to ~ sb down to doing sth** comprometer a uno a que haga algo; **~brush** n cepillo para las uñas; **~file** n lima para las uñas; **~ polish** n esmalte m or laca para las uñas; **~ polish remover** n quitaesmalte m; **~ scissors** npl tijeras fpl para las uñas; **~ varnish** (BRIT) n = **~ polish**
naïve [naɪ'iːv] adj ingenuo
naked ['neɪkɪd] adj (nude) desnudo; (flame) expuesto al aire
name [neɪm] n nombre m; (surname) apellido; (reputation) fama, renombre m ♦ vt (child) poner nombre a; (criminal) identificar; (price, date etc) fijar; **what's your ~?** ¿cómo se llama?; **by ~** de nombre; **in the ~ of** en nombre de; **to give one's ~ and address** dar sus señas; **~ly** adv a saber; **~sake** n tocayo/a
nanny ['nænɪ] n niñera
nap [næp] n (sleep) sueñecito, siesta
nape [neɪp] n: **~ of the neck** nuca, cogote m
napkin ['næpkɪn] n (also: **table ~**) servilleta
nappy ['næpɪ] (BRIT) n pañal m; **~ rash** n prurito
narcotic [nɑː'kɔtɪk] adj, n narcótico
narrow ['nærəu] adj estrecho, angosto; (fig: majority etc) corto; (: ideas etc) estrecho ♦ vi (road) estrecharse; (diminish) reducirse; **to**

have a ~ **escape** escaparse por los pelos; **to ~ sth down** reducir algo; **~ly** adv (miss) por poco; **~-minded** adj de miras estrechas

nasty ['nɑːstɪ] adj (remark) feo; (person) antipático; (revolting: taste, smell) asqueroso; (wound, disease etc) peligroso, grave

nation ['neɪʃən] n nación f

national ['næʃənl] adj, n nacional m/f; **~ dress** n vestido nacional; **N~ Health Service** (BRIT) n servicio nacional de salud pública; ≈ Insalud m (SP); **N~ Insurance** (BRIT) n seguro social nacional; **~ism** n nacionalismo; **~ist** adj, n nacionalista m/f; **~ity** [-'nælɪtɪ] n nacionalidad f; **~ize** vt nacionalizar; **~ly** adv (nationwide) en escala nacional; (as a nation) nacionalmente, como nación; **~ park** (BRIT) n parque m nacional

nationwide ['neɪʃənwaɪd] adj en escala or a nivel nacional

native ['neɪtɪv] n (local inhabitant) natural m/ f, nacional m/f ♦ adj (indigenous) indígena; (country) natal; (innate) natural, innato; **a ~ of Russia** un(a) natural m/f de Rusia; **a ~ speaker of French** un hablante nativo de francés; **N~ American** adj, n americano/a indígena, amerindio/a; **~ language** n lengua materna

Nativity [nə'tɪvɪtɪ] n: **the ~** Navidad f

NATO ['neɪtəʊ] n abbr (= North Atlantic Treaty Organization) OTAN f

natural ['nætʃrəl] adj natural; **~ly** adv (speak etc) naturalmente; (of course) desde luego, por supuesto

nature ['neɪtʃə*] n (also: N~) naturaleza; (group, sort) género, clase f; (character) carácter m, genio; **by ~** por or de naturaleza

naught [nɔːt] = nought

naughty ['nɔːtɪ] adj (child) travieso

nausea ['nɔːsɪə] n náuseas fpl

nautical ['nɔːtɪkl] adj náutico, marítimo; (mile) marino

naval ['neɪvl] adj naval, de marina; **~ officer** n oficial m/f de marina

nave [neɪv] n nave f

navel ['neɪvl] n ombligo

navigate ['nævɪgeɪt] vt gobernar ♦ vi navegar; (AUT) ir de copiloto; **navigation** [-'geɪʃən] n (action) navegación f; (science) náutica; **navigator** n navegador(a) m/f, navegante m/f; (AUT) copiloto m/f

navvy ['nævɪ] (BRIT) n peón m caminero

navy ['neɪvɪ] n marina de guerra; (ships) armada, flota; **~(-blue)** adj azul marino

Nazi ['nɑːtsɪ] n nazi m/f

NB abbr (= nota bene) nótese

near [nɪə*] adj (place, relation) cercano; (time) próximo ♦ adv cerca ♦ prep (also: ~ to: space) cerca de, junto a; (: time) cerca de a ♦ vt acercarse a, aproximarse a; **~by** [nɪə'baɪ]

adj cercano, próximo ♦ adv cerca; **~ly** adv casi, por poco; **I ~ly fell** por poco me caigo; **~ miss** n tiro cercano; **~side** n (AUT: in Britain) lado izquierdo; (: in US, Europe etc) lado derecho; **~-sighted** adj miope, corto de vista

neat [niːt] adj (place) ordenado, bien cuidado; (person) pulcro; (plan) ingenioso; (spirits) solo; **~ly** adv (tidily) con esmero; (skilfully) ingeniosamente

necessarily ['nesɪsrɪlɪ] adv necesariamente

necessary ['nesɪsrɪ] adj necesario, preciso

necessitate [nɪ'sesɪteɪt] vt hacer necesario

necessity [nɪ'sesɪtɪ] n necesidad f; **necessities** npl artículos mpl de primera necesidad

neck [nek] n (of person, garment, bottle) cuello; (of animal) pescuezo ♦ vi (inf) besuquearse; **~ and ~** parejos; **~lace** ['neklɪs] n collar m; **~line** n escote m; **~tie** ['nektaɪ] n corbata

née [neɪ] adj: **~ Scott** de soltera Scott

need [niːd] n (lack) escasez f, falta; (necessity) necesidad f ♦ vt (require) necesitar; **I ~ to do it** tengo que or debo hacerlo; **you don't ~ to go** no hace falta que (te) vayas

needle ['niːdl] n aguja ♦ vt (fig: inf) picar, fastidiar

needless ['niːdlɪs] adj innecesario; **~ to say** huelga decir que

needlework ['niːdlwɜːk] n (activity) costura, labor f de aguja

needn't ['niːdnt] = need not

needy ['niːdɪ] adj necesitado

negative ['negətɪv] n (PHOT) negativo; (LING) negación f ♦ adj negativo; **~ equity** n situación que se da cuando el valor de la vivienda es menor que el que de la hipoteca que pesa sobre ella

neglect [nɪ'glekt] vt (one's duty) faltar a, no cumplir con; (child) descuidar, desatender ♦ n (of house, garden etc) abandono; (of child) desatención f; (of duty) incumplimiento

negligee ['neglɪʒeɪ] n (nightgown) salto de cama

negotiate [nɪ'gəʊʃɪeɪt] vt (treaty, loan) negociar; (obstacle) franquear; (bend in road) tomar ♦ vi: **to ~ (with)** negociar (con); **negotiation** [-'eɪʃən] n negociación f, gestión f

neigh [neɪ] vi relinchar

neighbour ['neɪbə*] (US neighbor) n vecino/ a; **~hood** n (place) vecindad f, barrio; (people) vecindario; **~ing** adj vecino; **~ly** adj (person) amable; (attitude) de buen vecino

neither ['naɪðə*] adj ni ♦ conj: **I didn't move and ~ did John** no me he movido, ni Juan tampoco ♦ pron ninguno ♦ adv: **~ good nor bad** ni bueno ni malo; **~ is true** ninguno/a de los/las dos es cierto/a

329

neon → nitrogen

neon ['niːɔn] n neón m; **~ light** n lámpara de neón
nephew ['nɛvjuː] n sobrino
nerve [nəːv] n (ANAT) nervio; (courage) valor m; (impudence) descaro, frescura; **a fit of ~s** un ataque de nervios; **~-racking** adj desquiciante
nervous ['nəːvəs] adj (anxious, ANAT) nervioso; (timid) tímido, miedoso; **~ breakdown** n crisis f nerviosa
nest [nɛst] n (of bird) nido; (wasps' ~) avispero ♦ vi anidar; **~ egg** n (fig) ahorros mpl
nestle ['nɛsl] vi: **to ~ down** acurrucarse
net [nɛt] n (gen) red f; (fabric) tul m ♦ adj (COMM) neto, líquido ♦ vt coger (SP) or agarrar (AM) con red; (SPORT) marcar; **the N~** (Internet) la Red; **~ball** n básquet m
Netherlands ['nɛðələndz] npl: **the ~** los Países Bajos
nett [nɛt] adj = **net**
netting ['nɛtɪŋ] n red f, redes fpl
nettle ['nɛtl] n ortiga
network ['nɛtwəːk] n red f
neurotic [njuə'rɔtɪk] adj, n neurótico/a m/f
neuter ['njuːtə*] adj (LING) neutro ♦ vt castrar, capar
neutral ['njuːtrəl] adj (person) neutral; (colour etc, ELEC) neutro ♦ n (AUT) punto muerto; **~ize** vt neutralizar
never ['nɛvə*] adv nunca, jamás; **I ~ went** no fui nunca; **~ in my life** jamás en la vida; see also **mind**; **~-ending** adj interminable, sin fin; **~theless** [nɛvəðə'lɛs] adv sin embargo, no obstante
new [njuː] adj nuevo; (brand new) a estrenar; (recent) reciente; **N~ Age** n Nueva Era; **~born** adj recién nacido; **~comer** ['njuːkʌmə*] n recién venido/a or llegado/a; **~-fangled** (pej) adj modernísimo; **~-found** adj (friend) nuevo; (enthusiasm) recién adquirido; **~ly** adv nuevamente, recién; **~lyweds** npl recién casados mpl
news [njuːz] n noticias fpl; **a piece of ~** una noticia; **the ~** (RADIO, TV) las noticias fpl; **~ agency** n agencia de noticias; **~agent** (BRIT) n vendedor(a) m/f de periódicos; **~caster** n presentador(a) m/f, locutor(a) m/f; **~ flash** n noticia de última hora; **~letter** n hoja informativa, boletín m; **~paper** n periódico, diario; **~print** n papel m de periódico; **~reader** n = **~caster**; **~reel** n noticiario; **~ stand** n quiosco or puesto de periódicos
newt [njuːt] n tritón m
New Year n Año Nuevo; **~'s Day** n Día m de Año Nuevo; **~'s Eve** n Nochevieja
New York ['njuː'jɔːk] n Nueva York
New Zealand [njuː'ziːlənd] n Nueva

Zelanda; **~er** n neozelandés/esa m/f
next [nɛkst] adj (house, room) vecino; (bus stop, meeting) próximo; (following: page etc) siguiente ♦ adv después; **the ~ day** el día siguiente; **~ time** la próxima vez; **~ year** el año próximo or que viene; **~ to** junto a, al lado de; **~ to nothing** casi nada; **~ please!** ¡el siguiente! **~ door** adv en la casa de al lado ♦ adj vecino, de al lado; **~-of-kin** n pariente m más cercano
NHS n abbr = **National Health Service**
nib [nɪb] n plumilla
nibble ['nɪbl] vt mordisquear, mordiscar
Nicaragua [nɪkə'ræɡjuə] n Nicaragua; **~n** adj, n nicaragüense m/f
nice [naɪs] adj (likeable) simpático; (kind) amable; (pleasant) agradable; (attractive) bonito, mono, lindo (AM); **~ly** adv amablemente; bien
nick [nɪk] n (wound) rasguño; (cut, indentation) mella, muesca ♦ vt (inf) birlar, robar; **in the ~ of time** justo a tiempo
nickel ['nɪkl] n níquel m; (US) moneda de 5 centavos
nickname ['nɪkneɪm] n apodo, mote m ♦ vt apodar
nicotine ['nɪkətiːn] n nicotina
niece [niːs] n sobrina
Nigeria [naɪ'dʒɪərɪə] n Nigeria; **~n** adj, n nigeriano/a m/f
niggling ['nɪɡlɪŋ] adj (trifling) nimio, insignificante; (annoying) molesto
night [naɪt] n noche f; (evening) tarde f; **the ~ before last** anteanoche; **at ~, by ~** de noche, por la noche; **~cap** n (drink) bebida que se toma antes de acostarse; **~ club** n cabaret m; **~dress** (BRIT) n camisón m; **~fall** n anochecer m; **~gown** n = **~dress**; **~ie** ['naɪtɪ] n = **~dress**
nightingale ['naɪtɪŋɡeɪl] n ruiseñor m
night: **~life** n vida nocturna; **~ly** adj de todas las noches ♦ adv todas las noches, cada noche; **~mare** n pesadilla; **~ porter** n portero de noche; **~ school** n clase(s) f(pl) nocturna(s); **~ shift** n turno nocturno or de noche; **~-time** n noche f; **~ watchman** n vigilante m nocturno
nil [nɪl] (BRIT) n (SPORT) cero, nada
Nile [naɪl] n: **the ~** el Nilo
nimble ['nɪmbl] adj (agile) ágil, ligero; (skilful) diestro
nine [naɪn] num nueve; **~teen** num diecinueve, diez y nueve; **~ty** num noventa
ninth [naɪnθ] adj noveno
nip [nɪp] vt (pinch) pellizcar; (bite) morder
nipple ['nɪpl] n (ANAT) pezón m
nitrogen ['naɪtrədʒən] n nitrógeno

no [nəu] (pl **~es**) adv (opposite of "yes") no; are you coming? — ~ (I'm not) ¿vienes? — no; would you like some more? — ~ thank you ¿quieres más? — no gracias ♦ adj (not any): I have ~ money/time/books no tengo dinero/tiempo/libros; ~ other man would have done it ningún otro lo hubiera hecho; "~ entry" "prohibido el paso"; "~ smoking" "prohibido fumar" ♦ n no m

nobility [nəu'bɪlɪtɪ] n nobleza

noble ['nəubl] adj noble

nobody ['nəubədɪ] pron nadie

nod [nɔd] vi saludar con la cabeza; (in agreement) decir que sí con la cabeza; (doze) dar cabezadas ♦ vt: to ~ one's head inclinar la cabeza ♦ n inclinación f de cabeza; ~ off vi dar cabezadas

noise [nɔɪz] n ruido; (din) escándalo, estrépito; **noisy** adj ruidoso; (child) escandaloso

nominate ['nɔmɪneɪt] vt (propose) proponer; (appoint) nombrar; **nominee** [-'niː] n candidato/a

non... [nɔn] prefix no, des..., in...; **~alcoholic** adj no alcohólico; **~chalant** adj indiferente; **~committal** adj evasivo; **~descript** adj soso

none [nʌn] pron ninguno/a ♦ adv de ninguna manera; ~ of you ninguno de vosotros; I've ~ left no me queda ninguno/a; he's ~ the worse for it no le ha hecho ningún mal

nonentity [nɔ'nentɪtɪ] n cero a la izquierda, nulidad f

nonetheless [nʌnðə'les] adv sin embargo, no obstante

non-existent adj inexistente

non-fiction n literatura no novelesca

nonplussed [nɔn'plʌst] adj perplejo

nonsense ['nɔnsəns] n tonterías fpl, disparates fpl; ~! ¡qué tonterías!

non: **~smoker** n no fumador(a) m/f; **~smoking** adj (de) no fumador; **~stick** adj (pan, surface) antiadherente; **~stop** adj continuo; (RAIL) directo ♦ adv sin parar

noodles ['nuːdlz] npl tallarines mpl

nook [nuk] n: ~s and crannies escondrijos mpl

noon [nuːn] n mediodía m

no-one pron = nobody

noose [nuːs] n (hangman's) dogal m

nor [nɔː*] conj = neither ♦ adv see neither

norm [nɔːm] n norma

normal ['nɔːml] adj normal; **~ly** adv normalmente

north [nɔːθ] n norte m ♦ adj del norte, norteño ♦ adv al or hacia el norte; **N~**

Africa n África del Norte; **N~ America** n América del Norte; **~east** n nor(d)este m; **~erly** ['nɔːðəlɪ] adj (point, direction) norteño; **~ern** ['nɔːðən] adj norteño, del norte; **N~ern Ireland** n Irlanda del Norte; **N~ Pole** n Polo Norte; **N~ Sea** n Mar m del Norte; **~ward(s)** ['nɔːθwəd(z)] adv hacia el norte; **~west** n nor(d)oeste m

Norway ['nɔːweɪ] n Noruega; **Norwegian** [-'wiːdʒən] adj noruego/a ♦ n noruego/a; (LING) noruego

nose [nəuz] n (ANAT) nariz f; (ZOOL) hocico; (sense of smell) olfato ♦ vi: to ~ about curiosear; **~bleed** n hemorragia nasal; **~dive** n (of plane: deliberate) picado vertical; (: involuntary) caída en picado; **~y** (inf) adj curioso, fisgón/ona

nostalgia [nɔs'tældʒɪə] n nostalgia

nostril ['nɔstrɪl] n ventana de la nariz

nosy ['nəuzɪ] (inf) adj = nosey

not [nɔt] adv no; ~ that ... no es que ...; it's too late, isn't it? es demasiado tarde, ¿verdad or no?; ~ yet/now todavía/ahora no; why ~? ¿por qué no?; see also all; only

notably ['nəutəblɪ] adv especialmente

notary ['nəutərɪ] n notario/a

notch [nɔtʃ] n muesca, corte m

note [nəut] n (MUS, record, letter) nota; (banknote) billete m; (tone) tono ♦ vt (observe) notar, observar; (write down) apuntar, anotar; **~book** n libreta, cuaderno; **~d** ['nəutɪd] adj célebre, conocido; **~pad** n bloc m; **~paper** n papel m para cartas

nothing ['nʌθɪŋ] n nada; (zero) cero; he does ~ no hace nada; ~ new nada nuevo; ~ much no mucho; for ~ (free) gratis, sin pago; (in vain) en balde

notice ['nəutɪs] n (announcement) anuncio; (warning) aviso; (dismissal) despido; (resignation) dimisión f; (period of time) plazo ♦ vt (observe) notar, observar; to bring sth to sb's ~ (attention) llamar la atención de uno sobre algo; to take ~ of tomar nota de, prestar atención a; at short ~ con poca anticipación; until further ~ hasta nuevo aviso; to hand in one's ~ dimitir; **~able** adj evidente, obvio; ~ board (BRIT) n tablón m de anuncios

notify ['nəutɪfaɪ] vt: to ~ sb (of sth) comunicar (algo) a uno

notion ['nəuʃən] n idea; (opinion) opinión f

notorious [nəu'tɔːrɪəs] adj notorio

nougat ['nuːgɑː] n turrón m

nought [nɔːt] n cero

noun [naun] n nombre m, sustantivo

nourish ['nʌrɪʃ] vt nutrir; (fig) alimentar; **~ing** adj nutritivo; **~ment** n alimento, sustento

novel ['nɔvl] n novela ♦ adj (new) nuevo,

original; (*unexpected*) insólito; **~ist** *n*
novelista *m/f*; **~ty** *n* novedad *f*
November [nəu'vɛmbə*] *n* noviembre
m
novice ['nɔvɪs] *n* (*REL*) novicio/a
now [nau] *adv* (*at the present time*) ahora,
(*these days*) actualmente, hoy día ♦ *conj:*
~ (that) ya que, ahora que; **right ~** ahora
mismo; **by ~** ya; **just ~** ahora mismo; **~
and then, ~ and again** de vez en cuando;
from ~ on de ahora en adelante;
~adays ['nauədeɪz] *adv* hoy (en) día,
actualmente
nowhere ['nəuwɛə*] *adv* (*direction*) a
ninguna parte; (*location*) en ninguna parte
nozzle ['nɔzl] *n* boquilla
nuance ['nju:ã:ns] *n* matiz *m*
nuclear ['nju:klɪə*] *adj* nuclear
nucleus ['nju:klɪəs] (*pl* **nuclei**) *n* núcleo
nude [nju:d] *adj, n* desnudo/a *m/f*; **in the ~**
desnudo
nudge [nʌdʒ] *vt* dar un codazo a
nudist ['nju:dɪst] *n* nudista *m/f*
nuisance ['nju:sns] *n* molestia, fastidio;
(*person*) pesado, latoso; **what a ~!** ¡qué lata!
null [nʌl] *adj:* **~ and void** nulo y sin efecto
numb [nʌm] *adj:* **~ with cold/fear**
entumecido por el frío/paralizado de miedo
number ['nʌmbə*] *n* número; (*quantity*)
cantidad *f* ♦ *vt* (*pages etc*) numerar, poner
número a; (*amount to*) sumar, ascender a;
to be ~ed among figurar entre; **a ~ of** varios,
algunos; **they were ten in ~** eran diez;
~ plate (*BRIT*) *n* matrícula, placa
numeral ['nju:mərəl] *n* número, cifra
numerate ['nju:mərɪt] *adj* competente en la
aritmética
numerous ['nju:mərəs] *adj* numeroso
nun [nʌn] *n* monja, religiosa
nurse [nɜ:s] *n* enfermero/a; (*also:* **~maid**)
niñera ♦ *vt* (*patient*) cuidar, atender
nursery ['nɜ:sərɪ] *n* (*institution*) guardería
infantil; (*room*) cuarto de los niños; (*for
plants*) criadero, semillero; **~ rhyme** *n*
canción *f* infantil; **~ school** *n* parvulario,
escuela de párvulos; **~ slope** (*BRIT*) *n* (*SKI*)
cuesta para principiantes
nursing ['nɜ:sɪŋ] *n* (*profession*) profesión *f* de
enfermera; (*care*) asistencia, cuidado;
~ home *n* clínica de reposo
nut [nʌt] *n* (*TECH*) tuerca; (*BOT*) nuez *f*;
~crackers *npl* cascanueces *m inv*
nutmeg ['nʌtmeg] *n* nuez *f* moscada
nutritious [nju:'trɪʃəs] *adj* nutritivo,
alimenticio
nuts [nʌts] (*inf*) *adj* loco
nutshell ['nʌtʃel] *n:* **in a ~** en resumidas
cuentas
nylon ['naɪlɔn] *n* nilón *m* ♦ *adj* de nilón

O, o

oak [əuk] *n* roble *m* ♦ *adj* de roble
O.A.P. (*BRIT*) *n abbr* = **old-age pensioner**
oar [ɔ:*] *n* remo
oasis [əu'eɪsɪs] (*pl* **oases**) *n* oasis *m inv*
oath [əuθ] *n* juramento; (*swear word*)
palabrota; **on** (*BRIT*) or **under ~** bajo
juramento
oatmeal ['əutmi:l] *n* harina de avena
oats [əuts] *n* avena
obedience [ə'bi:dɪəns] *n* obediencia
obedient [ə'bi:dɪənt] *adj* obediente
obey [ə'beɪ] *vt* obedecer; (*instructions,
regulations*) cumplir
obituary [ə'bɪtjuərɪ] *n* necrología
object [*n* 'ɔbdʒɪkt, *vb* əb'dʒɛkt] *n* objeto;
(*purpose*) objeto, propósito; (*LING*)
complemento ♦ *vi:* **to ~ to** estar en contra
de; (*proposal*) oponerse a; **to ~ that** objetar
que; **expense is no ~** no importa cuánto
cuesta; **I ~!** ¡yo protesto!; **~ion** [əb'dʒɛkʃən] *n*
protesta; **I have no ~ion to ...** no tengo
inconveniente en que ...; **~ionable**
[əb'dʒɛkʃənəbl] *adj* desagradable; (*conduct*)
censurable; **~ive** *adj, n* objetivo
obligation [ɔblɪ'geɪʃən] *n* obligación *f*; (*debt*)
deber *m*; **without ~** sin compromiso
oblige [ə'blaɪdʒ] *vt* (*do a favour for*)
complacer, hacer un favor a; **to ~ sb to do
sth** forzar or obligar a uno a hacer algo; **to be
~d to sb for sth** estarle agradecido a uno por
algo; **obliging** *adj* servicial, atento
oblique [ə'bli:k] *adj* oblicuo; (*allusion*)
indirecto
obliterate [ə'blɪtəreɪt] *vt* borrar
oblivion [ə'blɪvɪən] *n* olvido; **oblivious** [-ɪəs]
adj: **oblivious of** inconsciente de
oblong ['ɔblɔŋ] *adj* rectangular ♦ *n*
rectángulo
obnoxious [əb'nɔkʃəs] *adj* odioso,
detestable; (*smell*) nauseabundo
oboe ['əubəu] *n* oboe *m*
obscene [əb'si:n] *adj* obsceno
obscure [əb'skjuə*] *adj* oscuro ♦ *vt*
oscurecer; (*hide: sun*) esconder
observant [əb'zɜ:vnt] *adj* observador(a)
observation [ɔbzə'veɪʃən] *n* observación *f*;
(*MED*) examen *m*
observe [əb'zɜ:v] *vt* observar; (*rule*) cumplir;
~r *n* observador(a) *m/f*
obsess [əb'sɛs] *vt* obsesionar; **~ive** *adj*
obsesivo; obsesionante
obsolete ['ɔbsəli:t] *adj:* **to be ~** estar en
desuso
obstacle ['ɔbstəkl] *n* obstáculo; (*nuisance*)
estorbo; **~ race** *n* carrera de obstáculos

obstinate ['ɔbstɪnɪt] adj terco, porfiado; (determined) obstinado

obstruct [əb'strʌkt] vt obstruir; (hinder) estorbar, obstaculizar; **~ion** [əb'strʌkʃən] n (action) obstrucción f; (object) estorbo, obstáculo

obtain [əb'teɪn] vt obtener; (achieve) conseguir

obvious ['ɔbvɪəs] adj obvio, evidente; **~ly** adv evidentemente, naturalmente; **~ly not** por supuesto que no

occasion [ə'keɪʒən] n oportunidad f, ocasión f; (event) acontecimiento; **~al** adj poco frecuente, ocasional; **~ally** adv de vez en cuando

occupant ['ɔkjupənt] n (of house) inquilino/a; (of car) ocupante m/f

occupation [ɔkju'peɪʃən] n ocupación f; (job) trabajo; (pastime) ocupaciones fpl; **~al hazard** n riesgo profesional

occupier ['ɔkjupaɪə*] n inquilino/a

occupy ['ɔkjupaɪ] vt (seat, post, time) ocupar; (house) habitar; **to ~ o.s. in doing** pasar el tiempo haciendo

occur [ə'kə:*] vi pasar, suceder; **to ~ to sb** ocurrírsele a uno; **~rence** [ə'kʌrəns] n acontecimiento; (existence) existencia

ocean ['əuʃən] n océano

o'clock [ə'klɔk] adv: **it is 5 ~** son las 5

OCR n abbr = **optical character recognition/reader**

October [ɔk'təubə*] n octubre m

octopus ['ɔktəpəs] n pulpo

odd [ɔd] adj extraño, raro; (number) impar; (sock, shoe etc) suelto; **60~** 60 y pico; **at ~ times** de vez en cuando; **to be the ~ one out** estar de más; **~ity** n rareza; (person) excéntrico; **~-job man** n chico para todo; **~ jobs** npl bricolaje m; **~ly** adv curiosamente, extrañamente; see also **enough**; **~ments** npl (COMM) retales mpl; **~s** npl (in betting) puntos mpl de ventaja; **it makes no ~s** da lo mismo; **at ~s** reñidos/as; **~s and ends** minucias fpl

odometer [ɔ'dɔmɪtə*] n (US) n cuenta-kilómetros m inv

odour ['əudə*] n (US **odor**) n olor m; (unpleasant) hedor m

---

of [ɔv, əv] prep **1** (gen) de; **a friend ~ ours** un amigo nuestro; **a boy ~ 10** un chico de 10 años; **that was kind ~ you** eso fue muy amable por or de tu parte

2 (expressing quantity, amount, dates etc) de; **a kilo ~ flour** un kilo de harina; **there were 3 ~ them** había tres; **3 ~ us went** tres de nosotros fuimos; **the 5th ~ July** el 5 de julio

3 (from, out of) de; **made ~ wood** (hecho de) madera

---

off [ɔf] adj, adv (engine) desconectado; (light) apagado; (tap) cerrado; (BRIT: food: bad) pasado, malo; (: milk) cortado; (cancelled) cancelado ♦ prep de; **to be ~** (to leave) irse, marcharse; **to be ~ sick** estar enfermo or de baja; **a day ~** un día libre or sin trabajar; **to have an ~ day** tener un día malo; **he had his coat ~** se había quitado el abrigo; **10% ~** (COMM) (con el) 10% de descuento; **5 km ~** (the road) a 5 km (de la carretera); **~ the coast** frente a la costa; **I'm ~ meat** (no longer eat/like it) paso de la carne; **on the ~ chance** por si acaso; **~ and on** de vez en cuando

offal ['ɔfl] (BRIT) n (CULIN) menudencias fpl

off-colour [ɔf'kʌlə*] (BRIT) adj (ill) indispuesto

offence [ə'fɛns] (US **offense**) n (crime) delito; **to take ~ at** ofenderse por

offend [ə'fɛnd] vt (person) ofender; **~er** n delincuente m/f

offensive [ə'fɛnsɪv] adj ofensivo; (smell etc) repugnante ♦ n (MIL) ofensiva

offer ['ɔfə*] n oferta, ofrecimiento; (proposal) propuesta ♦ vt ofrecer; (opportunity) facilitar; **"on ~"** (COMM) "en oferta"; **~ing** n ofrenda

offhand [ɔf'hænd] adj informal ♦ adv de improviso

office ['ɔfɪs] n (place) oficina; (room) despacho; (position) carga, oficio; **doctor's ~** (US) consultorio; **to take ~** entrar en funciones; **~ block** (US **~ building**) n bloque m de oficinas; **~ hours** npl horas fpl de oficina; (US: MED) horas fpl de consulta

officer ['ɔfɪsə*] n (MIL etc) oficial m/f; (also: **police ~**) agente m/f de policía; (of organization) director(a) m/f

office worker n oficinista m/f

official [ə'fɪʃl] adj oficial, autorizado ♦ n funcionario, oficial m

offing ['ɔfɪŋ] n: **in the ~** (fig) en perspectiva

off-: ~-licence (BRIT) n (shop) bodega, tienda de vinos y bebidas alcohólicas; **~-line** adj, adv (COMPUT) fuera de línea; **~-peak** adj (electricity) de banda económica; (ticket) billete de precio reducido por viajar fuera de las horas punta; **~-putting** (BRIT) adj (person) asqueroso; (remark) desalentador(a); **~-season** adj, adv fuera de temporada

offset ['ɔfsɛt] (irreg) vt contrarrestar, compensar

offshoot ['ɔfʃu:t] n (fig) ramificación f

offshore [ɔf'ʃɔ:*] adj (breeze, island) costera; (fishing) de bajura

offside ['ɔf'saɪd] adj (SPORT) fuera de juego; (AUT: in UK) del lado derecho; (: in US, Europe etc) del lado izquierdo

offspring ['ɒfsprɪŋ] n inv descendencia
off: ~**stage** adv entre bastidores; ~**-the-peg**
(US ~**-the-rack**) adv confeccionado; ~**-white**
adj color crudo
often ['ɒfn] adv a menudo, con frecuencia;
how ~ **do you go?** ¿cada cuánto vas?
oh [əu] excl ¡ah!
oil [ɔɪl] n aceite m; (petroleum) petróleo; (for
heating) aceite m combustible ♦ vt engrasar;
~**can** n lata de aceite; ~**field** n campo
petrolífero; ~ **filter** n (AUT) filtro de aceite;
~ **painting** n pintura al óleo; ~ **rig** n torre f
de perforación; ~ **tanker** n petrolero; (truck)
camión m cisterna; ~ **well** n pozo (de
petróleo); ~**y** adj aceitoso; (food) grasiento
ointment ['ɔɪntmənt] n ungüento
O.K., okay ['əu'keɪ] excl O.K., ¡está bien!,
¡vale! (SP) ♦ adj bien ♦ vt dar el visto bueno
a
old [əuld] adj viejo; (former) antiguo; **how**
~ **are you?** ¿cuántos años tienes?, ¿qué edad
tienes?; **he's 10 years** ~ tiene 10 años; ~**er**
brother hermano mayor; ~ **age** n vejez f; ~**-**
age pensioner (BRIT) n jubilado/a; ~**-**
fashioned adj anticuado, pasado de moda
olive ['ɒlɪv] n (fruit) aceituna; (tree) olivo
♦ adj (also: ~**-green**) verde oliva; ~ **oil** n
aceite m de oliva
Olympic [əu'lɪmpɪk] adj olímpico; **the**
~ **Games, the** ~**s** las Olimpíadas
omelet(te) ['ɒmlɪt] n tortilla (SP), tortilla de
huevo (AM)
omen ['əumən] n presagio
ominous ['ɒmɪnəs] adj de mal agüero,
amenazador(a)
omit [əu'mɪt] vt omitir

KEYWORD

on [ɒn] prep 1 (indicating position) en; sobre;
~ **the wall** en la pared; **it's** ~ **the table** está
sobre or en la mesa; ~ **the left** a la izquierda
2 (indicating means, method, condition etc):
~ **foot** a pie; ~ **the train/plane** (go) en tren/
avión; (be) en el tren/el avión; ~ **the radio/**
television/telephone por or en la radio/
televisión/al teléfono; **to be** ~ **drugs** drogarse;
(MED) estar a tratamiento; **to be** ~ **holiday/**
business estar de vacaciones/en viaje de
negocios
3 (referring to time): ~ **Friday** el viernes;
~ **Fridays** los viernes; ~ **June 20th** el 20 de
junio; **a week** ~ **Friday** del viernes en una
semana; ~ **arrival** al llegar; ~ **seeing this** al ver
esto
4 (about, concerning) sobre, acerca de; **a**
book ~ **physics** un libro de or sobre física
♦ adv 1 (referring to dress): **to have one's**
coat ~ tener or llevar el abrigo puesto; **she**
put her gloves ~ se puso los guantes

2 (referring to covering): **"screw the lid**
~ **tightly"** "cerrar bien la tapa"
3 (further, continuously): **to walk** etc ~ seguir
caminando etc
♦ adj 1 (functioning, in operation: machine,
radio, TV, light) encendido/a (SP), prendido/a
(AM); (: tap) abierto/a; (: brakes) echado/a,
puesto/a; **is the meeting still** ~? (in progress)
¿todavía continúa la reunión?; (not cancelled)
¿va a haber reunión al fin?; **there's a good**
film ~ **at the cinema** ponen una buena
película en el cine
2: **that's not** ~! (inf: not possible) ¡eso ni
hablar!; (: not acceptable) ¡eso no se hace!

once [wʌns] adv una vez; (formerly)
antiguamente ♦ conj una vez que; ~ **he had**
left/it was done una vez que se había
marchado/se hizo; **at** ~ en seguida,
inmediatamente; (simultaneously) a la vez;
~ **a week** una vez por semana; ~ **more** otra
vez; ~ **and for all** de una vez por todas;
~ **upon a time** érase una vez
oncoming ['ɒnkʌmɪŋ] adj (traffic) que viene
de frente

KEYWORD

one [wʌn] num un(o)/una; ~ **hundred and**
fifty ciento cincuenta; ~ **by** ~ uno a uno
♦ adj 1 (sole) único; **the** ~ **book which** el
único libro que; **the** ~ **man who** el único que
2 (same) mismo/a; **they came in the** ~ **car**
vinieron en un solo coche
♦ pron 1: **this** ~ éste/ésta; **that** ~ ése/ésa;
(more remote) aquél/aquella; **I've already got**
(**a red**) ~ ya tengo uno/a (rojo/a); ~ **by** ~
uno/a por uno/a
2: ~ **another** os (SP), se (+ el uno al otro,
unos a otros etc); **do you two ever see**
~ **another?** ¿vosotros dos os veis alguna vez?
(SP), ¿se ven ustedes dos alguna vez?; **the**
boys didn't dare look at ~ **another** los chicos
no se atrevieron a mirarse (el uno al otro);
they all kissed ~ **another** se besaron unos a
otros
3 (impers): ~ **never knows** nunca se sabe; **to**
cut ~**'s finger** cortarse el dedo; ~ **needs to eat**
hay que comer

one: ~**-day excursion** (US) n billete m de ida
y vuelta en un día; ~**-man** adj (business)
individual; ~**-man band** n hombre-orquesta
m; ~**-off** (BRIT: inf) n (event) acontecimiento
único
oneself [wʌn'self] pron (reflexive) se; (after
prep) sí; (emphatic) uno/a mismo/a; **to hurt** ~
hacerse daño; **to keep sth for** ~ guardarse
algo; **to talk to** ~ hablar solo
one: ~**-sided** adj (argument) parcial; ~**-to-**~

adj (relationship) de dos; **~-way** *adj (street)* de sentido único

ongoing ['ɔngəʊɪŋ] *adj* continuo

onion ['ʌnjən] *n* cebolla

on-line *adj, adv (COMPUT)* en línea

onlooker ['ɔnlukə*] *n* espectador(a) *m/f*

only ['əʊnlɪ] *adv* solamente, sólo ♦ *adj* único, solo ♦ *conj* solamente que, pero; **an ~ child** un hijo único; **not ~ ... but also ...** no sólo ... sino también ...

onset ['ɔnsɛt] *n* comienzo

onshore ['ɔnʃɔː*] *adj (wind)* que sopla del mar hacia la tierra

onslaught ['ɔnslɔːt] *n* ataque *m*, embestida

onto ['ɔntu] *prep* = **on to**

onward(s) ['ɔnwəd(z)] *adv (move)* (hacia) adelante; **from that time ~** desde entonces en adelante

onyx ['ɔnɪks] *n* ónice *m*

ooze [uːz] *vi* rezumar

opaque [əu'peɪk] *adj* opaco

OPEC ['əupek] *n abbr (= Organization of Petroleum-Exporting Countries)* OPEP *f*

open ['əupn] *adj* abierto; *(car)* descubierto; *(road, view)* despejado; *(meeting)* público; *(admiration)* manifiesto ♦ *vt* abrir ♦ *vi* abrir; *(book etc: commence)* comenzar; **in the ~ (air)** al aire libre; **~ on to** *vt fus (subj: room, door)* dar a; **~ up** *vt* abrir; *(blocked road)* despejar ♦ *vi* abrirse, empezar; **~ing** *n* abertura; *(start)* comienzo; *(opportunity)* oportunidad *f*; **~ing hours** *npl* horario de apertura; **~ learning** *n* enseñanza flexible a tiempo parcial; **~ly** *adv* abiertamente; **~-minded** *adj* imparcial; **~-necked** *adj (shirt)* desabrochado; sin corbata; **~-plan** *adj*: **~-plan office** gran oficina sin particiones

opera ['ɔpərə] *n* ópera; **~ house** *n* teatro de la ópera

operate ['ɔpəreɪt] *vt (machine)* hacer funcionar; *(company)* dirigir ♦ *vi* funcionar; **to ~ on sb** *(MED)* operar a uno

operatic [ɔpə'rætɪk] *adj* de ópera

operating table ['ɔpəreɪtɪŋ-] *n* mesa de operaciones

operating theatre *n* sala de operaciones

operation [ɔpə'reɪʃən] *n* operación *f*; *(of machine)* funcionamiento; **to be in ~** estar funcionando or en funcionamiento; **to have an ~** *(MED)* ser operado; **~al** *adj* operacional, en buen estado

operative ['ɔpərətɪv] *adj* en vigor

operator ['ɔpəreɪtə*] *n (of machine)* maquinista *m/f*, operario/a; *(TEL)* operador(a) *m/f*, telefonista *m/f*

opinion [ə'pɪnɪən] *n* opinión *f*; **in my ~** en mi opinión, a mi juicio; **~ated** *adj* testarudo; **~ poll** *n* encuesta, sondeo

opponent [ə'pəunənt] *n* adversario/a,

contrincante *m/f*

opportunity [ɔpə'tjuːnɪtɪ] *n* oportunidad *f*; **to take the ~ of doing** aprovechar la ocasión para hacer

oppose [ə'pəuz] *vt* oponerse a; **to be ~d to sth** oponerse a algo; **as ~d to** a diferencia de; **opposing** *adj* opuesto, contrario

opposite ['ɔpəzɪt] *adj* opuesto, contrario a; *(house etc)* de enfrente ♦ *adv* en frente ♦ *prep* en frente de, frente a ♦ *n* lo contrario

opposition [ɔpə'zɪʃən] *n* oposición *f*

oppressive [ə'presɪv] *adj* opresivo; *(weather)* agobiante

opt [ɔpt] *vi*: **to ~ for** optar por; **to ~ to do** optar por hacer; **~ out** *vi*: **to ~ out of** optar por no hacer

optical ['ɔptɪkl] *adj* óptico

optician [ɔp'tɪʃən] *n* óptico *m/f*

optimist ['ɔptɪmɪst] *n* optimista *m/f*; **~ic** [-'mɪstɪk] *adj* optimista

option ['ɔpʃən] *n* opción *f*; **~al** *adj* facultativo, discrecional

or [ɔː*] *conj* o; *(before o, ho)* u; *(with negative)*: **he hasn't seen ~ heard anything** no ha visto ni oído nada; **~ else** si no

oral ['ɔːrəl] *adj oral* ♦ *n* examen *m* oral

orange ['ɔrɪndʒ] *n (fruit)* naranja ♦ *adj* color naranja

orbit ['ɔːbɪt] *n* órbita ♦ *vt*, *vi* orbitar

orchard ['ɔːtʃəd] *n* huerto

orchestra ['ɔːkɪstrə] *n* orquesta; *(US: seating)* platea

orchid ['ɔːkɪd] *n* orquídea

ordain [ɔː'deɪn] *vt (REL)* ordenar, decretar

ordeal [ɔː'diːl] *n* experiencia horrorosa

order ['ɔːdə*] *n* orden *m*; *(command)* orden *f*; *(good ~)* buen estado; *(COMM)* pedido ♦ *vt* *(also: put in ~)* arreglar, poner en orden; *(COMM)* pedir; *(command)* mandar, ordenar; **in ~** en orden; *(of document)* en regla; **in (working) ~** en funcionamiento; **in ~ to do/** **that** para hacer/que; **on ~** *(COMM)* pedido; **to be out of ~** estar desordenado; *(not working)* no funcionar; **to ~ sb to do sth** mandar a uno hacer algo; **~ form** *n* hoja de pedido; **~ly** *n* *(MIL)* ordenanza *m*; *(MED)* enfermero/a (auxiliar) ♦ *adj* ordenado

ordinary ['ɔːdnrɪ] *adj* corriente, normal; *(pej)* común y corriente; **out of the ~** fuera de lo común

Ordnance Survey ['ɔːdnəns-] *(BRIT)* *n* servicio oficial de topografía

ore [ɔː*] *n* mineral *m*

organ ['ɔːgən] *n* órgano; **~ic** [ɔː'gænɪk] *adj* orgánico; **~ism** *n* organismo

organization [ɔːgənaɪ'zeɪʃən] *n* organización *f*

organize ['ɔːgənaɪz] *vt* organizar; **~r** *n* organizador(a) *m/f*

orgasm ['ɔ:gæzəm] n orgasmo
orgy ['ɔ:dʒɪ] n orgía
Orient ['ɔ:rɪənt] n Oriente m; **oriental** [-'ɛntl] adj oriental
orientate ['ɔ:rɪənteɪt] vt: **to ~ o.s.** orientarse
origin ['ɔrɪdʒɪn] n origen m
original [ə'rɪdʒɪnl] adj original; (first) primero; (earlier) primitivo ♦ n original m; **~ly** adv al principio
originate [ə'rɪdʒɪneɪt] vi: **to ~ from, to ~ in** surgir de, tener su origen en
Orkneys ['ɔ:knɪz] npl: **the ~** (also: **the Orkney Islands**) las Orcadas
ornament ['ɔ:nəmənt] n adorno; (trinket) chuchería; **~al** [-'mɛntl] adj decorativo, de adorno
ornate [ɔ:'neɪt] adj muy ornado, vistoso
orphan ['ɔ:fn] n huérfano/a
orthopaedic [ɔ:θə'pi:dɪk] (US **orthopedic**) adj ortopédico
ostensibly [ɔs'tɛnsɪblɪ] adv aparentemente
ostentatious [ɔstɛn'teɪʃəs] adj ostentoso
osteopath ['ɔstɪəpæθ] n osteópata m/f
ostracize ['ɔstrəsaɪz] vt hacer el vacío a
ostrich ['ɔstrɪtʃ] n avestruz m
other ['ʌðə*] adj otro ♦ pron: **the ~** (one) el/la otro/a ♦ adv: **~ than** aparte de; **~s** (~ people) otros; **the ~ day** el otro día; **~wise** adv de otra manera ♦ conj (if not) si no
otter ['ɔtə*] n nutria
ouch [autʃ] excl ¡ay!
ought [ɔ:t] (pt ought) aux vb: **I ~ to do it** debería hacerlo; **this ~ to have been corrected** esto debiera haberse corregido; **he ~ to win** (probability) debe or debiera ganar
ounce [auns] n onza (28.35g)
our ['auə*] adj nuestro; see also **my**; **~s** pron (el) nuestro/(la) nuestra etc; see also **mine**[1]; **~selves** pron pl (reflexive, after prep) nosotros; (emphatic) nosotros mismos; see also **oneself**
oust [aust] vt desalojar
out [aut] adv fuera, afuera; (not at home) fuera (de casa); (light, fire) apagado; **~ there** allí (fuera); **he's ~** (absent) no está, ha salido; **to be ~ in one's calculations** equivocarse (en sus cálculos); **to run ~** salir corriendo; **~ loud** en alta voz; **~ of** (outside) fuera de; (because of: anger etc) por; **~ of petrol** sin gasolina; **"~ of order"** "no funciona"; **~-and-~** adj (liar, thief etc) redomado, empedernido; **~back** n interior m; **~board** adj: **~board motor** (motor m) fuera borda m; **~break** n (of war) comienzo; (of disease) epidemia; (of violence etc) ola; **~burst** n explosión f, arranque m; **~cast** n paria m/f; **~come** n resultado; **~crop** n (of rock) afloramiento; **~cry** n protestas fpl; **~dated** adj anticuado, fuera de moda; **~do** (irreg) vt superar;

~door adj exterior, de aire libre; (clothes) de calle; **~doors** adv al aire libre
outer ['autə*] adj exterior, externo; **~ space** n espacio exterior
outfit ['autfɪt] n (clothes) conjunto
out: ~going adj (character) extrovertido; (retiring: president etc) saliente; **~goings** (BRIT) npl gastos mpl; **~grow** (irreg) vt: **he has ~grown his clothes** su ropa le queda pequeña ya; **~house** n dependencia; **~ing** ['autɪŋ] n excursión f, paseo
out: ~law n proscrito ♦ vt proscribir; **~lay** n inversión f; (US: ELEC) salida; (of pipe) desagüe m; (US: retail ~let) punto de venta; **~line** n (shape) contorno, perfil m; (sketch, plan) esbozo ♦ vt (plan etc) esbozar; **in ~line** (fig) a grandes rasgos; **~live** vt sobrevivir a; **~look** n (fig: prospects) perspectivas fpl; (: for weather) pronóstico; **~lying** adj remoto, aislado; **~moded** adj anticuado, pasado de moda; **~number** vt superar en número; **~-of-date** adj (passport) caducado; (clothes) pasado de moda; **~-of-the-way** adj apartado; **~patient** n paciente m/f externo/a; **~post** n puesto avanzado; **~put** n (volumen m de) producción f, rendimiento; (COMPUT) salida
outrage ['autreɪdʒ] n escándalo; (atrocity) atrocidad f ♦ vt ultrajar; **~ous** [-'reɪdʒəs] adj monstruoso
outright [adv aut'raɪt, adj 'autraɪt] adv (ask, deny) francamente; (refuse) rotundamente; (win) de manera absoluta; (be killed) en el acto ♦ adj franco; rotundo
outset ['autsɛt] n principio
outside [aut'saɪd] n exterior m ♦ adj exterior, externo ♦ adv fuera ♦ prep fuera de; (beyond) más allá de; **at the ~** (fig) a lo sumo; **~ lane** n (AUT: in Britain) carril m de la derecha; (: in US, Europe etc) carril m de la izquierda; **~ line** n (TEL) línea (exterior); **~r** n (stranger) extraño, forastero
out: ~size adj (clothes) de talla grande; **~skirts** npl alrededores mpl, afueras fpl; **~spoken** adj muy franco; **~standing** adj excepcional, destacado; (remaining) pendiente; **~stay** vt: **to ~stay one's welcome** quedarse más de la cuenta; **~stretched** adj (hand) extendido; **~strip** vt (competitors, demand) dejar atrás, aventajar; **~tray** n bandeja de salida
outward ['autwəd] adj externo; (journey) de ida
outweigh [aut'weɪ] vt pesar más que
outwit [aut'wɪt] vt ser más listo que
oval ['əuvl] adj ovalado ♦ n óvalo
ovary ['əuvərɪ] n ovario
oven ['ʌvn] n horno; **~proof** adj resistente al horno

over ['əuvə*] *adv* encima, por encima ♦ *adj* (*or adv*) (*finished*) terminado; (*surplus*) de sobra ♦ *prep* (*por*) encima de; (*above*) sobre; (*on the other side of*) al otro lado de; (*more than*) más de; (*during*) durante; ~ **here** (por) aquí; ~ **there** (por) allí or allá; **all** ~ (*everywhere*) por todas partes; ~ **and** ~ (*again*) una y otra vez; ~ **and above** además de; **to ask sb** ~ invitar a uno a casa; **to bend** ~ inclinarse

overall [*adj, n* 'əuvərɔːl, *adv* əuvər'ɔːl] *adj* (*length etc*) total; (*study*) de conjunto ♦ *adv* en conjunto ♦ *n* (*BRIT*) guardapolvo; ~**s** *npl* mono (*SP*), overol *m* (*AM*)

over: ~**awe** *vt:* **to be** ~**awed (by)** quedar impresionado (con); ~**balance** *vi* perder el equilibrio; ~**board** *adv* (*NAUT*) por la borda; ~**book** [əuvə'buk] *vt* sobrerreservar

overcast ['əuvəkɑːst] *adj* encapotado

overcharge [əuvə'tʃɑːdʒ] *vt:* **to** ~ **sb** cobrar un precio excesivo a uno

overcoat ['əuvəkəut] *n* abrigo, sobretodo

overcome [əuvə'kʌm] (*irreg*) *vt* vencer; (*difficulty*) superar

over: ~**crowded** *adj* atestado de gente; (*city, country*) superpoblado; ~**do** (*irreg*) *vt* exagerar; (*overcook*) cocer demasiado; **to** ~**do it** (*work etc*) pasarse; ~**dose** *n* sobredosis *f inv*; ~**draft** *n* saldo deudor; ~**drawn** *adj* (*account*) en descubierto; ~**due** *adj* retrasado; ~**estimate** [əuvər'estimeit] *vt* sobreestimar

overflow [*vb* əuvə'fləu, *n* 'əuvəfləu] *vi* desbordarse ♦ *n* (*also:* ~ *pipe*) (cañería de) desagüe *m*

overgrown [əuvə'grəun] *adj* (*garden*) invadido por la vegetación

overhaul [*vb* əuvə'hɔːl, *n* 'əuvəhɔːl] *vt* revisar, repasar ♦ *n* revisión *f*

overhead [*adv* əuvə'hed, *adj, n* 'əuvəhed] *adv* por arriba or encima ♦ *adj* (*cable*) aéreo ♦ *n* (*US*) = ~**s**; ~**s** *npl* (*expenses*) gastos *mpl* generales

over: ~**hear** (*irreg*) *vt* oír por casualidad; ~**heat** *vi* (*engine*) recalentarse; ~**joyed** *adj* encantado, lleno de alegría

overland ['əuvəlænd] *adj, adv* por tierra

overlap [əuvə'læp] *vi* traslaparse

over: ~**leaf** *adv* al dorso; ~**load** *vt* sobrecargar; ~**look** *vt* (*have view of*) dar a, tener vistas a; (*miss: by mistake*) pasar por alto; (*excuse*) perdonar

overnight [əuvə'nait] *adv* durante la noche; (*fig*) de la noche a la mañana ♦ *adj* de noche; **to stay** ~ pasar la noche

overpass ['əuvəpɑːs] (*US*) *n* paso superior

overpower [əuvə'pauə*] *vt* dominar; (*fig*) embargar; ~**ing** *adj* (*heat*) agobiante; (*smell*) penetrante

over: ~**rate** *vt* sobreestimar; ~**ride** (*irreg*) *vt* no hacer caso de; ~**riding** *adj* predominante; ~**rule** *vt* (*decision*) anular; (*claim*) denegar; ~**run** (*irreg*) *vt* (*country*) invadir; (*time limit*) rebasar, exceder

overseas [əuvə'siːz] *adv* (*abroad: live*) en el extranjero; (*: travel*) al extranjero ♦ *adj* (*trade*) exterior; (*visitor*) extranjero

overshadow [əuvə'ʃædəu] *vt:* **to be** ~**ed by** estar a la sombra de

overshoot [əuvə'ʃuːt] (*irreg*) *vt* excederse

oversight ['əuvəsait] *n* descuido

oversleep [əuvə'sliːp] (*irreg*) *vi* quedarse dormido

overstep [əuvə'step] *vt:* **to** ~ **the mark** pasarse de la raya

overt [əu'vəːt] *adj* abierto

overtake [əuvə'teik] (*irreg*) *vt* sobrepasar; (*BRIT: AUT*) adelantar

over: ~**throw** (*irreg*) *vt* (*government*) derrocar; ~**time** *n* horas *fpl* extraordinarias; ~**tone** *n* (*fig*) tono

overture ['əuvətʃuə*] *n* (*MUS*) obertura; (*fig*) preludio

over: ~**turn** *vt* volcar; (*fig: plan*) desbaratar; (*: government*) derrocar ♦ *vi* volcar; ~**weight** *adj* demasiado gordo or pesado; ~**whelm** *vt* aplastar; (*subj: emotion*) sobrecoger; ~**whelming** *adj* (*victory, defeat*) arrollador(a); (*feeling*) irresistible; ~**work** *vi* trabajar demasiado; ~**wrought** [əuvə'rɔːt] *adj* sobreexcitado

owe [əu] *vt:* **to** ~ **sb sth, to** ~ **sth to sb** deber algo a uno; **owing to** *prep* debido a, por causa de

owl [aul] *n* búho, lechuza

own [əun] *vt* tener, poseer ♦ *adj* propio; **a room of my** ~ una habitación propia; **to get one's** ~ **back** tomar revancha; **on one's** ~ solo, a solas; ~ **up** *vi* confesar; ~**er** *n* dueño/a; ~**ership** *n* posesión *f*

ox [ɔks] (*pl* ~**en**) *n* buey *m*; ~**tail** *n:* ~**tail soup** sopa de rabo de buey

oxygen ['ɔksidʒən] *n* oxígeno

oyster ['ɔistə*] *n* ostra

oz. *abbr* = **ounce(s)**

ozone ['əuzəun] *n:* ~ **friendly** *adj* que no daña la capa de ozono; ~ **hole** *n* agujero *m* de/en la capa de ozono; ~ **layer** *n* capa *f* de ozono

P, p

p [piː] *abbr* = **penny; pence**

P.A. *n abbr* = **personal assistant; public address system**

p.a. *abbr* = **per annum**

pa [pɑː] (*inf*) *n* papá *m*

pace [peis] *n* paso ♦ *vi:* **to** ~ **up and down**

pasearse de un lado a otro; **to keep ~ with** llevar el mismo paso que; **~maker** n (MED) regulador m cardíaco, marcapasos m inv; (SPORT: also: ~setter) liebre f

Pacific [pə'sɪfɪk] n: **the ~ (Ocean)** el (Océano) Pacífico

pack [pæk] n (packet) paquete m; (of hounds) jauría; (of people) manada, bando; (of cards) baraja; (bundle) fardo; (US: of cigarettes) paquete m; (back ~) mochila ♦ vt (fill) llenar; (in suitcase etc) meter, poner; (cram) llenar, atestar; **to ~ (one's bags)** hacerse la maleta; **to ~ sb off** despachar a uno; **~ it in!** (inf) ¡déjalo!

package ['pækɪdʒ] n paquete m; (bulky) bulto; (also: ~ deal) acuerdo global; **~ holiday** n vacaciones fpl organizadas; **~ tour** n viaje m organizado

packed lunch n almuerzo frío

packet ['pækɪt] n paquete m

packing ['pækɪŋ] n embalaje m; **~ case** n cajón m de embalaje

pact [pækt] n pacto

pad [pæd] n (of paper) bloc m; (cushion) cojinete m; (inf: home) casa ♦ vt rellenar; **~ding** n (material) relleno

paddle ['pædl] n (oar) canalete m; (US: for table tennis) paleta ♦ vt impulsar con canalete ♦ vi (with feet) chapotear; **paddling pool** (BRIT) n estanque m de juegos

paddock ['pædək] n corral m

padlock ['pædlɔk] n candado

paediatrics [piːdɪ'ætrɪks] (US **pediatrics**) n pediatría

pagan ['peɪgən] adj, n pagano/a m/f

page [peɪdʒ] n (of book) página; (of newspaper) plana; (also: ~ boy) paje m ♦ vt (in hotel etc) llamar por altavoz a

pageant ['pædʒənt] n (procession) desfile m; (show) espectáculo; **~ry** n pompa

pager ['peɪdʒə*] n (TEL) busca m

paging device ['peɪdʒɪŋ-] n = pager

paid [peɪd] pt, pp of **pay** ♦ adj (work) remunerado; (holiday) pagado; (official etc) a sueldo; **to put ~ to** (BRIT) acabar con

pail [peɪl] n cubo, balde m

pain [peɪn] n dolor m; **to be in ~** sufrir; **to take ~s to do sth** tomarse grandes molestias en hacer algo; **~ed** adj (expression) afligido; **~ful** adj doloroso; (difficult) penoso; (disagreeable) desagradable; **~fully** adv (fig: very) terriblemente; **~killer** n analgésico; **~less** adj que no causa dolor; **~staking** ['peɪnzteɪkɪŋ] adj (person) concienzudo, esmerado

paint [peɪnt] n pintura ♦ vt pintar; **to ~ the door blue** pintar la puerta de azul; **~brush** n (artist's) pincel m; (decorator's) brocha; **~er** n pintor(a) m/f; **~ing** n pintura; **~work** n

pintura

pair [pɛə*] n (of shoes, gloves etc) par m; (of people) pareja; **a ~ of scissors** unas tijeras; **a ~ of trousers** unos pantalones, un pantalón

pajamas [pə'dʒɑːməz] (US) npl pijama m

Pakistan [pɑːkɪ'stɑːn] n Paquistán m; **~i** adj, n paquistaní m/f

pal [pæl] (inf) n compinche m/f, compañero/a

palace ['pæləs] n palacio

palatable ['pælɪtəbl] adj sabroso

palate ['pælɪt] n paladar m

pale [peɪl] adj (gen) pálido; (colour) claro ♦ n: **to be beyond the ~** pasarse de la raya

Palestine ['pælɪstaɪn] n Palestina; **Palestinian** [-'tɪnɪən] adj, n palestino/a m/f

palette ['pælɪt] n paleta

pall [pɔːl] vi perder el sabor

pallet ['pælɪt] n (for goods) pallet m

pallid ['pælɪd] adj pálido

palm [pɑːm] n (ANAT) palma; (also: ~ tree) palmera, palma ♦ vt: **to ~ sth off on sb** (inf) encajar algo a uno; **P~ Sunday** n Domingo de Ramos

paltry ['pɔːltrɪ] adj irrisorio

pamper ['pæmpə*] vt mimar

pamphlet ['pæmflət] n folleto

pan [pæn] n (also: sauce~) cacerola, cazuela, olla; (also: frying ~) sartén f

Panama ['pænəmɑː] n Panamá m; **the ~ Canal** el Canal de Panamá

pancake ['pænkeɪk] n crepe f

panda ['pændə] n panda m; **~ car** (BRIT) n coche m Z (SP)

pandemonium [pændɪ'məʊnɪəm] n jaleo

pander ['pændə*] vi: **to ~ to** complacer a

pane [peɪn] n cristal m

panel ['pænl] n (of wood etc) panel m; (RADIO, TV) panel m de invitados; **~ling** (US **~ing**) n paneles mpl

pang [pæŋ] n: **a ~ of regret** (una punzada de) remordimiento; **hunger ~s** dolores mpl del hambre

panic ['pænɪk] n (terror m) pánico ♦ vi dejarse llevar por el pánico; **~ky** adj (person) asustadizo; **~-stricken** adj preso de pánico

pansy ['pænzɪ] n (BOT) pensamiento; (inf: pej) maricón m

pant [pænt] vi jadear

panther ['pænθə*] n pantera

panties ['pæntɪz] npl bragas fpl, pantis mpl

pantihose ['pæntɪhəʊz] (US) n pantimedias fpl

pantomime ['pæntəmaɪm] (BRIT) n revista musical representada en Navidad, basada en cuentos de hadas

pantry ['pæntrɪ] n despensa

pants [pænts] n (BRIT: underwear: woman's) bragas fpl; (: man's) calzoncillos mpl; (US: trousers) pantalones mpl

paper ['peɪpə*] n papel m; (also: news~) periódico, diario; (academic essay) ensayo; (exam) examen m ♦ adj de papel ♦ vt empapelar (SP), tapizar (AM); ~s npl (also: identity ~s) papeles mpl, documentos mpl; ~back n libro en rústica; ~ bag n bolsa de papel; ~ clip n clip m; ~ hankie ♦ pañuelo de papel; ~weight n pisapapeles m inv; ~work n trabajo administrativo

paprika ['pæprɪkə] n pimentón m

par [pɑ:*] n par f; (GOLF) par m; to be on a ~ with estar a la par con

parachute ['pærəʃu:t] n paracaídas m inv

parade [pə'reɪd] n desfile m ♦ vt (show off) hacer alarde de ♦ vi desfilar; (MIL) pasar revista

paradise ['pærədaɪs] n paraíso

paradox ['pærədɒks] n paradoja; ~ically [-'dɒksɪklɪ] adv paradójicamente

paraffin ['pærəfɪn] (BRIT) n (also: ~ oil) parafina

paragon ['pærəgən] n modelo

paragraph ['pærəgrɑ:f] n párrafo

parallel ['pærəlel] adj en paralelo; (fig) semejante ♦ n (line) paralela; (fig, GEO) paralelo

paralyse ['pærəlaɪz] vt paralizar

paralysis [pə'rælɪsɪs] n parálisis f inv

paralyze ['pærəlaɪz] (US) vt = **paralyse**

paramount ['pærəmaʊnt] adj: of ~ importance de suma importancia

paranoid ['pærənɔɪd] adj (person, feeling) paranoico

paraphernalia [pærəfə'neɪlɪə] n (gear) avíos mpl

parasite ['pærəsaɪt] n parásito/a

parasol ['pærəsɒl] n sombrilla, quitasol m

paratrooper ['pærətru:pə*] n paracaidista m/f

parcel ['pɑ:sl] n paquete m ♦ vt (also: ~ up) empaquetar, embalar

parched [pɑ:tʃt] adj (person) muerto de sed

parchment ['pɑ:tʃmənt] n pergamino

pardon ['pɑ:dn] n (LAW) indulto ♦ vt perdonar; ~ me!, I beg your ~! (I'm sorry!) ¡perdone usted!; (I beg your) ~?, ~ me? (US) (what did you say?) ¿cómo?

parent ['peərənt] n (mother) madre f; (father) padre m; ~s npl padres mpl; ~al [pə'rentl] adj paternal/maternal

parenthesis [pə'renθɪsɪs] (pl parentheses) n paréntesis m inv

Paris ['pærɪs] n París m

parish ['pærɪʃ] n parroquia

Parisian [pə'rɪzɪən] adj, n parisiense m/f

park [pɑ:k] n parque m ♦ vt aparcar, estacionar ♦ vi aparcar, estacionarse

parking ['pɑ:kɪŋ] n aparcamiento, estacionamiento; "no ~" "prohibido estacionarse"; ~ lot (US) n parking m; ~ meter n parquímetro; ~ ticket n multa de aparcamiento

parliament ['pɑ:ləmənt] n parlamento; (Spanish) Cortes fpl; ~ary [-'mentərɪ] adj parlamentario

parlour ['pɑ:lə*] (US parlor) n sala de recibo, salón m, living m (AM)

parochial [pə'rəʊkɪəl] (pej) adj de miras estrechas

parole [pə'rəʊl] n: on ~ libre bajo palabra

parquet ['pɑ:keɪ] n: ~ floor(ing) parquet m

parrot ['pærət] n loro, papagayo

parry ['pærɪ] vt parar

parsley ['pɑ:slɪ] n perejil m

parsnip ['pɑ:snɪp] n chirivía

parson ['pɑ:sn] n cura m

part [pɑ:t] n (gen, MUS) parte f; (bit) trozo; (of machine) pieza; (THEATRE etc) papel m; (of serial) entrega; (US: in hair) raya ♦ adv = partly ♦ vt separar ♦ vi (people) separarse; (crowd) apartarse; to take ~ in tomar parte or participar en; to take sth in good ~ tomar algo en buena parte; to take sb's ~ defender a uno; for my ~ por mi parte; for the most ~ en su mayor parte; to ~ one's hair hacerse la raya; ~ with vt fus ceder, entregar; (money) pagar; ~ exchange (BRIT) n: in ~ exchange como parte del pago

partial ['pɑ:ʃl] adj parcial; to be ~ to ser aficionado a

participant [pɑ:'tɪsɪpənt] n (in competition) concursante m/f; (in campaign etc) participante m/f

participate [pɑ:'tɪsɪpeɪt] vi: to ~ in participar en; **participation** [-'peɪʃən] n participación f

participle ['pɑ:tɪsɪpl] n participio

particle ['pɑ:tɪkl] n partícula; (of dust) grano

particular [pə'tɪkjʊlə*] adj (special) particular; (concrete) concreto; (given) determinado; (fussy) quisquilloso; (demanding) exigente; ~s npl (information) datos mpl; (details) pormenores mpl; in ~ en particular; ~ly adv (in particular) sobre todo; (difficult, good etc) especialmente

parting ['pɑ:tɪŋ] n (act of) separación f; (farewell) despedida; (BRIT: in hair) raya ♦ adj de despedida

partisan [pɑ:tɪ'zæn] adj partidista ♦ n partidario/a

partition [pɑ:'tɪʃən] n (POL) división f; (wall) tabique m

partly ['pɑ:tlɪ] adv en parte

partner ['pɑ:tnə*] n (COMM) socio/a; (SPORT, at dance) pareja; (spouse) cónyuge m/f; (lover) compañero/a; ~ship n asociación f; (COMM) sociedad f

partridge ['pɑ:trɪdʒ] n perdiz f

part-time adj, adv a tiempo parcial

party ['pɑːtɪ] n (POL) partido; (celebration)
fiesta; (group) grupo; (LAW) parte f interesada
♦ cpd (POL) de partido; ~ **dress** n vestido de
fiesta

pass [pɑːs] vt (time, object) pasar; (place)
pasar por; (overtake) rebasar; (exam)
aprobar; (approve) aprobar ♦ vi pasar; (SCOL)
aprobar, ser aprobado ♦ n (permit) permiso;
(membership card) carnet m; (in mountains)
puerto, desfiladero; (SPORT) pase m; (SCOL:
also: ~ mark): **to get a ~** in aprobar en; **to
~ sth through sth** pasar algo por algo; **to
make a ~ at sb** (inf) hacer proposiciones a
uno; ~ **away** vi fallecer; ~ **by** vi bajar ♦ vt
(ignore) pasar por alto; ~ **for** vt fus pasar
por; ~ **on** vt transmitir; ~ **out** vi desmayarse;
~ **up** vt (opportunity) renunciar a; ~**able** adj
(road) transitable; (tolerable) pasable

passage ['pæsɪdʒ] n (also: ~way) pasillo; (act
of passing) tránsito; (fare, in book) pasaje m;
(by boat) travesía; (ANAT) tubo

passbook ['pɑːsbʊk] n libreta de banco

passenger ['pæsɪndʒəʳ] n pasajero/a,
viajero/a

passer-by [pɑːsəˈbaɪ] n transeúnte m/f

passing ['pɑːsɪŋ] adj pasajero; **in** ~ de paso;
~ **place** n (AUT) apartadero

passion ['pæʃən] n pasión f; ~**ate** adj
apasionado

passive ['pæsɪv] adj (gen, also LING) pasivo;
~ **smoking** n efectos del tabaco en fumadores
pasivos

Passover ['pɑːsəʊvəʳ] n Pascua (de los
judíos)

passport ['pɑːspɔːt] n pasaporte m;
~ **control** n control m de pasaporte;
~ **office** n oficina de pasaportes

password ['pɑːswɜːd] n contraseña

past [pɑːst] prep (in front of) por delante de;
(further than) más allá de; (later than)
después de ♦ adj pasado; (president etc)
antiguo ♦ n (time) pasado; (of person)
antecedentes mpl; he's ~ forty tiene más de
cuarenta años; **ten/quarter ~ eight** las ocho y
diez/cuarto; **for the ~ few/3 days** durante los
últimos días/últimos 3 días; **to run ~ sb** pasar
a uno corriendo

pasta ['pæstə] n pasta

paste [peɪst] n pasta; (glue) engrudo ♦ vt
pegar

pasteurized ['pæstəraɪzd] adj pasteurizado

pastille ['pæstl] n pastilla

pastime ['pɑːstaɪm] n pasatiempo

pastry ['peɪstrɪ] n (dough) pasta; (cake) pastel
m

pasture ['pɑːstʃəʳ] n pasto

pasty¹ ['pæstɪ] n empanada

pasty² ['peɪstɪ] adj (complexion) pálido

pat [pæt] vt dar una palmadita a; (dog etc)

acariciar

patch [pætʃ] n (of material, eye ~) parche m;
(mended part) remiendo; (of land) terreno
♦ vt remendar; **(to go through) a bad ~**
(pasar por) una mala racha; ~ **up** vt reparar;
(quarrel) hacer las paces en; ~**work** n labor
m de retazos; ~**y** adj desigual

pâté ['pæteɪ] n paté m

patent ['peɪtnt] n patente f ♦ vt patentar
♦ adj patente, evidente; ~ **leather** n charol
m

paternal [pəˈtɜːnl] adj paternal; (relation)
paterno

path [pɑːθ] n camino, sendero; (trail, track)
pista; (of missile) trayectoria

pathetic [pəˈθetɪk] adj patético, lastimoso;
(very bad) malísimo

pathological [pæθəˈlɒdʒɪkəl] adj patológico

pathway ['pɑːθweɪ] n sendero, vereda

patience ['peɪʃns] n paciencia; (BRIT: CARDS)
solitario

patient ['peɪʃnt] n paciente m/f ♦ adj
paciente, sufrido

patio ['pætɪəʊ] n patio

patriot ['peɪtrɪət] n patriota m/f; ~**ic**
[pætrɪˈɒtɪk] adj patriótico

patrol [pəˈtrəʊl] n patrulla ♦ vt patrullar por;
~ **car** n coche m patrulla; ~**man** (US irreg) n
policía m

patron ['peɪtrən] n (in shop) cliente m/f; (of
charity) patrocinador(a) m/f; ~ **of the arts**
mecenas m; ~**ize** ['pætrənaɪz] vt (shop) ser
cliente de; (artist etc) proteger; (look down
on) condescender con; ~ **saint** n santo/a
patrón/ona m/f

patter ['pætəʳ] n golpeteo; (sales talk) labia
♦ vi (rain) tamborilear

pattern ['pætən] n (SEWING) patrón m;
(design) dibujo

pauper ['pɔːpəʳ] n pobre m/f

pause [pɔːz] n pausa ♦ vi hacer una pausa

pave [peɪv] vt pavimentar; **to ~ the way for**
preparar el terreno para

pavement ['peɪvmənt] n (BRIT) acera (SP),
vereda (AM)

pavilion [pəˈvɪlɪən] n (SPORT) caseta

paving ['peɪvɪŋ] n pavimento, enlosado;
~ **stone** n losa

paw [pɔː] n pata

pawn [pɔːn] n (CHESS) peón m; (fig)
instrumento ♦ vt empeñar; ~ **broker** n
prestamista m/f; ~**shop** n monte m de
piedad

pay [peɪ] (pt, pp **paid**) n (wage etc) sueldo,
salario ♦ vt pagar ♦ vi (be profitable) rendir;
to ~ attention (to) prestar atención (a); **to
~ sb a visit** hacer una visita a uno; **to ~ one's
respects to sb** presentar sus respetos a uno;
~ **back** vt (money) reembolsar; (person)

pagar; ~ **for** vt fus pagar; ~ **in** vt ingresar; ~ **off** vt saldar ♦ vi (scheme, decision) dar resultado; ~ **up** vt pagar (de mala gana); **~able** adj: **~able** to pagadero a; ~ **day** n día m de paga; **~ee** n portador(a) m/f; ~ **envelope** (US) n = ~ **packet**; **~ment** n pago; **monthly ~ment** mensualidad f; ~ **packet** (BRIT) n sobre m (de paga); ~ **phone** n teléfono público; **~roll** n nómina; ~ **slip** n recibo de sueldo; ~ **television** n televisión f de pago

PC n abbr = **personal computer**; (BRIT) = **police constable** ♦ adv abbr = **politically correct**

p.c. abbr = **per cent**

pea [pi:] n guisante m (SP), chícharo (AM), arveja (AM)

peace [pi:s] n paz f; (calm) paz f, tranquilidad f; **~ful** adj (gentle) pacífico; (calm) tranquilo, sosegado

peach [pi:tʃ] n melocotón m (SP), durazno (AM)

peacock ['pi:kɔk] n pavo real

peak [pi:k] n (of mountain) cumbre f, cima; (of cap) visera; (fig) cumbre f; ~ **hours** npl, ~ **period** n horas fpl punta

peal [pi:l] n (of bells) repique m; ~ **of laughter** carcajada

peanut ['pi:nʌt] n cacahuete m (SP), maní m (AM); ~ **butter** manteca de cacahuete or maní

pear [pɛə*] n pera

pearl [pə:l] n perla

peasant ['peznt] n campesino/a

peat [pi:t] n turba

pebble ['pebl] n guijarro

peck [pek] vt (also: ~ **at**) picotear ♦ n picotazo; (kiss) besito; **~ing order** n orden m de jerarquía; **~ish** (BRIT: inf) adj: **I feel ~ish** tengo ganas de picar algo

peculiar [pɪ'kju:liə*] adj (odd) extraño, raro; (typical) propio, característico; ~ **to** propio de

pedal ['pedl] n pedal m ♦ vi pedalear

pedantic [pɪ'dæntɪk] adj pedante

peddler ['pedlə*] n: **drug ~** traficante m/f; camello

pedestrian [pɪ'destrɪən] n peatón/ona m/f ♦ adj pedestre; ~ **crossing** (BRIT) n paso de peatones; ~ **precinct** (BRIT), ~ **zone** (US) n zona peatonal

pediatrics [pi:dɪ'ætrɪks] (US) n = **paediatrics**

pedigree ['pedɪgri:] n genealogía; (of animal) raza, pedigrí m ♦ cpd (animal) de raza, de casta

pee [pi:] (inf) vi mear

peek [pi:k] vi mirar a hurtadillas

peel [pi:l] n piel f; (of orange, lemon) cáscara; (: removed) peladuras fpl ♦ vt pelar ♦ vi (paint etc) desconcharse; (wallpaper)

despegarse, desprenderse; (skin) pelar

peep [pi:p] n (BRIT: look) mirada furtiva; (sound) pío ♦ vi (BRIT: look) mirar furtivamente; ~ **out** vi salir (un poco); **~hole** n mirilla

peer [pɪə*] vi: **to ~ at** esudriñar ♦ n (noble) par m; (equal) igual m; (contemporary) contemporáneo/a; **~age** n nobleza

peeved [pi:vd] adj enojado

peg [peg] n (for coat etc) gancho, colgadero; (BRIT: also: clothes ~) pinza

Pekingese [pi:kɪ'ni:z] n (dog) pequinés/esa m/f

pelican ['pelɪkən] n pelícano; ~ **crossing** (BRIT) n (AUT) paso de peatones señalizado

pellet ['pelɪt] n bolita; (bullet) perdigón m

pelt [pelt] vt: **to ~ sb with sth** arrojarle algo a uno ♦ vi (rain) llover a cántaros; (inf: run) correr ♦ n pellejo

pen [pen] n (fountain ~) pluma; (ballpoint ~) bolígrafo; (for sheep) redil m

penal ['pi:nl] adj penal; **~ize** vt castigar

penalty ['penltɪ] n (gen) pena; (fine) multa; ~ **(kick)** n (FOOTBALL) penalty m; (RUGBY) golpe m de castigo

penance ['penəns] n penitencia

pence [pens] npl of **penny**

pencil ['pensl] n lápiz m, lapicero (AM); ~ **case** n estuche m; ~ **sharpener** n sacapuntas m inv

pendant ['pendnt] n pendiente m

pending ['pendɪŋ] prep antes de ♦ adj pendiente

pendulum ['pendjuləm] n péndulo

penetrate ['penɪtreɪt] vt penetrar

penfriend ['penfrend] (BRIT) n amigo/a por carta

penguin ['peŋgwɪn] n pingüino

penicillin [penɪ'sɪlɪn] n penicilina

peninsula [pə'nɪnsjulə] n península

penis ['pi:nɪs] n pene m

penitentiary [penɪ'tenʃərɪ] (US) n cárcel f, presidio

penknife ['pennaɪf] n navaja

pen name n seudónimo

penniless ['penɪlɪs] adj sin dinero

penny ['penɪ] (pl **pennies** or (BRIT) **pence**) n penique m; (US) centavo

penpal ['penpæl] n amigo/a por carta

pension ['penʃən] n (state benefit) jubilación f; **~er** (BRIT) n jubilado/a; ~ **fund** n caja or fondo de pensiones

pentagon ['pentəgən] n: **the P~** (US: POL) el Pentágono

Pentecost ['pentɪkɔst] n Pentecostés m

penthouse ['penthaus] n ático de lujo

pent-up ['pentʌp] adj reprimido

people ['pi:pl] npl gente f; (citizens) pueblo, ciudadanos mpl; (POL): **the ~** el pueblo ♦ n (*nation, race*) pueblo, nación *f*; **several ~ came** vinieron varias personas; **~ say that ...** dice la gente que ...

pep [pep] (*inf*): **~ up** *vt* animar

pepper ['pepə*] *n* (*spice*) pimienta; (*vegetable*) pimiento ♦ *vt*: **to ~ with** (*fig*) salpicar de; **~mint** *n* (*sweet*) pastilla de menta

peptalk ['peptɔ:k] *n*: **to give sb a ~** darle a uno una inyección de ánimo

per [pə:*] *prep* por; **~ day/person** por día/persona; **~ annum** al año; **~ capita** *adj, adv* per cápita

perceive [pə'si:v] *vt* percibir; (*realize*) darse cuenta de

per cent *n* por ciento

percentage [pə'sentɪdʒ] *n* porcentaje *m*

perception [pə'sepʃən] *n* percepción *f*; (*insight*) perspicacia; (*opinion etc*) opinión *f*; **perceptive** [-'septɪv] *adj* perspicaz

perch [pə:tʃ] *n* (*fish*) perca; (*for bird*) percha ♦ *vi*: **to ~ (on)** (*bird*) posarse (en); (*person*) encaramarse (en)

percolator ['pə:kəleɪtə*] *n* (*also: coffee ~*) cafetera de filtro

perennial [pə'renɪəl] *adj* perenne

perfect [*adj, n* 'pə:fɪkt, *vb* pə'fekt] *adj* perfecto ♦ *n* (*also: ~ tense*) perfecto ♦ *vt* perfeccionar; **~ly** ['pə:fɪktlɪ] *adv* perfectamente

perforate ['pə:fəreɪt] *vt* perforar

perform [pə'fɔ:m] *vt* (*carry out*) realizar, llevar a cabo; (*THEATRE*) representar; (*piece of music*) interpretar ♦ *vi* (*well, badly*) funcionar; **~ance** *n* (*of a play*) representación *f*; (*of actor, athlete etc*) actuación *f*; (*of car, engine, company*) rendimiento *m*; (*of economy*) resultados *mpl*; **~er** *n* (*actor*) actor *m*, actriz *f*

perfume ['pə:fju:m] *n* perfume *m*

perhaps [pə'hæps] *adv* quizá(s), tal vez

peril ['perɪl] *n* peligro, riesgo

perimeter [pə'rɪmɪtə*] *n* perímetro

period ['pɪərɪəd] *n* período; (*SCOL*) clase *f*; (*full stop*) punto; (*MED*) regla ♦ *adj* (*costume, furniture*) de época; **~ic(al)** [-'ɔdɪk(l)] *adj* periódico; **~ical** [-'ɔdɪkl] *n* periódico; **~ically** [-'ɔdɪklɪ] *adv* de vez en cuando, cada cierto tiempo

peripheral [pə'rɪfərəl] *adj* periférico ♦ *n* (*COMPUT*) periférico, unidad *f* periférica

perish ['perɪʃ] *vi* perecer; (*decay*) echarse a perder; **~able** *adj* perecedero

perjury ['pə:dʒərɪ] *n* (*LAW*) perjurio

perk [pə:k] *n* extra *m*; **~ up** *vi* (*cheer up*) animarse

perm [pə:m] *n* permanente *f*

permanent ['pə:mənənt] *adj* permanente

permeate ['pə:mɪeɪt] *vi* penetrar, trascender ♦ *vt* penetrar, trascender a

permissible [pə'mɪsɪbl] *adj* permisible, lícito

permission [pə'mɪʃən] *n* permiso

permissive [pə'mɪsɪv] *adj* permisivo

permit [*n* 'pə:mɪt, *vt* pə'mɪt] *n* permiso, licencia ♦ *vt* permitir

perplex [pə'pleks] *vt* dejar perplejo

persecute ['pə:sɪkju:t] *vt* perseguir

persevere [pə:sɪ'vɪə*] *vi* persistir

Persian ['pə:ʃən] *adj, n* persa *m/f*; **the ~ Gulf** el Golfo Pérsico

persist [pə'sɪst] *vi*: **to ~ (in doing sth)** persistir (en hacer algo); **~ence** *n* empeño; **~ent** *adj* persistente; (*determined*) porfiado

person ['pə:sn] *n* persona; **in ~** en persona; **~al** *adj* personal; individual; (*visit*) en persona; **~al assistant** *n* ayudante *m/f* personal; **~al column** *n* anuncios *mpl* personales; **~al computer** *n* ordenador *m* personal; **~ality** [-'nælɪtɪ] *n* personalidad *f*; **~ally** *adv* personalmente; (*in person*) en persona; **to take sth ~ally** tomarse algo a mal; **~al organizer** *n* agenda; **~al stereo** *n* Walkman ® *m*; **~ify** [-'sɔnɪfaɪ] *vt* encarnar

personnel [pə:sə'nel] *n* personal *m*

perspective [pə'spektɪv] *n* perspectiva

Perspex ® ['pə:speks] *n* plexiglás ® *m*

perspiration [pə:spɪ'reɪʃən] *n* transpiración *f*

persuade [pə'sweɪd] *vt*: **to ~ sb to do sth** persuadir a uno para que haga algo

Peru [pə'ru:] *n* el Perú; **Peruvian** *adj, n* peruano/a *m/f*

perverse [pə'və:s] *adj* perverso; (*wayward*) travieso

pervert [*n* 'pə:və:t, *vb* pə'və:t] *n* pervertido/a ♦ *vt* pervertir; (*truth, sb's words*) tergiversar

pessimist ['pesɪmɪst] *n* pesimista *m/f*; **~ic** [-'mɪstɪk] *adj* pesimista

pest [pest] *n* (*insect*) insecto nocivo; (*fig*) lata, molestia

pester ['pestə*] *vt* molestar, acosar

pesticide ['pestɪsaɪd] *n* pesticida *m*

pet [pet] *n* animal *m* doméstico ♦ *cpd* favorito ♦ *vt* acariciar; **teacher's ~** favorito/a (del profesor); **~ hate** manía

petal ['petl] *n* pétalo

peter ['pi:tə*]: **to ~ out** *vi* agotarse, acabarse

petite [pə'ti:t] *adj* chiquita

petition [pə'tɪʃən] *n* petición *f*

petrified ['petrɪfaɪd] *adj* horrorizado

petrol ['petrəl] (*BRIT*) *n* gasolina; **two/four-star ~** gasolina normal/súper; **~ can** *n* bidón *m* de gasolina

petroleum [pə'trəʊlɪəm] *n* petróleo

petrol: ~ pump (*BRIT*) *n* (*in garage*) surtidor *m* de gasolina; **~ station** (*BRIT*) *n* gasolinera; **~ tank** (*BRIT*) *n* depósito (de gasolina)

petticoat ['petɪkəʊt] *n* enaguas *fpl*

petty ['petɪ] *adj* (*mean*) mezquino; (*unimportant*) insignificante; **~ cash** *n* dinero para gastos menores; **~ officer** n contramaestre m

petulant ['petjulənt] adj malhumorado

pew [pju:] n banco

pewter ['pju:tə*] n peltre m

phantom ['fæntəm] n fantasma m

pharmacist ['fɑ:məsıst] n farmacéutico/a

pharmacy ['fɑ:məsı] n farmacia

phase [feız] n fase f ♦ vt: **to ~ sth in/out** introducir/retirar algo por etapas

Ph.D. abbr = **Doctor of Philosophy**

pheasant ['feznt] n faisán m

phenomenon [fə'nɔmınən] (pl **phenomena**) n fenómeno

philanthropist [fı'lænθrəpıst] n filántropo/a

Philippines ['fılıpi:nz] npl: **the ~** las Filipinas

philosopher [fı'lɔsəfə*] n filósofo/a

philosophy [fı'lɔsəfı] n filosofía

phobia ['fəubjə] n fobia

phone [fəun] n teléfono ♦ vt telefonear, llamar por teléfono; **to be on the ~** tener teléfono; (be calling) estar hablando por teléfono; **~ back** vt, vi volver a llamar; **~ up** vt, vi llamar por teléfono; **~ book** n guía telefónica; **~ booth** n cabina telefónica; **~ box** (BRIT) n = **~ booth**; **~ call** n llamada (telefónica); **~card** n teletarjeta; **~-in** (BRIT) n (RADIO, TV) programa m de participación (telefónica)

phonetics [fə'netıks] n fonética

phoney ['fəunı] adj falso

photo ['fəutəu] n foto f; **~copier** n fotocopiadora; **~copy** n fotocopia ♦ vt fotocopiar

photograph ['fəutəgrɑ:f] n fotografía ♦ vt fotografiar; **~er** [fə'tɔgrəfə*] n fotógrafo/a; **~y** [fə'tɔgrəfı] n fotografía

phrase [freız] n frase f ♦ vt expresar; **~ book** n libro de frases

physical ['fızıkl] adj físico; **~ education** n educación f física; **~ly** adv físicamente

physician [fı'zıʃən] n médico/a

physicist ['fızısıst] n físico/a

physics ['fızıks] n física

physiotherapy [fızıəu'θerəpı] n fisioterapia

physique [fı'zi:k] n físico

pianist ['pi:ənıst] n pianista m/f

piano [pı'ænəu] n piano

pick [pık] n (tool: also: **~-axe**) pico, piqueta ♦ vt (select) elegir, escoger; (gather) coger (SP), recoger; (remove, take out) sacar, quitar; (lock) abrir con ganzúa; **take your ~** escoja lo que quiera; **the ~ of** lo mejor de; **to ~ one's nose/teeth** hurgarse las narices/limpiarse los dientes; **to ~ a quarrel with sb** meterse con alguien; **~ at** vt fus: **to ~ at one's food** comer con poco apetito; **~ on** vt fus (person) meterse con; **~ out** vt escoger; (distinguish) identificar; **~ up** vi (improve: sales) ir mejor;

(: patient) reponerse; (: FINANCE) recobrarse ♦ vt recoger; (learn) aprender; (POLICE: arrest) detener; (person: for sex) ligar; (RADIO) captar; **to ~ up speed** acelerarse; **to ~ o.s. up** levantarse

picket ['pıkıt] n piquete m ♦ vt piquetear

pickle ['pıkl] n (also: **~s:** as condiment) escabeche m; (fig: mess) apuro ♦ vt encurtir

pickpocket ['pıkpɔkıt] n carterista m/f

pickup ['pıkʌp] n (small truck) furgoneta

picnic ['pıknık] n merienda ♦ vi ir de merienda; **~ area** n zona de picnic; (AUT) área de descanso

picture ['pıktʃə*] n cuadro; (painting) pintura; (photograph) fotografía; (TV) imagen f; (film) película; (fig: description) descripción f; (: situation) situación f ♦ vt (imagine) imaginar; **~s** npl: **the ~s** (BRIT) el cine; **~ book** n libro de dibujos

picturesque [pıktʃə'resk] adj pintoresco

pie [paı] n pastel m; (open) tarta; (small: of meat) empanada

piece [pi:s] n pedazo, trozo; (of cake) trozo; (item): **a ~ of clothing/furniture/advice** una prenda (de vestir)/un mueble/un consejo ♦ vt: **to ~ together** juntar; (TECH) armar; **to take to ~s** desmontar; **~meal** adv poco a poco; **~work** n trabajo a destajo

pie chart n gráfico de sectores or tarta

pier [pıə*] n muelle m, embarcadero

pierce [pıəs] vt perforar

piercing ['pıəsıŋ] adj penetrante

pig [pıg] n cerdo (SP), puerco (SP), chancho (AM); (pej: unkind person) asqueroso; (: greedy person) glotón/ona m/f

pigeon ['pıdʒən] n paloma; (as food) pichón m; **~hole** n casilla

piggy bank ['pıgı-] n hucha (en forma de cerdito)

pig: ~-headed ['pıg'hedıd] adj terco, testarudo; **~let** ['pıglıt] n cochinillo; **~skin** n piel f de cerdo; **~sty** ['pıgstaı] n pocilga; **~tail** n (girl's) trenza; (Chinese, TAUR) coleta

pike [paık] n (fish) lucio

pilchard ['pıltʃəd] n sardina

pile [paıl] n montón m; (of carpet, cloth) pelo ♦ vt (also: **~ up**) amontonar; (fig) acumular ♦ vi (also: **~ up**) amontonarse; acumularse; **~ into** vt fus (car) meterse en; **~s** [paılz] npl (MED) almorranas fpl, hemorroides mpl; **~-up** n (AUT) accidente m múltiple

pilfering ['pılfərıŋ] n ratería

pilgrim ['pılgrım] n peregrino/a; **~age** n peregrinación f, romería

pill [pıl] n píldora; **the ~** la píldora

pillage ['pılıdʒ] vt pillar, saquear

pillar ['pılə*] n pilar m; **~ box** (BRIT) n buzón m

pillion ['pıljən] n (of motorcycle) asiento

trasero
pillow ['pɪləu] n almohada; **~case** n funda
pilot ['paɪlət] n piloto ♦ cpd (scheme etc)
piloto ♦ vt pilotar; **~ light** n piloto
pimp [pɪmp] n chulo (SP), cafiche m (AM)
pimple ['pɪmpl] n grano
PIN n abbr (= personal identification number)
número personal
pin [pɪn] n alfiler m ♦ vt prender (con alfiler);
~s and needles hormigueo; **to ~ sb down** (fig)
hacer que uno concrete; **to ~ sth on sb** (fig)
colgarle a uno el sambenito de algo
pinafore ['pɪnəfɔ:ᵇ] n delantal m; **~ dress**
(BRIT) n mandil m
pinball ['pɪnbɔ:l] n mesa americana
pincers ['pɪnsəz] npl pinzas fpl, tenazas fpl
pinch [pɪntʃ] n (of salt etc) pizca ♦ vt
pellizcar; (inf: steal) birlar; **at a ~** en caso de
apuro
pincushion ['pɪnkuʃən] n acerico
pine [paɪn] n (also: ~ tree, wood) pino ♦ vi: to
~ suspirar por; **~ away** vi morirse de
pena
pineapple ['paɪnæpl] n piña, ananás m
ping [pɪŋ] n (noise) sonido agudo; **~-pong** ®
n pingpong ® m
pink [pɪŋk] adj rosado, (color de) rosa ♦ n
(colour) rosa; (BOT) clavel m, clavellina
pinpoint ['pɪnpɔɪnt] vt precisar
pint [paɪnt] n pinta (BRIT = 568cc; US =
473cc); (BRIT: inf: of beer) pinta de cerveza,
≈ jarra (SP)
pin-up n fotografía erótica
pioneer [paɪə'nɪəᵇ] n pionero/a
pious ['paɪəs] adj piadoso, devoto
pip [pɪp] n (seed) pepita; **the ~s** (BRIT) la señal
pipe [paɪp] n tubo, caño; (for smoking) pipa
♦ vt conducir en cañerías; **~s** npl (gen)
cañería; (also: bag~s) gaita; **~ cleaner** n
limpiapipas m inv; **~ dream** n sueño
imposible; **~line** n (for oil) oleoducto; (for
gas) gasoducto; **~r** n gaitero/a
piping ['paɪpɪŋ] adv: **to be ~ hot** estar que
quema
piquant ['pi:kənt] adj picante; (fig) agudo
pique [pi:k] n pique m, resentimiento
pirate ['paɪərət] n pirata m/f ♦ vt (cassette,
book) piratear; **~ radio** (BRIT) n emisora
pirata
Pisces ['paɪsi:z] n Piscis m
piss [pɪs] (inf!) vi mear; **~ed** (inf!) adj (drunk)
borracho
pistol ['pɪstl] n pistola
piston ['pɪstən] n pistón m, émbolo
pit [pɪt] n hoyo; (also: coal ~) mina; (in
garage) foso de inspección; (also: orchestra
~) platea ♦ vt: **to ~ one's wits against sb**
medir fuerzas con uno; **~s** npl (AUT) box m
pitch [pɪtʃ] n (MUS) tono; (BRIT: SPORT) campo,

terreno; (fig) punto; (tar) brea ♦ vt (throw)
arrojar, lanzar ♦ vi (fall) caer(se); **to ~ a tent**
montar una tienda (de campaña); **~-black**
adj negro como boca de lobo; **~ed battle** n
batalla campal
pitfall ['pɪtfɔ:l] n riesgo
pith [pɪθ] n (of orange) médula
pithy ['pɪθɪ] adj (fig) jugoso
pitiful ['pɪtɪful] adj (touching) lastimoso,
conmovedor(a)
pitiless ['pɪtɪlɪs] adj despiadado
pittance ['pɪtns] n miseria
pity ['pɪtɪ] n compasión f, piedad f ♦ vt
compadecer(se de); **what a ~!** ¡qué pena!
pizza ['pi:tsə] n pizza
placard ['plækɑ:d] n letrero; (in march etc)
pancarta
placate [plə'keɪt] vt apaciguar
place [pleɪs] n lugar m, sitio; (seat) plaza,
asiento; (post) puesto; (home): **at/to his ~**
en/a su casa; (role: in society etc) papel m
♦ vt (object) poner, colocar; (identify)
reconocer; **to take ~** tener lugar; **to be ~d** (in
race, exam) colocarse; **out of ~** (not suitable)
fuera de lugar; **in the first ~** en primer lugar;
to change ~s with sb cambiarse de sitio con
uno; **~ of birth** lugar m de nacimiento
placid ['plæsɪd] adj apacible
plague [pleɪg] n plaga; (MED) peste f ♦ vt
(fig) acosar, atormentar
plaice [pleɪs] n inv platija
plaid [plæd] n (material) tartán m
plain [pleɪn] adj (unpatterned) liso; (clear)
claro, evidente; (simple) sencillo; (not
handsome) poco atractivo ♦ adv claramente
♦ n llano, llanura; **~ chocolate** n chocolate
m amargo; **~-clothes** adj (police) vestido de
paisano; **~ly** adv claramente
plaintiff ['pleɪntɪf] n demandante m/f
plait [plæt] n trenza
plan [plæn] n (drawing) plano; (scheme) plan
m, proyecto ♦ vt proyectar, planificar ♦ vi
hacer proyectos; **to ~ to do** pensar hacer
plane [pleɪn] n (AVIAT) avión m; (MATH, fig)
plano; (also: ~ tree) plátano; (tool) cepillo
planet ['plænɪt] n planeta m
plank [plæŋk] n tabla
planner ['plænəᵇ] n planificador(a) m/f
planning ['plænɪŋ] n planificación f; **family ~**
planificación familiar; **~ permission** n
permiso para realizar obras
plant [plɑ:nt] n planta; (machinery)
maquinaria; (factory) fábrica ♦ vt plantar;
(field) sembrar; (bomb) colocar
plaster ['plɑ:stəᵇ] n (for walls) yeso; (also:
~ of Paris) yeso mate; (BRIT: also: sticking ~)
tirita (SP), esparadrapo, curita (AM) ♦ vt
enyesar; (cover): **to ~ with** llenar or cubrir de;
~ed (inf) adj borracho; **~er** n yesero

plastic ['plæstɪk] n plástico ♦ adj de plástico;
~ **bag** n bolsa de plástico
Plasticine ® ['plæstɪsi:n] (BRIT) n plastilina
®
plastic surgery n cirujía plástica
plate [pleɪt] n (dish) plato; (metal, in book)
lámina; (dental ~) placa de dentadura postiza
plateau ['plætəʊ] (pl ~s or ~x) n meseta,
altiplanicie f
plateaux ['plætəʊz] npl of **plateau**
plate glass n vidrio cilindrado
platform ['plætfɔ:m] n (RAIL) andén m;
(stage, BRIT: on bus) plataforma; (at meeting)
tribuna; (POL) programa m (electoral)
platinum ['plætɪnəm] adj, n platino
platoon [plə'tu:n] n pelotón m
platter ['plætə*] n fuente f
plausible ['plɔ:zɪbl] adj verosímil; (person)
convincente
play [pleɪ] n (THEATRE) obra, comedia ♦ vt
(game) jugar; (compete against) jugar contra;
(instrument) tocar; (part: in play etc) hacer el
papel de; (tape, record) poner ♦ vi jugar;
(band) tocar; (tape, record) sonar; to ~ **safe**
ir a lo seguro; ~ **down** vt quitar importancia
a; ~ **up** vi (cause trouble to) dar guerra;
~boy n playboy m; **~er** n jugador/a m/f;
(THEATRE) actor/actriz m/f; (MUS) músico/a;
~ful adj juguetón/ona; **~ground** n (in
school) patio de recreo; (in park) parque m
infantil; **~group** n jardín m de niños; **~ing
card** n naipe m, carta; **~ing field** n campo
de deportes; **~mate** n compañero/a de
juego; **~-off** n (SPORT) (partido de)
desempate m; **~pen** n corral m; **~thing** n
juguete m; **~time** n (SCOL) recreo; **~wright**
n dramaturgo/a
plc abbr (= public limited company) ≈ S.A.
plea [pli:] n súplica, petición f; (LAW) alegato,
defensa; ~ **bargaining** n (LAW) acuerdo entre
fiscal y defensor para agilizar los trámites
judiciales
plead [pli:d] vt (LAW): to ~ **sb's case** defender
a uno; (give as excuse) poner como pretexto
♦ vi (LAW) declararse; (beg): to ~ **with sb**
suplicar or rogar a uno
pleasant ['plɛznt] adj agradable; **~ries** npl
cortesías fpl
please [pli:z] excl ¡por favor! ♦ vt (give
pleasure to) dar gusto a, agradar ♦ vi (think
fit): do as you ~ haz lo que quieras;
~ **yourself!** (inf) ¡haz lo que quieras!, ¡como
quieras!; **~d** adj (happy) alegre, contento;
~d (with) satisfecho (de); **~d to meet you**
¡encantado!, ¡tanto gusto!; **pleasing** adj
agradable, grato
pleasure ['plɛʒə*] n placer m, gusto; "**it's a
~**" "el gusto es mío"
pleat [pli:t] n pliegue m

pledge [plɛdʒ] n (promise) promesa, voto
♦ vt prometer
plentiful ['plɛntɪful] adj copioso, abundante
plenty ['plɛntɪ] n: ~ **of** mucho(s)/a(s)
pliable ['plaɪəbl] adj flexible
pliers ['plaɪəz] npl alicates mpl, tenazas fpl
plight [plaɪt] n situación f difícil
plimsolls ['plɪmsəlz] (BRIT) npl zapatos mpl
de tenis
plinth [plɪnθ] n plinto
plod [plɔd] vi caminar con paso pesado; (fig)
trabajar laboriosamente
plonk [plɔŋk] (inf) n (BRIT: wine) vino peleón
♦ vt: to ~ **sth down** dejar caer algo
plot [plɔt] n (scheme) complot n, conjura; (of
story, play) argumento; (of land) terreno, lote
m (AM) ♦ vt (mark out) trazar; (conspire)
tramar, urdir ♦ vi conspirar
plough [plaʊ] (US **plow**) n arado ♦ vt (earth)
arar; to ~ **money into** invertir dinero en;
~ **through** vt fus (crowd) abrirse paso por la
fuerza por; **~man's lunch** (BRIT) n almuerzo
de pub a base de pan, queso y encurtidos
pluck [plʌk] vt (fruit) coger (SP), recoger
(AM); (musical instrument) puntear; (bird)
desplumar; (eyebrows) depilar; to ~ **up
courage** hacer de tripas corazón
plug [plʌg] n tapón m; (ELEC) enchufe m,
clavija; (AUT: also: **spark(ing)** ~) bujía ♦ vt
(hole) tapar; (inf: advertise) dar publicidad a;
~ **in** vt (ELEC) enchufar
plum [plʌm] n (fruit) ciruela
plumb [plʌm] vt: to ~ **the depths of** alcanzar
los mayores extremos de
plumber ['plʌmə*] n fontanero/a (SP),
plomero/a (AM)
plumbing ['plʌmɪŋ] n (trade) fontanería,
plomería; (piping) cañería
plummet ['plʌmɪt] vi: to ~ (**down**) caer a
plomo
plump [plʌmp] adj rechoncho, rollizo ♦ vi: to
~ **for** (inf: choose) optar por; ~ **up** vt mullir
plunder ['plʌndə*] vt pillar, saquear
plunge [plʌndʒ] n zambullida ♦ vt sumergir,
hundir ♦ vi (fall) caer; (dive) saltar; (person)
arrojarse; to take the ~ lanzarse; **plunging**
adj: **plunging neckline** escote m pronunciado
pluperfect [plu:'pə:fɪkt] n pluscuamperfecto
plural ['plʊərl] adj plural ♦ n plural m
plus [plʌs] n (also: ~ **sign**) signo más ♦ prep
más, y, además de; **ten/twenty** ~ más de
diez/veinte
plush [plʌʃ] adj lujoso
plutonium [plu:'təʊnɪəm] n plutonio
ply [plaɪ] vt (a trade) ejercer ♦ vi (ship) ir y
venir ♦ n (of wool, rope) cabo; to ~ **sb with
drink** insistir en ofrecer a uno muchas copas;
~wood n madera contrachapada
P.M. n abbr = **Prime Minister**

345

p.m. → pop

p.m. *adv abbr* (= *post meridiem*) de la tarde or noche

pneumatic [nju:'mætɪk] *adj* neumático; **~ drill** *n* martillo neumático

pneumonia [nju:'məunɪə] *n* pulmonía

poach [pəutʃ] *vt* (*cook*) escalfar; (*steal*) cazar (*or pescar*) en vedado ♦ *vi* cazar (*or pescar*) en vedado; **~ed** *adj* escalfado; **~er** *n* cazador(a) *m/f* furtivo/a

P.O. Box *n abbr* = **Post Office Box**

pocket ['pɔkɪt] *n* bolsillo; (*fig: small area*) bolsa ♦ *vt* meter en el bolsillo; (*steal*) embolsar; **to be out of ~** (*BRIT*) salir perdiendo; **~book** (*US*) *n* cartera; **~ calculator** *n* calculadora de bolsillo; **~ knife** *n* navaja; **~ money** *n* asignación *f*

pod [pɔd] *n* vaina

podgy ['pɔdʒɪ] *adj* gordinflón/ona

podiatrist [pɔ'di:ətrɪst] (*US*) *n* pedicuro/a

poem ['pəuɪm] *n* poema *m*

poet ['pəuɪt] *n* poeta *m/f*; **~ic** [-'etɪk] *adj* poético; **~ry** *n* poesía

poignant ['pɔɪnjənt] *adj* conmovedor(a)

point [pɔɪnt] *n* punto; (*tip*) punta; (*purpose*) fin *m*, propósito; (*use*) utilidad *f*; (*significant part*) lo significativo; (*moment*) momento; (*ELEC*) toma (de corriente); (*also: decimal ~*): **2 ~ 3** (2.3) dos coma tres (2,3) ♦ *vt* señalar; (*gun etc*): **to ~ sth at sb** apuntar algo a uno ♦ *vi*: **to ~ at** señalar; **~s** *npl* (*AUT*) contactos *mpl*; (*RAIL*) agujas *fpl*; **to be on the ~ of doing sth** estar a punto de hacer algo; **to make a ~ of** poner empeño en; **to get/miss the ~** comprender/no comprender; **to come to the ~ al** meollo; **there's no ~** (**in doing**) no tiene sentido (hacer); **~ out** *vt* señalar; **~ to** *vt fus* (*fig*) indicar, señalar; **~-blank** *adv* (*say, refuse*) sin más hablar; (*also: at ~-blank range*) a quemarropa; **~ed** *adj* (*shape*) puntiagudo, afilado; (*remark*) intencionado; **~edly** *adv* intencionadamente; **~er** *n* (*needle*) aguja, indicador *m*; **~less** *adj* sin sentido; **~ of view** *n* punto de vista

poise [pɔɪz] *n* aplomo, elegancia

poison ['pɔɪzn] *n* veneno ♦ *vt* envenenar; **~ing** *n* envenenamiento; **~ous** *adj* venenoso; (*fumes etc*) tóxico

poke [pəuk] *vt* (*jab with finger, stick etc*) empujar; (*put*): **to ~ sth in(to)** introducir algo en; **~ about** *vi* fisgonear

poker ['pəukə*] *n* atizador *m*; (*CARDS*) póker *m*

poky ['pəukɪ] *adj* estrecho

Poland ['pəulənd] *n* Polonia

polar ['pəulə*] *adj* polar; **~ bear** *n* oso polar

Pole [pəul] *n* polaco/a *m/f*

pole [pəul] *n* palo; (*fixed*) poste *m*; (*GEO*) polo; **~ bean** (*US*) *n* ≈ judía verde; **~ vault** *n* salto con pértiga

police [pə'li:s] *n* policía ♦ *vt* vigilar; **~ car** *n* coche-patrulla *m*; **~man** (*irreg*) *n* policía, guardia *m*; **~ state** *n* estado policial; **~ station** *n* comisaría; **~woman** (*irreg*) *n* mujer *f* policía

policy ['pɔlɪsɪ] *n* política; (*also: insurance ~*) póliza

polio ['pəulɪəu] *n* polio *f*

Polish ['pəulɪʃ] *adj* polaco ♦ *n* (*LING*) polaco

polish ['pɔlɪʃ] *n* (*for shoes*) betún *m*; (*for floor*) cera (de lustrar); (*shine*) brillo, lustre *m*; (*fig: refinement*) educación *f* ♦ *vt* (*shoes*) limpiar; (*make shiny*) pulir, sacar brillo a; **~ off** *vt* (*food*) despachar; **~ed** *adj* (*fig: person*) elegante

polite [pə'laɪt] *adj* cortés, atento; **~ness** *n* cortesía

political [pə'lɪtɪkl] *adj* político; **~ly** *adv* políticamente; **~ly correct** políticamente correcto

politician [pɔlɪ'tɪʃən] *n* político/a

politics ['pɔlɪtɪks] *n* política

poll [pəul] *n* (*election*) votación *f*; (*also: opinion ~*) sondeo, encuesta ♦ *vt* encuestar; (*votes*) obtener

pollen ['pɔlən] *n* polen *m*

polling day ['pəulɪŋ-] *n* día *m* de elecciones

polling station *n* centro electoral

pollute [pə'lu:t] *vt* contaminar

pollution [pə'lu:ʃən] *n* polución *f*, contaminación *f* del medio ambiente

polo ['pəuləu] *n* (*sport*) polo; **~-necked** *adj* de cuello vuelto; **~ shirt** *n* polo, niqui *m*

polyester [pɔlɪ'estə*] *n* poliéster *m*

polystyrene [pɔlɪ'staɪri:n] *n* poliestireno

polythene ['pɔlɪθi:n] (*BRIT*) *n* politeno

pomegranate ['pɔmɪgrænɪt] *n* granada

pomp [pɔmp] *n* pompa

pompous ['pɔmpəs] *adj* pomposo

pond [pɔnd] *n* (*natural*) charca; (*artificial*) estanque *m*

ponder ['pɔndə*] *vt* meditar

ponderous ['pɔndərəs] *adj* pesado

pong [pɔŋ] (*BRIT: inf*) *n* hedor *m*

pony ['pəunɪ] *n* poney *m*, jaca, potro (*AM*); **~tail** *n* cola de caballo; **~ trekking** (*BRIT*) *n* excursión *f* a caballo

poodle ['pu:dl] *n* caniche *m*

pool [pu:l] *n* (*natural*) charca; (*also: swimming ~*) piscina (*SP*), alberca (*AM*); (*fig: of light etc*) charco; (*SPORT*) chapolín *m* ♦ *vt* juntar; **~s** *npl* (*football ~s*) quinielas *fpl*; **typing ~** servicio de mecanografía

poor [puə*] *adj* pobre; (*bad*) de mala calidad ♦ *npl*: **the ~** los pobres; **~ly** *adj* mal, enfermo ♦ *adv* mal

pop [pɔp] *n* (*sound*) ruido seco; (*MUS*) (música) pop *m*; (*inf: father*) papá *m*; (*drink*) gaseosa ♦ *vt* (*put quickly*) meter (de prisa)

♦ vi reventar; (cork) saltar; ~ **in/out** vi
entrar/salir un momento; ~ **up** vi aparecer
inesperadamente; ~**corn** n palomitas fpl
pope [pəup] n papa m
poplar ['pɒplə*] n álamo
popper ['pɒpə*] (BRIT) n automático
poppy ['pɒpɪ] n amapola
Popsicle ® ['pɒpsɪkl] (US) n polo
pop star n estrella del pop
populace ['pɒpjuləs] n pueblo, plebe f
popular ['pɒpjulə*] adj popular
population [pɒpju'leɪʃən] n población f
porcelain ['pɔːslɪn] n porcelana
porch [pɔːtʃ] n pórtico, entrada; (US) veranda
porcupine ['pɔːkjupaɪn] n puerco m espín
pore [pɔː*] n poro ♦ vi: **to ~ over** engolfarse
en
pork [pɔːk] n carne f de cerdo (SP) or chancho
(AM)
pornography [pɔː'nɔgrəfɪ] n pornografía
porpoise ['pɔːpəs] n marsopa
porridge ['pɒrɪdʒ] n gachas fpl de avena
port [pɔːt] n puerto; (NAUT: left side) babor m;
(wine) vino de Oporto; ~ **of call** puerto de
escala
portable ['pɔːtəbl] adj portátil
porter ['pɔːtə*] n (for luggage) maletero, -a;
(doorkeeper) portero, -a, conserje m/f
portfolio [pɔːt'fəulɪəu] n cartera
porthole ['pɔːthəul] n portilla
portion ['pɔːʃən] n porción f; (of food) ración
f
portrait ['pɔːtreɪt] n retrato
portray [pɔː'treɪ] vt retratar; (subj: actor)
representar
Portugal ['pɔːtjugl] n Portugal m
Portuguese [pɔːtju'giːz] adj portugués/esa
♦ n inv portugués/esa m/f; (LING) portugués
m
pose [pəuz] n postura, actitud f ♦ vi
(pretend): **to ~ as** hacerse pasar por ♦ vt
(question) plantear; **to ~ for** posar para
posh [pɒʃ] (inf) adj elegante, de lujo
position [pə'zɪʃən] n posición f; (job) puesto;
(situation) situación f ♦ vt colocar
positive ['pɒzɪtɪv] adj positivo; (certain)
seguro; (definite) definitivo
possess [pə'zɛs] vt poseer; ~**ion** [pə'zɛʃən] n
posesión f; ~**ions** npl (belongings)
pertenencias fpl
possibility [pɒsɪ'bɪlɪtɪ] n posibilidad f
possible ['pɒsɪbl] adj posible; **as big as** ~ lo
más grande posible; **possibly** adv
posiblemente; **I cannot possibly come** me es
imposible venir
post [pəust] n (BRIT: system) correos mpl;
(BRIT: letters, delivery) correo; (job, situation)
puesto; (pole) poste m ♦ vt (BRIT: send by
post) echar al correo; (BRIT: appoint): **to ~ to**

enviar a; ~**age** n porte m, franqueo; ~**age**
stamp n sello de correos; ~**al** adj postal, de
correos; ~**al order** n giro postal; ~**box** (BRIT)
n buzón m; ~**card** n tarjeta postal; ~**code**
(BRIT) n código postal
postdate [pəust'deɪt] vt (cheque) poner
fecha adelantada a
poster ['pəustə*] n cartel m
poste restante [pəust'rɛstɔnt] (BRIT) n lista
de correos
postgraduate ['pəust'grædjuət] n
posgraduado, -a
posthumous ['pɒstjuməs] adj póstumo
postman ['pəustmən] (irreg) n cartero
postmark ['pəustmɑːk] n matasellos m inv
post-mortem [-'mɔːtəm] n autopsia
post office n (building) (oficina de) correos
m; (organization): **the Post Office**
Administración f General de Correos; **Post**
Office Box n apartado postal (SP), casilla de
correos (AM)
postpone [pəs'pəun] vt aplazar
postscript ['pəustskrɪpt] n posdata
posture ['pɒstʃə*] n postura, actitud f
postwar [pəust'wɔː*] adj de la posguerra
posy ['pəuzɪ] n ramillete m (de flores)
pot [pɒt] n (for cooking) olla; (tea~) tetera;
(coffee~) cafetera; (for flowers) maceta; (for
jam) tarro, pote m; (inf: marijuana) chocolate
m ♦ vt (plant) poner en tiesto; **to go to ~**
(inf) irse al traste
potato [pə'teɪtəu] (pl ~**es**) n patata (SP), papa
(AM); ~ **peeler** n pelapatatas m inv
potent ['pəutnt] adj potente, poderoso;
(drink) fuerte
potential [pə'tɛnʃl] adj potencial, posible ♦ n
potencial m; ~**ly** adv en potencia
pothole ['pɒthəul] n (in road) bache m;
(BRIT: underground) gruta; **potholing** (BRIT)
n: **to go potholing** dedicarse a la espeleología
potluck [pɒt'lʌk] n: **to take** ~ tomar lo que
haya
potted ['pɒtɪd] adj (food) en conserva;
(plant) en tiesto or maceta; (shortened)
resumido
potter ['pɒtə*] n alfarero, -a ♦ vi: **to ~ around,**
~ **about** (BRIT) hacer trabajitos; ~**y** n
cerámica; (factory) alfarería
potty ['pɒtɪ] n orinal m de niño
pouch [pautʃ] n (ZOOL) bolsa; (for tobacco)
petaca
poultry ['pəultrɪ] n aves fpl de corral; (meat)
pollo
pounce [pauns] vi: **to ~ on** precipitarse sobre
pound [paund] n libra (weight = 453g or
16oz; money = 100 pence) ♦ vt (beat)
golpear; (crush) machacar ♦ vi (heart) latir;
~ **sterling** n libra esterlina
pour [pɔː*] vt echar; (tea etc) servir ♦ vi

correr, fluir; **to ~ sb a drink** servirle a uno una copa; **~ away** or **off** *vt* vaciar, verter; **~ in** *vi* (*people*) entrar en tropel; **~ out** *vi* salir en tropel ♦ *vt* (*drink*) echar, servir; (*fig*): **to ~ out one's feelings** desahogarse; **~ing** *adj*: **~ing rain** lluvia torrencial

pout [paut] *vi* hacer pucheros

poverty ['pɔvətɪ] *n* pobreza, miseria; **~-stricken** *adj* necesitado

powder ['paudə*] *n* polvo; (*face ~*) polvos *mpl* ♦ *vt* polvorear; **to ~ one's face** empolvarse la cara; **~ compact** *n* polvera; **~ed milk** *n* leche *f* en polvo; **~ room** *n* aseos *mpl*

power ['pauə*] *n* poder *m*; (*strength*) fuerza, (*nation*, *TECH*) potencia; (*drive*) empuje *m*; (*ELEC*) fuerza, energía ♦ *vt* impulsar; **to be in ~** (*POL*) estar en el poder; **~ cut** (*BRIT*) *n* apagón *m*; **~ed** *adj*: **~ed by** impulsado por; **~ failure** *n* = **~ cut**; **~ful** *adj* poderoso; (*engine*) potente; (*speech etc*) convincente; **~less** *adj*: **~less (to do)** incapaz (de hacer); **~ point** (*BRIT*) *n* enchufe *m*; **~ station** *n* central *f* eléctrica

p.p. *abbr* (= *per procurationem*): **~ J. Smith** p.p. (por poder de) J. Smith; (= *pages*) págs

PR *n abbr* = **public relations**

practical ['præktɪkl] *adj* práctico; **~ity** [-'kælɪtɪ] *n* factibilidad *f*; **~ joke** *n* broma pesada; **~ly** *adv* (*almost*) casi

practice ['præktɪs] *n* (*habit*) costumbre *f*; (*exercise*) práctica, ejercicio; (*training*) adiestramiento; (*MED*: of profession) práctica, ejercicio; (*MED, LAW: business*) consulta ♦ *vt, vi* (*US*) = **practise**; **in ~** (*in reality*) en la práctica; **out of ~** desentrenado

practise ['præktɪs] (*US* **practice**) *vt* (*carry out*) practicar; (*profession*) ejercer; (*train at*) practicar ♦ *vi* ejercer; (*train*) practicar; **practising** *adj* (*Christian etc*) practicante; (*lawyer*) en ejercicio

practitioner [præk'tɪʃənə*] *n* (*MED*) médico/a

prairie ['prɛərɪ] *n* pampa

praise [preɪz] *n* alabanza(s) *f(pl)*, elogio(s) *m(pl)* ♦ *vt* alabar, elogiar; **~worthy** *adj* loable

pram [præm] (*BRIT*) *n* cochecito de niño

prank [præŋk] *n* travesura

prawn [prɔːn] *n* gamba; **~ cocktail** *n* cóctel *m* de gambas

pray [preɪ] *vi* rezar

prayer [prɛə*] *n* oración *f*, rezo; (*entreaty*) ruego, súplica

preach [priːtʃ] *vi* (*also fig*) predicar; **~er** *n* predicador(a) *m/f*

precaution [prɪ'kɔːʃən] *n* precaución *f*

precede [prɪ'siːd] *vt, vi* preceder

precedent ['prɛsɪdənt] *n* precedente *m*

preceding [prɪ'siːdɪŋ] *adj* anterior

precinct ['priːsɪŋkt] *n* recinto; **~s** *npl* contornos *mpl*; **pedestrian ~** (*BRIT*) zona peatonal; **shopping ~** (*BRIT*) centro comercial

precious ['prɛʃəs] *adj* precioso

precipitate [prɪ'sɪpɪteɪt] *vt* precipitar

precise [prɪ'saɪs] *adj* preciso, exacto; **~ly** *adv* precisamente, exactamente

precocious [prɪ'kəuʃəs] *adj* precoz

precondition [priːkən'dɪʃən] *n* condición *f* previa

predecessor ['priːdɪsɛsə*] *n* antecesor(a) *m/f*

predicament [prɪ'dɪkəmənt] *n* apuro

predict [prɪ'dɪkt] *vt* pronosticar; **~able** *adj* previsible; **~ion** [-'dɪkʃən] *n* predicción *f*

predominantly [prɪ'dɔmɪnəntlɪ] *adv* en su mayoría

pre-empt [priː'ɛmt] *vt* adelantarse a

preen [priːn] *vt*: **to ~ itself** (*bird*) limpiarse (las plumas); **to ~ o.s.** pavonearse

preface ['prɛfəs] *n* prefacio

prefect ['priːfɛkt] (*BRIT*) *n* (*in school*) monitor(a) *m/f*

prefer [prɪ'fəː*] *vt* preferir; **to ~ doing** or **to do** preferir hacer; **~able** ['prɛfrəbl] *adj* preferible; **~ably** ['prɛfrəblɪ] *adv* de preferencia; **~ence** ['prɛfrəns] *n* preferencia; (*priority*) prioridad *f*; **~ential** [prɛfə'rɛnʃəl] *adj* preferente

prefix ['priːfɪks] *n* prefijo

pregnancy ['prɛgnənsɪ] *n* (*of woman*) embarazo; (*of animal*) preñez *f*

pregnant ['prɛgnənt] *adj* (*woman*) embarazada; (*animal*) preñada

prehistoric ['priːhɪs'tɔrɪk] *adj* prehistórico

prejudice ['prɛdʒudɪs] *n* prejuicio; **~d** *adj* (*person*) predispuesto

premarital ['priː'mærɪtl] *adj* premarital

premature ['prɛmətjuə*] *adj* prematuro

premier ['prɛmɪə*] *adj* primero, principal ♦ *n* (*POL*) primer(a) ministro/a

première ['prɛmɪɛə*] *n* estreno

premise ['prɛmɪs] *n* premisa; **~s** *npl* (*of business etc*) local *m*; **on the ~s** en el lugar mismo

premium ['priːmɪəm] *n* premio; (*insurance*) prima; **to be at a ~** ser muy solicitado; **~ bond** (*BRIT*) *n* bono del estado que participa en una lotería nacional

premonition [prɛmə'nɪʃən] *n* presentimiento

preoccupied [priː'ɔkjupaɪd] *adj* ensimismado

prep [prɛp] *n* (*SCOL: study*) deberes *mpl*

prepaid [priː'peɪd] *adj* porte pagado

preparation [prɛpə'reɪʃən] *n* preparación *f*; **~s** *npl* preparativos *mpl*

preparatory [prɪ'pærətərɪ] *adj* preparatorio,

preliminar; **~ school** n escuela preparatoria
prepare [prɪ'pɛəʳ] vt preparar, disponer;
(CULIN) preparar ♦ vi: **to ~ for** (action)
prepararse or disponerse para; (event) hacer
preparativos para; **~d to** dispuesto a; **~d for**
listo para
preposition [prɛpə'zɪʃən] n preposición f
preposterous [prɪ'pɒstərəs] adj absurdo,
ridículo
prep school n = **preparatory school**
prerequisite [priː'rɛkwɪzɪt] n requisito
Presbyterian [prɛzbɪ'tɪərɪən] adj, n
presbiteriano/a m/f
preschool ['priː'skuːl] adj preescolar
prescribe [prɪ'skraɪb] vt (MED) recetar
prescription [prɪ'skrɪpʃən] n (MED) receta
presence ['prɛzns] n presencia; **in sb's ~** en
presencia de uno; **~ of mind** aplomo
present [adj, n 'prɛznt, vb prɪ'zɛnt] adj (in
attendance) presente; (current) actual ♦ n
(gift) regalo; (actuality): **the ~** la actualidad,
el presente ♦ vt (introduce, describe)
presentar; (expound) exponer; (give)
presentar, dar, ofrecer; (THEATRE) representar;
to give sb a ~ regalar algo a uno; **at ~**
actualmente; **~able** [prɪ'zɛntəbl] adj: **to**
make o.s. ~able arreglarse; **~ation** [-'teɪʃən] n
presentación f; (of report etc) exposición f;
(formal ceremony) entrega de un regalo; **~-**
day adj actual; **~er** [prɪ'zɛntəʳ] n (RADIO, TV)
locutor(a) m/f; **~ly** adv (soon) dentro de
poco; (now) ahora
preservative [prɪ'zɜːvətɪv] n conservante m
preserve [prɪ'zɜːv] vt (keep safe) preservar,
proteger; (maintain) mantener; (food)
conservar ♦ n (for game) coto, vedado; (often
pl: jam) conserva, confitura
president ['prɛzɪdənt] n presidente m/f; **~ial**
[-'dɛnʃl] adj presidencial
press [prɛs] n (newspapers): **the P~** la prensa;
(printer's) imprenta; (of button) pulsación f
♦ vt empujar; (button etc) apretar; (clothes:
iron) planchar; (put pressure on: person)
presionar; (insist): **to ~ sth on sb** insistir en
que uno acepte algo ♦ vi (squeeze) apretar;
(pressurize): **to ~ for** presionar por; **we are**
~ed for time/money estamos apurados de
tiempo/dinero; **~ on** vi avanzar; (hurry)
apretar el paso; **~ agency** n agencia de
prensa; **~ conference** n rueda de prensa;
~ing adj apremiante; **~ stud** (BRIT) n botón
m de presión; **~-up** (BRIT) n plancha
pressure ['prɛʃəʳ] n presión f; **to put ~ on sb**
presionar a uno; **~ cooker** n olla a presión;
~ gauge n manómetro; **~ group** n grupo
de presión; **pressurized** adj (container) a
presión
prestige [prɛs'tiːʒ] n prestigio
presumably [prɪ'zjuːməblɪ] adv es de

suponer que, cabe presumir que
presume [prɪ'zjuːm] vt: **to ~ (that)** presumir
(que), suponer (que)
pretence [prɪ'tɛns] (US **pretense**) n
fingimiento; **under false ~s** con engaños
pretend [prɪ'tɛnd] vt, vi (feign) fingir
pretentious [prɪ'tɛnʃəs] adj presumido;
(ostentatious) ostentoso, aparatoso
pretext ['priːtɛkst] n pretexto
pretty ['prɪtɪ] adj bonito (SP), lindo (AM)
♦ adv bastante
prevail [prɪ'veɪl] vi (gain mastery) prevalecer;
(be current) predominar; **~ing** adj (dominant)
predominante
prevalent ['prɛvələnt] adj (widespread)
extendido
prevent [prɪ'vɛnt] vt: **to ~ sb from doing sth**
impedir a uno hacer algo; **to ~ sth from**
happening evitar que ocurra algo; **~ative** adj
= **preventive; ~ive** adj preventivo
preview ['priːvjuː] n (of film) preestreno
previous ['priːvɪəs] adj previo, anterior; **~ly**
adv antes
prewar [priː'wɔːʳ] adj de antes de la guerra
prey [preɪ] n presa ♦ vi: **to ~ on** (feed on)
alimentarse de; **it was ~ing on his mind** le
preocupaba, le obsesionaba
price [praɪs] n precio ♦ vt (goods) fijar el
precio de; **~less** adj que no tiene precio;
~ list n tarifa
prick [prɪk] n (sting) picadura ♦ vt pinchar;
(hurt) picar; **to ~ up one's ears** aguzar el oído
prickle ['prɪkl] n (sensation) picor m; (BOT)
espina; **prickly** adj espinoso; (fig: person)
enojadizo; **prickly heat** n sarpullido causado
por exceso de calor
pride [praɪd] n orgullo; (pej) soberbia ♦ vt: **to**
~ o.s. on enorgullecerse de
priest [priːst] n sacerdote m; **~hood** n
sacerdocio
prim [prɪm] adj (demure) remilgado; (prudish)
gazmoño
primarily ['praɪmərɪlɪ] adv ante todo
primary ['praɪmərɪ] adj (first in importance)
principal ♦ n (US: POL) (elección f) primaria;
~ school (BRIT) n escuela primaria
prime [praɪm] adj primero, principal;
(excellent) selecto, de primera clase ♦ n: **in**
the ~ of life en la flor de la vida ♦ vt (wood,
fig) preparar; **~ example** ejemplo típico;
P~ Minister n primer(a) ministro/a
primeval [praɪ'miːvəl] adj primitivo
primitive ['prɪmɪtɪv] adj primitivo; (crude)
rudimentario
primrose ['prɪmrəʊz] n primavera, prímula
Primus (stove) ® ['praɪməs-] (BRIT) n
hornillo de camping
prince [prɪns] n príncipe m
princess [prɪn'sɛs] n princesa

principal ['prɪnsɪpl] adj principal, mayor ♦ n director(a) m/f; **~ity** [-'pælɪtɪ] n principado

principle ['prɪnsɪpl] n principio; **in ~** en principio; **on ~** por principio

print [prɪnt] n (foot~) huella; (finger~) huella dactilar; (letters) letra de molde; (fabric) estampado; (ART) grabado; (PHOT) impresión f ♦ vt imprimir; (cloth) estampar; (write in capitals) escribir en letras de molde; **out of ~** agotado; **~ed matter** n impresos mpl; **~er** n (person) impresor(a) m/f; (machine) impresora; **~ing** n (art) imprenta; (act) impresión f; **~out** n (COMPUT) impresión f

prior ['praɪə*] adj anterior, previo; (more important) más importante; **~ to** antes de

priority [praɪ'ɔrɪtɪ] n prioridad f; **to have ~ (over)** tener prioridad (sobre)

prison ['prɪzn] n cárcel f, prisión f ♦ cpd carcelario; **~er** n (in prison) preso/a; (captured person) prisionero/a; **~er-of-war** n prisionero de guerra

privacy ['prɪvəsɪ] n intimidad f

private ['praɪvɪt] adj (personal) particular; (property, industry, discussion etc) privado; (person) reservado; (place) tranquilo ♦ n soldado raso; **"~"** (on envelope) "confidencial"; (on door) "prohibido el paso"; **in ~** en privado; **~ enterprise** n empresa privada; **~ eye** n detective m/f privado/a; **~ property** n propiedad f privada; **~ school** n colegio particular

privet ['prɪvɪt] n alheña

privilege ['prɪvɪlɪdʒ] n privilegio; (prerogative) prerrogativa

privy ['prɪvɪ] adj: **to be ~ to** estar enterado de

prize [praɪz] n premio ♦ adj de primera clase ♦ vt apreciar, estimar; **~-giving** n distribución f de premios; **~winner** n premiado/a

pro [prəʊ] n (SPORT) profesional m/f ♦ prep a favor de; **the ~s and cons** los pros y los contras

probability [prɒbə'bɪlɪtɪ] n probabilidad f; **in all ~** con toda probabilidad

probable ['prɒbəbl] adj probable

probably ['prɒbəblɪ] adv probablemente

probation [prə'beɪʃən] n: **on ~** (employee) a prueba; (LAW) en libertad condicional

probe [prəʊb] n (MED, SPACE) sonda; (enquiry) encuesta, investigación f ♦ vt sondar; (investigate) investigar

problem ['prɒbləm] n problema m

procedure [prə'siːdʒə*] n procedimiento; (bureaucratic) trámites mpl

proceed [prə'siːd] vi (do afterwards): **to ~ to do sth** proceder a hacer algo; (continue): **to ~ (with)** continuar or seguir (con); **~ings** npl acto(s) (pl); (LAW) proceso; **~s** ['prəʊsiːdz] npl (money) ganancias fpl, ingresos mpl

process ['prəʊses] n proceso ♦ vt tratar, elaborar; **~ing** n tratamiento, elaboración f; (PHOT) revelado

procession [prə'seʃən] n desfile m; **funeral ~** cortejo fúnebre

pro-choice [prəʊ'tʃɔɪs] adj en favor del derecho a elegir de la madre

proclaim [prə'kleɪm] vt (announce) anunciar

procrastinate [prəʊ'kræstɪneɪt] vi demorarse

procure [prə'kjuə*] vt conseguir

prod [prɒd] vt empujar ♦ n empujón m

prodigy ['prɒdɪdʒɪ] n prodigio

produce [n 'prɒdjuːs, vt prə'djuːs] n (AGR) productos mpl agrícolas ♦ vt producir; (play, film, programme) presentar; **~r** n productor(a) m/f; (of film, programme) director(a) m/f; (of record) productor(a) m/f

product ['prɒdʌkt] n producto

production [prə'dʌkʃən] n producción f; (THEATRE) presentación f; **~ line** n línea de producción

productivity [prɒdʌk'tɪvɪtɪ] n productividad f

profession [prə'feʃən] n profesión f; **~al** adj profesional ♦ n profesional m/f; (skilled person) perito

professor [prə'fesə*] n (BRIT) catedrático/a; (US, Canada) profesor(a) m/f

proficient [prə'fɪʃənt] adj experto, hábil

profile ['prəʊfaɪl] n perfil m

profit ['prɒfɪt] n (COMM) ganancia ♦ vi: **to ~ by or from** aprovechar or sacar provecho de; **~ability** [-ə'bɪlɪtɪ] n rentabilidad f; **~able** adj (ECON) rentable

profound [prə'faʊnd] adj profundo

profusely [prə'fjuːslɪ] adv profusamente

programme ['prəʊgræm] (US **program**) n programa m ♦ vt programar; **~r** (US **programer**) n programador(a) m/f; **programming** (US **programing**) n programación f

progress [n 'prəʊgres, vi prə'gres] n progreso; (development) desarrollo ♦ vi progresar, avanzar; **in ~** en curso; **~ive** [-'gresɪv] adj progresivo; (person) progresista

prohibit [prə'hɪbɪt] vt prohibir; **to ~ sb from doing sth** prohibir a uno hacer algo; **~ion** [-'bɪʃn] n prohibición f; (US): **P~ion** Ley f Seca

project [n 'prɒdʒekt, vb prə'dʒekt] n proyecto ♦ vt proyectar ♦ vi (stick out) salir, sobresalir; **~ion** [prə'dʒekʃən] n proyección f; (overhang) saliente m; **~or** [prə'dʒektə*] n proyector m

pro-life [prəʊ'laɪf] adj pro-vida

prolong [prə'lɒŋ] vt prolongar, extender

prom [prɒm] n abbr = **promenade**; (US: ball) baile m de gala

promenade [prɒmə'nɑːd] n (by sea) paseo

marítimo; **~ concert** (*BRIT*) *n* concierto (en que parte del público permanece de pie)
prominence ['prɒmɪnəns] *n* importancia
prominent ['prɒmɪnənt] *adj* (*standing out*) saliente; (*important*) eminente, importante
promiscuous [prə'mɪskjuəs] *adj* (*sexually*) promiscuo
promise ['prɒmɪs] *n* promesa ♦ *vt, vi* prometer; **promising** *adj* prometedor(a)
promote [prə'məut] *vt* (*employee*) ascender; (*product, pop star*) hacer propaganda por; (*ideas*) fomentar; **~r** *n* (*of event*) promotor(a) *m/f*; (*of cause etc*) impulsor(a) *m/f*; **promotion** [-'məuʃən] *n* (*advertising campaign*) campaña de promoción *f*; (*in rank*) ascenso
prompt [prɒmpt] *adj* rápido ♦ *adv*: **at 6 o'clock ~** a las seis en punto ♦ *n* (*COMPUT*) aviso ♦ *vt* (*urge*) mover, incitar; (*when talking*) instar; (*THEATRE*) apuntar; **to ~ sb to do sth** instar a uno a hacer algo; **~ly** *adv* rápidamente; (*exactly*) puntualmente
prone [prəun] *adj* (*lying*) postrado; **~ to** propenso a
prong [prɒŋ] *n* diente *m*, punta
pronoun ['prəunaun] *n* pronombre *m*
pronounce [prə'nauns] *vt* pronunciar; **~d** *adj* (*marked*) marcado
pronunciation [prənʌnsɪ'eɪʃən] *n* pronunciación *f*
proof [pru:f] *n* prueba ♦ *adj*: **~ against a** prueba de
prop [prɒp] *n* apoyo; (*fig*) sostén *m* ♦ *vt* (*also: ~ up*) apoyar; (*lean*): **to ~ sth against** apoyar algo contra
propaganda [prɒpə'gændə] *n* propaganda
propel [prə'pɛl] *vt* impulsar, propulsar; **~ler** *n* hélice *f*
propensity [prə'pensɪtɪ] *n* propensión *f*
proper ['prɒpə*] *adj* (*suited, right*) propio; (*exact*) justo; (*seemly*) correcto, decente; (*authentic*) verdadero; (*referring to place*): **the village ~** el pueblo mismo; **~ly** *adv* (*adequately*) correctamente; (*decently*) decentemente; **~ noun** *n* nombre *m* propio
property ['prɒpətɪ] *n* propiedad *f*; (*personal*) bienes *mpl* muebles; **~ owner** *n* dueño/a de propiedades
prophecy ['prɒfɪsɪ] *n* profecía
prophesy ['prɒfɪsaɪ] *vt* (*fig*) predecir
prophet ['prɒfɪt] *n* profeta *m*
proportion [prə'pɔːʃən] *n* proporción *f*; (*share*) parte *f*; **~al** *adj*: **~al (to)** en proporción (con); **~al representation** *n* representación *f* proporcional; **~ate** *adj*: **~ate (to)** en proporción (con)
proposal [prə'pəuzl] *n* (*offer of marriage*) oferta de matrimonio; (*plan*) proyecto
propose [prə'pəuz] *vt* proponer ♦ *vi*

declararse; **to ~ to do** tener intención de hacer
proposition [prɒpə'zɪʃən] *n* propuesta
proprietor [prə'praɪətə*] *n* propietario/a, dueño/a
propriety [prə'praɪətɪ] *n* decoro
pro rata [-'rɑːtə] *adv* a prorrateo
prose [prəuz] *n* prosa
prosecute ['prɒsɪkjuːt] *vt* (*LAW*) procesar; **prosecution** [-'kjuːʃən] *n* proceso, causa; (*accusing side*) acusación *f*; **prosecutor** *n* acusador(a) *m/f*; (*also: public prosecutor*) fiscal *m*
prospect [*n* 'prɒspekt, *vb* prə'spekt] *n* (*possibility*) posibilidad *f*; (*outlook*) perspectiva ♦ *vi*: **to ~ for** buscar; **~s** *npl* (*for work etc*) perspectivas *fpl*; **~ing** *n* prospección *f*; **~ive** [prə'spektɪv] *adj* futuro
prospectus [prə'spektəs] *n* prospecto
prosper ['prɒspə*] *vi* prosperar; **~ity** [-'spɛrɪtɪ] *n* prosperidad *f*; **~ous** *adj* próspero
prostitute ['prɒstɪtjuːt] *n* prostituta; (*male*) hombre que se dedica a la prostitución
protect [prə'tɛkt] *vt* proteger; **~ion** [-'tɛkʃən] *n* protección *f*; **~ive** *adj* protector(a)
protein ['prəutiːn] *n* proteína
protest [*n* 'prəutest, *vb* prə'test] *n* protesta ♦ *vi*: **to ~ about** or **at/against** protestar de/contra ♦ *vt* (*insist*): **to ~ (that)** insistir en (que)
Protestant ['prɒtɪstənt] *adj, n* protestante *m/f*
protester [prə'testə*] *n* manifestante *m/f*
protracted [prə'træktɪd] *adj* prolongado
protrude [prə'truːd] *vi* salir, sobresalir
proud [praud] *adj* orgulloso; (*pej*) soberbio, altanero
prove [pruːv] *vt* probar; (*show*) demostrar ♦ *vi*: **to ~ (to be) correct** resultar correcto; **to ~ o.s.** probar su valía
proverb ['prɒvəːb] *n* refrán *m*
provide [prə'vaɪd] *vt* proporcionar, dar; **to ~ sb with sth** proveer a uno de algo; **~d (that)** *conj* con tal de que, a condición de que; **~ for** *vt fus* (*person*) mantener a; (*problem etc*) tener en cuenta; **providing** [prə'vaɪdɪŋ] *conj*: **providing (that)** a condición de que, con tal de que
province ['prɒvɪns] *n* provincia; (*fig*) esfera; **provincial** [prə'vɪnʃəl] *adj* provincial; (*pej*) provinciano
provision [prə'vɪʒən] *n* (*supplying*) suministro, abastecimiento; (*of contract etc*) disposición *f*; **~s** *npl* (*food*) comestibles *mpl*; **~al** *adj* provisional
proviso [prə'vaɪzəu] *n* condición *f*, estipulación *f*
provocative [prə'vɒkətɪv] *adj* provocativo
provoke [prə'vəuk] *vt* (*cause*) provocar,

incitar; (*anger*) enojar
prowess ['prauɪs] *n* destreza
prowl [praul] *vi* (*also*: ~ about, ~ around)
merodear ♦ *n*: **on the ~** de merodeo; **~er** *n*
merodeador(a) *m/f*
proxy ['prɒksɪ] *n*: **by ~** por poderes
prudent ['pru:dənt] *adj* prudente
prune [pru:n] *n* ciruela pasa ♦ *vt* podar
pry [praɪ] *vi*: **to ~ (into)** entrometerse (en)
PS *n abbr* (= *postscript*) P.D.
psalm [sɑ:m] *n* salmo
pseudonym ['sju:dəunɪm] *n* seudónimo
psyche ['saɪkɪ] *n* psique *f*
psychiatric [saɪkɪˈætrɪk] *adj* psiquiátrico
psychiatrist [saɪˈkaɪətrɪst] *n* psiquiatra *m/f*
psychic ['saɪkɪk] *adj* (*also*: ~al) psíquico
psychoanalyse [saɪkəuˈænəlaɪz] *vt*
psicoanalizar; **psychoanalysis** [-əˈnælɪsɪs] *n*
psicoanálisis *m inv*
psychological [saɪkəˈlɒdʒɪkl] *adj* psicológico
psychologist [saɪˈkɒlədʒɪst] *n* psicólogo/a
psychology [saɪˈkɒlədʒɪ] *n* psicología
PTO *abbr* (= *please turn over*) sigue
pub [pʌb] *n abbr* (= *public house*) pub *m*, bar
m
puberty ['pju:bətɪ] *n* pubertad *f*
public ['pʌblɪk] *adj* público ♦ *n*: **the ~** el
público; **in ~** en público; **to make ~** hacer
público; **~ address system** *n* megafonía
publican ['pʌblɪkən] *n* tabernero/a
publication [pʌblɪˈkeɪʃən] *n* publicación *f*
public: **~ company** *n* sociedad *f* anónima;
~ convenience (*BRIT*) *n* aseos *mpl* públicos
(*SP*), sanitarios *mpl* (*AM*); **~ holiday** *n* día de
fiesta (*SP*), (día) feriado (*AM*); **~ house** (*BRIT*)
n bar *m*, pub *m*
publicity [pʌbˈlɪsɪtɪ] *n* publicidad *f*
publicize ['pʌblɪsaɪz] *vt* publicitar
publicly ['pʌblɪklɪ] *adv* públicamente, en
público
public: **~ opinion** *n* opinión *f* pública;
~ relations *n* relaciones *fpl* públicas;
~ school *n* (*BRIT*) escuela privada; (*US*)
instituto; **~-spirited** *adj* que tiene sentido del
deber ciudadano; **~ transport** *n* transporte
m público
publish ['pʌblɪʃ] *vt* publicar; **~er** *n* (*person*)
editor(a) *m/f*; (*firm*) editorial *f*; **~ing** *n*
(*industry*) industria del libro
pub lunch *n* almuerzo que se sirve en un pub;
to go for a ~ almorzar o comer en un pub
pucker ['pʌkə*] *vt* (*pleat*) arrugar; (*brow etc*)
fruncir
pudding ['pudɪŋ] *n* pudín *m*; (*BRIT*: *dessert*)
postre *m*; **black ~** morcilla
puddle ['pʌdl] *n* charco
puff [pʌf] *n* (*of smoke, air*) bocanada;
(*of breathing*) resoplido ♦ *vt*: **to ~ one's pipe**
chupar la pipa ♦ *vi* (*pant*) jadear; **~ out** *vt*

hinchar; **~ pastry** *n* hojaldre *m*; **~y** *adj*
hinchado
pull [pul] *n* (*tug*): **to give sth a ~** dar un tirón
a algo ♦ *vt* tirar de; (*press: trigger*) apretar;
(*haul*) tirar, arrastrar; (*close: curtain*) echar
♦ *vi* tirar; **to ~ to pieces** hacer pedazos; **to
not ~ one's punches** no andarse con bromas;
to ~ one's weight hacer su parte; **to ~ o.s.
together** sobreponerse; **to ~ sb's leg** tomar el
pelo a uno; **~ apart** *vt* (*break*) romper;
~ down *vt* (*building*) derribar; **~ in** *vi* (*car
etc*) parar (junto a la acera); (*train*) llegar a la
estación; **~ off** *vt* (*deal etc*) cerrar; **~ out** *vi*
(*car, train etc*) salir ♦ *vt* sacar, arrancar;
~ over *vi* (*AUT*) hacerse a un lado;
~ through *vi* (*MED*) reponerse; **~ up** *vi*
(*stop*) parar ♦ *vt* (*raise*) levantar; (*uproot*)
arrancar, desarraigar
pulley ['pulɪ] *n* polea
pullover ['pulauvə*] *n* jersey *m*, suéter *m*
pulp [pʌlp] *n* (*of fruit*) pulpa
pulpit ['pulpɪt] *n* púlpito
pulsate [pʌlˈseɪt] *vi* pulsar, latir
pulse [pʌls] *n* (*ANAT*) pulso; (*rhythm*)
pulsación *f*; (*BOT*) legumbre *f*
pump [pʌmp] *n* bomba; (*shoe*) zapatilla ♦ *vt*
sacar con una bomba; **~ up** *vt* inflar
pumpkin ['pʌmpkɪn] *n* calabaza
pun [pʌn] *n* juego de palabras
punch [pʌntʃ] *n* (*blow*) golpe *m*, puñetazo;
(*tool*) punzón *m*; (*drink*) ponche *m* ♦ *vt*
(*hit*): **to ~ sb/sth** dar un puñetazo o golpear
a uno/algo; **~line** *n* palabras que rematan un
chiste; **~-up** *n* (*BRIT*: *inf*) riña
punctual ['pʌŋktjuəl] *adj* puntual
punctuation [pʌŋktjuˈeɪʃən] *n* puntuación *f*
puncture ['pʌŋktʃə*] (*BRIT*) *n* pinchazo ♦ *vt*
pinchar
pungent ['pʌndʒənt] *adj* acre
punish ['pʌnɪʃ] *vt* castigar; **~ment** *n* castigo
punk [pʌŋk] *n* (*also*: ~ rocker) punki *m/f*;
(*also*: ~ rock) música punk; (*US*: *inf*: hoodlum)
rufián *m*
punt [pʌnt] *n* (*boat*) batea
punter ['pʌntə*] (*BRIT*) *n* (*gambler*)
jugador(a) *m/f*; (*inf*) cliente *m/f*
puny ['pju:nɪ] *adj* débil
pup [pʌp] *n* cachorro
pupil ['pju:pl] *n* alumno/a; (*of eye*) pupila
puppet ['pʌpɪt] *n* títere *m*
puppy ['pʌpɪ] *n* cachorro, perrito
purchase ['pə:tʃɪs] *n* compra ♦ *vt* comprar;
~r *n* comprador(a) *m/f*
pure [pjuə*] *adj* puro
purée ['pjuəreɪ] *n* puré *m*
purely ['pjuəlɪ] *adv* puramente
purge [pə:dʒ] *n* (*MED, POL*) purga ♦ *vt* purgar
purify ['pjuərɪfaɪ] *vt* purificar, depurar
purple ['pə:pl] *adj* purpúreo; morado

purpose ['pɜːpəs] n propósito; **on ~** a propósito, adrede; **~ful** adj resuelto, determinado

purr [pɜː*] vi ronronear

purse [pɜːs] n monedero; (US) bolsa (SP), cartera (AM) ♦ vt fruncir

pursue [pə'sjuː] vt seguir; **~r** n perseguidor(a) m/f

pursuit [pə'sjuːt] n (chase) caza; (occupation) actividad f

push [puʃ] n empuje m, empujón m; (of button) presión f; (drive) empuje m ♦ vt empujar; (button) apretar; (promote) promover ♦ vi empujar; (demand): **to ~ for** luchar por; **~ aside** vt apartar con la mano; **~ off** (inf) vi largarse; **~ on** vi seguir adelante; **~ through** vi (crowd) abrirse paso a empujones ♦ vt (measure) despachar; **~ up** vt (total, prices) hacer subir; **~chair** (BRIT) n sillita de ruedas; **~er** n (drug ~er) traficante m/f de drogas; **~over** (inf) n: **it's a ~over** está tirado; **~-up** (US) n plancha; **~y** (pej) adj agresivo

puss [pus] (inf) n minino

pussy(-cat) ['pusɪ-] (inf) n = **puss**

put [put] (pt, pp put) vt (place) poner, colocar; (~ into) meter; (say) expresar; (a question) hacer; (estimate) estimar; **~ about**, or **around** vt (rumour) diseminar; **~ across** vt (ideas etc) comunicar; **~ away** vt (store) guardar; **~ back** vt (replace) devolver a su lugar; (postpone) aplazar; **~ by** vt (money) guardar; **~ down** vt (on ground) poner en el suelo; (animal) sacrificar; (in writing) apuntar; (revolt etc) sofocar; (attribute): **to ~ sth down to** atribuir algo a; **~ forward** vt (ideas) presentar, proponer; **~ in** vt (complaint) presentar; (time) dedicar; **~ off** vt (postpone) aplazar; (discourage) desanimar; **~ on** vt ponerse; (light etc) encender; (play etc) presentar; (gain): **to ~ on weight** engordar; (brake) echar; (record, kettle etc) poner; (assume) adoptar; **~ out** vt (fire, light) apagar; (rubbish etc) sacar; (cat etc) echar; (one's hand) alargar; (inf: person): **to be ~ out** alterarse; **~ through** vt (TEL) poner; (plan etc) hacer aprobar; **~ up** vt (raise) levantar, alzar; (hang) colgar; (build) construir; (increase) aumentar; (accommodate) alojar; **~ up with** vt fus aguantar

putt [pʌt] n putt m, golpe m corto; **~ing green** n green m; minigolf m

putty ['pʌtɪ] n masilla

put-up ['putʌp] adj: **~ job** (BRIT) amaño

puzzle ['pʌzl] n rompecabezas m inv; (also: crossword ~) crucigrama m; (mystery) misterio ♦ vt dejar perplejo, confundir ♦ vi: **to ~ over sth** devanarse los sesos con algo; **puzzling** adj misterioso, extraño

pyjamas [pɪ'dʒɑːməz] (BRIT) npl pijama m

pylon ['paɪlən] n torre f de conducción eléctrica

pyramid ['pɪrəmɪd] n pirámide f

Pyrenees [pɪrə'niːz] npl: **the ~** los Pirineos

python ['paɪθən] n pitón m

Q, q

quack [kwæk] n graznido; (pej: doctor) curandero/a

quad [kwɔd] n abbr = **quadrangle; quadruplet**

quadrangle ['kwɔdræŋgl] n patio

quadruple [kwɔ'druːpl] vt, vi cuadruplicar

quadruplets [kwɔː'druːplɪts] npl cuatrillizos/as

quail [kweɪl] n codorniz f ♦ vi: **to ~ at** or **before** amedrentarse ante

quaint [kweɪnt] adj extraño; (picturesque) pintoresco

quake [kweɪk] vi temblar ♦ n abbr = **earthquake**

Quaker ['kweɪkə*] n cuáquero/a

qualification [kwɔlɪfɪ'keɪʃən] n (ability) capacidad f; (often pl: diploma etc) título; (reservation) salvedad f

qualified ['kwɔlɪfaɪd] adj capacitado; (professionally) titulado; (limited) limitado

qualify ['kwɔlɪfaɪ] vt (make competent) capacitar; (modify) modificar ♦ vi (in competition): **to ~ (for)** calificarse (para); (pass examination(s)): **to ~ (as)** calificarse (de), graduarse (en); (be eligible): **to ~ (for)** reunir los requisitos (para)

quality ['kwɔlɪtɪ] n calidad f; (of person) cualidad f; **~ time** n tiempo dedicado a la familia y a los amigos

qualm [kwɑːm] n escrúpulo

quandary ['kwɔndrɪ] n: **to be in a ~** tener dudas

quantity ['kwɔntɪtɪ] n cantidad f; **in ~** en grandes cantidades; **~ surveyor** n aparejador(a) m/f

quarantine ['kwɔrəntiːn] n cuarentena

quarrel ['kwɔrəl] n riña, pelea ♦ vi reñir, pelearse

quarry ['kwɔrɪ] n cantera

quart [kwɔːt] n ≈ litro

quarter ['kwɔːtə*] n cuarto, cuarta parte f; (US: coin) moneda de 25 centavos; (of year) trimestre m; (district) barrio ♦ vt dividir en cuartos; (MIL: lodge) alojar; **~s** npl (barracks) cuartel m; (living ~s) alojamiento; **a ~ of an hour** un cuarto de hora; **~ final** n cuarto de final; **~ly** adj trimestral ♦ adv cada 3 meses, trimestralmente

quartet(te) [kwɔː'tɛt] n cuarteto

quartz [kwɔ:ts] n cuarzo
quash [kwɔʃ] vt (verdict) anular
quaver ['kweɪvə*] (BRIT) n (MUS) corchea ♦ vi temblar
quay [ki:] n (also: ~side) muelle m
queasy ['kwi:zɪ] adj: **to feel ~** tener náuseas
queen [kwi:n] n reina; (CARDS etc) dama; **~ mother** n reina madre
queer [kwɪə*] adj raro, extraño ♦ n (inf: highly offensive) maricón m
quell [kwɛl] vt (feeling) calmar; (rebellion etc) sofocar
quench [kwɛntʃ] vt: **to ~ one's thirst** apagar la sed
query ['kwɪərɪ] n (question) pregunta ♦ vt dudar de
quest [kwɛst] n busca, búsqueda
question ['kwɛstʃən] n pregunta; (doubt) duda; (matter) asunto, cuestión f ♦ vt (doubt) dudar de; (interrogate) interrogar, hacer preguntas a; **beyond ~** fuera de toda duda; **out of the ~** imposible; ni hablar; **~able** adj dudoso; **~ mark** n punto de interrogación; **~naire** [-'nɛə*] n cuestionario
queue [kju:] (BRIT) n cola ♦ vi (also: ~ up) hacer cola
quibble ['kwɪbl] vi sutilizar
quick [kwɪk] adj rápido; (agile) ágil; (mind) listo ♦ n: **cut to the ~** (fig) herido en lo vivo; **be ~!** ¡date prisa!; **~en** vt apresurar ♦ vi apresurarse, darse prisa; **~ly** adv rápidamente, de prisa; **~sand** n arenas fpl movedizas; **~-witted** adj perspicaz
quid [kwɪd] (BRIT: inf) n inv libra
quiet ['kwaɪət] adj (voice, music etc) bajo; (person, place) tranquilo; (ceremony) íntimo ♦ n silencio; (calm) tranquilidad f ♦ vt, vi (US) **= ~en; ~en** (also: ~ down) vi calmarse; (grow silent) callarse ♦ vt calmar, hacer callar; **~ly** adv tranquilamente; (silently) silenciosamente; **~ness** n silencio; tranquilidad f
quilt [kwɪlt] n edredón m
quin [kwɪn] n abbr **= quintuplet**
quintet(te) [kwɪn'tɛt] n quinteto
quintuplets [kwɪn'tju:plɪts] npl quintillizos/as
quip [kwɪp] n pulla
quirk [kwə:k] n peculiaridad f; (accident) capricho
quit [kwɪt] (pt, pp quit or quitted) vt dejar, abandonar; (premises) desocupar ♦ vi (give up) renunciar; (resign) dimitir
quite [kwaɪt] adv (rather) bastante; (entirely) completamente; **that's not ~ big enough** no acaba de ser lo bastante grande; **~ a few of them** un buen número de ellos; **~ (so)!** ¡así es!, ¡exactamente!
quits [kwɪts] adj: **~ (with)** en paz (con); **let's**

call it ~ dejémoslo en tablas
quiver ['kwɪvə*] vi estremecerse
quiz [kwɪz] n concurso ♦ vt interrogar; **~zical** adj burlón(ona)
quota ['kwəutə] n cuota
quotation [kwəu'teɪʃən] n cita; (estimate) presupuesto; **~ marks** npl comillas fpl
quote [kwəut] n cita; (estimate) presupuesto ♦ vt citar; (price) cotizar ♦ vi: **to ~ from** citar de; **~s** npl (inverted commas) comillas fpl

R, r

rabbi ['ræbaɪ] n rabino
rabbit ['ræbɪt] n conejo; **~ hutch** n conejera
rabble ['ræbl] (pej) n chusma, populacho
rabies ['reɪbi:z] n rabia
RAC (BRIT) n abbr **= Royal Automobile Club**
rac(c)oon [rə'ku:n] n mapache m
race [reɪs] n carrera; (species) raza ♦ vt (horse) hacer correr; (engine) acelerar ♦ vi (compete) competir; (run) correr; (pulse) latir a ritmo acelerado; **~ car** (US) n **= racing car; ~ car driver** (US) n **= racing driver; ~course** n hipódromo; **~horse** n caballo de carreras; **~track** n pista; (for cars) autódromo
racial ['reɪʃl] adj racial
racing ['reɪsɪŋ] n carreras fpl; **~ car** (BRIT) n coche m de carreras; **~ driver** (BRIT) n corredor(a) m/f de coches
racism ['reɪsɪzəm] n racismo; **racist** [-sɪst] adj, n racista m/f
rack [ræk] n (also: luggage ~) rejilla; (shelf) estante m; (also: roof ~) baca, portaequipajes m inv; (dish ~) escurreplatos m inv; (clothes ~) percha ♦ vt atormentar; **to ~ one's brains** devanarse los sesos
racket ['rækɪt] n (for tennis) raqueta; (noise) ruido, estrépito; (swindle) estafa, timo
racquet ['rækɪt] n raqueta
racy ['reɪsɪ] adj picante, salado
radar ['reɪdɑ:*] n radar m
radiant ['reɪdɪənt] adj radiante (de felicidad)
radiate ['reɪdɪeɪt] vt (heat) radiar; (emotion) irradiar ♦ vi (lines) extenderse
radiation [reɪdɪ'eɪʃən] n radiación f
radiator ['reɪdɪeɪtə*] n radiador m
radical ['rædɪkl] adj radical
radii ['reɪdɪaɪ] npl of **radius**
radio ['reɪdɪəu] n radio f; **on the ~** por radio
radio... [reɪdɪəu] prefix: **~active** adj radioactivo; **~graphy** [reɪdɪ'ɔgrəfɪ] n radiografía; **~logy** [reɪdɪ'ɔlədʒɪ] n radiología
radio station n emisora
radiotherapy [-'θerəpɪ] n radioterapia
radish ['rædɪʃ] n rábano
radius ['reɪdɪəs] (pl radii) n radio
RAF n abbr **= Royal Air Force**

raffle ['ræfl] *n* rifa, sorteo

raft [rɑːft] *n* balsa; (*also: life ~*) balsa salvavidas

rafter ['rɑːftə*] *n* viga

rag [ræg] *n* (*piece of cloth*) trapo; (*torn cloth*) harapo; (*pej: newspaper*) periodicucho; (*for charity*) actividades estudiantiles benéficas; **~s** *npl* (*torn clothes*) harapos *mpl*; **~ doll** *n* muñeca de trapo

rage [reɪdʒ] *n* rabia, furor *m* ♦ *vi* (*person*) rabiar, estar furioso; (*storm*) bramar; **it's all the ~** (*very fashionable*) está muy de moda

ragged ['rægɪd] *adj* (*edge*) desigual, mellado; (*appearance*) andrajoso, harapiento

raid [reɪd] *n* (*MIL*) incursión *f*; (*criminal*) asalto; (*by police*) redada ♦ *vt* invadir, atacar; asaltar

rail [reɪl] *n* (*on stair*) barandilla, pasamanos *m inv*; (*on bridge, balcony*) pretil *m*; (*of ship*) barandilla; (*also: towel ~*) toallero; **~s** *npl* (*RAIL*) vía; **by ~** por ferrocarril; **~ing(s)** *n*(*pl*) vallado; **~road** (*US*) *n* = **~way**; **~way** (*BRIT*) *n* ferrocarril *m*, vía férrea; **~way line** (*BRIT*) *n* línea (de ferrocarril); **~wayman** (*BRIT irreg*) *n* ferroviario; **~way station** (*BRIT*) *n* estación *f* de ferrocarril

rain [reɪn] *n* lluvia ♦ *vi* llover; **in the ~** bajo la lluvia; **it's ~ing** llueve, está lloviendo; **~bow** *n* arco iris; **~coat** *n* impermeable *m*; **~drop** *n* gota de lluvia; **~fall** *n* lluvia; **~forest** *n* selvas *fpl* tropicales; **~y** *adj* lluvioso

raise [reɪz] *n* aumento ♦ *vt* levantar; (*increase*) aumentar; (*improve: morale*) subir; (: *standards*) mejorar; (*doubts*) suscitar; (*a question*) plantear; (*cattle, family*) criar; (*crop*) cultivar; (*army*) reclutar; (*loan*) obtener; **to ~ one's voice** alzar la voz

raisin ['reɪzn] *n* pasa de Corinto

rake [reɪk] *n* (*tool*) rastrillo; (*person*) libertino ♦ *vt* (*garden*) rastrillar

rally ['rælɪ] *n* (*POL etc*) reunión *f*, mitin *m*; (*AUT*) rallye *m*; (*TENNIS*) peloteo ♦ *vt* reunir ♦ *vi* recuperarse; **~ round** *vt fus* (*fig*) dar apoyo a

RAM [ræm] *n abbr* (= *random access memory*) RAM *f*

ram [ræm] *n* carnero; (*also: battering ~*) ariete *m* ♦ *vt* (*crash into*) dar contra, chocar con; (*push: fist etc*) empujar con fuerza

ramble ['ræmbl] *n* caminata, excursión *f* en el campo ♦ *vi* (*pej: also: ~ on*) divagar; **~r** *n* excursionista *m/f*; (*BOT*) trepadora; **rambling** *adj* (*speech*) inconexo; (*house*) laberíntico; (*BOT*) trepador(a)

ramp [ræmp] *n* rampa; **on/off ~** (*US: AUT*) vía de acceso/salida

rampage [ræm'peɪdʒ] *n*: **to be on the ~** desmandarse ♦ *vi*: **they went rampaging through the town** recorrieron la ciudad armando alboroto

rampant ['ræmpənt] *adj* (*disease etc*): **to be ~** estar extendiéndose mucho

ram raid *vt* atacar (*rompiendo el escaparate con un coche*)

ramshackle ['ræmʃækl] *adj* destartalado

ran [ræn] *pt of* **run**

ranch [rɑːntʃ] *n* hacienda, estancia; **~er** *n* ganadero

rancid ['rænsɪd] *adj* rancio

rancour ['ræŋkə*] (*US* **rancor**) *n* rencor *m*

random ['rændəm] *adj* fortuito, sin orden; (*COMPUT, MATH*) aleatorio ♦ *n*: **at ~** al azar

randy ['rændɪ] (*BRIT: inf*) *adj* cachondo

rang [ræŋ] *pt of* **ring**

range [reɪndʒ] *n* (*of mountains*) cadena de montañas, cordillera; (*of missile*) alcance *m*; (*of voice*) registro; (*series*) serie *f*; (*of products*) surtido; (*MIL: also: shooting ~*) campo de tiro; (*also: kitchen ~*) fogón *m* ♦ *vt* (*place*) colocar; (*arrange*) arreglar ♦ *vi*: **to ~ over** (*extend*) extenderse por; **to ~ from ... to ...** oscilar entre ... y ...

ranger [reɪndʒə*] *n* guardabosques *m inv*

rank [ræŋk] *n* (*row*) fila; (*MIL*) rango; (*status*) categoría; (*BRIT: also: taxi ~*) parada de taxis ♦ *vi*: **to ~ among** figurar entre ♦ *adj* fétido, rancio; **the ~ and file** (*fig*) la base

ransack ['rænsæk] *vt* (*search*) registrar; (*plunder*) saquear

ransom ['rænsəm] *n* rescate *m*; **to hold to ~** (*fig*) hacer chantaje a

rant [rænt] *vi* divagar, desvariar

rap [ræp] *vt* golpear, dar un golpecito en ♦ *n* (*music*) rap *m*

rape [reɪp] *n* violación *f*; (*BOT*) colza ♦ *vt* violar; **~ (seed) oil** *n* aceite *m* de colza

rapid ['ræpɪd] *adj* rápido; **~ity** [rə'pɪdɪtɪ] *n* rapidez *f*; **~s** *npl* (*GEO*) rápidos *mpl*

rapist ['reɪpɪst] *n* violador *m*

rapport [ræ'pɔː*] *n* simpatía

rapturous ['ræptʃərəs] *adj* extático

rare [reə*] *adj* raro, poco común; (*CULIN: steak*) poco hecho

rarely ['reəlɪ] *adv* pocas veces

raring ['reərɪŋ] *adj*: **to be ~ to go** (*inf*) tener muchas ganas de empezar

rascal ['rɑːskl] *n* pillo, pícaro

rash [ræʃ] *adj* imprudente, precipitado ♦ *n* (*MED*) sarpullido, erupción *f* (*cutánea*); (*of events*) serie *f*

rasher ['ræʃə*] *n* lonja

raspberry ['rɑːzbərɪ] *n* frambuesa

rasping ['rɑːspɪŋ] *adj*: **a ~ noise** un ruido áspero

rat [ræt] *n* rata

rate [reɪt] *n* (*ratio*) razón *f*; (*price*) precio; (: *of hotel etc*) tarifa; (*of interest*) tipo; (*speed*) velocidad *f* ♦ *vt* (*value*) tasar; (*estimate*) estimar; **~s** *npl* (*BRIT: property tax*) impuesto municipal; (*fees*) tarifa; **to ~ sth/sb as** considerar algo/a uno como; **~able value** (*BRIT*) *n* valor *m* impuesto; **~payer** (*BRIT*) *n* contribuyente *m/f*

rather ['rɑːðə*] *adv*: **it's ~ expensive** es algo caro; (*too much*) es demasiado caro; (*to some extent*) más bien; **there's a lot buy bastante, I would** *or* **I'd ~ go** preferiría ir; **or ~** mejor dicho

rating ['reɪtɪŋ] *n* tasación *f*; (*score*) índice *m*; (*of ship*) clase *f*; **~s** *npl* (*RADIO, TV*) niveles *mpl* de audiencia

ratio ['reɪʃɪəu] *n* razón *f*; **in the ~ of 100 to 1** a razón de 100 a 1

ration ['ræʃən] *n* ración *f* ♦ *vt* racionar; **~s** *npl* víveres *mpl*

rational ['ræʃənl] *adj* (*solution, reasoning*) lógico, razonable; (*person*) cuerdo, sensato; **~e** [-'nɑːl] *n* razón *f* fundamental; **~ize** *vt* justificar

rat race *n* lucha incesante por la supervivencia

rattle ['rætl] *n* golpeteo; (*of train etc*) traqueteo; (*for baby*) sonaja, sonajero ♦ *vi* castañetear; (*car, bus*): **to ~ along** traquetear ♦ *vt* hacer sonar agitando; **~snake** *n* serpiente *f* de cascabel

raucous ['rɔːkəs] *adj* estridente, ronco

ravage ['rævɪdʒ] *vt* hacer estragos en, destrozar; **~s** *npl* estragos *mpl*

rave [reɪv] *vi* (*in anger*) encolerizarse; (*with enthusiasm*) entusiasmarse; (*MED*) delirar, desvariar ♦ *vi* (*inf: party*) rave *m*

raven ['reɪvən] *n* cuervo

ravenous ['rævənəs] *adj* hambriento

ravine [rə'viːn] *n* barranco

raving ['reɪvɪŋ] *adj*: **~ lunatic** loco/a de atar

ravishing ['rævɪʃɪŋ] *adj* encantador(a)

raw [rɔː] *adj* crudo; (*not processed*) bruto; (*sore*) vivo; (*inexperienced*) novato, inexperto; **~ deal** (*inf*) *n* injusticia; **~ material** *n* materia prima

ray [reɪ] *n* rayo; **~ of hope** (rayo de) esperanza

raze [reɪz] *vt* arrasar

razor ['reɪzə*] *n* (*open*) navaja; (*safety ~*) máquina de afeitar; (*electric ~*) máquina (eléctrica) de afeitar; **~ blade** *n* hoja de afeitar

Rd *abbr* = **road**

re [riː] *prep* con referencia a

reach [riːtʃ] *n* alcance *m*; (*of river etc*) extensión *f* entre dos recodos ♦ *vt* alcanzar, llegar a; (*achieve*) lograr ♦ *vi* extenderse; **within ~** al alcance (de la mano); **out of ~** fuera del alcance; **~ out** *vt* (*hand*) tender ♦ *vi*: **to ~ out for sth** alargar *or* tender la mano para tomar algo

react [riː'ækt] *vi* reaccionar; **~ion** [-'ækʃən] *n* reacción *f*

reactor [riː'æktə*] *n* (*also: nuclear ~*) reactor *m* (nuclear)

read [riːd, *pt, pp* red] (*pt, pp* **read**) *vi* leer ♦ *vt* leer; (*understand*) entender; (*study*) estudiar; **~ out** *vt* leer en alta voz; **~able** *adj* (*writing*) legible; (*book*) leíble; **~er** *n* lector(a) *m/f*; (*BRIT: at university*) profesor(a) *m/f* adjunto/a; **~ership** *n* (*of paper etc*) (número de) lectores *mpl*

readily ['redɪlɪ] *adv* (*willingly*) de buena gana; (*easily*) fácilmente; (*quickly*) en seguida

readiness ['redɪnɪs] *n* buena voluntad *f*; (*preparedness*) preparación *f*; **in ~** (*prepared*) listo, preparado

reading ['riːdɪŋ] *n* lectura; (*on instrument*) indicación *f*

ready ['redɪ] *adj* listo, preparado; (*willing*) dispuesto; (*available*) disponible ♦ *n*: **at the ~** (*MIL*) listo para tirar; **to get ~** *vi* prepararse ♦ *vt* preparar; **~-made** *adj* confeccionado; **~-to-wear** *adj* confeccionado

real [rɪəl] *adj* verdadero, auténtico; **in ~ terms** en términos reales; **~ estate** *n* bienes *mpl* raíces; **~istic** [-'lɪstɪk] *adj* realista

reality [riː'ælɪtɪ] *n* realidad *f*

realization [rɪəlaɪ'zeɪʃən] *n* comprensión *f*; (*fulfilment, COMM*) realización *f*

realize ['rɪəlaɪz] *vt* (*understand*) darse cuenta de

really ['rɪəlɪ] *adv* realmente; (*for emphasis*) verdaderamente; (*actually*): **what ~ happened** lo que pasó en realidad; **~?** ¿de veras?; **~!** (*annoyance*) ¡vamos!, ¡por favor!

realm [relm] *n* reino; (*fig*) esfera

realtor ® ['rɪəltɔː*] *n* (*US*) *n* corredor(a) *m/f* de bienes raíces

reap [riːp] *vt* segar; (*fig*) cosechar, recoger

reappear [riːə'pɪə*] *vi* reaparecer

rear [rɪə*] *adj* trasero ♦ *n* parte *f* trasera ♦ *vt* (*cattle, family*) criar ♦ *vi* (*also: ~ up*) (*animal*) encabritarse; **~guard** *n* retaguardia

rearmament [riː'ɑːməmənt] *n* rearme *m*

rearrange [riːə'reɪndʒ] *vt* ordenar *or* arreglar de nuevo

rear-view mirror *n* (*AUT*) (espejo) retrovisor *m*

reason ['riːzn] *n* razón *f* ♦ *vi*: **to ~ with sb** tratar de que uno entre en razón; **it stands to ~ that** es lógico que; **~able** *adj* razonable; (*sensible*) sensato; **~ably** *adv* razonablemente; **~ing** *n* razonamiento, argumentos *mpl*

reassurance [riːə'ʃuərəns] *n* consuelo

reassure [riːə'ʃuə*] *vt* tranquilizar, alentar; **to ~ sb that** tranquilizar a uno asegurando que

rebate ['riːbeɪt] *n* (*on tax etc*) desgravación *f*

rebel [*n* 'rebl, *vi* rɪ'bel] *n* rebelde *m/f* ♦ *vi* rebelarse, sublevarse; **~lious** [rɪ'beljəs] *adj* rebelde; (*child*) revoltoso

rebirth [ˈriːbɜːθ] *n* renacimiento

rebound [*vi* rɪˈbaʊnd, *n* ˈriːbaʊnd] *vi* (*ball*) rebotar ♦ *n* rebote *m*; **on the ~** (*also fig*) de rebote

rebuff [rɪˈbʌf] *n* desaire *m*, rechazo

rebuild [riːˈbɪld] (*irreg*) *vt* reconstruir

rebuke [rɪˈbjuːk] *n* reprimenda ♦ *vt* reprender

rebut [rɪˈbʌt] *vt* rebatir

recall [*vb* rɪˈkɔːl, *n* ˈriːkɔl] *vt* (*remember*) recordar; (*ambassador etc*) retirar ♦ *n* recuerdo; retirada

recap [ˈriːkæp], **recapitulate** [riːkəˈpɪtjuleɪt] *vt*, *vi* recapitular

rec'd *abbr* (= *received*) rbdo

recede [rɪˈsiːd] *vi* (*memory*) ir borrándose; (*hair*) retroceder; **receding** *adj* (*forehead, chin*) huidizo; **to have a receding hairline** tener entradas

receipt [rɪˈsiːt] *n* (*document*) recibo; (*for parcel etc*) acuse *m* de recibo; (*act of receiving*) recepción *f*; **~s** *npl* (*COMM*) ingresos *mpl*

receive [rɪˈsiːv] *vt* recibir; (*guest*) acoger; (*wound*) sufrir; **~r** *n* (*TEL*) auricular *m*; (*RADIO*) receptor *m*; (*of stolen goods*) perista *m/f*; (*COMM*) administrador *m* jurídico

recent [ˈriːsnt] *adj* reciente; **~ly** *adv* recientemente; **~ly arrived** recién llegado

receptacle [rɪˈseptɪkl] *n* receptáculo

reception [rɪˈsepʃən] *n* recepción *f*; (*welcome*) acogida; **~ desk** *n* recepción *f*; **~ist** *n* recepcionista *m/f*

recess [rɪˈses] *n* (*in room*) hueco; (*for bed*) nicho; (*secret place*) escondrijo; (*POL etc*: *holiday*) clausura

recession [rɪˈseʃən] *n* recesión *f*

recipe [ˈresɪpɪ] *n* receta; (*for disaster, success*) fórmula

recipient [rɪˈsɪpɪənt] *n* recibidor(a) *m/f*; (*of letter*) destinatario/a

recital [rɪˈsaɪtl] *n* recital *m*

recite [rɪˈsaɪt] *vt* (*poem*) recitar

reckless [ˈrekləs] *adj* temerario, imprudente; (*driving, driver*) peligroso; **~ly** *adv* imprudentemente; de modo peligroso

reckon [ˈrekən] *vt* calcular; (*consider*) considerar; (*think*): **I ~ that ...** me parece que ...; **~ on** *vt fus* contar con; **~ing** *n* cálculo

reclaim [rɪˈkleɪm] *vt* (*land, waste*) recuperar; (*land: from sea*) rescatar; (*demand back*) reclamar

reclamation [rekləˈmeɪʃən] *n* (*of land*) acondicionamiento de tierras

recline [rɪˈklaɪn] *vi* reclinarse; **reclining** *adj* (*seat*) reclinable

recluse [rɪˈkluːs] *n* recluso/a

recognition [rekəgˈnɪʃən] *n* reconocimiento; **transformed beyond ~** irreconocible

recognizable [ˈrekəgnaɪzəbl] *adj*: **~ (by)** reconocible (por)

recognize [ˈrekəgnaɪz] *vt*: **to ~ (by/as)** reconocer (por/como)

recoil [*vi* rɪˈkɔɪl, *n* ˈriːkɔɪl] *vi* (*person*): **to ~ from doing sth** retraerse de hacer algo ♦ *n* (*of gun*) retroceso

recollect [rekəˈlekt] *vt* recordar, acordarse de; **~ion** [-ˈlekʃən] *n* recuerdo

recommend [rekəˈmend] *vt* recomendar

reconcile [ˈrekənsaɪl] *vt* (*two people*) reconciliar; (*two facts*) compaginar; **to ~ o.s. to sth** conformarse a algo

recondition [riːkənˈdɪʃən] *vt* (*machine*) reacondicionar

reconnoitre [rekəˈnɔɪtə*] (*US* **reconnoiter**) *vt*, *vi* (*MIL*) reconocer

reconsider [riːkənˈsɪdə*] *vt* repensar

reconstruct [riːkənˈstrʌkt] *vt* reconstruir

record [*n* ˈrekɔːd, *vt* rɪˈkɔːd] *n* (*MUS*) disco; (*of meeting etc*) acta; (*register*) registro, partida; (*file*) archivo; (*also: criminal ~*) antecedentes *mpl*; (*written*) expediente *m*; (*SPORT, COMPUT*) récord *m* ♦ *vt* registrar; (*MUS: song etc*) grabar; **in ~ time** en un tiempo récord; **off the ~** *adj* no oficial ♦ *adv* confidencialmente; **~ card** *n* (*in file*) ficha; **~ed delivery** (*BRIT*) *n* (*POST*) entrega con acuse de recibo; **~er** *n* (*MUS*) flauta de pico; **~ holder** *n* (*SPORT*) actual poseedor(a) *m/f* del récord; **~ing** *n* (*MUS*) grabación *f*; **~ player** *n* tocadiscos *m inv*

recount [rɪˈkaʊnt] *vt* contar

re-count [ˈriːkaʊnt] *n* (*POL: of votes*) segundo escrutinio

recoup [rɪˈkuːp] *vt*: **to ~ one's losses** recuperar las pérdidas

recourse [rɪˈkɔːs] *n*: **to have ~ to** recurrir a

recover [rɪˈkʌvə*] *vt* recuperar ♦ *vi* (*from illness, shock*) recuperarse; **~y** *n* recuperación *f*

recreation [rekrɪˈeɪʃən] *n* recreo; **~al** *adj* de recreo; **~al drug** droga recreativa

recruit [rɪˈkruːt] *n* recluta *m/f* ♦ *vt* reclutar; (*staff*) contratar

rectangle [ˈrektæŋgl] *n* rectángulo; **rectangular** [-ˈtæŋgjulə*] *adj* rectangular

rectify [ˈrektɪfaɪ] *vt* rectificar

rector [ˈrektə*] *n* (*REL*) párroco; **~y** *n* casa del párroco

recuperate [rɪˈkuːpəreɪt] *vi* reponerse, restablecerse

recur [rɪˈkəː*] *vi* repetirse; (*pain, illness*) producirse de nuevo; **~rence** [rɪˈkʌrəns] *n* repetición *f*; **~rent** [rɪˈkʌrənt] *adj* repetido

recycle [riːˈsaɪkl] *vt* reciclar

red [red] *n* rojo ♦ *adj* rojo; (*hair*) pelirrojo; (*wine*) tinto; **to be in the ~** (*account*) estar en números rojos; (*business*) tener un saldo

negativo; **to give sb the ~ carpet treatment**
recibir a uno con todos los honores;
R~ Cross n Cruz f Roja; **~currant** n grosella
roja; **~den** vt enrojecer ♦ vi enrojecerse
redeem [rɪ'diːm] vt redimir; (*promises*)
cumplir; (*sth in pawn*) desempeñar; (*fig, also*
REL) rescatar; **~ing** adj: **~ing feature** rasgo
bueno or favorable
redeploy [riːdɪ'plɔɪ] vt (*resources*) reorganizar
red: **~-haired** adj pelirrojo; **~-handed** adj: **to**
be caught ~-handed cogerse (*SP*) or pillarse
(*AM*) con las manos en la masa; **~head** n
pelirrojo/a; **~ herring** n (*fig*) pista falsa; **~-**
hot adj candente
redirect [riːdaɪ'rekt] vt (*mail*) reexpedir
red light n: **to go through a ~** (*AUT*) pasar la
luz roja; **red-light district** n barrio chino
redo [riː'duː] (*irreg*) vt rehacer
redress [rɪ'dres] vt reparar
Red Sea n: **the ~** el mar Rojo
redskin ['redskɪn] n piel roja m/f
red tape n (*fig*) trámites mpl
reduce [rɪ'djuːs] vt reducir; **to ~ sb to tears**
hacer llorar a uno; **to be ~d to begging** no
quedarle a uno otro remedio que pedir
limosna; "**~ speed now**" (*AUT*) "reduzca la
velocidad"; **at a ~d price** (*of goods*) (a precio)
rebajado; **reduction** [rɪ'dʌkʃən] n reducción
f; (*of price*) rebaja; (*discount*) descuento;
(*smaller-scale copy*) copia reducida
redundancy [rɪ'dʌndənsɪ] n (*dismissal*)
despido; (*unemployment*) desempleo
redundant [rɪ'dʌndnt] adj (*BRIT*: *worker*)
parado, sin trabajo; (*detail, object*) superfluo;
to be made ~ quedar(se) sin trabajo
reed [riːd] n (*BOT*) junco, caña; (*MUS*)
lengüeta
reef [riːf] n (*at sea*) arrecife m
reek [riːk] vi: **to ~ (of)** apestar (a)
reel [riːl] n carrete m, bobina; (*of film*) rollo;
(*dance*) baile m escocés ♦ vt (*also: ~ up*)
devanar; (*also: ~ in*) sacar ♦ vi (*sway*)
tambalear(se)
ref [ref] (*inf*) n abbr = **referee**
refectory [rɪ'fektərɪ] n comedor m
refer [rɪ'fəː*] vt (*send: patient*) referir;
(: *matter*) remitir ♦ vi: **to ~ to** (*allude to*)
referirse a, aludir a; (*apply to*) relacionarse
con; (*consult*) consultar
referee [refə'riː] n árbitro; (*BRIT*: *for job*
application): **to be a ~ for sb** proporcionar
referencias a uno ♦ vt (*match*) arbitrar en
reference ['refrəns] n referencia; (*for job*
application: *letter*) carta de recomendación;
with ~ to (*COMM*: *in letter*) me remito a;
~ book n libro de consulta; **~ number** n
número de referencia
refill [vt riː'fɪl, n rɪ'riːfɪl] vt rellenar ♦ n
repuesto, recambio

refine [rɪ'faɪn] vt refinar; **~d** adj (*person*) fino;
~ment n cultura, educación f; (*of system*)
refinamiento
reflect [rɪ'flekt] vt reflejar ♦ vi (*think*)
reflexionar, pensar; **it ~s badly/well on him** le
perjudica/le hace honor; **~ion** [-'flekʃən] n
(*act*) reflexión f; (*image*) reflejo; (*criticism*)
crítica; **on ~ion** pensándolo bien; **~or** n (*AUT*)
captafaros m inv; (*of light, heat*) reflector m
reflex ['riːfleks] adj, n reflejo; **~ive** [rɪ'fleksɪv]
adj (*LING*) reflexivo
reform [rɪ'fɔːm] n reforma ♦ vt reformar;
~atory (*US*) n reformatorio
refrain [rɪ'freɪn] vi: **to ~ from doing**
abstenerse de hacer ♦ n estribillo
refresh [rɪ'freʃ] vt refrescar; **~er course**
(*BRIT*) n curso de repaso; **~ing** adj
refrescante; **~ments** npl refrescos mpl
refrigerator [rɪ'frɪdʒəreɪtə*] n nevera (*SP*),
refrigeradora (*AM*)
refuel [riː'fjuəl] vi repostar (combustible)
refuge ['refjuːdʒ] n refugio, asilo; **to take ~ in**
refugiarse en
refugee [refju'dʒiː] n refugiado/a
refund [n 'riːfʌnd, vb rɪ'fʌnd] n reembolso
♦ vt devolver, reembolsar
refurbish [riː'fɜːbɪʃ] vt restaurar, renovar
refusal [rɪ'fjuːzəl] n negativa; **to have first**
~ on tener la primera opción a
refuse[1] ['refjuːs] n basura; **~ collection** n
recolección f de basuras
refuse[2] [rɪ'fjuːz] vt rechazar; (*invitation*)
declinar; (*permission*) denegar ♦ vi: **to ~ to**
do sth negarse a hacer algo; (*horse*) rehusar
regain [rɪ'geɪn] vt recobrar, recuperar
regal ['riːgl] adj regio, real
regard [rɪ'gɑːd] n mirada; (*esteem*) respeto;
(*attention*) consideración f ♦ vt (*consider*)
considerar; **to give one's ~s to** saludar de su
parte a; "**with kindest ~s**" "con muchos
recuerdos"; **~ing, as ~s, with ~ to** con
respecto a, en cuanto a; **~less** adv a pesar de
todo; **~less of** sin reparar en
régime [reɪ'ʒiːm] n régimen m
regiment ['redʒɪmənt] n regimiento; **~al**
[-'mentl] adj militar
region ['riːdʒən] n región f; **in the ~ of** (*fig*)
alrededor de; **~al** adj regional
register ['redʒɪstə*] n registro ♦ vt registrar;
(*birth*) declarar; (*car*) matricular; (*letter*)
certificar; (*subj: instrument*) marcar, indicar
♦ vi (*at hotel*) registrarse; (*as student*)
matricularse; (*make impression*) producir
impresión; **~ed** adj (*letter, parcel*) certificado;
~ed trademark n marca registrada
registrar ['redʒɪstrɑː*] n secretario/a (del
registro civil)
registration [redʒɪs'treɪʃən] n (*act*)
declaración f; (*AUT: also: ~ number*) matrícula

registry ['redʒɪstrɪ] *n* registro; **~ office** (*BRIT*) *n* registro civil; **to get married in a ~ office** casarse por lo civil

regret [rɪ'gret] *n* sentimiento, pesar *m* ♦ *vt* sentir, lamentar; **~fully** *adv* con pesar; **~table** *adj* lamentable

regular ['regjulə*] *adj* regular; (*soldier*) profesional; (*usual*) habitual; (*: doctor*) de cabecera ♦ *n* (*client etc*) cliente/a *m/f* habitual; **~ly** *adv* con regularidad; (*often*) repetidas veces

regulate ['regjuleɪt] *vt* controlar; **regulation** [-'leɪʃən] *n* (*rule*) regla, reglamento

rehearsal [rɪ'hɜːsəl] *n* ensayo

rehearse [rɪ'hɜːs] *vt* ensayar

reign [reɪn] *n* reinado; (*fig*) predominio ♦ *vi* reinar; (*fig*) imperar

reimburse [riːɪm'bɜːs] *vt* reembolsar

rein [reɪn] *n* (*for horse*) rienda

reindeer ['reɪndɪə*] *n inv* reno

reinforce [riːɪn'fɔːs] *vt* reforzar; **~d concrete** *n* hormigón *m* armado; **~ments** *npl* (*MIL*) refuerzos *mpl*

reinstate [riːɪn'steɪt] *vt* reintegrar; (*tax, law*) reinstaurar

reiterate [riː'ɪtəreɪt] *vt* reiterar, repetir

reject [*n* 'riːdʒekt, *vb* rɪ'dʒekt] *n* (*thing*) desecho ♦ *vt* rechazar; (*suggestion*) descartar; (*coin*) expulsar; **~ion** [rɪ'dʒekʃən] *n* rechazo

rejoice [rɪ'dʒɔɪs] *vi*: **to ~ at** or **over** regocijarse or alegrarse de

rejuvenate [rɪ'dʒuːvəneɪt] *vt* rejuvenecer

relapse [rɪ'læps] *n* recaída

relate [rɪ'leɪt] *vt* (*tell*) contar, relatar; (*connect*) relacionar ♦ *vi* relacionarse; **~d** *adj* afín; (*person*) emparentado; **~d to** (*subject*) relacionado con, **relating to** *prep* referente a

relation [rɪ'leɪʃən] *n* (*person*) familiar *m/f*, pariente/a *m/f*; (*link*) relación *f*; **~s** *npl* (*relatives*) familiares *mpl*; **~ship** *n* relación *f*; (*personal*) relaciones *fpl*; (*also*: **family ~ship**) parentesco

relative ['relətɪv] *n* pariente/a *m/f*, familiar *m/f* ♦ *adj* relativo; **~ly** *adv* (*comparatively*) relativamente

relax [rɪ'læks] *vi* descansar; (*unwind*) relajarse ♦ *vt* (*one's grip*) soltar, aflojar; (*control*) relajar; (*mind, person*) descansar; **~ation** [riːlæk'seɪʃən] *n* descanso; (*of rule, control*) relajamiento; (*entertainment*) diversión *f*; **~ed** *adj* relajado; (*tranquil*) tranquilo; **~ing** *adj* relajante

relay ['riːleɪ] *n* (*race*) carrera de relevos ♦ *vt* (*RADIO, TV*) retransmitir

release [rɪ'liːs] *n* (*liberation*) liberación *f*; (*from prison*) puesta en libertad; (*of gas etc*) escape *m*; (*of film etc*) estreno; (*of record*) lanzamiento ♦ *vt* (*prisoner*) poner en libertad; (*gas*) despedir, arrojar; (*from wreckage*)

soltar; (*catch, spring etc*) desenganchar; (*film*) estrenar; (*book*) publicar; (*news*) difundir

relegate ['relɪgeɪt] *vt* relegar; (*BRIT: SPORT*): **to be ~d to** bajar a

relent [rɪ'lent] *vi* ablandarse; **~less** *adj* implacable

relevant ['relɪvənt] *adj* (*fact*) pertinente; **~ to** relacionado con

reliable [rɪ'laɪəbl] *adj* (*person, firm*) de confianza, de fiar; (*method, machine*) seguro; (*source*) fidedigno; **reliably** *adv*: **to be reliably informed that ...** saber de fuente fidedigna que ...

reliance [rɪ'laɪəns] *n*: **~ (on)** dependencia (de)

relic ['relɪk] *n* (*REL*) reliquia; (*of the past*) vestigio

relief [rɪ'liːf] *n* (*from pain, anxiety*) alivio; (*help, supplies*) socorro, ayuda; (*ART, GEO*) relieve *m*

relieve [rɪ'liːv] *vt* (*pain*) aliviar; (*bring help to*) ayudar, socorrer; (*take over from*) sustituir; (*: guard*) relevar; **to ~ sb of sth** quitar algo a uno; **to ~ o.s.** hacer sus necesidades

religion [rɪ'lɪdʒən] *n* religión *f*; **religious** *adj* religioso

relinquish [rɪ'lɪŋkwɪʃ] *vt* abandonar; (*plan, habit*) renunciar a

relish ['relɪʃ] *n* (*CULIN*) salsa; (*enjoyment*) entusiasmo ♦ *vt* (*food etc*) saborear; (*enjoy*): **to ~ sth** hacerle mucha ilusión a uno algo

relocate [riːləu'keɪt] *vt* cambiar de lugar, mudar ♦ *vi* mudarse

reluctance [rɪ'lʌktəns] *n* renuencia

reluctant [rɪ'lʌktənt] *adj* renuente; **~ly** *adv* de mala gana

rely on [rɪ'laɪ-] *vt fus* depender de; (*trust*) contar con

remain [rɪ'meɪn] *vi* (*survive*) quedar; (*be left*) sobrar; (*continue*) quedar(se), permanecer; **~der** *n* resto; **~ing** *adj* que queda(n); (*surviving*) restante(s); **~s** *npl* restos *mpl*

remand [rɪ'mɑːnd] *n*: **on ~** detenido (bajo custodia) ♦ *vt*: **to be ~ed in custody** quedar detenido bajo custodia; **~ home** (*BRIT*) *n* reformatorio

remark [rɪ'mɑːk] *n* comentario ♦ *vt* comentar; **~able** *adj* (*outstanding*) extraordinario

remarry [riː'mærɪ] *vi* volver a casarse

remedial [rɪ'miːdɪəl] *adj* de recuperación

remedy ['remədɪ] *n* remedio ♦ *vt* remediar, curar

remember [rɪ'membə*] *vt* recordar, acordarse de; (*bear in mind*) tener presente; (*send greetings to*): **~ me to him** dale recuerdos de mi parte; **remembrance** *n* recuerdo; **R~ Day** *n* ≈ día en el que se recuerda a los caídos en las dos guerras mundiales

remind [rɪ'maɪnd] vt: **to ~ sb to do sth** recordar a uno que haga algo; **to ~ sb of sth** (of fact) recordar algo a uno; **she ~s me of her mother** me recuerda a su madre; **~er** n notificación f; (memento) recuerdo

reminisce [remɪ'nɪs] vi recordar (viejas historias); **reminiscent** adj: **to be reminiscent of sth** recordar algo

remiss [rɪ'mɪs] adj descuidado; **it was ~ of him** fue un descuido de su parte

remission [rɪ'mɪʃən] n remisión f; (of prison sentence) disminución f de pena; (REL) perdón m

remit [rɪ'mɪt] vt (send: money) remitir, enviar; **~tance** n remesa, envío

remnant ['remnənt] n resto; (of cloth) retal m; **~s** npl (COMM) restos mpl de serie

remorse [rɪ'mɔːs] n remordimientos mpl; **~ful** adj arrepentido; **~less** adj (fig) implacable, inexorable

remote [rɪ'məut] adj (distant) lejano; (person) distante; **~ control** n telecontrol m; **~ly** adv remotamente; (slightly) levemente

remould ['riːməuld] (BRIT) n (tyre) neumático or llanta (AM) recauchutado/a

removable [rɪ'muːvəbl] adj (detachable) separable

removal [rɪ'muːvəl] n (taking away) el quitar; (BRIT: from house) mudanza; (from office: dismissal) destitución f; (MED) extirpación f; **~ van** (BRIT) n camión m de mudanzas

remove [rɪ'muːv] vt quitar; (employee) destituir; (name: from list) tachar, borrar; (doubt) disipar; (abuse) suprimir, acabar con; (MED) extirpar

Renaissance [rɪ'neɪsãs] n: **the ~** el Renacimiento

render ['rendə*] vt (thanks) dar; (aid) proporcionar, prestar; (make): **to ~ sth useless** hacer algo inútil; **~ing** n (MUS etc) interpretación f

rendezvous ['rɒndɪvuː] n cita

renew [rɪ'njuː] vt renovar; (resume) reanudar; (loan etc) prorrogar; **~able** adj renovable; **~al** n reanudación f; prórroga

renounce [rɪ'nauns] vt renunciar a; (right, inheritance) renunciar

renovate ['renəveɪt] vt renovar

renown [rɪ'naun] n renombre m; **~ed** adj renombrado

rent [rent] n (for house) arriendo, renta ♦ vt alquilar; **~al** n (for television, car) alquiler m

rep [rep] n abbr = **representative**; **repertory**

repair [rɪ'pɛə*] n reparación f, compostura ♦ vt reparar, componer; (shoes) remendar; **in good/bad ~** en buen/mal estado; **~ kit** n caja de herramientas

repatriate [riːpætrɪ'eɪt] vt repatriar

repay [riː'peɪ] (irreg) vt (money) devolver, reembolsar; (person) pagar; (debt) liquidar; (sb's efforts) devolver, corresponder a; **~ment** n reembolso, devolución f; (sum of money) recompensa

repeal [rɪ'piːl] n revocación f ♦ vt revocar

repeat [rɪ'piːt] n (RADIO, TV) reposición f ♦ vt repetir ♦ vi repetirse; **~edly** adv repetidas veces

repel [rɪ'pel] vt (drive away) rechazar; (disgust) repugnar; **~lent** adj repugnante ♦ n: insect **~lent** crema (or loción f) anti-insectos

repent [rɪ'pent] vi: **to ~ (of)** arrepentirse (de); **~ance** n arrepentimiento

repercussions [riːpə'kʌʃənz] npl consecuencias fpl

repertory ['repətəri] n (also: ~ theatre) teatro de repertorio

repetition [repɪ'tɪʃən] n repetición f

repetitive [rɪ'petɪtɪv] adj repetitivo

replace [rɪ'pleɪs] vt (put back) devolver a su sitio; (take the place of) reemplazar, sustituir; **~ment** n (act) reposición f; (thing) recambio; (person) suplente m/f

replay ['riːpleɪ] n (SPORT) desempate m; (of tape, film) repetición f

replenish [rɪ'plenɪʃ] vt rellenar; (stock etc) reponer

replica ['replɪkə] n copia, reproducción f (exacta)

reply [rɪ'plaɪ] n respuesta, contestación f ♦ vi contestar, responder

report [rɪ'pɔːt] n informe m; (PRESS etc) reportaje m; (BRIT: also: school ~) boletín m escolar; (of gun) estallido ♦ vt informar de; (PRESS etc) hacer un reportaje sobre; (notify: accident, culprit) denunciar ♦ vi (make a report) presentar un informe; (present o.s.): **to ~ (to sb)** presentarse (ante uno); **~ card** n (US, Scottish) cartilla escolar; **~edly** adv según se dice; **~er** n periodista m/f

repose [rɪ'pəuz] n: **in ~** (face, mouth) en reposo

reprehensible [reprɪ'hensɪbl] adj reprensible, censurable

represent [reprɪ'zent] vt representar; (COMM) ser agente de; (describe): **to ~ sth as** describir algo como; **~ation** [-'teɪʃən] n representación f; **~ations** npl (protest) quejas fpl; **~ative** n representante m/f; (US: POL) diputado/a m/f ♦ adj representativo

repress [rɪ'pres] vt reprimir; **~ion** [-'preʃən] n represión f

reprieve [rɪ'priːv] n (LAW) indulto; (fig) alivio

reprisals [rɪ'praɪzlz] npl represalias fpl

reproach [rɪ'prəutʃ] n reproche m ♦ vt: **to ~ sb for sth** reprochar algo a uno; **~ful** adj de reproche, de acusación

reproduce [ri:prə'dju:s] vt reproducir ♦ vi reproducirse; **reproduction** [-'dʌkʃən] n reproducción f

reprove [rɪ'pru:v] vt: **to ~ sb for sth** reprochar algo a uno

reptile ['reptaɪl] n reptil m

republic [rɪ'pʌblɪk] n república f; **~an** adj, n republicano/a m/f

repudiate [rɪ'pju:dɪeɪt] vt rechazar; (violence etc) repudiar

repulsive [rɪ'pʌlsɪv] adj repulsivo

reputable ['repjutəbl] adj (make etc) de renombre

reputation [repju'teɪʃən] n reputación f

reputed [rɪ'pju:tɪd] adj supuesto; **~ly** adv según dicen or se dice

request [rɪ'kwest] n petición f; (formal) solicitud f ♦ vt: **to ~ sth of or from sb** solicitar algo a uno; **~ stop** (BRIT) n parada discrecional

require [rɪ'kwaɪə*] vt (need: subj: person) necesitar, tener necesidad de; (: thing, situation) exigir; (want) pedir; **to ~ sb to do sth** pedir a uno que haga algo; **~ment** n requisito; (need) necesidad f

requisition [rekwɪ'zɪʃən] n: **~ (for)** solicitud f (de) ♦ vt (MIL) requisar

rescue ['reskju:] n rescate m ♦ vt rescatar; **~ party** n expedición f de salvamento; **~r** n salvador(a) m/f

research [rɪ'sɜ:tʃ] n investigaciones fpl ♦ vt investigar; **~er** n investigador(a) m/f

resemblance [rɪ'zembləns] n parecido

resemble [rɪ'zembl] vt parecerse a

resent [rɪ'zent] vt tomar a mal; **~ful** adj resentido; **~ment** n resentimiento

reservation [rezə'veɪʃən] n reserva

reserve [rɪ'zɜ:v] n reserva; (SPORT) suplente m/f ♦ vt (seats etc) reservar; **~s** npl (MIL) reserva; **in ~** de reserva; **~d** adj reservado

reshuffle [ri:'ʃʌfl] n: **Cabinet ~** (POL) remodelación f del gabinete

residence ['rezɪdəns] n (formal: home) domicilio; (length of stay) permanencia; **~ permit** (BRIT) n permiso de permanencia

resident ['rezɪdənt] n (of area) vecino/a; (in hotel) huésped(a) m/f ♦ adj (population) permanente; (doctor) residente; **~ial** [-'denʃəl] adj residencial

residue ['rezɪdju:] n resto

resign [rɪ'zaɪn] vt renunciar a ♦ vi dimitir; **to ~ o.s. to** (situation) resignarse a; **~ation** [rezɪg'neɪʃən] n dimisión f; (state of mind) resignación f; **~ed** adj resignado

resilient [rɪ'zɪlɪənt] adj (material) elástico; (person) resistente

resist [rɪ'zɪst] vt resistir, oponerse a; **~ance** n resistencia

resolute ['rezəlu:t] adj resuelto; (refusal) tajante

resolution [rezə'lu:ʃən] n (gen) resolución f

resolve [rɪ'zɒlv] n resolución f ♦ vt resolver ♦ vi: **to ~ to do** resolver hacer; **~d** adj resuelto

resort [rɪ'zɔ:t] n (town) centro turístico; (recourse) recurso ♦ vi: **to ~ to** recurrir a; **in the last ~** como último recurso

resounding [rɪ'zaundɪŋ] adj sonoro; (fig) clamoroso

resource [rɪ'sɔ:s] n recurso; **~s** npl recursos mpl; **~ful** adj despabilado, ingenioso

respect [rɪs'pekt] n respeto ♦ vt respetar; **~s** npl recuerdos mpl, saludos mpl; **with ~ to** con respecto a; **in this ~** en cuanto a eso; **~able** adj respetable; (large: amount) apreciable; (passable) tolerable; **~ful** adj respetuoso

respective [rɪs'pektɪv] adj respectivo; **~ly** adv respectivamente

respite ['respaɪt] n respiro

respond [rɪs'pɒnd] vi responder; (react) reaccionar; **response** [-'pɒns] n respuesta; reacción f

responsibility [rɪspɒnsɪ'bɪlɪtɪ] n responsabilidad f

responsible [rɪs'pɒnsɪbl] adj (character) serio, formal; (job) de confianza; (liable): **~ (for)** responsable (de)

responsive [rɪs'pɒnsɪv] adj sensible

rest [rest] n descanso, reposo; (MUS, pause) pausa, silencio; (support) apoyo; (remainder) resto ♦ vi descansar; (be supported): **to ~ on** descansar sobre ♦ vt (lean): **to ~ sth on/against** apoyar algo en or sobre/contra; **the ~ of them** (people, objects) los demás; **it ~s with him to ...** depende de él el que ...

restaurant ['restərən] n restaurante m; **~ car** (BRIT) n (RAIL) coche-comedor m

restful ['restful] adj descansado, tranquilo

rest home n residencia para jubilados

restive ['restɪv] adj inquieto; (horse) rebelón(ona)

restless ['restlɪs] adj inquieto

restoration [restə'reɪʃən] n restauración f; devolución f

restore [rɪ'stɔ:*] vt (building) restaurar; (sth stolen) devolver; (health) restablecer; (to power) volver a poner a

restrain [rɪs'treɪn] vt (feeling) contener, refrenar; (person): **to ~ (from doing)** disuadir (de hacer); **~ed** adj (style) reservado; **~t** n (restriction) restricción f; (moderation) moderación f; (of manner) reserva

restrict [rɪs'trɪkt] vt restringir, limitar; **~ion** [-kʃən] n restricción f, limitación f; **~ive** adj restrictivo

rest room (US) n aseos mpl

result [rɪ'zʌlt] n resultado ♦ vi: **to ~ in** terminar en, tener por resultado; **as a ~ of a**

361   **resume → revolving**

consecuencia de

resume [rɪ'zju:m] vt reanudar ♦ vi comenzar de nuevo

résumé ['reɪzju:meɪ] n resumen m; (US) currículum m

resumption [rɪ'zʌmpʃən] n reanudación f

resurgence [rɪ'sə:dʒəns] n resurgimiento

resurrection [rezə'rekʃən] n resurrección f

resuscitate [rɪ'sʌsɪteɪt] vt (MED) resucitar

retail ['ri:teɪl] adj, adv al por menor; **~er** n detallista m/f; **~ price** n precio de venta al público

retain [rɪ'teɪn] vt (keep) retener, conservar; **~er** n (fee) anticipo

retaliate [rɪ'tælɪeɪt] vi: **to ~ (against)** tomar represalias (contra); **retaliation** [-'eɪʃən] n represalias fpl

retarded [rɪ'tɑ:dɪd] adj retrasado

retch [retʃ] vi dársele a uno arcadas

retentive [rɪ'tentɪv] adj (memory) retentivo

retire [rɪ'taɪə*] vi (give up work) jubilarse; (withdraw) retirarse; (go to bed) acostarse; **~d** adj (person) jubilado; **~ment** n (giving up work: state) retiro; (: act) jubilación f; **retiring** adj (leaving) saliente; (shy) retraído

retort [rɪ'tɔ:t] vi contestar

retrace [ri:'treɪs] vt: **to ~ one's steps** volver sobre sus pasos, desandar lo andado

retract [rɪ'trækt] vt (statement) retirar; (claws) retraer; (undercarriage, aerial) replegar

retrain [ri:'treɪn] vt reciclar; **~ing** n readaptación f profesional

retread ['ri:tred] n neumático (SP) or llanta (AM) recauchutado/a

retreat [rɪ'tri:t] n (place) retiro; (MIL) retirada ♦ vi retirarse

retribution [retrɪ'bju:ʃən] n desquite m

retrieval [rɪ'tri:vəl] n recuperación f

retrieve [rɪ'tri:v] vt recobrar; (situation, honour) salvar; (COMPUT) recuperar; (error) reparar; **~r** n perro cobrador

retrospect ['retrəspekt] n: **in ~** retrospectivamente; **~ive** [-'spektɪv] adj retrospectivo; (law) retroactivo

return [rɪ'tə:n] n (going or coming back) vuelta, regreso; (of sth stolen etc) devolución f; (FINANCE: from land, shares) ganancia, ingresos mpl ♦ cpd (journey) de regreso; (BRIT: ticket) de ida y vuelta; (match) de vuelta ♦ vi (person etc: come or go back) volver, regresar; (symptoms etc) reaparecer; (regain): **to ~ to** recuperar ♦ vt devolver; (favour, love etc) corresponder a; (verdict) pronunciar; (POL: candidate) elegir; **~s** npl (COMM) ingresos mpl; **in ~ (for)** a cambio (de); **by ~ of post** a vuelta de correo; **many happy ~s (of the day)!** ¡feliz cumpleaños!

reunion [ri:'ju:nɪən] n (of family) reunión f; (of two people, school) reencuentro

reunite [ri:ju:'naɪt] vt reunir; (reconcile) reconciliar

rev [rev] (AUT) n abbr (= revolution) revolución f ♦ vt (also: ~ up) acelerar

reveal [rɪ'vi:l] vt revelar; **~ing** adj revelador(a)

revel ['revl] vi: **to ~ in sth/in doing sth** gozar de algo/con hacer algo

revenge [rɪ'vendʒ] n venganza; **to take ~ on** vengarse de

revenue ['revənju:] n ingresos mpl, rentas fpl

reverberate [rɪ'və:bəreɪt] vi (sound) resonar, retumbar; (fig: shock) repercutir

reverence ['revərəns] n reverencia

Reverend ['revərənd] adj (in titles): **the ~ John Smith** (Anglican) el Reverendo John Smith; (Catholic) el Padre John Smith; (Protestant) el Pastor John Smith

reversal [rɪ'və:sl] n (of order) inversión f; (of direction, policy) cambio; (of decision) revocación f

reverse [rɪ'və:s] n (opposite) contrario; (back: of cloth) revés m; (: of coin) reverso; (: of paper) dorso; (AUT: also: ~ gear) marcha atrás; (setback) revés m ♦ adj (order) inverso; (direction) contrario; (process) opuesto ♦ vt (decision, AUT) dar marcha atrás a; (position, function) invertir ♦ vi (BRIT: AUT) dar marcha atrás; **~-charge call** (BRIT) n llamada a cobro revertido; **reversing lights** (BRIT) npl (AUT) luces fpl de retroceso

revert [rɪ'və:t] vi: **to ~ to** volver a

review [rɪ'vju:] n (magazine, MIL) revista; (of book, film) reseña; (US: examination) repaso, examen m ♦ vt repasar, examinar; (MIL) pasar revista a; (book, film) reseñar; **~er** n crítico/a

revise [rɪ'vaɪz] vt (manuscript) corregir; (opinion) modificar; (price, procedure) revisar ♦ vi (study) repasar; **revision** [rɪ'vɪʒən] n corrección f; modificación f; (for exam) repaso

revival [rɪ'vaɪvəl] n (recovery) reanimación f; (of interest) renacimiento; (THEATRE) reestreno; (of faith) despertar m

revive [rɪ'vaɪv] vt resucitar; (custom) restablecer; (hope) despertar; (play) reestrenar ♦ vi (person) volver en sí; (business) reactivarse

revolt [rɪ'vəult] n rebelión f ♦ vi rebelarse, sublevarse ♦ vt dar asco a, repugnar; **~ing** adj asqueroso, repugnante

revolution [revə'lu:ʃən] n revolución f; **~ary** adj, n revolucionario/a m/f; **~ize** vt revolucionar

revolve [rɪ'vɒlv] vi dar vueltas, girar; (life, discussion): **to ~ (a)round** girar en torno a

revolver [rɪ'vɒlvə*] n revólver m

revolving [rɪ'vɒlvɪŋ] adj (chair, door etc) giratorio

revue [rɪ'vjuː] n (THEATRE) revista

revulsion [rɪ'vʌlʃən] n asco, repugnancia

reward [rɪ'wɔːd] n premio, recompensa ♦ vt:
to ~ (for) recompensar or premiar (por);
~ing adj (fig) valioso

rewind [riː'waɪnd] (irreg) vt rebobinar

rewire [riː'waɪə*] vt (house) renovar la
instalación eléctrica de

rheumatism ['ruːmətɪzəm] n reumatismo,
reúma m

Rhine [raɪn] n: **the ~** el (río) Rin

rhinoceros [raɪ'nɔsərəs] n rinoceronte m

rhododendron [rəʊdə'dɛndrn] n
rododendro

Rhone [rəʊn] n: **the ~** el (río) Ródano

rhubarb ['ruːbaːb] n ruibarbo

rhyme [raɪm] n rima; (verse) poesía

rhythm ['rɪðm] n ritmo

rib [rɪb] n (ANAT) costilla ♦ vt (mock) tomar el
pelo a

ribbon ['rɪbən] n cinta; **in ~s** (torn) hecho
trizas

rice [raɪs] n arroz m; **~ pudding** n arroz m
con leche

rich [rɪtʃ] adj rico; (soil) fértil; (food) pesado;
(: sweet) empalagoso; (abundant) rico;
(in minerals etc) rico en; **the ~** npl los ricos; **~es**
npl riqueza; **~ly** adv ricamente; (deserved,
earned) bien

rickets ['rɪkɪts] n raquitismo

rid [rɪd] (pt, pp **rid**) vt: **to ~ sb of sth** librar a
uno de algo; **to get ~ of** deshacerse or
desembarazarse de

ridden ['rɪdn] pp of ride

riddle ['rɪdl] n (puzzle) acertijo; (mystery)
enigma m, misterio ♦ vt: **to be ~d with** ser
lleno or plagado de

ride [raɪd] (pt **rode**, pp **ridden**) n paseo;
(distance covered) viaje m, recorrido ♦ vi (as
sport) montar; (go somewhere: on horse,
bicycle, motorcycle, bus) viajar ♦ vt (a horse)
montar a; (a bicycle, motorcycle) andar en;
(distance) recorrer; **to take sb for a ~** (fig)
engañar a uno; **~r** n (on horse) jinete/a m/f;
(on bicycle) ciclista m/f; (on motorcycle)
motociclista m/f

ridge [rɪdʒ] n (of hill) cresta; (of roof)
caballete m; (wrinkle) arruga

ridicule ['rɪdɪkjuːl] n irrisión f, burla ♦ vt
poner en ridículo, burlarse de; **ridiculous**
[rɪ'dɪkjuləs] adj ridículo

riding ['raɪdɪŋ] n equitación f; **I like ~** me
gusta montar a caballo; **~ school** n escuela
de equitación

rife [raɪf] adj: **to be ~** ser muy común; **to be
~ with** abundar en

riffraff ['rɪfræf] n gentuza

rifle ['raɪfl] n rifle m, fusil m ♦ vt saquear;

~ through vt (papers) registrar; **~ range** n
campo de tiro; (at fair) tiro al blanco

rift [rɪft] n (in clouds) claro; (fig: disagreement)
desavenencia

rig [rɪg] n (also: **oil ~**: at sea) plataforma
petrolera ♦ vt (election etc) amañar; **~ out**
(BRIT) vt disfrazar; **~ up** vt improvisar; **~ging**
n (NAUT) aparejo

right [raɪt] adj (correct) correcto, exacto;
(suitable) indicado, debido; (proper)
apropiado; (just) justo; (morally good)
bueno; (not left) derecho ♦ n bueno; (title,
claim; not left) derecha ♦ adv bien,
correctamente; (not left) a la derecha;
(exactly): **~ now** ahora mismo ♦ vt enderezar;
(correct) corregir ♦ excl ¡bueno!, ¡está bien!;
to be ~ (person) tener razón; (answer) ser
correcto; **is that the ~ time?** (of clock) ¿es esa
la hora buena?; **by ~s** en justicia; **on the ~** a
la derecha; **to be in the ~** tener razón; **~ away**
en seguida; **~ in the middle** exactamente en
el centro; **~ angle** n ángulo recto; **~eous**
['raɪtʃəs] adj justado, honrado; (anger)
justificado; **~ful** adj legítimo; **~-handed** adj
diestro; **~-hand man** n brazo derecho; **~-
hand side** n derecha; **~ly** adv
correctamente, debidamente; (with reason)
con razón; **~ of way** n (on path etc) derecho
de paso; (AUT) prioridad f; **~-wing** adj (POL)
derechista

rigid ['rɪdʒɪd] adj rígido; (person, ideas)
inflexible

rigmarole ['rɪgmərəʊl] n galimatías m inv

rigorous ['rɪgərəs] adj riguroso

rile [raɪl] vt irritar

rim [rɪm] n borde m; (of spectacles) aro; (of
wheel) llanta

rind [raɪnd] n (of bacon) corteza; (of lemon
etc) cáscara; (of cheese) costra

ring [rɪŋ] (pt **rang**, pp **rung**) n (of metal) aro;
(on finger) anillo; (of people) corro; (of
objects) círculo; (gang) banda; (for boxing)
cuadrilátero; (of circus) pista; (bull ~) ruedo,
plaza; (sound of bell) toque m ♦ vi (on
telephone) llamar por teléfono; (bell) repicar;
(doorbell, phone) sonar; (also: **~ out**) sonar;
(ears) zumbar ♦ vt (BRIT: TEL) llamar,
telefonear; (bell etc) hacer sonar; (doorbell)
tocar; **to give sb a ~** (BRIT: TEL) llamar or
telefonear a alguien; **~ back** (BRIT) vt, vi (TEL)
devolver la llamada; **~ off** (BRIT) vi (TEL)
colgar, cortar la comunicación; **~ up** (BRIT) vt
(TEL) llamar, telefonear; **~ing** n (of bell)
repique m; (of phone) el sonar; (in ears)
zumbido; **~ing tone** n (TEL) tono de
llamada; **~leader** n (of gang) cabecilla m;
~lets ['rɪŋlɪts] npl rizos mpl, bucles mpl;
~ road (BRIT) n carretera periférica or de
circunvalación

rink [rɪŋk] n (also: ice ~) pista de hielo
rinse [rɪns] n aclarado; (dye) tinte m ♦ vt
aclarar; (mouth) enjuagar
riot ['raɪət] n motín m, disturbio ♦ vi
amotinarse; **to run ~** desmandarse; **~ous** adj
alborotado; (party) bullicioso
rip [rɪp] n rasgón m, rasgadura ♦ vt rasgar,
desgarrar ♦ vi rasgarse, desgarrarse; **~cord** n
cabo de desgarre
ripe [raɪp] adj maduro; **~n** vt madurar;
(cheese) curar ♦ vi madurar
ripple ['rɪpl] n onda, rizo; (sound) murmullo
♦ vi rizarse
rise [raɪz] (pt rose, pp risen) n (slope) cuesta,
pendiente f; (hill) altura; (BRIT: in wages)
aumento; (in prices, temperature) subida; (fig:
to power etc) ascenso ♦ vi subir; (waters)
crecer; (sun, moon) salir; (person: from bed
etc) levantarse; (also: ~ up: rebel) sublevarse;
(in rank) ascender; **to give ~ to** dar lugar or
origen a; **to ~ to the occasion** ponerse a la
altura de las circunstancias; **risen** ['rɪzn] pp
of **rise**; **rising** adj (increasing: number)
creciente; (: prices) en aumento or alza; (tide)
creciente; (sun, moon) naciente
risk [rɪsk] n riesgo, peligro ♦ vt arriesgar; (run
the ~ of) exponerse a; **to take** or **run the ~ of
doing** correr el riesgo de hacer; **at ~** en
peligro; **at one's own ~** bajo su propia
responsabilidad; **~y** adj arriesgado, peligroso
rissole ['rɪsəul] n croqueta
rite [raɪt] n rito; **last ~s** exequias fpl
ritual ['rɪtjuəl] adj ritual ♦ n ritual m, rito
rival ['raɪvl] n rival m/f; (in business)
competidor(a) m/f ♦ adj rival, opuesto ♦ vt
competir con; **~ry** n competencia
river ['rɪvə*] n río ♦ cpd (port) de río; (traffic)
fluvial; **up/down ~** río arriba/abajo; **~bank** n
orilla (del río); **~bed** n lecho, cauce m
rivet ['rɪvɪt] n roblón m, remache m ♦ vt (fig)
captar
Riviera [rɪvi'eərə] n: **the (French) ~** la Costa
Azul (francesa)
road [rəud] n camino; (motorway etc)
carretera; (in town) calle f ♦ cpd (accident) de
tráfico; **major/minor ~** carretera principal/
secundaria; **~ accident** accidente m de
tráfico; **~block** n barricada; **~hog** n loco/a
del volante; **~ map** n mapa m de carreteras;
~ rage n agresividad en la carretera; **~ safety** n seguridad f vial; **~side** n borde
m (del camino); **~sign** n señal f de tráfico;
~ user n usuario/a de la vía pública; **~way**
n calzada; **~works** npl obras fpl; **~worthy**
adj (car) en buen estado para circular
roam [rəum] vi vagar
roar [rɔ:*] n rugido; (of vehicle, storm)
estruendo; (of laughter) carcajada ♦ vi rugir;
hacer estruendo; **to ~ with laughter** reírse a

carcajadas; **to do a ~ing trade** hacer buen
negocio
roast [rəust] n carne f asada, asado ♦ vt asar;
(coffee) tostar; **~ beef** n rosbif m
rob [rɔb] vt robar; **to ~ sb of sth** robar algo a
uno; (fig: deprive) quitar algo a uno; **~ber** n
ladrón/ona m/f; **~bery** n robo
robe [rəub] n (for ceremony etc) toga; (also:
bath~, US) albornoz m
robin ['rɔbɪn] n petirrojo
robot ['rəubɔt] n robot m
robust [rəu'bʌst] adj robusto, fuerte
rock [rɔk] n roca; (boulder) peña, peñasco;
(US: small stone) piedrecita; (BRIT: sweet) ≈
pirulí ♦ vt (swing gently: cradle) balancear,
mecer; (: child) arrullar; (shake) sacudir ♦ vi
mecerse, balancearse; sacudirse; **on the ~s**
(drink) con hielo; (marriage etc) en ruinas;
~ and roll n rocanrol m; **~-bottom** n (fig)
punto más bajo; **~ery** n cuadro alpino
rocket ['rɔkɪt] n cohete m
rocking ['rɔkɪŋ]: **~ chair** n mecedora;
~ horse n caballo de balancín
rocky ['rɔkɪ] adj rocoso
rod [rɔd] n vara, varilla; (also: fishing ~) caña
rode [rəud] pt of **ride**
rodent ['rəudnt] n roedor m
roe [rəu] n (species: also: ~ deer) corzo; (of
fish): **hard/soft ~** hueva/lecha
rogue [rəug] n pícaro, pillo
role [rəul] n papel m
roll [rəul] n rollo; (of bank notes) fajo; (also:
bread ~) panecillo; (register, list) lista,
nómina; (sound: of drums etc) redoble m ♦ vt
hacer rodar; (also: ~ up: string) enrollar;
(: sleeves) arremangar; (cigarette) liar; (also:
~ out: pastry) aplanar; (flatten: road, lawn)
apisonar ♦ vi rodar; (drum) redoblar; (ship)
balancearse; **~ about** or **around** vi (person)
revolcarse; (object) rodar (por); **~ by** vi
(time) pasar; **~ over** vi dar una vuelta; **~ up**
vi (inf: arrive) aparecer ♦ vt (carpet) arrollar;
~ call n: **to take a ~ call** pasar lista; **~er** n
rodillo; (wheel) rueda; (for hair) rulo; **~erblade** n patín m
(en línea); **~er coaster** n montaña rusa; **~er
skates** npl patines mpl de rueda
rolling ['rəulɪŋ] adj (landscape) ondulado;
~ pin n rodillo (de cocina); **~ stock** n (RAIL)
material m rodante
ROM [rɔm] n abbr (COMPUT: = read only
memory) ROM f
Roman ['rəumən] adj romano/a; **~ Catholic**
adj, n católico/a m/f (romano/a)
romance [rə'mæns] n (love affair) amor m;
(charm) lo romántico; (novel) novela de
amor
Romania [ru:'meɪnɪə] n = **Rumania**
Roman numeral n número romano

romantic [rə'mæntɪk] *adj* romántico
Rome [rəum] *n* Roma
romp [rɒmp] *n* retozo, juego ♦ *vi* (*also:*
~ *about*) jugar, brincar
rompers ['rɒmpəz] *npl* pelele *m*
roof [ru:f] (*pl* ~**s**) *n* (*gen*) techo; (*of house*)
techo, tejado ♦ *vt* techar, poner techo a; the
~ **of the mouth** el paladar; ~**ing** *n* techumbre
f; ~ **rack** *n* (*AUT*) baca, portaequipajes *m inv*
rook [ruk] *n* (*bird*) graja; (*CHESS*) torre *f*
room [ru:m] *n* cuarto, habitación *f*, pieza (*esp
AM*); (*also: bed~*) dormitorio; (*in school etc*)
sala; (*space, scope*) sitio, cabida; ~**s** *npl*
(*lodging*) alojamiento; "~**s to let**", "~**s for
rent**" (*US*) "se alquilan cuartos"; **single/
double ~** habitación individual/doble o para
dos personas; ~**ing house** (*US*) *n* pensión *f*;
~**mate** *n* compañero/a de cuarto; ~ **service**
n servicio de habitaciones; ~**y** *adj* espacioso;
(*garment*) amplio
roost [ru:st] *vi* pasar la noche
rooster ['ru:stə*] *n* gallo
root [ru:t] *n* raíz *f* ♦ *vi* arraigarse; ~ **about** *vi*
(*fig*) buscar y rebuscar; ~ **for** *vt fus* (*support*)
apoyar a; ~ **out** *vt* desarraigar
rope [rəup] *n* cuerda; (*NAUT*) cable *m* ♦ *vt*
(*tie*) atar *or* amarrar con (una) cuerda;
(*climbers: also:* ~ *together*) encordarse; (*an
area: also:* ~ *off*) acordonar; **to know the ~s**
(*fig*) conocer los trucos (del oficio); ~ **in** *vt*
(*fig*): **to ~ sb in** persuadir a uno a tomar parte
rosary ['rəuzərɪ] *n* rosario
rose [rəuz] *pt of* **rise** ♦ *n* rosa; (*shrub*) rosal *m*;
(*on watering can*) roseta
rosé ['rəuzeɪ] *n* vino rosado
rosebud ['rəuzbʌd] *n* capullo de rosa
rosebush ['rəuzbuʃ] *n* rosal *m*
rosemary ['rəuzmərɪ] *n* romero
roster ['rɒstə*] *n*: **duty** ~ lista de deberes
rostrum ['rɒstrəm] *n* tribuna
rosy ['rəuzɪ] *adj* rosado, sonrosado; **a ~ future**
un futuro prometedor
rot [rɒt] *n* podredumbre *f*; (*fig: pej*) tonterías
fpl ♦ *vt* pudrir ♦ *vi* pudrirse
rota ['rəutə] *n* (sistema *m* de) turnos *mpl*
rotary ['rəutərɪ] *adj* rotativo
rotate [rəu'teɪt] *vt* (*revolve*) hacer girar, dar
vueltas a; (*jobs*) alternar ♦ *vi* girar, dar
vueltas; **rotating** *adj* rotativo; **rotation**
[-'teɪʃən] *n* rotación *f*
rotten ['rɒtn] *adj* podrido; (*dishonest*)
corrompido; (*inf: bad*) pocho; **to feel ~** (*ill*)
sentirse fatal
rotund [rəu'tʌnd] *adj* regordete
rouble ['ru:bl] (*US* **ruble**) *n* rublo
rough [rʌf] *adj* (*skin, surface*) áspero; (*terrain*)
quebrado; (*road*) desigual; (*voice*) bronco;
(*person, manner*) tosco, grosero; (*weather*)
borrascoso; (*treatment*) brutal; (*sea*) picado;

(*town, area*) peligroso; (*cloth*) basto; (*plan*)
preliminar; (*guess*) aproximado ♦ *n* (*GOLF*): **in
the** ~ en las hierbas altas; **to ~ it** vivir sin
comodidades; **to sleep ~** (*BRIT*) pasar la noche
al raso; ~**age** *n* fibra(s) *f(pl)*; ~**-and-ready**
adj improvisado; ~ **copy** *n* borrador *m*;
~ **draft** *n* = ~ **copy**; ~**ly** *adv* (*handle*)
torpemente; (*make*) toscamente; (*speak*)
groseramente; (*approximately*)
aproximadamente; ~**ness** *n* (*of surface*)
aspereza; (*of person*) rudeza
roulette [ru:'let] *n* ruleta
Roumania [ru:'meɪnɪə] *n* = **Rumania**
round [raund] *adj* redondo ♦ *n* círculo; (*BRIT:
of toast*) rebanada; (*of policeman*) ronda; (*of
milkman*) recorrido; (*of doctor*) visitas *fpl*;
(*game: of cards, in competition*) partida; (*of
ammunition*) cartucho; (*BOXING*) asalto; (*of
talks*) ronda ♦ *vt* (*corner*) doblar ♦ *prep*
alrededor de; (*surrounding*): ~ **his neck/the
table** en su cuello/alrededor de la mesa; (*in a
circular movement*): **to move** ~ **the room/sail**
~ **the world** dar una vuelta a la habitación/
circunnavigar el mundo; (*in various
directions*): **to move** ~ **a room/house** moverse
por toda la habitación/casa; (*approximately*)
alrededor de ♦ *adv:* **all** ~ por todos lados; **the
long way** ~ por el camino menos directo; **all
the year** ~ durante todo el año; **it's just** ~ **the
corner** (*fig*) está a la vuelta de la esquina;
~ **the clock** *adv* las 24 horas; **to go** ~ **to sb's
(house)** ir a casa de uno; **to go** ~ **the back**
pasar por atrás; **enough to go** ~ bastante
(para todos); **a** ~ **of applause** una salva de
aplausos; **a** ~ **of drinks/sandwiches** una ronda
de bebidas/bocadillos; ~ **off** *vt* (*speech etc*)
acabar, poner término a; ~ **up** *vt* (*cattle*)
acorralar; (*people*) reunir; (*price*) redondear;
~**about** (*BRIT*) *n* (*AUT*) isleta; (*at fair*) tiovivo
♦ *adj* (*route, means*) indirecto; ~**ers** *n*
(*game*) juego similar al béisbol; ~**ly** *adv* (*fig*)
rotundamente; ~ **trip** *n* viaje *m* de ida y
vuelta; ~**up** *n* rodeo; (*of criminals*) redada;
(*of news*) resumen *m*
rouse [rauz] *vt* (*wake up*) despertar; (*stir up*)
suscitar; **rousing** *adj* (*cheer, welcome*)
caluroso
route [ru:t] *n* ruta, camino; (*of bus*) recorrido;
(*of shipping*) derrota
routine [ru:'ti:n] *adj* rutinario ♦ *n* rutina;
(*THEATRE*) número
rove [rəuv] *vt* vagar *or* errar por
row[1] [rəu] *n* (*line*) fila, hilera; (*KNITTING*)
pasada ♦ *vi* (*in boat*) remar ♦ *vt* conducir
remando; **4 days in a** ~ 4 días seguidos
row[2] [rau] *n* (*racket*) escándalo; (*dispute*)
bronca, pelea; (*scolding*) regaño ♦ *vi*
pelear(se)
rowboat ['rəubəut] (*US*) *n* bote *m* de remos

rowdy ['raudi] adj (person: noisy) ruidoso; (occasion) alborotado

rowing ['rəuɪŋ] n remo; ~ **boat** (BRIT) n bote m de remos

royal ['rɔɪəl] adj real; **R~ Air Force** n Fuerzas fpl Aéreas Británicas; **~ty** n (~ persons) familia real; (payment to author) derechos mpl de autor

rpm abbr (= revs per minute) r.p.m.

R.S.V.P. abbr (= répondez s'il vous plaît) SRC

Rt. Hon. abbr (BRIT: = Right Honourable) título honorífico de diputado

rub [rʌb] vt frotar; (scrub) restregar ♦ n: to give sth a ~ frotar algo; to ~ sb up or ~ sb (US) the wrong way entrarle uno por mal ojo; ~ **off** vi borrarse; ~ **off on** vt fus influir en; ~ **out** vt borrar

rubber ['rʌbə*] n caucho, goma; (BRIT: eraser) goma de borrar; ~ **band** n goma, gomita; ~ **plant** n ficus m

rubbish ['rʌbɪʃ] n basura; (waste) desperdicios mpl; (fig: pej) tonterías fpl; (junk) pacotilla; ~ **bin** n (BRIT) n cubo (SP) or bote m (AM) de la basura; ~ **dump** n vertedero, basurero

rubble ['rʌbl] n escombros mpl

ruble ['ruːbl] (US) n = **rouble**

ruby ['ruːbɪ] n rubí m

rucksack ['rʌksæk] n mochila

rudder ['rʌdə*] n timón m

ruddy ['rʌdɪ] adj (face) rubicundo; (inf: damned) condenado

rude [ruːd] adj (impolite: person) mal educado; (: word, manners) grosero; (crude) crudo; (indecent) indecente; ~**ness** n descortesía

ruffle ['rʌfl] vt (hair) despeinar; (clothes) arrugar; to get ~d (fig: person) alterarse

rug [rʌg] n alfombra; (BRIT: blanket) manta

rugby ['rʌgbɪ] n (also: ~ football) rugby m

rugged ['rʌgɪd] adj (landscape) accidentado; (features) robusto

ruin ['ruːɪn] n ruina ♦ vt arruinar; (spoil) estropear; ~**s** npl ruinas fpl, restos mpl

rule [ruːl] n (norm) norma, costumbre f; (regulation, ruler) regla; (government) dominio ♦ vt (country, person) gobernar ♦ vi gobernar; (LAW) fallar; **as a ~** por regla general; ~ **out** vt excluir; ~**d** adj (paper) rayado; ~**r** n (sovereign) soberano; (for measuring) regla; **ruling** adj (party) gobernante; (class) dirigente ♦ n (LAW) fallo, decisión f

rum [rʌm] n ron m

Rumania [ruːˈmeɪnɪə] n Rumanía; ~**n** adj rumano/a ♦ n rumano/a m/f; (LING) rumano

rumble ['rʌmbl] n (noise) ruido sordo ♦ vi retumbar, hacer un ruido sordo; (stomach, pipe) sonar

rummage ['rʌmɪdʒ] vi (search) hurgar

rumour ['ruːmə*] (US **rumor**) n rumor m ♦ vt: it is ~**ed that** ... se rumorea que ...

rump [rʌmp] n (of animal) ancas fpl, grupa; ~ **steak** n filete m de lomo

rumpus ['rʌmpəs] n lío, jaleo

run [rʌn] (pt **ran**, pp **run**) n (fast pace): at a ~ corriendo; (SPORT, in tights) carrera; (outing) paseo, excursión f; (distance travelled) trayecto; (series) serie f; (THEATRE) temporada; (SKI) pista ♦ vt correr; (operate: business) dirigir; (: competition, course) organizar; (: hotel, house) administrar, llevar; (COMPUT) ejecutar; (pass: hand) pasar; (PRESS: feature) publicar ♦ vi correr; (work: machine) funcionar, marchar; (bus, train: operate) circular, ir; (: travel) ir; (continue: play) seguir; (: contract) ser válido; (flow: river) fluir; (colours, washing) desteñirse; (in election) ser candidato; **there was a ~ on** (meat, tickets) hubo mucha demanda de; **in the long ~** a la larga; **on the ~** en fuga; **I'll ~ you to the station** te llevaré a la estación (en coche); **to ~ a risk** correr un riesgo; to ~ **a bath** llenar la bañera; ~ **about** or **around** vi (children) correr por todos lados; ~ **across** vt fus (find) dar or topar con; ~ **away** vi huir; ~ **down** vt (production) ir reduciendo; (factory) ir restringiendo la producción en; (subj: car) atropellar; (criticize) criticar; **to be ~ down** (person: tired) estar debilitado; ~ **in** (BRIT) vt (car) rodar; ~ **into** vt fus (meet: person, trouble) tropezar con; (collide with) chocar con; ~ **off** vt (water) dejar correr; (copies) sacar ♦ vi huir corriendo; ~ **out** vi (person) salir corriendo; (liquid) irse; (lease) caducar, vencer; (money etc) acabarse; ~ **out of** vt fus quedar sin; ~ **over** vt (AUT) atropellar ♦ vt fus (revise) repasar; ~ **through** vt fus (instructions) repasar; ~ **up** vt (debt) contraer; **to ~ up against** (difficulties) tropezar con; ~**away** adj (horse) desbocado; (truck) sin frenos; (child) escapado de casa

rung [rʌŋ] pp of **ring** ♦ n (of ladder) escalón m, peldaño

runner ['rʌnə*] n (in race: person) corredor(a) m/f; (: horse) caballo; (on sledge) patín m; ~ **bean** n (BRIT) n judía verde; ~**-up** n subcampeón/ona m/f

running ['rʌnɪŋ] n (sport) atletismo; (business) administración f ♦ adj (water, costs) corriente; (commentary) continuo; **to be in/out of the ~ for sth** tener/no tener posibilidades de ganar algo; **6 days ~** 6 días seguidos; ~ **commentary** n (TV, RADIO) comentario en directo; (on guided tour etc) comentario detallado; ~ **costs** npl gastos mpl corrientes

runny ['rʌnɪ] adj fluido; (nose, eyes) gastante

run-of-the-mill adj común y corriente

runt [rʌnt] n (also pej) redrojo, enano

run-up n: ~ **to** (election etc) período previo a

runway ['rʌnweɪ] n (AVIAT) pista de aterrizaje

rural ['ruərl] adj rural

rush [rʌʃ] n ímpetu m; (hurry) prisa; (COMM) demanda repentina; (current) corriente f fuerte; (of feeling) torrente; (BOT) junco ♦ vt apresurar; (work) hacer de prisa ♦ vi correr, precipitarse; ~ **hour** n horas fpl punta

rusk [rʌsk] n bizcocho tostado

Russia ['rʌʃə] n Rusia; ~**n** adj ruso/a ♦ n ruso/a m/f; (LING) ruso

rust [rʌst] n herrumbre f, moho ♦ vi oxidarse

rustic ['rʌstɪk] adj rústico

rustle ['rʌsl] vi susurrar ♦ vt (paper) hacer crujir

rustproof ['rʌstpruːf] adj inoxidable

rusty ['rʌstɪ] adj oxidado

rut [rʌt] n surco; (ZOOL) celo; **to be in a** ~ ser esclavo de la rutina

ruthless ['ruːθlɪs] adj despiadado

rye [raɪ] n centeno

S, s

Sabbath ['sæbəθ] n domingo; (Jewish) sábado

sabotage ['sæbətɑːʒ] n sabotaje m ♦ vt sabotear

saccharin(e) ['sækərɪn] n sacarina

sachet ['sæʃeɪ] n sobrecito

sack [sæk] n (bag) saco, costal m ♦ vt (dismiss) despedir; (plunder) saquear; **to get the** ~ ser despedido; ~**ing** n despido; (material) arpillera

sacred ['seɪkrɪd] adj sagrado, santo

sacrifice ['sækrɪfaɪs] n sacrificio ♦ vt sacrificar

sad [sæd] adj (unhappy) triste; (deplorable) lamentable

saddle ['sædl] n silla (de montar); (of cycle) sillín m ♦ vt (horse) ensillar; **to be ~d with sth** (inf) quedar cargado con algo; ~**bag** n alforja

sadistic [sə'dɪstɪk] adj sádico

sadly ['sædlɪ] adv lamentablemente; **to be ~ lacking in** estar por desgracia carente de

sadness ['sædnɪs] n tristeza

s.a.e. abbr (= stamped addressed envelope) sobre con las propias señas de uno y con sello

safari [sə'fɑːrɪ] n safari m

safe [seɪf] adj (out of danger) fuera de peligro; (not dangerous, sure) seguro; (unharmed) ileso ♦ n caja de caudales, caja fuerte; ~ **and sound** sano y salvo; **(just) to be on the** ~ **side** para mayor seguridad; ~**-conduct** n salvoconducto; ~**-deposit** n (vault) cámara

acorazada; (box) caja de seguridad; ~**guard** n protección f, garantía ♦ vt proteger, defender; ~**keeping** n custodia; ~**ly** adv seguramente, con seguridad; **to arrive ~ly** llegar bien; ~ **sex** n sexo seguro or sin riesgo

safety ['seɪftɪ] n seguridad f; ~ **belt** n cinturón m (de seguridad); ~ **pin** n imperdible m (SP), seguro (AM); ~ **valve** n válvula de seguridad

saffron ['sæfrən] n azafrán m

sag [sæg] vi aflojarse

sage [seɪdʒ] n (herb) salvia; (man) sabio

Sagittarius [sædʒɪ'tɛərɪəs] n Sagitario

Sahara [sə'hɑːrə] n: **the** ~ (Desert) el (desierto del) Sáhara

said [sɛd] pt, pp of **say**

sail [seɪl] n (on boat) vela; (trip): **to go for a** ~ dar un paseo en barco ♦ vt (boat) gobernar ♦ vi (travel: ship) navegar; (SPORT) hacer vela; (begin voyage) salir; **they ~ed into Copenhagen** arribaron a Copenhague; ~ **through** vt fus (exam) aprobar sin ningún problema; ~**boat** n (US) velero, barco de vela; ~**ing** n (SPORT) vela; **to go ~ing** hacer vela; ~**ing boat** n barco de vela; ~**ing ship** n velero; ~**or** n marinero, marino

saint [seɪnt] n santo; ~**ly** adj santo

sake [seɪk] n: **for the** ~ **of** por

salad ['sæləd] n ensalada; ~ **bowl** n ensaladera; ~ **cream** n (BRIT) n (especie f de) mayonesa; ~ **dressing** n aliño

salary ['sælərɪ] n sueldo

sale [seɪl] n venta; (at reduced prices) liquidación f, saldo; (auction) subasta; ~**s** npl (total amount sold) ventas fpl, facturación f; **"for ~"** "se vende"; **on** ~ en venta; **on** ~ **or return** (goods) venta por reposición; ~**room** n sala de subastas; ~**s assistant** (US ~**s clerk**) n dependiente/a m/f; **salesman/woman** (irreg) n (in shop) dependiente/a m/f; (representative) viajante m/f

salmon ['sæmən] n inv salmón m

salon ['sælɒn] n (hairdressing ~) peluquería; (beauty ~) salón m de belleza

saloon [sə'luːn] n (US) bar m, taberna; (BRIT: AUT) (coche m de) turismo; (ship's lounge) cámara, salón m

salt [sɔːlt] n sal f ♦ vt salar; (put ~ on) poner sal en; ~ **cellar** n salero; ~**water** adj de agua salada; ~**y** adj salado

salute [sə'luːt] n saludo; (of guns) salva ♦ vt saludar

salvage ['sælvɪdʒ] n (saving) salvamento, recuperación f; (things saved) objetos mpl salvados ♦ vt salvar

salvation [sæl'veɪʃən] n salvación f; **S~ Army** n Ejército de Salvación

same [seɪm] adj mismo ♦ pron: **the** ~ el/la mismo/a, los/las mismos/as; **the** ~ **book as** el mismo libro que; **at the ~ time** (*at the ~ moment*) al mismo tiempo; (*yet*) sin embargo; **all** *or* **just the ~** sin embargo, aun así; **to do the ~ (as sb)** hacer lo mismo (que uno); **the ~ to you!** ¡igualmente!

sample ['sɑːmpl] *n* muestra ♦ *vt* (*food*) probar; (*wine*) catar

sanction ['sæŋkʃən] *n* aprobación *f* ♦ *vt* sancionar; aprobar; **~s** *npl* (POL) sanciones *fpl*

sanctity ['sæŋktɪtɪ] *n* santidad *f*; (*inviolability*) inviolabilidad *f*

sanctuary ['sæŋktjuərɪ] *n* santuario; (*refuge*) asilo, refugio; (*for wildlife*) reserva

sand [sænd] *n* arena; (*beach*) playa ♦ *vt* (*also: ~ down*) lijar

sandal ['sændl] *n* sandalia

sand: ~box (US) *n* = **~pit**; **~castle** *n* castillo de arena; **~ dune** *n* duna; **~paper** *n* papel *m* de lija; **~pit** *n* (*for children*) cajón *m* de arena; **~stone** *n* piedra arenisca

sandwich ['sændwɪtʃ] *n* bocadillo (SP), sandwich *m*, emparedado (AM) ♦ *vt* intercalar; **~ed between** apretujado entre; **cheese/ham ~** sandwich de queso/jamón; **~ course** (BRIT) *n* curso de medio tiempo

sandy ['sændɪ] *adj* arenoso; (*colour*) rojizo

sane [seɪn] *adj* cuerdo; (*sensible*) sensato

sang [sæŋ] *pt of* **sing**

sanitary ['sænɪtərɪ] *adj* sanitario; (*clean*) higiénico; **~ towel** (US **~ napkin**) *n* paño higiénico, compresa

sanitation [sænɪ'teɪʃən] *n* (*in house*) servicios *mpl* higiénicos; (*in town*) servicio de desinfección; **~ department** (US) *n* departamento de limpieza y recogida de basuras

sanity ['sænɪtɪ] *n* cordura; (*of judgment*) sensatez *f*

sank [sæŋk] *pt of* **sink**

Santa Claus [sæntə'klɔːz] *n* San Nicolás, Papá Noel

sap [sæp] *n* (*of plants*) savia ♦ *vt* (*strength*) minar, agotar

sapling ['sæplɪŋ] *n* árbol nuevo *or* joven

sapphire ['sæfaɪə*] *n* zafiro

sarcasm ['sɑːkæzm] *n* sarcasmo

sardine [sɑː'diːn] *n* sardina

Sardinia [sɑː'dɪnɪə] *n* Cerdeña

sash [sæʃ] *n* faja

sat [sæt] *pt, pp of* **sit**

Satan ['seɪtn] *n* Satanás *m*

satchel ['sætʃl] *n* (*child's*) cartera (SP), mochila (AM)

satellite ['sætəlaɪt] *n* satélite *m*; **~ dish** *n* antena de televisión por satélite; **~ television** *n* televisión *f* vía satélite

satin ['sætɪn] *n* raso ♦ *adj* de raso

satire ['sætaɪə*] *n* sátira

satisfaction [sætɪs'fækʃən] *n* satisfacción *f*

satisfactory [sætɪs'fæktərɪ] *adj* satisfactorio

satisfy ['sætɪsfaɪ] *vt* satisfacer; (*convince*) convencer; **~ing** *adj* satisfactorio

Saturday ['sætədɪ] *n* sábado

sauce [sɔːs] *n* salsa; (*sweet*) crema; jarabe *m*; **~pan** *n* cacerola, olla

saucer ['sɔːsə*] *n* platillo

Saudi ['saudɪ]: **~ Arabia** *n* Arabia Saudí *or* Saudita; **~ (Arabian)** *adj*, *n* saudí *m/f*, saudita *m/f*

sauna ['sɔːnə] *n* sauna

saunter ['sɔːntə*] *vi*: **to ~ in/out** entrar/salir sin prisa

sausage ['sɔsɪdʒ] *n* salchicha; **~ roll** *n* empanadita de salchicha

sauté ['sauteɪ] *adj* salteado

savage ['sævɪdʒ] *adj* (*cruel, fierce*) feroz, furioso; (*primitive*) salvaje ♦ *n* salvaje *m/f* ♦ *vt* (*attack*) embestir

save [seɪv] *vt* (*rescue*) salvar, rescatar; (*money, time*) ahorrar; (*put by, keep: seat*) guardar; (COMPUT) salvar (y guardar); (*avoid: trouble*) evitar; (SPORT) parar ♦ *vi* (*also: ~ up*) ahorrar ♦ *n* (SPORT) parada ♦ *prep* salvo, excepto

saving ['seɪvɪŋ] *n* (*on price etc*) economía ♦ *adj*: **the ~ grace of** el único mérito de; **~s** *npl* ahorros *mpl*; **~s account** *n* cuenta de ahorros; **~s bank** *n* caja de ahorros

saviour ['seɪvjə*] (US **savior**) *n* salvador(a) *m/f*

savour ['seɪvə*] (US **savor**) *vt* saborear; **~y** *adj* sabroso; (*dish: not sweet*) salado

saw [sɔː] (*pt* **sawed**, *pp* **sawed** *or* **sawn**) *pt of* **see** ♦ *n* (*tool*) sierra ♦ *vt* serrar; **~dust** *n* (a)serrín *m*; **~mill** *n* aserradero; **~n-off shotgun** *n* escopeta de cañones recortados

saxophone ['sæksəfəun] *n* saxófono

say [seɪ] (*pt, pp* **said**) *n*: **to have one's ~** expresar su opinión ♦ *vt* decir; **to have a** *or* **some ~ in sth** tener voz *or* tener que ver en algo; **to ~ yes/no** decir que sí/no; **could you ~ that again?** ¿podría repetir eso?; **that is to ~** es decir; **that goes without ~ing** ni que decir tiene; **~ing** *n* dicho, refrán *m*

scab [skæb] *n* costra; (*pej*) esquirol *m*

scaffold ['skæfəuld] *n* cadalso; **~ing** *n* andamio, andamiaje *m*

scald [skɔːld] *n* escaldadura ♦ *vt* escaldar

scale [skeɪl] *n* (*gen*, MUS) escala; (*of fish*) escama; (*of salaries, fees etc*) escalafón *m* ♦ *vt* (*mountain*) escalar; (*tree*) trepar; **~s** *npl* (*for weighing: small*) balanza; (: *large*) báscula; **on a large ~** en gran escala; **~ of charges** tarifa, lista de precios; **~ down** *vt* reducir a escala

scallop ['skɔləp] *n* (ZOOL) venera; (SEWING) festón *m*

scalp [skælp] *n* cabellera ♦ *vt* escalpar

scampi ['skæmpɪ] *npl* gambas *fpl*

scan [skæn] *vt* (*examine*) escudriñar; (*glance*

at quickly) dar un vistazo a; (*TV, RADAR*) explorar, registrar ♦ *n* (*MED*): **to have a ~** pasar por el escáner

scandal ['skændl] *n* escándalo; (*gossip*) chismes *mpl*

Scandinavia [skændɪ'neɪvɪə] *n* Escandinavia; **~n** *adj, n* escandinavo/a *m/f*

scant [skænt] *adj* escaso; **~y** *adj* (*meal*) insuficiente; (*clothes*) ligero

scapegoat ['skeɪpɡəʊt] *n* cabeza de turco, chivo expiatorio

scar [skɑ:] *n* cicatriz *f*; (*fig*) señal *f* ♦ *vt* dejar señales en

scarce [skɛəs] *adj* escaso; **to make o.s. ~** (*inf*) esfumarse; **~ly** *adv* apenas; **scarcity** *n* escasez *f*

scare [skɛə*] *n* susto, sobresalto; (*panic*) pánico ♦ *vt* asustar, espantar; **to ~ sb stiff** dar a uno un susto de muerte; **bomb ~** amenaza de bomba; **~ off** or **away** *vt* ahuyentar; **~crow** *n* espantapájaros *m inv*; **~d** *adj*: **to be ~d** estar asustado

scarf [skɑ:f] (*pl* **~s** or **scarves**) *n* (*long*) bufanda; (*square*) pañuelo

scarlet ['skɑ:lɪt] *adj* escarlata; **~ fever** *n* escarlatina

scarves [skɑ:vz] *npl of* **scarf**

scary ['skɛərɪ] (*inf*) *adj* espeluznante

scathing ['skeɪðɪŋ] *adj* mordaz

scatter ['skætə*] *vt* (*spread*) esparcir, desparramar; (*put to flight*) dispersar ♦ *vi* desparramarse; dispersarse; **~brained** *adj* ligero de cascos

scavenger ['skævəndʒə*] *n* (*person*) basurero/a

scenario [sɪ'nɑ:rɪəʊ] *n* (*THEATRE*) argumento; (*CINEMA*) guión *m*; (*fig*) escenario

scene [si:n] *n* (*THEATRE, fig etc*) escena; (*of crime etc*) escenario; (*view*) panorama *m*; (*fuss*) escándalo; **~ry** *n* (*THEATRE*) decorado; (*landscape*) paisaje *m*; **scenic** *adj* pintoresco

scent [sent] *n* perfume *m*, olor *m*; (*fig: track*) rastro, pista

sceptic ['skeptɪk] (*US* **skeptic**) *n* escéptico/a; **~al** *adj* escéptico

sceptre ['septə*] (*US* **scepter**) *n* cetro

schedule ['ʃedju:l, (*US*) 'skedju:l] *n* (*timetable*) horario; (*of events*) programa *m*; (*list*) lista ♦ *vt* (*visit*) fijar la hora de; **to arrive on ~** llegar a la hora debida; **to be ahead of/behind ~** estar adelantado/en retraso; **~d flight** *n* vuelo regular

scheme [ski:m] *n* (*plan*) plan *m*, proyecto; (*plot*) intriga; (*arrangement*) disposición *f*; (*pension ~ etc*) sistema *m* ♦ *vi* (*intrigue*) intrigar; **scheming** *adj* intrigante ♦ *n* intrigas *fpl*

schizophrenic [skɪtsə'frenɪk] *adj* esquizofrénico

scholar ['skɒlə*] *n* (*pupil*) alumno/a; (*learned person*) sabio/a, erudito/a; **~ship** *n* erudición *f*; (*grant*) beca

school [sku:l] *n* escuela, colegio; (*in university*) facultad *f* ♦ *cpd* escolar; **~ age** *n* edad *f* escolar; **~book** *n* libro de texto; **~boy** *n* alumno; **~ children** *npl* alumnos *mpl*; **~girl** *n* alumna; **~ing** *n* enseñanza; **~master/mistress** *n* (*primary*) maestro/a; (*secondary*) profesor(a) *m/f*; **~teacher** *n* (*primary*) maestro/a; (*secondary*) profesor(a) *m/f*

schooner ['sku:nə*] *n* (*ship*) goleta

sciatica [saɪ'ætɪkə] *n* ciática

science ['saɪəns] *n* ciencia; **~ fiction** *n* ciencia-ficción *f*; **scientific** [-'tɪfɪk] *adj* científico; **scientist** *n* científico/a

scissors ['sɪzəz] *npl* tijeras *fpl*; **a pair of ~** unas tijeras

scoff [skɒf] *vt* (*BRIT: inf: eat*) engullir ♦ *vi*: **to ~ (at)** (*mock*) mofarse (de)

scold [skəʊld] *vt* regañar

scone [skɒn] *n* pastel de pan

scoop [sku:p] *n* (*for flour etc*) pala; (*PRESS*) exclusiva; **~ out** *vt* excavar; **~ up** *vt* recoger

scooter ['sku:tə*] *n* moto *f*; (*toy*) patinete *m*

scope [skəʊp] *n* (*of plan*) ámbito; (*of person*) competencia; (*opportunity*) libertad *f* (*de acción*)

scorch [skɔ:tʃ] *vt* (*clothes*) chamuscar; (*earth, grass*) quemar, secar

score [skɔ:*] *n* (*points etc*) puntuación *f*; (*MUS*) partitura; (*twenty*) veintena ♦ *vt* (*goal, point*) ganar; (*mark*) rayar; (*achieve: success*) conseguir ♦ *vi* marcar un tanto; (*FOOTBALL*) marcar (un) gol; (*keep score*) llevar el tanteo; **~s of** (*very many*) decenas de; **on that ~** en lo que se refiere a eso; **to ~ 6 out of 10** obtener una puntuación de 6 sobre 10; **~ out** *vt* tachar; **~ over** *vt fus* obtener una victoria sobre; **~board** *n* marcador *m*

scorn [skɔ:n] *n* desprecio; **~ful** *adj* desdeñoso, despreciativo

Scorpio ['skɔ:pɪəʊ] *n* Escorpión *m*

scorpion ['skɔ:pɪən] *n* alacrán *m*

Scot [skɒt] *n* escocés/esa *m/f*

Scotch [skɒtʃ] *n* whisky *m* escocés

Scotland ['skɒtlənd] *n* Escocia

Scots [skɒts] *adj* escocés/esa; **~man/woman** (*irreg*) *n* escocés/esa *m/f*; **Scottish** ['skɒtɪʃ] *adj* escocés/esa; **Scottish Parliament** *n* Parlamento escocés

scoundrel ['skaundrl] *n* canalla *m/f*, sinvergüenza *m/f*

scout [skaut] *n* (*MIL, also: boy ~*) explorador *m*; **girl ~** (*US*) niña exploradora; **~ around** *vi* reconocer el terreno

scowl [skaul] *vi* fruncir el ceño; **to ~ at sb** mirar con ceño a uno

scrabble ['skræbl] vi (claw): **to ~ (at)** arañar; (also: **to ~ around**: search) revolver todo buscando ♦ n: **S~** ® Scrabble ® m

scraggy ['skrægɪ] adj descarnado

scram [skræm] (inf) vi largarse

scramble ['skræmbl] n (climb) subida (difícil); (struggle) pelea ♦ vi: **to ~ through/out** abrirse paso/salir con dificultad; **to ~ for** pelear por; **~d eggs** npl huevos mpl revueltos

scrap [skræp] n (bit) pedacito; (fig) pizca; (fight) riña, bronca; (also: **~ iron**) chatarra, hierro viejo ♦ vt (discard) desechar, descartar ♦ vi reñir, armar (una) bronca; **~s** npl (waste) sobras fpl, desperdicios mpl; **~book** n álbum m de recortes; **~ dealer** n chatarrero/a

scrape [skreɪp] n: **to get into a ~** meterse en un lío ♦ vt raspar; (skin etc) rasguñar; (~ against) rozar ♦ vi: **to ~ through** (exam) aprobar por los pelos; **~ together** vt (money) arañar, juntar

scrap: **~ heap** n(fig): **to be on the ~ heap** estar acabado; **~ merchant** (BRIT) n chatarrero/a; **~ paper** n pedazos mpl de papel

scratch [skrætʃ] n rasguño; (from claw) arañazo ♦ cpd: **~ team** equipo improvisado ♦ vt (paint, car) rayar; (with claw, nail) rasguñar, arañar; (rub: nose etc) rascarse ♦ vi rascarse; **to start from ~** partir de cero; **to be up to ~** cumplir con los requisitos

scrawl [skrɔ:l] n garabatos mpl ♦ vi hacer garabatos

scrawny ['skrɔ:nɪ] adj flaco

scream [skri:m] n chillido ♦ vi chillar

screech [skri:tʃ] vi chirriar

screen [skri:n] n (CINEMA, TV) pantalla; (movable barrier) biombo ♦ vt (conceal) tapar; (from the wind etc) proteger; (film) proyectar; (candidates etc) investigar a; **~ing** n (MED) investigación f médica; **~play** n guión m

screw [skru:] n tornillo ♦ vt (also: **~ in**) atornillar; **~ up** vt (paper etc) arrugar; **to ~ up one's eyes** arrugar el entrecejo; **~driver** n destornillador m

scribble ['skrɪbl] n garabatos mpl ♦ vt, vi garabatear

script [skrɪpt] n (CINEMA etc) guión m; (writing) escritura, letra

Scripture(s) ['skrɪptʃə*(z)] n(pl) Sagrada Escritura

scroll [skrəul] n rollo

scrounge [skraundʒ] (inf) vt: **to ~ sth off** or **from sb** obtener algo de uno de gorra ♦ n: **on the ~** de gorra; **~r** n gorrón/ona m/f

scrub [skrʌb] n (land) maleza ♦ vt fregar, restregar; (inf: reject) cancelar, anular

scruff [skrʌf] n: **by the ~ of the neck** por el pescuezo

scruffy ['skrʌfɪ] adj desaliñado, piojoso

scrum(mage) ['skrʌm(mɪdʒ)] n (RUGBY) melée f

scruple ['skru:pl] n (gen pl) escrúpulo

scrutinize ['skru:tɪnaɪz] vt escudriñar; (votes) escrutar; **scrutiny** ['skru:tɪnɪ] n escrutinio, examen m

scuff [skʌf] vt (shoes, floor) rayar

scuffle ['skʌfl] n refriega

sculptor ['skʌlptə*] n escultor(a) m/f

sculpture ['skʌlptʃə*] n escultura

scum [skʌm] n (on liquid) espuma; (pej: people) escoria

scurry ['skʌrɪ] vi correr; **to ~ off** escabullirse

scuttle ['skʌtl] n (also: **coal ~**) cubo, carbonera ♦ vt (ship) barrenar ♦ vi (scamper): **to ~ away**, **~ off** escabullirse

scythe [saɪð] n guadaña

SDP (BRIT) n abbr = Social Democratic Party

sea [si:] n mar m ♦ cpd de mar, marítimo; **by ~** (travel) en barco; **on the ~** (boat) en el mar; (town) junto al mar; **to be all at ~** (fig) estar despistado; **out to ~**, **at ~** en alta mar; **~board** n litoral m; **~food** n mariscos mpl; **~ front** n paseo marítimo; **~-going** adj de altura; **~gull** n gaviota

seal [si:l] n (animal) foca; (stamp) sello ♦ vt (close) cerrar; **~ off** vt (area) acordonar

sea level n nivel m del mar

sea lion n león m marino

seam [si:m] n costura; (of metal) juntura; (of coal) veta, filón m

seaman ['si:mən] (irreg) n marinero

seance ['seɪɔns] n sesión f de espiritismo

seaplane ['si:pleɪn] n hidroavión m

seaport ['si:pɔ:t] n puerto de mar

search [sə:tʃ] n (for person, thing) busca, búsqueda; (COMPUT) búsqueda; (inspection: of sb's home) registro ♦ vt (look in) buscar en; (examine) examinar; (person, place) registrar ♦ vi: **to ~ for** buscar; **in ~ of** en busca de; **~ through** vt fus registrar; **~ing** adj penetrante; **~light** n reflector m; **~ party** n pelotón m de salvamento; **~ warrant** n mandamiento (judicial)

sea: **~shore** n playa, orilla del mar; **~sick** adj mareado; **~side** n playa, orilla del mar; **~side resort** n centro turístico costero

season ['si:zn] n (of year) estación f; (sporting etc) temporada; (of films etc) ciclo ♦ vt (food) sazonar; **in/out of ~** en sazón/fuera de temporada; **~al** adj estacional; **~ed** adj (fig) experimentado; **~ing** n condimento, aderezo; **~ ticket** n abono

seat [si:t] n (in bus, train) asiento; (chair) silla; (PARLIAMENT) escaño; (buttocks) culo, trasero; (of trousers) culera ♦ vt sentar; (have room for) tener cabida para; **to be ~ed** sentarse; **~ belt** n cinturón m de seguridad

sea: ~ **water** n agua del mar; **~weed** n alga marina; **~worthy** adj en condiciones de navegar

sec. abbr = **second(s)**

secluded [sɪ'kluːdɪd] adj retirado

seclusion [sɪ'kluːʒən] n reclusión f

second ['sɛkənd] adj segundo ♦ adv en segundo lugar ♦ n segundo; (AUT: also: ~ gear) segunda; (COMM) artículo con algún desperfecto; (BRIT: SCOL: degree) título de licenciado con calificación de notable ♦ vt (motion) apoyar; **~ary** adj secundario; **~ary school** n escuela secundaria; **~-class** adj de segunda clase ♦ adv (RAIL) en segunda; **~hand** adj de segunda mano, usado; ~ **hand** n (on clock) segundero; **~ly** adv en segundo lugar; **~ment** [sɪ'kɔndmənt] (BRIT) n traslado temporal; **~-rate** adj de segunda categoría; ~ **thoughts** npl: to have ~ thoughts cambiar de opinión; **on** ~ **thoughts** or **thought** (US) pensándolo bien

secrecy ['siːkrəsɪ] n secreto

secret ['siːkrɪt] adj, n secreto; **in** ~ en secreto

secretarial [sɛkrɪ'tɛərɪəl] adj de secretario; (course, staff) de secretariado

secretary ['sɛkrətərɪ] n secretario/a; **S~ of State (for)** (BRIT: POL) Ministro (de)

secretive ['siːkrətɪv] adj reservado, sigiloso

secretly ['siːkrɪtlɪ] adv en secreto

sect [sɛkt] n secta; **~arian** [-'tɛərɪən] adj sectario

section ['sɛkʃən] n sección f; (part) parte f; (of document) artículo; (of opinion) sector m; (cross-~) corte m transversal

sector ['sɛktə*] n sector m

secular ['sɛkjulə*] adj secular, seglar

secure [sɪ'kjuə*] adj seguro; (firmly fixed) firme, fijo ♦ vt (fix) asegurar, afianzar; (get) conseguir

security [sɪ'kjuərɪtɪ] n seguridad f; (for loan) fianza; (: object) prenda

sedate [sɪ'deɪt] adj tranquilo ♦ vt tratar con sedantes

sedation [sɪ'deɪʃən] n (MED) sedación f

sedative ['sɛdɪtɪv] n sedante m, sedativo

seduce [sɪ'djuːs] vt seducir; **seduction** [-'dʌkʃən] n seducción f; **seductive** [-'dʌktɪv] adj seductor/a

see [siː] (pt **saw**, pp **seen**) vt ver; (accompany): **to** ~ **sb to the door** acompañar a uno a la puerta; (understand) ver, comprender ♦ vi ver ♦ n (arz)obispado; **to** ~ **that** (ensure) asegurar que; ~ **you soon!** ¡hasta pronto!; ~ **about** vt fus atender a, encargarse de; ~ **off** vt despedir; ~ **through** vt fus (fig) calar ♦ vt (plan) llevar a cabo; ~ **to** vt fus atender a, encargarse de

seed [siːd] n semilla; (in fruit) pepita; (fig: gen pl) germen m; (TENNIS etc) preseleccionado/

a; **to go to** ~ (plant) granar; (fig) descuidarse; **~ling** n planta de semillero; **~y** adj (shabby) desaseado, raído

seeing ['siːɪŋ] conj: ~ **(that)** visto que, en vista de que

seek [siːk] (pt, pp **sought**) vt buscar; (post) solicitar

seem [siːm] vi parecer; **there ~s to be ...** parece que hay ...; **~ingly** adv aparentemente, según parece

seen [siːn] pp of **see**

seep [siːp] vi filtrarse

seesaw ['siːsɔː] n subibaja

seethe [siːð] vi hervir; **to** ~ **with anger** estar furioso

see-through adj transparente

segment ['sɛgmənt] n (part) sección f; (of orange) gajo

segregate ['sɛgrɪgeɪt] vt segregar

seize [siːz] vt (grasp) agarrar, asir; (take possession of) secuestrar; (: territory) apoderarse de; (opportunity) aprovecharse de; ~ **(up)on** vt fus aprovechar; ~ **up** vi (TECH) agarrotarse

seizure ['siːʒə*] n (MED) ataque m; (LAW, of power) incautación f

seldom ['sɛldəm] adv rara vez

select [sɪ'lɛkt] adj selecto, escogido ♦ vt escoger, elegir; (SPORT) seleccionar; **~ion** [-'lɛkʃən] n selección f, elección f; (COMM) surtido

self [sɛlf] (pl **selves**) n uno mismo; **the** ~ **el yo** ♦ prefix auto...; **~-assured** adj seguro de sí mismo; **~-catering** (BRIT) adj (flat etc) con cocina; **~-centred** (US **~-centered**) adj egocéntrico; **~-confidence** n confianza en sí mismo; **~-conscious** adj cohibido; **~-contained** (BRIT) adj (flat) con entrada particular; **~-control** n autodominio; **~-defence** (US **~-defense**) n defensa propia; **~-discipline** n autodisciplina; **~-employed** adj que trabaja por cuenta propia; **~-evident** adj patente; **~-governing** adj autónomo; **~-indulgent** adj autocomplaciente; **~-interest** n egoísmo; **~-ish** adj egoísta; **~ishness** n egoísmo; **~-less** adj desinteresado; **~-made** adj: **~-made man** hombre m que se ha hecho a sí mismo; **~-pity** n lástima de sí mismo; **~-portrait** n autorretrato; **~-possessed** adj sereno, dueño de sí mismo; **~-preservation** n propia conservación f; **~-respect** n amor m propio; **~-righteous** adj santurrón/ona; **~-sacrifice** n abnegación f; **~-satisfied** adj satisfecho de sí mismo; **~-service** adj de autoservicio; **~-sufficient** adj autosuficiente; **~-taught** adj autodidacta

sell [sɛl] (pt, pp **sold**) vt vender ♦ vi venderse; **to** ~ **at** or **for £10** venderse a 10 libras; ~ **off** vt liquidar; ~ **out** vi: **to** ~ **out of tickets/milk**

vender todas las entradas/toda la leche; **~by
date** n fecha de caducidad; **~er** n
vendedor(a) m/f; **~ing price** n precio de
venta

Sellotape ® ['sɛləuteɪp] (BRIT) n cinta
adhesiva, celo (SP), scotch m (AM)

selves [sɛlvz] npl of **self**

semblance ['sɛmbləns] n apariencia

semen ['si:mən] n semen m

semester [sɪ'mɛstəʳ] n semestre m

semi... [sɛmɪ] prefix semi..., medio...; **~circle**
n semicírculo; **~colon** n punto y coma;
~conductor n semiconductor m;
~detached (house) n (casa) semiseparada;
~-final n semi-final m

seminar ['sɛmɪnɑ:ʳ] n seminario

seminary ['sɛmɪnərɪ] n (REL) seminario

semiskilled ['sɛmɪskɪld] adj (work, worker)
semi-cualificado

semi-skimmed (milk) n leche
semidesnatada

senate ['sɛnɪt] n senado; **senator** n
senador(a) m/f

send [sɛnd] (pt, pp sent) vt mandar, enviar;
(signal) transmitir; **~ away** vt despachar;
~ away for vt fus pedir; **~ back** vt devolver;
~ for vt fus mandar traer; **~ off** vt (goods)
despachar; (BRIT: SPORT: player) expulsar;
~ out vt (invitation) mandar; (signal) emitir;
~ up vt (person, price) hacer subir; (BRIT:
parody) parodiar; **~er** n remitente m/f; **~-off**
n: **a good ~-off** una buena despedida

senior ['si:nɪəʳ] adj (older) mayor, más viejo;
(: on staff) de más antigüedad; (of higher
rank) superior; **~ citizen** n persona de la
tercera edad; **~ity** [-'ɔrɪtɪ] n antigüedad f

sensation [sɛn'seɪʃən] n sensación f; **~al** adj
sensacional

sense [sɛns] n (faculty, meaning) sentido;
(feeling) sensación f; (good ~) sentido común,
juicio ♦ vt sentir, percibir; **it makes ~** tiene
sentido; **~less** adj estúpido, insensato;
(unconscious) sin conocimiento; **~ of
humour** n sentido del humor

sensible ['sɛnsɪbl] adj sensato; (reasonable)
razonable, lógico

sensitive ['sɛnsɪtɪv] adj sensible; (touchy)
susceptible

sensual ['sɛnsjuəl] adj sensual

sensuous ['sɛnsjuəs] adj sensual

sent [sɛnt] pt, pp of **send**

sentence ['sɛntns] n (LING) oración f; (LAW)
sentencia, fallo ♦ vt: **to ~ sb to death/to 5
years (in prison)** condenar a uno a muerte/a
5 años de cárcel

sentiment ['sɛntɪmənt] n sentimiento;
(opinion) opinión f; **~al** [-'mɛntl] adj
sentimental

sentry ['sɛntrɪ] n centinela m

separate [adj 'sɛprɪt, vb 'sɛpəreɪt] adj
separado; (distinct) distinto ♦ vt separar;
(part) dividir ♦ vi separarse; **~s** npl (clothes)
coordinados mpl; **~ly** adv por separado;
separation [-'reɪʃən] n separación f

September [sɛp'tɛmbəʳ] n se(p)tiembre m

septic ['sɛptɪk] adj séptico; **~ tank** n fosa
séptica

sequel ['si:kwl] n consecuencia, resultado; (of
story) continuación f

sequence ['si:kwəns] n sucesión f, serie f;
(CINEMA) secuencia

sequin ['si:kwɪn] n lentejuela

serene [sɪ'ri:n] adj sereno, tranquilo

sergeant ['sɑ:dʒənt] n sargento

serial ['sɪərɪəl] n (TV) telenovela, serie f
televisiva; (BOOK) serie f; **~ize** vt emitir como
serial; **~ killer** n asesino/a múltiple;
~ number n número de serie

series ['sɪəri:z] n inv serie f

serious ['sɪərɪəs] adj serio; (grave) grave; **~ly**
adv en serio; (ill, wounded etc) gravemente

sermon ['sə:mən] n sermón m

serrated [sɪ'reɪtɪd] adj serrado, dentellado

serum ['sɪərəm] n suero

servant ['sə:vənt] n servidor(a) m/f; (house
~) criado/a

serve [sə:v] vt servir; (customer) atender;
(subj: train) pasar por; (apprenticeship) hacer;
(prison term) cumplir ♦ vi (at table) servir;
(TENNIS) sacar; **to ~ as/for/to do** servir de/
para/para hacer ♦ n (TENNIS) saque m; **it ~s
him right** se lo tiene merecido; **~ out** vt
(food) servir; **~ up** vt = **~ out**

service ['sə:vɪs] n servicio; (REL) misa; (AUT)
mantenimiento; (dishes etc) juego ♦ vt (car
etc) revisar; (: repair) reparar; **the S~s** npl las
fuerzas armadas; **to be of ~ to sb** ser útil a
uno; **~ included/not included** servicio
incluido/no incluido; **~able** adj servible,
utilizable; **~ area** n (on motorway) area de
servicio; **~ charge** (BRIT) n servicio; **~man** n
militar m; **~ station** n estación f de servicio

serviette [sə:vɪ'ɛt] (BRIT) n servilleta

session ['sɛʃən] n sesión f; **to be in ~** estar en
sesión

set [sɛt] (pt, pp set) n juego; (RADIO) aparato;
(TV) televisor m; (of utensils) batería; (of
cutlery) cubierto; (of books) colección f;
(TENNIS) set m; (group of people) grupo;
(CINEMA) plató m; (THEATRE) decorado;
(HAIRDRESSING) marcado ♦ adj (fixed) fijo;
(ready) listo ♦ vt (place) poner, colocar; (fix)
fijar; (adjust) ajustar, arreglar; (decide: rules
etc) establecer, decidir ♦ vi (sun) ponerse;
(jam, jelly) cuajarse; (concrete) fraguar;
(bone) componerse; **to be ~ on doing sth**
estar empeñado en hacer algo; **to ~ to music**
poner música a; **to ~ on fire** incendiar, poner

fuego a; **to ~ free** poner en libertad; **to ~ sth going** poner algo en marcha; **to ~ sail** zarpar, hacerse a la vela; **~ about** vt fus ponerse a; **~ aside** vt poner aparte, dejar de lado; (money, time) reservar; **~ back** vt (cost): **to ~ sb back £5** costar a uno cinco libras; (: in time): **to ~ back (by)** retrasar (por); **~ off** vi partir ♦ vt (bomb) hacer estallar; (events) poner en marcha; (show up well) hacer resaltar; **~ out** vi partir ♦ vt (arrange) disponer; (state) exponer; **to ~ out to do sth** proponerse hacer algo; **~ up** vt establecer; **~back** n revés m, contratiempo; **~ menu** n menú m

settee [se'tiː] n sofá m

setting ['setɪŋ] n (scenery) marco; (position) disposición f; (of sun) puesta; (of jewel) engaste m, montadura

settle ['setl] vt (argument) resolver; (accounts) ajustar, liquidar; (MED: calm) calmar, sosegar ♦ vi (dust etc) depositarse; (weather) serenarse; (also: ~ down) instalarse; tranquilizarse; **to ~ for sth** convenir en aceptar algo; **to ~ on sth** decidirse por algo; **~ in** vi instalarse; **~ up** vi: **to ~ up with sb** ajustar cuentas con uno; **~ment** n (payment) liquidación f; (agreement) acuerdo, convenio; (village etc) pueblo; **~r** n colono/a, colonizador(a) m/f

setup ['setʌp] n sistema m; (situation) situación f

seven ['sevn] num siete; **~teen** num diez y siete, diecisiete; **~th** num séptimo; **~ty** num setenta

sever ['sevə*] vt cortar; (relations) romper

several ['sevərl] adj, pron varios/as m/fpl, algunos/as m/fpl; **~ of us** varios de nosotros

severance ['sevərəns] n (of relations) ruptura; **~ pay** n indemnización f por despido

severe [sɪ'vɪə*] adj severo; (serious) grave; (hard) duro; (pain) intenso; **severity** [sɪ'verɪtɪ] n severidad f; gravedad f; intensidad f

sew [səʊ] (pt sewed, pp sewn) vt, vi coser; **~ up** vt coser, zurcir

sewage ['suːɪdʒ] n aguas fpl residuales

sewer ['suːə*] n alcantarilla, cloaca

sewing ['səʊɪŋ] n costura; **~ machine** n máquina de coser

sewn [səʊn] pp of sew

sex [seks] n sexo; (lovemaking): **to have ~** hacer el amor; **~ist** adj, n sexista m/f; **~ual** ['seksjuəl] adj sexual; **~y** adj sexy

shabby ['ʃæbɪ] adj (person) desharrapado; (clothes) raído, gastado; (behaviour) ruin inv

shack [ʃæk] n choza, chabola

shackles ['ʃæklz] npl grillos mpl, grilletes mpl

shade [ʃeɪd] n sombra; (for lamp) pantalla;

(for eyes) visera; (of colour) matiz m, tonalidad f; (small quantity): **a ~ (too big/more)** un poquitín (grande/más) ♦ vt dar sombra a; (eyes) proteger del sol; **in the ~** en la sombra

shadow ['ʃædəʊ] n sombra ♦ vt (follow) seguir y vigilar; **~ cabinet** (BRIT) n (POL) gabinete paralelo formado por el partido de oposición; **~y** adj oscuro; (dim) indistinto

shady ['ʃeɪdɪ] adj sombreado; (fig: dishonest) sospechoso; (: deal) turbio

shaft [ʃɑːft] n (of arrow, spear) astil m; (AUT, TECH) eje m, árbol m; (of mine) pozo; (of lift) hueco, caja; (of light) rayo

shaggy ['ʃægɪ] adj peludo

shake [ʃeɪk] (pt shook, pp shaken) vt sacudir; (building) hacer temblar; (bottle, cocktail) agitar ♦ vi (tremble) temblar; **to ~ one's head** (in refusal) negar con la cabeza; (in dismay) mover o menear la cabeza, incrédulo; **to ~ hands with sb** estrechar la mano a uno; **~ off** vt sacudirse; (fig) deshacerse de; **~ up** vt agitar; (fig) reorganizar; **shaky** adj (hand, voice) trémulo; (building) inestable

shall [ʃæl] aux vb: **~ I help you?** ¿quieres que te ayude?; **I'll buy three, ~ I?** compro tres, ¿no te parece?

shallow ['ʃæləʊ] adj poco profundo; (fig) superficial

sham [ʃæm] n fraude m, engaño ♦ vt fingir, simular

shambles ['ʃæmblz] n confusión f

shame [ʃeɪm] n vergüenza ♦ vt avergonzar; **it is a ~ that/to do** es una lástima que/hacer; **what a ~!** ¡qué lástima!; **~ful** adj vergonzoso; **~less** adj desvergonzado

shampoo [ʃæm'puː] n champú m ♦ vt lavar con champú; **~ and set** n lavado y marcado

shamrock ['ʃæmrɔk] n trébol m (emblema nacional irlandés)

shandy ['ʃændɪ] n mezcla de cerveza con gaseosa

shan't [ʃɑːnt] = shall not

shantytown ['ʃæntɪtaʊn] n barrio de chabolas

shape [ʃeɪp] n forma ♦ vt formar, dar forma a; (sb's ideas) formar; (sb's life) determinar; **to take ~** tomar forma; **~ up** vi (events) desarrollarse; (person) formarse; **~d** suffix: **heart-~d** en forma de corazón; **~less** adj informe, sin forma definida; **~ly** adj (body etc) esbelto

share [ʃeə*] n (part) parte f, porción f; (contribution) cuota; (COMM) acción f ♦ vt dividir; (have in common) compartir; **to ~ out (among** or **between)** repartir (entre); **~holder** (BRIT) n accionista m/f

shark [ʃɑːk] n tiburón m

sharp [ʃɑːp] adj (blade, nose) afilado; (point)

puntiagudo; (*outline*) definido; (*pain*)
intenso; (*MUS*) desafinado; (*contrast*)
marcado; (*voice*) agudo; (*person: quick-
witted*) astuto; (: *dishonest*) poco escrupuloso
♦ *n* (*MUS*) sostenido ♦ *adv*: **at 2 o'clock ~** a
las 2 en punto; **~en** *vt* afilar; (*pencil*) sacar
punta a; (*fig*) agudizar; **~ener** *n* (*also: pencil
~ener*) sacapuntas *m inv*; **~-eyed** *adj* de vista
aguda; **~ly** *adv* (*turn, stop*) bruscamente;
(*stand out, contrast*) claramente; (*criticize,
retort*) severamente

shatter ['ʃætə*] *vt* hacer añicos or pedazos;
(*fig: ruin*) destruir, acabar con ♦ *vi* hacerse
añicos

shave [ʃeɪv] *vt* afeitar, rasurar ♦ *vi* afeitarse,
rasurarse ♦ *n*: **to have a ~** afeitarse; **~r** *n*
(*also: electric ~r*) máquina de afeitar
(eléctrica)

shaving ['ʃeɪvɪŋ] *n* (*action*) el afeitarse,
rasurado; **~s** *npl* (*of wood etc*) virutas *fpl*;
~ brush *n* brocha (de afeitar); **~ cream** *n*
crema de afeitar; **~ foam** *n* espuma de
afeitar

shawl [ʃɔːl] *n* chal *m*

she [ʃiː] *pron* ella; **~-cat** *n* gata

sheaf [ʃiːf] (*pl* **sheaves**) *n* (*of corn*) gavilla; (*of
papers*) fajo

shear [ʃɪə*] (*pt* **sheared**, *pp* **sheared** *or* **shorn**)
vt esquilar, trasquilar; **~s** *npl* (*for hedge*)
tijeras *fpl* de jardín

sheath [ʃiːθ] *n* vaina; (*contraceptive*)
preservativo

sheaves [ʃiːvz] *npl of* **sheaf**

shed [ʃed] (*pt, pp* **shed**) *n* cobertizo ♦ *vt*
(*skin*) mudar; (*tears, blood*) derramar; (*load*)
derramar; (*workers*) despedir

she'd [ʃiːd] = **she had; she would**

sheen [ʃiːn] *n* brillo, lustre *m*

sheep [ʃiːp] *n inv* oveja; **~dog** *n* perro pastor;
~skin *n* piel *f* de carnero

sheer [ʃɪə*] *adj* (*utter*) puro, completo; (*steep*)
escarpado; (*material*) diáfano ♦ *adv*
verticalmente

sheet [ʃiːt] *n* (*on bed*) sábana; (*of paper*)
hoja; (*of glass, metal*) lámina; (*of ice*) capa

sheik(h) [ʃeɪk] *n* jeque *m*

shelf [ʃelf] (*pl* **shelves**) *n* estante *m*

shell [ʃel] *n* (*on beach*) concha; (*of egg, nut
etc*) cáscara; (*explosive*) proyectil *m*, obús *m*;
(*of building*) armazón *f* ♦ *vt* (*peas*)
desenvainar; (*MIL*) bombardear

she'll [ʃiːl] = **she will; she shall**

shellfish ['ʃelfɪʃ] *n inv* crustáceo; (*as food*)
mariscos *mpl*

shell suit *n* chándal *m* de calle

shelter ['ʃeltə*] *n* abrigo, refugio ♦ *vt* (*aid*)
amparar, proteger; (*give lodging to*) abrigar
♦ *vi* abrigarse, refugiarse; **~ed** *adj* (*life*)
protegido; (*spot*) abrigado; **~ed housing** *n*

viviendas vigiladas para ancianos y
minusválidos

shelve [ʃelv] *vt* (*fig*) aplazar; **~s** *npl of* **shelf**

shepherd ['ʃepəd] *n* pastor *m* ♦ *vt* (*guide*)
guiar, conducir; **~'s pie** (*BRIT*) *n* pastel de
carne y patatas

sherry ['ʃeri] *n* jerez *m*

she's [ʃiːz] = **she is; she has**

Shetland ['ʃetlənd] *n* (*also: the ~s, the
~ Isles*) las Islas de Zetlandia

shield [ʃiːld] *n* escudo; (*protection*) blindaje *m*
♦ *vt*: **to ~ (from)** proteger (de)

shift [ʃɪft] *n* (*change*) cambio; (*at work*) turno
♦ *vt* trasladar; (*remove*) quitar ♦ *vi* moverse;
~ work *n* trabajo a turnos; **~y** *adj* tramposo;
(*eyes*) furtivo

shimmer ['ʃɪmə*] *n* reflejo trémulo

shin [ʃɪn] *n* espinilla

shine [ʃaɪn] (*pt, pp* **shone**) *n* brillo, lustre *m*
♦ *vi* brillar, relucir ♦ *vt* (*shoes*) lustrar, sacar
brillo a; **to ~ a torch on sth** dirigir una linterna
hacia algo

shingle ['ʃɪŋgl] *n* (*on beach*) guijarros *mpl*; **~s**
n (*MED*) herpes *mpl or fpl*

shiny ['ʃaɪnɪ] *adj* brillante, lustroso

ship [ʃɪp] *n* buque *m*, barco ♦ *vt* (*goods*)
embarcar; (*send*) transportar or enviar por vía
marítima; **~building** *n* construcción *f* de
buques; **~ment** *n* (*goods*) envío; **~ping** *n*
(*act*) embarque *m*; (*traffic*) buques *mpl*;
~wreck *n* naufragio ♦ *vt*: **to be ~wrecked**
naufragar; **~yard** *n* astillero

shire ['ʃaɪə*] (*BRIT*) *n* condado

shirt [ʃəːt] *n* camisa; **in (one's) ~ sleeves** en
mangas de camisa

shit [ʃɪt] (*infl*) *excl* ¡mierda! (!)

shiver ['ʃɪvə*] *n* escalofrío ♦ *vi* temblar,
estremecerse; (*with cold*) tiritar

shoal [ʃəʊl] *n* (*of fish*) banco; (*fig: also: ~s*)
tropel *m*

shock [ʃɒk] *n* (*impact*) choque *m*; (*ELEC*)
descarga (eléctrica); (*emotional*) conmoción
f; (*start*) sobresalto, susto; (*MED*) postración *f*
nerviosa ♦ *vt* dar un susto a; (*offend*)
escandalizar; **~ absorber** *n* amortiguador *m*;
~ing *adj* (*awful*) espantoso; (*outrageous*)
escandaloso

shoddy ['ʃɒdɪ] *adj* de pacotilla

shoe [ʃuː] (*pt, pp* **shod**) *n* zapato; (*for horse*)
herradura ♦ *vt* (*horse*) herrar; **~brush** *n*
cepillo para zapatos; **~lace** *n* cordón *m*;
~ polish *n* betún *m*; **~shop** *n* zapatería;
~string *n* (*fig*): **on a ~string** con muy poco
dinero

shone [ʃɒn] *pt, pp of* **shine**

shook [ʃʊk] *pt of* **shake**

shoot [ʃuːt] (*pt, pp* **shot**) *n* (*on branch,
seedling*) retoño, vástago ♦ *vt* disparar; (*kill*)
matar a tiros; (*wound*) pegar un tiro;

(*execute*) fusilar; (*film*) rodar, filmar ♦ *vi* (*FOOTBALL*) chutar; **~ down** *vt* (*plane*) derribar; **~ in/out** *vi* entrar corriendo/salir disparado; **~ up** *vi* (*prices*) dispararse; **~ing** *n* (*shots*) tiros *mpl*; (*HUNTING*) caza con escopeta; **~ing star** *n* estrella fugaz

shop [ʃɔp] *n* tienda; (*workshop*) taller *m* ♦ *vi* (*also: go ~ping*) ir de compras; **~ assistant** (*BRIT*) *n* dependiente/a *m/f*; **~ floor** (*BRIT*) *n* (*fig*) taller *m*, fábrica; **~keeper** *n* tendero/a; **~lifting** *n* mechería; **~per** *n* comprador(a) *m/f*; **~ping** *n* (*goods*) compras *fpl*; **~ping bag** *n* bolsa (de compras); **~ping centre** (*US* **~ping center**) *n* centro comercial; **~soiled** *adj* deteriorado; **~ steward** (*BRIT*) *n* (*INDUSTRY*) enlace *m* sindical; **~ window** *n* escaparate *m* (*SP*), vidriera (*AM*)

shore [ʃɔː*] *n* orilla ♦ *vt*: **to ~ (up)** reforzar; **on ~** en tierra

shorn [ʃɔːn] *pp of* **shear**

short [ʃɔːt] *adj* corto; (*in time*) breve, de corta duración; (*person*) bajo; (*curt*) brusco, seco; (*insufficient*) insuficiente; **(a pair of) ~s** (unos) pantalones *mpl* cortos; **to be ~ of sth** estar falto de algo; **in ~** en pocas palabras; **~ of doing ...** fuera de hacer ...; **it is ~ for** es la forma abreviada de; **to cut ~** (*speech, visit*) interrumpir, terminar inesperadamente; **everything ~ of ...** todo menos ...; **to fall ~ of** no alcanzar; **to run ~ of** quedarle a uno poco; **to stop ~** parar en seco; **to stop ~ of** detenerse antes de; **~age** *n*: **a ~age of** una falta de; **~bread** *n* especie de mantecada; **~change** *vt* no dar el cambio completo a; **~circuit** *n* cortocircuito; **~coming** *n* defecto, deficiencia; **~(crust) pastry** (*BRIT*) *n* pasta quebradiza; **~cut** *n* atajo; **~en** *vt* acortar; (*visit*) interrumpir; **~fall** *n* déficit *m*; **~hand** (*BRIT*) *n* taquigrafía; **~hand typist** (*BRIT*) *n* taquimecanógrafo/a; **~ list** (*BRIT*) *n* (*for job*) lista de candidatos escogidos; **~lived** *adj* efímero; **~ly** *adv* en breve, dentro de poco; **~sighted** (*BRIT*) *adj* miope; (*fig*) imprudente; **~staffed** *adj*: **to be ~staffed** estar falto de personal; **~ story** *n* cuento; **~tempered** *adj* enojadizo; **~term** *adj* (*effect*) a corto plazo; **~wave** *n* (*RADIO*) onda corta

shot [ʃɔt] *pt, pp of* **shoot** ♦ *n* (*sound*) tiro, disparo; (*try*) tentativa; (*injection*) inyección *f*; (*PHOT*) toma, fotografía; **to be a good/poor ~** (*person*) tener buena/mala puntería; **like a ~** (*without any delay*) como un rayo; **~gun** *n* escopeta

should [ʃud] *aux vb*: **I ~ go now** debo irme ahora; **he ~ be there now** debe de haber llegado (ya); **I ~ go if I were you** yo en tu lugar me iría; **I ~ like to** me gustaría

shoulder ['ʃəuldə*] *n* hombro ♦ *vt* (*fig*) cargar con; **~ bag** *n* cartera de bandolera;

~ blade *n* omóplato

shouldn't ['ʃudnt] **= should not**

shout [ʃaut] *n* grito ♦ *vt* gritar ♦ *vi* gritar, dar voces; **~ down** *vt* acallar a gritos; **~ing** *n* griterío

shove [ʃʌv] *n* empujón *m* ♦ *vt* empujar; (*inf*: *put*): **to ~ sth in** meter algo a empellones; **~ off** (*inf*) *vi* largarse

shovel ['ʃʌvl] *n* pala; (*mechanical*) excavadora ♦ *vt* mover con pala

show [ʃəu] (*pt* **showed**, *pp* **shown**) *n* (*of emotion*) demostración *f*; (*semblance*) apariencia; (*exhibition*) exposición *f*; (*THEATRE*) función *f*, espectáculo; (*TV*) show *m* ♦ *vt* mostrar, enseñar; (*courage etc*) mostrar, manifestar; (*exhibit*) exponer; (*film*) proyectar ♦ *vi* mostrarse; (*appear*) aparecer; **for ~** para impresionar; **on ~** (*exhibits etc*) expuesto; **~ in** *vt* (*person*) hacer pasar; **~ off** (*pej*) *vi* presumir ♦ *vt* (*display*) lucir; **~ out** *vt*: **to ~ sb out** acompañar a uno a la puerta; **~ up** *vi* (*stand out*) destacar; (*inf*: *turn up*) aparecer ♦ *vt* (*unmask*) desenmascarar; **~ business** *n* mundo del espectáculo; **~down** *n* enfrentamiento (final)

shower ['ʃauə*] *n* (*rain*) chaparrón *m*, chubasco; (*of stones etc*) lluvia; (*for bathing*) ducha (*SP*), regadera (*AM*) ♦ *vi* llover ♦ *vt* (*fig*): **to ~ sb with sth** colmar a uno de algo; **to have a ~** ducharse; **~proof** *adj* impermeable

showing ['ʃəuɪŋ] *n* (*of film*) proyección *f*

show jumping *n* hípica

shown [ʃəun] *pp of* **show**

show: **~-off** (*inf*) *n* (*person*) presumido/a; **~piece** *n* (*of exhibition etc*) objeto cumbre; **~room** *n* sala de muestras

shrank [ʃræŋk] *pt of* **shrink**

shrapnel ['ʃræpnl] *n* metralla

shred [ʃred] *n* (*gen pl*) triza, jirón *m* ♦ *vt* hacer trizas; (*CULIN*) desmenuzar; **~der** *n* (*vegetable ~der*) picadora; (*document ~der*) trituradora (de papel)

shrewd [ʃruːd] *adj* astuto

shriek [ʃriːk] *n* chillido ♦ *vi* chillar

shrill [ʃrɪl] *adj* agudo, estridente

shrimp [ʃrɪmp] *n* camarón *m*

shrine [ʃraɪn] *n* santuario, sepulcro

shrink [ʃrɪŋk] (*pt* **shrank**, *pp* **shrunk**) *vi* encogerse; (*be reduced*) reducirse; (*also: ~ away*) retroceder ♦ *vt* encoger ♦ *n* (*inf*: *pej*) loquero/a; **to ~ from (doing) sth** no atreverse a hacer algo; **~wrap** *vt* embalar con película de plástico

shrivel ['ʃrɪvl] (*also: ~ up*) *vt* (*dry*) secar ♦ *vi* secarse

shroud [ʃraud] *n* sudario ♦ *vt*: **~ed in mystery** envuelto en el misterio

Shrove Tuesday ['ʃrəuv-] *n* martes *m* de

carnaval

shrub [ʃrʌb] n arbusto; **~bery** n arbustos mpl

shrug [ʃrʌg] n encogimiento de hombros ♦ vt, vi: **to ~** (one's shoulders) encogerse de hombros; **~ off** vt negar importancia a

shrunk [ʃrʌŋk] pp of **shrink**

shudder ['ʃʌdə*] n estremecimiento, escalofrío ♦ vi estremecerse

shuffle ['ʃʌfl] vt (cards) barajar ♦ vi: **to ~** (one's feet) arrastrar los pies

shun [ʃʌn] vt rehuir, esquivar

shunt [ʃʌnt] vt (train) maniobrar; (object) empujar

shut [ʃʌt] (pt, pp shut) vt cerrar ♦ vi cerrarse; **~ down** vt, vi cerrar; **~ off** vt (supply etc) cortar; **~ up** vi (inf: keep quiet) callarse ♦ vt (close) cerrar; (silence) hacer callar; **~ter** n contraventana; (PHOT) obturador m

shuttle ['ʃʌtl] n lanzadera; (also: ~ service) servicio rápido y continuo entre dos puntos: (: AVIAT) puente m aéreo; **~cock** n volante m; **~ diplomacy** n viajes mpl diplomáticos

shy [ʃaɪ] adj tímido; **~ness** n timidez f

Sicily ['sɪsɪlɪ] n Sicilia

sick [sɪk] adj (ill) enfermo; (nauseated) mareado; (humour) negro; (vomiting): **to be ~** (BRIT) vomitar; **to feel ~** tener náuseas; **to be ~ of** (fig) estar harto de; **~ bay** n enfermería; **~en** vt dar asco a; **~ening** adj (fig) asqueroso

sickle ['sɪkl] n hoz f

sick: ~ leave n baja por enfermedad; **~ly** adj enfermizo; (smell) nauseabundo; **~ness** n enfermedad f, mal m; (vomiting) náuseas fpl; **~ pay** n subsidio de enfermedad

side [saɪd] n (gen) lado m; (of body) costado; (of lake) orilla; (of hill) ladera; (team) equipo; ♦ adj (door, entrance) lateral ♦ vi: **to ~ with sb** tomar el partido de uno; **by the ~ of** al lado de; **~ by ~** juntos/as; **from ~ to ~** de un lado para otro; **from all ~s** de todos lados; **to take ~s (with)** tomar partido (con); **~board** n aparador m; **~boards** (BRIT) npl = **~burns**; **~burns** npl patillas fpl; **~ drum** n tambor m; **~ effect** n efecto secundario; **~light** n (AUT) luz f lateral; **~line** n (SPORT) línea de banda; (fig) empleo suplementario; **~long** adj de soslayo; **~ order** n plato de acompañamiento; **~ show** n (stall) caseta; **~step** vt (fig) esquivar; **~ street** n calle f lateral; **~track** vt (fig) desviar (de su propósito); **~walk** (US) n acera; **~ways** adv de lado

siding ['saɪdɪŋ] n (RAIL) apartadero, vía muerta

siege [si:dʒ] n cerco, sitio

sieve [sɪv] n colador m ♦ vt cribar

sift [sɪft] vt cribar; (fig: information) escudriñar

sigh [saɪ] n suspiro ♦ vi suspirar

sight [saɪt] n (faculty) vista; (spectacle)

espectáculo; (on gun) mira, alza ♦ vt divisar; **in ~** a la vista; **out of ~** fuera de (la) vista; **on ~** (shoot) sin previo aviso; **~seeing** n excursionismo, turismo; **to go ~seeing** hacer turismo

sign [saɪn] n (with hand) señal f, seña; (trace) huella, rastro; (notice) letrero; (written) signo ♦ vt firmar; (SPORT) fichar; **to ~ sth over to sb** firmar el traspaso de algo a uno; **~ on** vi (BRIT: as unemployed) registrarse como desempleado; (for course) inscribirse ♦ vt (MIL) alistar; (employee) contratar; **~ up** vi (MIL) alistarse; (for course) inscribirse ♦ vt (player) fichar

signal ['sɪgnl] n señal f ♦ vi señalizar ♦ vt (person) hacer señas a; (message) comunicar por señales; **~man** (irreg) n (RAIL) guardavía m

signature ['sɪgnətʃə*] n firma; **~ tune** n sintonía de apertura de un programa

signet ring ['sɪgnət-] n anillo de sello

significance [sɪgˈnɪfɪkəns] n (importance) trascendencia

significant [sɪgˈnɪfɪkənt] adj significativo; (important) trascendente

signify ['sɪgnɪfaɪ] vt significar

sign language n lenguaje m para sordomudos

signpost ['saɪnpəʊst] n indicador m

silence ['saɪlns] n silencio ♦ vt acallar; (guns) reducir al silencio; **~r** n (on gun, BRIT: AUT) silenciador m

silent ['saɪlnt] adj silencioso; (not speaking) callado; (film) mudo; **to remain ~** guardar silencio; **~ partner** n (COMM) socio/a comanditario/a

silhouette [sɪluːˈet] n silueta

silicon chip ['sɪlɪkən-] n plaqueta de silicio

silk [sɪlk] n seda ♦ adj de seda; **~y** adj sedoso

silly ['sɪlɪ] adj (person) tonto; (idea) absurdo

silt [sɪlt] n sedimento

silver ['sɪlvə*] n plata; (money) moneda suelta ♦ adj de plata; (colour) plateado; **~ paper** (BRIT) n papel m de plata; **~-plated** adj plateado; **~smith** n platero/a; **~ware** n plata; **~y** adj argentino

similar ['sɪmɪlə*] adj: **~ (to)** parecido or semejante (a); **~ity** [-ˈlærɪtɪ] n semejanza; **~ly** adv del mismo modo

simmer ['sɪmə*] vi hervir a fuego lento

simple ['sɪmpl] adj (easy) sencillo; (foolish, COMM: interest) simple; **simplicity** [-ˈplɪsɪtɪ] n sencillez f; **simplify** ['sɪmplɪfaɪ] vt simplificar

simply ['sɪmplɪ] adv (live, talk) sencillamente; (just, merely) sólo

simulate ['sɪmjuːleɪt] vt fingir, simular; **~d** adj simulado; (fur) de imitación

simultaneous [sɪmlˈteɪnɪəs] adj simultáneo; **~ly** adv simultáneamente

sin [sɪn] n pecado ♦ vi pecar

since [sɪns] adv desde entonces, después ♦ prep desde ♦ conj (time) desde que; (because) ya que, puesto que; **~ then, ever ~** desde entonces

sincere [sɪnˈsɪə*] adj sincero; **~ly** adv: **yours ~ly** (in letters) le saluda atentamente; **sincerity** [-ˈsɛrɪtɪ] n sinceridad f

sinew [ˈsɪnjuː] n tendón m

sing [sɪŋ] (pt **sang**, pp **sung**) vt, vi cantar

Singapore [sɪŋəˈpɔː*] n Singapur m

singe [sɪndʒ] vt chamuscar

singer [ˈsɪŋə*] n cantante m/f

singing [ˈsɪŋɪŋ] n canto

single [ˈsɪŋgl] adj único, solo; (unmarried) soltero; (not double) simple, sencillo ♦ n (BRIT: also: **~ ticket**) billete m sencillo; (record) sencillo, single m; **~s** npl (TENNIS) individual m; **~ out** vt (choose) escoger; **~ bed** cama individual f; **~-breasted** adj recto; **~ file** n: **in ~ file** en fila de uno; **~-handed** adv sin ayuda; **~-minded** adj resuelto, firme; **~ parent** n padre m soltero, madre f soltera (o divorciado etc); **~ parent family** familia monoparental; **~ room** n cuarto individual

singly [ˈsɪŋglɪ] adv uno por uno

singular [ˈsɪŋgjulə*] adj (odd) raro, extraño; (outstanding) excepcional ♦ n (LING) singular m

sinister [ˈsɪnɪstə*] adj siniestro

sink [sɪŋk] (pt **sank**, pp **sunk**) n fregadero ♦ vt (ship) hundir, echar a pique; (foundations) excavar ♦ vi (gen) hundirse; **to ~ sth into** hundir algo en; **~ in** vi (fig) penetrar, calar

sinner [ˈsɪnə*] n pecador(a) m/f

sinus [ˈsaɪnəs] n (ANAT) seno

sip [sɪp] n sorbo ♦ vt sorber, beber a sorbitos

siphon [ˈsaɪfən] n sifón m; **~ off** vt desviar

sir [sə*] n señor m; **S~ John Smith** Sir John Smith; **yes ~** sí, señor

siren [ˈsaɪərn] n sirena

sirloin [ˈsəːlɔɪn] n (also: **~ steak**) solomillo

sister [ˈsɪstə*] n hermana; (BRIT: nurse) enfermera jefe; **~-in-law** n cuñada

sit [sɪt] (pt, pp **sat**) vi sentarse; (be sitting) estar sentado; (assembly) reunirse; (for painter) posar ♦ vt (exam) presentarse a; **~ down** vi sentarse; **~ in on** vt fus asistir a; **~ up** vi incorporarse; (not go to bed) velar

sitcom [ˈsɪtkɔm] n abbr (= situation comedy) comedia de situación

site [saɪt] n sitio; (also: building ~) solar m ♦ vt situar

sit-in n (demonstration) sentada

sitting [ˈsɪtɪŋ] n (of assembly etc) sesión f; (in canteen) turno; **~ room** n sala de estar

situated [ˈsɪtjueɪtɪd] adj situado

situation [sɪtjuˈeɪʃən] n situación f; **"~s vacant"** (BRIT) "ofrecen trabajo"

six [sɪks] num seis; **~teen** num diez y seis, dieciséis; **~th** num sexto; **~ty** num sesenta

size [saɪz] n tamaño; (extent) extensión f; (of clothing) talla; (of shoes) número; **~ up** vt formarse una idea de; **~able** adj importante, considerable

sizzle [ˈsɪzl] vi crepitar

skate [skeɪt] n patín m; (fish: pl inv) raya ♦ vi patinar; **~board** n monopatín m; **~boarding** n monopatín m; **~r** n patinador(a) m/f; **skating** n patinaje m; **skating rink** n pista de patinaje

skeleton [ˈskɛlɪtn] n esqueleto; (TECH) armazón f; (outline) esquema m; **~ staff** n personal m reducido

skeptic etc [ˈskɛptɪk] (US) = **sceptic**

sketch [skɛtʃ] n (drawing) dibujo; (outline) esbozo, bosquejo; (THEATRE) sketch m ♦ vt dibujar; (plan etc: also: **~ out**) esbozar; **~ book** n libro de dibujos; **~y** adj incompleto

skewer [ˈskjuːə*] n broqueta

ski [skiː] n esquí m ♦ vi esquiar; **~ boot** n bota de esquí

skid [skɪd] n patinazo ♦ vi patinar

ski: ~er n esquiador(a) m/f; **~ing** n esquí m; **~ jump** n salto con esquís

skilful [ˈskɪlful] (BRIT) adj diestro, experto

ski lift n telesilla m, telesquí m

skill [skɪl] n destreza, pericia; técnica; **~ed** adj hábil, diestro; (worker) cualificado; **~full** (US) adj = **skilful**

skim [skɪm] vt (milk) desnatar; (glide over) rozar, rasar ♦ vi: **to ~ through** (book) hojear; **~med milk** n leche f desnatada

skimp [skɪmp] vt (also: **~ on: work**) chapucear; (cloth etc) escatimar; **~y** adj escaso; (skirt) muy corto

skin [skɪn] n piel f; (complexion) cutis m ♦ vt (fruit etc) pelar; (animal) despellejar; **~ cancer** n cáncer m de piel; **~-deep** adj superficial; **~ diving** n buceo; **~ny** adj flaco; **~tight** adj (dress etc) muy ajustado

skip [skɪp] n brinco, salto; (BRIT: container) contenedor m ♦ vi brincar; (with rope) saltar a la comba ♦ vt saltarse

ski: ~ pass n forfait m (de esquí); **~ pole** n bastón m de esquiar

skipper [ˈskɪpə*] n (NAUT, SPORT) capitán m

skipping rope [ˈskɪpɪŋ-] n comba

skirmish [ˈskəːmɪʃ] n escaramuza

skirt [skəːt] n falda (SP), pollera (AM) ♦ vt (go round) ladear; **~ing board** (BRIT) n rodapié m

ski slope n pista de esquí

ski suit n traje m de esquiar

ski tow n remonte m

skittle [ˈskɪtl] n bolo; **~s** n (game) boliche m

skive [skaɪv] (BRIT: inf) vi gandulear

skull [skʌl] n calavera; (ANAT) cráneo

skunk [skʌŋk] n mofeta

sky [skaɪ] n cielo; **~light** n tragaluz m, claraboya; **~scraper** n rascacielos m inv

slab [slæb] n (stone) bloque m; (flat) losa; (of cake) trozo

slack [slæk] adj (loose) flojo; (slow) de poca actividad; (careless) descuidado; **~s** npl pantalones mpl; **~en** (also: **~en off**) vi aflojarse ♦ vt aflojar; (speed) disminuir

slag heap ['slæg-] n escorial m, escombrera

slag off (BRIT: inf) vt poner como un trapo

slam [slæm] vt (throw) arrojar (violentamente); (criticize) criticar duramente ♦ vi (door) cerrarse de golpe; **to ~ the door** dar un portazo

slander ['slɑːndə*] n calumnia, difamación f

slang [slæŋ] n argot m; (jargon) jerga

slant [slɑːnt] n sesgo, inclinación f; (fig) interpretación f; **~ed** adj (fig) parcial; **~ing** adj inclinado; (eyes) rasgado

slap [slæp] n palmada; (in face) bofetada ♦ vt dar una palmada o bofetada a; (paint etc): **to ~ sth on sth** embadurnar algo con algo ♦ adv (directly) exactamente, directamente; **~dash** adj descuidado; **~stick** n comedia de golpe y porrazo; **~-up** adj: **a ~-up meal** (BRIT) un banquetazo, una comilona

slash [slæʃ] vt acuchillar; (fig: prices) fulminar

slat [slæt] n tablilla, listón m

slate [sleɪt] n pizarra ♦ vt (fig: criticize) criticar duramente

slaughter ['slɔːtə*] n (of animals) matanza; (of people) carnicería ♦ vt matar; **~house** n matadero

Slav [slɑːv] adj eslavo

slave [sleɪv] n esclavo/a ♦ vi (also: ~ away) sudar tinta; **~ry** n esclavitud f

slay [sleɪ] (pt slew, pp slain) vt matar

sleazy ['sliːzɪ] adj de mala fama

sledge [sledʒ] n trineo; **~hammer** n mazo

sleek [sliːk] adj (shiny) lustroso; (car etc) elegante

sleep [sliːp] (pt, pp slept) n sueño ♦ vi dormir; **to go to ~** quedarse dormido; **~ around** vi acostarse con cualquiera; **~ in** vi (oversleep) quedarse dormido; **~er** n (person) durmiente m/f; (BRIT: RAIL: on track) traviesa; (: train) coche-cama m; **~ing bag** n saco de dormir; **~ing car** n coche-cama m; **~ing partner** (BRIT) n (COMM) socio comanditario; **~ing pill** n somnífero; **~less** adj: **a ~less night** una noche en blanco; **~walker** n sonámbulo/a; **~y** adj soñoliento; (place) soporífero

sleet [sliːt] n aguanieve f

sleeve [sliːv] n manga; (TECH) manguito; (of record) portada; **~less** adj sin mangas

sleigh [sleɪ] n trineo

sleight [slaɪt] n: **~ of hand** escamoteo

slender ['slendə*] adj delgado; (means) escaso

slept [slept] pt, pp of **sleep**

slew [sluː] pt of **slay** ♦ vi (BRIT: veer) torcerse

slice [slaɪs] n (of meat) tajada; (of bread) rebanada; (of lemon) rodaja; (utensil) pala ♦ vt cortar (en tajos); rebanar

slick [slɪk] adj (skilful) hábil, diestro; (clever) astuto ♦ n (also: oil ~) marea negra

slide [slaɪd] (pt, pp slid) n (movement) descenso, desprendimiento; (in playground) tobogán m; (PHOT) diapositiva; (BRIT: also: hair ~) pasador m ♦ vt correr, deslizar ♦ vi (slip) resbalarse; (glide) deslizarse; **sliding** adj (door) corredizo; **sliding scale** n escala móvil

slight [slaɪt] adj (slim) delgado; (frail) delicado; (pain etc) leve; (trivial) insignificante; (small) pequeño ♦ n desaire m ♦ vt (insult) ofender, desairar; **not in the ~est** en absoluto; **~ly** adv ligeramente, un poco

slim [slɪm] adj delgado, esbelto; (fig: chance) remoto ♦ vi adelgazar

slime [slaɪm] n limo, cieno

slimming ['slɪmɪŋ] n adelgazamiento

slimy ['slaɪmɪ] adj cenagoso

sling [slɪŋ] (pt, pp slung) n (MED) cabestrillo; (weapon) honda ♦ vt tirar, arrojar

slip [slɪp] n (slide) resbalón m; (mistake) descuido; (underskirt) combinación f; (of paper) papelito ♦ vt (slide) deslizar ♦ vi deslizarse; (stumble) resbalar(se); (decline) decaer; (move smoothly): **to ~ into/out of** (room etc) introducirse en/salirse de; **to give sb the ~** eludir a uno; **a ~ of the tongue** un lapsus; **to ~ sth on/off** ponerse/quitarse algo; **~ away** vi escabullirse; **~ in** vt meter ♦ vi meterse; **~ out** vi (go out) salir (un momento); **~ up** vi (make mistake) equivocarse; meter la pata; **~ped disc** n vértebra dislocada

slipper ['slɪpə*] n zapatilla, pantufla

slippery ['slɪpərɪ] adj resbaladizo

slip: **~ road** (BRIT) n carretera de acceso; **~-up** n (error) desliz m; **~way** n grada, gradas fpl

slit [slɪt] (pt, pp slit) n raja; (cut) corte m ♦ vt rajar; cortar

slither ['slɪðə*] vi deslizarse

sliver ['slɪvə*] n (of glass, wood) astilla; (of cheese etc) raja

slob [slɒb] (inf) n abandonado/a

slog [slɒg] (BRIT) vi sudar tinta; **it was a ~** costó trabajo (hacerlo)

slogan ['sləʊgən] n eslogan m, lema m

slope [sləʊp] n (up) cuesta, pendiente f; (down) declive m; (side of mountain) falda, vertiente m ♦ vi: **to ~ down** estar en declive;

to ~ up inclinarse; **sloping** adj en pendiente; en declive; (writing) inclinado

sloppy ['slɔpɪ] adj (work) descuidado; (appearance) desaliñado

slot [slɔt] n ranura ♦ vt: to ~ **into** encajar en

slot machine n (BRIT: vending machine) distribuidor m automático; (for gambling) tragaperras m inv

slouch [slautʃ] vi andar etc con los hombros caídos

Slovenia [sləu'viːnɪə] n Eslovenia

slovenly ['slʌvənlɪ] adj desaliñado, desaseado; (careless) descuidado

slow [sləu] adj lento; (not clever) lerdo; (watch): to be ~ atrasar ♦ adv lentamente, despacio ♦ vt, vi (also: ~ down, ~ up) retardar; "~" (road sign) "disminuir velocidad"; **~down** (US) n huelga de manos caídas; **~ly** adv lentamente, despacio; ~ **motion** n: **in** ~ **motion** a cámara lenta

sludge [slʌdʒ] n lodo, fango

slug [slʌg] n babosa; (bullet) posta; **~gish** adj lento; (person) perezoso

sluice [sluːs] n (gate) esclusa; (channel) canal m

slum [slʌm] n casucha

slump [slʌmp] n (economic) depresión f ♦ vi hundirse; (prices) caer en picado

slung [slʌŋ] pt, pp of **sling**

slur [sləː*] n: to cast a ~ **on** insultar ♦ vt (speech) pronunciar mal

slush [slʌʃ] n nieve f a medio derretir

slut [slʌt] n putona

sly [slaɪ] adj astuto; (smile) taimado

smack [smæk] n bofetada ♦ vt dar con la mano a; (child, on face) abofetear ♦ vi: to ~ of saber a, oler a

small [smɔːl] adj pequeño; ~ **ads** (BRIT) npl anuncios mpl por palabras; ~ **change** n suelto, cambio; **~holder** (BRIT) n granjero/a, parcelero/a; ~ **hours** npl: **in the** ~ **hours** a las altas horas (de la noche); **~pox** n viruela; ~ **talk** n cháchara

smart [smaːt] adj elegante; (clever) listo, inteligente; (quick) rápido, vivo ♦ vi escocer, picar; **~en up** vi arreglarse ♦ vt arreglar

smash [smæʃ] n (also: ~-up) choque m; (MUS) exitazo ♦ vt (break) hacer pedazos; (car etc) estrellar; (SPORT: record) batir ♦ vi hacerse pedazos; (against wall etc) estrellarse; **~ing** (inf) adj estupendo

smattering ['smætərɪŋ] n: **a ~ of** algo de

smear [smɪə*] n mancha; (MED) frotis m inv ♦ vt untar; ~ **campaign** n campaña de desprestigio

smell [smɛl] (pt, pp **smelt** or **smelled**) n olor m; (sense) olfato ♦ vt, vi oler; **~y** adj maloliente

smile [smaɪl] n sonrisa ♦ vi sonreír

smirk [sməːk] n sonrisa falsa or afectada

smith [smɪθ] n herrero; **~y** ['smɪðɪ] n herrería

smog [smɔg] n esmog m

smoke [sməuk] n humo ♦ vi fumar; (chimney) echar humo ♦ vt (cigarettes) fumar; **~d** adj (bacon, glass) ahumado; **~r** n fumador(a) m/f; (RAIL) coche m fumador; ~ **screen** n cortina de humo; ~ **shop** (US) n estanco (SP), tabaquería (AM); **smoking** n: **"no smoking"** "prohibido fumar"; **smoky** adj (room) lleno de humo; (taste) ahumado

smolder ['sməuldə*] (US) vi = **smoulder**

smooth [smuːð] adj liso; (sea) tranquilo; (flavour, movement) suave; (sauce) fino; (person: pej) meloso ♦ vt (also: ~ out) alisar; (creases, difficulties) allanar

smother ['smʌðə*] vt sofocar; (repress) contener

smoulder ['sməuldə*] (US **smolder**) vi arder sin llama

smudge [smʌdʒ] n mancha ♦ vt manchar

smug [smʌg] adj presumido; orondo

smuggle ['smʌgl] vt pasar de contrabando; **~r** n contrabandista m/f; **smuggling** n contrabando

smutty ['smʌtɪ] adj (fig) verde, obsceno

snack [snæk] n bocado; ~ **bar** n cafetería

snag [snæg] n problema m

snail [sneɪl] n caracol m

snake [sneɪk] n serpiente f

snap [snæp] n (sound) chasquido; (photograph) foto f ♦ adj (decision) instantáneo ♦ vt (break) quebrar; (fingers) castañetear ♦ vi quebrarse; (fig: speak sharply) contestar bruscamente; to ~ **shut** cerrarse de golpe; ~ **at** vt fus (subj: dog) intentar morder; ~ **off** vi partirse; ~ **up** vt agarrar; ~ **fastener** (US) n botón m de presión; **~py** (inf) adj (answer) instantáneo; (slogan) conciso; **make it ~py!** (hurry up) ¡date prisa!, ¡menéate!; **~shot** n foto f (instantánea)

snare [snɛə*] n trampa

snarl [snaːl] vi gruñir

snatch [snætʃ] n (small piece) fragmento ♦ vt (~ away) arrebatar; (fig) agarrar; to ~ **some sleep** encontrar tiempo para dormir

sneak [sniːk] (pt (US) **snuck**) vi: to ~ **in/out** entrar/salir a hurtadillas ♦ n (inf) soplón/ona m/f; to ~ **up on sb** aparecérsele de improviso a uno; **~ers** npl zapatos mpl de lona; **~y** adj furtivo

sneer [snɪə*] vi reír con sarcasmo; (mock): to ~ **at** burlarse de

sneeze [sniːz] vi estornudar

sniff [snɪf] vi sollozar ♦ vt husmear, oler; (drugs) esnifar

snigger ['snɪgə*] vi reírse con disimulo

snip [snɪp] n tijeretazo; (BRIT: inf: bargain) ganga ♦ vt tijeretear

sniper ['snaɪpə*] n francotirador(a) m/f
snippet ['snɪpɪt] n retazo
snob [snɔb] n (e)snob m/f; **~bery** n (e)snobismo; **~bish** adj (e)snob
snooker ['snu:kə*] n especie de billar
snoop [snu:p] vi: **to ~ about** fisgonear
snooze [snu:z] n siesta ♦ vi echar una siesta
snore [snɔ:*] n ronquido ♦ vi roncar
snorkel ['snɔ:kl] n (tubo) respirador m
snort [snɔ:t] n bufido ♦ vi bufar
snout [snaut] n hocico, morro
snow [snəu] n nieve f ♦ vi nevar; **~ball** n bola de nieve ♦ vi (fig) agrandarse, ampliarse; **~bound** adj bloqueado por la nieve; **~drift** n ventisquero; **~drop** n campanilla; **~fall** n nevada; **~flake** n copo de nieve; **~man** (irreg) n figura de nieve; **~plough** (US **~plow**) n quitanieves m inv; **~shoe** n raqueta (de nieve); **~storm** n nevada, nevasca
snub [snʌb] vt (person) desairar ♦ n desaire m, repulsa; **~-nosed** adj chato
snuff [snʌf] n rapé m
snug [snʌg] adj (cosy) cómodo; (fitted) ajustado
snuggle ['snʌgl] vi: **to ~ up to sb** arrimarse a uno

KEYWORD

so [səu] adv 1 (thus, likewise) así, de este modo; **if ~** de ser así; **I like swimming — ~ do I** a mí me gusta nadar — a mí también; **I've got work to do — ~ has Paul** tengo trabajo que hacer — Paul también; **it's 5 o'clock — ~ it is!** son las cinco — ¡pues es verdad!; **I hope/think ~** espero/creo que sí; **~ far** hasta ahora; (in past) hasta este momento
2 (in comparisons etc: to such a degree) tan; **~ quickly (that)** tan rápido (que); **~ big (that)** tan grande (que); **she's not ~ clever as her brother** no es tan lista como su hermano; **we were ~ worried** estábamos preocupadísimos
3: **~ much** adj, adv tanto; **~ many** tantos/as
4 (phrases): **10 or ~** unos 10, 10 o así; **~ long!** (inf: goodbye) ¡hasta luego!
♦ conj 1 (expressing purpose): **~ as to do** para hacer; **~ (that)** para que + sub
2 (expressing result) así que; **~ you see, I could have gone** así que ya ves, (yo) podría haber ido

soak [səuk] vt (drench) empapar; (steep in water) remojar ♦ vi remojarse, estar a remojo; **~ in** vi penetrar; **~ up** vt absorber
soap [səup] n jabón m; **~flakes** npl escamas fpl de jabón; **~ opera** n telenovela; **~ powder** n jabón m en polvo; **~y** adj jabonoso
soar [sɔ:*] vi (on wings) remontarse; (rocket, prices) dispararse; (building etc) elevarse

sob [sɔb] n sollozo ♦ vi sollozar
sober ['səubə*] adj (serious) serio; (not drunk) sobrio; (colour, style) discreto; **~ up** vt quitar la borrachera
so-called [-'kɔ:ld] adj así llamado
soccer ['sɔkə*] n fútbol m
social ['səuʃl] adj social ♦ n velada, fiesta; **~ club** n club m; **~ism** n socialismo; **~ist** adj, n socialista m/f; **~ize** vi: **to ~ize (with)** alternar (con); **~ly** adv socialmente; **~ security** n seguridad f social; **~ work** n asistencia social; **~ worker** n asistente/a m/f social
society [sə'saɪətɪ] n sociedad f; (club) asociación f; (also: high ~) alta sociedad
sociology [səusɪ'ɔlədʒɪ] n sociología
sock [sɔk] n calcetín m (SP), media (AM)
socket ['sɔkɪt] n cavidad f; (BRIT: ELEC) enchufe m
sod [sɔd] n (of earth) césped m; (BRIT: inf!) cabrón/ona m/f (!)
soda ['səudə] n (CHEM) sosa; (also: ~ water) soda; (US: also: ~ pop) gaseosa
sofa ['səufə] n sofá m
soft [sɔft] adj (lenient, not hard) blando; (gentle, not bright) suave; **~ drink** n bebida no alcohólica; **~en** ['sɔfn] vt ablandar; suavizar; (effect) amortiguar ♦ vi ablandarse; suavizarse; **~ly** adv suavemente; (gently) delicadamente, con delicadeza; **~ness** n blandura; suavidad f; **~ware** n (COMPUT) software m
soggy ['sɔgɪ] adj empapado
soil [sɔɪl] n (earth) tierra, suelo ♦ vt ensuciar; **~ed** adj sucio
solar ['səulə*] adj: **~ energy** n energía solar; **~ panel** n panel m solar
sold [səuld] pt, pp of **sell**; **~ out** adj (COMM) agotado
solder ['səuldə*] vt soldar ♦ n soldadura
soldier ['səuldʒə*] n soldado; (army man) militar m
sole [səul] n (of foot) planta; (of shoe) suela; (fish: pl inv) lenguado ♦ adj único
solemn ['sɔləm] adj solemne
sole trader n (COMM) comerciante m exclusivo
solicit [sə'lɪsɪt] vt (request) solicitar ♦ vi (prostitute) importunar
solicitor [sə'lɪsɪtə*] (BRIT) n (for wills etc) ≈ notario/a; (in court) ≈ abogado/a
solid ['sɔlɪd] adj sólido; (gold etc) macizo ♦ n sólido; **~s** npl (food) alimentos mpl sólidos
solidarity [sɔlɪ'dærɪtɪ] n solidaridad f
solitary ['sɔlɪtərɪ] adj solitario, solo; **~ confinement** n incomunicación f
solo ['səuləu] n solo ♦ adv (fly) en solitario; **~ist** n solista m/f
soluble ['sɔljuːbl] adj soluble

solution [sə'luːʃən] n solución f
solve [sɔlv] vt resolver, solucionar
solvent ['sɔlvənt] adj (COMM) solvente ♦ n (CHEM) solvente m

KEYWORD
---

some [sʌm] adj 1 (a certain amount or number of): ~ tea/water/biscuits té/agua/(unas) galletas; there's ~ milk in the fridge hay leche en el frigo; there were ~ people outside había algunas personas fuera; I've got ~ money, but not much tengo algo de dinero, pero no mucho
2 (certain: in contrasts) algunos/as; ~ people say that ... hay quien dice que ...; ~ films were excellent, but most were mediocre hubo películas excelentes, pero la mayoría fueron mediocres
3 (unspecified): ~ woman was asking for you una mujer estuvo preguntando por ti; he was asking for ~ book (or other) pedía un libro; ~ day algún día; ~ day next week un día de la semana que viene
♦ pron 1 (a certain number): I've got ~ (books etc) tengo algunos/as
2 (a certain amount) algo; I've got ~ (money, milk) tengo algo; could I have ~ of that cheese? ¿me puede dar un poco de ese queso?; I've read ~ of the book he leído parte del libro
♦ adv: ~ 10 people unas 10 personas, una decena de personas

some: ~body ['sʌmbədɪ] pron = **someone**; **~how** adv de alguna manera; (for some reason) por una u otra razón; **~one** pron alguien; **~place** (US) adv = **somewhere**
somersault ['sʌməsɔːlt] n (deliberate) salto mortal; (accidental) vuelco ♦ vi dar un salto mortal; dar vuelcos
some: ~thing pron algo; **would you like ~thing to eat/drink?** ¿te gustaría cenar/tomar algo?; **~time** adv (in future) algún día, en algún momento; (in past): **~time last month** durante el mes pasado; **~times** adv a veces; **~what** adv algo; **~where** adv (be) en alguna parte; (go) a alguna parte; **~where else** (be) en otra parte; (go) a otra parte
son [sʌn] n hijo
song [sɔŋ] n canción f
son-in-law n yerno
soon [suːn] adv pronto, dentro de poco; ~ afterwards poco después; see also as; **~er** adv (time) antes, más temprano; (preference): I would **~er** do that preferiría hacer eso; **~er or later** tarde o temprano
soot [sut] n hollín m
soothe [suːð] vt tranquilizar; (pain) aliviar
sophisticated [sə'fɪstɪkeɪtɪd] adj sofisticado

sophomore ['sɔfəmɔː*] (US) n estudiante m/f de segundo año
sopping ['sɔpɪŋ] adj: ~ (wet) empapado
soppy ['sɔpɪ] (pej) adj tonto
soprano [sə'prɑːnəu] n soprano f
sorcerer ['sɔːsərə*] n hechicero
sore [sɔː*] adj (painful) doloroso, que duele ♦ n llaga; **~ly** adv: I am **~ly** tempted to estoy muy tentado a
sorrow ['sɔrəu] n pena, dolor m; **~s** npl pesares mpl; **~ful** adj triste
sorry ['sɔrɪ] adj (regretful) arrepentido; (condition, excuse) lastimoso; **~!** ¡perdón!, ¡perdone!; **~?** ¿cómo?; **to feel ~ for sb** tener lástima a uno; I feel **~ for him** me da lástima
sort [sɔːt] n clase f, género, tipo ♦ vt (also: ~ out: papers) clasificar; (: problems) arreglar, solucionar; **~ing office** n sala de batalla
SOS n SOS m
so-so adv regular, así así
soufflé ['suːfleɪ] n suflé m
sought [sɔːt] pt, pp of **seek**
soul [səul] n alma; **~ful** adj lleno de sentimiento
sound [saund] n (noise) sonido, ruido; (volume: on TV etc) volumen m; (CEO) estrecho ♦ adj (healthy) sano; (safe, not damaged) en buen estado; (reliable: person) digno de confianza; (sensible) sensato, razonable; (secure: investment) seguro ♦ adv: ~ asleep profundamente dormido ♦ vt (alarm) sonar ♦ vi sonar, resonar; (fig: seem) parecer; to ~ like sonar a; ~ out sondear; ~ barrier n barrera del sonido; **~bite** n cita jugosa; ~ effects npl efectos mpl sonoros; **~ly** adv (sleep) profundamente; (defeated) completamente; **~proof** adj insonorizado; **~track** n (of film) banda sonora
soup [suːp] n (thick) sopa; (thin) caldo; ~ plate n plato sopero; **~spoon** n cuchara sopera
sour ['sauə*] adj agrio; (milk) cortado; it's ~ grapes (fig) están verdes
source [sɔːs] n fuente f
south [sauθ] n sur m ♦ adj del sur, sureño ♦ adv al sur, hacia el sur; **S~ Africa** n África del Sur; **S~ African** adj, n sudafricano/a m/f; **S~ America** n América del Sur, Sudamérica; **S~ American** adj, n sudamericano/a m/f; **~-east** n sudeste m; **~erly** ['sʌðəlɪ] adj sur; (from the ~) del sur; **~ern** ['sʌðən] adj del sur, meridional; **S~ Pole** n Polo Sur; **~ward(s)** adv hacia el sur; **~-west** n suroeste m
souvenir [suːvə'nɪə*] n recuerdo
sovereign ['sɔvrɪn] adj, n soberano/a m/f; **~ty** n soberanía
soviet ['səuvɪət] adj soviético; the S~ Union la Unión Soviética

sow¹ [səu] (*pt* **sowed**, *pp* **sown**) *vt* sembrar

sow² [sau] *n* cerda (*SP*), puerca (*SP*), chancha (*AM*)

soy [sɔɪ] (*US*) *n* = **soya**

soya ['sɔɪə] (*BRIT*) *n* soja; **~ bean** *n* haba de soja; **~ sauce** *n* salsa de soja

spa [spa:] *n* balneario

space [speɪs] *n* espacio; (*room*) sitio ♦ *cpd* espacial ♦ *vt* (*also:* ~ **out**) espaciar; **~craft** *n* nave *f* espacial; **~man/woman** (*irreg*) *n* astronauta *m/f*, cosmonauta *m/f*; **~ship** *n* = **~craft**; **spacing** *n* espaciado

spacious ['speɪʃəs] *adj* amplio

spade [speɪd] *n* (*tool*) pala, laya; **~s** *npl* (*CARDS: British*) picas *fpl*; (: *Spanish*) espadas *fpl*

spaghetti [spə'geti] *n* espaguetis *mpl*, fideos *mpl*

Spain [speɪn] *n* España

span [spæn] *n* (*of bird, plane*) envergadura; (*of arch*) luz *f*; (*in time*) lapso ♦ *vt* extenderse sobre, cruzar; (*fig*) abarcar

Spaniard ['spænjəd] *n* español(a) *m/f*

spaniel ['spænjəl] *n* perro de aguas

Spanish ['spænɪʃ] *adj* español(a) ♦ *n* (*LING*) español *m*, castellano; **the ~** *npl* los españoles

spank [spæŋk] *vt* zurrar

spanner ['spænə*] (*BRIT*) *n* llave *f* (inglesa)

spare [spεə*] *adj* de reserva; (*surplus*) sobrante, de más ♦ *n* = **~ part** ♦ *vt* (*do without*) pasarse sin; (*refrain from hurting*) perdonar; **to ~** (*surplus*) sobrante, de sobra; **~ part** *n* pieza de repuesto; **~ time** *n* tiempo libre; **~ wheel** *n* (*AUT*) rueda de recambio

sparingly ['spεərɪŋlɪ] *adv* con moderación

spark [spa:k] *n* chispa; (*fig*) chispazo; **~(ing) plug** *n* bujía

sparkle ['spa:kl] *n* centelleo, destello ♦ *vi* (*shine*) relucir, brillar; **sparkling** *adj* (*eyes, conversation*) brillante; (*wine*) espumoso; (*mineral water*) con gas

sparrow ['spærəu] *n* gorrión *m*

sparse [spa:s] *adj* esparcido, escaso

spartan ['spa:tən] *adj* (*fig*) espartano

spasm ['spæzəm] *n* (*MED*) espasmo

spastic ['spæstɪk] *n* espástico/a

spat [spæt] *pt, pp of* **spit**

spate [speɪt] *n* (*fig*): **a ~ of** un torrente de

spawn [spɔ:n] *vi* desovar, frezar ♦ *n* huevas *fpl*

speak [spi:k] (*pt* **spoke**, *pp* **spoken**) *vt* (*language*) hablar; (*truth*) decir ♦ *vi* hablar; (*make a speech*) intervenir; **to ~ to sb/of or about sth** hablar con uno/de or sobre algo; **~ up!** ¡habla fuerte!; **~er** *n* (*in public*) orador(a) *m/f*; (*also: loud~er*) altavoz *m*; (*for stereo etc*) bafle *m*; (*POL*): **the S~er** (*BRIT*) el Presidente de la Cámara de los Comunes; (*US*)

el Presidente del Congreso

spear [spɪə*] *n* lanza ♦ *vt* alancear; **~head** *vt* (*attack etc*) encabezar

spec [spek] (*inf*) *n*: **on ~** como especulación

special ['speʃl] *adj* especial; (*edition etc*) extraordinario; (*delivery*) urgente; **~ist** *n* especialista *m/f*; **~ity** [speʃɪ'ælɪtɪ] (*BRIT*) *n* especialidad *f*; **~ize** *vi*: **to ~ize (in)** especializarse (en); **~ly** *adv* sobre todo, en particular; **~ty** (*US*) *n* = **~ity**

species ['spi:ʃi:z] *n inv* especie *f*

specific [spə'sɪfɪk] *adj* específico; **~ally** *adv* específicamente

specify ['spesɪfaɪ] *vt, vi* especificar, precisar

specimen ['spesɪmən] *n* ejemplar *m*; (*MED: of urine*) espécimen *m* (: *of blood*) muestra

speck [spek] *n* grano, mota

speckled ['spekld] *adj* moteado

specs [speks] (*inf*) *npl* gafas *fpl* (*SP*), anteojos *mpl*

spectacle ['spektəkl] *n* espectáculo; **~s** *npl* (*BRIT: glasses*) gafas *fpl* (*SP*), anteojos *mpl*; **spectacular** [-'tækjulə*] *adj* espectacular; (*success*) impresionante

spectator [spek'teɪtə*] *n* espectador(a) *m/f*

spectrum ['spektrəm] (*pl* **spectra**) *n* espectro

speculate ['spekjuleɪt] *vi*: **to ~ (on)** especular (en); **speculation** [spekju'leɪʃən] *n* especulación *f*

speech [spi:tʃ] *n* (*faculty*) habla; (*formal talk*) discurso; (*spoken language*) lenguaje *m*; **~less** *adj* mudo, estupefacto; **~ therapist** *n* especialista que corrige defectos de pronunciación en los niños

speed [spi:d] *n* velocidad *f*; (*haste*) prisa; (*promptness*) rapidez *f*; **at full or top ~** a máxima velocidad; **~ up** *vi* acelerarse ♦ *vt* acelerar; **~boat** *n* lancha motora; **~ily** *adv* rápido, rápidamente; **~ing** *n* (*AUT*) exceso de velocidad; **~ limit** *n* límite *m* de velocidad, velocidad *f* máxima; **~ometer** [spɪ'dɔmɪtə*] *n* velocímetro; **~way** *n* (*sport*) pista de carrera; **~y** *adj* (*fast*) veloz, rápido; (*prompt*) pronto

spell [spel] (*pt, pp* **spelt** (*BRIT*) or **spelled**) *n* (*also: magic ~*) encanto, hechizo; (*period of time*) rato, período ♦ *vt* deletrear; (*fig*) anunciar, presagiar; **to cast a ~ on sb** hechizar a uno; **he can't ~** pone faltas de ortografía; **~bound** *adj* embelesado, hechizado; **~ing** *n* ortografía

spend [spend] (*pt, pp* **spent**) *vt* (*money*) gastar; (*time*) pasar; (*life*) dedicar; **~thrift** *n* derrochador/a *m/f*, pródigo/a

sperm [spə:m] *n* esperma

sphere [sfɪə*] *n* esfera

sphinx [sfɪŋks] *n* esfinge *f*

spice [spaɪs] *n* especia ♦ *vt* condimentar

spicy ['spaɪsɪ] *adj* picante

spider ['spaɪdə*] n araña

spike [spaɪk] n (point) punta; (BOT) espiga

spill [spɪl] (pt, pp spilt or spilled) vt derramar, verter ♦ vi derramarse; **to ~ over** desbordarse

spin [spɪn] (pt, pp spun) n (AVIAT) barrena; (trip in car) paseo (en coche); (on ball) efecto ♦ vt (wool etc) hilar; (ball etc) hacer girar ♦ vi girar, dar vueltas

spinach ['spɪnɪtʃ] n espinaca; (as food) espinacas fpl

spinal ['spaɪnl] adj espinal; **~ cord** n columna vertebral

spin doctor n informador(a) parcial al servicio de un partido político etc

spin-dryer (BRIT) n secador m centrífugo

spine [spaɪn] n espinazo, columna vertebral; (thorn) espina; **~less** adj (fig) débil, pusilánime

spinning ['spɪnɪŋ] n hilandería; **~ top** n peonza

spin-off n derivado, producto secundario

spinster ['spɪnstə*] n solterona

spiral ['spaɪərl] n espiral f ♦ vi (fig: prices) subir desorbitadamente; **~ staircase** n escalera de caracol

spire ['spaɪə*] n aguja, chapitel m

spirit ['spɪrɪt] n (soul) alma f; (ghost) fantasma m; (attitude, sense) espíritu m; (courage) valor m, ánimo; **~s** npl (drink) licor(es) m(pl); **in good ~s** alegre, de buen ánimo; **~ed** adj enérgico, vigoroso

spiritual ['spɪrɪtjuəl] adj espiritual ♦ n espiritual m

spit [spɪt] (pt, pp spat) n (for roasting) asador m, espetón m; (saliva) saliva ♦ vi escupir; (sound) chisporrotear; (rain) lloviznar

spite [spaɪt] n rencor m, ojeriza ♦ vt causar pena a, mortificar; **in ~ of** a pesar de, pese a; **~ful** adj rencoroso, malévolo

spittle ['spɪtl] n saliva, baba

splash [splæʃ] n (sound) chapoteo; (of colour) mancha ♦ vt salpicar ♦ vi (also: ~ about) chapotear

spleen [spliːn] n (ANAT) bazo

splendid ['splendɪd] adj espléndido

splint [splɪnt] n tablilla

splinter ['splɪntə*] n (of wood etc) astilla; (in finger) espigón m ♦ vi astillarse, hacer astillas

split [splɪt] (pt, pp split) n hendedura, raja; (fig) división f; (POL) escisión f ♦ vt partir, rajar; (party) dividir; (share) repartir ♦ vi dividirse, escindirse; **~ up** vi (couple) separarse; (meeting) acabarse

spoil [spɔɪl] (pt, pp spoilt or spoiled) vt (damage) dañar; (mar) estropear; (child) mimar, consentir; **~s** npl despojo, botín m; **~sport** n aguafiestas m inv

spoke [spəʊk] pt of **speak** ♦ n rayo, radio

spoken ['spəʊkn] pp of **speak**

spokesman ['spəʊksmən] (irreg) n portavoz m; **spokeswoman** ['spəʊkswʊmən] (irreg) n portavoz f

sponge [spʌndʒ] n esponja; (also: ~ cake) bizcocho ♦ vt (wash) lavar con esponja ♦ vi: **to ~ off** or **on sb** vivir a costa de uno; **~ bag** (BRIT) n esponjera

sponsor ['spɒnsə*] n patrocinador(a) m/f ♦ vt (applicant, proposal etc) proponer; **~ship** n patrocinio

spontaneous [spɒn'teɪnɪəs] adj espontáneo

spooky ['spuːkɪ] (inf) adj espeluznante, horripilante

spool [spuːl] n carrete m

spoon [spuːn] n cuchara; **~-feed** vt dar de comer con cuchara a; (fig) tratar como un niño a; **~ful** n cucharada

sport [spɔːt] n deporte m; (person): **to be a good ~** ser muy majo ♦ vt (wear) lucir, ostentar; **~ing** adj deportivo; (generous) caballeroso; **to give sb a ~ing chance** darle a uno una (buena) oportunidad; **~ jacket** (US) n = **~s jacket**; **~s car** n coche m deportivo; **~s jacket** (BRIT) n chaqueta deportiva; **~sman** (irreg) n deportista m; **~smanship** n deportividad f; **~swear** n trajes mpl de deporte or sport; **~swoman** (irreg) n deportista f; **~y** adj deportista

spot [spɒt] n sitio, lugar m; (dot: on pattern) punto, mancha; (pimple) grano; (RADIO) cuña publicitaria; (TV) espacio publicitario; (small amount): **a ~ of** un poquito de ♦ vt (notice) notar, observar; **on the ~** allí mismo; **~ check** n reconocimiento rápido; **~less** adj perfectamente limpio; **~light** n foco, reflector m; (AUT) faro auxiliar; **~ted** adj (pattern) de puntos; **~ty** adj (face) con granos

spouse [spaʊz] n cónyuge m/f

spout [spaʊt] n (of jug) pico; (of pipe) caño ♦ vi salir en chorro

sprain [spreɪn] n torcedura ♦ vt: **to ~ one's ankle/wrist** torcerse el tobillo/la muñeca

sprang [spræŋ] pt of **spring**

sprawl [sprɔːl] vi tumbarse

spray [spreɪ] n rociada; (of sea) espuma; (container) atomizador m; (for paint etc) pistola rociadora; (of flowers) ramita ♦ vt rociar; (crops) regar

spread [spred] (pt, pp spread) n extensión f; (for bread etc) pasta para untar; (inf: food) comilona ♦ vt extender; (butter) untar; (wings, sails) desplegar; (work, wealth) repartir; (scatter) esparcir ♦ vi (also: ~ out: stain) extenderse; (news) diseminarse; **~ out** vi (move apart) separarse; **~-eagled** adj a pata tendida; **~sheet** n hoja electrónica or de cálculo

spree [spriː] n: **to go on a ~** ir de juerga

sprightly ['spraɪtlɪ] adj vivo, enérgico

spring [sprɪŋ] (pt **sprang**, pp **sprung**) n (season) primavera; (leap) salto, brinco; (coiled metal) resorte m; (of water) fuente f, manantial m ♦ vi saltar, brincar; **~ up** vi (thing: appear) aparecer; (problem) surgir; **~board** n trampolín m; **~-clean(ing)** n limpieza general; **~time** n primavera

sprinkle ['sprɪŋkl] vt (pour: liquid) rociar; (: salt, sugar) espolvorear; **to ~ water** etc **on**, **~ with water** etc rociar or salpicar de agua etc; **~r** n (for lawn) rociadera; (to put out fire) aparato de rociadura automática

sprint [sprɪnt] n esprint m ♦ vi esprintar

sprout [spraut] vi brotar, retoñar; **(Brussels) ~s** npl coles fpl de Bruselas

spruce [spruːs] n inv (BOT) pícea ♦ adj aseado, pulcro

sprung [sprʌŋ] pp of **spring**

spun [spʌn] pt, pp of **spin**

spur [spəː*] n espuela; (fig) estímulo, aguijón m ♦ vt (also: **~ on**) estimular, incitar; **on the ~ of the moment** de improviso

spurious ['spjuərɪəs] adj falso

spurn [spəːn] vt desdeñar, rechazar

spurt [spəːt] n chorro; (of energy) arrebato ♦ vi chorrear

spy [spaɪ] n espía m/f ♦ vi: **to ~ on** espiar a ♦ vt (see) divisar, lograr ver; **~ing** n espionaje m

sq. abbr = **square**

squabble ['skwɔbl] vi reñir, pelear

squad [skwɔd] n (MIL) pelotón m; (POLICE) brigada; (SPORT) equipo

squadron ['skwɔdrn] n (MIL) escuadrón m; (AVIAT, NAUT) escuadra

squalid ['skwɔlɪd] adj vil; (fig: sordid) sórdido

squall [skwɔːl] n (storm) chubasco; (wind) ráfaga

squalor ['skwɔlə*] n miseria

squander ['skwɔndə*] vt (money) derrochar, despilfarrar; (chances) desperdiciar

square [skwɛə*] n cuadro; (in town) plaza; (inf: person) carca m/f ♦ adj cuadrado; (inf: ideas, tastes) trasnochado ♦ vt (arrange) arreglar; (MATH) cuadrar; (reconcile) compaginar; **all ~** igual(es); **to have a ~ meal** comer caliente; **2 metres ~** 2 metros en cuadro; **2 ~ metres** 2 metros cuadrados; **~ly** adv de lleno

squash [skwɔʃ] n (BRIT: drink): **lemon/orange ~** zumo (SP) or jugo (AM) de limón/naranja; (US: BOT) calabacín m; (SPORT) squash m, frontenis m ♦ vt aplastar

squat [skwɔt] adj achaparrado ♦ vi (also: **~ down**) agacharse, sentarse en cuclillas; **~ter** n persona que ocupa ilegalmente una casa

squeak [skwiːk] vi (hinge) chirriar, rechinar; (mouse) chillar

squeal [skwiːl] vi chillar, dar gritos agudos

squeamish ['skwiːmɪʃ] adj delicado, remilgado

squeeze [skwiːz] n presión f; (of hand) apretón m; (COMM) restricción f ♦ vt (hand, arm) apretar; **~ out** vt exprimir

squelch [skwɛltʃ] vi chapotear

squid [skwɪd] n inv calamar m; (CULIN) calamares mpl

squiggle ['skwɪgl] n garabato

squint [skwɪnt] vi bizquear, ser bizco ♦ n (MED) estrabismo

squirm [skwəːm] vi retorcerse, revolverse

squirrel ['skwɪrəl] n ardilla

squirt [skwəːt] vi salir a chorros ♦ vt chiscar

Sr abbr = **senior**

St abbr = **saint**; **street**

stab [stæb] n (with knife) puñalada; (of pain) pinchazo; (inf: try): **to have a ~ at (doing) sth** intentar (hacer) algo ♦ vt apuñalar

stable ['steɪbl] adj estable ♦ n cuadra, caballeriza

stack [stæk] n montón m, pila ♦ vt amontonar, apilar

stadium ['steɪdɪəm] n estadio

staff [stɑːf] n (work force) personal m, plantilla; (BRIT: SCOL) cuerpo docente ♦ vt proveer de personal

stag [stæg] n ciervo, venado

stage [steɪdʒ] n escena; (point) etapa; (platform) plataforma; (profession): **the ~** el teatro ♦ vt (play) poner en escena, representar; (organize) montar, organizar; **in ~s** por etapas; **~coach** n diligencia; **~ manager** n director(a) m/f de escena

stagger ['stægə*] vi tambalearse ♦ vt (amaze) asombrar; (hours, holidays) escalonar; **~ing** adj asombroso

stagnant ['stægnənt] adj estancado

stag party n despedida de soltero

staid [steɪd] adj serio, formal

stain [steɪn] n mancha; (colouring) tintura ♦ vt manchar; (wood) teñir; **~ed glass window** n vidriera de colores; **~less steel** n acero inoxidable; **~ remover** n quitamanchas m inv

stair [stɛə*] n (step) peldaño, escalón m; **~s** npl escaleras fpl; **~case** n = **~way**; **~way** n escalera

stake [steɪk] n estaca, poste m; (COMM) interés m; (BETTING) apuesta ♦ vt (money) apostar; (life) arriesgar; (reputation) poner en juego; (claim) presentar una reclamación; **to be at ~** estar en juego

stale [steɪl] adj (bread) duro; (food) pasado; (smell) rancio; (beer) agrio

stalemate ['steɪlmeɪt] n tablas fpl (por ahogado); (fig) estancamiento

stalk [stɔːk] n tallo, caña ♦ vt acechar, cazar al acecho; **~ off** vi irse airado

stall [stɔ:l] n (in market) puesto; (in stable) casilla (de establo) ♦ vt (AUT) calar; (fig) dar largas a ♦ vi (AUT) calarse; (fig) andarse con rodeos; **~s** npl (BRIT: in cinema, theatre) butacas fpl

stallion ['stælɪən] n semental m

stamina ['stæmɪnə] n resistencia

stammer ['stæmə*] n tartamudeo ♦ vi tartamudear

stamp [stæmp] n sello (SP), estampilla (AM) f; (mark, also fig) marca, huella; (on document) timbre m ♦ vi (also: ~ one's foot) patear ♦ vt (mark) marcar; (letter) poner sellos or estampillas en; (with rubber ~) sellar; **~ album** n álbum m para sellos or estampillas; **~ collecting** n filatelia

stampede [stæm'pi:d] n estampida

stance [stæns] n postura

stand [stænd] (pt, pp stood) n (position) posición f, postura; (for taxis) parada; (hall ~) perchero; (music ~) atril m; (SPORT) tribuna; (at exhibition) stand m ♦ vi (be) estar, encontrarse; (be on foot) estar de pie; (rise) levantarse; (remain) quedar en pie; (in election) presentar candidatura ♦ vt (place) poner, colocar; (withstand) aguantar, soportar; (invite to) invitar; **to make a ~** (fig) mantener una postura firme; **to ~ for parliament** (BRIT) presentarse (como candidato) a las elecciones; **~ by** vi (be ready) estar listo ♦ vt fus (opinion) aferrarse a; (person) apoyar; **~ down** vi (withdraw) ceder el puesto; **~ for** vt fus (signify) significar; (tolerate) aguantar, permitir; **~ in for** vt fus suplir a; **~ out** vi destacarse; **~ up** vi levantarse, ponerse de pie; **~ up for** vt fus defender; **~ up to** vt fus hacer frente a

standard ['stændəd] n patrón m, norma; (level) nivel m; (flag) estandarte m ♦ adj (size etc) normal, corriente; (text) básico; **~s** npl (morals) valores mpl morales; **~ lamp** (BRIT) n lámpara de pie; **~ of living** n nivel m de vida

stand-by ['stændbaɪ] n (reserve) recurso seguro; **to be on ~** estar sobre aviso; **~ ticket** n (AVIAT) (billete m) standby m

stand-in ['stændɪn] n suplente m/f

standing ['stændɪŋ] adj (on foot) de pie, en pie; (permanent) permanente ♦ n reputación f; **of many years' ~** que lleva muchos años; **~ joke** n broma permanente; **~ order** (BRIT) n (at bank) orden f de pago permanente; **~ room** n sitio para estar de pie

stand: **~point** n punto de vista; **~still** n: **at a ~still** (industry, traffic) paralizado; (car) parado; **to come to a ~still** quedar paralizado; pararse

stank [stæŋk] pt of stink

staple ['steɪpl] n (for papers) grapa ♦ adj

(food etc) básico ♦ vt grapar; **~r** n grapadora

star [stɑ:*] n estrella; (celebrity) estrella, astro ♦ vt (THEATRE, CINEMA) ser el/la protagonista de; **the ~s** npl (ASTROLOGY) el horóscopo

starboard ['stɑ:bəd] n estribor m

starch [stɑ:tʃ] n almidón m

stardom ['stɑ:dəm] n estrellato

stare [steə*] n mirada fija ♦ vi: **to ~ at** mirar fijo

starfish ['stɑ:fɪʃ] n estrella de mar

stark [stɑ:k] adj (bleak) severo, escueto ♦ adv: **~ naked** en cueros

starling ['stɑ:lɪŋ] n estornino

starry ['stɑ:rɪ] adj estrellado; **~-eyed** adj (innocent) inocentón/ona, ingenuo

start [stɑ:t] n principio, comienzo; (departure) salida; (sudden movement) salto, sobresalto; (advantage) ventaja ♦ vt empezar, comenzar; (cause) causar; (found) fundar; (engine) poner en marcha ♦ vi comenzar, empezar; (with fright) asustarse, sobresaltarse; (train etc) salir; **to ~ doing** or **to do sth** empezar a hacer algo; **~ off** vi empezar, comenzar; (leave) salir, ponerse en camino; **~ up** vi comenzar; (car) ponerse en marcha ♦ vt comenzar; poner en marcha; **~er** n (AUT) botón m de arranque; (SPORT: official) juez m/f de salida; (BRIT: CULIN) entrada; **~ing point** n punto de partida

startle ['stɑ:tl] vt asustar, sobrecoger; **startling** adj alarmante

starvation [stɑ:'veɪʃən] n hambre f

starve [stɑ:v] vi tener mucha hambre; (to death) morir de hambre ♦ vt hacer pasar hambre

state [steɪt] n estado ♦ vt (say, declare) afirmar; **the S~s** los Estados Unidos; **to be in a ~** estar agitado; **~ly** adj majestuoso, imponente; **~ly home** n casa señorial, casa solariega; **~ment** n afirmación f; **~sman** (irreg) n estadista m

static ['stætɪk] n (RADIO) parásitos mpl ♦ adj estático; **~ electricity** n estática

station ['steɪʃən] n (gen) estación f; (RADIO) emisora; (rank) posición f social ♦ vt colocar, situar; (MIL) apostar

stationary ['steɪʃnərɪ] adj estacionario, fijo

stationer ['steɪʃənə*] n papelero/a; **~'s (shop)** (BRIT) n papelería; **~y** [-nərɪ] n papel m de escribir, artículos mpl de escritorio

station master n (RAIL) jefe m de estación

station wagon (US) n ranchera

statistic [stə'tɪstɪk] n estadística; **~s** n (science) estadística

statue ['stætjuː] n estatua

status ['steɪtəs] n estado; (reputation) estatus m; **~ symbol** n símbolo de prestigio

statute ['stætjuːt] n estatuto, ley f; **statutory** adj estatutario

staunch [stɔːntʃ] *adj* leal, incondicional
stay [steɪ] *n* estancia ♦ *vi* quedar(se); (*as guest*) hospedarse; **to ~ put** seguir en el mismo sitio; **to ~ the night/5 days** pasar la noche/estar 5 días; **~ behind** *vi* quedar atrás; **~ in** *vi* quedarse en casa; **~ on** *vi* quedarse; **~ out** *vi* (*of house*) no volver a casa; (*on strike*) permanecer en huelga; **~ up** *vi* (*at night*) velar, no acostarse; **~ing power** *n* aguante *m*
stead [sted] *n*: **in sb's ~** en lugar de uno; **to stand sb in good ~** ser muy útil a uno
steadfast ['stedfɑːst] *adj* firme, resuelto
steadily ['stedɪlɪ] *adv* constantemente; (*firmly*) firmemente; (*work, walk*) sin parar; (*gaze*) fijamente
steady ['stedɪ] *adj* (*firm*) firme; (*regular*) regular; (*person, character*) sensato, juicioso; (*boyfriend*) formal; (*look, voice*) tranquilo ♦ *vt* (*stabilize*) estabilizar; (*nerves*) calmar
steak [steɪk] *n* (*gen*) filete *m*; (*beef*) bistec *m*
steal [stiːl] (*pt* **stole**, *pp* **stolen**) *vt* robar ♦ *vi* robar; (*move secretly*) andar a hurtadillas
stealth [stelθ] *n*: **by ~** a escondidas, sigilosamente; **~y** *adj* cauteloso, sigiloso
steam [stiːm] *n* vapor *m*; (*mist*) vaho, humo ♦ *vt* (*CULIN*) cocer al vapor ♦ *vi* echar vapor; **~ engine** *n* máquina de vapor; **~er** *n* (*buque m de* vapor *m*; **~roller** *n* apisonadora; **~ship** *n* = **~er**; **~y** *adj* (*room*) lleno de vapor; (*window*) empañado; (*heat, atmosphere*) bochorno
steel [stiːl] *n* acero ♦ *adj* de acero; **~works** *n* acería
steep [stiːp] *adj* escarpado, abrupto; (*stair*) empinado; (*price*) exorbitante, excesivo ♦ *vt* empapar, remojar
steeple ['stiːpl] *n* aguja; **~chase** *n* carrera de obstáculos
steer [stɪəʳ] *vt* (*car*) conducir (*SP*), manejar (*AM*); (*person*) dirigir ♦ *vi* conducir, manejar; **~ing** *n* (*AUT*) dirección *f*; **~ing wheel** *n* volante *m*
stem [stem] *n* (*of plant*) tallo; (*of glass*) pie *m* ♦ *vt* detener; (*blood*) restañar; **~ from** *vt fus* ser consecuencia de
stench [stentʃ] *n* hedor *m*
stencil ['stensl] *n* (*pattern*) plantilla ♦ *vt* hacer un cliché de
stenographer [steˈnɒɡrəfəʳ] (*US*) *n* taquígrafo/a
step [step] *n* paso; (*on stair*) peldaño, escalón *m* ♦ *vi*: **to ~ forward/back** dar un paso adelante/hacia atrás; **~s** *npl* (*BRIT*) = **~ladder**; **in/out of ~** (*with*) acorde/en disonancia (con); **~ down** *vi* (*fig*) retirarse; **~ on** *vt fus* pisar; **~ up** *vt* (*increase*) aumentar; **~brother** *n* hermanastro; **~daughter** *n* hijastra; **~father** *n* padrastro; **~ladder** *n* escalera

doble or de tijera; **~mother** *n* madrastra; **~ping stone** *n* pasadera; **~sister** *n* hermanastra; **~son** *n* hijastro
stereo ['stɛrɪəʊ] *n* estéreo ♦ *adj* (*also*: **~phonic**) estéreo, estereofónico
sterile ['sterail] *adj* estéril; **sterilize** ['sterɪlaɪz] *vt* esterilizar
sterling ['stɜːlɪŋ] *adj* (*silver*) de ley ♦ *n* (*ECON*) (*libras fpl*) esterlinas *fpl*; **one pound ~** una libra esterlina
stern [stɜːn] *adj* severo, austero ♦ *n* (*NAUT*) popa
stew [stjuː] *n* cocido (*SP*), estofado (*SP*), guisado (*AM*) ♦ *vt* estofar, guisar; (*fruit*) cocer
steward ['stjuːəd] *n* camarero; **~ess** *n* (*esp on plane*) azafata
stick [stɪk] (*pt, pp* **stuck**) *n* palo; (*of dynamite*) barreno; (*as weapon*) porra; (*walking ~*) bastón *m* ♦ *vt* (*glue*) pegar; (*inf: put*) meter; (*: tolerate*) aguantar, soportar; (*thrust*): **to ~ sth into** clavar or hincar algo en ♦ *vi* pegarse; (*be unmoveable*) quedarse parado; (*in mind*) quedarse grabado; **~ out** *vi* sobresalir; **~ up** *vi* sobresalir; **~ up for** *vt fus* defender; **~er** *n* (*label*) etiqueta engomada; (*with slogan*) pegatina; **~ing plaster** *n* esparadrapo
stick-up ['stɪkʌp] (*inf*) *n* asalto, atraco
sticky ['stɪkɪ] *adj* pegajoso; (*label*) engomado; (*fig*) difícil
stiff [stɪf] *adj* rígido, tieso; (*hard*) duro; (*manner*) estirado; (*difficult*) difícil; (*person*) inflexible; (*price*) exorbitante ♦ *adv*: **scared/bored ~** muerto de miedo/aburrimiento; **~en** *vi* (*muscles etc*) agarrotarse; **~ neck** *n* tortícolis *m inv*; **~ness** *n* rigidez *f*, tiesura
stifle ['staɪfl] *vt* ahogar, sofocar; **stifling** *adj* (*heat*) sofocante, bochorno
stigma ['stɪɡmə] *n* (*fig*) estigma *m*
stile [staɪl] *n* portillo, portilla
stiletto [stɪˈletəʊ] (*BRIT*) *n* (*also*: **~ heel**) tacón *m* de aguja
still [stɪl] *adj* inmóvil, quieto ♦ *adv* todavía; (*even*) aun; (*nonetheless*) sin embargo, aun así; **~born** *adj* nacido muerto; **~ life** *n* naturaleza muerta
stilt [stɪlt] *n* zanco; (*pile*) pilar *m*, soporte *m*
stilted ['stɪltɪd] *adj* afectado
stimulate ['stɪmjʊleɪt] *vt* estimular
stimulus ['stɪmjʊləs] (*pl* **stimuli**) *n* estímulo, incentivo
sting [stɪŋ] (*pt, pp* **stung**) *n* picadura; (*pain*) escozor *m*, picazón *f*; (*organ*) aguijón *m* ♦ *vt, vi* picar
stingy ['stɪndʒɪ] *adj* tacaño
stink [stɪŋk] (*pt* **stank**, *pp* **stunk**) *n* hedor *m*, tufo *m* ♦ *vi* heder, apestar; **~ing** *adj* hediondo, fétido; (*fig: inf*) horrible
stint [stɪnt] *n* tarea, trabajo ♦ *vi*: **to ~ on**

escatimar

stir [stə:*] n (fig: agitation) conmoción f ♦ vt
(tea etc) remover; (fig: emotions) provocar
♦ vi moverse; ~ **up** vt (trouble) fomentar

stirrup ['stɪrəp] n estribo

stitch [stɪtʃ] n (SEWING) puntada; (KNITTING)
punto; (MED) punto (de sutura); (pain)
punzada ♦ vt coser; (MED) suturar

stoat [stəut] n armiño

stock [stɔk] n (COMM: reserves) existencias fpl,
stock m; (: selection) surtido; (AGR) ganado,
ganadería; (CULIN) caldo; (descent) raza,
estirpe f; (FINANCE) capital m ♦ adj (fig: reply
etc) clásico ♦ vt (have in ~) tener existencias
de; ~s **and shares** acciones y valores; **in** ~ en
existencia or almacén; **out of** ~ agotado; **to**
take ~ **of** (fig) asesorar, examinar; ~ **up with**
vt fus abastecerse de; ~**broker** ['stɔkbrəukə*]
n agente m/f or corredor(a) m/f de bolsa;
~ **cube** (BRIT) n pastilla de caldo;
~ **exchange** n bolsa

stocking ['stɔkɪŋ] n media

stock: ~ **market** n bolsa (de valores); ~**pile**
n reserva ♦ vt acumular, almacenar; ~**taking**
(BRIT) n (COMM) inventario

stocky ['stɔkɪ] adj (strong) robusto; (short)
achaparrado

stodgy ['stɔdʒɪ] adj indigesto, pesado

stoke [stəuk] vt atizar

stole [stəul] pt of **steal** ♦ n estola

stolen ['stəuln] pp of **steal**

stomach ['stʌmək] n (ANAT) estómago;
(belly) vientre m ♦ vt tragar, aguantar;
~**ache** n dolor m de estómago

stone [stəun] n piedra; (in fruit) hueso; =
6.348 kg; 14 libras ♦ adj de piedra ♦ vt
apedrear; (fruit) deshuesar; ~**-cold** adj
helado; ~**-deaf** adj sordo como una tapia;
~**work** n (art) cantería; **stony** adj
pedregoso; (fig) frío

stood [stud] pt, pp of **stand**

stool [stu:l] n taburete m

stoop [stu:p] vi (also: ~ **down**) doblarse,
agacharse; (also: have a ~) ser cargado de
espaldas

stop [stɔp] n parada; (in punctuation) punto
♦ vt parar, detener; (break off) suspender;
(block: pay) suspender; (: cheque) invalidar;
(also: put a ~ to) poner término a ♦ vi
pararse, detenerse; (end) acabarse; **to** ~
~ **doing sth** dejar de hacer algo; ~ **dead** vi
pararse en seco; ~ **off** vi interrumpir el viaje;
~ **up** vt (hole) tapar; ~**gap** n (person)
interino/a; (thing) recurso provisional; ~**over**
n parada; (AVIAT) escala

stoppage ['stɔpɪdʒ] n (in strike) paro;
(blockage) obstrucción f

stopper ['stɔpə*] n tapón m

stop press n noticias fpl de última hora

stopwatch ['stɔpwɔtʃ] n cronómetro

storage ['stɔ:rɪdʒ] n almacenaje m; ~ **heater**
n acumulador m

store [stɔ:*] n (stock) provisión f; (depot: BRIT:
large shop) almacén m; (US) tienda; (reserve)
reserva, repuesto ♦ vt almacenar; ~**s** npl
víveres mpl; **in** ~ (fig): **to be in** ~ **for sb**
esperarle a uno; ~ **up** vt acumular; ~**room** n
despensa

storey ['stɔ:rɪ] (US **story**) n piso

stork [stɔ:k] n cigüeña

storm [stɔ:m] n tormenta; (fig: of applause)
salva; (: of criticism) nube f ♦ vi (fig) rabiar
♦ vt tomar por asalto; ~**y** adj tempestuoso

story ['stɔ:rɪ] n historia; (lie) mentira; (US) =
storey; ~**book** n libro de cuentos

stout [staut] adj (strong) sólido; (fat) gordo,
corpulento; (resolute) resuelto ♦ n cerveza
negra

stove [stəuv] n (for cooking) cocina; (for
heating) estufa

stow [stəu] vt (also: ~ **away**) meter, poner;
(NAUT) estibar; ~**away** n polizón/ona m/f

straggle ['stræɡl] vi (houses etc) extenderse;
(lag behind) rezagarse

straight [streɪt] adj recto, derecho; (frank)
franco, directo; (simple) sencillo ♦ adv
derecho, directamente; (drink) sin mezcla; **to**
put or **get sth** ~ dejar algo en claro; ~ **away,**
~ **off** en seguida; ~**en** vt (also: ~**en out**)
enderezar, poner derecho; ~**-faced** adj serio;
~**forward** adj (simple) sencillo; (honest)
honrado, franco

strain [streɪn] n tensión f; (TECH) presión f;
(MED) torcedura; (breed) tipo, variedad f ♦ vt
(back etc) torcerse; (resources) agotar;
(stretch) estirar; (food, tea) colar; ~**s** npl
(MUS) son m; ~**ed** adj (muscle) torcido;
(laugh) forzado; (relations) tenso; ~**er** n
colador m

strait [streɪt] n (GEO) estrecho; **to be in dire** ~**s**
pasar grandes apuros; ~**-jacket** n camisa de
fuerza; ~**-laced** adj mojigato, gazmoño

strand [strænd] n (of thread) hebra; (of hair)
trenza; (of rope) ramal m

stranded ['strændɪd] adj (person: without
money) desamparado; (: without transport)
colgado

strange [streɪndʒ] adj (not known)
desconocido; (odd) extraño, raro; ~**ly** adv
de un modo raro; see also **enough**; ~**r** n
desconocido/a; (from another area)
forastero/a

strangle ['stræŋɡl] vt estrangular; ~**hold** n
(fig) dominio completo

strap [stræp] n correa; (of slip, dress) tirante m

strategic [strə'ti:dʒɪk] adj estratégico

strategy ['strætɪdʒɪ] n estrategia

straw [strɔ:] n paja; (drinking ~) caña, pajita;

that's the last ~! ¡eso es el colmo!
strawberry ['strɔ:bəri] n fresa (SP), frutilla (AM)
stray [strei] adj (animal) extraviado; (bullet) perdido; (scattered) disperso ♦ vi extraviarse, perderse
streak [stri:k] n raya; (in hair) raya ♦ vt rayar ♦ vi: to ~ past pasar como un rayo
stream [stri:m] n riachuelo, arroyo; (of people, vehicles) riada, caravana; (of smoke, insults etc) chorro ♦ vt (SCOL) dividir en grupos por habilidad ♦ vi correr, fluir; to ~ in/out (people) entrar/salir en tropel
streamer ['stri:mə*] n serpentina
streamlined ['stri:mlaind] adj aerodinámico
street [stri:t] n calle f; ~car (US) n tranvía m; ~ lamp n farol m; ~ plan n plano; ~wise (inf) adj que tiene mucha calle
strength [strɛŋθ] n fuerza; (of girder, knot etc) resistencia; (fig: power) poder m; ~en vt fortalecer, reforzar
strenuous ['strɛnjuəs] adj (energetic, determined) enérgico
stress [strɛs] n presión f; (mental strain) estrés m; (accent) acento ♦ vt subrayar, recalcar; (syllable) acentuar
stretch [strɛtʃ] n (of sand etc) trecho ♦ vi estirarse; (extend): to ~ to or as far as extenderse hasta ♦ vt extender, estirar; (make demands of) exigir el máximo esfuerzo a; ~ out vi tenderse ♦ vt (arm etc) extender; (spread) estirar
stretcher ['strɛtʃə*] n camilla
strewn [stru:n] adj: ~ with cubierto or sembrado de
stricken ['strikən] adj (person) herido; (city, industry etc) condenado; ~ with (disease) afectado por
strict [strikt] adj severo; (exact) estricto; ~ly adv severamente; estrictamente
stride [straid] (pt strode, pp stridden) n zancada, tranco ♦ vi dar zancadas, andar a trancos
strife [straif] n lucha
strike [straik] (pt, pp struck) n huelga; (of oil etc) descubrimiento; (attack) ataque m ♦ vt golpear, pegar; (oil etc) descubrir; (bargain, deal) cerrar ♦ vi declarar la huelga; (attack) atacar; (clock) dar la hora; on ~ (workers) en huelga; to ~ a match encender un fósforo; ~ down vt derribar; ~ up vt (MUS) empezar a tocar; (conversation) entablar; (friendship) trabar; ~r n huelguista m/f; (SPORT) delantero; **striking** adj llamativo
string [striŋ] (pt, pp strung) n (gen) cuerda; (row) hilera ♦ vt: to ~ together ensartar; to ~ out extenderse; the ~s npl (MUS) los instrumentos de cuerda; to pull ~s (fig) mover palancas; ~ bean n judía verde,

habichuela; ~(ed) instrument n (MUS) instrumento de cuerda
stringent ['strindʒənt] adj riguroso, severo
strip [strip] n tira; (of land) franja; (of metal) cinta, lámina ♦ vt desnudar; (paint) quitar; (also: ~ down: machine) desmontar ♦ vi desnudarse; ~ cartoon n tira cómica (SP), historieta (AM)
stripe [straip] n raya; (MIL) galón m; ~d adj a rayas, rayado
strip lighting n alumbrado fluorescente
stripper ['stripə*] n artista m/f de striptease
strive [straiv] (pt strove, pp striven) vi: to ~ for sth/to do sth luchar por conseguir/hacer algo
strode [strəud] pt of stride
stroke [strəuk] n (blow) golpe m; (SWIMMING) brazada; (MED) apoplejía; (of paintbrush) toque m ♦ vt acariciar; at a ~ de un solo golpe
stroll [strəul] n paseo, vuelta ♦ vi dar un paseo or una vuelta; ~er (US) n (for child) sillita de ruedas
strong [strɔŋ] adj fuerte; they are 50 ~ son 50; ~hold n fortaleza; (fig) baluarte m; ~ly adv fuertemente, con fuerza; (believe) firmemente; ~room n cámara acorazada
strove [strəuv] pt of strive
struck [strʌk] pt, pp of strike
structure ['strʌktʃə*] n estructura; (building) construcción f
struggle ['strʌgl] n lucha ♦ vi luchar
strum [strʌm] vt (guitar) rasguear
strung [strʌŋ] pt, pp of string
strut [strʌt] n puntal m ♦ vi pavonearse
stub [stʌb] n (of ticket etc) talón m; (of cigarette) colilla; to ~ one's toe on sth dar con el dedo (del pie) contra algo; ~ out vt apagar
stubble ['stʌbl] n rastrojo; (on chin) barba (incipiente)
stubborn ['stʌbən] adj terco, testarudo
stuck [stʌk] pt, pp of stick ♦ adj (jammed) atascado; ~-up adj engreído, presumido
stud [stʌd] n (shirt ~) corchete m; (of boot) taco; (earring) pendiente m (de bolita); (also: ~ farm) caballeriza; (also: ~ horse) caballo semental ♦ vt (fig): ~ded with salpicado de
student ['stju:dənt] n estudiante m/f ♦ adj estudiantil; ~ driver (US) n aprendiz(a) m/f
studio ['stju:diəu] n estudio; (artist's) taller m; ~ flat (US ~ apartment) n estudio
studious ['stju:diəs] adj estudioso; (studied) calculado; ~ly adv (carefully) con esmero
study ['stʌdi] n estudio ♦ vt estudiar; (examine) examinar, investigar ♦ vi estudiar
stuff [stʌf] n materia; (substance) material m, sustancia; (things) cosas fpl ♦ vt llenar;

(CULIN) rellenar; (animals) disecar; (inf: push) meter; **~ing** n relleno; **~y** adj (room) mal ventilado; (person) de miras estrechas

stumble ['stʌmbl] vi tropezar, dar un traspié; **to ~ across, ~ on** (fig) tropezar con; **stumbling block** n tropiezo, obstáculo

stump [stʌmp] n (of tree) tocón m; (of limb) muñón m ♦ vt: **to be ~ed for an answer** no saber qué contestar

stun [stʌn] vt dejar sin sentido

stung [stʌŋ] pt, pp of **sting**

stunk [stʌŋk] pp of **stink**

stunning ['stʌnɪŋ] adj (fig: news) pasmoso; (: outfit etc) sensacional

stunt [stʌnt] n (in film) escena peligrosa; (publicity ~) truco publicitario; **~man** (irreg) n doble m

stupid ['stjuːpɪd] adj estúpido, tonto; **~ity** [-'pɪdɪtɪ] n estupidez f

sturdy ['stɜːdɪ] adj robusto, fuerte

stutter ['stʌtəʳ] n tartamudeo ♦ vi tartamudear

sty [staɪ] n (for pigs) pocilga

stye [staɪ] n (MED) orzuelo

style [staɪl] n estilo; **stylish** adj elegante, a la moda

stylus ['staɪləs] n aguja

suave [swɑːv] adj cortés

sub... [sʌb] prefix sub...; **~conscious** adj subconsciente; **~contract** vt subcontratar; **~divide** vt subdividir

subdue [səb'djuː] vt sojuzgar; (passions) dominar; **~d** adj (light) tenue; (person) sumiso, manso

subject [n 'sʌbdʒɪkt, vb səb'dʒɛkt] n súbdito; (SCOL) asignatura; (matter) tema m; (GRAMMAR) sujeto ♦ vt: **to ~ sb to sth** someter a uno a algo; **to be ~ to** (law) estar sujeto a; (subj: person) ser propenso a; **~ive** [-'dʒɛktɪv] adj subjetivo; **~ matter** n (content) contenido

sublet [sʌb'lɛt] vt subarrendar

submarine [sʌbmə'riːn] n submarino

submerge [səb'mɜːdʒ] vt sumergir ♦ vi sumergirse

submissive [səb'mɪsɪv] adj sumiso

submit [səb'mɪt] vt someter ♦ vi: **to ~ to sth** someterse a algo

subnormal [sʌb'nɔːməl] adj anormal

subordinate [sə'bɔːdɪnət] adj, n subordinado/a m/f

subpoena [səb'piːnə] n (LAW) citación f

subscribe [səb'skraɪb] vi suscribir; **to ~ to** (opinion, fund) suscribir, aprobar; (newspaper) suscribirse a; **~r** n (to periodical) subscriptor(a) m/f; (to telephone) abonado/a

subscription [səb'skrɪpʃən] n abono; (to magazine) subscripción f

subsequent ['sʌbsɪkwənt] adj subsiguiente,

posterior; **~ly** adv posteriormente, más tarde

subside [səb'saɪd] vi hundirse; (flood) bajar; (wind) amainar; **subsidence** [-'saɪdns] n hundimiento; (in road) socavón m

subsidiary [səb'sɪdɪərɪ] adj secundario ♦ n sucursal f, filial f

subsidize ['sʌbsɪdaɪz] vt subvencionar

subsidy ['sʌbsɪdɪ] n subvención f

subsistence [səb'sɪstəns] n subsistencia; **~ allowance** n salario mínimo

substance ['sʌbstəns] n sustancia

substantial [səb'stænʃl] adj sustancial, sustancioso; (fig) importante

substantiate [səb'stænʃɪeɪt] vt comprobar

substitute ['sʌbstɪtjuːt] n (person) suplente m/f; (thing) sustituto ♦ vt: **to ~ A for B** sustituir A por B, reemplazar B por A

subtitle ['sʌbtaɪtl] n subtítulo

subtle ['sʌtl] adj sutil; **~ty** n sutileza

subtotal [sʌb'təʊtl] n total m parcial

subtract [səb'trækt] vt restar, sustraer; **~ion** [-'trækʃən] n resta, sustracción f

suburb ['sʌbəːb] n barrio residencial; **the ~s** las afueras (de la ciudad); **~an** [sə'bəːbən] adj suburbano; (train etc) de cercanías; **~ia** [sə'bəːbɪə] n barrios mpl residenciales

subway ['sʌbweɪ] n (BRIT) paso subterráneo or inferior; (US) metro

succeed [sək'siːd] vi (person) tener éxito; (plan) salir bien ♦ vt suceder a; **to ~ in doing** lograr hacer; **~ing** adj (following) sucesivo

success [sək'sɛs] n éxito; **~ful** adj exitoso; (business) próspero; **to be ~ful (in doing)** lograr (hacer); **~fully** adv con éxito

succession [sək'sɛʃən] n sucesión f, serie f

successive [sək'sɛsɪv] adj sucesivo, consecutivo

succinct [sək'sɪŋkt] adj sucinto

such [sʌtʃ] adj tal, semejante; (of that kind): **~ a book** tal libro; (so much): **~ courage** tanto valor ♦ adv tan; **~ a long trip** un viaje tan largo; **~ a lot of** tanto(s)/a(s); **~ as** (like) tal como; **as ~** como tal; **~-and-~** adj tal o cual

suck [sʌk] vt chupar; (bottle) sorber; (breast) mamar; **~er** n (ZOOL) ventosa; (inf) bobo, primo

suction ['sʌkʃən] n succión f

Sudan [su'dæn] n Sudán m

sudden ['sʌdn] adj (rapid) repentino, súbito; (unexpected) imprevisto; **all of a ~** de repente; **~ly** adv de repente

suds [sʌdz] npl espuma de jabón

sue [suː] vt demandar

suede [sweɪd] n ante m (SP), gamuza (AM)

suet ['suɪt] n sebo

Suez ['suːɪz] n: **the ~ Canal** el Canal de Suez

suffer ['sʌfəʳ] vt sufrir, padecer; (tolerate) aguantar, soportar ♦ vi sufrir; **to ~ from** (illness etc) padecer; **~er** n víctima; (MED) enfermo/a; **~ing** n sufrimiento

sufficient [sə'fɪʃənt] adj suficiente, bastante; **~ly** ad suficientemente, bastante

suffocate ['sʌfəkeɪt] vi ahogarse, asfixiarse; **suffocation** [-'keɪʃən] n asfixia

sugar ['ʃugə*] n azúcar m ♦ vt echar azúcar a, azucarar; **~ beet** n remolacha; **~ cane** n caña de azúcar

suggest [sə'dʒest] vt sugerir; **~ion** [-'dʒestʃən] n sugerencia; **~ive** (pej) adj indecente

suicide ['suɪsaɪd] n suicidio; (person) suicida m/f; see also **commit**

suit [su:t] n (man's) traje m; (woman's) conjunto; (LAW) pleito; (CARDS) palo ♦ vt convenir; (clothes) sentar a, ir bien a; (adapt): **to ~ sth to** adaptar o ajustar algo a; **well ~ed** (well matched: couple) hecho el uno para el otro; **~able** adj conveniente; (apt) indicado; **~ably** adv convenientemente; (impressed) apropiadamente

suitcase ['su:tkeɪs] n maleta (SP), valija (AM)

suite [swi:t] n (of rooms, MUS) suite f; (furniture): **bedroom/dining room ~** (juego de) dormitorio/comedor

suitor ['su:tə*] n pretendiente m

sulfur ['sʌlfə*] (US) n = **sulphur**

sulk [sʌlk] vi estar de mal humor; **~y** adj malhumorado

sullen ['sʌlən] adj hosco, malhumorado

sulphur ['sʌlfə*] (US sulfur) n azufre m

sultana [sʌl'tɑːnə] n (fruit) pasa de Esmirna

sultry ['sʌltrɪ] adj (weather) bochornoso

sum [sʌm] n suma; (total) total m; **~ up** vt resumir ♦ vi hacer un resumen

summarize ['sʌmməraɪz] vt resumir

summary ['sʌmərɪ] n resumen m ♦ adj (justice) sumario

summer ['sʌmə*] n verano ♦ cpd de verano; **in ~** en verano; **~ holidays** npl vacaciones fpl de verano; **~house** n (in garden) cenador m, glorieta; **~time** n (season) verano; **~ time** n (by clock) hora de verano

summit ['sʌmɪt] n cima, cumbre f; (also: ~ conference, ~ meeting) (conferencia) cumbre f

summon ['sʌmən] vt (person) llamar; (meeting) convocar; (LAW) citar; **~ up** vt (courage) armarse de; **~s** n llamamiento, llamada ♦ vt (LAW) citar

sump [sʌmp] (BRIT) n (AUT) cárter m

sumptuous ['sʌmptjuəs] adj suntuoso

sun [sʌn] n sol m; **~bathe** vi tomar el sol; **~block** n filtro solar; **~burn** n (painful) quemadura; (tan) bronceado; **~burnt** adj quemado por el sol

Sunday ['sʌndɪ] n domingo; **~ school** n catequesis f dominical

sundial ['sʌndaɪəl] n reloj m de sol

sundown ['sʌndaun] n anochecer m

sundry ['sʌndrɪ] adj varios/as, diversos/as; **all and ~** todos sin excepción; **sundries** npl géneros mpl diversos

sunflower ['sʌnflauə*] n girasol m

sung [sʌŋ] pp of **sing**

sunglasses ['sʌnglɑːsɪz] npl gafas fpl (SP) or anteojos mpl de sol

sunk [sʌŋk] pp of **sink**

sun: ~light n luz f del sol; **~lit** adj iluminado por el sol; **~ny** adj soleado; (day) de sol; (fig) alegre; **~rise** n salida del sol; **~ roof** n (AUT) techo corredizo; **~screen** n protector m solar; **~set** n puesta del sol; **~shade** n (over table) sombrilla; **~shine** n sol m; **~stroke** n insolación f; **~tan** n bronceado; **~tan oil** n aceite m bronceador

super ['su:pə*] (inf) adj genial

superannuation [su:pərænju'eɪʃən] n cuota de jubilación

superb [su:'pə:b] adj magnífico, espléndido

supercilious [su:pə'sɪlɪəs] adj altanero

superfluous [su:'pə:fluəs] adj superfluo, de sobra

superhuman [su:pə'hju:mən] adj sobrehumano

superimpose ['su:pərɪm'pəuz] vt sobreponer

superintendent [su:pərɪn'tendənt] n director(a) m/f; (POLICE) subjefe/a m/f

superior [su:'pɪərɪə*] adj superior; (smug) desdeñoso ♦ n superior m; **~ity** [-'ɔrɪtɪ] n superioridad f

superlative [su:'pə:lətɪv] n superlativo

superman ['su:pəmæn] (irreg) n superhombre m

supermarket ['su:pəmɑːkɪt] n supermercado

supernatural [su:pə'nætʃərəl] adj sobrenatural ♦ n: **the ~** lo sobrenatural

superpower ['su:pəpauə*] n (POL) superpotencia

supersede [su:pə'si:d] vt suplantar

superstar ['su:pəstɑː*] n gran estrella

superstitious [su:pə'stɪʃəs] adj supersticioso

supertanker ['su:pətæŋkə*] n superpetrolero

supervise ['su:pəvaɪz] vt supervisar; **supervision** [-'vɪʒən] n supervisión f; **supervisor** ['su:pəvaɪzə*] n supervisor(a) m/f

supper ['sʌpə*] n cena

supple ['sʌpl] adj flexible

supplement [n 'sʌplɪmənt, vb sʌplɪ'mænt] n suplemento ♦ vt suplir; **~ary** [-'mentərɪ] adj suplementario; **~ary benefit** (BRIT) n subsidio suplementario de la seguridad social

supplier [sə'plaɪə*] n (COMM) distribuidor(a) m/f

supply [sə'plaɪ] vt (provide) suministrar; (equip): **to ~ (with)** proveer (de) ♦ n provisión f; (gas, water etc) suministro; **supplies** npl (food) víveres mpl; (MIL) pertrechos mpl; ~ **teacher** n profesor/a m/f suplente

support [sə'pɔːt] n apoyo; (TECH) soporte m ♦ vt apoyar; (financially) mantener; (uphold, TECH) sostener; ~**er** n (POL etc) partidario/a; (SPORT) aficionado/a

suppose [sə'pəuz] vt suponer; (imagine) imaginarse; (duty): **to be ~d to do sth** deber hacer algo; ~**dly** [sə'pəuzɪdlɪ] adv según cabe suponer; **supposing** conj en caso de que

suppress [sə'prɛs] vt suprimir; (yawn) ahogar

supreme [su'priːm] adj supremo

surcharge ['səːtʃɑːdʒ] n sobretasa, recargo

sure [ʃuə*] adj seguro; (definite, convinced) cierto; **to make ~ of sth/that** asegurarse de algo/asegurar que; ~**!** (of course) ¡claro!, ¡por supuesto!; ~ **enough** efectivamente; ~**ly** adv (certainly) seguramente

surf [səːf] n olas fpl

surface ['səːfɪs] n superficie f ♦ vt (road) revestir ♦ vi (also fig) salir a la superficie; **by ~ mail** por vía terrestre

surfboard ['səːfbɔːd] n tabla (de surf)

surfeit ['səːfɪt] n: **a ~ of** un exceso de

surfing ['səːfɪŋ] n surf m

surge [səːdʒ] n oleada, oleaje m ♦ vi (wave) romper; (people) avanzar en tropel

surgeon ['səːdʒən] n cirujano/a

surgery ['səːdʒərɪ] n cirugía; (BRIT: room) consultorio; ~ **hours** (BRIT) npl horas fpl de consulta

surgical ['səːdʒɪkl] adj quirúrgico; ~ **spirit** (BRIT) n alcohol m de 90°

surname ['səːneɪm] n apellido

surpass [səː'pɑːs] vt superar, exceder

surplus ['səːpləs] n excedente m; (COMM) superávit m ♦ adj excedente, sobrante

surprise [sə'praɪz] n sorpresa ♦ vt sorprender; **surprising** adj sorprendente; **surprisingly** adv: **it was surprisingly easy** me etc sorprendió lo fácil que fue

surrender [sə'rɛndə*] n rendición f, entrega ♦ vi rendirse, entregarse

surreptitious [sʌrəp'tɪʃəs] adj subrepticio

surrogate ['sʌrəgɪt] n sucedáneo; ~ **mother** n madre f portadora

surround [sə'raund] vt rodear, circundar; (MIL etc) cercar; ~**ing** adj circundante; ~**ings** npl alrededores mpl, cercanías fpl

surveillance [səː'veɪləns] n vigilancia

survey [n 'səːveɪ, vb səː'veɪ] n inspección f, reconocimiento; (inquiry) encuesta ♦ vt examinar, inspeccionar; (look at) mirar, contemplar; ~**or** n agrimensor(a) m/f

survival [sə'vaɪvl] n supervivencia

survive [sə'vaɪv] vi sobrevivir; (custom etc)

perdurar ♦ vt sobrevivir a; **survivor** n superviviente m/f

susceptible [sə'sɛptəbl] adj: ~ **(to)** (disease) susceptible (a); (flattery) sensible (a)

suspect [adj, n 'sʌspɛkt, vb səs'pɛkt] adj, n sospechoso/a m/f ♦ vt (person) sospechar de; (think) sospechar

suspend [səs'pɛnd] vt suspender; ~**ed sentence** n (LAW) libertad f condicional; ~**er belt** n portaligas m inv; ~**ers** npl (BRIT) ligas fpl; (US) tirantes mpl

suspense [səs'pɛns] n incertidumbre f, duda; (in film etc) suspense m; **to keep sb in ~** mantener a uno en suspense

suspension [səs'pɛnʃən] n (gen, AUT) suspensión f; (of driving licence) privación f; ~ **bridge** n puente m colgante

suspicion [səs'pɪʃən] n sospecha; (distrust) recelo; **suspicious** [-ʃəs] adj receloso; (causing suspicion) sospechoso

sustain [səs'teɪn] vt sostener, apoyar; (suffer) sufrir, padecer; ~**able** adj sostenible; ~**ed** adj (effort) sostenido

sustenance ['sʌstɪnəns] n sustento

swab [swɒb] n (MED) algodón m

swagger ['swægə*] vi pavonearse

swallow ['swɒləu] n (bird) golondrina ♦ vt tragar; (fig, pride) tragarse; ~ **up** vt (savings etc) consumir

swam [swæm] pt of **swim**

swamp [swɒmp] n pantano, ciénaga ♦ vt (with water etc) inundar; (fig) abrumar, agobiar; ~**y** adj pantanoso

swan [swɒn] n cisne m

swap [swɒp] n canje m, intercambio ♦ vt: **to ~ (for)** cambiar (por)

swarm [swɔːm] n (of bees) enjambre m; (fig) multitud f ♦ vi (bees) formar un enjambre; (people) pulular; **to be ~ing with** ser un hervidero de

swastika ['swɒstɪkə] n esvástica

swat [swɒt] vt aplastar

sway [sweɪ] vi mecerse, balancearse ♦ vt (influence) mover, influir en

swear [swɛə*] (pt **swore**, pp **sworn**) vi (curse) maldecir; (promise) jurar ♦ vt jurar; ~**word** n taco, palabrota

sweat [swɛt] n sudor m ♦ vi sudar

sweater ['swɛtə*] n suéter m

sweatshirt ['swɛtʃəːt] n suéter m

sweaty ['swɛtɪ] adj sudoroso

Swede [swiːd] n sueco/a

swede [swiːd] (BRIT) n nabo

Sweden ['swiːdn] n Suecia; **Swedish** ['swiːdɪʃ] adj sueco ♦ n (LING) sueco

sweep [swiːp] (pt, pp **swept**) n (act) barrido; (also: chimney ~) deshollinador(a) m/f ♦ vt barrer; (with arm) empujar; (subj: current) arrastrar ♦ vi barrer; (arm etc) moverse

rápidamente; (*wind*) soplar con violencia;
~ away *vt* barrer; **~ past** *vi* pasar
majestuosamente; **~ up** *vi* barrer; **~ing** *adj*
(*gesture*) dramático; (*generalized: statement*)
generalizado

sweet [swiːt] *n* (*candy*) dulce *m*, caramelo;
(*BRIT: pudding*) postre *m* ♦ *adj* dulce; (*fig:
kind*) dulce, amable; (: *attractive*) mono;
~corn *n* maíz *m*; **~en** *vt* (*add sugar to*)
poner azúcar a; (*person*) endulzar; **~heart** *n*
novio/a; **~ness** *n* dulzura; **~ pea** *n* guisante
m de olor

swell [swel] (*pt* **swelled**, *pp* **swollen** or
swelled) *n* (*of sea*) marejada, oleaje *m* ♦ *adj*
(*US: inf: excellent*) estupendo, fenomenal ♦ *vt*
hinchar, inflar *m* ♦ *vi* (*also: ~ up*) hincharse;
(*numbers*) aumentar; (*sound, feeling*) ir
aumentando; **~ing** *n* (*MED*) hinchazón *f*

sweltering [ˈsweltərɪŋ] *adj* sofocante, de
mucho calor

swept [swept] *pt, pp of* **sweep**

swerve [swɜːv] *vi* desviarse bruscamente

swift [swɪft] *n* (*bird*) vencejo ♦ *adj* rápido,
veloz; **~ly** *adv* rápidamente

swig [swɪg] (*inf*) *n* (*drink*) trago

swill [swɪl] *vt* (*also: ~ out, ~ down*) lavar,
limpiar con agua

swim [swɪm] (*pt* **swam**, *pp* **swum**) *n*: **to go
for a ~** ir a nadar o a bañarse ♦ *vi* nadar;
(*head, room*) dar vueltas ♦ *vt* nadar; (*the
Channel etc*) cruzar a nado; **~mer** *n*
nadador(a) *m/f*; **~ming** *n* natación *f*; **~ming
cap** *n* gorro de baño; **~ming costume**
(*BRIT*) *n* bañador *m*, traje *m* de baño; **~ming
pool** *n* piscina (*SP*), alberca (*AM*); **~ming
trunks** *n* bañador *m* (de hombre); **~suit** *n*
= **~ming costume**

swindle [ˈswɪndl] *n* estafa ♦ *vt* estafar

swine [swaɪn] (*inf!*) canalla (!)

swing [swɪŋ] (*pt, pp* **swung**) *n* (*in playground*) columpio; (*movement*) balanceo,
vaivén *m*; (*change of direction*) viraje *m*;
(*rhythm*) ritmo ♦ *vt* balancear; (*also:
~ round*) voltear, girar ♦ *vi* balancearse,
columpiarse; (*also: ~ round*) dar media
vuelta; **to be in full ~** estar en plena marcha;
~ bridge *n* puente *m* giratorio; **~ door** (*US
~ing door*) *n* puerta giratoria

swingeing [ˈswɪndʒɪŋ] (*BRIT*) *adj* (*cuts*) atroz

swipe [swaɪp] *vt* (*hit*) golpear fuerte; (*inf:
steal*) guindar

swirl [swɜːl] *vi* arremolinarse

Swiss [swɪs] *adj, n inv* suizo/a *m/f*

switch [swɪtʃ] *n* (*for light etc*) interruptor *m*;
(*change*) cambio ♦ *vt* (*change*) cambiar de;
~ off *vt* apagar; (*engine*) parar; **~ on** *vt*
encender (*SP*), prender (*AM*); (*engine,
machine*) arrancar; **~board** *n* (*TEL*) centralita
(de teléfonos) (*SP*), conmutador *m* (*AM*)

Switzerland [ˈswɪtsələnd] *n* Suiza

swivel [ˈswɪvl] *vi* (*also: ~ round*) girar

swollen [ˈswəulən] *pp of* **swell**

swoon [swuːn] *vi* desmayarse

swoop [swuːp] *n* (*by police etc*) redada ♦ *vi*
(*also: ~ down*) calarse

swop [swɒp] = **swap**

sword [sɔːd] *n* espada; **~fish** *n* pez *m* espada

swore [swɔːr] *pt of* **swear**

sworn [swɔːn] *pp of* **swear** ♦ *adj* (*statement*)
bajo juramento; (*enemy*) implacable

swot [swɒt] (*BRIT*) *vt, vi* empollar

swum [swʌm] *pp of* **swim**

swung [swʌŋ] *pt, pp of* **swing**

sycamore [ˈsɪkəmɔːr] *n* sicomoro

syllable [ˈsɪləbl] *n* sílaba

syllabus [ˈsɪləbəs] *n* programa *m* de estudios

symbol [ˈsɪmbl] *n* símbolo

symmetry [ˈsɪmɪtrɪ] *n* simetría

sympathetic [sɪmpəˈθetɪk] *adj*
(*understanding*) comprensivo; (*likeable*)
simpático; (*showing support*): **~ to(wards)**
bien dispuesto hacia

sympathize [ˈsɪmpəθaɪz] *vi*: **to ~ with**
(*person*) compadecerse de; (*feelings*)
comprender; (*cause*) apoyar; **~r** *n* (*POL*)
simpatizante *m/f*

sympathy [ˈsɪmpəθɪ] *n* (*pity*) compasión *f*;
sympathies *npl* (*tendencies*) tendencias *fpl*;
with our deepest ~ nuestro más sentido
pésame; **in ~** en solidaridad

symphony [ˈsɪmfənɪ] *n* sinfonía

symptom [ˈsɪmptəm] *n* síntoma *m*, indicio

synagogue [ˈsɪnəgɒg] *n* sinagoga

syndicate [ˈsɪndɪkɪt] *n* (*gen*) sindicato; (*of
newspapers*) agencia de noticias

syndrome [ˈsɪndrəum] *n* síndrome *m*

synopsis [sɪˈnɒpsɪs] (*pl* **synopses**) *n* sinopsis *f
inv*

synthesis [ˈsɪnθəsɪs] (*pl* **syntheses**) *n* síntesis
f inv

synthetic [sɪnˈθetɪk] *adj* sintético

syphilis [ˈsɪfɪlɪs] *n* sífilis *f*

syphon [ˈsaɪfən] = **siphon**

Syria [ˈsɪrɪə] *n* Siria; **~n** *adj, n* sirio/a

syringe [sɪˈrɪndʒ] *n* jeringa

syrup [ˈsɪrəp] *n* jarabe *m*; (*also: golden ~*)
almíbar *m*

system [ˈsɪstəm] *n* sistema *m*; (*ANAT*)
organismo; **~atic** [-ˈmætɪk] *adj* sistemático,
metódico; **~ disk** *n* (*COMPUT*) disco del
sistema; **~s analyst** *n* analista *m/f* de
sistemas

T, t

ta [tɑː] (*BRIT: inf*) *excl* ¡gracias!

tab [tæb] *n* lengüeta; (*label*) etiqueta; **to keep**

~s on (fig) vigilar

tabby ['tæbɪ] n (also: ~ cat) gato atigrado

table ['teɪbl] n mesa; (of statistics etc) cuadro,
tabla ♦ vt (BRIT: motion etc) presentar; **to lay**
or **set the ~** poner la mesa; **~cloth** n mantel
m; **~ of contents** n índice m de materias;
~ d'hôte [taːblˈdəut] adj del menú; **~ lamp**
n lámpara de mesa; **~mat** n (for plate)
posaplatos m inv; (for hot dish) salvamantel
m; **~spoon** n cuchara de servir; (also:
~spoonful: as measurement) cucharada

tablet ['tæblɪt] n (MED) pastilla, comprimido;
(of stone) lápida

table tennis n ping-pong m, tenis m de
mesa

table wine n vino de mesa

tabloid ['tæblɔɪd] n periódico popular
sensacionalista

tack [tæk] n (nail) tachuela; (fig) rumbo ♦ vt
(nail) clavar con tachuelas; (stitch) hilvanar
♦ vi virar

tackle ['tækl] n (fishing ~) aparejo (de
pescar); (for lifting) aparejo ♦ vt (difficulty)
enfrentarse con; (challenge: person) hacer
frente a; (grapple with) agarrar; (FOOTBALL)
cargar; (RUGBY) placar

tacky ['tækɪ] adj pegajoso; (pej) cutre

tact [tækt] n tacto, discreción f; **~ful** adj
discreto, diplomático

tactics ['tæktɪks] n, npl táctica

tactless ['tæktlɪs] adj indiscreto

tadpole ['tædpəul] n renacuajo

tag [tæg] n (label) etiqueta; **~ along** vi (or
venir) también

tail [teɪl] n cola; (of shirt, coat) faldón m ♦ vt
(follow) vigilar a; **~s** npl (formal suit) levita;
~ away vi (in size, quality etc) ir
disminuyendo; **~ off** vi = ~ away; **~back**
(BRIT) n (AUT) cola; **~ end** n cola, parte f
final; **~gate** n (AUT) puerta trasera

tailor ['teɪləˣ] n sastre m; **~ing** n (cut) corte
m; (craft) sastrería; **~-made** adj (also fig)
hecho a la medida

tailwind ['teɪlwɪnd] n viento de cola

tainted ['teɪntɪd] adj (food) pasado; (water,
air) contaminado; (fig) manchado

take [teɪk] (pt took, pp taken) vt tomar;
(grab) coger (SP), agarrar (AM); (gain: prize)
ganar; (require: effort, courage) exigir;
(tolerate: pain etc) aguantar; (hold:
passengers etc) tener cabida para;
(accompany, bring, carry) llevar; (exam)
presentarse a; **to ~ sth from** (drawer etc) sacar
algo de; (person) quitar algo a; **I ~ it that ...**
supongo que ...; **~ after** vt fus parecerse a;
~ apart vt desmontar; **~ away** vt (remove)
quitar; (carry off) llevar; (MATH) restar;
~ back vt (return) devolver; (one's words)
retractarse de; **~ down** vt (building) derribar;

(letter etc) apuntar; **~ in** vt (deceive)
engañar; (understand) entender; (include)
abarcar; (lodger) acoger, recibir; **~ off** vi
(AVIAT) despegar ♦ vt (remove) quitar; **~ on**
vt (work) aceptar; (employee) contratar;
(opponent) desafiar; **~ out** vt sacar; **~ over**
vt (business) tomar posesión de; (country)
tomar el poder ♦ vi: **to ~ over from sb**
reemplazar a uno; **~ to** vt fus (person) coger
cariño a, encariñarse con; (activity)
aficionarse a; **~ up** vt (a dress) acortar;
(occupy: time, space) ocupar; (engage in:
hobby etc) dedicarse a; (accept): **to ~ sb up
on** aceptar; **~away** (BRIT) adj (food) para
llevar ♦ n tienda (or restaurante m) de
comida para llevar; **~off** n (AVIAT) despegue
m; **~out** (US) n = ~away; **~over** n (COMM)
absorción f

takings ['teɪkɪŋz] npl (COMM) ingresos mpl

talc [tælk] n (also: ~um powder) (polvos de)
talco

tale [teɪl] n (story) cuento; (account) relación
f; **to tell ~s** (fig) chivarse

talent ['tælnt] n talento; **~ed** adj de talento

talk [tɔːk] n charla; (conversation)
conversación f; (gossip) habladurías fpl,
chismes mpl ♦ vi hablar; **~s** npl (POL etc)
conversaciones fpl; **to ~ about** hablar de; **to
~ sb into doing sth** convencer a uno para que
haga algo; **to ~ sb out of doing sth** disuadir a
uno de que haga algo; **to ~ shop** hablar del
trabajo; **~ over** vt discutir; **~ative** adj
hablador(a); **~ show** n programa m de
entrevistas

tall [tɔːl] adj alto; (object) grande; **to be 6 feet
~** (person) ≈ medir 1 metro 80

tally ['tælɪ] n cuenta ♦ vi: **to ~ (with)**
corresponder (con)

talon ['tælən] n garra

tambourine [tæmbəˈriːn] n pandereta

tame [teɪm] adj domesticado; (fig) mediocre

tamper ['tæmpəˣ] vi: **to ~ with** tocar, andar
con

tampon ['tæmpən] n tampón m

tan [tæn] n (also: sun~) bronceado ♦ vi
ponerse moreno ♦ adj (colour) marrón

tang [tæŋ] n sabor m fuerte

tangent ['tændʒənt] n (MATH) tangente f; **to
go off at a ~** (fig) salirse por la tangente

tangerine [tændʒəˈriːn] n mandarina

tangle ['tæŋgl] n enredo; **to get in(to) a ~**
enredarse

tank [tæŋk] n (water ~) depósito, tanque m;
(for fish) acuario; (MIL) tanque m

tanker ['tæŋkəˣ] n (ship) buque m cisterna;
(truck) camión m cisterna

tanned [tænd] adj (skin) moreno

tantalizing ['tæntəlaɪzɪŋ] adj tentador(a)

tantamount ['tæntəmaunt] adj: **~ to**

equivalente a

tantrum ['tæntrəm] *n* rabieta

tap [tæp] *n* (BRIT: *on sink etc*) grifo (SP), canilla (AM); (*gas ~*) llave *f*; (*gentle blow*) golpecito ♦ *vt* (*hit gently*) dar golpecitos en; (*resources*) utilizar, explotar; (*telephone*) intervenir; **on ~** (*fig: resources*) a mano; **~ dancing** *n* claqué *m*

tape [teɪp] *n* (*also: magnetic ~*) cinta magnética; (*cassette*) cassette *f*, cinta; (*sticky ~*) cinta adhesiva; (*for tying*) cinta ♦ *vt* (*record*) grabar (en cinta); (*stick with ~*) pegar con cinta adhesiva; **~ deck** *n* grabadora; **~ measure** *n* cinta métrica, metro

taper ['teɪpə*] *n* cirio ♦ *vi* afilarse

tape recorder *n* grabadora

tapestry ['tæpɪstrɪ] *n* (*object*) tapiz *m*; (*art*) tapicería

tar [tɑː] *n* alquitrán *m*, brea

target ['tɑːgɪt] *n* (*gen*) blanco

tariff ['tærɪf] *n* (*on goods*) arancel *m*; (BRIT: *in hotels etc*) tarifa

tarmac ['tɑːmæk] *n* (BRIT: *on road*) asfaltado; (AVIAT) pista (de aterrizaje)

tarnish ['tɑːnɪʃ] *vt* deslustrar

tarpaulin [tɑː'pɔːlɪn] *n* lona impermeabilizada

tarragon ['tærəgən] *n* estragón *m*

tart [tɑːt] *n* (CULIN) tarta; (BRIT: *inf: prostitute*) puta ♦ *adj* agrio, ácido; **~ up** (BRIT: *inf*) *vt* (*building*) remozar; **to ~ o.s. up** acicalarse

tartan ['tɑːtn] *n* tejido escocés *m*

tartar ['tɑːtə*] *n* (*on teeth*) sarro; **~(e) sauce** *n* salsa tártara

task [tɑːsk] *n* tarea; **to take to ~** reprender; **~ force** *n* (MIL, POLICE) grupo de operaciones

taste [teɪst] *n* (*sense*) gusto; (*flavour*) sabor *m*; (*also: after~*) sabor *m*, dejo; (*sample*): **have a ~!** ¡prueba un poquito!; (*fig*) muestra, idea ♦ *vt* (*also fig*) probar ♦ *vi*: **to ~ of** *or* **like** (*fish, garlic etc*) saber a; **you can ~ the garlic (in it)** se nota el sabor a ajo; **in good/bad ~** de buen/mal gusto; **~ful** *adj* de buen gusto; **~less** *adj* (*food*) soso; (*remark etc*) de mal gusto; **tasty** *adj* sabroso, rico

tatters ['tætəz] *npl*: **in ~** hecho jirones

tattoo [tə'tuː] *n* tatuaje *m*; (*spectacle*) espectáculo militar ♦ *vt* tatuar

tatty ['tætɪ] (BRIT: *inf*) *adj* cochambroso

taught [tɔːt] *pt, pp* of **teach**

taunt [tɔːnt] *n* burla ♦ *vt* burlarse de

Taurus ['tɔːrəs] *n* Tauro

taut [tɔːt] *adj* tirante, tenso

tax [tæks] *n* impuesto ♦ *vt* gravar (con un impuesto); (*fig: memory*) poner a prueba (: *patience*) agotar; **~able** *adj* (*income*) gravable; **~ation** [-'seɪʃən] *n* impuestos *mpl*; **~ avoidance** *n* evasión *f* de impuestos;

~ disc (BRIT) *n* (AUT) pegatina del impuesto de circulación; **~ evasion** *n* evasión *f* fiscal; **~-free** *adj* libre de impuestos

taxi ['tæksɪ] *n* taxi *m* ♦ *vi* (AVIAT) rodar por la pista; **~ driver** *n* taxista *m/f*; **~ rank** (BRIT) *n* = **~ stand**; **~ stand** *n* parada de taxis

tax: **~ payer** *n* contribuyente *m/f*; **~ relief** *n* desgravación *f* fiscal; **~ return** *n* declaración *f* de ingresos

TB *n abbr* = **tuberculosis**

tea [tiː] *n* té *m*; (BRIT: *meal*) ≈ merienda (SP); cena; **high ~** (BRIT) merienda-cena (SP); **~ bag** *n* bolsita de té; **~ break** (BRIT) *n* descanso para el té

teach [tiːtʃ] (*pt, pp* **taught**) *vt*: **to ~ sb sth**, **~ sth to sb** enseñar algo a uno ♦ *vi* (*be a teacher*) ser profesor(a), enseñar; **~er** *n* (*in secondary school*) profesor(a) *m/f*; (*in primary school*) maestro/a, profesor(a) de EGB; **~ing** *n* enseñanza

tea cosy *n* cubretetera *m*

teacup ['tiːkʌp] *n* taza para el té

teak [tiːk] *n* (*madera de*) teca

team [tiːm] *n* equipo; (*of horses*) tiro; **~work** *n* trabajo en equipo

teapot ['tiːpɒt] *n* tetera

tear¹ [tɪə*] *n* lágrima; **in ~s** llorando

tear² [tɛə*] (*pt* **tore**, *pp* **torn**) *n* rasgón *m*, desgarrón *m* ♦ *vt* romper, rasgar ♦ *vi* rasgarse; **~ along** *vi* (*rush*) precipitarse; **~ up** *vt* (*sheet of paper etc*) romper

tearful ['tɪəfəl] *adj* lloroso

tear gas ['tɪə-] *n* gas *m* lacrimógeno

tearoom ['tiːruːm] *n* salón *m* de té

tease [tiːz] *vt* tomar el pelo a

tea set *n* servicio de té

teaspoon *n* cucharita; (*also: ~ful: as measurement*) cucharadita

teat [tiːt] *n* (*of bottle*) tetina

teatime ['tiːtaɪm] *n* hora del té

tea towel (BRIT) *n* paño de cocina

technical ['teknɪkl] *adj* técnico; **~ college** (BRIT) *n* ≈ escuela de artes y oficios (SP); **~ity** [-'kælɪtɪ] *n* (*point of law*) formalismo; (*detail*) detalle *m* técnico; **~ly** *adv* en teoría; (*regarding technique*) técnicamente

technician [tek'nɪʃn] *n* técnico/a

technique [tek'niːk] *n* técnica

technological [teknə'lɔdʒɪkl] *adj* tecnológico

technology [tek'nɔlədʒɪ] *n* tecnología

teddy (bear) ['tedɪ-] *n* osito de felpa

tedious ['tiːdɪəs] *adj* pesado, aburrido

teem [tiːm] *vi*: **to ~ with** rebosar de; **it is ~ing (with rain)** llueve a cántaros

teenage ['tiːneɪdʒ] *adj* (*fashions etc*) juvenil; (*children*) quinceañero; **~r** *n* quinceañero/a

teens [tiːnz] *npl*: **to be in one's ~** ser adolescente

tee-shirt ['tiːʃəːt] n = T-shirt

teeter ['tiːtə*] vi balancearse; (fig): **to ~ on the edge of ...** estar al borde de ...

teeth [tiːθ] npl of tooth

teethe [tiːð] vi echar los dientes

teething ['tiːðɪŋ]: **~ ring** n mordedor m; **~ troubles** npl (fig) dificultades fpl iniciales

teetotal ['tiː'təʊtl] adj abstemio

telegram ['tɛlɪgræm] n telegrama m

telegraph ['tɛlɪgrɑːf] n telégrafo; **~ pole** n poste m telegráfico

telepathy [tə'lɛpəθɪ] n telepatía

telephone ['tɛlɪfəʊn] n teléfono ♦ vt llamar por teléfono, telefonear; (message) decir por teléfono; **to be on the ~** (talking) hablar por teléfono; (possessing ~) tener teléfono; **~ booth** n cabina telefónica; **~ box** (BRIT) n = ~ booth; **~ call** n llamada (telefónica); **~ directory** n guía (telefónica); **~ number** n número de teléfono; **telephonist** [tə'lɛfənɪst] (BRIT) n telefonista m/f

telesales ['tɛlɪseɪlz] npl televenta(s) f(pl)

telescope ['tɛlɪskəʊp] n telescopio

television ['tɛlɪvɪʒən] n televisión f; **on ~** en la televisión; **~ set** n televisor m

tell [tɛl] (pt, pp **told**) vt decir; (relate: story) contar; (distinguish): **to ~ sth from** distinguir algo de ♦ vi (talk): **to ~ (of)** contar; (have effect) tener efecto; **to ~ sb to do sth** mandar a uno hacer algo; **~ off** vt: **to ~ sb off** regañar a uno; **~er** n (in bank) cajero/a; **~ing** adj (remark, detail) revelador(a); **~tale** adj (sign) indicador(a)

telly ['tɛlɪ] (BRIT: inf) n abbr (= television) tele f

temp [tɛmp] n abbr (BRIT: = temporary) temporero/a

temper ['tɛmpə*] n (nature) carácter m; (mood) humor m; (bad ~) (mal) genio; (fit of anger) acceso de ira ♦ vt (moderate) moderar; **to be in a ~** estar furioso; **to lose one's ~** enfadarse, enojarse

temperament ['tɛmprəmənt] n (nature) temperamento

temperate ['tɛmprət] adj (climate etc) templado

temperature ['tɛmprətʃə*] n temperatura; **to have** or **run a ~** tener fiebre

temple ['tɛmpl] n (building) templo; (ANAT) sien f

tempo ['tɛmpəʊ] (pl **tempos** or **tempi**) n (MUS) tiempo, tiempo; (fig) ritmo

temporarily ['tɛmpərərɪlɪ] adv temporalmente

temporary ['tɛmpərərɪ] adj provisional; (passing) transitorio; (worker) temporero; (job) temporal

tempt [tɛmpt] vt tentar; **to ~ sb into doing sth** tentar or inducir a uno a hacer algo; **~ation** [-'teɪʃən] n tentación f; **~ing** adj

tentador(a); (food) apetitoso/a

ten [tɛn] num diez

tenacity [tə'næsɪtɪ] n tenacidad f

tenancy ['tɛnənsɪ] n arrendamiento, alquiler m

tenant ['tɛnənt] n inquilino/a

tend [tɛnd] vt cuidar ♦ vi: **to ~ to do sth** tener tendencia a hacer algo

tendency ['tɛndənsɪ] n tendencia

tender ['tɛndə*] adj (person, care) tierno, cariñoso; (meat) tierno; (sore) sensible ♦ n (COMM: offer) oferta; (money): **legal ~** moneda de curso legal ♦ vt ofrecer; **~ness** n ternura; (of meat) blandura

tenement ['tɛnəmənt] n casa de pisos (SP)

tennis ['tɛnɪs] n tenis m; **~ ball** n pelota de tenis; **~ court** n cancha de tenis; **~ player** n tenista m/f; **~ racket** n raqueta de tenis

tenor ['tɛnə*] n (MUS) tenor m

tenpin bowling ['tɛnpɪn-] n (juego de los) bolos

tense [tɛns] adj (person) nervioso; (moment, atmosphere) tenso; (muscle) tenso, en tensión ♦ n (LING) tiempo

tension ['tɛnʃən] n tensión f

tent [tɛnt] n tienda (de campaña) (SP), carpa (AM)

tentative ['tɛntətɪv] adj (person, smile) indeciso; (conclusion, plans) provisional

tenterhooks ['tɛntəhʊks] npl: **on ~** sobre ascuas

tenth [tɛnθ] num décimo

tent peg n clavija, estaca

tent pole n mástil m

tenuous ['tɛnjuəs] adj tenue

tenure ['tɛnjuə*] n (of land etc) tenencia; (of office) ejercicio

tepid ['tɛpɪd] adj tibio

term [təːm] n (word) término; (period) período; (SCOL) trimestre m ♦ vt llamar; **~s** npl (conditions, COMM) condiciones fpl; **in the short/long ~** a corto/largo plazo; **to be on good ~s with sb** llevarse bien con uno; **to come to ~s with** (problem) aceptar

terminal ['təːmɪnl] adj (disease) mortal; (patient) terminal ♦ n (ELEC) borne m; (COMPUT) terminal m; (also: air ~) terminal f; (BRIT: also: coach ~) (estación f) terminal f

terminate ['təːmɪneɪt] vt terminar

terminus ['təːmɪnəs] (pl **termini**) n término, (estación f) terminal f

terrace ['tɛrəs] n terraza; (BRIT: row of houses) hilera de casas adosadas; **the ~s** (BRIT: SPORT) las gradas fpl; **~d** adj (garden) en terrazas; (house) adosado

terrain [tɛ'reɪn] n terreno

terrible ['tɛrɪbl] adj terrible, horrible; (inf) atroz; **terribly** adv terriblemente; (very badly) malísimamente

terrier ['terɪə*] n terrier m

terrific [tə'rɪfɪk] adj (very great) tremendo; (wonderful) fantástico, fenomenal

terrify ['terɪfaɪ] vt aterrorizar

territory ['terɪtərɪ] n (also fig) territorio

terror ['terə*] n terror m; **~ism** n terrorismo; **~ist** n terrorista m/f

test [test] n (gen, CHEM) prueba; (MED) examen m; (SCOL) examen m, test m; (also: driving ~) examen m de conducir ♦ vt probar, poner a prueba; (MED, SCOL) examinar

testament ['testəmənt] n testamento; **the Old/New T~** el Antiguo/Nuevo Testamento

testicle ['testɪkl] n testículo

testify ['testɪfaɪ] vi (LAW) prestar declaración; **to ~ to sth** atestiguar algo

testimony ['testɪmənɪ] n (LAW) testimonio

test: **~ match** n (CRICKET, RUGBY) partido internacional; **~ tube** n probeta

tetanus ['tetənəs] n tétano

tether ['teðə*] vt atar (con una cuerda) ♦ n: **to be at the end of one's ~** no aguantar más

text [tekst] n texto; **~book** n libro de texto

textiles ['tekstaɪlz] npl textiles mpl; (textile industry) industria textil

texture ['tekstʃə*] n textura

Thailand ['taɪlænd] n Tailandia

Thames [temz] n: **the ~** el (río) Támesis

than [ðæn] conj (in comparisons): **more ~ 10/once** más de 10/una vez; **I have more/less ~ you/Paul** tengo más/menos que tú/Paul; **she is older ~ you think** es mayor de lo que piensas

thank [θæŋk] vt dar las gracias a, agradecer; **~ you (very much)** muchas gracias; **~ God!** ¡gracias a Dios!; **~s** npl gracias fpl ♦ excl (also: **many ~s**, **~s a lot**) ¡gracias!; **~s to** prep gracias a; **~ful** adj: **~ful (for)** agradecido (por); **~less** adj ingrato; **T~sgiving (Day)** n día m de Acción de Gracias

that [ðæt] (pl those) adj (demonstrative) ese/a, pl esos/as; (more remote) aquel/aquella, pl aquellos/as; **leave those books on the table** deja esos libros sobre la mesa; **~ one** ése/ésa; (more remote) aquél/aquélla; **~ one over there** ése/ésa de ahí; aquél/aquélla de allí

♦ pron **1** (demonstrative) ése/a, pl ésos/as; (neuter) eso; (more remote) aquél/aquélla, pl aquéllos/as; (neuter) aquello; **what's ~?** ¿qué es eso (or aquello)?; **who's ~?** ¿quién es ése/a (or aquél/aquélla)?; **is ~ you?** ¿eres tú?; **will you eat all ~?** ¿vas a comer todo eso?; **~'s my house** ésa es mi casa; **~'s what he said** eso es lo que dijo; **~ is (to say)** es decir

2 (relative: subject, object) que; (with preposition) (el/la) que etc, el/la cual etc; **the book (~) I read** el libro que leí; **the books**

~ are in the library los libros que están en la biblioteca; **all (~) I have** todo lo que tengo; **the box (~) I put it in** la caja en la que or donde lo puse; **the people (~) I spoke to** la gente con la que hablé

3 (relative: of time) que; **the day (~) he came** el día (en) que vino

♦ conj que; **he thought ~ I was ill** creyó que yo estaba enfermo

♦ adv (demonstrative): **I can't work ~ much** no puedo trabajar tanto; **I didn't realise it was ~ bad** no creí que fuera tan malo; **~ high** así de alto

thatched [θætʃt] adj (roof) de paja; (cottage) con tejado de paja

thaw [θɔ:] n deshielo ♦ vi (ice) derretirse; (food) descongelarse ♦ vt (food) descongelar

the [ðiː, ðə] def art **1** (gen) el, f la, pl los, fpl las (NB = el immediately before f n beginning with stressed (h)a; a+ el = al; de+ el = del); **~ boy/girl** el chico/la chica; **~ books/flowers** los libros/las flores; **to ~ postman/from ~ drawer** al cartero/del cajón; **I haven't ~ time/money** no tengo tiempo/dinero

2 (+ adj to form n) los; lo; **~ rich and ~ poor** los ricos y los pobres; **to attempt ~ impossible** intentar lo imposible

3 (in titles): **Elizabeth ~ First** Isabel primera; **Peter ~ Great** Pedro el Grande

4 (in comparisons): **~ more he works ~ more he earns** cuanto más trabaja más gana

theatre ['θɪətə*] (US **theater**) n teatro; (also: lecture ~) aula; (MED: also: operating ~) quirófano; **~-goer** n aficionado/a al teatro

theatrical [θɪ'ætrɪkl] adj teatral

theft [θeft] n robo

their [ðeə*] adj su; **~s** pron (el) suyo/(la) suya etc; see also **my**; **mine**[1]

them [ðem, ðəm] pron (direct) los/las; (indirect) les; (stressed, after prep) ellos/ellas; see also **me**

theme [θiːm] n tema m; **~ park** n parque de atracciones (en torno a un tema central); **~ song** n tema m (musical)

themselves [ðəm'selvz] pl pron (subject) ellos mismos/ellas mismas; (complement) se; (after prep) sí (mismos/as); see also **oneself**

then [ðen] adv (at that time) entonces; (next) después; (later) luego, después; (and also) además ♦ conj (therefore) en ese caso, entonces ♦ adj: **the ~ president** el entonces presidente; **by ~** para entonces; **from ~ on** desde entonces

theology [θɪ'ɔlədʒɪ] n teología

theory ['θɪərɪ] n teoría

therapist ['θerəpɪst] n terapeuta m/f
therapy ['θerəpɪ] n terapia

KEYWORD

there ['ðɛə*] adv 1: ~ is, ~ are hay; ~ is no-
one here/no bread left no hay nadie aquí/no
queda pan; ~ has been an accident ha habido
un accidente

2 (referring to place) ahí; (distant) allí; it's ~
está ahí; put it in/on/up/down ~ ponlo ahí
dentro/encima/arriba/abajo; I want that book
~ quiero ese libro de ahí; ~ he is! ¡ahí está!

3: ~, ~ (esp to child) ea, ea

there: ~abouts adv por ahí; ~after adv
después; ~by adv así, de ese modo; ~fore
adv por lo tanto; ~'s = there is; there has
thermal ['θə:ml] adj termal; (paper) térmico
thermometer [θə'mɒmɪtə*] n termómetro
Thermos ® ['θə:məs] n (also: ~ flask) termo
thermostat ['θə:məustæt] n termostato
thesaurus [θɪ'sɔ:rəs] n tesoro
these [ði:z] pl adj estos/as ♦ pl pron éstos/as
thesis ['θi:sɪs] (pl theses) n tesis f inv
they [ðeɪ] pl pron ellos/ellas; (stressed) ellos
(mismos)/ellas (mismas); ~ say that ... (it is
said that) se dice que ...; ~'d = they had;
they would; ~'ll = they shall; they will; ~'re
= they are; ~'ve = they have

thick [θɪk] adj (in consistency) espeso; (in size)
grueso; (stupid) torpe ♦ n: in the ~ of the
battle en lo más reñido de la batalla; it's 20
cm ~ tiene 20 cm de espesor; ~en vi
espesarse ♦ vt (sauce etc) espesar; ~ness n
espesor m; grueso; ~set adj fornido
thief [θi:f] (pl thieves) n ladrón/ona m/f
thigh [θaɪ] n muslo
thimble ['θɪmbl] n dedal m
thin [θɪn] adj (person, animal) flaco; (in size)
delgado; (in consistency) poco espeso; (hair,
crowd) escaso ♦ vt: to ~ (down) diluir
thing [θɪŋ] n cosa; (object) objeto, artículo;
(matter) asunto; (mania): to have a ~ about
sb/sth estar obsesionado con uno/algo; ~s
npl (belongings) efectos mpl (personales); the
best ~ would be to ... lo mejor sería ...; how
are ~s? ¿qué tal?
think [θɪŋk] (pt, pp thought) vi pensar ♦ vt
pensar, creer; what did you ~ of them? ¿qué
te parecieron?; to ~ about sth/sb pensar en
algo/uno; I'll ~ about it lo pensaré; to ~ of
doing sth pensar en hacer algo; I ~ so/not
creo que sí/no; to ~ well of sb tener buen
concepto de uno; ~ over vt reflexionar
sobre, meditar; ~ up vt (plan etc) idear;
~ tank n gabinete m de estrategia
thinly ['θɪnlɪ] adv (cut) fino; (spread)
ligeramente
third [θə:d] adj (before n) tercer(a); (following

n) tercero/a ♦ n tercero/a; (fraction) tercio;
(BRIT: SCOL: degree) título de licenciado con
calificación de aprobado; ~ly adv en tercer
lugar; ~ party insurance (BRIT) n seguro
contra terceros; ~-rate adj (de calidad)
mediocre; T~ World n Tercer Mundo
thirst [θə:st] n sed f; ~y adj (person, animal)
sediento; (work) que da sed; to be ~y tener
sed
thirteen ['θə:'ti:n] num trece
thirty ['θə:tɪ] num treinta

KEYWORD

this [ðɪs] (pl these) adj (demonstrative) este/a;
pl estos/as; (neuter) esto; ~ man/woman este
hombre/esta mujer; these children/flowers
estos chicos/estas flores; ~ one (here) éste/a,
esto (de aquí)

♦ pron (demonstrative) éste/a; pl éstos/as;
(neuter) esto; who is ~? ¿quién es éste/ésta?;
what is ~? ¿qué es esto?; ~ is where I live
aquí vivo; ~ is what he said esto es lo que
dijo; ~ is Mr Brown (in introductions) le
presento al Sr. Brown; (photo) éste es el Sr.
Brown; (on telephone) habla el Sr. Brown

♦ adv (demonstrative): ~ high/long etc así de
alto/largo etc; ~ far hasta aquí

thistle ['θɪsl] n cardo
thorn [θɔ:n] n espina
thorough ['θʌrə] adj (search) minucioso;
(wash) a fondo; (knowledge, research)
profundo; (person) meticuloso; ~bred adj
(horse) de pura sangre; ~fare n calle f; "no
~fare" "prohibido el paso"; ~ly adv (search)
minuciosamente; (study) profundamente;
(wash) a fondo; (utterly: bad, wet etc)
completamente, totalmente
those [ðəuz] pl adj esos/esas; (more remote)
aquellos/as
though [ðəu] conj aunque ♦ adv sin embargo
thought [θɔ:t] pt, pp of think ♦ n
pensamiento; (opinion) opinión f; ~ful adj
pensativo; (serious) serio; (considerate)
atento; ~less adj desconsiderado
thousand ['θauzənd] num mil; two ~ dos
mil; ~s of miles de; ~th num milésimo
thrash [θræʃ] vt azotar; (defeat) derrotar;
~ about or around vi debatirse; ~ out vt
discutir a fondo
thread [θred] n hilo; (of screw) rosca ♦ vt
(needle) enhebrar; ~bare adj raído
threat [θret] n amenaza; ~en vi amenazar
♦ vt: to ~en sb with/to do amenazar a uno
con/con hacer
three [θri:] num tres; ~-dimensional adj
tridimensional; ~-piece suit n traje m de tres
piezas; ~-piece suite n tresillo; ~-ply adj
(wool) de tres cabos

threshold ['θreʃhəuld] n umbral m

threw [θru:] pt of **throw**

thrifty ['θrɪftɪ] adj económico

thrill [θrɪl] n (excitement) emoción f; (shudder) estremecimiento ♦ vt emocionar; **to be ~ed** (with gift etc) estar encantado; **~er** n novela (u obra o película) de suspense; **~ing** adj emocionante

thrive [θraɪv] (pt, pp **thrived**) vi (grow) crecer; (do well): **to ~ on sth** sentarse muy bien a uno algo; **thriving** adj próspero

throat [θrəut] n garganta; **to have a sore ~** tener dolor de garganta

throb [θrɔb] vi latir; dar punzadas; vibrar

throes [θrəuz] npl: **in the ~ of** en medio de

throne [θrəun] n trono

throng [θrɔŋ] n multitud f, muchedumbre f ♦ vt agolparse en

throttle ['θrɔtl] n (AUT) acelerador m ♦ vt estrangular

through [θru:] prep por, a través de; (time) durante; (by means of) por medio de, mediante; (owing to) gracias a ♦ adj (ticket, train) directo ♦ adv completamente, de parte a parte; de principio a fin; **to put sb ~ to sb** (TEL) poner or pasar a uno con uno; **to be ~** (TEL) tener comunicación; (have finished) haber terminado; **"no ~ road"** (BRIT) "calle sin salida"; **~out** prep (place) por todas partes de, por todo; (time) durante todo ♦ adv por or en todas partes

throw [θrəu] (pt **threw**, pp **thrown**) n tiro; (SPORT) lanzamiento ♦ vt tirar, echar; (SPORT) lanzar; (rider) derribar; (fig) desconcertar; **to ~ a party** dar una fiesta; **~ away** vt tirar; **~ through** vt fus (book); (money) derrochar; **~ off** vt deshacerse de; **~ out** vt tirar; (person) echar; expulsar; **~ up** vi vomitar; **~away** adj para tirar, desechable; (remark) hecho de paso; **~-in** n (SPORT) saque m

thru [θru:] (US) = **through**

thrush [θrʌʃ] n zorzal m, tordo

thrust [θrʌst] (pt, pp **thrust**) vt empujar (con fuerza)

thud [θʌd] n golpe m sordo

thug [θʌg] n gamberro/a

thumb [θʌm] n (ANAT) pulgar m; **to ~ a lift** hacer autostop; vt fus (book) hojear; **~tack** (US) n chincheta (SP)

thump [θʌmp] n golpe m; (sound) ruido seco or sordo ♦ vt golpear ♦ vi (heart etc) palpitar

thunder ['θʌndə*] n trueno ♦ vi tronar; (train etc): **to ~ past** pasar como un trueno; **~bolt** n rayo; **~clap** n trueno; **~storm** n tormenta; **~y** adj tormentoso

Thursday ['θɜːzdɪ] n jueves m inv

thus [ðʌs] adv así, de este modo

thyme [taɪm] n tomillo

thyroid ['θaɪrɔɪd] n (also: ~ gland) tiroides m

---

inv

tic [tɪk] n tic m

tick [tɪk] n (sound: of clock) tictac m; (mark) palomita; (ZOOL) garrapata; (BRIT: inf): **in a ~** en un instante ♦ vi hacer tictac ♦ vt marcar; **~ off** vt marcar; (person) reñir; **~ over** vi (engine) girar en marcha lenta; (fig) ir tirando

ticket ['tɪkɪt] n billete m (SP), tíquet m, boleto (AM); (for cinema etc) entrada, boleto (AM); (in shop: on goods) etiqueta; (for raffle) papeleta; (for library) tarjeta; (parking ~) multa por estacionamiento ilegal; **~ collector** n revisor(a) m/f; **~ office** n (THEATRE) taquilla (SP), boletería (AM); (RAIL) despacho de billetes (SP) or boletos (AM)

tickle ['tɪkl] vt hacer cosquillas a ♦ vi hacer cosquillas; **ticklish** adj (person) cosquilloso; (problem) delicado

tidal ['taɪdl] adj de marea; **~ wave** n maremoto

tidbit ['tɪdbɪt] (US) n = **titbit**

tiddlywinks ['tɪdlɪwɪŋks] n juego infantil con fichas de plástico

tide [taɪd] n marea; (fig: of events etc) curso, marcha; **~ over** vt (help out) ayudar a salir del apuro

tidy ['taɪdɪ] adj (room etc) ordenado; (dress, work) limpio; (person) (bien) arreglado ♦ vt (also: ~ up) poner en orden

tie [taɪ] n (string etc) atadura; (BRIT: also: neck~) corbata; (fig: link) vínculo, lazo; (SPORT etc: draw) empate m ♦ vt atar ♦ vi (SPORT etc) empatar; **to ~ in a bow** atar con un lazo; **to ~ a knot in sth** hacer un nudo en algo; **~ down** vt (fig: person: restrict) atar; (: to price, date etc) obligar a; **~ up** vt (parcel) envolver; (dog, person) atar; (arrangements) concluir; **to be ~d up** (busy) estar ocupado

tier [tɪə*] n grada; (of cake) piso

tiger ['taɪgə*] n tigre m

tight [taɪt] adj (rope) tirante; (money) escaso; (clothes) ajustado; (bend) cerrado; (shoes, schedule) apretado; (budget) ajustado; (security) estricto; (inf: drunk) borracho ♦ adv (squeeze) muy fuerte; (shut) bien; **~en** vt (rope) estirar; (screw, grip) apretar; (security) reforzar ♦ vi estirarse; apretarse; **~-fisted** adj tacaño; **~ly** adv (grasp) muy fuerte; **~rope** n cuerda floja; **~s** (BRIT) npl panti mpl

tile [taɪl] n (on roof) teja; (on floor) baldosa; (on wall) azulejo; **~d** adj (roof) de tejas; embaldosado; (wall) alicatado

till [tɪl] n caja (registradora) ♦ vt (land) cultivar ♦ prep, conj = **until**

tilt [tɪlt] vt inclinar ♦ vi inclinarse

timber ['tɪmbə*] n (material) madera

time [taɪm] n tiempo; (epoch: often pl) época; (by clock) hora; (moment) momento; (occasion) vez f; (MUS) compás m ♦ vt calcular or medir el tiempo de; (*race*) cronometrar; (*remark, visit etc*) elegir el momento para; **a long ~** mucho tiempo; **4 at a ~ de** 4 en 4; **4 a la vez; for the ~ being de** momento, por ahora; **from ~ to ~** de vez en cuando; **at ~s a veces; in ~** (*soon enough*) a tiempo; (*after some time*) con el tiempo; (*MUS*) al compás; **in a week's ~** dentro de una semana; **in no ~** en un abrir y cerrar de ojos; **any ~** cuando sea; **on ~** a la hora; **5 ~s 5** 5 por 5; **what ~ is it?** ¿qué hora es?; **to have a good ~** pasarlo bien, divertirse; **~ bomb** n bomba de efecto retardado; **~less** adj eterno; **~ limit** n plazo; **~ly** adj oportuno; **~ off** n tiempo libre; **~r** n (*in kitchen etc*) programador m horario; **~ scale** (*BRIT*) n escala de tiempo; **~share** n apartamento (or casa) a tiempo compartido; **~ switch** (*BRIT*) n interruptor m (horario); **~table** n horario; **~ zone** n huso horario

timid ['tɪmɪd] adj tímido

timing ['taɪmɪŋ] n (*SPORT*) cronometraje m; **the ~ of his resignation** el momento que eligió para dimitir

tin [tɪn] n estaño; (*also: ~ plate*) hojalata; (*BRIT: can*) lata; **~foil** n papel m de estaño

tinge [tɪndʒ] n matiz m ♦ vt: **~d with** teñido de

tingle ['tɪŋgl] vi (*person*): **to ~ (with)** estremecerse (de); (*hands etc*) hormiguear

tinker ['tɪŋkə*] n: **~ with** vt fus jugar con, tocar

tinned [tɪnd] (*BRIT*) adj (*food*) en lata, en conserva

tin opener [-əupnə*] (*BRIT*) n abrelatas m inv

tinsel ['tɪnsl] n (guirnalda de) espumillón m

tint [tɪnt] n matiz m; (*for hair*) tinte m; **~ed** adj (*hair*) teñido; (*glass, spectacles*) ahumado

tiny ['taɪnɪ] adj minúsculo, pequeñito

tip [tɪp] n (*end*) punta; (*gratuity*) propina; (*BRIT: for rubbish*) vertedero; (*advice*) consejo ♦ vt (*waiter*) dar una propina a; (*tilt*) inclinar; (*empty: also: ~ out*) vaciar, echar; (*overturn: also: ~ over*) volcar; **~-off** n (*hint*) advertencia; **~ped** (*BRIT*) adj (*cigarette*) con filtro

Tipp-Ex ® ['tɪpeks] n Tipp-Ex ® m

tipsy ['tɪpsɪ] (*inf*) adj alegre, mareado

tiptoe ['tɪptəu] n: **on ~** de puntillas

tire ['taɪə*] n (*US*) = **tyre** ♦ vt cansar ♦ vi (*gen*) cansarse; (*become bored*) aburrirse; **~d** adj cansado; **to be ~d of sth** estar harto de algo; **~less** adj incansable; **~some** adj aburrido; **tiring** adj cansado

tissue ['tɪʃuː] n tejido; (*paper handkerchief*) pañuelo de papel, kleenex ® m; **~ paper** n papel m de seda

tit [tɪt] n (*bird*) herrerillo común; **to give ~ for tat** dar ojo por ojo

titbit ['tɪtbɪt] (*US* **tidbit**) n (*food*) golosina;

(*news*) noticia sabrosa

title ['taɪtl] n título; **~ deed** n (*LAW*) título de propiedad; **~ role** n papel m principal

TM abbr = **trademark**

to [tuː, tə] prep **1** (*direction*) a; **to go ~ France/ London/school/the station** ir a Francia/ Londres/al colegio/a la estación; **to go ~ Claude's/the doctor's** ir a casa de Claude/al médico; **the road ~ Edinburgh** la carretera de Edimburgo

2 (*as far as*) hasta, a; **from here ~ London** de aquí a or hasta Londres; **to count ~ 10** contar hasta 10; **from 40 ~ 50 people** entre 40 y 50 personas

3 (*with expressions of time*): **a quarter/twenty ~ 5** las 5 menos cuarto/veinte

4 (*for, of*): **the key ~ the front door** la llave de la puerta principal; **she is secretary ~ the director** es la secretaria del director; **a letter ~ his wife** una carta a or para su mujer

5 (*expressing indirect object*) a; **to give sth ~ sb** darle algo a alguien; **to talk ~ sb** hablar con alguien; **to be a danger ~ sb** ser un peligro para alguien; **to carry out repairs ~ sth** hacer reparaciones en algo

6 (*in relation to*): **3 goals ~ 2** 3 goles a 2; **30 miles ~ the gallon** ≈ 9,4 litros a los cien (kms)

7 (*purpose, result*): **to come ~ sb's aid** venir en auxilio or ayuda de alguien; **to sentence sb ~ death** condenar a uno a muerte; **~ my great surprise** con gran sorpresa mía

♦ with vb **1** (*simple infin*): **~ go/eat** ir/comer

2 (*following another vb*): **to want/try/start ~ do** querer/intentar/empezar a hacer; *see also relevant vb*

3 (*with vb omitted*): **I don't want ~** no quiero

4 (*purpose, result*) para; **I did it ~ help you** lo hice para ayudarte; **he came ~ see you** vino a verte

5 (*equivalent to relative clause*): **I have things ~ do** tengo cosas que hacer; **the main thing is ~ try** lo principal es intentarlo

6 (*after adj etc*): **ready ~ go** listo para irse; **too old ~ ...** demasiado viejo (como) para ...

♦ adv: **pull/push the door ~** tirar de/empujar la puerta

toad [təud] n sapo; **~stool** n hongo venenoso

toast [təust] n (*CULIN*) tostada; (*drink, speech*) brindis m ♦ vt (*CULIN*) tostar; (*drink to*) brindar por; **~er** n tostador m

tobacco [tə'bækəu] n tabaco; **~nist** n estanquero/a (*SP*), tabaquero/a (*AM*); **~nist's (shop)** (*BRIT*) n estanco (*SP*), tabaquería (*AM*)

toboggan [tə'bɔgən] n tobogán m

today [tə'deɪ] *adv, n (also fig)* hoy *m*
toddler ['tɒdlə*] *n* niño/a (que empieza a andar)
toe [təu] *n* dedo (del pie); *(of shoe)* punta; **to ~ the line** *(fig)* conformarse; **~nail** *n* uña del pie
toffee ['tɒfɪ] *n* toffee *m*; **~ apple** *(BRIT) n* manzana acaramelada
together [tə'geðə*] *adv* juntos; *(at same time)* al mismo tiempo, a la vez; **~ with** junto con
toil [tɔɪl] *n* trabajo duro, labor *f* ♦ *vi* trabajar duramente
toilet ['tɔɪlət] *n* retrete *m*; *(BRIT: room)* servicios *mpl* (SP), wáter *m* (SP), sanitario (AM) ♦ *cpd (soap etc)* de aseo; **~ paper** *n* papel *m* higiénico; **~ries** *npl* artículos *mpl* de tocador; **~ roll** *n* rollo de papel higiénico
token ['təukən] *n (sign)* señal *f*, muestra; *(souvenir)* recuerdo; *(disc)* ficha ♦ *adj (strike, payment etc)* simbólico; **book/record ~** *(BRIT)* vale *m* para comprar libros/discos; **gift ~** *(BRIT)* vale-regalo
Tokyo ['təukjəu] *n* Tokio, Tokío
told [təuld] *pt, pp of* **tell**
tolerable ['tɒlərəbl] *adj (bearable)* soportable; *(fairly good)* pasable
tolerant ['tɒlərnt] *adj*: **~ of** tolerante con
tolerate ['tɒləreɪt] *vt* tolerar
toll [təul] *n (of casualties)* número de víctimas; *(tax, charge)* peaje *m* ♦ *vi (bell)* doblar
tomato [tə'mɑːtəu] *(pl ~es) n* tomate *m*
tomb [tuːm] *n* tumba
tomboy ['tɒmbɔɪ] *n* marimacho
tombstone ['tuːmstəun] *n* lápida
tomcat ['tɒmkæt] *n* gato (macho)
tomorrow [tə'mɒrəu] *adv, n (also: fig)* mañana; **the day after ~** pasado mañana; **~ morning** mañana por la mañana
ton [tʌn] *n* tonelada (BRIT = 1016 kg; US = 907 kg); *(metric ~)* tonelada métrica; **~s of** *(inf)* montones de
tone [təun] *n* tono ♦ *vi (also: ~ in)* armonizar; **~ down** *vt (criticism)* suavizar; *(colour)* atenuar; **~ up** *vt (muscles)* tonificar; **~-deaf** *adj* con mal oído
tongs [tɒŋz] *npl (for coal)* tenazas *fpl*; *(curling ~)* tenacillas *fpl*
tongue [tʌŋ] *n* lengua; **~ in cheek** irónicamente; **~-tied** *adj (fig)* mudo; **~-twister** *n* trabalenguas *m inv*
tonic ['tɒnɪk] *n (MED, also fig)* tónico; *(also: ~ water)* (agua) tónica
tonight [tə'naɪt] *adv, n* esta noche; esta tarde
tonsil ['tɒnsl] *n* amígdala; **~litis** [-'laɪtɪs] *n* amigdalitis *f*
too [tuː] *adv (excessively)* demasiado; *(also)* también; **~ much** demasiado; **~ many** demasiados/as

took [tuk] *pt of* **take**
tool [tuːl] *n* herramienta; **~ box** *n* caja de herramientas
toot [tuːt] *n* pitido ♦ *vi* tocar el pito
tooth [tuːθ] *(pl teeth) n (ANAT, TECH)* diente *m*; *(molar)* muela; **~ache** *n* dolor *m* de muelas; **~brush** *n* cepillo de dientes; **~paste** *n* pasta de dientes; **~pick** *n* palillo
top [tɒp] *n (of mountain)* cumbre *f*, cima; *(of tree)* copa; *(of head)* coronilla; *(of ladder, page)* lo alto; *(of table)* superficie *f*; *(of cupboard)* parte *f* de arriba; *(lid: of box)* tapa; *(: of bottle, jar)* tapón *m*; *(of list etc)* cabeza; *(toy)* peonza; *(garment)* blusa; camiseta ♦ *adj* de arriba; *(in rank)* principal, primero; *(best)* mejor ♦ *vt (exceed)* exceder; *(be first in)* encabezar; **on ~ of** *(above)* sobre, encima de; *(in addition to)* además de; **from ~ to bottom** de pies a cabeza; **~ off** *(US) vt* = **~ up**; **~ up** *vt* llenar; **~ floor** *n* último piso; **~ hat** *n* sombrero de copa; **~-heavy** *adj (object)* mal equilibrado
topic ['tɒpɪk] *n* tema *m*; **~al** *adj* actual
top: **~less** *adj (bather, bikini)* topless *inv*; **~-level** *adj (talks)* al más alto nivel; **~most** *adj* más alto
topple ['tɒpl] *vt* derribar ♦ *vi* caerse
top-secret *adj* de alto secreto
topsy-turvy ['tɒpsɪ'tɜːvɪ] *adj* al revés ♦ *adv* patas arriba
torch [tɔːtʃ] *n* antorcha; *(BRIT: electric)* linterna
tore [tɔː*] *pt of* **tear²**
torment [*n* 'tɔːment, *vt* tɔː'ment] *n* tormento ♦ *vt* atormentar; *(fig: annoy)* fastidiar
torn [tɔːn] *pp of* **tear²**
torrent ['tɒrnt] *n* torrente *m*
tortoise ['tɔːtəs] *n* tortuga; **~shell** ['tɔːtəʃel] *adj* de carey
torture ['tɔːtʃə*] *n* tortura ♦ *vt* torturar; *(fig)* atormentar
Tory ['tɔːrɪ] *(BRIT) adj, n (POL)* conservador(a) *m/f*
toss [tɒs] *vt* tirar, echar; *(one's head)* sacudir; **to ~ a coin** echar a cara o cruz; **to ~ up for sth** jugar a cara o cruz algo; **to ~ and turn** *(in bed)* dar vueltas
tot [tɒt] *n (BRIT: drink)* copita; *(child)* nene/a *m/f*
total ['təutl] *adj* total, entero; *(emphatic: failure etc)* completo, total ♦ *n* total *m*, suma ♦ *vt (add up)* sumar; *(amount to)* ascender a; **~ly** *adv* totalmente
touch [tʌtʃ] *n* tacto; *(contact)* contacto ♦ *vt* tocar; *(emotionally)* conmover; **a ~ of** *(fig)* un poquito de; **to get in ~ with sb** ponerse en contacto con uno; **to lose ~** *(friends)* perder contacto; **~ on** *vt fus (topic)* aludir (brevemente) a; **~ up** *vt (paint)* retocar; **~-and-go** *adj* arriesgado; **~down** *n* aterrizaje

m; (on sea) amerizaje m; (US: FOOTBALL) ensayo; ~ed adj (moved) conmovido; ~ing adj (moving) conmovedor(a); ~line n (SPORT) línea de banda; ~y adj (person) quisquilloso

tough [tʌf] adj (material) resistente; (meat) duro; (problem etc) difícil; (policy, stance) inflexible; (person) fuerte; ~en vt endurecer

toupée ['tuːpeɪ] n peluca

tour ['tʊə*] n viaje m, vuelta; (also: package ~) viaje m todo comprendido; (of town, museum) visita; (by band etc) gira ♦ vt recorrer, visitar; ~ guide n guía m turístico, guía f turística

tourism ['tʊərɪzm] n turismo

tourist ['tʊərɪst] n turista m/f ♦ cpd turístico; ~ office n oficina de turismo

tousled ['tauzld] adj (hair) despeinado

tout [taut] vi: to ~ for business solicitar clientes ♦ n (also: ticket ~) revendedor(a) m/f

tow [təu] vt remolcar; "on or in (US) ~" (AUT) "a remolque"

toward(s) [tə'wɔːd(z)] prep hacia; (attitude) respecto a, con; (purpose) para

towel ['tauəl] n toalla; ~ling n (fabric) felpa; ~ rail (US ~ rack) n toallero

tower ['tauə*] n torre f; ~ block (BRIT) n torre f (de pisos); ~ing adj muy alto, imponente

town [taun] n ciudad f; to go to ~ ir a la ciudad; (fig) echar la casa por la ventana; ~ centre n centro de la ciudad; ~ council n ayuntamiento, consejo municipal; ~ hall n ayuntamiento; ~ plan n plano de la ciudad; ~ planning n urbanismo

towrope ['təurəup] n cable m de remolque

tow truck (US) n camión m grúa

toy [tɔɪ] n juguete m; ~ with vt fus jugar con; (idea) acariciar; ~shop n juguetería

trace [treɪs] n rastro ♦ vt (draw) trazar, delinear; (locate) encontrar; (follow) seguir la pista de; **tracing paper** n papel m de calco

track [træk] n (mark) huella, pista; (path: gen) camino, senda; (: of bullet etc) trayectoria; (: of suspect, animal) pista, rastro; (RAIL) vía; (SPORT) pista; (on tape, record) canción f ♦ vt seguir la pista de; to keep ~ of mantenerse al tanto de, seguir; ~ down vt (prey) seguir el rastro de; (sth lost) encontrar; ~suit n chandal m

tract [trækt] n (GEO) región f

traction ['trækʃən] n (power) tracción f; in ~ (MED) en tracción

tractor ['træktə*] n tractor m

trade [treɪd] n comercio; (skill, job) oficio ♦ vi negociar, comerciar ♦ vt (exchange): to ~ sth (for sth) cambiar algo (por algo); ~ in vt (old car etc) ofrecer como parte del pago; ~ fair n feria comercial; ~mark n marca de fábrica; ~ name n marca registrada; ~r n

comerciante m/f; ~sman (irreg) n (shopkeeper) tendero; ~ union n sindicato; ~ unionist n sindicalista m/f

tradition [trə'dɪʃən] n tradición f; ~al adj tradicional

traffic ['træfɪk] n (gen, AUT) tráfico, circulación f, tránsito (AM) ♦ vi: to ~ in (pej: liquor, drugs) traficar en; ~ circle (US) n isleta; ~ jam n embotellamiento; ~ lights npl semáforo; ~ warden n guardia m/f de tráfico

tragedy ['trædʒədɪ] n tragedia

tragic ['trædʒɪk] adj trágico

trail [treɪl] n (tracks) rastro, pista; (path) camino, sendero; (dust, smoke) estela ♦ vt (drag) arrastrar; (follow) seguir la pista de ♦ vi arrastrar; (in contest etc) ir perdiendo; ~ behind vi quedar a la zaga; ~er n (AUT) remolque m; (caravan) caravana; (CINEMA) trailer m, avance m; ~er truck (US) n trailer m

train [treɪn] n tren m; (of dress) cola; (series) serie f ♦ vt (educate, teach skills to) formar; (sportsman) entrenar; (dog) adiestrar; (point: gun etc): to ~ on apuntar a ♦ vi (SPORT) entrenarse; (learn a skill): to be a teacher etc estudiar para profesor etc; one's ~ of thought el razonamiento de uno; ~ed adj (worker) cualificado; (animal) amaestrado; ~ee [treɪ'niː] n aprendiz(a) m/f; ~er n (SPORT: coach) entrenador(a) m/f; (: shoe): ~ers zapatillas fpl (de deporte); (of animals) domador(a) m/f; ~ing n formación f; entrenamiento; to be in ~ing (SPORT) estar entrenando; ~ing college n (gen) colegio de formación profesional; (for teachers) escuela de formación del profesorado; ~ing shoes npl zapatillas fpl (de deporte)

trait [treɪt] n rasgo

traitor ['treɪtə*] n traidor(a) m/f

tram [træm] (BRIT) n (also: ~car) tranvía m

tramp [træmp] n (person) vagabundo/a; (inf: pej: woman) puta

trample ['træmpl] vt: to ~ (underfoot) pisotear

trampoline ['træmpəliːn] n trampolín m

tranquil ['træŋkwɪl] adj tranquilo; ~lizer n (MED) tranquilizante m

transact [træn'zækt] vt (business) despachar; ~ion [-'zækʃən] n transacción f, operación f

transfer [n 'trænsfə:*, vb træns'fə:*] n (of employees) traslado; (of money, power) transferencia; (SPORT) traspaso; (picture, design) calcomanía ♦ vt trasladar; transferir; to ~ the charges (BRIT: TEL) llamar a cobro revertido

transform [træns'fɔ:m] vt transformar

transfusion [træns'fju:ʒən] n transfusión f

transient ['trænzɪənt] adj transitorio

transistor [træn'zɪstə*] n (ELEC) transistor m;

~ **radio** n transistor m
transit ['trænzɪt] n: **in** ~ en tránsito
transitive ['trænzɪtɪv] adj (LING) transitivo
transit lounge n sala de tránsito
translate [træns'leɪt] vt traducir; **translation** [-'leɪʃən] n traducción f; **translator** n traductor(a) m/f
transmit [trænz'mɪt] vt transmitir; **~ter** n transmisor n
transparency [træns'pɛərnsɪ] n transparencia; (BRIT: PHOT) diapositiva
transparent [træns'pærnt] adj transparente
transpire [træns'paɪə*] vi (turn out) resultar; (happen) ocurrir, suceder; **it ~d that ...** se supo que ...
transplant ['trænsplɑːnt] n (MED) transplante m
transport [n 'trænspɔːt, vt træns'pɔːt] n transporte m; (car) coche m (SP), carro m (AM), automóvil m ♦ vt transportar; **~ation** [-'teɪʃən] n transporte m; **~ café** (BRIT) n bar-restaurant m de carretera
transvestite [trænz'vɛstaɪt] n travestí m/f
trap [træp] n (snare, trick) trampa; (carriage) cabriolé m ♦ vt coger (SP) or agarrar (AM) en una trampa; (trick) engañar; (confine) atrapar; **~ door** n escotilla
trapeze [trə'piːz] n trapecio
trappings ['træpɪŋz] npl adornos mpl
trash [træʃ] n (rubbish) basura; (pej): **the book/film is** ~ el libro/la película no vale nada; (nonsense) tonterías fpl; **~ can** (US) n cubo (SP) or balde m (AM) de la basura
travel ['trævl] n el viajar ♦ vi viajar ♦ vt (distance) recorrer; **~s** npl (journeys) viajes mpl; **~ agent** n agente m/f de viajes; **~ler** (US **~er**) n viajero/a; **~ler's cheque** (US **~er's check**) n cheque m de viajero; **~ling** (US **~ing**) n los viajes, el viajar; **~ sickness** n mareo
trawler ['trɔːlə*] n pesquero de arrastre
tray [treɪ] n bandeja; (on desk) cajón m
treacherous ['trɛtʃərəs] adj traidor, traicionero; (dangerous) peligroso
treacle ['triːkl] (BRIT) n melaza
tread [trɛd] (pt **trod**, pp **trodden**) n (step) paso, pisada; (sound) ruido de pasos; (of stair) escalón m; (of tyre) banda de rodadura ♦ vi pisar; **~ on** vt fus pisar
treason ['triːzn] n traición f
treasure ['trɛʒə*] n (also fig) tesoro ♦ vt (value: object, friendship) apreciar; (: memory) guardar
treasurer ['trɛʒərə*] n tesorero/a
treasury ['trɛʒərɪ] n: **the T~** el Ministerio de Hacienda
treat [triːt] n (present) regalo ♦ vt tratar; **to ~ sb to sth** invitar a uno a algo
treatment ['triːtmənt] n tratamiento

treaty ['triːtɪ] n tratado
treble ['trɛbl] adj triple ♦ vt triplicar ♦ vi triplicarse; **~ clef** n (MUS) clave f de sol
tree [triː] n árbol m; **~ trunk** tronco (de árbol)
trek [trɛk] n (long journey) viaje m largo y difícil; (tiring walk) caminata
trellis ['trɛlɪs] n enrejado
tremble ['trɛmbl] vi temblar
tremendous [trɪ'mɛndəs] adj tremendo, enorme; (excellent) estupendo
tremor ['trɛmə*] n temblor m; (also: **earth ~**) temblor m de tierra
trench [trɛntʃ] n zanja
trend [trɛnd] n (tendency) tendencia; (of events) curso; (fashion) moda; **~y** adj de moda
trespass ['trɛspəs] vi: **to ~ on** entrar sin permiso en; **"no ~ing"** "prohibido el paso"
trestle ['trɛsl] n caballete m
trial ['traɪəl] n (LAW) juicio, proceso; (test: of machine etc) prueba; **~s** npl (hardships) dificultades fpl; **by ~ and error** a fuerza de probar
triangle ['traɪæŋgl] n (MATH, MUS) triángulo
tribe [traɪb] n tribu f
tribunal [traɪ'bjuːnl] n tribunal m
tributary ['trɪbjutərɪ] n (river) afluente m
tribute ['trɪbjuːt] n homenaje m, tributo; **to pay ~ to** rendir homenaje a
trick [trɪk] n (skill, knack) tino, truco; (conjuring ~) truco; (joke) broma; (CARDS) baza ♦ vt engañar; **to play a ~ on sb** gastar una broma a uno; **that should do the ~** a ver si funciona así; **~ery** n engaño
trickle ['trɪkl] n (of water etc) goteo ♦ vi gotear
tricky ['trɪkɪ] adj difícil; delicado
tricycle ['traɪsɪkl] n triciclo
trifle ['traɪfl] n bagatela; (CULIN) dulce de bizcocho borracho, gelatina, fruta y natillas ♦ adv: **a ~ long** un poquito largo; **trifling** adj insignificante
trigger ['trɪgə*] n (of gun) gatillo; **~ off** vt desencadenar
trim [trɪm] adj (house, garden) en buen estado; (person, figure) esbelto ♦ n (haircut etc) recorte m; (on car) guarnición f ♦ vt (neaten) arreglar; (cut) recortar; (decorate) adornar; (NAUT: a sail) orientar; **~mings** npl (CULIN) guarnición f
trip [trɪp] n viaje m; (excursion) excursión f; (stumble) traspié m ♦ vi (stumble) tropezar; (go lightly) andar a paso ligero; **on a ~** de viaje; **~ up** vi tropezar, caerse ♦ vt hacer tropezar or caer
tripe [traɪp] n (CULIN) callos mpl
triple ['trɪpl] adj triple; **triplets** ['trɪplɪts] npl trillizos/as mpl/fpl; **triplicate** ['trɪplɪkət] n: **in triplicate** por triplicado

trite [traɪt] adj trillado

triumph ['traɪʌmf] n triunfo ♦ vi: **to ~ (over)** vencer; **~ant** [traɪ'ʌmfənt] adj (team etc) vencedor(a); (wave, return) triunfal

trivia ['trɪvɪə] npl trivialidades fpl

trivial ['trɪvɪəl] adj insignificante; (commonplace) banal

trod [trɒd] pt of **tread**

trodden ['trɒdn] pp of **tread**

trolley ['trɒlɪ] n carrito; (also: ~ bus) trolebús m

trombone [trɒm'bəʊn] n trombón m

troop [tru:p] n grupo, banda; **~s** npl (MIL) tropas fpl; **~ in/out** vi entrar/salir en tropel; **~ing the colour** n (ceremony) presentación f de la bandera

trophy ['trəʊfɪ] n trofeo

tropical ['trɒpɪkl] adj tropical

trot [trɒt] n trote m ♦ vi trotar; **on the ~** (BRIT: fig) seguidos/as

trouble ['trʌbl] n problema m, dificultad f; (worry) preocupación f; (bother, effort) molestia, esfuerzo; (unrest) inquietud f; (MED): **stomach etc ~** problemas mpl gástricos etc ♦ vt (disturb) molestar; (worry) preocupar, inquietar ♦ vi: **to ~ to do sth** molestarse en hacer algo; **~s** npl (POL etc) conflictos mpl; (personal) problemas mpl; **to be in ~** estar en un apuro; **it's no ~!** ¡no es molestia (ninguna)!; **what's the ~?** (with broken TV etc) ¿cuál es el problema?; (doctor to patient) ¿qué pasa?; **~d** adj (person) preocupado; (country, epoch, life) agitado; **~maker** n agitador(a) m/f; (child) alborotador m; **~shooter** n (in conflict) conciliador(a) m/f; **~some** adj molesto

trough [trɒf] n (also: drinking ~) abrevadero; (also: feeding ~) comedero; (depression) depresión f

troupe [tru:p] n grupo

trousers ['traʊzəz] npl pantalones mpl; **short ~** pantalones mpl cortos

trousseau ['tru:səʊ] (pl **~x** or **~s**) n ajuar m

trout [traʊt] n inv trucha

trowel ['traʊəl] n (of gardener) palita; (of builder) paleta

truant ['truənt] n: **to play ~** (BRIT) hacer novillos

truce [tru:s] n tregua

truck [trʌk] n (lorry) camión m; (RAIL) vagón m; **~ driver** n camionero; **~ farm** (US) n huerto

true [tru:] adj verdadero; (accurate) exacto; (genuine) auténtico; (faithful) fiel; **to come ~** realizarse

truffle ['trʌfl] n trufa

truly ['tru:lɪ] adv (really) realmente; (truthfully) verdaderamente; (faithfully): **yours ~** (in letter) le saluda atentamente

trump [trʌmp] n triunfo

trumpet ['trʌmpɪt] n trompeta

truncheon ['trʌntʃən] n porra

trundle ['trʌndl] vi: **to ~ along** ir sin prisas

trunk [trʌŋk] n (of tree, person) tronco; (of elephant) trompa; (case) baúl m; (US: AUT) maletero; **~s** npl (also: swimming ~s) bañador m (de hombre)

truss [trʌs] vt: **~ (up)** atar

trust [trʌst] n confianza; (responsibility) responsabilidad f; (LAW) fideicomiso ♦ vt (rely on) tener confianza en; (hope) esperar; (entrust): **to ~ sth to sb** confiar algo a uno; **to take sth on ~** aceptar algo a ojos cerrados; **~ed** adj de confianza; **~ee** [trʌs'ti:] n (LAW) fideicomisario; (of school) administrador m; **~ful** adj confiado; **~ing** adj confiado; **~worthy** adj digno de confianza

truth [tru:θ, pl tru:ðz] n verdad f; **~ful** adj veraz

try [traɪ] n tentativa, intento; (RUGBY) ensayo ♦ vt (attempt) intentar; (test: also: ~ out) probar, someter a prueba; (LAW) juzgar, procesar; (strain: patience) hacer perder ♦ vi probar; **to have a ~** probar suerte; **to ~ to do sth** intentar hacer algo; **~ again!** ¡vuelve a probar!; **~ harder!** ¡esfuérzate más!; **well, I tried** al menos lo intenté; **~ on** vt (clothes) probarse; **~ing** adj (experience) cansado; (person) pesado

T-shirt ['ti:ʃə:t] n camiseta

T-square n regla en T

tub [tʌb] n cubo (SP), balde m (AM); (bath) tina, bañera

tube [tju:b] n tubo; (BRIT: underground) metro; (for tyre) cámara de aire

tuberculosis [tjubə:kju'ləʊsɪs] n tuberculosis f inv

tube station (BRIT) n estación f de metro

tubular ['tju:bjʊlə*] adj tubular

TUC (BRIT) n abbr (= Trades Union Congress) federación nacional de sindicatos

tuck [tʌk] vt (put) poner; **~ away** vt (money) guardar; (building): **to be ~ed away** esconderse, ocultarse; **~ in** vt meter dentro; (child) arropar ♦ vi (eat) comer con apetito; **~ up** vt (child) arropar; **~ shop** n (SCOL) tienda; ≈ bar m (del colegio) (SP)

Tuesday ['tju:zdɪ] n martes m inv

tuft [tʌft] n mechón m; (of grass etc) manojo

tug [tʌɡ] n (ship) remolcador m ♦ vt tirar de; **~-of-war** n lucha de tiro de cuerda; (fig) tira y afloja m

tuition [tju:'ɪʃən] n (BRIT) enseñanza; (: private ~) clases fpl particulares; (US: school fees) matrícula

tulip ['tju:lɪp] n tulipán m

tumble ['tʌmbl] n (fall) caída ♦ vi caer; **to ~ to sth** (inf) caer en la cuenta de algo;

~down adj destartalado; **~ dryer** (BRIT) n secadora
tumbler ['tʌmblə*] n (glass) vaso
tummy ['tʌmɪ] (inf) n barriga, tripa
tumour ['tjuːmə*] (US **tumor**) n tumor m
tuna ['tjuːnə] n inv (also: ~ **fish**) atún m
tune [tjuːn] n melodía ♦ vt (MUS) afinar; (RADIO, TV, AUT) sintonizar; **to be in/out of ~** (instrument) estar afinado/desafinado; (singer) cantar afinando/desafinando; **to be in/out of ~ with** (fig) estar de acuerdo/en desacuerdo con; **~ in** vi: **to ~ in (to)** (RADIO, TV) sintonizar (con); **~ up** vi (musician) afinar (su instrumento); **~ful** adj melodioso; **~r** n: **piano ~r** afinador(a) m/f de pianos
tunic ['tjuːnɪk] n túnica
Tunisia [tjuːˈnɪzɪə] n Túnez m
tunnel ['tʌnl] n túnel m; (in mine) galería ♦ vi construir un túnel/una galería
turban ['təːbən] n turbante m
turbulent ['təːbjulənt] adj turbulento
tureen [təˈriːn] n sopera
turf [təːf] n césped m; (clod) tepe m ♦ vt cubrir con césped; **~ out** (inf) vt echar a la calle
Turk [təːk] n turco/a
Turkey ['təːkɪ] n Turquía
turkey ['təːkɪ] n pavo
Turkish ['təːkɪʃ] adj, n turco
turmoil ['təːmɔɪl] n: **in ~** revuelto
turn [təːn] n turno; (in road) curva; (of mind, events) rumbo; (THEATRE) número; (MED) ataque m ♦ vt girar, volver; (collar, steak) dar la vuelta a; (page) pasar; (change): **to ~ sth into** convertir algo en ♦ vi volver; (person: look back) volverse; (reverse direction) dar la vuelta; (milk) cortarse; (become): **to ~ nasty/forty** ponerse feo/cumplir los cuarenta; **a good ~** un favor; **it gave me quite a ~** me dio un susto; **"no left ~"** (AUT) "prohibido girar a la izquierda"; **it's your ~** te toca a ti; **in ~** por turnos; **to take ~s (at)** turnarse (en); **~ away** vi apartar la vista ♦ vt rechazar; **~ back** vi volverse atrás ♦ vt hacer retroceder; (clock) retrasar; **~ down** vt (refuse) rechazar; (reduce) bajar; (fold) doblar; **~ in** vi (inf: go to bed) acostarse ♦ vt (fold) doblar hacia dentro; **~ off** vi (from road) desviarse ♦ vt (light, radio etc) apagar; (tap) cerrar; (engine) parar; **~ on** vt (light, radio etc) encender (SP), prender (AM); (tap) abrir; (engine) poner en marcha; **~ out** vt (light, gas) apagar; (produce) producir ♦ vi (voters) concurrir; **to ~ out to be ...** resultar ser ...; **~ over** vi (person) volverse ♦ vt (object) dar la vuelta a; (page) volver; **~ round** vi volverse; (rotate) girar; **~ up** vi (person) llegar, presentarse; (lost object) aparecer ♦ vt (gen) subir; **~ing** n (in road)

vuelta; **~ing point** n (fig) momento decisivo
turnip ['təːnɪp] n nabo
turn: **~out** n concurrencia; **~over** n (COMM: amount of money) volumen m de ventas; (: of goods) movimiento; **~pike** (US) n autopista de peaje; **~stile** n torniquete m; **~table** n plato; **~up** (BRIT) n (on trousers) vuelta
turpentine ['təːpəntaɪn] n (also: **turps**) trementina
turquoise ['təːkwɔɪz] n (stone) turquesa ♦ adj color turquesa
turret ['tʌrɪt] n torreón m
turtle ['təːtl] n galápago; **~neck (sweater)** n jersey m de cuello vuelto
tusk [tʌsk] n colmillo
tutor ['tjuːtə*] n profesor(a) m/f; **~ial** [-ˈtɔːrɪəl] n (SCOL) seminario
tuxedo [tʌkˈsiːdəu] (US) n smóking m, esmoquin m
TV [tiːˈviː] n abbr (= television) tele f
twang [twæŋ] n (of instrument) punteado; (of voice) timbre m nasal
tweezers ['twiːzəz] npl pinzas fpl (de depilar)
twelfth [twelfθ] num duodécimo
twelve [twelv] num doce; **at ~ o'clock** (midday) a mediodía; (midnight) a medianoche
twentieth ['twentɪθ] adj vigésimo
twenty ['twentɪ] num veinte
twice [twaɪs] adv dos veces; **~ as much** dos veces más
twiddle ['twɪdl] vi: **to ~ (with)** sth dar vueltas a algo; **to ~ one's thumbs** (fig) estar mano sobre mano
twig [twɪg] n ramita
twilight ['twaɪlaɪt] n crepúsculo
twin [twɪn] adj, n gemelo/a m/f ♦ vt hermanar; **~-bedded room** n habitación f doble
twine [twaɪn] n bramante m ♦ vi (plant) enroscarse
twinge [twɪndʒ] n (of pain) punzada; (of conscience) remordimiento
twinkle ['twɪŋkl] vi centellear; (eyes) brillar
twirl [twəːl] vt dar vueltas a ♦ vi dar vueltas
twist [twɪst] n (action) torsión f; (in road, coil) vuelta; (in wire, flex) doblez f; (in story) giro ♦ vt torcer; (weave) trenzar; (roll around) enrollar; (fig) deformar ♦ vi serpentear
twit [twɪt] (inf) n tonto
twitch [twɪtʃ] n (pull) tirón m; (nervous) tic m ♦ vi crisparse
two [tuː] num dos; **to put ~ and ~ together** (fig) atar cabos; **~-door** adj (AUT) de dos puertas; **~-faced** adj (pej: person) falso; **~fold** adv: **to increase ~fold** doblarse; **~-piece (suit)** n traje m de dos piezas; **~-piece (swimsuit)** n dos piezas m inv, bikini m; **~some** n (people) pareja; **~-way** adj: **~-**

way traffic circulación f de dos sentidos

tycoon [tarˈkuːn] n: (business) ~ magnate m

type [taɪp] n (category) tipo, género; (model) tipo; (TYP) tipo, letra ♦ vt (letter etc) escribir a máquina; **~-cast** adj (actor) encasillado; **~face** n letra; **~script** n texto meca-nografiado; **~writer** n máquina de escribir; **~written** adj mecanografiado

typhoid [ˈtaɪfɔɪd] n tifoidea

typical [ˈtɪpɪkl] adj típico

typing [ˈtaɪpɪŋ] n mecanografía

typist [ˈtaɪpɪst] n mecanógrafo/a

tyrant [ˈtaɪərnt] n tirano/a

tyre [ˈtaɪə*] (US **tire**) n neumático (SP), llanta (AM); ~ **pressure** n presión f de los neumáticos

U, u

U-bend [ˈjuːˈbend] n (AUT, in pipe) recodo

udder [ˈʌdə*] n ubre f

UFO [ˈjuːfəu] n abbr = (unidentified flying object) OVNI m

ugh [əːh] excl ¡uf!

ugly [ˈʌglɪ] adj feo; (dangerous) peligroso

UHT abbr: ~ **milk** leche f UHT, leche f uperizada

UK n abbr = **United Kingdom**

ulcer [ˈʌlsə*] n úlcera; (mouth ~) llaga

Ulster [ˈʌlstə*] n Ulster m

ulterior [ʌlˈtɪərɪə*] adj: ~ **motive** segundas intenciones fpl

ultimate [ˈʌltɪmət] adj último, final; (greatest) máximo; **~ly** adv (in the end) por último, al final; (fundamentally) a o en fin de cuentas

umbilical cord [ʌmˈbɪlɪkl-] n cordón m umbilical

umbrella [ʌmˈbrelə] n paraguas m inv; (for sun) sombrilla

umpire [ˈʌmpaɪə*] n árbitro

umpteen [ʌmpˈtiːn] adj enésimos/as; **~th** adj: **for the ~th time** por enésima vez

UN n abbr (= United Nations) NN. UU.

unable [ʌnˈeɪbl] adj: **to be ~ to do sth** no poder hacer algo

unaccompanied [ʌnəˈkʌmpənɪd] adj no acompañado; (song) sin acompañamiento

unaccustomed [ʌnəˈkʌstəmd] adj: **to be ~ to** no estar acostumbrado a

unanimous [juːˈnænɪməs] adj unánime

unarmed [ʌnˈɑːmd] adj (defenceless) inerme; (without weapon) desarmado

unattached [ʌnəˈtætʃt] adj (person) soltero y sin compromiso; (part etc) suelto

unattended [ʌnəˈtendɪd] adj desatendido

unattractive [ʌnəˈtræktɪv] adj poco atractivo

unauthorized [ʌnˈɔːθəraɪzd] adj no autorizado

unavoidable [ʌnəˈvɔɪdəbl] adj inevitable

unaware [ʌnəˈweə*] adj: **to be ~ of** ignorar; **~s** adv de improviso

unbalanced [ʌnˈbælənst] adj (report) poco objetivo; (mentally) trastornado

unbearable [ʌnˈbeərəbl] adj insoportable

unbeatable [ʌnˈbiːtəbl] adj (team) invencible; (price) inmejorable; (quality) insuperable

unbelievable [ʌnbɪˈliːvəbl] adj increíble

unbend [ʌnˈbend] (irreg) vi (relax) relajarse ♦ vt (wire) enderezar

unbiased [ʌnˈbaɪəst] adj imparcial

unborn [ʌnˈbɔːn] adj que va a nacer

unbroken [ʌnˈbrəukən] adj (seal) intacto; (series) continuo; (record) no batido; (spirit) indómito

unbutton [ʌnˈbʌtn] vt desabrochar

uncalled-for [ʌnˈkɔːldfɔː*] adj gratuito, inmerecido

uncanny [ʌnˈkænɪ] adj extraño

unceremonious [ˈʌnserɪˈməunɪəs] adj (abrupt, rude) brusco, hosco

uncertain [ʌnˈsəːtn] adj incierto; (indecisive) indeciso

unchanged [ʌnˈtʃeɪndʒd] adj igual, sin cambios

uncivilized [ʌnˈsɪvɪlaɪzd] adj inculto; (fig: behaviour etc) bárbaro; (hour) inoportuno

uncle [ˈʌŋkl] n tío

uncomfortable [ʌnˈkʌmfətəbl] adj incómodo; (uneasy) inquieto

uncommon [ʌnˈkɔmən] adj poco común, raro

uncompromising [ʌnˈkɔmprəmaɪzɪŋ] adj intransigente

unconcerned [ʌnkənˈsəːnd] adj indiferente, despreocupado

unconditional [ʌnkənˈdɪʃənl] adj incondicional

unconscious [ʌnˈkɔnʃəs] adj sin sentido; (unaware): **to be ~ of** no darse cuenta de ♦ n: **the ~** el inconsciente

uncontrollable [ʌnkənˈtrəuləbl] adj (child etc) incontrolable; (temper) indomable; (laughter) incontenible

unconventional [ʌnkənˈvenʃənl] adj poco convencional

uncouth [ʌnˈkuːθ] adj grosero, inculto

uncover [ʌnˈkʌvə*] vt descubrir; (take lid off) destapar

undecided [ʌndɪˈsaɪdɪd] adj (character) indeciso; (question) no resuelto

under [ˈʌndə*] prep debajo de; (less than) menos de; (according to) según, de acuerdo con; (sb's leadership) bajo ♦ adv debajo, abajo; ~ **there** allí abajo; ~ **repair** en reparación

under... [' ʌndə*] prefix sub; **~age** adj menor de edad; (drinking etc) de los menores de edad; **~carriage** (BRIT) n (AVIAT) tren m de aterrizaje; **~charge** vt cobrar menos de la cuenta; **~clothes** npl ropa interior (SP) or íntima (AM); **~coat** n (paint) primera mano; **~cover** adj clandestino; **~current** n (fig) corriente f oculta; **~cut** vt irreg vender más barato que; **~developed** adj subdesarrollado; **~dog** n desvalido/a; **~done** adj (CULIN) poco hecho; **~estimate** vt subestimar; **~exposed** adj (PHOT) subexpuesto; **~fed** adj subalimentado; **~foot** adv con los pies; **~go** vt irreg sufrir; (treatment) recibir; **~graduate** n estudiante m/f; **~ground** n (BRIT: railway) metro; (POL) movimiento clandestino ♦ adj (car park) subterráneo ♦ adv (work) en la clandestinidad; **~growth** n maleza; **~hand(ed)** adj (fig) socarrón; **~lie** vt irreg (fig) ser la razón fundamental de; **~line** vt subrayar; **~mine** vt socavar, minar; **~neath** [ʌndə'ni:θ] adv debajo ♦ prep debajo de, bajo; **~paid** adj mal pagado; **~pants** npl calzoncillos mpl; **~pass** (BRIT) n paso subterráneo; **~privileged** adj desposeído; **~rate** vt menospreciar, subestimar; **~shirt** (US) n camiseta; **~shorts** (US) npl calzoncillos mpl; **~side** n parte f inferior; **~skirt** (BRIT) n enaguas fpl

understand [ʌndə'stænd] (irreg) vt, vi entender, comprender; (assume) tener entendido; **~able** adj comprensible; **~ing** adj comprensivo ♦ n comprensión f, entendimiento; (agreement) acuerdo

understatement ['ʌndəsteitmənt] n modestia (excesiva); **that's an ~!** ¡eso es decir poco!

understood [ʌndə'stud] pt, pp of **understand** ♦ adj (agreed) acordado; (implied) **it is ~ that** se sobreentiende que

understudy ['ʌndəstʌdɪ] n suplente m/f

undertake [ʌndə'teɪk] (irreg) vt emprender; **to ~ to do sth** comprometerse a hacer algo

undertaker ['ʌndəteɪkə*] n director(a) m/f de pompas fúnebres

undertaking ['ʌndəteɪkɪŋ] n empresa; (promise) promesa

under: ~tone n: **in an ~tone** en voz baja; **~water** adv bajo el agua ♦ adj submarino; **~wear** n ropa interior (SP) or íntima (AM); **~world** n (of crime) hampa, inframundo; **~writer** n (INSURANCE) asegurador(a) m/f

undesirable [ʌndɪ'zaɪrəbl] adj (person) indeseable; (thing) poco aconsejable

undo [ʌn'du:] (irreg) vt (laces) desatar; (button etc) desabrochar; (spoil) deshacer; **~ing** n ruina, perdición f

undoubted [ʌn'dautɪd] adj indudable

undress [ʌn'dres] vi desnudarse

undulating ['ʌndjuleɪtɪŋ] adj ondulante

unduly [ʌn'dju:lɪ] adv excesivamente, demasiado

unearth [ʌn'ə:θ] vt desenterrar

unearthly [ʌn'ə:θlɪ] adj (hour) inverosímil

uneasy [ʌn'i:zɪ] adj intranquilo, preocupado; (feeling) desagradable; (peace) inseguro

uneducated [ʌn'edjukeɪtɪd] adj ignorante, inculto

unemployed [ʌnɪm'plɔɪd] adj parado, sin trabajo ♦ npl: **the ~** los parados

unemployment [ʌnɪm'plɔɪmənt] n paro, desempleo

unending [ʌn'endɪŋ] adj interminable

unerring [ʌn'ə:rɪŋ] adj infalible

uneven [ʌn'i:vn] adj desigual; (road etc) lleno de baches

unexpected [ʌnɪk'spektɪd] adj inesperado; **~ly** adv inesperadamente

unfailing [ʌn'feɪlɪŋ] adj (support) indefectible; (energy) inagotable

unfair [ʌn'feə*] adj: **~ (to sb)** injusto (con uno)

unfaithful [ʌn'feɪθful] adj infiel

unfamiliar [ʌnfə'mɪlɪə*] adj extraño, desconocido; **to be ~ with** desconocer

unfashionable [ʌn'fæʃnəbl] adj pasado or fuera de moda

unfasten [ʌn'fɑ:sn] vt (knot) desatar; (dress) desabrochar; (open) abrir

unfavourable [ʌn'feɪvərəbl] (US **unfavorable**) adj desfavorable

unfeeling [ʌn'fi:lɪŋ] adj insensible

unfinished [ʌn'fɪnɪʃt] adj inacabado, sin terminar

unfit [ʌn'fɪt] adj bajo de forma; (incompetent): **~ (for)** incapaz (de); **~ for work** no apto para trabajar

unfold [ʌn'fəuld] vt desdoblar ♦ vi abrirse

unforeseen ['ʌnfɔ:'si:n] adj imprevisto

unforgettable [ʌnfə'getəbl] adj inolvidable

unfortunate [ʌn'fɔ:tʃnət] adj desgraciado; (event, remark) inoportuno; **~ly** adv desgraciadamente

unfounded [ʌn'faundɪd] adj infundado

unfriendly [ʌn'frendlɪ] adj antipático; (behaviour, remark) hostil, poco amigable

ungainly [ʌn'geɪnlɪ] adj desgarbado

ungodly [ʌn'gɔdlɪ] adj: **at an ~ hour** a una hora inverosímil

ungrateful [ʌn'greɪtful] adj ingrato

unhappiness [ʌn'hæpɪnɪs] n tristeza, desdicha

unhappy [ʌn'hæpɪ] adj (sad) triste; (unfortunate) desgraciado; (childhood) infeliz; **~ about/with** (arrangements etc) poco contento con, descontento de

unharmed [ʌn'hɑːmd] *adj* ileso
unhealthy [ʌn'helθɪ] *adj* (*place*) malsano; (*person*) enfermizo; (*fig*: *interest*) morboso
unheard-of *adj* inaudito, sin precedente
unhurt [ʌn'hɜːt] *adj* ileso
unidentified [ʌnaɪ'dentɪfaɪd] *adj* no identificado, sin identificar; *see also* UFO
uniform ['juːnɪfɔːm] *n* uniforme *m* ♦ *adj* uniforme
unify ['juːnɪfaɪ] *vt* unificar, unir
uninhabited [ʌnɪn'hæbɪtɪd] *adj* desierto
unintentional [ʌnɪn'tenʃənəl] *adj* involuntario
union ['juːnjən] *n* unión *f*; (*also*: trade ~) sindicato ♦ *cpd* sindical; **U~ Jack** *n* bandera del Reino Unido
unique [juːˈniːk] *adj* único
unison ['juːnɪsn] *n*: **in ~** (*speak, reply, sing*) al unísono
unit ['juːnɪt] *n* unidad *f*; (*section: of furniture etc*) elemento; (*team*) grupo; **kitchen ~** módulo de cocina
unite [juːˈnaɪt] *vt* unir ♦ *vi* unirse; **~d** *adj* unido; (*effort*) conjunto; **U~d Kingdom** *n* Reino Unido; **U~d Nations (Organization)** *n* Naciones *fpl* Unidas; **U~d States (of America)** *n* Estados *mpl* Unidos
unit trust (*BRIT*) *n* bono fiduciario
unity ['juːnɪtɪ] *n* unidad *f*
universe ['juːnɪvɜːs] *n* universo
university [juːnɪ'vɜːsɪtɪ] *n* universidad *f*
unjust [ʌn'dʒʌst] *adj* injusto
unkempt [ʌn'kempt] *adj* (*appearance*) descuidado; (*hair*) despeinado
unkind [ʌn'kaɪnd] *adj* poco amable; (*behaviour, comment*) cruel
unknown [ʌn'nəʊn] *adj* desconocido
unlawful [ʌn'lɔːful] *adj* ilegal, ilícito
unleaded [ʌn'ledɪd] *adj* (*petrol, fuel*) sin plombo
unless [ʌn'les] *conj* a menos que; **~ he comes** a menos que venga; **~ otherwise stated** salvo indicación contraria
unlike [ʌn'laɪk] *adj* (*not alike*) distinto de or a; (*not like*) poco propio de ♦ *prep* a diferencia de
unlikely [ʌn'laɪklɪ] *adj* improbable; (*unexpected*) inverosímil
unlimited [ʌn'lɪmɪtɪd] *adj* ilimitado
unlisted [ʌn'lɪstɪd] (*US*) *adj* (*TEL*) que no consta en la guía
unload [ʌn'ləʊd] *vt* descargar
unlock [ʌn'lɔk] *vt* abrir (con llave)
unlucky [ʌn'lʌkɪ] *adj* desgraciado; (*object, number*) que da mala suerte; **to be ~** tener mala suerte
unmarried [ʌn'mærɪd] *adj* soltero
unmistak(e)able [ʌnmɪs'teɪkəbl] *adj* inconfundible

unnatural [ʌn'nætʃrəl] *adj* (*gen*) antinatural; (*manner*) afectado; (*habit*) perverso
unnecessary [ʌn'nesəsərɪ] *adj* innecesario, inútil
unnoticed [ʌn'nəʊtɪst] *adj*: **to go** *or* **pass ~** pasar desapercibido
UNO ['juːnəʊ] *n abbr* (= *United Nations Organization*) ONU *f*
unobtainable [ʌnəb'teɪnəbl] *adj* inconseguible; (*TEL*) inexistente
unobtrusive [ʌnəb'truːsɪv] *adj* discreto
unofficial [ʌnə'fɪʃl] *adj* no oficial; (*news*) sin confirmar
unorthodox [ʌn'ɔːθədɒks] *adj* poco ortodoxo; (*REL*) heterodoxo
unpack [ʌn'pæk] *vi* deshacer las maletas ♦ *vt* deshacer
unpalatable [ʌn'pælətəbl] *adj* incomible; (*truth*) desagradable
unparalleled [ʌn'pærəleld] *adj* (*unequalled*) incomparable
unpleasant [ʌn'pleznt] *adj* (*disagreeable*) desagradable; (*person, manner*) antipático
unplug [ʌn'plʌg] *vt* desenchufar, desconectar
unpopular [ʌn'pɒpjulə*] *adj* impopular, poco popular
unprecedented [ʌn'presɪdəntɪd] *adj* sin precedentes
unpredictable [ʌnprɪ'dɪktəbl] *adj* imprevisible
unprofessional [ʌnprə'feʃnl] *adj* (*attitude, conduct*) poco ético
unqualified [ʌn'kwɒlɪfaɪd] *adj* sin título, no cualificado; (*success*) total
unquestionably [ʌn'kwestʃənəblɪ] *adv* indiscutiblemente
unreal [ʌn'rɪəl] *adj* irreal; (*extraordinary*) increíble
unrealistic [ʌnrɪə'lɪstɪk] *adj* poco realista
unreasonable [ʌn'riːznəbl] *adj* irrazonable; (*demand*) excesivo
unrelated [ʌnrɪ'leɪtɪd] *adj* sin relación; (*family*) no emparentado
unreliable [ʌnrɪ'laɪəbl] *adj* (*person*) informal; (*machine*) poco fiable
unremitting [ʌnrɪ'mɪtɪŋ] *adj* constante
unreservedly [ʌnrɪ'zɜːvɪdlɪ] *adv* sin reserva
unrest [ʌn'rest] *n* inquietud *f*, malestar *m*; (*POL*) disturbios *mpl*
unroll [ʌn'rəʊl] *vt* desenrollar
unruly [ʌn'ruːlɪ] *adj* indisciplinado
unsafe [ʌn'seɪf] *adj* peligroso
unsaid [ʌn'sed] *adj*: **to leave sth ~** dejar algo sin decir
unsatisfactory ['ʌnsætɪs'fæktərɪ] *adj* poco satisfactorio
unsavoury [ʌn'seɪvərɪ] (*US* **unsavory**) *adj* (*fig*) repugnante
unscrew [ʌn'skruː] *vt* destornillar

unscrupulous [ʌnˈskruːpjuləs] *adj* sin escrúpulos

unsettled [ʌnˈsetld] *adj* inquieto, intranquilo; (*weather*) variable

unshaven [ʌnˈʃeɪvn] *adj* sin afeitar

unsightly [ʌnˈsaɪtlɪ] *adj* feo

unskilled [ʌnˈskɪld] *adj* (*work*) no especializado; (*worker*) no cualificado

unspeakable [ʌnˈspiːkəbl] *adj* indecible; (*awful*) incalificable

unstable [ʌnˈsteɪbl] *adj* inestable

unsteady [ʌnˈstedɪ] *adj* inestable

unstuck [ʌnˈstʌk] *adj*: **to come ~** despegarse; (*fig*) fracasar

unsuccessful [ʌnsəkˈsesful] *adj* (*attempt*) infructuoso; (*writer, proposal*) sin éxito; **to be ~** (*in attempting sth*) no tener éxito, fracasar; **~ly** *adv* en vano, sin éxito

unsuitable [ʌnˈsuːtəbl] *adj* inapropiado; (*time*) inoportuno

unsure [ʌnˈʃuə*] *adj* inseguro, poco seguro

unsuspecting [ˈʌnsəsˈpektɪŋ] *adj* desprevenido

unsympathetic [ʌnsɪmpəˈθetɪk] *adj* poco comprensivo; (*unlikeable*) antipático

unthinkable [ʌnˈθɪŋkəbl] *adj* inconcebible, impensable

untidy [ʌnˈtaɪdɪ] *adj* (*room*) desordenado; (*appearance*) desaliñado

untie [ʌnˈtaɪ] *vt* desatar

until [ənˈtɪl] *prep* hasta ♦ *conj* hasta que; **~ he comes** hasta que venga; **~ now** hasta ahora; **~ then** hasta entonces

untimely [ʌnˈtaɪmlɪ] *adj* inoportuno; (*death*) prematuro

untold [ʌnˈtəʊld] *adj* (*story*) nunca contado; (*suffering*) indecible; (*wealth*) incalculable

untoward [ʌntəˈwɔːd] *adj* adverso

unused [ʌnˈjuːzd] *adj* sin usar

unusual [ʌnˈjuːʒuəl] *adj* insólito, poco común; (*exceptional*) inusitado

unveil [ʌnˈveɪl] *vt* (*statue*) descubrir

unwanted [ʌnˈwɔntɪd] *adj* (*clothing*) viejo; (*pregnancy*) no deseado

unwelcome [ʌnˈwelkəm] *adj* inoportuno; (*news*) desagradable

unwell [ʌnˈwel] *adj*: **to be/feel ~** estar indispuesto/sentirse mal

unwieldy [ʌnˈwiːldɪ] *adj* difícil de manejar

unwilling [ʌnˈwɪlɪŋ] *adj*: **to be ~ to do sth** estar poco dispuesto a hacer algo; **~ly** *adv* de mala gana

unwind [ʌnˈwaɪnd] (*irreg: like* wind²) *vt* desenvolver ♦ *vi* (*relax*) relajarse

unwise [ʌnˈwaɪz] *adj* imprudente

unwitting [ʌnˈwɪtɪŋ] *adj* inconsciente

unworthy [ʌnˈwəːðɪ] *adj* indigno

unwrap [ʌnˈræp] *vt* desenvolver

unwritten [ʌnˈrɪtn] *adj* (*agreement*) tácito; (*rules, law*) no escrito

---

> **KEYWORD**

up [ʌp] *prep*: **to go/be ~ sth** subir/estar subido en algo; **he went ~ the stairs/the hill** subió las escaleras/la colina; **we walked/climbed ~ the hill** subimos la colina; **they live further ~ the street** viven más arriba en la calle; **go ~ that road and turn left** sigue por esa calle y gira a la izquierda

♦ *adv* **1** (*upwards, higher*) más arriba; **~ in the mountains** en lo alto (de la montaña); **put it a bit higher ~** ponlo un poco más arriba or alto; **~ there** ahí or allí arriba; **~ above** en lo alto, por encima, arriba

2: **to be ~** (*out of bed*) estar levantado; (*prices, level*) haber subido

3: **~ to** (*as far as*) hasta; **~ to now** hasta ahora or la fecha

4: **to be ~ to** (*depending on*): **it's ~ to you** depende de ti; **he's not ~ to it** (*job, task etc*) no es capaz de hacerlo; **his work is not ~ to the required standard** su trabajo no a la talla; (*inf: be doing*): **what is he ~ to?** ¿que estará tramando?

♦ *n*: **~s and downs** altibajos *mpl*

---

upbringing [ˈʌpbrɪŋɪŋ] *n* educación *f*

update [ʌpˈdeɪt] *vt* poner al día

upgrade [ʌpˈgreɪd] *vt* (*house*) modernizar; (*employee*) ascender

upheaval [ʌpˈhiːvl] *n* trastornos *mpl*; (POL) agitación *f*

uphill [ʌpˈhɪl] *adj* cuesta arriba; (*fig: task*) penoso, difícil ♦ *adv*: **to go ~** ir cuesta arriba

uphold [ʌpˈhəʊld] (*irreg*) *vt* defender

upholstery [ʌpˈhəʊlstərɪ] *n* tapicería

upkeep [ˈʌpkiːp] *n* mantenimiento

upon [əˈpɔn] *prep* sobre

upper [ˈʌpə*] *adj* superior, de arriba ♦ *n* (*of shoe: also*: **~s**) empeine *m*; **~-class** *adj* de clase alta; **~ hand** *n*: **to have the ~ hand** tener la sartén por el mango; **~most** *adj* el más alto; **what was ~most in my mind** lo que me preocupaba más

upright [ˈʌpraɪt] *adj* derecho; (*vertical*) vertical; (*fig*) honrado

uprising [ˈʌpraɪzɪŋ] *n* sublevación *f*

uproar [ˈʌprɔː*] *n* escándalo

uproot [ʌpˈruːt] *vt* (*also fig*) desarraigar

upset [*n* ˈʌpset, *vb, adj* ʌpˈset] *n* (*to plan etc*) revés *m*, contratiempo; (MED) trastorno ♦ (*irreg*) *vt* (*glass etc*) volcar; (*plan*) alterar; (*person*) molestar, disgustar ♦ *adj* molesto, disgustado; (*stomach*) revuelto

upshot [ˈʌpʃɔt] *n* resultado

upside-down *adv* al revés; **to turn a place ~** (*fig*) revolverlo todo

upstairs [ʌpˈsteəz] *adv* arriba ♦ *adj* (*room*) de

arriba ♦ *n* el piso superior
upstart ['ʌpstɑːt] *n* advenedizo/a
upstream [ʌp'striːm] *adv* río arriba
uptake ['ʌpteɪk] *n*: **to be quick/slow on the ~** ser muy listo/torpe
uptight [ʌp'taɪt] *adj* tenso, nervioso
up-to-date *adj* al día
upturn ['ʌptəːn] *n* (*in luck*) mejora; (*COMM: in market*) resurgimiento económico
upward ['ʌpwəd] *adj* ascendente; **~(s)** *adv* hacia arriba; (*more than*): **~(s) of** más de
urban ['əːbən] *adj* urbano
urchin ['əːtʃɪn] *n* pilluelo, golfillo
urge [əːdʒ] *n* (*desire*) deseo ♦ *vt*: **to ~ sb to do sth** animar a uno a hacer algo
urgent ['əːdʒənt] *adj* urgente; (*voice*) perentorio
urinate ['juərɪneɪt] *vi* orinar
urine ['juərɪn] *n* orina, orines *mpl*
urn [əːn] *n* urna; (*also: tea ~*) *cacharro metálico grande para hacer té*
Uruguay ['juerəgwaɪ] *n* (el) Uruguay; **~an** [-'gwaɪən] *adj, n* uruguayo/a *m/f*
US *n abbr* (= *United States*) EE. UU.
us [ʌs] *pron* nos; (*after prep*) nosotros/as; *see also* **me**
USA *n abbr* (= *United States (of America)*) EE. UU.
usage ['juːzɪdʒ] *n* (*LING*) uso
use [*n* juːs, *vb* juːz] *n* uso, empleo; (*usefulness*) utilidad *f* ♦ *vt* usar, emplear; **she ~d to do it** (ella) solía *or* acostumbraba hacerlo; **in ~** en uso; **out of ~** en desuso; **to be of ~** servir; **it's no ~** (*pointless*) es inútil; (*not useful*) no sirve; **to be ~d to** estar acostumbrado a, acostumbrar; **~ up** *vt* (*food*) consumir; (*money*) gastar; **~d** *adj* (*car*) usado; **~ful** *adj* útil; **~fulness** *n* utilidad *f*; **~less** *adj* (*unusable*) inservible; (*pointless*) inútil; (*person*) inepto; **~r** *n* usuario/a; **~r-friendly** *adj* (*computer*) amistoso
usher ['ʌʃə*] *n* (*at wedding*) ujier *m*; **~ette** [-'ret] *n* (*in cinema*) acomodadora
USSR *n* (*HIST*): **the ~** la URSS
usual ['juːʒuəl] *adj* normal, corriente; **as ~** como de costumbre; **~ly** *adv* normalmente
utensil [juː'tɛnsl] *n* utensilio; **kitchen ~s** batería de cocina
uterus ['juːtərəs] *n* útero
utility [juː'tɪlɪtɪ] *n* utilidad *f*; (*public ~*) (empresa de) servicio público; **~ room** *n* ofis *m*
utilize ['juːtɪlaɪz] *vt* utilizar
utmost ['ʌtməust] *adj* mayor ♦ *n*: **to do one's ~** hacer todo lo posible
utter ['ʌtə*] *adj* total, completo ♦ *vt* pronunciar, proferir; **~ly** *adv* completamente, totalmente
U-turn ['juː'təːn] *n* viraje *m* en redondo

v. *abbr* = **verse**; **versus**; (= *volt*) v; (= *vide*) véase
vacancy ['veɪkənsɪ] *n* (*BRIT: job*) vacante *f*; (*room*) habitación *f* libre; **"no vacancies"** "completo"
vacant ['veɪkənt] *adj* desocupado, libre; (*expression*) distraído
vacate [və'keɪt] *vt* (*house, room*) desocupar; (*job*) dejar (vacante)
vacation [və'keɪʃən] *n* vacaciones *fpl*
vaccinate ['væksɪneɪt] *vt* vacunar
vaccine ['væksiːn] *n* vacuna
vacuum ['vækjum] *n* vacío; **~ cleaner** *n* aspiradora; **~flask** (*BRIT*) *n* termo; **~-packed** *adj* empaquetado al vacío
vagina [və'dʒaɪnə] *n* vagina
vagrant ['veɪgrnt] *n* vagabundo/a
vague [veɪg] *adj* vago; (*memory*) borroso; (*ambiguous*) impreciso; (*person: absent-minded*) distraído; (: *evasive*): **to be ~** no decir las cosas claramente; **~ly** *adv* vagamente; distraídamente; con evasivas
vain [veɪn] *adj* (*conceited*) presumido; (*useless*) vano, inútil; **in ~** en vano
valentine ['væləntaɪn] *n* (*also: ~ card*) tarjeta del Día de los Enamorados
valet ['væleɪ] *n* ayuda *m* de cámara
valid ['vælɪd] *adj* válido; (*ticket*) valedero; (*law*) vigente
valley ['vælɪ] *n* valle *m*
valuable ['væljuəbl] *adj* (*jewel*) de valor; (*time*) valioso; **~s** *npl* objetos *mpl* de valor
valuation [vælju'eɪʃən] *n* tasación *f*, valuación *f*; (*judgement of quality*) valoración *f*
value ['væljuː] *n* valor *m*; (*importance*) importancia ♦ *vt* (*fix price of*) tasar, valorar; (*esteem*) apreciar; **~s** *npl* (*principles*) principios *mpl*; **~ added tax** (*BRIT*) *n* impuesto sobre el valor añadido; **~d** *adj* (*appreciated*) apreciado
valve [vælv] *n* válvula
van [væn] *n* (*AUT*) furgoneta (*SP*), camioneta (*AM*)
vandal ['vændl] *n* vándalo/a; **~ism** *n* vandalismo; **~ize** *vt* dañar, destruir
vanilla [və'nɪlə] *n* vainilla
vanish ['vænɪʃ] *vi* desaparecer
vanity ['vænɪtɪ] *n* vanidad *f*
vantage point ['vɑːntɪdʒ-] *n* (*for views*) punto panorámico
vapour ['veɪpə*] (*US* **vapor**) *n* vapor *m*; (*on breath, window*) vaho
variable ['veərɪəbl] *adj* variable
variation [veərɪ'eɪʃən] *n* variación *f*
varicose ['værɪkəus] *adj*: **~ veins** varices *fpl*

varied ['veərɪd] *adj* variado

variety [və'raɪətɪ] *n* (*diversity*) diversidad *f*; (*type*) variedad *f*; ~ **show** *n* espectáculo de variedades

various ['veərɪəs] *adj* (*several: people*) varios/ as; (*reasons*) diversos/as

varnish ['vɑːnɪʃ] *n* barniz *m*; (*nail ~*) esmalte *m* ♦ *vt* barnizar; (*nails*) pintar (con esmalte)

vary ['veərɪ] *vt* variar; (*change*) cambiar ♦ *vi* variar

vase [vɑːz] *n* florero

Vaseline ® ['væsɪliːn] *n* vaselina ®

vast [vɑːst] *adj* enorme

VAT [væt] (*BRIT*) *n abbr* (= *value added tax*) IVA *m*

vat [væt] *n* tina, tinaja

Vatican ['vætɪkən] *n*: **the ~** el Vaticano

vault [vɔːlt] *n* (*of roof*) bóveda; (*tomb*) panteón *m*; (*in bank*) cámara acorazada ♦ *vt* (*also*: ~ *over*) saltar (por encima de)

vaunted ['vɔːntɪd] *adj*: **much ~** cacareado, alardeado

VCR *n abbr* = **video cassette recorder**

VD *n abbr* = **venereal disease**

VDU *n abbr* (= *visual display unit*) UPV *f*

veal [viːl] *n* ternera

veer [vɪə*] *vi* (*vehicle*) virar; (*wind*) girar

vegan ['viːgən] *n* vegetariano/a estricto/a, vegetaliano/a

vegeburger ['vedʒɪbəːgə*] *n* hamburguesa vegetal

vegetable ['vedʒtəbl] *n* (*BOT*) vegetal *m*; (*edible plant*) legumbre *f*, hortaliza ♦ *adj* vegetal; ~**s** *npl* (*cooked*) verduras *fpl*

vegetarian [vedʒɪ'teərɪən] *adj, n* vegetariano/a *m/f*

vehement ['viːɪmənt] *adj* vehemente, apasionado

vehicle ['viːɪkl] *n* vehículo; (*fig*) medio

veil [veɪl] *n* velo ♦ *vt* velar; ~**ed** *adj* (*fig*) velado

vein [veɪn] *n* vena; (*of ore etc*) veta

velocity [vɪ'lɔsɪtɪ] *n* velocidad *f*

velvet ['velvɪt] *n* terciopelo

vending machine ['vendɪŋ-] *n* distribuidor *m* automático

veneer [və'nɪə*] *n* chapa, enchapado; (*fig*) barniz *m*

venereal disease [vɪ'nɪərɪəl-] *n* enfermedad *f* venérea

Venetian blind [vɪ'niːʃən-] *n* persiana

Venezuela [venɪ'zweɪlə] *n* Venezuela; ~**n** *adj, n* venezolano/a *m/f*

vengeance ['vendʒəns] *n* venganza; **with a** ~ (*fig*) con creces

venison ['venɪsn] *n* carne *f* de venado

venom ['venəm] *n* veneno; (*bitterness*) odio; ~**ous** *adj* venenoso; lleno de odio

vent [vent] *n* (*in jacket*) respiradero; (*in wall*)

rejilla (de ventilación) ♦ *vt* (*fig: feelings*) desahogar

ventilator ['ventɪleɪtə*] *n* ventilador *m*

venture ['ventʃə*] *n* empresa ♦ *vt* (*opinion*) ofrecer ♦ *vi* arriesgarse, lanzarse; **business ~** empresa comercial

venue ['venjuː] *n* lugar *m*

veranda(h) [və'rændə] *n* terraza

verb [vəːb] *n* verbo; ~**al** *adj* verbal

verbatim [vəː'beɪtɪm] *adj, adv* palabra por palabra

verdict ['vəːdɪkt] *n* veredicto, fallo; (*fig*) opinión *f*, juicio

verge [vəːdʒ] (*BRIT*) *n* borde *m*; "**soft ~s**" (*AUT*) "arcén *m* no asfaltado"; **to be on the** ~ **of doing sth** estar a punto de hacer algo; ~ **on** *vt fus* rayar en

verify ['verɪfaɪ] *vt* comprobar, verificar

vermin ['vəːmɪn] *npl* (*animals*) alimañas *fpl*; (*insects, fig*) parásitos *mpl*

vermouth ['vəːməθ] *n* vermut *m*

versatile ['vəːsətaɪl] *adj* (*person*) polifacético; (*machine, tool etc*) versátil

verse [vəːs] *n* poesía; (*stanza*) estrofa; (*in bible*) versículo

version ['vəːʃən] *n* versión *f*

versus ['vəːsəs] *prep* contra

vertebra ['vəːtɪbrə] (*pl* ~**e**) *n* vértebra

vertical ['vəːtɪkl] *adj* vertical

verve [vəːv] *n* brío

very ['verɪ] *adv* muy ♦ *adj*: **the ~ book which** el mismo libro que; **the ~ last** el último de todos; **at the ~ least** al menos; ~ **much** muchísimo

vessel ['vesl] *n* (*ship*) barco; (*container*) vasija; *see* **blood**

vest [vest] *n* (*BRIT*) camiseta; (*US: waistcoat*) chaleco; ~**ed interests** *npl* (*COMM*) intereses *mpl* creados

vet [vet] *vt* (*candidate*) investigar ♦ *n abbr* (*BRIT*) = **veterinary surgeon**

veteran ['vetərn] *n* veterano

veterinary surgeon ['vetrɪnərɪ] (*US* **veterinarian**) *n* veterinario/a *m/f*

veto ['viːtəu] (*pl* ~**es**) *n* veto ♦ *vt* prohibir, poner el veto a

vex [veks] *vt* fastidiar; ~**ed** *adj* (*question*) controvertido

VHF *abbr* (= *very high frequency*) muy alta frecuencia

via ['vaɪə] *prep* por, por medio de

vibrant ['vaɪbrənt] *adj* (*lively*) animado; (*bright*) vivo; (*voice*) vibrante

vibrate [vaɪ'breɪt] *vi* vibrar

vicar ['vɪkə*] *n* párroco (de la Iglesia Anglicana); ~**age** *n* parroquia

vice [vaɪs] *n* (*evil*) vicio; (*TECH*) torno de banco

vice- [vaɪs] *prefix* vice-; ~-**chairman** *n*

vicepresidente m
vice squad n brigada antivicio
vice versa ['vaısı'vɜːsə] adv viceversa
vicinity [vı'sınıtı] n: **in the ~ (of)** cercano (a)
vicious ['vɪʃəs] adj (attack) violento; (words)
cruel; (horse, dog) resabido; **~ circle** n
círculo vicioso
victim ['vıktım] n víctima
victor ['vıktə*] n vencedor(a) m/f
victory ['vıktərı] n victoria
video ['vıdıəʊ] cpd video ♦ n (~ film)
videofilm m; (also: ~ cassette) videocassette f;
(also: ~ cassette recorder) magnetoscopio;
~ game n videojuego; **~ tape** n cinta de
vídeo
vie [vaı] vi: **to ~ (with sb for sth)** competir
(con uno por algo)
Vienna [vı'enə] n Viena
Vietnam [vjet'næm] n Vietnam m; **~ese**
[-nə'miːz] n inv, adj vietnamita m/f
view [vjuː] n vista; (outlook) perspectiva;
(opinion) opinión f, criterio ♦ vt (look at)
mirar; (fig) considerar; **on ~** (in museum etc)
expuesto; **in full ~ (of)** en plena vista (de); **in
~ of the weather/the fact that** en vista del
tiempo/del hecho de que; **in my ~** en mi
opinión; **~er** n espectador(a) m/f; (TV)
telespectador(a) m/f; **~finder** n visor m de
imagen; **~point** n (attitude) punto de vista;
(place) mirador m
vigour ['vıgə*] (US vigor) n energía, vigor m
vile [vaıl] adj vil, infame; (smell) asqueroso;
(temper) endemoniado
villa ['vılə] n (country house) casa de campo;
(suburban house) chalet m
village ['vılıdʒ] n aldea; **~r** n aldeano/a
villain ['vılən] n (scoundrel) malvado/a; (in
novel) malo; (BRIT: criminal) maleante m/f
vindicate ['vındıkeıt] vt vindicar, justificar
vindictive [vın'dıktıv] adj vengativo
vine [vaın] n vid f
vinegar ['vınıgə*] n vinagre m
vineyard ['vınjɑːd] n viña, viñedo
vintage ['vıntıdʒ] n (year) vendimia, cosecha
♦ cpd de época; **~ wine** n vino añejo
vinyl ['vaınl] n vinilo
viola [vı'əʊlə] n (MUS) viola
violate ['vaıəleıt] vt violar
violence ['vaıələns] n violencia
violent ['vaıələnt] adj violento; (intense)
intenso
violet ['vaıələt] adj violado, violeta ♦ n (plant)
violeta
violin [vaıə'lın] n violín m; **~ist** n violinista m/f
VIP n abbr (= very important person) VIP m
virgin ['vɜːdʒın] n virgen f
Virgo ['vɜːgəʊ] n Virgo
virtually ['vɜːtjuəlı] adv prácticamente
virtual reality ['vɜːtjuəl-] n (COMPUT)

mundo or realidad f virtual
virtue ['vɜːtjuː] n virtud f; (advantage)
ventaja; **by ~ of** en virtud de
virtuous ['vɜːtjuəs] adj virtuoso
virus ['vaıərəs] n (also: COMPUT) virus m
visa ['viːzə] n visado (SP), visa (AM)
visible ['vızəbl] adj visible
vision ['vıʒən] n (sight) vista; (foresight, in
dream) visión f
visit ['vızıt] n visita ♦ vt (person: US: also:
~ with) visitar, hacer una visita a; (place) ir a,
(ir a) conocer; **~ing hours** npl (in hospital
etc) horas fpl de visita; **~or** n (in museum)
visitante m/f; (invited to house) visita; (tourist)
turista m/f
visor ['vaızə*] n visera
visual ['vızjuəl] adj visual; **~ aid** n medio
visual; **~ display unit** n unidad f de
presentación visual; **~ize** vt imaginarse
vital ['vaıtl] adj (essential) esencial,
imprescindible; (dynamic) dinámico; (organ)
vital; **~ly** adv: **~ly important** de primera
importancia; **~ statistics** npl (fig) medidas
fpl vitales
vitamin ['vıtəmın] n vitamina
vivacious [vı'veıʃəs] adj vivaz, alegre
vivid ['vıvıd] adj (account) gráfico; (light)
intenso; (imagination, memory) vivo; **~ly** adv
gráficamente; (remember) como si fuera hoy
V-neck ['viːnek] n cuello de pico
vocabulary [vəʊ'kæbjulərı] n vocabulario
vocal ['vəʊkl] adj vocal; (articulate)
elocuente; **~ cords** npl cuerdas fpl vocales
vocation [vəʊ'keıʃən] n vocación f; **~al** adj
profesional
vodka ['vɔdkə] n vodka m
vogue [vəʊg] n: **in ~** en boga, de moda
voice [vɔıs] n voz f ♦ vt expresar; **~ mail** n
fonobuzón m
void [vɔıd] n vacío; (hole) hueco ♦ adj
(invalid) nulo, inválido; (empty): **~ of** carente
or desprovisto de
volatile ['vɔlətaıl] adj (situation) inestable;
(person) voluble; (liquid) volátil
volcano [vɔl'keınəʊ] (pl **~es**) n volcán m
volition [və'lıʃən] n: **of one's own ~** de su
propia voluntad
volley ['vɔlı] n (of gunfire) descarga; (of
stones etc) lluvia; (fig) torrente m; (TENNIS
etc) volea; **~ball** n vol(e)ibol m
volt [vəʊlt] n voltio; **~age** n voltaje m
volume ['vɔljuːm] n (gen) volumen m;
(book) tomo
voluntary ['vɔləntərı] adj voluntario
volunteer [vɔlən'tıə*] n voluntario/a ♦ vt
(information) ofrecer ♦ vi ofrecerse (de
voluntario); **to ~ to do** ofrecerse a hacer
vomit ['vɔmıt] n vómito ♦ vt, vi vomitar
vote [vəʊt] n voto; (votes cast) votación f;

(*right to* ~) derecho de votar; (*franchise*) sufragio ♦ *vt* (*chairman*) elegir; (*propose*): **to ~ that** proponer que ♦ *vi* votar, ir a votar; **~ of thanks** voto de gracias; **~r** *n* votante *m/f*; **voting** *n* votación *f*

vouch [vautʃ]: **to ~ for** *vt fus* garantizar, responder de

voucher ['vautʃə*] *n* (*for meal, petrol*) vale *m*

vow [vau] *n* voto ♦ *vt*: **to ~ to do/that** jurar hacer/que

vowel ['vauəl] *n* vocal *f*

voyage ['vɔıdʒ] *n* viaje *m*

vulgar ['vʌlgə*] *adj* (*rude*) ordinario, grosero; (*in bad taste*) de mal gusto; **~ity** [-'gærıtı] *n* grosería; mal gusto

vulnerable ['vʌlnərəbl] *adj* vulnerable

vulture ['vʌltʃə*] *n* buitre *m*

W, w

wad [wɒd] *n* bolita; (*of banknotes etc*) fajo

waddle ['wɒdl] *vi* anadear

wade [weıd] *vi*: **to ~ through** (*water*) vadear; (*fig: book*) leer con dificultad; **wading pool** (*US*) *n* piscina para niños

wafer ['weıfə*] *n* galleta, barquillo

waffle ['wɒfl] *n* (*CULIN*) gofre *m* ♦ *vi* dar el rollo

waft [wɒft] *vt* llevar por el aire ♦ *vi* flotar

wag [wæg] *vt* menear, agitar ♦ *vi* moverse, menearse

wage [weıdʒ] *n* (*also*: ~s) sueldo, salario ♦ *vt*: **to ~ war** hacer la guerra; **~ earner** *n* asalariado/a; **~ packet** *n* sobre *m* de paga

wager ['weıdʒə*] *n* apuesta

wag(g)on ['wægən] *n* (*horse-drawn*) carro; (*BRIT: RAIL*) vagón *m*

wail [weıl] *n* gemido ♦ *vi* gemir

waist [weıst] *n* cintura, talle *m*; **~coat** (*BRIT*) *n* chaleco; **~line** *n* talle *m*

wait [weıt] *n* (*interval*) pausa ♦ *vi* esperar; **to lie in ~ for** acechar a; **I can't ~ to** (*fig*) estoy deseando; **to ~ for** esperar (a); **~ behind** *vi* quedarse; **~ on** *vt fus* servir a; **~er** *n* camarero; **~ing** *n*: **"no ~ing"** (*BRIT: AUT*) "prohibido estacionarse"; **~ing list** *n* lista de espera; **~ing room** *n* sala de espera; **~ress** *n* camarera

waive [weıv] *vt* suspender

wake [weık] (*pt* **woke** *or* **waked**, *pp* **woken** *or* **waked**) *vt* (*also*: ~ **up**) despertar ♦ *vi* (*also*: ~ **up**) despertarse ♦ *n* (*for dead person*) vela, velatorio; (*NAUT*) estela; **waken** *vt, vi* = **wake**

Wales [weılz] *n* País *m* de Gales; **the Prince of ~** el príncipe de Gales

walk [wɔːk] *n* (*stroll*) paseo; (*hike*) excursión *f* a pie, caminata; (*gait*) paso, andar *m*; (*in park etc*) paseo, alameda ♦ *vi* andar, caminar; (*for pleasure, exercise*) pasear ♦ *vt* (*distance*) recorrer a pie, andar; (*dog*) pasear; **10 minutes' ~ from here** a 10 minutos de aquí andando; **people from all ~s of life** gente de todas las esferas; **~ out** *vi* (*audience*) salir; (*workers*) declararse en huelga; **~ out on** (*inf*) *vt fus* abandonar; **~er** *n* (*person*) paseante *m/f*, caminante *m/f*; **~ie-talkie** ['wɔːkı'tɔːkı] *n* walkie-talkie *m*; **~ing** *n* el andar; **~ing shoes** *npl* zapatos *mpl* para andar; **~ing stick** *n* bastón *m*; **W~man** ® ['wɔːkmən] *n* Walkman ® *m*; **~out** *n* huelga; **~over** (*inf*) *n*: **it was a ~over** fue pan comido; **~way** *n* paseo

wall [wɔːl] *n* pared *f*; (*exterior*) muro; (*city etc*) muralla; **~ed** *adj* amurallado; (*garden*) con tapia

wallet ['wɒlıt] *n* cartera (*SP*), billetera (*AM*)

wallflower ['wɔːlflauə*] *n* alhelí *m*; **to be a ~** (*fig*) comer pavo

wallow ['wɒləu] *vi* revolcarse

wallpaper ['wɔːlpeıpə*] *n* papel *m* pintado ♦ *vt* empapelar

walnut ['wɔːlnʌt] *n* nuez *f*; (*tree*) nogal *m*

walrus ['wɔːlrəs] (*pl* ~ *or* **~es**) *n* morsa

waltz [wɔːlts] *n* vals *m* ♦ *vi* bailar el vals

wand [wɒnd] *n* (*also*: **magic** ~) varita (mágica)

wander ['wɒndə*] *vi* (*person*) vagar; deambular; (*thoughts*) divagar ♦ *vt* recorrer, vagar por

wane [weın] *vi* menguar

wangle ['wæŋgl] (*BRIT: inf*) *vt* agenciarse

want [wɒnt] *vt* querer, desear; (*need*) necesitar ♦ *n*: **for ~ of** por falta de; **~s** *npl* (*needs*) necesidades *fpl*; **to ~ to do** querer hacer; **to ~ sb to do sth** querer que uno haga algo; **~ed** *adj* (*criminal*) buscado; **"~ed"** (*in advertisements*) "se busca"; **~ing** *adj*: **to be found ~ing** no estar a la altura de las circunstancias

war [wɔː*] *n* guerra; **to make ~ (on)** (*also fig*) declarar la guerra (a)

ward [wɔːd] *n* (*in hospital*) sala; (*POL*) distrito electoral; (*LAW: child: also*: ~ *of court*) pupilo/a; **~ off** *vt* (*blow*) desviar, parar; (*attack*) rechazar

warden ['wɔːdn] *n* (*BRIT: of institution*) director(a) *m/f*; (*of park, game reserve*) guardián/ana *m/f*; (*BRIT: also*: **traffic ~**) guardia *m/f*

warder ['wɔːdə*] (*BRIT*) *n* guardián/ana *m/f*, carcelero/a

wardrobe ['wɔːdrəub] *n* armario, guardarropa, ropero (*esp AM*)

warehouse ['wɛəhaus] *n* almacén *m*, depósito

wares [wɛəz] *npl* mercancías *fpl*

warfare ['wɔːfeə*] n guerra
warhead ['wɔːhed] n cabeza armada
warily ['weərɪlɪ] adv con cautela,
cautelosamente
warm [wɔːm] adj caliente; (thanks) efusivo;
(clothes etc) abrigado; (welcome, day)
caluroso; **it's ~** hace calor; **I'm ~** tengo calor;
~ up vi (room) calentarse; (person) entrar en
calor; (athlete) hacer ejercicios de
calentamiento ♦ vt calentar; **~-hearted** adj
afectuoso; **~ly** adv afectuosamente; **~th** n
calor m
warn [wɔːn] vt avisar, advertir; **~ing** n aviso,
advertencia; **~ing light** n luz f de
advertencia; **~ing triangle** n (AUT) triángulo
señalizador
warp [wɔːp] vi (wood) combarse ♦ vt
combar; (mind) pervertir
warrant ['wɔrnt] n autorización f; (LAW: to
arrest) orden f de detención; (: to search)
mandamiento de registro
warranty ['wɔrəntɪ] n garantía
warren ['wɔrən] n (of rabbits) madriguera;
(fig) laberinto
warrior ['wɔrɪə*] n guerrero/a
Warsaw ['wɔːsɔː] n Varsovia
warship ['wɔːʃɪp] n buque m o barco de
guerra
wart [wɔːt] n verruga
wartime ['wɔːtaɪm] n: **in ~** en tiempos de
guerra, en la guerra
wary ['weərɪ] adj cauteloso
was [wɔz] pt of **be**
wash [wɔʃ] vt lavar ♦ vi lavarse; (sea etc): **to
~ against/over sth** llegar hasta/cubrir algo ♦ n
(clothes etc) lavado; (of ship) estela; **to have a
~** lavarse; **~ away** vt (stain) quitar lavando;
(subj: river etc) llevarse; **~ off** vi quitarse (al
lavar); **~ up** vi (BRIT) fregar los platos, (US)
lavarse; **~able** adj lavable; **~basin** (US
~bowl) n lavabo; **~ cloth** (US) n manopla;
~er n (TECH) arandela; **~ing** n (dirty) ropa
sucia; (clean) colada; **~ing machine** n
lavadora; **~ing powder** (BRIT) n detergente
m (en polvo)
Washington ['wɔʃɪŋtən] n Washington m
wash: ~ing-up (BRIT) n fregado, platos mpl
(para fregar); **~ing-up liquid** (BRIT) n líquido
lavavajillas; **~-out** (inf) n fracaso; **~room**
(US) n servicios mpl
wasn't ['wɔznt] = **was not**
wasp [wɔsp] n avispa
wastage ['weɪstɪdʒ] n desgaste m; (loss)
pérdida
waste [weɪst] n derroche m, despilfarro; (of
time) pérdida; (food) sobras fpl; (rubbish)
basura, desperdicios mpl ♦ adj (material) de
desecho; (left over) sobrante; (land) baldío,
descampado ♦ vt malgastar, derrochar;

(time) perder; (opportunity) desperdiciar; **~s**
npl (area of land) tierras fpl baldías; **~ away**
vi consumirse; **~ disposal unit** (BRIT) n
triturador m de basura; **~ful** adj
derrochador(a); (process) antieconómico;
~ ground (BRIT) n terreno baldío; **~paper
basket** n papelera; **~ pipe** n tubo de
desagüe
watch [wɔtʃ] n (also: **wrist ~**) reloj m; (MIL:
group of guards) centinela m; (act) vigilancia;
(NAUT: spell of duty) guardia ♦ vt (look at)
mirar, observar; (: match, programme) ver;
(spy on, guard) vigilar; (be careful of)
cuidarse de, tener cuidado de ♦ vi ver, mirar;
(keep guard) montar guardia; **~ out** vi
cuidarse, tener cuidado; **~dog** n perro
guardián; (fig) persona u organismo encargado
de asegurarse de que las empresas actúan
dentro de la legalidad; **~ful** adj vigilante,
sobre aviso; **~maker** n relojero/a; **~man**
(irreg) n see **night**; **~ strap** n pulsera (de
reloj)
water ['wɔːtə*] n agua ♦ vt (plant) regar ♦ vi
(eyes) llorar; (mouth) hacerse la boca agua;
~ down vt (milk etc) aguar; (fig: story)
dulcificar, diluir; **~ closet** n wáter m;
~colour n acuarela; **~cress** n berro; **~fall** n
cascada, salto de agua; **~ heater** n
calentador m de agua; **~ing can** n regadera;
~ lily n nenúfar m; **~line** n (NAUT) línea de
flotación; **~logged** adj (ground) inundado;
~ main n cañería del agua; **~melon** n
sandía; **~proof** adj impermeable; **~shed** n
(GEO) cuenca; (fig) momento crítico; **~-
skiing** n esquí m acuático; **~tight** adj
hermético; **~way** n vía fluvial o navegable;
~works n central f depuradora; **~y** adj
(coffee etc) aguado; (eyes) lloroso
watt [wɔt] n vatio
wave [weɪv] n (of hand) señal f con la mano;
(on water) ola; (RADIO, in hair) onda; (fig)
oleada ♦ vi agitar la mano; (flag etc) ondear
♦ vt (handkerchief, gun) agitar; **~length** n
longitud f de onda
waver ['weɪvə*] vi (voice, love etc) flaquear;
(person) vacilar
wavy ['weɪvɪ] adj ondulado
wax [wæks] n cera ♦ vt encerar ♦ vi (moon)
crecer; **~ paper** (US) n papel m
apergaminado; **~works** n museo de cera
♦ npl figuras fpl de cera
way [weɪ] n camino; (distance) trayecto,
recorrido; (direction) dirección f, sentido;
(manner) modo, manera; (habit) costumbre
f; **which ~? — this ~** ¿por dónde?, ¿en qué
dirección? — por aquí; **on the ~** (en route) en
(el) camino; **to be on one's ~** estar en
camino; **to be in the ~** bloquear el camino;
(fig) estorbar; **to go out of one's ~ to do sth**

desvivirse por hacer algo; **under ~** en marcha; **to lose one's ~** extraviarse; **in a ~** en cierto modo or sentido; **no ~!** (*inf*) ¡de eso nada!; **by the ~ ...** a propósito ...; **"~ in"** (*BRIT*) "entrada"; **"~ out"** (*BRIT*) "salida"; **the ~ back** el camino de vuelta; **"give ~"** (*BRIT: AUT*) "ceda el paso"

waylay ['weɪleɪ] (*irreg*) *vt* salir al paso a

wayward ['weɪwəd] *adj* díscolo

W.C. *n* (*BRIT*) wáter *m*

we [wiː] *pl pron* nosotros/as

weak [wiːk] *adj* débil, flojo; (*tea etc*) claro; **~en** *vi* debilitarse; (*give way*) ceder ♦ *vt* debilitar; **~ling** *n* debilucho/a; (*morally*) persona de poco carácter; **~ness** *n* debilidad *f*; (*fault*) punto débil; **to have a ~ness for** tener debilidad por

wealth [welθ] *n* riqueza; (*of details*) abundancia; **~y** *adj* rico

wean [wiːn] *vt* destetar

weapon ['wepən] *n* arma

wear [wɛə*] (*pt* wore, *pp* worn) *n* (*use*) uso; (*deterioration through use*) desgaste *m*; (*clothing*): **sports/baby~** ropa de deportes/de niños ♦ *vt* (*clothes*) llevar; (*shoes*) calzar; (*damage: through use*) gastar, usar ♦ *vi* (*last*) durar; (*rub through etc*) desgastarse; **evening ~** ropa de etiqueta; **~ away** *vt* gastar ♦ *vi* desgastarse; **~ down** *vt* gastar; (*strength*) agotar; **~ off** *vi* (*pain etc*) pasar, desaparecer; **~ out** *vt* desgastar; (*person, strength*) agotar; **~ and tear** *n* desgaste *m*

weary ['wɪərɪ] *adj* cansado; (*dispirited*) abatido ♦ *vi*: **to ~ of** cansarse de

weasel ['wiːzl] *n* (*ZOOL*) comadreja

weather ['wɛðə*] *n* tiempo ♦ *vt* (*storm, crisis*) hacer frente a; **under the ~** (*fig: ill*) indispuesto, pachucho; **~-beaten** *adj* (*skin*) curtido; (*building*) deteriorado por la intemperie; **~cock** *n* veleta; **~ forecast** *n* boletín *m* meteorológico; **~man** (*irreg: inf*) *n* hombre *m* del tiempo; **~ vane** *n* = ~cock

weave [wiːv] (*pt* wove, *pp* woven) *vt* (*cloth*) tejer; (*fig*) entretejer; **~r** *n* tejedor(a) *m/f*; **weaving** *n* tejeduría

web [web] *n* (*of spider*) telaraña; (*on duck's foot*) membrana; (*network*) red; *f*; **the (World Wide) W~** el *or* la Web

website ['websaɪt] *n* espacio Web

wed [wed] (*pt, pp* wedded) *vt* casar ♦ *vi* casarse

we'd [wiːd] = we had; we would

wedding ['wedɪŋ] *n* boda, casamiento; **silver/golden ~** (*anniversary*) bodas *fpl* de plata/de oro; **~ day** *n* día *m* de la boda; **~ dress** *n* traje *m* de novia; **~ present** *n* regalo de boda; **~ ring** *n* alianza

wedge [wedʒ] *n* (*of wood etc*) cuña; (*of cake*) trozo ♦ *vt* acuñar; (*push*) apretar

Wednesday ['wednzdɪ] *n* miércoles *m inv*

wee [wiː] (*Scottish*) *adj* pequeñito

weed [wiːd] *n* mala hierba, maleza ♦ *vt* escardar, desherbar; **~killer** *n* herbicida *m*; **~y** *adj* (*person*) mequetréfico

week [wiːk] *n* semana; **a ~ today/on Friday** de hoy/del viernes en ocho días; **~day** *n* día *m* laborable; **~end** *n* fin *m* de semana; **~ly** *adv* semanalmente, cada semana ♦ *adj* semanal ♦ *n* semanario

weep [wiːp] (*pt, pp* wept) *vi, vt* llorar; **~ing willow** *n* sauce *m* llorón

weigh [weɪ] *vt, vi* pesar; **to ~ anchor** levar anclas; **~ down** *vt* sobrecargar; (*fig: with worry*) agobiar; **~ up** *vt* sopesar

weight [weɪt] *n* peso; (*metal~*) pesa; **to lose/put on ~** adelgazar/engordar; **~ing** *n* (*allowance*): (*London*) ~ing dietas (*por residir en Londres*); **~lifter** *n* levantador *m* de pesas; **~y** *adj* pesado; (*matters*) de relevancia *or* peso

weir [wɪə*] *n* presa

weird [wɪəd] *adj* raro, extraño

welcome ['welkəm] *adj* bienvenido ♦ *n* bienvenida ♦ *vt* dar la bienvenida a; (*be glad of*) alegrarse de; **thank you — you're ~** gracias — de nada

weld [weld] *n* soldadura ♦ *vt* soldar

welfare ['welfɛə*] *n* bienestar *m*; (*social aid*) asistencia social; **~ state** *n* estado del bienestar

well [wel] *n* fuente *f*, pozo ♦ *adv* bien ♦ *adj*: **to be ~** estar bien (de salud) ♦ *excl* ¡vaya!, ¡bueno!; **as ~** también; **as ~ as** además de; **~ done!** ¡bien hecho!; **get ~ soon!** ¡que te mejores pronto!; **to do ~** (*business*) ir bien; (*person*) tener éxito; **~ up** *vi* (*tears*) saltar

we'll [wiːl] = we will; we shall

well: **~-behaved** *adj* bueno; **~-being** *n* bienestar *m*; **~-built** *adj* (*person*) fornido; **~-deserved** *adj* merecido; **~-dressed** *adj* bien vestido; **~-groomed** *adj* de buena presencia; **~-heeled** (*inf*) *adj* (*wealthy*) rico

wellingtons ['welɪŋtənz] *npl* (*also*: wellington boots) botas *fpl* de goma

well: **~-known** *adj* (*person*) conocido; **~-mannered** *adj* educado; **~-meaning** *adj* bienintencionado; **~-off** *adj* acomodado; **~-read** *adj* leído; **~-to-do** *adj* acomodado; **~-wisher** *n* admirador(a) *m/f*

Welsh [welʃ] *adj* galés/esa ♦ *n* (*LING*) galés *m*; **the ~** *npl* los galeses; **the ~ Assembly** el Parlamento galés; **~man** (*irreg*) *n* galés *m*; **~ rarebit** *n* pan *m* con queso tostado; **~woman** (*irreg*) *n* galesa

went [went] *pt* of **go**

wept [wept] *pt, pp* of **weep**

were [wəː*] *pt* of **be**

we're [wɪə*] = we are

weren't [wəːnt] = were not

west [west] *n* oeste *m* ♦ *adj* occidental, del

oeste ♦ *adv* al *or* hacia el oeste; **the W~** el Oeste, el Occidente; **W~ Country** (*BRIT*) *n*: **the W~ Country** el suroeste de Inglaterra; **~erly** *adj* occidental; (*wind*) del oeste; **~ern** *adj* occidental ♦ *n* (*CINEMA*) película del oeste; **W~ Germany** *n* Alemania Occidental; **W~ Indian** *adj, n* antillano/a *m/f*; **W~ Indies** *npl* Antillas *fpl*; **~ward(s)** *adv* hacia el oeste

wet [wɛt] *adj* (*damp*) húmedo; (*~ through*) mojado; (*rainy*) lluvioso ♦ (*BRIT*) *n* (*POL*) conservador(a) *m/f* moderado/a; **to get ~** mojarse; **"~ paint"** "recién pintado"; **~suit** *n* traje *m* térmico

we've [wi:v] = **we have**

whack [wæk] *vt* dar un buen golpe a

whale [weɪl] *n* (*ZOOL*) ballena

wharf [wɔ:f](*pl* **wharves**) *n* muelle *m*

KEYWORD

what [wɔt] *adj* **1** (*in direct/indirect questions*) qué; **~ size is he?** ¿qué talla usa?; **~ colour/shape is it?** ¿de qué color/forma es?

2 (*in exclamations*): **~ a mess!** ¡qué desastre!; **~ a fool I am!** ¡qué tonto soy!

♦ *pron* **1** (*interrogative*) qué; **~ are you doing?** ¿qué haces *or* estás haciendo?; **~ is happening?** ¿qué pasa *or* está pasando?; **~ is it called?** ¿cómo se llama?; **~ about me?** ¿y yo qué?; **~ about doing ...?** ¿qué tal si hacemos ...?

2 (*relative*) lo que; **I saw ~ you did/was on the table** vi lo que hiciste/había en la mesa

♦ *excl* (*disbelieving*) ¡cómo!; **~, no coffee!** ¡que no hay café!

whatever [wɔt'ɛvə*] *adj*: **~ book you choose** cualquier libro que elijas ♦ *pron*: **do ~ is necessary** haga lo que sea necesario; **~ happens** pase lo que pase; **no reason ~** *or* **whatsoever** ninguna razón sea la que sea; **nothing ~** nada en absoluto

whatsoever [wɔtsəu'ɛvə*] *adj see* **whatever**

wheat [wi:t] *n* trigo

wheedle ['wi:dl] *vt*: **to ~ sb into doing sth** engatusar a uno para que haga algo; **to ~ sth out of sb** sonsacar algo a uno

wheel [wi:l] *n* rueda; (*AUT*: *also*: *steering ~*) volante *m*; (*NAUT*) timón *m* ♦ *vt* (*pram etc*) empujar ♦ *vi* (*also*: *~ round*) dar la vuelta, girar; **~barrow** *n* carretilla; **~chair** *n* silla de ruedas; **~ clamp** *n* (*AUT*) cepo

wheeze [wi:z] *vi* resollar

KEYWORD

when [wɛn] *adv* cuando; **~ did it happen?** ¿cuándo ocurrió?; **I know ~ it happened** sé cuándo ocurrió

♦ *conj* **1** (*at, during, after the time that*) cuando; **be careful ~ you cross the road** ten cuidado al cruzar la calle; **that was ~ I needed you** fue entonces que te necesité

2 (*on, at which*): **on the day ~ I met him** el día en qué le conocí

3 (*whereas*) cuando

whenever [wɛn'ɛvə*] *conj* cuando; (*every time that*) cada vez que ♦ *adv* cuando sea

where [wɛə*] *adv* dónde ♦ *conj* donde; **this is ~** aquí es donde; **~abouts** *adv* dónde ♦ *n*: **nobody knows his ~abouts** nadie conoce su paradero; **~as** *conj* visto que, mientras; **~by** *pron* por lo cual; **wherever** [-'ɛvə*] *conj* dondequiera que; (*interrogative*) dónde; **~withal** *n* recursos *mpl*

whether ['wɛðə*] *conj* si; **I don't know ~ to accept or not** no sé si aceptar o no; **~ you go or not** vayas o no vayas

KEYWORD

which [wɪtʃ] *adj* **1** (*interrogative: direct, indirect*) qué; **~ picture(s) do you want?** ¿qué cuadro(s) quieres?; **~ one?** ¿cuál?

2: **in ~ case** en cuyo caso; **we got there at 8 pm, by ~ time the cinema was full** llegamos allí a las 8, cuando el cine estaba lleno

♦ *pron* **1** (*interrogative*) cual; **I don't mind ~** el/la que sea

2 (*relative*: *replacing noun*) que; (: *replacing clause*) lo que; (: *after preposition*) (el/la) que *etc*, el/la cual *etc*; **the apple ~ you ate/~ is on the table** la manzana que comiste/que está en la mesa; **the chair on ~ you are sitting** la silla en la que estás sentado; **he said he knew, ~ is true/I feared** dijo que lo sabía, lo cual *or* lo que es cierto/me temía

whichever [wɪtʃ'ɛvə*] *adj*: **take ~ book you prefer** coja (*SP*) el libro que prefiera; **~ book you take** cualquier libro que coja

while [waɪl] *n* rato, momento ♦ *conj* mientras; (*although*) aunque; **for a ~** durante algún tiempo; **~ away** *vt* pasar

whim [wɪm] *n* capricho

whimper ['wɪmpə*] *n* sollozo ♦ *vi* lloriquear

whimsical ['wɪmzɪkl] *adj* (*person*) caprichoso; (*look*) juguetón/ona

whine [waɪn] *n* (*of pain*) gemido; (*of engine*) zumbido; (*of siren*) aullido ♦ *vi* gemir; zumbar; (*fig: complain*) gimotear

whip [wɪp] *n* látigo; (*POL*: *person*) *encargado de la disciplina partidaria en el parlamento* ♦ *vt* azotar; (*CULIN*) batir; (*move quickly*): **to ~ sth out/off** sacar/quitar algo de un tirón; **~ped cream** *n* nata *or* crema montada; **~-round** (*BRIT*) *n* colecta

whirl [wə:l] *vt* hacer girar, dar vueltas a ♦ *vi* girar, dar vueltas; (*leaves etc*) arremolinarse;

~pool n remolino; **~wind** n torbellino

whirr [wə:*] vi zumbar

whisk [wɪsk] n (CULIN) batidor m ♦ vt (CULIN) batir; **to ~ sb away** or **off** llevar volando a uno

whiskers ['wɪskəz] npl (of animal) bigotes mpl; (of man) patillas fpl

whiskey ['wɪskɪ] (US, Ireland) n = **whisky**

whisky ['wɪskɪ] n whisky m

whisper ['wɪspə*] n susurro ♦ vi, vt susurrar

whistle ['wɪsl] n (sound) silbido; (object) silbato ♦ vi silbar

white [waɪt] adj blanco; (pale) pálido ♦ n blanco; (of egg) clara; **~ coffee** (BRIT) n café m con leche; **~-collar worker** n oficinista m/f; **~ elephant** n (fig) maula; **~ lie** n mentirilla; **~ness** n blancura; **~ noise** n sonido blanco; **~ paper** n (POL) libro rojo; **~wash** n (paint) jalbegue m, cal f ♦ vt (also fig) blanquear

whiting ['waɪtɪŋ] n inv (fish) pescadilla

Whitsun ['wɪtsn] n pentecostés m

whizz [wɪz] vi: **to ~ past** or **by** pasar a toda velocidad; **~ kid** (inf) n prodigio

KEYWORD

who [hu:] pron 1 (interrogative) quién; **~ is it?**, **~'s there?** ¿quién es?; **~ are you looking for?** ¿a quién buscas?; **I told her ~ I was** le dije quién era yo
2 (relative) que; **the man/woman ~ spoke to me** el hombre/la mujer que habló conmigo; **those ~ can swim** los que saben or sepan nadar

whodun(n)it [hu:'dʌnɪt] (inf) n novela policíaca

whoever [hu:'evə*] pron: **~ finds it** cualquiera or quienquiera que lo encuentre; **ask ~ you like** pregunta a quien quieras; **~ he marries** no importa con quién se case

whole [həʊl] adj (entire) todo, entero; (not broken) intacto ♦ n todo; (all): **the ~ of the town** toda la ciudad, la ciudad entera ♦ n (total) total m; (sum) conjunto; **on the ~, as a ~** en general; **~food(s)** n(pl) alimento(s) m(pl) integral(es); **~hearted** adj sincero, cordial; **~meal** adj integral; **~sale** n venta al por mayor ♦ adj al por mayor; (fig: destruction) sistemático; **~saler** n mayorista m/f; **~some** adj sano; **~wheat** adj = **~meal**; **wholly** adv totalmente, enteramente

KEYWORD

whom [hu:m] pron 1 (interrogative): **~ did you see?** ¿a quién viste?; **to ~ did you give it?** ¿a quién se lo diste?; **tell me from ~ you received it** dígame de quién lo recibió
2 (relative) que; **to ~ a** quien(es); **of ~** quien(es), del/de la que etc; **the man ~ I**

saw/to ~ I wrote el hombre que vi/a quien escribí; **the lady about/with ~ I was talking** la señora de (la) que/con quien or (la) que hablaba

whooping cough ['hu:pɪŋ-] n tos f ferina

whore [hɔ:*] (inf: pej) n puta

KEYWORD

whose [hu:z] adj 1 (possessive: interrogative): **~ book is this?**, **~ is this book?** ¿de quién es este libro?; **~ pencil have you taken?** ¿de quién es el lápiz que has cogido?; **~ daughter are you?** ¿de quién eres hija?
2 (possessive: relative) cuyo/a, pl cuyos/as; **the man ~ son you rescued** el hombre cuyo hijo rescataste; **those ~ passports I have** aquellas personas cuyos pasaportes tengo; **the woman ~ car was stolen** la mujer a quien le robaron el coche
♦ pron de quién; **~ is this?** ¿de quién es esto?; **I know ~ it is** sé de quién es

KEYWORD

why [waɪ] adv por qué; **~ not?** ¿por qué no?; **~ not do it now?** ¿por qué no lo haces (or hacemos etc) ahora?
♦ conj: **I wonder ~ he said that** me pregunto por qué dijo eso; **that's not ~ I'm here** no es por eso (por lo) que estoy aquí; **the reason ~** la razón por la que
♦ excl (expressing surprise, shock, annoyance) ¡hombre!, ¡vaya! (explaining): **~, it's you!** ¡hombre, eres tú!; **~, that's impossible** ¡pero sí eso es imposible!

wicked ['wɪkɪd] adj malvado, cruel

wicket ['wɪkɪt] n (CRICKET: stumps) palos mpl; (: grass area) terreno de juego

wide [waɪd] adj ancho; (area, knowledge) vasto, grande; (choice) amplio ♦ adv: **to open ~** abrir de par en par; **to shoot ~** errar el tiro; **~-angle lens** n objetivo de gran angular; **~-awake** adj bien despierto; **~ly** adv (travelled) mucho; (spaced) muy; **it is ~ly believed/known that ...** mucha gente piensa/sabe que ...; **~n** vt ensanchar; (experience) ampliar ♦ vi ensancharse; **~ open** adj abierto de par en par; **~spread** adj extendido, general

widow ['wɪdəʊ] n viuda; **~ed** adj viudo; **~er** n viudo

width [wɪdθ] n anchura; (of cloth) ancho

wield [wi:ld] vt (sword) blandir; (power) ejercer

wife [waɪf] (pl wives) n mujer f, esposa

wig [wɪg] n peluca

wiggle ['wɪgl] vt menear

wild [waɪld] *adj* (*animal*) salvaje; (*plant*)
silvestre; (*person*) furioso, violento; (*idea*)
descabellado; (*rough: sea*) bravo; (: *land*)
agreste; (: *weather*) muy revuelto; **~s** *npl*
regiones *fpl* salvajes, tierras *fpl* vírgenes;
~erness ['wɪldənɪs] *n* desierto; **~life** *n*
fauna; **~ly** *adv* (*behave*) locamente; (*lash
out*) a diestro y siniestro; (*guess*) a lo loco;
(*happy*) a más no poder
wilful ['wɪlful] (*US* **willful**) *adj* (*action*)
deliberado; (*obstinate*) testarudo

KEYWORD
---

will [wɪl] *aux vb* **1** (*forming future tense*): **I
~ finish it tomorrow** lo terminaré *or* voy a
terminar mañana; **I ~ have finished it by
tomorrow** lo habré terminado para mañana;
~ you do it? — **yes I ~/no I won't** ¿lo harás?
— sí/no
2 (*in conjectures, predictions*): **he ~** *or* **he'll be
there by now** ya habrá *or* debe (de) haber
llegado; **that ~ be the postman** será *or* debe
ser el cartero
3 (*in commands, requests, offers*): **~ you be
quiet!** ¿quieres callarte?; **~ you help me?**
¿quieres ayudarme?; **~ you have a cup of tea?**
¿te apetece un té?; **I won't put up with it!** ¡no
lo soporto!
♦ *vt* (*pt, pp* **willed**): **to ~ sb to do sth** desear
que alguien haga algo; **he ~ed himself to go
on** con gran fuerza de voluntad, continuó
♦ *n* voluntad *f*; (*testament*) testamento

---

willing ['wɪlɪŋ] *adj* (*with goodwill*) de buena
voluntad; (*enthusiastic*) entusiasta; **he's ~ to
do it** está dispuesto a hacerlo; **~ly** *adv* con
mucho gusto; **~ness** *n* buena voluntad
willow ['wɪləu] *n* sauce *m*
willpower ['wɪlpauə*] *n* fuerza de voluntad
willy-nilly [wɪlɪ'nɪlɪ] *adv* quiérase o no
wilt [wɪlt] *vi* marchitarse
win [wɪn] (*pt, pp* **won**) *n* victoria, triunfo ♦ *vt*
ganar; (*obtain*) conseguir, lograr ♦ *vi* ganar;
~ over *vt* convencer a; **~ round** (*BRIT*) *vt* =
~ over
wince [wɪns] *vi* encogerse
winch [wɪntʃ] *n* torno
wind[1] [wɪnd] *n* viento; (*MED*) gases *mpl* ♦ *vt*
(*take breath away from*) dejar sin aliento a
wind[2] [waɪnd] (*pt, pp* **wound**) *vt* enrollar;
(*wrap*) envolver; (*clock, toy*) dar cuerda a
♦ *vi* (*road, river*) serpentear; **~ up** *vt* (*clock*)
dar cuerda a; (*debate, meeting*) concluir,
terminar
windfall ['wɪndfɔːl] *n* golpe *m* de suerte
winding ['waɪndɪŋ] *adj* (*road*) tortuoso;
(*staircase*) de caracol
wind instrument [wɪnd-] *n* (*MUS*)
instrumento de viento

windmill ['wɪndmɪl] *n* molino de viento
window ['wɪndəu] *n* ventana; (*in car, train*)
ventanilla; (*in shop etc*) escaparate *m* (*SP*),
vitrina (*AM*); **~ box** *n* jardinera de ventana;
~ cleaner *n* (*person*) limpiador *m* de
cristales; **~ ledge** *n* alféizar *m*, repisa;
~ pane *n* cristal *m*; **~ seat** *n* asiento junto a
la ventana; **~-shopping** *n*: **to go ~-shopping**
ir de escaparates; **~sill** *n* alféizar *m*, repisa
windpipe ['wɪndpaɪp] *n* tráquea
wind power *n* energía eólica
windscreen ['wɪndskriːn] (*US* **windshield**) *n*
parabrisas *m inv*; **~ washer** *n* lavaparabrisas
m inv; **~ wiper** *n* limpiaparabrisas *m inv*
windswept ['wɪndswept] *adj* azotado por el
viento
windy ['wɪndɪ] *adj* de mucho viento; **it's ~**
hace viento
wine [waɪn] *n* vino; **~ bar** *n* enoteca;
~ cellar *n* bodega; **~ glass** *n* copa (para
vino); **~ list** *n* lista de vinos; **~ waiter** *n*
escanciador *m*
wing [wɪŋ] *n* ala; (*AUT*) aleta; **~s** *npl* (*THEATRE*)
bastidores *mpl*; **~er** *n* (*SPORT*) extremo
wink [wɪŋk] *n* guiño, pestañeo ♦ *vi* guiñar,
pestañear
winner ['wɪnə*] *n* ganador(a) *m/f*
winning ['wɪnɪŋ] *adj* (*team*) ganador(a);
(*goal*) decisivo; (*smile*) encantador(a); **~s** *npl*
ganancias *fpl*
winter ['wɪntə*] *n* invierno ♦ *vi* invernar;
wintry ['wɪntrɪ] *adj* invernal
wipe [waɪp] *n*: **to give sth a ~** pasar un trapo
sobre algo ♦ *vt* limpiar; (*tape*) borrar; **~ off**
vt limpiar con un trapo; (*remove*) quitar;
~ out *vt* (*debt*) liquidar; (*memory*) borrar;
(*destroy*) destruir; **~ up** *vt* limpiar
wire ['waɪə*] *n* alambre *m*; (*ELEC*) cable *m*
(eléctrico); (*TEL*) telegrama *m* ♦ *vt* (*house*)
poner la instalación eléctrica en; (*also: ~ up*)
conectar; (*person: telegram*) telegrafiar
wireless ['waɪəlɪs] (*BRIT*) *n* radio *f*
wiring ['waɪərɪŋ] *n* instalación *f* eléctrica
wiry ['waɪərɪ] *adj* (*person*) enjuto y fuerte;
(*hair*) crespo
wisdom ['wɪzdəm] *n* sabiduría, saber *m*; (*good
sense*) cordura; **~ tooth** *n* muela del juicio
wise [waɪz] *adj* sabio; (*sensible*) juicioso
...wise [waɪz] *suffix*: **time~** en cuanto a *or*
respecto al tiempo
wish [wɪʃ] *n* deseo ♦ *vt* querer; **best ~es** (*on
birthday etc*) felicidades *fpl*; **with best ~es** (*in
letter*) saludos *mpl*, recuerdos *mpl*; **to ~ sb
goodbye** despedirse de uno; **he ~ed me well**
me deseó mucha suerte; **to ~ to do/sb to do
sth** querer hacer/que alguien haga algo; **to
~ for** desear; **~ful** *adj*: **it's ~ful thinking** eso
sería soñar
wisp [wɪsp] *n* mechón *m*; (*of smoke*) voluta

wistful ['wɪstful] adj pensativo
wit [wɪt] n ingenio, gracia; (also: ~s) inteligencia; (person) chistoso/a
witch [wɪtʃ] n bruja; **~craft** n brujería; **~hunt** n (fig) caza de brujas

---
KEYWORD
---

with [wɪð, wɪθ] prep **1** (accompanying, in the company of) con (con+ mí, ti, sí = conmigo, contigo, consigo); **I was ~ him** estaba con él; **we stayed ~ friends** nos quedamos en casa de unos amigos; **I'm (not) ~ you** (understand) (no) te entiendo; **to be ~ it** (inf: person: up-to-date) estar al tanto; (: alert) ser despabilado
2 (descriptive, indicating manner etc) con; de; **a room ~ a view** una habitación con vistas; **the man ~ the grey hat/blue eyes** el hombre del sombrero gris/de los ojos azules; **red ~ anger** rojo de ira; **to shake ~ fear** temblar de miedo; **to fill sth ~ water** llenar algo de agua

withdraw [wɪθ'drɔː] (irreg) vt retirar, sacar ♦ vi retirarse; **to ~ money (from the bank)** retirar fondos (del banco); **~al** n retirada; (of money) reintegro; **~al symptoms** npl (MED) síndrome m de abstinencia; **~n** adj (person) reservado, introvertido
wither ['wɪðə*] vi marchitarse
withhold [wɪθ'həuld] (irreg) vt (money) retener; (decision) aplazar; (permission) negar; (information) ocultar
within [wɪð'ɪn] prep dentro de ♦ adv dentro; **~ reach (of)** al alcance (de); **~ sight (of)** a la vista (de); **~ the week** antes de acabar la semana; **~ a mile (of)** a menos de una milla (de)
without [wɪð'aut] prep sin; **to go ~ sth** pasar sin algo
withstand [wɪθ'stænd] (irreg) vt resistir a
witness ['wɪtnɪs] n testigo m/f ♦ vt (event) presenciar; (document) atestiguar la veracidad de; **to bear ~ to** (fig) ser testimonio de; **~ box** n tribuna de los testigos; **~ stand** (US) n = **~ box**
witty ['wɪtɪ] adj ingenioso
wives [waɪvz] npl of **wife**
wk abbr = **week**
wobble ['wɔbl] vi temblar; (chair) cojear
woe [wəu] n desgracia
woke [wəuk] pt of **wake**
woken ['wəukən] pp of **wake**
wolf [wulf] n lobo; **wolves** [wulvz] npl of **wolf**
woman ['wumən] (pl **women**) n mujer f; **~ doctor** n médica; **women's lib** (inf: pej) n liberación f de la mujer; **~ly** adj femenino
womb [wuːm] n matriz f, útero

women ['wɪmɪn] npl of **woman**
won [wʌn] pt, pp of **win**
wonder ['wʌndə*] n maravilla, prodigio; (feeling) asombro ♦ vi: **to ~ whether/why** preguntarse si/por qué; **to ~ at** asombrarse de; **to ~ about** pensar sobre or en; **it's no ~ (that)** no es de extrañarse (que + subjun); **~ful** adj maravilloso
won't [wəunt] = **will not**
wood [wud] n (timber) madera; (forest) bosque m; **~ carving** n (act) tallado en madera; (object) talla en madera; **~ed** adj arbolado; **~en** adj de madera; (fig) inexpresivo; **~pecker** n pájaro carpintero; **~wind** n (MUS) instrumentos mpl de viento de madera; **~work** n carpintería; **~worm** n carcoma
wool [wul] n lana; **to pull the ~ over sb's eyes** (fig) engatusar a uno; **~en** (US) adj = **~len**; **~len** adj de lana; **~lens** npl géneros mpl de lana; **~ly** adj lanudo, de lana; (fig: ideas) confuso; **~y** (US) adj = **~ly**
word [wəːd] n palabra; (news) noticia; (promise) palabra (de honor) ♦ vt redactar; **in other ~s** en otras palabras; **to break/keep one's ~** faltar a la palabra/cumplir la promesa; **to have ~s with sb** reñir con uno; **~ing** n redacción f; **~ processing** n proceso de textos; **~ processor** n procesador m de textos
wore [wɔː*] pt of **wear**
work [wəːk] n trabajo; (job) empleo, trabajo; (ART, LITERATURE) obra ♦ vi trabajar; (mechanism) funcionar, marchar; (medicine) ser eficaz, surtir efecto ♦ vt (shape) trabajar; (stone etc) tallar; (mine etc) explotar; (machine) manejar, hacer funcionar; **~s** n (BRIT: factory) fábrica ♦ npl (of clock, machine) mecanismo; **to be out of ~** estar parado, no tener trabajo; **to ~ loose** (part) desprenderse; (knot) aflojarse; **~ on** vt fus trabajar en, dedicarse a; (principle) basarse en; **~ out** vi (plans etc) salir bien, funcionar ♦ vt (problem) resolver; (plan) elaborar; **it ~s out at £100** suma 100 libras; **~ up** vt: **to get ~ed up** excitarse; **~able** adj (solution) práctico, factible; **~aholic** [wəːkə'hɔlɪk] n trabajador(a) obsesivo a m/f; **~er** n trabajador(a) m/f, obrero/a; **~force** n mano f de obra; **~ing class** n clase f obrera; **~ing-class** adj obrero; **~ing order** n: **in ~ing order** en funcionamiento; **~man** (irreg) n obrero; **~manship** n habilidad f, trabajo; **~sheet** n hoja de trabajo; **~shop** n taller m; **~ station** n puesto or estación f de trabajo; **~-to-rule** (BRIT) n huelga de celo
world [wəːld] n mundo ♦ cpd (champion) del mundo; (power, war) mundial; **to think the ~ of sb** (fig) tener un concepto muy alto de

uno; **~ly** adj mundano; **~-wide** adj mundial, universal; **W~-Wide Web** n: **the W~-Wide Web** el World Wide Web

worm [wɔːm] n (also: earth~) lombriz f

worn [wɔːn] pp of wear ♦ adj usado; **~-out** adj (object) gastado; (person) rendido, agotado

worried ['wʌrɪd] adj preocupado

worry ['wʌrɪ] n preocupación f ♦ vt preocupar, inquietar ♦ vi preocuparse; **~ing** adj inquietante

worse [wɜːs] adj, adv peor ♦ n lo peor; **a change for the ~** un empeoramiento; **~n** vt, vi empeorar; **~ off** adj (financially): **to be ~ off** tener menos dinero; (fig): **you'll be ~ off this way** de esta forma estarás peor que nunca

worship ['wɜːʃɪp] n adoración f ♦ vt adorar; **Your W~** (BRIT: to mayor) señor alcalde; (: to judge) señor juez

worst [wɜːst] adj, adv peor ♦ n lo peor; **at ~** en lo peor de los casos

worth [wɜːθ] n valor m ♦ adj: **to be ~** valer; **it's ~ it** vale or merece la pena; **to be ~ one's while (to do)** merecer la pena (hacer); **~less** adj sin valor; (useless) inútil; **~while** adj (activity) que merece la pena; (cause) loable

worthy ['wɜːðɪ] adj respetable; (motive) honesto; **~ of** digno de

KEYWORD

would [wud] aux vb **1** (conditional tense): **if you asked him he ~ do it** si se lo pidieras, lo haría; **if you had asked him he ~ have done it** si se lo hubieras pedido, lo habría or hubiera hecho

2 (in offers, invitations, requests): **~ you like a biscuit?** ¿quieres una galleta?; (formal) ¿querría una galleta?; **~ you ask him to come in?** ¿quiere hacerle pasar?; **~ you open the window please?** ¿quiere or podría abrir la ventana, por favor?

3 (in indirect speech): **I said I ~ do it** dije que lo haría

4 (emphatic): **it WOULD have to snow today!** ¡tenía que nevar precisamente hoy!

5 (insistence): **she ~n't behave** no quiso comportarse bien

6 (conjecture): **it ~ have been midnight** sería medianoche; **it ~ seem so** parece ser que sí

7 (indicating habit): **he ~ go there on Mondays** iba allí los lunes

would-be (pej) adj presunto

wouldn't ['wudnt] = would not

wound¹ [wuːnd] n herida ♦ vt herir

wound² [waund] pt, pp of wind

wove [wəuv] pt of weave

woven ['wəuvən] pp of weave

wrap [ræp] vt (also: ~ up) envolver; **~per** n (on chocolate) papel m; (BRIT: of book) sobrecubierta; **~ping paper** n papel m de envolver; (fancy) papel m de regalo

wreak [riːk] vt: **to ~ havoc (on)** hacer estragos (en); **to ~ vengeance (on)** vengarse (de)

wreath [riːθ, pl riːðz] n (funeral ~) corona

wreck [rek] n (ship: destruction) naufragio; (: remains) restos mpl del barco; (pej: person) ruina ♦ vt (car etc) destrozar; (chances) arruinar; **~age** n restos mpl; (of building) escombros mpl

wren [ren] n (ZOOL) reyezuelo

wrench [rentʃ] n (TECH) llave f inglesa; (tug) tirón m; (fig) dolor m ♦ vt arrancar; **to ~ sth from sb** arrebatar algo violentamente a uno

wrestle ['resl] vi: **to ~ (with sb)** luchar (con or contra uno); **~r** n luchador(a) m/f (de lucha libre); **wrestling** n lucha libre

wretched ['retʃɪd] adj miserable

wriggle ['rɪɡl] vi (also: ~ about) menearse, retorcerse

wring [rɪŋ] (pt, pp wrung) vt retorcer; (wet clothes) escurrir; (fig): **to ~ sth out of sb** sacar algo por la fuerza a uno

wrinkle ['rɪŋkl] n arruga ♦ vt arrugar ♦ vi arrugarse

wrist [rɪst] n muñeca; **~watch** n reloj m de pulsera

writ [rɪt] n mandato judicial

write [raɪt] (pt wrote, pp written) vt escribir; (cheque) extender ♦ vi escribir; **~ down** vt escribir; (note) apuntar; **~ off** vt (debt) borrar (como incobrable); (fig) desechar por inútil; **~ out** vt escribir; **~ up** vt redactar; **~-off** n siniestro total; **~r** n escritor(a) m/f

writhe [raɪð] vi retorcerse

writing ['raɪtɪŋ] n escritura; (hand-~) letra; (of author) obras fpl; **in ~** por escrito; **~ paper** n papel m de escribir

written ['rɪtn] pp of write

wrong [rɒŋ] adj (wicked) malo; (unfair) injusto; (incorrect) equivocado, incorrecto; (not suitable) inoportuno, inconveniente; (reverse) del revés ♦ adv equivocadamente ♦ n injusticia ♦ vt ser injusto con; **you are ~ to do it** haces mal en hacerlo; **you are ~ about that, you've got it ~** en eso estás equivocado; **to be in the ~** no tener razón, tener la culpa; **what's ~?** ¿qué pasa?; **to go ~** (person) equivocarse; (plan) salir mal; (machine) estropearse; **~ful** adj injusto; **~ly** adv mal, incorrectamente; (by mistake) por error; **~ number** n (TEL): **you've got the ~ number** se ha equivocado de número

wrote [rəut] pt of write

wrought iron [rɔːt-] n hierro forjado

wrung [rʌŋ] pt, pp of wring

wt. abbr = weight

WWW n abbr (= World Wide Web) WWW m

X, x

Xmas ['eksməs] n abbr = **Christmas**
X-ray ['eksreɪ] n radiografía ♦ vt radiografiar, sacar radiografías de
xylophone ['zaɪləfəʊn] n xilófono

Y, y

Y2K abbr (= Year 2000): **the ~ problem** el efecto 2000
yacht [jɒt] n yate m; **~ing** n (sport) balandrismo; **~sman/woman** (irreg) n balandrista m/f
Yank [jæŋk] (pej) n yanqui m/f
Yankee ['jæŋkɪ] (pej) n = **Yank**
yap [jæp] vi (dog) aullar
yard [jɑːd] n patio; (measure) yarda; **~stick** n (fig) criterio, norma
yarn [jɑːn] n hilo; (tale) cuento, historia
yawn [jɔːn] n bostezo ♦ vi bostezar; **~ing** adj (gap) muy abierto
yd(s) abbr = **yard(s)**
yeah [jeə] (inf) adv sí
year [jɪə*] n año; **to be 8 ~s old** tener 8 años; **an eight-~-old child** un niño de ocho años (de edad); **~ly** adj anual ♦ adv anualmente, cada año
yearn [jɜːn] vi: **to ~ for sth** añorar algo, suspirar por algo
yeast [jiːst] n levadura
yell [jel] n grito, alarido ♦ vi gritar
yellow ['jeləʊ] adj amarillo
yelp [jelp] n aullido ♦ vi aullar
yes [jes] adv sí ♦ n sí m; **to say/answer ~** decir/contestar que sí
yesterday ['jestədɪ] adv ayer ♦ n ayer m; **~ morning/evening** ayer por la mañana/tarde; **all day ~** todo el día de ayer
yet [jet] adv ya; (negative) todavía ♦ conj sin embargo, a pesar de todo; **it is not finished ~** todavía no está acabado; **the best ~** el/la mejor hasta ahora; **as ~** hasta ahora, todavía
yew [juː] n tejo
yield [jiːld] n (AGR) cosecha; (COMM) rendimiento ♦ vt ceder; (results) producir, dar; (profit) rendir ♦ vi rendirse, ceder; (US: AUT) ceder el paso
YMCA n abbr (= Young Men's Christian Association) Asociación f de Jóvenes Cristianos
yog(h)ourt ['jəʊgət] n yogur m
yog(h)urt ['jəʊgət] n = **yog(h)ourt**
yoke [jəʊk] n yugo
yolk [jəʊk] n yema (de huevo)

you [juː] pron **1** (subject: familiar) tú, pl vosotros/as (SP), ustedes (AM); (polite) usted, pl ustedes; **~ are very kind** eres/es etc muy amable; **~ Spanish enjoy your food** a vosotros (or ustedes) los españoles os (or les) gusta la comida; **~ and I will go** iremos tú y yo
2 (object: direct: familiar) te, pl os (SP), les (AM); (polite) le, pl les, f la, pl las; **I know ~** te/le etc conozco
3 (object: indirect: familiar) te, pl os (SP), les (AM); (polite) le, pl les; **I gave the letter to ~ yesterday** te/os etc di la carta ayer
4 (stressed): **I told YOU to do it** te dije a ti que lo hicieras, es a ti a quien dije que lo hicieras; see also **3, 5**
5 (after prep: NB: con+ ti = contigo: familiar) ti, pl vosotros/as (SP), ustedes (AM); (: polite) usted, pl ustedes; **it's for ~** es para ti/vosotros etc
6 (comparisons: familiar) tú, pl vosotros/as (SP), ustedes (AM); (: polite) usted, pl ustedes; **she's younger than ~** es más joven que tú/vosotros etc
7 (impersonal: one): **fresh air does ~ good** el aire puro (te) hace bien; **~ never know** nunca se sabe; **~ can't do that!** ¡eso no se hace!

you'd [juːd] = **you had; you would**
you'll [juːl] = **you will; you shall**
young [jʌŋ] adj joven ♦ npl (of animal) cría; (people): **the ~** los jóvenes, la juventud; **~er** adj (brother etc) menor; **~ster** n joven m/f
your [jɔː*] adj tu; (pl) vuestro; (formal) su; see also **my**
you're [juə*] = **you are**
yours [jɔːz] pron tuyo; (pl) vuestro; (formal) suyo; see also **faithfully**; **mine**[1]; **sincerely**
yourself [jɔːˈself] pron tú mismo; (complement) te; (after prep) tí (mismo); (formal) usted mismo; (: complement) se; (: after prep) sí (mismo); **yourselves** pl pron vosotros mismos; (after prep) vosotros (mismos); (formal) ustedes (mismos); (: complement) se; (: after prep) sí mismos; see also **oneself**
youth [juːθ, pl juːðz] n juventud f; (young man) joven m; **~ club** n club m juvenil; **~ful** adj juvenil; **~ hostel** n albergue m de juventud
you've [juːv] = **you have**
Yugoslav ['juːgəʊslɑːv] adj, n yugo(e)slavo/a m/f
Yugoslavia [juːgəʊˈslɑːvɪə] n Yugoslavia
yuppie ['jʌpɪ] (inf) adj, n yupi m/f, yupy m/f
YWCA n abbr (= Young Women's Christian Association) Asociación f de Jóvenes Cristianas

Z, z

zany ['zeɪnɪ] *adj* estrafalario

zap [zæp] *vt* (*COMPUT*) borrar

zeal [ziːl] *n* celo, entusiasmo; **~ous** ['zɛləs] *adj* celoso, entusiasta

zebra ['ziːbrə] *n* cebra; **~ crossing** (*BRIT*) *n* paso de peatones

zero ['zɪərəu] *n* cero

zest [zɛst] *n* ánimo, vivacidad *f*; (*of orange*) piel *f*

zigzag ['zɪgzæg] *n* zigzag *m* ♦ *vi* zigzaguear,

hacer eses

zinc [zɪŋk] *n* cinc *m*, zinc *m*

zip [zɪp] *n* (*also:* ~ *fastener*, (*US*) ~*per*) cremallera (*SP*), cierre *m* (*AM*) ♦ *vt* (*also:* ~ *up*) cerrar la cremallera de; **~ code** (*US*) *n* código postal

zodiac ['zəudɪæk] *n* zodíaco

zone [zəun] *n* zona

zoo [zuː] *n* (jardín *m*) zoo *m*

zoology [zuːˈɔlədʒɪ] *n* zoología

zoom [zuːm] *vi*: **to ~ past** pasar zumbando; **~ lens** *n* zoom *m*

zucchini [zuːˈkiːnɪ] (*US*) *n(pl)* calabacín(ines) *m(pl)*

SPANISH VERB TABLES

1 Gerund. **2** Imperative. **3** Present. **4** Preterite. **5** Future. **6** Present subjunctive. **7** Imperfect subjunctive. **8** Past participle. **9** Imperfect. *Etc* indicates that the irregular root is used for all persons of the tense, *e.g.* **oír**: **6** oiga, oigas, oigamos, oigáis, oigan.

agradecer 3 agradezco **6** agradezca *etc*

aprobar 2 aprueba **3** apruebo, apruebas, aprueba, aprueban **6** apruebe, apruebes, apruebe, aprueben

atravesar 2 atraviesa **3** atravieso, atraviesas, atraviesa, atraviesan **6** atraviese, atravieses, atraviese, atraviesen

caber 3 quepo **4** cupe, cupiste, cupo, cupimos, cupisteis, cupieron **5** cabré *etc* **6** quepa *etc* **7** cupiera *etc*

caer 1 cayendo **3** caigo **4** cayó, cayeron **6** caiga *etc* **7** cayera *etc*

cerrar 2 cierra **3** cierro, cierras, cierra, cierran **6** cierre, cierres, cierre, cierren

COMER 1 comiendo **2** come, comed **3** como, comes, come comemos, coméis, comen **4** comí, comiste, comió, comimos, comisteis, comieron **5** comeré, comerás, comerá, comeremos, comeréis, comerán **6** coma, comas, coma, comamos, comáis, coman **7** comiera, comieras, comiera, comiéramos, comierais, comieran **8** comido **9** comía, comías, comía, comíamos comíais, comían

conocer 3 conozco **6** conozca *etc*

contar 2 cuenta **3** cuento, cuentas, cuenta, cuentan **6** cuente, cuentes, cuente, cuenten

dar 3 doy **4** di, diste, dio, dimos, disteis, dieron **7** diera *etc*

decir 2 di **3** digo **4** dije, dijiste, dijo, dijimos, dijisteis, dijeron **5** diré *etc* **6** diga *etc* **7** dijera *etc* **8** dicho

despertar 2 despierta **3** despierto, despiertas, despierta, despiertan **6** despierte, despiertes, despierte, despierten

divertir 1 divirtiendo **2** divierte **3** divierto, diviertes, divierte, divierten **4** divirtió, divirtieren **6** divierta, diviertas, divierta, divirtamos, divirtáis, diviertan **7** divirtiera *etc*

dormir 1 durmiendo **2** duerme **3** duermo, duermes, duerme, duermen **4** durmió, durmieron **6** duerma, duermas, duerma, durmamos, durmáis, duerman **7** durmiera *etc*

empezar 2 empieza **3** empiezo, empiezas, empieza, empiezan **4** empecé **6** empiece, empieces, empiece, empecemos, empecéis, empiecen

entender 2 entiende **3** entiendo, entiendes, entiende, entienden **6** entienda, entiendas, entienda, entiendan

ESTAR 2 está **3** estoy, estás, está, están **4** estuve, estuviste, estuvo, estuvimos, estuvisteis, estuvieron **6** esté, estés, esté, estén **7** estuviera *etc*

HABER 3 he, has, ha, hemos, han **4** hube, hubiste, hubo, hubimos, hubisteis, hubieron **5** habré *etc* **6** haya *etc* **7** hubiera *etc*

HABLAR 1 hablando **2** habla, hablad **3** hablo, hablas, habla, hablamos, habláis, hablan **4** hablé, hablaste, habló, hablamos, hablasteis, hablaron **5** hablaré, hablarás, hablará, hablaremos, hablaréis, hablarán **6** hable, hables, hable, hablemos, habléis, hablen 7 hablara, hablaras, hablara, habláramos, hablarais, hablaran 8 hablado 9 hablaba, hablabas, hablaba, hablábamos, hablabais, hablaban

hacer 2 haz 3 hago 4 hice, hiciste, hizo, hicimos, hicisteis, hicieron 5 haré *etc* 6 haga *etc* 7 hiciera *etc* 8 hecho

instruir 1 instruyendo 2 instruye 3 instruyo, instruyes, instruye, instruyen 4 instruyó, instruyeron 6 instruya *etc* 7 instruyera *etc*

ir 1 yendo 2 ve 3 voy, vas, va, vamos, vais, van 4 fui, fuiste, fue, fuimos, fuisteis, fueron 6 vaya, vayas, vaya, vayamos, vayáis, vayan 7 fuera *etc* 9 iba, ibas, iba, íbamos, ibais, iban

jugar 2 juega 3 juego, juegas, juega, juegan 4 jugué 6 juegue *etc*

leer 1 leyendo 4 leyó, leyeron 7 leyera *etc*

morir 1 muriendo 2 muere 3 muero, mueres, muere, mueren 4 murió, murieron 6 muera, mueras, muera, muramos, muráis, mueran 7 muriera *etc* 8 muerto

mover 2 mueve 3 muevo, mueves, mueve, mueven 6 mueva, muevas, mueva, muevan

negar 2 niega 3 niego, niegas, niega, niegan 4 negué 6 niegue, niegues, niegue, neguemos, neguéis, nieguen

ofrecer 3 ofrezco 6 ofrezca *etc*

oír 1 oyendo 2 oye 3 oigo, oyes, oye, oyen 4 oyó, oyeron 6 oiga *etc* 7 oyera *etc*

oler 2 huele 3 huelo, hueles, huele, huelen 6 huela, huelas, huela, huelan

parecer 3 parezco 6 parezca *etc*

pedir 1 pidiendo 2 pide 3 pido, pides, pide, piden 4 pidió, pidieron 6 pida *etc* 7 pidiera *etc*

pensar 2 piensa 3 pienso, piensas, piensa, piensan 6 piense, pienses, piense, piensen

perder 2 pierde 3 pierdo, pierdes, pierde, pierden 6 pierda, pierdas, pierda, pierdan

poder 1 pudiendo 2 puede 3 puedo, puedes, puede, pueden 4 pude, pudiste, pudo, pudimos, pudisteis, pudieron 5 podré *etc* 6 pueda, puedas, pueda, puedan 7 pudiera *etc*

poner 2 pon 3 pongo 4 puse, pusiste, puso, pusimos, pusisteis, pusieron 5 pondré *etc* 6 ponga *etc* 7 pusiera *etc* 8 puesto

preferir 1 prefiriendo 2 prefiere 3 prefiero, prefieres, prefiere, prefieren 4 prefirió, prefirieron 6 prefiera, prefieras, prefiera, prefiramos, prefiráis, prefieran 7 prefiriera *etc*

querer 2 quiere 3 quiero, quieres, quiere, quieren 4 quise, quisiste, quiso, quisimos, quisisteis, quisieron 5 querré *etc* 6 quiera, quieras, quiera, quieran 7 quisiera *etc*

reír 2 rie 3 río, ríes, ríe, ríen 4 rio, rieron 6 ría, rías, ría, riamos, riáis, rían 7 riera *etc*

repetir 1 repitiendo 2 repite 3 repito, repites, repite, repiten 4 repitió, repitieron 6 repita *etc* 7 repitiera *etc*

rogar 2 ruega 3 ruego, ruegas, ruega, ruegan 4 rogué 6 ruegue, ruegues, ruegue, roguemos, roguéis, rueguen

saber 3 sé 4 supe, supiste, supo, supimos, supisteis, supieron 5 sabré *etc* 6 sepa *etc* 7 supiera *etc*

salir 2 sal 3 salgo 5 saldré *etc* 6 salga *etc*

seguir 1 siguiendo 2 sigue 3 sigo, sigues, sigue, siguen 4 siguió, siguieron 6 siga *etc* 7 siguiera *etc*

sentar 2 sienta 3 siento, sientas, sienta, sientan 6 siente, sientes, siente, sienten

sentir 1 sintiendo 2 siente 3 siento, sientes, siente, sienten 4 sintió, sintieron **6** sienta, sientas, sienta, sintamos, sintáis, sientan **7** sintiera *etc*

SER 2 sé **3** soy, eres, es, somos, sois, son **4** fui, fuiste, fue, fuimos, fuisteis, fueron **6** sea *etc* **7** fuera *etc* **9** era, eras, era, éramos, erais, eran

servir 1 sirviendo **2** sirve **3** sirvo, sirves, sirve, sirven **4** sirvió, sirvieron **6** sirva *etc* **7** sirviera *etc*

soñar 2 sueña **3** sueño, sueñas, sueña, sueñan **6** sueñe, sueñes, sueñe, sueñen

tener 2 ten **3** tengo, tienes, tiene, tienen **4** tuve, tuviste, tuvo, tuvimos, tuvisteis, tuvieron **5** tendré *etc* **6** tenga *etc* **7** tuviera *etc*

traer 1 trayendo **3** traigo **4** traje, trajiste, trajo, trajimos, trajisteis, trajeron **6** traiga *etc* **7** trajera *etc*

valer 2 val **3** valgo **5** valdré *etc* **6** valga *etc*

venir 2 ven **3** vengo, vienes, viene, vienen **4** vine, viniste, vino, vinimos, vinisteis, vinieron **5** vendré *etc* **6** venga *etc* **7** viniera *etc*

ver 3 veo **6** vea *etc* **8** visto **9** veía *etc*

vestir 1 vistiendo **2** viste **3** visto, vistes, viste, visten **4** vistió, vistieron **6** vista *etc* **7** vistiera *etc*

VIVIR 1 viviendo **2** vive, vivid **3** vivo, vives, vive, vivimos, vivís, viven **4** viví, viviste, vivió, vivimos, vivisteis, vivieron **5** viviré, vivirás, vivirá, viviremos, viviréis, vivirán **6** viva, vivas, viva, vivamos, viváis, vivan **7** viviera, vivieras, viviera, viviéramos, vivierais, vivieran **8** vivido **9** vivía, vivías, vivía, vivíamos, vivías, vivían

volver 2 vuelve **3** vuelvo, vuelves, vuelve, vuelven **6** vuelva, vuelvas, vuelva, vuelvan **8** vuelto

VERBOS IRREGULARES EN INGLÉS

present	pt	pp	present	pt	pp
arise	arose	arisen	dream	dreamed, dreamt	dreamed, dreamt
awake	awoke	awaked			
be (am, is, are; being)	was, were	been	drink	drank	drunk
			drive	drove	driven
			dwell	dwelt	dwelt
bear	bore	born(e)	eat	ate	eaten
beat	beat	beaten	fall	fell	fallen
become	became	become	feed	fed	fed
begin	began	begun	feel	felt	felt
behold	beheld	beheld	fight	fought	fought
bend	bent	bent	find	found	found
beset	beset	beset	flee	fled	fled
bet	bet, betted	bet, betted	fling	flung	flung
			fly (flies)	flew	flown
bid	bid, bade	bid, bidden	forbid	forbade	forbidden
			forecast	forecast	forecast
bind	bound	bound	forget	forgot	forgotten
bite	bit	bitten	forgive	forgave	forgiven
bleed	bled	bled	forsake	forsook	forsaken
blow	blew	blown	freeze	froze	frozen
break	broke	broken	get	got	got, (US) gotten
breed	bred	bred			
bring	brought	brought	give	gave	given
build	built	built	go (goes)	went	gone
burn	burnt, burned	burnt, burned	grind	ground	ground
burst	burst	burst	grow	grew	grown
buy	bought	bought	hang	hung, hanged	hung, hanged
can	could	(been able)	have (has; having)	had	had
cast	cast	cast			
catch	caught	caught			
choose	chose	chosen	hear	heard	heard
cling	clung	clung	hide	hid	hidden
come	came	come	hit	hit	hit
cost	cost	cost	hold	held	held
creep	crept	crept	hurt	hurt	hurt
cut	cut	cut	keep	kept	kept
deal	dealt	dealt	kneel	knelt, kneeled	knelt, kneeled
dig	dug	dug			
do (3rd person; he/she/it/does)	did	done	know	knew	known
			lay	laid	laid
			lead	led	led
			lean	leant, leaned	leant, leaned
draw	drew	drawn			

424

present	pt	pp	present	pt	pp
leap	leapt, leaped	leapt, leaped	sink	sank	sunk
			sit	sat	sat
learn	learnt, learned	learnt, learned	slay	slew	slain
			sleep	slept	slept
leave	left	left	slide	slid	slid
lend	lent	lent	sling	slung	slung
let	let	let	slit	slit	slit
lie (lying)	lay	lain	smell	smelt, smelled	smelt, smelled
light	lit, lighted	lit, lighted	sow	sowed	sown, sowed
lose	lost	lost			
make	made	made	speak	spoke	spoken
may	might	—	speed	sped, speeded	sped, speeded
mean	meant	meant			
meet	met	met	spell	spelt, spelled	spelt, spelled
mistake	mistook	mistaken			
mow	mowed	mown, mowed	spend	spent	spent
			spill	spilt, spilled	spilt, spilled
must	(had to)	(had to)			
pay	paid	paid	spin	spun	spun
put	put	put	spit	spat	spat
quit	quit, quitted	quit, quitted	split	split	split
			spoil	spoiled, spoilt	spoiled, spoilt
read	read	read			
rid	rid	rid	spread	spread	spread
ride	rode	ridden	spring	sprang	sprung
ring	rang	rung	stand	stood	stood
rise	rose	risen	steal	stole	stolen
run	ran	run	stick	stuck	stuck
saw	sawed	sawn	sting	stung	stung
say	said	said	stink	stank	stunk
see	saw	seen	stride	strode	stridden
seek	sought	sought	strike	struck	struck, stricken
sell	sold	sold			
send	sent	sent	strive	strove	striven
set	set	set	swear	swore	sworn
shake	shook	shaken	sweep	swept	swept
shall	should	—	swell	swelled	swollen, swelled
shear	sheared	shorn, sheared			
			swim	swam	swum
shed	shed	shed	swing	swung	swung
shine	shone	shone	take	took	taken
shoot	shot	shot	teach	taught	taught
show	showed	shown	tear	tore	torn
shrink	shrank	shrunk	tell	told	told
shut	shut	shut	think	thought	thought
sing	sang	sung	throw	threw	thrown

present	pt	pp	present	pt	pp
thrust	thrust	thrust	wed	wedded, wed	wedded, wed
tread	trod	trodden			
wake	woke, waked	woken, waked	weep	wept	wept
			win	won	won
wear	wore	worn	wind	wound	wound
weave	wove, weaved	woven, weaved	wring	wrung	wrung
			write	wrote	written

LOS NÚMEROS

NUMBERS

un, uno(a)	1	one
dos	2	two
tres	3	three
cuatro	4	four
cinco	5	five
seis	6	six
siete	7	seven
ocho	8	eight
nueve	9	nine
diez	10	ten
once	11	eleven
doce	12	twelve
trece	13	thirteen
catorce	14	fourteen
quince	15	fifteen
dieciséis	16	sixteen
diecisiete	17	seventeen
dieciocho	18	eighteen
diecinueve	19	nineteen
veinte	20	twenty
veintiuno	21	twenty-one
veintidós	22	twenty-two
treinta	30	thirty
treinta y uno(a)	31	thirty-one
treinta y dos	32	thirty-two
cuarenta	40	forty
cincuenta	50	fifty
sesenta	60	sixty
setenta	70	seventy
ochenta	80	eighty
noventa	90	ninety
cien, ciento	100	a hundred, one hundred
ciento uno(a)	101	a hundred and one
doscientos(as)	200	two hundred
doscientos(as) uno(a)	201	two hundred and one
trescientos(as)	300	three hundred
cuatrocientos(as)	400	four hundred
quinientos(as)	500	five hundred
seiscientos(as)	600	six hundred
setecientos(as)	700	seven hundred
ochocientos(as)	800	eight hundred
novecientos(as)	900	nine hundred
mil	1 000	a thousand
mil dos	1 002	a thousand and two
cinco mil	5 000	five thousand
un millón	1 000 000	a million

LOS NÚMEROS

primer, primero(a), 1º, 1ᵉʳ (1ª, 1ᵉʳᵃ)
segundo(a) 2º (2ª)
tercer, tercero(a), 3º (3ª)
cuarto(a), 4º (4ª)
quinto(a), 5º (5ª)
sexto(a), 6º (6ª)
séptimo(a)
octavo(a)
noveno(a)
décimo(a)
undécimo(a)
duodécimo(a)
decimotercio(a)
decimocuarto(a)
decimoquinto(a)
decimosexto(a)
vigésimo(a)
vigésimo(a) primero(a)
trigésimo(a)
centésimo(a)
centésimo(a) primero(a)
milésimo(a)

Números Quebrados *etc*

un medio
un tercio
un cuarto
un quinto
cero coma cinco, 0,5
diez por cien(to)

NUMBERS

first, 1st

second, 2nd
third, 3rd
fourth, 4th
fifth, 5th
sixth, 6th
seventh
eighth
ninth
tenth
eleventh
twelfth
thirteenth
fourteenth
fifteenth
sixteenth
twentieth
twenty-first
thirtieth
hundredth
hundred-and-first
thousandth

Fractions *etc*

a half
a third
a quarter
a fifth
(nought) point five, 0.5
ten per cent

N.B. In Spanish the ordinal numbers from 1 to 10 are commonly used; from 11 to 20 rather less; above 21 they are rarely written and almost never heard in speech. The custom is to replace the forms for 21 and above by the cardinal number.

LA HORA

¿qué hora es?

es/son

medianoche, las doce (de la noche)

la una (de la madrugada)

la una y cinco
la una y diez
la una y cuarto *or* quince
la una y veinticinco

la una y media *or* treinta
las dos menos veinticinco, la una treinta y cinco
las dos menos veinte, la una cuarenta
las dos menos cuarto, la una cuarenta y cinco
las dos menos diez, la una cincuenta
mediodía, las doce (de la tarde)
la una (de la tarde)

las siete (de la tarde)

¿a qué hora?

a medianoche
a las siete

en veinte minutos
hace quince minutos

THE TIME

what time is it?

it's o *it is*

midnight, twelve p.m.

one o'clock (in the morning), one (a.m.)
five past one
ten past one
a quarter past one, one fifteen
twenty-five past one, one twenty-five
half-past one, one thirty
twenty-five to two, one thirty-five
twenty to two, one forty

a quarter to two, one forty-five

ten to two, one fifty

twelve o'clock, midday, noon
one o'clock (in the afternoon), one (p.m.)
seven o'clock (in the evening), seven (p.m.)

(at) what time?

at midnight
at seven o'clock

in twenty minutes
fifteen minutes ago

LA FECHA

hoy
todos los días
ayer
esta mañana
mañana por la noche
anteanoche; antes de ayer por la
  noche
antes de ayer; anteayer
anoche
hace dos días/seis años
mañana por la tarde
pasado mañana
todos los jueves, el jueves
va los viernes
"miércoles cerrado"
de lunes a viernes
para el jueves
un sábado de marzo
dentro de una semana
dentro de dos martes

el domingo que viene
esta semana/la semana que
  viene/la semana pasada
dentro de dos semanas
dentro de tres lunes
el primer/último viernes del mes
el mes que viene
el año pasado
el uno de junio, el primero de
  junio (LAM)
el dos de octubre
nací en 1987
su cumpleaños es el 6 de junio

el 18 de agosto

en el 96
en la primavera del 94
del 19 al 3
¿qué fecha es hoy?, ¿a cuanto
  estamos?
hoy es 15, estamos a quince

mil novecientos ochenta y ocho

hoy hace 10 años
a final de mes
a final de mes

DATES

today
every day
yesterday
this morning
tomorrow night
the night before last

the day before yesterday
last night
2 days/six years ago
tomorrow afternoon
the day after tomorrow
every Thursday, on Thursday
he goes on Fridays
"closed on Wednesdays"
from Monday to Friday
by Thursday
one Saturday in March
in a week's time
a week next/on Tuesday/Tuesday
  week
next Sunday
this/next/last week

in 2 weeks or a fortnight
two weeks on Monday
the first/last Friday of the month
next month
last year
the 1st of June, June first

the 2nd of October, October 2nd
I was born in 1987
his birthday is on June 6th (BRIT)
  or 6th June (US)
on 18th August (BRIT) or August
  18th (US)
in '96
in the Spring of '94
from the 19th to the 3rd
what's the date?, what date is it
  today?
today's date is the 15th, today is
  the 15th
1988 - nineteen (hundred and)
  eighty-eight
10 years to the day
at the end of the month
at the month end (ACCOUNTS)

LA FECHA

diariamente/semanalmente/
  mensualmente
anualmente
dos veces a la semana/dos veces
  al mes/dos veces al año
dos veces al mes
en el año 2006 (dos mil seis)
4 a. de C.
79 d. de C.
en el siglo XIII
en *o* durante los (años) 80
a mediados de la década de los 70
en mil novecientos noventa y
  tantos

HEADINGS OF LETTERS

9 de octubre de 1995

DATES

daily/weekly/monthly

annually
twice a week/month/year

bi-monthly
in the year 2006
4 B.C., B.C. 4
79 A.D., A.D. 79
in the 13th century
in *or* during the 1980s
in the mid seventies
in 1990 something

9th October 1995 *or* 9 October
  1995

PESOS YE MEDIDAS
CONVERSION CHARTS

In the weight and length charts the middle figure can be either metric or imperial. Thus 3.3 feet = 1 metre, 1 foot = 0.3 metres, and so on.

feet		metres	inches		cm	lbs		kg
3.3	1	0.3	0.39	1	2.54	2.2	1	0.45
6.6	2	0.61	0.79	2	5.08	4.4	2	0.91
9.9	3	0.91	1.18	3	7.62	6.6	3	1.4
13.1	4	1.22	1.57	4	10.6	8.8	4	1.8
16.4	5	1.52	1.97	5	12.7	11.0	5	2.2
19.7	6	1.83	2.36	6	15.2	13.2	6	2.7
23.0	7	2.13	2.76	7	17.8	15.4	7	3.2
26.2	8	2.44	3.15	8	20.3	17.6	8	3.6
29.5	9	2.74	3.54	9	22.9	19.8	9	4.1
32.9	10	3.05	3.9	10	25.4	22.0	10	4.5
			4.3	11	27.9			
			4.7	12	30.1			

°C	0	5	10	15	17	20	22	24	26	28	30	35	37	38	40	50	100
°F	32	41	50	59	63	68	72	75	79	82	86	95	98.4	100	104	122	212

Km	10	20	30	40	50	60	70	80	90	100	110	120
Miles	6.2	12.4	18.6	24.9	31.0	37.3	43.5	49.7	56.0	62.0	68.3	74.6

Liquids

gallons	1.1	2.2	3.3	4.4	5.5
litres	5	10	15	20	25

pints	0.44	0.88	1.76
litres	0.25	0.5	1